P9-CRB-822

OSWEGO CITY LIBRARY

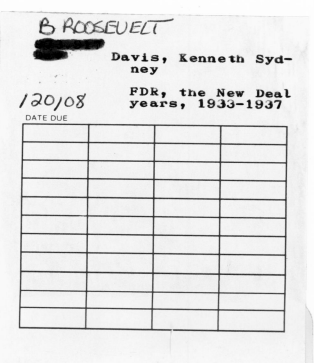

B ROOSEVELT

Davis, Kenneth Syd-
ney

FDR, the New Deal
years, 1933-1937

120/08

DATE DUE

OSWEGO CITY LIBRARY

28

DAY
BOOK

OTHER BOOKS BY KENNETH S. DAVIS

Fiction

IN THE FORESTS OF THE NIGHT

THE YEARS OF THE PILGRIMAGE

MORNING IN KANSAS

Nonfiction

SOLDIER OF DEMOCRACY
A Biography of Dwight Eisenhower

RIVER ON THE RAMPAGE

A PROPHET IN HIS OWN COUNTRY
The Triumphs and Defeats of Adlai E. Stevenson

THE HERO
Charles A. Lindbergh and the American Dream

WATER, THE MIRROR OF SCIENCE
(with John A. Day)

EXPERIENCE OF WAR
The U.S. in World War II

THE CAUTIONARY SCIENTISTS
*Priestley, Lavoisier, and the Founding
of Modern Chemistry*

THE POLITICS OF HONOR
A Biography of Adlai E. Stevenson

FDR
*The Beckoning of Destiny, 1882–1928
A History*

INVINCIBLE SUMMER
An Intimate Portrait of the Roosevelts

KANSAS
A Bicentennial History

FDR
The New York Years, 1928–1933

FDR
The New Deal Years
1933-1937

⁂ FDR ⁂
The New Deal Years
1933-1937
A History

———— ⫸⋈⫷ ————

Kenneth S. Davis

Random House New York

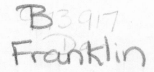

Copyright © 1979, 1983, 1986 by Kenneth S. Davis

All rights reserved under International and Pan-American Copyright Conventions.
Published in the United States by Random House, Inc., New York, and
simultaneously in Canada by Random House of Canada Limited, Toronto.

Library of Congress Cataloging-in-Publication Data

Davis, Kenneth Sydney, 1912–
FDR, the New Deal years, 1933–1937.
Includes index.
1. Roosevelt, Franklin D. (Franklin Delano), 1882–
1945. 2. Presidents—United States—Biography.
3. New Deal, 1933–1939. 4. United States—Politics and
government—1933–1945. I. Title.
E807.D37 1986   917.917′092′4   85-31704
ISBN 0-394-52753-4

A small portion of the epilogue appeared in "FDR as a Biographer's Problem,"
American Scholar, Winter 1983/84. Most of Chapter 11 and a small portion of
Chapter 14 first appeared as "The Birth of Social Security," *American Heritage,*
April/May 1979.

Manufactured in the United States of America
24689753
First Edition

In Memory
of
A Great Teacher
ALEXANDER MEIKLEJOHN
several of whose students played
active roles in the drama of the
New Deal, in ways influenced by
his teaching, and whose influence
upon the writing of this book has
been profound.

Contents

120108

PROLOGUE

❖

The State of the World,
March 2, 1933

IT was the evening of Thursday, March 2, 1933.

And it was the worst of times.

Everywhere evident in the Western world to those with knowledge of history were signs, even actual elements, of the death of civilization. Collapse and disintegration, tumult and turmoil, depression and despair, an increasing noise of ruinous violence—all these, stemming from and echoing the Great War of 1914–1918, were portentous of yet more horrendous quarrels in the making. The evening sun went down. Fading out of the western sky was that radiance of warm hope and bright faith and glowing love of man for man which is essential to the life of free societies. A dark night was falling. And its darkness deepened as the lights of reason were blown out by winds of passion all across the continent of Europe and began to dim, to flicker perilously near extinction in important parts of Great Britain and the United States, including parts where governing power resided. The very ground on which civilization stood—the richly fertile earth compounded of intelligence and morality and accumulated knowledge, whereby the institutions of civilization are nourished; that vital soil which has been so arduously produced through long centuries of creative effort —was being swiftly eroded and carried off into chaos by a rising tide of barbarism. Not in a thousand years had barbarism so threatened the most advanced societies of the West, and never before had the barbarians come as they now came, an overwhelming force rising up within, rather than an invading force from outside, the civilization they would destroy.

Who were they, these barbarians?

They were simply "mass man," according to a Spanish social philosopher much read in that worst of times—"average" men, who, however well trained technically or vocationally, remained uneducated, lacking moral commitment and intellectual discipline. They placed no unique value upon themselves as individuals, made no special demands of themselves, were perfectly content to be "just like everybody," and were consequently unfit to "direct their own personal destiny," much less "rule society in general," as José Ortega y Gasset wrote. He himself was committed to a kind of democracy in which excellence and the "select minority" are valued, yet was strongly influenced by the gloomy, doomful antidemocratic philosophy of Oswald Spengler, and for a dozen years and more he had been warning his fellow Europeans of catastrophe impending as mass man and his manipulators rose to supreme power over technologically advanced nations. Now, in his view, the catastrophe was at hand. All across the Western world, as he wrote his most famous book in

1929,* he saw increasingly the repudiation of excellence, the triumph of medi-
ocrity, the crushing of the individual person and all true individualism under
a "tyranny of the majority" and the "sovereignty of the unqualified."[1] In
nation after nation across the Continent, from Russia in the east and north to
Spain and Portugal in the south and west, he saw this sovereignty increasingly
identified with the state, and saw the state become, in proportion, ever more
militaristic and tyrannical. The situation had greatly worsened in this respect
during the four years since Ortega y Gasset completed his book—years of
deepening world depression and rising dictatorial governments in Europe.
Through saddened eyes the philosopher in Madrid must now look upon mass
man being armed with the most destructive weapons of modern science for a
fatal assault upon the civilization of the West.

Not wholly or necessarily inconsistent with the Spaniard's dark vision was
the view of those who, less inclined than he to cut off with passionate assertions
the quest for the reasons why, saw the darkness that fell and the barbarism
that rose in terms of patterned process. They saw it as an action-reaction the
root of which was the failure of modern men to respond intelligently to the
challenging implications of an explosively expanding technology—a failure to
make the kinds of social and economic arrangements that would tame this
monstrously growing physical power into the service of humane, life-enhanc-
ing, civilized purposes. Questions arose from this latter view. Was the failure
due to mass man's incapacities? If so, were the incapacities innate, inherent,
as Ortega y Gasset seemed sometimes to suggest? Or was the failure to master
technology the very cause or reason for this mass man, of whom so much more
was demanded, for self-government, than he seemed capable of supplying?

At any rate, the barbarians were now well on the way to taking over Germany,
one of the most scientifically, technologically advanced nations on earth. The
news that came out of that stricken land into the eyes and ears of liberty-loving
Americans on this Thursday evening was as dark as the wintry night now
falling westward across the Continent.

Barely a month ago Adolf Hitler had been named Chancellor of a German
republic he was sworn to abolish and replace with dictatorship. To most
Americans he was utterly incredible as political leader—a hysterical creature
whose scowling countenance, decorated with a Chaplinesque toothbrush mus-
tache, appeared comically absurd as it glared out of newspapers and magazines
and newsreels. To most educated Germans also he had been but a bad political
joke all through the 1920s—a half-educated mass man whose narrow mind was
closed over a few primitive, erroneous ideas, so tightly closed as to be impene-
trable by corrective knowledge, even by such teachings as painful experience
gives to normal human beings. "Think with your blood!" he cried, and no
doubt he himself did so of necessity, having no capacity for ratiocination. He

*La Rebelión de las Masas, published in Spain in 1930, was published in English translation in
1932 as The Revolt of the Masses.

was the most vicious of anti-Semites, the most fanatical of nationalists; he was a war addict with a passion for violence and destruction and the infliction of pain; he had an insatiable lust for coercive, terrifying power. He was so filled up with hate that there would have been no room in him for love if love had been, as it was not, possible for him. Yet he had enormous strength of will and a strangely powerful hypnotic influence upon most who came into direct contact with him. His influence over people in crowds—such people, at any rate, as came together in crowds to see and hear him—was overwhelming; he was a master of the kind of impassioned oratory that numbs minds and arouses religious frenzies. He appealed directly, also calculatedly (he had much animal shrewdness), to all that was most insanely egotistical in the German national soul, all that was meanest and cruelest in the German mass man. And his elevation could be viewed by reasonable men only as a measure of the depth of Germany's economic misery and psychic illness in this third year of world depression.

For in early 1929 the National Socialist (Nazi) party, which Hitler had largely made in his own image ten years before, remained the smallest of Germany's nine parties, with little prospect of much further growth. Then had come the cessation of American loans to Germany, a consequent collapse of the German prosperity, which had depended upon those loans, a swift upward surge of unemployment, and the abrupt creation of a mass of confused, miserable, frightened people who, having no notion why misery had come upon them, were filled with an inchoate, resentful, scapegoat-seeking anger. To these, Hitler offered a savior (himself) to be worshiped, a devil (the Jew-Communist) to be execrated, and the promise of a new and better life to be gained, not by thoughtful individual effort but by a letting go of self into mass hysterical emotionalism. All the same, the tide of Nazi popularity, swiftly rising through two and a half years, had apparently peaked in the summer of 1932. National Socialism had then emerged from an election as the largest of Germany's parties, with 230 of the Reichstag's 608 seats; but when another election was held just three months later,* the Nazis lost 34 seats while the Communists gained 11, bringing their total to 100. Hence an extremely complicated series of intrigues and double-dealings among various right-wing party leaders had been required before the Nazi Führer received from a reluctant Reich President Paul von Hindenburg his appointment as chancellor. He had promised Hindenburg he would obtain at once a governing Reichstag majority; he had been expected to do so through alliance with another right-wing party. Instead, with a boldness that seemed rash in view of the last election returns, he as chancellor persuaded the president to dissolve the Reichstag and call for new elections, to be held Sunday, March 5, just three days beyond this dark Thursday evening.

---

*The year 1932 was one of multiple German elections in swift succession as Nazi and Communist intransigence made impossible the formation of a coalition majority in the Reichstag. The Weimar Republic was thus sent tottering toward its grave.

Since then much world attention had been focused upon the Nazi election campaign, designed to give the party a clear majority. It was no edifying spectacle. Nazi Hermann Goering, now Prussian Minister of the Interior, had police control over two-thirds of the Reich; effective police control was in Nazi hands over much of the rest of the country. There was little interference from law enforcement officers as Nazi Brownshirts (the SA) routinely broke up meetings and engaged in all manner of brutal violence against the persons and property of Communists and other anti-Nazis, killing scores and injuring hundreds. Indeed, Prussian police operated as Nazi agents; six days ago they had raided abandoned Communist headquarters in Berlin, seizing documents "proving," as Goering announced, that the Communists were about to launch a revolutionary terror campaign, a veritable "blood bath." The climactic event had come just three days ago, on the night of February 27, when a fire of obviously incendiary origin destroyed the Reichstag Building. While the fire yet burned, Hitler and Goering proclaimed through a Nazi propaganda machine which was now a part of government that this ghastly deed had been done by Communists as the first act of their terror campaign, that a Communist agent (he was a feebleminded young Dutchman named Marinus van der Lubbe) had been caught by the SA inside the building in the very act of setting fire to a curtain, and that drastic defensive action must be taken by the government to save the life of the nation. A few hours later a decree prepared by Hitler and signed by Hindenburg was issued, suspending all constitutional articles guaranteeing freedom of speech, press, and assembly; assuring the secrecy of postal, telegraphic, and telephone communications; and protecting citizens against arbitrary arrest or searches and seizures of their property.

The latest news from Germany on this evening of March 2 was that all Communist newspapers throughout the Reich and all Socialist papers in Prussia had been shut down "until after the Reichstag elections next Sunday." Truckloads of Nazi Brownshirts were roaring through the streets of every German city to the homes of previously targeted anti-Nazis, who were violently seized, dragged off to SA barracks, and there beaten and tortured. Scores of prominent Socialists and Communists (some reports said hundreds) were more formally arrested by police and jailed. The outcome of Sunday's election was reported to be now a foregone conclusion: The Nazis were bound to win a huge majority.* Hitler, having for years proclaimed his purpose to be the scrapping of the Versailles Treaty and the remaking of Germany into a military power second to none, was then expected to demand constitutional revisions which would transfer from the Reichstag to himself all legislative power, all control over foreign affairs. There was reported speculation that Fascist

*In the event they didn't. Despite the terror and intimidation, 56 percent of the Germans who flocked to the polls in unprecedented numbers on March 5 voted against the Nazis. Out of a grand total of 37,943,627 ballots, 17,277,188 went to the Nazis, 20,666,447 to other parties. Even if one counted the Nationalist vote as a Nazi vote, since the Nationalists would vote with the Nazis in the Reichstag (this gave Hitler a sixteen-vote majority there), the Nazis fell short of a popular majority by a quarter million.

Italy's Mussolini and Nazi Germany's Hitler might soon form a military alliance which, with Germany rearmed, would dominate the Continent. The prospect, said this report, was viewed with alarm in Paris and London.

Black news, indeed, this of the conquest of power over one of the greatest nations on earth by some of the most brutish barbarians on earth, barbarians having in their hands all the vast coercive force which high technology provides.

Nor was the news that came to Americans from the other side of the world that evening of brighter hue.

One of the most amazing phenomena in all history had been the leap made by the Japanese people out of medieval feudalism into an advanced industrialism during the last half of the nineteenth century, after Japanese ports had been forcibly opened to foreign trade by the American commodore Matthew Perry. By 1900 the Japanese had become the most Westernized people by far in the Far East and one of the most scientifically technologically advanced in the world. Since then they had made great strides toward a political democracy modeled on Britain's constitutional monarchy. Under successive ministries following the Great War, the Diet in Tokyo had permitted, if not encouraged, trade union organization, had adopted universal male suffrage, had in general pursued a liberal internationalist policy. But industrialization had been accompanied by an explosive growth of population, greatly overcrowding Japan's island home and producing a wave of emigration which, washing high against America's Pacific shore, provoked the adoption, in 1924, of a United States immigration policy that totally excluded the Japanese. Industrialization and overpopulation also made Japan as dependent as Britain on overseas trade, but unlike Britain, it had no overseas empire to provide it with raw materials and assured markets for its manufactures. That it should acquire one, that it *must* do so by use of whatever force was necessary became an increasingly dominant theme of its political life as the onset of world depression caused everywhere a surge of economic nationalism. Import quotas were imposed by the nations with which Japan had to trade, especially after its abandonment of the gold standard had drastically depreciated the yen in late 1931 and early 1932. Tariff walls rose, those of America's Hawley-Smoot Act being especially harmful to Japan. And in Japan there was an abrupt growth of reactionary politics, a rapid turning away from democracy toward military dictatorship and a turning away, too, from the cultural and intellectual influences of the West toward feudalistic Japanese traditions, culture, religious belief. Here, as in Europe, internal miseries swelled a rising tide of barbarism. A Japanese premier was assassinated in November 1930, following which Japanese troops drove Chinese forces from Manchuria and set up there a puppet state, Manchukuo. Another premier was assassinated by military reactionaries in 1932, after which party government was wholly replaced in Tokyo by a government of generals and admirals. These then expanded and intensified the campaign of military conquest already launched upon the Asian mainland while curtailing civil liberties at home.

The latest news from the Far East which Americans read in their papers and listened to from their radios on this March 2 was of Japanese troops advancing upon the city of Jehol in China and, south of the Great Wall, into the Tientsin area, against sporadically brave but always ineffective Chinese resistance. There were reports of ghastly atrocities against civilians in the areas of Japanese occupation. From Nanking came loud protests against the ban which Britain had just imposed on arms shipments to either side of the Sino-Japanese conflict. This was no act of neutrality, cried the Chinese; it was an act of cruel discrimination against them, for it deprived them of desperately needed arms while doing nothing to halt the aggression of heavily armed Japan.

Thus barbarism was on the rise, barbarians were on the march, in the east as in the west.

Was there no bright offset, anywhere in the world, to all this dark news?

Some Americans claimed to see one when they looked toward that one-sixth of all the earth's land surface that stretches from the Baltic Sea to the seas of Okhotsk and Japan, bridging Occident and Orient. Socialism as practiced in the Union of Soviet Socialist Republics was said, in this early March 1933, to be scoring spectacular economic successes while democratic capitalist economies were everywhere in steep decline. Since 1929, according to the most reliable economic indices, the volume of industrial production had shrunk nearly 50 percent in the United States, more than 40 percent in Germany, more than 30 percent in France, and nearly 17 percent in England, the industrial economy of which had been chronically depressed since the Great War ended. But in Soviet Russia, by its own account, which Western economists seemed generally inclined to accept as accurate, industrial production had more than doubled during the last four years as goals set by the Five-Year Plan, announced by Joseph Stalin in 1928, were reached or surpassed.

Those Americans who saw this as great good news for mankind, however, proving that the "future" seen by Lincoln Steffens in the Russia of 1919 did indeed "work" toward a vast expansion of human happiness and well-being, had either ceased to be committed to human freedom and the basic tenets of democratic government or kept their eyes tightly closed against other facts about the Soviet Union. For instance, Russia's increased industrial production was almost wholly confined to *heavy* industry. Much of it was for national defense. The production of consumer goods evidently lagged well behind stated Gosplan (State Planning Commission) goals, which were themselves well below the requirements of a standard of living that was anywhere near as high as that of other industrial nations.

It must be remembered that what had first arisen out of the ruin of the czarist empire in the spring of 1917 had been a democratic government, joyously welcomed by Woodrow Wilson because it relieved him of the embarrassment of having one of the worst of despotic states fighting with him in the Great War "for democracy." But the democratic Russian Provisional Government had failed to heed the overwhelming popular demand for Russia's withdrawal from the war. It had proved incompetent to deal effectively with an increasingly violent quarrel between left and right factions of its Socialist majority. Its failure, a failure of democracy, was what had enabled Vladimir Lenin and his fellow ideological (Marxist) extremists to seize power in the Red October. And in their hands, working with a people who in all its long history had experienced little personal liberty and virtually no freedom of a political nature, socialism in Russia had become something very different from the democratic socialism of the Fabians in England or of the Social Democrats in central and western Europe or even the socialism (a "classless" society) which Marx saw emergent from "inevitable" class war between bourgeoisie and proletariat.* It was no extension of democracy from the political into the economic realm, now that meaningful distinction between the two realms was increasingly blotted out by the social effects of technological advance; it in no way resembled the kind of "industrial democracy" that the Socialist party of America aimed for: a cooperative system, democratically planned and administered, that would enhance personal liberty by increasing the number of opportunities for employment and ways of living among which individual choices might be made. Instead, Russian socialism was totalitarian communism, an iron dictatorship that employed terror with unprecedented efficiency to "liquidate the bourgeoisie" (meaning all who opposed the regime), nationalize industry, "collectivize" agriculture, stifle effective dissent, crush the individual person into mass man, and make of mass man the material of a machine state. Such economic success as this regime achieved was purchased at enormous cost in human suffering and lives—so enormous a cost that it could be neither wholly hidden behind the remarkably tight-woven screen of Soviet censorship nor wholly counteracted, discounted, by the equally effective (in view of a widely prevailing wish to believe) Communist propaganda. Mass executions, horrible tortures, widespread hunger, the forced labor of thousands under brutal guards in prison camps—these had been a running accompaniment of Soviet "progress" since the end of the Civil War in Russia, and they were markedly increased in scope and intensity since Stalin's capture of control over the ruling party machinery in the fall of 1926. Driblets of news about them, seeping through or around the censorship, had piled up to such persuasive height or depth in America's consciousness that Communist propaganda in this country now tempered its denials that the events occurred with assertions that they were necessary, made so by class war. The bourgeoisie was to blame!

On this very Thursday evening, in some American newspapers and magazines, there was a driblet of doubtful news, really no more than a puzzling hint, of what would eventually become known to all well-informed Americans as

*"Bolshevism triumphed in Russia . . . because there were in Russia no bourgeois," asserted Ortega y Gasset, going on to say that this "ought to be enough to convince us once and for all that Marxian Socialism and Bolshevism are two historical phenomena which have hardly a single common denominator."[2]

the worst famine in Russia's history and one of the worst in the history of the world.[3] This news was a report from *Pravda,* distributed by Tass, that the Soviet agricultural collectivization program was proceeding smoothly according to plan and that contrary to reports being currently circulated by certain foreign "enemies" of Communism, Soviet citizens not only were well fed but had produced a surplus of grain for export abroad. (Actually the Russian peasants and kulaks [well-to-do farmers], especially those of the Ukraine and northern Caucasus, had stubbornly resisted the taking of their land and persons into the collective farms. They had engaged in a kind of farm strike, deliberately producing in 1932 a crop much smaller than was called for by Gosplan and some 12 percent less than the production in an average year. To this, the government response had been punitive and merciless. Grain and other foodstuff were seized from their storage in the countryside and transported to industrial areas. A good deal of them went into foreign trade; Soviet grain exports in 1932 and 1933 were eight times as great as those of 1929 and 1930. A result was the "liquidation" by starvation of the peasants and kulaks. Between 3 and 5 million of them died of hunger in 1932. "The men died first," wrote a Soviet author matter-of-factly thirty years later, "then the children, and finally the woman."[4] Hundreds if not thousands of them had died since the sun rose on this first March Thursday of 1933. The final death toll would be ten million, according to Stalin himself.[5]

Surely there was no real bright offset here to the dark news out of Germany, China, Japan! Not for anyone committed to democracy. Not for anyone who placed supreme value on the individual person and consequently believed that the only proper aim of any social organization is the improved welfare, the increased happiness and creative self-expressiveness of the individuals involved in it. Certainly not for anyone who loathed violence and cruelty and dreaded the coming of new world war.

Virtually every bit of the solid information that came to Americans about Soviet Russia, good or bad, was discouraging to a faith in democracy. The bad news—of terror, of repression—was of a piece with the news of barbarism rising against civilization, of barbarians on the march, elsewhere in the world, and of the failure of human decency to organize effectively against this barbarism. The good news, indicating that Russian communism might ultimately succeed in its own terms, seemed also by this very fact to indicate that advancing scientific technology (and technology *must* advance since "progress is inevitable") implies an increasingly machinelike state of which the individual citizen is a cog and within which individual liberty is severely curtailed, if not abolished altogether. The issue seemed to have become freedom versus organization, with the latter bound to win out over the former as ever-closer, ever-tighter interdependencies were generated by the technological advance.

As for the horrendous broils the oncoming of which was so dreaded by the knowledgeable and civilized on this Thursday evening, there was a very real sense in which communism was historically responsible for them since it was responsible in this same sense for the rise of fascism, the rise of nazism. The fact became obvious when the Russian Revolution was viewed in its world-historical context. Revolutionary socialism had been for decades an international movement when the Bolsheviks seized power in the Red October of 1917, but this movement now became far more effectively organized. The Communists at once proclaimed their conquest of power in Russia to be but the first act of a world revolution which, in accord with Marxist tenets, must "inevitably" bring communism into power everywhere. They had continued to proclaim this through subversive international organization and propaganda ever since, if with a major shift of emphasis after Stalin, having defeated Trotsky in the struggle for power following Lenin's death, had begun to concentrate on "socialism in one country" and make of the Comintern an instrument of Soviet national interest. Communists did all they could, under the direction of Moscow, to foment revolutionary unrest in the capitalist countries of the West. And this initiated the process of action-reaction that now worked inexorably toward general war. Communism became a serious threat in postwar Italy and Germany especially. The reaction to it by the power elites of those nations was financial aid and political protection for Mussolini and Hitler, whose gangs of uniformed thugs waged street war on the Communists—aid and protection without which neither gangster leader could have survived grievous setbacks as he struggled toward power. Each countered Communist internationalism with the most extreme nationalism, each dedicated himself to the crushing of communism and the creation of a warrior state, each proclaimed his love of war as a breeder of all manly virtue, and each could be counted upon—would indeed be compelled by the manner in which he had obtained and now exercised ruling power—to launch as soon as possible aggressive, imperialistic adventures. There would be wars of conquest. These seemed certain to spread into new world war. And of this war, civilization's survival seemed highly doubtful.

Certainly the two leading democracies of Europe, those of France and Britain, gave little sign at that moment of the intelligent energy, the vital commitment and strength of will and steadiness of nerve that were obviously needed to scatter the falling darkness, to crush the rising barbarism, and so to reverse the prevailing trend. They appeared futile and ineffective, their minds dulled, their spirits broken, their energies exhausted by the Great War. Of the best of the generation now holding in its hands the reins of governing power, each country had lost a high percentage in the war, and if there had been no proportionate increase in the percentage of barbarians among the surviving national populations in general, as appeared to have happened in Germany and Italy, the percentage increase was substantial. It was sufficient to lower the average of competence, blur the definitions of national purpose, and prevent any bold national decisiveness. In both countries, especially in France, there were Communist and Fascist movements that made war on parliamentary democracy as they did on each other. In both countries, especially in France, there was a wavering weakness of government as party groupings were broken into special-interest blocs, which in turn became the

units of precarious coalition majorities. In France ministries had succeeded
one another with dizzying rapidity since the onset of world depression, a dozen
of them within the last twelve months. In Britain a Labor government under
Prime Minister Ramsay MacDonald had collapsed in 1931 under the pressure
of demands for drastic government economies in order to keep Britain on the
gold standard, economies that included deep cuts in the dole for the unemployed. This Labor government had been succeeded by a national coalition
government, inclusive of Conservative, Labor, and Liberal members, with
MacDonald as prime minister, though his own party bitterly opposed the
coalition and promptly expelled him from its ranks, along with all other party
leaders who joined him. Ambiguity was thus compounded in Whitehall. Clarity of mind and boldness of decision were made impossible there.

Evidently, then, as it seemed to millions of Americans and millions abroad on
this gloomy Thursday evening, the only hope for freedom and civilization was
the United States of America. If there was any bright offset to the prevailing
darkness, if there was any possibility of survival for personal liberty and
democratic government and for a reversal of the current world trend, it must
be sought and found and creatively realized here. Yet here, too, God knew,
were troubles enough to cloud any happy vision of things to come!
    For it was in America, after all, that the worldwide Great Depression had
been signaled and triggered by the stock market crash of '29, itself a manifestation of breakdown in the American mind and character. Everywhere one
looked, here in America, was apparent confirmation of the view that capitalism
had so totally failed it could never be revived and that the American democracy was going down with it. Factories produced at far less than their capacity
for production or ceased to produce at all, with the result that more than a
fourth of the total labor force was unemployed, and there was no new employment opportunity in sight for these dozen or more millions since industrial
prices and profits continued downward despite production cuts. Agricultural
prices and profits fell even farther and faster because agricultural production
remained as high as it had ever been. Farmers operating as individuals, though
continuously and loudly exhorted by government to grow less, were unable to
do so in the absence of guarantees that their neighbors would do the same. The
consequence was a market surplus of grain and fiber that overflowed storage
facilities while millions of shabbily dressed and poorly fed Americans, thousands of them within sight of the bulging bins and warehouses and elevators,
suffered for lack of processed fiber, processed grain, and the meat which grain
used as livestock feed would have nourished. Among the impoverished were
farmers who had produced these surpluses, some of whom in the corn belt that
winter were burning their corn to heat their homes because at prevailing prices
it was a cheaper fuel than coal. In every city were lengthening breadlines. In
every city was a proliferation of Hoovervilles—clusters of ramshackle huts,
tar-papered, roofed and walled sometimes with flattened tin cans, set down in
urban wastelands. In them huddled miserably, hopelessly, a discarded human-

ity. There was much aimless moving about, a restlessness of undirected, unpat-
terned energies. Every freight train moving across the land bore its quota of
homeless men and boys, who wandered from place to place, living on handouts
and odd jobs as they looked for steady work. Along every highway were
hitchhikers, thumbing their way from here to there, not knowing or much
caring where "there" might be. And conditions were not markedly better for
millions who still had jobs. They as individuals were as helpless to resist
exploitation by business organizations as farmers were in the face of exploitation through an allegedly "free" market that was actually rigged against them.
In factories, mines, steel mills, textile mills, they labored long hours for wages
well below those required to maintain a decent standard of living.

Nor was there any sign anywhere that the depression's bottom had been
reached, that things could not become worse and must therefore (in view of
the ceaselessness of change) become better soon. Indeed, the latest news of the
economy, glaring out through big headlines in the evening papers of this
March 2, outstripping by far in American reader interest the dark news from
abroad, was of yet further crackup and downturn, and this the most dreadful
and threatful of all to Americans of the middle and upper classes. Banks had
been failing at an unprecedented rate since the onset of the depression. Millions
of depositors had lost part or all of their savings. Now the whole of the national
credit structure, upon which all economic activity depended, was rapidly
collapsing and seemingly beyond any possibility of reconstruction. Ruinous
runs by scared depositors upon shaky banks, and the certainty of more such
runs in the immediate future, had caused half the states in the Union to close
by executive order all banks within their boundaries. Nearly all other state
governments had ordered severe restrictions on banking operations, drastically
limiting the amount of money any depositor could withdraw, and were now
seriously considering, or had already decided upon, total-closing orders. There
were printed rumors that Chicago and New York, the nation's two largest
cities, had suffered drains upon their banks so debilitating that the banks'
continued functioning beyond the coming weekend was doubtful. That such
rumors were of probable truth was indicated by a report from the Federal
Reserve, issued that day and printed in the evening papers—a report that the
Treasury's gold reserves had been reduced by $226 million during the last
week, while the amount of money in circulation had increased by $732 million,
and that nearly half the gold reserve depletion was due to domestic hoarding.
The report was certain to stimulate a rush of new gold withdrawals and
hoarding next day, along with new runs upon banks. All across America the
wheels of commerce were grinding to a complete stop; a total paralysis of the
national economy was imminent.

And in the face of this catastrophe, which had been developing with few and
brief interruptions for forty dreary months, and at an accelerating pace
through the last half year, the government in Washington had been and
remained impotent. Nothing could be done by government because nothing
should be done that would interfere with "free" market operations, operations

that would inevitably generate "natural" recovery if let alone. This, in sum and substance, had been the answer of the Hoover administration to increasingly loud pleas from the general public, and from much of its congressional representation, for a federal program of unemployment relief, for a program of concrete aid to individual farmers, and especially, overall, for strong and definite government action to start up again the engines of the national economy. Yet this same administration had not been loath to provide concrete aid to big business through a raising of tariff walls to their highest point in history and through massive low-interest government loans, a fact that had encouraged such economic class antagonisms, such acute sense of "class war" between the haves and have-nots, as had not been felt in America since the era of Andrew Jackson. A natural consequence had been the massive repudiation by the American electorate of Herbert Hoover and the Republican party in the national elections of last November.

Such national decisiveness had been almost wholly negative, however. Only very doubtfully, tentatively, could the repudiation of the Hoover administration be construed as an endorsement of President-elect Franklin D. Roosevelt and the administration to come. Few voters, after all, had had any notion what the new administration's programs and policies would be; there was strong suspicion among the knowledgeable that Roosevelt himself had no clear notion what they would be. Certainly the victor's campaign speeches had been notably lacking in sharp definitions and precise specifications as they dealt with issues between himself and his opposition, had evidently been designed far less to communicate information and ideas, and to stimulate thought, than to evoke favorable emotional responses and make pleasing personal impressions. They had evidently accomplished their primary image-making purposes, but no one could be sure that even this success was not in essence more a revulsion against Hoover's dour countenance and gloomy speech than an attraction toward Roosevelt's big smile,[6] his constant optimism of address. And save for those having to do with Muscle Shoals and the development of hydroelectric power, the President-elect's public utterances since election day had been as impressionistic, as unspecific, as his campaign addresses.

The outgoing President had had to work during the long and increasingly troubled interregnum with a recalcitrant lame-duck Congress of which Democrats were an elected majority in the House and, in the Senate, were but one vote shy of a majority and were often joined with dissident Republicans to deny presidential requests. Hoover had therefore made repeated efforts to associate the incoming President with him, publicly, in key policy decisions upon matters that had not been raised as issues during the campaign, such matters as war debts, foreign trade, international currency stabilization, and, latterly, the growing banking crisis. He had claimed that he could not act in these concerns without his successor's concurrence and support. These efforts had been rebuffed, their justifying claim denied, by Franklin Roosevelt. Responsibility and authority were indissolubly joined, he said; he would take no responsibility for deeds only the President had authority to perform.

Clearly the check-and-balance system of American democracy, with its built-in adversarial relationships among legislature, executive, and judiciary, had not been and was not now working for the benefit of the great mass of the citizenry during this time of crisis. And there were not wanting American voices proclaiming that democratic government, no matter how organized, is by its very nature incompetent to govern a great modern state, is unable to make the swift, substantial responses that are demanded by swift, substantial alterations of situation in this age of ceaseless, drastic change. In the very best of times, the most stable of times, political democracy is inefficient, these harsh voices said. In this worst of times it fails and is bound to fail utterly. It does so because its way of making decisions, through parliamentary procedure and debate ("wrangling" was commonly used as synonym for "deliberation" in descriptions of the workings of Congress), poured a flood of words into the gap between perception and conception and between conception and execution, widening these gaps so greatly that, often enough, conception and execution were prevented altogether. This could be fatal. It was likely to be in the immediate situation. More and more loudly, therefore, and more and more explicitly on the part of right-wing extremists, came calls for a wholesale transfer of legislative capacity from Capitol Hill to White House, enabling the incoming President to rule by decree, at least for the duration of the present acute emergency. A few extreme conservatives flatly publicly asserted the need for an American Mussolini, a concentration of power in the American executive as great as that given the executive in Italy (a constitutional monarchy) in 1922 and in process of being given the executive in Germany (a republic) in this third month of 1933. From the far left came more muted but gradually swelling cries for a social revolution which would end in a concentration of executive power as great as that called for by the extreme right but substantially different in that it would be not a dictatorship of the prevailing elite, the big businessmen who had been the most potent of all influences upon American government for the last dozen years, but a "dictatorship of the proletariat," modeled on the Soviet Union.

Such ultimate conclusions, however, were seriously considered by relatively few of America's citizens and concurred in by fewer still.

The overwhelming majority of Americans, despite their dismay and confusion over the way things were going and the anger they felt toward men of power, who had, they felt, betrayed and exploited them, remained committed to the American democracy defined by the Declaration of Independence, by the Constitution of the United States in its Bill of Rights and general welfare clauses, and by the most memorable words and historic deeds of the greatest Presidents—Jefferson and Jackson and Wilson, Teddy Roosevelt and Lincoln. Especially Abraham Lincoln, the Lincoln who, during a flag-raising ceremony at Independence Hall in Philadelphia on February 22, 1861, claimed he had "never had a feeling politically that did not spring from the Declaration of Independence," the Lincoln who had "often inquired" of himself "what great principle or idea" had kept the Union "so long together," his answer being that it was the "something" in the Declaration "giving liberty, not alone to the people of this country, but hope to the world for all future time."[7]

When Lincoln spoke these words, he was on his way to Washington for inauguration as President of a United States that was no longer united but split into two hostile nations, each a republic proclaiming its devotion to freedom (though in one of them it was the freedom of some people to enslave others), between which would soon rage bloody war.

And now, seventy-two years later, the continued commitment of the American people to freedom, to democracy bred hopes proportionate to the growing threat of death to all that civilized men hold dear.

Admittedly they were defiant hopes, shot through with fear and despair.

But they were as fervent as they were fearful and desperate.

And they focused massively upon a single man, the laughing, big, confident, physically crippled man who had been chosen to lead a crippled nation out of sick depression into a new order of prosperous good health and who at this very moment of a gloomy Thursday was journeying by rail toward Washington, toward the White House he would occupy on the day after tomorrow.

BOOK ONE

⇢⇢⫲⫷⫷

The New Deal Begins

Do I contradict myself?
Very well then I contradict myself.
(I am large, I contain multitudes.)
　　　　　　—WALT WHITMAN
　　　　　　　"Song of Myself"

I

->>X<<-

Inauguration amid Crisis

I

As the evening sun went down and wintry darkness fell upon this Thursday, March 2, 1933, Franklin Delano Roosevelt sat in pensive mood, though with no break in his show of confidence to those who conferred with him, in an easy chair in the rear car of the Baltimore & Ohio train that bore him southward, his steel-braced polio-withered legs often crossed but also often stretched out before him.

Ahead of him on this same train rode a considerable portion of the cast that would support his stellar role in the drama of history now about to begin.

Most of the members of his immediate family were aboard. The most important of them, measured in terms of influence upon his future career, was Anna Eleanor Roosevelt Roosevelt, his wife, who was also his fifth cousin and the niece of Teddy Roosevelt, the mother of his five children, two of whom —James with his wife, Betsey (née Cushing), and Elliott—were also on the train. So was the regal *grande dame* Sara Delano Roosevelt, the President-elect's mother, between whom and Eleanor was ceaseless psychological war, forever inconclusive and futile, for possession of the soul of Franklin Roosevelt. Virtually a member of the family, and in some ways closer to the President-elect than any having blood ties to him, was wizened, sickly, tiny, shrewd Louis McHenry Howe, by far the most intimate of Roosevelt's longtime friends, without whose selfless devotion to him of unusual abilities over more than two decades he almost certainly would not now be riding toward his presidential inauguration. Howe rode this train as one of the family; he would live with the family in the White House; he was appointed head of the White House secretariat and would have in that post an influence upon great events hard to define precisely but at least equivalent in strength to that of most cabinet ministers, for as long as his fading health permitted. Virtually of the family, too, riding this train, were sweet-faced and -tempered Marguerite "Missy" LeHand, Roosevelt's beloved and phenomenally skillful and efficient personal secretary (she had been for a dozen years), and her close friend, assistant, and fellow Roman Catholic Grace Tully, who these last years had taken and transcribed most of Roosevelt's dictation. (Tully's normally rosy complexion was pale this evening; she had a constant hacking cough; she would soon be forced to take a year's leave of absence to recuperate from active tuberculosis.) Somewhat less intimately of the innermost circle but very much a part of it were thin, cadaverous Marvin McIntyre, the former newspaper and newsreel journalist who was to be presidential appointments secretary, and

Stephen "Steve" Early, the fiery-tempered southerner who would become White House press secretary and whose white southerner racist attitudes would sometimes clash with Eleanor's championship of black rights but whose overall performance would prove of immense value to Roosevelt personally and to the New Deal.

Others aboard included Columbia University (Barnard College) Professor of Government Raymond Moley, acknowledged head of the informal group of Roosevelt "idea men" dubbed the Brain Trust, who had accepted appointment as assistant secretary of state, from which post he would continue to serve as Roosevelt's chief policy adviser; handsome, youthful, brilliant Rexford Guy Tugwell, a Columbia University economics professor who had been Moley's first choice for membership in the Brain Trust and had accepted appointment as assistant secretary of agriculture, from which post he, too, would continue to serve as Roosevelt policy adviser; and Henry Morgenthau, Jr., whose Hudson River estate was near Roosevelt's in Dutchess County and who with his wife, Elinor, was a longtime social friend of the Roosevelts, had headed the agricultural portion of Roosevelt's gubernatorial administration of New York, and was slated to head, and liquidate, the Federal Farm Board. Aboard, also, were broad-faced, stolid-appearing, but highly intelligent Samuel I. Rosenman, a first-class legal mind and a remarkably orderly mind, who had served Governor Roosevelt as speech writer and legal counsel and was destined to become the President's chief speech writer and editor in years to come; Josephus Daniels, the now-elderly North Carolina newspaperman whom the President-elect still called Chief because he had been secretary of the navy when Roosevelt was assistant secretary in the Wilson administration and who in years to come would serve the nation greatly as U.S. ambassador to revolutionary Mexico; and sensitive, retiring, intellectually sophisticated Edward "Ed" J. Flynn, who, incongruously, as it seemed, was tough Democratic "boss" of the Bronx Democratic organization in New York and had been only somewhat less valuable to presidential candidate Roosevelt than Howe had been during the latter part (the last four years) of the rocky road to the White House.

Three cabinet appointees rode on this train.

One was the former governor of Utah, George H. Dern, appointed secretary of war—a good solid man of conservative outlook and temperament, though classified as a "western progressive," who would play no key role in the coming New Deal but would serve the President well on matters assigned him during the next two years, until ill health limited his effectiveness.

Another was big, bald, immensely likable James A. Farley, the professional Irish-American politician (he signed all his letters in green ink) and devout Roman Catholic who had managed Roosevelt's hugely triumphant reelection campaign in 1930 and the Roosevelt presidential campaign last year. He would serve in the cabinet as postmaster general, a post with much patronage power that was traditionally assigned successful presidential campaign managers.

The third cabinet appointee aboard was sweet-natured little William H. Woodin, designated secretary of the treasury, whose elfin appearance and unassertiveness of manner belied a shrewdness and toughness that had served him well in big business (he had been president of the American Car and Foundry Company) and would, along with his conservative economic views and sweet reasonableness, be of determinative historical importance during the days and weeks just ahead. He had a creative passion for music that far exceeded his desire for personal power and was no doubt responsible in good part for the remarkable detachment, the disinterestedness, with which he wielded the power placed in his hands; it made the latter exercise seem to him, one suspects, comparatively dull and even boring. He was a composer as well as a talented performer on piano and guitar. Two of his compositions were to be featured during the inaugural festivities. The National Symphony Orchestra under the baton of Hans Kindler would present tomorrow evening, in Washington's Constitution Hall, a concert to be broadcast over a national radio network, and one of the compositions performed would be Will Woodin's "On the Prairie" from his *Covered Wagon Suite.* On the following day, in the inaugural parade, marching bands would play Will Woodin's newly composed "Franklin D. Roosevelt Inaugural March." And it is likely that these coming events were almost as much on his mind, were almost as absorptive of his interest as the banking crisis.

About this last he and Moley conferred with the President-elect, and at some length, at least once while on this train.

President Hoover in the White House had been pressed very hard all that day to take drastic federal executive action to halt a flight of gold into domestic hoarding and overseas which, if it continued at its present rate for many more hours, could totally ruin the national credit structure. The Treasury Department and the Federal Reserve Board urged him to issue at once an executive order closing for a stated period every bank in the country, using emergency powers assigned the executive by a Trading with the Enemy Act that had been adopted during the Great War and never repealed. Hoover had indicated his willingness to do this, though he personally thought it too drastic a move, preferring a declaration of national emergency whereby the President would be empowered, under the aforementioned act, to limit cash withdrawals from banks and to control all shipments of gold. He would take neither action, however, unless it were publicly concurred in by the President-elect—the stipulation he had stubbornly insisted upon all through the interregnum in his dealings with matters affecting international economic relations, despite Roosevelt's equally stubborn refusal to agree to it. Hoover was now more adamant on this point than ever before because of his cold fury over an incident that had occurred five days ago, on Saturday, February 25.

Rex Tugwell had lunched that Saturday with James H. Rand, Jr., of Remington Rand, Inc., and during the lunch he had talked indiscreetly, to say the least, about the Roosevelt camp's attitude toward the deteriorating banking situation. Rand, outraged by what he had heard, promptly reported the conversation by phone to Hoover's private secretary, who, of course, promptly reported it to Hoover. According to Rand, Tugwell had "said that they [those in the incoming administration] were fully aware" that the banking structure "would undoubtedly collapse in a few days" and that the impending event caused them no dismay since it "would place the responsibility in the lap of President Hoover" while giving the new administration "a free hand" and all credit for "rehabilitating the country after March 4th." By this Hoover's darkest suspicions concerning his successor in office had been confirmed. "When I consider this statement of Professor Tugwell's in connection with the recommendations we have made to the incoming administration," he had written to Rand, "I can say emphatically that it breathes with infamous politics devoid of every atom of patriotism."[1]

And as Hoover's determination not to act without Roosevelt's public concurrence was thus hardened, so in reaction was Roosevelt's determination to maintain to the end the noncommittal stance he had adopted four months before. He indicated as much to Will Woodin when the latter reported to him, on the train, Hoover's proposals, Woodin having kept in close touch by phone with the Treasury Department in Washington all day. Herbert Hoover was still President of the United States, said Franklin Roosevelt; he had full legal authority to act as he saw fit in this matter, whereas Roosevelt had no authority whatever. If there were doubts that the Trading with the Enemy Act remained in force, doubts, therefore, about the legal validity of any executive action taken under it—and admittedly there were such doubts, among Roosevelt's advisers as among Hoover's—it was up to Hoover to resolve them by decision, one way or the other. Roosevelt himself had pretty much made up his mind what to do; he would do it when he had the authority to do it, which would not be until midday of March 4. He would take no responsibility for anything Hoover did in the meantime.

After Woodin had left the stateroom Roosevelt occupied, the President-elect sat alone for a time. It had been near dusk when he and his party boarded the train on the New Jersey side of the Hudson River, across which they had been ferried. Now full night had come. Roosevelt looked out through the window beside him into a darkness punctuated by the lonely lights of farms, the clustered lights of villages, the solid islands of light that were the business sections of town and cities—looked out upon the night-shrouded body of a nearly paralyzed nation—and felt such emotion, thought such thoughts as Lincoln may have felt and thought when he, on the night of Washington's Birthday in 1861, rode the rear sleeping car of a train along this same route toward his tragic destiny in Washington. After a while Roosevelt felt a need to talk to someone, quietly, seriously—someone who might share, without intellectual assessment of it, some of the feeling that welled up in him. A religious feeling.

He pushed the bell button beside him. He asked the responding porter to find Jim Farley up ahead and invite him back here.

Some might think this a strange choice of companion for him to make at such a time, in his present mood. Farley was not, nor could he ever be, one of Roosevelt's intimate friends. But he was a restful companion who was naturally inclined to agree and affirm what was said to him. He was, to

Roosevelt, humbly subordinate. He listened well, without interjecting views of his own. And his religious faith, a Roman Catholicism not formally very different from Roosevelt's Anglicanism, was as strong and simple and unquestioned as Roosevelt's own. To Farley or (more probably) to himself, with Farley as vital sounding board, he talked of God, of the efficacy of prayer and the absolute need for it in this time of trouble, of a great nation's religious faith as the single most important prerequisite of its survival beyond this time (such faith was more important than carefully worked-out plans for dealing with the depression, he said), and of his own plan to begin his inaugural day with a prayer, a public, symbolic prayer. There would be a brief religious service for him and his family and associates in St. John's Episcopal Church, near the White House, shortly before he went to the White House to begin his ride to the inaugural platform on Capitol Hill.[2]

And as he talked, there may well have echoed through the nether corridors of his mind some of the words that Abraham Lincoln spoke in farewell to his Springfield friends and neighbors on the day of his departure for his own inauguration. "I now leave," Lincoln had then said, "not knowing when, or whether ever, I may return, with a task before me greater than that which rested on Washington. Without the assistance of that Divine Being who ever attended him, I cannot succeed. With that assistance, I cannot fail. Trusting in him who can go with me, and remain with you, and be everywhere for good, let us confidently hope that all will yet be well."

II

THOUGH the train was not scheduled to arrive until sometime after nine o'clock and though rain had begun to fall, a large crowd was gathered by eight o'clock on the platform beside the tracks of Washington's Union Station. It remained there, augmented by new arrivals, despite what soon became a steady downpour. Another large crowd was inside the building, gathered there in the belief (so slight was the public's knowledge of the extent of Roosevelt's physical disability) that the President-elect would climb the stairs into the station's central hall and pass through that hall on his way to the automobile that waited for him. The crowd was cheerful, determinedly so, despite the chill and damp and gloom of night. Its mood, though subdued, was "distinctly hopeful," as Arthur Krock of the New York *Times* described the general mood of the capital to be that day. Everyone who watched and waited was "ready to be enthusiastic over any display of leadership" after two long years miserably devoid of such display, eager to be convinced that the leader for whom he yearned, the messiah for whom he prayed, was indeed the man whose arrival was awaited.

At precisely 9:25 the section of the train containing the President-elect and his party backed into the station yard through rain that fell in slanting, slender lines of yellow light, reflecting the glow of electric sulfur lamps placed far apart along the tracks. An expectant hush settled over the crowd. The car in which Roosevelt rode was the farthest from the crowd when it came to a halt at the easternmost extremity of the station. At once, an automobile drove up beside this car. At once "a gangway with shining brass rails was put into place" at the rear platform steps of the çar. Roosevelt emerged onto the rear platform. As if on cue, while a roaring cheer burst from the crowd and photographers' flashbulbs exploded in thick cluster, the rain abruptly ceased. Not a drop fell on the President-elect as he made his way down the ramp to the waiting automobile where, having "made himself comfortable in the seat," he "leaned back" with a smile upon his face that was evidently enigmatic, since the *Times* reporter described it as "the smile of a man who is coming into his own, a smile with something of excitement in it, just a little nervous pleasure." Then the automobile moved off, very slowly, Louis Howe walking ahead of it "to aid the chauffeur in avoiding the protruding parts of all the other cars in the narrow way" until open space was reached and a motorcycle escort "roared into action." Within ten minutes after the train had appeared, the cavalcade of autos bearing the President-elect had "swept through the iron gates and into the night."[3]

Roosevelt was taken to the Mayflower Hotel, where he and his wife were assigned the Presidential Suite and where, from 10:30 P.M. until 12:30 in the morning of Friday, March 3, he conferred with, among others, Senators Joseph Robinson of Arkansas, James Byrnes of South Carolina, Key Pittman of Nevada, and Cordell Hull of Tennessee (Hull was to become secretary of state in the new cabinet), and with Jesse Jones of Texas, Democratic member and soon to be chairman of the board of the Reconstruction Finance Corporation, concerning the banking crisis and the action which must be taken with regard to it. He made clear to his conferees, as he was sure he had made clear to Herbert Hoover, that he would positively take no action whatever on this until he was inaugurated President of the United States.

Yet still Hoover persisted, going now well beyond the bounds of a decent respect for his successor.

At four o'clock in the afternoon of that Friday, March 3, Roosevelt with Eleanor and son James and James's wife, Betsey, paid the courtesy call upon the outgoing President which tradition prescribed. He came to the White House with no expectation of enjoyment. He knew that the Hoover invitation to tea had been grudgingly issued in lieu of the dinner which it was customary for an outgoing President to serve an incoming one on the eve of inaugural day. He did not, however, anticipate any such unpleasantness as actually occurred. His nephew Warren Delano Robbins, the State Department protocol officer, greeted him officially in the entrance hall and there whispered to him information conveyed by the White House usher, Ike Hoover*—to wit, that the President planned to take advantage of Roosevelt and the occasion to force a policy discussion of the banking crisis. Ogden Mills, secretary of the treasury, and Eugene Meyer, governor of the Federal Reserve Board, waited in an adjoining room; they would be called in as soon as the social amenities were

---

*Ike Hoover, no relation of Herbert Hoover, had an intense personal dislike of the latter, as did many, if not most, of the White House staff.

disposed of, while Mrs. Hoover entertained Eleanor and Betsey Roosevelt in another room. There would then be three against one, with the three thoroughly prepared to reinforce one another's pressure upon the one who was taken by surprise. "Call Moley!" Roosevelt whispered to Robbins. The professor, roused from a desperately needed catnap in his Mayflower Hotel room, appeared at Roosevelt's side within a minute or two after Meyer and Mills appeared at Hoover's.

The talk that followed, lasting an hour and ten minutes, far beyond the time that would have been consumed by a mere courtesy call, as reporters duly noted, was worse than useless. At its end Roosevelt, who believed it customary for an "outgoing President to return the call of an incoming one," remarked that he would "understand completely" if in the present instance, in view of the crisis situation, the custom was not honored. Hoover stiffened. For the first time that afternoon he looked his guest straight in the eye. "Mr. Roosevelt," he said coldly, "when you are in Washington as long as I have been you will learn that the President of the United States calls on nobody."

Roosevelt's polite smile abruptly faded. "I shall be waiting at my hotel, Mr. President, to learn what you decide," he said. Then, according to his own account of the incident, "I hustled my family from the room."[4]

That night Hoover made two phone calls to Roosevelt—one at 11:30 P.M., the other at 1:00 A.M. Again he asked Roosevelt to approve a presidential order controlling withdrawals and gold shipments. Again Roosevelt refused, then went to bed.

Moley was with Roosevelt when Hoover's second phone call came, and as he left the Presidential Suite, he met in the hallway a worried Will Woodin. At the topmost level of national decision, in this time of desperate crisis, the decision was to do nothing at all, and both Moley and Woodin were convinced that the "paramount interests of the nation" required a cooperation between the outgoing and incoming administrations which the personal animosity between Hoover and Roosevelt rendered seemingly impossible. They therefore agreed to "take a chance" and did so, at Woodin's instigation. Acting on no instructions from the President-elect, and even without his knowledge, acutely aware that what they were about to say and do could have only such decisive authority as their superior later conferred upon their words and deeds, they went "over to the Treasury . . . [to] see if we can give those fellows there a hand," as Woodin put it.[5]

Insured by this impulsive act was a continuity of technical administrative operation in Treasury which the Hoover-Roosevelt impasse threatened to disrupt. Insured also, and far more consequently, was a continuity of overall governmental purpose and policy.*

For at a moment in history when radical departures were not merely possible but widely expected of the new administration and were also widely favored

---

*Actually, the two kinds of continuity were inextricably joined; to preserve the existing technical administrative procedures through and beyond the crisis was to preserve the existing "system" without fundamental change.

among a distressed populace, at a moment when even any "unorthodoxy [in governmental dealings with the crisis] would have drained the last remaining strength from the capitalistic system," according to Moley, at this watershed moment the two men who undertook to speak and act for Roosevelt were as one with Herbert Hoover and Hoover's officers in their unquestioning commitment to a profit-oriented society, to "free enterprise," and to thoroughly conservative, wholly orthodox approaches to problems of money and banking. Insofar as they could prevent it, there would be no basic change whatever in the "system" or even any significant alteration of the prevailing pattern of property and income distribution. Ignored in practice was the central thesis of the "Forgotten Man" speech which Roosevelt had given during the campaign, a thesis which had at least seemed to point toward some revision of economic class structure to effect a wider distribution of power. Subscribed to instead was the "trickle-down" theory, as it came later to be called, applied now alike to the spread of material wealth and the creation of national psychological mood. No less than the Hoover men (Mills, Arthur Ballantine, Meyer), Woodin and Moley were, in the latter's words, "intent upon rallying the confidence, first, of the conservative business and banking leaders of the country and, then, through them, of the public generally."[6]

Such rallying required, however, "swift and staccato action" (Woodin's phrase) the initial moves of which the "conservative . . . banking leaders" were by no means all of a mind, or will, to make. Moley and Woodin's special contribution during the dark early-morning hours of March 4 was an effective pressure upon Governor Herbert Lehman of New York to order the closing of all banks in that state, despite insistence by New York City's leading bankers that the closing order wasn't necessary for their own survival, which, evidently, was all they cared about. Similar pressure upon Illinois's governor had similar results, overcoming similar resistance by Chicago's top bankers.

It was near dawn of inauguration day when Moley and Woodin, worn and haggard, emerged from the Treasury Building. By that time every bank in thirty-two states had been closed by state governmental edict; almost every bank was closed in six other states; and in the remaining ten states, plus the District of Columbia, bank withdrawals were limited to 5 percent of deposits or, in the case of Texas, no more than $10 in a single day. No bank anywhere in the country was performing its normal credit functions. America lay prostrate, economically, as Moley and Woodin made their way in a shared taxicab to their respective hotels.*

III

No bright sun rose up out of Chesapeake Bay to warm Prince Georges County and the District of Columbia at this dawning of Saturday, March 4, 1933. The weather in the nation's capital was as dreary as the national mood had been in recent weeks.

---

*Woodin had a room in the Carlton.

Franklin Roosevelt, awaking from sound sleep at his usual hour despite the lateness of his night before, saw through the windows of his room a leaden sky, a shadowless street, a leafless tree bough that shuddered spasmodically in gusts of chill gray wind, and though his own mood was by no means of a piece with the weather's, it was assuredly unwontedly solemn. His manner was grave, his face unsmiling, as he heard and read over his breakfast tray messages of utmost gravity. He joked not at all with bodyguard Augustus "Gus" Gennerich and valet Irvin McDuffie as these two helped him into the striped trousers, wing-collared shirt, and black coat of formal morning attire. He remained grave when, a few minutes after ten, with silk top hat on his head and black astra-khan-collared coat draped over his huge torso, he descended to the street and there entered an open car which bore him, his wife, his mother, his eldest son with Betsey, across the few blocks separating the Mayflower from St. John's Episcopal Church.

And his was a sober churchly mien as with his party he entered the church auditorium, though he briefly smiled and nodded in recognition of people he passed on his way to the forward pew assigned him. A hundred men and women stood up at his entrance—longtime friends, cabinet appointees, family relations, close working associates, each of them present by his or his wife's express invitation—and did not sit again until he, his leg braces unlocked at the knees, had done so. In the pulpit, in ecclesiastical robe, stood the revered and reverend mentor of his boyhood and youth, Rector Endicott Peabody of Groton School, who in his seventy-sixth year remained tall, erect, vigorous of voice and gesture. Religious music was played upon the organ. Selections were read from the Book of Common Prayer. Then he who was about to assume with pomp and ceremony the most powerful elective office on earth humbly bowed his head and closed his eyes as the Reverend Dr. Peabody prayed: "O Lord . . . most heartily we beseech Thee . . . to behold and bless Thy servant, Franklin, chosen to be President of the United States." He remained bowed in private prayer, face cupped in hands, for a half minute or so after the rector's loud amen. He rose then, his braces locked, and made his arduous way out of the church, on son James's arm, into the brightening day.

There had been a break in the clouds. The sun now shone upon Lafayette Square and the gleaming White House across the way. But it shone only on that narrow space, and there only briefly. By ten-forty, when Roosevelt arrived back at the Mayflower, the sky was again as solidly overcast, the light in the street as dreary as they had been when he awoke.[7]

Moley and Woodin awaited him in his suite, their faces pale with weariness, drawn with tension.

Roosevelt then listened with a close attention to Moley's succinct account of what had transpired at Treasury during the dark early-morning hours. He heartily approved what Woodin and Moley had done. Moley then presented for Roosevelt's consideration a tripartite recommendation for presidential action in which he and Woodin had concurred with the Hoover men. First, Roosevelt should at once invoke the powers of the Trading with the Enemy Act to declare a national bank holiday, something he had in fact already decided to do; secondly, as he had also already decided, he should call Congress into a special session to open at the earliest possible moment, this to legitimatize the bank-closing order and enact emergency legislation under which an orderly reopening of solvent banks might proceed; thirdly, he should summon to Washington the principal bankers of New York, Chicago, Philadelphia, Baltimore, and Richmond, asking them to assemble on Sunday, March 5, to give procedural advice and help in preparing the emergency legislation. Roosevelt promptly accepted these recommendations and asked his subordinates to see to it that the needed implementing documentation was at once prepared.[8]

As he did so, he again shrugged into his overcoat, held for him by McDuffie, and took his top hat in hand. Two minutes later he began his ride to the White House and the initiation of the inaugural ceremonies.

Seldom, if ever, had a mile seemed as long to Roosevelt, and no doubt to Herbert Hoover also, as the mile the two traversed together, seated side by side in the open car's back seat, up crowd-lined Pennsylvania Avenue to Capitol Hill. Hoover sat in cold, stony silence. He did not so much as glance at his companion after his perfunctory handshake, and he responded not at all to a conversational effort which grew more and more strained on Roosevelt's part (at one point, the President-elect heard himself commenting upon the "lovely steel" being used in a government building under construction) until at last Roosevelt gave it up and began to acknowledge with lifted hat the cheers and applause of the sidewalk crowds. Hoover continued to stare straight ahead.[9]

And Roosevelt himself was again somber, unsmiling, unwontedly abstracted when he entered the Senate Military Affairs Committee room in the Capitol and there sat in his wheelchair while the outgoing President, in the President's room next door, signed or pocket-vetoed the last bill of the last lame-duck congressional session in history.* So obviously was he withdrawn from those around him, absorbed into an inner world, that even the crassly exhibitionist senator from Louisiana, Huey Long, respected his privacy; having rushed up to greet him in typically exuberant fashion, the Kingfish, as he was called after a character in the radio show *Amos 'n' Andy,* halted abruptly and turned away. Then Roosevelt took out his reading copy of the inaugural address to check something that had been bothering him. Its very first sentence didn't seem to him, in his present mood, quite right as an opening. It was too long, too involved. He wanted something which abruptly grasped and focused attention, something in the nature of a religious exhortation, to set the tone of the address as a whole. His pen was in his hand. With it he scribbled atop the first page: "This is a day of consecration."

*The Twentieth Amendment to the Constitution had gone into effect on February 6, 1933, setting January 20 as presidential inauguration day and stipulating that "the Congress . . . assemble at least once in every year, and such meeting shall begin at noon on the third day of January, unless they shall by law appoint a different day." Thus the troublesome lame-duck session was abolished.

A few minutes later, after he had entered the Senate chamber to witness the oathtaking of John Nance Garner as Vice President of the United States, he became somewhat more his usual self, recognizing and smiling upon several of the men around him. But he was still withdrawn, remote.

Then came his own inauguration.

At one o'clock, on the arm of son James, he began his slow, stiff-legged march down a carpeted ramp under a Grecian-pillared canopy to the rostrum on the platform outside the Capitol, where the biblically bearded Charles Evans Hughes, Chief Justice of the United States, awaited him in judicial robe and where, immediately thereafter, right hand upraised and left hand resting upon the huge seventeenth-century Dutch Bible which had been in the Roosevelt family for at least seven generations, he "solemnly" swore in a firm, clear voice that he, Franklin Delano Roosevelt, would "faithfully execute the office of President of the United States and . . . to the best of my ability, preserve, protect, and defend the Constitution of the United States. So help me God." He turned then at once to the lectern. He glanced down at the battery of microphones through which his words would be broadcast to tens of millions of frightened, anxious people; looked out over a throng covering forty acres of Capitol lawn; and, unsmiling, even stern of face, spoke the opening sentence he had just penned, with one word added.

"This," he said with slow emphasis, "is a day of national consecration."

Thereafter he spoke somewhat more rapidly, saying he was "certain that my fellow Americans" expected him to "address them with . . . candor and decision" because now was "preeminently the time to speak the truth, the whole truth, frankly and boldly." The immense throng before him listened with a remarkable quiet, a remarkable lack of outward response;[10] but he seemed to feel its powerfully focused attention and to draw energy from it, for his voice gathered vibrant force as he went on:

> Nor need we shrink from honestly facing conditions in our country today. This great nation will endure as it has endured, will revive and will prosper. So, first of all, let me assert my firm belief that the only thing we have to fear is fear itself*—nameless, unreasoning, unjustified terror which paralyzes needed efforts to convert retreat into advance. In every dark hour of our national life a leadership of frankness and vigor has met that understanding and support of the people themselves which is essential to victory. I am convinced that you will again give that support to leadership in these critical days.

The national distress stemmed from no natural calamity, "no failure of substance," he continued, stressing the bitter paradox which leftist spokesmen

---

*These words had been inserted in the first paragraph of the Moley draft by Louis Howe, perhaps on the morning of February 28. He claimed to have seen them in a recent newspaper advertisement. Eleanor Roosevelt believed her husband paraphrased a famous sentence of Henry David Thoreau: "Nothing is so much to be feared as fear." She told Samuel Rosenman years later that someone had given her a copy of Thoreau's writings and that this volume lay on a table beside Roosevelt's bed in the Mayflower suite on March 3. Perhaps it did, but Roosevelt seems not to have derived the famous sentence from Thoreau.[11]

everywhere cited as proof of the need for radical social change. "Nature still offers her bounty and human efforts have multiplied it. Plenty is at our doorstep, but a generous use of it languishes in the very sight of the supply. Primarily this is because the rulers of the exchange of mankind's goods have failed through their own stubbornness and their own incompetence, have admitted their failure, and have abdicated. . . ." The fault, in other words, was not systemic but personal, was the evil of men without vision who had grossly mismanaged the paper symbols of wealth for their own selfish gain and were now swept out of the way by history's new broom. "The money changers have fled from their high seats in the temple of our civilization," proclaimed the new President of the United States, his voice dripping with scorn and indignation. "We may now restore that temple to the ancient truths." And he went on to say, as the preacher saith, that there are "social values more noble than monetary profit," that "[h]appiness lies not in the mere possession of money" but in the "joy of achievement, in the thrill of creative effort," and that "[t]hese dark days will be worth all they cost if they teach us that our true destiny is not to be ministered unto but to minister to ourselves and to our fellow men."

Yet "changes in ethics alone" could not effect "restoration."

"The Nation asks for action," said he in ringing tones, "and action now!"

When he went on to indicate the action he would take, however, he became, to some critically listening minds, distressingly vague, ambiguous, even self-contradictory. Apparently he was still without any clear, definite overall program, still lacked even the general ideas whereby a coherent overall program might be organized.

He proposed "to put people to work. . . . in part by direct recruitment by the Government itself" for "greatly needed projects to stimulate and reorganize the use of our natural resources." He said that "we must frankly recognize the over-balance of our population in our industrial centers and, by engaging on a national scale in redistribution [of population?], endeavor to provide a better use of the land for those best fitted for the land." But immediately thereafter he spoke of "definite efforts to raise the values of agricultural products and with this the power to purchase the output of our cities"—as if these "efforts" would not be immensely complicated by any such "redistribution" as his preceding sentence seemed to indicate. He spoke then of "preventing realistically . . . the growing loss through foreclosures of our small homes and our farms";* of "insistence that" the "cost" of "Federal, State, and local governments . . . be drastically reduced"; of "the unifying of relief activities" (which, critical minds noted, must certainly be curtailed if governmental "costs" were to be "drastically reduced"); and of "national planning for the supervision of all forms of transportation and communications and other

---

*Perhaps significant of the relative imprecision of Roosevelt's thought processes compared to Moley's is the difference between this sentence spoken on March 4, 1933, and the sentence originally composed by Moley. The latter speaks of "treating realistically the tragedy of" etc., which makes sense, whereas "preventing realistically" etc., does not.

utilities which have a definite public character." There must be "a strict supervision of all banking and credits and investments" to end "speculation with other people's money; and there must be provision for an adequate but sound currency." Uneasiness was bred in fiscal conservatives by his use of "adequate" in the latter phrase. Uneasiness was bred in those favoring inflation by his use of "sound."

As regards foreign affairs he was even less specific. He did seem to come down definitely on the side of the economic nationalists in their continuing controversy with internationalists, for he left unchanged the words nationalist Moley had written on this subject: "Our international trade relations, though vastly important, are in point of time and necessity secondary to the establishment of a sound national economy. I favor as a practical matter the putting of first things first. I shall spare no effort to restore world trade by international economic readjustment, but the emergency at home cannot wait on that accomplishment." Otherwise he would simply "dedicate this Nation to the policy of the good neighbor—the neighbor who resolutely respects himself and, because he does so, respects the rights of others—the neighbor who respects his obligations and respects the sanctity of his agreements in and with a world of neighbors." Here, too, the mind he spoke was that of nationalist, traditionally isolationist Ray Moley.

The words that followed, however, were quite definitely, exclusively his own. Essentially they were those he had spoken to Moley and Flynn on a train ride from Warm Springs, Georgia, to Jacksonville, Florida, just four weeks before—words Moley had then jotted down for speech draft purposes—and they were emphatically clear in their commitment of their speaker to bold leadership. The most critical and doubtful among his listeners were heartened by the impression he now gave of courage, optimistic faith, absolute self-confidence, and a determination to exercise to the fullest extent the great power of his office. These qualities, consistent with the President-elect's recent response to fatal danger in Miami, had been notably absent from the White House these last three years.*

"If I read the temper of our people correctly," Roosevelt said, "we now realize as we never realized before our interdependence on each other; that we cannot merely take but must give as well; that if we are to go forward, we must move as a trained and loyal army willing to sacrifice for the good of a common discipline. . . . We are . . . ready and willing to submit our lives and our property to such discipline, because it makes possible a leadership which aims at a larger good. This I propose to offer. . . ."

The risk here, of course, was of personal freedom as theretofore defined, and he hastened to reassure so far as possible those who, in his talk of a "loyal

---

*In Miami, where Roosevelt had just landed after a ten-day fishing cruise, a madman attempted to assassinate him as he spoke at a welcoming ceremony for him on the night of February 15, 1933. The cold nerve, the calm self-control he then manifested heartened a watching nation that had been theretofore somewhat doubtful of his personal quality. See Kenneth S. Davis, *FDR: The New York Years, 1928–1933* (New York, 1985), pp. 427–437.

army" and a "common discipline," heard ominous overtones, portentous of
fascism. The leadership he proposed could be exercised, he said, within the
framework of the Constitution he had just sworn to preserve, protect, and
defend, for "[o]ur Constitution is so simple and practical that it is always
possible to meet extraordinary needs by changes in emphasis and arrangement
without loss of essential form." But having said this, he went on to indicate
that the necessary "changes" just might amount to a temporary suspension of ·
the Constitution, a temporary resort to government by executive decree. He
"hoped that the normal balance of Executive and Legislative authority" would
prove "wholly adequate to meet the unprecedented task before us," but "it may
be that an unprecedented . . . need for undelayed action may call for temporary
departure from that normal balance of public procedure." If so, "I shall ask
the Congress for the one remaining instrument to meet the crisis—broad
Executive power to wage a war against the emergency, as great as the power
that would be given me if we were in fact invaded by a foreign foe."

This brought a loud burst of applause.

His peroration echoed in rhythm and tone the language Woodrow Wilson
had used when calling upon Congress to declare war against Germany in 1917.
Said Franklin Roosevelt:

> For the trust reposed in me I will return the courage and devotion that befit the time.
> I can do no less. We face the arduous days that lie before us in the warm courage
> of national unity; with the clear satisfaction that comes from the stern performance
> of duty. . . .* We do not distrust the future of essential democracy. The people of
> the United States have not failed. In their need they have registered a mandate that
> they want direct, vigorous action. They have asked for discipline and direction under
> leadership. They have made me the instrument of their wishes. In the spirit of the
> gift I take it.

He bowed his head over the lectern to speak in reverent tone his prayer for
God's blessing on America, for God's protection of each and every American,
for God's guidance "of me in the days to come."

There was an instant of silence.

Then, at last, the great crowd made full, overt response, with loud cheers
and applause, to the words they had listened to so quietly for the most part,
and to the man who had spoken them.

Roosevelt's facial expression since his oath taking had been of an unbroken
sobriety. Not once had he smiled. But now, suddenly, he did so. With his head
thrown back, his jaw outthrust, he smiled a great, wide, joyous, confident smile
as he raised high his right hand in a gesture of grateful acknowledgment, of
warm friendship, and of command.[12]

---

*". . . the right is more precious than peace," said Woodrow Wilson on April 2, 1917, "and we
shall fight for the things we have always held nearest our hearts. . . . To such a task we can dedicate
our lives and our fortunes . . . with the pride of those who know that the day has come when
America is privileged to spend her blood and her might for the principles that gave her birth.
. . . God helping her, she can do no other." Edmund Wilson, commenting on the inaugural in
the March 22, 1933, issue of the *New Republic,* heard in Roosevelt's words "echoes of Woodrow
Wilson's eloquence without Wilson's glow of life behind them."

IV

HE had refused to order any curtailment of planned inaugural festivities, which were very elaborate, though this had been urged upon him by some advisers during the last few days. To the argument that a prolonged, glittering, obviously expensive celebration, himself its focus, must strike distressed millions as a show of bad taste by the new executive, if not of a callous frivolity of mind, his commonsense reply had been that the monetary costs of the mammoth parade had been already incurred, along with those of the balls, the receptions, the other social functions; that the same was true of the travel, the new clothes, the hotel rooms for the many thousands of good Democrats who had swarmed into the national capital from every part of the nation, these last two days, anticipating historic holiday; and that, therefore, cancellation of any part of the great fete on its very eve would itself constitute a foolish extravagance. It would be a casting away without use of costly items bought and paid for—a deliberate waste for the sake of appearances. Nor did he believe that the latter were accurately assessed by those whose advice he rejected. He was convinced that actually the festivity would have, in the darkening circumstances, a wholesome, brightening psychological effect, being perceived by the great mass of citizens as a brave show of confidence in the Republic's essential strength and in the ability of the American people, under new leadership, to prevail over all that threatened them.

Besides, he personally hugely enjoyed great parades and public ceremony. He now gave himself over completely to that enjoyment.

After a hasty, crowded buffet luncheon at the White House where, at Eleanor Roosevelt's surprising order, hot dogs were served, he went out to the reviewing stand, which was a replica of the tall Grecian-pillared portico of The Hermitage of Andrew Jackson, and there he stood, bareheaded much of the time, through a long, cold, windy afternoon while mile after mile of parade passed before him. It was in its forward units a military parade: The commander in chief, with Army Chief of Staff General Douglas MacArthur at one side of him and Naval Operations Chief Admiral William V. Pratt at the other, received the salutes of Army, Navy, and Marine units, preceded by cavalry and marching bands, while squadrons of warplanes and the dirigible *Akron* flew low beneath the clouds overhead. There followed at intervals dozens of other bands, forty in all. Thirty-three governors, delegations from every state, and Al Smith passed by—Smith briskly footing it down the avenue, with the broad ribbons and medals of a sachem of Tammany Hall draped 'round his neck, lifting high above his head, in sweeping acknowledgment of his admirers' cheers, not the silk hat of his recent years but the brown derby of his years of greatness.

Daylight waned.

The parade's end was not in sight when Roosevelt at last left the stand, as unostentatiously as possible, to return to the White House, where a reception for thousands of guests was in progress and where he took his stand briefly beside his wife in the doorway between the Red and Blue rooms. Then he went upstairs to the Oval Room. There, seated behind a desk the top of which was bare, uncluttered with souvenirs as none at which he had worked for more than a day or so could ever be, he presided over the swearing in of his entire cabinet in one swoop—a precedent-shattering ceremony that dramatically emphasized his promise of "action now." He described the occasion, witnessed only by members of the appointees' families, as "a little family party," and his manner of conducting the formalities made them informal in tone and warmly human. As a happy paterfamilias, beaming with pride, he called out his appointees' names one by one, beginning with Cordell Hull; beaming, he watched their taking of the oath one by one, administered by Justice Benjamin N. Cardozo, then handed each of them, with affectionate handshake, a certificate of office; and he closed the proceedings with a graceful little speech expressing the hope that they all would be a truly happy family, working together without quarrel or friction for the general good. Downstairs again, where the huge reception was now drawing to a close, he went into the Red Room to greet with special warmth thirteen children on crutches, polio victims from Warm Springs, who were there by his special invitation. Supper was served buffet-style at eight o'clock for seventy-five of the Roosevelt clan. Among them were representatives of the Oyster Bay branch of the family, all of whom had voted for Hoover, including TR's headstrong acid-tongued daughter Alice Longworth, Eleanor's first cousin, who would soon repay such hospitality with malicious imitations at parties of Eleanor's public speaking voice and manner.

He did not attend the formal inaugural ball, deeming himself amply represented there by his wife, his daughter, his sons. Instead, he closed out the proudest, most historic day of his life thus far in private talk with the man who more than any other had helped him up the path to his present eminence and without whose fierce devotion, naysaying at decisive moments, and constant hard, skillful labor on his behalf, he almost certainly would have gone fatally astray. With Louis Howe he was alone for an hour or more, until bedtime, in the room Abraham Lincoln had used as a study. . . .[13]

V

IT would be difficult to exaggerate the extent of the change in national mood which took place during Franklin Roosevelt's first thirty-six hours in the White House. The gloomy compound of fear, anger, disgust, cynicism, and despair which had been as a lowering cloud upon the mind and spirit of the Republic at high noon on Saturday, March 4, rendering all hope defiant and desperate, was by the morning of Monday, March 6, greatly qualified by new confidence, new determination, a "warm courage of national unity." And for this dissipation of gloom, this sudden focus of resurgent energies in the light of renewed optimism, the tone of the inaugural address and the image projected by the new President of the United States were largely responsible.

During the preceding twenty-four hours he had been the active center of such a whirl of activity as had not swept through the White House and the whole of the executive branch since the Great War.

He had begun his hugely publicized first day as President by attending Sunday morning worship services at St. Thomas's. As he did so, there had gathered in the Treasury Building the great bankers whose summoning he had approved barely two hours before his public castigation of them or their ilk as "temple"-profaning "money changers." By noon these had been formed into a special Treasury advisory committee, though they at once proved themselves to be so utterly demoralized, so devoid of clear ideas that their "advice" was but a deafening "babble of tongues," as Moley disgustedly, and Woodin resignedly, reported to the President. Yet far into the night Woodin and Moley had labored with them, and with Ogden Mills and the other Hoover Treasury officials who remained to help, on bank crisis problems. Final drafts of two presidential proclamations had been completed. One, issued at once, called Congress into extraordinary session at noon on Thursday, March 9, by which time, Woodin promised, emergency banking legislation would be ready for enactment. The other, issued shortly after midnight on March 6, closed all banks until Friday, March 10, and placed prohibitions on gold exports, silver exports, and foreign exchange transactions. At a brief special meeting held in the Oval Room at two-thirty, Roosevelt had discussed with his cabinet the bank proclamation. He had explained it, too, in a meeting arranged by Press Secretary Steve Early, to representatives of the four major press associations, whom he immensely impressed with his sangfroid. "Sturdy-shouldered, smiling, calm, talking pleasantly with an occasional humorous sally, he was a picture of ease and confidence," wrote one of the correspondents in a dispatch which would be read by millions in Monday morning's papers. "As he talked, he deliberately inserted a fresh cigarette in an ivory holder. It was as if he was considering [nothing more important than] a bill for a bridge in some . . . rural county." To a huge national radio audience, early in the evening, he had made a brief speech specifically addressed to the American Legion but calling upon "all men and women who love their country" for such "sacrifice and devotion" as they would give in a war, "[t]o the end that the efforts I am giving in these first days of my Administration may be crowned with success and that we may achieve a lasting restoration of national well-being." It was "a mistake to assume that the virtues of war differ essentially from the virtues of peace," he had said. "All life is a battle. . . ."[14]

Thus the words he had spoken, the image he had projected were of a brave, resourceful commander in chief who mobilized armies. And the nation responded at once, emotionally, as to a call to arms against an invading foreign foe.

For the national mood, at this opening of one of the most fateful weeks in American history, had running through it a broad streak of messianic authoritarianism, as has been indicated, a longing for the Leader, the Messiah in whom a passionate communal faith could be invested and who would take responsibility for everything, obviating the necessity for individual thought and decision.

Walter Lippmann had been both expressive and determinative of this public mood when he said in his syndicated newspaper column a month and a half ago (January 17) that "[a]ny group of 500 men, whether they are called congressmen or anything else, is an unruly mob unless it comes under the strict control of a single will." Twelve days later Lippmann had visited in Warm Springs where, lunching alone with the President-elect, he had cited Hitler's assumption of the Reich chancellorship two days before as an example of what must inevitably happen in a democracy that fails to concentrate authority in an emergency—a democracy, in other words, that insists upon remaining democratic under crisis pressures. "The situation is critical, Franklin," he had said with utmost earnestness. "You may have no alternative but to assume dictatorial power." In his columns during the next two weeks he had reiterated this general view, saying that Congress must not be allowed "to obstruct, to delay, to mutilate, and to confuse" but should instead suspend debate and amendment of executive proposals for a year; that in the present situation the employment of " 'dictatorial powers,' if that is the name for it," was "essential"; and that the great danger was "not that Congress will give Franklin D. Roosevelt too much power, but that it will deny him the power he needs." Other voices chimed in. Al Smith, for instance, in public speech in early February, likened the present emergency to a war and asked rhetorically, then answered categorically a relevant question: "What does a democracy do in a war? It becomes a tyrant, a despot, a real monarch. In the World War we took our Constitution, wrapped it up, and laid it on the shelf and left it there until the war was over."[15]

Both Smith and Lippmann were among thirteen of the most influential citizens in the land who, on this morning of Monday, March 6, signed a letter addressed to a conference of governors* that was to meet an hour or so later in the East Room of the White House, pursuant of an invitation issued by the President-elect in early February. Other signers were Rear Admiral Richard E. Byrd, Newton D. Baker, Nicholas Murray Butler; Protestant clergyman Harry Emerson Fosdick, Roman Catholic George Cardinal Mundelein, Rabbi Stephen S. Wise; the presidents of the U.S. Chamber of Commerce, the American Federation of Labor, the American Farm Bureau Federation, the B&O Railroad; and the master of the National Grange. In their letter the "undersigned" said they were animated by "a spirit of cooperation with the President" and "convinced that there is throughout the nation a spontaneous spiritual uprising of confidence and hope in our chosen leader." They were further convinced of the necessity for "[p]rompt and decisive action of a national scope." The letter continued: "The ordinary operations of government that prevail and are suitable in time of prosperity with normal confidence, may be too slow to meet adequately this emergency and avoid the danger of this economic avalanche carrying all before it. We, a Coalition Committee of different groups and political and religious beliefs, respectfully request that you join . . . in the issuance of a Proclamation . . . in support of the President of the United States and our institutions, thus enabling the whole people to

---

*Twenty-five governors were present. A dozen others sent representatives.

declare in unison their confidence and faith in our President." Accompanying this declared faith in the executive was an evident lack of it in the legislature. For the letter went on to say that the declaration asked for "would constitute the people's appeal to the patriotism of Congress, *which we know they possess, in common with all,* * to cooperate with the President. . . ." The assembled governors and representatives of governors needed no urging along this line. Eighteen of them promptly signed a pledge expressing their "confidence and faith in our President" and begging "the Congress and all the people of our united country to cooperate with him. . . ." The conference as a whole then adopted a resolution which expressed not only "confidence in the leadership of the President" but also a "desire that he be granted immediately by the Congress such broad powers as may be necessary to enable the Executive to meet the present challenging emergency."[16]

Consistent with these words were those spoken by a leading journal in Mussolini's Italy when it commented on the "clear" import of the new President's inaugural address. "[T]he whole world feels the need for executive authority capable of acting with full powers of cutting short the purposeless chatter of legislative assemblies," said *Il Giornale d'Italia,* adding, "[T]his method of government may well be defined as Fascist."[17]

Such talk was far from pleasing, was indeed distressing, to Eleanor Roosevelt.

She, who on the eve of election day had told her close friend Associated Press reporter Lorena Hickok that the "responsibility he [her husband] may have to assume is something I hate to think about," found unhappy significance in the fact that her husband received his loudest applause during the inaugural address when he pledged himself to demand wartime executive powers if Congress failed to take the emergency actions he deemed necessary. Sharpened thereby was her already acute awareness that personal liberties to which she was committed with every atom of her being—the freedoms of speech, press, assembly, movement, even religion—were now gravely threatened in America. The disposition to purchase bread at the price of liberty, along with the belief that bread could now be obtained *only* at that price, grew strong among the great mass of citizens in proportion to the unsatisfied need for bread, while among the propertied classes the belief that personal liberties were antithetical to law and order grew in proportion to the fear of social revolution. And this acute awareness was joined, in Eleanor, with an unspoken doubt of her husband's ability, or of anyone's ability, to meet the threat successfully.

She gave some hint of this when Lorena Hickok interviewed her on the afternoon of March 4—the first interview ever granted a newspaper reporter in the White House. "It was very, very solemn and a little terrifying," Eleanor said of the inauguration ceremony. "The crowds were so tremendous, and you felt that they would do *anything*—if only someone would tell them *what* to

*Emphasis added to indicate the large element of doubt that the words were true.

do." Yet there was no way that anyone, however wise and good, could tell "them" what to do in any commanding way without destroying by that very act what her husband, in his address, had called "essential democracy." No way, at least, that Eleanor could see. And she was very sure that no one anywhere possessed the prescience whereby the future could be probed deeply enough to suggest with any clarity, any accuracy what must or ought now to be done. "One has the feeling of going it blindly," she said to the reporter, "because we're in a tremendous stream, and none of us knows where we're going to land."[18]

Yet there was this one man, her husband, who was at the very center of the swirling, tumultuous stream, the focus of everything, upon whom everything apparently depended, and who even to her, or especially to her, seemed absolutely self-secure, serenely in command, as he inspired a troubled nation with his show of calm confidence and cheerful courage.

Was he really that secure, that confident, that courageous?

On the evidence, a good part of Franklin Roosevelt's deepest feeling on this morning of Monday, March 6, was indicated by Eleanor's last-quoted words. He was, in fact, far more fatalistic than she expressed herself to be. For not only did he feel that he was borne toward unknown ends upon a "tremendous stream" the power of which he could not diminish and the main thrust or direction of which he could not change, but he also felt that even the choices among different ways of yielding to the stream, which were the only choices it was possible to make, must not be made by himself alone. Of course, his voice alone must speak the final yeas and nays. But these should never be the exclusive expressions of his single will, his uniquely personal idea. Always they must be the product of outside or "higher" forces impinging upon or working through him; this meant that the process of decision would, for him, consist of a calculation or intuition of the preponderance of force which emerged, and was measured by his abnormal sensitivity to pressure variations, out of the different forces operating in different directions that constantly played upon him. Or to put it another way, and a way more accurately descriptive of his general experience, his decisive acts would be indicated responses to cues, often very slight and subtle cues, whose significance he was uniquely equipped to grasp since according to his own feeling they were meant for him alone.

Thus many of the words which Prince Andrew used to describe General Kutuzov's essential attitude in Tolstoy's *War and Peace* could be applied to Roosevelt's sense of historic role. Like Kutuzov, whom Tolstoy flatly contrasted with Napoleon in this respect, Roosevelt understood that there was "something stronger than his own will"—namely, an "inevitable course of events"*—and that his primary assigned task was not "to bring in any plan of his own" or to "devise or undertake anything" but to "hear everything,

---

*Pure opportunists, of course, always lay heavy stress upon such "inevitability" when they strive to justify to themselves and others the compromises and contradictions of stated principle into which they are led "inevitably" by their opportunism.

remember everything, . . . put everything in its proper place"; it was to recognize and "grasp . . . [the] significance" of particular events in the overwhelming stream of them and then, "seeing that significance . . . [to] refrain from meddling," save insofar as he could encourage the happening of "anything useful" or discourage the happening of "anything harmful."[19] Moreover, like Kutuzov's, Roosevelt's fatalism was essentially a Christian religious faith —a profound and profoundly simple faith in God the Father of all Mankind who was also God the Author of all Event and whose instrument he, Franklin Roosevelt, was. Which is to say that Roosevelt's fatalism, like that of Tolstoy's Kutuzov, was at base absolutely optimistic.

And in this he differed radically from Eleanor.

Of the gloomy Calvinism which had pervaded the Tivoli (her mother's family place) of her childhood, Eleanor retained only the Puritan ethic, the Puritan conscience, having been "freed" (so she herself put it) from orthodox Christianity by the great teacher of her youth, Mlle. Marie Souvestre, the atheistic and politically liberal headmistress of Allenswood.* No such influence had operated on Roosevelt's youth, and in any case, since his childhood he had shied away from all speculations or introspections which might weaken his faith, doing so by instinctive reflex, it seemed, as if physically recoiling from a threatful knife or flame. Hence there was almost wholly absent from his present mood the grim foreboding, the dread of a future determined by historic processes beyond human control, which brooded behind Eleanor's quoted words. In his belief, the turbulent stream in which he was caught up was the eventful will of God, and since God was infinitely good, kind, and wise, the stream could not possibly be malevolent in motive, evil in substance, or cruel in end. If he knew and could know no better than another precisely "where we're going to land," he did know with the certainty of deepest faith that the ultimate landing would be a happy one. . . .

VI

THE accuracy of this psychological interpretation is attested to by something which seems at first glance to belie it—namely, a moment of pure terror which he suffered on this same morning of Monday, March 6. It was an experience he would often describe, in vivid circumstantial detail in afteryears, to people close to him and always with a kind of reverent wonder, as of a passage in his life that was wholly strange, profoundly shocking, rich in symbolism, and possessed of a significance more than personal.

The strangeness began for him when, in a bedroom for which he did not yet have any feeling of home (it was next door to the Oval Room), he awoke somewhat earlier than he usually did, though he really needed extra sleep, and was forced to lie waiting in his bed through what seemed to him quite a long time, unwontedly unoccupied, until McDuffie appeared at the normally sched-

*See Kenneth S. Davis, *FDR: The Beckoning of Destiny* (New York, 1972), pp. 186–88.

uled hour. When his breakfast tray came, it did not have upon it the several newspapers the contents of which he normally perused while eating his eggs and drinking his coffee. The papers were late that morning, nor were they, when they did finally arrive, quite the ones he wanted.

He was mildly irritated.

And this irritation, this queer sense of things going slightly but definitely wrong, was not diminished by the jolting he took as McDuffie wheeled him somewhat too rapidly over unfamiliar flagstones, along the enclosed terrace leading from the White House proper to the executive office wing. He entered for the first time the office of the President, which Herbert Hoover had vacated just thirty-six hours before, and was seated for the first time behind the President's desk.* McDuffie withdrew. All doors were closed. Roosevelt was alone in a chamber considerably larger than any he would personally have chosen as workplace, a chamber the wide, tall walls of which were as blank as the gaze he now bent upon them, for they had been stripped of Hoover's pictures and were not yet hung with his own. Bare, too, was the desktop, save for an empty incoming mail basket at one side and an empty outgoing one at the other. He opened the desk drawers; in them was nothing, not even a scrap of paper upon which a note might have been written. He looked along the desk's sides for a buzzer signal button; he could find none. He listened for some echo of human activity and heard none (he sat very still; the silence grew deafening) while he searched his mind in vain for some reason why, with so much of national crisis importance to be done, he had been abruptly left here in utter solitude, seemingly cut off from all the living world—he who could not have moved himself physically from that chair save as a crawling animal, a crippled animal dragging himself across the floor.

What had happened?

And then it was that the terror came. This that was happening to him was utterly impossible, it simply *couldn't* happen, and under the weight of that experienced impossibility his sanity gave way. Nowhere was there a vital connection he might grasp, nowhere a visible or audible cue for action, nowhere a sign of grace. He was thrown altogether inward upon himself, must draw wholly upon inner resources, and of these he found that he had at that moment none at all. He was achingly empty, his mind a blank, his will paralyzed. He felt such dread, such helpless despair, as he had not known, perhaps, since the darkest hour of his polio attack—and now, as then, he felt that God had abandoned him. . . .

His catatonic seizure (it amounted to that) could not have lasted for more than a few seconds of clock time, but it seemed forever in his immediate experience and very long in his remembrance of it, and its ending required a terrific wrench of his cramped, numbed will. He finally leaned back in his chair, threw back his head, and shouted for help—a shout whose tone had in it something of the terror he felt, evidently, for it brought Missy Le Hand

*His headquarters on Sunday, the fifth, had been the Oval Room.

rushing in from her office next door, extremely agitated, and Marvin McIntyre from his office on the other side, also extremely agitated. This broke the spell, of course. Vital connections were reestablished, normal proportions restored. The bustling wheels began at once to turn again in their normal fashion around him, the axis, and he was again his normal self, unruffled, good-humored, serenely in command.

Missy was rueful. It had been her idea that he might wish to be alone with his thoughts and feelings during these first few minutes of his first regular working day as President of the United States.[20]

→>>✕<<←

2

A Week of Fateful Decision

I

NOT again was there the slightest sign of qualm or doubt in him. There was every sign of perfect ease and security of self as he plunged, with evidently complete zest and joy, into a role he had long expected and prepared himself to play. It was by God's design that he was the axis, the focus, the radiant star. It was in fulfillment of divine purpose that he continued to emit vibratory waves of courage and confidence and good cheer which spread through the whole of the body politic.

On the eve of the national bank moratorium Yale Psychology Professor Edward S. Robinson, conversing with Yale Law School Professor Thurman W. Arnold, predicted that the closing of the banks would have no such dark, crushing effect upon American life and morale as was doomfully forecast by bankers, corporation executives, corporation lawyers. On the contrary, with suspense ended, the worst realized, a bottom reached whence the only possible turn was upward, "everyone will feel relieved. It will be a sort of national holiday. There will be general excitement and . . . everyone will have a lot of fun."[1] In the event, not *everyone* was "happy" or in "holiday" mood, of course. The bankers over whose endless wrangling Woodin presided in Washington were decidedly unhappy, were indeed distraught and miserable, as were bankers everywhere in the land. There were also instances of extreme physical hardship consequent upon the bank closing as the fateful week began, especially in Michigan, where the crisis was initiated and a state moratorium had been in effect for three weeks by the time the national one was ordered. In Detroit several day laborers employed by the city collapsed from hunger on the job, having been unable to cash their paychecks or use them in any other way to obtain food. But Postal Savings operations, exempt from the moratorium, continued in full force everywhere and mitigated somewhat the currency shortage. By Tuesday afternoon restrictions upon those banks still having cash in their vaults were sufficiently eased to permit the use of this cash against suffering: Individual depositors were permitted to withdraw enough to purchase vital necessities; employers were enabled to meet some payrolls; loans to finance food shipments were allowed. A pervasive mutual trust and goodwill among the general citizenry facilitated the continued performance of necessary tasks, the making of necessary exchanges, the direct sharing by the haves with the have-nots of essential goods. Hence most people, even in Michigan, suffered only inconveniences.

And of these they generally did make fun, literally, as they played with great good humor, with gusto even, the game of Making Do Without Money. There was much bartering, much use of local scrip, often in ways highly ingenious. The Dow Chemical Company stamped coins out of something called Dow-metal, a magnesium alloy, and used these to pay workers. Businesses normally conducted on a cash basis extended credit widely. R. H. Macy's, for instance, always a strictly cash store, honored for the time being the charge accounts of other department stores. IOUs were executed and accepted in huge quantity, were sometimes countersigned and used as endorsed checks; taxi dancers ("Ten Cents a Dance!") accepted them from customers who could show them personal checkbooks in New York City's famous Roseland Ballroom. Canadian dollars increasingly circulated through the northern tier of states, Mexican pesos through the Southwest, while in scattered hundreds of localities stamps became a medium of exchange, along with theater tickets, coupons, street car transfers, subway tokens, and soda pop bottles on which deposits had been made. Everywhere there was an exhilarating sense of living through one of the most memorable episodes in all American history, one whose happy issue (a happy outcome was now generally assumed) would enable its exciting experience to be recalled with pleasure in future years. Midway through the week Will Rogers asserted in his syndicated newspaper column, without excessive exaggeration, that the nation had become "united and happy, tickled with poverty."[2]

Thus did Professor Robinson's prophecy come true.

It came true, however, far less through the operation of such general "laws" of human behavior as the psychologist might have cited than it did through the particular vivid impress made upon the popular consciousness by the new President of the United States.

He made it consciously, deliberately, with a consummate actor's skill, made it in good part through the daily professional operations of Washington's newspaper correspondents. Which is to say that nothing he did during his first week in office was more important to his continued effectiveness than his initiation of a presidential relationship with the working press that was unprecedentedly frank, open, cordial, personal. With strong and cunning hand he thus grasped a lever of power whose potency had gone largely unrecognized, being measured far too small, by most earlier Presidents. Certainly none before him had manipulated that lever with anything like the skill he now employed.

It was on Wednesday, March 8—in a moment when every event of the fateful week seemed yet fluid, tentative, ambiguous in its historic meaning and direction, though the special session of Congress was to open at noon next day and every major element of the first draft legislation on which Congress was to act had been in fact decided—that Roosevelt held his first presidential press conference. At a little after ten in the morning Press Secretary Steve Early opened the presidential office door and whispered to veteran Doorkeeper Patrick McKenna a word which caused McKenna to clap his hands twice, the traditional signal for a rush by waiting reporters (there were 120-odd that day) into the room where Roosevelt, seated at his desk, greeted them with wide and warming smile. They crowded around his desk, notepads in hand, to hear him express the hope "that these conferences are going to be merely enlarged editions of the kind of very delightful family conferences I have been holding in Albany for the last four years," at which point, as if to emphasize the familial intimacy hoped for, he was interrupted by his two teenage sons, Franklin, Jr., and John, who pushed their way to his desk to kiss him good-bye. "These two boys are off to Arizona," he explained as they left the room. He then proceeded to implement his evident belief that the American people have not only the right but also a vital need, as citizens of a free society, to be fully informed of how their elected officials, their hired bureaucratic servants, are conducting the public's business.

He proposed to hold, normally, two press conferences each week—one at 10:00 A.M. on Wednesday, a time advantageous to evening paper reporters; the other at 4:00 P.M. Friday, a time advantageous to morning paper reporters, or so the White House at that time assumed. (The regularly scheduled conference days were soon changed in response to protests that newspapers were read less on Saturday than on any other day of the week.) He evoked broad smiles and murmurs of approval when he announced that he and Steve Early had decided *not* to require questions to be submitted in writing prior to each conference, as Harding and every President since had done.* He intended instead to converse freely, candidly with his conference guests. He could not promise to answer every question asked, of course. He would never answer hypothetical questions, " 'if' questions," as he called them, and there would inevitably be "others . . . which for various reasons I do not wish to discuss, or am not ready to discuss, or I do not know anything about." Neither would he permit direct quotation of him in straight news stories "unless direct quotations are given out by Steve in writing." As for his oral communications, they would be divided for use purposes into three categories: There would be "straight news for use from this office," which could be attributed to a White House source; there would be "background information," which reporters could use on their own authority and responsibility but without attribution to the White House; and there would be "off-the-record" information which must be regarded as privileged, confidential, and not to be published or divulged in any form to anyone not present at that conference—not even to colleagues absent because of illness or for some other compelling reason—but which would help those who heard it to report the permitted news in terms of its actual contextual importance.

Nearly all of that morning's oral communications were classified as "background" or "off-the-record." Virtually the only straight news given out was that the President's message to Congress on the morrow would be sent, not delivered in person, and would be brief. "The situation demands brevity." Also

---

*Answering off the cuff a reporter's question about the arms limitation conference under way in Washington, Harding in late 1921 made statements embarrassing to the U.S. government and humiliating to Secretary of State Charles Evans Hughes. It was then that the written-question requirement was imposed.

attributable to a White House source was Roosevelt's statement, in response to a specific question, that according to "what might be called 'present thought' because everything is subject to change within . . . twenty-four or even twelve hours," Congress would be asked to enact only "emergency" legislation at this special session and would then "recess for two or three weeks—to enable me to work out and draft more permanent legislation. . . ." It was, he explained, manifestly impossible "to write a permanent banking act . . . in three days."[3]

Roosevelt's smiling loquacity, in other words, during this first of his presidential news conferences, yielded a remarkably small percentage of hard, specific news, a smaller percentage, probably, than had emerged from many a meeting of Hoover with the press. Yet when the conference was ended at ten forty-five with what would become the traditional "Thank you, Mr. President" intoned by a press association correspondent, the reporters broke as one man into spontaneous, enthusiastic, grateful applause—something that assuredly had never happened at the close of a Hoover or Coolidge press meeting—and at least one of the reporters erroneously remembered a dozen years later that the new President in this single forty-five-minute session had "produced more sensational news than some of his predecessors had released in four years."[4] It had been a virtuoso performance certainly. Hoover's personal relations with the press had been characterized by cold stiffness, mutual distrust, an ill-concealed feeling on Hoover's part that he was being pilloried, a resentful feeling on the reporters' part that they were being snubbed. In total contrast was the attitude of this new man. Every correspondent in the room had a heady sense of being welcomed into the sanctum sanctorum of the new administration and there entrusted with state secrets; each had a sense of being dealt with by the President as a working partner in the enterprise of democratic government, a partner "as important . . . as a member of Cabinet or of Congress—even more important."[5] This, of course, influenced in ways favorable to Roosevelt the slant and tone of the news stories and "think pieces" which the reporters then wrote.

The stories, in turn, contributed to the general public impression of a President absolutely on top of his job, possessed of the most detailed information about a highly complex crisis situation to which he was intelligently, commandingly responsive, a man utterly confident of his ability to pilot the ship of state through dark and stormy seas to a shore of golden light. The self-confidence thus portrayed, along with its justification, was contagiously exemplary; it reinforced and intensified that popular confidence in him which the inaugural and its immediate aftermath had initiated. Seldom, if ever before in peacetime had Americans felt so closely interdependent, so emphatically members of a single human community, with shared fears, aspirations, dreams, troubles, as they did in these first days of a New Deal the personification of which was Franklin D. Roosevelt, and never in any time before, whether of war or peace, had Americans invested such passionate hope and faith in the strength, the will, the vision of one man.

Nor was their relationship with him remote or abstract in their feeling. It was, instead, direct, personal, concrete—a fact attested to by the unprecedented flood of written communications, some 450,000 letters and telegrams, which poured into the White House during the first half dozen days of the new administration. They were *personal* communications from individual men and women to *their* President; to handle them, a mailroom that had been adequately staffed by one man in Hoover's day was abruptly required to hire seventy people.[6]

II

AND generally prevailing among those millions most fervently committed to Roosevelt was the conviction that the historic process he personified, this New Deal, was a process of profound, even revolutionary change in American life and institutions. The old order had so obviously collapsed, its governors had so abundantly demonstrated their mental and moral unfitness to govern that a radically new order, headed by a new elite and infused with those "social values more noble than monetary profit" to which the new President in his inaugural had referred, seemed emphatically indicated if indeed it was not absolutely necessary for the survival of that "essential democracy" to which the President had also referred. What was under way at the very least, in the general view that week, was a restructuring of the nation's money and credit system whereby those "money changers" who had profaned and then ignominiously "fled" the "temple" would be forever barred from a return to it.

This latter view was to be found among members of Congress.

When Roosevelt on the evening of March 8 read to congressional leaders assembled in the White House the emergency draft legislation that would be formally introduced to them in special session next day (a first draft had been completed only an hour or two before; the final one would not be ready till late tomorrow morning), few of those present understood it in any detail. But several of them assumed it to be a stopgap measure which not only enabled the banks to reopen and function during an interim period but also prepared the way for permanent legislation creative of a truly new credit structure, one national in scope and strictly operative in the public interest. This assumption was evidently shared by journalist Ernest Lindley when he wrote a few weeks later that though the "banking system lay unconscious upon the table and the temptation to operate on it was strong," Roosevelt "chose instead to *postpone** the operation" because he did not yet have in hand a "completely worked out . . . permanent plan which commanded wide approval." Presumably a suitably drastic plan was in preparation, and few, that week, could doubt that the new President's proclamation of it as *his* proposal would be enough to gain for it the needed "wide approval." At one point during the meeting with congressional leaders in the White House, according to Frank Freidel, an agitated Senator Hiram Johnson of California rose to his feet, placed himself in front of Roosevelt's chair, and, having praised the President for the "strong

*Emphasis added.

tone" of his inaugural address, "proposed kicking the Wall Street bankers into oblivion and replacing them with a new banking system." There were nods and murmurs of approval from several in the room, and one who so nodded was Franklin Roosevelt.[7]

But all this was mere seeming, mere appearance.

What was actually under way was something very different.

Among Roosevelt's auditors at his first presidential press conference were one or two, surely, who sensed a couple of facts which to well-informed hindsight would become obvious: first, that Roosevelt had in reality, at that moment, but a slender grasp of mind upon the monetary crisis of the intricacies of which his superbly confident manner proclaimed him a master; secondly, that he, lacking any detailed knowledge of economics or any opinions of his own earned by hard thought in this field, followed an instinct, a sense of the force and direction of the flow of event that was profoundly conservative. When a reporter asked him if he favored "national scrip or scrip issued by clearing houses" to supply the shortage of cash, he replied, "Well, there . . . you are getting down to details and a very good illustration of why you cannot ask for too detailed legislation," thus reinforcing his stated intention to ask Congress for a broad grant of executive power. He went on to say that "by last night it looked possible to avoid" the "very, very wide use of scrip" which earlier in the week had seemed almost certainly necessary, but "I can't tell you any more than that, because we are still working on the details. . . ." Early in the conference he remarked: "As long as nobody asks me whether or not we are off the gold standard or gold basis, that is all right, because nobody knows what the gold basis or gold standard really is," though as "good a definition" as he knew of was economic journalist Ralph Robey's in last night's New York *Evening Post,* an article he then proceeded to read aloud, with interpolated commentary. Robey's "definition" (it was a description of the pure gold coin standard) listed four "requisites" of which the United States met two at that moment, according to Roosevelt—to wit, a gold "coin of definite weight and fineness" and "free and unlimited coinage of gold." As regards the third requisite, the full and free "convertibility of paper money into gold," the reporters were invited to "draw your own conclusions." Only in regard to the fourth requisite, which was the "free movement of gold" through domestic and foreign markets, was the United States definitely "off" gold as a result of the proclamation of "last Sunday night." In response to specific questions he said that a permanent solution of America's banking problem was *not* "intermeshed" with the work to be done by the upcoming World Economic Conference* (a reporter had suggested it might be), though there was, of course, linkage between

---

*The Hoover administration in the early summer of 1932 had committed the United States to full participation in a World Monetary and Economic Conference originally scheduled to open in London in January 1933. The opening was postponed because Hoover and Roosevelt had widely different views of what the conference could or should accomplish and so found it impossible to cooperate in conference preparations. See Kenneth S. Davis, *FDR: The New York Years* (New York, 1985), pp. 399–406, 409, 411–413.

domestic monetary policy and problems of international exchange with which the London Conference would deal; that he remained committed to a "sound" as well as an "adequate" currency, though "what you are coming to now really is a managed currency, the adequacy of which will depend on the conditions of the moment" (it might "expand one week" and "contract another week"); and that this management of the currency "ought to be part of a permanent system, so we don't run into this thing again. . . ." Asked if he didn't "want to define 'sound' " as applied to money, he replied flatly that he did not, though he would and did say that "the real mark of delineation between sound and unsound is when the Government starts to pay its bills by starting printing presses," an expedient to which he was clearly utterly opposed.

Came then a question upon a matter which greatly agitated the public mind that week.

"Can you tell us anything about guaranteeing of bank deposits?" asked a reporter, referring to the current widespread demand for a federal deposit insurance scheme.* Replied Roosevelt: "I can tell you . . . my own views." These were firmly *against* the proposal. Why? Because, he asserted, any general guarantee of deposits would mean that the government undertook to "guarantee bad banks as well as good banks." Typically he eschewed the long view, confining himself wholly to the immediate, concrete situation, as he said that deposit guarantee would mean "a definite loss to the Government" because "[t]here are undoubtedly some banks that are not going to pay one hundred cents on the dollar" and the government would be obligated to make up the difference. "We all know," he went on, using the form of words with which he habitually prefaced pronouncements of dubious or limited truth, especially his pronouncements of falsely exclusive alternatives, "it is better to have that loss taken [by individual depositors] than to jeopardize the credit of the United States Government or to put the Government further into debt. . . . We do not wish to make the United States Government liable for the mistakes and errors of individual banks, and put a premium on unsound banking in the future." These remarks, originally off-the-record, were reclassified as "background" after the reporter who had asked the question begged for the upgrading. The reclassification was made with a proviso: Reporters could use the information on their own responsibility, without attribution, but only "[a]s long as you don't write stories to give the average depositor the thought that his own particular bank isn't going to pay . . . because the average bank is going to pay. . . ."[8]

In sum, there emerged from a close look at this first press conference transcript and at other documented presidential words and deeds "no reason to believe . . . that the President himself had any idea of where to proceed"

*It was a demand in which were joined Senators Key Pittman, Robert La Follette, and Edward P. Costigan; Vice President Garner; Jesse Jones of the Reconstruction Finance Corporation (RFC); and many distinguished professors of economics, all of whom communicated their views to the White House via letter, telegraph, telephone, or personal call during this crisis week.

after his confidence-inspiring performance of March 4–5, as one of the most thorough and objective historians of the 1933 banking crisis wrote forty years later.[9]

Nor did he make any pretense to expert knowledge; neither did he evince the slightest awe of experts or their expertise in his dealings with those directly involved in emergency solutions. With a single exception he made no effort to feed substantive ideas of his own into the decision-making process. He presided. He made final choices between alternatives emergent from discussions deliberately exclusive of "unorthodox" ideas. And insofar as he exercised any controlling power over the event, he did so to *prevent* structural change, not to effect it.

In the afternoon of March 4, Hoover's secretary of the treasury, Ogden Mills, submitted to his successor a memorandum entitled "Tentative Outline of a Possible Line of Approach to the Solution of our Banking Problem." This, however, was no farewell address. Mills stayed on in Washington, along with Arthur Ballantine, F. G. Awalt, and other top officials of Hoover's Treasury, to work on crisis-solutions in full and equal partnership with Woodin, Moley, and others of the incoming administration and with the bankers who assembled in the Treasury, at Mills's original suggestion, on the morning of March 5. ("[W]e . . . had forgotten to be Republicans or Democrats," Moley recalled a half dozen years later. "We were just a bunch of men trying to save the banking system."[10]) At 10:00 A.M. that Sunday, Woodin's consultations with the assembled bankers began, to continue night and day for four long days thereafter. There were plenary sessions of this advisory group at first, then subcommittee sessions, and in almost every one of them sharp differences of opinion provoked quarrelsome words from tense, despairing, fear-soaked, bone-tired men. Chicago banker Melvin Traylor, who had been Illinois's favorite-son candidate for Democratic presidential nomination last summer, proved especially liable to nervous breakdown—he exploded in anger several times, was once reduced to tears, and was destined never to recover from this climactic week of a months-long ordeal (he died eleven months later, aged fifty-six) —but several others were almost equally out of control. Roosevelt's own special agents were by no means immune to acrimonious dispute. Will Woodin remained throughout patient and sweet-tempered, also mentally acute and effective as catalyst and leader, but there were nasty blowups between Moley and Adolf Berle, a key member of the famous Brain Trust, whom Moley had called into the deliberations. On one occasion, Berle accused Moley, bitterly, of attempting to assume in Roosevelt's administration the covertly powerful role which Colonel House had played in Wilson's.[11]

As for the bankers, some of them saw only stupid impracticality in every proposed alternative to the use of scrip. Some called loudly for deposit guarantees, which others as loudly opposed, while among those wanting guarantees was disagreement among those favoring a flat 50 percent guarantee and those favoring a sliding scale adjusted according to classifications of bank worth. There were vehement demands for the abolition of state banks, for the forcible inclusion of all banks in the Federal Reserve System; there were equally vehement protests against this. What there emphatically was *not* was any decisive consensus on any plan whatever. A few of the bankers were so totally drained of confidence in themselves and their colleagues, so demoralized by felt popular hostility to them, if not also by private feelings of guilt, private convictions of social justice, that they saw no way to avoid a socialization of the banking system—that is, a pooling of existing bank assets in a single central national bank having myriad local branches, the whole to be government-owned, government-operated. And this willingness to nationalize was far stronger throughout the banking community in general than it was among the big bankers called to Washington, as the latter well knew. The great majority of the nation's banks were insolvent, "and one thing our capitalists are always willing to socialize is a loss," as Kenneth Burke has remarked.[12]

Nationalization was, of course, being called for in the strongest terms by Norman Thomas and the Socialist party of New York. It was strongly favored by *Nation* editor Ernest Gruening, who, on March 9, in a letter to Norman Thomas, made wry comment on the "terrific confusion" in Washington, where "the money changers whom Mr. Roosevelt drove out of the temples . . . [are] congregating in the White House and telling him what to do." It was favored by Bronson Cutting, whom Roosevelt had tried to persuade into the cabinet and who, a year later, looked back upon the opening days of the New Deal with "a sick heart" because then "the nationalization of the banks by President Roosevelt could have been accomplished without a word of protest" and Roosevelt had failed to do it. "It was," Cutting then wrote, "President Roosevelt's great mistake." Nationalization was favored by Rex Tugwell, who as early as 1928 had publicly inveighed against the failure of the Federal Reserve System (the "Bankers' Bank") to operate in the public interest, had in early 1932 expressed in public speech his opinion that the government would be a more efficient banker than private profiteers could be, and had now in mind a rather vague scheme for a vastly expanded Postal Savings operation to alleviate the immediate crisis. Tugwell in future years was to reject with some asperity the contention of many New Deal historians that Roosevelt during the crisis week of 1933 could not "have done other than he did." Those making such assertions "minimize the . . . readiness of a paralyzed people to accept drastic solutions offered by a trusted leader," Tugwell said.[13]

But of course, the question of what was politically *possible* in this crisis was rendered forever academic by the fact that radical change in the credit structure, instinctively, sternly opposed by Roosevelt, was calculatedly opposed by the few men who had in hand the immediate task of bank reopening. And none other had any voice in the matter.

Late in the night of Monday, March 6, its having become obvious that the bankers talked in circles from which no straight line of advice would ever issue, Moley and Woodin, weary and disgusted with the endless, futile round of argument, retired to Woodin's room in the Carlton and there tried, in peace and quiet, "to see things in the large," as Moley would put it. They promptly agreed that the general plan outlined in the memorandum Mills had handed Woodin on Saturday afternoon was technically sound and workable. It should and would become the main substance of the emergency bill. (Thus was perfectly achieved that continuity between the two administrations for which Woodin, with Moley, had sought on the eve of the inauguration; Hoover's Treasury officials, the chief one being the archreactionary Ogden Mills, substantially wrote the first piece of New Deal legislation!) In other words, the technical problem, having to do with financial procedure and policy, was already essentially solved.

There remained, however, "a problem of public psychology," which was a problem "we were facing . . . more acutely than we were . . . a problem of finance," as Moley would say, and it was to this problem that the two men now addressed themselves. They were as one with Herbert Hoover in their definition of it: They saw it as a "crisis of confidence." They were also essentially at one with Hoover in their approach to a solution: New confidence must be instilled in the top echelon of the financial and business community, whence, with sufficient pumping pressure from the top echelon of government, it would spread swiftly downward and outward through the bulk of the body politic. In a sense, then, Woodin and Moley now operated as confidence men, plotting at midnight a strategy for winning tomorrow's confidence game, and insofar as they deemed a deceptive manipulation of appearances to be an essential ingredient, not only of the banking system they sought to save but also of the strategy for saving it, they themselves so regarded their labors.* By the time the professor left the secretary, in the dark first hour of March 7, and made his weary way to bed in the Mayflower, all the main strategical guidelines had been decided. There would be a "stressing of conventional banking methods and the avoidance of any unusual or highly controversial measures." There would be a "reopening of as many banks as possible" at holiday's end, including banks the solvency of which was dubious ("[W]here there was doubt about solvency, the decision should be weighted on the side of reopening . . ."), because this would increase the "probability of [public] confidence in banks generally." There would be a careful total exclusion from decision-making counsels of "all the reputedly radical and visionary individuals [Tugwell was among those named] who were hovering in the background with novel, even revolutionary, ideas." And there would be a "tremendous gesture by the President and Congress in the direction of [government] economy" joined with a "man-to-man appeal for public confidence by the President himself."[14]

As for this President himself, revealing of his basic mind-set is a reported conversation he had sometime during the crisis week with Senators La Follette of Wisconsin and Costigan of Colorado. When the two senators called upon him to urge bank nationalization or the creation of a national central banking

---

*"Woodin, by his earlier experience of banking, and I, by what I had learned in the last few days . . . had grasped an essential fact," writes Moley on page 171 of his *The First New Deal.* "We knew how much of banking depended on make-believe. . . ."

system so tightly controlled as to be virtually a government enterprise, he replied, "Oh, but that isn't necessary at all. I've had every assurance of cooperation from the bankers!"[15] Simultaneously he was much involved with Budget Director Lewis Douglas in shaping that "tremendous gesture" toward economy which was an essential of the Woodin-Moley confidence-restoring strategy and to which he was personally profoundly committed. Lunching with Douglas in his office on Tuesday, March 7, he approved the drastic spending cuts which Douglas proposed and saw to it that maximum publicity was at once given the fact, rendered ominous by the manner of its announcement, that the Treasury deficit inherited from the Hoover administration totaled some $2,934,000,000. Next day he gave final approval of the economy bill, entitled by Douglas "A Bill to Maintain the Credit of the United States Government," and decided to have it introduced at the earliest possible moment following adoption of the emergency banking measure.

Yet, strange to say, the single substantive idea he personally fed into the bank crisis deliberations was flatly contradictory of the policy he pursued with his budget director. It provoked cries of fearful outrage from the bankers and Treasury officials who learned of it.

On Monday he suggested to Woodin the possibility of avoiding a nationwide use of scrip by permitting holders of government bonds to cash these at par value, immediately, regardless of their maturity dates. This would have supplied the immediate need for currency, certainly, since some $21 billion of bonds were outstanding. It would also have been wildly inflationary, and irreversibly so, being accompanied by no suggested means for contracting the currency once the emergency was over. The credit of the U.S. government, cried horrified Treasury officials, would be completely destroyed! The effect of the suggestion, then—and this may well have been its *intended* effect, on Roosevelt's part—was to stimulate the Treasury conferees into quick agreement (within a few hours after the suggestion was made) upon a scrip-avoidance scheme of their own. Settled upon as a contingency device was a $200 million issue of Federal Reserve notes to be used to satisfy the need for currency if cash withdrawals continued in excess of deposits, for a time, after the bank holiday had ended—a proposal made in the memorandum Mills had given Woodin on Saturday afternoon, which Woodin, alone in his room at the Carlton, after Moley had left for the Mayflower, finally decided to accept, very early in the morning of Tuesday, March 7. "The Reserve Act lets us print all we'll need," said Woodin to Moley as the two breakfasted in the former's room a few hours later. "And . . . it won't look like stage money. It'll be money that looks like money."[16]

Settled upon also were (1) permission to the Reserve Banks to make cash loans to individuals and corporations that gave ninety-day notes backed by pledges of government securities, this permission being accompanied by Reserve bank authority to raise interest rates on such cash loans to force repayment if dangerous inflation threatened, and (2) permission to banks to issue preferred stock for purchase by the RFC, thus obtaining the working capital necessary for true solvency. (In the event, once the immediate crisis pressure was removed, the latter permission was one the bankers would be loath to avail themselves of, being fearful of a governmental control of their operations proportionate to governmental stock ownership. That this doorway to socialism would ever be opened, however, was rendered unlikely to the point of impossibility by the fact that Houston banker Jesse H. Jones, than whom there was no more fervent devotee of private enterprise, was now head of the RFC and would exercise over that increasingly powerful agency an autocratic authority. "In approaching the bank repair job," Jones remembered eighteen years later, "I discussed it freely with the President and recommended that we should not be too open-handed or too quick about the government putting in the needed capital, because if we did so the government would soon control too many banks." Instead, every effort should be made to encourage private individuals to buy stock in their local banks. "He [Roosevelt] agreed, and we decided that we would be liberal in valuing the assets of the banks."[17] Not until governmental deposit insurance imposed an absolute necessity for such action would Jones strongly press the bankers to sell enough preferred stock to the RFC to make their institutions at least minimally actually solvent.)

These major elements of a bank-reopening scheme were presented as a package to Roosevelt on Tuesday afternoon, he having earlier given his approval of the use of Federal Reserve notes instead of scrip. The package was promptly approved. Actual writing of the final bill was begun by Counsel Walter Wyatt of the Federal Reserve at eleven o'clock that night.

III

"WELL, Felix, they'll make a banker of me yet!"

Thus did Roosevelt greet Felix Frankfurter, next day, Wednesday, with a wry laugh, when the law school professor was ushered into the President's office by Marvin McIntyre at half past three in the afternoon.

The professor had been summoned to the White House from the I Street home (a four-story brick house near Lafayette Square) of retired Supreme Court Justice Oliver Wendell Holmes, Jr., who, on that March 8, was celebrating his ninety-second birthday. There had been a small luncheon party, enlivened in defiance of Prohibition by several glasses of champagne. (Among those at table had been two of Frankfurter's protégés, former law students of his, each sent down by him from Harvard to Washington to serve a highly educative year as Holmes's personal secretary. One was ebullient, brilliant Thomas G. "Tommy" Corcoran, rich in Irish charm, who had been Holmes's secretary in 1927 and 1928 and was now an RFC counsel; the other was Donald Hiss, Holmes's current secretary, whose elder brother, Alger, had been Holmes's secretary in 1929 and 1930 and would soon be recruited for service in Henry A. Wallace's Department of Agriculture.) Frankfurter had expected to remain

with Holmes until evening and to see the President there in the Holmes house
in late afternoon. For he knew that Roosevelt, with Eleanor and son James,
was scheduled to call upon the great justice at teatime—this in well-publicized
violation of Hoover's dictum that "the President of the United States calls on
nobody."

To Frankfurter, therefore, the midafternoon summons to the White House
was puzzling. And he was utterly taken aback when, without preliminary, the
President asked him to come into the administration as solicitor general,
launching into a plea for Frankfurter's acceptance before the professor had a
chance to reply. No man was better equipped to argue the government's cases
before the Supreme Court, said Roosevelt. Attorney General Homer Cummings heartily approved the proposed appointment. ". . . I want you down
here, because I need you for all sorts of things, and in all sorts of ways. As
you know, we are going in heavily for utility regulation, reorganization of the
various Commissions, amendment of the Sherman Law. . . ." Moreover,
Frankfurter as solicitor general would be available for appointment to the U.S.
Supreme Court—an appointment which Roosevelt wanted to make as soon as
a vacancy occurred but which it might not be possible for him to make unless
certain "objections to you" were overcome. Roosevelt ticked off the objections:
Frankfurter was a longtime professor who had "never practiced law"; he had
"never held judicial office," had indeed refused Governor Joseph B. Ely's
appointment of him to the Supreme Judicial Court of Massachusetts; he was
widely regarded as a "radical" because of his leading role in the protest against
the Sacco-Vanzetti convictions; and he was a Jew ("your race," as Roosevelt
put it). But all this would "be forgotten or disappear" once Frankfurter had
served as solicitor general.

The President's argument was formidable. It was not, however, persuasive.

Frankfurter refused the office, with proper expressions of gratitude. He said
he could render more important service to the government, and be of greater
use to the President personally, if he remained at Cambridge than if he spent
"sixteen hours a day" preparing briefs and arguing cases before the Court. He
could as Harvard professor continue in a consulting role and as a personnel
recruiting agent for the New Deal, and he could operate as a kind of New Deal
ambassador to British intellectual circles during the year he was scheduled to
spend as visiting professor at Oxford, beginning next September. As for the
Supreme Court possibility, "I really don't think I ought to take a post at which
I cannot be of the use that I can be by remaining where I am, simply because
it may promote my going elsewhere."[18]

From the White House Frankfurter returned to Holmes's I Street house. He
was there at five-thirty, when the White House limousine drew to the curb and
Gus Gennerich, with swift, practiced skill, lifted the crippled President to the
sidewalk, whence on locked braces and his son James's arm, he made his
painful way to the Holmes house door, his wife beside him.

Several remarks allegedly made during the half hour that Roosevelt and

Holmes were together that day would become famous in history. One story would have it that Holmes was in his library reading Plato's *Republic* when the President arrived. "Why do you read Plato, Mr. Justice?" asked Roosevelt, with quizzical smile. "To improve my mind, Mr. President," replied Holmes. Another story has Roosevelt saying, as he rose to take his leave of the Great Dissenter: "This is a dark hour, Justice Holmes. You have lived through half our country's history. You have seen its great men. What is your advice to me?" Said Holmes, without hesitation: "You are in a war, Mr. President. I was in a war, too.* And in a war there is only one rule. Form your battalions and fight!"[19]

After Roosevelt had left, Holmes sat in silence for a long moment, looking at the door. It was as if he shaped from fluid impressions a solid conclusion about the man who had just gone. What was it? Someone in the room— perhaps Tommy Corcoran—asked that question curiously.

"A second-class intellect," replied Holmes regretfully, then, with lifted head and in a louder firmer tone: "But a first-class temperament!"[20]

IV

THE emergency banking bill was sent to Congress shortly after it had convened at noon on Thursday, March 9.

The President's accompanying message was, as he had promised, brief. It stressed the strictly emergency nature of the measure. "Our first task is to reopen all sound banks," he said. "This is an essential preliminary to subsequent [*sic*] legislation directed against speculation with the funds of depositors and other violations of positions of trust." Stressed also was the "clear necessity for immediate action. A continuation of the strangulation of banking facilities is unthinkable."[21]

Certainly immediacy of action was achieved.

When the House began formal consideration of the bill at 2:55 P.M., printed copies of it were not yet available, Walter Wyatt having completed its drafting at 3 o'clock that morning, barely nine hours before its congressional introduction. Into the slotted box where bills are required to be deposited when introduced, was thrust a folded newspaper as substitute for the printed bill until copies of the latter arrived; it was from a typewritten copy that the bill was read aloud. Then Representative Joseph W. Byrns of Tennessee, the majority leader, elected to that post when the House organized itself immediately after convening (Representative Henry T. Rainey of Illinois was elected speaker), announced that, by action of the Rules Committee, no amendments and only

---

*Holmes, aged twenty, had in the spring of 1861 gone from Harvard College onto the battlefields of the Civil War as an officer of the 20th Massachusetts Infantry. He had fought at Balls Bluff, Fair Oaks, Malvern, Antietam, and in a dozen other bloody engagements. He had been thrice wounded, twice so dangerously his life was despaired.

forty minutes of debate would be allowed. As it turned out, there was no debate whatever; nobody spoke against the bill. It was passed by voice vote at 4:05 P.M.

Less swift, but still amazingly swift, was the Senate's action.

The bill was reported out of the Senate Banking and Currency Committee, favorably, with no amendments, at about the time the House was voting on it. Full Senate debate began a half hour later. Soon thereafter Huey Long proposed an amendment authorizing the President to declare the 14,000 state banks members of the Federal Reserve System and eligible as such to receive emergency measure benefits now limited, he somewhat inaccurately asserted, to 5,000 national banks. He made a fiery speech in defense of the "little banks" that had been ruined, he charged, by the worthless paper loaded into them by the "big banks." He was answered by Carter Glass of Virginia with scorn, indignation, and corrective factual information about the bill's provisions. The proposed amendment was then shouted down by voice vote. La Follette spoke at length against the bill. He feared its effect would be a relative strengthening of the New York City national banks over all other banks, the New York banks being now the most solvent, by far the strongest, in the country. There would follow mergers and consolidations into a few "group-banking units" that would control absolutely the national credit system. But he only hinted, and vaguely, at the alternative he favored when he said that there should be a pooling of liabilities as well as of assets of existing banks, evidently in separate categories or institutions (the resources and liabilities "should be merged respectively" were his actual confusing words); that the creation of new purchasing power by state action should be "permitted"; and that "if I could have my way," he would "insure control" by the President of all banks for the duration of the emergency. No one replied to his speech, perhaps because no one knew with any certainty what it meant.

After an amendment proposed by Oklahoma's blind Senator Thomas P. Gore had been put to voice vote and rejected, the bill itself came to a roll-call vote and was passed, 73 to 7. Of the sixteen senators who failed to vote, two who were absentees let it be known that they would have voted against. Bronson Cutting, Hiram Johnson, even Huey Long voted for it in the evident belief that it was an interim measure the adoption of which did not close the door against the permanent fundamental change which they favored. Those voting against included La Follette, Costigan, Farmer-Laborite Henrik Shipstead of Minnesota, Progressive Republican Gerald P. Nye of North Dakota, and Idaho's leonine Senator William E. Borah.

Then the Senate adjourned.

The time was 7:52 P.M. The whole of the enactment process had been completed in fewer than eight hours!

Precisely forty-five minutes later, seated at his desk in the Oval Room, with photographers recording the scene, Franklin Roosevelt signed into law the first bill to come before him as President of the United States. He used but one pen (often several are used for such ceremonial signings, so that several people will have souvenirs of the event), then handed it, with a broad smile, to Nancy Cook, who had been a White House guest since inauguration day.*

Immediately thereafter, under the authority given him by the act (this was a confirmation of the authority granted him by the Trading with the Enemy Act of 1917), he issued a proclamation extending the bank holiday indefinitely. His hope had been that some banks could reopen immediately, but Treasury and Reserve officials who, under the act, had to evaluate and classify banks as to their soundness before issuing them licenses to reopen, told him this was utterly impossible. He was assured, however, that thousands of banks would be licensed to reopen by Monday, enough of them to permit economic life to resume.

Next day (Friday, March 10) Congress received its second message from the new President: a request for authority to effect drastic economies in government. To it was attached the "Bill to Maintain the Credit of the United States Government."

Drafted by Lewis Douglas, with Moley, on Thursday afternoon (they worked on it in the Lincoln Room of the White House, whence they had easy access to Roosevelt), the message began with an expression of gratitude for the "immediate response given yesterday by the Congress to the necessity for drastic action to restore and improve our banking system"† but went on to say that a "like necessity exists with respect to the finances of the Government itself." The federal government had "for three long years . . . been on the road toward bankruptcy." To a deficit of $462,000,000 for fiscal 1931 had been added a deficit of $2,472,000,000 for fiscal 1932; the deficit for fiscal 1933 would probably exceed $1,200,000,000, and that for fiscal 1934 would probably be more than $1,000,000,000 "unless immediate action is taken" to prevent it. The "stagnation of the economic life of our people," the swelling of "the ranks of the unemployed," the bank collapse itself—all these had been in part effected by the horrendous increase in the national debt. "National recovery" accordingly depended upon an immediate "drastic retrenchment" of government

---

*Cook, with Marion Dickerman, had, of course, been close to Eleanor all through the inauguration day activities and had slept in the White House that Saturday night. Next day, Dickerman had returned to New York City to perform her Todhunter School duties, but Cook stayed on in the White House for eight days "to help Eleanor make the second floor into a living quarters for the Roosevelt family," to quote Dickerman. "They found that the brass bed in Franklin's room was too short, so Nan made, in the [Val-Kill Industries] shop, a fine four-poster bed of extra length when she got back to the cottage. The President used it for as long as he was in the White House. Nancy also made a four-poster for Eleanor's use in the White House."[22]

†A cynical hindsight might find significant the fact that the presidential message accompanying the emergency banking legislation had made no claim that it would either "restore" or "improve" the banking system. Instead, senators and representatives had been assured of the bill's limited purpose: that of "opening banks for the resumption of business," "an essential preliminary" to the truly substantial permanent legislation which would follow. "In the short space of five days it is impossible for us to formulate completed measures to prevent the recurrence of the evils of the past," the message had said. "This does not and should not, however, justify any delay in accomplishing this first step."[23]

expenditures. Hence the proposed legislation. It empowered the President to cut all government salaries, including congressional salaries and his own, by as much as 15 percent (the cuts were to be proportioned to the reduction in the cost of living resulting from price deflation since 1928); to slash severely veterans' pensions; to eliminate some categories of veterans' benefits altogether; and to curtail or eliminate other governmental activities, including scientific research and statistical services, without further reference to the legislature.

Because of its bold challenge to the theretofore irresistible veterans' lobby (the American Legion, the Veterans of Foreign Wars), which in the 1920's had forced much of the now-threatened benefit legislation onto the books over presidential vetoes and which now with swift efficiency, having had a day or so of "leaked" warning, loosed a flood of protesting telegrams upon members of Congress, this economy bill had far rougher going in Congress than the emergency banking bill had had. Indeed, it almost certainly encountered more congressional opposition than would have faced a Rooseveltian move to nationalize the credit structure in that week of closed banks, when the bankers themselves, viewed in the light of Ferdinand Pecora's continuing relentless investigation of their practices, were seen by myriads as a very low form of human life.*

The Democratic congressional leaders to whom Roosevelt outlined the bill on the night of March 9, in a meeting that opened in the White House barely an hour after the emergency banking bill's signing, were far from cheerfully acceptive of it, though the conservatives among them were grimly, determinedly so. Most, in fact, were dazed, some were angry, a few actually rebellious, when they left the White House shortly after midnight. And rebellion spread through the rank and file of the Democracy in the House next day. Majority Leader Byrns refused to sponsor the measure. House Speaker Rainey failed in an attempt to bind his party colleagues to an affirmative vote on the bill when he moved to do so in a caucus on Saturday morning, March 11; he could not obtain the necessary two-thirds vote. Not only that, but the caucus came close to gutting the measure. Skillful parliamentary maneuvering by conservative John McDuffie of Alabama, whom Byrns had defeated in the contest for House Speaker, was required to prevent caucus adoption of an amendment that would have drastically curtailed the President's power to cut pensions.

And it was only by a free and threatful use of the President's name, including reference to the fact that the President had patronage at his disposal and proposed *not* to dispose of it until the legislation he deemed necessary was on the books, that administration agents were enabled to achieve a modicum of

---

*The Senate Banking and Currency Committee had begun a mandated investigation of banks and banking practices in April 1932. The investigation was intensified after the committee acquired the brilliant and indefatigable Pecora as its counsel, following the election of 1932; it continued through 1933 into 1934. Its revelations embarrassed the financial community and outraged the general public. See Kenneth S. Davis, *FDR: The New York Years* (New York, 1985), p. 441.

control over unruly Democrats when, a few hours later, the bill was brought
up for action by the full House. Here, again, the conservative McDuffie was
economy's champion. Working in close alliance with archconservative Republican John Taber of New York, he led successful battles against motions to
recommit and motions to amend during the severely limited debating time (a
mere two hours) which was allowed by chair ruling. The bill then passed, 266
to 183. It might not have done so, however, if Republicans had not come to
its rescue: Sixty-nine of them crossed the aisle to support the measure while
ninety-two Democrats, seven of whom were party leaders, voted against it.[24]

Thus Roosevelt on Saturday evening had reason for concern over the fate
of this to him crucial measure in the Senate, where debate on it would begin
on Monday. Veterans' telegrams of protest flooded now onto senators' desks,
and their persuasive power, though offset by a flood of proeconomy messages,
was augmented by a conviction on the part of several influential senators that
the proposed measure, acutely deflationary in effect, could only delay a desperately needed increase in consumer purchasing power. This meant that the
upper chamber, in view of the Senate's tradition of unlimited debate, would
pass the bill (its ultimate passage appeared overwhelmingly probable) only
after dangerously prolonged deliberations. There was even the possibility of a
filibuster. The terrific momentum built up by the administration during its first
week was threatened, a momentum Roosevelt was now very anxious to maintain. For by Saturday night he had about decided not to permit a congressional
recess once the immediate emergency legislation was through but, instead, to
hold Congress in continuous session until a major portion of his program was
enacted.

This last was an exceedingly bold decision, considering the fact that he *had*
no prepared program as yet—not for public works or relief of the unemployed,
not for agricultural recovery, not for industrial recovery, not for bank and
securities market reform—but only loose collections of often contradictory
proposals. He would have to improvise a program while simultaneously presiding over its legislation, and the challenge was one before which a "first-class
intellect" would have quailed, even though joined to a "first-class temperament." Roosevelt, far from quailing, seemed to welcome the challenge as an
exciting game, an opportunity to exercise to the full his political skills.

He sought stratagems for the accomplishment of immediate purpose.

He found and employed two within the next forty-eight hours.

Already he had published an explanatory reassuring statement of the general method by which banks would be reopened, announcing in it his "intention, over the national radio networks, at ten o'clock on Sunday evening, to
explain clearly and in simple language to all of you just what has been achieved
and the sound reasons which underlie this declaration to you." Already a draft
of the announced radio speech had been prepared by Charles Michelson and
extensively revised (virtually rewritten) by Arthur Ballantine. And on Sunday,
Roosevelt, with the Ballantine-revised draft before him, dictated a final version, employing plain language of the kind he would have used had he ex-

plained things to his farmer Moses Smith at Hyde Park or to a worried housewife in Poughkeepsie.[25]

Meanwhile, radio network officials had agreed that the announcer of the presidential broadcast would be Robert Trout of the Columbia Broadcasting System's Washington station, whose manager was Harry C. Butcher. Two introductions were prepared; a formal one by Trout; a folksy one by Butcher.* Both were submitted for review in the White House, whence word came promptly back that Roosevelt much preferred the folksy one. So it was that, at ten o'clock in the evening of March 12, Bob Trout's mellow voice told some 60 million people, seated before nearly 20 million radios, that "the President wants to come into your home and sit at your fireside for a little fireside chat."[26]

And Roosevelt did so.

Riding his richly resonant tenor voice, he came as a smiling and reassuringly confident visitor into nearly 20 million homes to tell his friends there—a Buffalo shipping clerk, an elderly widow in Des Moines, a wheat farmer on the High Plains, a gas station operator in Birmingham, a secretary-typist in Memphis, an Oregon lumberman, a Chicago factory worker, a Kansas college professor, each in his or her own dwelling place—that they need have no fear. Everything that had gone wrong was being fixed up, and in a way that would keep things from going wrong again.

". . . [W]e start tomorrow, Monday, with the opening of the banks in twelve Federal Reserve Bank cities—those banks which on first examination by the Treasury have been already found to be all right," he said. "This will be followed on Tuesday by the resumption of all their functions by banks already found to be sound in cities where there are recognized clearing houses. . . . On Wednesday and succeeding days banks in smaller places all over the country will resume business, subject, of course, to the Government's physical capacity to complete its survey. . . . Let me make it clear . . . that if your bank does not open the first day you are by no means justified in believing it will not open. A bank that opens on one of the subsequent days is in exactly the same status as the bank that opens tomorrow. . . . I can assure you that it is safer to keep your money in a reopened bank than under the mattress. . . ."

To the prevailing popular antipathy to bankers as a class he made only such concession as was absolutely required by the circumstances, and his reference to it was designed to mitigate it:

"We had a bad banking situation," he said. "Some of our bankers had shown themselves either incompetent or dishonest. . . . They had used the money entrusted to them in speculations and unwise loans. This was, of course, not

---

*Born and reared on an Iowa farm, Butcher clinched his first job, that of editing a weekly issued by the Illinois Agricultural Association, after graduating in agricultural journalism from Iowa State College in 1924, when he told his prospective employer that one should write farm articles "as though you were chatting with the farmer beside a kerosene lamp in his home." This "theory," as Butcher called it, had been given him by editors of the *Iowa Homestead* for whom he had written pieces while an undergraduate at Ames.

true in the vast majority of our banks, but it was true in enough of them to shock people for a time into a sense of insecurity. . . . It was the Government's job to straighten out this situation. . . . And the job is being performed. . . . Confidence and courage are the essentials of success in carrying out our plan. You . . . must have faith; you must not be stampeded by rumors or guesses. Let us unite in banishing fear. . . . Together we cannot fail."[27]

Of all the dozens of "fireside chats* that would ultimately be made, none was more hugely successful, more utterly effective of its specific purpose than this first of them. It marked the end of the banking crisis, though grave problems yet remained unsolved, for there were no runs on the reopened banks, on Monday, the thirteenth. On the contrary, deposits far exceeded withdrawals as hoarded currency poured back into bank vaults all over the country. Some $15.5 million in coin and paper currency and $11.5 million in gold certificates, $27 million in all, had come into the Federal Reserve Bank in New York by day's end, while only $18 million had been paid out to member banks, and in other Reserve Banks across the land the story was much the same. It would continue the same during the weeks and months ahead as more and more banks were reopened. By the end of March 5,300 members of the Federal Reserve System and 7,600 state-chartered banks would be in virtually full operation, with reopenings to continue at the rate of about 100 a month until the end of the year, and practically all the $200 million of new Federal Reserve notes reposed unused in Treasury and bank vaults. They ultimately were retired unused. Simultaneously came a resurgence of activity in the securities markets, stimulated by the President's move toward government economy. An issue of $800 million of U.S. Treasury certificates of indebtedness was offered for bids on Wednesday, March 15, as part of the Treasury's refinancing program and was promptly oversubscribed by 100 percent. The event was encouraged by interest rates of 4 and 4½ percent, the highest for government securities since the Great War, but it was nonetheless indicative of a remarkable revival of business confidence. On the same day the New York Stock Exchange, closed since March 3, opened to record five hours later the greatest single-day rise in living memory. Stock prices advanced more than 15 percent on the largest volume of transactions (more than 3 million shares) since September 1932, when the market was steeply falling.

Thus there was and is justification for a dramatic declaration made by Raymond Moley seven years later. "Capitalism," declared Moley, "was saved in eight days. . . ."[29]

And waves of adulation lapped Roosevelt around, with the tallest and strongest rolling in from the right. An "incredible change" had "come over the face of things here in the United States in a single week," editorialized the *Wall Street Journal*, because "the new Administration in Washington has

---

*"The name 'fireside chat' seems to be used by the press even when the radio talk is delivered on a very hot mid-summer evening," Roosevelt commented in 1938.[28]

superbly risen to the occasion." If one admitted that only "a good beginning had been made" and that "incalculable tasks" remained, one must also acknowledge that "there are times when a beginning is nearly everything."[30]

Yet there *were* those remaining "incalculable tasks," and behind the scenes, in Washington, anxious men suffered moments of intense anxiety as they continued to make close, dangerous decisions. Perhaps the most momentous of these, certainly the most fortunate for Roosevelt's political future, was the very first one to follow the fireside chat: a decision on the morning of March 13 to permit the reopening of A. P. Giannini's giant Bank of America, in California.

With 410 branches and a million depositors, but with some $600 million in deposit liabilities also, the Bank of America was overwhelmingly the bank of "little people" on the West Coast. In this it was reminiscent of its ill-fated near namesake, the Bank of United States in New York City.* And no doubt Roosevelt's unhappy experience with the Bank of United States was what made him exceedingly wary of personally responsible involvement when a flat disagreement concerning the Giannini bank developed between the secretary of the treasury and the governor of the Federal Reserve Bank in San Francisco. This governor, John U. Calkins, representative of those long-established big bankers who resented, feared, even hated Giannini as an Italian immigrant upstart whose flamboyant expansionism threatened their hegemony, was emphatically of the opinion that the Bank of America was insolvent. He cited bank examiner reports in support of his contention. Woodin, on the other hand, was inclined to accept as valid Giannini's claim, supported by some statistical evidence, that the bank had grown considerably stronger since the last examiners' reports had been made, months ago. In any case, the risk of a license to reopen measured smaller in Woodin's mind than the certainty of vast economic distress along the West Coast if the license was refused, and he made this argument when he, with Awalt, called upon the President on Monday morning to urge a presidential order on the matter. Roosevelt demurred. Instead, he suggested that Woodin phone Calkins and either persuade him to acquiesce in a licensed reopening or force him to take full personal responsibility for a refusal of license. Woodin did so a few minutes later. Calkins, jarred by Woodin's stubborn insistence and by cited figures indicative of the Bank of America's solvency, refused the responsibility demanded of him. "Well, then," said Woodin, "the bank will open."[31]

Roosevelt himself would take full personal credit for this decision during the weeks and months ahead, as the Bank of America not only survived but greatly prospered, aided by large loans from the RFC. By May he would be telling a highly influential Californian, in dramatic circumstantial detail, how he had forced Calkins to shift ground by threatening to keep closed every bank in the San Francisco Federal Reserve District unless Giannini's bank was reopened. And the increasingly powerful Giannini was personally grateful; he became a

---

*See Kenneth S. Davis, *FDR: The New York Years* (New York, 1985), pp. 224–226.

devotee of Roosevelt and a staunch supporter of the administration, one of the very few bankers in the land to remain so through thick and thin.[32]

The President's persuasive power over a Senate that was just beginning its formal consideration of the economy bill was, of course, much augmented by the fireside chat's remarkable impress on the popular mind, by the success of the bank reopenings to which the talk contributed, and by the simultaneous resurgence of a general "business confidence" having promised government economy as a central theme. But Roosevelt could not be absolutely sure of this resounding success as he supped with a few intimates at the White House on Sunday evening, awaiting the time for his going on the air. Hence his second stratagem for the accomplishment of immediate purpose.

"I think now would be a good time for beer," he announced to his companions at table. He had been informed by legal experts that the Volstead Act could be constitutionally modified to permit the manufacture and sale of malt or vintage beverages having low (3.2 percent, or "nonintoxicating") alcoholic content. Louis Howe placed before him a copy of the 1932 Democratic platform, and from it, after he had completed his fireside chat, he derived the essential language of his third message to Congress, probably the shortest (a mere seventy-two words) ever delivered. "I recommend to the Congress the passage of legislation for the immediate modification of the Volstead Act, in order to legalize the manufacture and sale of beer and other beverages of such alcoholic content as is permissible under the Constitution," he wrote, "and to provide through such manufacture and sale, by substantial taxes, a proper and much-needed revenue for the Government. I deem action at this time to be of the highest importance."[33] When the House received this message at noon next day, it promptly changed its mind about recessing, as it had planned to do, until the Senate had completed action on the economy bill. There were loud demands for an immediate vote on the measure, the adoption of which was perfectly certain. Next day the beer-wine bill sailed through the lower chamber on a vote of 62 to 13.

This spurred swift action on the economy bill in the Senate since the upper chamber could not approve the enormously popular Volstead modification until economy was disposed of. Also, opposition to economy began to melt away from the Senate floor, and to so great an extent that the administration could safely refuse the slightest compromise with the measure's opponents. There was dissension within the ranks of the veterans themselves. Men who had fought overseas, especially those who had suffered battle wounds, had long resented the fact that they and the widows of battle-slain comrades often received less compensation through the Veterans Administration than did men who, drafted into uniform, had seen no action but had suffered disabling injury or illness months or years after the war's last shot had been fired. These bona fide veterans were perfectly willing to have "freeloaders" struck from benefit roles, so long as they themselves were protected; and, of course, veterans as a class were especially vulnerable to appeals to their "patriotism" in this "war" against depression.

A motion to recommit the economy bill was defeated, 60 to 20, on the Senate floor, late on Monday afternoon. Two days later the bill, without important amendment, was passed by the Senate, 62 to 13.

And on the day after that, Thursday, March 16, the Senate, whose composition rendered it much more susceptible to dry pressures than was the House, passed the beer-wine measure by a vote of 43 to 30.

V

So it was that Roosevelt, by the end of his first dozen days in the White House, had in "three quick blows . . . broken as many iron bands which were strangling the country actually or psychologically," to quote Ernest Lindley. "He had broken the banking panic and salvaged most of the banking system. He had beaten the most feared lobby in Washington. . . . He had beaten the remains of the once all-powerful dry lobby, and broken the fourteen-year grip of Volsteadism. The country surged with enthusiasm and hope."[34]

Embedded in this great triumph, however, or in the process from which it emerged, was a warning, if not the actual seed, of future troubles. And of this Roosevelt took heed, promptly.

The telegram which, on the day before the economy measure went to Congress, was dispatched by the American Legion lobby in Washington to Legion posts all over the nation said: "Wire your congressmen and Senators immediately opposing Congress abdicating its constitutional responsibility by granting to the President authority to repeal or amend existing veterans' benefits without approval of Congress." The wires came flooding back, as we have seen. And the danger of dictatorship implicit in this proposed new transfer of legislative authority from Capitol Hill to the White House, coming hard upon the broad grant of executive power made by the emergency banking bill, was then stressed by the economy bill's opponents during debate on the Senate floor. Alarmed senators described what was happening as a long first step in the direction taken by the Weimar Republic when the Reichstag acquiesced in a government that increasingly ruled by executive decree. Was this not the way to an American Hitler, or Mussolini, with Roosevelt as dictator?

Such talk alarmed Roosevelt himself. He, in the very act of reaching out for presidential powers unprecedented in times of peace, was acutely aware of the long-run political potency of the charge that he aspired to rule by fiat. To the extent it was believed, the charge, its negative force fed by the unfolding appalling spectacle of the new Nazi Germany, could generate only serious hazards to the President's future persuasive influence over populace and legislature. He was at some immediate pains, therefore, to counteract it.

For in truth it was only persuasive power, leadership power whereby things could be made or permitted to happen for the general good within the framework and through the processes of democracy, that Franklin Roosevelt really wanted for himself. The fun and excitement of politics as game would have been lost to him in a grant of despotic authority. Such a grant would have denied him opportunities to exercise manipulative skills of which he was very proud and from the exercise of which he derived great pleasure—his ability, for one thing, to locate and occupy pivotal points upon which countervailing forces were narrowly poised; his ability, for another, to make desired influential personal impressions upon many different kinds of people, charming them into an eagerness to do his bidding. Such a grant would also have imposed upon him burdens of personal responsibility from which he was now happily freed by his religion-rooted sense of historic mission and role within the American system of checks and balances. Moreover, his sense of decency, his human empathy and sympathy, his kindly temperament and open mind—all were combined in a strong aversion to any personal exercise of naked, intimidating coercive power over fellow human beings. The aversion could be overcome now and then by a well-camouflaged streak of vindictiveness in him —it would be in the case of Robert Moses, for instance, whenever opportunity occurred—but in general it was far greater and stronger in him than it commonly was in those most likely to damn him, in the future, for an insatiable power lust. Indeed, it was the latter's own power lust, the big businessman's common tendency to regard common folk as merely useful commodities or exploitable "resources" and to define "freedom" as a sacred "right" to exploit without governmental interference, that would constitute the greatest single threat, almost certainly, to the New Deal as servant of *all* the people.

Hence the swift reaction by which Roosevelt let it be known through the press, as from an authoritative White House source, that he had not the slightest intention to destroy the prevailing constitutional separation and balance of powers. He would call for no laws creative of a "constitutional dictatorship," said his agents to anxious senators.[35] He also encouraged Felix Frankfurter to "work" on Walter Lippmann in an effort to moderate the highly influential columnist's reiterated published contempt for Congress, harsh strictures upon legislative deliberations in general, and yearning toward a "concentration of authority" in the executive.

Sometime during his second or third week in the White House, Roosevelt reviewed with care copies of recent correspondence between Frankfurter and Lippmann, brought to him by the law professor. He heartily approved, he was himself influenced by, an argument Frankfurter addressed to Lippmann on March 11, the day following the introduction to Congress of the economy bill. Frankfurter the Brandeisian had written:

> Of course there are times for summary action and the pace for devising policies is properly more rapid at one time than at another. But all this is a very different thing from educating the public into the psychology of dictatorship. . . . The last week of course called for rapidity of deliberation and decision. But I think nothing but harm comes from talking about dictatorship, however euphemistically phrased, when all that we mean is responsibility appropriate to the specific situations. Before very long we shall, I think, be confronting this problem very concretely in the potential danger of too-hasty, too-ill-considered reorganizations of different activities of government,

derived from short-sighted notions of economy. . . . After all, the Lord doesn't create people sufficiently capacious in wisdom and detachment—no matter how disinterested—to run these vast organisms, whether of government or of finance, without ample opportunity for the corrective judgment of the deliberative process. And I strongly deplore the current tendency to assume that power as such generates wisdom and that the deliberative processes are drags upon wise action.

By such Brandeisian argument Lippmann was unpersuaded. Asked Lippmann of Frankfurter in a letter dated March 14: "[W]hat would you have done in the circumstances of the last two or three weeks? Do you really think, for example, that I should have urged Congress to consider carefully and attempt to understand thoroughly the provisions of the banking bill before passing it, or was it right to call upon Congress to take the thing on faith, suspending debate, suspending the process of education, suspending the deliberative method?" There were those, of course, who would have replied that Lippmann emphatically *should* have done these things he had deliberately refrained from doing, that Congress *should* have understood, should have been given the time and means for understanding, the legislation it had enacted on March 9. But Frankfurter replied on March 15:

The actions of Congress at this session offend none of my prejudices regarding the appropriate scope for reason in government or the appropriate role of Congress in our scheme of things. What I object to—and it goes to the very root of my political convictions—is the building up of opinion hostile to the need for Congress as a policy-making organ and as a critic of executive measures. It is one thing, in a time of great danger, to exact concentrated attention and a complete disregard of irrelevant or minor motives. It is quite another thing to ask Congress to abdicate its judgment. . . . I venture to suggest that the important thing [for you to do] is to explain . . . the reasons behind various proposals, rather than to inculcate the simple habit of expecting the White House to pull rabbits out of a hat.

Frankfurter predicted that "conflicts of interest now brewing beneath the surface" would "break out, and not too pleasantly, before this Administration has run its term. I have not the slightest fear," he went on, "that that tendency will be encouraged by Roosevelt himself. By temperament and experience he knows the importance of carrying the consent of the country—as far as may be—along with him, not merely generally and vaguely but by specific appeal on specific policies."

Roosevelt, who vividly remembered Lippmann's harshly negative judgments upon his (Roosevelt's) fitness to govern, published less than a year ago, derived only ironic amusement from the columnist's current demand that he be given more governing power than the Constitution allowed. He placed a low if not negative value upon a support he knew to be strictly temporary. For Lippmann seemed to him as much an elitist as the Herbert Hoover who believed, according to gubernatorial candidate Roosevelt in 1928, "that there exists at the top of our social system . . . a very limited group of highly able, highly educated people, through whom all progress in this land must originate . . . little tin gods on wheels up at the top who have got some kind of heavenly right to rule." Lippmann's contempt for Congress was part of his contempt for the intelligence of the common man whose mind, according to Lippmann's *Public Opinion,* was chock-full of fact-distorting, idea-resisting "stereotypes." And Lippmann would inevitably turn against the New Deal as the New Deal manifested respect for, and proved sympathetically responsive to, the views and interests and wishes of the ordinary citizen.

Roosevelt said as much to Frankfurter, who agreed with him.[36]

3

➵➤✕◀◄

Improvisations on Discordant Themes: The Opening Rush of the Hundred Days

I

TIME, in this opening spring of the New Deal, was so thick with event, so rich in excitements, so crowded with swift and seemingly profound change that a day of it was to the nation's immediate consciousness as a week or even several months of ordinary experience. There was an enormous speeding up of perceptions. Yesterday became years ago, tomorrow was a distant future, yet both pressed in so hard upon today, they thrust so much of residual possibility and potential reality into the present moment that *anything* might happen before the sun went down.

When Roosevelt opened his third presidential press conference on Wednesday morning, March 15, 1933, a few hours before the Senate's final action on government economy, he seemed to be in almost perfect step with the new rhythm of history. Indeed, he marched so closely to this rhythm that millions of his countrymen were convinced that he set it. He manifested no smug satisfaction over what had been accomplished since inauguration day. He sought, instead, to dispel euphoria or any trace of complacency by viewing the events of the last ten days in terms of national needs, national goals. There had been thus far, he indicated, a successful holding action against the enemy depression; a solid defensive position had been established, but there had been no attack, and without attack there could be no final victory. "Entirely just for background, the general thought has been this: that even if we can get through the three measures—banking economics, the economy bill and the beer bill—we still shall have done nothing on the constructive side, unless you consider the beer bill partially constructive." Hence his proposal of "two other matters that I would very much like to get started while the Congress is here —both of them constructive." One was "to put people to work in the national forests" in a way that "does not conflict with existing so-called public works." The other was an "effort to increase the value of farm products" through a reduction of crop acreages. This last must be done immediately, before next year's crops were planted, if it were to affect this year's prices.

Obviously he had thought a good deal about putting unemployed men to work in the forests. The ridicule heaped upon his ill-considered, ill-phrased reforestation proposal during the campaign had stimulated him to do so.* To reporters' questions about this proposed measure he could and did give cogent

*See Davis, *FDR: The New York Years,* pp. 334–335, 340.

answers. But about the proposed machinery for raising agricultural prices by reducing production, and allegedly in ways protective of family farming, he spoke with remarkable vagueness. Asked if all the "principal crops" would be included, he replied: "I think, entirely off the record, it will be something along the lines of leasing and certain features of the Smith cotton bills." Would it be permanent legislation? "No. Obviously a farm bill is in the nature of an experiment. . . . My position toward farm legislation is that we ought to try to do something to increase the value of farm products and if the darn thing doesn't work, we can say so quite frankly, but at least try it." In what order would the two proposals be made? "I don't know," he replied. "I haven't got to that yet or the time of sending the message up."[1]

Yet it was on the very next day (March 16) that he submitted to Congress the farm bill—a measure of unprecedented complexity and immense long-run implications, not just for agriculture but for the national economy, the national social structure as a whole. His accompanying message was as brief as the bill was long. It stressed the experimental nature of the proposal. "I tell you frankly," he said, "that this is a new and untrod path, but I tell you with equal frankness that an unprecedented condition calls for new means to rescue agriculture. If a fair administrative trial of it is made and it does not produce the hoped-for results I shall be the first to acknowledge it and advise you."[2] It was a message he himself had written, and it was considerably less committal than the one Wallace and Tugwell had brought him on the afternoon of the fifteenth, seeking and gaining his approval of its immediate introduction.

Such introduction settled once and for all the questions of congressional recess in the near future. There would be none. Democratic leaders, meeting at the White House on March 17, agreed to hold Congress in session indefinitely.

II

THE farm bill itself, under the threat of violent revolution in the rural Midwest, had evolved through a clash of alternative proposals into an omnibus measure which, in the words of agricultural journalist Russell Lord, "sought to legalize almost anything anybody could dream up." It was initially seen by Ray Moley, through spectacles provided him by Baruch's man Hugh Johnson, as an appalling hodgepodge the passage of which through Congress was as unlikely as it was undesirable.[3]

Candidate Roosevelt had indicated to farm leaders, and President-elect Roosevelt had reaffirmed, his willingness to accept as administration measure any agricultural recovery program upon which they all generally agreed. Late in the campaign he had said in the hearing of Clifford V. Gregory, *Prairie Farmer* editor, that his first act in the White House would be to summon the farm leaders to Washington, lock them in a room, and keep them there until they did arrive at a consensus.[4] But the main thrust of his own developing commitment, imposed upon him by external pressures, was toward the voluntary domestic allotment plan. This, it will be recalled,* was the complex plan for farm production controls the chief prophet of which was Montana State College's Milburn L. Wilson and which Candidate Roosevelt had subscribed to with studied vagueness, in his Chicago acceptance speech and in the farm program "specifications" set forth in his Topeka campaign speech. It became the essential substance of the Democratic farm bill, the so-called Agricultural Adjustment Act, which was introduced in the lame-duck congressional session.

By then domestic allotment was receiving strong support from leading farm journals (*Wallace's Farmer, Prairie Farmer,* several others); from distinguished economists led by the brilliant Mordecai Ezekiel of the U.S. Department of Agriculture; and, most important, from the American Farm Bureau Federation, by far the largest of the national farm organizations (though the Farmers' Union was growing rapidly). But the plan had also strong enemies. These included the yet-numerous and vociferous exponents of McNary-Haugenism, with its reliance on "marketing agreements," a "two-price" system, and government disposal of surpluses on the foreign market. Especially bitter was George N. Peek of the now-defunct Moline Plow Company, a coauthor of McNary-Haugen, who, identifying himself with hardheaded "dirt farmers," condemned domestic allotment as a typically complicated, impractical, theoretic scheme of the "professors." From a different angle, in good part because of badly blurred delegations of authority by the President-elect,† came destructive fire by Henry Morgenthau, Jr., who had not been disabused of his notion that he was Roosevelt's chief spokesman on agricultural matters and who, through all the early part of the interregnum, aspired to become secretary of agriculture. Generally accompanied to farm policy meetings by Professor William I. Myers of Cornell, Morgenthau had majored in agriculture as a Cornell undergraduate, had been a pupil of Cornell economist George Warren, and was much under the influence of Warren's theory of prices.‡ He proposed in place of domestic allotment a kind of shotgun approach to farm relief, an approach including marginal land retirement, aid to farm cooperatives, aid in farm mortgage refinancing, expansion of farm credit, elimination of speculation in commodity futures, and, as key basic element, the raising ("reflation") of commodity prices, and the ultimate achievement of a stable "commodity dollar" through governmental manipulations of the price of gold. Yet another line of fire came from John Simpson of the Farmers' Union and Milo Reno

---

*See Davis, *FDR: The New York Years,* pp. 363–365.

†"F.D.R. does not realize what the issues are and is careless in his commitments," complained Tugwell in his diary entry for January 12, 1933. "He tells several of us to do the same things even though we may have opposing views and then forgets." Tugwell was referring to the developing policy disagreement between himself and Henry Morgenthau, Jr.[5]

‡Warren's theory was that the price of gold determined other prices and that, therefore, the government could raise commodity prices by buying gold at prices arbitrarily set somewhat (not too much) higher than the prevailing gold price. See Davis, *FDR: The New York Years,* p. 359.

of the Farmers' Holiday Association. Like Peek, these men saw domestic allotment as an excessively complicated, unworkable, misdirected scheme—"worse than silly," as Reno put it. Was not the aim to increase farm prices and incomes relative to those of industry? Well, then, why not do so with simple directness? asked Simpson. There should be governmental price-fixing whereby the farmer would be guaranteed a "cost of production" price considerably higher than that aimed for in the proposed measure. And since the problem was clearly not "overproduction but underconsumption" resulting from the "monopolization and manipulation of our circulating medium," there must be a very substantial inflation of the currency.[6]

Such opposition had not prevented Agricultural Adjustment's passage through the House on January 12. It had gone through then on a vote of 203 to 150—an event largely consequent upon Speaker (Vice President-elect) Garner's coercive leadership of the House's Democratic majority, but aided by Progressive Republican votes rounded up (strange to say) by a politician as invincibly urban as Al Smith, though of very different stripe—namely, Representative Fiorello La Guardia of New York.* In the Senate, where conservatives were outraged by it, however, the proposal had gone nowhere. It was yet unreported by the Agriculture Committee when the lame-duck session ended.

But there remained the spur of threatened farm violence, and it now dug ever more deeply into Congress's left flank. "Unless something is done for the American farmer we will have revolution in the countryside within twelve months," Edward A. O'Neal, Farm Bureau Federation president, had predicted to a Senate committee hearing in January. At about the same time John Simpson had expressed to Roosevelt in a letter his "candid opinion . . . that unless you call a special session of Congress, after the fourth of March, and start a revolution in government affairs there will be one started in the country," and by "country" he evidently meant rural America.[7] Since then there had been growing evidence that farmers were preparing, psychologically and through organized action, to use whatever force seemed to them necessary to defend what they conceived to be their rights. They banded together to prevent foreclosures of mortgages on their neighbors' properties, to prevent competitive bidding at auction sales held to satisfy the claims of creditors (in several instances the farmer threatened with displacement was enabled to buy back his land, his buildings, his equipment for a dollar or so), and to prevent the delivery of farm produce to market. In the second week of the New Deal, Milo Reno announced that a farmers' strike would begin on May 3 if Congress had not by that time enacted a relief measure satisfactory to the Farmers' Holiday Association. There loomed the possibility, even the probability, of pitched and bloody battles between angry farmers and law enforcement agents as spring came on.

---

*La Guardia was himself a lame duck, his vote-attracting liberalism having proved incapable of overcoming his vote-repelling Republican label in the 1932 Democratic landslide. He was making plans to run for mayor of New York City in the fall.

Hardly less than the banking crisis, then, was this developing storm an immediate emergency. Clearly there must be government action on the farm front, "and action now!"

So on the evening of March 8, within an hour of his meeting with congressional leaders to explain the banking bill on which they would act on the morrow, Roosevelt, called upon in the Oval Room by Wallace and Tugwell, acquiesced in their suggestion that they proceed at once with farm legislation. Roosevelt also acquiesced in the Wallace-Tugwell suggestion that to insure the necessary swift agreement among farm leaders upon a draft bill, a wide range of program proposals be included in it, with the secretary of agriculture empowered to decide which among them would be emphatically implemented, which played down, which ignored altogether.

It was a suggestion toward which important farm leaders themselves were naturally gravitating.

Thus with Clifford Gregory. The *Prairie Farmer* editor was one of fifty-odd men summoned to the capital by telegram and telephone to join with U.S. Department of Agriculture (USDA) officials in an agricultural bill-drafting conference to begin on Friday morning, March 10. On the evening of March 9, while on a train to Washington, he read in an afternoon paper the provisions of the emergency banking bill. He was at once struck by the bill's wholesale transfer of power from legislature to executive; it was a device surely as applicable to governmental dealings with the farm crisis as it was to governmental dealings with the financial crisis. "There was the answer to the problem," he promptly concluded, "—a broad grant of authority to an administrative agency."[8]

The expansively revised Agricultural Adjustment bill which emerged from all this had domestic allotment at its heart. It proposed to raise farm prices and individual farm incomes by *paying* farmers to produce less, an arrangement deemed equivalent in justice, and a necessary offset, to the high tariff protection and special subsidies which government had long given manufacturers. Federal paychecks, called "benefit payments," were to go to individual farmers who "cooperated" in the program by entering into written agreements to reduce their crop acreages and hog production to specified "quotas," such cooperation to be entirely voluntary. Indeed, "democracy" was, in M. L. Wilson's conception, the key descriptive word of the whole enterprise, and Wilson's conception was destined to become a guiding principle of program administration. All farmers directly affected by an "adjustment" policy were to be involved in its determination, and administration was to be highly decentralized. Before any particular crop control program could go into effect —for cotton, say, or wheat, tobacco, or corn-hog—it must be approved by a large majority of that commodity's producers, voting in a national referendum; and local committees of farmers, county committees for the most part, elected by local "cooperators," were to oversee the actual applications of the program to the land, insuring "compliance" through direct visual knowledge of how each of their neighbors was handling his acreage. The declared aim was to achieve a "parity" of farm and industrial prices, with "parity" defined as the ratio of farm to factory prices that had prevailed in the halcyon years of 1909–1914. The payments were *not* to be made out of general tax revenues; Roosevelt set his face as flint against any such drain on the Treasury. They would instead be financed by a special "processing tax" levied on processors of farm produce into consumer goods. That such tax would be automatically passed on to the consumer in higher prices was assumed but unstressed by the plan's proponents, though Republican opponents soon charged that the bill, if enacted, would impose $1 billion tax on consumers.

Around this heart of the matter were grouped, for the secretary of agriculture's selection as regards application and emphasis, proposals derived from McNary-Haugen, from the laissez-faire economists of Cornell, and from other sources. Marketing agreements, the subsidization of exports of surpluses, the leasing of marginal land to withdraw it from agricultural production, loans on crops stored under seal and so withheld from market, the licensing of processors as a means of enforcing compliance—all these were authorized, though not mandated, in this omnibus bill.

Never before in all American history had there been proposed as an administration measure so direct, deep, and pervasive an intervention of government in production and marketing activity, never before so wholesale a transfer of lawmaking power from elected officials to a bureaucracy, never before so intricate a design for direct individual participation in the local application of federal law.

There was enough here, surely, to give Congress pause!

III

AND Congress *did* pause on this matter, to an extent that became highly worrisome to the administration—this despite Roosevelt's urgent reminder "that spring crops will soon be planted," despite his further plea that "action at this time" would place the United States "in a better position to discuss problems affecting world surpluses at the proposed [*sic*] World Economic Conference," despite the dangerously rising unrest in the countryside, and despite a flood of mail to Washington from ordinary citizens who, without pretending to understand the bill, favored its prompt passage because it was a *Roosevelt* measure.[9]

True, the bill went through the House, with its huge Democratic majority, almost as rapidly as had the three preceding bills. Though its initial reception by House leaders on farm affairs was a cold one (Representative Marvin Jones of Texas, chairman of the House Agriculture Committee, declined to sponsor it; the second-ranking Democratic member on the committee had to introduce it), the rank and file meekly submitted to the gag rule imposed by Speaker Rainey, limiting debate to four hours and prohibiting amendments, then passed the bill 315 to 98 on March 22, just six days after its introduction. But

the story was far different in the Senate. There hearings did not begin before
the Agriculture Committee, the chairman of which was Ellison D. "Cotton
Ed" Smith of South Carolina, until two days after the House had acted, and
the hearings at once promised to be prolonged.

For by March 24 the opponents of domestic allotment were massed and
ready for attack upon it. They included lobbyists for the canners, the millers,
the packers, the textile manufacturers, the big cotton brokers, and other commodity exchange operators, all of whom descended in full force upon Capitol
Hill to do battle against the processing tax provision. According to a former
president of the New York Cotton Exchange, the proposed tax, "oppressive
and almost confiscatory," would "demoralize all markets for agricultural products." According to spokesmen for the Chicago Board of Trade and the
Omaha Grain Exchange, the bill as a whole was the "most fantastic ever
proposed by any country in peacetime," a weird concoction by a "crowd of
professional farm racketeers," whose claim to speak for agriculture was an
outrageous presumption. Chairman Smith himself, acting in accordance with
his sobriquet, proposed to slash from the bill all that did not pertain to his
single interest, cotton; to this end he drafted a substitute bill. Republican
Charles McNary of Oregon and McNary-Haugen fame proposed to limit crop
acreage controls to wheat *and* cotton. Simpson of the Farmers' Union, with
the support of Nebraska's George Norris, bitterly opposed in his testimony
all production controls; he inveighed on grounds of common decency and
common sense against the proposal to create artificial scarcities of food and
fiber by means of a highly regressive tax in a time of hunger, ragged clothing,
and unparalleled deflation. "These farmers are not producing too much," cried
he. "We need all this. What we have overproduction of is empty stomachs and
bare backs." Simpson pressed again, more strongly than before, for adoption
of his cost of production scheme and found sympathetic listeners: George
Norris promptly moved a cost of production amendment to the pending bill.[10]

So as March drew toward a close, it appeared to Roosevelt that the bill
might remain in committee for weeks to come—far beyond the time when its
enactment could have any effect on this year's farm production—and was then
likely to be reported out in a form unacceptable by him.

He was challenged to a full exercise of his political skills.

On March 27 he submitted to Congress a message and an executive order
consolidating nine federal agencies dealing primarily with agricultural credit
(they included the Federal Farm Board, the Federal Farm Loan Board, units
of the RFC, and units of the office of the secretary of agriculture) in a single
agency to be called the Farm Credit Administration (FCA). The "immediate
effect," said the message, would be a "saving of more than $2,000,000" in
administrative costs, but "of greater and controlling importance is the maintenance of the long-standing policy of the Federal Government to maintain and
strengthen a sound and permanent system of cooperative agricultural credit
. . . for the purpose of meeting the credit needs of agriculture at minimum

cost." It was understood that this order presaged a request very soon for legislation to refinance farm mortgages and thereby alleviate one of the most grievous symptoms of agriculture's deep sickness. It was further understood that the Farm Credit Administration would administer whatever mortgage relief program was enacted and that Henry Morgenthau, Jr., currently chairman of the practically moribund Farm Board, would become the FCA's first governor.

On April 3 Roosevelt sent to Congress the expected request for farm mortgage relief legislation. "That many thousands of farmers in all parts of the country are unable to meet indebtedness incurred when their crop prices had a very different money value is known to all of you," he said. ". . . I seek an end to the threatened loss of homes and productive capacity now faced by hundreds of thousands of American farm families." He added that the suggested legislation would impose no "heavy burden upon the national Treasury." It would simply provide means whereby farm owners could "refinance themselves on reasonable terms" through existing government agencies. He also announced his intention soon to ask (this in distinct appeal to McNary-Haugenites) "for legislation enabling us to initiate practical reciprocal tariff agreements to break through trade barriers and establish foreign markets for farm and industrial products."[11] At once the Emergency Farm Mortgage Act was introduced as bill, proposing to refinance farm mortgages at 4½ percent. By amendment in the Agriculture Committee it was attached to the Agricultural Adjustment Act as Title II of an overall farm relief bill and this, of course, markedly increased the chances of Agricultural Adjustment's early passage without undue change since the demand for farm mortgage relief was overwhelming.

Bribe was followed by threat.

Next day, April 4, Cotton Ed Smith and other members of the Agriculture Committee were summoned to the Executive Office. There it was made clear to them by the President that his and the nation's patience with their dilatory tactics was at an end. The farm bill must be reported for floor action *at once.* Smith perforce yielded. He agreed to withdraw his proposed substitute measure. And on the morrow, April 5, the farm bill did at last reach the floor, favorably reported. It did so with major domestic allotment and processing tax provisions intact, but with several amendments in addition to Title II, one of them the cost of production proposal which Norris had moved and to which Roosevelt, though he deemed it unwise to say so at that moment out loud, was unalterably opposed for reasons of government economy.

Hence there yet loomed the hazard of prolonged debate, this time by the full Senate: debate of cost of production as a contradiction of domestic allotment, debate of domestic allotment as immoral and impractical, debate of the processing tax as unfair to processor and consumer, and debate in general of the wisdom or foolhardiness of creating a bureaucratic monster which, designed to implement professorial "theories," would no doubt be administered by radical professors or lawyers of like crimson hue. (Tugwell, already become the favorite target of conservatives who dared not attack the President directly, was much mentioned in this connection. Had he not visited the Soviet Union? Had he not written books and articles espousing national economic planning? Had he not said in public speech that business and businessmen were obsolete, rendered so by technological advance? And was he not a principal sponsor of domestic allotment?)

Roosevelt therefore let it be known that the top administrator of the new agency would assuredly *not* be a radical or even a professed liberal but, instead, a practical conservative man of business. As April opened, it was rumored that Bernard Baruch had been offered the post. And on the very day the farm bill was reported out of Senate committee, George Peek, a Baruch disciple ever since his service with Hugh Johnson on Baruch's War Industries Board, came with Wallace to the White House to be offered the post which Baruch had by then declined—or so Roosevelt said (one somehow doubts that the offer to Baruch was very firm or definite). Peek did not see how he could accept either. He bluntly said so, and why: There was a fundamental policy disagreement between him and the secretary of agriculture. He opposed acreage reduction, which Wallace favored; he favored essential features of McNary-Haugen, which Wallace opposed. Wallace nodded; there was indeed this disagreement. Roosevelt proceeded to minimize its importance. He turned the full force of his personal charm upon the shrewd, able, stubborn, single-minded, elderly man (Peek was sixty) who sat before him. He marshaled also persuasive arguments. There was, of course, no way, he said, by which acreage reduction could now be struck from the bill; political support of it was far too great for that. But surely this constituted no insurmountable obstacle to Peek's acceptance of the proffered post since the bill *also* authorized much, if not most, of the approach Peek favored. Roosevelt saw no reason why any or all of the designated options could not be exercised to greater or lesser degree—and no man in America was better equipped to exercise them judiciously, hardheadedly than George Peek. In the end Roosevelt had his way; it became public knowledge before many days had passed that Peek had agreed to head the agency the farm bill would create.

By this knowledge the bill's enactment in a form acceptable to Roosevelt was greatly aided. The worst fears of the processors and other devotees of private enterprise were soothed. Cut off as abruptly as water from a faucet was effective opposition by Baruch and Hugh Johnson, the latter of whom, at Baruch's behest, had warned Roosevelt that assignment to the new agency of processing tax collections was an obviously unconstitutional "delegation of the taxing power."[12]

These were great immediate advantages.

For them, however, a high price had to be paid. Peek's appointment made it perfectly predictable that bitter rending quarrels would torment and frustrate the policy-making procedures and program applications of the (as it would be called) Agricultural Adjustment Administration.

IV

MEANWHILE, operating on the principle that *any* action was preferable to none in these parlous times, Roosevelt drove ahead with a legislative program the only discernible rationale of which was the Democratic national platform of 1932 (he referred to it again and again in published statements, reiterating that he subscribed to it "one hundred percent") and the elements of which, having no internal relations one with another, were introduced helter-skelter as fast as draft bills could be prepared. Message after message went up the Hill from the White House. Enactment after enactment came down the Hill for White House signature. And the world watched with amazement and even awe this demonstration of the resiliency of American institutions, this proof of a great democracy's ability to respond swiftly to crisis under strong leadership, this development of what some were already calling a "revolution."*

On March 21 Roosevelt asked Congress for "three types of legislation" to provide unemployment relief. One, which "should be immediately enacted," would enable him "to create a civilian conservation corps to be used in simple work, not interfering with normal employment, and confining itself to forestry, the prevention of soil erosion, flood control and similar projects." "Existing machinery of the departments of Labor, Agriculture, War, and Interior" would control and direct the corps and its work. "I estimate that 250,000 men can be given temporary employment by early summer if you give me authority to proceed within the next two weeks." The CCC bill, introduced at the conclusion of the President's message by Senate Majority Leader Robinson on behalf of himself and New York Senator Robert Wagner, was promptly opposed by William Green of the AFL on the ground that the proposed pay of $30 a month for each corps enrollee was too low and would undermine pay scales in general. The argument was unpersuasive: Fewer than 2 percent of the 12 million unemployed would enter the corps, and those who did would receive food, clothing, and lodging in addition to their dollar a day—a total rather greater than the going rate for the kind of work they would be doing. The bill was also opposed, by both Green and liberal spokesmen, as an attempt to "solve" unemployment by putting unemployed youth into the Army, à la Mussolini and Hitler. To this Roosevelt replied that the corps was precisely what its name said it was—a *civilian* corps—with the Army involved only because it was the one agency that could swiftly organize and efficiently administer the transportation, supply, housing, and obviously necessary work camp discipline which were involved. "[T]alk about military control and militarization . . . is just utter rubbish," he told his press conference on March 22.[14] He won his way, and well within the time limit he had set. In just ten days the bill sailed through both houses on voice vote, and on the day the farm

---

*Ernest Lindley was writing that spring chapters of a book to be entitled *The Roosevelt Revolution* when it was published next fall. It was dedicated to his wife "who doesn't think the Roosevelt revolution is a real revolution yet. (And she may be right.)"[13]

bill at last emerged from Senate committee (April 5) Roosevelt signed an executive order establishing the Civilian Conservation Corps and naming as its head Robert Fechner, whose official title became Director of Emergency Conservation Work. The choice of director had as one purpose the smoothing of Green's ruffled feathers, for Fechner was an AFL man; he was vice-president of the machinists' union. Assistant Secretary of the Navy Roosevelt had become slightly acquainted with him, Louis Howe well acquainted with him, during the Great War.

The launching of no New Deal agency received a closer personal attention from Roosevelt than the launching of the CCC. The corps was *his* idea. His original proposal of it, in general terms, had been greeted with stinging, scornful ridicule. And he now assigned to Louis Howe, as his personal deputy, the task of assuring for his imaginative conception a swift and resounding practical success. It would prove an arduous task, one that drew heavily upon the sickly Howe's slender reserves of strength; it would also prove a mistaken assignment, ultimately, for Howe-and-Roosevelt's insistence upon the clearance of detail in the White House soon created a logjam in a stream that had to flow freely and swiftly if it were to carry the novel enterprise to its stated goal of a quarter million young men at work, in wood and field, by July. Not until mid-May would the logjam be broken, Roosevelt then delegating full, untrammeled authority to Labor for recruitment, to War for camp organization and management, to Agriculture (the Forest Service) and Interior (the Soil Erosion Service) for work projects, and to Fechner for overall CCC direction. Thereafter the new agency would quickly become and forever remain in history a shining triumph of the New Deal.[15]

Indeed, CCC proved immensely useful even before its first work camps became fully established, for it helped defuse a social bomb which, in view of the passions then being fanned among war veterans by the government economy drive, could have very dangerously exploded in the late spring of 1933. On May 9 the first contingent of a new Bonus Expeditionary Force—some hundreds of desperately poor, embittered men descended upon Washington. Within two weeks nearly 3,000 had arrived. Roosevelt's dealings with them measured the difference between his personality, his political acumen, and Herbert Hoover's.* He deputized Louis Howe to see to it that the veterans were decently sheltered at Fort Hunt, an old and practically abandoned Army camp across the Potomac from the capital; that they were given three meals a day and an abundance of coffee to drink; that they were provided with medical service; even that they were serenaded by the Navy Band. Their leaders were welcomed into the White House for consultations. One rainy day Howe took Eleanor Roosevelt to the encampment, unannounced and unaccompanied by the Secret Service or anyone else, since Howe remained in the

---

*In the summer of 1933, Hoover had used the Army to drive the first BEF out of Washington. The large shanty town the veterans had erected on the Anacostia Flat, and to which many of them had brought their wives and children, was burned by troops commanded by General Douglas MacArthur. See Davis, *FDR: The New York Years,* pp. 344–350.

car, dozing. She sloshed through the mud, inspecting the facilities with a practiced eye, talked with the men individually, addressed them collectively with reminiscences of her own experiences in wartime Washington and of her tour of American battlefields in France in 1929, then finally led them in the singing of a haunting song of the war years, "There's a Long, Long Trail." Shortly after her visit the veterans voted to disperse, as they had been gently but firmly urged by the administration to do, and there is no doubt that her visit encouraged this decision. The dispersal could not have been so smoothly effected, however, had there been no CCC into which the men could be enrolled, if they chose, through a waiving of the corps' normal age limit rules, the veterans being middle-aged. More than 2,600 *did* so choose, and the remaining 350 or so accepted free rail transportation to their homes.[16]

The second "type of legislation" asked for in the March 21 message was largely the brainchild of Harry Hopkins.

When Herbert Lehman took over as New York governor in January 1933, Hopkins was continued in the post to which Roosevelt had appointed him, that of chairman of the state's Temporary Emergency Relief Administration (TERA). It was as New York relief administrator, acutely aware of his state's crying need for massive federal relief assistance, that in company with Director William Hodson of the Welfare Council of New York he came down to Washington a few days after the inauguration to present to the President a plan for grants-in-aid to states for direct unemployment relief. The plan, a sharp break with Hoover policy, was also a considerable revision of the Democratic platform plank which Roosevelt would soon be citing in justification of it, a plank advocating "extension of federal *credit**" to the states to provide unemployment relief whenever the diminishing resources of the states make it impossible for them to provide for the needy." Marvin McIntyre, who at that time was driven "almost frantic trying to arrange [presidential] appointments," as Frances Perkins would remember, could or would make no appointment for Hopkins. So Hopkins turned to the secretary of labor. She arranged to meet the two men at the Women's University Club, which was so jammed with people that the only quiet place available was (again in Perkins's words) "a hole under the stairs." It was in these "cramped, unlovely quarters" that Hopkins and his companion "laid out their plan." The labor secretary then had in her office, by her own hyperbolic count, "over two thousand plans for federal action to cover unemployment." None she had thus far read, however, seemed to her as well informed and thoroughly practical as the one to which she then listened. Promptly she took it upon herself (it is significant of Roosevelt's administrative style that she felt perfectly "certain of my ground" as she "cut across the usual formalities") to insist to McIntyre that an appointment with the President be arranged for Hopkins and his companion "immediately," because "these people knew how to operate and had a concrete proposal."[17]

The upshot was Roosevelt's request of Congress "that you establish the

*Emphasis added.

office of Federal Relief Administrator whose duty it will be to scan requests
for grants and to check the efficiency and wisdom of their use"—a job description that may have been deliberately designed to minimize the power and
authority which the projected office would actually have. Soon thereafter, at
Roosevelt's request, Senators La Follette, Wagner, and Costigan conferred
with Hopkins and Secretary Perkins, then drafted a federal emergency relief
bill which would authorize a $500 million appropriation for relief grants to
states and give to the relief administrator broad supervisory power over the
states' use of these grants. Introduced on March 28, the bill at once encountered opposition from Republicans who had discovered in themselves during
the last few years, especially in the last few days (since the introduction of the
farm bill), a profound commitment to Jeffersonian principles. "Is there anything left of our Federal system?" cried one of them. Another could "hardly
find parliamentary language to describe" his outrage at the notion that states
and cities "cannot take care of the conditions in which they find themselves
but must come to the Federal Government for aid." Ohio's Senator Simeon
D. Fess begged his colleagues not to permit "our hearts to overcome our
judgment" and deplored the alleged fact that "Uncle Sam is looked upon as
a Santa Claus to give alms." Massachusetts Representative Robert Luce said
flatly that the bill was "socialism" and might even be "communism," though
of this last he was not sure. Such protests, however, were relatively few and
wholly futile. The bill went through the Senate in ten days on a vote of 55 to
17, through the House three weeks thereafter on a vote of 320 to 42, and was
signed into law on May 12.[18]

Ten days later, having resigned his $13,500 TERA salary in New York,
Harry Hopkins took over an $8,500 job as head of the new Federal Emergency
Relief Administration in Washington. He established his office in a dingy,
shabby, uncarpeted room (he refused to have it redecorated) on the top floor
of the badly run-down Walker-Johnson building on New York Avenue, just
a block and a half from the White House. Then and there he was as much in
his element as Franklin Roosevelt was in the President's office. Within two
days, drawing upon his wide acquaintance among social workers and aided by
soft-spoken, hardworking forty-two-year-old Aubrey Williams, who became
his chief assistant, he threw together a remarkably efficient staff, whose members were not only fanatically devoted to him personally but also imbued with
his determination to bring relief to suffering humanity *fast*, at a minimum
overhead cost. Within two weeks he had made his impress upon official Washington and, through the Washington press corps, upon the nation as a distinctly different kind of federal bureaucrat if, indeed, he was not one of a kind.
Within two months, initially sponsored by Eleanor Roosevelt, Hopkins was to
be introduced into the inner circle of presidential advisers, becoming recognized soon thereafter as "one of the guiding intelligences of the New Deal,"
as journalist Jay Franklin (J. F. Carter) wrote. A closely watching national
public would then see him to be what many observant New Yorkers had seen
him to be during the last year and a half: a pragmatic idealist or idealistic

pragmatist who uniquely blended dark cynicism with shining faith, operational toughness with tenderness of heart, bohemian tastes with austere moral commitment, and empathic sensitivity with a steel-hard, knife-sharp practical intellect. His cadaverous, burning-eyed countenance, perpetually wreathed in cigarette smoke, was to become famous in the land, the focus of immense admiration and virulent hatred, and famous, too, was the snarling, sardonic speech, "lousy" his favorite adjective, wherewith he expressed his contempt for smugness, callousness, selfishness, his loathing of privilege and all who deemed privilege their natural right. To the common argument of affluent conservatives that the economically distressed would benefit "in the long run" if the depression were permitted to run its "natural" course, uninterfered with by government, he replied with biting scorn that "people don't eat in the long run, they have to eat every day."[19]

The "third type of legislation" asked for on March 21 "extends to a broad public works labor-creating program," as Roosevelt put it, though he could not press for immediate action on this at the time. He had not yet in hand the necessary bill. ". . . I am studying the many projects suggested and the financial conditions involved," he said. "I shall make recommendations to the Congress presently."[20]

V

HE did have in hand at that time draft legislation to reform the conduct of the nation's financial markets.

This was not, properly speaking, emergency legislation—it was permanent legislation called for by a plank in the 1932 Democratic platform,* also by the Columbus speech of Roosevelt's election campaign—and its passage now could do little or nothing to speed economic recovery through the near future. It might even slow such recovery by discouraging the flotation of new securities issues necessary to finance a restoration of production—by provoking, in other words, a "capital strike" on the part of those who resented the government's "intrusion" upon a field in which they had theretofore operated with untrammeled "freedom." And Roosevelt would not have introduced this legislation now had other emergency legislation been ready and had he not "needed something to keep the House busy while the Senate . . . hesitated over the farm relief bill," to quote Ernest Lindley.[21]

Such introduction was seriously complicated, however, by the fact that the financial reform draft legislation now in Roosevelt's hand consisted, not of a single proposed bill but of two bills, each having politically potent authorship, each presumably prepared at his order, yet each so different from the other as

---

*"We advocate protection of the investing public by requiring to be filed with the Government, and carried in advertisements, of all offerings of foreign and domestic stocks and bonds, true information as to bonuses, commissions, principal invested, and interests of the sellers," said the 1932 Democratic platform.

to render impossible that "weaving together" of the two which was, of course, attempted.

Moley, in mid-December 1932, had suggested to the President-elect that Samuel Untermyer, who had been counsel for the House Committee on Banking and Currency (Louisiana's A. P. Pujo its chairman) during the famous investigation of J. P. Morgan and the "money trust" in 1912, might be useful in shaping legislation to regulate securities marketing and the operations of stock and commodity exchanges. Roosevelt had no fondness for the seventy-four-year-old Untermyer, a prima donna type whose love of personal publicity had augmented difficulties and hazards for the governor of New York during the long months of the Seabury investigation.* But there was no denying that Untermyer was a renowned expert in financial law. He was also one of the most influential Old Wilsonians. The President-elect, therefore, quickly acquiesced in Moley's suggestion, and Untermyer was so informed.

A month later the lawyer sent Moley a draft bill modeled closely on one which he had prepared in 1914 but which, when then introduced in Congress, had died in Senate committee after Wilson had declined to endorse it. To Moley, no expert in this field, the draft seemed generally satisfactory in its regulatory proposals; Untermyer's thorough knowledge of financial technicalities seemed everywhere evident in it. But it proposed to place the regulatory machinery in the Post Office Department, and *this,* in Moley's judgment, was not satisfactory at all. Untermyer's justification was that the exchanges and securities-issuing firms conducted their business through the U.S. mails. Hence violations of the law could be effectively enforced by threatened denials of mailing privileges. And since none could deny that the postal service operated across state lines, was engaged in interstate commerce, none could successfully challenge on states' rights grounds the constitutionality of the legislation. Moley's objection was that the Post Office, a service bureau, ought not to be encumbered with complex regulatory and policing functions. (Imagine Jim Farley in charge of these!) He voiced this objection to Untermyer, who dismissed it cavalierly. He voiced it to Roosevelt, who agreed with it. But Roosevelt also agreed with Moley that Untermyer, despite this objection, should be encouraged to proceed with the drafting of a bill the administration could sponsor and that Moley should continue in correspondence with the famous lawyer toward this end.

A few days after the inaugural, however, without informing Moley of the fact, Roosevelt asked Secretary of Commerce Daniel Roper, who was also an Old Wilsonian, and Attorney General Cummings to assume responsibility for a securities-regulating bill. Roper, in turn, asked Huston Thompson to work with a couple of designated Commerce Department officials in the drafting enterprise.

---

*Untermyer was District Attorney Thomas Crain's attorney during the 1931 investigation by Seabury of Crain's fitness for his office, had been a staunch and vociferous defender of Jimmy Walker against Seabury's harsh probe. His Palm Springs estate was Walker's favorite winter vacation resort. See Davis, *FDR: The New York Years,* p. 232.

A kindly, courtly elderly gentleman, a Colorado native whose youthful ideas had been tinctured by western Populism and Bryan Democracy, Thompson was yet another Old Wilsonian. Wilson had appointed him assistant attorney general of the United States in 1913 and, in 1918, had named him to a seven-year term on the Federal Trade Commission (FTC), of which he became chairman in 1920 and 1921 and, again, in 1923 and 1924. His approach to economic and social problems was Brandeisian. He, with Brandeis, deemed giant organizations, whether of business or government (the two kinds of bigness were causally linked, in his view), to be inherently evil, as corrupting of morals as they were practically inefficient, being rooted not in the imperatives of technological advance but in the human greed and power lust that created and then fed upon "special privilege." Destroy such privilege! cried he. He urged the strictest enforcement of the Sherman Act, which he described as "the greatest law . . . that has ever been enacted."[22] And it was in acute awareness of the role of securities marketing in the building up of monopoly power, though with no clear, direct application *to* this role, that he now drafted the requested bill.

It turned out to be essentially a disclosure bill, limited wholly to securities marketing; it had nothing to do with exchange operations, in which respect, measured against administration specifications, it was less satisfactory than the Untermyer bill. But Thompson's was much preferable to Untermyer's bill in that it placed administration of the law in the Federal Trade Commission, where it logically belonged. Designed more to prevent than to punish fraudulent transactions, though recognizing the deterrent effect of threatened punitive action, the bill required corporations issuing securities for interstate sale to register such issues with the FTC prior to their public offer, disclosing in registration statements, the substance of which must be repeated in prospectuses submitted to the public, information about capitalization, funded debt, current balance sheets, last year's income, commissions to underwriters, and so on. For the accuracy of these statements, which executive officers and directors must sign, the signers would be legally responsible—they would be liable to damage suits by securities purchasers who believed themselves to have been misled—and, of course, the FTC was empowered to revoke registrations containing false information, thus rendering illegal any sale of the securities.

Not until this draft bill had actually been completed did Moley learn, to his astonishment and chagrin, for his relations with Untermyer were embarrassed by the fact, that others had been assigned to work in a legislative field for which he had believed himself to be, as Roosevelt's agent, solely responsible.

Here was dilemma of the unhappiest kind!

Moley went at once to the White House to present Roosevelt with it, stressing its seriousness. It was bound to cause pain, to provoke acrimony, and as it did so, in view of the personalities and political influence of those on its opposite horns, it would multiply hazards to the success of any administration effort toward financial market reform. (These hazards were already sufficiently numerous, as any astute observer from the left could see. The response of urban conservatives to the farm relief bill made it clear that the New Deal would find its "honeymoon" with the right at an abrupt end if and when it proposed meaningful business reforms. Certainly the financial community, standing generally at the farthest reaches of the right, could be expected to oppose financial reforms with every ounce of the strength it recovered following the banking crisis.)

Roosevelt reacted typically and, by that token, quite possibly disingenuously.

He was all apologies, of course. He had completely forgotten about the Moley-Untermyer assignment when he made the Roper-Thompson one! But no damage that could not be repaired had been done. The thing to do now was get Untermyer and Thompson together, with the other principals involved, in a peace conference over which he, the President, would preside, a conference that would iron out differences and produce, in the end, a better bill than either of the two now in hand.

The conference was held. Indeed, two conferences were held—one in the Oval Room on Sunday, March 19; the other in the Oval Room on Sunday, March 26. They failed to produce the desired result, in good part because the egoistic and inflexible Untermyer was temperamentally incapable of collaborating with anyone.[23]

Roosevelt then decided to divide in two what had been originally conceived as a single enterprise. Moley was to continue working with Untermyer on a draft bill to regulate stock and commodity exchanges while the Thompson bill to reform securities marketing was at once submitted to Congress. Moley protested that if such division were made, exchange regulation should logically precede issues regulation, especially since the increasingly loud demands by western members of Congress for currency inflation was likely to spark very soon a dangerous speculative splurge on unregulated exchanges. Roosevelt replied that there was no need for such worry since there would be ample time to get both kinds of legislation on the books before the special session ended.

So on March 29 there went to Congress from the President a special message, drafted by Moley "with some misgivings," recommending "legislation for Federal supervision of traffic in investment securities in interstate commerce." Said the message:

> Of course, the Federal Government cannot and should not take any action which might be construed as approving or guaranteeing that newly issued securities are sound in the sense that their value will be maintained or that the properties which they represent will earn profit. There is, however, an obligation upon us to insist that every issue of new securities to be sold in interstate commerce shall be accompanied by full publicity and information, and that no essentially important element attending the issue shall be concealed from the buying public. This proposal adds to the ancient rule of *caveat emptor,* the further doctrine "let the seller also beware." It puts the burden of telling the whole truth on the seller. It should give impetus to honest dealing in securities and thereby bring back public confidence.[24]

The Thompson bill was introduced in both houses a few days later.

In the House, whose Interstate Commerce Committee was chaired by the remarkably able and politically powerful Sam Rayburn of Texas, the bill soon ran into serious difficulties. It was very long (thirty-five pages); its uneven drafting rendered imprecise much of its excessive detail; in its limitation of liability to directors and executive officers it ignored the general procedures and specialized expertise whereby securities were actually developed and issued for public sale; and it was more expressive of Thompson's anti-big-government bias than it was of realistic common sense in that it was intended to be largely self-enforcing, with limited enforcement powers assigned the FTC. After two weeks of hearings, during which the bill was vehemently opposed by financially experienced men of progressive mind who favored securities marketing reform (Averell Harriman, for one) as well as by Wall Street defenders of the status quo, Rayburn concluded that the bill was a hopeless mess. A new one must be prepared if there were to be any securities legislation in the present session. And Rayburn asked Moley not only "to persuade the Chief that this Thompson bill won't do" but also "to get me a draftsman who knows this stuff" to write the needed bill "under my direction." Moley, probably at Roosevelt's suggestion and certainly with his concurrence, turned for help to Felix Frankfurter who, promptly accepting the assignment, arrived in Washington on the morning of Friday, April 7, and, having checked in at the Carlton, breakfasted immediately thereafter with Moley in the latter's Carlton suite.[25]

He brought with him as his draftsmen, whose work he would direct from Cambridge, two of his former students.

One was a short, blond, thin-faced, sharp-eyed man named James M. Landis, who had been born in Tokyo thirty-four years before, the son of a Presbyterian missionary to Japan. He had come from Japan to the United States for prep schooling, aged fourteen, in 1912; had been graduated from Princeton at the top of his class seven years later; had been graduated from Harvard Law School in 1924, again at the top of his class; and, after a year of graduate study and another year as Justice Brandeis's secretary, had joined the Harvard Law School faculty and become a full professor in the incredibly short time of two years. He was as brilliant a teacher as he had been a student, and his teaching experience had provided him with a deep and wide knowledge, if as yet an exclusively theoretic knowledge, of the legislative process.

The other of the two was thirty-nine-year-old Benjamin V. Cohen. Born of a prominent and well-to-do Jewish family in Muncie, Indiana (the "Middletown" of the Lynds' famous sociological study), educated at the University of Chicago, from which he received a Ph.D. in economics in 1914 and a J.D. degree a year later (he was "the most brilliant student I ever taught," said Harold G. Moulton, Chicago professor in 1914 and head of the Brookings Institute in 1933), Cohen had been Frankfurter's most brilliant student in the Harvard Law School class of 1916, had been an attorney with the U.S. Shipping Board during the Great War, had become counsel for the American Zionists, and at the Paris Peace Conference, where he met John Maynard Keynes, had negotiated, with others, the Palestine mandate. He was a gentle-mannered, soft-spoken religious idealist, yet also possessed of a mind as tough as it was informed and incisive and with a great deal of practical experience in property law, especially in the intricacies of corporate reorganization. He was unimpressive in appearance; he had no evident wish to make deep personal impressions. The opposite of aggressive and assertive in his human relations, retiring in manner, inclined toward solitudes, he differed from Landis in that he had remarkably little strictly personal ambition—remarkably little desire, at any rate, to acquire and exercise power—whereas Landis was eager to influence directly large affairs.

And so was the third man who, at once brought into the drafting project, worked night and day thereafter with Cohen and Landis. This third man was thirty-three-year-old Tommy Corcoran.

A Rhode Island native who had received his B.A. degree in 1921 from Brown University, where Alexander Meiklejohn had been his great teacher, Corcoran had become Frankfurter's star pupil in the Harvard Law School class of 1925 and, after his year as Holmes's secretary, had joined the corporate law firm of Cotton & Franklin in New York City. His ideal commitment, directly influenced by Meiklejohn and Frankfurter, indirectly (through Frankfurter) by Brandeis, was to the law as servant of the public good. He had been quick to abandon the potentially lucrative private practice of corporate law in order to come down to Washington, just a year ago, as RFC counsel, a post for which Eugene Meyer, RFC head in 1932, had hired him on Frankfurter's recommendation. Corcoran's personal charm, as has been indicated, was immense. He was affectionate, high-spirited, witty, sentimental; he loved to sing sweet sad ballads, and funny ones, too, in his rich Irish tenor, accompanying himself on an accordian. He was a hero worshiper who formed strong emotional attachments and developed equally strong personal antipathies, quickly. He had a rare ability to spread around him the energizing excitement of his dramatic view of the world as a war of opposites—light versus dark, good versus evil, truth versus falsehood—with each warring element multitudinously personalized. In full force he possessed the Irishman's allegedly typical love of combat and consequent taste for factional politics; he proved remarkably adept in political rough-and-tumble and not overly squeamish about the employment of ruthless means to reach ends he deemed benign.

There were two common denominators among these three very different men, apart from their intellectual brilliance and shared dedication to public service.

One was a generally Brandeisian approach to socioeconomic problems that was considerably more sophisticated, more up-to-date than was either Thompson's or Untermyer's. They were more realistic than the two older men in their assessment of causal relations between technological advance and economic combination, more cognizant of the actual nature and workings of corporate financial structures, and they were acutely aware, as the older men seemed not to be, that any such return to "free competition" as the Sherman Act envisaged was a practical impossibility. Why attempt to stream banners against the wind? they might have asked. At the present moment, certainly, the prevailing wind of history—the predominant pressures of the business community and of such "national planners" within the administration as Rex Tugwell—was *against* antitrust law. That wind would, if it could, blow such law away. At the same time the three draftsmen were more cynical in their view of the morals and methods of corporate management, and consequently less inclined to trust it to regulate itself in the public interest, than were Thompson and Untermyer. They were very sure that any regulatory law worthy of the name must provide the federal regulatory agency with explicit and extensive coercive powers.

The other common denominator among these three was an uncommon capacity for hard, prolonged, intensely concentrated intellectual effort. And of this they had need during the immediately following days and weeks. Inevitably there were disagreements over detail and relative emphasis; inevitably these fused with personality differences to produce psychological tensions. They did so especially between Cohen and Landis. At one point the gentle but tough-minded Cohen found himself so at odds with Landis concerning the regulatory specifications needed in the bill (he favored more of them than Landis did) and so irritated by Landis' overbearing manner that he tried to withdraw from the enterprise. "Teamwork is impossible," said he to Frankfurter over the telephone. He had to be talked into staying by Frankfurter, who sternly addressed his sense of duty, and by Moley, who also forcefully advised Landis to be less abrasive, more respectful, more accommodating. Such flare-ups, however, had no deleterious effect upon the end product of the drafting enterprise.[26]

Far more important, as it was far happier—indeed, of major importance to the New Deal as a whole—was the simultaneous development under pressure of personal friendship between Corcoran and Cohen. It was a friendship that astonished and amused those who viewed it juxtaposed with the traditionally bigoted Irish Catholic's hatred of "Christ-killer" Jews; it would sustain through the years ahead a working partnership of rare creativity. The two men complemented each other. The gregarious Corcoran stimulated the solitary Cohen into social contacts which the latter would not otherwise have made but which enriched his life. He adopted toward the peaceably disposed Cohen a protective attitude; he was concerned to see that Cohen's quiet brilliance was recognized, was properly used, was properly appreciated. And Cohen helpfully moderated Corcoran's sometimes excessive enthusiasms, his sometimes dangerous tendency to overcommit to a perceived hero while overreacting against a perceived villain.

In the present instance, the triumvirate's task, which must be accomplished within a painfully constricted time span, was harshened and much increased in technical difficulty by acrimonies growing out of Roosevelt's initial overlapping of assigned responsibilities.

To soothe Thompson's sensibilities, already ruffled by the cold contempt with which he and his work had been treated by Untermyer in the President's presence, the three new draftsmen felt compelled at the outset to deprecate their effort as merely "perfecting amendments" of the Thompson measure; they so described it to Thompson himself when they breakfasted with him on

Monday, April 10, after their first weekend of drafting. Roosevelt also undertook to soothe Thompson; within an hour or so after he had talked with Frankfurter, on April 7, about the latter's new drafting assignment, he summoned Thompson to the White House and there flattered him by talking freely about his problems, foreign and domestic, then asking Thompson's help in dealing with alleged chicanery involving the Army Engineers and the sale of electric power from the government generating facilities at Muscle Shoals. Thereafter the Landis-Cohen-Corcoran team consulted with Thompson not at all. They labored behind a curtain of secrecy, in the lowering of which Frankfurter and Rayburn cooperated, to produce what was in effect a wholly new bill (though some of the Thompson language was retained for conciliatory reasons), a bill modeled on the British Companies Act of the mid-nineteenth century, if considerably more strict and inclusive than the Companies Act in its schedule of penalties and liabilities. Introduced in the House by Rayburn on May 3, this bill was rushed to House passage, without further hearings, two days later. By then Thompson, for all his natural amiability, was hurt and angered. He resented especially the secrecy with which Rayburn and Frankfurter had cloaked their operation—it was personally insulting to him—and he said so to them during an acrimonious meeting in the White House on May 5. He also damned the liability schedule in the House bill just passed, claiming it was designed to please "investment bankers" and, by that token, could "never work" for the protection of the investing public.[27] (Actually the investment bankers as a group were opposed to *any* effective regulatory legislation but found the Thompson bill somewhat more palatable than the Landis-Cohen-Corcoran draft.)

There ensued a parliamentary snarl the untangling of which required of Senate Majority Leader Robinson, aided by Senator James F. Byrnes, the utmost manipulative skill.

Thompson had a considerable following in the upper chamber, several of whose older members, rendered powerful by seniority, were personal friends, and the Fletcher committee had favorably reported his bill some days before the House acted upon the Rayburn-Frankfurter measure. Robinson and Byrnes, informed that Rayburn-Frankfurter was actually the administration bill, yet knowing that the superseded Thompson bill would certainly pass the Senate if it came to floor vote, nevertheless decided to permit such vote and then quietly maneuver to have Rayburn-Frankfurter substituted for Thompson in the joint conference committee which had to compromise the issue between the House and Senate bills. Accordingly the Thompson bill was presented to the full Senate for vote on May 8 and passed with a handsome majority. Rayburn became chairman of the joint committee. This rendered relatively easy the substitution of the House bill for the main substance of the Senate bill in the final conference report.

A grave complication arose, however.

Attached to the Thompson bill when it passed the Senate was an amendment, proposed by Hiram Johnson, which would establish an independent federal agency, called the Corporation of Foreign Security Holders, initially supervised by the FTC and having no banker participation in it (this was expressly forbidden). Its assigned duty would be to negotiate with foreign governments that had defaulted on their financial obligations, the purpose being to recover for bilked Americans at least some of the billions they had "invested" in foreign "securities," largely Latin American, whose current market value, if any, was but a fraction of the original purchase price. Johnson's proposal was, of course, extremely popular among the holders of such paper, and these totaled some 700,000 individuals and institutions, virtually all of them small investors (the average holding was around $800).[28] The proposal also found favor among a general public whose outrage against the financial community was almost daily fed that spring by new revelations of their greed and mendacity made by the financiers themselves in sworn testimony before the Senate Banking and Currency Committee, Duncan U. Fletcher its chairman, Ferdinand Pecora its counsel. Every newspaper reader now knew that many of the greatest, most prestigious bankers had joined in what amounted to a gigantic conspiracy to deceive and defraud, had marketed with false advertising and high-pressure salesmanship foreign paper they knew or strongly suspected to be worthless, reaping huge commissions for themselves in the process, and it was assumed that the new agency proposed by Johnson, as it negotiated with foreign governments, would necessarily call to account the American underwriters through whom those governments had operated. It was further assumed that the new agency, operating outside the State Department, might curb the latter's notorious tendency to conduct diplomatic operations, especially in Latin America, as if American ministers were foreign business agents of large American corporations.

As for the State Department, it, of course, vehemently opposed the Johnson amendment. If a "quasi-official body" were set up "outside the control" of State's diplomatic officers to deal directly with foreign governments, "the whole conduct of the Department's work would be complicated and confused," complained State economic adviser Herbert Feis to Louis Howe, two days after the Senate vote on the amended Thompson bill. Howe passed the objection on to Roosevelt, who weighed it in a balance that also included Secretary of State Hull's eagerness to implement at the earliest possible moment the promised Good Neighbor policy in Latin America. Certainly a Corporation of Foreign Security Holders, as it tried to force Latin American governments to meet their financial obligations, was unlikely to promote friendly relations between those governments and the United States. So Roosevelt, shortly before the conference committee met, voiced Feis's objection as his own in identical letters to Fletcher and Rayburn, though at the same time assuring Johnson of his profound sympathy with Johnson's aims. Johnson seems to have got wind of Roosevelt's yielding to Feis's argument. At any rate he wrote to his son on May 14 that the "Administration is going to kick it [the amendment] to pieces in the conference" because Roosevelt, knowing "nothing of the details," was "accepting the advice of a lot of little two-by-four individuals in the State Department."[29]

Rayburn as conference chairman, however, refused to involve himself in any such "kicking" or even to condone it. He told Johnson to confer with Roosevelt on the matter; he promised to do whatever Johnson and Roosevelt agreed should be done. But Johnson was unable to obtain decisive word from the President. And after the conference had approved the House bill (i.e., Rayburn-Frankfurter) as Title I of the bill to be reported for final action, Rayburn still refused to take a stand one way or the other on Title II, which the Johnson amendment had now become. An urgent phone call was made to the White House in search of decision. Still Roosevelt remained indecisive; Rayburn, he replied, should use his own judgment; whereupon Landis, who listened in on this conversation, suggested what should by then have been the obvious answer —namely, the inclusion of Title II as a discretionary measure, an option to be exercised only if and when the President concluded that doing so was in the public interest. Immediately thereafter Landis wrote a new section into the bill, implementing this idea, and Johnson promptly accepted it, to Landis-Cohen-Corcoran's astonishment and relief (Johnson seems not to have understood its implications). In this form the bill was finally reported.

The House passed it on May 22. The Senate passed it on May 23. Roosevelt signed it on May 27.

VI

MEANWHILE, Roosevelt had followed through resoundingly on the promise made on January 21, in public speech at Montgomery, Alabama, immediately following his tour of Muscle Shoals.

On April 10, in a special message to Congress, he said:

It is clear that the Muscle Shoals development is but a small part of the potential usefulness of the entire Tennessee River. Such use, if envisioned in its entirety, transcends mere power development; it enters the wide fields of flood control, soil erosion, afforestation, elimination from agricultural use of marginal lands, and distribution and diversification of industry. In short, this power development of war days leads logically to national planning for a complete river watershed involving many states and the future lives and welfare of millions. It touches and gives life to all forms of human concern.

He therefore called upon Congress for "legislation to create a Tennessee Valley Authority, a corporation clothed with the power of Government but possessed of the flexibility and initiative of a private enterprise." The authority not only should be charged with the broadest duty of planning for the proper use, conservation and development of the natural resources of the Tennessee Valley drainage basin" but "should also be clothed with the necessary power to carry these plans into effect."[30]

Here, indeed, was a bold new departure of enormous significance, "probably the most far-reaching adventure in regional planning ever undertaken outside Soviet Russia," as Ernest Lindley wrote a few weeks later.[31] It was far more grandly imaginative than any George Norris had envisaged in the eight ill-fated Muscle Shoals bills he had submitted since 1920, and the conception, in its grandeur, was very much Roosevelt's own. For it he had prepared with more than usual care. For it he had himself *been* prepared by a lifelong love of trees and water, of fields and meadows and open country living; by his experience of profitless farming on Pine Mountain above Warm Springs; and by his adult concern to halt, if not reverse, that trend of population from country to city which he deemed inimical to the good health of American civilization.

He had absorbed a remarkable amount of the information that poured in upon him from those having special interests in Muscle Shoals and the Tennessee Valley generally. He had listened carefully to engineers primarily concerned with river navigation and flood control; to Alabama Senators John H. Bankhead and Hugo Black, who, representing the farmers of the area, were primarily concerned with the manufacture of cheap fertilizers; to George Norris, of course, that grand old champion of public power, whose primary concern was the generation and transmission of cheap electricity.

But to his organismic conception of a vast multipurposed watershed project that wove together economic and human concerns in a seamless web, one reflective of that continuous web of water (surface and subterranean) which is the unifying principle of a river basin—a conception very different in kind from those he normally had in fields other than conservation—he was perhaps most greatly helped by a long talk he had one day with Arthur E. Morgan of Yellow Springs, Ohio, president there of the small but highly prestigious and experimentally progressive Antioch College. The fifty-five-year-old Morgan was by professional training a civil engineer. He had been in charge of planning and dam construction for the Miami Conservancy District, which, created to prevent any recurrence of the disastrous 1913 inundation of Dayton, Ohio, by the Miami River, had become a world model of successful engineering flood control. But he had a breadth of interest and human concern far from typical of the American engineer—he was indeed the quintessential ingenious Yankee of the moral- and social-uplift stripe, a believer in the possibility of human perfectibility through education, like Antioch founder Horace Mann—and he was intimately familiar with the people, the economy, the natural resources, and the river problems of that portion of the immense Ohio basin which comprises both the Miami and the Tennessee watersheds.

Morgan was precisely the man most likely to be set afire imaginatively by a musing question Roosevelt put to him during their talk together and to respond to it knowledgeably in ways that encouraged Roosevelt's developing conception. The Tennessee and its tributaries drained an area of some 41,000 square miles sprawled across seven states—Kentucky, Tennessee, Alabama, Mississippi, Georgia, Virginia, and a small piece of North Carolina. It had been repeatedly robbed of natural resources—forests, oil, gas—by exploitive capitalists, who moved in and out of the valley, taking wealth with them and leaving poverty behind. Scores of thousands of small farmers in the uplands scratched a miserable living out of soil which every year was less productive, being unfertilized and unprotected against erosion under a rainfall that averaged more than fifty inches. Even on the relatively fertile lowlands, even in the most prosperous of the small towns, the abundant life was rare indeed: More than 98 percent of all farms and an abnormally high percentage of town dwellings were without electricity. Every social and economic trend was downward. Could these trends be reversed? Could the valley be so transformed by regional planning as to support not only those now living in it, and at a decent standard of living, but also others who moved in, myriads of others who now, jobless and hopeless, walked city streets? "[I]s it possible," asked Roosevelt specifically of Morgan, "for us to develop small industries, where the people can produce what they use, and where they can use what they produce, and where, without dislocating the industry of America, we can absorb a lot of this unemployment, and give population a sound footing on which it can live . . . soundly and in a self-supporting way until we can work our way into a new economy?"[32]

This, then, was the frame of mind in which Roosevelt, nine days after his inauguration, asked Senator Norris to consult with him on the Tennessee Valley development. "[I]f the Congress should take recess for three weeks," he wrote, "I think we should have the bill ready as soon as the Congress returns."[33] There followed two such consultations. To the first of them, on April 1, Norris came in company with Representatives Lister Hill of Alabama and John J. McSwain of South Carolina (McSwain was chairman of the House Military Affairs Committee, to which the bill would be assigned). Roosevelt called in Wallace and Ickes. For nearly two hours the six men discussed the draft bill Norris had brought with him, at the end of which time all save the two southern congressmen, both of whom favored a more conservative, less comprehensive measure, were firmly agreed on the form the bill should have. Roosevelt approved a final draft in consultation with Norris on April 7, and it was introduced by Norris in the Senate, by John E. Rankin of Mississippi in the House, on the day after Roosevelt's message.

Roosevelt had learned from his experience with the New York Power Authority. He now thoroughly agreed with Norris that the TVA must be authorized not only to produce electricity but also to distribute it directly to users over its own transmission lines. It was, of course, this feature of the bill which was most protested by executives of the three major utilities companies operating in the Tennessee Valley—Georgia Light and Power, Alabama Light and Power, Tennessee Electric Power—all of which, in the aftermath of the Insull collapse, had come under the control of a new Wall Street-organized holding company, Commonwealth and Southern. The president of this last was a forty-year-old corporation lawyer, a large, heavy, tousle-haired, pleasant-faced, open-mannered Indiana native named Wendell Willkie, a rare bird among utilities executives in that he was a Democrat who had voted for Roosevelt last fall, despite Roosevelt's power record.* He had gained a reputa-

---

*He had *not* been a preconvention supporter of Roosevelt; he had been among the Indiana delegates to the 1932 Democratic convention who voted for Newton D. Baker on the first three ballots, though Baker had not been formally nominated.

tion for progressivism, if not his present post, by daring publicly to oppose in 1929 the then all-powerful Samuel Insull on a civil liberties issue. And he it was who now led the parade of utilities witnesses before the House Military Affairs Committee (only the House held hearings on the Tennessee proposal), declaring "that no one has read . . . with more gratification than we have of this magnificent proposed development. . . ." But the proposed construction of transmission lines would be tantamount to the confiscation of some $400 million of Commonwealth and Southern securities, he went on to say, for it would take away the C&S market, and to "take our market is to take our property." The power developed at Muscle Shoals should be sold at the site to the private utilities for delivery through such lines as *they* chose to build, and that these would be relatively few and far between was made abundantly clear by Willkie's further testimony. The Tennessee Valley market for electricity was already more than adequately served, he and his followers argued, citing an alleged 66⅔ percent excess generating capacity; they refused to concede that the existing market was but a small fraction of the potential which could and would be developed by TVA.[34]

Such testimony was rendered unpersuasive of any very large public by those who gave it, however. The utilities companies were in generally bad odor, thanks to Insull and other utilities magnates very like him in moral quality. Roosevelt himself continued firm in his support of the original conception. And when the House passed, 306 to 91, an amended bill which severely curtailed power line construction, while the Senate passed the Norris bill virtually intact, 63 to 20, Roosevelt exerted effective pressure upon the joint conference committee to report out for final floor action the Senate bill. He signed the bill in a joyous ceremony, George Norris at his side, on May 18.

The law provided that the authority be directed by a three-member board appointed by the President, and even before the bill was passed, Roosevelt knew whom he wanted as board chairman. He wanted Arthur E. Morgan, who promptly accepted the appointment. Soon thereafter Roosevelt appointed the other two board members. One was sixty-six-year-old Harcourt A. Morgan, president of the University of Tennessee for the last fourteen years and, before that, dean of agriculture at the same institution. He had long worked on farm problems in the closest cooperation with that most conservative branch of the USDA, namely, the Extension Service, and with Extension's all too closely linked partner in service of what in future years would become known as agribusiness, the American Farm Bureau Federation. Neither he nor Arthur Morgan had any inclination toward war with utilities companies; both favored the maximum possible cooperation with existing institutions, including the utilities. But in another important respect the two Morgans were very different: Harcourt Morgan was a practical-minded man who distrusted large generalities and had therefore little sympathetic understanding of the kind of idealistic broad-sweep organismic thinking in which Arthur Morgan habitually indulged.

The third appointed board member was David E. Lilienthal, who, at age thirty-four, was young enough to be the son of either of his fellow directors but whose abilities and conceptions fully qualified him as their professional equal. He was another of Felix Frankfurter's protégés and, like the others, was possessed of a generally Brandeisian scale of priorities and values. Upon graduation from De Pauw University in the early 1920s he had entered Harvard Law School, whence, upon Frankfurter's recommendation, he had gone into Donald Richberg's Chicago law firm. Lilienthal had established a lucrative law practice of his own when, in 1931, à la Frankfurter and Brandeis, he entered public service at a very considerable sacrifice of income. He accepted appointment by Wisconsin's young Governor Philip La Follette to the chairmanship of the Wisconsin Public Service Commission. In the two years since, he had made a distinguished and nationally recognized record in utilities regulation. To Lilienthal it was perfectly obvious, being in the very nature of the circumstances, that TVA's relationship with the Commonwealth and Southern companies would be, at least for many years, an adversary one.

Equally obvious to hindsight is the fact that grave risks to the authority's happy operation were inherent in the differences among its initial directors in outlook and conviction, for out of these differences would flare, two years later, bitter quarrels over TVA power and agricultural policy. But in the summer of 1933, as the three began their work together, these differences seemed more fortunate than otherwise. They determined a division of labor that, perfectly consistent with each man's professional training, seemed also perfectly complementary overall. To Lilienthal was assigned the development and administration of power policy; to Harcourt Morgan, the development and administration of fertilizer manufacture and agricultural policy; to Chairman Arthur Morgan, the administration of dam construction and the development of general socioeconomic policy governing the authority's dealings with the people of the valley.

VII

FOR so momentous a proposal, one that pointed toward significant changes in the relationships between federal, state, and local governments and might ultimately transform the whole of the national structure (did not Roosevelt speak in his April 10 message of marching "step by step" from TVA to "a like development of other great natural territorial units"?),* a proposal having truly revolutionary implications, the TVA bill attracted what in retrospect would appear a remarkably small amount of popular attention during the period of its congressional debate and passage. The reason becomes clear when TVA is considered in context. The public mind was on other things in this first spring of the New Deal. It was on a crowd of other things that came rushing out of March into April through a wide gap that had been left in Roosevelt's

---

*When the three TVA directors came to Washington for consultations in the fall of 1933, writes Arthur Schlesinger, Jr., they "asked Tugwell what Roosevelt meant TVA to be—a public corporation confined to specified tasks, or a planning and coordinating agency, or a new kind of regional government. Tugwell replied that TVA, in *his* view [emphasis added], must approximate a government. In certain matters, it might even supersede the states."[35]

yet-building wall of improvisations. And some of these other things had vividly immediate revolutionary implications, whereas those of TVA lay in a dimly perceived future. Indeed, it was in good part because congressional attention was divided among these other things that the Tennessee Valley legislation went through as easily as it did. As for the President who in mid-March had moved in such perfect step with the rhythm of current history that he seemed to be setting it and who addressed his enormous task and the watching nation every day with a show of perfect self-confidence, this same President was in fact, by mid-April, stumbling so badly out of step that even the semblance of his dominance over Congress was gravely threatened. He must move yet more swiftly and audaciously than he had before, and with a closer reckoning of the preponderant weight and direction of historic forces, if he were to achieve some measure of control (in his case this meant a dissipating or moderating control) over what Ernest Lindley described as "revolution boiling up from the bottom."[36]

Hugh Johnson had warned Moley of the developing legislative gap when, five days after the inauguration, he and the professor sat side by side on the train going down from New York to Washington. Johnson spoke of the pressures that were then forcing the administration toward early submission of a farm relief bill, pressures that were poking and prodding the draft legislation into monstrous shapes, in his emphatic opinion. But his main concern that day was with the catastrophe that impended if the administration, yielding to farm organization pressures, simultaneously failed to recognize and respond to pressures from the industrial sector of the economy. These last were less clearly focused and less effectively organized for immediate political action than agriculture's, but they were of even greater danger to the body politic than a farmers' revolt insofar as they included the fateful pressure of mass unemployment. By the time the train pulled into Washington's Union Station, Johnson at Moley's request had written into Moley's notebook the essence of his argument, stressing "his conviction that to increase the cost of farm products *without a parallel stimulation of industrial activity* would be fatal: the farm program, possibly coupled with inflation, would increase . . . [the cost of living] so fast that a crushing burden would fall upon the urban population."[37]

Moley was sufficiently impressed by this to ask banker James P. Warburg, who was assisting in preparations for the World Economic Conference, to review the numerous plans for industrial rehabilitation which had accumulated over the last two years, to talk with some of the authors of these proposals and with others who had ideas, and then to come up with a recommendation of his own. Young Warburg (he was thirty-eight), son of Paul M. Warburg of the great international banking house of Kuhn, Loeb, and Company,* was an expert in international finance, a board member of many corpo-

*Paul Warburg had been one of the organizers of the Federal Reserve System, and one of the few big bankers who in early 1929 publicly warned of the "bust" which must follow a continued stock market "boom."

rations, an officer of the International Acceptance Bank, and a highly intelligent conservative who, though in general agreement with the economic views of his good friend Budget Director Lewis Douglas, had a mind considerably more open and flexible than Douglas's. Working nights and weekends, while his normal working days were wholly occupied by intricate economic conference preparations, he managed to produce in four weeks a memorandum proposing to stimulate industrial production by means of a governmental guarantee against industry losses in the marketplace for a stipulated period, during which the government would share in whatever industrial profits were made. To the memorandum was attached a draft message to Congress in which the President was to describe the proposed legislation as "a bill for the regimentation of industry!" Moley, reading this on April 4 (the day he received it), was wholly unimpressed by the recommendation but strongly impressed by the evident lack of agreement upon clear and practical programmatic ideas among those whom Warburg had consulted. He concluded that "thinking in business and government circles on the subject had not yet crystallized sufficiently to justify further moves at this time." He said so to Roosevelt later that day.

Roosevelt was even less taken with Warburg's recommendation than Moley was. For one thing, there was his intuitive recognition of, his instinctive aversion to any suggestion of fundamental change in the economic structure whereby power-and-property would be transferred from haves to have-nots, and Warburg's recommendation that government become the funding partner of private business in profit-making enterprise just might open the door to such change. It might well result in an effective demand that government become more than an underwriter of business. Having "bought into" industry, must not the government join in "running" it on behalf of the people as a whole? But his main immediate fear, which he soon expressed to Warburg himself, was that there would be, in fact, no profits to share during the stipulated profit-sharing period—that the government bailout of business would cost a great deal of tax money.

For despite the billions of appropriations he was beginning to call for in relief and other "emergency" legislation, Roosevelt's commitment to rigorous government economy and a balanced budget remained firm. So he told himself at least—and others. Actually it was a commitment which his human generosity, joined to perceived political necessity, would permit him to fulfill only in appearance and then only by a species of double-dealing—namely, a dual budget arrangement which he had not and would never officially announce as administration policy. In the only loophole he had left in his campaign pledge to balance the budget, at Pittsburgh last October, he had said: "If starvation and dire need on the part of any of our citizens make necessary the appropriation of additional sums which would keep the budget out of balance, I shall not hesitate to tell the American people the full truth and to ask them to authorize the expenditure of that additional amount." But his nearest approach to telling the "full truth" now was his response to a question asked him by a reporter during his sixth press conference, on March 24. To Lew Douglas's dismay, which would increase, he made a distinction between the "normal" budget, which was in process of being balanced, and an "extraordinary" or "emergency" one, which must be financed by borrowing. "You cannot let people starve," said he to the assembled reporters, "but this starvation charge is not an annually recurring charge." (Inevitably, when news stories based on this "background" appeared, editorials in the conservative press recalled Roosevelt's lambasting of Hoover, in Pittsburgh, for incurring huge government deficits, specifically one of $903 million in 1932. By the "new" and "painless arithmetic" which Roosevelt now employed, as the New York *Times* caustically pointed out, Hoover had incurred no deficit at all in 1932! He had instead accumulated a *surplus* of $360 million!)

Exceedingly delicate, then, was the balance maintained in Roosevelt's mind or feeling between principle and expediency in this matter, and acceptance of Warburg's proposal would upset it.

So Roosevelt and Moley agreed, on this April 4, that legislation for industrial recovery, though greatly needed and important, would have to wait until the next regular session of Congress.[38]

It was at this point that the President began to be overtaken and overruled by events.

Alabama's Senator Hugo Black had introduced in the lame-duck session of the Seventy-second Congress a bill described by journalists and denounced by employers as more "radical" than the Adamson Act of 1916, which had imposed an eight-hour workday for railroad employees. Black's bill prohibited interstate commerce in goods produced in "any mine, quarry, mill, cannery, work-shop, factory, or manufacturing establishment" that worked its employees more than thirty hours a week. The proposal was in keeping with the then-prevailing view, immensely publicized during the Technocracy furor and persuasively argued in Arthur Dahlberg's *Jobs, Machines and Capitalism* (1932), that technological advance must inevitably result in permanent massive unemployment unless the government stepped in to insure that the necessary machine-tending employment was fairly distributed among the available labor force. There must be federal wages and hours legislation, enabling government to reduce hours and increase wages in proportion to the increasing productive efficiency of the machine. As it was, in these early months of 1933, greedy, conscienceless employers were taking ruthless advantage of the current labor "oversupply" and, through the operations of a "free market," forcing their more decent competitors to do much the same. This was especially obvious in those areas of the economy dominated by small business; the "sweatshop" of the garment industry became again notorious. But it was equally if sometimes less obviously so in many economic areas (textiles, mining, steel, automobiles) where big business was the rule. Since 1929 there had been an appalling increase in work hours (up to seventy a week in some states), an appalling decrease in wage rates (down to a few pennies an hour in textile mills), along with a breakdown of those safeguards which Progressivism had established, in the first two decades of the century, against child labor and filthy, dangerous working conditions. The only alternative to such crushing exploitation was, for helpless millions, no jobs at all.

Thus Black's thirty-hour bill had great immediate popular appeal. It had also the surprisingly fervent support of the generally cautious and conservative William Green, head of the American Federation of Labor, whose fervency may have been fed by his antipathy toward a proposal made by Sidney Hillman, president of the Amalgamated Clothing Workers. Hillman, whose pressure toward labor organization on an industry-wide rather than craft union basis was stubbornly opposed by Green, was calling for the establishment of federal labor boards authorized to regulate hours and wages in all industries in which decent standards were not maintained by industrial self-government. This was far too "socialistic" for Green, who, emphatically a free-marketeer, wanted no government interference with free bargaining between his craft unions and employers, and it was perhaps because of the labor leader's known antipathy to minimum wage proposals that Black included none in his bill. Certainly Black wanted, he felt he had to have, Green's support. And just as certainly he received it. In Senate committee hearings during the lame-duck session Green went so far as to predict a "universal strike" if the thirty-hour bill failed to pass. The listening senators were startled. Wouldn't that be "class war, practically"? asked a pleased Black, after a pause. And Green, if a bit nervous at finding himself on such controversial ground, perforce stood his ground. "Whatever it would be, it would be that . . . [a general strike]," said he, adding, "That is the only language a lot of employers ever understand—the language of force."[39]

But of course, there had been no chance of the bill's passage through the Seventy-second Congress—had it done so, President Hoover would have vetoed it—and Roosevelt had deemed highly unlikely its favorable consideration by the Seventy-third Congress when Black reintroduced it at the beginning of the special session. He personally opposed the measure. It was too rigid, too restrictive: during talk about it with Secretary of Labor Perkins, who was inclined to favor the measure, he wondered aloud how a thirty-hour week could apply in, say, the dairy industry, where, said he, "[t]here have to be hours adjusted to the rhythm of the cow." He doubted that so drastically shortened a workweek would actually spread employment. It was certain to reduce the incomes of those employed unless prevailing hourly wage rates were increased by more than 25 percent; he saw no reason to believe they would be in the absence of minimum wage guarantees. In any case, according to the attorney general and every other of his legal advisers, the proposed legislation was unconstitutional. Once when he and Moley were discussing his forthcoming relief message, he spoke of the Black bill as a "threat" (Black had asked him in writing on March 10 to call for this "imperatively necessary" legislation in his relief message), and Moley had then listed it in his notebook under the heading "Threats." But to both men the threat had then seemed relatively distant. It was something that could be dealt with later.[40]

Hence the shock of surprise in the White House when, on the very day Roosevelt and Moley agreed that industrial recovery legislation should be postponed, the Black bill came onto the Senate floor for debate, having been favorably reported out, 11 to 3, by the Judiciary Committee. On the same day a companion thirty-hour bill, introduced by Massachusetts Congressman William P. Connery, Jr., was favorably reported in the House, and this bill was even more drastic than the Senate version in that it proposed an embargo on all foreign goods produced in establishments working employees more than thirty hours a week! Two days later, after an amendment proposed by Majority Leader Robinson had been defeated, 48 to 41 (it would have lengthened the workweek to thirty-six hours), the Senate passed the bill by a vote of 53 to 30. The victory margin was, from Roosevelt's point of view, distressingly wide; it presaged a much wider margin of victory in the House.

Obviously, then, action on the industrial front could *not* be postponed. Obviously the executive must act *now* if it were to maintain or restore control over legislature or situation. And in the absence of any strategic plan for attack on this front, the action must necessarily be tactically defensive. Moreover, the action could not be limited to tactical maneuvers whereby the Black bill was blocked or drained of potency. For the bill's unexpected political momentum was but one of several current expressions of "revolution boiling up from the bottom," a revolutionary discontent whose energies must be somehow dispersed or redirected. Otherwise, the end would be a planned national economy radically different from that aimed for by business planners Gerard Swope and Henry I. Harriman (it accorded better with Tugwell's insistence upon national planning in terms of a "concert of interests") and outrageous of Roosevelt's own guiding principles in that it involved the actual nationalization or socialization of major portions of America's productive enterprise.*

The direness of the threat was impressed upon Roosevelt's mind by the fact that nationalization's advocacy was no longer confined to collectivists of the political left; a substantial part of it came from demoralized elements of the business community itself.

He had noted how some of the big bankers summoned by the White House to Washington during the New Deal's first days were of the opinion that the whole of the credit structure must be nationalized, that there was no other solution to the banking crisis. During that same week a large group of coal operators, including leading figures of that desperately sick industry, called personally upon the President to urge a government takeover of the mines. Roosevelt, wholly absorbed in the banking problem, turned them over to Frances Perkins and Harold Ickes (the Bureau of Mines was in the Department of the Interior), who listened, outwardly "solemn as owls" but inwardly

---

*"The government really ought to take over immediately large blocks of paralyzed industries, in my opinion, to make certain that production is set going," wrote Tugwell in his diary on April 21, 1933. "At the very least we ought to take them on lease. . . ."[41] Such advice only increased the urgency with which Roosevelt sought for means to avoid such takeovers without serious reduction of his political capital.

perturbed by the weight of responsibility suddenly thrust upon them, as one mineowner after another poured out "catastrophic stories" from the minefields, stories that ended with pleas for the nationalization of those fields. "The operators will sell the mines to the government at any price fixed by the government," they said, according to Perkins's remembrance. "Anything so we can get out of it."[42] There were less loud and urgent cries, but cries nevertheless, from some railroad executives for either a nationalization of their distressed industry or a government regulation so rigorous and complete as to be tantamount to government operation. Repeatedly referred to was the U.S. experience of "wartime socialism" in 1918, when the railroads were run as a single integrated enterprise by William Gibbs McAdoo's Railroad Administration, when all industry was brought under government control through Baruch's War Industries Board, and the nation produced as it had never produced before.

Even longtime public servants of lifelong Brandeisian convictions now veered toward a New Nationalism more extreme, more socialistic, than that envisaged in Herbert Croly's *Promise of American Life*. One of them was Joseph B. Eastman, chairman of the Interstate Commerce Commission and long recognized by both Republicans and Democrats as the nation's leading expert in the field of transportation. He had been appointed to the ICC by Wilson, acting on Brandeis's recommendation. Eastman's fervent belief at that time and for a dozen years thereafter had been that monopoly control is wicked, leading to "dry rot," while "competition is a stimulus to alert, aggressive management." But he was now driven by harsh experience to conclude that so far as the desperately troubled railroads were concerned, "the evils and wastes of competition outweigh its advantages" and that, therefore, "competition among railroads should be eliminated. . . ." They ought to be operated as a single national unit. "But I do not believe the country will stand for that without government ownership," he said to Frankfurter as he had said to Roosevelt himself, early in the year, "and it is also clear that this is the simplest road to unification."[43]

Roosevelt's response to the threat was typically vigorous and various: He moved swiftly in several different directions, scattering his shots in the expectation that at least one of them would be lucky, enabling him thereafter to concentrate his fire.

On Tuesday, April 11, he instructed Moley to consult with people outside government, in Washington, who were known to be working on industrial recovery plans. One of those whom he specifically mentioned was Harold G. Moulton of the Brookings Institute; another was Henry I. Harriman of the U.S. Chamber of Commerce. On Wednesday, April 12, Roosevelt dispatched identical telegrams to the governors of thirteen industrial states, calling their attention to a minimum wage law just passed by the New York legislature and approved by Governor Lehman, declaring it "against public policy for any employer to pay women or minors a wage which is 'both less than the fair and reasonable value of services rendered and less than sufficient to meet the ultimate cost of living necessary for health.'" He urged the governors to initiate similar legislation in their own states. (In the event, six states did so.) On Thursday, April 13, he sent Congress a message calling for legislation, modeled on the farm mortgage refinancing bill, to save small homes in towns and cities from mortgage foreclosure—a proposal that would encounter virtually no opposition (the need for it was obvious and desperate: Urban home foreclosures mounted to more than 1,000 a day; new home-financing loans were simply not being made; new home construction was down to 10 percent of the 1929 volume) and resulted in the Home Owners' Loan Act, to be signed in the second week of June. On the same Thursday, April 13, he received from his uncle Frederic A. Delano, whose reputation as city planner was deservedly high, a memorandum outlining a sweeping plan for business-government cooperation toward full production and employment; he referred the memorandum to Secretary of Commerce Roper with a cover note saying he thought his uncle "right but perhaps a little ahead of his time"—a reservation possibly less expressive of his own cautious conservatism than revelatory of his sensitivity to Roper's. This was tantamount to a suggestion that Roper proceed along the general lines of the Delano memorandum in the preparation of an administration bill.

Next morning (Friday, April 14), during his breakfast-tray perusal of newspapers, he had again impressed upon him the necessity for a swift, bold move if he was to stay on top of the developing situation, the impressive fact being a story by Arthur Krock displayed under big headlines on the front page of the New York *Times.* Roosevelt read it with some annoyance.

Obviously Krock's information came from a thoroughly knowledgeable source, for his story not only was an accurate account of general ideas which Tugwell, Donald Richberg, and other national planning advocates had been pressing upon Roosevelt, and which were contained in the Delano memorandum, but also took cognizance of the relationship, as twin pressures upon the executive, of the industrial planning and public works approaches to the unemployment problem. In the Senate the clamor for a massive federal public works program grew deafening, encouraged by Roosevelt's relief message of March 21. Senators La Follette, Costigan, and Cutting had already introduced, when the relief message was delivered, a bill calling for a $6 billion federal building program (the figure appalled Lewis Douglas, who opposed *any* federal construction). Senator Wagner had already developed, through his contacts with federal construction agencies and other members of Congress, a lengthy list of specific projects to be included in such a program. Hence the cogency of Krock's saying that there was "being developed by the President's closest advisers" a plan "to mobilize private industry under the government for expansion of the production of articles and materials in usual demand, this expansion to be coeval with the administration's public works activities. . . ." Krock went on: "Certain types of industry, under the plan, would be assembled and regulated by a governmental agency reminiscent of the War Industries Board. Competition would be regulated; hours of work and mini-

mum rates of pay would be fixed. . . . The thought behind the plan is that a
public works program, standing by itself, even if five billions is expended on
it, will not sufficiently reduce employment or make use of new purchasing
power." Who was the source for all this? Specifically and prominently mentioned was "Assistant Secretary of State Raymond Moley, who is represented
as being 'sold' on the general idea." If so, concluded Krock, the plan's "adoption [by the President] is but a step away. . . ."[44]

What annoyed Roosevelt about this was not its exposure to the public gaze
of a main current of administration thought; this he might welcome since
public reaction would help him toward final decisions. No, what annoyed him
was the strong hint that Professor Moley was the real maker of administration
policy, that the President simply followed the professor's lead on substantive
matters, coupled with the strong suggestion that someone or some group,
possibly Moley himself, was attempting to force his hand. The suggestion was
implicit in the fact of the story's appearance at this moment, in so influential
a paper, under so prestigious a by-line. And it was perhaps a resentment at
being thus pushed which caused Roosevelt, during his press conference in the
afternoon of that day, to reply as he did to a reporter's question about the
government's public works plans. "I have not talked about it at all yet," said
he dismissively.[45]

But soon thereafter he learned that it was not from Moley that Krock had
obtained his information. It was from Robert Wagner, with whom Krock had
lunched the day before the story appeared.

When Moley conferred with Moulton, he was told and obtained a copy of
a proposed national economic recovery act that had been drawn up by Moulton and a fellow Brookings Institute economist, Meyer Jacobstein. The latter,
formerly a congressman representing the Rochester district of New York, was
a close friend of Wagner's. And it was perhaps from Jacobstein that Wagner
learned of Moley's call upon the institute, with whose recovery plan Wagner
was already familiar, and that Moley's reaction to that plan was favorable.
According to Krock's own remembrance, Roosevelt's annoyance then focused
on Wagner, whose volubility he deplored, but if so, the annoyance was not
great enough to prevent his giving Wagner, a week later, the assignment to
prepare concrete industrial recovery legislation for the administration—precisely the assignment which Moley had thought was made to him exclusively
and which he now, on Tuesday, April 25, after trying for two weeks to come
to grips with it, assigned in turn to Hugh Johnson, probably with Roosevelt's
advance permission, certainly with Roosevelt's subsequent approval. (By his
own account, Moley was desperate when he accidentally encountered Johnson
in the Carlton lobby, for he was overwhelmed by other work assignments of
major importance. He then and there begged Johnson to "come over to my
office and take all the material I've got and do this job for F.D.R." Nobody
could do it better, said Moley. "You're familiar with the only comparable thing
that's ever been done—the War Industries Board"[46]).

Three days later John Dickinson, undersecretary of commerce, to whom

Roper had assigned what he thought was *his* responsibility for preparing the industrial recovery bill, addressed to Moley a letter fervently protesting testimony Frances Perkins had presented in House committee hearings on the thirty-hour bill.

For while Roosevelt cast around for legislative proposals that would head off the threat represented by the Black bill, concerning which he said publicly nothing at all, he permitted his secretary of labor to testify in favor of the bill, if with major amendments which she had talked over with him. The amendments called for somewhat greater flexibility in the matter of work hours: The thirty-hour week should generally prevail, said Madame Perkins, but in some industries the week might be lengthened to a maximum of forty hours. Moreover, the secretary of labor should be authorized to set up minimum wage boards, with members representing management, labor, and government, and should be authorized to order into effect the recommendations these boards made. Finally, the secretary should be enabled to relax those portions of antitrust law prohibiting such trade agreements as the secretary might deem necessary to achieve the purposes of the act.

Dickinson's letter to Moley was generally expressive of the views of the business community, whose outcry against the Perkins amendments was every bit as loud as it had been against the Black bill originally—louder, even, since the Perkins testimony seemed to indicate that the bill was to become an administration measure. This last, wrote Dickinson, would be "politically disastrous" since the measure would create a "monster bureaucracy" to direct operations bound to be "economically unfortunate for the country." Dickinson proposed, instead, certain elements of the plan on which he had been working, at Secretary Roper's behest.[47]

But by the time Moley read this, he knew that Dickinson's expressed fear was groundless. There was not the slightest chance that Roosevelt would adopt as his own the Black bill, however it might be amended. The whole effect of the furor over it was to make sure that attention to wages and hours would be paid in the industrial recovery legislation the prompt submission of which to Congress was now imperative.

4

➵➤✕◆◆◆

Improvisations Continue as Pressures Increase: To the End of the Hundred Days

I

MEANWHILE, the "revolution boiling up from the bottom" operated on the agricultural front with growing effectiveness, greatly agitating deliberations of the farm relief bill in the Senate. And there, in the Senate, farm policy became mixed up, inextricably, with considerations of monetary policy which, in turn, joined it inseparably with basic foreign policy considerations, for an announced objective of the upcoming World Monetary and Economic Conference, to open in London in June, was international currency stabilization on the basis of a renewed international gold standard.

It will be recalled that John Simpson of the Farmers' Union, in pressing for inclusion of a cost of production guarantee in the farm bill, joined this with a demand for substantial currency inflation. It will be further recalled that Senator Norris, immediately following Simpson's testimony in the farm bill hearings, moved a cost of production amendment to that bill. On April 13 this amendment came to a vote on the Senate floor, where, despite Roosevelt's strongly expressed opposition to it (on "economy" grounds) and despite furious efforts to block it by his floor leaders, it passed by a vote of 47 to 41. Here was rebellion indeed—the first clear defeat Roosevelt had suffered in Congress.

Obviously a farm bill acceptable to him could now be passed only if he yielded in some degree to the increasingly strong demand of western and farm belt senators for an inflation of the currency. Proof of this came four days later (Monday, April 17), when a farm bill amendment proposed by Senator Burton K. Wheeler of Montana came to a vote. This amendment was straight out of 1890s Bryanism in that it called for the remonetization of silver and its free and unlimited coinage in a ratio to gold of 16 to 1. When Wheeler first proposed it in the lame-duck session, as an amendment of the farm bill then before the Senate, it had fared poorly; only eighteen senators had voted for it. Now, despite strongly voiced opposition by Majority Leader Robinson as Roosevelt's spokesman, the amendment was defeated by a much narrower margin, 43 to 33. This emboldened Oklahoma's Senator Elmer Thomas, Congress's archinflationist, to introduce at once an inflationary amendment of his own. He did not limit himself to silver; in that omnibus spirit which the New Deal fostered, he proposed several inflationary devices among which the President *must* choose to effect a stated increase in the money supply. One was simply (in Roosevelt's disparaging words) "to start the printing presses," grinding out greenbacks as legal tender—the device used during the Civil War. Another was to remonetize silver and provide for its free coinage, as Wheeler proposed. A third was to manipulate the gold content of the dollar, as Cornell's George Warren was proposing. The expressed approval which this amendment received, orally from the senators as soon as they heard it, was loud enough to assure absolutely its prompt passage by a sizable majority when it came to floor vote, probably on the morrow.

And of this Ray Moley was informed early in the following morning (Tuesday, April 18).

He, Moley, was yet abed in the Carlton when he received in quick succession two urgent phone calls. One was from Ohio's Senator Robert J. Bulkley; the other, from South Carolina's Senator James F. Byrnes. Both told him that the Thomas amendment would certainly pass in precisely its present form unless the administration moved at once to modify it and that the limit of such possible modification was a weakening of the amendment's mandatory features, a proportionate widening of the assigned discretionary powers. Two hours later Byrnes accompanied Moley to the White House, where following his reading of the morning papers, the President routinely began his workday at nine o'clock with bedside conferences in which Howe, McIntyre, Early, and Moley always, in these opening months of the New Deal, participated and to which were invited such others as had special information or advice useful to that day's decision making.

On this Tuesday morning it was obvious that the essential decision regarding the day's most important action had already been made. Roosevelt could only ratify the inflationary action which the Senate, said Byrnes, was bound to take in any case. Otherwise he'd be faced by a Congress in *full* rebellion; he'd go down to a defeat gravely injurious, if not fatal, to his effective leadership in the months ahead. His single choice now was in the *manner* of his ratification.

As he always did in such cases, he chose to ratify with a flourish, giving the impression that the inevitable happened in accord with, if not as an actual expression of, his personal wish and will. There was a proviso. Thomas must be persuaded to consent to a thorough rewriting of the amendment, rendering it more flexible, more discretionary, in its provisions. Byrnes was assigned the task of obtaining this consent. Two or three hours later he brought Thomas to the Executive Office, where "the President . . . did an excellent sales job," as Byrnes would remember. Its conclusion was Thomas's acquiescence in whatever revision of language seemed to the President desirable, so long as the "big principle" was retained.[1]

That night there was scheduled a meeting in the White House to discuss the line the President should take in the talks he would have in a few days, face-to-face, with British Prime Minister J. Ramsay MacDonald concerning the upcoming World Monetary and Economic Conference. Roosevelt had invited MacDonald to Washington for this purpose (he had invited eleven countries, including France, Germany, Italy, Canada, Japan, to send representatives for bilateral conversations in preparation for the conference), and MacDonald with a considerable staff was at that moment on the high seas en route to America. As it turned out, there was very little discussion that night of any side of the specific topic for whose consideration the meeting had been called, and that little had to do with the probable effect upon British government attitudes of the announcement with which Roosevelt opened the meeting.

He made it as soon as the conferees were assembled in the Oval Room, immediately after dinner, and he made it in a way calculated to provoke a maximum of shock, outrage, and dismay in several of those who heard him. All in the administration having important parts in economic conference preparations were present: Hull, Woodin, Moley, Warburg, Lew Douglas, Herbert Feis, Charles Taussig (the continued involvement of this "molasses man" in top New Deal councils continued to irk Moley), Nevada's Key Pittman (he was chairman of the Senate Foreign Relations Committee), and the highly dramatic, inveterately conspiratorial William C. Bullitt, whose appointment as special assistant to the secretary of state was to be formally announced two days hence.* Of all those present, Bullitt may have been the one who most thoroughly appreciated and fully enjoyed the spectacle as Roosevelt, after holding up a copy of the Thomas amendment for all to see, handed it to Moley, saying, "Here, Ray, you act as a clearing house to take care of this. Have it thoroughly amended and then give them word to pass it." Thus he made definite and total the theretofore ambiguous and limited departure from the gold standard proclaimed in his order of a national bank holiday last March 6. He turned back to the others, broadly smiling. "Congratulate me!" he said.

They didn't, of course.

Woodin, Moley, and Pittman already knew of Roosevelt's decision, having been involved in its making that day. Woodin had accepted it with resignation; Pittman (a senator from a silver state, hence a fervent bimetallist), with enthusiasm. But among the others—especially Douglas, Warburg, and Feis—there was stunned surprise and consternation, followed by angry, vehement protest. "[H]ell broke loose in the room," Moley remembered, and this "hell" surged

---

*Bullitt had become part of the Roosevelt presidential campaign staff in September 1932, thanks largely to Louis B. Wehle, a nephew of Brandeis's and a coeditor with Roosevelt of the *Crimson* when the two were Harvard undergraduates. Wehle, instrumental in persuading Roosevelt to become a vice presidential candidate in 1920, was instrumental, too, in arranging for Bullitt to serve Roosevelt as adviser and information-gathering agent during two tours of European capitals, made at his own expense, one in November–December 1932, the other in January 1933. Bullitt conferred with many leading governmental figures in Europe, in evident violation of the Logan Act, which prohibits private citizens from conducting conversations with members of foreign governments about matters affecting relations between those governments and the United States, unless prior permission has been granted by the State Department. He had been obliged to cut short his second European tour when, in late January 1933, a wire service reported him to be in London as the President-elect's "secret agent." This caused a furor in the Senate and caused Roosevelt to seem, in the eyes of Sir Ronald Lindsay, British ambassador to the United States, "rather shame-faced" when, during Lindsay's visit to Warm Springs, the Bullitt matter was mentioned. "I imagine he [Roosevelt] is in an equivocal position," reported Lindsay to the Foreign Office. In earlier weeks Bullitt had sent telegrams, in private code, to Wehle for decoding and transmittal, through Missy LeHand, to Roosevelt. His last telegram, dated January 31, went to Missy directly and said in part: "Full reliance can be placed on French and German support for return of England to gold standard."[2]

and eddied around Roosevelt for two solid hours. He was unperturbed by it. He replied calmly and good-naturedly, or he merely smiled and shrugged in response, to charges that he didn't know what he was doing, that out of his abysmal ignorance of monetary intricacies he was destroying the (gold) foundations of world order. Warburg actually scolded him as a schoolmaster might a delinquent schoolboy. Warburg and Douglas both scoffed at the notion that there could ever be a "mild" or "controlled" inflation; public knowledge that greenback issuance was an available executive option would of itself alone set off wild inflation, leading to "complete chaos," they insisted. Feis stressed the international implications—U.S. abandonment of gold was bound to increase immensely the difficulty of international exchange stabilization—and he pointed again ("sound money" men invariably did so in those days) to the horrible example of Germany in 1923. Roosevelt remained unmoved when, shortly after ten o'clock, the meeting broke up.

The reaction of Douglas and Warburg to all this was one of utter horror. Moley went from the White House with Pittman to the latter's home to discuss the next day's Senate floor strategy. When he arrived in his Carlton suite shortly after midnight, he found Douglas and Warburg waiting for him. They were "in a state." They had to talk. They did talk, passionately and at length. When at last they left, to walk Washington's deserted streets until dawn, Douglas's parting words were ominous. "This," said he, "is the end of Western civilization."[3]

Roosevelt's nearest approach to a defensive posture, under the fire poured upon him during that night session of April 18, was his remark that the only alternative to his acceptance of discretionary inflationary powers was a congressional mandate to inflate, a mandate with specific inflexible terms. His mollifying implication was that he accepted under duress the lesser of two evils, that for all his brave show of decisiveness ("Congratulate me!"), he was really being forced into inflation against his will. And credence was given this interpretation by the fact that during the few days immediately preceding his acceptance of the Thomas amendment, he had authorized shipments by New York bankers of some $20 million of gold abroad, for the first time since his March 6 proclamation of an embargo on international gold shipments, to bolster a dollar that sagged in terms of foreign currencies. It sagged because monetary speculators believed some concessions would have to be made to congressional inflationists if the administration's farm bill were to pass, and the dollar *continued* to weaken despite the gold shipments, which were an earnest of the administration's determination to use gold reserves to maintain that dollar at its present value against alleged raids being made upon it by a consortium of well-heeled speculators in Amsterdam. There was actually a licensed gold shipment on the morning of April 18, seemingly indicative of the administration's continued commitment to the gold standard, though this license was granted in fulfillment of an oral promise made some days before.

But there is abundant evidence that the cheerfulness with which Roosevelt accepted discretionary inflationary powers was by no means all mere show, that in actual fact the Senate's impending action *did* accord to a considerable degree with his personal wish and will. His commitment to "sound money" as most fiscal conservatives defined the term had been far from absolute even at the time of his Pittsburgh campaign speech, and since the first of the year he had kept his mind wide open to suggestions that *some* inflation might be required to halt the continuing erosion of commodity prices, else there be violent revolt in the farm belt. Hence his refusal to give Carter Glass the absolute pledge against inflation which Glass had asked for. Hence his refusal to give his own definition of "sound money" when, in his very first presidential press conference, he was asked what he meant by it in his inaugural address; he had gone on to say, it will be recalled, that what America was "coming to" was a "managed currency" and that this "ought to be part of the permanent system." In his tenth press conference, on April 7, he had said, "So much of the legislation we have had this spring is of a deflationary character, in the sense that it locks up money or prevents the flow of money, that we are faced with the problem of offsetting that in some way."[4]

And only an hour or less before Moley came to his bedside with Byrnes in tow on the decisive morning of April 18, Roosevelt had been confirmed in his inflationary predilections by his reading of Walter Lippmann's column of that day, in the New York *Herald Tribune.*

Through that column the New Deal drew inspiration, ironically enough (or so it would have seemed to the general public), from 23 Wall Street, the home of J. P. Morgan's bank, where Lippmann had lunched a couple of days before with Morgan partners Thomas Lamont and Russell Leffingwell. Both bankers were terribly worried by the growing farmer revolt; both regarded a rise in commodity prices as absolutely necessary to the nation's political stability; and both were convinced that this could be achieved only if the administration gained full control of the currency. Such views were not uniquely heretical, that spring, in the big business world. A good many very prominent business-men argued and even organized to press for counteraction against the prevail-ing deflation. Among them were Robert E. Wood, president of Sears, Roebuck; Lessing Rosenwald, board chairman of Sears, Roebuck; and James H. Rand, Jr., of Remington Rand, all of whom had joined with others early in 1933 to form a Committee for the Nation to Rebuild Prices and Purchasing Power for the express purpose of inciting a controlled inflation by means of gold manipu-lations, the ultimate aim being a stable "commodity dollar." Rand was chair-man of this committee, whose chief economic advisers were George Warren and Irving Fisher. Thus Lamont and Leffingwell spoke for a highly respectable and sophisticated minority of the business community when, over lunch, they urged upon an already convinced Lippmann the need to free the U.S. currency from its bondage to gold. "Walter," said Leffingwell earnestly at luncheon's end, "you've got to explain to the people why we can no longer afford to chain ourselves to the gold standard. Then maybe Roosevelt, who I am sure agrees, will be able to act."[5]

And the resultant column, persuasive of millions of influential Americans, *did* certainly ease Roosevelt's immediate task with its remarkably clear statement of the historic choice America faced at that moment. It was the choice between economic nationalism and economic internationalism, a "choice," wrote Lippmann, ". . . between keeping up prices at home and keeping up the gold value of the currency abroad." For in the circumstances no nation could defend *both* the gold standard and its internal price level. The evidence on that point was conclusive. Britain, for instance, going off gold in the face of dangerously developing social unrest, had improved its internal economic situation enough to achieve political stability. Germany, remaining on gold, was now a Nazi dictatorship. As for the United States, if it now clung to the gold standard, it must abandon unemployment relief, credit expansion, public works, and, in the end, its present political structure, for assuredly this structure would be torn apart by Americans who preferred revolutionary change to abject starvation. Clearly, then, the price of gold was too high![6]

On Wednesday, April 19—the morning following his endorsement of a revised Thomas amendment—Roosevelt commented to his press conference* on the decision, which went into effect that day, to prohibit the "exporting of gold, except earmarked gold for foreign governments . . . and balances of commercial exchange." This meant, he explained, that the administration would no longer attempt "artificially to support" the dollar at its present value in terms of foreign currencies but would instead "let the dollar take care of itself," seeking "its own natural level." Dollar value would go down, commodity prices should therefore go up, and "[t]he whole problem before us is to raise commodity prices." A reporter, agreeing that "this policy would raise prices here at home," wondered what effect it would have on the World Economic Conference, the agenda of which included "an item for raising prices all over the world." The effect, said Roosevelt, would be "constructive." The new policy "puts us in the same position with nearly all the other nations of the world" and would "emphasize the necessity for all nations getting together on a more stable basis." What would this "stable basis" be? a reporter wanted to know. "[I]s it still the desire of the United States to go back on an international gold standard?" Absolutely, replied Roosevelt; "one of the things we hope to do is get the whole world back on some form of gold standard. . . ." Did the President have "any other ideas in mind . . . as to the steps to be taken" in this matter? "Nothing else," said Roosevelt. "It is a little bit like a football team that has a general plan of game against the other side," he went on. "Now, the captain and the quarterback of that team know pretty well what the next play is going to be and they know the general strategy of the team; but they cannot tell you what the play after the next play is going to be until the next play is run off. If the play makes ten yards, the succeeding play will

---

*This thirteenth press conference was held in the Oval Room instead of (as usual) the Executive Office, because Roosevelt had a cold. "I have gotten to the point where even a cigarette tastes bad," he told the reporters ruefully.

be different from what it would have been if they had been thrown for a loss.
. . . Here is a team that has a perfectly definite objective, which is to make a
touchdown, so far as commodity prices go. The basis of the whole thing really
comes down to commodity prices."[7]

The revised Thomas amendment came to a vote in the Senate on April 28,
passing by 64 to 21. It passed the House on May 3 by 307 to 86. By its terms
the President had opened to him five options for achievement of the desired
level of inflation. He could attempt to persuade Federal Reserve Banks to buy
in the open market up to $3 billion of government securities. If the banks
refused to do this, he could order the issuance of up to $3 billion of fiat money
("greenbacks"), using this to retire government bonds; 4 percent of the fiat
notes were to be retired annually. In lieu of either of these options he could
(1) remonetize silver at whatever value ratio to gold he desired; (2) reduce the
dollar's gold content by as much as 50 percent; or (3) buy silver at up to fifty
cents an ounce, which was 10 percent more than its current market price.
Necessarily implied by this was annulment of the clause in all outstanding
public and private contracts whereby debt payments were pledged to be made
in dollars each containing 23.32 grains of gold, and on June 5, in response to
Roosevelt's request and after debate in which fiscal conservatives gave full
voice to their moral outrage, Congress was to adopt the needed specific resolution, by overwhelming majority. (In his second fireside chat, on Sunday evening, May 7, a radio talk as successful as the first chat had been, Roosevelt,
explaining "what we have been doing and what we are planning to do,"
devoted considerable attention to monetary policy. "The Administration has
the definite objective of raising commodity prices to such an extent that those
who have borrowed money will, on the average, be able to repay that money
in the same kind of dollar which they borrowed," he explained. "We do not
seek to let them get such a cheap dollar that they will be able to pay back a
great deal less than they borrowed. In other words, we seek to correct a wrong
and not to create a wrong in the opposite direction."[8])

Adoption of the Thomas amendment effectively stymied the Norris cost of
production amendment and cleared the way for passage of the overall farm
relief bill. Such passage was spurred, too, by new violence in the Iowa countryside and by the imminent national farmers' strike which Milo Reno had called.
At Le Mars, Iowa, on April 27, a federal judge who had refused to suspend
mortgage foreclosure proceedings as demanded by angry farmers in his courtroom was dragged from the bench, slapped, pummeled, thrown into a truck,
and taken to a spot a mile from town where he was choked nearly to death
with a rope noose and smeared with grease and dirt after his trousers had been
removed. A few days later, after another farmer mob had violently prevented
foreclosure on a farm near Denison, Iowa's governor placed a half dozen
counties under martial law and called out the National Guard to enforce it.

So on May 12, at long last, the Agricultural Adjustment Act and the conjoined (as Title II) Emergency Farm Mortgage Act, having gone through both
houses with big majorities, went from Capitol Hill to White House and were

there promptly signed into law. The President issued a signature statement: "I urge upon mortgage creditors . . . until full opportunity has been given to make effective the provisions of the mortgage refinancing sections . . . that they abstain from bringing foreclosure proceedings and making any effort to dispossess farmers who are in debt to them. I invite their cooperation . . . to effect agreements which will make foreclosures unnecessary.[9]

II

WHILE all this was going on, Roosevelt was also presiding, with decisive yeas and nays, over the blockage and scattering of those historic forces which drove toward a nationalization of the railroads and, beyond this, toward a rational, humanly purposive control of advancing technology's applications in the field of transportation as a whole.

In the early spring of 1933 no industry save the coal industry was in deeper economic trouble than the railroads—in some part because of the water pumped into securities when railroad mergers were formed early in the century, in growing part because of the competition for freight and passenger traffic provided by the automobile and airplane, and most acutely, of course, because depression had drastically reduced all freight shipments and passenger travel. There had been a 50 percent drop in operating revenues, an equivalent drop in railroad employment (750,000 railroad workers had been laid off) since 1929. Dividend payments were down 70 percent. And for many roads bankruptcy was imminent despite the Railroad Bankruptcy Act passed by the lame-duck session in early 1933 to avert such catastrophe (Eastman, and Berle as Roosevelt's agent, had been involved in the act's drafting). This was bad news for the national credit structure in general, for railroad securities had long been a preferred "safe" investment for savings banks, trust funds, and other financially conservative institutions and individuals. Moreover, the RFC had made huge loans of taxpayers' money to the rail companies, and many of the notes for these were due during the coming summer. There were, therefore, loud cries from the creditor class for drastic government action to increase railroad operating efficiency, to eliminate competition that employed duplicative or redundant facilities, and to provide a just economic balance between rail lines, which were legally private property, privately maintained, and other means of transportation (highways, waterways) created and maintained with tax money.*

In these demands the creditors were by no means alone. A good many others saw in the current situation a rare opportunity not only to correct grievous errors in public policy made when the rails built westward after the Civil War

---

*It is not irrelevant to note that though the railroads were privately owned, most of the cost of building them had been borne by federal and state treasuries. Huge were the grants of public land and money given the railroad "barons" by bought-and-paid-for congressmen and state legislators in the 1860s, '70s, and '80s. It has been estimated that the western railroads cost the American people ten times as much as they would have cost had they been built by government directly.

but also to achieve through government a truly national, truly integrated and balanced transportation system, inclusive of railroads, interstate highways, air routes, inland waterways, coastwise shipping, and pipe lines. It would be, in the eyes of some, a system whose planned development and operation took account of and affected the design of new automobiles, new ships, new airplanes, new locomotives, new rail types (the monorail was then much talked of) while *also* taking account of the need for swift cheap U.S. mail delivery and of the ruinous effect which the rampant automobile was having on American community life, especially that village community life which Roosevelt, as squire of Hyde Park and Warm Springs, personally loved.

As President-elect, Roosevelt himself had talked of creating a single national transportation agency to regulate all transportation, including pipe lines and coastal shipping, an agency that would take over the administrative and quasi-judicial functions of the present Interstate Commerce Commission, whose inability to fulfill its original congressionally assigned role was notorious among those who paid close attention to such matters. For hardly ever since its establishment had the ICC won a rate dispute case in the courts; generally the courts, the presiding judges of which were often former corporation lawyers, ruled the way attorneys for the carriers asked them to rule. There should be, said Roosevelt, a reduction of excessive railroad capitalization and, to quote Lindley's description of Roosevelt's view, an "integration of highway, air, and water transportation with the railroads on an equitable basis, with the elimination of superfluous railroad mileage and unnecessary competition, and the establishment of a new rate-making base."[10] Upon entering the White House, Roosevelt had reiterated this as his aim. He could cite in support of it the recent report of a National Transportation Committee, whose membership had included several prestigious public figures of distinctly conservative hue (Calvin Coolidge was the committee's chairman when he died in January 1933; Bernard Baruch was vice-chairman; Al Smith was a member) as well as representatives of insurance companies and major universities having large railroad securities holdings. Drafted mostly by Moulton, with some help from Berle as Roosevelt's deputy, the report caused a considerable stir with its proposal to consolidate hitherto competitive lines and to regulate strictly, federally, not only these but every other kind of commercial transport. (Al Smith dissented from this, to a degree; he proposed outright abolition of the ICC and establishment of a U.S. Department of Transportation.)

But though, in this early spring of 1933, most students of the problem, including several top railroad executives (Carl Gray, president of the Union Pacific, was one), and every historic circumstance thus favored fundamental railroad reforms—and though Roosevelt himself did so, or said he did—none was made.

In early March the railroad problem was assigned by Roosevelt to a committee whose chairman was Eastman and whose membership included Berle and representatives of railroad securities holders and railroad management. This committee, which operated under the aegis of the Commerce Department and had on it no representative of either the shippers or the railroad brotherhoods, met with Roosevelt on April 1, presenting him then with four plans. The most striking and innovative of these, devised by a Boston banker named Frederick H. Prince, called for consolidation of all of America's railroads into seven or, at most, eight regional systems. These, by eliminating the wastes of competition and by increasing efficiency, would operate at a saving of $700 million annually, compared to present operating costs, and would enable the lines to show a profit even if traffic remained at the low 1932 level. For this bailing out of shareholders a price would have to be paid, of course—by others. A quarter million more men would be thrown out of work, for one thing. For another, the government would have to lend the railroads upwards of $2 billion. And the latter fact caused economy-minded Roosevelt, initially strongly attracted by the plan, to lose interest in it abruptly and completely. He turned to the other three plans, all of which had at their core a scheme devised by Berle for a federal transportation coordinator but which differed from one another in their specifications of the scope and kind of power this coordinator would have.

Out of these differences sprang angry disputes, settled by Roosevelt invariably in favor of the more conservative of two opposing views. Eastman and Secretary Roper, for instance, became entangled in a bureaucratic quarrel when Roper pressed for a dismantling of the ICC as an independent agency and the absorption of its functions by the Commerce Department, this to give the executive that authority over transportation which Roosevelt had said he wanted and which was certainly necessary for national transportation planning. Eastman, cast now in a thoroughly conservative role,* fought stubbornly for maintenance of the ICC in its historic integrity. Frankly and flatly he opposed Roosevelt himself when the latter talked of issuing an executive order that would have effected Roper's (and his own stated) purposes. And in the end, such was Eastman's prestige-engendered political potency with Republicans and Democrats alike, Roosevelt yielded to Eastman's view. A new transportation committee was appointed, this one inclusive, if on a distinctly minority basis, of shipper and labor union representatives. Berle accepted appointment as a special assistant to the RFC board, his intended function that of managing RFC loans to the railroads in a way that would force them to squeeze some of the water out of their fraudulent capitalization. There followed a series of seemingly endless, inconclusively wrangling conferences whence emerged, at last, stamped with Roosevelt's approval, a thoroughly compromised legislative proposal, one bound to be further compromised in the legislative process.

Roosevelt sent it to Congress with a special message on May 4. He said that though "steam railways still constitute the main arteries of commerce in the United States," they could not "profitably" operate competitively with "new

---

*In railroad management-labor disputes, Eastman stood firmly on the side of management, sympathetically, blaming labor executives (they "are drunk with power!" he said privately) for many of the roads' gravest economic troubles.[11]

forms of transportation" in terms of the presently "available traffic." Hence the "broad problem" was "to coordinate all agencies of transportation" in the interests of "adequate service." The President, however, was "not yet ready to submit to the Congress a comprehensive plan for permanent legislation." He submitted, instead, a stopgap measure, one that would place "railway holding companies . . . definitely under the regulation and control of the Interstate Commerce Commission in like manner as the railways themselves" and create "a Federal Coordinator of Transportation who, working with groups of railroads, will be able to encourage, promote or require action on the part of the carriers, in order to avoid duplication of service, prevent waste, and encourage financial reorganizations." There was an afterthought, imposed by the railroad brotherhoods after Roosevelt, on April 28, had made public the provisions of the administration bill. "Such a coordinator should also, in carrying out this policy, render useful service in maintaining railroad employment at a fair wage." The message closed with the hopeful assertion that "[t]he experience gained during the balance of this year will greatly assist the government and the carriers in preparation for a more permanent and a more comprehensive national transportation policy at the regular session of the Congress in 1934."[12]

As for the bill itself, it proposed, in effect, self-regulation by the railroads. There would be established three regional groups of lines—eastern, southern, western—each group of which would elect a committee of five railroad men. Over these committees the federal coordinator would exert what was seen to be, when obscuring verbiage was removed, an almost wholly nominal authority; his pay and that of his staff were to come from the railroads themselves, they being assessed for this purpose $1.50 annually for every mile of line they operated. The politically powerful railroad brotherhoods, with Donald Richberg arguing their case before the Senate, succeeded in preventing a legislated elimination of featherbedding practices,* and no coercive power was given government to effect the line consolidations which, if the traffic level of that early spring had continued, would have been absolutely essential to an even minimally profitable operation of the nation's railroads as a whole. But as a matter of fact, that low traffic level did *not* continue. By mid-May an upturn in the general economy, stimulated by the promise of large relief and public works expenditures and by the promise or threat of inflation, was reflected in increasing carloadings. By June, when the railroad bill went through both houses on voice vote (Roosevelt signed it on June 16), the carriers themselves had lost interest in the basic reforms, in the governmental action toward those reforms, for which they had loudly clamored early in the year.

Joseph B. Eastman was promptly appointed federal coordinator by the President, under the terms of the new law, as it had been long known he would be.

---

*That is, the forced employment of superfluous labor, such as firemen on electric- or diesel-powered locomotives, to avert technological unemployment.

III

By late April, as has been said, prompt submission to Congress of major industrial recovery legislation was of imperative importance to the administration. Such submission continued to be delayed, however, as April yielded to May. Three different bill-drafting operations were under way. And since the participants in each of them had reason to believe that *theirs* was the assigned responsibility for preparing the administration measure, there was inevitably a somewhat rancorous rivalry among them when they discovered each other's existence; inevitably there were disagreements the resolution of which was time-consuming.

The group headed by Senator Wagner held the first of its drafting conferences in his office on April 25. Present were three big business representatives (Fred I. Kent of the Bankers Trust Company of New York, Virgil D. Jordan of the National Industrial Conference Board, Rand of Remington Rand); two economists, one in the employ of the United Mine Workers, the other an industrial economist; an attorney specializing in trade associations; and a congressman, Clyde Kelley of Pennsylvania, who had sponsored legislation to stabilize the coal industry through abolition of cutthroat competition. The substantive proposal upon which they agreed, and sought to transform with necessary revisions into a bill, was the Moulton-Jacobstein plan, and both Moulton and Jacobstein were, of course, very actively present at this and subsequent drafting sessions.

The group headed by Undersecretary of Commerce Dickinson, as Roper's deputy, included Tugwell and a brilliant forty-four-year-old lawyer named Jerome N. Frank, another of Frankfurter's protégés, who had helped draft the agricultural adjustment bill in March and had become at that time a close associate of Tugwell's. Others were Leon H. Keyserling, a young Harvard Law School graduate, destined soon to become Wagner's legislative assistant, and, strange to say, Frances Perkins, who by her own somewhat dubious account invited herself into the discussions, with Roosevelt's blessing, evidently a day or so after Dickinson had addressed on April 28 the above-quoted letter to Moley. (A dozen years later Madame Perkins remembered that it was Tugwell and Hugh Johnson who were drafting partners and that they had been "working for many weeks under a mutual pledge of secrecy" when, having got wind of their enterprise, she called upon them in a top-floor office of the Treasury Building to find out what they were up to. The two men "were anything but pleased to see me," she wrote.)[13]

As for Hugh Johnson, having been told by Lewis Douglas that Roosevelt wanted a bill wide in scope but short in language, he drafted one in longhand on just two yellow pages of a legal-size tablet furnished him by Moley. This, completed within twenty-four hours, became the essential substance of subsequent lengthier drafts on which Johnson worked with Donald Richberg. As former legal counsel for railroad labor unions, Richberg had had much experience with labor legislation, had helped draft the Railway

Act of 1926, and it was upon the labor side of the recovery measure that he now worked.

Then, in the first week of May, the three bill-drafting operations became two.

On April 29 the New York *Times* carried a story outlining the plan put on paper by a subcommittee of three (Moulton was one of the three) appointed by Wagner to draft a bill. It called for antitrust-law relaxation to permit the formation of trade associations which, under a federal board's supervision, would draw up codes of "fair practices" applicable to association members and enforced by association and government in partnership. The codes would govern ("regularize") production, pricing, and competitive practice. The federal board would have regulatory authority, in close collaboration with industry, over wages and hours, but on an industry by industry basis, thereby assuring far greater flexibility in this matter than Black proposed. There were also provisions for large government loans to industry and, as a separate title, for a massive public works program. Finally, thanks to the decisive priorities of Wagner and Clyde Kelley, though with no support from the big businessmen whom Wagner had initially consulted, the bill included a guarantee of labor's right to organize and bargain collectively with employers, who were expressly forbidden to interfere in any way with the organizing process. This seemed to Wagner required by simple justice: If business were to be permitted to organize for price- and profit-raising purposes, labor must be permitted to organize for wage-raising purposes, and it was the one feature of the developing proposal which distinguished it sharply and fundamentally from those "corporative laws of Fascist Italy"* at which, according to Lindley, the bill drafters "glanced" as they did their work.[14] In other respects the Wagner group's approach was consistent, even in good part identical, with the approach Dickinson and his group were making. And immediately after the *Times* story had appeared, some of those who had been meeting with Dickinson (Frank for one, Keyserling for another, Tugwell [most important] for a third) began to meet also with Wagner. The latter then called and, with Dickinson, presided over a series of liaison conferences in Dickinson's Commerce Building office.

Thus the two groups coalesced to produce what became known as the Wagner-Dickinson draft bill.

It was a highly complex and legalistic measure designed to accomplish the

---

*Explained Fausto Pitigliani in a 1933 book, *The Italian Corporative State,* written with the cooperation and blessing of the Italian Ministry of Corporations: ". . . Fascism desires to build up . . . the economic collaboration of the various categories engaged in production. . . . The different categories of producers are represented officially by various Occupational Associations. . . . grouped in Corporations for purposes of protection and development of some specific branch of production. These advisory [sic] bodies are organs of the State, and they embody all the elements involved in a given branch of production, namely, capital, labor, and technical direction." Quoted by R. Palme Dutt, *Fascism and Social Revolution* [1935], p. 218.) But independent labor organizations were, of course, the first casualties of the capitalist-backed Fascist and Nazi "revolutions." In both Italy and Germany the trade union movement was utterly destroyed.

kind of "national planning" by business *for* business at which the big business community had been aiming more and more exclusively for the last three years. In effect it would, in the process of substituting industrial "cooperation" for "competition," confer upon giant business combines legislative and executive powers formerly belonging wholly to government itself: There would be legalized price-fixing and other monopolistic practices, though this fact was obscured, evidently in some degree from Wagner himself, by the descriptive language which defenders of the proposal employed against its critics, language that spoke of the "open listing" of prices—i.e., the sharing of price schedules among industrial firms prior to marketing—out of which would emerge "uniform price schedules." (Ironically, Secretary of the Interior Ickes loudly protested one glaring instance of "uniform" pricing at the very time Wagner-Dickinson was being put into final shape. On Saturday, May 6, the nation's newspapers carried Ickes's announcement that Interior had "had to reject bids for 400,000 barrels of cement for the Boulder Dam project* because, except for a variation due to [*sic*] different freight rates, all the bids were identical." Ickes was outraged by the obvious collusion; the businessmen involved were dismayed by collusion's exposure. "I am receiving many telegrams and letters from manufacturers of cement uttering loud wails and protesting their high virtues . . ." noted Ickes in his diary on May 8.[15]) The draft bill sought to expand the area of cooperation along lines followed by Bismarck's Germany, to include not only theretofore competing corporations but also these now supraorganized corporations and the federal government —this in the "partnership" spirit expressed by Roosevelt during his May 7 fireside chat. ("It is wholly wrong," said Roosevelt on that occasion, "to call the measures that we have taken Government control of farming, industry, and transportation. It is rather a partnership between Government and farming and industry and transportation, not a partnership for profits, for the profits still go to the citizen, but rather partnership in planning, and a partnership that sees that the plans are carried out."[16])

Far shorter and less complex was the draft bill produced by Johnson-Richberg. It was originally conceived by Johnson not as a permanent modification of the nation's economic structure (Wagner-Dickinson *was* so conceived) but as a strictly emergency measure. It was wholly designed for an immediate uplifting impact upon prices, wages, employment, an impact to be made by industrial collaboration involving, of course, antitrust-law suspensions, joined with swift expenditures by government for public works, and once the bill became law, if Johnson had his way, the vast emergency operation it authorized would be conducted in that fervently emotional martial spirit which had animated the nation in 1918. Employed would be much the same kind of

---

*Ickes had changed the project's name from Hoover to Boulder on his own authority because, to quote his diary entry for May 17, "Hoover had very little to do with the dam and in fact was supposed to be opposed to it." The name Hoover was restored to the dam by congressional action in the 1950s.

symbolic devices, overwhelming propaganda, and spectacular rallies as Mussolini and Hitler used to woo the masses. Consistent with this was Johnson's insistence upon "teeth" in his and Richberg's draft bill. The Wagner-Dickinson draft, assigning to trade associations the initiative for preparing industry codes, assigned to government a severely limited role, as regards not only code preparation but also code enforcement. Tugwell managed to insert in the draft a device borrowed from the Agricultural Adjustment Act—namely, a processing tax to be collected from each code-signing firm and then, at stated intervals, paid back to those firms and *only* those firms that complied fully with their industry codes. This would make it more profitable for a firm to comply than not to comply, and it was the nearest approach made by Wagner-Dickinson to compulsion. Johnson-Richberg, on the other hand, relied considerably less on the trade association per se and considerably more on government to effect the desired industrial "cooperation." It would have government involved in code-making initiatives; it would have government enforce code compliance by the threat or exercise of a rigorous licensing power.

On the face of it, the differences between the two drafts were more complementary than oppositional to each other and should have been fairly easily and quickly resolved. They became identified, however, with the clashing wills and temperaments of John Dickinson and Hugh Johnson in ways that delayed for several days that agreement upon a single draft which Roosevelt, by the end of the first week of May, was impatiently demanding. Chiefly it was over the "teeth" provided government in the Johnson-Richberg draft—the greater coercive "power" and "clearer compulsions" of this draft—that Johnson and Dickinson "came to loggerheads," as Tugwell wrote in his diary. Tugwell himself, though approving Wagner-Dickinson in other respects (after all, it "embodied my ideas"), favored the tougher Johnson approach to compliance, especially "if we cannot have my own method of making compliance profitable." But Dickinson, strongly if not exclusively committed to business self-government, was also irritated by Johnson's flamboyance of manner and extravagance of language. He stubbornly refused to concede the point, and this despite an expressed general agreement among business spokesmen, when they assembled on May 4 for the annual meeting of the U.S. Chamber of Commerce in Washington, "that some sort of federal supervision [of business] would have to be established insofar as the anti-trust laws were relaxed," as the New York *Herald Tribune* reported.[17]

(Roosevelt, addressing the Chamber of Commerce on May 4, took note of "a slight but definite upturn in most industries" during the preceding few weeks, accompanied by "a rise in most commodity prices," and asked employers not merely "to refrain from further reduction in the wages of your employees" but "also to increase your wage scales in conformity with and simultaneous with the rise of . . . commodity prices insofar as this lies within your power." For, he went on, it was "a simple fact that the average of the wage scale of the nation has gone down the past four years more rapidly than the cost of living"; this meant it was but simple justice to have the "wage scale

... brought back to meet the cost of living and that this process ... begin now and not later." Upon this plea Chamber of Commerce spokesmen made no published comment, but they did comment favorably upon the President's following words: "You and I acknowledge the existence of unfair methods of competition, of cut-throat prices and of general chaos. You and I agree that this condition must be rectified and that order must be restored. The attainment of that objective depends upon your willingness to cooperate with one another to this end and also your willingness to cooperate with your government."[18])

On May 10 the House Labor Committee *unanimously* favorably reported for floor action the thirty-hour bill which the Senate had already passed in different form. Organized industry at once protested, loudly, desperately. For there could now be not the slightest doubt that in the absence of a strongly persuasive counterproposal by the administration, Black-Connery would pass through the whole Congress in a few days with majorities large enough, probably, to overcome a presidential veto. Events, clearly, not only were out of hand, from the executive's point of view, but were about to burst through the outermost limit of the administration's power to control them.

And so, acting on Moley's suggestion, Roosevelt on this same May 10 presided in the White House over a joint conference of the two drafting groups, listening then to vehement and lengthy expositions of both sides of the quarrel between Dickinson and Johnson. He was asked to decide between the two. Characteristically he declined to do so. Characteristically he at conference's end ordered the disputants to lock themselves into a room somewhere and not come out until *they* had decided (agreed) upon a single draft.* And characteristically, or typically as regards the early New Deal in general, what emerged from this procedure, after Dickinson's opposition to Johnson's licensing provision had been overruled, was another omnibus measure whose approach to an allegedly new order was wholly designed to please or appease distinct pressure groups, distinct vested interests, of the order now prevailing. It was thus insured that the New Deal's industrial policy would be determined, overall, not by logic in the service of humane commitments but by simple inertia and action-reaction—those properties of bodies described in Newton's first and third laws which, in the body politic, operate as compounds of individual selfishness uninformed by that disinterested intelligence whose concern is with a *general* welfare.

For the dominating intent of the enormously complicated national industrial recovery bill that was at last delivered into Roosevelt's hand, and that he sent to Congress under a special message on May 17, was to legitimatize and render

---

*"Wagner, Dickinson, Frances Perkins, Johnson and I fought over the thing in Lew Douglas's office for some time," wrote Tugwell in his diary, as quoted by Frank Freidel in his *Franklin D. Roosevelt: Launching the New Deal,* p. 424. "I failed to get them to adopt my tax and reserve-fund scheme. I argued for it strongly but dropped it for the sake of harmony. But I sided with Johnson on his demand for more teeth in the penalty provisions if we could not have the tax. Dickinson was compelled to give way."

universal collusive big business practices that had increasingly, if covertly, vitiated a nominally "free market" since late in the nineteenth century. This was as obvious to astute observers at the time as it would become to all in hindsight. Yet there was an offset to this big business design. Thanks largely to Wagner and Frances Perkins, who in the finally decisive drafting sessions kept restoring it after their colleagues had removed it, the bill's Title I, authorizing "cooperative" code making by industrial firms, had in it a section, Section 7, which not only required each code to contain an "acceptable" provision for maximum hours, minimum wages, and healthful working conditions but also, in the at-once famous Section 7(a), outlawed yellow-dog contracts* and guaranteed labor's right to organize and bargain collectively. The bill, though foresightful labor leaders would hail 7(a) as labor's Magna Carta, was thus actually designed to continue into the new "cooperative" order approximately the same balance of power between management and labor as had previously obtained, a balance that would otherwise have been tipped decisively toward management.

The special message requesting passage of this legislation had not been easily composed. Roosevelt was at some pains to clothe in obscuring language the fact that the bill would in effect flatly repeal essential portions of antitrust law. Naked, that fact would offend the eyes of yet-numerous and -fervent supporters of the Sherman and Clayton acts. He therefore described the bill, at the outset, as primarily designed to benefit workers. It would provide the "machinery necessary for a great cooperative movement throughout all industry in order to obtain wide reemployment, to shorten the working week, to pay a decent wage for the shorter week and to prevent unfair competitition and disastrous overproduction." A great obstacle to "such cooperative efforts up to this time has been our anti-trust laws." These laws had been "properly designed as a means to cure the great evils of monopolistic price-fixing" and "should certainly be retained as a permanent assurance that the old evils of unfair competition shall never return." All the same, "the public interest will be served if, with the authority and under the guidance of Government, private industries are permitted to make agreements and codes insuring fair competition." On the other hand, "it is necessary, if we thus limit the operation of anti-trust laws to their original purpose, to provide a vigorous licensing power in order to meet rare cases of non-cooperation and abuse. Such a safeguard is indispensable." (He laid no stress on the fact that the "safeguard" was a wholly discretionary power; he was not mandated to exercise it and, in the event, never would.)

---

*In a yellow-dog contract the employee, as a condition of his employment, pledged himself not to join a union during the term of his employment. During the Progressive Era Kansas and several other states enacted laws prohibiting such contracts. Each of these had been declared in violation of the Fourteenth Amendment by federal courts, which freely issued injunctions against attempts by labor organizers to persuade employees to breach their signed promises. In 1932 the Norris-La Guardia Act, reluctantly signed by Hoover, specifically prohibited such injunctions if neither fraud nor violence had been used by union organizers. Employers promptly attempted to circumvent Norris-La Guardia by coercing their employees into company unions and by threats to fire them if they joined an independent union. Section 7(a) aimed to prevent such action.

Nor were Roosevelt's message-drafting difficulties confined to his dealings with the bill's Title I. Title II flagrantly violated Roosevelt's own budget-balancing economy pledge and personal commitment (it flatly contradicted the central thrust of his economy message of March 10) in that it called for the establishment of an emergency Public Works Administration authorized to spend up to $3.3 billion for the construction of federal buildings, dams, bridges, highways, and other public facilities, *including* U.S. Navy facilities, the needed money to be obtained by government borrowing. He described this expenditure as an "investment" in needed "public construction" whereby "the largest possible number of people" would be given employment. He said that states, counties, and municipalities would receive grants from the appropriation "to undertake useful public works." Such grants must be "subject, however, to the most effective possible means of eliminating favoritism and wasteful expenditures. . . ." And though it was imperative that this work begin at once, it was equally "imperative that the credit of the United States Government be protected and preserved." This meant, he went on, "that at the same time we are making these vast emergency expenditures there must be provided sufficient revenue to pay interest and amortization on the cost and that the revenues so provided must be adequate and certain rather than inadequate and speculative." It had been estimated that at least $220 million "of additional revenue" would "be needed to service the contemplated borrowings of the Government," an expenditure that would "of necessity involve some form or forms of new taxation." As for what the "forms" would be, he would say nothing "at this time." Instead, he asked the House Ways and Means Committee to study various revenue proposals "and be prepared by the beginning of the coming week to propose the taxes . . . they judge to be best. . . ." If the committee failed to do this, he would "transmit to the Congress my own recommendations. . . ."[19]

The decision to defer his "own recommendations" had been fortunately essentially made for him, only a few days before his delivery of this message, by those who had to legislate them. At the urging of Lew Douglas he had let it be known that he personally favored imposition of a "reemployment tax" (so Douglas labeled it), which was, in fact, the manufacturer's sales tax he had emphatically rejected, on principle, if after some hesitation, during the lame-duck session.* Douglas was sure that the proposed vast public works program was part and parcel of that "death of Western civilization" which must follow the abandonment of the gold standard, yet he remained manfully determined to preserve for as long as possible against impending catastrophe whatever bits and pieces of "civilization" might still be maintained, including especially that income of the affluent now threatened by an increase in its taxation. Far better (more "civilized") to have the new tax burden borne by the general consuming public. But congressmen took a different view. A delegation of congressional leaders, including Speaker Rainey and Majority Leader Robinson, promptly called at the White House to tell the President that a federal sales tax could

*See Davis, *FDR: The New York Years,* pp. 407–8.

not possibly pass unless he personally waged an all-out fight for it and that his victory in such a battle would be highly expensive of his personal popularity, his persuasive capital. He would do better, they suggested, to leave the matter in their hands. If he did so, they promised, Title III of the National Industrial Recovery Act, when it reached his desk for signature, would contain satisfactory revenue-raising provisions.[20]

IV

WITH his acquiescence in the NIR bill, following hard upon the AAA enactment, Roosevelt locked himself and the New Deal irrevocably into an implemented policy of economic nationalism, arriving thus at the culmination of a process begun with his final refusal, in his second meeting with Hoover during the interregnum, to permit an operative linkage of war debt, stabilization, and disarmament problem solving. It was a process which, in the absence of any overall principled planning or of much careful forethought in individual cases, was largely characterized by inadvertence, as we have seen. Roosevelt's final word to Hoover in the White House meeting of January 20,* his partial suspension of the gold standard on March 6, his total abandonment of gold on April 19, his approval of huge relief and public works programs involving deficit financing in April and May, his acceptance of agricultural nationalism and inflationary powers with his AAA signature of May 12, his acceptance now of industrial nationalism (this last would be further implemented in early June with his acceptance of an NIR amendment giving him discretionary powers to raise tariffs and impose import quotas to protect, against lower-priced imports, the rising American prices and wages which the bill was designed to protect)—all these were improvisational responses to immediate pressures, made in terms of feelings, intuitions that had never been shaped into logically consistent ideas in his mind.

Certainly his increasingly exclusive commitment to nationalism had not been accompanied, in private thought or public deed, by any clear-cut disavowal of internationalism. He seemed still to proceed on the assumption that a "weaving together" of the contradictions between nationalism and internationalism in some kind of creative compromise was a practical possibility, enabling him (as major instance) to manipulate dollar values in the exclusive interest of the domestic economy while simultaneously joining in an international effort to prevent precisely such manipulation. Having given his blessing to American participation in the World Monetary and Economic Conference, he personally did nothing publicly to discourage the great popular excitement and extravagant hopes which the onset of that conference, amid the glooms and despairs of world depression, aroused everywhere. On the contrary, he who had a decisive power over conference deliberations greater than anyone else's spoke publicly of the meeting's "vital importance to mankind," asserted

*See Davis, *FDR: The New York Years*, pp. 411–12.

that the "future of the world" demanded its success, and proclaimed the conference's duty to "establish order in place of the present chaos by a stabilization of currencies, and by international action to raise price levels." The latter statement went on to manifest his wishful belief in "weaving together" possibilities. Said he: "It [the conference] must, in short, supplement individual domestic programs for economic recovery, by wise and considered international action."[21]

Moreover, as the world was informed, it was by Roosevelt's personal initiative and invitation that British Prime Minister MacDonald and former French Premier Edouard Herriot came to Washington to consult with him on war debts and conference plans (the two must be kept separate as subjects of discussion, he continued to insist), and these were but the first of the long list of high-ranking foreign emissaries who came to the White House during the following weeks, similarly invited for preconference talks. To each of these he gave assurances of his personal commitment to international cooperation and to the upcoming conference's specific aims, assurances which were promptly repeated in joint statements issued to the public and the import of which seemed confirmed when, acceding to his secretary of state's urgent desire, he named Cordell Hull chairman of the six-member U.S. delegation to London. All the world knew of Hull's religious conviction that untrammeled freedom of trade among the nations of the world (this implied a stable international exchange) was an indispensable condition of permanent world peace and order.

And the vivid impression thus made of Roosevelt as internationalist, Roosevelt as world leader was sharpened and deepened on May 16. On that Tuesday he addressed to the heads of state of fifty-four nations a dramatic appeal for "peace by disarmament and for the end of economic chaos," a personal appeal that linked in common cause the international economic discussions soon to begin and the international disarmament discussion that had been going on, in evident futility, for more than a year, in Geneva. (Was this a tacit admission, as some thought, that Hoover had been right to insist that armaments, war debts, exchange stabilization, and a general lowering of trade barriers were problems internally related and not merely "parallel," as Roosevelt had insisted?)

Roosevelt's appeal had as its immediate incitement intense and growing anxiety over the course being pursued by Adolf Hitler in his management of Germany's domestic and foreign affairs. On April 1, under Nazi auspices, a national boycott of Jewish businesses and professions had been declared in Berlin, initiating weeks of ugly violence during which gangs of uniformed Nazi thugs roamed city streets, as they had done prior to the March 5 election, though this time they confined their brutal attentions to helpless Jews. These they often beat mercilessly while the police again looked on in seeming approval. On April 7, under powers granted him by the Enabling Act, Hitler promulgated a law creating a Reich governor *(Reichsstaathalter)* for each

German state, armed with authority to dissolve diets and appoint or dismiss local governmental officials as well as those of the state, including judges. Each appointed governor was, of course, a Nazi personally approved by Hitler, and he must govern in accordance with "the general policy laid down by the Reich chancellor."[22] Thus at one stroke the federal constitution of Germany, established by Bismarck in 1870, maintained against Wilhelm II's lust for power and glory, maintained even through Erich von Ludendorff's virtual dictatorship in the last year of the Great War, was abolished in favor of absolute national dictatorship by a single man, Adolf Hitler, though this last fact could not be officially formally recognized until the aged President Paul von Hindenburg, now obviously dying, died. On May 2, within twenty-four hours after stupendous May Day rallies organized by Nazi Propaganda Minister Joseph Goebbels, rallies designed to prove "how unjust and untrue is the statement that the [Nazi] revolution is directed against the German workers," as Hitler told a workers' delegation on May 1, Nazi law enforcement officers occupied trade union headquarters, arrested union leaders, and confiscated union funds and other property. The unions were declared dissolved.[23] Near midnight on May 10 Nazi students enrolled in the University of Berlin, after a torchlight parade through the streets, piled some 20,000 books in the center of a square, doused the pile with gasoline, then torched it, sending up in flames published works of Thomas Mann, Heinrich Mann, Stefan Zweig, Arnold Zweig, Albert Einstein, Erich Maria Remarque, Jakob Wassermann, and virtually every other German author of high world reputation, along with translated works of Emile Zola, Marcel Proust, André Gide, Sigmund Freud, Havelock Ellis, H. G. Wells, Upton Sinclair, and dozens of others whose commitment to humane values was infuriating to Nazis. There were other book bonfires in other cities, on this and following evenings, all of them carried out with the blessing of Goebbels, who said in public speech: "The soul of the German people can again express itself. These flames not only illuminate the final end of an old era; they also light up the new."[24]

Simultaneously and ominously, Hitler indicated in word and deed his intention to rearm Germany in defiance of Versailles and of the purposes of Geneva, where the German delegates deadlocked discussions by insisting that the war veteran Steel Helmet organization and other paramilitary groups in Germany, though obviously operating under central governmental direction and numbering in the hundreds of thousands, could not be counted as a part of Germany's armed forces for purposes of arms reduction. Utterly blocked by this was consideration of an appeasement plan proposed by MacDonald, on March 16, to revise the Versailles Treaty, "not at the point of the bayonet but at the point of reason," in order to assure Germany of "justice and freedom." The disarmament conference had been brought to the verge of collapse when, in the second week of May, Roosevelt held his final inconclusive conversation with Reichsbank President Hjalmar Schacht, who had come to Washington as Hitler's agent for pre-London consultations. Immediately thereafter Roosevelt read with alarm newspaper reports of a speech given by Reich Vice-Chancellor

Franz von Papen to a huge Steel Helmet rally, an extremely bellicose pronouncement in which Germany's situation "today" was compared to that of
1914 and which sought "to make clear to the world" the fact that the German
nation, on January 31, 1933, when Hitler became chancellor, had "blotted out
of its vocabulary the term pacifism." Cried the notoriously false, vain, crafty,
blunderingly stupid Papen,* "The battlefield is for a man what motherhood
is for a woman!"† The next day Hitler had summoned the Reichstag to
assemble in special session on May 17 for the purpose of hearing a statement
of German policy with regard to armaments and foreign affairs. Britain,
through its war minister, had recently more than hinted its willingness to join
with France in the employment of sanctions against Germany if Hitler decisively repudiated Versailles, and it seemed likely that Hitler would do this on
May 17. Hence the possibility of immediate general European war seemed very
real, despite Germany's relative military weakness, a weakness which might
in any case be more apparent than real, some feared, because of secret and
illegal war preparations. As long as six weeks ago Roosevelt had found "the
situation . . . alarming," saying then to French Ambassador Paul Claudel that
"Hitler is a madman and his counsellors, some of whom I personally know,
are even madder than he is."[26] His alarm was now intensified.

Such were the circumstances of Roosevelt's Appeal to the Nations.

He prepared it with more than his usual care. On Friday, May 12, having
called to his office the secretary of state, Undersecretary William Phillips,
William C. Bullitt, and Louis Howe, he began the drafting process by writing
out in their presence sentences and groups of sentences, which he then at once
read aloud for their revisionary criticism. There were further drafting sessions
during the next two days in the State Department, sessions in which J. Pierre-
pont Moffat, who occupied the department's West European desk, very actively participated. On Monday, May 15, the chaos of ideas and incoherent
language thus accumulated was turned over to Moley for final succinct drafting, he having been out of town for the weekend. Moley agreed that the "full
mellow tones of a pipe organ" rather than the "lighter tone of stringed instruments" should be employed in "a message from sovereign to sovereigns" (the
quotations are from Moffat's diary[27]), and it was in organ style that he composed through most of that day, working with his usual swift efficiency. In
Roosevelt's hand by nightfall was a message highly pleasing to him and to all
who then reviewed it. It was dispatched to fifty-four national capitals next
morning and published to all the world a few hours later.

Though it stressed the urgent importance of the economic conference, which
"will meet soon and must come to its conclusions quickly," the bulk of the

---

*Papen was in bad odor in the United States. During the Great War he was military attaché in
Washington until his complicity in attempted sabotage of American transportation facilities was
discovered. He was then expelled by a U.S. government not yet at war with Germany.
†Said Mussolini, as quoted in the New York *Herald Tribune* just a year later (May 27, 1934): "War
is to a man what maternity is to a woman."

message was concerned with peace through disarmament. The President asked why it was that armaments, despite "the lessons and tragedies of the World War, are today a greater burden upon the people of the earth than ever before." He answered that the chief reason was "the fear of nations that they will be invaded. I believe," he went on, "that the overwhelming majority of peoples feel obliged to retain excessive armaments because they fear some act of aggression against them and not because they themselves seek to be aggressors." The way to remove this fear was to eliminate wholly the weaponry of offense. He then repeated a recommendation which General Douglas MacArthur had rather surprisingly made two months ago to the State Department, for the instruction of U.S. delegates to Geneva.[28] He said, as MacArthur in substance had said: "Modern weapons of offense are vastly stronger than modern weapons of defense. Frontier forts, trenches, wire entanglements, coast defenses—in a word, fixed fortifications—are no longer impregnable to the attack of war planes, heavy mobile artillery, land battleships called tanks, and poison gas. If all nations will agree wholly to eliminate from possession and use the weapons which make possible a successful attack, defenses will automatically become impregnable, and the frontiers and independence of every nation will become secure. The ultimate objective of the Disarmament Conference must be the complete elimination of all offensive weapons. The immediate objective is a substantial reduction of some of these weapons and the elimination of many others." He proposed in very general terms three steps to reach this goal, plus a fourth step to assure "the peace of the world during the whole period of disarmament." The latter was "a solemn and definite pact of non-aggression".*[29]

To this appeal the responses were immediate for the most part, and predictably approving of Roosevelt's ultimate aim. Every nation, it seemed, "abhors war" (so spoke Queen Wilhelmina for her nation, the Netherlands) and welcomed the leadership of the President of the United States toward the final goal of total disarmament, including Fascist Italy, whose King Victor Emmanuel on May 18 thanked Roosevelt for his "noble message" (it "meets with full response in my spirit and in that of my Government"), including also, and most important, Nazi Germany, whose President Hindenburg on May 18 said that Roosevelt's "declaration, in which you show the world the way to eliminate the international crisis, has met with hearty approval throughout Germany." Proof of this, Hindenburg went on to say, was provided by "the statements which the German Reich chancellor made yesterday, with the unanimous agreement of the German Reichstag. . . ."[30]

For Hitler's speech of May 17, remodeled in response to Roosevelt's message, "of which I learned last night," surprised everyone with its conciliatory

*This had of course already been signed by most of the nations he addressed. The Kellogg-Briand Pact of 1928, "outlawing war"—a pact Roosevelt himself had deemed but a pious gesture, essentially meaningless, at the time it was proposed—had been signed by every major power and virtually all minor ones.

tone. The Reich chancellor welcomed the President's appeal as "a ray of comfort for all who wish to cooperate in the maintenance of peace" and described the German nation as most emphatically one of these. Papen had spoken out of turn, it appeared; his views were utterly repudiated. Far from being a nurturer of healthy, heroic manhood, as the vice-chancellor had asserted, war was "unlimited madness," which would "cause the collapse of the present social and political order." Wholly "alien to" the new Germany was that "mentality of the last century, which led people to believe that they could make Germans out of Poles and Frenchmen." As for the President's specific proposals, the Reich chancellor accepted them all wholeheartedly: "Germany is entirely ready to renounce all offensive weapons if the armed nations, on their side, will destroy their offensive weapons. . . . Germany would also be perfectly ready to disband her entire military establishment and destroy the small amount of arms remaining to her, if the neighboring countries will do the same. . . . Germany is prepared to agree to any solemn pact of nonaggression, because she does not think of attacking but only of acquiring security."[31]

The world sighed with relief. The world showered upon Roosevelt expressions of gratitude. He himself was delighted. "I think I have averted a war," he said to Morgenthau.[32]

And among internationalists at home and abroad the thanksgiving swelled into a chorus almost worshipful—there briefly descended upon Roosevelt's broad shoulders that radiant mantle of The Messiah which had enwrapped Woodrow Wilson in the eyes of Europe's masses for some five months after the armistice—when he supplied a few days later what the French, who had little inclination to trust Hitler's naked word, regarded as a glaring deficiency of the appeal: Roosevelt had made no promise of American collaboration in collective security arrangements, though he had made it to Herriot informally during the bilateral conversations. He now made it formally to the whole world through the mouth of Norman H. Davis, head of the U.S. delegation to the Geneva Disarmament Conference, who on May 22 addressed to that conference highly significant words that could not have been spoken, as the world knew, without prior White House approval.

The United States, said Davis, was willing "to consult the other states in case of a threat to peace with a view to averting conflict." Further, "in the event that the states, in conference, determine that a state has been guilty of a breach of the peace in violation of its international obligations and take measures against the violator, then, if we concur in the judgment rendered as to the responsible and guilty party, we will refrain from any action tending to defeat the collective effort which such states may make to restore peace." The diplomatic lawyer's prose was typically turgid with qualifying clauses, but out of it emerged a single clear meaning: The United States would not insist automatically and absolutely, as always before, upon a neutral's trading rights upon the high seas in case of war; the United States was renouncing the extreme isolationism which had for the last dozen years prevented American participation in the League or in any of the League's affiliates.

The language was so interpreted, in America as in Europe. "This is the end of isolation, or it is nothing," editorialized the San Francisco *Chronicle,* while in London, where representatives of dozens of nations were at work on final economic conference preparations, the consensus was that "the United States will now finally assume full obligations of membership in the League of Nations without actually becoming a member," to quote a dispatch from the London correspondent of the *Christian Science Monitor.*[33] The rejoicing was great among all who believed that, with firm U.S. support, the League would yet become an effective agency of world peace.

But, alas for the internationalists, New Deal deeds spoke far louder than Roosevelt's hopeful words in the realm of foreign affairs, and the words themselves were soon rendered dubious of meaning by the man who had spoken them. Within twenty-four hours after issuing his appeal, Roosevelt had beclouded its clear import, along with that of the upcoming Davis speech, in regard to American participation in international peacekeeping efforts. He made a statement for domestic consumption, in response to the expressed alarm of isolationists (he was particularly anxious to retain Hiram Johnson's support of New Deal legislation), saying that the United States was obligating itself to no more than consultation with other nations in situations threatful of war, that it certainly would scrap no weapons of its own unless other nations simultaneously scrapped theirs—in sum, that the appeal, and Davis's then-impending speech, effected "no change from . . . long-standing and existing policy."[34]

Moreover, on the very day of the appeal's issuance, Roosevelt read and approved, in Moley's presence, an article the professor had written from an economic nationalist's point of view about the impending World Economic Conference, an article which was to be syndicated in early June to newspapers throughout the country and which was bound to receive close and widespread critical attention because of its author's role as principal presidential adviser. It stressed the extreme difficulty of doing at all, even over a long period of time, what the appeal declared the conference "must" do "quickly."* People should not be led "to feel that the world is going to be transfigured by the Conference," wrote Moley, or that a "vast new commerce on the seven seas" would immediately result from even the most successful possible of London meetings, for beyond the realm of possibility, or even of desirability, in the circumstances, was any swift drastic lowering of international trade barriers:

> Tariffs and other restrictive devices are deeply rooted in the policies of the various countries and are closely integrated parts of their lives. All of the nations, including our own, have been moving toward self-support for a long time. Industrial and agricultural life has been developed in that direction with remarkable rapidity of late. Manufacturing has grown in even such remotely industrial countries as China and India. American capital and industry, by the establishment of factories abroad, have

---

*Moley as presidential draftsman spoke Roosevelt's mind when writing the appeal; he spoke his own mind in this signed syndicated article.

themselves gone far toward the acceleration of this tendency. . . . Thus a combination of forces is arrayed against extensive attacks upon trade barriers. Moderate results must be anticipated.[35]

Moley could hardly have been surprised if Roosevelt had objected to public dissemination of this on the ground that, given its authorship, it would confuse the public and be resented by Cordell Hull. After all, Moley bore the official title of Assistant Secretary of State; his article disparaged as naïve and dangerously unrealistic the repeatedly published free-trade sentiments of the secretary of state, and this secretary had been appointed chairman of the U.S. delegation to London. However, Roosevelt not only raised no objection to the article's argument, but heartily approved its publication, under Moley's name, and went on to say that "[a]s a matter of fact," it would be "a grand speech for Cordell to make at the opening of the Conference!" Moley received this comment with astonishment and, perceiving no irony to be intended, an incredulous silence. (When the substance of his piece was broadcast by Moley over a national radio network a few days later [on May 20], numerous newspapers, including the New York *Times,* at once remarked and deplored the revelation of a wide policy rift, possibly filled with personal ill feeling, between the secretary and the assistant secretary of state. Moley was impelled to express personal regrets to Hull when the two happened to meet in the lobby of the Carlton on May 22. The regrets were courteously accepted, the secretary giving no sign of being seriously disturbed. But, as Moley recalled seven years later, subsequent events would leave "no doubt that he [Hull] was deeply offended.")[36]

As for Hull's appointment to the delegation chairmanship, the sharp impression it had made upon the general public mind of Roosevelt as economic internationalist was badly blurred by the other delegate choices, all of which were obviously made with only domestic political considerations in mind. It was as if Roosevelt were still reacting, emotionally, against Herbert Hoover. It was as if he were motivated by a wish to show contempt for his predecessor by doing the precise opposite of what Hoover had so urgently insisted should be done—namely, choose well in advance of the conference a delegation of strong, prestigious men, who were then carefully prepared to carry out, in London, a clear and consistent policy. Certainly the men actually chosen were remarkably poor instruments of the purpose they ostensibly served. Not one of them had had prior experience of an international conference. No two of them fully agreed on any of the major questions the conference was called to decide.

Chosen in early May were James M. Cox, former governor of Ohio, who had headed the ticket on which Roosevelt ran as vice presidential candidate in 1920 (Cox became the delegation's vice-chairman); Nevada's Key Pittman, chairman of the Senate Foreign Relations Committee; and Tennessee's Samuel D. McReynolds, chairman of the House Foreign Affairs Committee. Cox was a monetary conservative and a low-tariff man but by no means as fervent a free trader as Hull. Pittman, a heavy drinker who was often incapacitated by drink, was a high-tariff man and an inflationist, primarily concerned to boost the price of silver. McReynolds, a low-tariff man, knew virtually nothing about monetary intricacies and had no curiosity concerning them. A prolonged effort was made to persuade Hiram Johnson—a man whose nationalism (isolationism) was every bit as fervent, and religiously so, as Hull's internationalism—to accept appointment. When Johnson, though tempted, finally refused,[37] Roosevelt hastily turned to Michigan's Progressive Republican Senator James Couzens, who accepted as a patriotic duty. Couzens, a man rather excessively fond of having his own way, was like Pittman a high-tariff man and an inflationist, but in different degree from Pittman and with no such commitment as the Nevadan had to silver. The final appointee was named only a day or so before the bulk of the delegation sailed from New York. He was a wealthy Texan named Ralph W. Morrison, whose views on monetary and economic matters were wholly unknown but who had been a large campaign contributor and was strongly recommended by both Garner and Jim Farley. In London he would prove a nonentity.

Only somewhat smaller were the differences in temperament and point of view among the principal members of the delegation staff, the whole of which was much too large (some fifty experts, clerks, advisers, etc. were on it) for swift, efficient operation. The chief executive officer was William C. Bullitt, whose commitment to a managed dollar was uninformed by any expert knowledge and whose brilliant abilities were often misapplied or frustrated by his excessively eager, romantic, dramatic temper. The financial adviser was Warburg, whose banker's pieties with regard to money, especially with regard to exchange stabilization, were increasingly outraged by Roosevelt's blithe disregard of them. The chief technical adviser was Feis, who was remarkably able but evidently unsure of himself and therefore inclined to act in accordance with a very strict, narrow definition of "subordinate"; he seldom forcefully promoted opinions of his own or opposed those of official superiors. The chief press officer was Charlie Michelson. Not actually members of the staff and, as such, subject to such discipline as Hull and Cox and Bullitt could impose, yet soon to be very actively present upon the London scene, were Harvard Economics Professor Oliver M. W. Sprague, a Treasury adviser, and George L. Harrison, the governor of the New York Federal Reserve Bank. Operating without written instructions and with no official authority, Sprague was "simply told" to do what he could toward "some sort of arrangement"[38] to halt the wild exchange fluctuations now occurring as the floating dollar, in process of "finding" its "natural level" under heavy speculative pressures, declined in value week by week.

Yet the disabilities under which Sprague would labor were not appreciably greater than those imposed upon official delegates by presidential instructions that were the opposite of clear and definite.

In his final meeting with the delegation and its staff, on May 29, the only thing the President was precisely emphatic about was the importance of completing the conference agenda with dispatch. "I wish to urge upon you that delay in conferences of this nature usually make it more difficult to secure results," he said. ". . . I can see no reason why its work cannot be completed by the middle of August." He read aloud four draft resolutions constituting a "memorandum of policy" subsequently sent over Roosevelt's signature to each delegate (Warburg had prepared them, in some perplexity), resolutions which, when formally introduced in London, were to define the overall American negotiating position. They did so in terms so broad and vague as to be of no help to minds unprepared to grasp contextual implications or subtle nuances of meaning. "The conference should confine itself to a few major problems and not diffuse its efforts over too wide a field," said Roosevelt in his summing-up. "It should proceed as rapidly as possible to adopt the principles of a solution to these problems, appointing immediately such committees as may be necessary to work out the details."[39]

Hull, Pittman, McReynolds, Morrison, and the bulk of the delegation staff sailed on May 31 aboard the *President Roosevelt*. Cox, with Warburg, Harrison, and Sprague, sailed two days later aboard the *Olympic*.

While the delegation was on the high seas, Roosevelt abruptly announced his decision to postpone action on the reciprocal trade bill whose early submittal to Congress he had promised in his special message calling for farm mortgage relief legislation, on April 3.* Reciprocal trade was, of course, Hull's beloved "baby." Its expected immediate passage was "one of the chief bases . . . for hoping that real results could be achieved at the Conference," in Hull's words. Its abandonment at that moment was, therefore, "a terrific blow" to him, as he would say in his *Memoirs*. He crumpled under it in what Bullitt described to Roosevelt, via "ultra-confidential" cable, as a "complete collapse," during which he wrote out "his immediate resignation to be telegraphed" to the President. Roosevelt, warned of this by Cox and Bullitt, sent at once (on June 11) a soothing message. Reciprocal trade was being put off solely because "eleventh hour rows in Congress over domestic problems made general tariff debate dangerous to our whole program," cabled Roosevelt to Hull, and represented "no alteration of your policy or mine." "I am squarely behind you and nothing said or done here will hamper your efforts," which might include, Roosevelt went on to say, the negotiation of individual reciprocal trade treaties the signatures of which could be ratified in a "special session of Senate alone in the autumn. . . ."[40] The latter suggestion was, as Hull well knew, an empty promise since treaty ratification requires a two-thirds majority and special-interest lobbying had prevented ratification of *any* trade treaty in the past.

Hull did not resign but, demoralized, he lapsed into sad-faced passivity. He was only too acutely aware that he lacked real authority, he felt that he had been publicly humiliated, and he now made no effort to exercise leadership over a delegation that had grown quarrelsome and unruly by the time it arrived in London.

*See page 75.

V

MEANWHILE, the industrial recovery bill was provoking the most intense debate and encountering the strongest opposition of all the administration measures thus far submitted to legislative action.

Introduction of it at once accomplished its inciting purpose—namely, the sidetracking of the Black-Connery thirty-hour bill—and for several days thereafter its swift and easy passage seemed assured. The proposed huge grant of powers to the executive, larger, on the face of it, than the grants already made by the Emergency Banking and Agricultural Adjustment acts, was disturbing to many and terrifying to some. It sparked new expressed fears of a developing "presidential dictatorship." But this new grant came as no great immediate shock to the general public, which had been well prepared for it by advance publicity, and, in any case, a large majority of the American people remained manifestly willing to accept an emergency dictatorship so long as the dictator was Franklin Roosevelt, a leader whose "charming personality and high motives" were conceded even by the Republican congressman who protested most often and vehemently against giving more power to him. Otherwise, as an omnibus measure with something in it for each of several large organized special interests, the bill commanded wide and disparate support. The Chamber of Commerce praised it as a "Magna Carta of industry and labor," and was not gainsaid by Green of the AFL or John L. Lewis of the United Mine Workers, both of whom so regarded at least Section 7 of the measure. The National Association of Manufacturers, though expressing grave doubts about the licensing provision and outright opposition to Section 7, hailed the measure as, overall, a brave long step into a hopeful future. *Business Week* magazine pointed out that the bill certainly should be welcomed by industry since it was substantially what industry had been pressing for "ever since Senator Black first confronted it with the threat of rigid control from above."[41]

Simultaneously Roosevelt made use of the same device as had helped soothe conservative fears of the agricultural adjustment bill when it was before the Senate: He permitted word to spread from the White House, unofficially but authoritatively, that the top executive of the agency which the act would create had already been chosen and was certainly no professorial advocate of social change, was most emphatically no left-winger. He was tough-talking hard-driving General Hugh S. Johnson, affectionately known as Old Ironpants—a former career Army officer, a former big business executive, currently a top aide to the eminently "practical" Bernard Baruch. This leaked information had at once the desired effect of an Arthur Krock column in the New York *Times* (May 20, 1933) wherein Roosevelt was praised for "drawing a distinction between planners and executives." Though the President drew freely upon "educators" for planning ideas, wrote Krock, he wisely chose practical men of affairs to implement these ideas, men like Johnson, George Peek, Joseph Eastman, Fechner, Lew Douglas, and Harry Hopkins, men who had no university connections whatever. (The inclusion in this list of Hopkins, destined to become one of Krock's major hates, was due to the accidental fact that Hopkins's appointment to the post of federal relief administrator was announced on the day the column was written, and Krock knew nothing about him save that he was a career social worker who had never been a professor. Significantly omitted from Krock's list, as Frank Freidel points out,[42] was Arthur E. Morgan of Antioch College, whose appointment as TVA board chairman was also announced that day.)

Yet one doubts that this leaked news of Johnson's impending appointment had its intended effect in Congress. If some conservatives were reassured by it, others were rendered uneasy, and all liberals who knew the general or knew much about him were definitely alarmed. None doubted his rare abilities. He was a first-rate writer and public speaker, with a genius for the pungent, colorful, memorable phrase. He was a first-rate organizer of work and had a truly amazing capacity for long concentrated bouts of it. He had an enormous fund of knowledge about industrial organization. He was personally immensely likable in somewhat the same way as Tommy Corcoran was, with boyish enthusiasms, a broad streak of sentimentality, and a tendency to see or feel the world as a dramatic conflict between heroism and villainy. But by the same token he went easily to extremes and could remain poised between them only with difficulty. He was also a blustering, swaggering authoritarian personality, basically insecure, who frankly admired Mussolini the man and saw much merit in fascism; only a year ago he had circulated among Wall Street financiers an only partially spoofing program for America, authored by himself, signed "Muscleinny, dictator pro tem" and calling for absolute "singleness of control" over the economy (Congress was to be "deported") as the "sole cure" for depression. Baruch himself, though generally assumed to be Johnson's sponsor in this as in other enterprises, reacted with alarm to rumors of his protégé's advancement. He was not in direct communication with Roosevelt at that moment (the two were at odds over monetary inflation), but he undertook to warn the President indirectly, through the secretary of labor. During a social evening in Frances Perkins's home he took her aside to tell her flatly that "Hugh," of whom he was very "fond," was wholly unfit to head a vast recovery program. "He's been my number three man for years," said Baruch. "I think he's a good number three man, maybe a number two man. But he's not a number one man. He's dangerous and unstable. He gets nervous and sometimes goes away for days without notice."[43] Baruch probably added, though Frances Perkins in her memoirs does not record, that what Johnson "went away" on when "nervous" were extended stupendous drinking sprees.

And the general now at once lent some credence to such strictures by proceeding, behind no discreet veil of secrecy, to establish a headquarters, draw up organization charts, lay specific project plans, consult with big businessmen, and recruit personnel for the new agency, as if the organic act were already on the books. This did not go down well with members of Congress who had not yet made up their minds about the bill or even with many who already had; it struck them as a tasteless display of executive arrogance, a violation of legislative prerogatives that was implicitly contemptuous of the legislators themselves. Moreover, driving ahead with characteristically excessive zeal, Johnson proceeded on the assumption that he would administer both Title I and Title II of the act, an assumption grounded in his conviction that public works must march hand in hand with codified industrial cooperation, their movements closely coordinated under a single direction, if the goal of national recovery were to be swiftly reached. And this did not go down well with Franklin Roosevelt. The President was even inclined to regard the general's assumption as something of a presumption.

For in Roosevelt's mind the linkage of the two titles in a single bill had been determined not by logical consistency but by accidental political expediency. The two were joined because public works was a virtually noncontroversial proposal the inevitable acceptance of which by a large congressional majority would help pass the industrial recovery measure in the same way as farm mortgage relief had helped pass the Agricultural Adjustment Act. Personally Roosevelt was far more committed to Title I than to Title II (the former was permanent legislation of immense importance, in his view; the latter a strictly emergency measure into which he was pushed by circumstances against his budget-balancing will), and far from seeing any necessity for a single administrative direction of the two, he saw good reason for keeping them separate. Each executive burden would be heavy enough of itself alone for any one man to bear, God knew. The weight of both could be crushing on a man like Hugh S. Johnson who, impetuous and high-strung, seemed always to operate a little out of control and was sometimes wholly so. For doubts about the general's administrative capacities were now growing in Roosevelt's mind, fed not only by the warnings of Baruch and others but also by his own direct observations.

Some hint of these doubts he gave to his cabinet at a meeting on Tuesday, June 6. He then expressed dissatisfaction over certain personnel choices Johnson was said to have made and even greater dissatisfaction over the fact they were being made by the general on his own initiative, with no prior approval from the White House. The President told the commerce secretary to tell the general that *no* personnel commitment for the new agency was valid that had not been cleared in advance in the Executive Office. This emboldened Roper to suggest that since industrial recovery operations were bound to overlap with the already established functions of at least four executive departments— Commerce, Labor, Agriculture, Interior—the secretaries of these four might well be constituted an interdepartmental committee of oversight, to review both Johnson's selection of personnel and his "work in general." Frances Perkins and Henry Wallace evidently raised no initial objections to this proposal, but by his own account, Harold Ickes did. He thought the interdepartmental committee device would prove as "cumbersome and ineffectual" in this case as it had in the case of the Civilian Conservation Corps and that it would be better to attach the new agency "to the Department of Commerce in some manner," thereby giving the general "a cabinet officer to represent him at the cabinet table" and "someone to whom he could come when he had decisions to make." Roosevelt was inclined to think this suggestion sound. Perkins, however, now expressed a doubt that Johnson "with his temperament would be able to work under a secretary," whereupon Ickes grew impatient. ". . . I asked her how he [Johnson] could work for four secretaries if he could not work with one."[44]

Roosevelt, fixing an amused gaze upon his testy, truculent, clamp-jawed, fiercely righteous fifty-nine-year-old interior secretary, may well have come close to concluding, at that moment, a process of decision whereby Harold Ickes would become, ultimately, Title II's administrator. Certainly, during the three months since inauguration day, Ickes had demonstrated professional abilities and personal qualities that were of immense value to the New Deal. In Roosevelt's mind, in the public's mind, he had solidly established himself as a remarkably efficient and honest administrator of a vast department whose reputation for honesty, sadly reduced during the Taft administration, had been virtually destroyed by the Teapot Dome scandal of the Harding years. He had proved himself a stubborn and effective foe of official corruption, an equally stubborn and effective champion of civil liberties and human rights. One of his first acts as interior secretary was the abolition of racial segregation in the rest rooms and dining areas of his department. His commitment to a politics of conscience, and liberalism, was implemented by shrewd, practical political skills of no mean order. His capacity for hard, concentrated work was awesome.

But of course this talk and thought about administrative arrangements presumed a passage of the national industrial recovery bill, and such event was by no means certain in early June.

Indeed, by that time the bill was in such serious trouble that harried congressional leaders advised the President to give it up for the present session, permitting Congress to wind up its business in two or three days and go home. Adjournment should have occurred a month ago, they said. They were being forced to do far too much in far too little time, they said. And was not Roosevelt himself pressing for adjournment by June 10, at the latest, because the World Economic Conference was to open on the twelfth? The advice was flatly rejected at the Oval Room meeting where it was given on the evening of June 4. For one thing, the threat of Black-Connery's passage remained; here was a piece of "business" that Congress might easily "wind up" in two or three days if the administration's industrial bill were withdrawn. Congressional leaders might, and now did, pledge themselves to prevent this catastrophe, but would they be able to redeem their pledge against the pressures for a thirty-hour week? These pressures had been demonstrably immense in early April; they would be overwhelming in early June if they again came together in concentrated focus. No, said Roosevelt, there could be no postponement of action on the industrial recovery bill, and that action *must* be affirmative.

All the same, as Roosevelt himself might have been willing to admit, the cogency of the rejected advice was considerably easier to deny in the air-conditioned White House than it was in the sweltering streets outside or in the dwelling places, offices, corridors and chambers of the Capitol, where the legislators must live and work. Washington was then in the throes of one of its worst heat waves. There were few places, virtually none, in fact, save for movie theaters and drugstores, where a taut-nerved, work-fatigued, heat-exhausted member of Congress could escape the humid fervency. Such weather militated powerfully against the patience, the willingness to compromise, the steadiness of mood and mind which sound dealings with exceedingly complex matters required. Nerves frayed. Tempers shortened.

Nor was this the only hazard to the executive's continued dominance over the legislature. A more serious one developed, in accordance with a familiar historical irony, out of the very success which this executive control was or seemed to be achieving. . . .

The "slight but definite upturn" in general business conditions, noted by Roosevelt in his Chamber of Commerce speech of May 4, had by the first week of June become more "definite," less "slight." On the morrow of the gold standard's abandonment, as the dollar lost 12 percent of the gold value it had had the day before, commodity and other prices rose moderately. They continued to rise. So did the physical volume of industrial production as indexed by the Federal Reserve Board. Having stood at 110 for the year 1929 as a whole (at one point in 1929 it had reached 125), industrial production stood at 59 in March 1933, was up to 69 a month later, and, by the end of May, had risen to 78. It continued swiftly to rise (it was 91 by the end of June, reached 100 in July). And simultaneously the stock market reacted in a way confirmative of Moley's belief, expressed to Roosevelt, that exchange operation reform should precede securities issuance reform if the two were to be legislated separately, for there now developed, had begun to develop by April 1 in anticipation of inflation, a speculative boom in stocks that was invested with all the ethical malpractices (pools, churnings, etc.) that had characterized the great bull market of the late 1920s, malpractices that could have been prevented during the upcoming summer had the administration been armed, in late May, with proper regulatory powers. Abandonment of the gold standard sparked, on the day after its announcement, a 5-million-share day on the New York Stock Exchange. This was one of the largest single-day volumes since 1930. In following weeks there were a good many 5-, even 6-million-share days, while stock prices shot upward, increasing nearly 65 percent between April 1 and June 1. It was a rise that was to continue through June and July, if with violent fluctuations reminiscent of the summer and early autumn of 1929.

Roosevelt himself, though naturally pleased by these signs of recovery, was by no means elated by them. Were the signs valid? Was the indicated recovery truly solid and substantial? These questions were very much in his mind when, on Monday, May 29, he renewed his outwardly cordial but always inwardly wary personal relations with Baruch by having the great financier as his luncheon guest, along with Morgenthau, in the White House. By then it was all too clear that the increase in industrial production and in commercial activity was effecting no proportionate decrease in unemployment. Indeed, the ranks of the totally unemployed remained virtually undiminished, and overall labor income showed no significant rise. One reason was that factories and businesses that had been employing people part-time now simply employed them full-time and tended to work them harder. Another reason was that the depression had encouraged the installation of laborsaving machinery, enabling the production of more goods in fewer man-hours of work. Far more worrisome than gratifying, in these circumstances, was the sharp rise in stock prices. Roosevelt indicated as much to his two luncheon guests. "I do not want to see the stock market go up too fast," he said, after having expressed the opinion that it had already risen too fast, and he reiterated the view, expressed a week before to Morgenthau, that steel production was also "going up too fast" when measured against the overall increase in construction activity. He saw renewed danger, here and elsewhere, of what he called "foolish overproduction."[45]

But his chief worry on this and following days, as regards the evident economic resurgence, might well have been over its effect upon the psychology of Congress and, in turn, upon the enactment of administration bills yet pending. For as crisis fear was lessened, as the threat of social revolution was reduced, so was the willingness of Congress to suspend its own judgment and accept executive dictation. Senators and representatives reasserted their independence. The conservatives among them increasingly resisted anything that smacked of business regulation or reform, anything that might change economic class relationships, claiming that what now took place was a "natural" recovery, a working out of the "natural law" of a "free" market, and that the process must be permitted to proceed with no further "governmental interference." The liberals among them, on the other hand, increasingly insisted that more and more positive government action was needed to ensure that there was no return to the big-business rule that had wrecked the nation before and would assuredly do so again were it permitted. And from both left and right and in between came increasing protest against the way in which the administration was handling patronage. Roosevelt's policy, implemented by Farley, had been to withhold official appointments until his legislative program was through, the clear implication being that in the ultimate distribution of offices, account would be taken of whether or not, and to what degree, individual legislators had acceded to administration wishes. Moreover, Roosevelt had made some major appointments without bothering to consult senators from the states of which the appointees were citizens. (He had had so much to do, so little time in which to do it.) Such procedure, along with the general "method of distributing patronage," would have to "change," fumed Cotton Ed Smith to Morgenthau in late April, else "the President will soon have a revolution on his hands."[46] On May 17 Roosevelt was attacked by House Democrats in floor speech (it was the first time he had been thus assailed by Democrats) for his management of the patronage, especially his delay of it. This, of course, did nothing to help the passage of the national industrial recovery bill, introduced that day.

It is true that House action on the measure immediately thereafter, as viewed from the Executive Office, was gratifyingly prompt and affirmative, made so through adherence to the pattern established during the emergency banking legislative process and generally followed in the lower chamber ever since. Assigned on the day of its introduction to the House Ways and Means Committee, of which North Carolina's Robert L. Doughton was chairman, the bill was favorably reported on May 23 and, three days later, after the adoption of rules severely limiting debate and banning amendments, passed by a vote of 325 to 76. Roosevelt well knew, however, that this passage had not been as smooth, as unprotested as its swiftness would suggest. Troublesome opposition arose, not to the bill's Title I or Title II (only a small portion of the permitted debate was devoted to these) but to the writing of Title III. This last was the revenue-raising measure whose initiation was the House's constitutional duty and prerogative but whose shaping was normally helped or determined by firm administration guidelines. No such guideline was now provided. During committee hearings the ever-consistent and -persistent Lew Douglas, appearing in his capacity as budget director, presented four new revenue-raising possibilities. The first of these was (he thus implied that the administration preferred) a general manufacturers' sales tax of 1½ percent. Doughton and the committee brusquely refused even to consider it. They settled, instead, upon proposals for an increase in individual income tax rates, for the inclusion of theretofore exempted corporate dividends in taxable income, and for an increase in the gasoline tax. These were the least objectionable to the general populace of available new tax options, and in view of Roosevelt's absolute insistence upon the raising of an additional $220 million annually, in view also of his now forced reiteration of personal opposition to a federal sales tax,* their easy passage through the House seemed assured. Instead, there arose a small but violent storm, shot through with lightning bolts of wrath, against the imposition upon the common citizenry of *any* new tax whatever!

The reason for this outburst was not far to seek. It was emblazoned on the front page of every newspaper that week as Ferdinand Pecora, the Fletcher committee's counsel, in a Senate committee hearing room, turned his investigative spotlight upon the great House of Morgan and thereby made sensational disclosures to the general public. Chief among his witnesses was the namesake son of that lordly founder of J. P. Morgan and Company who had so disdainfully, though revealingly, replied to Untermyer's questions during the Pujo investigation twenty years before. The present J. P. Morgan appeared rather less than lordly—he fidgeted; he flushed with annoyance and embarrassment†—when fact-armed Pecora relentlessly pursued a line of questioning that began

*Roosevelt made this renewed opposition known through Senator Byrnes after Massachusetts Representative John W. McCormack, a Democrat evidently misled by Douglas's hearings testimony, proposed on the House floor, as the substance of Title III, a manufacturers' sales tax of 2½ percent.
†Morgan had good reason to be furious, though he instead betrayed only surprise and reacted with good-humored courtesy, when a circus publicity agent suddenly placed in his lap as he sat in the witness chair a female midget, one of the circus's attractions.

with a seemingly casual question about Morgan's income tax. Had the banker paid any in 1930? Morgan couldn't remember; his income tax returns were prepared for him "at the office," and though he, of course, signed them, he paid them little heed. Pecora then spread upon the record documentary proof that Morgan had in fact paid no income tax in 1930, 1931, or 1932 and could legally avoid paying any in 1933. Nor had any of Morgan's partners paid a penny of income tax in 1931 (their aggregate payment in 1930 had been less than $50,000), though the most junior of these partners received at least $100,000 a year.[47] All this was because the law permitted capital losses incurred in 1929 to be used as tax write-offs year after year thereafter until the whole of the loss was written off—a tax dodge commonly employed by those who could afford tax lawyers but theretofore unknown to the public at large.

Vociferous congressmen reflected popular anger and disgust. Why, they asked, should the general citizenry be required to pay *more* taxes when the wealthiest in the land paid none at all? The rhetorical question was potent enough to reduce to a mere 19 votes the majority (213 to 194) by which House Democratic leaders pushed through the special rules of procedure on the industrial recovery bill, and among those who voted against the President on the issue were eighty-five Democrats and five Farmer-Laborites. Roosevelt took note of this disturbing fact and reacted to it at once. He summoned to the White House Secretary of the Treasury Woodin and Undersecretary of the Treasury Dean Acheson;* he agreed with them that the use of a capital loss as an income tax write-off should thereafter be permitted only for the year in which the loss occurred; he saw to it that administration leaders wrote this provision into the pending bill's Title III, increasing thereby the huge majority by which the bill was then passed by the House.

And on the afternoon of the day of this passage (May 26), as the result of yet another and even more sensational disclosure made by the Pecora investigation of J. P. Morgan operations, there was presented to the weekly cabinet meeting in the White House a very serious question concerning the secretary of the treasury, a question not without bearing upon the Senate's consideration of the industrial recovery bill and of two other important pending measures, insofar as the answer made to it might affect the executive's persuasive prestige, its reputation as champion of the "forgotten man."

Pecora had, of course, subpoenaed files from the House of Morgan. Among them he had found a "preferred list" of prominent men to whom the Morgan bank had offered for sale, in 1929, at prices substantially below their current market value, common stock in three holding companies which it had helped form—namely, Standard Brands, Inc., the Alleghany Corporation, and the United Corporation. Each of these men, in accepting the offer, accepted what amounted to a cash gift from Morgan and, by so doing, obviously, if tacitly, placed himself under obligation to the House. Woodin's name was on the list.

---

*Acheson had been appointed undersecretary of the treasury on May 3.

So was the name of Norman H. Davis.* The letter to Woodin from a Morgan partner had offered him, as one of "our close friends," 1,000 shares of Alleghany common at its cost to the firm of $20 a share, Alleghany being "not the class of security we wish to offer publicly." The partner went on to explain, "I believe that the stock is selling in the market for around $35 to $37 a share, which means very little, except that people wish to speculate. . . . There are no strings attached to this stock, so you can sell it whenever you wish. . . ."[49]

The disclosure of this cozy arrangement loosed a flood of public condemnation, both of the Morgan bank and of those who had accepted Morgan's largess. Said Republican Governor Alfred M. Landon of Kansas: "It is nothing more or nothing less than bribery. . . . I confidently expect the President to demand the resignation of Secretary of the Treasury Woodin."[50] Roosevelt did nothing of the sort. It was Woodin himself who, at the cabinet meeting of May 26, raised the question of whether or not he should resign. Vice President Garner expressed the opinion that he should since otherwise, "people . . . would believe that the Morgan interests were dominating this Administration," as they had allegedly dominated the government in the past. (Indeed, at that very moment on the floor of the Senate Huey Long was delivering a set speech blasting Roosevelt for staffing the Treasury Department with appointees from the Morgan company and its affiliates, this after promising to "drive the money changers from the temple." Cried Long: "[I]nstead of being out of the temple, they not only inject themselves in the temple but they sit in the seats of the mighty and pass judgment on the balance of us who waged that fight to deliver the country back to the American people. . . . We can enact all the laws we wish to regulate the conduct of financiers, the bloated masters of fortune and power, but it does not make any difference what kind of law we write on the books so long as we make them the masters of the law." Long's address was entitled "Our Constant Rulers."[51])

But Attorney General Cummings disagreed with Garner. So did the secretary of the interior. For one thing, Ickes pointed out, Woodin in 1929 had never held public office and did not expect to hold any; the Morgan offer to him could therefore not be interpreted as a bribe to influence "legislation or administrative acts." The case was different, however, with Norman Davis, in Ickes's

---

*Other leading Democrats on the list were Newton D. Baker, Bernard Baruch, John W. Davis, William Gibbs McAdoo, and John J. Raskob, who told a Morgan partner he hoped there would be in the future "opportunities for me to reciprocate." (Woodin, it might be noted, was still nominally a Republican in 1929; he was so as late as January 1932, though he'd supported Al Smith for President and Roosevelt for governor in 1928.) Republicans listed included Charles Francis Adams, Hoover's secretary of the navy; Owen J. Roberts, Hoover appointee to the U.S. Supreme Court; utilities magnate Henry E. Machold, Roosevelt's power policy foe; Silas H. Strawn, Republican leader in Chicago and former president of the U.S. Chamber of Commerce; and Calvin Coolidge, whose term as President ended only a few weeks before he received Morgan's inviting letter. Military hero General John J. Pershing and aviation hero Charles A. Lindbergh were also on the list.

stern judgment. ". . . Davis had been in public life, was in public life, and expected to be in public life" when he accepted Morgan's gift, and as ambassador-at-large, with a large role in shaping American relations with foreign governments, he was in a unique position to serve the special interests of a great international banker. Davis continued in this role, representing the United States in disarmament negotiations and in preparations for the World Economic Conference; he was, in this role, "a distinct liability to the Administration" and should be removed. But the final decision was the President's, of course, and Roosevelt made it clear that he would neither ask for Davis's resignation nor accept Woodin's. Noted Ickes in his diary that evening: "The President took the position that many of us did things prior to 1929 that we wouldn't think of doing now; that our code of ethics had radically changed."[52] From the White House thereafter came no official comment on the matter.

And whether or not this presidential tolerance of ethically dubious conduct on the part of administration conservatives had the effect of raising doubts among Senate liberals about Roosevelt's basic commitments and about the overall direction of the New Deal, thereby reinforcing the hot weather and the upturn in the economy as factors encouraging congressional opposition attitudes, whether or not this is true, there certainly did develop at this time a "struggle between Executive and Congress . . . [which] kept Washington in turmoil for two weeks," as Ernest Lindley has recorded. Veterans' benefit payments and the national industrial recovery bill were the two "main bones of contention," to quote Lindley again,[53] but hardly less contentious was a key provision in the permanent banking reform measure, the Glass-Steagall bill, passage of which was spurred by Pecora investigation disclosures.

VI

NOT until June 7 did the Senate Finance Committee report the industrial recovery bill favorably for full floor action, and it did so then only after making major revisions: Struck from the bill, by a vote of 12 to 7, was the provision for that "vigorous licensing power" which Roosevelt had described as an "indispensable safeguard"; added was an amendment mandating an embargo on all imports which might "interfere" with industrial recovery, an amendment opposed by the White House because it would drastically reduce the flexibility of the administration's negotiating stance during the upcoming London Conference. Both revisions were strongly favored by the National Association of Manufacturers, which, meeting in annual convention at this time, adopted resolutions saying so and also calling for a striking from the bill of its Section 7(a). To the latter proposal the AFL's President Green reacted instantaneously: He threatened to mobilize House and Senate labor opposition to the entire measure unless 7(a) remained, and since it was clear there was enough labor support to tip the balance against affirmative action on the bill, Green's move stymied the NAM's.

Far more worrisome to the administration than hit-and-run attacks from the right, however, was a major offensive from the left against the central provisions of Title I.

On June 8, an extremely hot day (the temperature of the Senate chamber's muggy air rose above ninety-five degrees), in an effort to meet Roosevelt's deadline of June 10 for congressional adjournment, the Senate debated national industrial recovery for thirteen long and weary hours. Wagner opened the debate with a carefully prepared argument in which he deprecated antitrust law as a deterrent of corporate giantism. Obviously it had been no deterrent. There was no evidence that it had even slowed the process by which economic power was concentrated in fewer and fewer hands, but there were abundant instances of its use against labor organization and against small business. The present bill was designed to accomplish *in fact* what the Sherman and Clayton acts had been intended by their creators to do: It would protect small business against the crushingly "unfair" competition of big business (no code, asserted Wagner bravely, could possibly be approved that discriminated against small business), and it would protect labor against exploitation by management. As for the loudly expressed fear of "dictatorial powers" being placed in the President's hands, it was rendered groundless by the sterling character of the great man in the White House; the practical effect would be that the act was administered "with the humane sympathies, level-headed judgment, and splendid valor which the President has shown in all his actions."[54]

Idaho's Progressive Republican William Borah was unconvinced. No President, however wise and good, could possibly exercise directly, personally, the enormous powers this bill would place in his hands. How on earth could anyone supervise the details of thousands of businesses as this bill, on its face, would have the President do? Roosevelt would perforce delegate his powers to individuals "unknown to Congress," and these "unknown" individuals would thereafter exercise not merely an executive authority but also a legislative authority properly belonging only to elected representatives of the general public. Borah was very sure that code making would in actual fact be dominated by the larger industries, the larger businesses to the detriment of small business and labor, and that the effect would be the creation of industrial combines powerful enough to "regulate the regulators."

Borah was more than ably seconded by Huey Long, whose two-hour tirade against the bill, delivered in his usual oratorical style (he paced the floor, tore his hair, waved his arms, laughed with scorn, and shouted with anger), began with a lament of Roosevelt's sidetracking of Black-Connery and continued with an embarrassing reference to that 1932 Democratic platform which Roosevelt had accepted "100 percent" in Chicago and had so often cited in justification of recent legislative proposals. No plank in that platform was more emphatic and less equivocal than the one promising a "strengthening and impartial enforcement" of the very antitrust law which the present iniquitous bill would suspend. In fact, the bill would suspend the Constitution itself. For surely the approving of codes of fair competition having the force of law was a legislative function constitutionally assigned to Congress, and surely the wholesale transfer of such power to the chief executive made this bill a reversion to that tyrannical government against which the American Colonies had rebelled. "Every fault of socialism is to be found in this bill, without one of its virtues," cried Huey Long. "Every crime of monarchy is in here, without one of the things that would give it credit. . . . It is . . . worse than anything proposed under the Soviet. . . ." Long also bitterly denounced Roosevelt's evident intention to appoint a close associate of Bernard Baruch's to administer the act. This was the same Baruch who a few months ago, at the very bottom of the depression, had called for the imposition of a national sales tax upon a suffering people (the point was sharpened by new disclosures of the fact that many of those who cried most loudly for a balanced budget were avoiding payment of tax on their own ample incomes), the same Baruch who had always aligned himself with the most reactionary elements of the Democratic party and would now be enabled, through Hugh Johnson, to exert upon the present administration the same pernicious influence he had exerted upon the administrations of Woodrow Wilson and Herbert Hoover.[55]

Yet when the Senate acted on the bill next day, only four Democrats voted against it (the bill passed 58 to 24)—and Long was not one of them! He switched his vote from nay to yea at the last moment. "How should a vote be cast when a senator is half against and half in favor of a bill?" he had asked of the chair, receiving from Vice President Garner a tart reply: "The senator would have to cut himself in two, which would be difficult to do." Indeed, every Democrat who voted in opposition was a conservative; liberals had been persuaded into a reluctantly affirmative vote by amendments adopted during floor debate. The licensing provision, stripped from the bill by the Finance Committee, had been restored to it. The embargo of competing imports, mandated in the committee-reported bill, had been rendered optional. An amendment adopted by a large majority made taxable as personal income the dividends of theretofore tax-exempt state and municipal bonds, and another amendment, proposed by La Follette and adopted by a two to one vote, required publication of corporation and personal income tax returns. (Clearly the Pecora disclosures were having their effect.) Most important, a Borah amendment providing that no industry code could "permit combinations in restraint of trade, price fixing or other monopolistic practices" had been adopted.

This last, of course, struck at the heart of Title I, destroying its very *raison d'être* in the view of big business, which reacted to it instantaneously, as to an electric shock, deluging with protests a White House disposed to listen to them sympathetically. How could industry decrease working hours and increase wages if it were denied the possibility of establishing "fair, just, and reasonable price levels?" asked industrial spokesmen in telegrams and phone calls. With price-fixing removed from the bill, National Industrial Recovery became a phony name for the act, said other messages in effect, since the act would then be "nothing more than an unsatisfactory labor measure."[56] In the big business view, every one of the Senate floor amendments of the House-passed bill *ought* to be removed in the joint conference committee to which the bill was now referred, but the Borah amendment simply *must* be! Roosevelt agreed. Administration leaders promptly moved to make sure that this happened.

Designated as Senate managers of the conference committee, to the loudly expressed disgust of Senate liberals, were three of the most conservative Democrats—Pat Harrison of Mississippi, Walter F. George of Georgia, and William H. King of Utah—each of whom had voted against the amendments, and under their leadership Senate conferees joined with those from the House to knock out Borah's amendment, knock out the proposal to tax income from state and municipal bonds, and revise the La Follette amendment into meaninglessness. This conference report was then promptly ratified by an again docile House, which, indeed, by the evening of June 10 had completed action on *all* the administration legislation before it, thus meeting Roosevelt's deadline for congressional adjournment. On the Senate floor, however, there was angry resistance. It was sparked not only by the bill as now reported but also by a remarkably ill-timed presidential message asking congressional approval of an executive order to consolidate several federal agencies and to eliminate others, at an estimated saving of $25 million. The order continued what had by this time become a decidedly unpopular government economy drive, and the message concerning it struck senators, and representatives also, as an attempt by the White House to take unfair advantage of their near exhaustion, their now almost desperate wish to go home. So it was that liberal senators who had been resigned to an immediate final vote on industrial recovery, the passage of which they knew was assured, and to an immediately following end of the session (this would postpone until the regular session action on Glass-Steagall and veterans' benefits, as the administration wished), now rebelled. Some of them started to filibuster. They forced an adjournment that was not sine die but only pro tem, until Monday, June 13.

And on Monday five liberal senators in quick succession (Wheeler, Long, Borah, Cutting, Black) took the floor to denounce those who had betrayed them in conference committee and to proclaim their now rock-hard opposition to the bill. A harassed, unhappy Wagner, normally to be found in the vanguard of Senate liberalism, tried in vain to reassure those who now *knew* that the main intent of this bill was to effect industrial combinations and price-fixing on an unprecedented scale that Section 7 was at best but a sop and bribe of dubious practical worth, and that the aims of that section could be much more certainly achieved by legislation exclusively concerned to achieve them. Black, speaking on the bill for the first time, poured scorn on the notion that it would accomplish a single purpose of his own thirty-hour bill. Altogether absurd, in his view, was the expectation that sweatshops would be abolished, wages raised, and work hours reduced by associations of the very industrialists who had created the sweatshops and who had kept wages so low, work hours so high that total purchasing power lagged disastrously behind production— behind even a production deliberately curtailed by business, as Black might have added, to maintain "profitable" scarcities. In any case, he went on to say, wage increases would not of themselves alone restore the economic balance needed for recovery; they must be matched by *decreases* in capital's exorbitant earnings, for clearly a root cause of depression was precisely this prevailing distorted pattern of income distribution. La Follette, having spoken against the reported bill in similar vein, then moved its recommittal to conference committee, a motion which would almost certainly have been adopted had it been put to a vote. But it was *not* put to a vote. The chair (Garner) ruled that since the House had already approved the reported measure, Senate recommittal of it was a parliamentary impossibility. La Follette's motion was declared out of order.[57]

The question was then moved.

This time the Senate vote was much closer, and the division between liberals and conservatives was far less blurred in the eyes of observers than had been the case four days earlier. National industrial recovery was passed 46 to 39, or by a majority of seven, compared with a majority of thirty-four in favor of the bill as revised by the full Senate on June 9. Voting against the conference report were eighteen liberal and antitrust senators who, on June 9, had voted *for* the earlier version. They were joined in their opposition by three senators who, the first time around, had not voted at all. Much smaller was the shift from opposition to approval—a mere two votes, joined by three not formerly recorded. Six senators remained unrecorded on the final roll call.

Obviously Title I, standing by itself, would have been voted down by the Senate. It was saved, as it had been designed to be saved, by its linkage to Title II.

VII

THERE followed not the congressional adjournment that Roosevelt wanted but three days of bitter warfare between Congress and White House over the two bones of contention which adjournment would have at least temporarily buried. Of these, the more contentious was the matter of reduced veterans' benefit payments.

Budget Director Lewis W. Douglas, who celebrated his thirty-eighth birthday in 1933, was lean and rangy as an Arizona cowboy and, with his homely, widemouthed grin and warm friendliness of manner, personally charmed even those who most abhorred his rigidly Tory views. Roosevelt, who had no little sympathy with his views, was initially much taken with him, regarding him as "in many ways the greatest 'find' of the Administration" (so Roosevelt wrote Colonel House in April), a young man who in a dozen years "would make a good Democratic candidate for President," as Roosevelt said to Moley on a morning in early March.[58] But as spring advanced and Douglas continued to practice the most extreme fiscal conservatism in the face of political challenges demanding flexible responses, Roosevelt's estimate of his value to the administration was revised downward. As early as April 1, when executive orders published the veterans' pension regulations which Douglas and Veterans Administrator Walker D. Hines had worked out under the terms of the Economy Act,* Roosevelt manifested qualms concerning the political effects of his budget director's single-minded budget-balancing zeal. Douglas was himself a combat veteran. He had fought with recognized valor on Flanders fields and in the Argonne. But as scion of a family rich in copper mines and ranchland and as an Anglophile who identified with the English aristocracy, he had neither personal need for a government pension nor any visible or audible sympathy with those whose need was great. "[B]orn to the purple, loves the English . . . and has a heart of stone" was Hiram Johnson's judgment upon him as a man; "shameful, outrageous, and cruel" was Johnson's judgment upon his dealings as director of the budget with veterans' affairs. Certainly his published regulations were draconian. They slashed from the pension budget some $480 million, which was nearly $100 million more than the reduction originally aimed for. They called for the closing of Veterans Administration regional offices; they clearly implied the closing of government hospitals for veterans. And they caused Roosevelt to issue a special personal message to veterans denying that they were "being singled out to make sacrifices. On the contrary," he went on, "I want them to know that the regulations issued are but an integral part of our economy program embracing every department and agency of the government to which every employee is making his or her contribution."[59]

But this presidential statement, issued on April Fools Day, persuaded no veterans who knew (and all of them were promptly informed by veterans' organizations) that men who had suffered wounds or been gassed overseas were having their disability allowances cut not by the 25 percent which the Economy Act prescribed but by as much as 60 percent and, in some cases, even more. Myriads, indeed tens of myriads, whose disabilities were only "presumed" to have originated in the service were being struck from the rolls altogether, without the investigation needed to determine the justice or injustice of individual cases. For Douglas's mind, typically ideological, was ruled by generalized abstractions; individual facts that varied from statistical averages were to the extent of their variance "unreal," in his tacit view; and veterans were by no means the only people, they were not even a majority of those who found the consequences outrageous in the present instance. Predictably, Socialist Norman Thomas in repeated public statement inveighed against the published schedule; he joined with his condemnation of Douglas's ruthlessness toward the needy an acid comment on Douglas's tender concern for the rich when these were threatened by increased taxation. But even conservative journals editorialized upon the unfairness of reducing monthly payments to war-maimed veterans by 65 percent (from $97 to $36) in the interests of a balanced budget while leading bankers, who had admittedly defrauded the

*General Hines, who had been director-general of the integrated railroad system during the war and had counselled the President-elect on government economy during the interregnum, was a principal one among those who had helped Douglas draft the Economy Act.

public (if generally in perfectly legal ways), were permitted to escape all taxation of their fat incomes. Rising winds of protest swept into the corridors of power in Washington all through April. They reached gale force by the second week of May, when Roosevelt perforce bent to them, though to the smallest possible extent.

On May 10, after conferring with Douglas and the national commander of the American Legion, Louis A. Johnson, he issued a statement admitting administration error. "[I]t now seems that the cut in compensations of service-connected World War veterans with specific injuries has been deeper than was originally intended," the President said. "The regulation and schedules in this respect will, therefore, be reviewed so as to effect more equitable levels of payment. Careful study will also be made of the other regulations and their effects." There would be, he went on to say, no closing of Veterans Administration regional offices, "as has been reported, except where it has been clearly demonstrated that regional facilities are not necessary," and it was "not contemplated that Government hospitals will be closed pending a careful, studious survey of the entire hospital situation."[60]

But this proved to be too little and too late to accomplish its soothing purpose, followed as it was a week later by the highly controversial, acrimony-producing industrial recovery bill. By the second week of June organized veterans' pressure on Congress was far more intense than it had been at the time the economy bill was passed. Moreover, there was at hand a legislative vehicle to carry protesting pressure easily onto the statute books, a vehicle provided, ironically enough, by Herbert Hoover when he had pocket-vetoed an independent offices bill passed by the Seventy-second Congress and thereby imposed upon the Seventy-third Congress the need to enact one. To this bill was now proposed an amendment to restore $170 million to the budget for disabled veterans and place an absolute limit of 25 percent on cuts made in the pensions of such veterans. The proposal was promptly strongly opposed by the administration, but when it came to a vote, the Senate divided evenly upon it, 42 to 42, whereupon Garner as presiding officer cast the deciding vote in favor of it. The Vice President justified his action on the ground that had he not taken it, a rebellious Senate would have made even more devastating attacks on the schedule and regulations. And, indeed, there impended another amendment, proposed by Bronson Cutting, which was an even more drastic proposal in that it would definitely restore to the benefit rolls all 154,000 of the veterans whom Douglas and Hines proposed to remove because their disabilities were only "presumed" to be service-connected. Nor could the administration have much hope for succor in this case from the House, where the veterans' bloc was stronger than in the Senate.

Roosevelt, though Douglas begged him to stand firm,* felt forced into another retreat.

He accepted the limitation to 25 percent of cuts in disability pensions, he

---

*The Budget Director urged Roosevelt to veto the amended bill, give his reasons for doing so to the country, and then keep Congress in session until it did his will.

agreed to leave the 154,000 "presumptives" on the disability rolls pending individual reviews of their cases, and he promised that in any case of doubt the benefit of doubt would go to the veteran. But he made it clear that this was the absolute limit of compromise; he would resort to veto, not a pocket veto but a "good worded" one, if the compromise were not accepted. The House then did accept it. Cutting, however, refused to withdraw his Senate amendment, thereby provoking Roosevelt's wrath as none other had done since the election—a cold fury frightening to witness; it was the only time during all the pressure-packed weeks of the special session that Raymond Moley "saw him lose his poise, self-confidence, and good-humor. . . ."[61] (Roosevelt seems earlier to have been ill at ease in his personal contacts with Progressive Republican Cutting, whose liberalism was profound and unwavering and whose privileged class background, Groton-Harvard schooling, and long, harsh struggle against crippling illness [Cutting's tuberculosis had been nearly fatal] were akin to his own. Was this because he sensed that Cutting, measuring him by standards of behavior to which he himself subscribed, found him wanting? If so, Roosevelt's resentment would have been fed by his conviction that Cutting made little effort to understand, much less sympathize with, the kinds of yieldings, the kinds of submissions, out of which the chief executive of a democracy must shape his leadership power.) Cutting's intransigence led to dangerous trouble for the executive. His amendment was adopted by a Senate in full rebellion against administration leadership, encouraging a movement in the House to renege on its acceptance of the Roosevelt compromise. Only by reiterations of Roosevelt's refusal to budge, joined with coercive tactics on the part of the House's administration leaders, was a majority of the lower chamber persuaded into a rejection of the Senate amendment. In the Senate, it was only physical and emotional exhaustion which at last assured the majority needed to pass a veterans' bill that Roosevelt could sign. Led by Hugo Black, nine senators switched from opposition to support of the Roosevelt compromise, enabling its passage by 45 to 36 at one-twenty in the morning of June 16, following which the Congress adjourned sine die.

Side by side with this contention over veterans' pensions, through the final days of the special session, marched an only somewhat less rancorous contention between White House and Capitol Hill over the inclusion in the permanent banking reform bill, the Glass-Steagall bill, of a federal guarantee of bank deposits.

On other major provisions of the bill—the absolute separation of commercial from investment banking (i.e., the total divorce of deposit handling from securities selling) and the granting to Federal Reserve of controls over interest rates, to curb speculation—there was sufficient agreement to assure easy passage. Even bankers, many of them, chastened by the Pecora exposures and the public's reaction to these, expressed themselves in favor of these reforms. But deposit insurance had been initially strongly opposed by Carter Glass himself, after a bill incorporating it, sponsored by Chairman Henry B. Steagall of the

House Banking and Currency Committee, had passed through the lower chamber with a large majority in 1932. Glass's acceptance of it had been recent and forced. The proposal continued to be sternly opposed not only by the American Bankers Association and ranking individual officers of the Federal Reserve System but also by the President of the United States, who still clung in early June to the views he had expressed on this matter to the first of his press conferences, in early March.

The division here was less between liberals and conservatives (though far more of the former than of the latter were in favor of insurance) than it was between Wall Street and the rest of the financial community, and between East and West. Texans Jesse Jones and John N. Garner, both bankers, both conservative, very actively favored the measure. So did Michigan's Republican Senator Arthur H. Vandenberg. It was Vandenberg who, with presiding officer Garner's connivance, introduced as an amendment to Glass's bill, suddenly, unexpectedly, on May 19, the proposal to guarantee deposits to a maximum of $2,500 in all member banks of the Federal Reserve System and in such other banks as met specific standards. The amendment was at once overwhelmingly accepted by the Senate.

Roosevelt was dismayed.

"It won't work, Jack," he had said to Garner when the latter, during the bank holiday, pressed for the inclusion of deposit guarantee in the emergency banking bill. "The weak banks will pull down the strong."[62]

And he moved now against the measure as strongly as he could. When the Glass and Steagall bills went into conference committee, he addressed a note to the conferees urging them to remove deposit insurance and threatening a veto if they did not. The threat was ineffective; deposit insurance obviously commanded a majority support great enough to overcome a veto. Roosevelt perforce retreated, but not without rearguard action. He proposed that the needed temporary insurance fund of $150 million be raised at least in part by a tax of one-sixteenth to one-fourth of 1 percent of the insured deposits. His proposal received no support.

Glass-Steagall sailed through the House on a vote of 262 to 19. It passed the Senate by acclamation and, on the morning of June 16, awaited the President's signature. Its final terms established a Federal Deposit Insurance Corporation which, beginning on January 1, 1934, would totally insure something over 95 percent of all individual deposits in the banks covered, for less than 5 percent of all deposits in America were then individually more than $2,500. Thanks in good part to Huey Long, who argued for it with loud persuasiveness, state banks not members of the Federal Reserve System (there were some 8,600 of these) were admitted to the deposit insurance fund, upon application and submission to examination. All Federal Reserve members were included automatically. On July 1, 1934, when the permanent insurance scheme went into effect, the FDIC would totally insure all deposits up to $10,000, 75 percent of all deposits of $10,000 to $50,000, and 50 percent of all deposits over $50,000. (Meanwhile, Jesse Jones was enabled to employ as whip and spur the requirements a bank must meet to be eligible for deposit insurance, thereby coercing reluctant bankers into borrowing enough working capital from the RFC to become actually solvent, such loans being secured by preferred stock and debentures deposited with the RFC. Most banks, though they had been permitted by a lenient administration of the Emergency Banking Act to open and operate, were *not* truly solvent in September 1933.) Beginning on July 1, 1936, no state bank which was not a member of the Federal Reserve could be admitted to the FDIC fund—a stipulation which pointed toward that unified banking system, privately managed, for which Carter Glass had been struggling for two decades.

So it was that despite Roosevelt's stubborn opposition, joined to that of the leading organization of American bankers, there was achieved the "structural change [in the banking system] most conducive of monetary stability since state bank note issues were taxed out of existence immediately following the Civil War," according to the authoritative monetary historians Milton Friedman and Anna Jacobson Schwartz.* The peril of bank panic was abruptly and almost totally removed; the incidence of commercial bank failure was dramatically reduced. Friedman and Schwartz write:†

> From 1921 through 1933, every year requires at least three digits to record the number of banks that suspended; from 1934 on, two digits suffice, and from 1943 through 1960, one digit, for both insured and non-insured banks. For the thirteen-year period 1921 to 1933, losses borne by depositors average $146 million a year or 45 cents per $100 of adjusted deposits in all commercial banks. For the twenty-seven years since [until 1960] losses have averaged $706,000 a year, or less than two-tenths of 1 cent per $100 of adjusted deposits in all commercial banks; moreover, over half the total losses during the twenty-seven years occurred in the very first year of the period and were mostly a heritage of the pre-FDIC period.

Of all New Deal reform legislation, this was the most resoundingly and unqualifiedly successful, measured in terms of its specific purpose.

VIII

EVEN by the standard set during the New Deal's first 103 days, the 104th (Friday, June 16, 1933) was an extraordinarily busy one for Franklin D. Roosevelt.

He signed into law that day four major enactments: Glass-Steagall, Farm Credit, Railroad Coordination, and National Industrial Recovery. With regard to the last, he issued a signature statement, a lengthy explanatory statement, and two executive orders. Said his signature statement: "History probably will record the National Industrial Recovery Act as the most important and far-reaching legislation ever enacted by the American Congress. It represents a supreme effort to stabilize for all time the many factors which make

---

*Friedman and Schwartz, *A Monetary History of the United States, 1867–1960,* p. 434.
†*Ibid.,* p. 437.

for the prosperity of the nation, and the preservation of American standards. . . . Obviously, if this project is to succeed, it demands the whole-hearted cooperation of industry, labor, and every citizen of the United States." The tone of his explanatory statement was at once challenging and defensive. "The challenge of this law is whether we can sink selfish interest and present a solid front against a common peril," he said. "It is a challenge to industry which has long insisted that, given the right to act in unison, it could do much for the general good which has hitherto been unlawful. From today it has that right. Many good men voted this new charter with misgivings. I do not share these doubts." He himself had had a part "in the great cooperation of 1917 and 1918," and he now employed Wilsonian rhetoric, a typically convoluted Wilsonian period, to proclaim "my faith that we can count on our industry once more to join in our general purpose to lift this new threat and to do it without taking advantage of the public trust which has this day been reposed without stint in the good faith and high purpose of American business." The new law also challenged labor. "Workers, too, are here given a new charter of rights long sought and hitherto denied. But they know that the first move expected by the nation is a great cooperation of all employers, by one single mass-action, to improve the case of workers on a scale never attempted in any nation. Industries can do this only if they have the support of the whole public and especially of their own workers." Finally, the new law challenged the administration. "We are relaxing some of the safeguards of the anti-trust laws. The public must be protected against the abuses that led to their enactment. . . . [T]he anti-trust laws still stand firmly against monopolies that restrain trade and price-fixing which allows inordinate profits or unfairly high prices."[63]

But these presidential statements were not published until late in the afternoon of that incredibly crowded day. Their publication had to await completion of the most painfully difficult, for Roosevelt, of all his cabinet meetings thus far.

General Hugh Johnson was summoned from his steaming Commerce Building office to the air-conditioned White House. He waited outside the cabinet room for a half hour or more, happily expectant of his official appointment to administer the NIRA. While he waited, one cabinet member after another, seated around the long mahogany table in the cabinet room, endorsed heartily Roosevelt's final decision to divorce the administration of the act's Title II utterly from the administration of Title I. There would be a National Recovery Administration, headquartered in the Commerce Department, but there would also be a Public Works Administration, headquartered in Interior, with Harold Ickes slated ultimately to become its head, a post temporarily assigned Colonel Donald H. Sawyer. For each agency there would be an advisory and review board consisting almost wholly of cabinet officials. Roosevelt "made it clear that he did not want any overlapping" of the NRA and PWA as organizational entities, according to Ickes's diary entry that night, a flat contradiction of Johnson's well-known contention that public works and codified industrial cooperation must proceed in tandem, under a single firm executive direction, if immediate recovery purposes were to be achieved. (Johnson proposed to use the allocation of public works contracts as industrial stimulant and as a means of securing industry's acceptance of what Frances Perkins called "the stern realities of the codes he expected to propose.") Roosevelt may have believed he could achieve whatever NRA-PWA coordination was truly needed by means of his appointed boards for these agencies since the two boards *did* definitely "overlap" constitutively (on both were the secretaries of commerce, interior, agriculture, and labor, the attorney general, the director of the budget), but he certainly knew that this decision, of which the general had been given no prior inkling, would cause great pain.

"It will be hard on Johnson," said the President to his cabinet, ruefully. "He won't like it. . . ."[64]

All the same he greeted the general with the broadest and happiest of smiles when the latter, upon call, entered the cabinet room. The national industrial recovery bill was about to be signed, said the beaming President. Its administrator would be Hugh S. Johnson. To this expected news the general, also smiling, responded with what Frances Perkins described as a "pleasant little speech of thanks" during which he pledged "his life to the great project." Not until then did a still-beaming Roosevelt communicate his decision. All the cabinet agreed with him, he said in a casual, matter-of-course tone, that it would be unfair and even "inhuman" to ask any single man to bear the burden of administering both titles. Johnson's smile abruptly faded. Hurt dismay was registered upon his countenance, which grew red, then purple as the President turned away to dictate the necessary executive orders. "I don't see why, I don't see why," he muttered in what Frances Perkins heard as "a strange, low voice that came from deep within him." Roosevelt seemed not to notice. Assuming that bland imperviousness of manner, that calculated unawareness which he customarily employed in the bosom of his family whenever the chronic deep-seated quarrel between his mother and his wife flared into the open, he calmly completed his dictation, then dismissed his cabinet. But he then at once beckoned the secretary of labor to his side.

"Stick with Hugh," he whispered to her while gazing compassionately upon the general, who now stood alone with bowed head at one side of the room. "Keep him sweet! Don't let him explode!"

And Frances Perkins did manage to carry out successfully what seemed to her at first a hopeless assignment. She managed to keep the general away from the press while he was yet distraught, sneaking him out of the White House by a side door, her arm linked in his. She soothed his hurt and gently countered his passionate argument during a long automobile ride through Washington's streets and parks. She pleaded with him not to "blow up," not to "pull out," but to continue to serve his country as "a good soldier." She praised somewhat extravagantly the organization job he had done thus far. At last he agreed ("very fatuously," he later said) to continue in an administrative role which was, he remained sure, disastrously flawed.[65]

As for Roosevelt, having gone through the painful experience of the cabinet meeting, he could have given but little further thought to Hugh Johnson's hurt feelings that day.

Even before he had been wheeled from cabinet room to executive office, his attention was drawn, as it had been recurrently since early morning, to a problem that had occupied the very first hour of his workday. Immediately following his breakfast, in bedside conference with Woodin and Acheson and Moley, he had critically reviewed a long cable from James Warburg in London, where the World Monetary and Economic Conference, the focus of such mass hopes as had attended no international meeting since Versailles in 1919, had been opened with great fanfare and pageantry just four days before (on June 12, a day when Roosevelt's face "was drawn with fatigue, I have never seen him look more exhausted," as Morgenthau noted in his diary[66]). Warburg's cable was reflective of the sad fact that already, even before all the ceremonial opening speeches were completed, the conference in general and the American delegation in particular were stumbling badly.

IX

A question of enormous practical difficulty was involved in the reestablishment of an international gold standard—that is, in the re-creation of stable currency ratios by making the basic unit of each currency a fixed, unvarying weight of gold, whose untrammeled international trade movement, after a period of adjustment, would then maintain the stabilized ratios automatically. This question was: At what levels should the various currencies be stabilized in terms of gold?

For one thing, gold was now very unevenly distributed among the nations, some of which (notably the United States) had excessive amounts while others had virtually none at all. Yet obviously the gold standard could not work unless *every* country on it had gold reserves sufficient to back its currency in adequate amount, and this meant that that there must now be for a time, until reserve deficiencies were supplied, a fairly massive movement of gold from the haves to the have-nots. The latter, during this opening period, must build up their reserves through an excess of exports over imports, aided by judicious loans from the haves. But once the formerly have-not nation had acquired the gold it needed, the rules of the game required it (1) to cease importing gold, accepting, instead, imports of goods and services in payment for its exports, and (2) to permit international gold movements to exert, without restraint or impediment, their "natural" influence upon internal prices. All this necessarily implied, of course, an immediate drastic revision of tariffs, quota restrictions, and all other barriers to international trade, this to initiate the transition from present "chaos" to future "order."

For another thing, the unevenness of gold distribution among the nations was matched to a degree by an unevenness in the depth and rate of domestic price decline, such decline being both a measure and a cause of general economic contraction. Statistically evident by the spring of 1933 was the fact that

the nations that had gone off gold were suffering considerably less economic
contraction than those that remained on it. Two of the three leading countries
that had gone off were Great Britain and Sweden. In both countries the
wholesale price index, with 1913 prices equaling 100, had by early 1933 fallen
but a few points (from 106 to a little more than 100 in Britain; from 115 to 106
in Sweden) since their abandonment of gold. In Japan, the third leading
country off gold, wholesale prices had actually risen, from around 120 to nearly
140, though currency depreciation was, of course, not wholly or perhaps even
chiefly responsible for this: Japan's domestic economy was boosted by governmental expenditures for the war with China. In France and Germany, however, which maintained the gold parity of their currencies, the same price index
fell from around 540 to around 385 and from 115 to 90, respectively. More
drastic still had been the fall in the United States until halted and reversed by
the presidential proclamation of April 19, abandoning gold. With the 1923 price
level being set at 100, wholesale prices in the United States declined from 77.7
in January 1931 to 59.6 in early March 1933 while farm commodity prices, taken
by themselves, were down to 40.6.[67]

In these circumstances there was ample room for acrimonious disagreement
among the nations as they attempted to decide upon ratios of value among
their currencies as a basis for a reinstituted gold standard. "In devaluing its
currency, that is, in reducing the gold content of the monetary unit, each
country will undoubtedly attempt to choose the new gold parity with a view
to strengthening its international position, favoring its exports, and protecting
its domestic market from foreign competition," predicted a memorandum
issued by the New York office of the National Industrial Conference Board a
few weeks before the economic conference opened. The issue was especially
acute between Great Britain and the United States. According to the memorandum:

> Great Britain is the greatest market for American exports, one of the largest export-
> ers to the United States, and one of the leading competitors of the United States in
> the world market. Neither country can afford, therefore, to permit the other to obtain
> even a temporary advantage through depreciation of the currency or through its
> stabilization at a point that would give advantage to one country over the other in
> international trade. . . . If [for instance] the exchange rate of the pound were
> stabilized at a point where its external purchasing power would be appreciably lower
> than its internal purchasing power, British exporters would be favored at the expense
> of American exporters, and all countries . . . would find it more profitable to sell in
> the United States and to buy in Great Britain than the other way around.[68]

The long cable which Roosevelt received from Warburg in the early morn-
ing of June 16 was the fruit of five days of negotiation between Harrison-
Sprague-Warburg and top officials of the Bank of England and the Bank of
France.

The British and French were naturally distressed by the downward trend
in the dollar's value since early April and especially since Roosevelt's monetary decision of April 19; it wiped out the competitive advantage Britain had

gained over America on the world market from its devaluation of the pound sterling and that which France had gained by its drastic devaluation of the franc before it returned to the gold standard. The British and French deplored, too, as everyone deplored, the wild speculative fluctuations in money, stock, and commodity markets, worldwide, that accompanied the dollar's downward trend. At the start of the negotiations they pressed hard for a dollar stabilized at about $3.50 to the pound. The proposed stabilization point was highly disadvantageous to the United States (on that very day, June 12, the pound was trading for around $4.18) in that it would make the dollar too expensive, thereby depressing the domestic prices which the New Deal struggled to raise. Mere published rumor that stabilization at around $4 was being considered caused a sharp rise in the dollar's value on June 15 (the pound traded that day for $4.02) with an almost equally sharp drop in stock prices. The rumor also prompted the issuance that day of a blunt warning statement by Secretary of the Treasury Woodin. "Any proposal concerning stabilization would have to be submitted to the President and to the Treasury and no suggestion of such a proposal has been received here," said Woodin to the world. "The discussions in London in regard to this subject must be exploratory only and any agreement on this subject will be reached in Washington, not elsewhere."[69]

A few hours later the Warburg cable arrived. It proposed active cooperation between the Bank of England and the Federal Reserve Bank of New York to stabilize the dollar within a narrow spread above or below $4 to the pound, with each central bank pledging expenditure of up to 60 million gold dollars to maintain this ratio and with the U.S. Treasury guaranteeing the Federal Reserve of New York against possible loss.* Along with the stabilization agreement there would be a declaration of intent by the United States and Great Britain to restore a gold basis to their currencies at the earliest practicable moment. Warburg, endorsing this proposal, indicated that it was in his view the best bargain the United States could make in the circumstances and that the alternative to its acceptance was likely to be the loss of America's power of leadership toward the goal of world economic peace and prosperity.[70]

Roosevelt reacted irritably to this message, and for a congeries of reasons.

The climactic last week of quarrel with Congress had drained nearly dry even his huge reservoir of patience, good humor, and zestful energy. Black half-moons of weariness were beneath his eyes; he badly needed the recreative holiday on which he was to embark on the morrow. Simultaneously with the onset of weariness had come (been forced upon him) an increasingly sharp awareness that any truly meaningful international economic collaboration was bound to involve a considerable curtailment of his freedom to act on the domestic scene and that this curtailment, undefined by any careful planning of his own, was almost certain to prove intolerable. From the first he had been impatient with the stubborn intricacies of the international exchange problem

*The guarantee was not explicit in the Warburg cable but was clearly implied by the language employed.

(they required for their comprehension a concentrated attention he was not prepared to give), and impatience became now exasperation. He angrily resented the pressure put abruptly upon him to make the hard either/or choice he had so long postponed in the hope that changing circumstances would obviate its necessity. (A month before he had written Colonel House that events were moving "so fast that what is a problem one day is solved or superseded the next. As you will realize, snap judgments have had to be made.["71]) Moreover, his experience of the banking community since 1928 had encouraged in him no great respect for either the general intelligence or public-spiritedness of big bankers or of the orthodox economists of academia who served banking interests, and it annoyed him that two American bankers and a Harvard professor in London, only one of whom was officially a member of the U.S. delegation staff, should, without specific instructions from Washington, have engaged in stabilization talks aimed at producing governmentally binding agreements—agreements which, for one thing, would require a tacit pledge by the President not to employ the powers granted him by the Thomas amendment.

Yet it must be said that Roosevelt was himself directly responsible for the belief of Sprague and Harrison that in London "stabilization would be handled by representatives of Treasury and Federal Reserve" independently of the U.S. delegation. Sprague had said as much, in the assertively authoritive (authoritarian) manner which was his classroom habit, during Roosevelt's last meeting with delegation and staff, and Warburg had then "asked the President whether this met with his approval and he said that it did."[72] Roosevelt's evident developing belief, not yet finally formulated, was that the stabilization problem could be dealt with in installments—first, temporary stabilization; second, permanent stabilization—and that the first installment was properly a problem for private international bankers, to be handled through cooperation among central banks, including the Federal Reserve, in ways that neither required U.S. government action nor imposed U.S. government obligations as regards shipments of gold. The conference, relieved of this vexatious problem, was to concern itself with matters of greater importance, though it must also be said that Roosevelt was far from clear in his mind what these matters precisely were.

His one firm conclusion, emergent from his preconference discussions, was that the overriding purpose at London should be "to raise the world price level." The other nations represented at the conference must "go along and work in our [New Deal] direction" of debtor relief, price raising, and the increase of purchasing power if there was to be anything "to cooperate about" in London. And in this context, as he said to his bedside conferees that Friday morning, the stabilization figure concurred in by Harrison-Sprague-Warburg was nowhere near the mark; those who agreed to it were more concerned with the special interests of international banking than committed to New Deal economic recovery programs, for the success of the AAA and NRA, at this moment of their launching, obviously required a dollar considerably cheaper than Warburg's cable proposed. How cheap? Roosevelt was reluctant even to hint at even a temporary stabilization point at this time, but since the current total uncertainty regarding the dollar's future would, if it continued, be no doubt deleterious to conference deliberations, he just *might* be willing to promise the worried British and French, in highly qualified fashion, that the United States would act unilaterally to keep the dollar from sinking much lower than $4.25 to the pound. He might authorize shipments of up to $80 million in gold for such purpose.

As for the proposed statement of intent by the United States and Great Britain to return to gold, it was wholly improper. Warburg and the others needed to be reminded that sixty-six nations had delegations in London and that the international gold standard to whose restoration the United States was in principle committed had to be agreed to by all or nearly all of these, not by merely two or three of them.[73]

It was along these lines that the cable replying to Warburg was drafted by Roosevelt, in collaboration with Moley and others, during moments snatched from the multitude of other demands upon his attention during that hectic day. The draft was completed and dispatched that evening, at which time it was agreed between Roosevelt and Moley that the latter should sail as soon as possible for England as presidential emissary, to see what could be done to straighten out the tangled situation there. (From the "very start" the plan had been for Moley "to go over sometime" for a week or two, Roosevelt had said off-the-record, in response to a question, at his press conference that morning.[74] Serving at the moment as Roosevelt's personal liaison officer in London, sending him reports on mood etc., was his cousin Warren Delano Robbins. No doubt his justification to himself for the haphazard way in which he chose the official delegates was that their roles would not be very important anyway; he himself, keeping every rein of power in his own hands, would provide the general guidance and make all the key decisions. He seems not to have considered the difficulty of doing this while on a sailing holiday, for it was a cruise along the New England coast that he was about to begin, and during it he would be denied direct telephone or telegraphic communication with London or Washington or New York City; he would have to rely instead upon exceedingly roundabout and inefficient arrangements for the receipt and transmittal of messages.) The tone of the cable, which flatly rejected the proposal Warburg had endorsed, was intentionally brusque, intentionally revealing of displeasure. Deliberately omitted, because it would mitigate the harshness, was a statement of the possibility that gold shipments might be authorized to peg the dollar at $4.25 to the pound.

All three men to whom the missive was directed were stung by it. George Harrison was so angered that he promptly packed his bags, checked out of his hotel, and boarded a steamer for home.

5

-->>><<<-

The Wrecking of the London Conference

I

AND Franklin Roosevelt boarded his special train in Washington's Union Station on Saturday morning, June 17, 1933, to begin his first vacation trip since becoming President of the United States.

The world had been told in early June, and the Secret Service had been galvanized into intense, anxious preparatory activity by the news, that the President's son James had chartered a forty-five-foot schooner, *Amberjack II,* on which the President would embark, as soon as Congress had adjourned, for a cruise along the New England coast. He himself would be the skipper of the craft; his sons James and John and Franklin, Jr., would be his crew; he would sail from the little Massachusetts town of Marion on Buzzards Bay around Cape Cod and north-northeast along the coasts of Massachusetts and New Hampshire and Maine to the little town of Welshpool on Campobello Island in the Bay of Fundy, completing there a leisurely voyage of some 360 nautical miles. The chosen points of embarkation and disembarkation had psychological significance. They signified that this voyage, though (alas) the most pressing of his immediate problems would be a constant, nagging accompaniment of it, was to be both a journey into his past and a defiant coming to terms with it, a voyage deliberately undertaken not only to renew his energy and refresh his spirit but also to remove dark shadows cast upon and into his naturally sunny buoyant spirit by the horror he had suffered after his last coasting way down east.

A dozen years ago that had been—in August 1921. He had stood then for long, tense hours at the wheel of a luxury power yacht, the *Sabalo,* as it thrust its way under his guidance through swirling curtains of mist, and within three days after his arrival on the beloved summer island of his childhood, his youth, his young manhood he had been struck down to within an inch of death by the polio that had forever crippled him. His last sight of the Roosevelt cottage on Campobello's shore had been from a stretcher as he was borne in sweating, jolting agony down the slope to the Roosevelt dock (somehow he had managed a wide smile and cheery wave of reassurance to his fearfully watching seven-year-old son Franklin, Jr.), whence he was taken by boat, a totally helpless paralytic, to Eastport. He knew that very few of those who then saw him believed it possible he could be restored to any active life. Most, including his rock-hard, imperious, ageless mother, whom he was now soon to greet, were convinced he was condemned to lifelong invalidism. He himself had doubted. As Missy LeHand and Louie Howe had glimpsed and Eleanor surmised, he had known black hours of utter despair, of total despondency, hours when he had huddled away from the sight of the world until he could raise again what had then been, though flawlessly bright, only a façade of confident optimism. He need huddle secretively no more. Out of the triumphs of the last five years, especially of the last incredible year, had come abundant confirmation of his deepest faith. He was nerved to confront that which had almost destroyed him. He could even feel honest gratitude for that which had almost destroyed him, for from it he had indeed learned "infinite patience and never-ending persistence," as Eleanor would say,[1] and out of it and in terms of it he had proved up to the hilt his possession of a rare, if not unique, stoic courage. Compared to what he had already borne, no burdens seemed now unbearable. Most seemed relatively easy. And he knew that he could "take it" and keep on "taking it" far beyond the possibilities of anyone with whom he was in contact.

As for the village of Marion, it, too, was a part of the past that had shaped this President of the United States who would come to it, briefly, in mid-June 1933. He had come here in the autumn of 1925 and again in the summer of 1926 to take a course of strenuous and painful exercises devised and supervised by a neurological doctor, exercises the purpose of which was to revive inert nerves and restore muscular tissue to his withered legs. They had failed to produce the results hoped for; in late August 1926 Roosevelt had decided not to renew these treatments but to concentrate, instead, on swimming in the thermal mineral waters of Warm Springs.

Boston was in the midst of a celebration of the 158th anniversary of the Battle of Bunker Hill when Roosevelt's train arrived there that Saturday afternoon. Crowds estimated to number a quarter million people cheered him as he rode in an open car from the railroad station through the city and its northwestward suburbs. Beyond the city, though the summer sun shone brightly, the New England country air was delightfully cool after Washington's humid heat. Roosevelt thoroughly enjoyed the ride through a green, lovely countryside across which the "embattled farmers" had harried British redcoats back from Concord to Boston in April 1775. He came to Groton Village. He came to Groton School. He gazed again upon the red-brick dormitory (Hundred House) and the red-brick classroom building (Brooks House) and upon the gymnasium and playing fields where, under the stern, righteous, measuring eye of Rector Endicott Peabody, the creator and absolute ruler of this exclusively masculine and muscularly Christian little world, he had been tested and found not wanting during the years of his adolescence, if found not particularly outstanding either. At the school was his mother, who was much like the rector in her absolute certainties of right and wrong and the order of the universe, in her overpowering force of personality, and in her unquestioning commitment to a society dominated by an aristocratic elite of which, of course, she was emphatically a member. She was visiting the two of her grandsons, his sons, who were now enrolled in the school. And she came with Franklin, Jr., out to the touring car in whose backseat he remained and stood there for a few minutes, talking with him about his vacation plans. A photograph was taken of the three of them, all of them smiling into the camera's lens—the father and son broadly, delightedly; stout Sara less broadly, more tentatively. He rode then southeastward from Groton across almost the whole width of Massachusetts to Marion and through Marion to a secluded cove beyond the village, a secret place closely guarded by the Secret Service, where *Amberjack II* rocked at anchor. He and his familial amateur crew went aboard.

He sailed early next morning, seated at the wheel in an open cockpit. He sailed under cloudy skies from which a chill rain soon fell, whereupon he donned a yellow slicker over his warm sweater and a floppy canvas hat, and he experienced there and then, in the rain, a rare sense of privacy, of solitude amid the immensities of sea and sky, though he was, of course, aware that this privacy was severely limited and could indeed be deemed such only by comparison with the endlessly crowded, hectic life he had been leading, without interruption, for many months. Of true physical solitude he could have none at all, now or at any time during this voyage into his past. Navy planes constantly patrolled the sky above him. Navy vessels escorted him: two destroyers and the cruiser USS *Indianapolis,* each possessed of facilities for receiving and transmitting coded wireless messages, plus a Coast Guard cutter having aboard a small White House staff and a Secret Service contingent. By Roosevelt's order these vessels remained as far off *Amberjack II* as the performance of their assigned duties permitted, but they were always visibly *there.* A quarter mile away cruised the *Mary Alice,* a motor-powered thirty-eight-foot ketch (she was a much more comfortable boat than Roosevelt's; with sails set, in rough seas, she hardly rolled at all), on which rode at their ease eight picked members of the White House press corps, including Lindley of the New York *Herald Tribune* and Charles Hurd of the New York *Times,* and from the deck of which a constant, watchful eye was kept, through binoculars, upon the President of the United States. Nearer by cruised a patrol boat bearing a Secret Service detail—a boat that continuously circled the little schooner during its night anchorages.[2]

On the first night the anchorage was in Nantucket Harbor. This was not according to plan. As he sailed into the afternoon, past Naushon and Martha's Vineyard, Roosevelt ran into heavy weather, and though he thoroughly enjoyed the swift hoistings and takings in of sail which the blow demanded, and though he welcomed the opportunity to display his sailing skills before the anxiously watching eyes of his naval guardians (he did so convincingly), he issued no foolhardy challenge to the elements. He turned southward from the planned course. He sought refuge in those safe waters from which the fictional Captain Ahab sailed the *Pequod* in quest of Moby Dick on a Christmas Day in the 1840s and whence in that and preceding years scores of real-life whaling captains sailed in competition with those of New Bedford, the latter including Roosevelt's own great-grandfather Warren Delano.

Messages were delivered to him while he was in that harbor. One was a cablegram from Warburg, concurred in by Sprague and Cox, in London (Cox

had just become chairman of the monetary committee of the economic conference), routed to him through Undersecretary of State Phillips in Washington.
It expressed regrets over the displeasure caused by the earlier Warburg cable
yet went on to repeat, essentially, the proposal Roosevelt had so irritably
rejected three days before, for Warburg inquired whether the President could
agree to a temporary stabilization of the dollar within a range of 10 percent
of $4 to the pound—that is, at some point between $3.80 and $4.20—this ratio
to be maintained "for the life of the conference." Roosevelt felt now more
relaxed than he had for months. All the same he replied to Warburg only
somewhat less irritably than he had before. In a message sent in Navy code
from the destroyer *Ellis* to Washington, thence to London in diplomatic code,
he said it was "still my personal thought that a range with upper and lower
limits is unnecessary," that in any case "the $4 medium point is in my judg-
ment too low," but that "a final medium point of $4.15 with maximum point
of 4.25 and minimum 4.05" might be "worth considering," though "I hesitate
to go even that far. . . ." Also, "We should ascertain whether life of conference
means August 12 or December 12. There is a vast difference."[3]

He remained in Nantucket Harbor that night. In the morning of Tuesday,
June 20, a glorious, golden day with not a cloud overhead and a gentle wind,
he again set sail. And as he headed out into the sound, slanting toward the
elbow of Cape Cod, he was informed that Moley, who was scheduled to sail
for England from New York aboard the *Manhattan* on the morrow, had just
landed at Martha's Vineyard after an early-morning flight in a Navy hydro-
plane from Washington and was requesting permission to consult with him
face-to-face on a matter of "vital importance." Roosevelt may well have been
startled, if not annoyed, by this abrupt, highly dramatic intrusion upon his
recreational activities (it was bound to produce large headlines and much
agitated speculation in the world's newspapers); he seems subsequently privately to have complained that it was not necessary; but he of course promptly
granted the request. He ordered the destroyer *Ellis* to bring Moley up from
the Vineyard. He welcomed his visitor aboard *Amberjack II,* then anchored
off Pollock Light, with every sign of cordiality at ten o'clock. And for two
hours thereafter the two men* engaged in serious if, on Roosevelt's part,
lighthearted and frequently bantering talk.

The matter of "vital importance" turned out to be grave last-minute doubts
raised in Moley's mind concerning the wisdom of his going as presidential
envoy, now or ever, to the World Economic Conference. Senator Byrnes, who
enjoyed a close temperamental rapport with Moley ("I had come to think a
lot of Moley . . ." writes Byrnes in his memoirs[4]), was very sure the trip should
not be made. He had come with Marvin McIntyre to the Carlton last night
to tell Moley so in utmost earnestness. No good and much harm could come

---

*Actually there was present a third man, J. A. Mullen, who was Moley's chief assistant and was
to go with him to London. He was the son of Arthur Mullen, the Democratic national committeeman from Nebraska.

from it. The delegations from other governments would be convinced that the official U.S. delegation had lost, if it had ever possessed, the President's confidence, for they would never believe that this closest, most influential, most publicized of Roosevelt's advisers could have come over as other than spokesman for the presidential mind, as instrument of the presidential will, superseding Hull and the other official U.S. delegates. The same conclusion would be reached by Hull and his colleagues; their morale, already reportedly low, would sink lower still as they were henceforth contemptuously ignored. They would be utterly incapacitated for the service of their government. Nor was this all. Byrnes expressed a friend's concern for Moley's own welfare. The professor's public career would be placed at fatal risk: He would be saddled with public responsibility for events (in Byrnes's opinion they would almost certainly be sad events) over which he had no controlling authority.

All this, or most of it, Moley repeated to Roosevelt, crediting it to Byrnes and McIntyre, as he sat with the President in the morning sun. He did not say flatly that he himself was convinced, absolutely, that he should not go, or even that he absolutely did not want to go. He simply, according to his own later remembrance, "asked to be excused from going" and was gaily refused. "F.D.R. laughed at my fears" and agreed to remove one cause of them by issuing a White House statement to the press down-playing the importance of Moley's mission. He wrote it out upon a scratch pad, saying in part: "Asst. Secretary Moley is sailing tomorrow for London at the request of the President. He will act in a sense as a messenger or liaison officer on this short trip, giving the American delegates first hand information of the various developments . . . in the country since the Delegation left and conveying the President's views of the effect of these developments on the original instructions given the Delegation before they sailed." As regards stabilization, over which Moley was assigned no specific negotiating authority whatever, he said again to Moley that if nothing else could be worked out, he "would consider stabilizing at a middle point of $4.15, with a high and low of $4.25 and $4.05. I'm not crazy about it, but I think I would go that far." At which point Moley handed him a brief memorandum, "essentially an argument against rigid and arbitrary stabilization," written by Herbert Bayard Swope in consultation with Baruch* the day before. Roosevelt, tucking the memorandum in his pocket for future reading, looked then far out across the sea and said: "The essential thing is that you impress on the delegation and the others that my primary international objective is to raise the world price level." He was convinced that "banker-influenced cabinets" in other countries attached "far too much importance . . . to exchange stability," which, though highly desirable, should not be the conference's main concern.[5]

*Swope, at Moley's suggestion, and as a sop to Baruch, who was also to occupy Moley's office in Washington while Moley was away, had been asked by Roosevelt to accompany Moley to London. Swope had begun serving Baruch as public relations man while editor of the New York *World*. It was typical of Baruch as "sure thing" speculator that he should privately associate himself with *opposition* to a proposal aimed to assure "sound money" while simultaneously preaching publicly "sound money" doctrine.

Moley departed. He went to New York City, where that evening Joseph P. Kennedy called upon him in his hotel room. Kennedy, himself disgruntled by Roosevelt's ignoring him since the election (he had rather counted upon becoming secretary of the treasury), emphatically warned the professor to "watch out" because Roosevelt was beginning to resent the prominence given his role by the press. Standing with Swope and Mullen on the *Manhattan*'s deck during the noon hour next day, watching the Statue of Liberty fade into the distance behind him, Raymond Moley was unhappily aware that there were many in high places who did not love him, some of whom awaited his arrival in London; it required a conscious act of will for him to erase a faint suspicion, encouraged by the Kennedy warning, that he was being deliberately "set up" by the President of the United States—either that or given rope in the belief he would probably hang himself.[6]

And this President, in high good humor, having sailed the *Amberjack* around the westward-bending finger of Cape Cod to an anchorage in Province-town Harbor for the night, sailed on the next day (Wednesday, June 21) across Massachusetts Bay to Gloucester, where in the late afternoon, by prior invitation, Colonel House and Lew Douglas came aboard. The colonel came bearing gifts. One was a lengthy letter from a convert to Warren's monetary theories; it argued strongly against even temporary stabilization. Another was a just published book by Sir Basil Blackett entitled *Planned Money;* it argued that national economic planning was essential to a healthy modern economy and that a rationally managed currency, the unit purchasing power of which remained constant "from year to year and decade to decade," was absolutely essential to the success of such planning. Next day the President received reassuring news from London via Phillips in Washington, news that convinced him he had been dead right to reject the Warburg-cabled proposal of tempo-rary stabilization. Warburg and Cox now believed, said Hull, that the conference crisis which had prompted their earlier cable had been "surmounted"; the "American position" was now understood by European representatives, and temporary stabilization was no longer an absolute requirement for continuance of the conference. Warburg warned, however, that there would be another crisis if there were a renewal of violently fluctuating drops in dollar value; he recommended the authorization of "Federal Reserve banks to take such ac-tions to limit fluctuations as may from time to time be desirable and practica-ble."[7]

There followed a couple of days of easy sailing for Roosevelt under sunny skies along the coast of Maine, during which he welcomed the White House correspondents aboard his boat each afternoon for cocktail-enlivened conver-sation (the reporters furnished the liquor) but made no real news. On the third day he had a stormy time of it, running through heavy seas under dark skies from Portland to North Haven Island at the entrance to Penobscot Bay, where at eight in the evening he cast anchor in Pulpit Harbor. He sailed into the weekend among the islands of Penobscot, where he sent a message to Phillips by way of the *Ellis* asking the undersecretary to confer with Baruch, Acheson, and Woodin about possible action to keep the dollar from going much higher than $4.25 to the pound, asking them also to draft another message on this subject for him to transmit to London if they deemed this desirable. He himself doubted that it was, since "the situation seems quieting down so well. . . ."[8] Beyond Penobscot Bay he loafed his way eastward through a sparkling, bright Sunday (June 25) on waters that beat gently but incessantly against the green-crowned cliffs of granite he closely passed. He read and approved, sometime that day, a press statement Moley proposed to issue when the *Manhattan* docked at Plymouth two days hence. It was a statement reiterating that Moley was to "act in a sense as messenger or liaison officer," and it reminded Roosevelt of the unhappy psychological situation which he had encouraged or permitted when he sent Moley across the seas. In transmitting to Phillips his approval of what Moley wished to release, he said: "I am inclined to think that from now on he [Moley] should give out no further statement or talk with press because he is under the Secretary and is not a member of the delegation. The same should apply to Swope. You might suggest this to Moley and inform the Secretary."[9] Some slight worry, in Roosevelt's mind, was indicated by this, but his mood that day was in general as serene as the sky.

And as he sailed on, there drove toward him an automobile bearing his wife and her two close friends, Nancy Cook and Marion Dickerman, who began their journey shortly after dawn, that morning, at Val-Kill Cottage in Hyde Park. They were on their way to Lubec, Maine, whence they would ride the car ferry to Campobello. They were to open the Roosevelt cottage on Campobello and prepare for a large picnic, a characteristically Rooseveltian affair, crowded with visiting dignitaries and island friends, exuberantly informal, to be held on the cottage grounds when the President arrived. A goodly number of island women were to be recruited for these preparations. Some would bake rolls and great pots of beans. Others would cook a huge ham. Yet others would make heaping bowls of potato salad and green salad. And the whole of the enterprise would be organized and directed by Nancy Cook, whose expertise in such matters had been developed and triumphantly demonstrated by numerous big picnics, not a few of them politically important, run by her and hosted by Franklin Roosevelt at Val-Kill. The three women, however, did not intend to make the whole of this long drive in a single day. They were to stop for the night on Mount Desert Island, at the summer home of Eleanor's longtime friend Mary Dreier in Southwest Harbor, only a few hours' sailing time east from Penobscot Bay.

Of his wife's travel plan Roosevelt had, of course, been informed. He put in at Southwest Harbor. She, looking out her upstairs bedroom window when she awoke on Monday morning, saw great activity in the harbor. A Navy cruiser and destroyer stood out in the channel between Mount Desert and the Cranberry Isles; a flotilla of smaller craft was in the harbor itself. And anchored just offshore was *Amberjack II*! The surprise, for her, was great. She had had no notion where her husband might be that day. When she went downstairs to the breakfast table, she found waiting for her three of her sons, James and John and Franklin, Jr., all beautifully tanned by sun and wind, young Franklin clad in the lettered sweater he had won in Groton School sports (he had been senior prefect at Groton that year; he would enter Harvard next fall). After breakfast the whole party went aboard the *Amberjack* for a brief but joyous reunion with the skipper of that craft.[10]

Then the *Amberjack* again set sail.

II

SURELY Eleanor Roosevelt, too, had earned a vacation by the end of the Hundred Days! Her activities had been no less strenuous, her impact on the national consciousness had been hardly less vivid than her husband's, and she had made of her public self, within the limits of its possible development, every bit as great a success as her husband had made of his—and far more of a success than any of her predecessors in the White House had made. In the process she had overcome formidable obstacles. Many of these were circumstantial, but the most difficult were inward, psychological.

She had been more than reluctant to become First Lady, had, in fact, flared up in passionate rebellion against the fate (she identified it with a ruthlessly antifeminist masculinity) which imposed this role upon her. She had so flared up, and most emphatically, in a letter she wrote Nancy Cook while awaiting in Hyde Park the outcome of the Chicago presidential nominating convention.* But she had done so with an only slightly lessened energy of desperation on other occasions and in other communications, oral and written, with her most intimate associates, including Louie Howe.

It was a rebellion having one of its main roots in the unhealing psychic wound inflicted by her discovery of her husband's infidelity with Lucy Mercer a decade and a half ago; it was nourished by the resentments, the aching sense of injustice, the bitter knowledge of personal failure and betrayal and rejection, which still oozed out of that yet-festering wound. But it had also other and deeper roots that were already growing when Lucy Mercer first entered the Roosevelt household and already feeding by that time a rebellion so deep-seated and secret that she herself did not recognize it as such. She knew only that she was not satisfied with herself or with the life she led, that she felt repressed, incomplete, inadequate, victimized. Indeed, though her husband's infidelity was certainly a root cause of her present rebellion, that infidelity could itself have been at least partially caused by, or partially a reaction to, the earlier, older rebellion which it now consequentially augmented.

Had it been?

Eleanor herself must have asked this question of herself in moments of anguished introspection. Certainly her daughter, Anna, asked it, and answered it affirmatively in later years, if not as early as the winter of 1932–1933.

She, Anna, who by the autumn of 1932 was deep in emotional problems of her own, for her marriage to Curtis Dall had been a ghastly mistake, she could

*See Davis, *FDR: The New York Years,* pp. 329–31.

not bear to live with him, her separation from him must end in a divorce whose publicity was bound to be detrimental to her father's public life—Anna ultimately divided her sympathy between her parents in this matter of Lucy, blaming neither, though her sympathy for her mother was different in quality from, and perhaps somewhat less in quantity than, the sympathy she had for her father. For one thing, she could more closely empathize with him than with her, even in such a concern as this, for she more closely resembled him in several ways of temperament and outlook. For another, it must be admitted that though she had learned greatly to love and admire her mother, she had for her father a greater personal respect, a respect having love and admiration at its base but an awareness of danger, a hint of fear, at its heart. Her father did not permit himself to be completely known, ever. He had, for instance, never advertently revealed to her any part of the horrible physical and psychological pain he had suffered, must have suffered during and for a long time after his acute polio attack. Anna could not even imagine his breaking down or out in any tearful personal confession or, indeed, in any that made any strong emotional demand upon his confessor. He was profoundly reticent. Always he kept himself closely to himself; always one had in one's dealings with him a vague but strong sense of knowledge withheld, of possibilities hidden, of secret recesses of being wherein power was held in reserve, tightly leashed by an almost incredible patience and self-control, a potential force which, actualized, would be tremendous and could be terrible. In this, his difference from Eleanor was total.

For part of Eleanor's need to love and be loved was her need to know and be known by other people, certain other people, in a way that made for an intense community of feelings. To this end she continuously ran vital risks, herself at stake, of a kind her husband never ran. She was by no means the extrovert that many believed her to be, of course. (When Washington *Herald* publisher Eleanor "Cissy" Patterson, interviewing Eleanor in the spring of 1933, opined in question form that she was "a complete extrovert," Eleanor made no reply but "just glanced up over her knitting needles with those clever grey eyes of hers," leading Patterson to conclude that Eleanor found the question mildly offensive.[11]) The impression she generally made of utter frankness, utter simplicity of being, or of an extroversion that left nothing hidden away inside her, was a false impression, and quite often deliberately so. Reporters interviewing her on the night of election day were impressed by her "incredible" composure, her "profound calm," though the tide of her rebellious unhappiness then ran at its seething height, as one of the reporters knew. To questions about her "feelings" that night she gave deceiving answers. No, she would not find burdensome the hostessing of White House social functions because "I love people, I love having them in my house," and she would simply entertain socially as she had always done ("I don't think I know what 'functions' are"). No, she would not regret the ending of her New York life because "I'm very much a person of circumstance. I've found I never miss anything after it's gone. The present is enough to deal with."[12] But if she was by no means the simple, open person she seemed in public to be, she certainly did have a self-revelatory honesty to which, among intimates, she gave frequent expression. She had an urgent need, if not an actual compulsion, to tell all, to give herself away completely to those she loved. And she encouraged, though, of course, she very often did not receive, an equivalence of confession on the part of those she loved.

Thus Anna's conclusion that responsibility for the affair of Lucy Mercer was divided equally between her parents, canceling out all blame, was the result of her ruminations of things her mother told her in profoundly revealing talk when she was seventeen and eighteen.[13] One memorable day Eleanor poured out to Anna the whole story of her husband and Lucy, bursting into tears as she did so. Some months later, in another heart-to-heart talk, she confessed to Anna that she had never really enjoyed the sexual act, had in fact found it distasteful, though her manner of saying this caused Anna to doubt that the thing said was truly a "confession" in the sense of being an intended acknowledgment of error or abnormality. It seemed to Anna that her mother, who was then in the opening stage of her long struggle for liberation and self-realization, believed her experience of sex and her attitude toward it to be the normal ones for a woman, that her mother at that time still accepted as true the Victorian notion that women were not supposed to enjoy sex per se, had not been designed by nature (God) to do so, but must submit to it, deriving from it only such satisfaction as came from the performance of duty, because it gave pleasure to their husbands and was necessary for procreation.

Since then, of course, Eleanor had come a long way toward her personal goal of a liberated woman leading an independent creative life—which only increased her dreadful apprehension as she viewed the prospect now before her: She was, she felt, on the verge of losing most or all of that which she had gained so arduously and valued so highly. Louie Howe reminded her that she had felt precisely the same way in 1928, when Franklin was elected governor, yet had experienced, in the event, not a contraction but an expansion of her interests, her activities, her effective influence for good. She was unpersuaded. Would she have succeeded in making a satisfactory life for herself as governor's wife, *could* she have so succeeded, if Albany had not been within easy travel distance of Hyde Park and New York City? She didn't think so. All the personal and material resources of her independent life were in New York. Val-Kill Cottage, Val-Kill Industries, Todhunter School, the Women's Division of the New York Democratic party, the *Women's Democratic News,* which the Women's Division issued, the Women's Trade Union League, the Consumers' League —with all these, and others important to her, her active connections must be severed by her removal to Washington, and so must be, or at least greatly attenuated, her relations with nearly all her closest friends. Nancy Cook, Marion Dickerman, Caroline O'Day, Esther Lape, Earl Miller, among others close to her, would remain in New York. Also, as Eleanor protested to Louis, the role of First Lady of the state was by no means as demanding, as narrowly defined by tradition, as bound up in ritual ceremony as was the role of First

Lady of the nation. Her hopeless dread remained. It darkly flooded into every gap in her fall campaign activity; it packed with gloom her every rare moment of idle solitude as fall gave way to winter.

She made two serious public relations mistakes during the interregnum, both of them products of her rebellious insistence upon continuing, with no concessions to changed circumstance, the journalistic activities she had initiated in earlier years and continued through the governorship. Both were concurred in by her husband and Louis, who approved the undertakings after much family discussion pro and con. And each was characterized by a lack of ethical sensitivity strange in one whose sense of right and wrong was generally more acute and more determinative of personal conduct than it was with most people.

She signed a contract with publisher Bernarr Macfadden to become editor in chief of a new magazine entitled *Babies—Just Babies.* Her labor would be well paid. Also, she would be enabled to give employment to her daughter, as assistant editor, at a time when troubled Anna badly needed occupation and the remuneration of several hundred dollars a month, which this occupation would provide. It was stipulated in the contract and announced to the public that Eleanor's control over the magazine's contents would be total.[14] But, alas, the tasteless vulgarity of several of Macfadden's earlier publishing ventures (notably *True Story* magazine, *True Romances* magazine, and the luridly sensational New York *Daily Graphic*) inevitably attached in the public mind to this new one, the very name of which provoked derisive laughter and ridicule. This ridicule inevitably focused on Eleanor, who was stung by it, and so, using as her excuse an editorial disagreement with Macfadden, she soon exercised her option to withdraw from the enterprise, an act of infanticide on her part, for *Babies—Just Babies* then promptly consequently died.

Her other mistake was no less vulgar. She signed a contract to give radio talks for pay on a national network program series commercially sponsored by a cosmetics firm, a huckstering of the position of First Lady that was but little less reprehensible than Republican Senator (later Vice President) Charles Curtis's notorious advertising endorsement of Lucky Strike cigarettes at the height of the New Era. She was severely censured for it on the editorial pages of leading newspapers and by moralizing public speakers, including ministers of the Gospel, especially after she had said in her first broadcast that the failure of Prohibition imposed upon most girls today the necessity of "learning, very young," how much they could safely partake "of such things as whiskey and gin," and of then "sticking to the proper quantity."[15] This provoked howls of shocked protest from members of the Woman's Christian Temperance Union and other dry organizations. She, whose loathing of alcohol derived from much tragic experience of alcoholism in her native family (her younger brother, Hall, was at that moment threatening to go the way of their drunkard father, their drunkard uncle Vallie Hall), was charged with encouraging drinking by young girls. She was forced onto the defensive. Far from advising girls to drink, said she, who herself drank not at all, she was warning them against the dangers of excessive drinking; her counsel was one of moderation, temperance, self-control. She also let it be known that virtually none of the money earned by her journalism went into her own purse; nearly all of it was donated to worthy causes. But she made no more cosmetics-advertising radio talks; she quietly canceled the radio contract she should not have signed in the first place.

Yet even while she made her mistakes, she offset their bad effects with public relations successes, and these continued in almost unbroken series as inauguration day came and passed. They soon assumed the proportions of triumph. She gained them, moreover, not by any calculated effort to create a favorable impression but simply by being her natural self; which is to say that the motivational root of her overall success was precisely the same as that of her failures, namely, her desperate fear of being crushed into the mold of passive symbolic personage "with nothing to do except stand in line and receive visitors and preside over official dinners,"[16] her stubborn determination to retain all that could possibly be retained of her freedom, her individuality. She insisted upon remaining "plain, ordinary Mrs. Roosevelt" (as she described herself to Lorena Hickok), a woman who had not the slightest impulse toward intimidating grandeur or coercive power but asked only to be allowed to be truly useful, doing work of her own and speaking her own mind for the edification (she was, by natural vocation, a *teacher*) of humankind.

She flatly refused to alter her style of living.

It was a style decidedly *un*stylish.

When she traveled by train between Washington and New York City, or Hyde Park, she rode as an ordinary day-coach passenger, unless she took a late-night train, and she took taxis from the railway station to wherever she was going. It was on the midnight train that she came down from New York to Washington a month before inauguration day to be shown over the White House by Mrs. Hoover and to decide the room assignments and furniture placement for her family when they moved in. Mrs. Hoover had asked by telegram where Mrs. Roosevelt would like to be met by the White House limousine and whether Mrs. Roosevelt wished her military aide to be in uniform or in civilian clothes. Eleanor's reply had been that no White House transportation would be needed and she wanted no military escort, in or out of uniform. Arrived in Washington, she, with Lorena Hickok beside her, took a taxi to the Mayflower, where, to her manifest annoyance, she was assigned the presidential suite. Three hours later she was called for in a State Department car by the department's protocol chief, Warren Robbins, and his wife, come to drive her to the executive mansion since she had refused the presidential limousine. She was again and more greatly annoyed. She was even angry, taking offense because her clearly expressed wish was being contemptuously ignored, her judgment implicitly questioned, her right of choice denied. She firmly declined the proffered ride. The Mayflower was but a couple of blocks from the White House. The weather was fine. She would walk over with Miss Hickok. And she did, overruling Robbins's horrified protests. She walked back to the hotel, too, with the reporter beside her, outlining on the way her plans for the family living quarters on the second floor. It was on that day that the decision was made to transform the oval room, used by "Uncle Ted" and his family as a sitting room, into a "study for Franklin," whose bedroom and bath would be next door.

When she traveled by plane—and she was to become an inveterate air traveler, doing much thereby to overcome the public's fearful doubts about airplane safety—she did so on regularly scheduled commercial flights. Thus in that first spring of the New Deal she made two flights across the continent, to Los Angeles and back, to visit Elliott, who was separating from his wife, was soon to be divorced, and had gone West "to make a new start," vowing he would never again live in the East. (Eleanor was grief-stricken by this simultaneous failure of two of her children's marriages, confessing in a confidential letter that she couldn't "shake the feeling of responsibility for Elliott and Anna." Obviously she had been "a pretty unwise teacher as to how to go about living," and now that it was "[t]oo late to do anything" about it, she was "disgusted" with herself. "I feel soiled. . . ."[17]) The flights, which in that year had to be made in stages of a few hundred miles each, attracted major press attention, all of it favorable to the First Lady. She was "out at every stop, day or night, standing for photographers by the hour, being interviewed, talking over the radio, no sleep," commented Will Rogers in print, though in point of fact she had a remarkable ability to snatch restful catnaps and went often sound asleep for an hour or more in her seat while on trains or planes.* "And yet they say she never showed one sign of weariness or annoyance of any kind. No maid, no secretary—just the First Lady of the land on a paid ticket on a regular passenger flight."[18]

Her insistence upon walking when she went to the White House for the first time as wife of the President-elect was by no means unique. She liked to walk, swinging along on her long legs at a pace so fast that few, male or female, found it easy to keep up with her. When in New York City, if her normally tight time schedule permitted and the distance to be covered was no more than a few blocks, she commonly moved about on foot. She also commonly took the Fifth Avenue bus if she was going very far downtown or up from East Sixty-fifth Street, and someone remarked in the public prints that the hats she wore "looked as though she had rushed in and bought them while her bus waited for the traffic light to change."[19] The remark, significantly, did not offend or annoy her; she thought it "funny." Nor did she give any sign of being at all bothered by other published comment, including some complaint on the part of commercial purveyors of high fashion, about the no-nonsense plainness of her everyday attire. This was a virtual uniform of tweed skirt, white silk blouse, and plain-toed low-heeled shoes. Dressed up, she was likely to wear a formless

---

*During the 1932 campaign, as an AP news story told the world, Eleanor slept through an entire World Series baseball game played in Chicago between the New York Yankees and the Chicago Cubs. It was a game in which Babe Ruth and Lou Gehrig each hit two home runs! She remained upright in her Wrigley Field seat only because she was tightly wedged between her husband and her son James.

flower print, preferably blue, that hung down from her high shoulders as loosely almost as from a clothes hanger, a dress that was as much or as little in style in that year as it had been three years before or would be three years later. The example thus set did no good, certainly, for those whose pocketbooks fattened upon annual changes in women's fashions.

But then plainness would be the hallmark of her public physical image in any case, no matter how fancy her dress, as she said to close associates matter-of-factly, having been accustomed from early childhood to regard herself as hopelessly ugly. She said it in a tone that relegated her "mere" appearance to the realm of the unimportant, though she was a great admirer of physical beauty in others and had made one major concession to appearances and to those who told her (chiefly Earl Miller in this case) what she in her position ought to do. For all its toothiness, her widely smiling face was more attractive, or less unattractive, than was her face in repose, its lips imperfectly closed. She could recognize this fact as well as another. And so she had acquired a public smile. It was by no means as constant as her husband's, but she had learned to switch it on automatically when news photographers focused upon her, the result being that her published image was of a cheerfully self-secure, outgoing personality rather than the tense, withdrawn, unhappy woman she had often appeared in earlier photographs to be. The basic homeliness remained, of course. "My dear," she said, with a shrug, to her most intimate friend of that year, "if you haven't any chin and your front teeth stick out, it's going to show on a camera plate."[20]

Her absolute personal democracy became proverbial. In this she and her husband were alike. They both looked upon people, and related to them, as individual persons, each unique; neither of the two, in a free choice of associates or social guests, paid much heed to categories of high or low, rich or poor, race or religion. And all kinds of people were invited by Eleanor into the White House. Some became dinner guests solely because they had information to impart or attitudes to express which she felt her husband should hear. Many were invited simply out of a personal human concern. These last included, as Joseph P. Lash has written,[21] "the shy, almost speechless parents of a young hitchhiker to whom Eleanor had given a lift in upstate New York and had undertaken to get into a CCC camp. . . ." In this as in other respects the contrast between the Roosevelt and Hoover White Houses could not have been greater. There had raged through the Hoover years a bitter protocol battle between the wife of Speaker of the House Nicholas Longworth (Alice Roosevelt Longworth) and the sister of Vice President Curtis (Dolly Gann), who was her brother's official hostess. All social Washington had been divided on the burning question of which of these two ladies should take precedence at formal White House functions. Eleanor's natural inclination was to pay no attention whatever to protocol, which struck her as ridiculous in itself and outrageous of democractic principles. A considerable effort on the part of her social secretary was required to make her see that protocol *had* to be adhered to at formal state functions and that she ought really to be grateful for it since it prevented far more social hurt than it caused, promoted orderly and efficient procedures, and relieved her of the need to make onerous, even hazardous decisions.

This social secretary was Edith Benham (Mrs. James M.) Helm, daughter of an admiral, widow of an admiral, who had been Mrs. Woodrow Wilson's secretary when Franklin Roosevelt was assistant secretary of the navy and who, within a week after 1933's inauguration day, had become for Eleanor one of an indispensable trio of White House assistants and friends. The other two were Malvina (Tommy) Thompson,* who continued as her personal secretary, and Henrietta Nesbitt, a Hyde Park neighbor whom Eleanor brought down to serve as housekeeper of the White House despite the fact that, as Chief Usher Ike Hoover protested, Mrs. Nesbitt had had no professional training for so difficult, so demanding a job.

It must be admitted that Ike Hoover's initial doubts proved justified to the extent that Mrs. Nesbitt was responsible for the planning and preparation of White House meals. She, of course, did no cooking herself, but the chef operated under her supervision, she "saw to it that the food was prepared her way," and she was herself, writes James Roosevelt, "the worst cook I've ever encountered." Robert E. Sherwood, who dined often with the President in later years, tells of a particularly awful "fancy salad" resembling the "productions one finds in the flossier types of tea shoppe," consisting of "a mountain of mayonnaise, slices of canned pineapple, carved radishes, etc.," a concoction frequently served despite the fact that Roosevelt invariably refused to touch it and had so refused for eight years. The President, who had gourmet tastes, complained again and again about the food he was served and expressed to intimates a wish that Mrs. Nesbitt could be fired.[22] She couldn't be. Strong-willed Eleanor, who herself had little interest in food save as nourishment and to whom the menus were submitted for approval (when she was at home) before going to the chef, was determined to have as housekeeper someone with whom she was altogether at ease and who would remain willingly wholly subordinate to her. This was a requirement of her strategy for maintaining a maximum possible degree of independence, and Mrs. Nesbitt fulfilled it. The housekeeper was also a conscientious woman, unpretentious, industrious, efficient in her work, possessed of a considerable administrative and managerial ability. She could rise to occasions; she could cope with sudden emergencies.

She did so, with Eleanor, on their very first day as White House residents, when 3,000 guests appeared at the inaugural day tea, to which only 1,000 had been invited. Somehow enough sandwiches, cakes, and tea were obtained to serve everybody, after most had been individually greeted by Eleanor.

The publicity given this inaugural tea was the beginning of Eleanor's reputa-

---

*Tommy had by now become Mrs. Frank Scheider, wife of a high school industrial arts teacher, but her husband seems never to have become a very important part of her life, and after her move to Washington, while he stayed in New York, the marriage lapsed toward the quiet divorce in which it ended a few years later.

tion as perhaps the most successful hostess, when measured by standards of human warmth and graciousness, that the White House had ever had. She shattered precedent in ways that helped her husband dispel every last wisp of the gloom, the funereal formality, that had characterized 1600 Pennsylvania Avenue when Herbert Hoover lived there. (Weeks before the inauguration Roosevelt had said to Eleanor's cousin Susie [Mrs. Henry Parish] that he and Eleanor intended to make the White House what it had been "when Uncle Ted was there— . . . gay and homelike."[23]) She refused, for instance, to make ceremonial entrances into rooms in which guests had already assembled, as had been customary for First Ladies, but instead met her guests at the door, welcoming them as family guests to the family home. She paid to each guest as much individual attention as she possibly could, went to whatever length was necessary to thaw out guests (there were a good many) who were initially frozen into a rigid, tongue-tied self-consciousness by their awe in the presence of so much Power and History, was concerned to discover and satisfy any special needs and wishes her overnight guests might have. Her hospitality, her ability to put people at their ease became as proverbial as the personal democracy of which, indeed, it was a part.

Proverbial, too, by the time she made her first airplane flight as First Lady was her seeming utter fearlessness, and a good part of this was also causally related to her profoundly democratic attitudes. "One cannot live in fear," she said to reporters who flocked around her in Ithaca, New York, on the morning after the assassination attempt upon her husband in Miami. Later that same morning, when her husband phoned her from Miami to tell her he had decided she should accept the Secret Service protection legally provided members of a President or President-elect's family, she reacted with indignation. If he "dared" to "do such a thing" as assign a a guard for her, she would "send him [the guard] straight back where he came from." When her husband argued with her about it on the phone, pointing out that he himself had constant Secret Service protection (and what good had it done him down there? she might have asked), her protests became vehement. Of course *he* had to be guarded, "and I'm *so* sorry for you!" But she didn't. "I'm not going to have any Secret Service man following me around," she said flatly. "*I simply will not have it.*" And Roosevelt, who essentially shared her attitude, pressed the matter no further. Others did. Two weeks after the inauguration she was in New York City, where, as it had been announced she would do, she visited the headquarters of the Women's Trade Union League, of which she had become an associate member in 1922 and of which her longtime friend Rose Schneiderman remained the active head. She found four policemen waiting for her outside the headquarters building, placed there, they said, for her protection. She asked them to go away. When they refused, saying they were under their captain's orders, she telephoned Louie Howe, who in turn called the captain. The latter came at once to the headquarters building, tried in vain to persuade her of her need of a guard detail, and then, reluctantly, retired with his men. The American people, said she to the reporters gathered there were "wonderful" and "I simply can't imagine being afraid to go among them as I have always done, as I always will."[24]

In Washington a day or so later, unguarded, she toured the nauseating, crime-infested, disease-stricken back-alley slums into which much of the capital's black population was crowded. She drove her own roadster, its top down, through these alleys, stopping now and again to inspect on foot, and to talk to the people who lived there. With her was an eighty-one-year-old member of Washington's social elite, Mrs. Archibald Hopkins, who for decades had crusaded for passage of a truly effective local slum clearance bill, one that would provide decent housing to replace the hovels that lined mile after mile of back street, and who now hoped to persuade Eleanor to emulate the first Mrs. Woodrow Wilson in this concern.* She succeeded to the extent that Eleanor, having expressed to reporters the shock and horror she felt at what she had just seen and heard, made it clear, without precisely saying so, that she favored passage through Congress of the bill which Mrs. Hopkins and her group were sponsoring—this despite her oft-repeated pledge *not* to make public comment on any specific piece of pending legislation.[25] Soon it was everywhere known that Mrs. Roosevelt might turn up anywhere, even deep in a coal mine, as a famous *New Yorker* cartoon suggested, to talk with common folk about their interests and problems, that she would often come by herself, and that she would *never* come with Secret Service or police protection. Already mentioned† has been the mid-May visit she made to the bonus army encampment at Fort Hunt. She walked then alone and unafraid among thousands of poor and desperate men whose sense of social injustice and proneness to violent correctives were being encouraged by the Communist agitators, few but well organized, among them, and the effects were not only that defusing of an explosive situation, which was Howe's purpose in arranging the visit, but also a personal public relations triumph for Eleanor of the largest proportions.

The impression made on this occasion was in its nature of a piece with that made upon reporters and through them upon the general public by her weekly press conferences: an impression of selflessness, of human sympathy and moral goodness and total honesty, joined with political shrewdness and a very considerable intellectual sophistication.

The holding of press conferences was wholly unprecedented for a First Lady. Eleanor herself had grave doubts about attempting them when Lorena Hickok suggested that she do so. She was in part persuaded by the argument that by meeting with women reporters and *only* women reporters on a weekly basis she would encourage the hiring of more women journalists by newspapers

---

*Ellen Axson Wilson, lying on her deathbed in the White House in August 1914, was told by Joe Tumulty, just before she sank into the final coma, that the Washington back-alley slum clearance bill which she was personally sponsoring had just been assured of passage through Congress. See Kenneth S. Davis, *FDR: The Beckoning of Destiny*, pp. 381–82.

†See pp. 78–79.

and magazines. She was finally persuaded when both her husband and Howe enthusiastically endorsed the Hickok suggestion. Her press conferences, which were to continue for as long as she lived in the White House, were a success. She announced at the outset that she would make no comments and answer no questions about current political issues, yet from the first she expressed personal opinions on matters out of which political issues must inevitably arise: the necessity for better housing of the poor; the iniquity of sweatshops; the wickedness of child labor; the foolishness and immorality of an isolationist foreign policy. She waxed vehement on the latter subject in a late-April press conference, when she was questioned about the series of dinners for foreign dignitaries over which she was presiding as White House hostess. Her husband's almost daily avowals during those weeks of his commitment to international cooperation in general, and to the purposes of the London and Geneva conferences in particular, justified her restatement of the internationalism to which she had been unwaveringly committed from the moment Woodrow Wilson unveiled the Covenant of the League of Nations in February 1919. "We ought to realize what the people are up against in Europe," she said, and went on to deplore the refusal of the United States to accept the role of leadership in world affairs that had been thrust upon it at the close of the Great War. This country had then been, and it yet remained, in "an ideal position to lead . . . because we have suffered less." But "[o]nly a few years are left to work in. Everywhere over there is the dread of this war which may come."[26]

By the end of the Hundred Days Eleanor Roosevelt was everywhere recognized, and was by a large majority of Americans greatly admired, as a potent influence within the New Deal, operating toward civic and social reforms: an ardent feminist who fought for the liberty and justice of all now discriminated against, not just for women's rights; a political liberal whose personal example did much to define the difference between liberal and conservative as essentially that between generosity (a primary concern for the general good) and selfishness (a primary concern for one's own private gain). She was, it was generally agreed, the most remarkable First Lady the nation had ever known.

III

A secret life nourished her public one, providing the emotional stability, the surcease from mental anguish which, during these crucial transitional months, was necessary for the maintenance of the public self.

We have remarked the rare sensibility whereby Lorena Hickok, alone among the reporters assigned to cover the candidate's wife, perceived Eleanor's profound unhappiness on the day Franklin Roosevelt won the presidential nomination. We have remarked the unexpectedness of such sensibility in a woman of so gross an appearance, so tough a manner (though Lorena, who had fine expressive blue eyes, could when she chose be charming of manner), have told how, during the election campaign, a rapport was established between the reporter and Eleanor when the latter learned, through Tommy Thompson, something of the horror of Lorena's childhood.* The growth of this rapport toward what had become by election day an intimate friendship was encouraged by the preference Hickok gained when, at some expense of strict journalistic ethics, she promised Howe early in the campaign that she would submit none of her important copy about the candidate's wife to the Associated Press without first showing it to him. This assured her of exclusive interviews. These in turn opened the way to personal contacts far closer, more intimate than the AP assignment required, so close, indeed, and so intimate as to constitute at last a wedge of contradiction driven hard between Hickok the reporter and Lorena the person.

For instance, on October 12, 1932, her forty-eighth birthday, Eleanor in exclusive interview made a cryptic remark that was of little value to Hickok the reporter (". . . it didn't make particularly good newspaper copy") but was intensely interesting to Lorena the woman (". . . I thought a good deal about it afterward"). Said Eleanor: "I'm a middle-aged woman, It's good to be middle-aged. Things don't matter so much. You don't take it so hard when things happen to you that you don't like." The remark raised, it was perhaps intended to invite, questions of a personal nature. Lorena longed to ask them but didn't quite dare, for at that time the friendship between the two women was yet in its developmental stage.

A clue to the answers was given, however, and a long step toward the final intimacy was taken a few days later.

Missy LeHand's mother died at her home in Potsdam, in far northern New York. Lorena, to her surprise, was invited to accompany Eleanor and Missy to Potsdam, where the funeral was held, an invitation given her, obviously, not as reporter but as friend. She returned to New York City with Eleanor (Missy remained in Potsdam for a few days) on a train so crowded that every Pullman berth on it was taken; they perforce shared the only available sleeping space, a drawing room. And while the train ran southward through red evening light across a landscape flaming with October foliage, then roared on into a darkness of frosty night, the two women had their first heart-to-heart talk. By the time she went to bed Lorena, who was now "Hick" in Eleanor's nomenclature, as she was in all others', had been told of Eleanor's unhappy childhood, its centerpiece the alcoholism and tragic death of a beloved father, and of the miseries of Eleanor's love-starved girlhood amid the glooms of Oak Terrace at Tivoli and of the Hall town house in New York City. She had been given, too, more than an inkling of the emotional estrangement of Eleanor from her husband, of the lack of marital relationship between the two. And finally, perhaps in sympathetic response to revealing confidences of her own, and certainly as a sign and seal of faith in her loyal friendship, her discretionary judgment, she was given permission to write whatever she felt should be published of what she had just heard.

*See Davis, *FDR: The New York Years 1928–1933*, pp. 331–32, 374.

"I trust you," said Eleanor softly.[27]

From that moment on the two women—each of ardent, passionate nature, each strong-willed and highly intelligent, each possessed of enormous physical vitality (though Lorena tended to dissipate hers through excessive indulgences in cigarettes and food, as ascetic Eleanor emphatically did not), each remarkably sensitive and responsive to the moods and especially the pain of others (if Eleanor was the more self-sacrificial of the two, she was but slightly so), each deeply injured by past experience of masculine sexuality, yet each forever longing to give and receive a totality of personal commitment, suffering in consequence a sense of rejection and deprivation, since the emotional demand was greater than others could supply—were as powerfully drawn to each other as particles of opposite electrical charge. They needed each other, desperately.

For both the experience was unprecedented in its overall intensity and in the depth and spread of its significance. If Eleanor had been attracted in somewhat the same way to Nancy Cook—tense, tough-talking, chain-smoking Nancy, with her mannish haircut and mannish clothes and amazing manual skills—it was less strongly, with less awareness of the nature of the attraction and perhaps with less responsiveness on the part of Cook, who, after all, had formed her lifelong attachment to Marion Dickerman years before she met Eleanor. The "E.M.N." of Val-Kill had been and remained a friendship of rare intimacy, had been a working partnership of rare creativity, but it had never been an actual fused unity of three-as-one; always it had remained a linkage of two distinct primary elements, "E" and "M-N"; and Eleanor had never derived from it the kind of emotional fulfillment she was beginning to derive from her relationship with Hick.

As for Hick . . .

In Minneapolis, where she became a star reporter on that city's *Tribune,* she had lived for several years with a pale, plain, slender, rather excessively feminine girl, heiress to a large fortune, who was very "literary" (she wrote poetry, unpublished) and who had seemed wholly to reciprocate Hick's devotion until, one day, shortly after the two had moved to San Francisco, she abruptly severed the connection. She eloped with a man; she married that man in Yuma, Arizona. Hick, who had had no warning, was utterly devastated. She fled San Francisco. She came to New York City and, with an aching void at the center of her life, became for a few months a by-lined "sob sister" on Hearst's sensational tabloid *Daily Mirror* before switching to the Associated Press, thus launching the big-time career that had brought her now, aged thirty-nine, near the top of her profession. After a while the void had become just that, an emptiness, a "well of loneliness" with but a floating vestige in it of specific yearning for the lost girl; now and again even this vestige had been briefly drowned as the well was temporarily filled by secret desperate encounters. For in the immediate aftermath of what she could not but deem a betrayal of her, she frankly "said to herself, what the hell?" She had this "tendency"; she had opportunities to "surrender" to it without scandal amid the vast indifferent anonymity of the metropolis. And so she did. She "went off the deep end about various women."[28]

None of these, however, or the girl in Minneapolis was a match for Eleanor Roosevelt by any measure of personal force, intelligence, strength of character, general ability, or capacity to give and receive love. *All* the pain in Hick's memory of her first love could not but have been erased, the memory itself rendered pale and relatively insignificant, by the onrush of this new relationship.

During the interregnum the two women were constantly together. Often, astonishingly so in view of Eleanor's crowded schedule and the public attention focused on her daily activities, they were alone in utter privacy.

It was a privacy Eleanor defended, on occasion, with stubborn, angry determination.

Thus, on a Sunday afternoon soon after the election, instead of the evening train she usually took, she rode an afternoon train down from Albany to New York City, where she was to meet her Todhunter School class next morning. She did so because she was to dine alone with Hick that evening, in Hick's apartment a few doors east of the Beekman Tower Hotel. A reporter, a girl reporter, newly assigned by a press service competitive with the AP, lay in wait at the Albany station. Eleanor brushed her off. The girl was incredibly persistent; she boarded the same train as Eleanor and, arrived at Grand Central, accosted Eleanor again, wanting to know the latter's plans for the evening. When Eleanor said she was dining with a friend, the girl asked the name of the friend. Eleanor flatly refused to give it; the engagement was "purely private and personal," and there would be no story. Still, the girl persisted, asking if she might follow and wait outside the dining place. Eleanor grew furious. "I will *not* be followed," she said, "by you or anyone else—and if you don't go away and leave me alone we'll both spend the whole evening right here in Grand Central!" Thereupon the girl at last gave up.

Eleanor was still angry when she arrived at Hick's.

"But why didn't you just tell her where you were going?" asked Hick. "She'd probably have been satisfied and gone away."

"I was afraid it might embarrass you," said Eleanor.[29]

The two were often together in Eleanor's third-floor sitting room at 49 East Sixty-fifth, where Hick became a frequent guest at meals. They attended plays together, and concerts. (It was following an evening of Wagner that one door to greater intimacy was opened between them, for Eleanor manifested awe at the capacity to feel, to care deeply, which Hick normally hid behind a façade of toughness but revealed under the spell of music—awe and a kind of yearning admiration, expressive of need. Hick, who had a beautiful contralto singing voice, was passionately fond of music as Eleanor could never be.) They ate often alone together in out-of-the-way restaurants that had become favorites of Hick's. On the evening of the Miami attempt on Roosevelt's life they dined in a little Armenian restaurant, far downtown, going afterward to the Warner Club, where Eleanor made her brief talk to a group of motion-picture executives, and the two women were with Louis Howe in the East Sixty-fifth Street house when Roosevelt's reassuring phone call to Eleanor came through, at last, from Florida. Within an hour thereafter Hick and Eleanor boarded the night train for Ithaca, where Eleanor made her speech to the Farm and Home Week crowd at Cornell next day.

They stayed over the night of February 16 in Ithaca.

And there is evidence that that night in Ithaca, in the aftermath of the emotional shock of the incident in Miami, was of climactic or culminating importance to the relationship between Eleanor and Hick. A ring, a symbolic ring, was given. Hick had worn it for seventeen years, ever since it had been impulsively pressed upon her as a gift by Madame Ernestine Schumann-Heink in grateful appreciation of a heartwarming story which Hick, then a Milwaukee *Sentinel* reporter, had written about that great singer. It was a beautiful ring, and expensive, a large brilliant sapphire surrounded by diamond chips. Eleanor was wearing it when the two returned to New York City next day.[30]

Thereafter the contradiction between Hick's professional commitment to the AP and her personal commitment to Eleanor was increasingly sharp and troublesome. On the weekend immediately following their return from Ithaca, for instance, Eleanor and Hick drove together in Eleanor's roadster, with Eleanor at the wheel, to Groton School, to visit the Roosevelt sons there. On the day before the trip began, which was very early on Saturday morning, Hick somewhat defiantly informed her office that she would file no story about it because Mrs. Roosevelt did not want one. "No one except members of the family knows I am going with her," said Hick's office memo. ". . . I believe the understanding is that I don't have to put out anything unless a really good story breaks. About the only really good stories I can think of are: an automobile accident, attempted kidnapping of her, or something of that sort: or a folo [follow-up] from her should anything happen to the Governor or any member of the family." In such case, of course, she "would be in a position to get a good clean beat. She understands that, if anything of the sort happened, I would . . . have to get on it." Since the two would be staying together at the school and "[n]o reporters are allowed at the school, she is not telling them I am a reporter." The office, therefore, would be well advised "not . . . to try to reach me unless it is vitally important."[31]

Often, however, she could not assuage her increasingly troubled conscience by any such frank prior disclosure to her bureau chief. She was, as a matter of fact, in continuous possession of confidential information which she had to regard as privileged but which her office would have regarded, she knew, as legitimate news of large value, news the AP had every right to demand that she deliver.

On what Eleanor bitterly described as her "last night out of captivity," Wednesday, March 1, 1933, she dined alone with Hick in the latter's apartment. Twenty-four hours later Hick was a passenger on the Roosevelt special train which pulled through rainy, chilly darkness into Washington's Union Station.

Into her care had been confided Eleanor's pet Scottish terrier, Meggie,* and
when she delivered the dog to Eleanor just before the train came to a stop, she
and Eleanor had a brief, soft-voiced conversation. Eleanor said that there was
"something I'd like to show you . . . something that used to mean a very great
deal to me when we [the Franklin Roosevelts] were in Washington before,"
and that she would do so if Hick would pick her up in a taxi at a side entrance
of the Mayflower shortly after eight o'clock next morning.

Hick did so, of course.

Eleanor was out of the hotel and into the taxi almost before the cab came
to a stop. She directed the driver to go, first, out along R Street past the house
where she had suffered the trauma of Lucy Mercer, then far out (a long drive)
to Rock Creek Cemetery. There, while the cab waited, Eleanor led Hick to a
seat on a curved stone bench before the famous statue, "Grief," executed by
Augustus Saint Gaudens on commission from his great friend Henry Adams
as a memorial to Adams's wife, dead by her own hand. It is a larger-than-life
bronze figure of a seated woman clad in long flowing robes, her face hooded,
and Hick, gazing upon it through long moments of silence, with Eleanor beside
her, "felt that all the sorrow humanity had ever had to endure was expressed
in that face," along with "something almost triumphant," as if this woman
"had experienced every kind of pain, every kind of suffering . . . and had come
out of it serene—and compassionate."

Eleanor felt the same way.

"In the old days, when we lived here, I was much younger and not so very
wise," she said in a soft, remote voice, as if talking to herself. "Sometimes I'd
feel very unhappy and sorry for myself. When I was feeling that way, if I could
manage it, I'd come out here, alone, and sit and look at that woman. And I'd
always come away somehow feeling better. And stronger."[32]

Two days later, on the afternoon of inauguration day, Hick functioned as
reporter for the last time in her relationship with Eleanor, being granted the
exclusive White House interview already quoted.† Thenceforward Eleanor
was covered for the AP by Bess Furman of the Washington bureau. On the
evening of Sunday, March 5, Hick returned to her AP assignment in New York
City.

But the two women remained in close communication through daily phone
calls, daily letters, with Eleanor's first one written on White House stationery
only a few hours after she had kissed Hick good-bye. "Hick, my dearest," it
began, "I cannot go to bed tonight without a word to you. I felt a little as
though a part of me was leaving tonight, you have grown so much to be a part
of my life. . . . These are strange days & very odd to me but I'll . . . try to plan
pleasant things & count the days between our times together!" There followed,

*The highly temperamental, jealous Meggie was destined to be banished to Hyde Park after only
a few weeks in the White House because of her distressing tendency to nip important people
angrily. The climactic episode was her biting of AP reporter Bess Furman on the lip.
†See pp. 37–38.

as would become customary in these letters, notations for the diary she had promised Hick she would keep from now on, notations of a kind that would become famous in later years, when Eleanor contributed to a national newspaper syndicate a column entitled "My Day." Then: "Oh! darling, I hope on the whole you will be happier for my friendship. I felt I had brought you so much discomfort & hardship today & almost more heartache than you could bear. . . ." On Tuesday, March 7, Hick's fortieth birthday, Eleanor wrote: "Hick, darling. All day long I've thought of you & another birthday I *will* be with you." On the afternoon of that day she had attended a concert where, she said, "I thought only of you. . . . Oh! I want to put my arms around you, I ache to hold you close. Your ring is a great comfort. I look at it & think she does love me or I would not be wearing it!" Clearly, these letters were not so much written as gushed onto paper, a torrent of feeling somewhat diluted by items of factual information but hardly ever by a concept or analysis, and they were very long, often covering a half dozen pages or more with Eleanor's hasty and, for most people, almost indecipherable scrawl. They manifested, certainly, a marvelous energy, being produced late at night, frequently after midnight, following jam-packed days crowned by hours of labor, with Tommy Thompson, over her daily correspondence, which was huge. "My pictures are nearly all up & I have you in my sitting room where I can look at you most of my waking hours!" she wrote to Hick on the night of March 9. "I can't kiss you so I kiss your picture good night and good morning!" She noted "one more day marked off" the time separating them from their next meeting, for she was to come to New York during the following week. "My dear, if you meet me may I forget there are other people present or must I behave? I shall want to hug you to death! I can hardly wait."[33]

Hick, too, had a calendar. Mounted on her bedroom wall, it became a record of her meetings with Eleanor and of whether the meeting had been wholly happy or flawed by something, for she circled the dates when they were together and crossed out with black X's the dates of separation, sometimes both circling and X-ing a date to indicate that they had been together but that the meeting had not been altogether satisfactory. She, too, wrote lengthy nightly letters.

Even before the inauguration they had begun to plan for a vacation trip together, just the two of them, sometime during the summer. By the time Eleanor departed on her flying trip to the West Coast these plans were firm. Hick would not accompany Eleanor to Campobello to greet Roosevelt at the end of the sailing cruise he wanted to make once the special session of Congress had ended. Eleanor had asked her to, but when Hick learned that Nancy Cook and Marion Dickerman were also going, she promptly, flatly declined. Predictably, Hick and the "Val-Kill ladies," as she derisively called them, had loathed one another on sight; after a weekend at Val-Kill Cottage, during which she felt she had been continuously snubbed and patronized, she vowed never again to permit herself to be put in a position where such insult from them was possible. So it had been arranged that their vacation together, hers and Eleanor's, would not begin until after Eleanor had returned from Campobello. They would then have three weeks alone together, on a motor trip north to Quebec and then around the Gaspé Peninsula, spending their nights in out-of-the-way places, often in private homes that took in tourists, and stopping off for a few days on Campobello, at the Roosevelt cottage there, on the way home. The very idea of such a trip was horrifying, of course, to Secret Service men, but since the President tolerantly, smilingly permitted it, there was nothing they could do to prevent it. They had already insisted that the gallivanting First Lady be armed with a pistol; they had presented her with one and a license to carry it. But she seldom did. She would not take it on this upcoming expedition to Canada.

By that time, too, Hick had finally arranged her resignation, to be effective at the end of June, from the Associated Press. She had done so with considerable anguish of spirit, for she loved newspaper journalism and was very proud of having become just about the "top gal reporter in the country." But she had been forced to face the fact that her relationship with Eleanor, so long as she continued to accept an AP salary, involved her in a fundamental integrity-shredding conflict of loyalties. She had talked about it with Louis Howe one day, she remembered nearly three decades later, but "he did not give me any comfort. 'A reporter,' he commented drily, 'should never get too close to the news source.' "[34]

It was with Howe's help, however, after Eleanor had suggested it, that Hick obtained employment as a confidential field investigator for Harry Hopkins in his capacity as head of the Federal Emergency Relief Administration. She was "to travel about the country, watching what was happening to people on relief —physically, mentally, and emotionally."[35] She was also to observe the operations of local relief administrators, the human effects of FERA policies. And she was to report what she saw and heard, and felt about what she saw and heard, in lengthy memorandums addressed to Hopkins personally, exclusively. It was a job for which she was uniquely qualified by her natural talent for vivid accurate descriptive writing, by her empathic compassion for human beings down on their luck, and, of course, by her long professional training as news reporter. It was also a job that would prove of some historical importance insofar as it produced one of the most perceptive of all eyewitness accounts of the depression as a human experience, an account influential to some indeterminate degree of New Deal relief policy, for Hopkins paid close attention to the reports and passed them on to Roosevelt, who sometimes read portions of them aloud at cabinet meetings.

Hick was to go on the FERA payroll at the end of July.

IV

ROOSEVELT'S run of generally good luck with the weather on his cruise was ended a few hours after *Amberjack II* had sailed out of Southwest Harbor on the morning of Monday, June 26. Fog closed in. The whole coast of Maine was blanketed by it. The *Amberjack* dropped anchor off Roque Island in Lakeman Bay. She remained there, fogbound in a spot as remote as it was dreary, for three nights and two days. Roosevelt, isolated thus in a narrow room whose walls of mist muffled all sound and denied all distant sight, had ample time in which to read or reread the two memorandums Moley and House had given him, to skim through Blackett's book *Planned Money,* and, for probably the first time, to ponder deeply the dilemma in which he found himself (had placed himself) with regard to the World Monetary and Economic Conference.

As for the news from that conference, it now turned as dismal as the Maine coast weather.

On Tuesday, June 27, the dollar price of the pound reached $4.30, well above the point at which, according to the Roosevelt message to Warburg of ten days before, unilateral action to stabilize might be taken by the United States. The "exchange situation" was "getting out of hand and [there was] increasing possibility that other countries now on gold would be forced to abandon gold, which would have the effect of putting the dollar up in relation to these countries," said a message to Roosevelt from Undersecretary of the Treasury Acheson, who spoke not only for himself but for Baruch, Lew Douglas, and the now-returned George Harrison ("Secretary Woodin," said Acheson, "is now ill in New York"). Confirmative of this was a message from Hull in London: The French, the Dutch, the Italians, the Swiss, the Belgians were wailing in panicky chorus that they might be forced off gold, France perhaps as early as next week, unless the United States acted at once to bolster the dollar and halt the frenzy of monetary exchange speculation. But it was not unilateral action that the advisory group, speaking through Acheson, recommended. Such action, consisting of the "purchase of dollars by export of gold," would mean a steady and possibly disastrous drain of U.S. gold reserves if the French and British did not act simultaneously "to keep the pound or franc up." Hence the group's "present thought . . . is that it would be better to work along the lines of the loose temporary tripartite agreement" with Britain and France. This would be "much safer now than two weeks ago" because of "increasing strength in commodity and security market."[36] For the dollar devaluation was indeed having its intended effect upon domestic prices: The rise that day of American commodity and stock prices was steep, and wheat, which had been as low as 30 cents a bushel a few months ago, went above $1.

Roosevelt also received the same day excerpted newspaper reports of Hull's gloomy, wrathful, doomful mood as he awaited Moley's imminent arrival in London. Though the secretary of state publicly denied that he had ever considered resignation, there were renewed rumors that he was about to resign and even that he had already prepared his resignation statement. These rumors were increasingly plausible. There could be no doubt that he had been repeatedly hurt, angered, disappointed, humiliated during the four weeks since he embarked for England, it was an open secret that he bitterly regretted having given up his U.S. Senate seat for a cabinet post that had come to seem more and more like a whipping post, and one newspaper correspondent reported that the secretary's hatred of Moley had become "psychopathic." Obviously an explosive psychological situation had developed within the American delegation in London, and it remained to be seen if Moley would or could defuse it.

Next day the London news was no better; if anything, it was worse. While American commodity and stock prices continued to rise, the dollar value of the pound reached a high of $4.43 on a violently fluctuating exchange, closing at $4.37½ (the 100-cent dollar of early April was now worth 77.3 cents), provoking yet louder wails of anguish from the gold bloc countries. The leaders of these last, who had pressed hard for stabilization at around $4 just two weeks ago, were now willing, were even desperately eager to settle for far less, as Moley was about to discover.

For it was upon Raymond Moley that all attention was now focused.

Upon landing in Plymouth, the professor had issued his self-deprecating press statement, but he had not been content with that. Instead of following Roosevelt's suggestion that he thenceforth avoid all meetings with the press, he had presented himself on his first day in London (Wednesday) before a huge press conference, with Hull at his side, and there made a great display of personal humility and subordination, repeatedly referring to Hull as "my chief," telling Hull before the assemblage how pleased the President was with his performance, and reiterating that he himself came here as mere messenger and liaison. The ostentatiousness of this display emphasized the spuriousness of the thing displayed; the news conference, while doing nothing to reduce the public's estimate of the professor's importance, did much to make the professor's public image more attractive. Thus the New York *Times* would report that "of the day's incidents the . . . debut of Professor Moley was the most interesting and provocative of most comment, all favorable to the newcomer." The United Press dispatch would say that "Moley deflated himself . . . completely, willingly, heartily . . . [and] made his act of deflation short and sharp and unmistakable . . . with the sure skill and efficiency of a great surgeon."[37] Surely Hull, if he did not already feel that he had been insultingly condescended to and patronized by the professor, would feel so very soon, for everyone in London continued to assume that Moley came armed with a negotiating authority greater than that of the official delegation. There was not the slightest diminution of the eagerness, the anxiety even, with which the British prime minister and the heads of other delegations sought conference with the special emissary while virtually ignoring the secretary of state.

In the afternoon of that Wednesday, June 28, Norman H. Davis aboard the destroyer *Bernardou* (the *Ellis*'s companion vessel) came through the fog on Lakeman Bay to the anchored *Amberjack*, ostensibly to report to the President on latest developments of the Geneva Disarmament Conference, from which Davis had just returned. He sat for a couple of hours with Roosevelt in the little schooner's cabin before going back aboard the destroyer, which would take him on to Campobello. What the two talked about remained unpublicized, but Davis, according to Louis Howe, was urgently pressing for a stabilization agreement, and it seems unlikely that this subject went entirely unmentioned. After Davis had left, Roosevelt wrote out an answer to Hull's message of the day before, manifesting in it his refusal to be frightened into stabilization by this latest threat, for so he viewed it, of the gold bloc countries. He was inclined to doubt that France would remain long on gold in any case, and "I do not greatly fear setback to our domestic price level restoration even if all these nations go off gold." Neither did he believe that their going off would greatly affect for better or worse an "ultimate permanent settlement" of international economic problems. The U.S. delegation, he concluded, should continue to reject all international stabilization proposals.

To Phillips, in his cover message to this one to Hull, Roosevelt said, significantly: "I suggest that special care be taken by delegation and Moley and those close to it to insure no publicity of any kind except through Secretary Hull."[38] But he also asked Phillips to show the draft instructions to Acheson and Baruch in Washington and to send them on at once *if* these advisers expressed "no serious disagreement." They did express disagreement. Moreover, they had been informed that Moley was at that moment at work with Sprague and others in London on a stabilization proposal along the lines Roosevelt had laid down in his June 17 and June 24 messages to Warburg. In consequence, these June 28 instructions, which might conceivably have warned Moley away from negotiations he had no clear authority to engage in, were never transmitted to London!

The next morning, Thursday, June 29, dawned as dismally off Roque Island as the preceding two had done. This was too much even for Roosevelt's vast patience. At breakfast in the *Amberjack* cabin he announced that he would remain immobilized here no longer. Fog or no fog, he would sail within the hour, and at eight-thirty he did so, seated at the wheel in the open cockpit under loosely filling sails, steering slowly, cautiously eastward, thereafter, into Englishman Bay. For hours his large, skilled, sensitive hands gripped the wheel spokes, his eyes strained to discern shapes of danger through swirling mists, while his craft headed inexorably toward narrow passages the hazards of which were increased by the ebb and flow of huge tides.

Vivid in his mind were memories of his last voyage through these treacherous waters, when his landing had been made in a fog as thick as this one—a gloom premonitory, as it seemed, of the malignant fate awaiting him.

Happily different was his landing this time.

For as the schooner, after hours of slow, blind running, arrived off Quoddy Head, turning there due north toward the Lubec Narrows, the curtain of fog was abruptly lifted, as if by the hand of God. It was in golden sunlight under a sky of brightest blue that Roosevelt sailed through Quoddy Bay and waved his acknowledgment of the cheers of thousands assembled along the shore at Eastport. In golden sunlight he sailed into Friar Bay, where the USS *Indianapolis* gave him a twenty-one-gun salute while he was circled by a parade of Canadian and American yachts. At Welshpool he moved in golden light from boat to land, he having not been on land for eleven days, and it was in a spotlight of gold that he stood on steel-braced legs, the sun slanting down through a gap in the foliage above him, while he briefly, informally addressed the islanders who had gathered (virtually every man, woman, and child on Campobello was present) to greet him, on the lawn of the yacht club.

Surely, if the darkness attending his last landing here was an evil omen, this present brightness following prolonged gloom must be a good one. So, at least, Roosevelt himself, who habitually inferred providential admonitory significances from chance events, might believe. He might even see it as a sign of God's blessing upon the difficult decision he had at last made regarding stabilization, finally, definitely, and must soon announce to the world.

He did so the very next day.

The big picnic for about a hundred guests was held on the seashore below the Roosevelt cottage in the early morning of Friday, June 30. Just as Roosevelt was about to go down to it, McIntyre came to him from the *Indianapolis* to say that a long, "extraordinarily important cable from Moley" (so it was described in a radiogram from Steve Early in Washington) was about to be forwarded from the State Department in diplomatic code (a State Department code clerk was now aboard the *Indianapolis* to decode messages). After the picnic, but before the cable had come in, Roosevelt invited the four correspondents from the *Mary Alice* to come up to the house, where, after desultory conversation and a few hands of cut-in bridge, he "pushed back his chair and said, 'I think it might be more interesting just to talk for awhile,' " as Hurd of the New York *Times* remembered three decades later.

He talked then for more than an hour about the problems of the London Conference.

No doubt he was influenced somewhat, Louis Howe was influenced greatly, by the fact that mere hints that a stabilization agreement might be in the offing had substantially strengthened the dollar that day. The price of the pound had fallen from over $4.40 to $4.25, and with it had fallen the prices of American commodities and securities. At any rate, Roosevelt manifested anger at attempts of leading European nations to trick the United States into a monetary agreement that would give them a market advantage over this country. He made it clear that the attempts had failed: The United States would *not* "at this time" subscribe either to a stabilization agreement or to any tariff arrangement that would hamper New Deal domestic programs or "allow the dumping of products by any cheap producer on American markets."

The reporters soon realized there was nothing casual or inadvertent about this session with them. It was a press conference. The President wanted the gist of what he said to be published, but without direct attribution and in such a way as to permit him to back off from it if that proved advisable. The canny, wary reporters, their professional reputations at stake, were reluctant to oblige him. There was an impasse. Why couldn't they do the story as a "think piece"? Roosevelt asked. "If you were to discuss this among yourselves might you not reach the same conclusion?" They might, answered the reporters, but their conclusion would not be news: "No one cares one whit what *we* think."

Roosevelt was at last compelled to indicate that his repudiation of their reports of what they had heard was highly unlikely. "Isn't a Campobello dateline a pretty good hedge?" he asked. Thereupon one of the reporters intoned the "Thank you, Mr. President!" which traditionally ended press conferences, and all of them departed in high excitement for the *Mary Alice,* there to write stories informing the world, tomorrow morning, that "President Roosevelt will not obligate the United States at this time to any form of stabilization of the dollar," this having been learned from the "highest authority" on Campobello Island.[39]

There was unpleasantness at the Roosevelt cottage dinner table that Friday evening.

On the night before, in the living room after dinner, Eleanor, in the presence of Howe and Morgenthau and Missy LeHand, also of Marion Dickerman and Nancy Cook, had let her husband know in no uncertain terms that his sending of Moley to London was, in her opinion, a major mistake. Not only did it "belittle Hull and weaken Hull's position," but it also further elevated the already excessively high reputation of Professor Moley, whose arrogant assumption of presidential powers was becoming, in her judgment, a threat to the President's own power and prestige. Roosevelt had defended his action "but . . . was not very convincing about it," Morgenthau noted in his diary. Tonight the quarrel between husband and wife was more personal and hence, for those who witnessed it, more embarrassing, Roosevelt had presided over a gay cocktail party for family and houseguests, in the living room, after the reporters had left him, a party so prolonged that dinner was delayed a full half hour, and during it he had served a cocktail to his teenage namesake son. Eleanor was horrified. When they arrived at the dinner table, she upbraided her husband for it and for his tardiness, harshly, angrily, as if he were a naughty little boy. The President of the United States was provoked into a rather petulant, shame-faced response.

"You can't scold me this way," he said to her who had just done so. "It is not my fault and I didn't know what time supper was."[40]

After dinner, again in the living room, while Louis Howe dozed upon a davenport and Eleanor with her two Val-Kill friends listened, Morgenthau expounded to Roosevelt more fully than he had ever done before the price theory of George Warren and Frank Pearson. He had with him, this time, charts and graphs, which he displayed to show how purchases of gold by the government at variable prices somewhat higher than the going market rate might be used not only to raise commodity prices but also to manipulate them in such a way as to achieve, ultimately, a permanently stable "commodity dollar."

There was lively discussion of all this and (though vaguely) of the possibility of establishing a new international monetary system along the same lines.

Before the conversation ended, after a couple of hours or so, Roosevelt had been handed and had read two messages, delivered by McIntyre from the *Indianapolis.* One was the decoded cable from Moley, transmitting a proposed "joint declaration by the countries on the gold standard and by those which are not on the gold standard," though the latter portion of this phrase seems to have arrived in garbled form. The other was from Steve Early in Washington saying that the special advisory group (Baruch, Harrison, Woodin) now assembled at Moley's request at Woodin's bedside in New York City recommended "acceptance Moley proposal"; that they had been trying "to reach the President" (there was no telephone connection between Campobello and the mainland); and that Moley had also "called again" to say that "every minute" was "vital" and that the "Economic Conference's fate is in the balance" (that is, Roosevelt must approve the declaration, else the conference would fail).[41]

Alas for the persuasiveness of this last. Roosevelt, having already suffered one severe scolding that evening, was in no mood to endure passively what had for him the earmarks of another. He was, in fact, more than normally inclined to resent and rebel against any attempt to force him into any path he had not himself chosen to follow. And in his present mood it probably did not displease him that Professor Moley, usually so self-assured, so totally confident of his special relationship with the President (never mind that Roosevelt was himself responsible for that confidence) was now evidently in a state of nerves.

And indeed, in London, Moley, during these hours of, for him, mysteriously prolonged presidential silence, began to suffer the most excruciating anxiety. His psyche, stripped of the certainties which normally clothed it, became exposed, naked and dangling, to rising bitter winds of doubt.

Disinterested observers of the conference scene, fully informed concerning it, might see no compelling reason why Moley must directly participate in negotiations with delegates and high officials of other nations or even why he must make himself the sole conduit or transmitter of official proposals from the conference to the President of the United States. They might see several excellent reasons why he should *not* do this, why he should instead operate wholly through the official delegation of his own country, and with extreme circumspection, keeping himself as far behind the scene as possible. But Moley was neither disinterested nor an observer. He notably lacked Roosevelt's ability to stand outside himself, to view himself objectively and pass judgment upon his own performance as actor on history's stage, yet he possessed a capacity for self-deception even greater than Roosevelt's, which was immense. This exercised ability to hide from himself, from his own recognition, a basic motivation rendered obvious by his own published words to all who can read, nourished and protected a self-esteem that, great to begin with, had been much inflated by his experience of the last two years. Dearly did he love power— the fawning attentions now paid him by the highest foreign dignitaries went to his head like wine—and if he did not actually crave (certainly he did not consciously seek) the kind of fame that had latterly come to him, he did thoroughly enjoy it.

Shortly after his press conference in London on the twenty-eighth he was informed that the gold bloc nations, reacting to Roosevelt's latest rebuff of their stabilization attempts, had prepared a draft declaration for signature by the nations represented at the conference; that the British had indicated a willingness to go along, if the United States did so; that Britain's Chancellor of the Exchequer Neville Chamberlain had arranged a meeting with the gold bloc representatives to discuss the matter at eleven o'clock next morning; and that Cox, Warburg, and Sprague were scheduled to attend that meeting. "It was apparent that Thursday would be a critical day," writes Moley. "As I reflected Wednesday night on just what it would involve, it seemed to me indispensable that Cox and Warburg be kept out of the impending negotiations." Why? Because they were members of the delegation, meaning that any "messages signed" by them "would have to be shown to the entire delegation," and this, as sad recent experience had demonstrated, was tantamount to publishing them to the world. Sprague was free of this necessity. He was not a delegation member; he had been sent to London to deal with monetary exchange problems, and as special Treasury representative he "might well handle communications back to Woodin and Acheson." It was at once obvious to Moley, however, that he himself, of all the Americans in London, was best equipped to manage this affair. His transatlantic communications could be kept confidential, he "had last-minute instructions from F.D.R. on the subject of stabilization to impart," and he "had a direct means of communication, through the Embassy, not only to Woodin but, presumably, to F.D.R. . . ." He therefore asked Hull to "invest me with . . . responsibility" for "negotiations over the proposed declaration," keeping away from these "everyone connected with the delegation," a request he deemed "merely a gesture of courtesy" since "Hull's authorization was neither needed nor, if given, valid." The secretary promptly complied. To the assembled delegation shortly after nine next morning he announced that Moley, with Sprague, would conduct the "negotiations concerning what he [Hull] called 'temporary stabilization' " and that Cox and Warburg, after briefing Moley "on the course of the negotiations thus far, would devote themselves . . . exclusively to the business of the delegation." (Hull "added smilingly," according to Moley, "that while he himself, as a member of the delegation and as Secretary of State, had no authority to touch the negotiations into which I was stepping he could authorize me to call on anyone in the delegation . . . for assistance.")[42]

Immediately thereafter Moley saw for the first time a copy of the draft declaration. He was, in his own words, "amazed" to find that it was "brief, simple, and wholly innocuous." It was in perfect accord with one of the four draft resolutions constituting the "memorandum of policy" which Roosevelt had signed and given each delegate just before the delegation sailed,* a resolution that Pittman had actually introduced to the conference on June 19. The "undersigned governments" were simply to agree that international monetary stability should "be attained as quickly as possible" and that "gold should be reestablished as the international measure of exchange value," though with the all-important proviso "that the parity and the time at which each of the

*See p. 131.

countries now off gold could undertake to stabilize must be decided by the respective governments concerned." Each of the undersigned governments was also to agree "to ask its central banks to cooperate with the central banks of other signatory governments in limiting speculation in the exchanges and when the time comes in reestablishing a general international gold standard."* Certainly this was not per se a stabilization agreement, immediate or otherwise; it was but a statement of intent to do at some future date what Roosevelt had repeatedly, publicly said he wanted ultimately to do. And it definitely committed the President "to absolutely nothing" in the way of action "except to ask the Federal Reserve to cooperate in limiting fluctuations due to [sic] speculation," as Moley later insisted. Yet for all its innocuousness, the declaration was of crucial psychological importance. So said every European leader with whom Moley talked. The Continental gold countries were said to be now swept by a panicky fear that they would soon be forced to abandon gold as monetary base and that uncontrollable inflation would follow, a fear fed by the growing belief that Roosevelt had lately decided to permit dollar devaluation and its accompanying speculation to continue indefinitely. By endorsing the proposed mild declaration, Roosevelt could soothe this fear, enabling the conference to turn its attention to constructive economic concerns.[43]

It did not take Moley long to make up his mind and to act upon it.

Having told the British and the French and the Italians that he "could not submit to Roosevelt anything I felt he would reject" and knowing as he said this that his listeners believed him to know Roosevelt's mind absolutely since he himself was said to be a large part of it, he cabled the declaration to Roosevelt and to the advisory group, asking the latter to assemble next day (at 11:00 A.M. New York time; 4:00 P.M. London time) at Woodin's house for transatlantic phone conversation. His doing this unmistakably implied his personal recommendation that the declaration be approved; he soon, in further communications, made this recommendation explicit and urgent. Nor did he have any doubt, at the outset, that his recommendation would be followed. So sure was he of Roosevelt's approval that he spoke of it as a *fait accompli* when, on Friday morning, June 30, he told Hull and the assembled delegation what he had done. He then suggested, "impulsively perhaps," he later said, that when the approval message was received, "Hull himself" should "meet with the foreign representatives and tell them the news."† His confidence was reinforced by his phone talk with Baruch and the others in Woodin's house,

---

*These quotations are from the finally revised draft, in the revision of which Moley had a hand (the official text is in *Foreign Relations, 1933*, vol. I, pp. 670–71), but the original provisions were substantially the same.

†In his *After Seven Years*, p. 250, published in 1939, Moley says he made this suggestion "out of the most generous impulse in the world" because "[w]hoever announced the news would receive the accolade of Europe and the United States" and "I wanted Hull, who had suffered so many disappointments . . . to take the bows." In his *First New Deal*, p. 458, published in 1966, he says: "In making this suggestion I was acting with the utmost precision. For it was not my function to act as a means of communicating such information to the foreign representatives. It was the prerogative of the chief of the delegation and the Secretary of State."

for they emphatically agreed with his recommendation of approval and told him they'd sent a message to Roosevelt saying so.

But the period of waiting that ensued in London became increasingly suspenseful as it extended beyond the time in which Roosevelt's approval message should have been received, even allowing for a maximum of transmittal difficulties. Moley's mood, initially smugly self-congratulatory, became uneasy, then worried, then anxious, and finally dreadfully so. The professor and Swope haunted the embassy code room, smoking one cigarette after another as they sat there.

Not until midafternoon (London time) of Saturday, July 1, did Roosevelt's reply begin to come in, and its first words told a now-distraught Moley that the declaration had been rejected. . . .[44]

It was near midnight of June 30 on Campobello Island when Roosevelt, with the Morgenthau argument of Warren's price theory yet ringing in his ears, dashed off his reply (it went as coded radiogram from the *Indianapolis* to Washington, whence it was not dispatched for several hours), and if he understood what it was that he rejected, the language he employed obscured the fact.

He spoke of the "suggested joint declaration" as if it were a definite stabilization agreement, saying he "gravely doubted" its alleged assumption "that immediate stabilization in international monetary field will create permanent stability." Such stabilization "would still allow a country to continue unbalanced budgets and other financial operations tending to eventually unsound currencies." He insisted "we must be free if gold and silver are reestablished as international measure of exchange to adopt our own method of stabilizing our own domestic price level in terms of the dollar regardless of foreign exchange rates," a statement that makes no sense on first reading and becomes increasingly incomprehensible upon analysis. He went on to say that he knew "of no appropriate means here to limit exchange speculation by governmental action" but it was "clear that this is not at the present time at least a government function but is one that could be undertaken only as a private banking function and only if governmental action is not implied or contemplated thereby" (that is, no gold shipments could be implied). When the "economic conference was initiated and called to discuss and agree on permanent solutions of world economics," the need for it "was obvious although problem of stabilizing of American dollar was not even in existence."[45]

Moley was devastated. There could be no hiding the fact that he had been personally repudiated, his most urgent advice rejected, by the man who was the sole source of his power and prestige. A damaging, possibly fatal blow had been dealt his position as the President's closest adviser on substantive matters. Desperately, one must assume, since it was a role he was singularly, temperamentally ill equipped to play, he attempted the role of courtier, cabling Roosevelt: "Personally bow to your judgment with no inconsiderable relief."* Yet

---

*"This meant, in a term so often used by Roosevelt, simply 'it is your baby now,' " explains Moley, unconvincingly, in his *First New Deal,* page 461.

he later remembered that his and Swope's "first thought, once we had collected ourselves, was that we must protect him [Roosevelt] at all costs" against the embarrassment, the damage to White House prestige, which publication of this presidential message would have. Hence the decision that the smallest possible number of people should be shown the message; Charlie Michelson was to (and did) tell the press only that the President had rejected the joint declaration "in its present form." Walter Lippmann was then in London, observing the conference for his column. He was called upon to exercise that genius for creative exposition which had enabled him to shape a clear, persuasive, self-consistent argument out of Woodrow Wilson's incoherently propagandistic Fourteen Points in 1919; he joined with Moley and Swope, in Claridge's Hotel, on that night of July 1, to draft a statement for presentation to the conference delegations on Monday morning, "explaining Roosevelt's position without revealing the error of Roosevelt's message and without controverting views Roosevelt had recently expressed"—a virtually impossible task which was nevertheless accomplished, to a surprising degree, during a dark early-morning hour of Sunday, July 2.[46]

This statement, however, was never issued.

Some seventeen hours later, on Sunday afternoon in Campobello, Franklin Roosevelt, amid pomp and circumstance, boarded the *Ellis* at the Welshpool wharf. The destroyer took him out to the USS *Indianapolis,* where he was received aboard with great ceremony. The cruiser's captain and officers, the ranked sailors, all in white uniform, stood at attention while the band played "The Star-Spangled Banner" and the President's flag was unfurled. The cruiser's guns fired a twenty-one-gun salute. Then, as the ship which was to take him back to Washington sailed southwestward through the Grand Manon Channel, to begin a voyage that would end in rough water at Annapolis next day, Roosevelt, alone in the captain's cabin, composed almost as rapidly as his hand could write another message to London. Immediately upon its completion he read it aloud, proudly, to Howe and Morgenthau and Franklin, Jr. (none other of his personal or official family was aboard), made at their suggestions a few slight revisions, then sent it on its way for Hull's "use Monday morning as a message from me to you." If Hull did not wish to release it in London, "let me know and . . . I will release it here as a White House statement."

He employed a lofty, lecturing, schoolmasterish tone.

"I would regard it as a catastophe amounting to world tragedy," he began, "if the great Conference of Nations, called to bring about a more real and permanent financial stability and a greater prosperity for the masses of all nations, should, in advance of any serious effort to consider these broader problems, allow itself to be diverted by the proposal of a purely artificial and temporary experiment affecting the monetary exchange of a few nations only. . . . The sound internal economic system of a nation is a greater factor in its well being than the price of its currency in changing terms of the currencies of other nations." He contemptuously dismissed the emphasis upon stabilization as one of the "old fetishes of so-called international bankers," which were "now being replaced by efforts to plan national currencies with the objective of giving these currencies a continuing purchasing power which does not vary in terms of the commodities and need of modern civilization." Though "our broad purpose is [still] the permanent stabilization of every nation's currency," he went on, the achievement of this purpose must await a restoration to good health of the several nations' domestic economies and a return by national governments to "balanced budgets."[47]

The statement exploded next day upon world consciousness as a bombshell; it was at once labeled the "bombshell message."

It destroyed the World Monetary and Economic Conference.

V

IN Europe the predominant immediate reaction was one of angry outrage and utter dismay. It is true that John Maynard Keynes, then in process of completing the argument he was to publish three years later as *The General Theory of Employment, Interest, and Money*, proclaimed Roosevelt to be "magnificently right," and there were other English economists who made a similar assessment. But these last were a small percentage of their country's professional economists, most of whom, like most of the European citizenry and virtually all the European press, were for the moment agreed with an enraged Philip Snowden,* who damned the message in print as both insulting and stupid. ("No such message was ever before sent by the head of a government to representatives of other nations," wrote Snowden. "It will be filed for all times as a classic example of conceit, hectoring, and ambiguity.")[48] As for European statesmen, they were generally convinced they had been deliberately deceived and misled by the President of the United States. They had reason. In his joint statement with Ramsay MacDonald on April 26 Roosevelt had spoken of the "ultimate re-establishment of equilibrium in the international exchanges" and the reestablishment of "an international monetary standard" as a conference aim and had said that economic and monetary problems were so "inter-related" they could not be solved separately or "by any individual country acting by itself." In his joint statement with M. Herriot of France two days later he had said that "the object" of the conference "must be to bring about a rapid revival of world activity and the raising of world prices by diminishing all sorts of impediments to international commerce . . . and by the re-establishment of a normal financial and monetary situation." In his joint statement with Italy's finance minister, Guido Jung, on May 6, he had said "that a fixed measure of exchange values must be re-established in the world

---

*Snowden had been chancellor of the exchequer in MacDonald's first and brief Labor government, in 1924. He had joined with MacDonald and others to form a new National Labor group in 1931, after the old Labor party expelled former party leaders who favored the National Coalition government (with Conservative, Liberal, and Labor members) of which MacDonald became prime minister.

and . . . this measure must be gold," also that economic and monetary questions "must be attacked as a unit," with the restoration of "stability in international exchanges" going "hand in hand" with the removal of "obstacles [i.e., tariffs, import quotas, and the like] to the flow of international commerce." In his joint statement with Nazi Germany's Hjalmar Schacht on May 12 he had said that "the creation of stable conditions in the monetary field" was of equal importance with the settlement of general economic questions; since "[e]conomic and monetary questions are so interdependent . . . the adjustment of both must necessarily go hand in hand." Small wonder that an almost weeping Prime Minister MacDonald, whose political life depended upon a successful conference outcome, wailed to Moley in the early morning of Tuesday, July 4, "This doesn't sound like the man I spent so many hours with in Washington. This sounds like a different man. I don't understand."⁴⁹

But in the United States, among the general electorate, whose majority was isolationist and to whose response Roosevelt (with Howe) gave priority over all other responses, the reaction was overwhelmingly one of approval. Editorialists in some eastern papers, more attuned than most Americans to U.S. links to Europe, were only slightly less condemnatory of the message than the Europeans were, but for the most part the "statement . . . got a grand press over here," as Roosevelt said to Moley when the professor returned from London. Ernest K. Lindley spoke the opinion of millions of Americans, especially in the Midwest and West (though Lindley wrote for the New York *Herald Tribune*), when he expressed gratitude for the fact that the "internationalist tendencies in the Administration" had been brought against the "hard realities of world politics" by Roosevelt "with enough force to bring most of the daydreamers to their senses," also that Roosevelt had shown the world "that the United States has a President whose first regard is the national interest." The latter sentiment was echoed in chorus across the land by popular commentators. For once, spoke Will Rogers for myriads, Uncle Sam had taken part in an international conference without being himself "taken" by wily Europeans. ("Franklin hasn't done anything so popular as his rejection of the declaration since the bank crisis," a chortling Louis Howe said to a hurt and angry Moley when the latter returned to Washington.)⁵⁰

As for Moley, he in London, in the immediate aftermath of the "bombshell," did his valiant best to retrieve the situation and repair the damage done himself. Very early in the morning of Tuesday, July 4, he sent through embassy facilities a message "to the President alone and exclusively, with no distribution in the Department," intended to serve as a kind of agenda for a transatlantic telephone conversation with Roosevelt in the White House next day.* In

---

*The *Indianapolis* dropped anchor off Annapolis in the morning of July 3. Roosevelt hosted a luncheon for six of his cabinet members aboard the cruiser that day, discussing "the international situation for two hours or more." He reported on conference developments. "It seemed to all of us," wrote Ickes in his diary, "that he had handled the matter with admirable skill and foresight. He has established a strictly American position which he has been adhering to firmly, in spite of all the blandishments and threats from the European countries."⁵¹

it Moley suggested a conference "recess for from 2 to 10 weeks permitting formulation of your ideas into resolutions" and a "reconstituted delegation" to handle these, since of the present delegation "Pittman is only member ... able intellectually and aggressively to present your ideas to the Conference" and the "[e]xpert group" also needed "strengthening." He closed with another attempt to play the courtier. "I consider your message splendid," he said. "It was the only way to bring people to their senses, and do not be disturbed by complaints about severity of language. It was true, frank and fair." He then, after meetings with MacDonald, Hull, and the U.S. delegates, set about reducing the bitterness provoked by the "severity of language" he had praised; in collaboration with Lippmann and Keynes, he and Swope prepared an "explanation" of the "bombshell" couched in "reasonable and conciliatory" terms, for Roosevelt's release to the conference and the world.[52]

Roosevelt, however, back in the White House in the evening of July 4, was opposed to a conference recess. If one could not be prevented, it should be limited to "10 days or say till July 17," he said in a message for "Hull and Delegation," and "should distinctly be labeled a recess to allow committees to work." Acquiescence in a longer recess would be "in my judgment a defeatist gesture." Next day, in telephone conversation with Moley and Hull, he approved the Lippmann-Keynes-Moley-Swope draft statement with minor revisions, most of them for the purpose of changing it from first person into third because, as he said, it would be in his view "a mistake to make it as a statement from me"; it ought instead to be issued as "a statement from the delegation."[53] This was done a few hours later and with a good deal of the hoped-for mollifying effect. It became a factor in Hull's thwarting of a concerted effort by the gold bloc countries to force immediate conference adjournment, placing the blame for failure squarely on Roosevelt.

For the secretary of state now became—suddenly, briefly—surprisingly effective as a leader, not only of the U.S. delegation but of the conference in general, his spirits having been raised and his normal energies somewhat restored by his witnessing Professor Moley's discomfiture—this despite the fact that his own great dream of using the conference to turn the world toward free trade had been crushed. It was due to Hull that the conference remained uninterruptedly in session for another three weeks, if to no clear purpose beyond a saving of face for the President of the United States. Certainly nothing that would improve world economic conditions was accomplished. Indeed, only one definite action was taken, this under the leadership of Key Pittman, and it was more harmful than helpful in its general effect. Pittman was drunk every day he was in London, sometimes roaringly, violently so, but he possessed a forceful personality and some expert knowledge of money along with a single mind of above-average ability, and by the exercise of these he obtained conference approval of a scheme whereby the governments of silver-producing nations (the United States, Canada, Mexico, Argentina, Australia, Peru) obligated themselves to purchase annually 35 million ounces of silver for coinage and for the metallic backing of paper currencies. The ostensible purpose was to help raise the general price level over the world (it failed to have any such effect); the actual purpose was to obtain a very substantial government subsidization of silver interests in Pittman's Nevada, and in other western states, a purpose that was achieved, especially after passage of the Silver Purchase Act signed by Roosevelt in June 1934.*

On July 27 the conference "recessed," never to meet again.

By that time it had become abundantly clear to Moley that the very special working relationship he had had with Roosevelt for nearly two years was coming to an end, had, as a matter of fact, already ended. During his last days in London he had desperately hoped that Roosevelt, returned to the White House, would issue a statement denying that he, Moley, was in disgrace, that he had been repudiated, if not rebuked, and was now "through," as the press reported under large headlines. During his voyage home (he sailed from Southampton on July 6) he had hoped against hope that Roosevelt would at least express to him privately "some slight regret for the false impression that had grown up." The President did nothing of the sort. He greeted Moley warmly but casually when the latter came to his White House bedside at nine o'clock in the morning of Bastille Day (Friday, July 14), listened in smiling silence to Moley's succinct account of the London situation, then turned the conversation to other topics, the chief of these being the current inundation of the White House by draft NRA codes. Moley came close to resigning his government post that very day. He decided not to only because doing so would confirm in the public mind the truth of all those stories about his fall from grace, and this might militate against the success of a journalistic venture to which he had been tentatively committed for several weeks and to which he now committed himself absolutely—namely, the editorship of a weekly journal of news and opinion, to be entitled *Today* and backed financially by Vincent Astor, Averell Harriman, and Averell's older sister Mary Harriman Rumsey. He sought a more propitious time and way of departure.

But the worst of his public humiliation was yet to come.

When members of the delegation returned from London, they seethed with anger over the "gross insult" given them by Moley's supposedly totally confidential message to Roosevelt, sent in the early morning of July 4. Despite its "top secret" classification, a copy had come into the hands of Robert W. Bingham, U.S. Ambassador to the Court of St. James's, presumably because it had been sent over embassy facilities, and Bingham, disliking Moley and actually loathing "Baruch's man" Swope,† had seen fit to pass it on to his close friend Cordell Hull. Hull, naturally, was incensed by the message's characteri-

---

*The principal silver-using nations—China, India, and Spain—were to suffer from the overpriding of silver that resulted from U.S. silver purchase operations. China was eventually forced to abandon its historic silver standard and adopt a managed currency.

†Wealthy publisher of the Louisville (Kentucky) *Courier-Journal,* Bingham made large financial contributions to Roosevelt's presidential campaign at the behest of his longtime friend Colonel House. He had sided with House in a bitter quarrel between Baruch and House during the Versailles peace conference.

zation of Pittman as the only delegate "able intellectually . . . to present" Roosevelt's "ideas" and by the recommendation that the delegation be "reconstituted" ("That piss-ant Moley!" he spluttered to Warburg shortly after he'd first read the message; "Here he curled up at mah feet and let me stroke his head like a hunting dog and then he goes and bites me in the ass!"). He promptly read or showed the offending sentences to others of the delegation. He then fired off to Roosevelt, on July 11, a confidential cable of his own, one whose tone and general substance were soon widely known and reported by the press, despite its strict "secret" classification.[54]

"It is most painful," Hull began, ". . . to have to report an attitude and course of conduct on the part of Professor Moley which has been utterly dumbfounding to me." He went on to present a bill of particulars, the most serious of these being Moley's "definite request that I announce to the delegation that he, Moley, would in company with Doctor Sprague take custody of the temporary stabilization matter to the entire exclusion, again at his express request, of Warburg." Hull, assuming that the professor acted on specific authorization from the President, had done as the professor requested. Then "after his failure [to obtain presidential approval] he pretended to claim that I on my initiative directed him to assume the task" and "likewise represented . . . that he was not expressing any personal views about the matter but was merely acting ad referendum." The climactic outrage "I only discovered . . . after he sailed." Immediately upon receipt of the President's July 2 message, Britain and the gold bloc nations had prepared a formal "resolution" to adjourn the conference and "charge sole responsibility for its wrecking on you." Adoption of the resolution had seemed virtually inevitable when Hull undertook "to deal with this crisis single-handed, and was lucky enough if I may say so to be the chief single factor in preserving the life of the Conference. . . ." Yet at the very time Hull was successfully performing this almost impossible task, and while Moley was "pretending absolute loyalty of friendship and official attitude toward me," the professor "was secretly sending code messages to you about my incapacity to function here." Concluded Hull: "My regret only equals my amazement. . . ."[55]

Roosevelt at once recognized this communication as, in effect, an ultimatum. Either Moley departed Washington or the secretary of state would resign his post acrimoniously along with, almost certainly, the ambassador to the Court of St. James's. The former event would be unregretted, if not actually welcomed, by most of official Washington; the latter would do great and possibly irreparable damage to the President's relations with Congress, especially the Senate. Since Moley could (and would) continue to be called upon for drafting and other chores, even though no longer an official part of the administration, the President's choice was easily made, was, indeed, no real choice at all.

Yet Roosevelt, characteristically, could not bring himself to face Moley with the naked fact that he must go. In late July Howe suggested to the professor a three-month assignment to the Hawaiian Islands, there to study the administration of criminal justice in the territory, a proposal Moley rejected with indignation; he was *damned* if he, having served for months as the President's right-hand man, would accept handouts from the likes of Louie Howe. Then Roosevelt himself proposed directly that Moley, without resigning as assistant secretary of state, go over to the Department of Justice for an indefinite period to work on ways and means of curbing the wave of kidnappings then sweeping the country. This proposal Moley accepted.

On September 7, after the furor over London had died down, the professor submitted his resignation, giving as his reason his wish to join in the launching of a new national weekly magazine. The President accepted it with "a sense of deep personal regret," gratitude for "a very definite service to your country," and the assurance that the "ending of our official relations will in no way terminate our close personal association."[56]

VI

IN his *Depression Decade* economic historian Broadus Mitchell describes Roosevelt's rejection of the London joint declaration as "probably the most momentous" decision he ever made yet finds it to have been made with an utterly appalling frivolity. "[W]as his decision reasoned, did he seek earnestly to strike a balance between immediate gain and later loss?" asks the historian rhetorically. "Or, infatuated with the prospect of rising prices at home, did he hastily condemn others to frustration, discord, and the appeal to arms? There was a lighthearted suddenness in his behavior which spoke of ignorance or . . . of the little knowledge which is a dangerous thing."[57]

Certainly there remained, there yet remains, of the London fiasco a haunting question of what might have been.

Suppose Roosevelt had worked from the start, clearly and definitely, toward international agreements whereby domestic price raising and unemployment reduction were joined to ultimate international currency stabilization at an agreed point of fairness for all. Suppose he had had in mind specific schemes for an international public works program. Suppose he had announced these as his aim in a way that left him and Congress free to take the emergency steps necessary to prevent U.S. economic collapse and had then carefully selected and instructed his conference delegation in terms of it. Might not the conference have then achieved at least something of what had been so desperately hoped for it—enough, perhaps, to stem or slow the tide of vicious aggressive nationalism which was then rising so ominously in Hitler's Germany, in Mussolini's Italy, in militaristic Japan?

The question must remain forever open.

All that is certain is that the effort was never made and that the conference failed in a way that encouraged a rampant economic nationalism and a resurgent militaristic imperialism pointed unmistakably, if not inevitably, in both Europe and the Far East, toward a renewal of world war.

BOOK TWO

⋙✕⋘

A Pattern Emerges from the Initial Surge of the New Deal

6

The Personality and Mind of the New Deal

I

THE afore-quoted Broadus Mitchell, writing only a few years after the events he describes in his *Depression Decade,* makes wise comment upon the relative values of the near view and the far to anyone who would truly understand what happened in history. Granting that later historians "will . . . discern forces at work in this time which now, so close to the event, do not reveal themselves," granting, too, the increase of wisdom that will accompany this later knowledge, Mitchell goes on to say: "But also something will be lost when the influence of vibrant personalities is obscured as it is bound to be by distance and philosophy. While acknowledging the limitations of present judgment, one makes no apology for ascribing potency to leaders. The future, in substituting pattern for persons, will miss, if not the truth of these times, then much of their spirit."[1] Mitchell's remark is perhaps more precisely applicable to the New Deal of which he writes than it is to any other period in American history. For whether or not it is true that the evil men do lives after them whereas the good is oft interred with their bones (the precise opposite of this may be as easily proved), it is certainly true that the charisma of a charismatic leader dies with him into the grave, that it is all too likely to be overly discounted by later historians as an influence upon great events, and that of no other "times" in America was the "spirit" so closely, so exclusively identified with a single "vibrant personality" as was the New Deal with Franklin Roosevelt. In certain respects of tone, of color, of feeling, the New Deal *was* the personality of this President, who in early July 1933 returned to the White House refreshed, zestful, his prestige and popularity at their highest pitch, and, freed for the first time of immediate legislative pressures and so enabled for the first time to function exclusively as chief executive, plunged without a qualm, with gaiety even, into what almost any eyes but his would have seen as a raging, overwhelming sea of troubles. Roosevelt as President, like Roosevelt as governor, ruled by charm and force of personality, and he had by this time fully developed the kind of presidential leadership he was to continue to the end of his days in the White House.

His daily White House routine remained as it had been during the Hundred Days, though it was followed with more regularity than had in those first days been possible: breakfast in bed, with swift perusal of a half dozen or so morning papers; bedside conferences with immediate aides; dressing with the aid of his valet; wheelchair transport to the Executive Office; the handling there of his correspondence, with Missy LeHand and Grace Tully; a series of conferences with scheduled visitors, generally timed to last fifteen minutes each (Howe and McIntyre had trouble holding him to schedule); lunch at his desk, always with one or more guests, during which much business was transacted; another series of conferences; a late-afternoon swim in the White House pool; a session with his personal physician, Dr. Ross T. McIntire, who cleared his sinuses with a spray in what to some doctors would seem, later, a mistaken treatment of chronic sinus trouble; swift perusal in the Oval Room of a half dozen evening papers; conviviality with intimates over cocktails in the Oval Room; dinner, at which there were almost always several guests and often many; more conferences and paperwork after dinner; and finally, bed at a little before midnight.

To those who observed or experienced it, the tonic effect of exposure to his personality bordered often on the miraculous. Every day, in steady stream, people came to him with troubling problems and because of their troubles. Often enough, waiting in the anteroom for their appointed times, they showed themselves unhappy; they were tense, anxious, despairing, angry, their faces drawn with fatigue, their gestures nervous. But almost always, after a quarter hour in his presence, they departed his office smiling and refreshed, their spirits uplifted, their confidence restored, as if they had taken a bath in liquid sunlight and been soaked through by it. How did he do it? In part it was by a conscious exercise (or had long habit made it by now a virtually *un*conscious exercise?) of psychological managerial techniques, he being empathically aware of words, gestures, approaches that would please his visitor and that he took care to employ to the greatest possible extent. He saw himself through his visitor's eyes, he heard his voice through his visitor's ears, and he played the role best calculated to produce upon his visitor the effect he wanted. Admittedly, too, much of the charm he had for his visitors derived as much from his high office as it did from his personality. Thus TVA's David Lilienthal tells of Roosevelt's "offering me a cigarette and lighting it for me—a trick which certainly gets you, having the most powerful man in the world casually lighting your cigarette." Of the same order was Roosevelt's calling people by their first names almost from the moment of his introduction to them, his regaling them with stories more or less apropos of the topic under discussion, the seemingly utter candor with which he talked about presidential problems, and the encouragement he gave others to express *their* views, *their* opinions.[2]

But it was by no means all "tricks," all technique.

There was nothing fake about the hearty, laughing good humor, the optimistic faith (he *knew* everything would come out right in the end!), the indomitable courage, the incessant, stupendous *joie de vivre* which he exuded and which others, needful of it, soaked up as parched earth does water. He genuinely liked people, all kinds and conditions of people, and not merely or chiefly as objects of his manipulation. He delighted in their foibles, their unexpectedness, their endless variety. He seemed to derive from his contacts with them as much uplift and stimulation as they did from their contacts with him, if of different nature. The bulk of his working day was filled, as has been said, with fifteen-minute conferences with individuals or small groups on (always) matters of importance for whose handling he had major ultimate personal responsibility. Three successive hours of these would have left any ordinary man tired out. But he generally emerged from them as fresh as he had entered, or more so, for often he was actually exhilarated. He was endlessly gregarious. He had neither desire nor need for contemplative solitudes.

In his dealings with others he always assumed at the outset that the best rather than worst possible interpretation of their characters, their behavior was true, an assumption that was part of his optimistic faith as it was also an essential element of the tonic effect he had upon people: It made them feel good about themselves; it tended to bring out in them, actively, that best in which he so manifestly believed. He was remarkably tolerant of personality types and traits and behavior that varied from the norm or even violated prevailing mores, and he maintained such tolerance despite the risks it sometimes imposed upon him, risks to his public standing, to his efficiency as public man. Thus his wife's private life had in it elements which, publicized, might have done much harm to his public career. He could not but have known that malicious rumor was likely to spread from her close relationship with handsome Earl Miller and could spread even more dangerously from her connection with Lorena Hickok, linked as this would be, in gossip, with the fact that so many of Eleanor's closest women friends were couples living together in evident lesbian relationships. He must at least have suspected (Howe seems frankly to have recognized) that Eleanor's love for Hick was of a passionate nature, meaning that such episodes as the vacation trip Eleanor had insisted upon taking alone with Hick might result in horrendous scandal. Yet with respect to these matters he seems to have uttered no word of protest or even of warning. In part this may have been due to a feeling that because of his own past relationship with Lucy Mercer, and continuing one with Missy LeHand, he personally was in no position to protest, but it was more deeply rooted in a profound and general belief that no human being has the right to exert coercive authority over the private, personal life of another adult human being —not, at any rate, in matters of this kind. Doing so would be an interference with the workings of Deity. "Vengeance is mine, saith the Lord."

It was at some risk to the administration that he extended his tolerance, his permissiveness to questionable personal conduct on the part of high government officials: to Woodin and Norman Davis, as we have seen, when their past acceptance of special favors from the Morgan bank was publicly exposed; to recurrent alcoholic binges and a notorious sexual affair with a secretary on the part of Hugh Johnson, later on; simultaneously, to a less obvious but potentially more scandalous affair between Ickes, of all people, and a young divorcée in his department. Concerning this last, there began to circulate in Washington in the late summer of 1933, scurrilous anonymous letters, some of which came into the hands of newspaper editors, who, fearing libel suits, refused to print them. Roosevelt must have heard of them at that time or soon afterward, for a worried Ickes spoke of them to Louis Howe in August 1933 without admitting, of course, that the allegations they made had any truth whatever. Months later, in the spring of 1934, Ickes talked directly to Roosevelt, and defensively, about his relationship with the woman the letters named, explaining that she was a family friend whom he had known since she was a small child in Altoona, Pennsylvania, where Ickes had grown up. He intimated that if he must choose between a maintenance of longtime friendships and the retention of his cabinet post, he was prepared to give up the latter. Roosevelt promptly replied that, of course, no such choice was necessary; he gave no sign of a suspicion that the relationship between Ickes and the young woman might be less innocent than Ickes claimed, though he could hardly have failed, by that time, to suspect this.[3]

There was nothing fake, either, about Roosevelt's frequent willingness to share or assume burdens of administrative responsibility that were crushing to his subordinates. Paul Appleby, the agriculture secretary's administrative assistant, was deeply impressed in the late summer or early autumn of 1933 when Henry Wallace phoned the President to warn him of an action the Department of Agriculture was about to take, a necessary action but one bound to cause sharp criticism of the executive. Wallace had little talent for swift, succinct oral communication, especially over a telephone. He fumbled for words, and from these Roosevelt drew the impression that Wallace himself was in some kind of trouble. "I was standing a few feet away," Appleby remembered years later, "but I could have heard what the President said if I had been across the room, and what I heard out of the receiver was 'Bring it over to me, Henry. My shoulders are broad.' "[4]

Endearing to almost everyone who witnessed it, and eliciting profound admiration, was his way of dealing with his infirmity. Representative was Lilienthal's experience of this one night in Warm Springs in late November 1934, when he and Morris L. Cooke, the nationally known management engineer and electric power expert, were two of a party dining with the President in a small dining room of the resort hotel. The gathering had been arranged by the President to discuss the proposition he presented over scotch and soda after the meal had ended—namely, that utilities holding companies created for the sole purpose of controlling operating companies were "against the public interest" and, since they "couldn't be regulated, should be abolished." He dominated the discussion, which, after possible approaches to the needed abolition had been reviewed, "went in a dozen different directions." At midnight "two great big men, part of the Secret Service detail," entered the dining room. Lilienthal never forgot the scene that followed. He wrote into his journal the next day:

> When the President sits at a table or even stands speaking, you are entirely unconscious of his disability because of his magnificent head and his tremendously powerful shoulders and arms. So it was quite a shock to see these men help get the President into his overcoat and then lean over and with the President still talking vivaciously to us put his arms [sic] over the shoulders of these . . . men, while they scooped him up much as you would a child and carried him out of the door and out into the night, with him turning his head around and calling good nights to us. I have never seen

such complete unself-consciousness or anything quite so touching as the contrast between this indomitable and really gay spirit and this ghastly invalidism.

Ickes tells in his diary of a conference on PWA problems he had in the bathroom next to the President's bedroom one morning, he seated on the toilet seat while the President sat before a mirror shaving himself. "When he was through shaving he was wheeled back to his room where he reclined on his bed again while his valet proceeded to help him dress," he talking all the time, as Ickes recorded. ". . . I was struck all over again with the unaffected simplicity and personal charm of the man. He was President of the United States but he was also a plain human being, talking over with a friend matters of mutual interest. . . . His disability didn't seem to concern him in the slightest degree nor disturb his urbanity."[5] By such conduct, men who came to him full of criticism and complaint were often disarmed—were made ashamed that they could have considered adding their troubles, relatively minor after all, to those so gallantly borne by a man so handicapped.

But though he ruled by charm and force of personality, and his personal leadership had in it relatively little of original idea or force of intellect, there *was* a kind of acumen, a species of intuitive intelligence that commanded respect, and even, sometimes, awe. Moley's "bow . . . with no inconsiderable relief" to Roosevelt's "judgment" on the London joint agreement was by no means *wholly* a courtier's gesture. For all his disparagement of Roosevelt's dealings with contradictory ideas, the professor, as is evident from the way he tells his story, was far from certain that the action that issued from these dealings was itself stupid. Deep within him was a suspicion that Roosevelt had ends in view that were hidden from others, one of these being, quite possibly, a calculated diminishment of Professor Moley. And such doubt-ridden judgments of Roosevelt as a mind were common among the intellectuals whom this President brought into government in greater number than any earlier President had done. These people might come to know that he who was their leader was ignorant of and incurious about the general (abstract) ideas and basic principles whereby factual information is transformed into an organized body of knowledge. They might deplore, with frequent exasperation and occasional disgust, what seemed to them his incredibly slovenly and erratic thought processes. But not one of them was actually contemptuous of him as a mind, ever, or even absolutely sure that his intelligence was not, overall, superior to their own, he being possessed of ways of knowing and understanding and reaching decisions that were beyond their ken.

Consistent with his gregariousness was the faculty he had of shifting his attention swiftly, easily, from one thing to another, one activity to another; seldom was he so deeply engaged by a problem or project in hand as to make his turning away from it a painful wrench. He could and did mingle work with play, the deadly serious with the utterly trivial, in a continuous flow that often baffled associates and sometimes dismayed them since it often delayed or prevented hard decisions, firm conclusions. As Lindley had noted of him in

Albany, he also had an amazing faculty for doing two or more things at once with equal efficiency: conversing about stock market regulation while swimming in the White House pool; stating his case against deposit insurance and listening to the answer to it while pasting stamps into one of his collection books; discussing war debts while reviewing and signing correspondence; or, as we have seen, preparing his mind for a momentous press conference while exuberantly socializing at a picnic on the seashore. "If these quick transitions, these smooth changes of pace did not make for a maximum efficiency in the short pull, they were certainly a clue to Roosevelt's staying power," Moley observed.[6] His working hours were thus rendered recreative; he was enabled to conduct public business late into the night, then drop at once to sleep when he lay his head upon the pillow, awaking in the morning eager to encounter whatever his new day might bring.

He had also his hours of pure recreation, of course.

An important part of his daily routine was what he called the "children's hour," when his secretaries and others of the innermost White House circle, with occasional White House guests, gathered in the Oval Room for cocktails at seven-fifteen in the evening, dinner being scheduled for eight o'clock. He himself mixed the drinks, from a large tray brought to his desk, doing so with elaborate ceremony but a minimal concern for precise measurement, or so it seemed to his guests, for he mixed without benefit of a jigger, talking a steady stream all the while. There is testimony that his bourbon old-fashioneds were "excellent," his martinis "awful," he making the latter of "two kinds of vermouth . . . and sometimes a dash of absinthe," according to Robert Sherwood. He was himself a very moderate consumer of alcohol. Drinking in little sips, he never downed more than two cocktails before dinner, often only one, while urging seconds and even thirds upon his guests. What was important to him about the cocktail hour was its bantering camaraderie and stream of small talk. He himself did most of the talking. He had favorite anecdotes, "which some of us . . . heard time and again," writes Sam Rosenman, "but which always seemed to gather additional embellishments as well as additional charm" with each new telling.[7]

He was fond of poker, had frequent poker sessions with members of his official family, and posed (it was probably frankly a pose) as a poker expert. In actual fact, though he delighted in winning money from such frequent fellow players as Ickes and Morgenthau, he lost more than he won. He bluffed excessively. Moreover, when dealer, he was likely to provoke groans from his fellow players, especially from those who loved poker as a game of skill, by calling a game in which so many cards were wild that the odds became incalculable. Here again, though he played always with gusto, it was the bantering camaraderie and light talk that were important to him. Indeed, Jack Garner, himself a serious poker player, thought Roosevelt played *just* for conversation," since the stakes he set were far too small to give any real importance to a game's outcome.[8]

His principal diversion continued to be his stamp collection, to which additions were made almost daily through all his years in the White House. He also enjoyed crossword puzzles and games of solitaire. But his recreations included no active enjoyment of the arts. Painting, sculpture, music—these communicated to him little emotion save, perhaps, if the music was aggressively "modern" and the painting abstract, a mingling of boredom with irritation. When sculptor Jo Davidson created in the spring of 1935 a scale wooden model of a gigantic monumental sculpture which he proposed to place on the Norris Dam spillway or on some other canyon dam—the figure of a man "in the position . . . [of] holding back the water, his body thrust back against the dam and more or less lost in the concrete itself"—David Lilienthal and Harry Hopkins were much taken with the idea. Hopkins promptly promised to provide federal relief money to sculptors now on relief, to work under Davidson's supervision, if the TVA "would permit the figure to be put on the dam." But Roosevelt, who had the final say, was not interested.[9] (Davidson's dream came to naught; no such sculpted figure was placed on any New Deal dam.) Jazz had no interest for the President, but he was fond of nostalgic, sentimental melody. He once told White House correspondents that his favorite song was "Home on the Range," they informed the world of that fact, and abruptly what had theretofore been a composition of modest fame became one of the most widely played and sung of all American songs. He took an active interest in architecture; he even fancied himself something of an architect. But his interest here was not artistic; he was concerned to design useful and comfortable buildings along strictly traditional, conventional lines, as in the remodeling of the Big House and the erection of Val-Kill Cottage at Hyde Park, for both of which projects he provided the basic design, the former Georgian, the latter Dutch Colonial, and which were closely personally supervised by him.

"Franklin always read a great deal, chiefly biography and history," writes Eleanor Roosevelt in her *This I Remember,* but the testimony of others is that he read very few serious books of any kind after he became governor of New York. He gave no sign of familiarity with the works of Thorstein Veblen, Bertrand Russell, the Webbs, Joseph Wood Krutch, Charles Beard, Harold Laski, H. G. Wells, John Dewey, Oswald Spengler, Reinhold Niebuhr (his *Moral Man and Immoral Society* came out in 1932), or any of the other writers of history, socioeconomics, or philosophy who had great influence on the mental life of America as it entered the 1930's. There is no clear evidence even that he read the books of Walter Lippmann, whose A *Preface to Morals* created a great stir in 1929; or of Felix Frankfurter, whose *The Public and Its Government* was sent him by the author soon after its publication in late 1930;* or

---

*"Ever so many thanks for sending me the copy . . ." wrote Roosevelt to Frankfurter in January 1931. "I am looking forward to reading it." But if he ever did, he made no mention of it in later letters to "Dear Felix." In late June 1931 Frankfurter inscribed a copy of his *Mr. Justice Holmes* to Roosevelt and, in the cover note, expressed a wish that Roosevelt would manage "to steal three-quarters of an hour to read the last essay in . . . *The Public and Its Government,* 'Expert Administration and Democracy.'" (See pp. 54, 56 of Max Freedman, ed., *Roosevelt and Frankfurter; Their Correspondence, 1928–1945.*)

of Stuart Chase, whose popular essays in economics were best-sellers in those years. The same is true as regards the fiction and poetry of Ernest Hemingway, Thomas Wolfe, William Faulkner, John Steinbeck, Ezra Pound, T. S. Eliot, Robert Frost, Carl Sandburg, and the "proletarian" writers who caused such controversy in the literary world of that time. His private talk and public speech were singularly barren of literary allusions. If he later perused the poetry of Archibald MacLeish, it was for other than aesthetic reasons. He did apparently read *Gone with the Wind* after it had become an enormous best-seller in 1936. Eleanor pressed the novel upon him; he took it to bed with him one night and, within a couple of days afterward, handed it back to her, saying he'd finished it. She didn't believe him (he could not have devoted as much as three hours to the book amid his crowded schedule; not even the legendary speed-reading of Uncle Ted could have gone through 1,000 pages that fast), but he parried her disbelief by answering correctly her every question about the story and characters. His chief recreational reading seems to have been of detective stories; he was almost as addicted to these as was Louie Howe and even, on one occasion, greatly publicized by a magazine editor, tried his hand at plotting one.

He was also a motion-picture addict. Others found it incomprehensible that he who was daily immersed in real-life dramas of fascinating interest and major importance could be for a moment intrigued by Hollywood make-believe, yet he had movies shown him two or three times a week, in the White House as in Albany's Executive Mansion, and seemed to lose himself in them completely from opening scene to last. "He always had a *Mickey Mouse,* which amused him greatly," according to Eleanor. "Though he rarely asked for a particular movie, he hated a picture to be too long, and it must not be sad." He refused for these reasons to view the motion-picture version of *Gone with the Wind.* [10]

He traveled a great deal. This was part of his gay defiance of his disability, his absolute refusal to surrender to adversity. But it was also a felt necessity of his job; it was required for his success, by his own standards of success, as political leader. The fact that he was physically immobilized, dependent upon other people for even his movement around a room,* meant that he was also more dependent than most upon other people's initiatives for such information as could come only through direct personal contacts. He could not casually, unexpectedly drop in on someone at work in an office or at ease in home or club. People had to come to him. And most of those who came unsummoned, having asked for appointments, did so because they wanted something from him for themselves, for their own operations. The information they gave him about facts and events and persons was therefore all too likely to be distorted and colored, wittingly or unwittingly, by their particular interests. It had to be checked for accuracy against information derived in other ways, from other

---

*He had to be helped by brawny men as he shifted from desk or table to wheelchair. His "walking" upon steel-braced legs was a balancing act, as has been noted; to remain upright on his braces, he had to lean heavily upon a strong man's arm.

sources, and this was facilitated, as his spirit was refreshed and renewed, by his seeing and talking with people in their own settings, far away from the capital. ("Get out of Washington if you want to know what is going on in America," he said in effect to many a subordinate; people in Washington "are the last people in the world to listen to."[11]) So he himself was away from Washington far more often and for longer periods of time than any of his White House predecessors had been, here again fusing work with recreation. He spent days, even weeks at a time in Warm Springs and Hyde Park. He went far across the country to inspect New Deal projects and make speeches, traveling always by train or automobile, never by plane. (Of a piece with his aversion to abstractions was his aversion to air travel; from the window of a high-flying plane all landscapes are abstract, empty of people.) He took lengthy cruises aboard Navy ships. And everywhere he went he made a point of talking to people, lots of people in all walks of life. His exclusively recreational trips were relatively few. But he continued to take, when he could, wholly fun-filled, sun-soaked fishing-and-cardplaying cruises off Florida in Vincent Astor's yacht with the hugely wealthy members of the original *"Nourmahal* gang," every one of whom, save Astor himself, was fervently, unwaveringly Republican in his politics and none of whom was notable for intellect.

Impressed upon all who had prolonged close contacts with him, being of a piece with his remarkably cheerful, even temper, his seemingly endless patience, were Roosevelt's aforementioned human kindness and eagerness to please. He kept close watch for signs of overwork and excessive fatigue in those he worked with, sometimes ordering them to take vacations, and always expressed great concern and was as helpful as possible when they suffered injury or illness. When Ickes was hospitalized with a severe back injury (he had slipped on ice in his driveway) in the second week of December 1933, Roosevelt immediately sent the White House physician over to Ickes's room in the Naval Hospital to make sure the patient received the best of care. He also sent over a warmly sympathetic handwritten note and, next day, went himself to Ickes's room for a half hour visit. Lilienthal tells in his journal of coming to Roosevelt's office after a serious illness, in mid-March 1939. Roosevelt "gave me ample reward for being ill, for the dreary trip to Washington, and a good many other things, by the warmest possible greeting. It really rather overcame me for a moment—the wide smile, the look of *really* being glad to see me, the powerful handshake of that massive hand of his, and the great booming voice: 'How ah you? You look grrand!' etc. I am fairly sophisticated about the 'charm' for which he is famous, but usually it is exerted when there is some ruction to smooth out, or some distinguished person to greet. Anyway, I was convinced he was genuinely glad to see me apparently well again, and back on the job."[12]

A concomitance was his extreme reluctance to cause pain or to be perceived as the cause of pain; this made it extremely difficult, sometimes even impossible for him to remove unfit subordinates in any direct, straightforward fashion. Elaborate and devious to the point of absurdity were some of the devices he employed to obtain resignations he desired without personally directly hurting the resignees. And if these didn't work, he often, in the early years of his administration, used Howe as hatchet man; the acerbic Howe had no personal concern whatever for the feelings of anyone who hindered, advertently or inadvertently, the triumphant progress of his beloved Franklin. As we shall see, General Johnson's temperamental administrative operations ultimately added up to what Ickes in his diary described as a "serious load for the Administration," so serious "that the President ought to get rid of him at once." And the President, Ickes went on, "has been trying to lose him, but he is so tender-hearted that he has not been able to say the final word . . . hasn't been able to tell him point blank that he has to go."[13] Considerable damage was done the administration in an election year before Roosevelt managed to obtain, without specifically asking for it, Johnson's letter of resignation, and he accepted this in a way that not only soothed the general's hurt but also retained his personal friendship for some time to come. One of the very few of whom Roosevelt himself emphatically, angrily demanded a resignation was Dean Acheson, whom he suspected, unjustly as he later learned, of leaking to the press information detrimental to the administration's gold policy, to which Acheson was strongly opposed.

Yet, surprisingly, there also ran through the complicated Roosevelt personality a thin, steel-edged cruelty, a narrow and deeply buried streak of sadism which seemed to contradict his empathic sensitivity,* which did flatly contradict his general kindliness, but which was consistent with his instinct for power and with the masked vindictiveness of his dealings with those (they were very few) who had shamed him or otherwise made him feel small.

The sadism was manifested in certain of his ways of maintaining and exercising power. Take, for instance, his notorious penchant for blurred or actually duplicative assignments of authority among those who served him, as in the drafting of securities marketing and industrial recovery legislation during the Hundred Days and in the establishment of rival agencies to deal with public works, industrial cooperation, and unemployment relief, though none of these could realize its full potential without close cooperation from the other two. This caused, as he could not but have known that it would, much pain and suffering for those involved in the turmoil; it brought the sufferers often into his office for personal applications of his soothing charm. Witness, too, his assurance of bitter administrative quarrel *within* an agency, notably in the AAA and the NRA, by his appointment to key posts of people who violently disagreed with one or another of the purposes of the organic act and, consequently, about operating policy. Perhaps, as some Roosevelt apologists were to claim, his intent was in part to foster creative competition whereby, in self-defense and the service of their ambitions, subordinates were forced to be tough and innovative while working to the limit of their capacities. One may cite that in some areas and at some times there did result a competition of ideas

---

*Actually, of course, a species of empathic sensitivity is an essential ingredient of sadomasochism.

leading to useful innovations that might not otherwise have been achieved, and there is no denying that the seemingly endless quarrels kept popular attention focused upon the processes of government, which were rendered by them dramatically exciting. We have seen, however, that Roosevelt's legislative operations were for the most part opportunistic responses to unforeseen challenges, very seldom were they expressions of his own deep-laid plans, and this fact casts doubt upon the notion that his own conscious intent was as his apologists claim. Moreover, the preponderance of evidence is that his way of organizing the execution of legislative mandates, far from maximizing creative efficiency, had overall precisely the opposite effect: It commonly diverted into unproductive and even counterproductive effort, through hurt and anxiety and anger and despair, human energies that might have been otherwise concentratedly devoted to the public good. An especially glaring example would be the angry dispute between Ickes and Harry Hopkins which raged in 1934 and 1935 over control of federal unemployment relief fund expenditures. Rooted in Roosevelt's failure to make a clear-cut decision on funding priorities, it provoked bitter comment from relief field investigator Lorena Hickok in the fall of 1935. "Months and months of rowing over who is going to run the show," wrote Hick to Eleanor. "And hence—no show running," this while "out here [Hick wrote from Toledo, Ohio] thousands of people *aren't* getting enough to eat, are facing evictions, begging for little jobs at a 'security wage' that none of us could live on. . . ."[14] Insofar as such arrangements clearly had a definite conscious purpose in Roosevelt's mind, it was to keep decisive power exclusively in his own hands—to make himself the final arbiter of every conflict, the court of last appeal. And this conscious purpose was certainly consonant with an unconscious sadism the essence of which was an urgent need to dominate other human beings and which derived a peculiar pleasure, wholly unadmitted, of course, from the pain and suffering, the anguished turmoil, that accompanied the quarrels he tacitly encouraged.

We know, too, that Roosevelt liked to shock and surprise, frankly enjoying the outrage provoked, from those committed to them, by his flouting of conventions, his violation of deeply held beliefs. He did so on the night he gaily announced to Warburg, Lew Douglas, and Feis his abandonment of the gold standard. He did so again, in a somewhat different but even more painful way, in his final dealings with Moley at the London Conference.

He also liked to tease. Generally this teasing was a harmless, if embarrassing, "kidding." Thus Roosevelt never let Howe forget his demonstrated inability to balance a checkbook during Roosevelt's 1912 state senatorial reelection campaign or let Lorena Hickok forget the summer night she, sleeping in Eleanor's White House sitting room, opened wide all the windows, triggering thereby a dehumidifier which, running full blast all night, spread three inches of water by morning over a lovely and expensive blue rug of which Eleanor was especially fond. Roosevelt again and again referred to the dehumidifier, in front of other people in Hickok's presence, as "Hick's rugwashing machine." Similarly with Sam Rosenman's attempt to hide his dislike of the cocktails Governor Roosevelt pressed upon him during cocktail hours in the Albany Executive Mansion, an attempt that involved Rosenman's surreptitious pouring of unwanted drinks into the soil of potted plants. "A peculiar thing happened to our potted plants in Albany when I was governor," Roosevelt in the White House would begin the story, concluding, "and that's why Sam is never offered a second drink."[15] But by no means all his kidding was of this happy nature. He was fond of teasing those who had no defense against it, people close to him who were especially vulnerable to hurts from him, their sensitivities being nakedly exposed to him by their yearning for his affection and good opinion. The notably humorless Henry Morgenthau, who was especially privileged in many ways by his long personal friendship with Roosevelt (it became standard procedure for him to lunch with the President, often alone, each Monday), was by the same token the most frequent target of a teasing that hurt, that was sometimes actually cruel. There were occasions when Morgenthau, at cabinet meetings, was so terribly, obviously hurt by things Roosevelt said that even those who resented and envied Morgenthau's special position vis-à-vis the President became embarrassed by Roosevelt's ill behavior and sympathetic with his victim. Another frequent victim of Roosevelt's teasing was the extremely touchy, vain, self-righteous, self-centered, but also extremely able Harold Ickes, though "Honest Harold," to judge from his diary, never realized how many of the things Roosevelt said and did to him during their long association were deliberately designed to "get a rise" out of him. (The pugnacious Ickes, one should add, never failed to "rise.")

As for Roosevelt's familial relationships, with both his blood family and "official family," they remained in the White House as they had been in Albany and before. Sara Delano Roosevelt continued to preside over the Big House at Hyde Park, with visits to Washington now and then, and the tensions between her and Eleanor, who, when in Hyde Park, continued to headquarter at Val-Kill Cottage, were of the same kind and intensity as before, with Roosevelt continuing blandly to ignore their existence. There was no more emotional intimacy between him and his wife than there had been for the last decade. He remained closer to Missy LeHand, who was far more a sympathetic companion and helpmeet for him, than to Eleanor. On occasion he was intensely irritated, for all his patience, by his wife's attempts to influence him on policy matters and displayed his irritation before others. But such occasions were, on the evidence, very rare. His respect for Eleanor as a person, his respect for her moral judgment on current affairs remained of the very highest, and the two of them continued to function as a remarkably effective team of Chief Executive and First Lady, complementing each other, supplementing each other, and presiding with grace and ease over White House social functions. Those who dined at the White House table generally agreed that the conversation there, during which strong contrary opinions were freely expressed and vehemently argued, more than made up for the mediocre quality of the food.

During his White House years Roosevelt, when occasion required it, publicly affirmed his Christian faith. (Once, when a questioner asked him for a statement of his "philosophy," he abruptly drew a psychological curtain between himself and his interlocutor. "My philosophy?" he replied dismissively with just a hint of rebuke. "I am a Christian and a Democrat."[16]) He commonly referred to lucky chances as providential: it was Divine Providence, divine intervention that had preserved him from the assassin's bullets at Miami, for instance. But he continued to make, in Washington as in Albany, very slight display of his religious belief, seldom attending church services because, as he had said, he hated to be "stared at" while he said his prayers. Of religious fervor, religious feeling of any strength, he displayed none at all.

Thus was the "vibrant personality" of the leader who dominated American political life during the 1930s—to return for a moment to Broadus Mitchell's terminology.

And certainly this unique temperament, magnificent in so many ways, had a significant influence upon mighty events.

II

THE influence, however, was not the kind that can be precisely, objectively measured, either during the time of its exertion or later. It was atmospheric. It was a weather of the national spirit. As such it created or shaped no institutions, no organized ways of doing things which remained after the direct influence was itself withdrawn.

Indeed, it is a general truth of political history that the "pattern" which remains after perspective has rendered "persons" no longer important, they being seen by a distant vision as mere elements or agents of "inevitable" developments, this pattern or scheme of relationships is *never* determined by personality or temperament. It is always a pattern of mind; it is determined by mental operations. It is a residue of thoughtful procedure, the product of a logic, if very often a flawed logic, whereby concepts and specific ideas were given practical application. Which is to say that every shape we now see in the enduring pattern resulted originally from a design of political intelligence upon challenging force within a context of uncontrollable or, at any rate, uncontrolled circumstances.

And in the 1930s, as in every other period of Western history since the seventeenth century, the challenging force was the physical energy released by science through technology into the realm of human purpose, where it had to be rationally controlled by human beings through their social and economic institutions and used thereby to enhance the quality of individual human lives, if it were not to be permitted by mindless selfishness to become a blind, inhuman determinant of human affairs. A Frankenstein's monster. Even amid the adversities of the Great Depression, as if possessed of a will of its own, scientific technology continued to advance at an accelerating pace. It snatched more and more power out of the natural world into the human world, power that bred in living men and women a mingling of hopeful happiness with anxious dread, a mingling of increased creature comfort and security with an increased creature misery and insecurity, the dread and misery being latterly predominant. For it was accompanied, this technological advance, by a swelling abundance of unsolved socioeconomic problems.

In other words, two factors were operating and interacting within that weather of the national spirit, that climate of attitude and feeling and opinion, which Franklin Roosevelt's "vibrant personality" so greatly influenced.

One factor was mind—the mind of the New Deal.

The other factor was force—the force of scientific progress and technological development.

Each must be taken account of by anyone who would accurately appreciate Roosevelt as political leader and the New Deal as historical event or process.

Hence we do not interrupt our story, we but provide a useful preface to our consideration of the mind of the New Deal in action, when we pause here for a brief look at what was happening in science and technology during the years of Roosevelt's presidential election and the launching of the New Deal.

III

THESE years happened to be a period of remarkably fruitful research into the nature of the atom. Discoveries pregnant with meaning for Roosevelt's future, and our own, were made one after another with breathtaking speed.

Thirty-odd years before, in the late 1890s, shortly after Henri Becquerel's discovery of radioactivity, two different rays—or particles, for they manifested both wave and particle properties—were identified among the emissions from radioactive substance. One was the alpha ray, having a positive electrical charge; the other was the beta ray, negatively charged. Also emitted were gamma rays, which resemble X rays but have a shorter wavelength. Because alpha rays have high energy—that is, they travel very fast, at a significant fraction of the speed of light—they have a penetrative power that was amazing to early-twentieth-century physicists. The great Ernest Rutherford in Cambridge University's Cavendish Laboratory promptly used them to bombard thin sheets of metal in a series of landmark experiments that discovered the atomic nucleus and led Danish theoretical physicist Niels Bohr to describe the structure of the atom as a nucleus the diameter of which is a tiny fraction of the whole atom's diameter but which comprises almost all of the atom's mass and the positive charge of which holds in thrall one (as in hydrogen) or more negatively charged electrons in somewhat the same way as the sun holds the planets in orbit.

Ever since, physicists had been using subatomic particles to bombard elements, proving that the nucleus is itself a composite, that in fact, radioactivity is nuclear disintegration whereby component particles are shot out, and two German physicists, Walther Bothe and H. Becker, were using alpha rays on beryllium in 1930 when they jarred loose from the bombarded element a mysterious radiation having a penetrative power greater than even the most powerful gamma rays, which until then were the most penetrative radiation known. In early 1932 British physicist James Chadwick discovered that the new radiation, which could easily pass through *several inches* of lead, consisted of particles that had the same mass as protons but that, unlike the positively charged proton or any other known subatomic particle, bore *no* electrical charge. Hence the name "neutron" bestowed upon it.[17] Hence, too, its penetrative power, despite the fact that it had in this experiment no remarkably high energy, the neutron, being uncharged, was unaffected by the atomic electrical fields through which it passed.

And Chadwick's was but the first of three tremendously exciting discoveries made by physical scientists in the year of Roosevelt's election. The second was American physicist Carl D. Anderson's laboratory observation of a subatomic particle, an "antielectron," the existence of which had been predicted by British theoretical physicist P. A. M. Dirac in 1930. Anderson conducted an experiment designed to determine whether the cosmic rays continuously raining down on earth from outer space (they had been first detected during high-altitude balloon experiments in 1911) were charged particles, as was strongly suggested by the research results of American physicist Arthur H. Compton, or were electromagnetic radiation, as was strongly asserted by American physicist Robert A. Millikan. Anderson placed a quarter-inch-thick sheet of lead over a Wilson cloud chamber,* which was in turn placed in a strong magnetic field, the purpose of the lead screen being to slow the tremendously energetic cosmic rays sufficiently to permit their paths through the cloud chamber to be tracked. He found that the cosmic ray tracks did indeed curve as those of charged particles should, but he also found that certain of the particles knocked out of the screening lead's atoms by the cosmic rays made tracks of precisely the kind electrons make; only they curved toward the *negative* instead of the positive side of the magnetic field. Clearly they were Dirac's predicted "antielectrons," they were electrons of *positive* charge, and Anderson promptly dubbed them positrons. Highly significant was the fact that no positron had more than a flashing instant of existence as an individual entity. When it encountered an electron, both it and the electron were annihilated in an explosion of gamma radiation. This was evidential confirmation of the validity of Einstein's mass-energy equation with its conjoined suggestion of the convertibility of matter into energy, and vice versa, though the Anderson experiment did nothing directly to prove the latter.

The third exciting discovery of 1932 was the only one greatly publicized in

---

*Some 30 million Americans viewed a Wilson cloud chamber in operation in an exhibit in the Hall of Science of Chicago's Century of Progress Exposition in 1933 and 1934, most of them for the first time, though this device had been a major research tool of physicists for nearly four decades, having been invented in 1895 by Scottish physicist C. T. R. Wilson. The chamber, made of transparent glass, is filled with a thick water fog, and as charged particles shoot through this fog, they leave in it tracks of ionized atoms. Different kinds of particles leave different kinds of tracks, enabling the physicist to identify many of them merely by studying their tracks.

the popular press, largely because of the nomenclature applied to it by scientists. This discovery was American chemist Harold C. Urey's isolation of a hydrogen isotope having twice the atomic weight of ordinary hydrogen, "heavy hydrogen," scientists called it, which linked with oxygen to form "heavy water" $(H^2)_2O$. Urey proposed the name "deuterium" for the heavy hydrogen atom, "deuteron" for the nucleus. There was at once a great flurry of experimentation to determine the incidence of deuterium in nature, the peculiar properties of heavy water, and the most efficient means of concentrating it. Predictably it proved to have a higher boiling point than ordinary water (101.42 C, as compared with 100 C), was found to occur in nature in a ratio of 1 part to about 6,000 of common H_2O, and could be best concentrated by electrolysis. Living creatures had difficulty using heavy water in their vital processes and sometimes couldn't use it at all. Thus tobacco seeds which promptly sprouted in ordinary water failed to do so after two weeks of contact with heavy water only.

The year 1932 had also been a year of marked advance in the development of a new atomic research tool known as the accelerator because its purpose was to increase the speed (energy) of particles focused in a beam directed at elementary substances, thus increasing the beam's efficiency as "atom smasher." British physicists J. D. Cockroft and E. T. S. Walton in 1928 had invented a voltage multiplier, which, improved in 1932, could impart to a proton beam an energy of nearly a half million electron volts. Using such a beam, they achieved, simultaneously with the three major discoveries we've described, the first ever human-induced disintegration of an atomic nucleus; they shattered the nuclei of lithium atoms. But already the Cockroft-Walton machine was being surpassed in efficiency. In the radiation laboratory of the University of California, E. O. Lawrence and his team of researchers were putting the finishing touches on a small model of a so-called cyclotron, a particle accelerator the design of which had been conceived by Lawrence some years before. In October 1932 this small model gave to a beam of protons an energy of 1.2 million electron volts (1.2 Mev)—the highest energy ever produced up to that time—and by then the plan to build a full-scale cyclotron, capable of producing immensely greater particle energies, was being implemented. Yet another and wholly different kind of accelerator, which had been invented around 1930 by R. J. Van de Graff at Princeton University and which caught the public's attention in the year of Roosevelt's election because its operation provided the press with spectacular photographs, was a so-called electrostatic generator. Improved and greatly enlarged in 1933 and 1934, it could then produce a 4 Mev beam of protons.

These research-tool developments clearly meant that basic experimental research in atomic physics must soon become almost exclusively a function of large-scale, massively financed organizations employing people by the score in ever-larger, ever more expensively equipped research facilities, for the efficiency of the new accelerators varied directly with their size and cost. The latter would soon amount to millions of dollars per machine.* Evidently, here, as in virtually every other realm of human activity in technologically advanced and advancing countries, the individual was being increasingly immersed or submerged in the collective.

Eagerly, rapidly physicists and chemists moved forward in 1933 and 1934 along the paths opened up to them by the discoveries of 1932. There was an explosive expansion of knowledge about the physical world.

The heavy-hydrogen nucleus, deuteron, was at once recognized as an extremely effective "bullet" for shooting at nuclei, perhaps more efficient for this purpose than the protons and alpha particles used theretofore, and simultaneously with Roosevelt's launching of the New Deal, deuterons were being so used in several laboratories. Lawrence and colleagues, employing the small cyclotron, managed to impart an energy of 3 Mev to deuterons and demonstrated among other things that a deuteron consists of a proton and a neutron (the alpha ray or particle was found to consist of two protons and two neutrons). In England in 1934, physicist M. L. E. Oliphant and a co-worker used deuterons to bombard deuterium itself, producing a "super heavy" hydrogen (tritium it was called, at Urey's suggestion), the nucleus of which consisted of a proton and two neutrons and which had, consequently, an atomic weight of 3. It proved to be unstable; having emitted an electron, tritium was transmuted into a stable but, in nature, extremely rare isotope of helium, helium 3.

In Paris a few weeks later the husband and wife team of Frédéric and Irène Joliot-Curie (she was the daughter of Marie and Pierre Curie, discoverers of radium), aided by Anderson's identification of the positron, demonstrated conclusively that radioactivity could be induced in naturally stable elements by particle bombardment. The universally prevailing assumption among scientists had been that the nuclear disintegration which occurred under bombardment did so only at the instant of impact, or immediately thereafter. The Joliot-Curies found, however, that aluminum bombarded with alpha particles not only emitted positrons as well as protons at the instant of impact but continued to emit positrons for several minutes after the bombardment had ceased. A similar temporary radioactivity was induced, in the same way, in boron and magnesium.

Meanwhile, at the University of Rome, Enrico Fermi was completing a paper arguing on theoretical grounds that neutrons, because of their lack of charge, would be much more effective of nuclear disintegrations than protons

*By 1939 the University of California had a cyclotron with magnets five feet across, which could accelerate particles to 20 million electron volts (20 Mev). By 1946 California had a synchrocyclotron capable of imparting 400 Mev to particles. A half dozen years later the Soviet Union had what it called a phasotron which could accelerate to 10 billion electron volts (10 Bev), and two years after that, in Geneva, an international agency having a dozen nation members (the European Committee for Nuclear Research, or CERN) began operating a "strong-focusing" cyclotron that achieved 30 Bev. Some 300 yards in diameter, with a circular track a fifth of a mile long, this giant machine cost $30 million, and the drive toward yet larger machines capable of achieving yet higher energies continued apace.

or deuterons or alpha particles, a paper published only a few weeks after the Joliot-Curies had announced the results of their experiments. By that time Fermi and his colleagues had worked out a way to produce neutrons in sufficient quantity to test his hypothesis (they used a sealed tube about six millimeters in diameter containing beryllium powder and radon), whereupon, stimulated to do so by the news from Paris, they focused neutron beams on some sixty elements, inducing radioactivity in forty of them.

A pregnant question at once arose. What would happen if a *naturally* radioactive element, such as uranium, were bombarded with neutrons? Fermi and his colleagues, in the immediately following years, were to do repeated experiments designed to answer this question and were quickly followed by others along this fateful path, notably by Austrian physicist Lise Meitner and German physicist Otto Hahn working together in Berlin. The latter two were in the midst of a tremendously significant series of experiments which produced highly puzzling results—experiments continued by Hahn cooperating with German physicist Fritz Strassmann—when Hitler incorporated Austria into the Third Reich and so forced Meitner, a Jewess (her Austrian citizenship had theretofore protected her against Nazi anti-Semitic law), to flee to Stockholm. From Stockholm, Meitner, having pondered the puzzling experimental results she, Hahn, and Strassmann had obtained, was to announce their meaning in a letter published in the British journal *Nature* in January 1939, perhaps the most ominously fateful letter ever written. . . .

But already, before the first year of the New Deal had ended, this new atomic information, especially in view of the amazing rate at which it piled up, was arousing more dark apprehension than joyous anticipation among the few aware of its implications. Already it suggested a possible realization, perhaps within the next half century or so, of what had long been but a fantasy dream of science fictioneers (H. G. Wells for one; perhaps Jules Verne, even earlier, with his mysteriously powered submarine in *Twenty Thousand Leagues Under the Sea*)—namely, the unlocking and harnessing to human purposes, for good or evil, of the incredibly vast energy contained in atoms.[18] Albert Einstein's mass-energy equation, $E = mc^2$, which defines matter as intensely concentrated energy, was not in 1933 and 1934 the common knowledge it later became. Probably Roosevelt had never heard of it when he entered the White House; certainly he perceived no relevance of it to his own role, his own responsibilities. But those who did know of it, and of the accumulating experimental proof of its validity, were aware that a mere ounce of matter totally converted into energy would yield as much of it as, say, the burning of 52,702 *tons* of gasoline, were aware, too, that if the ounce's conversion were rendered instantaneous, the explosive force would equal that of thousands of tons of TNT. They were also painfully, even agonizingly aware of the vast disproportion between this awesome physical power and the social intelligence available to determine its uses.

Sensitive, knowledgeable, and humane minds, committed to the general welfare, could not but contemplate with horror even a remote possibility of atomic energy's release, either as controlled power applied to economic ends or as explosive force applied to war, within the "capitalist system" and conjoined anarchy of unlimited national sovereignties that now prevailed over the Western world. They shuddered at the very thought of placing physical power of these dimensions at the disposal of the kind of man who normally rose to posts of decisive authority over corporate business or political government, the two being organically linked, in even a politically democratic society, so long as that society assumed a passion for private profit, bodily pleasures, and "getting ahead" to be the prime and proper motive for individual human behavior. One could only hope that as Einstein himself then believed, the unleashing of atomic energy, even if all the requisite knowledge were at hand, could not be accomplished within the lifetime of anyone now on earth because of its enormous technical difficulty, that in the meantime there would become dominant the "new manner of thinking" required "if mankind is to survive," as Einstein later said,[19] and that as a concomitant of this development, a new social order would be created out of the elements freed by the breakdown of the old one. Clearly it must be an order based on principles radically different from those now generally operative, an order that encouraged not aggressive competitiveness but the spirit of cooperation, not acquisitive selfishness but compassionate generosity, not professional lying for personal profit but a plain and simple speaking of the truth for the good of all. And to minds thus aware and sensitive and humane, the success of Roosevelt's New Deal was to be measured by the progress it made toward the establishment of this new order.

IV

BUT if knowledge of what was going on in basic science stimulated such apocalyptic vision as has been here indicated, it was certainly no indispensable prerequisite to an advocacy of fundamental social change. For this, a common knowledge of what was going on in applied science (technology) sufficed.

Consider, first, the advance being made in communications technology.

In 1928 the general public had been amazed to learn of photographs being transmitted by radio from Oakland, California, to Schenectady, New York. By the first year of the New Deal such transmission was a common occurrence, and it was widely known that swift progress was being made in television, the development of which had been initiated by British inventor J. L. Baird in 1926. In 1933 a special type of cathode-ray tube, called an iconoscope, was being used to scan (pick up for broadcast) scenes illuminated by natural light only and used also for the reproduction of such scenes in receiving sets, with the result that by the end of 1934 research into mechanical systems for this purpose had been virtually abandoned. The technology now existed, as well-informed people knew, for the publication of a truly national newspaper. Identical editions could be simultaneously issued in every city of the land, every word and picture the same save for local advertisements (blanks could be left for these by the national broadcaster). But well-informed people also knew that the potency of print journalism of any kind, which Roosevelt believed to be already signifi-cantly reduced by radio, might become negligible as "inevitable progress" led to nationwide television broadcasts, with television sets to receive them in most American homes.

Such prospect, viewed in relation to the current business control of press and radio in America and of the alarmingly rapid concentration of this control in ever-fewer and -larger corporations, was less pleasing than anxious for those few Americans who were well informed on this matter and who greatly valued individual freedom, especially freedom of thought, expression, and access to accurate information. Insofar as human freedom has two aspects or necessary conditions—namely, an inward capacity to choose and an outward environ-ment containing multiple objects among which choices may be made—free-dom can be lost in two different ways. It can, of course, be lost to brute force, whereby the inward capacity for choice is frustrated, the bodily self being incarcerated and coerced, but it can also be lost insidiously through a degrad-ing or impoverishment of the environment—through a removal from the environment, deliberately or inadvertently, of all objects of choice save those conforming to the ideas or wishes of some special interest or group of interests. And it was the latter kind of human bondage, a completely standardized mental environment for the whole of the nation, created and maintained by businessmen or by politicians or bureaucrats, in conformity with their special interests and values, an environment in which minds would wither for lack of stimulating nourishment or exercise—it was this kind of insidious bondage that seemed likely to result from practical applications of the developing communications technology within the prevailing system of social and eco-nomic relationships.

Already, within the lifetimes of most Americans, there had been a considera-ble reduction in the diversity of easily available printed news and opinion sources—a considerable erosion, in other words, of the average citizen's free-dom in this field. At the opening of the twentieth century, when the population of the United States was around 76,000,000, 2,226 daily newspapers were being published in the nation. The great majority were of mediocre quality, many were positively bad, but they were individually owned and hence inclined to express on their editorial pages, more widely read then than now, individual points of view upon matters which a well-informed public opinion must decide in any healthy democracy. Nine years later, when the U.S. population totaled 90,000,000, the number of daily papers being published had risen to 2,600; the number of different dailies had increased at a rate faster than population growth till then. However, 1909 was the peak year for number of dailies, as it was a peak year for the Progressive movement; thereafter the number of dailies fell as population rose. By 1920, when the U.S. population had risen to 106,021,537, the number of dailies had fallen to 2,326, a loss of 276 papers within a decade, and a larger proportion of those published than ever before were elements of newspaper chains or "empires" (Munsey's, Hearst's, Scripps's, etc.) and expressive, therefore, of a single point of view and standard of values. By 1933, when U.S. population had climbed to nearly 126,000,000, the number of dailies had shrunk to 1903, and nearly 80 percent of these (more than 1,500) were published in towns or cities having but one paper or, if two, a single owner of the two.[20] The increase in multiple newspaper ownership, along with the national syndication of opinion columns and other features on an unprecedented scale, ensured a reduction in the diversity of printed news source and points of view considerably greater than in the number of papers. So did the fact that increased size in the surviving papers tended to make these in themselves big business, increasing the degree of subordination of newsroom and editorial chamber to the business office.

Certainly the rise of radio journalism and entertainment had done nothing to halt the trend toward mental standardization among the American populace. Radio network broadcasting had had, in fact, a precisely opposite effect. Nominally regulated in the public interest by a Federal Communications Commission which in 1934 assumed functions formerly performed by a Federal Radio Commission (it issued licenses to broadcast on prescribed wavelengths), radio networks were actually wholly controlled by the business interests that owned them. These made very sure that network broadcast programs were keyed to the lowest common denominator of popular interest and taste, that little of a "controversial" nature was aired at all, and that the presumed government "regulators" were rendered powerless effectively to regulate, even if they were so inclined, as most of them, in the circumstances, could not be. Moreover, the use of radio as an advertising medium—a development opposed at its outset by many prominent Americans, including Herbert Hoover who, as secretary of commerce, favored government action to prevent it—seemed bound to have some erosive effect upon the advertising revenues of the print media, thus encouraging a further decline in the number of newspapers and magazines published.

As for the "radio commercial" per se, though passively endured by most Americans as the price they had to pay for such entertainments as *Amos n' Andy* or Fred Allen or Jack Benny, it provoked angry outrage in virtually all concerned with the life of the mind, being deemed by these a nauseating pollutant of the cultural environment which should be outlawed forthwith. Especially outrageous during the opening years of the New Deal were two innovations reputedly introduced by the American Tobacco Company's George Washington Hill, innovations all too promptly adopted by other admen. One was the use of endless and endlessly irritating reiteration ("L.S.M.F.T., Lucky Strike Means Fine Tobacco") to drive a chanted "commercial message" so deeply into the mind it could not be got out in a lifetime thereafter. The other was the replacing of the lyrics of some familiar song with lyrics extolling some commercial product so that, forever after, the song was identified with that product. The crass and thieving vulgarity of the latter appalled millions when the practice first began; it meant that one long-beloved tune after another, transformed into a "singing commercial," would be destroyed as any kind of aesthetic experience.

Small wonder that millions of Americans longed for a U.S. equivalent of the British Broadcasting Corporation—a public nonprofit corporation having in its charge all radio broadcasting, whose employees were rigorously protected against outside pressures, political or otherwise, as they did their work; whose openness to diverse points of view was as rigorously insured; and which broadcast no commercials at all.

Yet obviously, in the circumstances, it was the American experience of radio over the last decade that foretold the American experience of television a decade or two hence. And those who hated what had happened to the marvelous technology of radio when it came under the businessman's control were bound to hate even more strongly, were bound to fear as an impending social disaster of measureless proportions what would happen as television, a yet more marvelous technology, marched inevitably and inexorably into the same dominion. For one thing, further hundreds of newspapers and dozens of magazines might be forced to suspend publication as commercial television drained away from the print media an increasingly large proportion of the total advertising budgets of firms making and selling consumer goods. For another, the crushing impact of the lowest common denominator upon American cultural and political life would be immensely increased by the addition of sight to sound over the airwaves. Witness the tremendous augmentation of vivid impact and attention absorption that accrued to the motion picture when sound tracks were added to reels!

So it was that the developing television technology lent urgency to the arguments of those who had long favored fundamental change in the management of America's communications facilities. Numerous critics of the American press, convinced that a totally free flow of information on all matters of public concern is a, if not *the,* prime necessity of any truly free society, had for years inveighed in published writings and public speech against the distortions and suppressions of the news that inevitably resulted from the press proprietor's dependence upon advertising revenue as well as from the buying and selling of the news as if it were a physical commodity of the same order as pig iron, or soap, or groceries. For years they had argued that communications in a democracy ought not to be controlled by business or any other special interest, political or bureaucratic or religious, whose adherents might gain power or wealth through manipulations of the popular mind, but should instead be entirely controlled by professional communicators—men and women whose basic commitment was to the communications job itself, to the gathering and interpretation of news of all kinds, in the same way as a scholar is committed to scholarship, a scientist to science, an artist to art, a teacher to teaching. "A sound system of communication, such as lies at the roots of civilization, cannot be built upon a structure of economic warfare," Kenneth Burke was writing during the first year of the New Deal. "It must be economically as well as spiritually Communistic—otherwise the wells of sociality are poisoned. . . . A sound communicative medium arises out of cooperative enterprises. And the mind, so largely a linguistic product, is constructed of combined cooperative and communicative materials. Let the system of cooperation become impaired, and the communicative equipment is correspondingly impaired, while this impairment of the communicative medium in turn threatens the structure of rationality itself." And one of America's great teachers was suggesting in that same year a possible solution to the problem of freeing the press from what he called its commercial bondage without imposing upon it that political or coercive governmental bondage which "Communistic" implied to most Americans. Since the "motives" of the investigative reporter "are essentially the same as those of the scholar," said Alexander Meiklejohn, and since "the work of the editor and reporter is, in the fullest sense, educational," it might be well to "make the newspaper [and radio] a part of the university," thereby "joining together in the same enterprise the advancement of learning and the spreading of the news." This would avoid the danger involved in any direct ownership and control of the press by government, the danger that the press would become a propaganda arm of government, as in Soviet Russia and Fascist Italy; it would enable editors and reporters to become "a self-governing, independent guild, just as is the university faculty," committed to "standards of excellence."[21]

Those who argued in this way, their anxiety growing insofar as they were aware of the rapid developments being made in television, could only hope that the New Deal with its greatly publicized Brain Trust recognized the communications problem to be of crucial long-term importance and placed efforts to solve it high on the agenda of reform. They would be inclined to use as one measure of the validity of the "Roosevelt Revolution" the progress made under Roosevelt's leadership toward the kind of communications arrangement they favored.

Such people were few in number, however, compared with the Americans who were rendered anxious and eager for social change by their belief that within the prevailing system, technological innovations had caused and threatened to increase "technological unemployment."

All through the 1920s the ratio of labor to capital in the overall production process, along with the ratio of wages to profits, had tended sharply downward, thanks to profit-motivated applications of new technology. In the flour-milling industry, for instance, the dollar value of the total product was the same in 1929 as it had been in 1923, but the number of workers in the industry had gone down during these half dozen years from 35,094 to 27,154 (a decline of 23 percent) and wages had gone down from $41,704,000 to $35,409,000 (a decline of 15 percent) while profits had risen from $160,000,000 to $185,000,000 (an increase of 16 percent). There had been similar developments during these same years in the chemical, steel, tobacco, and gas manufacturing industries, among many others.[22] The advent of the Great Depression had not called a halt to this general trend. On the contrary, the ratio of labor to capital and of wages to profits appeared to go down more swiftly. Profits had declined or disappeared at an appalling rate, certainly, but it was at an even more appalling rate that total wages declined and jobs disappeared.

There was no evident slackening of creative effort in applied science, no evident reduction of inventiveness in the field of technology as the depression deepened. Every year since the crash had seen some 118,000 patent applications pour into the U.S. Patent Office, which, every year, had issued patents in a number approximating 49,000. For the most part the patented inventions were improvements upon existent machines, designed to increase their efficiency and so to reduce labor costs. Increasingly applied to the same end were patents issued in earlier years but neglected until now. An example was the recent introduction of the diesel oil engine to locomotives; it reduced the hourly wage cost of locomotive operation by 64 percent—that is, from $2.75 per hour on steam locomotives to 99 cents on diesels.[23]

Much emphasis was being placed by industrialists upon increased automation, and much of the automation involved use of the photoelectric cell or electric eye.

> An unusual variety of uses has been found for this mechanical eye, which never knows fatigue, is marvelously swift and accurate, can see with invisible light, and coordinates with all the resources of electricity. It sorts beans, fruit, and eggs, measures illumination in studios and theaters, appraises color better than the human eye, classifies minerals, counts bills and throws out counterfeits, counts people and vehicles, determines thickness and transparency of cloth, detects and measures strains in glass, sees through fog, is indispensable in facsimile telegraphy, television and sound on film pictures, directs traffic automatically, and serves as an automatic train control.[24]

Thus W. F. Ogburn and S. C. Gilfallen on the photoelectric cell, in their "The Influence of Invention and Discovery," a section of the report of the Hoover-appointed President's Committee on Recent Social Trends, published in two volumes in 1933 under the title *Recent Social Trends in the United States.* The authors' evident enthusiasm for this new technological marvel, which might have been less evident had they written a few months after they did, was most emphatically not shared by those who made their livings out of sorting, or counting, or opening doors, or operating elevators, or doing any of the other things which the electric eye did or helped do better. The same lack of enthusiasm greeted for the same reason news of the increased use of electron tubes as industrial control devices and news of such typical developments as the changing of substations along the Panama Canal from manual to supervisory control. "Not only are dispatchers' orders more accurately and promptly obeyed," said the electrical engineer who reported this change with enthusiasm, "but decreased labor charges will pay for the installation in three years."[25]

The sum result of these technological developments was that America's industrial plant, by the end of Roosevelt's first year and a half in the White House, could produce considerably more goods than it had in 1928 when running full blast, and could do so with a smaller labor force. Moreover, every sign was that productive capability would continue to expand while the market for labor continued to contract. There were, of course, spokesmen for science and technology who claimed to see no such sign, spokesmen who were themselves of conservative political bent, hence reluctant to see any need for systemic change. "Every labor-saving device creates in general as many, oftentimes more, jobs than it destroys," asserted physicist Robert A. Millikan in public speech in February 1934. From the same platform on the same day, the president of the Massachusetts Institute of Technology, Karl A. Compton, stated an undoubted historical fact as if it were a present fact and future event, to wit: "Science has made jobs, not taken them away."[26] But the promise implicit in these pronouncements rang hollow in the ears of myriads who feared for their jobs. Where were the wonderful new inventions or technologies that would spawn new industries employing millions, as had the automobile, the airplane, the motion picture, the radio? They were desperately needed *now*!

At Chicago's Century of Progress Exposition, which opened in the spring of 1933, one of the featured exhibits in the Hall of Science, central to the whole exposition, was a three-room apartment wholly constructed of a new synthetic resin called Vinylite. Unlike Bakelite, which in 1933 was the most widely used synthetic resin, Vinylite could be cast and stamped and molded and sheeted and even used in solutions as a lacquer. Its use in combs, toothbrushes, and the new long-playing phonograph records, wherein sound grooves were much closer together than they could be in the waxes of which the great bulk of the records were currently made, was assured. But would it, would plastics in general, and *could* they in a profit-motivated society, create more jobs than were destroyed by them? What would happen to the carpenters, the bricklayers, the plasterers, the painters, the stonemasons currently employed in the making of walls and ceilings and floors if Vinylite became a major construction material? As for television, its development to the point of commercial feasibility was yet many years, perhaps decades away, and its economic impact when it reached that point might be but little more happy and fortunate than its virtually certain direct cultural impact within the current context of ownership and control. Its manufacture and sale and installation in American homes would, of course, create jobs. But would it not also take away jobs from, say, the motion-picture industry, motion-picture theaters, the legitimate theater, and, quite possibly, newspapers and magazines and book publishers?

Thus there was at hand no new invention or technological innovation that gave clear and definite promise of an increase in employment in the near future. There were several that threatened an opposite effect. And there was one that did this so ominously that its very inventors were reluctant to introduce its use on any large scale. This new machine, invented in 1927 by John Daniel Rust and his brother, Mack Donald Rust, was the mechanical cotton picker. Reportedly it was practically perfected by 1933, though it was not officially test-demonstrated until 1936. With its attached mechanical chopper it must render abruptly obsolete the small cotton farm and the small cotton farmer, (the tenant farmer who sharecropped, the man possessed of "forty acres and a mule," even the man possessed of four or five times as much) along with the labor of hundreds of thousands of seasonal hired hands. The making and selling of cotton pickers would employ but a tiny fraction of the number of people the machine would displace. What was to happen to the rest? Must they be forced off the land into the cities, there to swell the already swollen ranks of the urban unemployed?

V

ALL this added fuel to the fiery belief of those who raged against the Machine as enemy of Man—the Machine being identified with a scientific intelligence cold as death, Man being identified with warm, instinctual, passionate, com-passionate life. It was a belief that provided thematic material for many an impassioned essay and not a few novels, stories, and plays during the 1920s and early 1930s. Among these were the famous manifesto of the southern agrarian writers, *I'll Take My Stand;* fiction by the American Sherwood Anderson, the English D. H. Lawrence; and such plays as Karel Capek's *RUR,* wherein robots made their first appearance, and Eugene O'Neill's *Dynamo,* the central character of which worships electricity ("There is no God . . . but Electricity!") and dies embracing a dynamo. It was a belief providing general encouragement of the anti-intellectualism which is inevitably consequent upon an experiential splitting off of the analytical, thinking self from the willful, feeling self in the individual person and which had grown everywhere in the West, since the Great War, toward the dark flowering it actually achieved in the Italy of Mussolini, the Germany of Hitler.

But, of course, the belief was fallacious, said most of those who tried to see clearly the facts of the modern world through the eyes of reason and insisted upon thinking about the facts instead of just reacting to them.[27]

"Technological unemployment" was a misnomer, these people said, insofar as it implied that technology of itself alone caused permanent and absolute labor displacement; the permanent displacement occurred because the increase that the new technology made in per worker productivity was greater than the increase in total production and because wages were not raised, nor work hours lowered, in any just proportion to the increase of per hour worker production. Which is to say that it was not the machine, certainly it was not the scientific intellect from whose creative enterprise the machine emerged, which threat-ened humanity. The threat was born of the unhappy relationship between machine and prevailing socioeconomic system; it was the machine applied to the making of money for business rather than to the making of desired goods and services for human beings that became a Frankenstein's monster. For not only did the machine in this context make for a dangerously unjust distribution of wealth and power, even denying employment to millions, it also imposed upon society a tyranny of technology.

Consider how the system worked.

Any new technology that would make money for an entrepreneur, however harmful it might be in the long run to environment or general welfare, was likely to be applied even if the entrepreneur had monopoly control of it and so need not fear its use by a competitor; it was virtually certain to be applied if available to many, since market competition would then tend to force the event. Contrariwise, if a new technology were *not* privately profitable, it would *not* be applied, regardless of the benefits it might confer upon the general public. Such an economy denied to human beings, and to society as a whole, practically all power of choice among technological possibilities the realization of which would have immense social impact. Prevented was any orderly rational procedure whereby those possessed of the requisite expert knowledge— men freed of the pressures of special interest, men professionally committed to objective truth and the general good—could advise society of the possible, probable, or certain consequences of a given technological application, thus enabling society to decide beforehand, in terms of human values, what technologies were to be stressed, what played down, and which were to be rejected altogether. Such decisive control as now existed was severely limited by the fact that those who exercised it were themselves at the mercy of market-imposed technological imperatives; it was also concentrated in precisely the hands least likely to be moved by generous impulses, least likely to be guided by ideal concerns, they having generally come to the levers of power through the operations of a selective principle that richly rewarded energetic selfishness in pursuit of immediate gain while discouraging the taking of long views or any profound musings upon reasons why.

The practical result was a species of technological tyranny, as has been said, and a tyranny terrifying in its nature. The very fact that something *could* be done, was technically feasible, became a probability that it *would* be done sooner or later, willy-nilly—including the blowing up of the world with atomic weaponry in some not too distant future. Meanwhile, because the machine was out of rational control, it was likely to become increasingly *in* control of human lives, if the present system managed somehow to survive. People might find themselves doing more and more things, not of their own conscious volition but in simple reaction to technological stimuli and because technological process, or the organizational routines imposed by such process, demanded that they be done.

It was in part for this reason, if more effectively for other related reasons, that a good portion of the American intellectual community insisted upon *fundamental* social change. Even if the present economic system could be "patched up" and made to "run" awhile longer, it ought not to be but should instead be transformed at its roots. "The following . . . is written on the assumption that capitalism is dying and with the conviction that it ought to die," began a magazine article by Reinhold Niebuhr, published three days after Roosevelt's presidential inauguration. "It is dying because it is a contracting system which is unable to support the necessities of an industrial system that requires mass production for its maintenance. . . . It ought to die because it is unable to make the wealth created by modern technology available to all who participate in the productive process in terms of justice. . . ."[28] In the closing paragraph of his *Nation* review (February 1, 1933) of Adolf Berle and Gardiner Means's *The Modern Corporation and Private Property*, Ernest Gruening exclaimed: "Sing us no song of property rights!" For such "rights" had as their essence a decisive control over what one "owned," subject "only to the police power of the state," and "private ownership in America," so defined, had been already largely eliminated in regard to the most important property—namely, capital goods, by the rise of increasingly huge corporations. These were necessarily run not by a multitude of widely scattered and largely indifferent stockholders but by a management personnel that ruled by proxy and tended to be self-selected and self-perpetuating. Capitalism, then, was virtually at an end since "[p]rivate property is the cornerstone" of capitalism. Gruening made explicit statement of what seemed to most readers an inescapable conclusion of the highly factual Berle-Means argument, though a conclusion from which Berle himself shied away.* This conclusion was that the state must assume the corporate control now exercised irresponsibly, so far as the public was concerned, by private managers. Wrote Gruening: "[It is] inevitable . . . that in a self-governing democracy the people will proceed from control of the political State, and by means of it, to control of the economic super-power [the giant corporations]. . . ."[29]

But how viable, how permanent was "self-governing democracy" itself in the face of the present crisis? To this question there were flatly opposed answers from avant-garde American intellectuals who generally agreed with one another that capitalism was dead or dying.

Marxists and conservatives, including such relatively enlightened conservatives as Herbert Hoover, were as one in their assertion that democracy as institutionalized and practiced in America was the political manifestation of a private-property, private profit economic system and must therefore go down if or when this system went down. Extreme left and extreme right were also agreed that a regime of naked force, an iron dictatorship that suspended civil liberties and ruled by decree and coercion, must necessarily arise out of the current American crisis, as it had already arisen out of crisis in Russia, Italy, Germany. The two groups differed, of course, on the nature and purpose of the "inevitable" dictatorship. Fascists had no logical ideology, no clear conception of the historic end their dictatorship was to serve; their concern was simply to prevent by force, through the creation of a warrior and war-making state, any wholesale transfer of economic and political power away from the class now holding it, though their mass propaganda employed, cynically, a socialistic jargon. Communists, on the other hand, had an elaborate ideology derived from the premises of a so-called dialectical materialism. The coming dictatorship was dubbed by them a dictatorship of the proletariat and described by them as a transitional stage between capitalism and communism; it was to last only so long as was required for the "liquidation" of the "bourgeoisie" and the establishment of a "classless society" wherein, presumably, all men would be truly free and equal for the first time in recorded history— though the Marxists were notably obscure in their discussions of human freedom, a subject they were inclined to ignore.[30]

*See Davis, *FDR: The New York Years,* pp. 281–86.

The Fascist approach had little appeal to the American intellectual community, the bulk of whose members were now more alienated than ever before from the businessman and the business world. The one Fascist convert of any intellectual stature whatever, if one excepts the eccentric poet Ezra Pound, was a darkly romantic and baleful Wall Street economist named Lawrence Dennis. Dennis's first book, *Is Capitalism Doomed?* (1932), answered the title question with an emphatic yes. It was doomed because "our frontier days are over" and capitalism could maintain itself only if it had "new worlds to conquer." Lacking these, it must turn to war as the only "solution" to the problem of increasing unemployment. "Keeping six to eight million men unemployed . . . is the best known way to prepare for war." In *The Coming American Fascism* (1936) Dennis argued that fascism was preferable to communism, these being the only two choices open to America, because it would preserve private property and the market system and provide for a highly disciplined and efficient welfare state ruled by a "natural" elite. But Dennis found few readers, most of whom were repelled by his overassertiveness and by the brutal elitism, a passionate mood rather than a clear idea, which was his major premise and which, like Pound's political "philosophy," seemed rooted in self-hatred and sick despair.[31]

The case was different with the Communist approach. For this, ground was prepared by two American books published in the second and third years of the new decade. One was Lincoln Steffens's *Autobiography* (1931). In it, one of the greatest of the old muckrake journalists told in wonderfully vivid prose how, in a journey through the twentieth century during which he had known virtually every important person and witnessed virtually every important event, he had been abundantly confirmed in a conclusion he had reached soon after the century opened—namely, that America's "business civilization" was so corrupt and, by its very nature, corrupting that it could not possibly be reformed. It must be abolished. It *would* be abolished. All signs were that the United States must soon go in the direction pointed by Soviet Russia, where Steffens had seen the "future" in 1919 and been delighted to find that it "works." In public speech a few months after his book's publication, Steffens explicitly indicated his belief that America was headed for revolution and would then be guided by a few thousand dedicated revolutionaries into the "future." Similar was the conclusion reached by young John Chamberlain whose *Farewell to Reform* came out in 1932 and had tremendous immediate impact. In a style very different from Steffens's but highly effective, Chamberlain described the Progressive movement as an exercise in futility, its failure caused by a false view of the modern world and a foolishly optimistic assessment of human nature. Worse than useless now was the Progressive tradition, the Progressive heritage. For anyone who looked clear-eyed at the present "situation," said Chamberlain, the only alternative to personal cynicism was a commitment to social revolution.[32]

This conclusion was powerfully reinforced by British Marxist John Strachey, whose *The Coming Struggle for Power* was issued in its American edition in 1933. Writing with much of the ironic bite and all the sweeping force of his relative Lytton Strachey, John Strachey compelled thousands of American intellectuals to reexamine, reevaluate, and redefine against Marxist argument the "liberalism" to which most of them subscribed. Some were persuaded to do as Steffens and Chamberlain had already largely done: abandon altogether the historic liberal position, with its insistence upon the individual person as the primary initiating unit, and upon an exercised personal liberty as both means and end, of all valid political process.

The Marxist argument against gradualism in general, against institutionalized democracy in particular as a way of transition from old order to new, was disturbingly plausible. Anyone who believed in such painless evolution must believe, said the Marxists, that two economic systems flatly basically opposed to each other not only could exist peaceably in piecemeal side by side but also cooperate with each other in endeavors the end of which meant the "liquidation" of one of the two. Such wishful thinking was a "bourgeois" compound of cowardice and intellectual dishonesty that, if not itself Fascist in nature, was bound to lead in practice to fascism. (Chamberlain reached the same conclusion, saying that Progressive reforms were but a preparing of "ground for an American Fascism."[33]) For fascism was the final, desperate effort of an exploitive and obsolete "ruling class" to maintain itself against the effects of capitalism's fatal flaw, which was the contradiction between private property and modern production technique. It was an attempt to prevent by force and violence the onrush of that socialism which modern technique necessarily implied, and it was the *only* alternative to socialism (communism) as the outcome of the "coming struggle," in America as in the the rest of the Western world. Of course, fascism was a temporary phenomenon, doomed by history. Socialism was certain to come in the end if civilization survived, being a necessary condition of that survival. But *there* was the rub! Would or could civilization survive if America "went Fascist"? As the ultimate extreme of nationalism, fascism meant war, and the survival of civilization beyond a new world war more horrible, more devastating than the last was at best problematic.

All this was jarring, to say the least, to those who had theretofore accepted the tenets of liberalism unquestioningly. As an analysis and portrayal of the nature of capitalist crisis, Marxism, especially as written by Strachey, was powerfully persuasive.

It did not, however, persuade more than a small minority of American intellectuals into becoming avowed "fellow travelers" of the Communist party. It persuaded but a tiny handful into actual party membership. The reasons are not far to seek. The crudity with which party members interpreted and applied Karl Marx's relatively subtle and intellectually sophisticated materialism;* the consequent denigration of individual personality by the Communists as they

---

*As Bertrand Russell points out in his *History of Western Philosophy* (p. 783), Marx's "dialectical materialism" is more akin to the pragmatism of William James, the instrumentalism of John Dewey, than it is to traditional materialism. It in effect makes "true" an adverb instead of an adjective, the "truth" of an idea being determined by the consequences of that idea in action.

inordinately emphasized economic determinism, inevitability, and mass movements; the equally consequent arrogance and ruthless contempt for every form of civility which Communists displayed in arguments always, on their part, polemical; the inability of most Communists to explain how it happened that, everything being so predetermined and inevitable, everyman experienced such excruciating anguish of choice or decision as he indubitably did experience, or how it happened that consciousness itself had arisen in its present human form; the increasingly evident total identification of American Communism with the national interests of Stalin's Russia; above all, the jesuitical discipline and conspiratorial temper and eagerness to foment violence which characterized the Communist party and which, however necessary for the "radicalization" of the "masses" and the subversion of existing institutions, was wholly alien to the American spirit and outrageous of a common sense of decency—these were as a wall between the American intellectual community and any *total* commitment to Marxism in theory or communism in practice. Even those who felt compelled to accept the Marxist concept of class struggle as history's central dynamic and who therefore despaired of traditional democratic process as means to the necessary end, even these Americans retained, almost always, a stubborn, defiant belief in the primacy of the individual person, in the sacredness of the individual life, conjoined with a profound aversion to violent revolution. (They wanted their omelet, sneered the dedicated Communist, but were "morally" opposed to breaking eggs.)

Representative of one segment of the intellectual community, in this respect, was Reinhold Niebuhr in the magazine article already quoted. Niebuhr agreed with the Marxists that in the present crisis "liberalism" was the opposite of "political realism." He agreed also with the Marxist "judgment . . . that capitalism will not reform itself from within," there being "nothing in history to support the thesis that a dominant class ever yields its position or privileges in society because its rule has been convicted of ineptness or injustices." He did not, however, attribute this fact to the workings of some inexorable "law" of history that was itself *outside* history and humanity. Instead, he attributed it to the "stubborn inertia and blindness of collective egoism." The root cause of the social ill, in other words, was psychological. The evil was *human* evil; it was a failure of individual conscience. And the single specific prescription Niebuhr suggested for the illness's cure was also in essence psychological, having at its heart an appeal to individual conscience. He wrote:

> [I]t is important to recognize that neither the parliamentary nor the revolutionary course offers modern society any easy way to the mastery of technological civilization. . . . [I]t [therefore] becomes very important to develop such forms of resistance and mass coercion as will disturb the intricacies of an industrial civilization as little as possible, and as will preserve the temper of mutual respect within the area of social conflict. . . . Once the realities of this struggle are freely admitted, there is every possibility of introducing very important ethical elements into the struggle in the way, for instance, that Gandhi introduces them in India.

The strategy and tactics of organized nonviolent mass protest, of a passive resistance that aroused potent guilt feelings in the oppressor who sought to overcome it by forceful coercions—this *might* realize the always present possibility "that the old will capitulate and the new assume social direction without internecine conflict."[34]

Most American intellectuals, however, rejected altogether the class struggle tactic, nonviolent or no, as a means to desired ends.

Stuart Chase, no champion of civil liberties, did so only because the tactic was "unrealistic." It aimed toward "socialism or communism," which were (so Chase wrote, confusingly, if not confusedly) "production-age systems," whereas the present crisis was in his view transitional between a "production system" and a "distribution system." Nor had Chase "been able to find any hope in an enlightened or reformed capitalism" or to find any "body of doctrine competent to deal with this trend." So he was "thrown . . . back on the experimental method" as a way of developing the "philosophy and . . . social program for the age of production that is coming."[35] To run the system shaped by this "philosophy and program," Chase favored "an industrial general staff with dictatorial powers covering the smooth technical operation of all the major sources of raw material and supply. Political democracy can remain if it confines itself to all but economic matters. . . ." So he wrote in 1934, as Technocratic disciple of Veblen, in *The Economy of Abundance.*[36]

In his acceptance of experimental method, though it was a tentative and halfhearted acceptance, Chase was influenced by John Dewey. Dewey himself, reexamining the "philosophy of liberalism" in the early 1930s, saw no reason to abandon liberalism's commitment to "individuality" and "liberty" but every reason to redefine these in ways that realistically connected them with their social and economic conditions. Needed was a general realization "that an individual is nothing fixed, given ready-made" but is instead "something achieved . . . with the aid and support of conditions, cultural and physical, including in 'cultural' economic, legal, and political institutions as well as science and art." As for liberty, a prerequisite of any genuine individualism, "it is absurd to conceive . . . [it] as that of the business entrepreneur and ignore the immense regimentation to which workers are subjected, intellectual as well as manual workers." True individual liberty, though it, of course, involved freedom of bodily activity and economic choice, was most concerned with "liberty of mind, freedom of thought and its expression in speech, writing, print, and assemblage" and with the opportunity of the individual "to share in the cultural resources of civilization." So defined, freedom and individuality were now obviously denied or drastically curtailed for millions of Americans by existing economic conditions, and since these conditions came out of the existing economic system, and did so because of the system's very nature, the system must be *radically* transformed. Not by violent means, however. There is, Dewey insisted, a "complete correlation between means used and . . . consequences." Wholly mistaken, therefore, were "[d]octrines, whether proceeding from Mussolini or Marx, which assume that because certain ends are desirable therefore [*sic*] those ends and nothing else will result from the use of force to attain them. . . ." Actually, in the "degree in which mere force is resorted to, . . . consequences are themselves so compromised that the ends originally in view have in fact to be worked out afterwards [if achieved at all] by the method of experimental intelligence." So why not use the experimental method, the "method of intelligence," in the first place? Dewey advocated doing so, though he was concerned lest the nature of true experiment be misunderstood. Perhaps with an eye on the New Deal, which was then some eighteen months old, he wrote: "Experimental method is not just messing around nor doing a little of this and a little of that, in the hope that things will improve. Just as in the physical sciences, it implies a coherent body of ideas, a theory, that gives direction to effort. What is implied, in contrast to every form of absolutism, is that ideas and theory be taken as methods of action tested and continuously revised by the consequences they produce in actual social conditions."[37]

VI

WITH what Dewey said here, the mind of the New Deal was in general agreement.

This mind was, of course, a composite or conglomerate, a mixture and mingling of mental tendencies and points of view that differed from one another to the point, often enough, of direct contradiction. Its practical parameters were set by Franklin Roosevelt's unexamined commitments to capitalism and democracy and Christianity, fused into one within his intuitive conception.

Very much a part of it, within these limits, were Felix Frankfurter and his protégés, whose approach, as we know, was Brandeisian. (Not until 1982 did it become public knowledge that Brandeis, who had become a millionaire as corporation lawyer before turning "people's advocate," provided Frankfurter with an annual stipend of $3,500 during these years to enable Frankfurter to promote political causes Brandeis favored but could not, as Supreme Court justice, actively espouse.[38]) These people abhorred or at least profoundly distrusted giantism in anything, including government. Atomistic, they were sure that the general is but a simple sum of particulars; they therefore opposed any policy that made or seemed to make the particular derivative from the general. They stressed individualistic libertarian principles to the maximum degree possible, regulation being required to maintain freedom, within the interdependencies of a technologically advanced society.

These Brandeisian atomists, however, were not predominant over the composite mind in the months immediately following the Hundred Days. They were less determinative of what would become known to history as the First New Deal[39] than were the national planners, of whom Rex Tugwell was a leading representative. And these, with their emphasis upon the need for a social discipline commensurate with the requirements of modern machine production, were less concerned with individual liberty than with overall efficiency. They even manifested on occasion a distinctly totalitarian temper as, in the face of the "sentimental," they vaunted their "hard-headed realism." (It was a "realism" which, of course, struck Marxists as itself "sentimental" in its faith in the possibilities of capitalist reform.)

In between these opposing views were Adolf Berle and Henry Wallace. Berle's incisive boldness of diagnosis and blurring timidity of prescription for social ills were fully shared by Wallace, otherwise a very different kind of man. In one aspect, the secretary of agriculture was emphatically a modern Western man—a scientist whose concern was to make accurate observations of objective fact guided by hypotheses based on objective fact, then to handle these with analytical precision, and finally to draw from them, by logical inference, the knowledge that is power. In his special field of plant genetics, which requires a mastery of statistical and inductive method, he had made major contributions to the development of hybrid corn, becoming in the process a millionaire. But in another aspect he was equally emphatically a timeless Eastern man—a mystic whose deeply religious Christianity was rendered unorthodox, even dubious by his fascination with the occult; a more than half believer in prophetic vision and the potent magic of symbols; a faddist whose shifting commitments among various dietary and exercise regimens seemed to others, at times, evidence of emotional instability.

Tying together and providing common denominators for the otherwise divergent tendencies of thought (the atomistic, the organismic, the mediatory) was a broad strand of social conscience, of generous human concern. This rendered the New Deal mind radically different from that of the immediately preceding administrations. All those whom we have named or classified, beginning with Roosevelt himself, had this strand running through them; in all of them it worked as a spring or principle of action, though with a strength that varied greatly between individuals. But it worked most effectively through Eleanor Roosevelt, whose every social and political idea was rooted in moral feeling and who, in these opening months of the New Deal, had as her allies or agents Louis Howe, Harry Hopkins, Frances Perkins, M. L. Wilson, and scores of immensely capable women friends, in and out of government, who had some influence on policy making.

Finally, there were the out-and-out conservatives—Lewis Douglas, Jesse Jones, Warburg, Morgenthau (to a lesser degree), Moley, et al.—whose primary aim was to revive what they called "free enterprise" within a context of "sound money"* and balanced budgets and who, reinforcing Roosevelt's own basic conservatism, operated as a dead weight upon truly innovative decisiveness.

Thus the New Deal mind *in toto,* necessarily a compromising mind, was also in essential ways a compromised mind as it faced the technological future. It had become by the summer of 1933 a vibrant, intensely busy revival of the Progressivism that, unable to make fundamental decisions between New Free-

---

*Though Jones's definition of "sound money" had marked differences from Douglas's or Warburg's.

dom and New Nationalism in domestic affairs, or between nationalism and internationalism in foreign affairs, had so often permitted circumstance to make policy during the Wilson years. Its parameters and internal divisions inclined it always and strongly toward halfway measures and middle grounds, inclined it to measure the difference between opposing proposals only in terms of immediate political pressure and then, in action decision, to split the difference as precisely in half as possible, this even when one of the two "extremes" demonstrably possessed far more of truth and justice than the other.

A case in point, typically expressive of the overall mind, was Henry Wallace's 14,000-word essay *America Must Choose,* published early in 1934, first (in part) as an article in the *New York Times Magazine,* then as a pamphlet jointly issued by the Foreign Policy Association and the World Peace Foundation. (It had immediate major impact on public opinion: Some 150,000 copies of the pamphlet had been sold at twenty-five cents apiece by year's end, and Wallace's argument had by then been much commented upon editorially.) America's choice in this hour of world history, said Wallace, was between economic nationalism and economic internationalism, and he proceeded to describe and assess in vigorous prose what each choice would ultimately involve, for agriculture in particular and for the American people in general.

Nationalism (isolationism) meant that American agriculture would produce almost exclusively for domestic consumption, and this meant the "permanent retirement" from production of 50 million acres of cropland. In the South "only 25 to 30 million acres of cotton" would be grown "instead of 40 or 45 million." This meant a population shift in the South, which raised the question of where and to what occupations this population was to be shifted. The question's difficulty increased with the realization that there would also have to be reductions of acreage in the corn and wheat belts only somewhat less drastic than those of cotton. Compulsory marketing controls, licensing of plowed land ("Every plowed field would have its permit sticking up on a post"), and "base and surplus quotas for every farmer for every product for each month of the year"—all these would become necessary, along with an immense government bureaucracy (Wallace didn't stress this), a massive, reason-drowning government propaganda of the "patriotic" variety, and, almost certainly, severe curtailments of the freedoms of speech, press, and assembly. Behind prohibitively high tariff walls, America would become a regimented society, living virtually in a state of siege, with a consequently developing siege (paranoid) mentality.

Far better for America to go the internationalist way! This would involve difficulties, too. A drastic lowering of tariffs, to permit an additional billion dollars of goods from abroad to enter the country annually, would require major reorganizations of theretofore protected industry. But internationalism would also involve an opening out rather than a closing in of American attitudes and enterprise. It would point the way toward a "world neighborhood" instead of toward a world war. And being in accord with the traditional generosity and sense of decency of the American people as a whole, it would encourage growth rather than shrinkage of the American spirit.

Thus the choice, as Wallace presented it with rude eloquence, was that of freedom or totalitarian dictatorship in domestic affairs, quarrelsomeness or neighborliness in world affairs. It was ultimately, in sum, a choice between good and evil. But Wallace, who had begun by saying that the choice *must* be made, ended by saying that it need not be, that America might instead, and should, take a stand upon a "middle ground" as it engaged in "new dealing with the world." Instead of retiring 50 million acres of cropland, as nationalism would require, he proposed retiring 25 million; instead of cutting tariffs to permit the entry of another billion dollars of goods, as internationalism would require, he proposed a cut permitting the entry of a half billion dollars' worth. "The planned middle course I propose is one precisely halfway between . . . [the] extremes."[40]

Yet for all its internal divisions and compromised nature, or perhaps because of them and the cue-following role-playing tentativeness of Franklin Roosevelt, the composite New Deal mind did agree, as we have said, with Dewey in his advocacy of social experiment as means of social change. It agreed with a difference, of course. Dewey himself would deplore the excess of pure empiricism, the deficiency or reasoning, especially the failure to shape logical hypotheses, in much of what the New Deal called "experiment." Often it seemed to him that the administration's psychology was more that of a cautious gambler than of a research scientist, that the New Deal was inclined to use so-called experimental method not as a way and test of thinking but as a way of avoiding thought. All the same, the Dewey impact upon the overall mind was substantial.

It was especially so through Rex Tugwell.

As we have seen,* Tugwell's intellectual development had been greatly influenced by both Veblen and Dewey, and the influence of both was evident in the book *The Industrial Discipline,* which Tugwell was completing when he first met Roosevelt. He extensively revised the work during the winter of the interregnum, rendering it considerably less strident, more conciliatory in tone than it had originally been, to avoid embarrassing an administration of which he was to become a part. The book was published in June 1933. And inevitably most readers deemed its central argument to be a statement of the hypothesis (the "ideas," the "theory") by which the New Deal's industrial recovery legislation had been "given direction" and which the NRA under Hugh S. Johnson was about to test in action.

It was on this assumption that Paul H. Douglas reviewed the work for the *Nation,* which published his review under the title "Rooseveltian Liberalism" on June 21, 1933. Douglas summarized as follows:

Mr. Tugwell's central thesis is that while machine industry has compelled close and scientific organization within individual plants and companies, there has been almost

---

*See *FDR: The New York Years,* pp. 268–69. Tugwell had been particularly impressed by Dewey's *Reconstruction in Philosophy.*

complete anarchy between these concerns. The economic mechanism as a whole, therefore, works badly. . . . What Mr. Tugwell in essence proposes is that society should . . . launch out upon a program of so integrating these plants and industries that they may best serve society as a whole. . . . The specific method of control which is suggested . . . is the integration of each industry through a government board which would make and execute plans for that industry, together with a central body, composed primarily of the associated industries, which would seek to introduce a common policy between industries and coordinate them with each other. These two sets of groups would have . . . control over the quantities to be produced, the conditions of competition, the division of markets, wages and working conditions, the pooling of patents, and finally prices. . . . In short, Mr. Tugwell is proposing a planned and liberalized capitalism as the next step in social development; and such, indeed, seems to be the program of the Roosevelt Administration.[41]

In a concluding paragraph of his book Tugwell wrote: "Selectivity is still possible; we can experiment now, and we ought to do it before it is too late. Otherwise we are surely committed to revolution. The essential contrast between the liberal and the radical view of the tasks which lie before us is that liberalism requires this experimenting and that radicalism rejects it for immediate entry on the revolutionary tactic. Liberals would like to rebuild the station while the trains are running; radicals prefer to blow up the station and forgo service until the new structure is built. Their ultimate objectives may not be so very different. . . ."[42]

Douglas in his review quoted this "final and moving passage," appending to it his own hope that the New Deal would "accomplish real reform without revolution." But he had doubts.

The real ultimate difficulty with their program of legalized cartels lies . . . in the assumption that there is a sufficiently strong and independent force outside of capitalism which can control it. At the moment we have a progressive President and an able body of advisers . . . who have no personal axes to grind. Moreover, industry in its despair is uttering words of repentance. But if prosperity should return, capitalism would once again wish to throw off effective control, and the question would then arise whether Rooseveltian liberalism would be strong enough to check it. We have thus far been unable to regulate our public utilities in the interests of consumers, and it will be even more difficult to regulate industry as a whole. The owners of industry will struggle for high prices and for low costs [i.e., low wages] and will try to break or discredit anyone who gets in their way. . . . Along with the Rooseveltian program must go, therefore, the organization of those who are at present weak. . . . Trade unions need to be built up and farmers' cooperatives as well. Finally, the urban and rural workers of hand and brain need a strong party of their own.

For the Democratic party could not be counted upon in the long run to provide good government, being largely based "in the East and in some of the Midwest States . . . upon [political] machines which are in league with the worst forces of the under and upper world."[43]

7

→→>X<←←
Recovery Through Planned Scarcity:
NRA and AAA

I

Upon his return to the White House from his New England coastal cruise on Independence Day 1933, Roosevelt plunged zestfully, with no sign of doubt or fear, into a sea of troubles that was streaked with cross- and undercurrents and by these rendered turbulent.

During his absence from Washington there had arisen between Lew Douglas and Rex Tugwell a policy disagreement that was almost, if not quite, a quarrel. Its object was public works. Douglas, in his unabating passion for government economy, having struggled vainly against the inclusion of Title II in the National Industrial Recovery Act, struggled now to prevent executive implementation of this law. If there had ever been a plausible excuse for huge public works expenditures, there was certainly none now, he argued at a meeting of the Special Board of Public Works* held in Ickes's office on July 1. The economy was in process of making a "natural" correction of imbalance. The "spiral of deflation" was halted; prices were rising. To inject "an artificial factor [public works] into the situation" would be to delay, or even place at fatal risk, the very recovery it was intended to promote. For was not excessive debt load a principal cause of depression? And would not public works expenditures increase the federal deficit, which was the most dangerous debt of all?[1] Tugwell, attending the meeting as Wallace's deputy, almost snorted with impatience. He had no such faith as Douglas expressed in the current signs of recovery; he had no belief whatever in what Douglas deemed a natural recovery process.

True, the index of industrial production had risen spectacularly since inauguration day. It had stood at 56 in March, it would reach 101 in July, and the rise was especially steep for steel, automobiles, construction, and textiles. Manufacturing employment had gone up from 58.9 in March to 71.5 in July, with payrolls rising from 37.1 to 50.8. Farm prices, standing at 55 in March, would reach 87 in July. The stock exchange during this same period experienced what was, in percentage terms, one of the most stupendous bull markets in all history, with industrial stocks rising from an average of 63 in March to 109 in July and the monthly volume of shares traded increasing sixfold, from 20 million in February to 125 million in June.[2]

*This was the board set up by law to oversee the operations of the Public Works Administration (see p. 152). It had the following members: the secretary of the interior, chairman; the secretary of war; the attorney general; the secretary of agriculture; the secretary of commerce; the director of the budget; Colonel George R. Spaulding; and Assistant Secretary of the Treasury Laurence Roberts.

But Tugwell, among other consumption economists, saw no validity in these alleged signs of recovery. Purchasing power was not rising at anything like the rate of rise in production and in prices (retail food prices, for instance, had gone up from 59.8 to 71 in four months[3]), meaning that it was actually relatively *shrinking;* this in turn meant to Tugwell that this current "boom" was nearly as speculative and spurious as that of 1928 and 1929. Its causes were obvious. Industrialists, anticipating inflation under the Thomas amendment and price raising through production controls (i.e., production limitation) under the NRA, aided also by low interest rates, hastened to pile up manufactured goods for sale at the coming higher prices. At that point they could be expected to reduce both their production and their payrolls unless or until real recovery was under way—a possibility which Tugwell continued to hope would be realized through planned government-industry cooperation, though he had growing doubts about the NRA in practice. Merchants similarly hedged against inflation by increasing their inventories. As for the stock exchange, it vastly overdiscounted what business in general foresaw, as the market often did, and in ways designed to profit "insiders" at the expense of those who, speculating as individuals, were unarmed with special information. For the stock market remained free of government regulation, thanks to Roosevelt's decision in March to postpone the submission to Congress of exchange control legislation.* What Tugwell anticipated, therefore, was an early "flattening out of markets and maybe a precipitous drop."[5]

He did not say so, however, at that July 1 meeting of the Public Works Board. He confined himself to pointing out that Congress had spoken on this matter and that its word was law. The assigned task of the board was to see to it that the $3.3 billion appropriated under Title II was efficiently and expeditiously spent to achieve its stated purpose. Tugwell was backed in this by Ickes, who intervened between him and Douglas to say that "after all, the Act has been passed and we are called upon to administer it." This failed to budge Douglas a single inch. The act, insisted the budget director, was "entirely permissive, and not mandatory at all"—an interpretation that seemed to a coldly angry Tugwell willfully contemptuous of both Congress and truth.[6]

Yet Ickes himself soon appeared to Tugwell and many others to be but slightly less inclined than Douglas, if for different reasons, to ignore what had clearly been Congress's main intent when it adopted Title II.

The huge congressional majority that had voted for a massive public works program had done so because it wanted to give the ailing economy a "shot in the arm." It wanted to provide public works jobs for the unemployed, stimulate markets through public works expenditures, promote in general through

---

*See p. 84. Joseph P. Kennedy was one of the "insiders" who profited on the exchange in that summer of 1933. With other speculators he formed a pool to trade Libbey-Owens-Ford stock while spreading false rumors that the glass manufacturer would produce liquor bottles and so cash in on the allegedly huge demand for such bottles which would follow Prohibition's repeal. Trading back and forth among themselves, churning upward their stock's price, Kennedy and the others eventually *sold short* to hapless "outsiders," making for themselves a profit that was handsome indeed.[4]

"ripple effect" the increased consumption that would in turn engender increased industrial production—and it wanted to do these things *fast*.[7] So did General Hugh S. Johnson, the NRA administrator. Johnson's chief policy adviser was a longtime personal friend, Alexander Sachs, whom he had brought down to Washington on leave of absence from Lehman Brothers to head the NRA's Research and Planning Division. A polymath if ever there was one, the forty-year-old Russian-born Sachs had formal education in science, philosophy, jurisprudence, sociology, economics (he served Lehman Brothers as economic counseler); he habitually saw and thought in terms of connections most people are unaware of, as did Johnson to a lesser degree; and in early 1933 he had sharply defined for Johnson the latter's originally vague perception of organic connection between federal public works and government-industry cooperation toward the goal of a permanently healthy national economy. He thereby encouraged Johnson's preparation of a detailed organization chart for public works while the industrial recovery bill was yet being debated in the Senate, and he, of course, fully shared the general's dismay when Roosevelt abruptly divorced Title I from Title II for administrative purposes. This sadly mistaken decision, agreed Johnson and Sachs, immensely increased the difficulty of the general's assigned task since it denied him the use of public works directly, in a consistent, coordinated fashion, to induce code making and enforce code compliance. All was not *necessarily* lost, however. A swift initiation by the PWA of large-scale federal construction projects could greatly help create an economic climate favorable to the desired codification of industry, and Johnson (with Sachs) prayed for this to happen.

It didn't.

"Honest Harold" Ickes had no more intention of moving fast on public works than he had of cooperating with Johnson in ways that would enable the PWA and NRA to operate in tandem. Nor was any pressure put upon him by the President to do so. Indeed, within an hour of his signing the executive orders establishing the PWA and NRA as separate entities, Roosevelt had made it clear that he wanted the two to be kept entirely separate in their operations. He told Ickes "he hoped . . . space in the Interior Building" could be found for the PWA "because he didn't want that office to be in the Commerce Building where General Johnson would be," as Ickes noted in his diary. And at a nine o'clock meeting that same evening in the Oval Room, Roosevelt had agreed with Howe, Farley, and Ickes "that it was absolutely necessary, to prevent a major scandal, to put only high-class men in . . . [PWA state administrative posts] and so safeguard the work done as to prevent any graft or anything of an improper nature."[8] Returned from his coastal cruise, he continued to regard Title II as a merely temporary emergency relief measure. He deemed it far less important than Title I, which was "a supreme effort to stabilize" the economy for "all time," as he had said when he signed the bill. He seemed also more than half-inclined, now, to share Douglas's belief that recovery was already under way and that therefore, whatever public works money remained unspent a few months hence would be "money saved to the

Treasury."[9] At any rate, in seeming rejection of both Tugwell's proposal that *all* the $3.3 billion be spent as quickly as possible and Douglas's that *none* of it be spent at all, Roosevelt announced that the money would be ultimately spent, all of it, but that utmost care would be taken to ensure that it was prudently spent, for projects only of preproved worth. Naturally, Ickes, formally appointed head of the PWA on July 5, manifested thereafter far more concern with assuring the "soundness" and "legitimacy" of proposed projects and with "safeguarding" those approved against the slightest taint of scandal than he did with speedy action.

It would probably have been impossible in any case to launch public works on a scale and with the rapidity needed to provide a real "shot in the arm," as Tugwell himself later admitted. Very few were the projects for which plans had been already drawn up when Ickes took over as PWA administrator, though public works had been agitated for, and loudly, ever since the crash. A number of highway construction projects had been planned by the various states under the supervision of the Bureau of Public Roads. The Navy, spurred by its former assistant secretary from his present White House post, quickly submitted plans for the largest naval building program ever undertaken as a unit in the nation's history. On August 3 contracts for the building of twenty-three ships in private shipyards and allocation of PWA funds to build sixteen other vessels in Navy shipyards were approved by the President. (The event provoked protest from pacifists, who saw contradiction between it and Roosevelt's continued insistence that the United States was committed to the stated aims of the Geneva Disarmament Conference, where, he also continued to insist, "progress" was "being made.") Otherwise, Ickes had to start from scratch. Federal departments and state agencies must be induced to develop project plans, these must be carefully reviewed, tentative contracts must be drawn up and opened to competitive bidding, land must be acquired, materials must be purchased, and every step of this process was across weeks of time. Hence the "building of a power or sewage-treatment plant for a city in Nebraska or Nevada could scarcely be got under way, with the best will in the world, for two years," as Tugwell later said.[10]

But Ickes could certainly have moved far more rapidly than he did. He was endlessly suspicious. He insisted upon reviewing personally, in detail, every project proposal, every plan, every contract. He instituted an elaborate Interior Department undercover investigative program to forestall any possible Treasury-raiding connivance of PWA personnel with private building contractors, whose proneness as a class to corrupt activity was notorious, then as now. And he was from first to last entirely successful in his effort to prevent fraud while enriching the national estate, at last, with a multitude of permanently valuable constructions, including post offices, schools, auditoriums, water systems, tunnels, highways, bridges, sewage treatment plants. The petty pace at which he moved toward this goal, however, in the summer and autumn of 1933, was maddening to those whose overriding concern was to reduce unemployment and stimulate the economy. Letters complaining about him poured into the office of Senator Wagner, chief author of public works legislation. Typical was one from Father John O'Grady of the National Conference of Catholic Charities. Thanks to the dilatoriness of the PWA administrator, asserted Father O'Grady on August 23, 1933, things were now no better as regards public works than they had been in the Hoover years, "and at the present pace we simply are not going to have any worthwhile public works program."[11]

II

THIS dilatoriness had a "ripple effect" of its own.

By it Hugh Johnson's handling of his NRA job was importantly influenced.

For having been denied the use of public works contracts to reward through their granting, or to coerce through their withholding, the business cooperation with government which the NRA was designed to achieve, the general was now denied that solid market uplift which a swift launching of massive public works would have produced and which would have made relatively easy the acceptance by business of the minimum wage and maximum hour provisions that, by the terms of the act, must be written into every code. As things now were, and would remain until general recovery was under way, there could be only a redistribution of current income; Johnson, who had emphatically expressed his opposition to price-fixing in the codes, must expect business to insist upon precisely this in compensation for its wage and hour concessions to labor. The pressures for profit guarantees through higher prices cooperatively set, joined with agreed production quotas, must become intense.

Would the general resist them? *Could* he?

The key staff which he had assembled by the time the NIRA was on the statute books, and which he publicly announced three days later, resembled that of the War Industries Board of 1918 insofar as it was recruited almost wholly from the ranks of big business. All six of his principal deputies had business backgrounds, conjoined in one or two instances with a military background. Three advisory boards were established to guide NRA policy, though it was "no easy task to persuade General Johnson to agree to this," according to Frances Perkins. ("He didn't want to be bothered with them," she writes, adding that her uneasiness about him had been increased by his giving her a short time before, as a book she ought to read, Italian Fascist Raffaello Viglioni's glowing description of *The Corporate State*.)[12] One of the three was an Industrial Advisory Board, appointed by the secretary of commerce and chaired by Walter C. Teagle of Standard Oil of New Jersey. All its members were big businessmen;* they would be actively represented in code-making operations by a permanent staff of specialists, most of whom were on loan from business. This board was presumably balanced in the overall organization by a seven-member Labor Advisory Board appointed by the secretary of labor and

---

*Among the most active were Gerard Swope of General Electric and Louis E. Kirstein of Boston's Filene and Company.

headed by her. Its members included William Green, John L. Lewis of the United Mine Workers, and Sidney Hillman of the Amalgamated Clothing Workers as well as Rose Schneiderman of the Women's Trade Union League, Eleanor's longtime friend. The third board, the Consumers' Advisory Board, was "a last minute thought" on the part of Frances Perkins, according to her own account,[13] it having suddenly occurred to her that the "community" should be protected "against a combination of labor and industry which might . . . [be] adverse." Johnson agreed to it only after Mary Rumsey,* who was a friend of his, promised to serve as chairman. She in turn appointed or helped appoint, as original board members, the soon-to-be president of the University of North Carolina, Frank P. Graham; two officers of the League of Women Voters; the director of the Food Research Institute of Stanford University; the president of the American Arbitration Association; and the famed social scientist friend of Tugwell's, W. F. Ogburn of the University of Chicago, who became executive director of the board's staff but soon resigned, to be replaced by economist Dexter Keezer.

In the event, the Labor Advisory Board had practical effect upon the code-making process. Its members were as single-minded as industry's representatives as they pressed the interests of a clearly defined constituency, and they were aided by the language of Section 7. But their success was always severely limited; it tended to vary with the strength of existing trade union organization within the industries being codified, i.e., with the potency of threats to strike, which is to say it was small indeed over large areas of industry and even larger areas of commerce. As for the Consumers' Advisory Board, though it was from first to last composed of remarkably able and persuasive people,† it lacked any defined organized constituency; it, therefore, could not exert the pressure that gets things done in politics. It could be safely ignored by Johnson, or so he obviously believed. He never sought its advice during these opening months; he ignored its advice when this was volunteered. The board and its highly competent staff could only register protests and hope that these, spread abroad, would generate effective popular agitations for desired policy changes.

In sum, then, the NRA was structured and staffed in such a way as to ensure a strong big business bias as it approached what were bound to be adversarial relationships of big business versus labor, big business versus small business, big business versus the consumer. Nor was this bias at all offset, as many had initially believed it would be, by the influence of Donald Richberg, who, as general counsel, was the NRA's second-in-command.

Over the years few men in public life had been as caustic as Richberg in commentary upon the mentality and morality of American big businessmen, variously described by him as "pawn-brokers" and "slave-drivers" and "trad-

---

*This was the elder sister of Averell Harriman, who was joining with Vincent Astor to finance the new weekly newsmagazine *Today* (later to become *Newsweek*), which Moley was to edit. She shared a house in Washington with Frances Perkins.
†Among those who later served upon it were Paul H. Douglas, Gardiner C. Means, Walton H. Hamilton of the Yale Law School, and sociologist Robert S. Lynd, coauthor of *Middletown*.

ers," whose overriding "witless purpose" was to "squeeze more money" for themselves "out of more men."[14] Moreover, an original Bull Mooser, he had earned under fire his reputation as a champion of Progressivism, notably in his fight as railroad labor lawyer against the use of federal court injunctions to break strikes in 1922, his leading role as draftsman and lobbyist in the enactment of the Railway Labor Act of 1926 and the Norris-La Guardia Anti-Injunction Act of 1932, and his fight in partnership with Ickes for municipal reform in Chicago against such powerful foes of the public weal as Samuel Insull and Mayor William "Big Bill" Thompson. But Richberg was also ambitious for personal prestige and power—inordinately so, some thought. He had reason to consider himself a Roosevelt favorite. He continued to have direct, frequent access to the President after becoming officially Johnson's subordinate, a fact not pleasing to the general; Richberg was evidently encouraged by Roosevelt to regard one of his NRA functions to be the sober-minded moderation of the general's flightiness, the general's tendency to go to extremes. And he clearly saw that for one who wanted to gain and permanently to retain preferment in the New Deal, especially if one was a liberal, the only way to go was the middle way, with the middle defined or located by an equivalence of conflicting pressures. This, therefore, was the way he went, both in his drafting contribution to the NIRA and in his role as administrator of the act. He assumed the stance of a "neutral," he stood as impartial referee upon a middle ground, and this, in view of the prevailing distribution and relative weight of pressures, effectively allied him with big business at almost every crucial juncture. Thus, though Richberg, with Jerome Frank, was largely responsible for the inclusion in the NIRA of Section 7(a), he, with Johnson, soon interpreted its practical meaning in ways that denied majority rule to the process whereby employees determined their bargaining agency, and chose their bargaining representatives, for labor-management negotiations. It was an interpretation highly pleasing to management, highly distressing to labor, in that it placed roadblocks in the way of effective independent union organization.

But even if Johnson (with Richberg) had been truly neutral in the struggle of conflicting interests and had chosen NRA's personnel accordingly—or if (better still) he had conceived his role to be truly *governmental,* a coercive and creative exercise of the general will on behalf of the general welfare—even then he would have been severely handicapped in his pursuit of success. In his own view, at least, he lacked the necessary disciplinary tools.

There was, of course, that licensing provision for which he had fought so furiously, against Dickinson, when the industrial recovery bill was being drafted.* Roosevelt, it will be recalled, when sending the bill to Congress, had publicly supported Johnson's side of this argument, *after* Johnson had won it. He had stressed the need for "a rigorous licensing power" wherewith "to meet rare cases of non-cooperation and abuse" of that freedom from antitrust law, that governmental permission "to make agreements and codes insuring fair

*See pp. 118–119.

competition," which the act would grant "private industries."[15] On the face of it, this power to license, amounting to a power of life or death over any private enterprise, was more than enough to compel satisfactory code making and to enforce code compliance. There now arose, however, a question the answer to which had a lowering effect upon the general's morale and a sad effect upon his administrative operation. Was this licensing provision, so potent on paper, a real power in the real world? Would it stand up in court? An outside observer might assume this question to have been thoroughly canvassed and firmly answered in the affirmative, by both proponents and opponents of the licensing proposal, well before the bill went into its final drafting stage. Why, otherwise, the intensity of the battle over its inclusion in the bill? But this had evidently *not* been done, and Johnson, by the time the bill was signed into law, had been convinced by Alexander Sachs that this portion of the law, if not (as was probable) the whole of it, was unconstitutional. Just last year, as Sachs may have pointed out, the U.S. Supreme Court had ruled in an Oklahoma case (it involved a company selling ice for refrigeration) that a licensing system violated "due process" as guaranteed by the Fifth and Fourteenth Amendments.

To Johnson, therefore, the licensing power he so stubbornly insisted upon in mid-May had become, by mid-June, but a paper sword. As NRA administrator he never for a moment considered drawing that sword from its paper scabbard. And hardly more substantial was the presidential power, conferred by the act, to impose codes upon industries that failed to adopt them on their own. This last was at best a wooden sword; it might work on occasion as a threat over quarreling industrialists, moving them toward compromise agreement, but it would almost certainly splinter in the hand that tried actually to use it as a weapon, for it seemed little if any less vulnerable than licensing to a charge of unconstitutionality. Hence the general's forcible-feeble approach to his job. He had to rely almost exclusively, he felt, upon moral suasion to win his way, this joined with what he later called "a strong surge of public opinion behind" the act, and through the weeks and months ahead he would employ much argument and even more bluster and bombast, bluff and cajolery, as he appealed to emotion, to reason, and (finally, most effectively) to those pocketbook interests of which the businessman's social "principles" and "ideas" are generally flat reflections. He shuddered when false rumor told him in the third week of June that a group of leading industrialists plotted an immediate test of the NIRA's constitutionality. And his awareness that such a test, though it might be postponed for a year or two, was inevitable, that the government itself must take the law into court sooner or later, else code violators go unpunished and the law become a mockery, encouraged his natural tendency to plunge straight ahead at breakneck speed, with no adequate reconnaissance of the hazardous terrain into which he moved. It became his overriding purpose to achieve a tremendous and irreversible *fait accompli,* namely, the codification of all American industry, all American business, with a consequent expanding national prosperity, before the Supreme Court had a chance to render a final verdict upon the act which made all this possible.

Time, therefore, was of the essence! The success or failure of this mighty effort would be determined within the next two months, said the general in mid-June. He hoped by the end of that time to have under code all ten of the nation's largest industrial and commercial segments: steel; automobiles; lumber; coal; petroleum; textiles; garment making; building construction; wholesale trade; retail trade. He chafed, in June and July, at the slowness with which industry moved toward NRA cooperation. He chafed, too, at the slowness (so he deemed it) of the procedure whereby draft codes were transmuted into federal law.

Preparation and submission of a tentative draft code were, of course, the first step of the code-making process. It had to be taken by business or industry for, as Johnson said, the NRA did not impose codes but only accepted them from those who were to be ruled by them. And in practice this initial step was taken either by an existing trade association or group of these or by an association specifically formed for the purpose, the prime initial mover usually being a corporation lawyer who became secretary, first, of the sponsoring committee and, later, of the code authority by which the code was administered. In NRA headquarters this tentative draft went first to the Control Division, which docketed it and assigned it to a deputy administrator. Then it went to the Code Analysis Division; there it was reviewed to make sure it contained the mandated provisions but, especially as time went on, was subjected, generally, to little else in the way of analysis. So reviewed, the draft became the subject of preliminary (prehearing) conferences presided over by the assigned deputy administrator and attended by the sponsoring committee and others of the industry. Here it was that the advisory boards exerted such influence as they had upon code making, for the deputy administrator in his presiding chair was flanked by representatives from the three boards. As has been indicated, by far the most influential of the three was the expertly staffed Industrial Advisory Board; less so was the Labor Advisory Board, while the consumers' board had virtually no influence whatever. Next came an advertised public hearing, a formal hearing, in Washington, with full stenographic record, presided over by the deputy administrator and open to all interested parties. Such differences as were unresolved at the end of this public hearing were ironed out in posthearing conferences with the sponsoring committee, and it was at this stage of the proceedings that the threat of a presidential imposition of some version of the developing code was occasionally effective of an industry-wide agreement which might otherwise have been indefinitely delayed. The agreed draft code was then referred by the deputy administrator, with his recommendations concerning it, and with dissenting opinions, if any, from his advisers, to the NRA administrator, who, if he approved it, submitted it to the President. With the latter's signature, the code became law.

All this, for any single code, and especially for the earliest of them, took time, would have taken many weeks, if not months, had it been carried out with a careful concern for relevant fact, for consistency of means with stated ends, and for overall fairness in service of the general welfare. But time was not allowed in any sufficiency; it was cut short by the general's relentless pressure for speed and more speed.

During these hectic opening moments of his most important hour upon history's stage, Johnson's psychology was somewhat akin to that of Woodrow Wilson in Paris in 1919. NRA codification assumed in his mind much the same supreme value as the Covenant of the League of Nations had had in Wilson's. He convinced himself (not wholly; at the root of his morale gnawed stubborn doubts) that every concession now made to business, however unfair to other conflicting interests in the short run, would be abundantly justified in the long run, for the public as a whole, by a resultant economy-reviving, prosperity-breeding "industrial self-government" under Washington's aegis. But *all* would be lost if codes were not got into operation at once! This attitude gravely weakened him, as he stood officially for the public interest against single-minded exponents of special interest, in precisely the same way as Wilson had been weakened in 1919 when, representing the world-historical drive toward world government, he was faced by single-minded exponents of national sovereignty (notably Clemenceau). The passion for speed could be used against the general, and it was, by men whose ruling passion was for selfish advantage and private profit; they wrung from him crucially important concessions by playing upon his fear of losing all through loss of time.

This happened during the making of the very first code to be adopted, the Cotton Textile Code, which set the pattern for all the rest.

All through the Republican Prosperity of the 1920s the cotton textile industry, plagued by every evil consequent upon cutthroat competition, had suffered acutely from market overproduction. No industry save coal mining had been or remained more brutally exploitive of labor, including child labor, especially after millowners had moved the bulk of their operations out of New England into the South, to take advantage there of the lowest wage rates in the nation, and no industry save coal had suffered more grievously from the depression. It had cut its labor force by well over one-fourth between 1929 and 1933 (it remained one of the large industrial employers, however, with 314,000 on its payrolls in 1933), and those it continued to employ worked longer hours for less pay, sometimes receiving $5 or less for a fifty- to sixty-hour workweek. This labor was unorganized. Not one in twenty textile employees over the nation as a whole, and hardly anyone at all in the South, was a member of the United Textile Workers of America, whose leadership was in any case notably weak and incompetent.[16] These circumstances had made the industry especially eager for industry-wide cooperation to halt overproduction and prevent price-lowering competitions. By the time the NIRA was signed, the Cotton Textile Institute, headed by George A. Sloan, had a draft code ready for submission, and despite Johnson's urgings and pleadings with industry for speedy action, this draft remained the only one that was in process of becoming a code when Roosevelt returned to his desk from Campobello.

Five days later (July 9, 1933), the Cotton Textile Code was signed by the President, who issued a statement in glowing praise of it and of the "great industry" which, by instituting it, had "proved itself the leader of a new thing in economics and government." The industry had thereby demonstrated "faith and courage and patriotism of the highest order." The code specifically out-

lawed child labor! This, it seemed to President and public, was a landmark
event of immense hopeful significance. Roosevelt said:

> After years of fruitless effort and discussion, this ancient atrocity went out in a day,
> because this law permits employers to do by agreement that which none of them
> could do separately and live in competition. In the eyes of the public, there was a
> great conference among the leaders of our industry, labor and social service, presided
> over by Government. It considered the most controverted question in the whole
> economic problem—wages and hours of labor—and it brought that question to a
> definite conclusion. It dealt with facts and facts only. There was not one word of
> accusation. And most remarkable of all it arrived at a solution which has the
> unanimous approval of these conferring leaders on all three sides of the question at
> issue. . . . I can think of no greater achievement of cooperation, mutual understand-
> ing and good-will.[17]

Actually, as Roosevelt (being then out of Washington) may or may not have
known, a considerable accusatory acrimony had been expressed during the
conferences preceding the June 27 opening of the formal public hearings on
this code as well as during the hearings themselves. The draft originally
presented by Sloan, perforce inclusive of collective bargaining guarantees
(these could and would be circumvented or ignored in mill after mill), called
for a minimum wage of $11 in the North, $10 in the South in payment for an
average workweek of forty hours. It said nothing whatever about child labor.
Sloan claimed this was unnecessary; the new wage scale would automatically
halt the employment of workers under sixteen years of age. Only under harsh
criticism and heavy pressures from labor and liberal congressional leaders, and
only following an emergency meeting held at Johnson's insistence after the
public hearings had ended, did Sloan agree to raise the weekly minimum wage
by a couple of dollars (to $13 in the North, $12 in the South) and to write into
the code a specific prohibition of child labor. Successfully resisted by Sloan
were pressures by Alabama's Senator Black and by William Green for a
codified thirty-hour week, to spread employment.

Moreover, the concessions which the industry had made to the public good,
hailed as generous and statesmanlike by the President himself, had been made
only after Johnson had paid for them with a crucial concession of his own, one
which Consumers' Advisory Board members were inclined to view as a betrayal of public trust.

Firm opposition to the writing of price-fixing and production restriction
permissions into the codes had been reiterated by the general as basic NRA
policy at the outset of textile code negotiations. But at the same time Johnson
had revealed to such shrewd eyes as Sloan's his mounting anxiety and fuming
impatience over the slowness with which industry as a whole was moving to
cooperate in the recovery program. Sloan, therefore, had only to make it clear
to the general that a major cause of the distressing slowness was precisely the
NRA's price policy, a policy which certainly militated against swift adoption
of the Cotton Textile Code (for how could manufacturers be expected to agree
to increased manufacturing costs, consequent upon increased wages, unless

assured of an offsetting increase of income?),—Sloan had only to do this to force an abrupt flat reversal of policy. On June 23, Johnson announced that price-fixing *would* be permitted after all; the erstwhile market competitors might make agreements among themselves not to sell at a price lower than the "cost of production." How this last was to be determined was left in the air.*
And the final Cotton Textile Code, drawn up under this changed policy, not only permitted agreements not to sell below cost but also stipulated that there be no plant expansion or installation of new machinery, save as replacements of existing units, without NRA permission and, most important, that no textile plant could operate production machinery for more than two shifts of a forty-hour week! The latter stipulation, which caused immediate worker layoffs in several plants, "including a third of the employees of a large textile concern," according to Bernard Bellush,[19] squared not at all with the June 16 presidential statement about the NRA, a statement which began, "The law I have just signed was passed *to put people back to work* [italicized by Roosevelt]. . . ."

As for code administration, it was entrusted to a Cotton Textile Industry Committee whose composition did nothing to assure workers or consumers that in the practical interpretation and application of code law, their interests would be protected against the predatory interests of business. The committee's membership consisted of the Cotton Textile Institute plus a few representatives of other textile trade associations. Its chairman was George Sloan. Thus the committee, or code authority, though a public agency insofar as it was an official arm of the NRA, was yet a private agency insofar as it was, in Johnson's later description, "an agency of the employers in . . . [the] industry."[20]

In this way were established fateful precedents.

III

BUT the textile code's adoption was not immediately followed, as Johnson urgently desired, by a rush of code applications. Days passed, a week, then two weeks with no decisive action. Six weeks after the NIRA's signing, cotton textiles remained the only industry codified.

By then, however, the general had found a way, he was convinced, to loose the codification flood which NRA's success, in his view, required. He had prepared what he called a blanket code, formally named the President's Reemployment Agreement, which was to be mailed to every business establishment, every employer in the land. By signing it, each employer would become an NRA "member" who, as such, was pledged to abide by basic NRA standards as regards wages and hours—that is, a maximum thirty-five- to forty-hour week for a minimum wage of $12 to $15—until such time as a national code

---

*If industrialists used the "code to fix extortionate prices," Johnson added, he would "have to step in immediately in conformance with the law."[18]

for his own industry or business area was adopted. The insignia of membership would be the Blue Eagle—actually the Navaho thunderbird redrawn to clutch a cogwheel in one claw, a half dozen lightning bolts in the other, with "NRA Member" printed above it and "WE DO OUR PART" printed below. This thunderbird Blue Eagle would be launched into roaring flight by a thunderous thirty-day propaganda drive modeled on the Liberty Loan drives of the Great War,* complete with mass rallies, brass bands, parades, four-minute speakers, and vast publicity over press and radio. It would be the greatest peacetime "mass movement" in the nation's history, arousing such a frenzy of emotional popular support for NRA that no recalcitrant could stand against it.

The general's enthusiasm for such theatrics was emphatically *not* shared by members of the Special Industrial Recovery Board, which was supposedly empowered to oversee and, if need be, to overrule the NRA administrator. As a matter of fact, the board was almost unanimously negative in its reactions to the plans the general outlined during meetings held on July 18 and 19. Board members pointed to the disgust and cynicism that had colored the long-term popular reaction to the propaganda fervors of the Great War. They pointed to unwholesome similarities between the Blue Eagle and the fasces of Mussolini's Italy, the swastika of Hitler's Germany. Commerce's John Dickinson flatly rejected the general's contention that a swift universal codification was vital to NRA success, saying it was more likely to be fatal since it "would almost certainly destroy at the outset the great advantages which may be expected from organizing the industries of the country one by one." Tugwell expressed fear of what might happen to the President's personal prestige and leadership power if he were identified in the way Johnson proposed to identify him with a campaign that promised swift, vast reemployment within a resurgent economy, then failed to deliver on this promise. What if there were a "precipitous drop" in the markets "right in the midst of a ballyhoo campaign"? This was a very likely possibility, in Tugwell's view. Wouldn't the administration then "look like ten cents"?[21]

But the President had, or expressed, no such fear. If aware of risks, he was more acutely aware of great political advantages to be gained from a mass emotional involvement in the New Deal, and in any case, he knew how to minimize the risks as involvements of his personal prestige. He had himself no little anxiety deep down, regarding the Supreme Court's ultimate judgment upon the NIRA, was also disturbed by the fact that the rise in the prices of commodities and securities, and in production, since early March was unaccompanied by an equivalent rise in employment and total wages; he was, therefore, easily persuaded by the general's essential argument for swift, widespread code adoptions. He himself was an activist by temperament, impatient of the postponements of action that are imposed by careful preliminary surveys of possible consequences. He himself was a theatrical role player, hence

---

*Indeed, one of its chief planners and organizers, called upon by Johnson for this patriotic service, was the man who had directed bond sales drives in 1918, Charles F. Horner of Kansas City.

strongly attracted by the general's theatricality, the general's promise of an exciting show on the national stage. And as a teleological gambler he vibrated sympathetically to the general's assertion that the proposed campaign, if admittedly "a gamble," was a "good gamble" ("I think I can put this thing over," said the general),[22] though Roosevelt himself, it should be added, would never have used the word "gamble." He would have called Johnson's proposal an experiment.

For all these reasons, he overruled the Special Industrial Advisory Board. He told the general to go ahead.

And on June 24, in his third fireside chat, he personally opened the great campaign.

He began his talk with brave assertions about the New Deal's "careful planning." He "set forth the fundamentals of this planning" in order to "make it abundantly clear to you that all of the proposals and all of the legislation since the fourth day of March have not been just a collection of haphazard schemes, but rather the orderly component parts of a connected and logical whole." He spoke of the Economy Act, asserting that it was not "inconsistent for a government to cut down its regular expenses and at the same time to borrow and to spend billions for an emergency . . . because a large portion of the emergency money has been paid out in the form of sound loans which will be repaid to the Treasury over a period of years; and to cover the rest of the emergency money we have imposed taxes to pay the interest. . . ." He swiftly reviewed the banking acts, the farm and home mortgage acts, the CCC, public works, and agricultural adjustment, before concentrating on the industrial recovery program. Again he praised the Cotton Textile Code, with its abolition of child labor, going on to say that the Industrial Recovery Act* "gives us the means to conquer unemployment with exactly the same weapon that we have used to strike down child labor." For the NIRA enabled "all employers to act together to shorten hours and raise wages. . . . No employer will suffer, because the relative level of competitive cost will advance by the same amount for all. But if any considerable group should lag or shirk, this great opportunity will pass us by and we shall go into another desperate winter. This must not happen."

To arrive at NRA codes "industry by industry," however, was "naturally" a time-consuming task. It involved "a great many hearings and many months . . . and we cannot wait for all of them to go through." But the blanket agreements "will start the wheels turning now. . . ." He was, therefore, "now asking the cooperation that comes from opinion and conscience. These are the only weapons we shall use in this great summer offensive against unemployment. But we shall use them to the limit to protect the willing from the laggard and to make the plan succeed." He waxed poetic. "In war, in the gloom of night attack, soldiers wear a bright badge on their shoulders to be sure that

---

*Strangely, in the speech as reprinted in *The Public Papers and Address . . . 1933* (p. 300), he calls it the recovery *bill*.

comrades do not fire on comrades. On that principle those who cooperate in this program must know each other at a glance. That is why we have provided a badge of honor for this purpose, a simple design with a legend, 'We do our part,' and I ask that all those who join with me shall display that badge prominently."[23]

The ensuing ballyhoo was blinding and deafening in its intensity.

Abruptly the Blue Eagle appeared everywhere. It was on the walls of manufacturing plants, in every store window, and in the windows of millions of private homes, for consumers were invited to sign pledges to buy only from merchants displaying the symbol. ("When every American housewife understands that the Blue Eagle on everything that she permits to enter her home is a symbol of its restoration to security, may God have mercy on the man or group of men who attempt to trifle with this bird!" cried the general in public speech.[24]) It was on billboards and magazine covers, in newsreels and full-page newspaper advertisements. It was stamped on commercial products by the million and on the bare thighs of bathing beauty contestants (were they also articles of commerce?) at Atlantic City. When a Mrs. Collins of Upper Darby, Pennsylvania, christened her newborn daughter Nira, after the NIRA, in late July, she received a letter from the President of the United States complimenting her on the choice of name, "[s]ignifying, as it does, the faith, confidence and cooperation necessary in any great human endeavor."[25] There were mass rallies and parades in 1,000 towns during which the placarded Blue Eagle was held aloft while dignitaries extolled it in orations and brass bands blared "Happy Days Are Here Again." The climax was a mammoth parade down Fifth Avenue in New York City on September 13. From early afternoon till midnight that day there flowed an unbroken stream of humanity along the street past a reviewing stand on which stood, through much of that long time, New York's Governor Lehman, New York's NRA Chairman W. Averell Harriman, and General Hugh S. Johnson, whose mood that day was one of religious exaltation. A quarter million people marched; 2 million watched from the sidewalks. It was the greatest parade in the city's history.*

By then the general himself, "Old Ironpants," had become something of a folk hero. He had been the star of the show. He remained the star of a show he continued to produce for months thereafter—the central figure of the whole recovery effort of the New Deal, in the eyes of millions. He looked the part he played. In sternness of countenance and muscular stockiness of figure he was remarkably similar to the actors who portrayed Captain Flagg in stage and movie versions of *What Price Glory?*, as one commentator wrote. His gruff, bearlike charm; the torrential energy with which he rushed about the country in airplanes, exhorting the public and prodding local officials into swifter action; the sense of mingled toughness and harassed sensitivity conveyed by

---

*Greatest in number of people actively participating, that is. Its spectators numbered less than half the number who had watched the Lindbergh parade down the same avenue a half dozen years before, when the aviator hero returned from his solo flight to Paris.

his continuously disheveled appearance (his clothes always looked as though they had been slept in); especially his genius for colorful invective (he was forever "cracking down" linguistically, if *only* linguistically, on "slackers" and "chiselers" and "pygmies" who posed as "giants of industry")—these made as vivid an impression upon the popular mind, for the time being, as did the very different personality of Franklin Roosevelt.

And measured in terms of Johnson's immediate purpose, his campaign was a huge success.

Within a few weeks well over 2 million employers had signed the blanket code. Many millions had signed the consumers' code. And the latter fact was in some part effective of the former since it threatened a national boycott of businesses not signed up, a pressure to sign that was augmented by executive orders requiring purchases of federal governmental supplies to be made only from blanket code signers. Yet employers, by signing, pledged themselves to increases in their labor costs with no assurance that they, without being undercut by competitors, could offset higher costs with price increases *unless* they joined with these competitors in cooperative price arrangements. This they could do legally, and in most cases practically, only by means of an NRA code of "fair competition." The desired effect was a sudden flood of draft codes into NRA headquarters, beginning on the morrow of the Blue Eagle's takeoff into roaring flight. During the closing days of July 144 draft codes were submitted; 546 came in during the following month. There would be over 500 more by the end of the year. The initial handling of them forced an abrupt huge expansion of the NRA's staff and budget (these increased tenfold in little more than a year), despite which the agency perforce processed draft codes into law far more rapidly, with far less concern for a rational overall balance of interests, than service of the general welfare required. Basic codes were signed by the President at the rate of several a week in August and September 1933. Between October 1 and February they were signed at the rate of two a day.

The shipbuilding code, signed on July 26, 1933, was the single major instance in which public works had the kind of effect upon NRA operations that Johnson and Sachs believed all public works should have had, for pending naval construction contracts proved to be powerful inducements to swift code making. Even so, the shipbuilders were permitted to write into the code a minimum price provision. Also signed on July 26 was the Wool Textile Code, modeled after the cotton code. On August 4 were signed the electrical manufacturers' code (it, too, contained a minimum price provision) and the code for the coat and suit industry. Ten days later Roosevelt, who had gone up to Hyde Park for his usual August stay, came back to Washington to take a personal hand in troubled negotiations over draft codes for oil, steel, lumber, and coal. He remained in the capital for six whirlwind days.

He authorized Johnson to use the threat of presidential imposition of a petroleum code to force quarreling oilmen into agreement. The general barked orders, brooked no backtalk. The tactic worked.

Roosevelt summoned to the White House Myron C. Taylor, board chairman of U.S. Steel, and Charles M. Schwab, board chairman of Bethlehem Steel, for a long morning hour of conference. Weeks before, Roosevelt had agreed to Secretary Perkins's unorthodox proposal that the Department of Labor represent the steelworkers in the steel code negotiations since the workers had no organizations of their own. Frances Perkins had then personally toured the steel towns of Pennsylvania and West Virginia to talk to workers face-to-face. She was appalled by what she saw and heard. She, of course, knew that the steel companies for a half century had maintained the open shop in their mills by means of force, fraud, and violence against employees who attempted union organization. She now saw at first hand the consequence of this labor policy: thousands of men forced to perform the heaviest kind of physical labor through twelve-hour days and, on occasion, seven-day weeks, for bare-subsistence wages. She now also personally experienced the denial to steelworkers of their citizen rights of free speech and free assembly: The burgess (mayor) of Homestead, Pennsylvania, scene of the bloody Homestead strike of 1892, refused to let her hear in a town hall or in a town park the grievances of a couple of hundred labor "malcontents" or "reds," as the burgess called them; she was compelled at last to hold the meeting in the local post office, under the American flag. Thus she was prepared to protest vigorously, and she did, if vainly, when Johnson in negotiations yielded to the steel industry one disputed point after another of the original draft NRA code that had been prepared by the employers' Iron and Steel Institute. Industry's representatives, however, had not been able to replace the language of Section 7(a), as they wished to do, with language *specifying* company unions as acceptable employee collective bargaining agents, language aimed at forestalling independent unionization. And this was the point upon which negotiations were stalled when the President called the two most powerful men of steel into the Executive Office. He was disposed to be firm, if not stern, for Frances Perkins had reported to him her personal observations of the steel towns and mills, along with her outrage over them, and he had measured this information against recent revelations of the huge salaries and bonuses which top steel executives had routinely voted themselves at annual board meetings during the palmy days of the Republican Prosperity. He listened unsympathetically as Charlie Schwab explained his reluctance to agree to the NRA code labor clause as being the result of his obligation to Bethlehem's stockholders. "Were you looking after your stockholders when you paid those million-dollar bonuses to my friend 'Gene Grace?"* asked Roosevelt, "smiling sweetly," according to Ernest Lindley.[26]

Schwab and Taylor were grim-faced and unresponsive to reporters' questions when they left the White House a few minutes later. Soon thereafter they with their colleagues agreed upon a code that included the disputed labor

---

*Eugene Grace was the president of Bethlehem Steel.

clause, though they made it clear as they did so that they intended to fight tooth and nail against the unionization of their industry. The code, providing for an eight-hour day and a forty-hour week, with a minimum wage of twenty-five to forty cents an hour (far too low to promote recovery, said Secretary Perkins), was not to go into effect until November 1 for a ninety-day trial period, and not then unless the industry was operating at 60 percent of its capacity. The code was to remain in effect only so long as the industry continued to operate at 60 percent or more. Also, at peak periods a forty-eight-hour week was permitted. The severely limited concessions to labor were paid for with code clauses permitting cooperative price-fixing and other specific exemptions from antitrust law and assuring an administrative code authority firmly under the control of Big Steel.

Less immediately fruitful was Roosevelt's meeting that week with top coal company executives. Here much of the trouble he dealt with was due to John L. Lewis, who saw in Section 7(a) a golden opportunity to revitalize his United Mine Workers of America. This once-powerful industrial union had become almost moribund and, moreover, had become so in good part *because* of Lewis's leadership—a fact whose realization by Lewis himself may well have increased the zeal with which he now set about retrieving the situation. It was also a fact that would soon seem exceedingly strange to those of the general public who knew of it. For Lewis was about to erupt upon the national scene as the most potent of all labor leaders. Within two years he would become principal agent of an important historical development.

We perhaps do well, therefore, to pause here for a look at him.

He was personally immensely impressive. He had a massively powerful physique, deep-chested and broad-shouldered, heavily mantled with muscular tissue developed by youthful years of hard physical labor. He had a strong, rugged countenance dominated by coal black brows as thick as mustaches above blue eyes whose gaze was always piercing, sometimes almost hypnotic. It was a countenance often set in a scowl hard as iron, black as a thundercloud, but also a countenance that could relax in warm smiles and, indeed, register an unusually wide range of emotions, including tender ones, in swift succession. He was a master of orotund oratory, with a Welshman's gift for lyrical phrases. His deep musical voice, unamplified, carried easily to the farthest corner of an auditorium and his habitual employment of Shakespearian language, Shakespearian rhythms, soon provided the press with an abundance of memorable quotations. All in all, he was a figure every bit as theatrically colorful as Hugh Johnson and far tougher, far braver, far more certain of the objects he pursued and of the best ways to attain them.

Yet he had presided over a sad fall of his union's power, as we have said. When he became its head in 1919, aged thirty-nine, the UMW had more than 400,000 members who, among them, mined all the anthracite and more than two-thirds of the bituminous coal produced nationally. Fourteen years later the UMW had fewer than 100,000 members and was too weak effectively to protect its rank and file against the most viciously exploitive labor practices in all American industry. How had this happened? Much of the answer was rooted in Lewis's mind and character, wherein an inordinate lust for personal power was joined with laissez-faire political attitudes in a way far more generally typical of big businessmen than of labor leaders. He was a conservative Republican when he became his union's head. He remained so, allying himself with men and interests the most hostile to organized labor. He soon gained and thereafter maintained an iron dictatorship over his union, not hesitating to use goon squads in brutal violence against miners who challenged his authority. All through the 1920s he had ignored those majority resolutions of miner conventions which happened not to jibe with his own views, especially those resolutions (there were several) calling for an outright nationalization of coal. He had encouraged the owners to install laborsaving machinery in their mines, justifying the reduced employment as a trade-off for an increase in wage rates. His political support of Coolidge and Hoover in 1924 and 1928 had included serving them as labor adviser during their election campaigns. He had voted for Hoover again in 1932. It is no wonder, therefore, that he was more liked by business and industry than by rank-and-file labor at the outset of the New Deal. ("[N]o one thought John L. Lewis 'a menace' in those days," writes Frances Perkins. "He was regarded [by employers, she implies] as an intelligent, capable labor leader who was famous for living up to his contracts."[27]) Among the miners he was supposed to represent there were grave doubts about his integrity, grave suspicions that he may have "sold out" to the operators during the great soft-coal strike of 1922. There had arisen a rival union, the Progressive Miners of America, especially strong in Illinois, which gave signs of becoming the dominant union of the coalfields.

But Lewis, drastically revising his laissez-faire views to admit the need for government intervention in the economy, now met the threat to him head-on and effectively. He had played some part in the NIRA drafting. Within a day or two after the act had been signed he had scores of experienced UMW organizers in the coalfields, using for this purpose almost the last resource of the shrunken UMW treasury. Within thirty days he had added 150,000 new members to his union's rolls. When the Blue Eagle took flight, he was flooding the coalfields with leaflets asserting that "The President Wants You to Join the Union," an assertion whose truth it would have been impolitic for Roosevelt publicly to deny. By early August the stubborn resistance of the mineowners to signing any code that complied with Section 7(a), coupled with a drive on their part to pile as much mined coal as possible aboveground at prevailing low wage rates, before higher rates were forced upon them, was provoking a rash of strikes to which the mineowners were responding in time-honored fashion: using company police to club and shoot strikers who refused to yield to shows of force.

Especially serious was violence at mines of the Frick Coke Company in southwestern Pennsylvania—captive mines they were called, to distinguish them from commercial mines, for the Frick company was a subsidiary of U.S. Steel whose total coal output was consumed by the steel corporation and whose labor policy was determined by that corporation. The violence was fatal to one striker and injurious to many on August 1. Pennsylvania's governor, Progressive Republican Gifford Pinchot, called out the National Guard—the first call-out of militia to deal with coalfield troubles since 1922—and a temporary truce was arranged, announced by Roosevelt on August 5, whereby the 27,000 miners on strike agreed to go back to work pending arbitration. On the same day Roosevelt responded to an "appeal to management and labor for industrial peace" signed by members of both the labor and the industrial advisory boards of the NRA; he established a seven-member National Labor Board as a "tribunal to pass promptly on any case of hardship or abuse that may arise from interpretation or application of the President's Reemployment Agreement."[28] Chaired by Senator Wagner, who cut short a European vacation to accept the assignment,* the "tribunal" consisted of three labor representatives (William Green, John L. Lewis, Leo Wolman) and three industry representatives (Walter C. Teagle, Gerard Swope, Louis E. Kirstein). Its mandate was vague, its specified authority nil, yet the NLB had a very considerable success as moderator and arbitrator of labor-management disputes during the immediately following weeks.

This, then, was the context in which Roosevelt lectured the coal operators in the Executive Office during his whirlwind mid-August week in Washington. He passed in review, impressing them with his detailed knowledge of, the troubles plaguing their industry. He told them they were riding a "dying horse," that their attitudes and tactics were making the coalfields a breeding ground of communism. He was impressive. They returned to code negotiations in a somewhat chastened mood.

Meanwhile, finishing touches were put upon the lumber code. It granted to the industry a price-fixing authority, including a guarantee not to sell below an ill-defined "cost of production," which Tugwell thought outrageous. Roosevelt accepted it without demur.

Shortly before midnight on Saturday, August 19, he signed the oil, steel, and lumber codes, then boarded his train for a return to Hyde Park.

There was much trouble over the automobile code.

Henry Ford, that blindly stubborn individualist, refused even to consider compliance with a law that might force wage and hour concessions and collective bargaining upon him. When Hugh Johnson flew to Detroit to plead with him face-to-face in late July, Ford relented to the extent of permitting company representatives to join with the representatives of other companies in code-drafting operations. He soon backed out, however; he would have no part of

---

*Was Wagner's appointment to a post in the executive branch a violation of the constitutional separation of powers since he continued to serve in the Senate? The question was raised in several minds and never answered.

the Blue Eagle, he announced, though he promised to meet or better the minimum wage and maximum hour provisions of the code.* Yet even to him it should have been obvious in the third week of August that he would lose nothing by signing the code, then in appoximately its final shape. On July 28, meeting with top auto executives in Detroit, Johnson had told them he was "on the whole sympathetic with the industry's point of view" and had then proved this to be so by interpreting Section 7(a) in ways that gutted it as a guarantee of collective bargaining. The section did not mean that employers could not bargain with employees as individuals, he said. It meant simply that they must not refuse to bargain with the agents of those employees who were organized—that is, in actual practice, with agents of the small fraction of the industry's total labor force which a timidly led AFL had enrolled in craft unions. "The fact that you bargain with the men doesn't mean that you have to agree," Johnson added, significantly. Finally, after some *pro forma* resistance, the general concurred in the executives' insistence that the selection, retention, and promotion of employees must continue to be "on the basis of individual merit without regard to their membership or nonmembership in any organization"—in other words, that the prevailing open-shop policy of the industry would remain in force. He permitted the writing of this "merit clause" into the final draft code.[29]

The outcry of labor leaders and liberals across the land was immediate, loud, and angry. The Labor Advisory Board protested to the President vigorously, though meek and mild William Green, in White House conference, was quickly charmed by Roosevelt into acquiescence in the presidential decision. This last, being essentially an assessment of the strength of immediate opposing pressures, was, of course, to back General Johnson. Where, after all, could labor and the liberals go if they withdrew their support from the administration? Nowhere, at that moment. And was not automobile manufacture virtually the keystone of the American industrial arch, a prime employer of labor directly, a prime consumer of steel, rubber, glass, fabrics, and a multitude of other products? Clearly an automobile code, however imperfect, was indispensable to any overall NRA success.

So the code, unsigned by Henry Ford, was signed by the President on August 27. By then a merit clause modeled after the one in the auto code was being written into one draft code after another. Twenty-nine draft codes contained it by September 1. (By then, or shortly afterward, in response to the swelling outcry, Johnson was publicly admitting that his original permission of an open-shop code clause had been a mistake. On October 5 Roosevelt

---

*Asked what punitive action he would take against Ford, Johnson replied in effect that none would be needed: Denial of the Blue Eagle insignia to Ford products would prove a sufficient chastisement. Ford was declared ineligible to receive government contracts because of his refusal to comply with the NRA, this on October 27, but on November 11 the comptroller general announced that Ford *was* eligible for such contracts after all. Action against him was rendered difficult by the fact that he did keep his promise as regards wage and hour standards whereas a great many code signers flouted them.

removed this clause from the farm equipment, boot and shoe, and boiler manufacturing codes before signing them.)

There remained to be codified, of key industries, bituminous coal.

Strikes and slowdowns spread again through the coalfields in early September. The response of mine operators to them continued surly and forceful. Again the most serious trouble was in southwestern Pennsylvania, where the strike leader was John Ryan, a far more militant labor leader than Lewis had theretofore been and a man who, along with a great many of those he led, had little use for Lewis because of vivid remembrances of events in 1922. Yet their action greatly benefited Lewis as UMW head, for the strikers enrolled en masse in his union and enticed miners in other areas to do the same. Hugh Johnson complicated the situation by repeatedly and needlessly intervening personally, imposing "upon the strained . . . negotiations his own particular blend of bluster, bombast, bourbon, and baloney," to quote labor historian Irving Bernstein,[30] but by mid-September the UMW had enrolled miners nationwide in a number approximating the membership of 1919 (ultimately the union had 700,000 on its rolls, making it by far the largest industrial union the nation had thus far seen), and John Lewis was strong enough to stand tall and firm against any combine of mineowners and top NRA administration. Pragmatic Franklin Roosevelt recognized the fact. He again called the mine operators to the White House. He again lectured them sternly. This time he gave them just twenty-four hours in which to reach an agreement on an acceptable code, else he would impose one by executive fiat.

And so, at last, the operators came to terms. The Bituminous Coal Code was placed on the President's desk and signed by him, on September 18, to become effective on October 2.

It did not establish the closed shop that the UMW had pressed for. Otherwise, it represented a solid victory for the UMW. It provided for an eight-hour day, a five-day week, a minimum wage of $3.36 a day, and the checkoff of union dues. It eased or abolished requirements that miners live in company houses, buy in company stores;[31] established machinery for the arbitration of labor-management disputes; and conceded to the union a half dozen other points, less important but initially strongly opposed by the operators. Moreover, it was a wedge whereby the first crack was opened in the steel industry's wall of steel against independent industrial unionism. For though the coal code did not directly apply to the captive mines, owned by steel companies that had their own NRA code, Ryan insisted that the captive mines adopt the coal code's labor provisions, and he was substantially backed in this by Lewis and the National Labor Board. In late November employee elections in the captive mines were won in most cases by UMW representatives. When the mine operators refused to bargain with them, there was another crippling strike. In arbitration proceedings conducted by the labor board, Roosevelt personally, presidentially intervened. In a strike-settling agreement on January 19, 1934, many of the captive mines accepted as their own the labor terms earlier accepted by the commercial mines.

IV

IN general, then, from its very inception as administrative agency, NRA proceeded along the lines that had been predicted for it, *not* by its proponents but by its opponents, during the Senate debate of the industrial recovery bill. The largest businesses dominated the writing of the codes; they dominated the code authorities whereby the codes were administered; and they employed their power in ways that actualized the "ultimate difficulty" Paul Douglas had seen in the system of "legalized cartels," or "planned capitalism," which Tugwell proposed in *The Industrial Discipline* and which the administration seemed to be embracing.* Inevitably and unwaveringly big businessmen fixed their gaze upon what a later generation would call the bottom line. "I am fully aware that wage increases will eventually raise costs," the President had said in his June 16 statement on the NIRA, "but I ask that managements give first consideration to the improvement of operating figures by greatly increased sales to be expected from the rising purchasing power of the public. . . . The aim of this whole effort is to restore our rich domestic market by raising our vast consuming capacity. If we now inflate prices as fast and as far as we increase wages, the whole project will be set at naught."[32] But though they paraded their patriotism down Fifth Avenue and issued statements of their concern to increase employment and mass purchasing power in accordance with the presidential appeal, big businessmen in practice abundantly demonstrated that their *real* primary concern was to advantage themselves in the immediate marketplace by raising prices to a maximum while keeping costs (wages) as low as possible. It often seemed that in their view, any business competition at all was "unfair competition," to be prevented by code, whereas a maximum of "free competition" was to be maintained in the labor market no matter what the code said. And it must be added that Johnson-Richberg, with Roosevelt's active aid at crucial junctures, did far more to assist than to hinder the practical implementation of this view.

First, as regards labor . . .

In the fireside chat with which he launched the Blue Eagle into flight, Roosevelt said: "While we are making this great common effort there should be no discord or dispute. . . . The workers of this country have rights under the law which cannot be taken away from them, and nobody will be permitted to whittle them away but, on the other hand, no aggression is now necessary to attain these rights. The whole country will be united to get them for you."[33] But of course, big businessmen (notably from steel, coal, automobiles) were at that very moment "whittling away" at what labor deemed its "rights under the law," during prehearing code conferences. They had already obtained, would continue to obtain, concessions from Johnson-Richberg that practically nullified Section 7(a), and in those cases in which they failed of this, they would

*See p. 237.

obviously soon be denying that 7(a) meant in practice what it said in words. Truly effective labor leaders could only conclude that it was *absolutely* necessary for workers to employ what the President chose to call aggression (that is, the strike weapon) if they were to "attain" their "rights." Certainly the government, presumably representing the "whole country," showed no disposition to employ its police power to this end. Hence the wave of strikes that was sweeping the country, though actually it was not a very high wave in the circumstances. By the end of the first four months following the signing of the NIRA there had been a total of 1,100 strikes, countrywide, with an estimated loss of some 7 million workdays and some $24 million in wages, according to a November 17 announcement of the National Association of Manufacturers.[34]

Simultaneously with this announcement, the NAM declared war upon the National Labor Board, this despite the membership on the board of General Electric's Swope, Standard Oil's Teagle, and Filene's Kirstein. If these three were not deliberately betraying the business interest, in the evident judgment of the NAM, they were being outargued in debate and outvoted in decision by Senator Wagner and the three labor members.

Until then, as has been said, the board had achieved a considerable success in its effort to arbitrate disputes and end strikes. On August 10, just five days after its creation, it had announced a formula for dealing with labor-management quarrels. It was known as the Reading Formula because it was originally promulgated to settle a strike by 10,000 workers, incited by management's refusal to recognize as bargaining agent a newly formed independent employees' union, in the Berkshire Knitting Mills headquartered at Reading, Pennsylvania. The formula called for the strike's immediate termination, the rehiring of all strikers by management without discrimination, the subsequent holding of an election under NLB auspices wherein workers by secret ballot selected representatives to negotiate for them with management, and agreement by both sides to submit to the NLB's decision, which would be final, all differences remaining after full labor-management negotiations had been conducted. The formula assumed "majority rule"—that is, the union voted for by a majority of the workers in a plant would represent *all* the workers of that plant in labor-management negotiations—and under the formula the NLB, directly or through the twenty regional boards it established, settled during its first three months of existence not only the Berkshire Mills dispute but also a silk manufacturing strike in Paterson, New Jersey, a tool-and-die shop strike in Detroit, and hundreds of other, lesser disputes. It was under the Reading Formula that the NLB, with presidential assistance, succeeded in bringing many of the captive mines into conformity with the labor provisions of the Bituminous Coal Code.

But an abrupt drastic reduction of NLB effectiveness followed the declaration of war by the manufacturers' association.

Two major employers, Weirton Steel, with three large plants, and Budd Manufacturing of Philadelphia, flatly refused to abide by an NLB ruling that they permit their employees to hold secret-ballot elections to determine who would represent them. Despite loud protests from Wagner, and a warning from Johnson that "[i]n my opinion you are about to commit a deliberate violation of federal laws,"[35] Ernest T. Weir conducted in his plants private elections in which those employees who voted (most did not) could vote *only* for company union representatives. Edward G. Budd of the Budd company followed suit. And this twin defiance exposed to all watchful eyes the fundamental weakness of the NLB: the fact that operating under the vaguest of mandates as regards jurisdiction and procedure, the board had no enforcement powers whatever. The President called Weir to the White House for personal conference, but, unlike the AFL's William Green, the industrialist proved invulnerable to the Roosevelt charm, remaining adamant in his refusal to "cooperate." No punitive action was taken against him. Neither he nor Budd was even formally deprived of the right to display the Blue Eagle insignia, though there were several instances in which small businesses were so deprived by action of local NRA compliance boards.

(On this, Cornelia Pinchot, wife of Pennsylvania's governor, made acid public comment: "Until men like Mr. Weir and Mr. Budd are made to obey the law, I see no sense in taking the Blue Eagle away from a little beauty shop or small restaurant." Especially since a great many small businesses, unlike larger firms, were simply financially unable to meet NRA wage and hour standards, Lorena Hickok would have added. "Hotels, for instance," wrote Hick to Eleanor Roosevelt from Ottumwa, Iowa, in late November 1933. "You see the same crew on all day and far into the night. Clerks—some hotels seem to have only one. Waitresses. Dick [an otherwise unnamed relief official] and I had dinner at 8 o'clock in the coffee shop of the Warrior in Sioux City one night last week, and at breakfast at 6:30 next morning the same waitress served us [the Warrior flew the Blue Eagle on its walls and windows]. I doubt if the Warrior *could* take on any more help and remain solvent. There couldn't have been more than a dozen guests in the place when we were there, and . . . it's a very good hotel.")[36]

Thus, as 1933 ended and 1934 began, the NLB's position had become hopeless, in the view of Senator Wagner. Not only was it under attack by industry, but it was also under attack by labor, whose leaders increasingly viewed it as an agency to prevent or break strikes rather than as an agency of social justice. So in December Wagner assigned Leon Keyserling, his new legislative assistant, to the task of drafting a bill which would spell out 7(a)'s meaning in specifics and provide for its effective enforcement. He also let it be known that he had considered resigning his NLB chairmanship. Roosevelt then issued an executive order reiterating the labor board's original terms of reference and saying that all "action heretofore taken by this Board . . . is hereby ratified and approved,"[37] an order that helped persuade Wagner not to give up publicly on the NLB but did nothing to resolve the issue of majority rule versus proportional representation or to provide for the enforcement of NLB rulings.

The situation was not improved when, on February 1, 1934, under pressure from Wagner, the President issued another executive order, saying that the

NLB had authority to conduct representation elections when these were requested by a "substantial majority" of a company's employees. The order *seemed* an endorsement of the majority rule principle, especially since it was accompanied by a White House remark to reporters that the government wished to halt the formation of company unions. It also *seemed* to give the NLB some measure of enforcement backing, saying that cases of noncompliance with its rulings were to be referred to the NRA administrator, the implication being that the latter would from now on be required to take punitive action on these, with criminal prosecution through the Department of Justice as an ultimate recourse. For these reasons, the order was initially received by labor and liberals with cries of joy, by businessmen with howls of rage. The rage and joy both were short-lived. Within forty-eight hours after the order's issuance, Johnson-Richberg formally, publicly "interpreted" it as actually an endorsement of proportional representation! It simply meant, said Johnson-Richberg, that a majority of the employees of any company had the right to choose their own collective bargaining representatives; it did *not* deny to any employee minority *their* right to conduct bargaining negotiations on *their* own, either in organized groups or as individuals. This was, of course, a contradiction of NLB policy. It meant that management bargained as a single unit, if it condescended to bargain at all, with a labor representation divided into competing, disputatious units—a labor force unable to speak with a single voice. And since the President let the "interpretation" pass without comment, it became in effect a statement of NRA and general governmental policy.

The policy was emphatically confirmed in practice a few weeks later.

With little help from Green's AFL headquarters, and despite ruthless firings and blacklistings of labor "agitators" by management, a union had been organized in recent months in the automobile manufacturing plants of General Motors and Hudson, in Detroit. It was without money, it lacked experienced leadership, but its membership was very angry. On the first anniversary of Roosevelt's presidential inauguration this union announced its intention to strike unless a 20 percent wage increase was granted all workers, management rehired without prejudice all who had been discharged for union activity, and the union was recognized as collective bargaining agent. Simultaneously, the head of the union, knowing his new organization to be far too weak to prevail in any direct trial of strength against its powerful antagonists, sent the President a telegram asking for government aid in settling the dispute. Roosevelt, anxious to prevent interruption of the recovery which by then was being signaled by some economic indicators, and worried by information that the threatened strike might become industry-wide, at once asked the NLB to request strike postponement so that hearings might be held. The NLB did so on March 5. Nine days later the union, having postponed the strike, requested that the Reading Formula be applied to the dispute, enabling elections to be held for employee collective bargaining representatives. When General Motors, Hudson, and the National Automobile Chamber of Commerce flatly refused to permit such elections or to deal at all with any labor organization, the union called a strike to begin on March 21. On March 20 the President directly intervened. At his request the strike was again postponed, labor and management representatives were called to Washington for conference, and since the automobile manufacturing representatives refused to sit at the same table with labor's representatives, Roosevelt, with Johnson, dealt with the two groups separately in long conferences held between March 21 and 25.

The settlement announced by the President on the latter date virtually destroyed the fledgling auto workers' union.

It absolutely destroyed what little was left of the NLB's effectiveness.

For it accepted completely the automobile industry's interpretation, which was a nullifying interpretation, of Section 7(a). It endorsed proportional representation and gave legal sanction to the formation of company unions (employer-dominated unions) as bargaining agents for labor, saying, in presidential statement, "The Government makes it clear that it favors no particular union or particular form of employee organization or representation." It also established as an NRA agency, wholly independent of the NLB, an Automobile Labor Board made up of three members, one representing industry, one representing labor, and the third "neutral." The new board would emphatically *not* apply the Reading Formula. Sitting in Detroit, it would "pass on all questions of representation, discharge and discrimination." Its decisions were to be "final and binding on employer and employees."[38]

Embittered rank-and-file auto workers now proclaimed that NRA stood for "National Run Around." Columnist Heywood Broun, who had organized the American Newspaper Guild as the trade union of professional newspaper people in the fall of 1933, ridiculed those labor leaders who, having succumbed to the charm of that slippery, devious man in the White House, now had their proper reward.

Secondly, as regards prices . . .

To sell cheaply was to commit a crime. This was the general practical effect of the NRA's definition of "unfair competition."

There were a few cases in which a direct price-fixing authority, without reference to cost, was granted the code authority. This was true in the lumber and coal codes, among the major industry codes. But in most cases—indeed, in some 85 percent of the hundreds of codes adopted during the NRA's first year—what was written into the code was a minimum price provision in the form of a cost of production or cost of operation guarantee, a provision plausibly justifiable to the general public on the ground that it prevented the kind of predatory price cutting that enabled large businesses to crush small ones. Prohibited, in other words, were sales at a price below cost.

This last was arrived at, for code purposes, in a number of different ways. Sometimes cost was identified as the average of the individual costs of the enterprises covered by the code. Sometimes it was identified as the actual specific cost for the particular firm, determined by a formula of cost accounting approved by the code authority. At other times it was called simply the "lowest representative cost" or the "lowest reasonable cost" and, as such, was arbitrarily set by the code authority. Always, however, what was really meant by "cost" was "price." Always the design was to widen (by no accident was it ever to narrow) the overall margin of profit. And always, therefore, the cost figure tended to be set at or near the uppermost limit of the range from low to high of the actual costs within the codified industry or businesses. Price inflation was encouraged, too, and even more, by the system of open filing of prices provided for in a large majority of the codes, generally in addition to minimum price stipulations. Open filing, or open pricing, as it was commonly called, involved a number of collusive practices prohibited by antitrust law. It required every firm to list its current and proposed future prices with the code authority, as information open to all code members, and any price change was required to be announced long enough in advance of its going into effect to enable other firms to adjust to it or, during the "waiting period," to protest and possibly prevent it if, as rarely happened, the change was a price reduction.[39]

Nor were these forms of more or less direct price control the only means by which such control was effected through NRA codes. It was also effected indirectly by means of industrial production controls—controls exerted always to *limit* production or, in other words, to ensure that the available productive capacity (the available technology) was not so efficiently used as to prevent a profitable scarcity in the marketplace. We have seen how such controls were written into the Cotton Textile Code. The code for the furniture manufacturing industry similarly prohibited the construction of new plants or the expansion of existing ones without the express permission of the code authority, or the operation of factory machinery by more than one work shift in any twenty-four-hour period save when necessary to balance production among the divisions within a single plant. In a few cases, specific production quotas were set, always to obtain a drastic curtailment of production in an industry especially cursed by market oversupply. Thus, ostensibly for "conservation" purposes, the petroleum code had the immediate effect of cutting crude oil production by nearly 25 percent, or from between 2.8 million barrels and 3 million barrels a day before September 2, 1933 (the day the code went into effect) to between 2.2 million and 2.3 million barrels daily from then to year's end.[40]

Limitation of production had, of course, a limiting effect upon that reemployment which was the chief purpose of the NRA as proclaimed by presidential statement and Blue Eagle ballyhoo. When the Blue Eagle was launched, Hugh Johnson, intoxicated by his own rhetoric, if not, as was distinctly possible, by his own bourbon, publicly predicted that the President's Reemployment Agreement would result in the rehiring of between 5 million and 6 million of the currently unemployed by Labor Day, then a little more than a month away.* Nothing so dramatic occurred. The NRA *did* effect a considera-

---

*Sobering up, a day or so later, he revised his prediction downward. The NRA would reduce unemployment by 3 million within two months, he now said.

ble reemployment in the months immediately following the Blue Eagle's takeoff. The steep rise in industrial production between March and July of that year had been accompanied by but a moderate increase in employment, as has been said. While factory production went up 67.2 percent, factory employment went up only 22.1 percent,[41] meaning a much smaller percentage decrease in the overall employment figure, and this lag of employment behind production, caused in some part by increased per worker productivity resulting from new and improved technology, was due in greater part to management's tendency to lengthen the workweek instead of hiring new workers. The tendency was reversed, overall, by the NRA's insistence upon a shorter workweek. The existent work load was thereafter distributed more widely over the available work force. Consequently, despite a sharp *decrease* in production between July and November, industrial employment continued to increase. Total unemployment, standing at 13,687,000 in March, was down to 10,076,000 in October, according to AFL estimates (reliable government figures on such matters were still not available).[42] In November, however, unemployment began to go up again instead of continuing to decline, as it might have done (indeed, the decline between July and November would have been considerably steeper) if NRA code authorities had not imposed production controls in order to raise prices.

As for the price-raising efficiency of the NRA, there could be no slightest doubt by year's end, or even by early autumn, that it was very great.

On July 19, 1933, the second of the two days during which the Special Industrial Recovery Board gave Johnson's Blue Eagle plans a disapproving review, there occurred or began to occur that "precipitous drop" in the markets of which Tugwell had expressed fear only the day before. On both the stock and commodity exchanges, prices plummeted in what the press described as a "violent break." Average stock prices fell five points that day, and December wheat went down from $1.24 to $1.08½ per bushel. The decline continued next day, with stocks going down another six points on large volume and December wheat sinking to 93¾ cents. Cotton went down $4 per bale. On July 22, with the grain market closed in defense against panic, New York Stock Exchange transactions totaled nearly 10 million shares, the largest trading volume since October 30, 1929, and average stock prices went down yet another ten points. In four days stock prices were deflated nearly 20 percent, and commodity prices by considerably more. Thus was terminated the speculative boom that had begun with Roosevelt's inauguration. Nor was it only the gambling splurge that ended: More serious, more worrisome to the administration was the aforementioned decline in production. From a high of 101 in July, the index of production fell to 71 in November.[43]

Yet there was no such fall in prices as had always theretofore accompanied declines in stock prices and production. Farm prices, initially rising faster than industrial prices, having now fallen, stayed down. But industrial and retail prices rose. They continued to rise through the months that followed. And the cause was identified unmistakably, by means of comparative statistics, as the sum total of those various price-elevating devices which business had written into the NRA codes and now exercised without stint through the code authorities.

Data collected by the Mail Order Association of America (E. J. Condon of Sears, Roebuck was its chief spokesman) showed that in mid-December 1933 the prices of articles not covered by NRA codes, or covered by codes wholly lacking price provisions, were between 17 and 18 percent below those of 1926, the peak year for prices under the Republican Prosperity; they were nearly 10 percent below those of 1929. On the other hand, the prices for articles under codes containing outright price-fixing provisions were but a little more than 1 percent below 1926 prices and were 3 percent above the prices for 1929. By far the most potent uplifter of prices, however, to judge from Mail Order Association data, was the price collusion effected through open pricing. On December 15, 1933, the prices of articles under codes containing open price provisions (a large majority of all codes did, as has been said) were 11.2 percent higher than those of peak year 1926. They were well over 23 percent above those for 1929. And the distortion of the economy as a whole that was caused by this business price raising was indicated by the fact that farm produce sold in mid-December 1933 for only a little more than half as much as it had sold for in 1926.[44]

All this was viewed with great and growing alarm by most members of the Special Industrial Recovery Board, especially by those (Wallace and Wallace's deputy, Tugwell) whose primary concern was with agriculture.

We have noted Tugwell's belief, at the opening of the 1930s, that it made little difference whether industrial collectives were publicly or privately owned, because it was not owners but managers who made the controlling decisions.* By the spring of 1933 he had considerably modified this view. As he helped with the drafting of the NIRA, he was convinced that any such "national collectivism" as the act envisaged "would . . . make it necessary for government rather than business to make final determinations and ultimately to regulate the process of conjuncture in the public interest." In other words, since the necessary "determinations" and "process regulation" were exercises of essential property rights, the government had to assume a good measure of actual ownership of the collectives. What had happened, however, during the blind rush toward universal codification, encouraged by the President with his blanket Reemployment Agreement, was the precise opposite of what Tugwell now thought *ought* to happen. Power properly belonging to government had been surrendered wholesale to private business-dominated code authorities, which, moreover, were not fairly representative of the business interest as a whole. Only the largest or larger businesses were effectively represented on them; small and scattered businesses were grossly underrepresented. Labor and the consuming public were not represented at all. "[E]ven omitted," as Tugwell later complained, was that "governmental representation" which was "irredu-

*See Davis, *FDR: The New York Years,* pp. 270–71.

cibly necessary . . . to see to it that industry behaved in the civilized manner envisioned by the self-government theory."[45]

Again and again, that summer and fall, in written communications to Johnson and in oral argument to others, Tugwell warned that the NRA was bound to fail, dragging down into ruin the whole recovery effort, unless the greed of big businessmen as manifested by their collaborative price raising was restrained. "[T]o all intents and purposes industries are now free to set up what prices they please," there having "been a complete abrogation of either protection to the public from price increases by competition, or by public authority," said a representative Tugwell statement to a meeting of the Special Industrial Recovery Board. And he pointed more and more definitely to what seemed to him an inescapable conclusion: Since self-restraint, that essential ingredient of self-government, was evidently not in the businessman's nature, restraints would simply have to be forcibly imposed by government. There would have to be government price controls. In this conclusion an outraged Federal Trade Commission emphatically concurred. The President was informed by the FTC chairman, himself a board member, that there was "no middle ground discernible" between protection of the public through price competition and "protection through government price-fixing." If the former were to remain effectively abolished by the codes, the latter must be instituted.[46]

But in the view of an increasingly harassed, increasingly exasperated General Johnson, government price-fixing would be a far more vicious evil than was the private price-fixing now under way. On occasion he, with Richberg, defended the prevailing price policy by pointing to the horrendous consequences of cutthroat price competition—sweatshops, slums, child labor, all manner of brutal human exploitation—as if competition of this sort were the only possible alternative to what was now going on. On occasion, too, he issued public pleas to businessmen "to keep prices down—for God's sake keep prices down!"[47] Reluctantly he agreed to appoint public members to some of the code authorities. Still more reluctantly he agreed to permit the Consumers' Advisory Board to organize public hearings on price policy, to be held in December, then abruptly postponed them when businessmen expressed fear of the impact the hearings would have on Christmas buying. The postponement brought into his office one Saturday evening (December 17) a delegation of dismayed consumer advocates led by Mary Rumsey and including economist Leon Henderson of the Russell Sage Foundation. Typically the general sought to intimidate his critical visitors with a display of roaring wrath, but to the delight of onlookers and to Johnson's own astonishment, not unmingled with delight, he was answered roar for roar, and finally actually shouted down, by economist Henderson. Johnson then and there challenged Henderson, "if you're so goddamned smart," to come into NRA as the administrator's assistant on consumer problems, a challenge Henderson promptly accepted, to the general's surprise and subsequent regret.[48] (In February 1934 Henderson became head of the Research and Planning Division, which Alexander Sachs had initially headed and staffed with academic economists but which had been rendered virtually impotent, deliberately, by Sachs's successor, a Johnson appointee named Stephen Dubrul, formerly a General Motors sales manager.) Otherwise, the chief effect upon Johnson of the special board's persistent protests against rising prices was to increase the resentment he had felt from the outset toward the board's very existence. He was determined to rid himself of this "meddling" oversight at the earliest opportunity.

The opportunity came within two days after the famous Johnson-Henderson shouting match.

The special board, whose members were already overburdened with other heavy responsibilities, overreached itself by proposing that from now on every draft code be submitted to it for critical review before being sent to the White House. Johnson interpreted this as an insulting commentary upon his administrative competence, a direct challenge to his administrative authority. He went in a rage to the White House. He demanded that the board be abolished forthwith.

And Roosevelt did as the general wished.

To his bewildering array of vaguely supervisory, vaguely advisory, vaguely coordinative executive agencies, Roosevelt had added by executive order on December 6 a National Emergency Council. It was another cabinet committee —which is to say that its primary membership was for the most part identical with that of the original oversight committees for both Title I and Title II of the NIRA. Its specified functions were to "set up in Washington a central information bureau for the purpose of conveying to the general public all factual information with reference to the various governmental agencies" and to "provide machinery, temporary in character, for the adjustment of such controversies as may arise from the operations of the National Industrial Recovery Act and the Agricultural Adjustment Act."[49] All save three of the members of the Special Industrial Recovery Board were original members of the emergency council, and these three (the attorney general, the budget director, the FTC chairman) became council members on December 19 via an executive order which transferred the special board's functions to this council.

This meant, in effect, that the functions would be no longer performed. The general's NRA operations would thenceforth be free of any official committee oversight; the chief restraining influence upon his service to big business in the matter of prices would be exercised by the NRA's Consumers' Advisory Board.

V

INDUSTRY, through the NRA, could use production controls to create price-raising scarcities in ways not blatantly obvious to the general public. Agriculture, through the AAA, could not in 1933. It was in full sight of a public, including myriads of hungry and ragged Americans, that pigs were slaughtered by the million, that acres of cotton were plowed up by the million, in the summer and early fall of that year—a deliberate, laborious destruction of potential food and fiber that was organized and subsidized by government at a direct, immediate cost to taxpayers of between $100 million and $200 million.

The spectacle struck a great many who watched it as both insane and obscene. It came close to being regarded in this light by not a few of those directly involved in its administration, including Secretary of Agriculture Henry Wallace.

But by the overwhelming logic (illogic) of the prevailing economic order (disorder), what other could be done? As Wallace truly said, those who decried this organized wastefulness in a world filled with needy people were "not really criticizing the farmers or the AAA but the profit system."[50] For if the system were to survive the present emergency, if violent revolution were not to sweep the farm belt, a workable balance simply must be struck very soon between the agricultural and industrial economies, and such balance required an immediate drastic curtailment of farm production.

It will be remembered that when the agricultural adjustment bill was introduced in the Seventy-third Congress in mid-March, Roosevelt had pressed Congress for its speedy enactment so that it could have effect before spring planting of crops had been completed. Congress had not been able to move at anything like that speed upon a measure so complicated and controversial. By May 12, when the bill was at last signed into law, corn was growing on nearly 106,000,000 acres, wheat (most of it winter wheat, planted in 1932) on nearly 50,000,000 acres, and cotton on nearly 40,000,000 acres. These were far larger acreages than were needed, if per acre production was anywhere near normal and if need was defined as effective market demand. The last year, from nearly 58,000,000 acres, wheat farmers had harvested 756,000,000 bushels, and of this huge crop almost half (360,000,000 bushels) remained unconsumed—a carryover three and a half times that of former years. Last year from nearly 36,000,000 acres, cotton farmers had harvested a little more than 13,000,000 bales, and 8,000,000 bales were still warehoused—a carryover three times that of former years. For corn, the story was much the same, if more complicatedly told, since the bulk of the corn crop was fed to hogs on the farms where it was raised, then marketed as pork. Last year 71,425,000 hogs had been slaughtered, and the price per hundredweight had gone down from $6.16 the year before to $3.83. This year nearly 80,000,000 hogs were being prepared for market, and the market forecast was that if sold, they would bring farmers but $2.50 a hundredweight, a good deal less than the cost of production.

Drastic "production control" was indicated for each of these major crops, but it was the surplus cotton acreage which presented AAA with its most immediate operative problem in late May, this while the newborn agency was struggling to organize itself administratively.

The price of cotton was rising at that time. It was to rise steeply during the weeks just ahead, reaching 10.6 cents a pound in July, compared with 5.5 cents in March.* But this was clearly due to a general anticipation of currency inflation, especially after the passage of the Agricultural Adjustment Act with its Thomas amendment, and to an abnormal, strictly temporary demand for cotton by textile manufacturers who wanted to process as much as possible of

---

*In 1923 cotton sold for 29 cents a pound.

it into cloth before the NRA code with its wage and hour provisions went into effect. Even steeper than the rise, obviously, and to depths beyond plumbing, would be the fall of cotton price as the "emergency" buying ended and the already huge cotton market oversupply was hugely augmented. For estimates were that the cotton now growing would produce upon maturity 16,651,000 bales—and there was already enough cotton in warehouses to supply the whole of the world market for a year ahead! Much of it was owned by the federal government, of course, having been purchased through Hoover's Federal Farm Board to keep it off the market, but it definitely existed, and its very existence was an actual or potential price depressor of crushing weight. A total cotton price collapse was in the offing.

In the deep shadow of this immediately impending event, on May 23 in Washington, a conference of AAA, Bureau of Agricultural Economics, and Extension Service representatives decided there must be a plow-up of a full fourth of the growing cotton crop—some 10,304,000 acres in all. It was an easy decision to make, being, on the premises, a virtually automatic reaction to circumstance. It was *not* an easy decision to carry out, however. Indeed, the practical difficulties, as viewed in late May and early June, were enormous. The agreed plan called for the secretary of agriculture to "rent" the "surplus" cotton acreage, paying individual farmers from $6 to $20 an acre for it. By the terms of the rental agreement, each farmer was then to do the plow-up job himself, under such governmental supervision as was needed to make sure the job was thoroughly done, using for this purpose his own plow, his own tractor, or (more commonly) mules.* A large AAA field staff of professional caliber was obviously needed, just to handle this immediate cotton program, and there would be thereafter hundreds of thousands of production-controlling contracts with cotton farmers for next year's crop and the crops of following years. Similarly for the wheat, corn-hog, tobacco, and other AAA programs to be initiated that summer. Yet the AAA in early June 1933 had no field staff whatever. It consisted then wholly of a core or skeleton national headquarters staff, the size of which had to be swiftly multiplied to deal with the enormous volume of administrative work soon to descend upon it.

Inevitably, if probably at M. L. Wilson's original suggestion, the AAA turned for active help to the Extension Service, a thoroughly decentralized cooperative federal-state organization headed in each state by a director who was a member of the administrative staff of the land-grant college.† Under the

---

*Tractors were far better for such work, as farmers would discover. Mules initially refused with typical mulish stubbornness to trample down rows of growing crops.

†So called because established in consequence of the Morrill Act of 1862, an enactment of immense importance to American higher education and, indeed, to the development of American democracy. The act provided for the endowment with land from the public domain of state colleges dedicated to the "practical" education of "farmers and mechanics." The endowment consisted of 30,000 acres for each congressman the state sent to Washington. In some states—Wisconsin, Illinois, Minnesota, Nebraska, for instance—the agricultural college became a part of the university. In other states—Michigan, Iowa, Kansas, Colorado, etc.—the two institutions were separate and became, inevitably, more or less bitter rivals, with the agricultural college inferior in social prestige and overall educational quality, assuming "education" to mean something other than

director's general supervision were county agricultural agents charged with the duty of spreading among local farmers scientific agricultural information developed by the land-grant colleges and their attached agricultural experiment stations—information about agronomy, animal husbandry, fertilizers, cultivation methods, farm management, and so on. These agents were personally acquainted with the farmers; they were intimately knowledgeable about the farm problems of their respective localities. They were looked up to by the farmers, who often sought their advice and were accustomed to their frequent leadership in agricultural community affairs. Hence the proposal that the extension director in each state become the AAA administrator for that state, the county agents then becoming the AAA's field staff, was soon made and was quickly accepted by Henry Wallace. In no other way could the AAA obtain so swiftly, so painlessly a staff of such high professional, technical competence.

There were, however, serious drawbacks to this arrangement, disadvantages so heavy they outweighed the advantages in the view of many, including Rex Tugwell. To link the AAA with the Extension Service in so organic a fashion was to link it thus with the American Farm Bureau Federation, giving to "that anomalous, powerful, semi-public organization," as Gladys Baker has called it,[51] a yet greater and growing power, including a possibly decisive voice in the shaping of AAA policies, if not the policy of the Department of Agriculture as a whole.

The story of how this state of affairs had come to be, like the story of the relationship of the U.S. Army Corps of Engineers with the National Rivers and Harbors Congress, provides a classic case study of the way political pressure groups are developed and of how democracy is ultimately denied or distorted when the distinction between special private interests and the general public interest is blurred in institutionalized ways at the outset of the developmental process. The Smith-Lever Act of 1914, which established the Extension Service, specifically recognized private donations as legitimate sources of state-matching funds to pay county agent salaries and to finance the agents' work. County farm bureaus having dues-paying members were organized for this purpose, their organization encouraged by the Extension Service as an arm of the land-grant college. Such organization became almost an act of patriotism during the great "Food Will Win the War" campaign of 1917–18. Also encouraged by the Extension Service in those years was the joining together of county farm bureaus to form state farm bureau federations, a development that was viewed askance by some of the county agents themselves and that definitely alarmed leaders of the Grange, the Farmers' Union, and other long-existent farm organizations. These last protested what seemed to them a governmental sponsorship of a developing rival organization. They were told by the Extension Service that such fears were groundless: The county agents and the

---

specialized vocational training. In recent decades, of course, as the agricultural economic interest has decreased in importance relative to other segments of the economy, the former agricultural colleges have themselves become universities—Kansas State University at Manhattan as distinct from the University of Kansas at Lawrence, Michigan State University at Lansing as distinct from the University of Michigan at Ann Arbor, etc.

bureaus were engaged purely and exclusively in educational activity and would be aided in this by statewide affiliation. But already, in 1916, one state farm bureau federation had been organized primarily for frankly stated legislative and business purposes, and this organization, calling itself the Illinois Agricultural Association, was from the first, in terms of its purpose, immensely successful. It attracted a large membership as an organization in its own right (one could become a member without prior membership in a county bureau or even without being actually a farmer), and it became the model for, as it was the most powerful of, the state farm bureaus which in 1919 and 1920, again with Extension Service encouragement, came together to form the American Farm Bureau Federation. The latter action, it should be added, was deemed "nothing less than tragic" at the time by some Extension Service leaders, *including* Montana's M. L. Wilson.[52]

So it was that in each state, by 1933, the Extension Service and the county and state farm bureaus were inextricably joined together, functioning often as a virtually single organism, while at the same time the state farm bureaus and the national Farm Bureau as a federation of these state bodies were *private* organizations and, as such, among the most potent special interest lobbies operating on state legislatures and the U.S. Congress. As lobby, however, thanks to the Illinois Agricultural Association model, the American Farm Bureau Federation did not accurately represent the interests of the average American "dirt farmer"; it did not at all represent the tenant farmer, North or South. It represented the landlord, the relatively prosperous farmer, the farmer who could afford expensive farm machinery and who operated with such machinery a large and expanding acreage, the kind of farmer who in future years became known as an agribusinessman, being involved not just in farming but in all manner of related business enterprises, especially banking and insurance. He was as a type extremely conservative politically, hostile to social legislation, automatically opposed to any governmental proposal that might change the prevailing pattern of landownership or farmer-income distribution. Which is to say he opposed any proposal likely to halt or slow the prevailing trend toward larger and fewer farms. Thus the linkage of the Extension Service to the AAA organically by means of a shared field staff militated against Franklin Roosevelt's personal desire to preserve and revitalize the small family farm as an important part of America's cultural and economic life, a desire which was generally presumed to be a principal long-range purpose of the AAA.

The immediate practical advantages of this linkage, however, were very great. Within a day or so following public announcement of the cotton plan on June 19, a veritable army of men—some 22,000 county agents, agricultural college employees, experiment station workers, high school vocational agriculture teachers,* and "leading farmers" who had been mobilized by the county agents and designated as AAA committeemen—swarmed through 956 coun-

---

*Under the terms of the Smith-Hughes Act of 1917 these received a substantial portion of their salaries from the federal government.

ties to explain the program, "sell" it, and obtain farmer signatures upon government contracts. Within a little over three weeks (by July 14) a total of 1,026,514 contracts between individual farmers and the secretary of agriculture had been executed. And in August the great plow-up was carried out, overseen by the county agents and the local AAA committeemen. There was much fanfare, governmentally organized—more than was wise, considering the unpopularity of this whole enterprise among city dwellers and the consuming public in general. The first government check issued in payment of participation in the program was presented in the President's office by the President personally to a tall, lean southerner who carried in his left hand a broad-brimmed hat and a cotton plant loaded with white-bursting bolls, while news cameras clicked and a tentatively smiling Henry Wallace looked on. The first farmer actually to accomplish his assigned quota of destruction (he happened to be a black farmer from Georgia) was brought to Washington and honored for his exemplary deed by the President in a ceremony on the White House lawn.[53]

Even greater than the publicity attending the cotton plow-up, but much less a product of government "information specialists" and much more disapproving, was the publicity given the vast pig slaughter of late summer and early fall.

The inevitable decision for this undertaking was arrived at by means of a National Corn-Hog Committee, whose members included Ed O'Neal of the national Farm Bureau, and the heads of the national Grange and Farmers' Union (John Simpson), as well as representatives of committees of corn-hog producers, local committees of "leading farmers" organized by county agents operating as AAA staff. Most of the general public, nearly all of it not directly involved in the agricultural economy, watched thereafter with shock and outrage as the government purchased from farmers more than 6.2 million pigs weighing from 25 to 100 pounds apiece,* plus 220,000 hogs soon to farrow, and supervised their destruction in packers' abattoirs. The negative popular reaction was encouraged by newspapers, notably the Hearst chain and the Chicago *Tribune,* whose publishers' initial enthusiasm for the New Deal swiftly curdled into hostility when abortive efforts were made to apply NIRA wage and hour provisions to reporters and newsboys. But outrage would have been great in any case among people who, themselves impoverished, acutely aware of the poverty around them, contemplated what happened to the quarter billion pounds of meat which the vast slaughter yielded. A portion of it was simply thrown away as pure waste. Hundreds of millions of pounds of it were processed into fertilizer, a procedure that was "practical" in that it enabled packers

---

*Some of the popular horror seemed to derive from the fact that it was "little pigs" rather than full-grown hogs that were slaughtered. Wallace was provoked into defensive sarcasm. Did people really believe that "every little pig" has a natural right "to attain before slaughter the full pigginess of his pigness"? Or did they (though they ate pork) believe it wrong to kill pigs at any age? "Perhaps they think that farmers should run a sort of old-folks home for hogs and keep them around indefinitely as barnyard pets."[54]

to be handsomely paid for their pig-killing labor, at no cost to the federal Treasury, but which was also bitterly and nonsensically ironical insofar as it was part of a program designed to *limit* agricultural production.[55]

A bare tenth of the meat was distributed as food to hungry families on relief.

VI

THAT any of it at all was so distributed was largely due to Jerome Frank, who had by this time become one of the brightest stars in the galaxy of New Deal liberals and, as such, was now a focus of the quarrelsome administrative turmoil that had predictably arisen from Roosevelt's appointment of George Peek to be AAA administrator.*

Aged forty-four in 1933, a slender, handsome man of medium height, vividly alive, tirelessly energetic, possessing an immense and a wide-ranging erudition (he read at a phenomenal speed) and a genius for leadership of the bright young men whom he brought into the New Deal, Frank himself had been invited to Washington originally by Tugwell to serve as solicitor of the Department of Agriculture. The son of a prosperous Jewish lawyer in Chicago, he had been graduated from the famously progressive Hyde Park High School in that city and had taken both his A.B. and law school degrees at the University of Chicago, where sociologist and social reformer Charles E. Merriam had fired him with an idealistic zeal for public service, a zeal which remained undiminished during the twenty years of Frank's successful career as corporation lawyer, first in Chicago, then on Wall Street. Merriam had also impressed upon him the importance of psychological factors in political organization, political process, and Frank's own 1930 book, *Law and the Modern Mind,* stressed the importance of individual personal psychology in the making of judicial decisions, in the shaping of judicial interpretations. His literary interests were intense. He was a close friend of Harriet Monroe, to whose *Poetry* magazine his wife contributed verse. He had been a member of an informal luncheon club in Chicago which included Carl Sandburg, Lloyd Lewis, Sherwood Anderson. As corporation lawyer he was unusual in that instead of concentrating on profit for bankers and lawyers during business reorganizations, he concentrated upon protecting small security holders, inventing special techniques for this purpose. It was as stockholder representative that he first encountered George Peek, who, as head of the failed Moline Plow Company, was Frank's opponent in reorganization court battles which Peek, a poor loser, lost.

This last did him no good, indeed caused him much trouble, in Washington.

When his appointment as solicitor was blocked by Jim Farley, who was under the misapprehension that Frank's father-in-law was a Tammanyite political enemy of Farley in New York City (actually Frank's father-in-law, now dead, had lived the whole of his life in Kansas and Chicago), Frank was named general counsel of the AAA, a post over which the postmaster general

*See pp. 75–76.

had no patronage power and which paid a higher salary than that of solicitor ($10,000 instead of $8,000).* He was installed as general counsel some days before the official appointment of Peek as AAA administrator. Peek was infuriated by it; almost his first act, upon assuming his official duties, was to insist upon Frank's removal. A big-city lawyer who was also a Jew would be wholly unacceptable to farmers and farm organization leaders, said Peek emphatically to the President, in Wallace's presence, and Roosevelt seems to have accepted Peek's judgment, perhaps felt compelled to do so, since Peek was nominally the general counsel's superior officer. Wallace, too, went along. When Wallace explained this to Frank, however, very apologetically, with a shrug of helplessness ("Well, there it is, Jerry"), the latter, in his own words, "got mad" and "fought back." His popularity or lack of it with farmers seemed to him irrelevant to the technical legal job, a huge and hugely important job, which he as counsel would have to do, and he was *damned* if he'd passively yield to Peek's personal animosity and anti-Semitism. He had Tugwell's firm support. Tugwell promptly took the case back to the White House and there, arguing forcefully, persuaded the President that Frank was far too valuable a man to be lost to government in this way. Frank, therefore, stayed on.[56]

But this did not end the matter, alas. Tough and stubborn George Peek flatly refused to have anything to do with the general counsel. He insisted upon bringing in his own personal lawyer, in violation of all manner of government rules and regulations, paying this lawyer out of his own pocket (that is, he turned over to him his own $10,000 government salary), and the man he chose was one for whose legal abilities Frank had slight regard. He was Frederic P. Lee, who, while yet on the legal staff of the American Farm Bureau Federation, had been a principal draftsman of the Agricultural Adjustment Act and from whose "sloppy draftsmanship," in Frank's contemptuous view, much trouble had come and would continue to come. Certainly Lee's operations at Peek's side did nothing to prevent and much to provoke administrative battles between Peek and Wallace, battles in which Frank, on frequent occasion, being caught in the middle, suffered wounding fire from both sides.

As for the inevitable power struggle between Wallace and Peek, a struggle rooted in fundamental disagreements about national agricultural policy and exacerbated by clashing temperaments, it had begun even before, weeks before, the agricultural adjustment bill was enacted. It had begun, in fact, within a few hours after Roosevelt, seeking to spur the bill's passage, had let it be known that Peek was slated to be the act's administrator.

By that time Paul Appleby, whom Wallace had summoned to Washington a few days after the inauguration to serve as secretary to the secretary of agriculture and who had initially accepted the job for a thirty-day trial period only, was firmly established as Wallace's indispensable right-hand man, his administrative arm, the man chiefly responsible, with Tugwell, for imposing efficient order upon an already immensely sprawling and now rapidly expand-

---

*Frank had been making more than $35,000 per annum as a member of the Wall Street firm of Chadbourne, Stanchfield & Levy.

ing department. He was superbly equipped for the job. A graduate of Grinnell College in Iowa, where Harry Hopkins had been a fellow student (so had been Chester Davis, who became Peek's second-in-command at the AAA), Appleby had been for twenty-odd years a newspaperman in the West and Midwest—in country towns, where he became intimately acquainted with farmers and farm problems, and on the *Register-Tribune* in Des Moines where he became one of Wallace's few close friends. In his early forties, Appleby was quiet, unassuming, highly intelligent, if not especially creative, remarkably selfless, yet shrewd in his assessment of power, of its location, its relative distribution, and the power motivations of other people. (He himself was more disturbed than pleased by the great and undefined delegations of authority which Wallace made to him; he moved as rapidly as he could toward an institutionalization of this authority, depersonalizing it within the bureaucratic structure.)

Appleby reacted, therefore, with instant alarm when Peek, having just been submitted to Roosevelt's blandishments, told reporters he "was not going to take a job subordinate to the Secretary of Agriculture." If this were a truculent assertion of Peek's willful intent, a blunt statement of the terms on which he would take the job Roosevelt wanted him to take, it might also be Peek's understanding of what Roosevelt had told him. Certainly Wallace's authority was being gravely threatened. Appleby took immediate defensive action. He drafted on his own typewriter a letter to the President, for Wallace's signature, "making the point that the country would expect the Secretary of Agriculture to be the responsible man in the agricultural field and that if Peek came in he should come in with the clear understanding that he was heading a big, new [but] subordinate organization in the Department."

Thus alerted to danger, Wallace proposed to sign this missive immediately and have Appleby deliver it at once, in person, to the White House. Appleby himself, however, counseled patience. Tugwell was in New York City that day. Surely the advice of Tugwell, who was so experienced in Rooseveltian psychology, should be sought upon so important a matter. And when Tugwell read the letter next morning, he, acutely aware of Roosevelt's aversion to clear-cut irrevocable decisions and of Roosevelt's tendency to "get his Dutch up" when someone tried to force him into such a decision, suggested the deletion of the concluding sentence Appleby had written, a sentence saying, "What I hope you will do in the circumstances, Mr. President, is to write me a letter affirming." Suppose Roosevelt made no reply? With that sentence in, his silence must be construed as disapproval of Wallace's position; with that sentence out, his silence could be construed as per se affirmative. So the sentence was removed, the letter retyped, and Appleby personally placed it in Marvin McIntyre's hand at the White House within the hour.

There was a cabinet meeting that afternoon. When Wallace returned from it to his office, he called in Paul Appleby.

"Well, Paul," he said, "I got my answer to the letter. At the end of the meeting as I was leaving the President he said, 'That was a good letter you wrote, Henry."[57]

But this was no conclusive answer certainly.

Some days later, after it was certain that the agricultural adjustment bill was about to be passed, there was another cabinet meeting, a special evening one for the purpose of explaining the new legislation to cabinet members. A few hours before it began, newsmen warned Appleby that Peek had prepared an AAA organization chart which had him, as administrator, reporting directly to the President rather than through the secretary of agriculture and that Peek planned to present this for approval by the President as soon as the cabinet meeting had ended. At once Appleby with Wallace prepared their own organization chart, placing the AAA administrator definitely under the secretary. That night, after the meeting had been adjourned, Peek and Wallace both approached the President's desk, their respective charts under their respective arms. Peek got there first. Roosevelt, with a show of great interest, perused Peek's chart and made a few meaningless check marks on it with his pen, then handed it back with a smile. He did precisely the same with Wallace's chart. A stalemate. But the upshot was that Peek, like his former business associate Hugh Johnson, *did* gain direct access to the President. And within three days after the act had been signed, Wallace was writing Roosevelt that "Mr. Peek's insistence on using you as an umpire between him and myself . . . will prove to be a fundamental handicap to the unified administration of the Farm Adjustment Act."[58]

Through the summer and fall of 1933 there were, in effect, *two* Agriculture departments, with the AAA divided acrimoniously between them. After Roosevelt in early June had decisively approved the Wallace-Tugwell-Wilson emphasis upon production control as the chief means of raising farm prices, Peek perforce accepted the decision—but only insofar as it applied to 1933's cotton, corn, and hogs and only reluctantly, halfheartedly, as a strictly temporary emergency measure. He remained opposed, if futilely, to M. L. Wilson's program for a drastic reduction in the acreage planted to winter wheat in the fall of 1933. He still had no faith whatever in the price-raising efficacy of subsidized acreage reductions in general. His own fervent faith continued to be placed in marketing agreements, with surplus disposal abroad, and he chose as his principal subordinates men who had fought at his side for McNary-Haugen in the 1920s (Chester Davis had done so, though Davis was now more than half persuaded of the merits of domestic allotment). On June 26 a presidential executive order, issued by Roosevelt from *Amberjack II* as he sailed into fog off the coast of Maine, facilitated Peek's vigorous implementation of his faith: It transferred code-making authority, under Title I of the NIRA, from the NRA to the Department of Agriculture "with respect to trades, industries, or subdivisions thereof engaged principally in the handling of milk and its products, tobacco and its products, and all foods and food-stuffs."[59]* Thereafter Peek was able to make marketing agreements with processors in the

---

Not transferred, but remaining under the NRA's jurisdiction, were "the determination and administration of provisions relating to hours of labor, rates of pay, and other conditions of employment," to quote the executive order.

form of presidentially approved codes of fair competition, and he did so as rapidly as he could.

He also continued to complain about Jerome Frank's "unfitness" for his post, continued to raise the "issue" of anti-Semitism. He asserted that businessmen and farmers from the South and West found it hard, if not impossible, to deal with the Jewish lawyers with whom Frank had staffed the Office of the General Counsel.

In point of fact, the number of Jews on Frank's staff was disproportionately small in view of his insistence upon high intelligence, high professional competence, and personal sympathy with the liberal aims of the New Deal. There were no more than a half dozen, including Frank himself, among the 100 or so attorneys whose work he administered. But it was true, and it outraged Peek, that a prior knowledge of agricultural problems, much less a direct acquaintance with farmers and farming, was not among Frank's criteria for staff selection. He wanted "brilliant young men with keen legal minds and imagination."[60] He obtained them—young men of immense ability and ambition who could and did swiftly learn all that their jobs required them to know about agriculture. Several of their names were destined to become nationally known, if not happily so in every instance, including Abe Fortas, Thurman Arnold, Alger Hiss, Lee Pressman, Adlai Stevenson, and all of them were inspired by Frank's leadership and example to work at the highest pitch of their energies and talents for incredibly long hours.

Thus young Adlai Stevenson, on leave from a corporate law firm in Chicago, sharing bachelor quarters with his brother-in-law in the home of a Washington friend (the wives of all three men remained away from the humid Washington summer heat), was caught up in such a fever of work that he had scarcely a glimpse of either his relative or his host from mid-July to mid-September. He was designated a special attorney on the staff of the general counsel of the AAA, and in an early August letter to his wife he explained what he was doing. "In essence, we're creating gigantic trusts in all the food industries, to raise prices and eliminate unfair competition, thereby increasing returns to farmers ultimately," he wrote. "Everyone from flour millers to mayonnaise manufacturers are [sic] here and each day I hear about the troubles of a different industry in conferences, then spend the night drafting a marketing agreement to correct them."[61]

This indicates why Frank's commitment to the general welfare led him into AAA activities that increased the bitterness of Peek's aversion to him. He was concerned to balance on the scales of justice the effect of such labors as Stevenson and others like him performed under, perforce, his own administrative direction. For what about the "troubles" of common folk who, out of meager incomes, had to pay the "raised prices" which just *might* "ultimately," in the general counsel's dubious view, increase "returns to farmers"? Who was to protect ordinary consumers against government-sponsored profiteering by processors? Frank did all he could to strengthen the role of the Consumers Division which, to Peek's disgust and against Ed O'Neal's opposition,* he had established within the Office of the General Counsel. It was headed by sixty-six-year-old Frederic C. Howe, who had been an indefatigable warrior for progressive causes since the turn of the century. Howe's top assistant was Gardner "Pat" Jackson, a former Boston newspaperman who had headed a defense committee for death-sentenced Sacco and Vanzetti. And Frank was as delighted as Peek (with Hugh Johnson) was infuriated when Fred Howe "began to get out simple exhibits showing how much of the increased price of a pair of overalls or of a housewife's apron was due to the processing tax on cotton, how much to higher wages in cotton mills, how much to better prices for raw cotton, and how much for increased profit," to quote Jay Franklin.[63] These exhibits made public knowledge of the fact that under the Cotton Textile Code as administered by George Sloan, whose industrial statesmanship the President had praised, the cotton industry was price-gouging and profiteering unmercifully while continuing, as other evidence showed, to exploit labor unmercifully, having devised various schemes for circumventing the code's wage and hour provisions. And what the cotton industry was doing under the NRA was being done by other processors of agricultural products under the AAA, as Howe also demonstrated.

In line with Frank's concern for the consumer was his proposal, as the pig slaughter began, that the meat obtained by government be turned over to Harry Hopkins for distribution to the needy through the Federal Emergency Relief Administration.

The idea encountered opposition from Peek and from O'Neal, who argued that giving meat to Hopkins would prevent his buying meat on the open market; it would thus reduce price-raising demand, militating against the very purpose of the pig slaughter. But as Frank quickly ascertained, Hopkins was buying no meat. He had no plans for doing so. And he was enthusiastic about Frank's idea, the immediate implementation of which seemed to him dictated by common sense and common decency. So, on a Sunday afternoon, the relief administrator came to the apartment which Tugwell and Frank shared through these months, and there and then the three worked out on paper the proposal of a Federal Surplus Relief Corporation, to be integrated with the FERA, a nonprofit corporation to which the AAA could transfer title to all the surplus pork obtained. The FERA could then use its own funds to process these raw products into food—mostly salt pork. Nor need the corporation's activities be limited to the distribution of this immediate pig-kill pork; it could also be used to distribute other agricultural surpluses to the destitute during the months and years ahead, if unemployment remained an unsolved problem despite the New Deal's efforts to solve it.

Next day the three men journeyed together to Hyde Park to present the idea

---

*The farm organization leaders "generally didn't give a damn about consumers," Frank sourly remembered in a later year. Their concern was exclusively with the economic welfare of commercial farmers.[62]

to the President. They found Roosevelt in a receptive mood (for one thing, he was acutely aware of political danger in the current popular revulsion against the AAA's organized destructiveness) and he promptly approved the proposal. On September 21 he announced his authorization of the purchase of $75 million of surplus food and clothing for distribution among the destitute unemployed, the distribution to be made by the FERA in cooperation with state and local relief agencies. This was an authorization for which Hopkins had been pressing for days, if not weeks, before his visit to Hyde Park with Frank and Tugwell. On October 1 announcement of the decision to create the Surplus Relief Corporation was made in the form of a presidential "instruction" to Hopkins.[64] Within a few days the new organization was incorporated in Delaware.* Its directors were Wallace as agriculture secretary, Ickes as public works administrator, and Hopkins as FERA administrator, with the last becoming corporation president. It continued to operate with high efficiency as a relief agency for some two years thereafter, receiving from the AAA, for distribution to the impoverished, a very considerable bulk of pork, flour, dairy products, cornmeal, and other food.

It also continued to be viewed askance by top AAA officialdom, however, and by the conjoined Extension Service-Farm Bureau officialdom, men who saw it as an at least potential threat to the maximization of commercial agricultural profit. They maneuvered to gain control of it. In 1935 they succeeded. By presidential order the agency was transferred from the FERA to the Department of Agriculture and renamed the Surplus Commodities Corporation. Its directorship was changed. The secretary of agriculture, of course, continued on the board, but the farm credit administration's governor replaced the PWA administrator, and the relief administrator was replaced by the AAA administrator, who became the corporation's president. From that time onward the corporation operated not as a relief organization "but as an agency to assist in the program being conducted by the AAA to remove farm surpluses," as the President explained in 1938.[65]

VII

THERE was, in that same month of October 1933, a spin-off from the original idea for the Federal Surplus Relief Corporation which, though it initially horrified Jerome Frank, turned out to be highly effective of its purpose, which was to increase immediate income for the producers of certain basic agricultural commodities. The brainchild of Oscar Johnston, manager of one of the world's largest cotton plantations,† whom Peek had brought into the AAA to play a key role in both the enforcement and the financial procedures of the

---

*Frank paid the $40 incorporation fee out of his own pocket to avoid the complication which would result if the comptroller general disapproved such expenditure of federal funds.
†Located at Scott, Mississippi, and owned by the Delta and Pine Mine Company, the huge plantation had been largely financed by Dutch and English capital.

organization, it was given legal form by Stanley Reed, the RFC's general counsel, who used as his model Frank's Delaware-incorporated nonprofit surplus relief agency.

Johnston's ingenious idea was to have the government lend cotton farmers 10 cents a pound on their cotton, at 4 percent interest, though cotton was then selling on the open market for only a little more than 8 cents. The loans were to be fully secured by the cotton itself. This meant, of course, that all the cotton on which the government had lent money would remain off the market and that the government would own it outright unless the price of cotton had gone above 10 cents plus interest before the expiration date of the loan. To Frank, this "monetizing" of cotton, as he called it, was the "most shocking idea" he'd "ever heard of," and he wrote a memorandum to Peek and Wallace saying so. ("If there was any virtue in the gold system, it was that your average congressman couldn't understand it and therefore couldn't monkey with it," said Frank in a later year. "But anybody could understand this. If you started with this, where were you going to stop? Next you'd monetize coal, lumber, and whatnot. . . . You'd just have logrolling over monetizing commodities the way you did over the tariff."[66]) But Roosevelt, whose felt need to funnel money into farmers' pockets at once was at that moment acute, liked the idea. Perhaps on the very afternoon it was first presented to him, he phoned Jesse Jones to tell him about it and order its implementation with Reconstruction Finance Corporation funds.

Thus was created the Commodity Credit Corporation, by executive order on October 16. Incorporated in Delaware on the following day, it began operations at once, operations which had immediate price-sustaining and -raising effect. By mid-November cotton was selling for 9.6 cents a pound, and by the end of the year the cash income of cotton farmers had been increased by more than 50 percent over that received in 1932, or in 1931. Commodity credit extensions also greatly and immediately facilitated "voluntary compliance" by cotton farmers with the acreage reductions specified for the 1934 crop, for to be eligible for a loan, the farmer had to agree to participate in the AAA's cotton production control program. Similarly with regard to corn-hogs. On October 25 Wallace announced that the Commodity Credit Corporation would lend farmers 30 to 35 cents (significantly more than the current on-farm market price) for each bushel of corn sealed and stored in bins on their farms, charging 4 percent interest but accepting the corn itself as full security for the loan, *provided* the farmer signed up for participation in the 1934 corn-hog production control program, a program which called for an overall 20 percent reduction in corn acreage and a 25 percent reduction in litters farrowed and marketed in 1934.

Frank's worst fears about Commodity Credit proved to be unjustified by the event, if perhaps in part because these fears had been so emphatically expressed and thus transformed into potent warnings and because Frank himself remained in his post of legal authority until early 1935. It is true that in 1934, with cotton selling at 10 cents a pound, farmers demanded and obtained a

12-cent loan, a procedure pointing unmistakably toward the piling up by decade's end of huge amounts of government-owned and, till then, unmarketable cotton. Also in 1934 Commodity Credit began to make contracts with private lending agencies, which in turn made loans to farmers, at profit to themselves, of course, in addition to those made directly by government, and if such contracts were not actually illegal, as Frank believed them to be, they were certainly an unwise risk of the general public's interest. But the great bulk of the commodity loans made during the corporation's first two years of operation—*all* the $134 million lent on corn; nearly three-fourths of the $464 million directly lent on cotton by the government—was liquidated on schedule.[67] As for the dire prediction that lumber, coal, et al. would be "monetized," too, with consequent uncontrollable and disastrous congressional logrolling, it did not come true. Moreover, and most important in terms of Roosevelt's most immediate concern as he initially approved Johnston's proposal, Commodity Credit helped defuse what had again become, in the fall of 1933, a dangerously explosive situation among the embittered corn-hog farmers of the Middle West. On November 25, just one month after Wallace's announcement that corn loans would be made, the first loan check was delivered to a farmer in Pocahontas County, Iowa. Next day the second check was delivered, to a farmer in Woodbury County, Iowa.[68] Thereafter such checks were poured as rapidly as possible into the countryside around Sioux City, where the Farmers' Holiday Association was strongest and farmer unrest most violent. The effect was soothing.

8

–>>X<<–

A Hazardous Passage Across Winter into Spring and Summer 1934

I

ON the evening of October 30, 1933, solitary in a cheerless hotel room in the small town of Dickinson, North Dakota, Lorena Hickok addressed to Harry Hopkins, her boss, a report-letter about her "first day's work" in that state: "I must say there was nothing particularly joyous about it."

She told of driving that afternoon with a couple of county commissioners "over a road so full of ruts that you couldn't tell it from ploughed fields up to a shabby little country church, standing bleakly alone in the center of a vast tawny prairie land." She found grouped around the church entrance "a dozen or more men in shabby denim, shivering in the biting wind that swept across the plain." They were farmers whose 1933 crops had been destroyed by hail in late June and early July, and they had come to this church because a relief investigator had established headquarters there that day and they were applying for federal relief. Most of them had been accounted well-to-do, by Dakota farm standards in the early 1920s; they owned on the average 640 acres (a square mile) of land. Yet they were utterly destitute. They'd had a good wheat crop the year before, but wheat in North Dakota had brought in 1932 "about 30 cents a bushel," and it had cost "77 cents to raise it." They and their families were in desperate need of everything, especially clothing:

> "How about clothes?" the investigator asked one of them. He shrugged. "Everything I own I have on my back," he said. He then explained that, having no underwear, he was wearing two pairs of overalls, and two, very ragged, denim jackets. . . . With one or two exceptions none of the men hanging around the church had overcoats. Most . . . were in denim—faded, shabby denim. Cotton denim doesn't keep out the wind very well. It was cold enough today so that I, in a woolen dress and warm coat, was by no means too warm when I stood out in the wind. When we came out to the car, we found it full of farmers, with the windows closed. They apologized and said they had crawled in there to keep warm. . . .[1]

On the following night Hick was in Bottineau, North Dakota, just twelve miles south of the Canadian border. From a shabby hotel room that stank of "stale soapsuds, old wet rags, some sort of disinfectant," she wrote a long, anguished letter to Eleanor Roosevelt. Hers had been, she said, a "dreadful day. Not from the standpoint of the weather. That has been perfect, though cold—deep blue, cloudless sky and sunlight that brings out all the gold and blue and reds and orchid shades in the prairie landscape. These plains are beautiful. But, oh, the terrible crushing drabness of life here. And the suffering, for both people and animals." No less appalling than the physical misery were the psychological effects of Bottineau County's destitution, which was alleged to be the worst in the state. "The people up here—farmers, people on relief, and those administering relief—are in a daze. A sort of nameless dread hangs over the place." But in point of fact, this dread in its most potent form *did* have a name, and that name was winter. "Up here, dear lady, they have winters! It was down to zero today. . . . Last winter the temperature went down to 40 below zero and stayed there ten days, while a 60-mile wind howled across the plains. And entering that kind of winter we have between 4,000 and 5,000 human beings—men and women and children—without clothing or bedding, getting just enough food to keep them from starving. No fuel. Living in houses that a prosperous farmer wouldn't put his cattle in. . . . They now have 850 families on relief, and applications are coming in at the rate of 15 or 20 a day." She told of visiting that afternoon, with a relief investigator, one of the "better" homes among those of people on relief. "Out on the windswept prairie it stood —what had once been a house. No repairs had been made in years. The kitchen floor was all patched up with pieces of tin—a wash boiler cover, ten can lids, some old automobile license plates. . . . Newspapers had been stuffed in the cracks around the windows." In that cold, drafty dwelling lived husband, wife, and two small children, and the wife was expecting her third child in January. "The investigator asked her about her bedding. She hesitated a moment, then led us upstairs. One bed. A filthy ragged mattress. . . . She said the last of her sheets and pillowcases gave out two years ago. . . . 'Do you and your husband and the children all sleep together?' the investigator asked. 'We have to,' she replied simply, 'to keep warm.' This, dear lady, is the stuff that farm strikes and agrarian revolutions are made of. Communists are in here now, working among these people, I was told."[2]

And in South Dakota a few days later Hick found abundant evidence that Communists, whose purpose was not to improve the situation but "to make everybody as miserable as possible to get a revolution," were "very, very busy . . . [g]etting right down among the farmers and working like beavers." They might well be "responsible for the more violent activities of the Farm Holiday crowd"—such violence as had occurred "near Milbank the other day," where a sheriff and his deputies were badly beaten by a "Farm Holiday gang gathered to stop a foreclosure sale."[3]

Hopkins and Eleanor, who were increasingly close friends and allies in that year, made sure that the essence of Hickok's field reports reached Roosevelt's eyes and ears. Sometimes the reports themselves came to his desk. More often he read excerpts from them or heard oral summaries of them from Eleanor. (Indeed, Hick as roving reporter was working not only for the relief administrator but also directly for the White House at that time insofar as she carried out a special assignment which Louis Howe had given her, with Hopkins's permission. "[H]e is interested in finding out what sort of treatment people are getting from government representatives who deal with them directly when they ask for help," explained Hick to Hopkins in a letter written on a train en route from Chicago to Minneapolis on October 24. "This includes representatives of NRA, the Farm Credit Administration, Home Loan Board, and so on. He feels that it is a matter of great importance, and I certainly agree

with him. . . . As I go about, I shall probably hear a good deal on the subject.
I could very easily pass on to Colonel Howe on that matter the same information I would give you on the relief show—a general picture, without citing
specific cases or individuals."[4]

And we may be sure that Roosevelt paid close attention to those portions
of Hick's reports which were specifically concerned with political repercus-
sions—her report, for instance, of an interview she had with Floyd B. Olson,
Minnesota's Farmer-Laborite governor, in Minneapolis on October 28. Olson,
she said, was "bitter" about an appointment Jesse Jones had just made to a
key post in the RFC—the appointment of one C. T. Jaffray, chairman of the
board of the First National Bank of Minneapolis, a man who had been "for
years . . . a sort of overlord among the financial interests that have pretty much
run the Northwest." Farmers loathed him. So did Olson. And Olson emphatically confirmed Hickok's general impression that here in the upper Mississippi
Valley, time was rapidly running out for the New Deal. Farmers, even those
of the Farmers' Holiday Association, generally still believed "in the sincerity
and good faith of the President." But they no longer believed in the administration as it related to them; they were convinced that Roosevelt was "getting a
lot of silly advice from 'theorists.' " They had "a violent hatred of the so-called
'brains trust.' " (This last reflected the loudly proclaimed opinions of George
Peek, loudly echoed by Milo Reno, for Peek, with his simplistic insistence that
the single aim of agricultural policy should be to raise farm prices enough to
provide a decent profit margin, was far more popular among the more militant
farmers than Wallace was. The antipathy to "theorists" also reflected increasingly harsh attacks now being made upon New Deal "professors," notably
Tugwell, by newspapers the proprietors of which deemed it as yet unseemly
and imprudent to attack directly, personally, a President who on frequent
occasion gave signs of being on *their* side of basic issues.) "The feeling seems
to be that the Public Works crowd, NRA, the Department of Agriculture,
A.A.A. and so on—'are trying to do a lot of funny things but aren't getting
anywhere.' " Governor Olson "gives the President thirty days more," wrote
Hickok. "If there isn't a change in that period, the President's prestige will
have crumbled, too. . . ."[5]

Other items of her reports were worth Roosevelt's particular attention. In
her November 3 letter to Hopkins, reporting the ghastly relief problem in
Bottineau County, she laid heavy stress upon the county's "desperate" fuel
need as winter came on. It was estimated by local relief officials that 10,000
tons of coal would be required to supply relief needs that winter. "They have
little wood to burn in this state, you know. It's all coal. It's mined right here
in the state, but in Bottineau—because of freight rates and *a rise in price
attributed to NRA*—it now costs $4 a ton."[6]

A price rise attributed to the NRA!

In Washington, in that late summer and autumn of 1933, there was added

*Emphasis added.

to the already abundant incitements of quarrel between George Peek and Wallace the effort of Wallace, Tugwell, and Frank, the latter two especially, to "reduce the spread." What was the "spread"? It was, explained Tugwell in a syndicated newspaper column, "that vast uncharted region between the six cents a pound the farmer gets for beef cattle and the fifteen to seventy cents a pound the consumer pays for it."[7] The "region" *should* be charted, indeed *must* be by public servants if the NRA and AAA were to operate in the public interest. To both Tugwell and Frank it was a practical necessity, as it was also simple justice, for packers, canners, and other processors, in return for their exemption from antitrust law, to give the government access to their company records. They must "open the books." How otherwise could the public be protected against exorbitant profiteering? How otherwise could the New Deal employ what Tugwell called controlled monopoly (a planned capitalism, mingling private and public economic activity) to achieve recovery and permanent prosperity? But to the processors, of course, the proposal was anathema. They damned it as un-American, "socialistic" if not "communistic"; they fought against it tooth and nail, as they did against Frank's and Frederic Howe's attempts to write into marketing agreements consumer-protecting provisions regarding quality standards, labeling, package fill, and the like. George Peek, sharing the outlook of the processors, fought at their side. He had announced when he first took over as AAA administrator that his agency's operations would involve "as little interference with established institutions and methods . . . as is consistent with the fixed purpose of the law; namely, to raise farm prices."[8] (His *sole* concern was to raise farm prices. It was as if the concept of parity were beyond the grasp of his mind, for he gave no sign of understanding that the most dramatic possible rise in commodity prices could do the farmer no good if other prices rose as fast or faster.) What Tugwell and Frank and, less consistently, Wallace now proposed struck Peek as "interference" of the most radical kind. He reacted vehemently against it.

The quarrel, or a significant segment of it, reached Roosevelt's desk in early October. Frank, to Peek's disgust, insisted upon a creative participation by his Legal Division in every marketing agreement negotiation, and during the negotiation of an agreement for flue-cured tobacco one of Frank's assistants, a young man whose zealous commitment to public good was interpreted by industry representatives (probably accurately) as an antibusiness attitude, wrote into the draft a provision designed to limit the spread between the purchase price of raw tobacco and the selling price of processed tobacco. The provision, of course, required for its enforcement government access to company books. The tobacco industry was furious. George Peek was furious. He went storming to the White House, where he accused Frank, and Frank's young lawyers, of conspiring to use the AAA to transform "radically" the nation's economic structure. He demanded that the whole price-limiting portion of the draft agreement be struck from it. And Roosevelt, having listened sympathetically (so it seemed) to both sides of the quarrel and having assessed the relative weights of the opposing pressures as they translated into political terms, decided in Peek's favor.[9]

He was considerably less disposed to back Peek in this way during the weeks that followed. Events forced a change in his assessment of the relative weights of the opposing pressures. He found himself being shifted toward the Wallace-Tugwell side of the price controversy.

For in the aftermath of the July collapse of the commodity market, as farmers watched with growing, bitter anger the steady, steep rise in cost of practically everything they had to buy—farm implements, clothing, household appliances, fuel, processed foods, automobiles, railway transport—while the price of everything they had to sell remained far below what it had been in early July and, as regards corn, wheat, cattle, hogs, well below the cost of production, their perception of the NRA as a price-raising conspiracy on the part of big businessmen became as a flaming match dropped upon interlocking trails of gunpowder all across the dairy and corn-hog regions of the upper Mississippi Valley, all across the cattle and spring wheat region of the northern Great Plains. As early as September 11 Wallace was warning Roosevelt that NRA price-fixing "by apparently fiat methods" might "soon make it necessary to adopt price fixing for agriculture or else start inflation in the very near future," though he himself was appalled by the degree of governmental regimentation which direct farm price controls would entail and was acutely aware of the danger that inflation might go out of control. He concluded: "The political temper of the dairy and livestock farmers of the middlewest at the present time is far worse than you realize."[10]

It grew worse still in late September and all through October.

Milo Reno moved forcefully to make capital out of flaming discontents, political pressure capital wherewith to buy or compel abandonment of domestic allotment as major national agricultural policy and the adoption in its place of the farm program he, with Simpson, had advocated from the beginning. There was a meeting of the national executive committee of the Farmers' Holiday Association on September 22. From it emerged two demands upon the administration. One was for a halt to all farm mortgage foreclosures pending the farmers' receipt of assistance commensurate with the advantages the NRA conferred upon big business. The other was a new idea, highly plausible and hard to counter in argument—namely, a demand for an agricultural production code of the same kind as that which industrialists fashioned for themselves under the NRA, a code including cost of production price guarantees along with marketing and production control agreements. Three Farmers' Holiday representatives were dispatched at once to Washington to present the demands in person. In a threatful announcement of their coming, Reno wired the President: "National Farm Strike held in abeyance pending acceptance of this code." Three days later he addressed a letter to the President saying, "If you have any reason(s) why the farmer should not be given the same consideration as banks, insurance companies, and, by edict, protected in the possession of their [sic] property . . . I would be interested in hearing them."[11] The tone of these communications was ill suited to their purpose, if that purpose was to persuade or otherwise obtain affirmative action from Franklin

Roosevelt. ("I do not like to have anybody hold a pistol to my head and demand that I do something," said a wrathful President to Morgenthau.) All the same, the three Farmers' Holiday emissaries were given a cordial and sympathetic reception in Washington by Wallace, Peek, Morgenthau in his capacity as farm credit administrator, and Roosevelt himself. Especially Roosevelt. They returned to the Midwest to report that farmers had a legal right to submit a draft code of fair competition under the NIRA, the same right as other producers had, according to Washington officialdom, and that such a draft, if submitted, "would receive favorable consideration." They also reported assurances from "official Washington" that agriculture was "entitled to receive cost of production prices."[12]

Reno was somewhat encouraged. Nevertheless, or consequently, he increased the pressure. In early October he polled his organization's membership to see if it favored "an immediate holding action"—that is, a farm strike. He also persuaded Iowa's Governor Clyde L. Herring to invite to Des Moines, for conference on October 30, thirteen governors of important agricultural states, to act upon an agenda which Reno himself would prepare. In mid-October he made a highly emotional speech to a crowd of 5,000 in Shenandoah, Iowa, following which a group of farmers delighted the throng by paddling the stuffing out of an effigy of Henry Wallace. Then, on October 21, after Governor William Langer of North Dakota had declared an embargo on all wheat sales in his state at less than a cost of production price and had asked other wheat state governors to follow suit, Reno issued his formal strike proclamation.

He called upon the nation's farmers to withhold their produce from market until four specific demands upon government had been met. The principal one of these was for the agricultural code containing cost of production price guarantees. The others were for "adequate" currency "reflation," a national moratorium on farm mortgage foreclosures, and the removal of bankers from control of the national monetary system. "We have been patient and long suffering," he polemicized in a public letter to his organization's local presidents, a letter quoted in every major daily newspaper in the land. "We have been made a political football for jingo politicians, who are controlled by the money-lords of Wall Street. . . . We were promised a new deal. . . . Instead we have the same old stacked deck and, so far as the Agricultural Act is concerned, the same dealers."[13] (The "same dealers" were in Reno's view, the American Farm Bureau Federation, the state farm bureaus, the Extension Service, and the land-grant colleges.) Violence flared in following days, such violence as Lorena Hickok took note of in South Dakota. A farmer picket was shot by a milk truck driver near Madison, Wisconsin. A farmer who persisted in shipping milk in defiance of the strike was beaten near to death outside Marshfield, Wisconsin. Truckers attempting to bring farm produce into Council Bluffs and Sioux City, encountering roadblocks, were forcibly turned back. The great stockyards of Omaha reported a 50 percent decline in truck deliveries to them of cattle and hogs.

Four of the thirteen governors whom Herring had invited came to Des

Moines for the October 30 conference. They were Olson of Minnesota, Albert G. Schmedeman of Wisconsin, Langer of North Dakota, and Thomas Berry of South Dakota. They came with their minds made up. Farmers, many of them Holiday members, packed the auditorium in which public sessions were held. They listened in stony silence, interspersed with boos, as Charles Hearst, president of the Iowa Farm Bureau, argued against the resolutions Reno had prepared—the only speaker to do so. They loudly cheered when the five governors adopted the resolutions, by unanimous vote.[14] Yet the program proposal thus made was a radical departure from the American political tradition, calling for an extreme of governmental control, a degree of regimentation in the service of private profit, that accorded better with Fascist dictatorship than with the economic planning of a free, cooperative society. In addition to government price-fixing, there would be compulsory production and marketing controls, enforced through a licensing of all farmers, all processors. . . .

The five governors promptly departed in a body for the nation's capital, there to urge the program's acceptance by the administration.

II

BUT even before Reno issued his strike call, Washington was responding to the challenge.

Roosevelt personally was responding.

All through late August and September he had presided over renewed heated debate within the administration concerning monetary policy. On one side was Warburg, his basic economic views unchanged (indeed, he considered their validity confirmed) by what had happened at the London Conference and after. He spoke for the bankers who continued to press for a stable, gold-backed dollar and for a return to an international gold standard at the earliest possible moment; only thus could confidence in the currency be restored to the investing public, and only through such restoration could recovery be achieved. On the other side was Cornell University's George Warren with his theory that the price of gold determines commodity prices, the latter rising or falling in direct proportion to the dollar value of gold. What Warren aimed for was a dollar the value of which was constant in terms of commodities; it would have to be considerably cheaper in terms of gold than it was at the moment. Warren's plea that the theory be tried in practice became urgent in the aftermath of the July market crash. In between these two views but inclining strongly toward Warren's insofar as this meant currency inflation was Jesse Jones, representing the entrepreneur capitalists of the South and West, men (Garner was among them) whose demand was for easy money, easy credit, and whose consequent hostility to traditional Wall Street control of the money market came close to matching in intensity that of the old-time Populists.

To Roosevelt the pragmatist, as September wore on, the central issue of the debate became more and more that of an action possibly hurtful, probably helpful versus an inaction that would be certainly overwhelmingly disastrous in the face of mounting crisis in the farm belt.

On September 20 both Warburg and Warren addressed letters to him. Warren again advised him to order the Treasury "to buy a certain amount of gold at a certain price" and then continue to buy, raising the price "at frequent intervals." In this way he could raise commodity prices in measured steps, effecting a precisely controlled inflation, and such "rise in prices is essential" to the ultimate achievement of a permanently stable "commodity dollar." Warburg urged him to cease all action upon the currency; he should issue a statement of flat opposition to further depreciation of the dollar and then stand aside while the price situation was automatically corrected by free market operations. That this corrective process would be slow and painful, Warburg conceded, but it was the only way to sound, permanent recovery.[15]

A few days later Warburg's advice was reiterated in the formal report of a monetary advisory committee which Roosevelt had appointed sometime before, at Warburg's urging, and of which Warburg was a member, along with Lew Douglas, George Harrison, O.M.W. Sprague, and Dean Acheson, among others. (Nominal chairman of the committee was Secretary of the Treasury Woodin, but he was now virtually incapacitated by the throat cancer which had been diagnosed during the summer and for which surgery was impossible. He had offered his resignation following the breakdown of his health during the London Conference, but Roosevelt had asked him to stay on.) The President was by this time acutely aware of the growing number of farmers who showed no disposition to suffer quietly while the market made its slow "automatic" adjustments—who showed every disposition to march, instead, to the barricades of revolution. Moreover, he was increasingly convinced that it was *not* a lack of confidence in the currency on the part of any large investing public which was hampering recovery but, rather, a "deliberate conspiracy" on the part of bankers to block the administration's program and force a return to gold. They were conducting what amounted to a strike by capital, he was soon to say to his cabinet, citing numerous reports that had come to him of bankers' refusing to lend money to businesses even on excellent security. And the Chicago banks were said to be the worst in this regard, were said to be "tighter on credit than any other banks in the country,"[16] an alleged fact that was highly relevant to the growing unrest of midwestern farmers. Roosevelt, therefore, reacted to the monetary committee's recommendation as irritably as he had to Harrison-Sprague-Warburg's communication from London three months before.* "I do not like or approve the report," he wrote Woodin on September 30. Obviously the bankers had no notion of the "seriousness of the situation." Commodity prices, "especially agricultural prices," simply *must* go up, and what he wanted from the committee was a "recommendation of how to obtain that objective and that objective only."[17]

---

*See pp. 155–57. Did Roosevelt regret in the fall of 1933 that the banks had not been nationalized in the spring? He may have, in fleeting moments at least, then and later.

But he, of course, knew that this committee could, or would, make no such recommendation.

Hence his decision in the first days of October to act upon Warren's advice.

He was blocked for a couple of weeks by Dean Acheson, Treasury's acting secretary in Woodin's absence. Acheson's principled opposition to the whole idea was joined to a conviction that Treasury had no legal authority to buy gold at a price higher than the current statutory limit, a view with which Woodin agreed in phone conversation. In other words, Roosevelt proposed to violate the law. But Morgenthau's lawyers in the Farm Credit Administration had a different view. They found legal precedent established during the Civil War emergency for, roughly, what Roosevelt wanted to do. Stanley Reed, the RFC general counsel, gave it as his opinion that this precedent combined with the powers conferred upon the executive by the RFC act to give the President a sufficient legal authority. And the upshot was a scheme whereby the RFC would make the actual gold purchases and then use the bought gold as collateral for loans from the Treasury.

Roosevelt presented this scheme to a White House meeting of top officials on October 19, a meeting approximately as stormy as the one at which he'd announced his acceptance of the Thomas amendment last May. Acheson vehemently argued that the RFC had no more legal authority to make these gold purchases than the Treasury had, which is to say it had none. RFC lawyers argued, less vehemently, to the contrary. Most in the room indicated their agreement with the President and the RFC lawyers.

"I say it is legal," said Roosevelt at last, closing the discussion.[18]

Three days later, on the morning of Sunday, October 22, Ray Moley was in the White House for the first time since his resignation from the State Department in early September. He had been summoned from New York by phone, to serve not as presidential adviser but solely as speech-writing technician. He participated in a conference that morning of ten or so men, including Acheson and Warren and Morgenthau, gathered in the Oval Room to help decide the language in which Warren's gold thesis would be presented to the public in a fireside chat, the fourth of these, on the evening of that very day. When the conference ended shortly before noon, Moley began carpentering into succinct, coherent form the notes on this matter that had accumulated on the President's desk, while "Warren fluttered over the creation much as he might have watched a hatching experiment in the poultry laboratory at Cornell." (Moley himself believed that an egg was being laid, though one for which he personally "had no responsibility. . . . My conscience was clear. I had repeatedly argued against the scheme to F.D.R.")[19]

A few hours later, seated before a small forest of microphones in the Diplomatic Reception Room on the ground floor of the White House, Roosevelt delivered his speech in tones of warm, friendly intimacy, making it a personal communication to every listener, individually, in a radio audience numbering tens of millions.

Leftist-sounding rhetoric was, as usual, scattered in phrases throughout the speech draft. There was a reference to the "edifice of recovery" as a "temple which, when completed, will no longer be a temple of money changers or of beggars, but rather a temple dedicated to and maintained for a greater social justice." There was a reference, if a vague one, to "chiselers," both "big" and "petty," who took advantage of NRA codes. There was even a reference to the kind of information Fred Howe was developing with regard to price gouging in the cotton textile industry, though Roosevelt carefully refrained from any mention of the industry itself in this connection. He spoke, instead, "of the salesman in a store in a large Eastern city who tried to justify the increase in the price of a cotton shirt from one dollar and a half to two dollars and a half by saying that it was due to the cotton processing tax. Actually in that shirt there was about one pound of cotton and the processing tax amounted to four and a quarter cents on that pound of cotton."*

But his main emphasis was upon the government's "definite policy . . . to restore commodity price levels," a restoration which had to be made *before* there was any "permanent revaluation [i.e., stabilization] of the dollar. . . ." Once "we have restored the price level, we shall seek to establish and maintain a dollar which will not change its purchasing and debt-paying power during the succeeding generations. I said that in my message to the American delegation in London last July. And I say it now once more." Since the dollar had long been far too much at the mercy of "accidents of international trade, . . . the internal policies of other nations and . . . political disturbances in other continents," it must now be brought "firmly" under the control of the government of the United States, which would of itself alone determine the "gold value," the aim being "the continued recovery of our commodity prices." To this end he was "authorizing the Reconstruction Finance Corporation to buy gold newly mined in the United States at prices to be determined from time to time after consultation with the Secretary of the Treasury and the President. Whenever necessary to the end in view, we shall also buy and sell gold in the world market. My aim in taking this step is to establish and maintain continuous control. This is a policy and not an expedient."[20]

Some sixty-odd hours later, on the morning of October 25, which was the day of Henry Wallace's announcement that Commodity Credit loans would be made on corn, Jesse Jones and Henry Morgenthau came to the President's bedroom for the first of what became, during the weeks ahead, daily meetings to decide the price of gold for that day. It was significant that Morgenthau, but not the acting secretary of the treasury, was invited to these sessions. On this first morning, having talked matters over with his two guests while, propped up in bed, he ate his breakfast from a tray, Roosevelt ordered the RFC to buy gold at the agreed price of $31.36 an ounce when the market opened —a whopping increase of $1.56 over the price for the preceding day.

---

*Some of Roosevelt's listeners may have been astonished to learn that the processing tax levied per pound of cotton amounted to half the open market price of that pound in the late summer of 1933.

No single price change thereafter was anywhere near as great. It varied from 10 to 22 cents between daily fixes until November 14 (the price was then $33.56; the gold value of the dollar had by then declined from 65.91 cents on October 25 to 61.59 cents), following which there was no price change at all for several days. A yet longer period of no change occurred in December. For the price setters, the only important considerations were that no single change be so drastic as to disrupt markets, that the change be always an increase in price, and that the changes follow no pattern the discernment of which by speculators might enable them to reap windfall profits. Accordingly Roosevelt made a kind of numbers game out of these sessions. One morning (it was Friday, November 3), when Morgenthau came to the bedside tense with worry over some pressing problem and suggested that the price change that day be considerably greater than the 10 to 15 cents of immediately preceding days, Roosevelt promptly announced that the increase would be 21 cents. Why *that* figure? Because "three times seven" is a lucky number, said Roosevelt, his face straight but his blue eyes twinkling at Morgenthau's recoil from such frivolous dealing with a serious matter.[21]

Morgenthau's momentary dismay was as nothing compared with the prolonged outrage felt by most of the financial community and most academic economists as they contemplated what appeared to them a reckless defiance of natural economic law, a shattering assault upon the very foundation of the existing order. The press was full of expressions of this outrage on the morrow of the gold purchase announcement, initiating such lengthy, fervent, and highly educative national public debate of monetary policy as there had not been since Bryan's Cross of Gold campaign in 1896.

Loud voices were raised in support of the program, including those of big businessmen associated with the Committee for the Nation.* Several farm leaders spoke up again in vehement espousal of inflationary policy, and so did Father Charles E. Coughlin, both in his radio broadcasts and at a mass meeting in New York City's Hippodrome on November 27. But louder still, being greatly amplified by a business-controlled press, were the doomful voices of bitter opposition. On November 12 a group of Chicago businessmen formed an association for the express purpose of publicly demanding an end to "monetary experimentation" and a "prompt return to the gold standard." The same demand was made in even more urgent tones by the national Chamber of Commerce on November 18. Three days later the Federal Reserve Advisory Council appealed for a return to gold, saying that uncertainty over the value of the currency was militating against business recovery. Three days after that, Al Smith blasted Roosevelt's "baloney dollars" and his turning of "130,000,000 Americans into guinea pigs for experimentation." Cried Smith, "I am for experience against experiment." (Roosevelt himself, in a speech at Savannah, Georgia, on November 18, he having come South to begin his annual Thanksgiving stay at Warm Springs, confessed that his administration was indeed

*See p. 108.

"guilty of great experimentation," as charged by certain "modern Tories," but reminded his listeners that the founding of "thirteen new colonies in the American wilderness" had also been an "experiment," that "during the period of 1776 . . . the Washingtons, the Adams, the Bullocks . . . conducted another experiment," and that then, as now, "there were doubting Thomases . . . who feared change, . . . who wanted to let things alone.")[22]

There were two greatly publicized defections from the administration by the last of November. Professor Sprague resigned as official adviser to the Treasury on November 21 because of his "fundamental disagreement" with Roosevelt's monetary policies, policies which threatened a collapse "of the credit of the government" and a "drift into unrestrained inflation." Two or three days later Warburg severed all his connections with the administration and issued a public statement similar to Sprague's. It surprised many that Lew Douglas did *not* resign his post of budget director, though he made no secret of his desperate unhappiness; evidently he remained stubbornly determined to fight within the administration for whatever bits and pieces of "civilization" might yet be salvaged.[23]

Dean Acheson may have shared this stubborn determination. Nevertheless, he departed the administration in mid-November.

Some of the earliest criticisms of the President's action, during this monetary debate, were attributed by the press to an anonymous "high official" in the administration who was said to be convinced that the gold buying was unconstitutional. Assuming Acheson to be this official (it was probably Douglas), Roosevelt summoned the acting treasury secretary and all others involved in the program to a White House meeting on October 29. No charm was exercised on this occasion. Grim-faced, coldly angry, Roosevelt told the men before him that the gold program was a settled policy, no longer debatable; he invited anyone present who disliked the "boat" they were "all in" to "get out of it." And as he said these things, he looked directly at one after another of those in the room, his gaze resting longest and hardest upon Dean Acheson. Acheson could not but have felt its weight, and it seemed to Morgenthau that the acting treasury secretary looked "very miserable and very sick through the whole thing."[24] Others saw no sign of guilt feeling or other perturbation in Acheson.

But a few days later he and Jesse Jones had angry words over an RFC procedural matter that was connected with gold buying, whereupon Acheson submitted to the President a handwritten and undated letter of resignation, to be accepted if and when the President pleased to do so. Subsequently, there appeared more press stories in which criticisms of the gold program were attributed to a "high official." On November 13 Roosevelt definitely decided that Acheson must go, and go without the usual letter of thanks and appreciation from the President.

He talked privately that morning with Morgenthau, immediately following the bedside meeting on gold (the decision was made to up the price that day from $33.32 to $33.45 per ounce), telling Morgenthau of Acheson's impending departure and of "a very interesting and confidential conversation" he had just had with Woodin. The desperately ill secretary had again asked to be officially relieved of his duties. Instead, Roosevelt was going to ask him to take an indefinite leave of absence without pay. This left the problem of finding "some person" to become acting secretary who was capable of filling the post of full secretary in, almost certainly, a near future.

"I have decided that that person is Henry Morgenthau, Jr.," said Roosevelt. "You made good for me in Albany, and you are one of the two or three people who have made an outstanding success in Washington, so let's you and I go on to bigger things. . . . We will have lots of fun doing it together."[25]

Acheson's resignation was announced on November 15.

III

At the conclusion of his angry lecturing of Acheson and the others in the White House on October 28, Roosevelt said, very seriously: "Gentlemen, if we continued another week or so longer without my having made this move on gold, we would have had an agrarian revolution in this country."[26]

And certainly the gold program, joined with other recent administration moves toward the elevation of agricultural prices, took much stormy wind out of the sails which swept the five disgruntled farm state governors into Washington from Des Moines on November 2.

The governors had an interview with the President in the White House that day, departing from it with the distinct impression, if he did not actually say, that he was wholly sympathetic with the proposals they made. Olson left the meeting convinced that the President was personally in favor of agricultural price-fixing; he indicated as much to a reporter.[27]

They had an interview with George Peek, who also indicated sympathy with Farmers' Holiday objectives, though without specifically endorsing cost of production price guarantees, and who declared that the gold purchase program proved the President to be the farmer's friend. ("[A]ll these people are trying to do is save their homes," Peek had said to reporters on the day before Reno issued his farm strike call. "I, too, would fight to save my home. We have been warning the east for twelve years that things like this would happen unless the incomes of farmers were increased." Reno himself evidently feared the negative impact which the gold program would have upon the farmer movement he led, for on the day after the program had been announced, he declared in public statement that he saw "no ray of hope" in it, that it was perfectly in line with the policies of "the money-changers who have well-nigh wrecked this republic."[28])

They had an interview with Morgenthau, who stressed the steps already taken, and the additional steps now being taken, to ease the farm credit situation and delay or prevent farm mortgage foreclosures. He also pointed to the fact that for the last two weeks, as governor of the Farm Credit Administration, in which were vested the purchasing powers of Hoover's Federal Farm

Board, he had been buying more than $1 million worth of wheat every day on the open market. ("We've got to do something about the price of wheat!" Roosevelt had said to Morgenthau on October 16. "Can't you buy 25,000,000 bushels for Harry Hopkins and see if you can't put the price up?" Next day Morgenthau had initiated the wheat buying, spending some $1,250,000 and putting the price up three cents a bushel. On the evening of that same day Ickes, Wallace, and Morgenthau, meeting as directors of the Surplus Relief Corporation, agreed to buy $10,000,000 of wheat, $10,000,000 of surplus butter, and "to make a bid for the surplus apple crop of the Northwest," as Ickes noted in his diary.[29])

They had an interview with Harry Hopkins, who had just returned from a swing through the Midwest, was more knowledgeable about the economic distress of that region as it translated into human terms than the governors were, and may well have at least hinted to his visitors that a bold new approach to unemployment relief would soon be announced, one that would do much to prevent the horrible human suffering that had characterized the winter of 1932–1933, and do it in a way that would help the market for farm produce. (Hopkins had just obtained presidential approval of this new approach during a luncheon he'd had alone with Roosevelt in the Oval Room on the day of his return to Washington.[30] The coming of the five governors was undoubtedly a factor in Roosevelt's decision in favor of Hopkins's proposal.)

But the truly decisive interviews which the governors had were with Henry Wallace. He told them that contrary to what the three Farmers' Holiday emissaries had been led to believe (probably by Peek), such a code of fair competition as they proposed for agriculture was *not* legal; it was forbidden by an amendment Huey Long had tacked onto the Industrial Recovery Act to protect individual farmers and laboring men against assaults on their free marketing rights. He corrected their obvious misconceptions and -perceptions of AAA policy and operation. He proved to them with statistical evidence that the cost of production price they called for was, thanks to the current rise in industrial prices, considerably lower than the parity price which agricultural adjustment aimed to achieve, information which at once caused the governors to revise their proposal, substituting parity for cost of production as the price to be fixed. Wallace's most jarring argument, however, was that compulsory marketing controls would require the creation of what amounted to a police state: "[I]t would be necessary to go to Congress to get a very large appropriation so as to have a police force of half a million men to keep down the racketeering." For all these reasons, Wallace turned down the governors' proposals, flatly.[31]

And so did the President, reversing himself under pressure from Wallace, in Olson's belief, when the governors had their second and final session with him. "It is . . . my earnest conviction that we should not try to impose compulsion on the farmers and that compulsion should not be adopted until farmers know all that is involved and willingly accept it," said Roosevelt.[32]

Thus the mission of the five governors became a failed mission, necessarily publicly humiliating to them in some degree. Yet they had been so adroitly handled that only one of the five departed Washington in a mood personally bitterly hostile to Roosevelt or to the administration's farm program. Herring confessed himself completely won over. Olson expressed admiration and respect for the President, though he continued to doubt that the farm problem could be solved by "voluntary means" in a way that would preserve the small family farm. Berry, soon after his return to South Dakota, described to Lorena Hickok the talk he'd given to a Farmers' Holiday crowd in Watertown just the day before: "I told 'em not to get the idea this bird Roosevelt wasn't for 'em or that he hadn't given us a fair hearing. Why, good Lord, we had one conference with him that lasted three hours and another that lasted an hour. And he told us any time we had an idea he wanted to know about it—to bring it down there and it would get a hearing. The whole crowd of 'em had that same attitude. They couldn't take ours—not this one—but that don't mean they didn't listen to us or won't listen to us again."[33] Only Langer remained wholly unpersuaded. He publicly asserted that the turndown "means the farmer is the forgotten man in this Administration." He made contemptuous reference to the "professors" who had allegedly "surrounded" the governors "when Secretary Wallace called [in] his assistants. . . ." And he was said to have "snarled" to associates, "We just voted one son of a bitch out of office and we can do it again!"[34] But Langer himself was regarded with contempt by a good many who shared his general political views, including Tom Berry. "[H]e's scared to death," said Berry to Hickok in the afore-quoted conversation. "The Communists got a big vote in North Dakota last fall. And they've got a recall law up there. . . . He knows he ain't going over so very big, and he's scared."[35]

The farm strike spluttered out in sporadic acts of violence, which also marked the death throes of the Farmers' Holiday movement, during the week following the five governors' return to their home states. On November 5 an interstate cattle train was brought to a crashing halt by a barricade across the tracks near Lawton, Iowa, and 100 men, "unidentified" but "said to be mostly communists from Sioux City," as the press reported, broke the seals of eight cattle cars, releasing the animals. They then burned a railway bridge six miles north of Sioux City. During the darkness of night, on November 6 and 7, several railway bridges were burned in western Iowa and eastern Nebraska— a senseless vandalism, obviously counterproductive, which Reno was compelled publicly to deplore, saying "the people have been admonished to carry on by peaceful picketing."[36] But it was by then obvious even to Reno, who was much embittered by the fact, that the size and depth of commitment of his following had been greatly overestimated. His own "people" simply quietly withdrew from the farm strike. They declined to "carry on." No farmer pickets, peaceful or otherwise, appeared on the wintry, windswept roads over which farm produce was trucked to market during the first days of November. None subsequently appeared. And all furtive violence had ceased, too, by November's second week.

When Henry Wallace delivered an anxiously prepared address in Des Moines on Armistice Day, he was surprised and delighted to find himself facing a friendly audience. He never knew that the meeting's organizers had guaranteed friendliness in the front rows by reserving these for Farm Bureau members, preventing their occupancy by hostile Holiday adherents, but there was no heckling from elsewhere in the auditorium either as Wallace likened Reno's movement to the ache in a diseased tooth, a symptom useful for diagnostic purposes but, of itself alone, wholly pernicious. "[L]et a few more heads be cracked, and a few more milk trucks upset," said he, "and I fear the reaction among consumers will be anything but helpful to farmers generally." Loud applause greeted his remark that he himself had always "insisted that the best way to stop this kind of ruckus was to get more money into farmers' hands," and he was yet more loudly applauded when he went on to speak of the corn loan money and AAA benefit checks that were soon to come flowing into the corn belt and of the higher farm prices, the increased farm income, bound to ensue from the administration's "reflation" of the currency and from the acreage controls that would be fully in effect for the next crop year— provided the farmers, having accurately informed themselves of AAA programs (he admitted that the corn-hog program was of necessity "complicated"), fully cooperated in them.[37]

A few days later Governor Langer lifted North Dakota's wheat embargo, which had been almost totally ineffective in any case. Five days after that a handful of Holiday officers, in attendance at a National Farmers' Union convention in Omaha, formally called off a farm strike that had in fact petered out weeks before.

So came to an end 1933's threat of "agrarian revolution."

And almost simultaneous with this climax and this dissolution of trouble in the cornbelt were a climax and a dissolution of trouble at the top of the administrative machinery of the AAA.

When Wallace returned to Washington, he found on his desk a memorandum from Peek, dated November 15, requesting the immediate dismissal of Jerome Frank, who, said Peek, had in the last few weeks become utterly "impossible." To this memo Wallace made no reply; nor did he to another from Peek, dated November 25, making the same request. Meanwhile, Peek continued in blind stubbornness to press not only the marketing agreement device, though his chief enterprise of this sort, his network of milk agreements in the Chicago area, was obviously falling apart, but also the two-price method of dealing with farm surpluses à la McNary-Haugen. He formally requested approval by the secretary of a $500,000 advance from processing tax revenues, to finance the export of surplus butter—that is, to make up the difference between the current domestic butter price, which would be paid dairy processors, and the lower price at which the butter would be disposed of (dumped) on the European market. "Henry went out of town on that one," Tugwell later said dryly. The secretary entrained for a visit with the President in Warm

Springs, leaving Tugwell in charge of the Agriculture Department. And Tug-well as acting secretary, convinced that a final showdown with Peek was long overdue and having discussed the matter by long-distance phone with Wallace, turned down the Peek request, flatly, giving his reasons in a lengthy memoran-dum addressed jointly to Wallace and the AAA administrator. His stated reasons were cogent, certainly. "This practice [of dumping]," he wrote, "has been condemned by every international conference; it was the subject of special treatment in our recent tariff truce agreement [for the duration of the London Conference]; it is recognized as provocative of retaliation. . . ."[38]

Peek responded according to form. The dispute went to the White House a day or so after Roosevelt's return from Warm Springs. Roosevelt, too, responded according to form. He listened with seeming warm sympathy to Peek's side of the story—so sympathetically that Peek, leaving the Executive Office, was convinced he had presidential support. Then Roosevelt summoned Tugwell in order to express presidential displeasure, mild but real, over the trouble Tugwell had caused by an action possibly in excess of his official authority and certainly overly precipitous.

Tugwell, however, did *not* respond according to form.

Normally a mild-mannered man, so unemphatic of statement and devoid of self-importance as to limit his effectiveness, often, in decisive conferences (so noted Paul Appleby, for one[39]), he was on this day fighting mad, according to his own account. He told the President that he and Wallace were being constantly forced to defend the President's own policy and program against sabotage by Peek and were being constantly let down by the President at crucial moments. For had not the President himself definitely decided that domestic allotment, *not* marketing agreements with processors, would be the centerpiece of AAA operations? It was a decision Peek had never in practice accepted. He had continued to impose such obstacles as he could to acreage reduction programs, and it was now abundantly clear that the marketing agreements which he had so assiduously promoted, though they raised con-sumer prices and increased processor profits, did nothing to increase the income of the average farmer.

The situation had become intolerable, Tugwell concluded. A truly final decision could be no longer postponed.

Roosevelt was doubtless taken aback by Tugwell's unwonted vehemence. But it is a measure of the quality of his leadership, specifically of his ability to stand outside himself and view his own performance objectively, that he was not angered by it or offended. Instead, he tacitly disarmingly admitted the justice of Tugwell's strictures by beginning, almost at once, to canvass aloud possible solutions to the problem before him. "Must I fire Peek?" he asked himself aloud. Or could another post be found for the old war-horse? From an outright firing, which would have satisfied both Tugwell and Wallace, Roosevelt shied away, not only because of the personal pain he would thus inflict and suffer but also because, in his estimation, the political costs could be substantial. Peek had a considerable following in the Midwest, among influential farmers, businessmen, politicians, and his relationship with Baruch, who was reputed to "own" so many senators and congressmen, added to his political clout. This meant that, outside the administration, having been forced out in a humiliating way, he could become an active foe, and a formidable foe, of the farm program. Tugwell broke into Roosevelt's musings at this point to suggest that since Peek was so eager to dispose of farm surpluses abroad, perhaps he should be assigned some official responsibility in the field of foreign economic policy. Tugwell must have made the suggestion with ironical intent; in view of Peek's fervent economic nationalism and the secretary of state's profound commitment to free trade, it was outrageous. Roosevelt greeted it with a shout of laughter.

"Lordy, Lordy!" he cried. "How Cordell Hull would love that."[40]

Nevertheless, he acted on the suggestion a few days later.

The secretary of state was out of the country at that time; as head of the U.S. delegation to the Inter-American Conference at Montevideo, Paraguay, he was endeavoring with some success to implement the New Deal's Good Neighbor policy. So it was with Undersecretary of State William Phillips, a longtime personal friend of his,* that Roosevelt arranged what he called, in strictest confidence, a "window-dressing" assignment "to save the face of Peek."[41]

And a very red face it was that Peek carried into the Oval Room on the night of December 6, there to confer at length with Wallace, Hugh Johnson, and the President.

Only a few hours before, he had endured a press conference during which, seated at Wallace's side in the office of the secretary of agriculture, he had heard his Chicago milk agreements "calmly" described in detail by Wallace as "a failure," his "work . . . a total loss," to quote one of the reporters present. "Yet it was done too impersonally and too adroitly for Peek to take offense," according to this same reporter.[42] Actually, of course, Peek was furious, and in the conference that night he, with the support of Johnson, fully vented his fury. Much of it focused on Jerome Frank and the way Frank and his lawyers dealt with the codes (marketing agreements), which the AAA administered in accordance with the President's executive order of last June 26. Peek spoke the mind and will of processors who bitterly resented Frank's ruthless examination of every draft code, Frank's insistence that the marketing agreements conform with consumer and general public-interest standards, Frank's efforts to "open the books" as the price of exemption from antitrust law. Largely because of Frank and Fred Howe, the processors had been pressing hard for a return of their codes to the NRA which, under Johnson-Richberg, had no such concern with the price spread as Tugwell-Frank-Howe manifested, and Peek himself along with Johnson now urged the same thing. If Wallace made

---

*While Roosevelt served as assistant secretary of the navy under Woodrow Wilson, Phillips served as assistant secretary of state, and during those years the two young men, with their families, did much socializing together.

any effort to counter this onslaught, his effort broke futilely against Roosevelt's determination to conciliate and appease.

In the last hour of that day Steve Early gave the news to White House correspondents: "Following a conference tonight with Secretary Wallace, George Peek and General Johnson, the President authorized the statement that, for the purpose of coordination, all codes under the N.I.R.A. including those under negotiation by the A.A.A. will be turned over to the Administrator of the N.R.A."[43]

Peek formally resigned his post as AAA administrator on December 11, his departure eased for him by the fact that his longtime friend and associate Chester Davis was chosen by Wallace to succeed him. An able administrator who conceived his new role to be exclusively that of administrator—which is to say he was no innovator, certainly no reformer—Davis was a man with whom Wallace could work easily and with whom Tugwell, if somewhat less easily, could get along. On December 15 came the announcement that Peek had accepted the chairmanship of a temporary committee to plan a permanent organization "to coordinate all government relations to American foreign trade." It was generally assumed that Peek was being eased out of the administration, gradually, as painlessly as possible. But when Export-Import Banks were established by executive order in early February 1934, Peek was made president of them. And on March 23, 1934, he was named the President's special adviser on foreign trade, a role in which he was to cooperate closely with the State Department.

Utterly dumbfounded by this last was Cordell Hull, who at that time was deeply involved in the struggle for passage of the reciprocal trade legislation which Roosevelt had postponed while Hull was on the high seas, bound for the London Conference, in June 1933. A quarter century later Hull remembered that "if Mr. Roosevelt had hit me between the eyes with a sledgehammer he could not have stunned me more than by this appointment."[44]

IV

By the time of Peek's departure from Agriculture—following which, it may be said, the New Deal's farm program had smooth passage into the spring of 1934, with no recurrence of politically dangerous farmer unrest—Roosevelt realized that his gold purchase program was not having the effect Warren had predicted it would have. The lowering of the gold value of the dollar was *not* reflected in rising commodity prices; as a matter of fact, these prices declined slightly in November, with farm prices going down the most, and this process of slight decline continued through December. Reasons for this ineffectiveness were given in a "private and confidential" letter from "an influential group of Oxford economists," forwarded to Roosevelt on November 23 by Oxford's visiting Professor Felix Frankfurter. The economists agreed that the "scheme for stabilizing the commodity value of the dollar by varying its gold content" might well have worked when it was first propounded by Irving Fisher "many years ago." But it could not work in current circumstances. "Two conditions are necessary for its effectiveness. (i) Action must be taken as soon as any tendency to deflation (or inflation) appears, so that the forces of slump or boom may be counteracted before they have gathered strength. (ii) The rest of the world, or most of it, must be on the gold standard."[45]

A month later Roosevelt received from Frankfurter an advance copy of an article by John Maynard Keynes, scheduled for publication in the New York *Times* for Sunday, December 31. Composed in the form of "An Open Letter to President Roosevelt," the article contained expressions of great admiration for Roosevelt personally and warm sympathy with the President's general mode of operation.

> You have made yourself the Trustee for those in every country who seek to mend the evils of our condition by reasoned experiment within the framework of the existing social system. . . . You remain for me the ruler whose general outlook and attitude to the tasks of government are the most sympathetic in the world. You are the only one who sees the necessity for a profound change of methods and is attempting it without intolerance, tyranny or destruction. You are feeling your way by trial and error, and are felt to be, as you should be, entirely uncommitted in your own person to the details of a particular technique. In my country, as your own, your position remains singularly untouched by criticism of this or the other detail.

All the same, Keynes was sharply critical of Roosevelt's gold program, the theoretic roots of which he traced back to "a crude economic doctrine known as the Quantity Theory of Money." From this theory "some people" inferred that "income can be raised by increasing the amount of money," which was rather "like trying to get fat by buying a larger belt," and it was "an even more foolish application of the same ideas to believe that there is a mathematical relation between the price of gold and the prices of other things." Actually governmental gold buying to raise prices was worse than futile, and Roosevelt's way of doing it as a "game of blind man's buff with exchange speculators . . . is extremely undignified. It upsets confidence, hinders business decisions, occupies the public attention in a measure far exceeding its real importance, and is responsible both for the irritation and for a certain lack of respect which exists abroad." This "experiment," therefore, should be abandoned at once. Then "you can announce that you will definitely control the dollar exchange by buying and selling gold and foreign currencies so as to avoid wide or meaningless fluctuations, with the right to shift the priorities at any time but with the declared intention only so to do either to correct a serious want of balance in America's international receipts and payments or to meet a shift in your domestic price level relatively to price levels abroad."

This last is substantially what Roosevelt soon decided to do.

When the Seventy-third Congress opened its first regular session, the White House had in preparation legislation "to organize a sound and adequate currency system." The bill was sent up the Hill with a special presidential message on January 15. It proposed to place the upper limit of the President's power to devalue at 60 percent of the dollar's former weight in gold; to transfer to

the Treasury the title to all gold now owned by Federal Reserve Banks; to
establish, out of the "profit" (the extra dollars) generated by devaluation, a $2
billion fund "for the purpose of stabilizing the exchange value of the dollar";
and to strengthen and clarify the power already granted the secretary of the
treasury "to buy and sell gold." The bill passed swiftly through both houses
and was signed into law as the Gold Reserve Act of 1934 on January 30, the
President's fifty-second birthday. Next day a presidential proclamation fixed
the weight of the gold dollar at 15⁵⁄₂₁ grains, which was 59.06 percent of its
former weight. The price of gold was set at $35 an ounce.[46]

But both Keynes and the Oxford economists deemed their monetary advice
of slight importance compared with their positive proposals for recovery. A
"great campaign of Public Works" along with "a great drive" for "unemployment relief and other social services" was urged by the Oxonians, to be
financed "with borrowed money." They wrote: "It is essential that these
schemes should not be financed by taxation. If they are, the income that is put
into one pocket is taken out of another, and there is no net increase in purchasing power* nor [sic] tendency for prices to rise." Keynes said the same thing:

[A]s the prime mover in the first stage of the technique of recovery I lay overwhelming emphasis on the increase of national purchasing power resulting from governmental expenditure which is financed by Loans and not by taxing present incomes.
Nothing else counts in comparison with this. In a boom, inflation can be caused by
allowing unlimited credit to support the excited enthusiasm of business speculators.
But in a slump, governmental Loan expenditure is the only sure means of securing
quickly a rising output at rising prices. . . . In the past orthodox finance has regarded
a war as the only legitimate excuse for creating employment by governmental
expenditure. You, Mr. President, having cast off such fetters, are free to engage in
the interests of peace and prosperity the technique which hitherto has only been
allowed to serve the purposes of war and destruction. The set-back which American
recovery experienced this autumn was the predictable consequence of the failure of
your administration to organize any material increase in new Loan expenditures
during your first six months in office. The position six months hence will entirely
depend on whether you have been laying the foundations for larger expenditures in
the near future.

Keynes was "not surprised that so little has been spent up-to-date." He realized there were "many factors . . . which render especially difficult in the
United States the rapid improvisation of a vast program of public works. I do
not blame Mr. Ickes for being cautious and careful. But the risks of less speed
must be weighed against those of more haste. He must get across the crevasses
before it is dark."[47]

On the evidence, these letters had little persuasive impact upon the mind of

*There were, of course, labor economists in 1933 who asserted that taxing money out of the pockets
of the rich, who were few, into the pockets of the poor, who were many, would result in a "net
increase" of market-effective purchasing power, if done in a rational fashion. They argued that
such taxes would pump money out of excess savings and an economically unimportant luxury
market into the great market for mass-produced consumer goods. No doubt they would have
agreed with the Oxonians, however, that the "net increase" so achieved would be too small to
affect significantly the American economy in 1933.

Franklin Roosevelt; there is even doubt he understood the argument they made. Writing "Dear Felix" on the day after his receipt of the Keynes piece, he said: "The memorandum from your economist colleagues was read by me to one of my little confidential meetings—Morgenthau, Cummings, Governor [Eugene] Black [of Federal Reserve], George Harrison, [James Harvey] Rogers [of Yale], and [Herman] Oliphant—and the comment was that the Oxonians are thinking much in our terms and that since their memorandum was written we have already put several suggestions into practical effect. . . . You can tell the professor [Keynes] that in regard to public works we shall spend in the next fiscal year nearly twice the amount we are spending this fiscal year, but there is a practical limit to what the Government can borrow—especially because the banks are offering passive resistance in most of the large centers." (If Frankfurter did report the last sentence verbatim to the "professor," Keynes must have been fairly maddened by it. Twice the small amount of public works money being spent in the current fiscal year was but a fraction of what was needed, in Keynes's view. As for the notion that the borrowing power of the government of the United States remained at the mercy of a handful of bankers whose past performance had contributed substantially to the present great emergency, it was utterly appalling.) Roosevelt also implied in his letter that in consequence of actions he'd already taken, recovery was now well under way and that his political opposition was by this fact undermined. "About December 10th the pack of Tories was in full cry, but for some strange, rather obscure reason—possibly the advent of the Christmas buying —the Tories have become extraordinarily silent for the moment," he wrote. ". . . The Christmas buying is beyond belief—streets jammed, stores sold out —more like the boom days than anything since 1928. Even Congress looks almost lamblike. There will be speechmaking, of course, and probably two or three big rows . . . but on the whole I really believe they will be businesslike (comparatively). . . ."[48]

V

OF course, there *was* causal connection between 1933's Christmas buying and Roosevelt's management of the presidency. Such buying was encouraged by the mood of confident optimism which spread as a radiant energy from the White House to every corner of the land. It was encouraged much more by commodity loans, credit easing through the Farm Credit Administration and the Home Owners' Loan Corporation, and *especially* the effects of the aforementioned major decision made during the Harry Hopkins luncheon in the Oval Room a few days after the gold buying began, a few days before the five farm state governors arrived. The decision was in accord with the relief spending advice received from the Oxford economists a month later, but it was made primarily, if not wholly, as a temporary emergency relief measure, out of motives that mingled humanitarian with political considerations, and *not* for the recovery purposes stressed by the Oxonians and Keynes. Only later did

Roosevelt discover, in public statement, that one reason for his decision was the recognized need to inject "a great quantity of purchasing power . . . into the economic system in a short time."[49]

As for the thing decided, it was rooted in a profound aversion to direct "handout" relief ("the dole") to men and women able and willing to work, an aversion Harry Hopkins shared with Franklin Roosevelt. Hopkins saw it as certainly morally degrading of its recipients and likely to become so of its administrators, if continued over any long period of time. He had seen it so since well before he took charge of New York's Temporary Emergency Relief Administration. And in the late summer of 1933, as it became clear that NRA was not going to reduce unemployment at anything like the rate Hugh Johnson had publicly predicted and that PWA under Ickes would reduce it not at all during the next few months, Hopkins and Aubrey Williams, his chief FERA assistant, began laying plans for a huge federal jobs program, to be administered by or in conjunction with FERA, a program which would do what public works proponents had hoped PWA would do—namely, shift millions of people off relief rolls onto payrolls—and do it *fast*. By mid-October, with winter just ahead and the number of people on relief actually rising again, Hopkins and Williams were convinced their planned program was an urgent immediate necessity. Nevertheless, Hopkins hesitated to present the idea to the President; he feared a Roosevelt rejection of it not only because the program would cost a great deal of money, and Lew Douglas was still listened to in the White House, but also because a negative reaction to it by William Green and other leaders of organized labor was likely, and Roosevelt in that season, anxious to weld labor firmly into the NRA structure, was sensitive to the attitude of labor leaders.

But when Hopkins returned from his late-October swing through the Midwest, he was armed with a factual argument which the labor leaders would be hard put to overcome. From the voluminous newspaper clipping files of John R. Commons, the University of Wisconsin's famous institutional and labor economist, there had come into Aubrey Williams's hand, and thence into Hopkins's, the information that Samuel Gompers, principal founder and first president of the American Federation of Labor, had in 1898 advocated a so-called Day Labor Plan which was essentially identical with the jobs program now proposed. Hopkins was in Kansas City at the time. He promptly put through a long-distance phone call to the White House and arranged through Marvin McIntyre that luncheon date with the President, on the day of his return to Washington, which we have already twice mentioned.

And at lunch in the Oval Room he found the President astonishingly easy to persuade. How many federal jobs would be needed to get through the winter? Roosevelt wanted to know. About 4 million, Hopkins replied. "Let's see," said the President, thinking aloud. "Four million people—that means roughly $400 million." He was thinking of a sixty-day emergency job period, and that the $400 million would be in addition to the direct relief money which the FERA would shift over to workers' wages. Where was the extra money to come from? Obviously from PWA's appropriation, in which little more than a dent had been thus far made.[50]

Nor did Ickes object to this when, at noon on November 6, "Secretaries Wallace and Perkins and Harry Hopkins . . . came in [to Ickes's office] for a conversation by direction of the President." He was hardly in a position to object: The jobs proposal already had presidential approval, and Ickes was assured it was a strictly temporary expedient, to be ended, probably, in sixty days. Of the need for it there could be no doubt. Obviously mass suffering during the coming winter would be at least as severe as that of last winter unless strong preventive action was taken by the federal government, and there was a very real possibility of revolutionary violence on city streets and country roads if the hopeful expectations Roosevelt had raised up among the dispossessed with his New Deal were now shatteringly cast down upon frozen earth. So, though the transfer of appropriation "would put a serious crimp in the balance of our public works fund, we all thought it ought to be done," as Ickes noted in his diary.[51]

Three days later the Civil Works Administration was established by executive order, with the FERA administrator designated its administrator. "Its organization and operation was [sic] essentially different from that of the F.E.R.A.," Roosevelt explained in a later year. FERA was a highly decentralized operation, its state and local administration only loosely supervised by the federal government.* CWA was a truly *national* operation. Headquartered in Washington, it was subdivided organizationally into state, county, and city CWAs, each operating under national supervision in conformity with national directives. "All of the State Civil Works Administrations . . . were appointed by the Federal Administrator, and were actually sworn federal officials."[52] Hopkins promptly transferred a large portion of his FERA headquarters staff to CWA and transformed local relief agencies into CWA subdivisions, adding such new personnel as was absolutely necessary.

There ensued such a whirlwind of effective administrative activity as has seldom been seen in Washington, before or since. Hopkins and his associates had to start from scratch. They had no overall program to guide their labors and no stockpile of developed project plans from which to draw those that met the job specifications imposed by necessity on the CWA, specifications of simplicity (there was no time for the teaching of complicated new skills), brevity of duration (the jobs must be of a kind that could be completed in a few weeks), and seasonal suitability (the jobs must be performed under wintry conditions). Yet Hopkins had pledged himself to put 2,000,000 people to work within ten days and 2,000,000 more by the end of two weeks thereafter! What he pledged was utterly impossible; of course. But what he actually accom-

---

*Such decentralization was encouraged by political considerations. Southern senators and representatives, Democrats all, their legislative potency enhanced by the seniority they derived from single-party rule of their region, were much concerned lest federal relief upset prevailing race relations. Local control of relief helped southern whites ensure that "their" Negroes were not "corrupted" and rendered "uppity" by too much of it.

plished was only somewhat less so. More than 800,000 were on CWA payrolls by the end of the first ten days. Nearly 2,000,000 were on a fortnight later. And during the week ending January 18, 1934, the week in which CWA employment was at its peak, 4,263,644 men and women were at work on CWA projects.

Nor were this haste and magnitude of operation one whit greater than circumstances required of a humane government. The winter of 1933–1934 turned out to be one of the worst on record. In parts of New England, across the northern Midwest, and in the western mountains, temperatures sank to fifty degrees below zero, and even lower (to fifty-six degrees below in Caribou, Maine), on several ghastly days. There were hard frosts in parts of the South that had not suffered them within living memory. In Washington, D.C., a record low temperature of six below gave certain members of Congress who badly needed it some hint of what was suffered by fellow Americans who, through no fault of their own, were deprived of adequate food, clothing, shelter, fuel. When CWA's initial funding was virtually exhausted in mid-January and Hopkins went to Congress to ask for a direct $950 million appropriation to carry CWA and FERA through the winter, Washington's bitter weather augmented the persuasive power, with Congress, of Roosevelt's emphatic approval of the request. The National Republican Committee harshly attacked CWA and Hopkins personally on every ground of efficiency and morality and viewed with horror the size of the appropriation asked for, but such sounds were very faintly echoed in the legislative chambers, and Hopkins got his money, quickly.[53]

The new program's impact upon the lives of the dispossessed was immediate and fortunate.

"Three loud cheers for CWA!" wrote Lorena Hickok to Hopkins from Lincoln, Nebraska, on November 18, just nine days after the agency's creation. ". . . I think probably it's the smartest thing that has been tried since we went into the relief business. It is actually getting out some of that Public Works money I've been yowling about all these weeks. (In Lincoln today I actually saw, with my own eyes, my first public works project under way, with the exception of a few highway jobs. It's a sewer project.)" Five days later she wrote Hopkins from Sioux City: "I spent most of the morning . . . having a look at PWA and CWA projects. . . . The CWA gangs, some 20 men, were putting shoulders along an old and rather narrow paved road. It was a nasty morning. Cold. And sleet. But they looked cheerful. Thirty-hour week. 40 cents an hour—CASH, instead of grocery orders." And two days later (November 25) she reported from Des Moines on "the first CWA pay day in the state of Iowa." A happy day. "Something over 5,000 men, who went to work with picks and shovels and wheelbarrows last Monday morning, lined up and got paid—MONEY. It was for only half a week's work. The payrolls were made up as of Thursday night, but for many, many of them it was the first money they'd seen in months. They took it with wide grins and made bee-lines for the grocery stores, NOT to shove a grocery order across the counter but to go where they pleased and buy what they pleased, with cash. And along about a week from today these and many thousands more will be dropping into drygoods stores, too, and clothing stores. I wonder if you have any idea of what CWA is doing for the morale of these people and the communities. Officials, like the mayor of Sioux City, tell me it's almost beyond belief. And they wouldn't have to tell me. I can see for myself.[54]

Similar reports came to Roosevelt directly a couple of months later from Frank C. Walker, the politically astute, sweet-tempered, notably fair-minded Montana lawyer whom Roosevelt had appointed to preside over the National Emergency Council.

Walker and Roosevelt alike were disturbed by reports that came in through the emergency council's field offices during the CWA's early days. Often hysterical in tone, they were reports of wholesale graft, corruption, and incompetency in the jobs program's local administration. Hopkins had not yet become one of Roosevelt's intimate associates; he was much closer to Eleanor Roosevelt, who, at his request, was at that time taking the lead in establishing a specific CWA program devoted to unemployed women. Hence Roosevelt could not but be concerned lest Hopkins, a political novice, pay insufficient attention to the threat which a venal politics inevitably posed to any such enterprise as this. It was with the President's blessing therefore, if not at the President's suggestion, that Walker made a cross-country inspection tour to see with his own eyes what was happening.

What was happening, he found, was wonderfully good on the whole. In his home state he saw "old friends of mine, men I had been to school with— digging ditches and laying sewer pipe. They were wearing their regular business suits as they worked because they couldn't afford overalls and rubber boots. If ever I thought, 'There but for the grace of God—' it was right then." Yet these men counted themselves fortunate to be doing what they were doing. "Do you know, Frank," said one of them, "this is the first money I've had in my pockets for a year and a half? Up to now I've had nothing but tickets that you could exchange for groceries." When he returned to Washington, Walker in written report advised the President to "pay little attention to those who criticize the creation of CWA or its administration." Hopkins and company were doing "a magnificent job," an "amazing" job. "You have every reason to be proud of CWA and its administration." Walker's report concluded: "It is my considered opinion that this has averted one of the most serious crises in our history. Revolution is an ugly word to use, but I think we were dangerously close to at least the threat of it." (Confirmative in major part of Walker's judgment was a report that came to Roosevelt's desk, some weeks later, from an observer for the War Department, Lieutenant Colonel John C. H. Lee of the Army Corps of Engineers. Himself an authoritarian personality, rigidly hierarchical in his administrative attitudes and techniques,* Lee, in the words of Arthur Schlesinger, Jr., "watched Hopkins's unorthodox methods with astonished admiration." Wrote Lee: "Mr. Hopkins's loose fluidity of organiza-

---

*He served as Major General Lee, commander of the Services of Supply of the ETO in England in 1942–1943, and his personal operation was almost as notable for its imperious nature as for its practical efficiency.

tion . . . enabled him to engage for employment in two months nearly as many persons as were enlisted and called to the colors during our year and a half of World War mobilization, and to disburse to them, weekly, a higher average rate of wage than Army and Navy pay." The young administrator and "the group of able young assistants which he has assembled and inspired . . . have worked daily long into the night with a morale easily comparable to that of a war emergency." Lee was particularly impressed by the fact that these assistants were on familiar egalitarian terms with their superior, addressing him "fondly as 'Harry,' " and that there was "no rigidity or formality in their staff conferences with him, yet he holds their respect, confidence, and seemingly whole-souled cooperation."[55])

As a "shot in the arm" for the ailing economy, CWA was highly effective. Nearly 80 percent of the agency's total expenditure of close to $1 billion went directly into wages and salaries, with the bulk of the remainder, or approximately $120 million, being paid out for work materials—which is to say that almost the whole of the agency's appropriation, all save a few percent of it, went directly into the market for consumer goods.

In addition to the work relief it provided—and despite the wastefulness, including a high percentage of "made work" and some (though surprisingly little) graft, which inevitably accompanied the incredible speed with which the program was put into effect—CWA's concrete accomplishments were substantial, overall, and remain, many of them, to be seen to this day. It was initially agreed between Ickes and Hopkins that CWA would "undertake no contract work," would build "no sewers or waterworks or incinerators or bridges," confining itself to "projects of a minor character," to quote the Ickes diary. It was also agreed, however and perforce, that PWA might turn over to CWA projects on which work had not yet begun and which the CWA might begin and advance, if not complete, within its allotted life span.[56] There were many such projects. So it was that within a little more than four months CWA's 180,000 projects, including those transferred from PWA, had built or improved a half-million miles of city street and secondary road, constructed or remodeled 40,000 school buildings, created more than 450 airfields and improved as many existing ones, laid scores of miles of sewer line, and constructed or improved hundreds of parks, playgrounds, stadiums, swimming pools. Nor was practical physical construction the only kind of employment which CWA provided. Acting on a suggestion from artist George Biddle (he was of the Philadelphia Biddles, a Groton graduate whose brother Francis, also a Grotonian, was destined for high place in the later Roosevelt administration), Hopkins used CWA money to fund a Public Works Arts Project, administered by the Treasury Department, which employed painters and sculptors at wages of up to $46.50 a week to embellish with artwork government buildings in each of the forty-eight states. He also established within CWA itself a Federal Arts Program which gave employment to 3,000 writers, musicians, painters, sculptors who, as Hopkins said in irritable response to critics, have "got to eat just like other people."[57] Needy unemployed scholars, some hundreds of them, under the classification of "writer," were provided by CWA with what were in effect research grants, enabling them to receive wages while pursuing their scholarly interests.

As for conservative opposition to CWA, it was at the outset unwontedly weak and soft-spoken. There was widely quoted ridicule from Al Smith. He had become nominal editor of the magazine *New Outlook;* he contributed to each monthly issue a signed editorial. And in the December 1933 issue he wrote that "one of the absent-minded professors" in Washington had been playing "anagrams with the alphabet soup" and, while "the soup got cold," had "unconsciously" invented this "new game" of identifying agencies by initials. To CCC, AAA, TVA, NRA, FCA, PWA, FERA, etc. etc., was now added CWA, which was to administer "civil works." And what was a "civil work" as distinct from a "public work" or a "relief work"? No one could say, "except that it is some sort of minor construction or repair . . . which can be finished before February 15, when the money gives out." The *reason* for the new agency, however, was "crystal clear." CWA was created "to hide the failure of" PWA, a "crazy, topheavy structure, choked with red tape and bureaucracy," which nevertheless "is being left as it is. . . ." Smith also had plausible explanation of the otherwise strange dearth of hostile comment on this new departure from conservative politicians: "[N]o sane local official who has hung up an empty stocking over the municipal fireplace is going to shoot Santa Claus just before a hard Christmas."[58]

But this dearth of hostile comment did not last beyond the holiday season. In its headlong progress across what was for a national agency new ground, yet a ground crowded with old and vested interests, CWA inevitably trod upon many tender toes, including those of members of political organizations who resented Hopkins's total disregard of what they deemed their patronage rights. And in early 1934, as liberal pressures increased for CWA's continuance beyond its initially scheduled expiration date and even for its establishment as a permanent federal agency, so did conservative pressures for its immediate termination. There began to swirl about the agency a whirlwind of controversy that matched in intensity the agency's whirlwind of activity.

From the South came bitter complaints because Hopkins insisted upon an equality of CWA wages between black and white workers, such wages being considerably higher than southern whites were accustomed to paying "their niggers." These complaints were necessarily listened to, if not fully shared, by the South's generally conservative congressional delegation, all of it Democratic. The southern white was not without recourse on his home ground, of course. Since the local CWA staff was generally identical with that which had formerly administered local relief, it was easy for local sentiment to vitiate national policy. If blacks must be paid the same as whites, then jobs that should go to them on any basis of fair proportional representation would be given instead to whites. This happened throughout the South. (In Atlanta in the winter of 1934 Norman Thomas "found much bitterness among Negroes who said they could not get jobs on relief projects even when the relief projects involved work on a colored school."[59]) All the same, there *was* this published national policy. It was an "insulting" commentary upon white southern practice, a commentary known to the black community, and as a legal regulation it even made such practice actually criminal. It was furiously resented.

From leaders of business and industry who were basically opposed to relief of any kind yet dared not say so publicly in the circumstances came the usual expressions of solicitude for the spiritual well-being, the "moral fiber" of those whose physical selves were being nourished through CWA paychecks. If a "civil work" was truly useful, said these leaders, it constituted unfair governmental competition with private industry. Thus mattress manufacturers raised howls of protest when some hundreds of women on CWA payrolls were set to work making mattresses out of 250,000 bales of surplus cotton, for distribution free of charge to the desperately needy. The howls subsided after it was pointed out that not one of these mattresses would ever go on the market,[60] but there remained in the business mind, from this demonstration of governmental cooperative production for human use in place of private production for business profit, a horrific vision of coming socialism, with CWA its precursor. On the other hand, if a "civil work" was *not* useful, it simply mitigated or removed the onus of "going on relief" and did so at a greater cost to the taxpayer than direct relief involved. Actually, "going on relief" *ought* to be a humiliation and a misery. If it were not, those going on would make insufficient effort to get off; they would embrace the pernicious notion that "society owes every man a living," and their individual initiative and self-reliance, the very core of "moral character," would atrophy for lack of exercise. Far better for all relief to be administered frankly *as* relief, its amount limited to "a bare subsistence allowance," as Sears, Roebuck executive Robert E. Wood put it in a private letter.[61]

Nor was it only from avowed conservatives that pressure came for a swift termination of CWA as the new year wore on. Rather surprisingly, Lorena Hickok, who had greeted the advent of the new agency with such enthusiasm (though even then as "an emergency measure"), became convinced by direct observation of the agency's field operations that if it were continued for long beyond its originally specified term, its harmful effects would outweigh the good it was doing. Trouble arose from the fact that CWA's wage and hour provisions did not conform with those of the NRA codes "for the different communities," as she said in a letter to Hopkins from Raleigh, North Carolina, on February 14. In the South CWA workers were receiving only a little less for a twenty-four- to thirty-hour week than cotton mill workers were supposed to get for a forty-hour week under the cotton industry code, yet much of CWA's work was of a "boondoggling" variety* and CWA workers were "too

---

*Originally, according to *American Heritage Dictionary*, "boondoggle" was the name of "the plaited leather cord worn around the neck by Boy Scouts" in uniform and was coined in 1925 by an American scoutmaster named R. H. Link. It was given wide currency as a label for "pointless, unnecessary, time-wasting work" of the kind the New Deal sometimes provided through its work relief programs.

often of the 'unemployable,' indigent type." Naturally, the mill employees and managers were unhappy. This was not, however, the most serious trouble, in Hick's opinion, since it was relatively easy to correct. From her direct observation she derived reasons for CWA termination that were closely akin to those business conservatives derived from selfish interest and ideological preconception. "With regard to the people who are actually at work on CWA wages, the story seems to be pretty much the same everywhere," she wrote. "I get it from engineers, administrators, social workers. When CWA came in, the men were 'tickled to death.' Their morale jumped up about a hundred points. They went to work with a will. Now they are beginning to be bitten by the urge to get even more. They want to get 65 cents an hour instead of 40. They want to be foremen, at $1.10, and they suspect every foreman of having got his job through political pull. I guess it's true that, the more you do for people, the more they demand." Her conclusion: "CWA should be stopped, and as quickly as possible without causing too much disturbance," though "we may as well face the fact that there'll have to be something else" and that "the gap between CWA and this 'something else' should not be too great."[62]

But Hick's view, as she herself pointed out, was at odds with the views of the University of North Carolina sociology professor who was chairman of the state CWA and Emergency Relief Committee; of the chairman of North Carolina's National Emergency Council; of Jonathan Daniels, Josephus's son, now editor of the Raleigh *News and Observer;* of the collector for the Internal Revenue Service for North Carolina; and of "many of the [CWA] administrators." All these wanted CWA continued, "with some changes."[63] And this was certainly the opinion and desire of an overwhelming majority of liberals and New Deal supporters across the land. While Hickok was in Raleigh, Norman Thomas was in the lead-mining area of Missouri, where, he found, more than 50 percent of the population was "dependent upon CWA or other forms of relief." He deemed it outrageous that an allegedly liberal and humane administration in Washington should even consider abandoning CWA until something better was available to replace it or until there was, as Thomas doubted there ever would be, a sufficient private industrial recovery to give jobs to all who were now unemployed. Returned to New York City from his travels, Thomas organized a "march on Washington" to urge CWA's continuance. Simultaneously a deluge of letters and telegrams urging continuance (more than 60,000 within a week) descended upon Roosevelt in the White House, upon Hopkins in the Walker-Johnson Building. And all over the country there were demonstrations by CWA workers protesting the impending loss of their jobs. Hopkins himself, with Williams and all others of the headquarters staff, believed that CWA should go on, with appropriate changes in structure and procedure; he saw no sure sign that the need for it would be significantly less next winter than it was right now.

By such pleading and protest and expressed belief, however, Roosevelt was unpersuaded. And the final decision was, of course, his to make.

Here was an instance, of a piece with his pushing through Congress of his

Economy Act, when he acted from conviction on a basis of principle, not from impulse, or by intuition, or out of a calculation of immediate pressure weights. The voice of conscience (it was also the voice of long-suffering Lew Douglas) continued to preach the iniquity of deficits, the virtue of thrift; it did so so loudly in this instance that it drowned out all contrary-speaking voices, being amplified by Roosevelt's belief that the recovery process which had been renewed in December, after a few weeks of interruption, continued apace and should soon render possible a drastic reduction of relief expenditures. CWA "was not designed as a continuing program," he explained in a later year. It "was relatively costly," compared with FERA. So he ordered its winding down to the point of almost total abandonment by the end of March 1934 "in favor of a work relief program hiring only destitute unemployed on a budgetary deficiency basis."[64] They were orders which Hopkins promptly carried out, efficiently, uncomplainingly, though it required him to deal harshly on occasion with protesting members of his own staff. His was a demonstration of total loyalty to the President that matched Louis Howe's; it contrasted sharply with the behavior of George Peek, Hugh Johnson, Donald Richberg, Lew Douglas, Harold Ickes, and others when, then and later, their policy proposals were rejected, their ambitious desires thwarted. Roosevelt would not forget it.

From the wreckage of CWA were saved certain ongoing white-collar projects, including several that gave employment to artists, writers, musicians, scientists, scholars.

VI

THERE were remarkably few and mild popular disturbances—no riots in the streets, no dangerously threatful mass demonstrations—following and consequent upon CWA's discontinuance. If Roosevelt himself was not surprised by this, others high in his administration were. Yet Roosevelt's decision on this matter became another item, and a major one, upon a lengthening bill of particulars being compiled on the left, during the winter and spring of 1934, in condemnation of the President and his New Deal.

Other items, of which some have already received mention, derived from NRA's price policy. We have told* of Hugh Johnson's reluctant permission of public hearings on this policy, to be organized by the Consumers' Advisory Board, and of his abrupt postponement of these when business complained of the effect the publicity they generated might have upon Christmas shopping. The consumers' board made good use of the extra preparatory time thus given it. When the rescheduled hearings were opened in the Commerce Building on January 9, 1934, representatives of farm organizations, consumer groups, small business, large retailers (mail-order houses especially), and the purchasing divisions of governmental agencies were lined up to testify in factual detail

*See p. 268.

against the price effects of nearly three dozen codes, with special attention to the codes for such major industries as lumber, steel, textiles, electrical appliances, bituminous coal. The board itself had in hand a report for each of a considerable number of industries and, most important, a summary report wherein many hundreds of individual complaints were carpentered into a coherent indictment, replete with statistical citations and illustrative charts and graphs.

In the interests of fair play, having nothing to fear from it and everything to gain, the board sent out to leaders of each of the codified industries concerned, in advance of the hearings date, a brief summary of the report for that industry. Industry's response, implemented by NRA officialdom, was an effort to prevent knowledge of the reports' contents from reaching the public. From among his key subordinates, Johnson chose to preside over the hearings, precisely the man most hostile to the consumers' board and to consumerism in all its forms. Arthur D. Whiteside was a former president of Dun & Bradstreet. Strongly committed to the trade association idea, he was very weakly committed, if at all, to First Amendment principles. And just before the hearings opened, he, as chairman of the proceedings, informed the board that because of businessmen's objections, its reports could not be admitted as hearings evidence. It was a ruling that, predictably, greatly deepened the impress of the board's findings upon the public mind. News reporters quickly, inevitably learned of it; their story that the board was being "gagged" received a bigger play in the nation's press than a full and frank disclosure of the board's findings would have received. Moreover, the Seventy-third Congress was now well into its first regular session, and either a full copy of the board's report or the excerpted substance of it was soon in the hands of Senator Gerald Nye. By the time Whiteside had reversed himself to the extent of permitting the board to present summary statements at the hearings, the popular impression was that NRA officialdom had a great deal to hide. This added force to the lambasting Nye gave NRA on the Senate floor as a conspiracy on the part of large corporations to strangle small business and gain monopoly control of the national marketplace. (The Blue Eagle, cried Nye, was "a bird of prey upon the masses!") And what Nye had to say was at once loudly seconded by Idaho's Senator Borah, who claimed to have received more than 9,000 specific complaints from small businessmen and who proposed a resolution to investigate price-fixing by the steel and oil industries, a resolution that was adopted.[65]

These were attacks which the White House could not ignore. They clearly expressed a prevailing opinion among the constituencies of Progressive Republicans (Norris, La Follette, Hiram Johnson, as well as Nye and Borah) whom Roosevelt sought to join with liberal Democracy to form a dependable congressional "Roosevelt coalition." On January 20 he issued an executive order "to provide a practical and rapid way" of handling specific complaints against "monopolistic practices" which, allegedly sanctioned by NRA codes, tended "to eliminate, oppress or discriminate against small enterprises." A complainant "dissatisfied with the disposition of his case" by NRA might "press his case before the Federal Trade Commission." FTC, in dealing with such complaints, "will follow the procedure set forth in the organic act—a procedure that is informal, not costly to the complainant, and expeditious."[66] But this, hardly more than a symbolic gesture, did nothing to stem the rising tide of complaint, since prices continued to rise inordinately.

On February 19 Johnson announced the creation of a six-member National Recovery Review Board to examine the codes and ascertain whether they were designed to foster monopoly or to discriminate in any way against small business. The announcement came after a series of conferences between Johnson and Nye, in one of which Johnson himself, acting upon a sudden impulse to display his open-mindedness (he later called it "a moment of total aberration"), suggested that Clarence Darrow, the famous labor and criminal lawyer, be named board chairman. This was done, the board being then at once dubbed the Darrow Board in the press. Other members of it, subsequently appointed, were a retail merchant from Nye's North Dakota, a North Carolina hosiery manufacturer, a druggists' association executive, a New York banker named John F. Sinclair, and Darrow's former law partner, William O. Thompson, who shared Darrow's social views.

Eight days later, in further forced response to growing pressures, the general convened a so-called Field Day of Criticism, which, because of the number of people who wished to testify, had to be extended over four days, with a Sunday intervening. The Commerce Department auditorium was jammed as a long parade of witnesses reiterated and expanded upon criticisms already made through the consumers' board, notably in a report just issued, entitled *Suggestions for Code Revision* (Johnson had tried and failed to prevent its publication). In it were statistics showing that, under NRA codes, seven industries had increased the ultimate consumer prices of their products by from 17 percent to 250 percent, the former increase being for coal, the latter for copper boilers.[67]

The Field Day ended on March 3.

On March 5 there opened in Washington a conference of some 600 NRA code authorities, more than 5,000 businessmen in all, and to its first session, Roosevelt delivered an address surveying NRA's progress thus far. He strove to wring the last full measure of optimistic hope from the rage of criticism that had come to a close in this same hall only two days before. He did so, characteristically, by asserting a complete divorcement of means from ends or of grand totality from the "mere" detail of its composition. "I am sure it will hearten you to know," he declared, "that the great majority of the complaints [during the Field Day] were directed not at the codes but at errors or omissions in what was done under the codes. The great bulk of complaint or criticism of the Recovery Act does not go to the Act itself or its basic principles, but rather to the details of mere method. In this we should feel encouraged . . . that we are on the right track and can go forward." But to what must "we" now "go forward"? Men who had abundantly manifested in practical ways their eagerness to cooperate in price-fixing listened with no visible enthusiasm to the President's "inescapable conclusion that we must now consider immediate cooperation to secure increase in wages and shortening of hours" and "to get more people to work." Nor was there any audience enthusiasm as Roosevelt went on to qualify his assertive optimism with a vague threat. "I have never believed that we should violently impose flat, arbitrary and abrupt changes on the economic structure," he said, "but . . . the Government cannot forever continue to absorb the full burden of unemployment." And he followed this with words far more expressive of his personal wish than of objective fact, words capable of being perceived as deliberately ironical: "Your self-governing groups are not here to devise ingenious plans to circumvent the purposes of the Act. You are here in a patriotic spirit to effect these purposes. With few exceptions industry will give wholehearted compliance. It is only in the case of rare exceptions where industrial self-government may fail that the Government itself must and will, under the law, move firmly and promptly to prevent failure."[68]

Two days after that, Roosevelt formally established by executive order the National Recovery Review Board (the Darrow Board), the creation of which had been announced by Johnson two weeks before.

Clarence Darrow, veteran of many a sensational court battle in which he fought for liberal views against efforts to restrict free thought and free speech, one such battle being the Scopes "monkey trial" in Dayton, Tennessee, in 1925, was now an old man. He celebrated his seventy-seventh birthday in April 1934. But it was with a youthful zest and energy, as well as a youthful eagerness to dismay and confound exponents of the Prevailing View, the Established Order, that he plunged into his assigned labors. He spurned Hugh Johnson's offer of office space in the Commerce Building adjacent the general's own, establishing his headquarters, instead, in the Willard Hotel. He also ignored Johnson's wish that he submit his reports to the NRA administrator ("I am the big cheese here," General Johnson told him, with boyish grin); he insisted upon reporting instead directly to the President. It was to the White House, then, that Darrow delivered in early May his first report, signed by five of the six review board members. Dealing with eight major codes, this report summarized and drew conclusions from hundreds of pages of testimony accumulated in a crowded series of public hearings during the preceding seven weeks, hearings to which very little had been contributed by NRA's top administrators or by code authorities.* Its overall conclusion was that gross "monopolistic practices" on the part of "bold and aggressive" code authorities were indeed oppressing small businesses and creating, or tending toward the creation of, national monopoly controls. Its overall recommendation was a total reversal of basic NRA price policy, with a drastic revision of codes, to eliminate virtually all the present pricing and production control provisions. There was a dissenting minority report, submitted by banker Sinclair, who protested the "sloppy,

---

*Since the board had no subpoena power, it could obtain testimony only from those who wished or were willing to testify, and the great majority of these were complainants against NRA.

one-sided half information" on which the majority allegedly based its conclusions, though he agreed with several of its specific recommendations. There was also a five-page supplementary statement by Darrow and Thompson, who said that the real choice now facing America was not between private monopoly and governmentally guaranteed "free competition" but between governmentally sponsored monopoly and socialism, with the latter infinitely preferable to the former. The technology already available could and would create an age of abundance for everyone "when industry produces for use and not for profit."[69]

Roosevelt was not pleased. "Unfortunately," he complained in a later year, "the Board, in its investigation, proceeded rather as a prosecuting agency to prove a case against big business, than as an impartial investigating body. . . ." He was himself convinced—he asserted "it was a demonstrated fact"—that "innumerable small and independent business men were greatly helped in their struggle to survive by the establishment [through NRA] of fair competition and the elimination of such monopolistic practices as destructive price cutting."* He was further convinced that "[m]any of the complaints of monopoly by big business" came from "smaller business men" who had formerly profited from "sweatshop practices" and were now compelled by code labor provisions "to pay decent wages for decent hours of labor." At the request of an outraged General Johnson, who claimed never to have seen a "more superficial, intemperate and inaccurate document," Roosevelt delayed issuance of the report for two weeks so that Johnson and Richberg would have time in which to prepare a rebuttal for simultaneous issuance.[70]

And so it was that the report's publication on May 20 initiated at once a war of words, of furiously angry and vituperative words, such as Washington had seldom seen or heard since another Johnson, Andrew, warred with Radical Republicans over Reconstruction in the late 1860s. In a seventeen-page "analysis" Donald Richberg, formerly a friend and ally of Darrow, with whom he had sided against railroad labor exploitation and Chicago political corruption, damned the board and its chairman for conducting "a haphazard, one-sided investigation" wherein factual evidence was tortured into the service of "preconceptions" fundamentally opposed to the theory, the purpose, of NRA. Darrow personally was accused of petty-mindedness and prejudice; having obtained the bulk of his testimony from those whose selfish interests were hampered by NRA, he now supported with his report, wittingly or no, "chiselers" and the very "monopolists" to whom he was ostensibly opposed. He thereby provided "ammunition for the malicious sniping of political partisans. . . ." And to confuse the picture as viewed from the left, the Johnson-

---

*It was also "a demonstrated fact," in the eyes of such direct observers as Lorena Hickok (see p. 262), that innumerable small-business enterprises in the Midwest would have been forced into bankruptcy in the fall and winter of 1933–1934 had they actually obeyed the wage and hour provisions of the codes they had signed. They did not obey, of course. Nor were the employees of such enterprises in a position to protest such disobedience. Their jobs were at stake.

Richberg position in this matter was substantially supported by NRA's Labor Advisory Board, whose members, though bitterly unhappy about the Johnson-Richberg interpretation of Section 7(a), still deemed this to be labor's Magna Carta and were greatly concerned lest it go down in the wreckage of NRA, bringing a return of cutthroat competition with its implacable, invincible hostility on the part of employers to labor union organization.[71]

Darrow, who had been engaged in polemics through all his long professional life, replied in kind, and effectively, so far as impact on the popular mind was concerned.

It was while this war of words raged most loudly that John Maynard Keynes came to Washington for what a few knowledgeable people deemed at the time, as many people later assumed it to have been, a historically important face-to-face meeting with Franklin Roosevelt.

The way to this meeting had been opened by Felix Frankfurter. In Oxford on May 7, 1934, he addressed to the President a letter saying that Keynes was about to depart for America, where he would receive "an honorary degree from Columbia," and planned a week's visit in Washington. "I am giving him a note to Miss LeHand in the hope it may be possible for you to find time to see him," said Frankfurter, going on to advance arguments shrewdly designed to ensure that the "time" would indeed be "found." Keynes was "perhaps the single most powerful supporter of the New Deal in England." He not only wielded "a trenchant economic pen" but was also the "head of an important insurance company" (he had been chairman of the National Mutual Insurance Company since 1921), and as such "he exercises considerable influence in the City." This fact gave him prestige on Wall Street, "and various Wall Street correspondents of his are seeking to reach his mind, with all the misrepresentations of which lower New York has such mastery. Therefore I believe it is doubly important that he hear about the Administration's efforts and purposes at first hand. . . ." Keynes, added Frankfurter, "is accompanied by his very charming wife, Lydia Lopokova, the famous dancer and actress [she had been a ballerina in Sergei Diaghilev's ballet company]."[72]

Keynes checked into Washington's Mayflower Hotel on May 25, was invited with his wife to the White House for tea three days later, and, either on that occasion or the day following, had a lengthy private talk with the President. He attempted to impart to Roosevelt in capsule form, with evidently some use of mathematical formulae, the gist of the wisdom he would publish two years later in his *General Theory of Employment, Interest, and Money* (the first draft of this immensely influential work was being completed in this spring of 1934). Immediately thereafter Keynes wrote Frankfurter: "I had an hour's tête-à-tête with the President which was fascinating and illuminating." Roosevelt wrote Frankfurter: "I had a grand talk with Keynes and liked him immensely." But in point of fact, the meeting was less than satisfactory for both its participants —and actually a disappointment to Keynes—as was indicated in the remarks both made orally, separately, to Frances Perkins. "I saw your friend Keynes," said Roosevelt to Perkins. "He left a whole rigamarole of figures. He must be a mathematician rather than a political economist." And Keynes "cautiously" confessed to Perkins some disillusionment with a man whose operations he had watched from afar with the greatest admiration. He said, with regret, that he had "supposed the President was more literate, economically speaking."[73]*

A few days later Keynes, always a close observer of the hands of people with whom he talked, for he believed hands to be "the best guide to character,"† expressed in a letter his disappointment in Roosevelt's hands. "Firm and fairly strong," he wrote of them, "but not clever or with finesse, shortish round nails like those at the end of a businessman's fingers." (In his *Economic Consequences of the Peace* Keynes describes Woodrow Wilson's hands as "capable and fairly strong" but "wanting sensitiveness and finesse.") They were, to Keynes, "oddly familiar." Where had he seen them before? "At last it came to me. Sir Edward Grey [Sir Edward was British foreign secretary at the outbreak of the Great War; Keynes had scant respect for him as mind or character]. A more solid and Americanized Sir Edward Grey. . . . Much cleverer, much more fertile, sensitive, and permeable, but something, all the same, which corresponded to those finger nails and carried me back to Sir Edward Grey."[74]

In sum, the interview would seem to have been less a meeting of minds than a clash of temperaments. Roosevelt was never wholly at ease when conversing on matters of moment with intellectuals, unless the latter made an effort to put him at ease through flattery and ostentatious self-subordination, as Frankfurter always did. Often he felt decidedly uncomfortable in the company of such as Marriner Eccles, Norman Thomas, Walter Lippmann, though he generally managed to hide the fact from them, perhaps also from himself to some degree, through his exercise of remarkable empathic sensitivities joined with a genius for convincing role playing. And since Keynes, one of the most brilliant and powerful intellects of the twentieth century, came into Roosevelt's presence with an exaggerating preconception of the President's acumen and intellectual sophistication, he no doubt played up rather than down an elitist manner, insouciant, cocksure, disdainful, that was as if designed to irritate all who were not members of the Bloomsbury set to which Keynes himself belonged or of some equivalent set.

Arthur Krock in the New York *Times* for June 5 devoted a long column to the Keynes visit to Washington. He chided his fellow newsmen for their ignoring of this visit, their failure to recognize its importance. Keynes's inter-

---

*"It was true that Keynes delivered himself of a mathematical approach to the problems of national income, public and private expenditure, purchasing power, and the fine points of his formula," writes Perkins, who regretted that Keynes had not been more "concrete when he talked to Roosevelt, instead of treating him as though he belonged in the higher echelons of economic knowledge."

†Keynes had had casts made of his and his wife's hands.

views with high government officials, and especially his "long interview" with Roosevelt just before the President "departed for Gettysburg,"* were alleged by Krock to have influenced the administration toward increased government spending. Actually Keynes had no influence whatever upon Roosevelt's decision making at that time or, directly, ever.

Fortunately the war of words between Johnson and Darrow was over in a few weeks. It ended with the release on June 28 of the Darrow Board's third and final report, a last word that reiterated the criticisms made in earlier reports and blasted Johnson-Richberg for failure "to remove or even restrain" the monopolistic practices earlier revealed. But by that time irreparable damage had been done NRA's standing with the public, whose well-informed portion now generally regarded the "experiment" as a failure. The agency was in forced and faltering retreat from its initial price policy. On June 5 it had issued a policy memorandum declaring a restored competitive market to be NRA's goal, a declaration the consistency of which with the original trade association (industrial self-government) idea was difficult to discern. To this end, the memorandum went on to say, open price provisions must contain specific safeguards against price-fixing; also, code prohibitions of price cutting must apply only to such cuts as were *truly* destructive of fair competition, *truly* a threat to the survival of small enterprises, *truly* inimical to fair labor standards. This, the first general policy statement ever issued by NRA, and virtually the last, was an instant sensation. Within twenty-four hours big businessmen had flooded NRA headquarters with protests against it. And characteristically, General Johnson issued or ordered issued at the end of that twenty-four-hour period an "interpretation" of the new policy which was, in practical effect, its nullification. There had been, said he, some "misunderstanding" of the announcement; it did not apply to codes already approved, as protesters feared, but only to future codes. Since 90 percent of all American industry, including virtually every major corporation save Henry Ford's, was already under approved codes (there were some 460 by then), the net result of the announcement as interpreted was to open to the public gaze a wide gap, filled with contradictions, between stated NRA policy and actual NRA practice.

By that time, too, the topmost echelon of NRA administration was in disarray. General Johnson, personally, was in total disarray. His administrative flounderings and vacillations had cost him the support of much of his principal constituency, the leaders of business organizations, who were in any case more and more unhappy over the pernicious workings, as they saw it, of Section 7(a). The Kiplinger monthly newsletter, speaking and helping to shape

*In his Gettysburg address on May 30, 1934, Roosevelt spoke of the battlefield there as a symbol of the "doom of sectionalism," saying that the "selfishness of sectionalism has no place in our national life." He concluded: "Here, here at Gettysburg, here in the presence of the spirits of those who fell on this ground, we give renewed assurance that the passions of war are moldering in the tombs of Time and the purposes of peace are flowing today in the hearts of a united people."[75]

the business view of public affairs, flatly blamed NRA's troubles upon the "temperamental incompetence of the man at the top." Notorious in Washington had become the general's increasingly frequent resort to alcohol in excess as an escape from his mounting woes, notorious, too, his allegedly too intimate personal relations with, and dependence upon, his confidential secretary, Frances "Robbie" Robinson. She was a bright, attractive, aggressive young woman of some twenty-eight years who did her best to moderate the general's drinking and to hold the fort for him when he was incapacitated, to the angry disgust of key NRA officials, for at such times she exercised, or strove to exercise, an administrative power that went well beyond her official authority or personal competence. Writes Ickes in his diary: "She went with him everywhere, sat in all conferences, and was as obtrusive as a certain type of wife in the private affairs of her husband."[76] (Her salary was considerably higher than the highest prescribed by Civil Service for secretaries. When criticism of this appeared in the press, the general "begged the newspapermen to lay off, saying she was no 'mere stenographer or secretary,' " writes the Unofficial Observer [Jay Franklin]. "When the newspapers headlined this as 'more than a stenographer,' Johnson growled, 'Boys, you're hitting below the belt'—an observation with which the wise-guys of the tabloids made merry."[77])

There were other disturbing signs of the general's mental and emotional instability, including a marked tendency to embrace in public "fascistic" authoritarian ideas he had formerly been content, for the most part, to entertain in private. He publicly envisioned for NRA a future grand and, to democratic minds, terrifying. He wrote in late spring an article, to be published in the *Saturday Evening Post*, wherein he indicated a development of NRA into *the* central agency of both the national government and the national economy, an agency which, having absorbed the departments of Commerce and Labor, would effect that "[o]rganization of both Industry and Labor to the ultimate" (there would be strict "regulation of production" accompanied by price-fixing) which was the "only way to meet the serious economic problems with which we are faced."[78]

There now poured into the Executive Office and Oval Room a stream of written and oral complaints against the general and of recommendations that he be at once removed from office.

Still, as summer advanced, Roosevelt kept him on.

VII

ON that lengthening bill of particulars being compiled on the left as an indictment of Roosevelt's handling of the presidency, yet other items had to do with labor policy.

Leading spokesmen for the administration were continuously stressing "balance" as the key word to be used in any accurate description of the New Deal's approach to recovery and reform. "What we seek is balance in our economic system—balance between agriculture and industry, and balance between the wage earner, the employer and the consumer," said Roosevelt in his March 5 address to the conference of NRA code authorities. Hugh Johnson echoed this in his 1935 book *The Blue Eagle from Egg to Earth:* "Always the answer is balance—balance of supply to demand, balance of prices at fair exchange parity throughout the whole economic structure, and balance of benefits among great economic areas." But what about the balance of *power* among these "areas" or, as the left would put it, among the economic "classes"? This was the basic question asked by those leftist critics who, viewing Roosevelt's operations, saw him as far too sensitive and immediately responsive to prevailing pressures, pressures which were against his doing what they, with Paul Douglas, deemed it absolutely necessary to do— namely, achieve through government a redistribution of power or, to put it more accurately, a creation of *new* power through the "organization of those who are at present weak. . . ."* Only thus could be shaped a truly, justly balanced thrust of overall social power toward the good of all. "Trade unions need to be built up," Douglas had said. And this buildup, far from being encouraged by Roosevelt through the first half of 1934, was actively discouraged by him.

On March 1, a little more than three weeks before the automobile strike settlement of which we have told, Senator Wagner introduced in the Senate his Labor Disputes Act of 1934, the bill which Leon Keyserling had prepared in January and which he and Wagner had repeatedly revised during February. In echo and counterbalance of the "unfair competition" specifications of NRA codes, the bill specified a number of "unfair labor practices" which were henceforth to be prohibited, including (1) the initiation and financing by management of company unions, (2) employer interference of any kind in employee elections to determine collective bargaining agents, and (3) refusal by employers to recognize and bargain with the agents so selected by majority vote of the employees. It would establish, as the act's administrative agency, a permanent national labor board having essentially the same powers as the Federal Trade Commission and other federal regulatory bodies: the power of subpoena; the power of enforcement through the federal courts.

From the outset Wagner had expected strong big business opposition to this proposal. He was surprised, however, by the vehemence, the passion with which the proposal and its author were attacked as hearings on it began in mid-March before the Senate Education and Labor Committee, chaired by Massachusetts's David I. Walsh. If the measure were adopted, it would "place the AF of L in control of every manufacturing industry" in the country. It would destroy the "happy and peaceful relationships" between labor and management that were now fostered by company unions,† would prohibit "the

---

*See p. 237.

†"A tranquil relationship between employer and employed, while eminently desirable, is not a sole desideratum," said Wagner in a *New York Times Magazine* article published on March 11, 1934. "It all depends upon the basis of tranquillity. The slave system of the Old South was tranquil as a summer's day. . . ."

practice of Christian brotherhood," would incite "class warfare." It would place "loyalty to labor unions above loyalty to God" and "out-Stalin Stalin, out-Soviet the Russian Soviets, and create a despotism." Thus the general tone and substance of full-page newspaper advertisements, letters to stockholders, handbills, speeches, press interviews, and hearings testimony by industry spokesmen, several of whom expressed the belief that labor disputes in an industry ought to be assigned for settlement to the NRA code authority for that industry. The proposal was also and similarly abused editorially by most large newspapers, though the arch-Republican New York *Herald Tribune* attacked it (March 26, 1934) not as communistic but as the road to fascism— a judgment in which, ironically, the American Communist press concurred. As for Wagner himself, though his courtesy, scrupulous fairness, and obviously sincere concern for his fellowman had theretofore rendered him largely immune from personal attack, they did not do so in this case. He was angrily assailed as a follower of Karl Marx (the irony of the Communist press judgment is thus sharpened), an exponent of the "Leftist Left in the Left wing of all Demo-Socialists in . . . Washington."[79]

Unexpected, too, and profoundly disappointing to the New York senator was the administration's attitude toward his bill. Asked about it at his press conference on March 2, Roosevelt said he hadn't read it. He remained publicly silent about it during the days and weeks of controversy over it which followed, though his statement of settlement of the automobile dispute was, of course, in effect a proclaimed White House disapproval of Wagner's proposal, at least in its present form, and was everywhere so interpreted.[80] Roosevelt wavered somewhat in his attitude during April and May, as the preliminary moves were made of that year's midterm election campaign and as an almost unprecedented labor militancy was manifested throughout the land, notably in Minneapolis and San Francisco, rendering impossible any precise measurement of the relative weights of the opposing pressures focused on Wagner's bill. Wagner himself displayed a willingness to compromise in order to get the gist of his proposal on the statute books, a foundation stone on which to build next year. After Hugh Johnson, having declined invitations to testify in person before the Walsh committee, had issued a public statement saying that employers should be permitted to *initiate* company unions but not to *dominate* them,* Wagner, to the dismay of his fellow liberals, publicly agreed to the indicated drastic change in his handiwork. He agreed to other revisions almost as drastic during conferences with Johnson, Richberg, Hopkins, Frances Perkins, and Labor Department Solicitor Charles E. Wyzanski, Jr.—conferences held in late April at the behest of the President. He, for instance, yielded to Secretary Perkins's insistence that the proposed labor board be set up not as an independent agency reporting directly to the President but as an integral part of the Labor Department. Roosevelt then told his press conference (April 30, 1934)

---

*"[T] the government should not favor any particular form of [labor] organization," said the NRA administrator, reiterating a central phrase of the auto dispute settlement statement.

that he "very much" wanted the Wagner bill to pass, though he stopped short of placing it on his list of "must" legislation.

In early June, however, he again changed his mind.

He was anxious in this election year to prevent any explosive growth of business hostility through the gap that had opened that spring in the theretofore generally amicable relations between the business community and the administration. It had been opened in part by a tragically dramatic controversy over airmail subsidization, occurring almost simultaneously with a battle over securities exchange legislation, the stories of which will be later told;* but a more important cause was the encouragement of labor organization by 7(a) and the increasing tendency of the business community bitterly to blame the White House for this. Roosevelt, therefore, viewed with some alarm the evident distinct possibility that the measure reported out by the Walsh committee in emasculated form (it was now called the National Industrial Adjustment Act) might have its original potency restored during full Senate debate of it. Amendments to this effect were ready for introduction. La Follette, Norris, Nye, Cutting, perhaps Wagner himself were prepared to do battle for such amendments. And there were signs that a Senate majority was disposed to accept them, then pass the measure approximately in its original form, *unless* the White House came out in flat opposition to it—something politician Roosevelt was loath to do.

He resorted to stratagem.

On June 13, 1934, he submitted to Congress, as substitute for the reported Wagner bill, a draft joint resolution that had been prepared by Richberg and Wyzanski at his orders. It proposed essentially nothing beyond a preservation of the status quo; it simply gave to the President, and this for a period of a single year, the power to appoint a "Board or Boards authorized and directed to investigate issues, facts, practices or activities of employers or employees in any controversy arising under Section 7(a)."[81] Wagner, under pressures personally exerted by the President and after two full days of hesitation, acquiesced unhappily in this move.

The New York senator, in consequence, found himself compelled to speak against his own measure when, on June 16, the joint resolution, having gone through the House on voice vote, came to the Senate floor for action. Bob La Follette at once called for action instead upon the committee-reported Wagner bill, and everyone knew he was armed with corrective amendments. Feeling ran high, tensions were great when Wagner rose to speak. He admitted that this was "one of the most embarrassing moments of my whole political life." He assured his fellow liberals that he remained absolutely committed to the principles of the original bill, saying, "Again we are failing to maintain a balance among production, profits, and wages. In order that the strong may not take advantage of the weak, every group must be equally strong." But the President was convinced that a time empty of new reforms was now needed

*See pp. 358–71.

"so that the processes of education and understanding may catch up with the social program that has been inaugurated," and since "[n]o one is better prepared than . . . [the President] to weigh the program in its entirety," he, Wagner, was "prepared to go along with him." He concluded on a pleading note: The fight was not ended; it would be continued next year.

Unpersuaded, La Follette and the others continued for some time their argument for the floor action they had proposed. But in the end they had to give up and permit the resolution, Public Resolution No. 44, to be adopted.

Bronson Cutting did so in a blaze of anger. From the outset, the Progressive Republican from New Mexico had sharply distinguished the New Deal, which he identified with a compassionate heart and a liberal mind, from Franklin Roosevelt, whom he increasingly identified with the duplicitous, the shallowly opportunistic, the essentially unprincipled. And Cutting, shortly before the final vote was taken, spoke the bitterness of myriads who saw things as he did.

"The New Deal," he cried out on the Senate floor, "is being strangled in the house of its friends!"[82]

VIII

CERTAINLY there was being violently demonstrated at that very moment in the streets of Minneapolis and on the streets and waterfront of San Francisco the crying need for new federal legislation, rigorously enforced, which resolved the issue of majority rule versus proportional representation, established firm guidelines for the conduct of employee organization elections and for subsequent labor-management negotiations, and in other respects clarified the practical meaning of Section 7(a).

Both Minneapolis and San Francisco were historically notoriously hostile to labor unions and union organizers. In each city the employers had been long and well organized (in Minneapolis the organization was called the Citizens' Alliance; in San Francisco, the Industrial Association) to maintain the open shop by whatever forceful means were required. And in each there had been since the Great War a full use of the yellow-dog contract, the blacklist, the forced membership in a company union, and the court injunction implemented by police power to crush out in its initial stage every effort toward genuine collective bargaining. Then had come the Norris-La Guardia Act of 1932. It struck from the employers' hands, at long last, what had theretofore been a virtually invincible injunction weapon. And this weakening of the employer relative to the employee in labor-management confrontations had seemingly been not merely confirmed but dramatically increased by the launching of the Blue Eagle, with its 7(a), in 1933.

It was in the shadow of the Blue Eagle's wings, in the fall of 1933, that Minneapolis's truck drivers began to organize themselves into Teamsters Union Local 574 under leadership that was radical (Trotskyite), tough, fearless, thoroughly honest, and remarkably able, being far more concerned to gain concrete benefits for the workers it represented and far less concerned with ideological purity as defined by some party line, hence far more flexible in negotiating procedures, than radicals of those years commonly were. The organization drive had the blessing of Minnesota's Farmer-Labor Governor Olson. It was highly successful. By early 1934 almost every truck driver in the city was a Teamster member.

Yet when Local 574 made to the employers a contract proposal for higher pay, shorter hours, better working conditions in general, and, above all, recognition of the union as exclusive employee bargaining agent, the employers through their Citizens' Alliance refused even to negotiate. They persisted in this after it had been pointed out to them by a powerless Regional Labor Board that such refusal was in clear violation of the NRA code they all had signed. So in mid-May the truckers went out on strike, virtually paralyzing a city the industrial and commercial life of which was more dependent upon transportation than the lives of most cities are. Still the alliance, determined to destroy the union, refused to negotiate. Instead, it employed forceful tactics of a kind that had succeeded for it in the past: It organized a "citizens' army" of some 150 of the city's young elite, each sworn in as a special police deputy, and with them attempted on May 22 to run trucks through striker picket lines into the city's central marketplace. The result was a pitched battle fought with clubs and lead pipes and baseball bats, at the end of which two men, both of them special deputies, lay dead and dozens were seriously injured. Other labor unions in the city now declared their solidarity with the Teamsters, and this pressure, plus the shock of bloodshed and Governor Olson's threat of martial law (he ordered the mobilization of the National Guard), forced the alliance to enter into negotiations, not *directly* with the Teamsters but through federal mediators, thereby *indirectly* recognizing the union. This was enough to cause the Teamster leadership to agree to a truce. The truckers went back to work, pending the outcome of the talks. But the talks dragged on for weeks, getting nowhere, until the alliance, still bent on crushing the union, abruptly withdrew from them. The strike was then (July 16) renewed, again with paralyzing effect upon the city and again with fatal violence. When a strikebreaker truck convoyed by police armed with shotguns was sent into a street blocked by a Teamster truck parked broadside, the police, without warning, opened fire upon the unarmed pickets in the truck and upon the street crowd. Sixty-seven people were shot down in a few minutes. Two of them died.[83]

Governor Olson then did what his oath of office required him to do: He moved forcefully to restore law and order. Again he threatened martial law, ordering both Teamsters and employers to accept a "compromise" proposal that had been worked out by federal mediators. It was a proposal that accorded closely with what the Teamsters had originally demanded, and the union promptly accepted it. The employers refused to do so. Thereupon Olson called out the National Guard and, with it, ruled the city by martial law. He ruled evenhandedly. When the Teamsters threatened renewed violence in the streets because he issued special permits for certain kinds of trucking (this, shouted the strike leaders, was strike breaking!), he ordered a dawn raid upon strike headquarters, with the arrest of several strike leaders. A similar raid was ordered against the Citizens' Alliance headquarters a couple of days later. But such evenhandedness was a notable departure from the local government's traditional siding with business in such situations, and the Teamsters gained from it at the expense of the alliance. Cracks opened in the employers' theretofore solid wall of opposition to union recognition. Two or three employers accepted the federal settlement plan, signing contracts with the Teamsters that embodied it. Then more employers did so. Finally, in the third week of August the alliance as a whole caved in—a resounding victory for labor in a year when it could count few victories of any kind. Its price was high, however. Minneapolis as a community had been torn asunder by what amounted to a class war, and the gaping, throbbing wound thus opened would require years to heal. . . .

In San Francisco the militant labor organization hatched under the Blue Eagle was a local of the International Longshoremen's Association (ILA) led by a thirty-three-year-old Australian immigrant named Harry Bridges. If not actually a member of the Communist party, Bridges, who had not become a U.S. citizen, was certainly a fervent Marxist who adhered closely to the party line on all political issues. Physically he was unimpressive—"a small, thin, somewhat haggard man in a much-worn overcoat, the collar turned up and pinned around the throat, and with a cap in his hand," as Frances Perkins saw him when first she met him,[84] but he was highly intelligent, selfless, a lion in courage, utterly convinced (correctly, in the present instance) of the employer's implacable, ruthless enmity to the workingman and absolutely incorruptible in an area of the labor movement that was rife with corruption.

The major grievance of the longshoremen, as it was the major exploitive device of the shipowner, was the prevailing system of hiring. The longshoreman was not hired on a weekly or monthly basis; he was hired anew, if at all, every day, on an hourly basis, with no firm assurance on any workday that he would have work on the next. Early each morning large crowds of men gathered in the street or in employer-run hiring halls along the Embarcadero for what was called the shape-up, each man hoping that some foreman would hire him for a day's work on a crew loading or unloading cargo, and often those hired had to pay for their jobs with kickbacks to the foreman of 10 to 20 percent of their wages, since this labor market was most emphatically a buyers' market. Always the number of applicants greatly exceeded the number of jobs, the ranks of the applicants being swollen by men who were not properly longshoremen at all but casual workers, drifters, men unskilled or, if skilled, unable to find work they were trained to do. As for the longshoreman's work, it was heaviest kind of physical labor. It was also dangerous; of all occupations, only mining had a higher rate of serious accidental injury.

From the employer's point of view, this system had the gratifying effect of keeping the pay scale at a rock-bottom low (a San Francisco longshoreman made less than $45 a month on the average in 1933) and of enabling expenditures for the comfort and safety of workers to be reduced to virtually nothing.

Proportionately degrading and dehumanizing was the system's effect upon longshoremen. These saw the fog-enshrouded Embarcadero in the chill of dawn as a "slave market," themselves slaves on the auction block, and indeed, the treatment they commonly received on the job was little, if any, better than that commonly accorded black field hands on plantations in the antebellum South. This had been so in the best of times. But with the depression working conditions had become much worse, for the employers, their profits reduced to paper-thin margins or wiped out altogether, resorted to the speedup in an effort to keep down labor costs, with the result that the very huskiest of longshoremen were worked to near exhaustion, while the accident rate was sharply increased.

In late February 1934 Harry Bridges pushed through the Pacific Coast ILA convention, against the convention's conservative leadership, resolutions calling for replacement of the shape-up with a union hiring hall, a substantial pay increase, a six-hour day, a thirty-hour week, and recognition of the union as the longshoremen's sole collective bargaining agency. The San Francisco local presented these resolutions to the shipowners a few days later as a set of demands which must be met by March 23, else a strike would begin on that date. But the employers of longshoremen in San Francisco were, in one major respect, like the employers of truck drivers in Minneapolis insofar as their overriding purpose, for the achievement of which they were willing to pay the cost of a strike, was the destruction of the burgeoning union. They were even eager for a showdown they were convinced they would win. They were aided in their purpose by the federal executive's own stated labor policy: When they refused to consider any change in the shape-up, they pointed out that the proposed union hiring hall, being tantamount to a closed shop, was illegal according to Johnson-Richberg's reiterated interpretations of 7(a), in which the President had concurred. This employer attitude was by no means uniquely San Franciscan as applied to longshoremen; it was manifestly shared by employers all along the Pacific shore, from San Diego to Seattle, as one local after another of the Pacific Coast ILA endorsed the Bridges demands and prepared to strike also, closing down the entire West Coast, if the demands were not met.

In the third week of March, Roosevelt made direct appeal to the San Francisco ILA local for a postponement of the strike until a special board composed of the chairmen of the three coast labor boards had a chance to investigate the issues and propose a basis for settlement. The union did as the President asked. And on April 1, after four days of hearings, this board, having suggested that the wage and hour question be arbitrated by yet another board, made two specific recommendations: (1) that the present shape-up be replaced by hiring halls that were *jointly* controlled by longshoremen and employers and (2) that representation elections be conducted among the longshoremen in each port, under the auspices of the regional labor boards, whereby the majority would decide who spoke for them all at the bargaining table. Alas, this latter recommendation came hard and shatteringly against the terms of settlement of the auto dispute, announced by Roosevelt only a few days before (March 25), a policy statement that rejected majority rule while embracing proportional representation. San Francisco's employers would recognize the ILA as bargaining agent for those, and *only* those, who voted for ILA candidates in the representation election. Minority representatives would also be recognized. Since this virtually assured the ineffectiveness of labor in any allegedly joint control of hiring (ILA activists would almost certainly be blacklisted), Bridges and his men flatly rejected this proposal even after the national president of the ILA, Joseph P. Ryan, joined with conservative Assistant Labor Secretary Edward McGrady to urge its acceptance.*

And so, on May 9, the strike began, closing every port on the Pacific coast, though the central focus of the whole effort remained on Bridges's San Francisco union.

In San Francisco at the outset, and for many weeks thereafter, there was little violence. But as the shutdown extended into late June, well beyond the point at which its cost could be easily borne by shipowners, the Industrial Association, which on June 5 had assumed command of the employers' side of the dispute, announced to local officials its intention to employ whatever strikebreaking force was needed to open warehouses and move cargo. In great alarm, for there would be no doubt this action would precipitate fatal violence on streets and docks, San Francisco's mayor and California's Senator Hiram Johnson sent urgent messages to the White House begging for preventive action by the President.

Roosevelt was then about to embark aboard the USS *Houston* (he was to sail on July 1) for a 14,000-mile six-week cruise down the Atlantic coast to the Panama Canal and through the Canal to the Hawaiian Islands and back, and as part of his desk-clearing preparations for this holiday he was in process of setting up by executive order a National Labor Relations Board—this under the authority of the resolution, Public Resolution No. 44, which he had pushed through Congress two weeks before to prevent the otherwise probably affirmative action upon Wagner's labor bill. He would issue the order on June 29. But in prompt response to the appeal from San Francisco, he now anticipated this action by ordering the creation on June 26 of a National Longshoreman's Board† of three members (a Catholic archbishop, a prominent San Francisco attorney, Assistant Labor Secretary McGrady) which was to conduct another investigation of the issues and, if authorized to do so by the disputants, arbitrate the hiring hall question, with special attention to the employers' use of the blacklist.

This presidential action gave the employers pause, but only for a few days. On July 3, a Tuesday, the Industrial Association made a tentative yet strong

---

*Ryan, it should be added, had no standing with rank-and-file ILA members anywhere. As labor boss of the notoriously corrupt New York City waterfront, himself a close associate of organized crime figures, Ryan was reputed to win his elected office by fraudulent means and to keep his union members in line by brutal means while selling them out, repeatedly, to the employers.

†Though nominally a "national" board, its jurisdiction was specifically limited by Roosevelt to the West Coast.

probe of the striking longshoremen's will to fight for their cause. Escorted by some 700 policemen, strikebreaking truckers attempted a run through the picket lines on the Embarcadero; they were turned back after a four-hour street fight in which scores were injured, more than two dozen seriously enough to require hospitalization. The next day there was quiet in the city, save for the fireworks noise of Independence Day celebrations. The quiet, however, was ominous. Both the association and the longshoremen, who were now joined by the Teamsters and by members of some other local unions on the picket lines, prepared for renewed violent struggle. It came on the morrow, July 5. The association then sent hundreds of strikebreakers into the dock area, convoyed by 800 heavily armed police, in an all-out effort to open the port—and there was "war in San Francisco . . . blood ran red in the streets," to quote the San Francisco *Chronicle*'s account of what became known to the nation as Bloody Thursday.[85] With brickbats, clubs, stones, tear gas, and, at last, blazing guns in the hands of police, running battles were fought in a series extending through a long afternoon into evening. At nightfall the port remained closed. But scores of men lay seriously injured, some of them critically. Two pickets were dead. And at midnight, by order of California's Republican governor, Frank F. Merriam, national guardsmen, 5,000 strong, occupied the waterfront. Their bayoneted ranks patrolled the Embarcadero thereafter—a show of seemingly irresistible force predominantly exerted, of course, on the side of the employers.

All the same, Bloody Thursday proved to be, in ultimate effect, a victory for the longshoremen.

On July 9 many thousands marched up Market Street behind the coffins of the two slain pickets, grimly demonstrating labor solidarity in the city and arousing the sympathy of a considerable portion of the general populace not normally concerned with labor's cause. During the following two days several of San Francisco's unions, including some under highly conservative leadership, went out on sympathy strikes. On July 12, in defiance of their own national officers, the local Teamsters extended their dock strike into a strike of the whole city. The next day the San Francisco Central Labor Council voted by overwhelming majority in favor of Harry Bridges's proposal of a general strike. And three days after that, on Monday, July 16, this general strike, involving 130,000 workers, formally began.

It effected no such paralysis of the community, hence constituted no such social revolutionary action, as local Communists had called for. The central strike committee, as it exempted all essential services from the shutdown, gave to "essential" a liberal definition. Not only were light and power supply, water supply, and medical and hospital service permitted to continue uninterrupted, but so were milk and bread delivery, ferry operation, newspaper publication, and the serving of meals by nineteen restaurants. Moreover, the strike committee's members were themselves more than a little frightened by the power they now wielded, having no idea of what to do next—a fact obvious by Tuesday morning to all close and clear-eyed observers.

The event, nevertheless, sent shock waves of pure terror through the employing class all along the Pacific shore. Vividly recollected were Big Bill Haywood with his "One Big Union" and his Wobblies and the general strike of Seattle in 1919. There could be no doubt that the general strike was the most potent of all the weapons that workers could employ to subvert the social order —and had not Communists in San Francisco issued the first call for this present action? What was happening, therefore, must be the beginning of a social revolution which, unless the government acted promptly against it, would soon engulf every West Coast state and possibly involve the whole of the United States in civil war. Such was the immediate conclusion of San Francisco's mayor, California's governor, California's senior U.S. senator, and the governor of Oregon. Old Progressive Hiram Johnson, once himself regarded by conservatives as a dangerous radical, wired his friend Harold Ickes, "Here is revolution not only in the making but with initial actuality," a "disaster" for San Francisco and the "possible ruin of the Pacific Coast." California's Governor Merriam published his intention to ask the President to send federal troops to crush rebellion. Oregon's Governor Julius Meier, directly addressing Roosevelt by means of the *Houston*'s radio, not only asked for federal troops "to prevent insurrection which if not checked will develop into civil war" but also requested, or strongly recommended, that Roosevelt "delegate to General Johnson the power of your great office . . . to enforce settlement"—presumably with the U.S. Army.[86]

IX

It was by unhappy coincidence that Hugh S. Johnson was on the West Coast at that time.

One of the things Roosevelt had tried to do as he prepared to embark on his long vacation was persuade the harried, obviously unwell NRA administrator to take an extended holiday of his own. An earlier attempt to persuade him into a European trip, ostensibly to survey the handling of industrial recovery problems there, had foundered on the hard mistrust, the actual enmity which had by then developed between the general and Donald Richberg. With good reason, Johnson suspected that Richberg, intending to succeed to his job, was attempting to undermine his standing in the White House; he saw this proposed European trip as an element of Richberg's plot; and he promptly carried to the White House this suspicion, along with his profound hurt over the President's seeming concurrence in the machinations. There had ensued showdown scenes in the Executive Office and the Oval Room. Almost unanimously Roosevelt's advisers were of the opinion that he should accept the resignation which Johnson was prepared to submit, if not also the resignation which Richberg did in fact submit. Instead, typically, he smoothed things over with a temporary patchwork arrangement. In an executive order issued on June 30 he appointed Richberg the executive secretary of the Executive Council and the executive director of National Emergency Council "from and after July 1, 1934," replacing Frank C. Walker, "who is hereby, at his request, temporarily relieved of the duties of said offices." He also created an Industrial Emergency Committee (on it were the interior secretary, the labor secretary, the relief administrator, the NRA administrator) the "duty" of which was "to make recommendations to the President, through its director, with respect to problems of relief, public works, labor disputes and industrial recovery. . . ." He then appointed Richberg this committee's director and ordered that he, Richberg, "be given leave of absence as General Counsel of the National Recovery Administration until September 1. . . ."[87] As for Johnson, he was presidentially persuaded of his indispensability and so stayed on in his NRA post, though, as has been said, he was urged to take at once an extended recreational leave.

Instead, in the second week of July, the general went off on a speaking tour.

White House secretaries Louis Howe and Marvin McIntyre almost tearfully begged him not to go. They also sent urgent coded messages to Roosevelt aboard the *Houston,* insisting that it was "highly undesirable" for the general to make public speeches at this time and that an immediate vacation was "essential" for him. But Johnson himself assured the President that the upcoming speeches were to be on a "purely noncontroversial and constructive basis," he promised to take two weeks of vacation as soon as the speaking tour was completed, and so Roosevelt permitted him to proceed.

Thus it came about that Johnson, having delivered himself of a couple of characteristically colorful but uncharacteristically innocuous addresses in the Midwest, was in Portland, Oregon, on the eve of the general strike, and there, in his agitation over the impending event (it was an agitation which naturally augmented the already excessive fears of Oregon's Governor Meier), departed from his prepared text to say it was "madness" not to settle this dispute at the bargaining table, that "strikes never got anything for anybody." The latter remark, so obviously historically untrue, served to fortify labor's conviction that in this dispute, as in all other labor-management confrontations, the NRA administrator stood on the employers' side. He arrived in San Francisco on the afternoon of the day the general strike began. He checked in at the Palace Hotel. There he learned that the emergency had caused University of California administrators to cancel his speech, which was to have been delivered next day on the Berkeley campus. He was dismayed in proportion to his wish to speak, which was very great. But his dismay was short-lived. The Palace happened to be the hotel in which California's newspaper publishers had established strike emergency headquarters. From them, who were among the most reactionary of their generally illiberal breed, he obtained biased up-to-the-minute information concerning the issues, the prevailing attitudes, the events of the strike (he seems not to have conferred with any strike leader), and he easily persuaded them to exert pressure upon university authorities to rescind the speech cancellation order. The pressure was effective.

So on the afternoon of Tuesday, July 17, riding one of the ferries whose operators had been exempted from the strike, Johnson crossed the Bay and was driven to the Greek open-air theater on the university campus. There, to the large crowd before him and through microphones to a radio audience that

constituted a majority of the entire Bay Area population, he addressed words
that were as verbal oil poured upon social conflagration.* Attempting to drive
a wedge between AFL conservatives and the Bridges leadership of San Francisco labor, he added fuel to flames of terror among the propertied class as he
asserted that Communists had seized opportunities presented them by the
"extreme and unreasonable" stand the shipping industry had initially taken
against collective bargaining, had managed to employ labor's just grievances
as a means of gaining control of the unions, and had then maneuvered rank-
and-file workingmen into a general strike which they, the Communists, had
planned and which they now directed—a strike that was a "threat to the
community . . . a menace to government." The clear duty of "patriotic" and
"responsible labor organization" was to "run these subversive influences out
of its ranks like rats." Otherwise, "[i]f the federal government did not act, the
people would act, and it would wipe out this subversive element as you clean
off a chalk mark on a blackboard with a wet sponge."[88]

On that same afternoon, in the streets of San Francisco, there was a resurgence of the vigilante activity to which this city had been peculiarly prone ever
since the gold rush days of the mid-nineteenth century. Well-organized bands
of violent men invaded union headquarters and the office of the local Communist newspaper. They shattered windows, smashed office equipment, destroyed
files, and beat up scores of people with fists and clubs so severely they required
medical treatment or, in dozens of cases, hospitalization. There were thousands of national guardsmen patrolling the streets that afternoon; they made
no move to prevent or halt the violence. As for the police, well-armed squads
of them actually aided and abetted the vigilante activity, "mopping up" after
the mob had departed and arresting for "vagrancy" well over 300 of those who
had been attacked. Not a single vigilante was arrested. . . .

But this continuation or renewal of the violence of Bloody Thursday, a
renewal that seemed to many causally linked with the inflammatory demagoguery of Hugh S. Johnson, had an effect contrary to its intention. A popular
aversion to Industrial Association tactics was increased, as was a popular
sympathy for the longshoremen and their allies, and the violence did *not* lead
to that federal intervention to "restore law and order," with the U.S. Army
as strikebreaker, at which the employers aimed.

Such intervention was strongly favored by Secretary of State Hull and
Attorney General Homer Cummings in Washington; it was urged upon the
President in a number of wireless messages delivered to him aboard the *Hous-
ton,* which was then in the Pacific, heading northwest toward Hawaii. As
Roosevelt himself put it seven weeks later in an off-the-record comment to
reporters, "In the San Francisco strike a lot of people completely lost their

---

*There was perhaps a causal connection between the general's West Coast posturings and the fact
that he was accompanied on this trip, as on most he made, by his confidential secretary, Robbie.
He seems always to have been inordinately anxious to appear in her eyes the most masterfully
masculine of tough fighting men.

heads and telegraphed me, 'For God's sake, come back; turn the ship around.'
. . . Everybody demanded that I sail into San Francisco Bay, all flags flying
and guns double shotted, and end the strike." But of course, not "everybody"
made such demand. Quite as emphatic was advice precisely to the contrary,
given by administration officials long experienced in labor relations. On the day
before the general strike began, Louis Howe and Labor Secretary Perkins
insisted to the President that the "only danger [of] San Francisco strike is that
mayor is badly frightened and his fear has infected entire city." Frances
Perkins was convinced that labor in the troubled city was not out to subvert
lawful government but rather to compel employer obedience of the law as labor
understood it—the law guaranteeing the right of collective bargaining. If the
President cut short his trip in order to intervene directly, she warned, his
action would "start the very panic it is necessary to avoid."[89] And of the truth
of this Roosevelt was easily persuaded, his remarkable ability to stay calm and
cool amid crisis being one of the major assets of his leadership.

So the *Houston* sailed on to a joyous welcome in Honolulu for a President
who said and did nothing at all about the strike while in San Francisco the
weight of events tipped the overall balance definitely toward labor's side of the
argument and toward a localized partial correction of the Johnson-Richberg
labor policy. Within a few hours after Johnson's Berkeley speech, San Francisco's Central Labor Council voted 207 to 180 in favor of asking for federal
arbitration of the dispute. Two days later, responding to a request by the new
Longshoremen's Board, and despite protests from Bridges, the council voted,
191 to 174, to call off the general strike and submit the issues to binding
arbitration by the board. San Francisco's longshoremen then voted to end the
dock strike as soon as the employers agreed also to binding arbitration. So did
other ILA locals up and down the coast. And these actions resulted in such
pressure upon the employers to go along that reluctantly, after some days of
hesitation, they did so. The long strike came to an end. On July 27, as Roosevelt prepared to sail from Hawaii aboard the *Houston* next day, ILA members
moved cargo on San Francisco's waterfront for the first time in more than
eleven weeks.

And when the Longshoremen's Board handed down its decision on October
12, 1934, the longshoremen won most of what they had originally struck for:
abolition of the brutal shape-up, its replacement by hiring halls "maintained
and operated jointly" by union and employer (the union selected the dis-
patcher, thus preventing blacklisting), a shortening of the workweek but (with
overtime pay) a substantial increase in total wage, various improvements in
working conditions, and recognition of the union as bargaining agent.

9

⇥⫸✕⫷⇤

The View from Russian Hill:
An Interlude and Retrospect

I

IT was near half past ten on a night in late July in San Francisco, and a nearly full moon rode high in the sky, when the two women walked into a tiny park atop Russian Hill and seated themselves upon a bench. There had been no published word of the First Lady's presence in the city; there were no prying eyes, no cocked ears, to violate the privacy of the two friends; they felt very close to each other and very happy, utterly at peace with themselves in a lovely, peaceful world as they sat there looking far out across the town and the Bay, talking quietly. Below them, in the moon-silvered streets, there was no sign of the labor strife that had lately racked the city, and even the fortress-island of Alcatraz, which was at the center of their distant view and on which rose up blackly the newest and grimmest of federal prisons, was beautiful in moonlight. Lorena Hickok saw it as "a big, lighted battleship floating" in the sea.[1]

Eleanor Roosevelt may have had a different metaphor. She could have been reminded of two visual experiences she had had in the late summer of 1929 (how long ago that seemed!)*—one of them in that balconied hotel on the Rhine whence she had looked out across the great river, itself remindful of the mighty Hudson, upon the grim fortress of Coblenz on the opposite bank; the other in that fisherman's rowboat in a shallow sea just off the Normandy shore whence she had looked out across a shimmering expanse of water upon the towering fortress-abbey of Mont-St.-Michel.

Then, as now, the summer night had been soft and warm, with a gentle breeze.

Then, as now, the world had been filled with moonlight.

And now, as then, the radiance of the moon was as the Blessed Virgin's blessing upon all that it illuminated, the feminine principle dissolved in liquid light and poured down with soothing softening effect upon emphatically masculine constructions. The outline of the fortress prison of Alcatraz, unforgivingly hard in the blazing light of noon, was now in the light of the moon mysteriously shadowed, softly blurring into a darkly silvered sea, a darkly silvered sky, as the outline of the fortress-church of St. Michael had seemed to melt into the Norman sea and sky while yet retaining all its strength, all its firmness of line, in moonlight a half decade (ages) ago.

---

*See Davis, *FDR: The New York Years,* pp. 133–40.

II

THE intertwining of harsh reality with a dream of love, the fusing of tender feeling with practical toughness, had been characteristic of the linked lives of these two women ever since the end on Campobello of their three-week holiday trip together, almost precisely a year before.

Most of the time they had been physically separated by hundreds of miles, sometimes by thousands.

Hickok's itinerary as Harry Hopkins's investigative field reporter had been a wide-ranging zigzag across the continent, and none other in all the land now had a personal view of America in depression that was more sweepingly comprehensive or more individually detailed. She had traveled through Pennsylvania and West Virginia and Kentucky in August 1933; through upstate New York into northern New England, all the way to Eastport on the Bay of Fundy and back, in September; from New York City westward into the upper Mississippi Valley, the northern Great Plains, the corn belt, in October, November, December; deep into the Deep South in the first months of 1934; through Texas into the far Southwest and then back again through the southern border states in the spring; then again westward, all the way to the West Coast, with a pause to view the progress and human effects of TVA, another pause to view the progress and human effects of the great drouth which, by the summer of 1934, was transforming much of the high plains into a dust bowl. From Los Angeles, in the first days of July, she had gone southeastward into the Imperial Valley, where she was appalled by a pervasive and wholly vicious "fear of Communist agitators"* and whence, from El Centro, where the temperature was 120 degrees in the shade, she moved northward through California's great central valley to Sacramento, there to meet Eleanor, who was flying in (incognito, she hoped) from Chicago. Some thousands of miles of this travel had been in a secondhand Chevrolet convertible, nicknamed Bluette, which Eleanor had purchased as a gift for her friend but which Hick had insisted upon paying for in monthly installments sent by check to the White House. Bluette, alas, had no long life in Hick's inexperienced hands (she had had to learn to drive *after* the car was given her); the car was demolished in an accident on the road in the late spring of 1934, an accident from which Hick emerged unscathed. Eleanor had then lent Hick her Buick (Hick drove it to

---

*"If you don't agree with them, you are a Communist, of course," wrote Hick to Eleanor from El Centro on July 3, 1934, referring to the Associated Farmers, whose utterly ruthless exploitation of migrant labor, especially as regards housing, had provoked labor trouble. "There is a rumor here that they beat General [Pelham G.] Glassford up before he left the valley. There is also a story that they gave him knockout drops in a cocktail. He himself told one of our field people that the county agent—representing the Department of Agriculture in the valley, if you please —threatened him with the possibility of being 'taken for a ride' if he didn't agree with 'public opinion' in the valley!" This was the same Glassford who had been superintendent of the Metropolitan Police Department of Washington, D.C., and who had befriended the bonus marchers, in the summer of 1932. (See Davis, *FDR: The New York Years,* pp. 346–49.) He had come into the Imperial Valley as a federal labor conciliator.[2]

Dayton, Ohio, to report on a rural cooperative project there in late May), and it was with money advanced by Eleanor, while insurance claims from the wreck were being settled, that Hick now bought a brand-new Plymouth.

As for Eleanor's travels through the year, they had been only somewhat less constant and far-ranging than Hick's. She made frequent speaking trips, including one to Chicago, where she spoke at the Century of Progress Exposition. She was often in New York City, often at Hyde Park, where her headquarters continued to be Val-Kill Cottage; she was in Warm Springs with her husband in late autumn of 1933 and was there again, briefly, in late February; she was many times back and forth between Washington and a major project of hers in West Virginia; she visited her son James in Boston, her stuffy Cousin Susie (Susan Parish) in stuffy Newport; she drove from Hyde Park to Groton with her mother-in-law and husband to attend the fiftieth anniversary celebration of the founding of Groton School ("F. spoke well," she informed Hick, "& it was a nice evening with well-deserved praise for the Rector & Mrs. Peabody. 451 graduates were back. . . ."[3]); and she managed to snatch from her crowded schedule a few days spent with Louis Howe, whose health was now fading fast (his cigarette-induced emphysema was slowly smothering him to death), at Howe's seaside cabin on Horseneck Beach in Massachusetts.

But amid these separate journeyings the two friends had had several direct contacts during the year, had spent an amount of time alone together that was, in the circumstances, astonishing, if by no means as much time as they both longed for. When Hick was in Washington, she stayed in the White House. Indeed, at Eleanor's insistence, 1600 Pennsylvania Avenue became her official legal residence, the address to which her tax forms and, when she was in Washington, her paychecks were directed. She was there for many days at a time in September, October, and December 1933, in February and May and June 1934. On three memorable occasions the two had met and spent days together far away from Washington. They were together for several days in West Virginia in mid-August 1933. They had a weekend together at Warm Springs late in the following February. They were together, too, on Hick's forty-first birthday (March 7, 1934), if not in the way Hick had hoped they would be or that Eleanor, in her original planning for the event, had intended. Hick was a little-publicized member of the party (it included reporters and photographers and, part of the time, Rex Tugwell) that accompanied Eleanor on a greatly publicized eleven-day trip from Washington to Puerto Rico and back, March 4 through March 15.

The two would have been in close daily communication anyway, no matter what the physical distance between them, for they kept the promises they had made each other during the last days of the interregnum, when a reluctant, almost distraught Eleanor was preparing to move into the White House. By telegram and long distance phone, whenever necessary, the two kept each other informed of where each would be during the week or so immediately ahead, and every night, no matter how weary she was after a day crowded with activity, and no matter how late the hour (it was sometimes 2:00 A.M.), each wrote a letter to the other. Often these letters, dashed off as rapidly as the writing hand could move, were ten or more pages long.

This correspondence, treasured by Lorena Hickok throughout her life, was deposited by her (out of what motive? for what intended effect?) in a research library for Roosevelt scholars as her life drew to a close. By the terms of her bequest, it would be opened to researchers ten years after her death, and by it, scholars were then to be given, among other things, tangential, highly personalized glimpses of historic events.

One such was of the diplomatic recognition of the Soviet Union by the United States, nine months after Roosevelt's inauguration.

The initiative was Roosevelt's; he took it a few weeks after the collapse of the World Monetary and Economic Conference. He proceeded cautiously. A survey of press opinion told him in September that, of 1,139 newspapers, less than 27 percent opposed recognition, many of them not strongly, whereas 63 percent favored recognition, most of them quite strongly out of a belief that it would open up a big market for American exports while reducing the danger of military aggression by Japan against Russia. An assessment of general public opinion revealed indifference on the part of most and, among those concerned, a majority in favor of recognition. This was true even among conservatives. The only really serious opposition came from the Roman Catholic hierarchy, and this opposition Roosevelt greatly reduced, indeed almost eliminated, through one of his most amazing exercises of personal charm. He called to him, for warm, friendly conference, Father Edmund A. Walsh of Georgetown University. (Georgetown, a Catholic institution in Washington, was the only university to train young men specifically for the Foreign Service; this resulted in a church influence over State Department operations that was as powerful as it was subtle.) Within an hour Walsh, the outspoken leader of opposition to recognition, was persuaded by Roosevelt to make a public statement saying that the President could and should be trusted to do what was right in this matter.

As Roosevelt's agent William Bullitt had by then made an informal approach to Moscow through the chief representative in the United States of Amtorg, the Soviet trade corporation. Letters were subsequently exchanged between the President of the United States and Mikhail Kalinin, president of the All Union Central Executive Committee in Moscow. In early November Maxim Litvinov, people's commissar for foreign affairs, came from Moscow to Washington for negotiations. And by mid-November these negotiations, including two lengthy face-to-face meetings between Roosevelt and Litvinov, were completed. The various agreement documents, including one that guaranteed U.S. nationals in Russia full freedom of religious worship, were ready for signature by the evening of November 16, the evening of the Roosevelts' official dinner for cabinet members. After dinner the fifty people who had sat at table went into the East Room for music and were joined there by other guests, including Maxim Litvinov.

Shortly after midnight, on the morning of Friday, November 17, Roosevelt and Litvinov, in the Oval Room, signed simultaneously the recognition papers.[4]

A great many people at the time regarded this event as of earthshaking importance. Eleanor's comments upon it, to Hick, were casual, offhand. On Saturday, November 18, when telephone communications between the White House and the Kremlin, via shortwave radio, were ceremoniously inaugurated with a call to Moscow by Litvinov, Eleanor wrote Hick: "It was a busy & rather fruitless day. I started to ride and then Litvinoff was late & Henry Morgenthau wanted a ceremony to swear him in [as treasury secretary] so by 12 that took place & it was too late to ride. Well, Russia is recognized, Bullitt goes as Ambassador. I wonder if that is why F.D.R. has been so content to let Missy play with him! She'll have another embassy to visit next summer anyway! I hope Henry will do well in the Treasury. . . ." In a following letter she commented upon what seemed to her a remarkable lack of popular excitement over the development: "How quietly everyone takes resumption of intercourse with Russia."[5]

More representative of the correspondence in general, if also more frankly expressive of passionate desire than most, was a letter from Hickok dated December 5, 1933. It covered fourteen pages, the bulk of them devoted to descriptions of what she had seen and heard that day, first on the flat cultivated plain of the Red River Valley, then on the flat cutover timberland south of Red Lake, in northern Minnesota. "Tonight it's Bemidji . . ." Hick began, "not a bad hotel, and one day nearer you. Only eight more days. Twenty-four hours from now and it will be only seven more—just one week! I've been trying today to bring back your face—to remember just *how* you look. Funny how even the dearest face will fade away in time. Most clearly I remember your eyes, with a kind of teasing smile in them, and the feeling of that soft spot just northeast of the corner of your mouth against my lips. I wonder what we'll do when we meet—what we'll say. Well—[here the words become cryptic, and all the more revealing for being so] I'm rather proud of us, aren't you? I think we've done rather well." The letter closed: "Goodnight, dear one. I want to put my arms around you and kiss you at the corner of your mouth. And in a little more than a week from now—I shall!"[6]

Eleanor's letter to Hick from the White House on the following night, which was before she had received Hick's from Bemidji, told of going "to hear F. speak to the Federated Council of Churches & it really was a good speech." Speaking to several hundred delegates from twenty-five Christian denominations in a convention auditorium and to millions via national radio hookup, Roosevelt had said:

> From the bottom of my heart I believe that this beloved country of ours is entering upon a time of great gain. That gain can well include a greater material prosperity if we take care that it is a prosperity for a hundred and twenty million human beings and not a prosperity for the top of the pyramid alone. It can be a prosperity socially controlled for the common good. It can be a prosperity built on spiritual and social

values rather than on special privilege and special power. . . . The churches, while they remain wholly free from even the suggestion of interference in Government, can at the same time teach their millions of followers that they have the right to demand of the Government of their choosing, the maintenance and furtherance of "a more abundant life."

Had Hick listened to this? Eleanor wondered in her letter. "Funny everything I do my thoughts fly to you, never are you out of them dear & just one week from tomorrow I hope I'll be meeting you. Of course the long separation has been hardest on you because so much of the time you've been with strangers but on the other hand your job is more stimulating than mine."[7]

On the night after that Hick was in Hibbing, Minnesota, where she addressed to Eleanor a long letter that described the towns of the Mesabi iron range, the mines of which were under the control of U.S. Steel, as shining islands of prosperity in the dark sea of depression that spread across northern Minnesota. The letter ended: "Oh, my dear—I can hardly wait to see you! Day after tomorrow, Minneapolis and letters from you. A week from now—right this minute—I'll be with you! Good night, my dear. God keep you." Next night, in the White House, Eleanor wrote Hick of a meeting she had arranged between Harry Hopkins and actress-producer Eva Le Gallienne to discuss the development of a federal theater project, funded with federal relief money, to provide employment for presently unemployed, or misemployed, actors, actresses, producers, directors, playwrights. But she spoke of this dismissively. "Dear," she concluded, "nothing is important except that my last trip will be over tomorrow morning before you come & I hope the next one will be with you. Less than a week now. Take care of yourself. I know I won't be able to talk when we first meet but though I can remember just how you look I shall want to look long & very lovingly at you."[8]

There was a great mutual emotional dependence. Yet there was a difference in quantity and kind between the dependencies, considered separately, and of this they both were aware, Hick more strongly so than Eleanor. Eleanor retained and continuously, actively nourished her intimate friendships with Nancy Cook, Marion Dickerman, Elinor Morgenthau, Caroline O'Day, Esther Lape, Elizabeth Read, Earl Miller, among many others less intimate —friendships formed years before she met Hick. She had a constant abundance of parental concerns. Currently she was deeply involved with her daughter Anna's troubled marital affairs. Estranged but not yet divorced from Curtis Dall, Anna had fallen passionately in love with a handsome, moody young newspaperman named John Boettiger, assistant chief of the Washington bureau of the Chicago *Tribune* (of all papers!), whose own first marriage ended in divorce in November 1933,* and Eleanor, who was very fond of Boettiger

---

*Writes Doris Faber on p. 160 of her *Life of Lorena Hickok:* "[W]hen Louis Howe told the First Lady that the White House press room was buzzing over John Boettiger's divorce it provoked a remarkable little outburst [on Eleanor's part] to Hick. 'One cannot hide things in this world can one? How lucky you are not a man!' After Hick glumly replied that there was probably some gossip about them anyway, E.R. dismissed Hick's fear with an airy comment that anyway 'they' must think the two of them stood separation rather well."

and thoroughly approved of her daughter's plan to marry him, went so far as to aid and abet secret rendezvous of the lovers, defying the expressed wish of her husband, who had said that Anna should not see Boettiger until she herself was divorced. Eleanor wrote of this to Hick in early December: "I've been glibly telling F.D.R. she [Anna] spent her holiday in N.Y. May I be forgiven!" (She added: "I must write Earl & sign a mountain of mail so goodnight sweet one. Eleven days from now!")[9] For Hick there were no such distractions from, or mitigations of, her one great love. She resented and feared her beloved's other attachments; she suffered a constant nagging sense of insecurity in her love, a chronic fear of impending rejection. And on occasion this suffering burst forth to envelop Eleanor in bitter, angrily accusatory flames of anguish.

It did so during Hick's stay in the White House in the week before Christmas 1933, the time together toward which both of them had looked so longingly during their six full weeks of separation. Eleanor, with a multitude of obligations to fulfill daily, was unable to spend as much time alone with Hick as Hick had counted on, and Hick, increasingly hurt, finally blew up when Eleanor, having positively promised that she would spend a certain evening with her, spent it instead with Anna. Eleanor was abjectly apologetic. There was a scene of reconciliation. Hick then went up to her apartment in New York City, where she was to hostess a party for friends on Christmas Eve. Eleanor managed a brief visit with her there a couple of days before Christmas, writing immediately upon her return to Washington: ". . . I went to sleep saying a little prayer, 'God give me depth enough not to hurt Hick again.' Darling, I know I'm not up to you in many ways but I love you dearly. . . ." At one o'clock on Christmas morning she wrote: "Darling, I'm just back from midnight service & it was lovely & I was glad I went alone & now dear I will call you in a minute. . . . I wished & prayed for many things for you as I knelt in the dark tonight. May you have your heart's desire & be happy & at peace this day & forever more." There followed words which some might find incongruous with the overall impression, as regards the nature of the relationship between these two, made upon readers of this correspondence four decades later. "Darling the love one has for one's children is different & not even Anna could be to me what you are," wrote Eleanor. "I want to protect her, but I know her life must claim her & I must only touch it where I can help. There is a difference with friends of our own age & with you there is a much deeper understanding and quality of companionship not possible with youth. . . ."[10]

Fewer than twenty-four hours later she was again writing Hick, about Christmas in the White House, mentioning at the outset that she had talked to her husband about the possibility of her accompanying Hick to Puerto Rico when Hick went there, as planned, to report on the island's relief problems. "Franklin said I could ask Harry Hopkins . . . & he said nothing about not flying when I said we'd go that way. I only wonder if I'll be a nuisance for you for of course we can't keep it quiet & there will be reporters & press. . . ." She continued: "We started [Christmas] with stockings, then breakfast, church & Anna & the boys & I walked home. After lunch which the kids had with us we opened presents nearly all afternoon. . . . Dinner was jolly & then F.D.R.

read parts of the Christmas Carol. . . . The young ones then went dancing including Fjr. who has had & still has a sore throat! . . . It was good to hear your voice & you shall dine in bed & sleep all you want if you'll just stay here and be happy. Don't think I don't know what it is like to be jealous, or to want to be alone, because I know both emotions tho I succeed as a rule in subduing them with laughter! When I don't, I give you & myself a pretty bad time, don't I, but I promise I'll be quite reasonable & in hand before you get here Friday![11]

Hick departed for her travels into the Deep South in the second week of January 1934, after a weekend in the White House. On Wednesday, January 24, she was in Florida, after an intensely busy week in Georgia, and of Florida's general life, CWA operation, and relief problems, her reports to Hopkins in following days were as anxious and disturbing as they were vivid. "[T]his state seems to be chock full of politics and petty graft," she wrote from Miami on January 28. Next day, from the same city, she wrote: ". . . I'll tell you right off the bat for being mean-spirited, selfish, and irresponsible, I think Florida citrus growers have got the world licked. . . . Do you know what happened just before Christmas this year? Two weeks before Christmas the whole citrus industry just closed down for the holidays and turned everybody loose—without money or jobs. No wonder there is an 'outlaw union' in the citrus belt and a strike." Her letters to Eleanor, and Eleanor's to her, were of the same passionately yearning tone as before, with Eleanor[1] continuing to blame herself for Hick's pre-Christmas outbreak. "Darling, I love you deeply," said one from Eleanor. "I never want to hurt you. You are dearer to me than you can guess. I kiss your photograph & ask every blessing for you." Another of Eleanor's letters exclaimed "How you can write!" It also said, "I love you deeply, tenderly, darling & I would like to put my arms around you." She spoke of Florida with distaste; she'd been generally miserable down there when she visited her husband aboard the *Larooco* in 1925 and 1926.* "How well I know that Florida landscape," she wrote. "I might like it with you, it may just be that I knew it best in my stormy years & the associations are not so pleasant."[12]

On Tuesday, January 30, her husband's fifty-second birthday, she wrote Hick that she felt "a bit aggrieved," evidently with Hick, because she had received "no letter" that day, though she knew this aggrievement to be "foolish" since the mailroom was swamped with birthday messages to the President and had, in consequence, "sent up no mail" at all to her that day. "You have gathered I expect," she went on, "that all the preparations for F's party etc. are a bit on my nerves & I am missing you far away. What shall I do when you are West, oh, well, sufficient unto the day etc.!"[13]

III

CERTAINLY she had sufficient reason, at that time, for jangled nerves. The wonder is that she found a single moment to devote to Hick amid a day as hectic as any she had spent in the White House, in part the result of the

*See Davis, *FDR: The Beckoning of Destiny,* pp. 776, 795–96.

working out of an idea which, insofar as it was a generous idea, productive of social good, had an unlikely source.

Henry L. Doherty was board chairman of the giant holding company called Cities Service. He was "a dapper little gentleman with a closely trimmed beard" (so Harold Ickes saw him[14]), who was afflicted physically with recurrent acute arthritis and, morally, with his full share of that ruthless greed which then seemed especially characteristic of oil and utilities magnates. He was much in the news in late 1933 and 1934, and not in ways that endeared him to a depression-ridden public. The Federal Trade Commission accused him of possibly illegal and certainly dishonest manipulations of a Cities Service subsidiary's stock to gain a profit for himself, at a loss to other people, of $17 million. A congressman, speaking on the floor of the House, accused him of being the "biggest tax evader in the country."

He was, therefore, highly susceptible to a suggestion for the garnering of favorable personal publicity which was made to him by Keith Morgan, an insurance man who had become chief fund-raiser for the Georgia Warm Springs Foundation,* the suggestion that he actively, publicly associate himself with the raising of money for polio victims, an indubitably worthy cause. In pursuit of this suggestion he came down to Warm Springs on November 24, 1933, to attend the ceremonial dedication of a new sanatorium headquarters building, Georgia Hall, built at a cost of more than $125,000, all of it privately subscribed, and sometime during that day, meeting with foundation trustees, including Roosevelt himself, who was to deliver the dedicatory address that evening, Doherty proposed the raising of money by means of birthday parties or balls, with paid admissions, to be held nationwide on the President's birthday. He pledged a substantial monetary contribution of his own to help defray the cost of preparing for the event. The idea, at once enthusiastically adopted, was soon thereafter publicly announced as a definite plan, to be carried out under the aegis of a distinguished special committee (Governor Lehman, John L. Lewis, Harvey Firestone were on it). There was initiated a flurry of preparatory activity in every city and almost every town in America, to the accompaniment of a rising tide of publicity.[15]

And so it happened that Franklin Roosevelt's fifty-second birthday became a much more celebrated event, nationally, in 1934 than were the birthdays of Washington or Lincoln or Jefferson. No fewer than 6,000 birthday balls were held on the night of January 30 (they raised for the foundation something over $1,016,000 after $800,000 for expenses had been deducted), the grandest of them costing $25 per admission at the Waldorf-Astoria in New York City and having the President's mother, who now approached her own eightieth birthday, as honored guest. The merrymakers were addressed over a national radio hookup by Roosevelt. "I wish I could divide myself by six thousand and attend

---

*It was Keith Morgan who had engineered the $560,000 insurance policy on Roosevelt's life, with the Georgia Warm Springs Foundation named the beneficiary, in 1930. (See Davis, *FDR: The New York Years,* p. 185.)

in person each and every one of these birthday parties," he said. "I cannot do that, but I can be and I am with you all in spirit and in the promotion of this great cause [the aiding of the victims of crippling illness] for which we are all crusading. No man has ever had a finer birthday remembrance from his friends. . . . I thank you but I lack the words to tell you how deeply I appreciate what you have done and I bid you goodnight on what is for me the happiest birthday I ever have known."[16] Three of the birthday balls were in Washington. Eleanor made a brief speaking appearance at each of them. And this impending effort was very much on her mind as she dashed off her "aggrieved" note to Hick.

As for "F's party," which preceded the balls, it was the annual Cuff Links Club affair; it had been held on each of Roosevelt's birthdays, now, for more than a decade. Originally composed of men (McIntyre, Early, Thomas Lynch, Howe, of course, a handful of others) to whom Roosevelt had presented gold cuff links in token of his appreciation of their service during his run for the vice presidency in 1920, the Cuff Links "gang" had since been enlarged to include the women of the innermost circle, all of whom were very actively involved in Rooseveltian politics. As a matter of fact, Eleanor and her Val-Kill friends, especially Nancy Cook, had become the chief organizers of the annual event, and Missy LeHand, Grace Tully, Tommy Thompson, and Margaret "Rabbit" Durand were often called upon to help in the preparations. A standard party format was followed. After cocktails and dinner came an elaborate skit, acted in costume (generally), written in mingled prose and rhyming verse by Howe, who also directed the production. Space was left in the script for original contributions by those in attendance. ("I finally wrote two stunts," said Eleanor's letter of January 30 to Hick. "Louis was paraphrasing hymns & that seemed to me possible so we will have something to do when called upon.") The end of the skit was the end of the party for the women, but the men retired to a private room for a poker session that lasted into the following morning.

The party for 1934 was held in the upper hall of the White House, its theme suggested by the increasingly loud charge of conservatives that Roosevelt designed to become a dictator, transforming republic into empire, himself the emperor, as Julius Caesar and Augustus had done in ancient Rome. (It was a charge that prompted Adolf Berle, in the late summer of 1933, to begin using "Dear Caesar" as the salutation of almost his every letter to Roosevelt, a practice he continued until early March 1937 when Roosevelt, worried lest some hostile columnist learn of it, asked him to stop.) Everyone was clad as an ancient Roman. McIntyre, Early, and Howe were helmeted and armored as members of the Praetorian Guard. Other men wore senatorial togas. The women were gowned as Roman maidens and matrons were supposed to be; each wore around her neck a garland that extended to her waist. Eleanor "represented the Delphic Oracle—it was a crazy, mixed-up kind of skit, you see—and issued strange prophecies regarding the New Deal," as Marion Dickerman remembered. Roosevelt himself, clad in a toga of royal purple, crowned with laurel, entered with gusto into the spirit of his role; he was haughty and imperious in his every word, every facial expression, every gesture, enjoying himself hugely and spreading joy around him. It was a hilarious evening. Eleanor, however, in her report of it to Hick next day, wrote merely that it had "gone off well" and that she believed that "Louis enjoyed it."[17]

In their communications with each other the two women continued to be mutually emotionally supportive, almost desperately so at times, as winter passed and spring came on. First one, then the other expressed bitter resentment of their forced separation; first one, then the other spoke words meant to soothe and inspire with hope. "I just talked to you darling, it was so good to hear your voice," said a February letter from Eleanor. "If I could just take you in my arms. Dear, I often feel rebellious too & yet I know we get more joy when we are together than we would have if we lived apart in the same city & I could only meet for short periods now and then. . . . Dearest, we are happy together & strong relationships have to grow deep roots. We're growing them now, partly because we are separated. The foliage & the flowers will come, somehow I'm sure of it." Said another Eleanor letter, after the two had been together: "I believe it gets harder to let you go each time but that is because you grow closer. It seems as though you belonged near me, but even if we lived together we would have to separate sometime & just now what you do is of such value to the country that we ought not to complain only that doesn't make me miss you less or feel less lonely." They dreamed of making a home together, of sharing a cottage permanently, if perhaps on a part-time basis, in some unspecified future. Repeated reference was made to this dream in their correspondence, mostly by Eleanor. "[W]e'll have years of happy times so bad times will be forgotten," she wrote to Hick a few hours after the latter had departed for her long western trip—an especially difficult parting for both of them. When she viewed the annual (1934) New York City show of the colonial furniture that had been handcrafted at Val-Kill, she took special note of a "corner cupboard I long to have for our camp or cottage or home, which is it to be? I've always thought of it in the country. . . ."[18] But the realization of this dream would mean a drastic revision of Eleanor's vital longtime commitments to Nancy Cook and Marion Dickerman, would probably mean a complete severance of her relations with Val-Kill Cottage, the furniture factory, Todhunter School, to all of which she was bound by legal ties, and Hick seems never to have believed, really, that it would ever happen.

Instead, as Hick traveled westward in late May and through June, with frequent extended stops and one wide zigzag that took her up to Lansing, Michigan, and down to Florence, Alabama, she seems to have felt more and more darkly premonitory, more and more convinced of the probability that the tide of her loving relationship with Eleanor had already peaked and must soon, now, begin to ebb. For months, almost since the end of their highly successful trip around the Gaspé Peninsula in 1933, the two friends had been vaguely planning a similar adventure in delicious anonymity for the summer of 1934.

Eleanor "was still confident that she could travel about unnoticed most of the time," Hick remembered decades later, and stubbornly clung to this belief despite her husband's emphatic warning that she would "never get away with it." When Roosevelt decided to take a cruise to Hawaii as soon as Congress adjourned, the vacation plan for Eleanor and Hick became definite. They would meet in Sacramento after Eleanor's unpublicized flight from Chicago and then spend three weeks motoring northward in leisurely fashion, stopping (as last year) in out-of-the-way places and camping in national parks on the way to Portland, where Roosevelt was to debark from the *Houston.* But as the time for this meeting approached, Hick became increasingly anxious; she expressed anxiety in her letters. Eleanor was puzzled. "Dear one, why should you feel shy and worried about seeing me?" she wrote. "You don't feel that way about your old friends [Eleanor classified herself as a *"new"* friend]." She urged Hick to "try to feel you just saw me yesterday & we will just pick up where we left off." A following letter said: "I can't understand why you are so worried dear, why can't you just be natural? Of course we are going to have a good time together & neither of us is going to be upset."[19]

Thus the yearning, the passion, the anxiety . . .

IV

BUT concerning this voluminous correspondence as a whole (nearly 600 letters, totaling 2,000 or more holograph pages, were exchanged during the first sixteen months of the New Deal), a highly significant point must be made—namely, that a far greater portion of it had to do with the public affairs in which these two remarkable women were caught up than had to do with their personal feelings, their private plans. Expressions of these last actually bulked little larger, proportionately, than a few silken threads weaving their way in binding fashion through wide swatches of, say, a cotton fabric. The fact is well worth stressing. It suggests a causal connection between the secret emotional life which these two shared and the work they were doing in the great world, a connection that frequently determined the nature of, the direction taken by, their worldly efforts. And to the extent that this happened, and that the work they were doing was historically important, their love became an energy of history. Hick would not have become Hopkins's and Howe's field reporter, would never have written her vivid policy-influencing accounts of New Deal relief and recovery operations in every section of the country but for her relationship with Eleanor. Eleanor would not have made as wonderfully well as she did her painful transition from New York to Washington, where she had suffered so horribly in the past, had it not been for Hick's profoundly sympathetic understanding, her morale-sustaining influence. She might never have initiated a regularly held press conference of her own—a device enabling her to contribute a good deal over the years to the progress of feminism, civil liberty, racial equality, and liberalism in general—if Hick had not urged her to do so. And there were at least two instances during the New Deal's first year when specific enterprises of some historic import issued directly from the love these two women had for each other.

One of these was the aforementioned trip to Puerto Rico. Eleanor prepared for it carefully, after Hopkins had decided that the island dependency must be an object of Hick's investigative reporting and Hick had proposed, Roosevelt accepting the proposal when Eleanor relayed it to him, that the two friends make the journey together. Eleanor saw to it that the press reported in word and picture the human consequences of the island's economic woes. She insisted that photographs be taken of her when visiting slum areas, photographs revelatory of the misery amid which she stood, though photographs could not give an adequate sense of what these slums were like, as Hick reported to Hopkins, because "they don't give you the odors." Hick went on:

> Imagine a swamp, with stagnant, scum-covered, muddy water everywhere, in open ditches, pools, backed up around and under the houses. Flies swarming everywhere. Mosquitoes. Rats. Miserable, scrawny, sick cats and dogs and goats, crawling about. Pack into this area, over these pools and ditches as many shacks as you can, so close together that there is barely room to pass between them. Ramshackle, makeshift affairs, made of bits of board and rusty tin, picked up here and there. Into each *room* put a family, ranging from three or four persons to eighteen or twenty. Put in some malaria and hookworm, and in about every other house somebody with tuberculosis, coughing and spitting around, probably occupying the family's only bed. And, remember, not a latrine in the place. No room for them. No place to dispose of garbage, either. Everything dumped right out in the mud and stagnant water. And pour down into that mess good, hot sun—that may be good for rickets but certainly doesn't help your stomach any as you plod through the mud followed by swarms of flies. . . .[20]

An effect was to focus more popular and presidential attention on Puerto Rican economic problems than had perhaps been focused there since the Puerto Rican Children's Feeding Fund had been inaugurated by Theodore Roosevelt early in the century. Political ground was prepared for those changes, including a deemphasis of sugar as the mainstay of economic life which Rex Tugwell, who came down to the island while Eleanor was there, insisted were absolutely necessary. Soon thereafter the island's territorial administration, transferred from the War Department to Interior, was greatly liberalized. A division of territories and island dependencies was established in Interior, directed by former *Nation* editor Ernest Gruening, who also (1935–1939) headed the Puerto Rican Reconstruction Administration. When Ickes visited the island in January 1936, he remarked upon the failure of Puerto Rico's former attorney general, a mainland lawyer, "to break up the big sugar estates into five-acre holdings, as provided by the law of Congress," and upon his own and Gruening's successful effort to secure the forced retirement of this attorney general and his replacement by a liberal native Puerto Rican lawyer. Ickes also noted that in "various parts of the island subsistence homestead developments are already in progress or have been projected."[21]

The latter remark may here serve to introduce the other and earlier of the two enterprises, historically of some importance, that stemmed directly from the relationship between Hick and Eleanor.

Responsive to Roosevelt's expressed wish, Congress during the Hundred Days had written into Title II of the Industrial Recovery Act a provision for what he called subsistence homesteads, a provision funded by a $25 million appropriation. Its aim, in Roosevelt's view, was to encourage the shift of population from city to country, a "back-to-the-land movement," some called it, which had become statistically noticeable by the Census Bureau, if barely so, during the last three years. The original idea was to demonstrate by means of pilot projects (the smallness of the initial appropriation permitted no more than this) how economically distressed people could become self-sustaining family units by establishing themselves on small-acreage farms, bought on easy credit terms, on which they would grow most or all of their own food, with perhaps some surplus for sale, while obtaining cash income from part-time employment in nearby industrial and business concerns. There was for this move on Roosevelt's part a Bismarckian motive. He revealed it when interviewed by Anne O'Hare McCormick for a *New York Times Magazine* piece shortly before he began his long cruise aboard the *Houston*. [22] He then referred to an event of February 1934 which had profoundly shocked liberal sentiment throughout the world. It was the destruction of Austrian socialism by armed government force, including the deliberate ruin by shell fire of the great Socialist cooperative housing development known as the Karl Marx Hof in central Vienna—this on orders from Austrian Chancellor Engelbert Dollfuss, who had by decree dissolved all political parties save his own Fatherland Front and who evidently hoped by this piece of viciousness to moderate Hitler's demand, implemented by violent Austrian Nazi agitation, for the incorporation of Austria in the Third Reich.* Roosevelt, when he talked with the *Times* correspondent, had just been told that Austrian Socialists who lived on privately owned one-acre garden plots in the Vienna environs had refused to join with the central-city Socialists in resistance to the Dollfuss decree. Some people might view this refusal as humanly contemptible, a cowardly betrayal of principles and comrades. Roosevelt viewed it as admirable. And he pointed to it as evidence of the soundness of his own subsistence homestead approach whereby, at slight long-term cost to the taxpayer, potential subversives of the profit system could be transformed into its supporters.

But since this subsistence homestead provision had not even been mentioned in congressional floor debate of the industrial recovery bill, and since the President had subsequently said nothing about it to Ickes, who was to administer it as an item of Title II, Ickes had done nothing about it for many weeks.

---

*Five months later, Dollfuss was murdered by Austrian Nazis who invaded his office and shot him through his throat, whereupon Roosevelt sent to Vienna from the *Houston* a message of condolence: "It is with horror and deep regret that I learn of the assassination of Engelbert Dollfuss, Minister of Foreign Affairs and Chancellor of Austria. I extend . . . to the Austrian people sincere sympathy. . . . Mrs. Roosevelt joins me in expressing to Madame Dollfuss our deepest sympathy in this great sorrow which has come to her."[23]

The PWA administrator moved with the speed of flowing molasses, as we have seen, even with regard to the much-debated major public works program, where speed was loudly called for by the program's proponents, and we may assume that his delay in initiating subsistence homesteads would have been further prolonged, and that the direction taken would have been very different from that actually taken, if Lorena Hickok at the outset of her first field trip for Hopkins had not called in Philadelphia upon Clarence Pickett, executive secretary of the American Friends Service Committee, for advice on where she should go for a direct view of the problems the FERA must address. "[T]o see just how bad things are," Pickett told her, "go down into the southwestern part of the state and into West Virginia."[24] She did so, with Pickett's brother-in-law accompanying her as guide; was profoundly shocked by the poverty she encountered in southwestern Pennsylvania, where the steel mills and coal mines had virtually ceased to operate, and was absolutely appalled by what she saw and heard and smelled in West Virginia, where the coal-town slums rivaled in human misery the slums she later visited in Puerto Rico.

"Scotts Run, a coal-mining community, not far from Morgantown, was the worst place I'd ever seen," she remembered decades later. "In a gutter, along the main street through the town, there was stagnant, filthy water, which the inhabitants used for drinking, cooking, washing, and everything else imaginable. On either side of the street were ramshackle houses, black with coal dust, which most Americans would not have considered fit for pigs. And in those houses every night children went to sleep hungry, on piles of bug-infested rags, spread out on the floor. There were rats in those houses." As she went on through the state, she "found other places just as bad. Everywhere, grimy, undernourished, desperate people—so hungry that they could not wait for vegetables to mature in the pathetic little gardens they tried to raise on mountainsides so steep they must have had to shoot the seeds in to make them stick. [Garden planting had been heavily promoted by the Agricultural Extension Service of the University of West Virginia, in Morgantown.] They would dig up the tiny potatoes long before they had reached their full size and pick the tomatoes and eat them while they were still green." Near Logan in southwestern West Virginia she visited a tent camp where lived, with their families, scores of miners whom the coal operators had blacklisted following a failed strike. They "had been living in tents for years when I was there—and the tents were so old and tattered they provided practically no shelter at all."[25]

It was as the hottest of sparks shot into the driest of tinder that Hick's long, vividly reportive letter, written "in a kind of state of shock" a few hours after her visit to Scotts Run, penetrated Eleanor's yearning, questing spirit in the White House. It caused Eleanor to phone Hick at once. Hick then promptly phoned Pickett in Philadelphia. And on August 18, 1933, the three met in Morgantown, West Virginia, Eleanor having driven over, alone in her Buick, from Washington. On that and succeeding days, unintroduced and unrecognized as First Lady, Eleanor in company with Hick, Pickett, and two Quaker women who had been doing social work in the area, visited Scotts Run and other like communities in the vicinity. She talked as warmly sympathetic friend with a dozen or more families whose miserable dwellings she entered, she closely questioned her Quaker guides for their ideas of what could and should be done, she discussed everything with Hick, and she returned to Washington with an abundance of horror stories and corrective ideas to pour into the receptive ears of her husband and Louis Howe. The latter, who had a surprisingly effective radio voice, deep, resonant, with a cultured accent, was making that summer a series of weekly national radio broadcasts, each cleared in advance with the President, under the sponsorship of RCA Victor, nine-minute broadcasts for which he was paid $100 per minute.* His talk for Sunday, August 22, dealt with rural resettlement as an "experiment" in industrial decentralization, one that might "revolutionize the manufacturing industry," providing a steady livelihood to the worker "who has now [in the city] to go into the breadline whenever work is slack."[26] And he and Roosevelt were easily persuaded that the portion of Appalachia visited by Eleanor should be the location of the first subsistence homestead project. Nowhere else was a demonstration of the government's concern for a suffering humanity more needed to stave off revolutionary agitations, though as a matter of fact, and as the Quakers had said to Hick when she inveighed against the Communists, these poor people of West Virginia were much too far beaten down, too crushed into hopeless passivity to respond actively to revolutionary propaganda.

Already, at his wife's suggestion, the President had prevailed upon Ickes to name M. L. Wilson the head of the PWA's Subsistence Homestead Division, which meant a shifting of Wilson away from his post as head of the AAA's wheat program. (Some irony attaches to the fact that Wilson's shift to subsistence homesteading for hungry people was eased by the drouth conditions developing in that summer of 1933 across the plains states. Drouth promised to effect the reduction in wheat production which the AAA might otherwise have been "forced" to effect through a fall plow-up of planted wheat acreage.) Wilson now, in turn, also at Eleanor's suggestion, named Clarence Pickett his principal assistant. Both men were at once caught up in a whirlwind of activity the prime generative force of which was the close working partnership between Eleanor and Louis. Wilson, Pickett, Ickes, and everyone else associated with this West Virginia enterprise were driven people. Howe himself was driven, in part by a desperate desire to regain some of the practical importance to his beloved Franklin which he had lost after Roosevelt had become the presidential candidate and even more by his realization that he personally had little time left in which to act at all. For his breathing grew almost daily more

---

*The dubious ethicality of the arrangement, quietly deplored by many liberals, was loudly proclaimed and denounced by Senator Arthur Vandenberg, the New York *Sun*, and other voices of conservative opinion.

difficult; his prostrating illnesses became more frequent; his slender strength ebbed more and more away; his nervous irritability consequently increased.

On October 13 a press release from Ickes's office announced the purchase by the Subsistence Homestead Division of a 1,200-acre tract known as the Arthur Farm, adjacent to the village of Reedsville (it was fifteen miles southeast of Morgantown; Scotts Run was nearby) and the launching there of the nation's pioneering subsistence homestead project.[27] Its official name would be Arthurdale. It was intended to be the model for scores of government-sponsored settlements scattered throughout the nation (fifty other homestead projects had received official approval by the summer of 1934), and the plans being made for it, some of them indicated in the press release, glowed with hope and promise.

Arthurdale was to become vital as a human community and self-sufficient as an economic unit through a creative mingling of country and small-town living, of individualistic and cooperative economic activity. Each family would have its own house, at an initial cost to the government of $2,000, but this cost was a government loan; it would be paid off by the homesteader over a thirty-year period. Each family would have from two to five acres of land, the plot size varying inversely with estimated per acre productivity. On this, vegetables, chickens, eggs, milk, beef, pork might be produced, though it was Eleanor's opinion, shared by Wilson, that the values of community as well as of economic efficiency would be best served if individual home production were at least supplemented by community gardens and community livestock herds. There would be local industry to provide cash incomes; PWA was allocating to the Post Office Department $525,000 for the establishment at Arthurdale of a small factory for the making of such post office equipment as mailboxes. The children of Arthurdale were to attend a progressive experimental school whose principal, personally selected by Eleanor, would be one of John Dewey's protégés, Elsie Clapp. Dewey himself would become a member of an advisory committee for the school which, in accordance with ideas developed in Dewey's *School and Society* and *Democracy and Education,* * would become the center and focus of community activity. There would be a great deal of such activity—practical, recreational—including furniture making, weaving, other handicrafts, along with dramatic presentations, folk singing and dancing, and instrumental music. Nancy Cook would be hired by Eleanor as special consultant, to organize and supervise the handicraft center; she would thereafter divide her time and energy between Arthurdale and the Val-Kill shop. The government of the community would be in the hands of its members and would be of the town meeting type, to the maximum degree possible for a federally funded enterprise.

Thus Arthurdale as model aimed to realize a dream Eleanor had had ever

---

*In his Preface to *Democracy and Education*, dated 1915, Dewey writes: "Hearty acknowledgements are due . . . to Miss Elsie Ripley Clapp for many criticisms and suggestions."

since the construction of Val-Kill Cottage and the establishment of the Val-Kill shop, a dream manifested in repeated bursts of social experimentation by considerable groups of people in every American generation since the beginning of the Industrial Revolution (there would be especially vivid, if inchoate, manifestations of it during the 1960s and early 1970s). It was the dream of a kind of social organization in which the individual person was *truly* the end and master, through voluntary cooperative activity, and not the mere means and puppet, of economic processes, a social organization which defined "efficiency" in concrete personal terms rather than in terms of overall statistical abstraction, a highly decentralized social organization whose components were small enough to permit the people in them to know one another as whole human beings, as unique multidimensional, multifaceted living organisms, not merely as one-dimensional creatures or elements of huge single-purpose, single-standard economic enterprises whose operations were technologically determined. This dream was the very essence of the enormous popular appeal, which is to say it was the very basis of the growing demagogic power in 1933 and after, of "Radio Priest" Charles E. Coughlin and "Kingfish" Huey Long. Collectivism was involved in it, to a degree, but the degree was severely limited; the collective was to be of *individual* people, for the purpose of preserving and strengthening individuality. It was person-oriented. It was cooperative in its form. It was, in essential nature, a community whose vital unit was the individual and whose ultimate purpose was the enhancement and enlargement of freedom for the individual. Thus small local industry was necessary to the dream's realization, and this might well be communally owned and cooperatively operated, but each family was to own "a home and the comforts of home," as Huey Long stressed, and each person was to have far greater economic freedom, far more control over the ways and means with which he made a living, than the average person now had. Not at all out of line with community so defined was Father Coughlin's stated belief that the "sensible, socially just and American" approach to economic problems was "to multiply private ownership and not impede it."[28]

So far as Arthurdale was concerned, there was some danger to the long-term realization of this dream in the very fact that Eleanor was so directly, so intimately involved in its working out.

The First Lady became Arthurdale's very active patroness in somewhat the same way as her husband was patron of Warm Springs. (For instance, in the fall of 1934 she was to risk renewed public censure by making a half dozen fifteen-minute radio broadcasts under commercial sponsorship, the pay for these [$18,000] going to Arthurdale by way of the Friends Service Committee: $8,000 for Nancy Cook's handicraft center; $6,000 for Elsie Clapp's first-year salary; $6,000 for community medical services. She also obtained generous financial support of the school from Bernard Baruch, whose first check was for $22,000. Baruch's motives seem fairly transparent—he very assiduously cultivated the friendship of Eleanor, Nancy, Marion because only through them could he hope to gain access to the White House inner circle—but he does seem also to have become genuinely interested in Arthurdale and committed to it.) The project "was 'her baby,' the critics would say" (so Hick remembered it), and the First Lady devoted to it the kind of mother love that often stultifies, as indeed, patronage in general stultifies to the extent that it is a "we-them" relationship, with "we" doing *for* "them." Insofar as Eleanor's ideas were imposed on Arthurdale's residents instead of becoming their own through persuasion, they had to fail in long-term practice. And they did fail as regards progressive education. "I'm afraid [the school] . . . was a bit *too* progressive for the homesteaders," said Marion Dickerman long afterward, and ruefully, for her Todhunter School was notably progressive. "They began to feel that their children were not being taught the fundamentals—the three R's—as they should be. So Elsie, with her teaching staff, had to move out— to another community. The Arthurdale school then became part of West Virginia's public education system."[29]

V

YES, patronage was a danger.

But a far greater danger was the one Marxists stressed in their repudiation of gradualism—namely, the fundamental hostility of a highly organized system of private profit to the principles upon which Arthurdale was founded.

This would prove ultimately fatal to the enterprise as a whole.

Industrial firms manufacturing items purchased by the Post Office Department promptly and loudly protested the allocation of PWA funds to establish at Arthurdale (Reedsville) a government plant that would, they claimed, reduce their market and so force them to curtail production, laying off workers. Furniture manufacturers protested, too, the establishment with government funds of a workshop in which Arthurdale's residents would make their own furniture instead of buying it, or having it bought for them, from existing private plants. Especially loud, as voiced upon the floor of Congress in January 1934 by Congressman Louis Ludlow of Indiana, a Democrat, were the anguished cries of the Keyless Lock Company of Indianapolis, which made locks for post office boxes. Nothing of the sort would be made at Arthurdale, Howe assured the congressman in private conference. Keyless Lock, therefore, in Ludlow's district, had nothing to fear, Howe insisted. But the company, hence Ludlow, remained unpersuaded, the latter proclaiming in floor speech that Arthurdale's government plant pointed the way toward a sovietized America and the "death . . . of individual liberty in the United States," this last being, according to Republican Representative John Taber of New York, precisely the aim of the present administration.[30] In late January Ludlow managed to attach to a Treasury appropriation bill a rider specifically forbidding the Post Office Department to purchase any equipment manufactured in Arthurdale.

Nor would it be possible to attract private industry to Arthurdale, or to any other subsistence homestead project, by means of government subsidy, according to a ruling by the director of the General Accounting Office, Comptroller General J. R. McCarl.* Such subsidies for such purpose would, in the absence of a specific legislative grant of authority to make it, be a violation of Section 9 of Article I of the Constitution, which says, "No Money shall be drawn from the Treasury, but in Consequence of Appropriations made by Law"—or so McCarl evidently believed.

Yet the Arthurdale cause, insofar as its success required government financial help to establish local industry, appeared by no means hopeless as January gave way to February. Eleanor, replying to an excited telegram from Upton Sinclair, five days after Ludlow's rider was attached, did not overstate the case when she assured the famous Socialist writer that "the chance for a government factory is still possible" and that, in her opinion, "a great deal has been made of this prematurely."[31] Indeed, it then appeared not merely possible but probable that Congress, instead of specifically forbidding the already announced PWA allocation, would in the end specifically approve it. Congressional sentiment in favor of such action was by no means confined to liberals. Tennessee's Senator Kenneth McKellar, chairman of the Senate Committee on Post Offices and Post Roads, was a notably conservative Democrat, though one whose imagination had been fired by TVA, and McKellar, whose opinion in general carried weight with conservatives of both parties and might well (in view of his committee chairmanship) be decisive in the present controversy, argued strongly for a Post Office factory at Arthurdale. When Ickes told a press conference in the third week of February that the Arthurdale plant would be "used as a yardstick to determine if the government has been paying too much for post office equipment, and thereby hangs a tale and may be the reason why some are opposing it,"[32] McKellar agreed with him.

Certainly the general public was being given at that time good reason to doubt that the public interest was invariably better served by the Post Office's purchase of goods and services from private contractors than it would be by a direct ownership and operation of the key facilities of mail delivery.

---

*It should perhaps be noted here that, in the belief of many New Dealers, McCarl's interpretation of the law invariably favored the business interest over the public interest whenever and wherever the language of statutes affecting business was sufficiently vague to permit such interpretation. He was a Republican. He had been appointed in 1921 to the fifteen-year term prescribed for his office by the Budget and Accounting Act of 1921, which meant that he would remain until 1936 in what Tommy Corcoran once described as the "most powerful office in the government barring only the presidency," for by law a comptroller general could be removed only for specific cause, by joint resolution of Congress. His power derived from his legally assigned task of preauditing executive expenditures—that is, before any specific payment was made by an administrative agency, it must be reviewed by the comptroller general to make sure it was authorized by law. Such preauditing by an office responsible to Congress, operating as a kind of police arm of the legislature, was a violation of the constitutional separation of powers, many students of government believed. Certainly it significantly reduced the President's control over the executive. In 1937 the President's Committee on Administrative Management was to recommend that the GAO as then constituted be abolished, that its authority to settle accounts be transferred to the Treasury Department, and that a General Auditing Office be established outside to conduct postaudits and report on them to Congress. Nothing came of this recommendation.

Almost simultaneous with the launching of the Arthurdale project in the late summer and autumn of 1933 had been the launching of an investigation of airmail and ocean mail contracts, with major public emphasis on the former, by a special Senate investigative committee chaired by Alabama's redoubtable Hugo Black. It had been established as a subcommittee of McKellar's post office committee by the lame-duck session of the Seventy-second Congress, some weeks before Roosevelt's inauguration. Soon thereafter Black learned that a Hearst reporter in Washington named Fulton Lewis, Jr., had for two years been gathering material upon the official conduct of Hoover's postmaster general, Walter F. Brown; that the Hearst newspapers, on orders from William Randolph Hearst himself, had flatly refused publication of Lewis's reports of his information;* and that the information itself was of sensational import. So it proved to be, after Black had been presented with it by the reporter. The senator, forewarned and forearmed by it, was enabled to pry from reluctant witnesses sworn testimony in abundance of fraud, bribery, and collusion in the awarding of airmail contracts, a body of evidence that accorded only too perfectly, in the public mind, with those peculiar ethics of big business which Pecora's investigations had revealed and continued to reveal.

The Hoover administration, obviously, had come into office with a clear and definite federal aeronautics policy, shaped by corporation lawyers and approved in corporate boardrooms, without benefit or hazard of popular debate. Its aim was to replace competition with cooperation among large airlines— that is, to destroy the free market in commercial air transport—to the maximum degree possible and with a maximum of profitability to huge financial concerns. Implementation of this policy by Postmaster General Brown involved the use of airmail contracts, which made the difference between an airline's financial success and failure, to ensure that certain big and therefore favored companies, those with Wall Street connections, survived and grew while their smaller competitors, regardless of the cost efficiency of their operations, were crushed or forced into mergers in which their identities were lost. This in turn involved blatant violations of antitrust law and of the laws requiring open, competitive bidding for government contracts and their award to the lowest bidder that met specifications. The decisive action had been taken in the spring of 1930, when Brown presided over a series of secret meetings in the Post Office Building ("spoils conferences" they were frankly dubbed by some who participated in them) to which only officials of the larger airlines were invited or admitted. From them had emerged, abruptly, an efficient

---

*Hearst colleague and syndicated columnist Arthur Brisbane was a close personal friend of Brown's. Reporter Lewis, it should be noted, was no crusader for good government or against big business chicanery; he was well on his way to becoming one of the most reactionary and mendacious of American journalists. But he had personal family reasons for hostility toward Brown, who was a political enemy of his father-in-law, Colonel Claudius Huston. In 1930, possibly in consequence of covert action by Brown, Huston, charged with an "unwise" use of party funds, had been forced out of the chairmanship of the Republican National Committee. See Henry Ladd Smith, *Airways, the History of Commercial Aviation in the United States* (pp. 215–16).

cooperative order in place of the theretofore prevailing chaos of competition: Three Wall Street-organized aviation holding companies—the North American-General Motors group, United Aircraft, and Aviation Corporation—walked off with twenty-four of the twenty-seven federal airmail contracts then available, whereupon a number of aviator-entrepreneurs went swiftly under. Nor was his disposition of mail contracts the only direct contribution Brown made to the new order. He personally involved himself in at least one of the mergers that were encouraged or forced by his policy—namely, the "shotgun wedding" of Transcontinental Air Transport (TAT) with Western Air Express, whose issue was Transcontinental and Western Airline (TWA). And he, who seems not to have personally profited in a monetary way from official acts which profited others hugely, was very sure that the end achieved more than justified the means he had employed. By July 4, 1931, as he said with pride, there had been hustled into being a stable, coordinated, passenger-carrying transcontinental airline system, replacing an airmail hazardously and uncertainly "carried in an open-cockpit ship with a young lad of twenty-five years of age sitting on a parachute."[33]

But Senator Black had a different order of priorities, hence a less flattering description of what had happened.

"The control of American aviation," said he in late 1933, "has been ruthlessly taken away from men who could fly and bestowed upon bankers, brokers, promoters, and politicians, sitting in their inner offices, allotting to themselves the taxpayers' money."[34]

They allotted themselves a considerable amount of it.

Black concluded, on the basis of documentary evidence and sworn testimony presented to his committee, that favored airlines had robbed the U.S. Treasury of some $46,800,000 between July 1930 and January 1934. The contract for airmail transport between Washington and New York City, for example, had gone to a company charging three times the amount bid by a rival concern. TWA's bid for a contract had been some $5,000,000 higher than that of a competitor, yet TWA had won the award. TWA had also used personal bribes to prevent competitive bidding. Under oath, a high official of that company admitted that his firm had paid one Erle Halliburton $1,400,000 not to bid for a contract TWA wanted and got, a deal whereby not only the government but probably also the stockholders in Halliburton's company were cheated. And thievery had been compounded through lying reports to the Post Office of the amount of mail carried. American Airways had received payment of $5,308,958 for mail it should have carried for only $3,338,673, according to the very generous terms of its contract—an overcharge of nearly $2,000,000, despite the allegedly watchful eye of Comptroller General McCarl.[35]

Not one of the airmail contracts made during the Brown regime was technically legal, said Black to Roosevelt when the two lunched together in the Oval Room in late January. Most were grossly fraudulent. All should be canceled immediately. A few days later Roosevelt asked for an opinion from his attorney general upon this matter. Was a blanket cancellation justified by the evidence the Black committee had in hand? It was, definitely, opined Homer Cummings on the morning of February 9. The Post Office Department counseled a less precipitous action. Postmaster General Farley, who was alleged by Brown to have expressed privately an intense dislike of the investigation by "publicity hound" Black while this was going on, an allegation Farley flatly denied, now recommended that cancellation be postponed until June 1, enabling the present airmail service to be continued uninterrupted while new specifications were drawn up, and new bids taken. It was advice which Roosevelt's normal prudence and tolerance of dubious business ethics must have inclined him to accept. Prudence, however, was outweighed in this instance by other considerations. Here was a golden opportunity for highly dramatic action whereby honesty in government was championed, the Hoover administration further discredited, and it was in any case surely wrong, and politically dangerous, to condone for four months longer the fraud, the thievery which Black had publicly exposed.

So Roosevelt inquired whether the U.S. Army, the pilots of which had flown the first airmail a decade and a half ago, was prepared to resume such service for the duration of what he was prepared to declare "an emergency." The Army *was* prepared, and eager to do the job, replied the chief of the Army Air Corps, Major General Benjamin D. Foulois, promptly, rashly. Roosevelt would have done well at that point to check the accuracy of the general's judgment against the expert opinion of such as Colonel Billy Mitchell, former assistant chief of what had then been called the Army Air Service. Mitchell asserted that the present Air Corps was "not properly equipped for any kind of duty," in peace *or* war, because of "machinations of . . . [the] aviation profiteers" who had gained control of the aircraft and airline industries, and of the Army and Navy air arms as well, to a sad degree, through "service politicians" whose policy decisions were made in anticipation of lucrative posts in big business when they retired from the service.[36] But Mitchell was not consulted. Instead, Roosevelt accepted Foulois's optimistic assurance at face value. He told Farley to issue at once a blanket cancellation order, to be effective ten days hence. And within an hour after Farley had done so (all this decisive action occupied but little more than two hours of that Friday morning, February 9), Roosevelt himself issued an executive order directing the Army to fly the mail from February 19 until further notice.

This hasty action proved a major, tragic blunder.

For one thing, it immediately brought into direct public opposition to the President the "single American personality who might match Franklin Roosevelt in national popularity" at that time, as Arthur Schlesinger, Jr., has written. In June 1928, a little more than a year after his solo flight from New York to Paris and only a few weeks after TAT had been established through the cooperation of two large railroads, five big investment houses, the Wright Aeronautical Company, and the Curtiss Aeroplane and Motor Corporation, Charles A. Lindbergh had become chairman of the technical committee of the corporation. The corporation's president* had then presented the flier with a check for $250,000, which Lindbergh, by prior agreement, endorsed and returned to the company in payment for 25,000 shares of TAT stock at $10 a share, most of which he sold soon thereafter, as the corporation head advised him to do. What was, of course, purchased by this transaction, of which the Black committee had obtained detailed information, was mostly the Lindbergh name, the commercial use of that heroic fame whose commercialization in more vulgar and less lucrative ways the flier had ostentatiously refused. First TAT, then TWA became identified in the public mind, through incessant national advertising, as the "Lindbergh Line." So it was that Lindbergh, "the one authentic hero of the 1920s," had reason to feel personally offended by the President's action, and on Saturday evening, February 11, in a telegram which he released to the press simultaneously with its dispatch to the White House (it made big headlines in Monday morning's papers), the hero charged the President with gross injustice. The blanket cancellation "condemns the largest portion of our commercial aviation without just trial . . . does not discriminate between innocence and guilt and places no premium on honest business . . . will unnecessarily and greatly damage all American aviation." It also risked needlessly and greatly the lives of Army pilots, according to Lindbergh's "known belief" (so reported the New York *Times*), for they would be using planes and landing field equipment unsuited to the airmail job, and they were themselves inadequately trained in cross-country flying, night flying, instrument flying.[37]

The "known belief" at once proved to be tragic prophecy.

The winter weather that year, as has been said, was approximately the worst on record for the nation as a whole. There was much heavy fog, much freezing rain, many raging blizzards, and, across the northern half of the country, day after day of sub-zero temperatures. Even before the Army had begun the actual carrying of mail, three of its pilots had been killed in crashes as they made test runs over the routes they were to cover. By the end of the first week of Army mail flying, two more pilots had been killed, six had been critically injured, eight planes had been destroyed. There was a rising storm of public outrage and protest, focused on Jim Farley, who manfully publicly assumed full responsibility for the original airmail decision, when Roosevelt on March 10, by which date ten Army pilots had lost their lives, ordered the Army to stop flying the mail "except on such routes, under such weather conditions and under such equipment and personnel conditions as will insure . . . against constant recurrence of accidents."[38]

On the following day Lindbergh had a personal conference with Secretary of War George Dern, at the latter's request. He was asked for his opinion of Dern's proposal to establish a special committee "to study and report on the performance of the Army Air Corps in its mission to carry the air mail." When

---

*He was neither aviator nor aeronautical engineer but an investment counsel named C. M. Keys.

the conference ended, Dern believed that his appeasement effort had succeeded, believed that Lindbergh (he held the rank of full colonel in the Air
Corps Reserve) not only had approved the proposal but had agreed to accept
committee appointment. Either Dern was mistaken or the flier quickly
changed his mind. Two days later Lindbergh dispatched to the secretary of war
and (again) simultaneously released to the press a telegram reiterating his
conviction that "use of the Army Air Corps to carry the air mail was unwarranted and contrary to American principles . . . unjust to the airlines . . . unfair
to the personnel of the Army Air Corps" and concluding that he could not
"serve on a committee whose function is to assist in following out an executive
order to take over the commercial air mail system of the United States." To
Dern's prompt request that he reconsider, the flier returned a prompt, flat no.

Remarked Senator George Norris, coldly: "Now Colonel Lindbergh is earning his $250,000." And Billy Mitchell contemptuously dismissed the hero as
" 'front man' for the Air Trust," a "commercial flier" whose "motive is principally profit."[39]

But the shining heroism of the Lone Eagle remained untarnished in the eyes
of the vast majority of Americans. His repeated charge of "condemnation
without trial" was not only plausible but persuasive. And his strictures upon
the administration's action were given constantly increasing weight by the fact
that the plane crashes continued, in almost the same proportion to miles flown
as before. By April twelve Army pilots had been killed and there had been
forty-six forced landings.

"The Army," said Billy Mitchell bitterly, "has lost the art of flying. It can't
fly." For that sad fact he again blamed the businessmen who, having gained
control of American aviation, used it for private profit only. He pointed out
that in the present instance the Air Corps was denied the use of the radio
system, the blind-flying instruments, the safety equipment of the commercial
airlines, though taxpayers' dollars had paid for the development of all these.
It was Mitchell's conviction that the airmail should not have been taken out
of the Army's hands in the first place. He favored a drastic restructuring of
the whole of the American aviation enterprise, with one major element of the
process being the *permanent* assignment to the Army Air Corps of airmail
transport. This, said he, "would result in a much more efficient Air Corps and
it would aid in the proper development of aviation as a means of national
defense."[40]

Roosevelt never for an instant considered the idea. Nor did it occur to him
that the Black committee disclosures, coupled with the tragic revelation of Air
Corps incompetence, an incompetence easily proved to be causally related to
big business domination of American aviation, might present another opportunity to move toward that integrated national transportation system, inclusive
of, and rationally balanced between, highway, rail, water, air, and pipeline
transport, which he had stated as goal while a presidential candidate.* Instead,

*See pp. 111–12.

in what was bound to seem to the general public a tacit admission of grievous administration error, he simply gave up on the Air Corps as mail carrier. In May almost all letters bearing airmail stamps were again being carried by commercial airlines.

The episode as a whole was, of course, no such clear demonstration of the inherent incapacity of government to manage efficiently an economic enterprise, it was certainly no such clear-cut triumph of the allegedly "private" aviation industry over "socialistic" efforts toward governmental control and reform, as it was made to appear by a business-controlled press now increasingly openly hostile to Roosevelt and the New Deal.

In consequence of the Black committee investigation there was a considerable reorganization and a quite drastic change in the operating procedures of the airlines and of the aviation industry in general. There was an abrupt drastic reduction in the size of the airmail subsidy (the 1934 subsidy was but 40 percent the size of 1933's). And on June 12 the President signed the Air Mail Act of 1934, the legislative fruit of Black's inquiry, the passage of which Roosevelt had recommended in identical letters dated March 7 to Senator McKellar, Senator Black, and the chairman of the House Committee on Post Offices and Post Roads. It was legislation designed (in the language of the letter) to prevent "combinations, agreements, or understandings" that would inhibit or deny true competitive bidding and to prohibit the "award of an air-mail contract to any company" having direct or indirect ties, through subsidiary or affiliate or holding company, with other companies engaged "in the operation of competitive routes or in the manufacture of aircraft, or other materials or accessories generally used in the aviation industry." It was also designed to prevent the selling or subletting of an airmail contract by any company "to any other contracting company" and to prevent mergers or consolidations of companies holding mail contracts.[41]

But there was no blinking the fact that the entire affair, which had attracted a concentrated popular attention, constituted a personal defeat for Roosevelt in the court of public opinion—not a grave or permanently damaging defeat, certainly, but the first since his taking of office that affected in any way his popularity with the great mass of Americans. And there was significance for the future in the fact that the defeat had been in part administered by Charles Augustus Lindbergh, a personality and mind and temperament as antithetical to Roosevelt's as can easily be imagined. The aviator hero and Franklin Roosevelt had apparently come together in head-on collision, and it was Roosevelt who had been forced to back down.

Nor was there any blinking the fact that this episode, which had at its beginning augured well for the establishment of a Post Office factory at Arthurdale, contributed in the end to a climate of opinion unfavorable to any such enterprise. The arguments of opponents of "government in business" were given increased plausibility; the "versus" between conservative and liberal, between business and New Deal, was given increased emphasis; and in consequence, it was somewhat harder than it had been before for congressional conservatives to go along with the White House on any program that smacked of "socialism."

VI

CONTRIBUTING also to a change in opinion climate that was deleterious to Arthurdale was an impassioned controversy over securities-exchange regulation. It began, as a public row, some five weeks after the Seventy-Third Congress had assembled for its first regular session, and it reached its acrimonious height or depth in March, at precisely the time when popular indignation over the continuing Army airmail crashes was at its peak.

It will be remembered* that Roosevelt, during the Hundred Days, had divided in two a legislative proposal originally aimed both at reform of securities marketing and at regulation of the exchanges, the former to protect buyers against false and misleading statements by sellers, the latter to prevent exchange practices that had contributed heavily to the stock market crash of 1929. The first part of this proposal had become the Securities Act of 1933; the latter part had not even achieved satisfactory draft as a bill when the special session of Congress ended in June. Yet before all eyes not blinded by interested preconceptions and prejudices, evidence of the acute, immediate need for stiff regulatory legislation was piled up high and ever higher as Pecora continued his investigations. Especially was this so in the aftermath of the collapse of 1933's bull market in securities, a month after congressional adjournment.

For it was then revealed that every malpractice of exchange operators during the New Era was being repeated in full force through the opening months of the New Deal. Indeed, the essential fact of the July collapse was a huge wave of short selling on the New York Stock Exchange, orchestrated by a number of highly potent bear pools, including one of which Joseph P. Kennedy was a key figure, as has been mentioned. Nor was public confidence in the efficacy of exchange self-regulation at all enhanced by the feeble gesture toward "reform" which the exchange governors made immediately after the collapse, in response to angry denunciations of them by a good part of the business community itself. Quite the contrary. For one thing, the "new reform" announced in August by Richard Whitney, the arrogantly aristocratic president of the New York Stock Exchange, called upon exchange members to report to the governors all pools, syndicates, and joint trading accounts "of which they have knowledge beginning on August 4." Why August 4? So asked a cynical and disgusted John T. Flynn in his *New Republic* column, "Other People's Money," for August 16, 1933. "Why did not the Exchange date the period for information from July 4 to July 20 when the market was honeycombed with pools and syndicates . . . ?" By August 4 "the pools [were] fairly well liquidated." Not at all surprising, therefore, was the fact that the holders

---

*See pp. 81–84.

of New York Stock Exchange seats reported not a single pool or syndicate or joint account. Clearly, exchange self-regulation worked and must continue to work in the same fashion as did industrial self-regulation through NRA code authorities, and toward the same end, which was the maximization of immediate private profit at whatever cost to long-term general welfare. Such conclusion was clear, at least, to such as John T. Flynn, and Flynn, a principal assistant of Pecora as counsel for Senator Duncan V. Fletcher's Banking and Currency Committee, would have a hand in the drafting of the exchange control legislation.[42]

Raymond Moley was in the White House a few days after Christmas 1933, called there to discuss, among other matters, exchange regulation, which, he was told, would be must legislation for the coming session of Congress. According to Moley's own account, the President "suggested that I get someone . . . to prepare" a bill, whereupon "somewhat reluctantly, I called in Tom Corcoran and Ben Cohen," who, with Landis, had drafted the Securities Act. A week later, which was some four days after the regular congressional session had opened, Moley, again in the White House and again according to his own account, "carefully described . . . to the President" the abilities and limitations of the Cohen-Corcoran team, stressing Cohen's genius as legal draftsman and Corcoran's as a supplier of Fletcher and Rayburn "with arguments when the fight over the bill began." Both, however, "would require watching, or their exuberance [what conservative Moley referred to was their zeal for genuine reform] would get out of hand." The President, according to Moley, "agreed and asked me to direct the fight for the Act."[43]

Actually Cohen and Corcoran had by late December virtually completed drafting the bill, which was introduced in the Senate by Fletcher, in the House by Sam Rayburn, on February 10, the day after Roosevelt had sent up the Hill a special message recommending exchange regulatory legislation to protect investors, safeguard values, and eliminate "so far as it may be possible . . . unwise and destructive speculation."[44]

The drafting process had been unusually prolonged and difficult. In the late summer or early autumn of 1933 Roosevelt had appointed a committee to evaluate the workings of the new Securities Act and, on the basis of that evaluation, make proposals for exchange regulation legislation. The size and composition of this committee (Roosevelt had chosen fervent exponents of "all points of view") rendered impossible a final majority report favoring any important change in the status quo. The committee's chairman was Secretary of Commerce Roper. The vice-chairman was Commerce's Assistant Secretary John Dickinson. Landis and Berle were on it, but so were corporation lawyers whose primary commitment was to the special interests of their clients. One of these was Henry Richardson, who circulated a draft bill of his own "drawn on the theory that insofar as possible each exchange will discipline its own members and conduct its own affairs." Richardson's chief concern was to prevent the assignment of exchange regulatory power to the Federal Trade Commission; he proposed, instead, an independent stock exchange commission consisting of seven members appointed by the President, but under a legislated directive insuring a composition precisely in accord with what Felix Frankfurter, writing from Oxford University, would soon describe to Roosevelt as the inevitable "game" of the current governors of the exchanges— "namely, to have the 'right' kind of regulatory body . . . devoid of the necessary courage and resourcefulness for making the legislation effective." Of the seven commissioners, two were to represent the "general investing public." Two were to be members of "some stock or commodity" exchange. One would be "engaged in agriculture," and one "shall represent business." Perpetual chairman of the commission would be the governor of the New York Federal Reserve Bank. The "game" was as clearly perceived by Frankfurter's protégés in Washington as it was by their mentor, of course. The notion that a federal regulatory body must have on it interested representatives of the private institutions to be regulated seemed preposterous to James Landis, who had been appointed to the FTC by Roosevelt in the early fall to administer the Securities Act and who was encouraged by Pecora and by Max Lowenthal, also a member of Fletcher's staff, to suggest to Cohen and Corcoran that they have ready by January a draft bill that would do what *really* needed to be done.[45]

When Cohen-Corcoran received through Moley a mandate from the White House to do this job, their draft bill had gone through no fewer than thirteen rewritings, being put at last into final shape during the Christmas holidays, chiefly by Cohen, but with help from Corcoran and Landis and with some input from Flynn. Frankfurter, having reviewed in Oxford the printed bill (it was fifty pages long), wrote Roosevelt that it was "an astonishingly careful and acute piece of draftsmanship," achieving "a fine blend . . . between fixity and flexibility, between the things that specifically should be enumerated by legislation . . . and the things as to which discretionary power must be left to the Federal Trade Commission."[46] The bill aimed at three broad reforms which were generally deemed essential to national economic health, even by the business community—Richard Whitney and his ilk to the contrary notwithstanding. It aimed to provide federal control over the sources and volume of credit for exchange trading, this being needed (for one thing) to prevent such massive flow of call money into the stock market, much of it from undistributed corporate profits, as had made a shambles of Federal Reserve money market controls, while contributing disastrously to the great bull market, in 1928 and 1929. Secondly, the bill aimed to prevent such manipulative practices as pools, wash sales, and the like, whereby "insiders" fleeced the small and uninformed purchaser of stocks. Thirdly, the bill aimed to increase the effectiveness of 1930's Securities Act in preventing the selling of "blue sky" to the uninformed or deliberately misinformed: Every corporation the stock of which was listed would be required to provide the public with a financial report that was full, accurate, and, because of uniform reporting procedures, comparable to those of other listed firms.

But if the Fletcher-Rayburn bill, viewed by an expert legal craftsman and judged in terms of the general welfare, was beautifully drafted, and though there was wide agreement, even among businessmen, on the need for the broad reforms at which it aimed, the bill was also intricately technical to a degree that denied to most members of Congress any detailed understanding of it. And among those who did understand it, there was wide disagreement concerning the means it employed to reach desired goals.

Especially controversial were four of these means.

One was the provision for stringent margin controls, exercised by the FTC to insure that there would never again be such trading on dangerously thin margins, such frenzied gambling with borrowed money, as had played havoc with the exchanges in the past. Carter Glass and the Federal Reserve, though in favor of margin controls, objected to their imposition through FTC; they saw this last as an invasion by FTC of the domain of national credit control that properly belonged exclusively to Federal Reserve.

A second controversial provision specified in considerable detail what the required financial disclosure statements must contain. This was opposed by virtually the entire business community, including large retailers who deplored the past performance and loathed the present management of the New York Stock Exchange. They deemed it an outrageous governmental invasion of privacy and a long step toward business regimentation. The reaction of Sears, Roebuck's Robert E. Wood, who had been generally strongly supportive of the New Deal in general up to now, was representative. Wood wrote Roosevelt on February 28 that Fletcher-Rayburn in its present form would place "every corporation in the land under the supervision of the Federal Trade Commission, loading it with reports and subjecting it to . . . bureaucratic control."[47]

A third controversial provision was one upon which John T. Flynn had vehemently insisted—namely, the strict segregation of brokers and dealers. Section 10 of the original bill prohibited brokers from operating as dealers or underwriters "whether or not registered on any national securities exchange"; this meant that exchange members could no longer engage in floor trading on their own account. This was naturally displeasing to most exchange members —they must either confine themselves to brokerage operations or sell their exchange seats—but it was especially obnoxious to members of the regional exchanges, whose incomes in any depression year had to be drastically reduced by the proposed segregation and who saw the ultimate effect to be a further concentration of financial power in the hands of the "big boys" of the New York Stock Exchange.

The fourth controversial provision was the one assigning administration of the law to FTC. The exchange governors objected strenuously to this; they advocated establishment of a new regulatory agency, a board that would include at least two exchange members and "would be confined to exchange problems only and would not . . . be bound by congressional limitations," as the president of the New York Curb Exchange put it.[48] The new board or commission, in other words, would be given a broad mandate to "regulate" and would be left free to determine for itself how this would be done.

Richard Whitney organized and led opposition to the bill.

Within days after Roosevelt's recommendation of the legislation, the New York Stock Exchange president had formed an *ad hoc* national organization, with committees in key industrial cities, to wage war on Fletcher-Rayburn. He moved down to Washington for the duration of this war, renting a house from which to direct the struggle, and he was the first of a parade of witnesses who marched against the bill in mental uniform and in perfect emotional step with one another through several weeks of House and Senate committee hearings. Far from being an evil thing, speculation was the very essence of the American Way, the very foundation of the American system, and could not be prevented by statute in any case, since it was "human nature."* Such was the conviction of Richard Whitney; such was the conviction of those who followed him to the witness table.

They were not without effect.

Under intense hostile pressures, and in the knowledge that the White House had not endorsed the stringent requirements of the original bill but had instead evinced a willingness to compromise, Cohen, Landis, and Corcoran, the last of whom proved to be a remarkably able defender of the bill in Senate and House hearings, again rewrote the measure completely. In so doing, they weakened it considerably. Jurisdiction over margin requirements was shifted from FTC to Federal Reserve, though limits were placed on the board's discretionary power here. Several provisions dealing with broker-dealer segregation and exchange practices, mandatory in the original bill, were rendered discretionary on the part of the administrative agency. All the same, the measure retained enough strength to effect drastic change in the way business and industry were financed; it would greatly reduce the operating freedom which the exchanges had formerly had. And when the revised bill was presented to Congress on March 19, it pleased Whitney no more than had the original draft. He promptly said as much, as did many of his colleagues. Financial columnist Fred I. Kent spoke for these when, in a March 23 letter to Roosevelt, he asserted that the second bill "is just as unfortunate as the first and will be just as harmful to this country if it is passed. It has a positive tendency to separate men in Government and men out of Government into two opposing camps, which is most unfortunate for a people."[49]

But Roosevelt would compromise no further. The growth and hardening of business hostility toward him and the New Deal, a process which first came into full view of the general public in that March 1934, provoked a counter-hardening of his own mood. He now, on March 26, addressed to Fletcher and Rayburn a letter in which he strongly, unequivocally endorsed the revised measure.

"It has come to my attention that a more definite and more highly organized

---

*"Those who argue that social and moral reform is impossible on the ground that the Old Adam of human nature remains forever the same, attribute . . . to native activities the permanence and inertia that in truth belong to acquired customs," writes John Dewey in his *Human Nature and Conduct* (p. 109 of 1930 Modern Library edition).

drive is being made against effective legislation [to regulate the national traffic in securities] . . . than against any similar recommendation made by me during the past year," he wrote, in words read by millions. "Letters and telegrams bearing all the earmarks of origin at some common source are pouring into the White House and the Congress." Yet the "people of this country . . . in overwhelming majority" were fully aware that unregulated speculation in securities and commodities had contributed greatly to the "terrible conditions of the years following 1929," and they would "not be satisfied with legislation" on this matter which did not have "teeth in it." He himself was convinced "that speculation, even as it exists today," was dangerously excessive and must be "drastically curtailed" through the imposition of high margin requirements and that the federal government must have vested in it "definite powers of supervision over exchanges" sufficient "to correct abuses." He concluded: "The bill, as shown to me this afternoon by you, seems to meet the minimum requirements. I do not see how any of us could afford to have it weakened in any shape, manner, or form."[50]

Next day Roosevelt entrained for Miami, where, on March 28, he boarded Vincent Astor's *Nourmahal* for a ten-day fishing cruise off the Bahama Islands —the same area in which he had cruised immediately preceding the attempt upon his life a year before and with the same "gang" of immensely wealthy men. (One may safely assume there was no serious talk of politics on that cruise.)

While he was away, the Washington scene was enlivened, and the nation as a whole entertained, if not edified, by the antics of a certain Dr. William A. Wirt, superintendent of schools in Gary, Indiana. An excessively loquacious gentleman, elderly, and possessed of an excessively dramatic and con- spiratorial imagination, Wirt was also a monetary crank who had been a paid propagandist (a lecturer, a pamphleteer) for the Committee for the Nation, of which James H. Rand, Jr., of Remington Rand, was chairman.* In the sum- mer of 1933 Wirt had attended a dinner party in Washington. His companions at table had all been, by his own account, New Deal "brain trusters"; the table talk had all been, by his own account, of a Communist conspiracy to overthrow the existing order, a conspiracy in which all present, save the shocked and outraged Dr. Wirt, were actively involved. Roosevelt, it seems, was a figure- head, a puppet of the conspirators. He was "only the Kerensky of this revolu- tion," to be kept in seeming power until the conspirators were "ready to supplant him with a Stalin."† Meanwhile, his key decisions were not really his own, though he believed that they were; they were made for him by the secret Communists (Tugwell was one) who surrounded him, who had "control [of] the avenues of influence," and who manipulated him by means of this control.

*See p. 108.
†The Russian historical anology was faulty, of course, insofar as it was not Stalin but Lenin who "supplanted" Kerensky, and Kerensky was not the puppet but the victim of Lenin and fellow conspirators.

(Specifically cited by Wirt in later public testimony as an instance of communistic plot was the Arthurdale project. The resettlement of miners away from Morgantown, West Virginia, said the doctor, was a deliberate design to reduce Morgantown's rents and undermine its tax base. Actually, as Eleanor Roosevelt promptly publicly replied, not one of those resettled had paid either rent or taxes for years.)

All this and more of the same were recorded by Wirt in a bulky manuscript, which eventually found its way into the hands of Rand, and when Rand appeared before Rayburn's House committee to testify against the revised exchange bill, on March 23, he used this manuscript to support his own charge that the bill under consideration was the product of a deep, dark plot to point the nation "down the road from Democracy to Communism."

Rand's testimony created a national sensation. It was being played up to the greatest possible height by the press when Roosevelt left Washington for his holiday. But the sensation was short-lived. A select House committee was at once appointed to look into the matter. Wirt was called before it in early April for questioning. And at the witness table he proved himself to be either the dupe of practical jokers or a remarkably inept liar, if not both. Of the guests at that notorious dinner party, none had any close connection with the White House or with anyone of Roosevelt's inner circle, and none, by his or her own testimony (each was called to testify before the select committee), had spoken more than a few words all evening long. It was the voluble Dr. Wirt who had done all the talking, said the other guests; he had inflicted upon them a virtually unbroken five-hour discourse on his monetary views. . . .[51]

By the time Roosevelt returned to Washington on Friday, April 13 (he would never begin a journey on a Friday the thirteenth if he could avoid it, according to Grace Tully,[52] but evidently had no aversion to ending one on the "unlucky" date), the whole absurd affair had blown over in a way that did more to help than to hinder the exchange bill's passage.

To this last, the only obstacle now became certain quite wide discrepancies between House and Senate versions of the bill as reported out by the respective committees, for floor action, in early May. Retained in the House version, which passed through the lower chamber by a vote of 280 to 84 on May 5, were the original bill's designation of FTC as administrative agency and its mandatory margin requirements, though there was a secret willingness on the part of Rayburn, Roosevelt, and all the original chief draftsmen save Cohen to compromise as regards the administrative agency. The Senate version, which passed through the upper chamber by a vote of 62 to 13 on May 12, assigned administration of the act to a new five-man regulatory commission, to be appointed by the President, and gave this commission power to fix margin requirements for brokers' loans to customers while assigning to the Federal Reserve power to fix margin requirements for bank loans to brokers—a cumbersome division of power and authority between commission and Federal Reserve which was itself divisive of the financial community, with many brokers strongly opposed to it. It therefore became relatively easy, and adroit and discrete leadership by Roosevelt greatly helped, to remove the discrepancies in joint conference committee.

The conference-reported bill incorporated the Senate's proposal of a five-member Securities and Exchange Commission (SEC) to administer, in place of FTC, both the last year's Securities Act and the present measure, but it also incorporated the House's upper limit on the amount of money a broker could lend a stock buyer and on the amount of money a bank could lend a broker, with the Federal Reserve to have full power to fix margin requirements below these mandated limits. Of this final bill there was no floor debate; it was passed through both houses by a large majority. Roosevelt signed it into law on June 6.

There remained the highly important question of who should be appointed to the new commission. "The extent and effectiveness of the powers conferred by the legislation will depend largely upon the understanding of the possibilities under the statute by those charged with its administration . . ." wrote Frankfurter to Roosevelt. "And so, plainly, you need administrators who are equipped to meet the best legal brains whom Wall Street always has at its disposal, who have the stamina and do not weary of the fight, who are moved neither by blandishments nor [by] fears, who, in a word, unite public zeal with unusual capacity."[53] Four of the five whom Roosevelt soon appointed, with the advice and counsel of Ray Moley, met these specifications in the judgment of all New Dealers and most knowledgeable observers. Three were shifted over from FTC—a Progressive (La Follette) Republican from Wisconsin named George C. Mathews; an able Vermont Republican, Judge Robert Healy, who had been serving as FTC's general counsel; and James Landis. The fourth was Ferdinand Pecora.

But Roosevelt's choice of SEC's chairman, for a five-year term, astonished most of his cabinet when he announced it at a meeting on June 29; it raised a storm of protest from liberals everywhere when it became known to the world at large. For the man chosen was none other than Joseph P. Kennedy, the notorious "stock market plunger," as Ickes described him, whose valuable services to the Roosevelt 1932 campaign, financial and otherwise, had for so long gone unrewarded and who now stubbornly, adamantly insisted upon this reward.[54] "The President has great confidence in him because he has made his pile, has invested all his money in Government securities, and knows all the tricks of the trade," confided Ickes to his diary. "Apparently he is going on the assumption that Kennedy would now like to make a name for himself for the sake of his family, but I have never known many of these cases to work out as expected." To Howe, Eleanor, Marion Dickerman, and others of the innermost circle, nearly all of whom deemed the appointment outrageous, Roosevelt merely said, with shrug and smile, "Set a thief to catch a thief."[55]

And it may be said here, in forecast, that Roosevelt's expressed confidence in Kennedy's performance of his new role was justified by the event.

By word and deed, Kennedy soon convinced his colleagues on the commission and the financial community generally that he intended SEC to execute the law firmly and fairly, in the public interest, if not in the punitive, reformist way which Pecora (for one) favored. In his maiden address as SEC chairman, broadcast over national radio on the afternoon of July 25, he said: "We of the SEC do not regard ourselves as coroners sitting on the corpse of free enterprise. On the contrary, we think of ourselves as the means of bringing new life into the body of the securities business.... Everybody says that what business needs is confidence. I agree—confidence that if business does the right thing, it will be protected and given a chance to live, make profits and grow, helping itself and helping the country." He did indeed know all the tricks of the trade. His quick perceptions of attempted wrongdoing were born of his own active experience of churnings, bear raids, and the like, and so was his willingness to forgive past misdeeds. He spoke not as moralist but as hardheaded realist in the face of changed conditions when he said in public statement: "The days of stock manipulation are over. Things that seemed all right a few years ago [to such as himself, one assumes] find no place in our present-day philosophy."[56]

At the outset he faced that "strike by capital" of which Roosevelt had taken bitter note in the fall of 1933 and which intensified in the immediate aftermath of 1934's exchange legislation. There was what seemed to some a concerted refusal by industrial corporations and financial institutions to float new stock and bond issues, their evident purpose being to force the administration to nullify in practice the new regulatory law. Kennedy was at pains, therefore, to persuade bankers and industrialists and brokers that New Deal securities law, far from being inimical to long-term corporate financing, was designed to work strongly in favor of it, and since the facts argued on his side, he was convincing. In the early spring of 1935 there was a $43 million bond issue by Swift and Company, an opening up of credit which was encouraged in the following month, when the rules against stock manipulation which SEC had adopted were announced by Kennedy and, to the surprise of many, promptly endorsed by the New York Stock Exchange. Other exchanges quickly followed suit. By September 21, when Kennedy resigned his post, he having told Roosevelt to begin with that he would stay only a year, or until SEC was on solid footing, the volume of new corporate financing had climbed toward $1 billion (it reached $2 billion by the end of the year).[57] By then the new commission was generally acknowledged by the financial community to be a boon to exchange business, having through its operations generated confidence in the exchanges on the part of the investing public and having given the financial community increased confidence in itself. Lawful order had replaced chaotic chicanery.

The solid foundations laid during Kennedy's chairmanship were built upon under the chairmen who succeeded him during the next half dozen years: first Landis, then William O. Douglas, then Jerome Frank. All these successors were politically liberal. The last two were generally damned by the business community as "dangerous radicals." Yet each subscribed to Kennedy's expressed view, in a trade publication article, that SEC's great responsibility was that "of giving all the aid of which Government is capable to the better organization of the mechanism through which the savings of the people find their way into securities. . . . Domestic tranquillity is as essential to business as it is to our political system." Echoed Chairman Landis, warningly, in a speech to the Investment Bankers Association, a year later: "[I]f we [of SEC] fail, others will take charge; their sanctions, their mechanisms will be different." Chairman Douglas described SEC, in a 1938 address to a convention of social scientists, as "one of the outposts of capitalism" whose concern was "with the preservation of capitalism." And Jerome Frank in 1939, defending himself in private letter against a published charge that he was a "revolutionary" whose purpose as SEC chairman was "to lay the ground for . . . federal control of almost every activity of American life," proclaimed his fervent belief that "America will go to hell in a hack if there is a drive away from the essentials of our profit system." SEC existed, said he in another letter, "primarily to preserve the capitalist form."[58]

VII

So viewed, the Securities and Exchange Commission epitomized in nature and intent the whole of the New Deal as seen through history's eyes.

Of all New Deal agencies, it was perhaps the purest single expression of the central purpose, the overall endeavor of the Roosevelt presidency as Roosevelt himself conceived it to be: He would revive a failing capitalism; he would restore it to healthy growth.

And surely this was a purpose and enterprise to which the business community must enthusiastically subscribe!

Yet, ironically, it was out of the legislative battle from which there emerged the SEC, an agency soon recognized as beneficent by the very men who fought so furiously against its creation, that there arose also the first strong, open manifestation of a general business hostility toward the New Deal and toward Roosevelt personally which, simultaneously encouraged by the perceived growing "threat" of labor organization under the NIRA's Section 7(a), became soon as monstrous as it was adamant.

It was well on the way to becoming so by the Saturday night (it was July 28, 1934) that Eleanor sat with Hick, in soft moonlight, upon a park bench atop San Francisco's Russian Hill.

And by then Roosevelt was reacting to it, mentally, emotionally, against his own will.

He was at sea aboard USS *Houston* on that Saturday night, having sailed only a few hours before from Pearl Harbor toward his holiday's end in Portland. It had been a grand holiday. He was relaxed and suntanned; he was in the best of good humors as he looked out from the *Houston*'s deck across a mild, moon-silvered Pacific. Yet even in that moment of rare peace there was working through his thought and feeling a change of attitude, a shifting of emphasis, which presaged the end of what historians have come to call the First New Deal.

During the 1932 campaign and since entering the White House, he had now and then said, in public speech, things harshly critical of the way business had been conducted by businessmen during the years of Republican Prosperity. But at the same time, in the same speeches, he had been conciliatory, had expressed an eagerness to forgive and forget and to believe in the wholehearted cooperation of business with government in the solution of depression problems. His actual decisive deeds had been quite generally heavily weighted on the side of the big business interest against the competing interests of labor and the consumer as he dealt with the issues that rose to him out of the operations of AAA and NRA and out of the opposing demands of human compassion and governmental thrift (to keep taxes upon the affluent down) amid national economic distress. He had acted upon an assumption of basic human decency and commitment to American democratic principles on the part of American businessmen. Especially big businessmen.

And what was his reward from those whom he had favored?

The ingratitude that is more bitter than winter's wind, sharper than the serpent's tooth.

There began for him a period and process of emotional, attitudinal transition. Strongly suggested was the possibility that the most dangerous enemy of American capitalism, the most subversive of all subversives of the profit system, was the American capitalist—the big businessman with his myopic greed, his primary concern for his own immediate profit, his secondary concern for the immediate profit of his corporation's shareholders, his almost total disregard of the general good. And Roosevelt—That Man in the White House, as he was beginning to be hatefully dubbed by the affluent generally—could not but resent with growing disgust and contempt "the failure of those who have property to realize that I am the best friend the profit system ever had," as he said in a letter to Frankfurter, "even though I add my denunciation of unconscionable profits."[59] Alas, it was "unconscionable profits" that these men of property insisted upon and even demanded as their God-given right.

The letter quoted above was not written until early 1937. But even before he boarded the *Houston* at Annapolis on July 1, 1934 he expressed in public speech a developing sense and resentment of the hostilities directed against him. His fifth fireside chat, which was his first of that year, delivered on Thursday, June 28, was a defense of his administration's overall accomplishments against those who denigrated them because they sought and were being denied "special political privilege" and "special financial privilege." He asked each of his listeners to compare his or her "own individual situation" with what it had been a year ago. Was it not markedly improved? And "have you as an individual paid too high a price for these gains" in terms of "a loss of individual liberty?" He asked each listener to read the Bill of Rights of the Constitution, which he as President had "solemnly sworn to maintain," and then ask himself or herself "whether you personally have suffered the impairment of a single jot of these great assurances." He poured scorn upon the efforts of "plausible self-seekers and theoretical die-hards" to confuse and mislead the people by applying "new and strange names" to what the New

Deal was doing. Sometimes the name was "Fascism," sometimes "Communism"; sometimes it was "Regimentation," sometimes "Socialism." But in actual fact, "what we are doing today is a necessary fulfillment of what Americans have always been doing—a fulfillment of old and tested American ideals."

He resorted to extended metaphor:

> While I am away from Washington this summer, a long-needed renovation of and addition to our White House office building is to be started. The architects have planned a few new rooms built into the present all too small one-story structure. We are going to include in this addition and in this renovation modern electric wiring and modern plumbing and modern means of keeping the offices cool in the hot Washington summers. But the structural lines of the old Executive office building will remain. The artistic lines of the White House buildings were the creation of master builders when our Republic was young. The simplicity and strength of the structure remain in the face of every modern test. But within this magnificent pattern, the necessities of modern government business require constant reorganization and rebuilding. . . . The architects and builders are men of common sense and of artistic American tastes. They know that the principles of harmony and of necessity itself require that the new structure shall blend with the essential lines of the old. It is this combination of the old and the new that marks orderly peaceful progress, not only in building buildings but in building government itself. Our new structure is a part of and a fulfillment of the old.[60]

Within a week after his return to Washington from his holiday he was to manifest in a letter to Adolf Berle his further hardening of mood, was to give vent to his increase in irritation by business hostility and obstructionism.

Berle had written "Dear Caesar" to ask if it would be all right for him to serve as public member of an unpaid advisory board of the New York Stock Exchange which Richard Whitney was forming. Berle was inclined to think it a good idea: "At least we could try it until we discovered whether all they wanted was a whitewash committee, in which case I could pull out." Roosevelt replied at once: "I think it is absolutely all right to go on that Stock Exchange Board. As a matter of fact . . . the fundamental trouble with this whole Stock Exchange Crowd is their complete lack of elementary education. I do not mean lack of college diplomas, etc., but just inability to understand the country or the public or their obligations to their fellow man. Perhaps you can help them to acquire a kindergarten knowledge of these subjects."[61]

VIII

To the general deleterious effects upon the Arthurdale project of this change in opinion climate, this polarization of attitudes by the developing, highly emotional conflict of business versus New Deal, were added the specific effects of a bad mistake made by Louis Howe at the very outset of this subsistence homestead "experiment."

We have remarked the desperate urgency with which this desperately ill man, sensing that there might be for him no tomorrow, drove himself and others into a remarkably swift, a dangerously swift launching of this unprece-dented governmental enterprise. One element of his haste was his ordering by telephone, for shipment to Reedsville, of fifty prefabricated houses originally designed for summer residence on Cape Cod. The price was right. They cost only $1,000 apiece. And Howe let be known his optimistic belief that at least some of the thirty-six miners and their families who had been moved from coal town slums to Arthurdale by the third week in November 1933 (most were temporarily quartered in the old Arthur mansion, others encamped in tents on the mansion lawn) would eat their Thanksgiving dinners in the prefabs they had by then erected with their own hands. The rest would be housed by Christmas. In any event, it was not until June 7, 1934, that the homesteaders were enabled to move into their new homes. For when the prefabs were delivered, they proved to be too small for the concrete foundations which, by some incredible mischance, had already been poured for them. They also proved to be far too flimsy to provide adequate shelter against Appalachian winters. It became necessary to hire architect Eric Gugler, a long-time friend of Marion Dickerman's who by that token had become a warm friend of Eleanor's in the 1920s,* to redesign the houses and supervise a complete rebuilding of them. He did what all who understood his problem regarded as a superb job. The completed houses were "attractive indeed," as Ickes noted in his diary when he reviewed the design portraits of them. But the cost per house soared. It was estimated in excess of $10,000, more than five times the original housing estimate, when Ickes, in the White House with Gugler and Director M. L. Wilson of the subsistence homestead division, reviewed with Roosevelt the final design—this on March 10, 1934. "The President said that we could justify the cost . . . by the fact that it is a model for other homestead projects," wrote Ickes into his diary that evening. "My reply was to ask what it was a model of, since obviously it wasn't a model of low-cost housing for people on the very lowest rung of the economic order. . . . I don't see how we can possibly justify ourselves on this project. It worries me more than anything else in my whole department. . . . I am afraid we are going to come in for a lot of justifiable criticism."[62]

What Ickes fearfully anticipated, a headline-making journalistic expose of outrageous waste and extravagance in the conduct of this pilot project, had not yet come to pass when Eleanor and Hick made their way to that park bench on Russian Hill. But by then the Arthurdale project had already suffered a severe blow. In the closing days of its 1934 session Congress passed the ap-proriations bill to which Ludlow had attached his rider specifically forbidding the establishment of a Post Office factory at Arthurdale—and the rider re-mained intact. This boded ill for the project's future. Indicated was Arthur-

---

*Gugler had been a draftsman with the famed architectural firm of McKim, Mead & White, as had been Henry Toombs of the historically famous Toombs family of Georgia (General Robert Toombs was secretary of state of the Confederate States of America during the Civil War). A cousin of Eleanor's close friend Caroline O'Day, Toombs worked with Roosevelt in the design and construction of Val-Kill Cottage in 1925.

dale's destiny never to become the self-sustaining economic unit, mingling agriculture with factory employment, that was initially envisaged. At no time in its history would more than a third of the community's work force find employment in local industry, and most of the time the industrial employment level would be much lower than this, despite Eleanor's prolonged and determined efforts to persuade one or another large corporation to establish a permanent branch factory in the locality.

By that night, too, the blow Ickes most feared was about to be delivered. Already written was an article attacking Arthurdale from an all too solid factual base and employing a highly effective ammunition of sarcasm and ridicule. It was scheduled for publication in the August 4 issue of the weekly *Saturday Evening Post,* the most widely read magazine in America, whose editor in chief, George Horace Lorimer, an extreme conservative of advanced years and authoritarian temper, had declared open war upon Roosevelt and the New Deal as early as the autumn of 1933.*

When Eleanor arrived back in Washington, she found upon her desk a copy of the *Post* issue featuring this article, derisively entitled "The New Homesteader." Its author, Wesley W. Stout, fully shared Lorimer's political views —as a matter of fact, he succeeded Lorimer as the magazine's editor in chief in 1936—and the story of Howe's prefabs and their costly remodelling lost nothing of its absurdity in his telling of it. He also told of eight wells that had been expensively drilled and then abandoned because, allegedly, the architect had whimsically decided to relocate eight houses. (Actually this relocation was consequent upon a failure to make percolation tests of the proposed building sites at the time the Arthur tract was purchased, this being in turn consequent upon Howe's driving haste to get the project under way. The substratum proved to be a porous rock through which sewage easily flowed considerable distances to contaminate water supplies.) The story, as Stout told it, had a moral. It typified the ghastly bungling of the New Deal; it thus demonstrated the inevitable failure of any planned economy. And this moral would be at once reiterated in newspaper features and editorials, dozens of them, of which clippings would be sent Eleanor in a bundle soon after her return to Washington.[63]

She would be hard put to defend the project at her next news conference. The "girls" of the press corps would be under orders from their editors to question her rigorously.

But on this Saturday night in San Francisco neither past nor impending Arthurdale troubles disturbed either her or Hick as they sat together, looking far out over the moonlit Bay.

Their holiday together had not begun well. Reporters and photographers

---

*In the year of Roosevelt's election Lorimer, upon the retirement of Cyrus Curtis, had become president of the Curtis Publishing Company, which owned both the *Post* and the *Ladies' Home Journal.* Yet he retained his position as editor of the *Post.*

had jammed the lobby of the Sacramento hotel where Eleanor and Hick were to stay on the night of Eleanor's arrival, by plane, from Chicago, though her destination when she left Chicago was supposed to be secret. Doubtless an airline press agent had, as Hick believed, tipped off the press. The next morning, when Eleanor continued flatly to refuse to give them her holiday itinerary, reporters and photographers had followed the two women in a dangerously high-speed chase as a California state trooper drove Hick's new Plymouth north from Sacramento toward the little town of Colfax, where the two were to spend a few days, in total anonymity they hoped, with an old friend of Hick's. Eleanor had been forced finally to abandon the hazardous escape attempt. She had dismissed the state trooper, had seated herself in the shade of a tree with her knitting in hand, and had told her tormentors that she was perfectly willing to sit there all day, knitting, if necessary, "but I am not going to tell you where we are going." In the end, it was the newsmen who had been forced to give up.

Good times had followed. There had been no invasion of the two women's privacy in Colfax or on the ranch at Pyramid Lake in Nevada, to which the two had driven over the High Sierra to visit daughter Anna, who was staying on this ranch (it was owned by friends of hers) while establishing the state residency required for her obtaining a Reno divorce from Curtis Dall. Good times had continued as the two camped in Yosemite National Park, though Hick had been angered there one day when a crowd of tourists unexpectedly converged upon them, with clicking cameras, while they were feeding chipmunks that ate from their hands.

But the best time of all, the two agreed, was this night together in San Francisco.

They had checked into "a small inconspicuous hotel back of the St. Francis" whose manager, a friend of Hick's since the days when she had lived in this city, was respectful of their wish for privacy and protective of their right to it. They had dined in a nearby restaurant, a small place and unknown to tourists, which served, in Hick's words, "the best French food I'd ever eaten anywhere." No one in the restaurant had paid any special attention to them, nor had anyone on the cable car which took them up Russian Hill. And to climax it all was this loveliness of quiet solitude and silver light and soft, warm air, with the Bay shimmering in moonlight below them. They felt more intimately *together,* more in tune with each other, than they had felt at any time since their tour of the Gaspé Peninsula last year.

It was after eleven when they left the tiny park and rode a cable car down the hill. In a drugstore near the St. Francis they had ice cream sodas, then walked back toward their hotel, happily agreeing that "it had been a perfect evening."

But it ended abruptly.

They were met a half block from their hotel by the hotel manager, who agitatedly warned them that his hotel's lobby was filled with reporters. He was distraught. He kept protesting that he had told no one of the First Lady's presence. Hick believed him. Probably the hotel's single bellboy was responsible for the crowd of reporters and flash-exploding photographers through which the two women had to push their way to reach, in angry dismay, the privacy of their room. And there was a continuation of this misery for them the next morning when they breakfasted in the Hotel Clift's coffee shop (their own hotel had none); all day long it continued as they moved about the city and, by ferry, across the Bay to Sausalito. "We were able to exchange hardly a dozen words in private," Hick remembered long afterward, but bitterly still.

They managed to escape early next morning. In Hick's Plymouth they drove northward along the coast, in leisurely fashion, staying in out-of-the-way places. They visited Crater Lake National Park. They visited Muir Woods. They were undisturbed in their privacy until they checked into a hotel in Bend, Oregon, some hundred miles southeast of Portland, for the last night of their holiday together. While they dined that evening, word spread of the First Lady's presence in the town. When they entered the lobby from the hotel dining room, they found it packed with people, among them Bend's mayor at the head of a reception line. Hick fled to the suite which the manager had annoyingly assigned them. She left Eleanor to her fate—a fate which, as Hick realized in a spasm of utter despair, must forever prevent that mutual happiness they both had dreamed of, she and Eleanor.

It was a furious First Lady for whom Hick opened the door of their suite a long half hour later and who, in a loss of self-control unprecedented and unsucceeded in all Hick's experience of her, slammed the door hard behind her. Her cheeks flamed as she went into Hick's assigned room and dropped down on Hick's bed. She spoke then those words of finality, an acknowledgment of the end of dreams, which Hick had known from the first must at last be spoken but which sounded, all the same, as a death knell in her ears.

"Franklin said I'd never get away with it, and he was right!" said Eleanor. "I can't."

She paused, breathing out a long sigh.

Then she said, in words reminiscent of those she had spoken to her mother-in-law when she abandoned her plans for a European camping trip with Marion Dickerman and Nancy Cook and her two youngest sons in the summer of 1929: "From now on I shall travel as I'm supposed to travel, as the President's wife, and try to do what is expected of me."[64]

BOOK THREE

※✕※

The New Deal Ebbs,
Then Flows to
Its Highest Tide

→>>X<<←
Into a Land of Quandary:
The Elections of 1934, and After

I

IT was in the dawn's early light—a gray light on that cloudy morning of
Friday, August 3, 1934—that the cannon-bristled warship *Houston* sailed out
of the Pacific into the Columbia's mouth and began to plow its way, at reduced
speed, upstream and eastward. Shortly thereafter a suntanned Franklin Roosevelt, looking and feeling remarkably fit as he rose up from his bed in the
admiral's quarters,* saw through portholes the first land he'd seen in five days
and knew that his ocean voyage, with its laze of sun and fun and tangy salt
air, had already ended, that the open sea was already miles behind him and
receding at a steady rate of several knots into spatial distance and time past.
His mood, however, was not regretful. His mind did not dwell upon that which
was passing away. He looked ahead, his mind and mood thrusting forward in
zestful anticipation. And especially was this so as regards his *immediate*
future. For he entered this morning, and would traverse during the days just
ahead, a mental landscape and field of endeavor through which he could move
with greater confidence, perhaps, than he could through any other that was
not primarily political, he being remarkably well prepared for travel in it and
knowing himself to be.

From the quarterdeck, where he sat after breakfast facing the prow, he saw,
a mile to the left of him, a dark slope of green-forested earth interspersed with
rock cliff rising above placid waters, saw another such slope rising a half mile
to his right, saw upon the river's bosom a cargo ship moving toward him,
passing him on his left, and he was "reminded a good deal of another river,
a river on which I was born and brought up," as he was to say a few hours
hence in public speech. "It has been my conception, my dream," he was also
to say, "that while most of us are alive we would see great sea-going vessels
come up the Columbia River as far as The Dalles," where cargo would be
transferred from ship to barge, from barge to ship, the river and certain of its
main tributaries having by then been so engineered that barge transportation
extended north "into the wheat country" of eastern Washington, and even
"into the State of Idaho." He admitted, he was to reiterate in his speech, that
this "is a dream, my friends. . . ." It was, however, no "idle dream." So far
did it lie within the limits of "what men can do to improve the conditions of
mankind" that he could and did restate it as a practical problem for the
Columbia not unlike one already triumphantly solved in his own home state,

---

*The *Houston* was a flagship.

on his own home river. "It was only a comparatively few years ago—within the last ten years—that through the action of the Federal Government the channel of the Hudson River was so deepened that Albany, 140 miles from the sea, was made into a seaport."[1] An unbroken line of water transport, by river and barge canal, ran now all the way from New York City to Buffalo. . . .

And as he sat there dreaming of the Columbia's future and made an imaginative leap toward his dream's practical realization, the battle cruiser he rode made a right turn with the river's channel, a slight turn at first (the bend was only somewhat more acute than that of the Hudson at Crum Elbow) but soon a sharper one until, heading into the stream, he traveled almost directly south toward the confluence of the Columbia and the Willamette. The mouth of the Willamette was reached and entered a little after ten o'clock. By eleven or thereabouts the *Houston* was warped and tied to a dock on the Willamette's bank, in Portland, while a huge crowd upon the waterfront looked on. From thousands of throats burst a roaring cheer when a little later the President of the United States appeared on deck beside the ship's officers to welcome aboard, with ceremony, the secretary of war and the secretary of the interior.

Two hours later, after a buffet luncheon had been served on ship, the President appeared again before a crowd that, far from shrinking, had increased in size and manifest enthusiasm during the long wait. The roaring cheer was louder than before when he, his steel leg braces locked and with one hand tightly gripping a brawny arm beside him, came slowly, stiffly down the gangplank. There was upon his suntanned face not the slightest sign of the strain, much less of the dully throbbing pain, which he always felt when he "walked." He broadly smiled, head held high, he gaily waved to the cheering thousands as he approached the automobile awaiting him at the gangplank's foot. After entering the car while others of his party entered other cars lined up behind his, he began a processional tour of the city. What followed was a most happy, gratifying experience for those who rode in the procession. Despite lowering skies from which showers now intermittently fell, "everyone in Portland" was "lined up along the right of way, and many besides"—or so it seemed to Secretary Ickes, who was mightily impressed by this demonstration of Roosevelt's personal popularity.[2]

Out of Portland, then, the presidential cavalcade drove at moderate speed for two hours eastward over a road beside the river to Bonneville and through that little town to the site of the great Bonneville Dam, on which construction had been recently begun by the Army Engineers. There, at the damsite, had gathered another huge crowd, and to it Roosevelt spoke extemporaneously for a brief quarter hour, including in his remarks the analogy of Columbia and Hudson which had occurred to him that morning. Then back to Bonneville. Parked there on a siding, and boarded at once, was a special train of five Pullmans to accommodate the governors, cabinet ministers, senators, congressmen, newspaper correspondents, and working assistants of various kind, who now constitute the presidential party or would during coming days. At the train's rear was the President's private car where his wife, Louis Howe, and three Roosevelt sons—James, Franklin, Jr., and John—would ride with him. The train pulled out in the late afternoon.

Thus began, just three months before the midterm elections, a triumphant progress across the Northwest and the western Midwest to Chicago, a slow but busy and crowded passage through five days, on every one of which save Sunday Roosevelt was seen and heard by thousands upon thousands of people.

On Saturday, October 4, he spoke at the Grand Coulee damsite on the Columbia, in Washington, to a crowd estimated at more than 20,000—this in a desert country! Many in the crowd had driven 200, even 300 miles to be there. He spoke also that day in Spokane and in the little town of Bonners Ferry, in Idaho, only a few miles south of the Canadian line. Dinner guests at the Roosevelt family table in the President's private car that night were Secretary of War Dern, Secretary of Interior Ickes, and Montana's Senator Burton Wheeler. They found little need or, indeed, opportunity to converse. Soon after all were seated at table, Eleanor, very much in character, opened a torrent of exclusively familial argument by remarking the need for a more equitable distribution of the national income among American citizens and proposing to achieve it through "a strict limitation of income, whether earned or not." This accorded far more closely with Huey Long's published views than with those of the Roosevelt sons, all of whom were, in fact, outraged by their mother's "subversive" idea, being themselves convinced of every American's God-given right to "earn" as much as he could and keep it. They said so, vehemently. Thereafter they and she monopolized, and loudly, the dinner conversation, with the President making but slight contribution and, when he did, being shouted at by his excited sons. At one point Ickes managed to raise his voice above the din to opine that his host must have learned how to manage Congress from his dealings with his own family.

"But Congress," objected an amused Wheeler, "is never as bad as this."[3].

The next day, Sunday, Roosevelt spoke to the whole nation via network radio from Glacier National Park, in Montana, spoke in praise of the National Park Service and, with special emphasis, "of the work of the Civilian Conservation Corps boys," some of which he had seen that day. He said, in words prepared for him by Louis Howe:

Of the 300,000 young men in these [CCC] camps, 75,000 are at work in our national parks. Here, under trained leadership, we are helping these men to help themselves and their families and at the same time we are making the parks more available and more useful for the average citizen. Hundreds of miles of firebreaks have been built, fire hazards have been reduced on great tracts of timberland, thousands of miles of roadside have been cleared, 2,500 miles of trails have been constructed and 10,000 acres have been reforested. Other tens of thousands of acres have been treated for tree disease and soil erosion.

He went on in words of his own:

This is just another example of our efforts to build not for today alone, but for tomorrow as well. . . . We are definitely in an era of building, the best kind of building —the building of great public projects for the benefit of the public and with the definite objective of building human happiness. I believe, too, that we are building a better comprehension of our national needs. People understand, as never before, the splendid public purpose that underlies the development of great power sites, the improving of navigation, the prevention of floods and of the erosion of our agricultural fields, the prevention of forest fires, the diversification of farming and the distribution of industry. We know, more and more, that the East has a stake in the West and the West has a stake in the East, that the nation must and shall be considered as a whole and not as an aggregate of disjointed groups.

On Monday, August 6, he spoke at Fort Peck, on the upper reaches of the Missouri River, in Montana, where the largest earthen dam in the world (the Gatún Dam in the Panama Canal Zone "is a pygmy compared with Fort Peck") was under construction. Again he stressed interdependencies and connectedness, referring

> to the fact that when this dam is completed, it is going to be an important factor in the navigation of the Missouri River. It is going to maintain a nine-foot channel. This channel will connect with the Mississippi. It will enable the wheat growers and farmers of the Northwest to get cheaper transportation rates from the middle of the country to the south and the east and to foreign countries. Then, of course, there are other features: the power that will be generated; the effect on flood control and soil erosion. One of the things that makes me happiest is that downstream from this point they are going to be able to place under irrigation some 84,000 acres of land —land which today is not particularly fit for human habitation and which, when we get water on it, will be the means of support and honest livelihood for thousands of American families.

He was aware of contradiction between this opening of new land for farming at a time when "overproduction" was the bane of the agricultural economy and the justification for AAA production controls, but this contradiction he passed over, slurred over with the suggestion that the newly watered land would be populated by families who moved of their own volition off the land on which they now lived miserably because it was marginal, or submarginal, and "ought not . . . be used for agriculture." Fort Peck Dam, then, would be, when completed, the "fulfillment of a dream" but of a dream which "is only a small percentage of the whole dream covering" all the "watershed of the Missouri River, not only the main stem of the Missouri but countless tributaries that run into it and countless other tributaries that run into these tributaries. Before American men and women get through with this job, we are going to make every ounce and every gallon of water that falls . . . count before it makes its way down to the Gulf of Mexico." And even this was but a part of the "whole dream," for he would have similar planned development for "all the important watersheds of the nation."[4]

He entered now a drought-stricken land.

It was no such blasted, blighted region as extended south of him for hundreds of miles and across 200 miles or so from east to west, through the western Dakotas and western Nebraska, all across the high plains of western Kansas and eastern Colorado, down through Oklahoma into the Texas panhandle. There, with the end of three decades of abundant or sufficient rain and the onset of a cycle of increasingly dry years, men began three years ago to pay, and they now paid with compounded interest, the price of the stupendous plains plow-up and wheat planting of the early years of the century, especially of the war years. Millions of acres had been stripped of the ground-hugging grasses (buffalo, gamma) which had carpeted them for thousands of years. They now lay naked, defenseless against winds that blew almost constantly, often furiously, their force unmitigated or uninterrupted for mile on mile by any such obstacle as hill or tree. The consequences were bitter, acrid with dust. Every living plant and every human hope paled and withered, if it did not perish, as the fierce sun glared down out of a sky of brass and dusty death claimed day by day a greater dominion. It began to extend far beyond the plains and the people of the plains. Almost every major dust storm since 1931 had increased in intensity, and in the area covered, until, just two and a half months before, on May 11, 1934, one of them raised an 8,000-foot wall of dust that swept on a west wind all across the eastern half of the United States, almost blotting out the noonday sun in the nation's capital.

But if the North Dakota countryside he saw on this Tuesday was not as parched as the Great Plains west and south of him, it was thirsty enough. When he descended from his train in a hot blaze of afternoon sun and toured the farm country around Devils Lake in an automobile for a couple of hours, he saw at one point along the road he traveled a crudely lettered sign addressed to him in wry, ironic prayerfulness: "You gave us beer, now give us water."

He referred to this last a short time later when he spoke to another astonishingly large crowd, in Devils Lake. He said, "[T]he beer part was easy," its being clear that "the people of this country . . . wanted beer" and that he had legal authority to give it to them. "But when you come to this water problem . . . you are up against" natural forces that were beyond the control of man "in his present stage of development." This was not to say, however, that *nothing* could be done over the long run. For more than a year he had personally concerned himself with soil and water conservation as it affected agriculture, had had technical experts hard at work on various aspects of the problem. He had taken special interest in a proposal by one forest scientist* to make 100-foot-wide shelterbelt or windbreak plantings of drought-resistant trees and shrubs, running crosswise to the prevailing winds, as a means of conserving moisture and reducing soil blowing on the Great Plains. He had been told that such "forest-strip planting" proved effective of its purpose in the Ukraine, in Russia, fifty years ago and that Nebraska experiments proved such plantings to be effective "over an area ten times as wide as the trees were tall."[5] He persisted in his espousal of this idea despite the lack of enthusiasm for it on the part of most professional foresters and against the strong objections of Lew Douglas to any adequate funding of such enterprise, on the ground of

*Raphael Zon, director of the Lake States Forest Experiment Station in St. Paul, Minnesota, who did most of the planning for the shelterbelt and was placed in charge of its technical aspects when it got under way in the summer of 1934.

"government economy." He was to continue to press stubbornly along this line until, by the end of the decade, shelterbelts established by the Forest Service had become a prominent feature of the plains landscape, achieving all the success predicted for them by their proponents. "Soon after I get back to Washington many of the studies being made this summer . . . will be completed," he now told his Devils Lake audience. "I expect to confer within the next few weeks with all the experts. I shall give an opportunity to people who do not agree with their conclusions to come and be heard. As you know, I believe in action."[6]

His listeners did know it. They cheered him to the echo when, his brief remarks ended, he waved his farewell and turned away.

He entered his private car. The train pulled out.

And as we observe him unlocking his leg braces and seating himself in easy chair, there to take his ease in usual fashion (that is, very busily: He had paperwork constantly in hand; he had consultations constantly in progress) until he spoke again from the rear platform of his train a couple of hours later to another great crowd, in Fargo, we may also observe that the action he had taken and would take with regard to natural resource conservation and hydroelectric power was more deeply rooted in informed thought, more abundantly nourished by studiously earned ideas, than action he normally took in any area outside that of pure elective politics. By innate character and formative experience he was a country gentleman, invincibly, personally rural in his outlook upon a gigantically mechanized and urbanized America. Stronger in him than in most men was a profound instinctive feeling for living nature. Something deep in his spirit vibrated in rare sympathy with the rhythms of seasonal change and weather change, of river flow and sea tide, and the growth of green-growing things, trees and grass, food plants and flowers (especially strong had always been his love of trees), thrusting their way out of the living soil into sunlight and air, ripening there in open air, then dying back into the soil whence they came. Since his earliest childhood in Hyde Park and Algonac on the Hudson, in Fairhaven and Campobello on the sea, he had so vibrated.

Of this deep feeling he had shaped with unwonted mental effort concepts which served him now as guides to policy. Some of the most basic emerged twenty-odd years ago from his laborious drafting of a speech he presented to a People's Forum in Troy, New York, on March 3, 1912, barely a month after his thirtieth birthday.*[7]

He sought then to define two kinds of freedom in terms of "what we today call Conservation," one the "liberty of the individual," the other the "liberty of the community." He said: "It was recognized in Germany . . . one hundred years ago that the trees on the land were necessary for the preservation of water power and indeed for the health of the people" and that therefore, the individual owners of wooded land could not be permitted to denude it at will. "Today . . . the land-owner must cut only in a manner scientifically worked out. They

*See Davis, *FDR: The Beckoning of Destiny,* pp. 266–67.

[the Germans] have passed beyond the liberty of the individual to do as he pleased with his property and found it necessary to check this liberty for benefit of the freedom of the whole people." Nothing of the sort was done 500 years ago in what was then "one of the most prosperous provinces in [northern] China," an area famous as "both a lumber exporting center and . . . an agricultural community." At its heart was a populous walled city. Today that city was abandoned. "There is not a human being within its walls. There are but few human beings in the whole region. Rows upon rows of bare ridges and mountains stretch back from the city without a vestige of tree life, without a vestige of flowing streams and with the bare rocks reflecting the glare of the sun. Below in the plains the little soil which remains is parched and unable to yield more than a tiny fraction of its former crops. This is the best example I know of the liberty of the individual without anything further."

And had there not been in some sad degree a repetition in New York State of the mistake those northern Chinese made half a millennium ago? Had not New York forests been leveled for immediate profit by lumber companies that paid no heed to selective harvesting or reproductive planting? And why "are so many of the farms in the State of New York abandoned? The answer is easy. Their owners fifty or one hundred years ago took from the land without returning any equivalent to the soil [by means of] . . . fertilizers and other methods of soil regeneration. Today the people of the cities and the people on the farms are suffering because these early farmers gave no thought to the liberty of the community." This process of soil ruination must be halted; the "liberty of the community" must prevail over the "liberty of the individual." The time might soon come "when the government of the State will rightly and of necessity compel every cultivator of land to pay back to that land some quid pro quo."[8]

Thus did a normally pragmatic, empirical collector's mind struggle to think organismically about environmental problems in relation to political action. It was a struggle that prepared Roosevelt's mind to accept organismic concepts that would be presented to it after the state senator of 1912 had become the President of 1933.

II

ONE such concept had come to him, via Rex Tugwell, from a big, rumpled, homely, blue-eyed fifty-two-year-old dynamo of a man named Hugh Hammond Bennett—a man direct and simple in all his dealings with the world, single-minded, forceful in personality yet selfless in his conception of public service—who in the spring of 1933 had been for three decades a soils scientist in the U.S. Department of Agriculture's Bureau of Chemistry and Soils. H. H. Bennett was a soil erosion alarmist; his USDA pamphlet *Soil Erosion: A National Menace,* with its stress upon the insidious but stupendous loss of topsoil through sheet erosion on sloping fields conventionally cultivated (only gully erosion is immediately obvious to untrained eyes), created something of a sensation upon its publication in 1928, and not only among agriculturists. He was also, and consequently, a soil conservation evangelist; two of his recent published papers (1930, 1931) called for a national program of soil and water conservation wherein research and education were fused in ways immediately effective of actual widespread erosion control on farming land.

And it was both as alarmist and as evangelist that Hugh Bennett made an agitated appearance before the desk of a newly installed assistant secretary of agriculture one spring day to protest a proposed so-called soil conservation program that was to be funded with $5 million of PWA funds and to consist exclusively of terrace construction on farmland. The proposal, cried Bennett, was outrageous. For 100 years terraces had been built in the United States to prevent erosion and, on the whole, they had done more harm than good because "we haven't known how . . . or where to build them, or how to maintain them," and have failed to support them with such other soil-saving practices as contour plowing, strip cropping, grassed waterways, crop rotations, and the assignment to permanent vegetative cover (pasture, meadow, woodlot) of land the erosibility of which rendered it unsuited to row-crop cultivation. The practicality of these last measures was attested to by the prosperous farms of the Mennonites of Lancaster County, Pennsylvania, who had used them since the mid-eighteenth century on rolling erosible land that yet remains highly fertile. What Bennett proposed to Tugwell is use of the available $5 million to initiate "demonstration projects" which would be exemplary displays ("show-cases") of *true* soil conservation. In these demonstrations individual farmers would cooperate with government conservationists to plan and carry out on their farms integrated programs based on soil survey maps, employing, not just terraces (often no terraces at all) but whatever combination of erosion control practices was best suited to the land's need and the farmers' interests.[9]

Rex Tugwell was easily persuaded, and persuaded Ickes, or so he believed, to set up at once an erosion control agency, with Bennett its director, in PWA. Tugwell's plan was to incorporate the new agency eventually as a permanent bureau in the Department of Agriculture, where it obviously belonged. But Ickes was a bureaucratic empire builder of limitless ruthless ambition (he was bound and determined to make Interior *the* conservation department of government despite its dreary record of sellout of the public's to special interests), and Ickes had control of the only money immediately available to this present enterprise. So it was in Interior, not in PWA, that a Soil Erosion Service (surely an infelicitous name for it!) was established in the late summer of 1933, under Bennett's dynamic leadership.

Bennett's labors were immense and immediately productive. He knew precisely what needed to be done at the topmost executive level and where to find the men to do it, knew also where and how to lay his hands upon the kind of men best equipped to staff field offices and there work directly with farmers and on the land. Within a few weeks he assembled a staff notable, even among New Deal agencies, for zealous, youthful dedication to its job. Within a few months forty erosion control projects encompassing 4 million acres were operating in thirty-one states, and scores of CCC camps were devoting full time to soil conservation work. It was an enterprise in which Roosevelt took great personal interest. At its very outset he said to Tugwell or, it may be, Ickes: "Tell Bennett to be sure to select areas, wherever possible, on a watershed basis. If his conservation should show important effects on the reduction of flood heights and the deposition of silt from rolling uplands, it will help his program [so far as congressional appropriations are concerned] as nothing else is likely to do."[10] This was good advice, expressive of the organismic thinking Roosevelt now habitually did in this field of conservation; but it was advice that encouragingly confirmed rather than directly determined Bennett's plan of action. For Hugh Bennett was wise, indeed, in the ways of running water, the water that stole soil away; he knew well that runoff paid not the slightest heed to property lines or to political boundary lines but followed always and only the physical lines of least resistance along the steepest gradients. He knew, too, the connection of upland runoff and erosion with downstream problems of floods and the silting that inhibits navigation. All his demonstration projects, from the first, were watershed projects. . . .

Bennett and his staff were moving in highest gear by the midsummer days of Roosevelt's cross-country progress from Portland toward Chicago. And from this night (August 7, 1934) of presidential train ride from Fargo down across southwestern Minnesota toward Rochester, where next day he was to pay public tribute to the brothers Mayo of the Mayo Clinic, we may look ahead eight months to a day when he conferred with Hugh Bennett, whom he had abruptly, unexpectedly summoned to the White House at a time when, as he well knew able, touchy, pugnacious, empire-building Harold Ickes was out of the capital, in Florida.

On that day Bennett remained somewhat longer in the Executive Office than the normally scheduled quarter hour. And within an hour after his departure Roosevelt dictated to Ickes a memorandum, the contents of which were at once phoned to the interior secretary by a highly disturbed administrative assistant. The memo said:

> Mr. Bennett is most appreciative of the splendid cooperation he has had from the Department of the Interior and I want to make it perfectly clear to you that he has not in any shape, manner or form, advocated a transfer of the Soil Erosion Service to the Department of Agriculture. Nevertheless, after full consideration . . . I have definitely concluded that as a matter of function, the Soil Erosion Service should be transferred to the jurisdiction of the Department of Agriculture. . . . In view of this will you be good enough to ask the Public Works' administrative body to pass the necessary Resolution making the transfer? I think no Executive Order is necessary since the Soil Erosion Service was originally set up in the Department of Interior by Resolution of the Public Works Administration.

He knew as he dictated this last sentence that Ickes might interpret it as a rebuke of his grabbing the Soil Erosion Service into Interior in the first place —an interpretation which might make the transfer seem, to Ickes, a disciplinary action. Roosevelt fully expected to receive, as he did in fact receive at once, a lengthy telegram from the interior secretary vehemently protesting the transfer and begging for, at the very least, a postponement of final action until he was back in Washington. Instead, at Roosevelt's personal insistence, the PWA board met at four o'clock on a Friday afternoon (March 22, 1935) and took the ordered action, though Ickes was due back in Washington, and was indeed in his office, before noon next day. Upon his desk he found a "Dear Harold" missive from the President saying, with what its recipient deemed a bland mendacity:

> I would certainly have waited in the matter of the Soil Erosion Bureau except for the fact that a very difficult situation started to come to a head on the hill. [*What* "difficult situation"? asked Ickes of himself; he could discover none.] I had already talked with Bennett, who, I think, preferred personally to stay in Interior because of the splendid treatment you have given them. Nevertheless, I had to decide the matter from the point of view of common sense administrative layout and charting and there is no question that Soil Erosion has more to do with Agriculture activities than with Interior activities. I am sure you will understand.[11]

And Ickes did understand, only too well. Or thought he did.

His anger and hurt were greater by far than they would have been had Roosevelt consulted him forthrightly and face-to-face in this matter, had listened to his opposition with due respect, then overruled it on the grounds ultimately stated. As it was, he felt he had been slapped in the face in contemptuous, humiliating reprimand. ". . . I have no disposition to submit to . . . incidents of this sort," he fumingly wrote in his diary. ". . . [Roosevelt] had no right to go over my head in my absence. It looks like disciplinary action." And his bitter resentment of insult grew until, ten days later, it burst forth in what he himself described as "a pretty savage letter to write to the President of the United States," a letter setting forth "the complete record" regarding the Soil Erosion Service and making most "vigorous comment" not so much upon the transfer itself, though Ickes continued to oppose it, as upon "the manner in which . . . [it] was effected. . . ." The letter, however, was never mailed. Its author prudently submitted it to the judgment of two of his top subordinates, both of whom urged him to "file it away with other similar letters that have had no effect except somewhat to relieve my feelings," though in "this particular instance my feelings have not been relieved. I resent very much the way the President has treated me . . . and I am not likely to forget it."[12]

Thus did Ickes indicate his awareness, vague but strong, that in "this particular instance" (there were many others, one of them the presidential dealings with Moley during the London Conference), Roosevelt's devious conduct was determined primarily not, as it often was, by human kindness, but by his instinct for power—for the gaining and keeping of it. No man possessed of Roosevelt's empathic sensitivities could fail to know that Ickes's sufferings would be augmented by the doubts, the uncertainties, which his chief's bland indirections would plant in his normally cocksure mind. The anguish must therefore be deliberately provoked for, as Ickes suspects, "disciplinary" purposes, Roosevelt being acutely aware that Ickes, like Moley in 1933, was inclined to be a little too sure of himself and of his special standing with the White House and had a love of power that, unchecked, could become a threat to Roosevelt's own exercise of it. His present operation knocked Ickes off-balance. It shrank Ickes's self-assurance and self-righteousness to manageable proportions, creating a need for reassurance from on high that measured as it increased Roosevelt's personal power and authority over him. Moreover, this operation enabled Roosevelt to exercise those skills of "charm," of smoothing out initially rough differences, the exercise of which he thoroughly enjoyed.

A portion of Ickes's diary entry for Wednesday, April 10, 1935, is revealing. In it he tells of a full half hour of talk he had with the President in the morning. Ickes, who had come "with the full intention of discussing matters frankly," found the President "looking well and in good spirits." He bluntly asked the President "whether he was trying to discipline me in transferring Soil Erosion to Agriculture. He said, 'Certainly not,' and wanted to know why I felt that way. I told him . . . that the transfer was made late of a Friday afternoon and I was due back in Washington the following morning. He said he had found a bad legislative situation and had to take quick action. I told him I knew all about the legislative situation and that if it had been let alone, Congress would have passed a bill making Soil Erosion a permanent function of this Department." One might imagine Roosevelt's response to this—a shrug of his powerful shoulders, perhaps, and a broad but rueful smile in tacit admission that he had been caught out. He then stated that his real reason for acting as he did was precisely the one given in his written communications to Ickes—namely, that erosion control belonged "functionally" in Agriculture. For one thing, much such work must be done in the national forests; these were under the jurisdiction of the Forest Service, which was in Agriculture. So it was, said Ickes, but it "belongs in Interior" as per the bill to transform Interior into a Department of Conservation which, as Roosevelt knew, was being drafted under Ickes's direction. Ickes asked now if he "should go ahead with my bill," and Roosevelt said, "All right, go ahead." Ickes pressed: "Will you make it an administration measure?" Roosevelt "hesitated and then said that perhaps he might." Thus Ickes accomplished really nothing, nothing solid, of what he had been bound and determined to accomplish in this interview, yet found the President so cordial, "his manner . . . most friendly" that he was disarmed, mollified despite himself. As he was about to take his leave, "I remarked that I didn't find it easy to get into an argument with him this morning, and he laughed."[13]

By this time the House had passed (April 1) against no opposition a bill, H.R. 7054, establishing as a bureau in the Department of Agriculture a Soil Conservation Service, replacing the Soil Erosion Service. Hearings on it were conducted in the Senate Office Building where, on an April day, H. H. Bennett was the chief witness before the Senate Committee on Public Lands and Surveys. And on that day he drew out his expert testimony unconscionably, as it seemed to several weary senators, piling statistic on statistic and fact on fact to a top-heavy height, did so deliberately because he had been informed that an immense cloud of dust, larger and denser than the one of May 11 last year and far more so than two that came over Washington only a few weeks past (all three were statistically described at excessive length in Bennett's testimony), was on its way from the Dust Bowl and should sweep into the capital sometime during the afternoon. It did so, at last, abruptly, and it was in its effect almost as theatrically dramatic as the prose in which Bennett's hero-worshiping biographer presents the episode: "The group [of senators] gathered at a window.... The skies took on a copper color. The sun went into hiding. The air became heavy with grit.... Here was Texas for every congressman to grind between his teeth. Here was Oklahoma reddening the eyes and making breathing difficult. Here were tons and tons of fertile soils—farms from Kansas and Colorado and New Mexico—swirling in from a 2,000-mile journey to tell the committee that this man Bennett was right, tragically right, urging them to accept his assurance that enormous folly was on the land and in the air [4 million acres had been ruined by erosion; 60 million more, severely damaged] and that something must be done immediately to stem it."[14] At once the committee reported the bill favorably, unanimously, to the full Senate; on April 15 the Senate passed the bill unanimously;* on April 27 the President signed it into law. The Soil Conservation Service director was H. H. Bennett; its staff, that of the Interior agency it replaced. . . .

All this, to repeat, was yet eight months and more in the future as the President's special train carried him on Wednesday, August 8, 1934, from Rochester to Lake City and Wabasha on the Minnesota bank of the Mississippi and then on across the river into Wisconsin.

But already, as he rode east toward Green Bay, where on the morrow he was to give the one speech of his cross-country tour that had definite political overtones, he had a vision of America that can be described in terms of the organismic watershed concept—the concept which the two Morgans and Lilienthal applied on a grand scale in TVA and which H. H. Bennett applied on a much smaller scale, with much more limited means, in each of his soil conservation demonstration projects. There was in Roosevelt's mind a vivid, though vaguely defined, sense of water, flowing water, as means and organizing principle of Union. The watershed became metaphor. It bespoke the unity of nature and the bitter wages of man's sinning against this unity. By the same token, it bespoke the natural necessity and the basis in nature for defining *individual* freedom as a *cooperative* enterprise in any truly civilized human society, especially one of advanced technology. The America it stood for would be possessed of that "liberty of the community" based on principles of natural resource conservation which a young Franklin Roosevelt, inspired by the

---

*One senator introduced the next day a motion to reconsider, but he withdrew his motion after making the point that administration of the new law *ought* to be by the Interior Department.

example of Cousin Theodore,* struggled so hard to describe two decades ago, a "liberty" that did not destroy or even truly limit the "liberty of the individual" but incorporated and validated and enhanced it.

Coon Valley in southwestern Wisconsin, where the very first of Bennett's projects, a model for all the rest, was established, might be taken as example. It was a steeply sloping 92,000-acre watershed the soil of which was abnormally erosible. Within it everything was so connected up and rendered interdependent by running water that the failure of one strategically placed upland farmer to reduce runoff and soil loss from his land must complicate, if it did not wholly frustrate, the conservation efforts of his neighbors downstream. And as running water thus created interdependencies and compelled cooperation among those who farmed the land—this, or ruin—it also created interdependencies and compelled cooperation among those experts, those scientific specialists, whom Bennett recruited as his field staff. Agronomists, soil chemists, foresters, wildlife specialists, agricultural engineers, agricultural economists (farm management specialists)—these came into Coon Valley in the fall of 1933 to make a concerted attack, in cooperation with individual farmers, upon soil erosion. Each had the pride of his profession, his specialized knowledge. Each was committed to his particular expertise and convinced of its crucial importance in the world. Yet by Bennett's administrative policy—a policy directly determined by the needs of the land—no agronomist operated exclusively or primarily as an agronomist in Coon Valley, no forester as forester or engineer as engineer, but each and every one operated primarily as "soil conservationist," a new breed of professional man in Bennett's conception.

There had been effected in less than a year a marked change in Coon Valley's physical appearance, a marked growth of community among its inhabitants, when Roosevelt spoke informally from the rear platform of his train to a great crowd at Sparta, Wisconsin, only a few miles from the watershed project's northern boundary, on the afternoon of Wednesday, August 8, 1934. Four years hence the change would be dramatic. By then well over half the farms in the watershed, including virtually all those upland farms most susceptible to erosion damage, were operating in accordance with complete farm conservation plans. Every acre of each "cooperating" farm was assigned to the use for which it was best suited; this meant that much formerly plowed land was now under permanent vegetative cover, used as meadow, pasture, woodlot. Not one steeply sloping acre was cultivated in straight rows; all were contourtilled, most of them in alternating strips of grain and grass (or clover, or alfalfa). CCC camp labor, of which a high percentage was under Soil Conservation Service direction nationally, had planted in this watershed hundreds of thousands of trees on formerly denuded, rapidly eroding slopes; scores of miles

*TR's very first presidential message to Congress declared "forest and water problems" to be "perhaps the most vital internal problems of the United States" and called for a federal program of conservation and reclamation that was, for that time, of huge dimensions.

of soil-saving, water-saving terraces had been built; gullying had been halted by scores of check dams, streamback erosion by scores of wing dams. And a grateful land thanked its stewards with an enhanced crop and dairy productivity, a resurgence of wildlife (quail, ruffed grouse, pheasant populations increased with the increase in cover), and improved trout fishing as the streams in the watershed flowed more brightly, cleanly. Downstream the effect of all this was a distinct lessening of the silt burden borne by Coon Creek into the Mississippi. The frequency and height of Coon Creek's floods during wet seasons was reduced, while the level of stream flow during drought seasons was somewhat higher than in former years. As for the people of Coon Valley, their cooperative effort toward harmony with the natural environment had joined them together in community spirit, community pride, as never before.[15]

It was natural for Roosevelt, as he thought about America's rivers and river policy, to begin, as Bennett perforce did in his conservation labors, with "small waters" far upstream—with the natural integrity, water being the integrator, of small watersheds that were organically joined together by water flowing into river systems which were in turn joined together, fused, into gigantic river basins containing hundreds of thousands and even millions of square miles. He temperamentally preferred the small particular, the definitely concrete, to the general and abstract. But in public speech, from the perspective of his high office, he proceeded from "great waters" to small: He began with that "main stem" of his Fort Peck speech and envisaged "countless" tributaries branching out from it into other "countless" tributaries in a sequence extending to the outermost margin of the whole immense valley. The end was the same, however one began (sound river thinking *has* to be holistic), for every acre and every square mile of every river basin is linked with every other by a continuous network or "seamless web" of water—surface water, topsoil water, subsoil water—flowing fast or slow, or merely seeping, but always in the same direction ultimately, its final destination the mouth through which the central river pours its substance into the sea.

And Franklin Roosevelt, thinking thus of America's major river basins, found notable a commonality of economic and social interests, of attitudes and ways of life among the people of these basins which accorded fairly closely with the basin's unity of water and pointed toward *natural* community of the kind emergent, on small scale, in Coon Valley. His sense of this was at the root of his developing dream of river valley authorities, modeled on TVA, for "all the important watersheds of the nation"—the Columbia, the Missouri, the Colorado, the Upper Mississippi, the Arkansas, the Connecticut, et al.—with each authority a government corporation set up to do a unified, multipurpose, valley-wide job. This would do away with the prevailing wasteful chaos of bureaucratic rivalries whereby a half dozen federal agencies operated as sovereign powers upon a half dozen artificially designated portions of, say, the Missouri Valley's overall river problem. For Roosevelt, during his journey eastward, had been made sharply aware, had been sharply reminded of the bureaucratic war now being waged between the Bureau of Reclamation and the Army Engineers for control of the Missouri Valley's limited and widely fluctuating water supply.

Many of his presidential dealings with both agencies had been and were to continue to be unhappy. They were especially so with the Corps of Engineers, which, he was finding out, was more submissive to the desires of big contractors, big business in general, than to policy directives of the President whenever the desires and the directives conflicted. This overweening power of the Engineers, militating against wise river planning and frustrating democratic process, derived in large part from the fact that the National Rivers and Harbors Congress, a special-interest pressure group, numbered among its members many who were the objects of its pressure—namely, U.S. senators and representatives and all Army Engineer officers engaged in rivers and harbors work —as well as representatives of state and local governments, industrial organizations, trade associations, labor unions, and private contractors. When the National Resources Board* presented to Roosevelt a few months later a proposal to combine in a single national agency all elements of river planning, a proposal the President was eager to implement, he received from Secretary of War Dern a letter opposing the move, evidently because it would undermine the Army Engineers' privileged position vis-à-vis Congress. Dern's letter spoke of "noteworthy and praiseworthy achievements of the Corps of Engineers, acting *in pursuance of law as an agency of the legislative* [*not* the executive] *branch.*"†[16] In the summer of 1934, the corps and the Reclamation Bureau were each developing bit by bit their own Missouri Valley plans, ultimately to become the Pick Plan for the Engineers, stressing flood control and navigation, and the Sloan Plan for Reclamation, stressing irrigation and power development. They were contradictory of each other in terms of water supply: If either was carried out fully, the other could not be. There just wasn't enough water.

III

THE language of conservation, devoid of divisive ideological overtones, its words referring to things and facts rather than issues and ideas, was a language for agreement and cooperation. It was in essential nature and useful purpose the very language of Roosevelt's highly conscious effort during his first year

*The board was established by an executive order prepared just before Roosevelt embarked on his *Houston* cruise and issued on July 3, 1934. The same order abolished the National Planning Board. The new board's members were the secretary of the interior (chairman), the secretary of war, the secretary of agriculture, the secretary of commerce, the federal relief administrator, Frederic A. Delano (Roosevelt's Uncle Fred), Charles E. Merriam (he was chairman of the political science department at Chicago University), and economist Wesley C. Mitchell (he was director of research for the National Bureau of Economic Research). The last three named constituted the original advisory committee of the board, to which other members were subsequently appointed. The committee was, in effect, the board as a functioning body; the other members constituted, in effect, the board's oversight committee. See Edgar D. Nixon, ed., *Franklin D. Roosevelt and Conservation,* (Franklin D. Roosevelt Library, Hyde Park, N.Y., 1957), v.1, pp. 317–18.
†Emphasis added.

in the White House to present himself to the electorate as personally above the
battles of partisan politics—as President of All the People, in James MacGregor Burns's phrase. He had employed during these months, to the maximum
extent possible within his political situation, in public speech, words that
named matters of fact obvious to common sense and concepts plainly derived
from such matters of fact. On occasion the concepts were directly those of
conservation, as in the draft speech he was reviewing on that August 8, on his
way across Wisconsin:

> Year after year, as science progressed and mastery of the mysteries of the physical
> universe increased, man has been turning nature, once his hard master, into useful
> servitude. That is why, on this trip across the northern part of this continent, I have
> been so moved by the distressing effects of a widespread drouth and at the same time
> so strengthened in my belief that science and cooperation can do much from now
> on to undo the mistakes that men have made in the past and to aid the good forces
> of nature and the good impulses of men instead of fighting against them. Yes, we
> are but carrying forward the fundamentals behind the pioneering spirit of the fathers
> when we apply the pioneering methods to the better use of vast land and water
> resources. . . ."[17]

He addressed himself again and again to the "average citizen," the "average
man"—to provide "a wider opportunity" to the "average man" was the New
Deal's purpose, he said—for the average was in his conception the very essence
of All. On occasion, if generally off-the-record, he deprecated use of the party
label: It was divisive, and it failed accurately to indicate the basic views of the
individual so labeled; these views and their position on a measuring scale
between right and left were what was truly important politically. He equated,
was even inclined to identify, "neutrality" with "middleness." He himself
strove for balance upon a fulcrum of neutrality, himself the fulcrum, at a point
"a little left of center," but only because of his conviction that the overall drift
of current history was slowly leftward and that therefore, the position he
occupied at any given moment, though it *seemed* leftish, was actually, in terms
of the long run, precisely of the middle. "My best judgment is that I should
take part in no Jefferson Day celebrations this year," he wrote Colonel House
on March 10, 1934, rejecting an invitation to do so from one of the colonel's
friends. "Our strongest plea to the country in this particular year of grace is
that the recovery and reconstruction program is being accomplished by men
and women of all parties—that I have repeatedly appealed to Republicans as
much as to Democrats to do their part. . . . Therefore I think you will agree
with me that much as we love Thomas Jefferson we should not celebrate him
in a partisan way. It would be a fine thing if non-partisan Jefferson Dinners
should be held, but there should be as many Republicans as Democrats on the
banquet committees."[18] (As we have seen and as Burns points out, Roosevelt
cooperated fully in the balls celebrating his *own* birthday. He was, however,
at great pains to make these absolutely nonpartisan, nonpolitical; he addressed
the celebrants as a President of All the People who happened to have suffered
polio and now used his high office to help other polio victims and promote

research which might wipe out this dread disease—a cause favored by every-one.)

Yet if he occasionally deprecated use of the party label under the conditions then prevailing, he constantly strove to change these conditions in a way that would make the label truly meaningful. He continued a course of action upon which he had entered during his first term as state senator in New York and which he emphatically defined in a banquet address to the Democratic National Committee in Chicago in May 1919. Then and there he pointed to the disastrous defeat the Democratic party had suffered in 1904 when, reacting against Bryanism, it tried "to reconcile the conservative wing of the party" in the face of Theodore Roosevelt's Progressive Republicanism. He said that "from that day, it became evident that the Democracy of the United States was and is and must be a progressive Democracy." Ever since, whenever opportunity presented itself, he had done what he could toward a party realignment whereby the Republicans were clearly and exclusively defined as conservative and reactionary, the Democrats as progressive and liberal. During the current midterm election campaign, whenever and wherever there was a close race between a Progressive Republican and a reactionary Democrat, he would do nothing to help the latter and sometimes, if his persuasive weight could decide the contest, would let it be known, without actually saying out loud, that his personal preference was the Progressive Republican. He would do the same with regard to contests in states having third parties whose candidates ran to the left of the New Deal's main line but closer to it, in Roosevelt's estimation, than regular Democratic candidates did on the right.

Thus it was in Minnesota, where by Roosevelt's specific written order Farley did and would do nothing to aid regular Democrats running against Farmer-Laborite Senator Henrik Shipstead and Farmer-Laborite Governor Olson. Thus, too, in the Wisconsin across which Roosevelt rode on this August day. Last May, under the leadership of the La Follette brothers, Young Bob and Phil, the Progressive wing of the Wisconsin Republican party broke away from the GOP, with which it had long had in actual fact nothing in common, and established itself as a new party, or restoration of the elder La Follette's party of 1924, the Progressive party. The incentive for doing so was the disaster that befell Governor Phil La Follette when he sought reelection as a Republican in 1932. The popular reaction against Hoover, the popular attraction toward Roosevelt had then caused numerous Wisconsin Progressives to swing over into the Democracy during the primaries, and Phil had failed of renomination as a Republican. Democrat A. G. Schmedeman had won the governorship that fall and now sought reelection, running against Progressive Phil La Follette, while Young Bob ran for reelection to the U.S. Senate as a Progressive, against a regular Democratic opponent. Roosevelt would let reporters know "off-the-record" that he wanted Bob La Follette to win yet yielded to pleas of regular Democrats in Wisconsin that he not publicly endorse Young Bob. At Green Bay on August 9, in his address to the huge throng gathered before him and to the nation, he was ostentatiously evenhanded, recognizing no issue between

Progressives and Democrats. He spoke of Wisconsin's two senators, Bob La Follette and [Democrat] Ryan Duffy, as "both old friends of mine," who "worked with me in maintaining excellent cooperation . . . between the executive and legislative branches of government." He also thanked "Governor Schmedeman, another old friend of mine, for his patriotic cooperation with the national administration."

Cooperation was, indeed, the central theme of this Green Bay address— cooperation to improve the conditions of life for the "average man"—and it was in terms of their refusal of such cooperation that he expressed his impatience with, his resentment of "certain types of so-called 'big business' " (big businessmen) who now declared their hostility to the New Deal and to him personally more and more openly, more and more fervently. He spoke of the "long and bitter fight" which "the average man in Wisconsin waged" not only against wilderness, the "blind powers of "Nature," but also "against those forces which disregard human cooperation and human rights in seeking that kind of individual profit which is gained at the expense of his fellows. It is just as hard to achieve harmonious and cooperative action among human beings," he went on, speaking from sad experience, "as it is to conquer the forces of Nature. Only through the submerging of individual desires into unselfish and practical cooperation can civilization grow." He poured scorn upon the notion that the essential ingredient of recovery and prosperity for the nation was what big businessmen called "confidence," by which they meant assurance that their own exploitive economic privileges would be maintained or restored.

> Before I left on my trip . . . I received two letters from important men, both of them pleading that I say something to restore confidence. To both of them I wrote identical answers: "What would you like to have me say?" From one of them I have received no reply at all. . . . The other man wrote me frankly that in his judgment the way to restore confidence was for me to tell the people of the United States that all supervision by all forms of government, federal and state, over all forms of human activity called business should be forthwith abolished. Now, my friends, . . . that man was frank enough to imply that he would repeal all laws . . . which regulate business —that a utility could henceforth charge any rate, unreasonable or otherwise; that the railroads could go back to rebates and other secret agreements; that the processors of food stuffs could disregard all rules of health and of good faith; that the unregulated wild-cat banking of a century ago would be restored; that fraudulent securities and watered stock could be palmed off on the public; that stock manipulation which caused panics and enriched insiders could go unchecked. In fact, my friends, if we were to listen to him and his type the old law of the tooth and the claw would reign in our nation once more. The people of the United States will not restore that ancient order. There is no lack of confidence on the part of those businessmen, farmers and workers who clearly read the signs of the times. Sound economic improvement comes from the improved conditions of the whole population and not a small fraction thereof. Those who would measure confidence in this country in the future must look first to the average citizen.[19]

There followed a few sentences specifically intended to reassure men of property. They had been inserted in the draft at the last moment upon the insistence of Ray Moley, who had told Eleanor that he was "worried about certain things in the Wisconsin speech" and been told by her he should communicate his worry to her husband.[20] Hence the words: "This Government intends no injury to honest business. The processes we follow in seeking social justice do not, in adding to general prosperity, take from one and give to another. In this modern world, the spreading out of opportunity ought not to consist of robbing Peter to pay Paul. In other words, we are concerned with more than mere subtraction and addition. We are concerned with multiplication also—multiplication of wealth through cooperative action, wealth in which all can share."[21]

The conciliatory note was not, however, the dominant note of this speech, so far as the business community was concerned. It was the note of irritation with big businessmen that sounded most loudly and clearly in the ears of these businessmen, and to it they reacted negatively, angrily in public comment. They thereby ensured that this Green Bay presentation would become in retrospect a pivotal address, pivotal in its precarious tipping balance between those basic attitudes which Roosevelt had maintained during his first year in the White House and the very different attitudes, as regards business, which had in the last few months begun to replace them. The change was, from Roosevelt's point of view, a forced one. It was made necessary by the businessman's resurgent and wholly unrepentant rapacity, his refusal to admit any responsibility for the debacle of 1929 now that the New Deal had removed the imminent threat of social revolution, and by his insistence that there be restored to him, as a "right" which he identified with "freedom," the prestige and the privileged power to exploit without hindrance which were his during the New Economic Era.

IV

A few days after his arrival back in Washington on August 10, Roosevelt received a visit from Jouett Shouse, the conservative former director of the National Democratic Committee headquarters, who told him of a new organization, called the American Liberty League, which was in process of formation and which Shouse was to head. It was, stressed Shouse, a "non-partisan" body the purpose of which was "educational"—namely, to teach respect for property and property rights and to teach the duty of government to protect property and encourage private enterprise. Did Roosevelt object to this? asked Shouse. Roosevelt, of course, did not. As President he had no authority to interfere with any such private organization, he smilingly replied, and as private person he had no wish to do so, being himself committed to the very general economic views Shouse had stated.[22]

But he had no illusions about the new organization's real purpose—nor did anyone else after the league was incorporated on August 22 and a public announcement of it made next day. Its members were prominent conservative Democrats of the same stripe as Shouse, Democrats whose economic views were indistinguishable from those of right-wing Republicans and who were at one with the Republicans in increasingly active hostility toward Roosevelt and the New Deal. Among them were Al Smith, John W. Davis, John J. Raskob, Irénée du Pont, and Pierre S. du Pont. Associated with these Democrats were such wealthy Republicans as former New York Governor Nathan L. Miller, Representative James W. Wadsworth, steelman Ernest T. Weir, oilman J. Howard Pew, Alfred P. Sloan of General Motors, and Sewell L. Avery of Montgomery Ward. It very soon became clear that the league's "educational" purpose was that of political propaganda—propaganda designed to convince the public that every salient feature of the New Deal, every measure which encouraged labor organization, promoted social security, provided for slum clearance and public housing, regulated business in protection of the public against malpractices, and sought for a more equitable distribution of the national income through use of the taxing power was an element of an overall conspiracy to subvert the Constitution and establish a Socialist or Communist state.

This rising organized animosity on the right was far less worrisome to Roosevelt, however, as he looked beyond the midterm elections toward those of 1936, than was the growing popular discontent and organized opposition on the left. For one thing, the Liberty League, in its original conception and in its actions from the outset, was characterized by that "lack of political instinct," that "spectacular amateurishness," which Walter Lippmann had noted in Raskob's operations as Democratic National Committee chairman at the close of 1931.* Expressive of this and of its root in the big businessman's contempt for the intelligence of common folk was a "confidential memorandum" circulated among Liberty League organizers during the summer of 1934 by W. H. Stayton. "However strong or efficient such an organization [as the league] may be," Stayton had written, "it will have great difficulty in accomplishing its purpose unless it has a moral or emotional purpose. Nor do I believe that many issues could command more support or evoke more enthusiasm among our people than the simple issue of the 'Constitution.' Public ignorance concerning it is dense and inexperienced but, nevertheless, there is a mighty, though vague, affection for it. The people, I believe, need merely to be led and instructed, and this affection will become almost worship."[23] Within the Republican party itself, the league's advent was greeted with a severely limited enthusiasm (only the denizens of Wall Street seemed thoroughly to approve) and a considerable measure of opposition. Astute William Allen White deplored the league's use of "free enterprise" as a disguise for monopoly capitalism. "The right of every man to go his own economic way and play his own selfish, sordid or silly economic game according to the dictates of his own stupidity or his own ignorant cupidity—that day is gone," said a White editorial in his Emporia (Kansas) *Gazette* in mid-August 1934. The "restriction of men who now use their liberties for economic license" would gain a "larger

*See Davis, *FDR: The New York Years,* p. 126.

economic liberty," White opined.[24] More surprising was the response of White's good friend Herbert Hoover when he was invited by Raskob to join the new organization. Hoover, who in the popular perception was the personification of all the Liberty League stood for, was unlikely to forget that Raskob had "financed the Democratic smearing campaign" directed against him by Charlie Michelson. Raskob and his fellows were, "therefore, hardly the type of men to lead the cause of Liberty," wrote Hoover, adding that he had "no more confidence in the Wall Street model of human liberty, which this group so well represents, than I have in the Pennsylvania Avenue model upon which the country now rides."[25]

No such political ineptitude had characterized Huey Long's organization of a so-called Share Our Wealth Society, with a slogan of "Every Man a King," in January 1934, or his launching of it as a national enterprise with a highly effective network radio broadcast a month later. Long proposed that the federal government impose a capital levy tax that would be confiscatory beyond $5 million for any one family, or beyond 300 times the average American family fortune, and an income tax that would prevent any family's receiving more than $1 million a year, or more than 300 times the average American family income. Out of the taxes thus collected, the federal government would provide every family with a $5,000 "homestead"; guarantee a family income of $2,000 to $3,000 annually, or of one-third of the average family income, whichever was larger; provide each elderly person with an "adequate" pension; give generous bonuses to veterans; and finance the college education of all youths of proved ability. Long further proposed increased government regulation of the economy, a thirty-hour week for an eleven-month work year, and government purchase and storage of agricultural surpluses to balance supply and demand in the farm marketplace.[26]

Also launched in January 1934, by a mild-mannered, modestly circumstanced sixty-six-year-old medical doctor named Francis E. Townsend, had been a nonprofit corporation called Old-Age Revolving Pensions, Ltd., to promote what soon became known nationwide as the Townsend Plan. Dr. Townsend, after decades of meagerly paid service to impoverished rural communities in the Black Hills of South Dakota, had wearied of the harsh Dakota winters and gone into semiretirement (he held a minor health department post) in Long Beach, California, where, one day, through a window of his modest home, he had watched with horror as three old women searched through a garbage can in an alley for bits of food—this in America, the wealthiest nation on earth! Horror had given way to mighty wrath, though he was by nature a remarkably gentle, patient man. Out of wrath had come the determination "to do something about it." And of this determination had been born his inspiration. He proposed to provide for the aged, restore mass purchasing power, cure unemployment, and revive business prosperity by giving $200 a month to every person over sixty years of age, regardless of personal means, *provided* (1) that the recipient retired from active employment and (2) that he or she spent the full $200 within a month after its receipt. The scheme was to be financed by a 2 percent tax on all "transactions"—by a general sales tax, in other words. Anyone who critically examined Townsend's arithmetic could see that his plan, which would require a police state for its enforcement, must lead to economic disaster. Between 8 million and 10 million old people would receive between $20 billion and $24 billion (the latter figure was more than thrice the total federal and state tax bill for 1934), all of it to be raised by a sales tax that pressed most heavily upon those least able to pay it and that would promptly pyramid to ruinous heights as it was compounded from one "transaction" to another. Such critical examination was not encouraged, however, was indeed actively discouraged by the leaders of what was destined to become virtually a religious crusade.

Neither of these grand schemes (not Townsend's, not Long's) had yet sparked a mass movement of truly major national proportions, but each was clearly well on the way to doing so, by the late spring of 1934. Already 1,000 or more Townsend Clubs with hundreds of thousands of elderly members had been formed. Already these clubs, the first effective pressure group for the elderly over organized in America, had become a political force in California. And the movement grew nationally by geometric progression. By year's end the Townsend movement was to number more than 5,000 clubs, with some 2 million members. As regards Share Our Wealth Clubs, the story was much the same. The first of these were formed in Louisiana, as an integral part of Long's state machine, but soon clubs were being organized in other southern states and throughout the Midwest, with a heavy concentration of them in the "radical" north-central states. Long had hired as professional organizer one Gerald L. K. Smith, an ordained minister of the Disciples of Christ, who had rare talents as a rabble-rouser, and with Smith's aid, the Share Our Wealth movement was growing by leaps and bounds. Its enrolled membership was well over 7 million by year's end, and its fellow-traveling converts numbered millions more. The two movements together had been a major incitement of that portion of a lengthy special message to Congress from Roosevelt, on June 8, which not only reaffirmed the administration's commitment to social insurance but also took the first definite steps toward its implementation.

Yet another pressure from the left against Roosevelt's centrism came out of the fertile mind of author Upton Sinclair, who had been a resident of Southern California (he lived now in Beverly Hills) since 1915.

Sweet-tempered yet continuously outraged by perceived social injustices; puritanical in his attitudes toward sex and alcohol yet unusually strongly sexed and occasionally adulterous; selfless yet self-centered and immensely ambitious; incurably sentimental yet also often hardheaded and clear-eyed, Sinclair, aged fifty-five in 1933, was an addict of causes, each of which became for him a passionate moral crusade. His indefatigable journalistic muckrake had exposed, among other evils, a filthy and labor-exploitive meat-packing industry (*The Jungle*, 1906), a business-dominated and hence unfree press (*The Brass Check*, 1919), colleges and universities that were business-dominated and hence falsely educative (*The Goose-Step*, 1919), a criminal justice system perverted by business interests in the case of Sacco and Vanzetti (*Boston, 1928**), and a motion-picture industry that was rife with financial chicanery (*Upton Sinclair Presents William Fox, 1933*). He had been a member of the Socialist party for thirty years. But he had grown unutterably weary of the endless ideological quarrels which split the party into factions following the death of Eugene Debs in 1926 and denied it the possibility of becoming a truly decisive force in American politics. He had become convinced that the needed social changes could be effected only from within one of the two major parties. So when a wealthy Santa Monica friend urged him to run for the Democratic nomination for governor of California, he, who had been the Socialist gubernatorial candidate in 1930, was quickly persuaded. On September 1, 1933, he changed his party registration from Socialist to Democrat, and he announced his candidacy shortly thereafter. The event was national front-page news. Among Socialists and their sympathizers it created a sensation and vast consternation. A telegram to Sinclair from his son in New York City cried out: "Almost collapsing [with] grief [over your] insane opportunism. Is it possible you have lost all integrity as man and Socialist?" From Norman Thomas came a letter saying, "You alone, or you with the help of a certain number of California voters, cannot make the word Democratic a symbol for Socialism. That word with its capital D is a symbol for the party which bitterly discriminates not only against Negroes but white workers in the South, for the party of Tammany Hall in New York, and [Frank] Hague in New Jersey." But Sinclair never considered withdrawing from what both his son and Thomas regarded as a hopeless contest, one which could only injure the cause of socialism. (Thomas spoke ruefully of Sinclair's "sublime naïvete.")[27] Instead, he promptly wrote, published himself, and sold by the 100,000, a short book entitled *I, Governor of California, and How I Ended Poverty: A True Story of the Future,* announcing therein a program to End Poverty in California (EPIC) that would, by peaceful means, replace capitalism with a cooperative Socialist society.

It was based upon a dozen stated principles. The salient ones were that "private ownership of tools, a basic liberty when tools are simple, becomes a basis of enslavement when tools become complex"; that "the present depression is one of abundance, not scarcity"; that "the destruction of food or other wealth, or the limitation of production [as in the AAA and NRA programs] is economic insanity"; and that "the remedy is to give the workers access to the means of production and let them produce for themselves, not for others." Sinclair proposed to do this by having the state acquire, through purchase or rental, idle industrial plants which would then be turned over to unemployed workers. By means of the plants the workers would cooperatively manufacture their own clothing, shelter, food products, and other necessary goods, ex-

---

*Sinclair's two-volume novel concentrated upon the obvious unfairness of the Sacco-Vanzetti trial. His research convinced him against his will that the Sacco-Vanzetti defense had made use of perjured testimony and that Sacco, at least, was probably guilty of the crime for which he was convicted.

changing these things among themselves through use of a scrip that was valid money only within the cooperative system. This last would soon spread out in a network of "production-for-use" communities which, as they expanded and demonstrated their superiority over "production-for-profit" units, while the latter continued to falter and fail, must soon transform capitalist California into a cooperative commonwealth the example of which other states would be bound to follow. In the meantime, Sinclair as governor would repeal the state sales tax; institute a graduated income tax on all incomes above $5,000, with a 50 percent tax on all incomes above $50,000; and greatly increase inheritance taxes and property taxes on large real estate holdings, while exempting from property taxes all houses and farms valued at less than $3,000.[28]

The EPIC program proved at once surprisingly popular. So eager were "average" Californians to learn about it from its author that Sinclair was enabled to pay nearly all his campaign expenses by selling his signed campaign literature and by charging admission to campaign rallies at which he spoke. Moreover, by the summer of 1934 EPIC as a program had won endorsements from influential people far outside California's borders, among them John Dos Passos, Theodore Dreiser, David Dubinsky of the International Ladies 'Garment Workers' Union, and Emil Reive of the hosiery worker's union, the latter two of whom were members of the Socialist party. By then, too, Sinclair's candidacy had long ceased to be a joke to the propertied classes of California (they were definitely alarmed) or to Sinclair's eight Democratic primary opponents, the chief of whom was George Creel, Woodrow Wilson's war propagandist in 1917 and 1918, who was supported by Wilson's son-in-law, Senator William Gibbs McAdoo. All the same, the Democratic administration in Washington was as astonished as the rest of the country when, on primary day in late August, Sinclair won the gubernatorial nomination decisively. He received, in fact, more votes than all his rivals put together, a total of 436,000 compared to their 377,000 (George Creel won only 288,000), and since his vote total exceeded that won by incumbent Governor Merriam in the Republican primary, his chances for election seemed excellent. Here was an embarrassment for the national Democracy! It was a rueful, reluctant Jim Farley who said on the morrow of the primary that "there's nothing else we can do but congratulate him [Sinclair]," then signed in green ink a letter endorsing the entire California state Democratic ticket. "The party has never failed to support its nominee," said Farley defensively. And it was a wary, cautious, challenged, yet very curious Roosevelt who, shortly after the primary, agreed to a visit from Sinclair. The visit would have to be "nonpolitical," though, said Roosevelt through Marvin McIntyre; the President was taking no part in state elections.[29]

To these pressures from the left (Long's Share Our Wealth, the Townsend Plan, EPIC) was added that summer an increasingly radical leadership of an increasingly militant labor movement, this in reaction to the adamant, violent refusal of employers to permit the union organization and collective bargaining presumably guaranteed by the NIRA's Section 7(a). We have seen how this happened in Minneapolis, where the leadership was Trotskyite, and in San

Francisco, where the leadership was Communist in sympathy, if not in party membership. There was a similar radicalization of labor in Toledo, where Ohio national guardsmen fired into a crowd of striking workers at the Electric Auto-Lite Company, killing two and wounding hundreds; in Seattle, where clubs and tear gas were used to rout strike pickets; in the "model" company town of Kohler, Wisconsin, where deputy police shot twenty-one strikers, killing one of them; and in other towns whose labor-management strife was less widely publicized.

In mid-August, almost simultaneously with Jouett Shouse's call at the White House to tell Roosevelt about the Liberty League, delegates to a national convention of the United Textile Workers of America (UTWA), whose membership had grown from a few thousand to nearly a quarter million since the enactment of the NIRA, voted for a nationwide strike to begin on September 1. The action, taken against the advice of most of the union's own national leadership, had a sufficient cause surely. Under the leadership of George A. Sloan, whose industrial statesmanship had been so greatly praised when the Cotton Textile Code became the first NRA code to be signed, and whose Cotton Textile Institute was in effect the code authority for his industry,* millowners and managers consistently and almost universally violated every provision of the industry code designed to increase employment, raise wages, improve working conditions, and guarantee independent union organization —especially the latter. Admittedly the employers, too, had a problem: The industry as a whole continued to suffer greatly from a production capacity much in excess of market demand. But the employer "solution" to this problem involved no cooperation with labor, no sharing with workers of gains as well as losses; it consisted, instead, almost wholly of a continued brutal labor exploitation. The employers offset the reduction of work hours to eight-a-day by imposing speedups and a stretch-out work schedule. They made the minimum wage of the code virtually the maximum wage by various means, not infrequently discharging skilled workers in order to rehire them as "learners" at *less* than the minimum wage. The result was that thousands of textile workers were being paid considerably less in 1934 than they had been in 1932. When excess inventories piled up in warehouses, the employers imposed through the code authority, with Hugh Johnson's approval, a reduction of weekly machine hours by 25 percent, from eighty to sixty, for June, July, and August 1934, with consequent reduction in employment and weekly wage. (The *official* weekly wage was reduced that summer from $12 to $9 in the South, from $13 to $9.75 in the North.) When complaints of employer code violation were made to the Cotton Textile National Industrial Relations Board—and there was increased use of company detectives, worker firings for union activity, and the blacklist, especially in the South, in flagrant violation of the letter and spirit of Section 7(a)—the board simply passed them along to the code authority, which, since it consisted essentially of Sloan's Cotton Textile Institute, naturally invariably found the complaints unjustified. On June 2, in a

*See pp. 248–49.

worker appeasement effort, Hugh Johnson arranged an "understanding" between the union and the government whereby the former agreed to postpone
a then-imminent walkout in return for union representation on the industrial
relations board for cotton textiles; but the arrangement was entered into by the
union with the stipulation that it be "without prejudice to the right to strike,"
it touched upon none of the basic issues between management and labor, and
it gave no assurance that George Sloan would actually sit down at a negotiating
table with any UTWA member. In the event, he flatly refused to do so.

Grievances enough! They cried out for redress.

All the same, the timing and circumstances of this strike call could hardly
have been less propitious for the UTWA, or more favorable for the employers.
The latter generally welcomed a shutdown that would enable them to reduce
inflated inventories at the expense of the workers, whose union they were
determined to crush. The press, choosing to interpret the June 2 arrangement
as an ironclad agreement by the union *not* to strike, generally denounced
UTWA leadership as "false," "irresponsible," "radical," "subversive." And the
Roosevelt administration proved to be no more an effective friend of organized
labor in this crucial instance than it had in other crucial instances over the last
seventeen months, despite Roosevelt's own growing disillusionment with the
business community.

From the moment the strike was called for, Roosevelt was directly involved
in futile efforts to avert it. It was in response to White House pressure conjoined with that of Secretary Perkins, and in recognition of the utter impotence
of the industrial relations board for cotton textiles, that the National Labor
Relations Board sought to intervene in the dispute, in the third week of
August, by offering to mediate the differences between union and employers.
The union promptly indicated its willingness to arbitrate. Sloan and his Cotton
Textile Institute as promptly refused the offer; there was no need for "outside"
arbitrators, said Sloan, since the industry's code authority was fully competent
to deal with the matter. In that same week, on August 21, Roosevelt issued an
executive order approving amendments to the Code of Fair Competition for
the Cotton Garment Industry whereby the weekly wage of some 200,000
textile workers was raised by 10 percent while the workweek was cut by 10
percent. The order might have postponed the strike if the millowners to whom
it applied had not at once denounced it as "unwarranted" and challenged the
President to enforce it.

So the nationwide strike began as scheduled, on Saturday of the Labor Day
weekend.

V

ROOSEVELT had by then gone from Washington to Hyde Park, where he
would remain until September 25.

On the evening of Thursday, August 30, in his study at Hyde Park, he had
a private talk with Budget Director Lew Douglas. The occasion was unhappy

for both. Douglas had borne for as long as he could official burdens in an administration the words and deeds of which daily outraged his conservative principles—had for many months been convinced he could do nothing to halt or even to curtail a public works program he deemed ruinous or to change monetary policies he deplored. He therefore placed in Roosevelt's hand his written resignation, to be effective immediately. Roosevelt was more taken aback by this than one might have expected him to be. Acutely aware of the mollifying influence upon the business community of Douglas's continued presence in the administration, anxious about the effect Douglas's departure at this time might have upon the upcoming midterm elections, he appealed to his budget director, "as a patriot and . . . as a Democrat," to stay on until December 1. He appealed in vain. Lewis Douglas, his hard single mind made up, stood solid as a rock upon the highest "moral" ground. He would not be moved. And Roosevelt was not only "terribly upset and hurt," or so it seemed to Morgenthau some dozen hours later, but also angry. Since January 1934 he had suspected that Douglas's practice of addressing to him lengthy argumentative memorandums on policy questions, a practice initiated immediately after Acheson's dismissal, was motivated by a wish "to make a written record" whereby to prove at a later time, with dated documentation, that grievous presidential actions were taken against Douglas's urgent advice. (It was a tactic Roosevelt himself, as assistant secretary of the navy, had employed when he was in strong disagreement with his superior officer, Navy Secretary Josephus Daniels, during the Great War.*) He now suspected that Douglas's resignation was *deliberately* timed to hurt the New Deal at the polls.[30]

Next morning Morgenthau, at Hopewell Junction, was called over to neighboring Hyde Park, where, directed to an upstairs bathroom, he was received by a stark-naked President of the United States, lying in a bath. When Morgenthau entered, the President "sat up straight in the bathtub," fixed a stern gaze upon the secretary of the treasury, and said with great emphasis, "Henry, in the words of John Paul Jones, we have just begun to fight!" He then told of the Douglas resignation and went on to say, also with great emphasis, "Henry, I give you until midnight to get me a new Director of the Budget." Cautious, conservative Henry Morgenthau, who himself "wanted a scheduled tapering off of spending so that we could look forward to a balancing of the budget" and who knew that Roosevelt hoped for this, too, yet whose compassionate nature (like Roosevelt's) would never permit him to favor balancing the budget by denying help to the desperately needy, asked, cautiously, if the President himself had anyone in mind for the post. What about Tom Corcoran? asked Roosevelt. The suggestion "took my breath away," Morgenthau later said; Corcoran was so obviously "absolutely out of the question" as budget director, for all his talents as "a first-class lawyer, a first-class political operator, a first-class accordion player!" "So I hastily suggested Daniel [W.] Bell, then my Commissioner of Accounts and Deposits in the Treasury Department," Mor-

*See Davis, *FDR: The Beckoning of Destiny,* pp. 474–76.

genthau recorded. It was a suggestion Roosevelt promptly accepted and promptly acted upon. He wrote out in longhand a press release which stressed not Douglas's departure but Bell's appointment and saw to it that the release was made during the Labor Day weekend, when it was little likely to make much of an impression on the public mind.

That evening Roosevelt was guest of honor at a clambake at the Morgenthau home in Hopewell Junction. "As the evening wore on he began to sing songs and you could tell from the way he acted that a great load and worry was off his mind," wrote Morgenthau in his diary. "As a matter of fact the people closely associated with him [it seems curious that Morgenthau evidently did not number himself among these since few were as close to the President as he] said that they had never seen him sing and be so jolly as he was that night since he became President."[31]

He was in the same exuberant mood the following evening, at the dinner table at the Big House in Hyde Park. Seated at the table were Missy Le Hand, of course, and Marion Dickerman, who had come up from New York City that afternoon, also Eleanor, Nancy Cook, and Earl Miller, who had come down a day or so before from ten days in a hideaway wilderness vacation spot, Chazy Lake, in the Adirondacks. (Eleanor had arranged this holiday with her "old" friends before going West to be with her "new" friend, Hick; had left Washington for Chazy Lake only a few days after her return to Washington. From the Adirondacks her written reports of the "fun" she was having caused Hick to writhe with jealousy.) Dickerman commanded the attention of those at table when she presented to the President the gift of a just-published little book entitled *Frankie in Wonderland*. Written by Latham R. Reed, "A Tory, with Apologies to Lewis Carroll," the book had come into Dickerman's hand that morning when she called upon a friend of hers, and of Todhunter School, in his financier's office on Wall Street. Her friend, who was no friend of the New Deal, had received with incredulity her statement that Roosevelt would "love" to have this book and had then given her his copy to pass on, with the proviso that she report back to him what the President "*really* said" after he'd looked through it. As it turned out, Dickerman had no need to report back: Roosevelt's reaction to this work was national news within forty-eight hours.

For Roosevelt not only read the parody delightedly aloud to his houseguests after dinner that evening but also read it aloud on the following afternoon to newsmen assembled for the annual picnic he gave them at Val-Kill Cottage. With gusto, with great histrionic effectiveness, he told (read) how Little Frankie, "tired of having only one state to play with" and also eager to "get rid of the rowdy little Smith boy who always wanted to play with his toys," was inspired by the sight of the "White Rabbit with pink eyes" dashing past him through the garden into "a large rabbit hole under the hedge. . . . What the country really needs, thought Little Frankie, is a few rabbit tricks—and if I could catch a nice white rabbit, especially one with pink eyes, I could throw my hat into the ring and then pull the rabbit out of the hat. . . . So, without considering how in the world he would ever get out of it again, he popped into the hole after the rabbit." Thereafter Little Frankie was involved in a series of absurdities, each unmistakably analogous to a specific New Deal event. By the time the reading was done, the newsmen, most of whom worked for papers hostile to the New Deal, had laughed themselves limp, and their reports of the episode in their papers next day rendered *Frankie* forever ineffective as anti-Roosevelt propaganda.[32]

This same zestfulness and high good humor carried him triumphantly through his visit with Upton Sinclair, who came to Hyde Park for the scheduled hour of talk a couple of days later, on Tuesday, September 4. Not but what he could have easily managed Sinclair in any case. For though it would be difficult to imagine a mind, a personality more unlike Franklin Roosevelt than was this crusading author, it would be equally difficult to conceive of anyone more vulnerable to the Roosevelt charm or less resistant to the kind of human manipulation of which Roosevelt was past master. Sinclair quite predictably emerged from his conference, which had stretched out to two full hours, in an elated, exalted mood, as the reporters who promptly interviewed him noted in their news stories. "I think I have had the most interesting two hours' talk I ever had," he told the reporters. "I talked with one of the kindest and most genial and frank and open-minded and lovable men I have ever met. . . . We folks out in California speculate as to what he is doing and how much he knows about it. I am very happy to tell the people of California that he knows. . . ." Sinclair also left Hyde Park convinced that Roosevelt had promised to come out in favor of production-for-use, in a radio address, before the end of October. The author's happy mood was sustained by the warm reception given him by leading administration figures in Washington. "I've been taken into the family," he told reporters. ". . . Mr. Morgenthau said to me: 'Whatever you need, just ask for it.' " By the time he arrived back in California he had, or believed that he had, the endorsement of the EPIC program by Father Coughlin, whom he had stopped off to see in Detroit, and he had indeed received the public endorsement of, among other intellectuals, Archibald MacLeish, liberal lawyer Morris Ernest, Stuart Chase, Clarence Darrow, and Dorothy Canfield Fisher, all of whom had signed an appeal to the nation for support of him.[33]

On the day of Sinclair's visit with him, it appeared to Roosevelt that the textile union had the upper hand in its strike against the textile industry. The response to the strike call was of a magnitude unprecedented in all American history, with some 375,000 textile workers out by that Tuesday evening, September 4, and with virtually every textile mill in the South and New England closed down.

The next day Roosevelt appointed a three-man board of inquiry into the dispute.

This was a move more heartening than otherwise to the strike leadership, for the board's appointed chairman was Governor John G. Winant of New

Hampshire, a notably able and fair-minded man, who was familiar with textile industry problems (southern New Hampshire was dotted with mill towns*) and far more sympathetic to New Dealish social aims than to those of the Republican party of which he was nominally a member. With such an inquiry board the union could and did readily cooperate. Indeed, only three days after the board had been announced, Vice-president Francis J. Gorman of the UTWA, who was the actual national leader of the strike, submitted to Winant a request that the board serve as arbiter of the dispute.

But arbitration, or any settlement of the issues in terms of overall fairness, was the last thing the employers wanted at that juncture. By that time they, who had been initially surprised and a little disconcerted by the magnitude of the response to the strike call, had mobilized and begun to exert the vast superiority of naked force which was theirs in this conflict. Sloan told Winant, as he had told the NLRB, that "outsiders" were not needed; the code authority could take care of everything.

Immediately thereafter bloody violence followed a savage trail down from Rhode Island into the Deep South as state and local governments used their police power in the employers' interest, to break the strike and crush the union. In Rhode Island 2 strikers were killed and scores were seriously injured in street clashes with state troopers. In North Carolina "the governor called out the State Guard, at the request of the owners," who were then, in effect, the commanders of the troops, as Josephus Daniels complained to Roosevelt in a letter from Raleigh.[34] In South Carolina deputies killed 6 strikers and injured scores in a clash at Honea Path. In other violent incidents in the South 3 other strikers were killed, and dozens injured. In Georgia the governor, an obscene gallus-snapping racial bigot and total reactionary named Eugene Talmadge (he loathed Franklin Roosevelt; Franklin Roosevelt loathed him), declared martial law and used the National Guard and state police to prevent forcibly the exercise by the strikers of their civil rights. More than 100 Georgia citizens, men and women, were placed in a military stockade on trumped-up charges or no charge at all "for the duration of the war," as Talmadge put it.

Against this array of brute force the UTWA found itself almost totally defenseless and undefended. Its leadership was compelled to admit as much as the strike went into its third week.

Timid William Green and the other craft union conservatives of the AFL's executive council chose to stand aside from this conflict; they did nothing to provide the organizational and financial help for which the strikers, through Gorman, pleaded. Some help came from John L. Lewis and his United Mine Workers, from David Dubinsky's garment workers' union, and from Norman Thomas's faction-torn Socialist party, but it was in sum far less than was needed. As for the Roosevelt administration, insofar as it took any action at all in this matter, it was action that strengthened the employers' already

---

*Many of the mills had closed, however, during the last decade, as cheap, unorganized labor in the South sucked the textile industry out of unionized New England.

mighty hand. Hugh Johnson, whose forced resignation as NRA head had been confidently expected by all knowledgeable observers when Roosevelt returned from his *Houston* cruise and who had in fact offered two resignations which Roosevelt (incredibly) had refused to accept in late August,* now repeated in essence his lamentable performance at the time of the San Francisco general strike. Addressing some thousands of representatives of 400 code authorities in New York City's Carnegie Hall in mid-September, he departed from his announced topic (he was to present to the code authorities his NRA reorganization plans) in order to denounce the textile strike as an "absolute violation of . . . [the] understanding" of June 2. The strike, he went on, had a "political" motivation which, he more than hinted, was subversive, citing the fact that Socialist Norman Thomas had been present at the UTWA national convention when the strike vote was taken.† All this was bound to raise doubts about labor unions in general as "responsible" organizations, said Johnson. Nor did he confine himself to condemnation of the striking workers, increasing numbers of whom now went hungry as local relief agencies in the South, run by antiunionists, cut them off from federal aid; he also expressed his great personal sympathy with George A. Sloan, for whom, he cried, "my heart weeps." Why? Because Sloan, who had had a hard struggle to persuade his fellow industrialists to accept the NRA code's "concessions for labor," was now forced to "take the rap for the dissension between labor and management." Johnson's words were bitterly assailed by spokesmen for organized labor, who damned him for prejudiced partisan "intrusion into the textile situation," and by Norman Thomas, who spoke darkly of the possibility "that under your [Johnson's] leadership NRA may degenerate into a quasi-Fascist scheme for standardizing work and workers."[36] But those same words were loudly cheered by the audience of businessmen in Carnegie Hall and by the textile employers, who were by then further confirmed in their conviction of an inevitably swift and crushing victory over the striking union. It was a conviction shared, despairingly, by the union leadership itself—and by the Winant board, whose task became that of mitigating to the greatest possible degree (it proved a very small degree) the harshness of the surrender terms imposed by the victors.

On Thursday, September 20, Winant went to Hyde Park to present the terms to the President in a formal board report. With Roosevelt's prompt acceptance, the report became the federal government's recommended settlement of the dispute, and as such it was at once released to the press. Felix Frankfurter now back in Cambridge, Massachusetts, after his year in Oxford,

---

*He did so against the urgent advice of Morgenthau, Ickes, Tugwell, Frances Perkins, Richberg, and numerous Democratic politicos who saw Johnson as a menace to liberal Democracy's success at the polls in the upcoming elections.

†Thomas had been invited to speak by the convention's organizers. In his speech he "expressly told the convention that not even the friendliest outsider had a right to decide the momentous question of whether or not to strike." He also warned his listeners that they could not count on local relief committees, in a South whose Democracy was reactionary, to provide food for the strikers and their families, however well intentioned the relief administrator in Washington might be. He offered to help raise relief funds by soliciting private donations.[35]

at once sent the President a typical courtier's telegram: "Have just read admirable text Winant Report. It wholly confirms wisdom your appointment of that board and should lead to early constructive settlement of strike. Congratulations."[37] What the report actually did, upon Roosevelt's acceptance of it, was identify the administration with a catastrophic defeat not only for organized labor but for the general cause of social progress in the South—and in an approving way that heightened antiadministration feeling on the left and doubts about Roosevelt's personal quality. For the settlement which a helpless strike leadership perforce accepted on September 22 was in every essential a return to the status quo ante. Union recognition was denied. Wages, hours, and the stretchout remained unchanged, though of the last a "study" by the government which *might* lead to change was promised. The settlement made no effective guarantee that striking workers would be rehired, and, in the event, thousands upon thousands were not, having been replaced during the strike by scabs when police and militia forcibly reopened mills. Some 300 millowners in the Cotton Texile Institute openly declared their intention to deny reemployment to *any* striker. A new Textile Labor Relations Board, which Roosevelt soon appointed, proved in the event but another instrumentality whereby employers gained a government stamp of approval upon their antilabor decisions and actions.

Roosevelt himself was uneasy about this settlement at the time it was made; he feared that what it cost him in goodwill on the left was offset by no equivalent gain in goodwill on the right. And his unease seems indicated by the fact that he made written reply to Frankfurter's congratulatory wire, something he often deemed it unnecessary to do. Moreover, the note he sent "Dear Felix" seems in context a note of relief, as if he had expected in this instance no commendation from the professor but, more likely, silent censure. "Many many thanks to you for your kind message," he wrote. "I am delighted to have it."[38]

VI

CERTAINLY the Roosevelt who returned to Washington from Hyde Park on September 25 evinced no such zest, no such buoyancy as had been his when he left the capital in the last week of August and which remained his in early September. His month of nominal "vacation" beside the great thematic river of his life had been no vacation at all and had done him no good. During that month anxieties had been born of the harsh pressure of events upon a mind suspended, wavering, undecided, between fundamental alternatives, and these anxieties weighed heavy upon his spirit. Ickes was not alone in remarking how tired the President appeared, "more tired than at any time except the end of a long winter." And the winter of 1934–35 had not yet begun! "He looks far differently [*sic*] than he did when I met him at Portland on his return from Hawaii," and he seemed notably to lack the "carefree spirit which has been so characteristic of him."[39]

And anxieties continued to accumulate.

Upon his desk in the Oval Room, which served as presidential headquarters while the Executive Office wing was being remodeled, Roosevelt found, on that Wednesday of his return, a letter from General Hugh S. Johnson resigning as NRA administrator. This was the third resignation Johnson had submitted in the last six weeks. Two were submitted in August, as indicated. One was orally made a few days after Roosevelt's return from the *Houston* cruise. This offer had been made in a theatrically self-sacrificial, almost tearfully emotional fashion which caused a softhearted President to beg him to stay on until his plans for an NRA reorganization were completed. It was a softheartedness the effect of which Roosevelt himself at once regretted and tried to mitigate. A few days later he called Johnson into the Oval Room, where, in the presence of Donald Richberg, whom Johnson now virulently hated, and Frances Perkins, he proposed that Johnson head a commission to study economic recovery in European nations, a proposal the general at once recognized as a means of easing him out of NRA. He was deeply hurt. He showed his hurt as he said, stiffly, that there was "of course . . . nothing for me to do but resign immediately"—a statement whose truth Roosevelt did not then and there deny. But that night, when he received by hand delivery a lengthy letter of resignation from Johnson that was every bit as theatrical and emotional as his oral resignation had been, Roosevelt reacted as before. He begged Johnson to forget the letter and remain at his post until NRA reorganization plans were in place. Johnson, too, responded as before. He stayed on to review with the President, in quiet and friendly conference a day or two later, the reorganization ideas he was developing, and he did not object to the President's proposal to take over the running of NRA himself for the next several weeks, to familiarize himself with its problems.[40]

This third of Johnson's resignations, however, proved to be his last. Roosevelt promptly accepted it, could, indeed, do no other in view of a highly confidential report made orally to him by Adolf Berle at Hyde Park,* a few days after Sinclair's visit there, and in view of the strong negative reaction, the

---

*Berle's report was the outcome of an informal meeting he had had in Washington on August 2 with Tugwell, Assistant Secretary of State Sumner Welles, molasses manufacturer Charles Taussig, who had become committed to Roosevelt during the 1932 campaign, and Robert Straus, who was the son of Jesse Straus and held a high NRA post. During the meeting, the five men "reviewed the state of the nation," finding it not good. "Bobby Straus reported that N.R.A. was practically over," wrote Berle in a memo to himself on August 3; "about half the men were resigning, largely because of the affair between Johnson and 'Robby,' which has now reached an acute stage. A somewhat similar situation on rather the same lines seems to be going on in Interior [Berle evidently referred to Ickes's passionate involvement with a divorcee, the daughter of a family friendly with Ickes's native family in Pennsylvania, an affair mentioned on pp. 203–4]. . . . The intrigues are growing; many of them turn on the activities of George Peek . . . as head of the Export and Import Bank. . . . In other words, we have an Administration in very bad shape indeed; at least partially corrupt and headed for a crisis. . . . It was agreed that as soon as the President gets back I was to see him and ask him to call a conference of Sumner Welles, Rexford Tugwell, Charles Taussig, myself, and possibly one or two others and simply attack the situation on all phases. There is no point in declining to face the issue."[41].

almost complete absence of positive public reaction, to the general's Carnegie Hall performance, climaxing as it did an unbearably long list of Johnson errors. Yet Roosevelt managed this acceptance in such a way, with a letter of such personal warmth and affection and gratitude for services rendered, that he retained Johnson's personal friendship and loyalty; the general would not follow, for months to come, the path that Lew Douglas was at that moment following into overt opposition to the New Deal. (By year's end Douglas was prominently enrolled as a member of the Liberty League.)

On the following afternoon, Wednesday, September 26, there was a secret meeting of the National Emergency Council in the Oval Room to consider an NRA reorganization plan (it was *not* Johnson's) whereby the council, of which Richberg was executive director, would determine NRA policy while an Industrial Recovery Board of presidential appointees would become the agency's executive, replacing the single top administrative office, the "one-man rule," which Johnson's erratic performance had discredited.

The new arrangement was announced the next day in an executive order which also, in its naming of the appointees to the new board, manifested Roosevelt's growing, reluctant realization that big businessmen, as sole or major determiners of federal industrial recovery policy or as chief executors of that policy, would not be trusted by the general public to serve the general welfare and *could* not be trusted in actual performance to do so. Only two of the five appointees—Arthur D. Whiteside of Dun and Bradstreet and Clay Williams of Reynolds Tobacco—were businessmen. One was a labor leader— Sidney Hillman, president of the Amalgamated Clothing Workers. Two were college professors—Walton Hamilton, Leon C. Marshall. And there would soon be three university men on the board if Roosevelt had his way for, during the Wednesday afternoon meeting, he accepted with enthusiasm a suggestion from the Labor Department representative, strongly seconded by Ickes, that Robert M. Hutchins, the youthful, dynamic, innovative chancellor of the University of Chicago, be asked to take a leave of absence from his present post in order to serve as the new board's chairman. This would make him, in effect, the chief administrative officer of NRA. (The suggestion came to naught in the end. It was opposed by Whiteside, Williams, and a preponderance of the code authority personnel. Richberg, who was himself ambitious for supreme power over NRA, told Roosevelt that business confidence would be destroyed if Hutchins came in, whereas confidence would be restored if Clay Williams became board chairman. And Roosevelt, for all his publicly expressed contempt for the big businessman's definition of "confidence," was impressed by Richberg's insistence that hostility to Hutchins was so great among those who dominated the code authorities that he would not be able to operate at all in a decisive NRA post. So Roosevelt drew back or fell back into the wavering attitude and line of conduct which marked his passage through the closing months of 1934 into the opening months of 1935. Having personally proposed the appointment to Hutchins, who then obtained permission from the university's board of trustees to take the necessary leave of absence, Roosevelt now hesitated to make the appointment official. He delayed for so long a time that Hutchins, humiliated and disgusted, finally withdrew his name from consideration.[42])

In his second fireside chat of 1934, delivered on September 30, there was further manifestation of Roosevelt's growing impatience with the business community's lack of commitment to the general good, of his growing, if ill-defined, doubts about that wholesale transfer of power from the legislative and executive branches of government to the private business sector which had been effected through NRA code making and code authorities. He said:

> Let me call your attention to the fact that the National Industrial Recovery Act gave businessmen the opportunity they had sought for years to improve business conditions through what has been called self-government in industry. If the codes which have been written are too complicated, if they have gone too far in such matters as price fixing and limitation of production, let it be remembered that so far as possible, consistent with the immediate public interest of this last year and the vital necessity of improving labor conditions [this latter "consistency" seemed, of course, nonexistent to most liberals], the representatives of trade and industry were permitted to write their own ideas into the codes. It is now time to review these actions as a whole to determine . . . whether the methods and policies adopted in the emergency have been best calculated to promote industrial recovery and a permanent improvement of business and labor conditions. There may be serious question as to the wisdom of many of those devices to control production, or to prevent destructive price cutting which many business organizations have insisted were necessary, or whether their effect may have been to prevent that volume of production which would make possible lower prices and increased employment. Another question arises as to whether in fixing minimum wages on the basis of an hourly or weekly rate we have reached the heart of the problem, which is to provide such annual earnings for the lowest paid worker as will meet his minimum needs. We also question the wisdom of extending code requirements suited to the great industrial centers and to large employers to the great number of small employers in the smaller communities [the influence of Lorena Hickok's FERA field reports from the Middle West seems here evident].

All this added up, in effect, to a fairly sweeping indictment of what a big business-dominated NRA had done thus far.

And he went on to endorse, for the first time in any definite, emphatic way, publicly, that portion of the Industrial Recovery Act upon which the business community focused unremitting fire:

> When the businessmen of the country were demanding the right to organize themselves adequately to promote their legitimate interests; when the farmers were demanding legislation which would give them opportunities and incentives to organize themselves for a common advance, it was natural that the workers should seek and obtain a statutory declaration of their constitutional right to organize themselves for collective bargaining as embodied in Section 7(a). . . . It is time that we made a clean-cut effort to bring about that united action of management and labor, which is one of the high purposes of the Recovery Act. . . . Step by step we have created all the Government agencies necessary to insure, as a general rule, industrial peace, with justice for all those willing to use these agencies whenever their voluntary bargaining fails to produce a necessary agreement. There should at least be a full and fair trial given to these means of ending industrial warfare. . . .

Without mentioning the Liberty League, he spoke scornfully of its "awesome pronouncements concerning the unconstitutionality of some of our measures of recovery and relief and reform. We [Americans] are not frightened. . . . All these cries have been heard before." He quoted the "great Chief Justice White" of the Supreme Court, who, in 1913, had seen "great danger" in the "constant habit which prevails where anything is opposed or objected to, of referring without rhyme or reason to the Constitution as a means of preventing its accomplishment, thus creating the general impression that the Constitution is but a barrier to progress instead of being the broad highway through which alone true progress may be enjoyed." He closed with a defense of the New Deal as middle way:

> [W]e have avoided, on the one hand, the theory that business should and must be taken over into an all-embracing Government. We have avoided, on the other hand, the equally untenable theory that it is an interference with liberty to offer reasonable help when private enterprise is in need of help. . . . I am not for a return to that definition of liberty under which for many years a free people were being gradually regimented into the service of the privileged few. I prefer and I am sure you prefer that broader definition of liberty under which we are moving forward to greater freedom, to greater security for the average man than he has ever known before in the history of America.[43]

It was the middle way he sought to follow through October as he awaited the verdict which the citizenry would render upon his administration in the midterm elections, but he did so with an unwontedly irritable uncertainty about where, precisely, the middle was to be found in the stream of current history.

In late August, when his spirits and morale were high, he calmly advised Democrats worried about the upcoming elections to remain calm. "[W]e have to keep our tempers in the next couple of months," he said, for to react in kind to the provocations of the opposition would be to abandon the high ground, above partisan battle, where he was determined the administration must remain that autumn. He was then pretty well convinced that the New Deal was precisely and properly balanced between the "extremes." He told a meeting of the National Emergency Council that in his opinion, opposition to the administration comprised "about ten to fifteen percent of people whose mental slant might be described as being at the extreme right of modern philosophy, and that the rest of it is from ten to fifteen percent of the mental slant that belongs to the extreme left."[44]

But now, as October wore on, he was not so sure, was, in fact, very unsure.

Within his own official family he was subjected to strong opposing pressures.

Ray Moley, though a very busy editor in chief of *Today* magazine,* continued in the role of presidential speech writer which he had resumed in the

---

*By autumn of 1934 *Today* had become perhaps the most widely quoted magazine in America, but it had a circulation of only 75,000. In 1937 it was merged with *News-Week,* which had a circulation of 250,000 but was losing money, to form *Newsweek,* with Moley its first editor.

fall of 1933, and Moley argued forcefully that the time had come "to slow down the pace of reform while business caught its breath and acquainted itself with the new order of things." He further urged the President toward a major effort to conciliate big businessmen, and Roosevelt did invite a number of them to confer with him at Hyde Park in September. On the day of Upton Sinclair's visit with him, for instance, he had among his other visitors the president of the New York, New Haven, & Hartford Railroad and Joseph P. Kennedy. He subsequently conferred in series with partners in the Morgan bank, various retail and industrial corporation executives, and the dean of the Harvard Business School, than whom there was no more fervent exponent of "business confidence" as the one indispensable ingredient of economic recovery. But, alas for the Moley position, the net result of these talks was to confirm Roosevelt's reluctantly developed view of the business mind as ill informed, wholly self-centered, devoid of generous ideas (or, indeed, ideas of any kind), and hopelessly rigid. He complained that he received "not one single concrete answer" to any of the "concrete" problem situations he presented to these leaders of business and industry. Their sole concern was to balance the budget, not through increased taxation, of course (taxes should be cut), but through reduction in governmental expenditures, while regulation of business was also reduced. Moley himself sought to build a bridge of sympathetic understanding between government and big business through a series of dinners, hosted by him but paid for by an affluent pro-New Deal businessman, at which allegedly representative New Dealers and more certainly representative big businessmen exchanged views in a friendly atmosphere. The dinners did little, if any, of what Moley hoped for them. His guests from the administration tended to be probusiness types, like Richberg and Dan Roper, between whom and the business mind there were no basic issues. When Hopkins was the chief New Deal guest, there was a surprising amount of goodwill around the dining table but a very limited meeting of minds. On the night Tugwell was guest, the dialogue degenerated into acrimonious dispute.[45]

Precisely opposed to Moley's was the advice, the urging of Roosevelt's liberal advisers, including Tugwell, Corcoran, Hopkins, Ickes, Eleanor, even Louie Howe to a degree. These argued that the pace of reform, far from being slowed down, must be speeded up if there was not to be in the near future a dangerous explosion of social unrest. Myopic big businessmen might be satisfied that recovery was well under way simply because *they* were better off than they had been two years ago and no longer felt immediately threatened by social revolution, thanks to the governmental programs of federal relief, public works, and currency inflation against which most of them bitterly inveighed, but in actual fact all that had been accomplished thus far by the New Deal, said the liberals, was a holding action, a buying of time in which rationally considered moves might be made against the catastrophe which yet impended. Unchanged were the basic conditions—notably an unbearably high unemployment and a growing misery among tenant farmers, out of which social unrest grew toward revolutionary violence through such movements as

Long's, Townsend's, and (less certainly) Sinclair's and through the much more amorphous demagoguery of Father Coughlin. Such violence would almost certainly mean the death of American democracy; there would emerge from it a totalitarian dictatorship, Communist or Fascist.

Ickes expressed this view, and revealed the essentially conservative motivation of New Deal liberalism in general, in a diary entry for September 15, 1934. He told of a dinner party he had attended with his wife at the home of Cissy Patterson,* a dinner at which the other guests were the general manager of the Hearst publications and a leading Hearst writer, with their wives. "We talked quite a lot about the recent [primary] elections," wrote Ickes. "I pointed out that the trend was distinctly radical. I expressed the opinion that the country is much more radical than the Administration and that it was my judgment that the President would have to move further to the left in order to hold the country. I said . . . that if Roosevelt can't hold the country within reasonably safe limit, no one else can possibly hope to do so, and that a breakdown on the part of the Administration would result in an extreme radical movement, the extent of which no one could foresee." Ickes further opined that "a lot of newspapers that are now so busy attacking the Administration, if they had any regard for their own interests, would be supporting it because a wide swing to the left would engulf us all. . . . I said that I would a whole lot rather give up half of whatever property I might possess than be forced to give up all of it, and that the latter was a distinct possibility if affairs were permitted to get out of hand."[46]

Other administration liberals had more positive motivation than Ickes here expressed, but virtually all on the liberal side were now agreed that it was a bad mistake to regard recovery and reform as distinct and separate enterprises and then to give the former precedence over the latter, either in time or in "emergency" importance. Instead, the two should be seen as fused in a single enterprise of recovery and reform.† A more just and free society was the only kind within which a true, permanent economic recovery could be achieved, and from the very first the emergency ought to have been used as opportunity and justification for the major reforms required to create such a society. Certainly the emergency (for it continued) ought *now* to be so used. Roosevelt should simply accept the fact that business hostility to him was not only inevitable but bound to increase if he did what needed to be done, should take political advantage of it as a "common enemy" which, menacing alike to

---

*She, the sister of Joseph M. Patterson of the New York *Daily News* and a first cousin of Colonel Robert M. McCormick of the Chicago *Tribune,* was in that year publisher of Hearst's two Washington papers, the *Herald* and the *Times.* She eventually bought and merged these into the Washington *Times-Herald,* which became one of the most virulently anti-New Deal of all American papers.

†Roosevelt himself expressed this view in his special message to Congress of June 8, 1934, in a way suggesting, falsely, that the view had prevailed in the New Deal from the outset. "It is childish to speak of recovery first and reconstruction afterward," he then said. "In the very nature of the processes or recovery we must avoid the destructive influences of the past." See p. 287 of the *Public Papers and Addresses of Franklin D. Roosevelt, 1934.*

himself and to the multitudinous "forgotten man" or "average man," must bind these to him in a "common defense." The loss of upper-class support would be in this way more than offset by the increased size and fervor of his mass support.

Thus the opposing pressures, from left and right, upon Franklin Roosevelt. He tried hard to measure their relative weights. He increasingly doubted that he did so accurately. And day by day the harsh rightist forces, thrusting with growing strength against his personal wish and will, pushed him leftward in mood and thought, step by reluctant step. For the time being, he seemed wholly deprived of an inward capacity to choose, in consequence of which deprivation, and in the absence of clues or cues from on high, he lived more and more in quandary, amid a forest of uncertainties.

An instance of his difficulty occurred on Tuesday, October 23.

In conference that day with Moley, Frank Walker, Hopkins, and Morgenthau, in the Oval Room, he discussed the attitude, the tone he should take in an address he was to make on the morrow to the annual meeting of the American Bankers Association, in Washington's Constitution Hall. He also attempted to determine some of the actual language of the speech. His acceptance of the invitation to speak had been in accord with Moley's views on the need for establishing harmonious relationships between the administration and big business, and the bankers who programmed the meeting had let the White House know that they wanted the session at which the President appeared to be "a hatchet-burying ceremony," as Moley later put it. Alas for such happy harmony, the bankers who had been so panicky in February and March 1933 had now recovered not only a sense of security but also an excessive portion of that vast self-esteem which had been theirs during the Republican Prosperity. This showed in the speech with which Jackson Reynolds, president of the First National Bank of New York City, proposed to introduce the President of the United States. In the speech draft, which had come into the hands of Morgenthau and Hopkins and was read aloud in the Oval Room, Reynolds did say that the "banking fraternity" as a result of events of the last two years was "in such a chastened and understanding mood that you can accept with hospitality any overture of cooperation," but he went on to make clear his notion that the cooperation was to be of equals, a kind of truce between sovereign powers. He did so by means of an analogous reference to the failure of negotiations between the Carthaginians under Hannibal and the Romans under Scipio in North Africa in 202 B.C., a breakdown of talks that was followed by the Battle of Zama, in which the Romans suffered grievous losses while the Carthaginian army was destroyed.

Morgenthau and Hopkins found this outrageous. So did Roosevelt.

Roosevelt was further angered by Reynolds's reference (the banker intended a jocular reference) to the fact that he, Roosevelt, as "an eager youth" had been a student in one of Reynolds's classes when the latter was a professor in the Columbia Law School and had not always been able to answer correctly the questions put to him, a subtle insult, Roosevelt felt, which would be recognized as such by all who knew that he had failed to complete his work toward a Columbia law degree. He at once proceeded to dictate a rough speech draft which seemed to the listening Moley rough indeed, alarmingly belligerent in tone; and on the following morning, even though Reynolds had at Morgenthau's request deleted the two offensive references from his speech, Moley was hard put to persuade Roosevelt to accept a much softened speech draft which he, Moley, had prepared overnight.[47]

The softened version had steel in it; a good many of the bankers were well aware of this as they listened that evening. "[G]overnment is not merely one of many coordinate groups in the community or the Nation, but government is essentially the outward expression of the unity and the leadership of all groups," said the President of the United States. "Consequently the old fallacious notion of the bankers on one side and the government on the other side as being more or less equal and independent units, has passed away. Government by the necessity of things must be the leader, must be the judge of conflicting interests of all groups in the community, including bankers. The government is the outward expression of the common life of all citizens." He also made oblique reference to that "strike by capital" which had provoked his ire repeatedly, within the bosom of his official family, during the last year. He said: "Government should assert its leadership in encouraging not only the confidence of the people in banks, but the confidence of the banks in the people. In March, 1933, I asked the people of this country to renew their confidence in the banks of the country. They took me at my word. Tonight I ask the bankers of this country to renew their confidence in the people of this country. I hope you will take me at my word."[48]

The newspapers reported next morning that Roosevelt had indeed been conciliatory and that his words had been enthusiastically welcomed by his audience. Moley disagreed. "[T]he atmospheric conditions in which the speech was perfunctorily delivered approached the frigid," he recalled in a later year. "The President was scarcely pleasant either to his audience or to Reynolds."[49]

Eight days later, on the evening of November 1, during a White House conference with Hopkins, Morgenthau, and Ickes concerning the administration's public works plans for the coming year, Roosevelt spoke grimly of "definite information" that had come to him of a conspiracy by big business to "sabotage the Administration." He had been told, he evidently believed "that big business is carefully planting its own people wherever it can in various government agencies," people who "not only keep big business advised of what is going on but block the program whenever they can."[50]

And if such paranoia jarred discordantly with the happy, optimistic attitudes Roosevelt normally displayed to the world, it was not inconsistent with the streak of vindictiveness, normally deeply buried in his character, which was being manifested at that time with regard to Bronson Cutting. Ickes vigorously protested against this manifestation, or against the effect it was having, on that night of the public works conference in the White House. He remained, after the others had left, to report to the President his observations of the political situation in the West, from which he had just returned, and he said with emphasis that what the administration was doing in New Mexico was as offensive as it was incomprehensible to Hiram Johnson of California, to William E. Borah of Idaho, to friends of the New Deal everywhere in the West, and to Ickes himself. Surely the liberal Cutting, running on the Republican ticket for reelection as U.S. senator from New Mexico, should have the same administration support, covert and open, as was being given Wisconsin's Bob La Follette and Progressive Republicans in every other state. Instead, at Roosevelt's specific order, full administration backing was being given Dennis Chavez, a relatively undistinguished congressman who ran as a regular Democrat for Cutting's seat, and this changed what would have been an easy contest for Cutting into a very close and difficult one, so potent was Roosevelt's personal popularity among Cutting's normal supporters.[51] If Ickes hoped that Roosevelt would change his mind and tactics at this late date, however, he was disappointed. Five days hence, after a closing burst of covert administration support of his opponent and at the end of a campaign notable even in New Mexican politics for viciousness and money fraud, Bronson Cutting won reelection, but by so narrow a margin (barely 1,000 votes) that Dennis Chavez contested the outcome, again with Roosevelt's support. . . .

VII

TUESDAY, November 6, 1934, was a day of huge triumph for Franklin Roosevelt personally and for New Deal liberalism over its conservative opposition. A truism of American politics was that the party in office lost congressional seats in the midterm elections. Generally the loss was substantial, especially in the House. If the opposition's gain was small, if it amounted to, say, but 37 seats, which is what Garner on October 1 predicted the Republicans would gain that year, the outcome could be deemed, as Garner said, a "complete victory" for the administration. If there was no loss at all of House seats to the Republicans, which Jim Farley regarded on the eve of the election as a distinct possibility, the administration victory had to be deemed overwhelming. In the event, the Democrats actually *gained* seats in the House: The party's strength rose there from 313 to 322, with the Republican strength declining from 117 to 103 (some formerly Republican seats were won by Progressives and Farmer-Laborites, 10 of whom would be in this Seventy-fourth Congress's lower chamber). In the Senate the Democratic strength increased from 59 to 69 (one of the freshman Democratic senators in the new Congress was Missouri's Harry Truman), giving the Democrats three-fourths of the seats, the widest margin ever held in the upper chamber by any party in the history of the Republic. Equally disastrous for the Republicans was the overall outcome of the state elections: After 1935's inauguration days, only seven state governors would be Republicans, thirty-nine would be Democrats, the other two being Progressive Phil La Follette in Wisconsin and Farmer-Laborite Olson of Minnesota, each of whom won handsomely.

Among conservatives the magnitude of their repudiation by the general electorate produced for the moment consternation, dismay, a considerable measure of despair. Seasoned and allegedly objective observers of the political scene opined that the Republican party was about through as a major force in American life. It lacked dynamic leadership. It had no program or program ideas. The concerns it so vehemently expressed through the mass communications facilities which its members largely owned were utterly at variance with those that were predominant among the American people in general. Unless it made drastic changes in its own nature, the party seemed doomed to go the way, to extinction, of the Whig party of the 1850s. "The trouble with our beloved party is that it is shot through with the plutocratic conquest," Progressive Republican William Allen White had written to a longtime newspaperman friend in mid-September 1934. "If it can get rid of that, the party can revive. But it cannot live with fatty degeneration of the heart." White now viewed the outcome of the 1934 elections as not only a vindication of this view but also as an unprecedented personal triumph for Franklin Roosevelt. "He has been all but crowned by the people," wrote White. And journalists and publishers far to the right of White essentially agreed with him in this assessment. Roosevelt, wrote Arthur Krock of the Washington bureau of the New York Times, had won "the most overwhelming victory in the history of American politics." William Randolph Hearst, who had read The Party Battles of the Jackson Period and Jefferson and Hamilton by Claude G. Bowers, whom he had hired as editor of one of his New York City papers, said, "There has been no such popular endorsement since the days of Thomas Jefferson and Andrew Jackson."[52]

To Roosevelt, this election triumph was, of course, gratifying, exhilarating, reassuring. All the same, it raised certain questions and difficulties.

For one thing, so huge a party majority in Congress was far from being an unmitigated blessing, if a blessing at all, as politician Roosevelt well knew. "Some of our friends think the majority top heavy," Garner wrote him immediately after the election, "but if properly handled, the House and Senate will be all right and I am sure you can arrange that."[53] This meant implicitly that Garner was not sure of it absolutely. Nor could Roosevelt be. In normal circumstances, when the numerical difference between the majority and minority parties was relatively small, minority party opposition operated as a unifying force upon the majority party. This would not happen in the Seventy-fourth Congress. And in the absence of such unifying opposition the Democratic majority was all too likely to split into fractions, whose quarrels would be much harder to deal with, presidentially, than a normal division between the major parties would have been. The President would have to prevent such factionalism through active leadership, providing thus that unifying force which normally consisted of party reaction to minority opposition, and since the deficiency he had to supply was intimidatingly large, his problem was difficult.

The difficulty was increased by the complexion this Congress-elect presented to the watching world, a complexion considerably ruddier than that of the Congress it replaced.

No close, analytical look by him at the election returns, no objective assessment of their significance could fail to increase Roosevelt's doubt that he had accurately located the middle way. During the first months of his administration it had been more obvious to him than it was to such as Ickes that the country was indeed more radical than he was—more radical, by a good deal, than Congress, which was itself more radical than he. But he had thought this fact a temporary phenomenon, a momentary deviation from the main line of American historical development. Accordingly, in his dealings with the Seventy-third Congress, as we have seen, especially during the special session, his leadership role had been in essence more negative than positive. His instinctive concern had been to limit social and economic change to the bare minimum required to prevent immediate social revolution. It had been to put the brakes on what seemed to him headlong congressional tendencies toward a fundamental alteration of the traditional American economic system, to pull the country back and away from left "extremism" into what he deemed the mainstream (the central portion of the long-term flow) of current history—in short, to preserve the profit system essentially intact against the consequences of profiteering capitalists' excesses and failures, these last having constituted, as he saw or felt it, a grievous deviation to the *right* of the central mainstream. The main purpose and, indeed, achievement of all the tremendous flurry of the Hundred Days had thus been preventive, defensive, diffusive of radical energies. And this remained his own essential purpose. He clung to it stubbornly as he strove to determine, through inquiry into the meaning of these midterm elections, just what constituted the necessary minimum of social change and just where lay the narrowest boundaries of a middle way that was, obviously, somewhere to the left of the one he had been following.

Few members of this new Congress had stressed the need for government economy, or inveighed against business regulation, during their election campaigns. Many had laid heavy stress instead upon the need for *increased* government spending for relief and public works. A significant number had come out in favor of production for use. And clearly this new Congress, its composition a more accurate reflection of the national mood than that of its predecessor, would have stood farther to the left still, and by a good deal, if public issues had been fairly presented to the electorate during the campaign instead of distortedly through mass media controlled by conservatives and reactionaries. In instance after instance, in state after state, leftist candidates had had their victory margins reduced or wiped out altogether by hostile propaganda which they lacked the means to counter effectively.

Consider, for instance, the progress and ultimate fate of Upton Sinclair's EPIC campaign in California.

The probability of Sinclair's election to the governorship appeared overwhelming in the first weeks after his thumping primary victory. His Republican opponent, the incumbent Governor Frank Merriam, was as dull a personality as he was a mind, a complete reactionary whose ideological principles, however, did not prevent his endorsement, soon, of the Townsend Plan, so desperate became his quest for mass support. Sinclair's campaign, on the other hand, had all the enthusiasm, the moral fervor, the popular excitement of a great religious revival; it attracted huge crowds of adherents in California and much national and even international attention (Socialist writer Harold Laski, in London, commented favorably upon it).

And Roosevelt during these weeks maintained a far more open-minded, tolerant attitude toward EPIC than did many of his liberal advisers. He seems even to have welcomed it, not only as a means of determining more accurately than he could otherwise have done the amount of effective radicalism in the country and the amount of effective hostility to it but also as an interesting and valuable idea in its own right. It struck him as analogous to the Dayton Association of Cooperative Production Units in Dayton, Ohio, which his administration was aiding with subsistence homestead funds and of which he had read, late last spring, a glowing report by Lorena Hickok. He said as much to Sinclair personally. When an agitated Frances Perkins, just returned from a visit to California, told him that "sober liberals" in that state were begging his help "to stem the tide of votes for Sinclair," his unruffled reply was a reiteration of his intention to remain aloof from all state contests. "Perhaps they'll get EPIC in California," said he to his labor secretary. "What difference, I ask you, would that make in Dutchess County, New York, or Lincoln County, Maine? The beauty of our state-federal system is that people can experiment. If it has fatal consequences in one place, it has little effect upon the rest of the country. If . . . [it] works well, it will be copied." He dismayed California Democratic politician J.F.T. O'Connor, now comptroller of the Treasury, by remarking that Sinclair the man had at Hyde Park made a "favorable impression" upon him. He dismayed Moley even more by indicating that he might soon publicly endorse the Sinclair candidacy. (One suspects he was teasing, though he may truly have intended at that time to come out for production-for-use in a carefully worded statement in late October, as Sinclair believed he would.) EPIC made more sense than the Townsend Plan, which Merriam had embraced, said Roosevelt to Moley, adding, as clincher, "Besides, they tell me Sinclair's sure to be elected."[54]

Of this last he himself was less certain by the time Moley had editorialized in *Today* magazine (the issue of October 4) that "Sinclair's production-for-use program . . . is a call for blessed retreat—back beyond industrial civilization, back beyond the established national financial structure, back beyond the use of gold and silver and currency, back to barter, back to nature" and attacked Sinclair personally as a visionary "with no experience in practical administration." This became at once a highly effective piece of anti-EPIC propaganda in California, in good part because of the widespread assumption that Moley, believed still to be a close Roosevelt adviser, was speaking the President's mind in this case. It was an assumption Roosevelt did nothing to correct, though Sinclair at once begged him, in wires and letters, to do so, reminding him, in a letter dated October 5, of his "promise to come out in favor of production for use about the 25th of this month." On October 9, responding to a communication from Key Pittman in which the Nevada senator asserted that Sinclair presumed upon Roosevelt's personal kindness to the extent of claiming he had the President's campaign support, Roosevelt wrote warily "that if matters come to a head and he takes my name in vain the only possible answer is the one we have used before—'The President has taken no part in . . . any State election . . . and will take no part.' " He retreated somewhat from his earlier conviction that the probability of Sinclair's winning approached certainty, saying to Pittman, "At this distance it looks as though Sinclair will win if he stages an orderly, common sense campaign but will be beaten if he makes a fool of himself."[55]

He was drawing back. Within a week or so thereafter he was effectively dissociating himself and the administration, absolutely, from Sinclair and EPIC, "The President's instructions on Sinclair's candidacy in California are (1) Say nothing and (2) Do Nothing," said a note from Steve Early to Eleanor Roosevelt. A telegram, plaintive and desperate, came on October 18 from Sinclair to Roosevelt: "Respectfully remind you of that promise to broadcast in favor of production for use."[56] But no reply went from Roosevelt to Sinclair on that day or later, and October 25 came and passed with no broadcast, no comment of any kind by the White House about production-for-use. On the following day Jim Farley suddenly discovered and announced in a tone of rueful dismay that a form letter endorsing the entire state ticket in California, including Sinclair, had been sent out "by mistake" on the morrow of the primary, with Farley's signature affixed to it by rubber stamp. On the same day Roosevelt refused comment upon a statement by Sinclair, whose hurt bewilderment was now patent, that he (Sinclair), during his campaign, had said nothing and done nothing with regard to his relationship with Roosevelt that was not in strict accord with an understanding the two men had reached at Hyde Park. "I cannot take part in any state campaign" was all that Roosevelt would say. On the night of November 1 "it seemed clear" to a somewhat surprised Ickes (he had been away from Washington for nearly two weeks, on his trip to the West Coast) that the President "had swung clear over from his earlier attitude of tolerance of the Sinclair candidacy. . . ."[57]

For by then it was clear that Sinclair was not going to win.

There had been mounted by mid-September against this gentle soul, this tender conscience, this honorable if inordinately vain man a campaign rarely matched in American politics for malicious mendacity or utter viciousness of personal attack—and a campaign wholly unprecedented, for a single state, in its money cost. This last amounted to something over $10 million, or approximately twice the amount spent by both major parties nationally in 1932's presidential campaign. Movie mogul Louis B. Mayer of Metro-Goldwyn-Mayer was Republican state chairman, and among the devices he and his fellow movie industrialists used to raise money was the simple one of assessing each movie actor, each contract writer, each director, a day's salary and assigning it to the Merriam campaign.* Little of this money was spent, however, upon the positive promotion of Frank Merriam. The great bulk went into the production and distribution of fake newsreels, fake still photographs, phony affidavits (displayed in newspaper ads), upon handbills and pamphlets, propagandistic "news" stories and feature articles, "proving" Sinclair to be an atheist, an idiotic food faddist, an enemy of the Boy Scouts, an exponent of free love, and, above all, a Communist (though also an anarchist), whose election would mean a wholesale outflow of California industry, including motion pictures (these would move to Florida), and a wholesale influx of bums from all over America. Sinclair's own voluminous published writings over the years, on all manner of controversial subjects, provided an abundance of quotations for a leaflet entitled *Out of His Own Mouth Shall He Be Judged,* quotations whose damning effect was increased when they were torn from context and thus stripped of qualifications. Also, simultaneously, Sinclair's speeches, public statements, and campaign rallies ceased to be news reported in California's newspapers, which incessantly viciously attacked him on their editorial and feature pages and in manufactured "news."

That this massive assault upon the popular mind was effecting a substantial reduction of Sinclair's support became evident by mid-October. All indications then were that Sinclair was now likely to win only if Roosevelt at least tacitly endorsed him or EPIC's central idea. Instead, if Roosevelt did not definitely approve what J.F.T. O'Connor was doing at this time in California to ensure Sinclair's defeat, he certainly raised no objection to it—and politician O'Connor must have known that Roosevelt would not object after the deed was done. This deed was a secret deal with Merriam whereby, in return for the aid of the regular California Democratic organization, which was controlled by the conservative wing of the party, Republican Merriam promised to issue a statement saying that his victory could not be construed as a defeat for Roosevelt or the New Deal since it was won with Democratic help.

The final bitter blow to Sinclair was delivered in the last week of October with the publication of the results of a poll of the California citizenry conducted by the then highly respected *Literary Digest* magazine, a poll showing that Merriam would win 62 percent of the vote while Sinclair won only 25 percent, with the remaining 13 percent going to the Progressive candidate, Raymond Haight. This "did us irreparable harm," said Sinclair at a later date. "It encouraged our enemies, it weakened our friends, and it shifted the betting odds. . . . Many people were waiting to know which band wagon to climb onto, and now they knew." Later research proved this poll to be as phony, if perhaps inadvertently so, as the newsreels and still photos and affidavits linking Sinclair to Moscow. Some 75 percent of the poll ballots went to registered Republicans; one California employer distributed 200 of them to his employees.[58]

---

*There was backfire to this when a number of Hollywood celebrities, including James Cagney, Charlie Chaplin, Jean Harlow, Morrie Ryskind, and Nunnally Johnson, organized in support of Sinclair, but the backfire could make small headway against the studio-promoted anti-Sinclair conflagration.

On election day Sinclair did indeed lose to his Republican opponent, by the substantial margin of a quarter million votes. The outcome, however, did nothing to point the way Roosevelt should follow, between left and right "extremes," through 1935 into the election year 1936. Certainly it meant no massive repudiation of Sinclair's radicalism, no massive endorsement of Merriam's conservatism, by the people of California. It might merely indicate the power that could be exerted over the popular mind, especially in the short term, by mass media wholly controlled by extreme conservatives, and though this was a power Roosevelt would have to take careful account of as he planned his course through the coming year, California's demonstration of it would not be precisely quantified.

The signals given were in all respects blurred, confused.

It must be borne in mind, for one thing, that Merriam himself had switched signals in the midst of the campaign. Under the threat from Sinclair he had abandoned his theretofore consistently held rightist position to the extent of embracing the Townsend heresy, as has been said, and of permitting himself to be presented to the electorate, by the advertising men who ran his campaign, as a staunch bold Progressive! Even his warmest friends could hardly deny among themselves that he had been given every supportive advantage, and an unfair advantage, over his opponent. Yet even so, running as a Republican in a state that was traditionally overwhelmingly Republican (primary registrations by Republicans normally outnumbered those by Democrats three to one), Merriam had won reelection with a minority of the popular vote! He had received 1,138,620 votes as against 879,537 for Sinclair and 302,519 for Haight. The majority against him totaled 43,436.

Which is to say that despite the $10 million campaign of lies thunderously proclaimed against EPIC and its author by every art and means of mass propaganda; despite the coercive pressures to vote for Merriam that were blatantly exerted by employers upon their employees; despite the shiftiness of Roosevelt's dealings with Sinclair, whereby the latter was made to appear a foolish dupe or a liar; despite the phony *Literary Digest* poll and the secret, traitorous arrangement with the opposition entered into by O'Connor and other state Democratic leaders—despite all these hazards and dire misfortunes, Upton Sinclair would almost certainly have become governor of California if Progressive Haight had dropped out of the race in late October as Sinclair had asked him to do. It could be taken for granted that few of the votes Haight won would have gone to Frank Merriam.

(It should perhaps be added, as a typical instance of how action-reaction operates to make history, that many thousands of Sinclair's supporters were not only infuriated and embittered by the manner of EPIC's defeat but also permanently radicalized by it, some of them to the extent of becoming Communists. Especially was this true of Hollywood's contract writers. Among these there grew up a pathological hatred of the likes of Louis B. Mayer and of themselves for accepting fat checks from hands so slimy, in payment for trashy work. As for Sinclair himself, he was personally more relieved than dismayed by the election's outcome. Cheerfully he returned to his writing desk, where he whipped out in a few weeks a book recounting his experiences, entitled *I, Candidate for Governor—and How I Got Licked.*)

VIII

BUT if the election returns were thus of ambiguous meaning as a guide to future action, they were clear and definite in their indication of the President's vast personal popularity and its potency at the ballot box—a popularity and potency far greater than any earlier occupant of the White House had enjoyed at midterm. His knowledge of this possession had a tonic effect upon Franklin Roosevelt. Dark circles were erased from beneath his eyes, lines were smoothed out of his face, and all his normal buoyancy returned to him. It was as if he had just returned from that Thanksgiving trip to Warm Springs upon which, in actual truth, he was not to embark until November 15.

Of course, he yet remained undecided and indecisive about fundamental matters. From his reading, cold-eyed, of statistical descriptions of the state of the economy, in that autumn of 1934, he could derive no smug self-satisfaction over the New Deal's effect thus far upon the Great Depression. There had been some improvement: The net national product, which had totaled $48.6 billion in 1933, was to total $58.2 in 1934. But this was $37 billion less than the $95.2 billions of product in 1929. Similarly with regard to national income, which would be $49.5 billion as compared with $40.3 in 1933 but remained $37.3 billion below the 1929 figure of $85.9 billion. (Roosevelt noted, however, that "despite the worst drouth of record," farm income for 1934 "is running about a billion dollars above last year.") Less satisfactory still, in the optimistic view —and positively alarming in the pessimistic one—were the figures on unemployment. Having climbed from an estimated 1,550,000, or 3.2 percent of the labor force, in 1929, to 12,836,000, or about 25 percent of the labor force, in 1933, unemployment remained very near this last disastrous figure; it was to total 12,060,000 for 1934, or but slightly less than 22 percent of the labor force. Nor were conditions in general getting better that fall, according to leading indicators of economic trends. As noted before, the Federal Reserve Board's Adjusted Index of Industrial Production, which fell from 125 in 1929 to 56 in March 1933, shot upward to 101 in July 1933, at which point it started to fall and continued to fall until it reached 71 in November that year. Thereafter it had climbed steadily, reaching 86 in the spring of 1934. But then had begun another decline, and this yet continued. Fifteen points had been knocked off the index figure since June; it stood now at 71—precisely where it had stood one year ago.[59]

Thus a view of the economic facts gave no firm assurance that Roosevelt was going the right way as President. From these, as from the election returns, the one sure conclusion he could draw was that if he were to "hold the country," in Ickes's phrase, he would have to veer somewhat to the left of what had formerly seemed to him the proper line. Yet the election's outcome, or the dimensions of personal popularity and power which it revealed, *did* seem a clear sign that God the Cosmic Author was generally approving of his personal performance thus far in the role that had been assigned him. And the approval of his performance could only mean a continued divine approval of that performance's central thematic purpose, which was to revive and preserve democratic capitalism against the forces of radical change. He had been clinging to this purpose with blind obstinacy these latter weeks; now he could embrace it wholeheartedly again, with hope and faith renewed. This, in turn, encouraged him to believe that the problem of basic choice the nagging insistence of which had wearied him, rendering him unwontedly introspective and covertly irritable since early September, just might not require a painfully effortful solution by him after all. It might just go away, having been dissolved by the flowing "logic of the situation" or cast off by a natural "straightening out" of things, while he dealt with the Seventy-fourth Congress in essentially the same way and to the same end as he had dealt with the Seventy-third. This would involve on his part a continued braking of tendencies toward headlong change, a repeated throwing of his weight to the right on specific matters which might otherwise be settled too far to the left, while he pressed forward resolutely in those areas of work relief, taxation, community development, conservation, and electric power development and distribution where, in part *because* of big business opposition, he felt reasonably sure of his ground.

He felt sure of his ground in the Tennessee Valley.

He rode into the valley in his special train on the morning of November 16, journeying to Warm Springs by circuitous route from Washington, which he had left the night before. Eleanor was on the train, and Missy LeHand; so were Secretary of State Hull, though he would leave the train at Knoxville, and Ickes, who came aboard in Cincinnati that Friday morning. At Coal Creek, Tennessee, Roosevelt was met by Arthur E. Morgan, Harcourt A. Morgan, and David Lilienthal of the TVA board, and motored with them to the abuilding Norris Dam, where he briefly spoke to an immense crowd. He went on then to Knoxville, where his train awaited him. At Nashville, next morning, he left the train for a visit to The Hermitage, where he and his party were served a huge breakfast by the women whose organization had charge of this historic mansion, to whom he suggested that they solve their organization's financial problems by deeding The Hermitage to the federal government, which could then assign its management to them. ("The more I learn about old Andy Jackson the more I love him," wrote Roosevelt to John Garner a few days later.) From Nashville the presidential special slanted southwestward across Tennessee through a long lazy afternoon, toward Corinth, Mississippi. "President thoroughly enjoying himself," noted Lilienthal in his journal as the train approached the Mississippi line,"—no sign of fatigue. Talked [at dining table] about many things: electric rates, beech trees for textiles, humus, fertilizers; on every score keenest interest. Very great humor, tremendous laugh and voice. Mrs. Roosevelt with crinkly-eyed smile—charming, gracious, simple. . . . Impossible to reproduce the vitality and joy of living." As they neared

Corinth, the county seat of Alcorn County, Lilienthal told the President about the Alcorn County Electric Power Association, a Lilienthal idea which was destined to become the prototype for hundreds of government-sponsored cooperatives whereby electricity was wired into farmsteads theretofore denied it. Roosevelt was immensely impressed. Addressing extemporaneously a vast throng in Corinth a couple of hours later, he spoke "a special word of commendation for the way you in Alcorn County have worked out an experiment that is going to succeed." He went on: "There are two points in regard to what you have done that should be known all over the United States. . . . The first is that you are treating your county as a unit and, in treating it that way, you are giving an opportunity to the people who live on the farm equal with the people who live in the city. The other interesting fact, I am told, is that with cheaper rates of electricity than any you have ever had before, you are going to pay off in five and a half years the money you have borrowed."*[60]

He again spoke of cheap power as a cooperative community enterprise next morning, November 18, during extemporaneous remarks to yet another immense crowd in Tupelo, Mississippi. He said that "the most important thing of all" about what was being done in Tupelo and Corinth and other Tennessee Valley communities, under the aegis of TVA, was

> it is being done by the communities themselves. This is not coming from Washington. It is coming from you. You are not being Federalized. We still believe in the community; and things are going to advance in this country exactly in proportion to the community effort. This is not regimentation; it is community rugged individualism. It means no longer the kind of rugged individualism that allows an individual to do this, that or the other thing that will hurt his neighbor. He is forbidden to do that from now on. But he is going to be encouraged in every known way from the national capital and the state capital and the county seat to use his individualism in cooperation with his neighbor's individualism so that he and his neighbors may improve their lot in life.

Later that day he spoke in Birmingham, Alabama, where he urged the citizenry (another vast crowd was on hand), in view of the "many economic and social relationships" which industrial Birmingham had with the "great territory which lies north of you," to cooperate actively with TVA. He arrived that evening in Warm Springs, where next day he entered zestfully upon the activities which always so thoroughly recreated him in this world which he himself had made and upon which he himself bestowed, as sun-god, a vivifying radiant energy. He sunbathed; he bathed for hours in the thermal pool; he picnicked; he socialized with sanatorium patients and neighboring farmers and invited dignitaries; he presided in his usual wonderfully life-affirming way over the Thanksgiving feast.

In his informal talk to the sanatorium patients and guests, some 300 people,

---

*The money was borrowed from TVA. This pioneering electric cooperative made the final payment on its original debt, and on an additional $100,000 borrowed for the installation of rural power lines, in late May 1939. (See p. 109 of David E. Lilienthal, *The TVA Years, 1939–1945*, which is volume 1 of his published journals.)

in the Georgia Hall dining room on that Thanksgiving Day, Roosevelt spoke of Warm Springs as a "sanctuary" where "wars of the body and wars of the mind are absolutely taboo," thanks to that "Spirit of Warm Springs" which "has been here at least as long as I have been here" and of which he himself was the principal creator, though he did not say so. He did say that "tonight marks the tenth anniversary of my coming to Warm Springs" and went on to tell "the story . . . of the origin of the Foundation." In the late fall of 1924 there had been national publicity about Roosevelt's progress toward walking again, in consequence of his swimming in the resort pool, and shortly after his return here in the spring of 1925, he said, polio cripples from various parts of the nation began showing up, unexpectedly, at the Warm Springs railroad station.

> We did not know what to do with them so I sent for Doctor Johnson. He came and looked them over and guaranteed that they did not have heart trouble or something from which they would suddenly die. . . . And then I undertook to be doctor and physio-therapist, all rolled into one. I taught Fred Botts to swim. I taught them all at least to play around in the water. I remember there were two quite large ladies; and when I was trying to teach them an exercise which I had really invented, which was the elevating exercise in the medium of water, one of the ladies found great difficulty in getting both feet down to the bottom of the pool. Well, I would take one large knee and I would force this large knee and leg down until the foot rested firmly on the bottom. And then I would say, "Have you got it?" and she would say, "Yes," and I would say, "Hold it, hold it." Then I would reach up and get hold of the other knee very quickly and start to put it down and then number one knee would pop up. This used to go for half an hour at a time; but before I left in the spring, I could get both those knees down at the same time.

He told of the launching of the Warm Springs Foundation in 1927 and of its "continuous growth" through the seven years since. The growth would be more rapid still because of the birthday party of last January 30. "The Birthday Party will give 70 percent of all funds raised to the care of infantile paralysis in the various localities throughout the country where they have Birthday Balls; the other 30 percent is going to be spent to do something we have always had in mind. It is going to further the cause of research."[61]

He also transacted at Warm Springs much public business and made plans for future public business.

He dealt with a public row that erupted between Ickes and the man who had been appointed to head the Federal Housing Administration established under the National Housing Act of 1934—presidentially appointed to that post for no apparent good reason since the man had no concern to supply human housing needs but every concern for the private profit of bankers and businessmen in the housing industry and every concern to protect business against government "interference." He was James A. Moffett, an extremely wealthy oil company executive (he had been director of Standard Oil of New Jersey when named to the NRA's Industrial Advisory Board in 1933; he was currently vice-president of Standard Oil of California) whose agency's assigned function was to insure loans made by private lending agencies to middle-income people for home modernization or new home construction. Ickes as head of PWA, in which was a Housing Division, proposed a massive federal program to clear slums and construct low-cost housing for people who could never qualify for an FHA-insured loan—and there were many millions who could not. Ickes conceived his proposal to lie wholly outside Moffett's jurisdiction, and technically it did; but Moffett strongly, publicly objected to it just the same, claiming it would "wreck a $21 billion mortgage market and undermine the nation's real estate values." Roosevelt sided with Ickes when the latter protested Moffett's making public a dispute that could and should have been handled quietly within the administration. Roosevelt said as much to Moffett face-to-face when the latter came down, by invitation, to Warm Springs. He said so, too, in a warmly sympathetic letter to Ickes. But on the substantive matter at issue between the two men he sided tacitly, effectively with Moffett, for he refused to support Ickes's housing plans, which got nowhere as a result.[62]

With Lilienthal, Tugwell, and Morris L. Cooke, the President made plans to free the technology of electricity from holding companies (strangle-holding companies) the sole purpose of which was to profit businessmen at the expense of the general good. In one of the most psychologically revealing and significant, historically, of his press conferences, though nearly all of it was off the record, he told of "a certain friend of mine" who "in about 1928" began buying utilities bonds with his savings for old age because the bankers this friend went to recommended such bonds highly. For one thing, they paid 6 or 7 percent instead of the 4 percent paid by other securities. But he bought them "at 102, 103 and 104," and "today the average of those bonds is about 40; . . . he has lost over half" of the $20,000 or so he invested. Why? Because the banker-recommended bonds were holding company bonds, "none of them operating companies," and the holding companies existed simply and solely to provide rake-offs to their organizers:

> Let us take Associated Gas & Electric, for example, or Commonwealth & Southern, or any of the big holding companies. Those bonds have printed on them that behind them is so much stock. Let us call the first company the A company, and its bonds state that it has so much stock of B Company, C Company, D Company, as security for those bonds. Then you analyze and you ask, what is the common stock of B, C, and D Companies? You will find that they are holding companies. And you will also find that they have outstanding certain bonds which are backed by the common stocks of E, F, G, H, and I Companies. And then you will come down to those companies and perhaps they are operating companies or perhaps they are holding companies too. . . . The banker who does the merging gets a lot of common stock and dumps it off on the market. Now . . . if the utility companies in this country could capitalize [fairly] on the basis of the money put into them, every one of them would be making a profit today and every one of them could reduce rates.

In the same press conference he spoke again of the Alcorn County Electric Power Association. "There they had Corinth . . . and they found they could distribute in Corinth . . . household power at about two cents a kilowatt hour. But if they were to run an electric line out to a farm, they would have to charge [the farmer] three cents. . . . What did the Corinth people do? . . . Voluntarily they agreed . . . to pay for two-and-a-half-cent power which enabled the farmer to get two-and-a-half-cent power. . . . That is community planning." This splitting of the difference between town and country rates made every kind of sense; not only would it spread the blessings of electricity to those heretofore denied them, but it would also increase the overall profit of a profit-motivated distributor. And "there was no reason in God's world why the Mississippi Power Company could not have gone to Corinth" and made this arrangement. But the company "just never thought of it." Instead, "it was the T.V.A. that went down and . . . said, 'Let us have a uniform rate for the man next to the powerhouse and the . . . man who lives twenty-five miles up the Valley. We don't want to concentrate any more people in Corinth. We want to increase the rural population.' The result of that operation is that they . . . have [already] nearly doubled the consumption of power." An eight-year-old child would find obvious the profit-generating arithmetic: 2 times 3 is 6, but 4 times 2½ is 10. "Furthermore, they [in Alcorn County] have gone ahead and formed another [cooperative] association, tied to this county one, by which the people can buy refrigerators and electric cookstoves and all the other gadgets at a figure which is somewhere around 60 and 70 percent of what they were paying before." The cooperative did so by buying direct at wholesale prices from manufacturers instead of from a Mississippi Power Company subsidiary "generally owned by a son of a president of a power company—there is a lot of that nepotism."

As regards TVA as a whole, however, "Power is really a secondary matter," said Roosevelt. "What we are doing there is taking a watershed with about three and a half million people in it, almost all of them rural" and desperately poor. TVA was "primarily intended to change and improve the standard of living of the people in the valley. Power is . . . of course . . . important . . . because if you can get cheap power to those people, you hasten the process of raising the standard of living." But TVA was also doing a great many other things to improve the quality of life in the valley. "For instance, take fertilizer. . . . Dr. H. A. Morgan is running the fertilizer end of it and at Muscle Shoals he is turning out, not a nitrate—the plant was originally built [during the Great War] for a nitrate plant—but . . . a phosphate. He is conducting a very fine experiment with phosphate of lime." The immediate response of the National Fertilizer Association was, of course, an outraged protest against government in the fertilizer business. Yet the answer to that protest was "a very simple one." The TVA operation on fertilizers was experimental, designed to determine a yardstick for fertilizer prices. TVA would "take this year a thousand acres" of government-owned land, "worn-out land typical of the locality," and "use this phosphate of lime on these thousand acres and show what can be done with the land. . . . They will compare it with other fertilizers, putting them in parallel strips, and they will see [demonstrate] which works out best and at lowest cost. Having the large plant, they will be able to figure out [and tell farmers] what is a fair price for the best type of fertilizer." Then it would be "up to the National Fertilizer Association and its affiliated companies" to meet the demonstrated fair price. "Now, if these gentlemen fail to avail themselves of this magnificent opportunity to conduct a sound business and make a profit, well, it is just too bad." The implicit threat was noted by one of the reporters. The aim of this whole procedure was to provide "just a little guiding light," commented this reporter in a tone of voice conveying doubt. "An intimation," said a smiling Eleanor Roosevelt, who sat through that conference at her husband's side. Roosevelt protested this. "No, it is not even an intimation," he said. "No, it is a generous offer."[63]

He dealt, too, at Warm Springs, as November ended and December began, with plans for the unemployed.

By late October, after a series of night conferences in the White House with Harry Hopkins, Ickes, Morgenthau, and occasional others, he had been persuaded by the stubborn persistence of the unemployment problem and by the innovative and articulate Hopkins to revive the idea out of which the Civil Works Administration had come last year. He decided to abolish direct federal relief altogether, substituting for it a public works program massive enough to provide work directly, and stimulate private industry to provide jobs, for all the jobless who were willing and able to work. The estimated cost for fiscal 1935–1936 was $5 billion—a figure staggering to Joseph Kennedy and Undersecretary of the Treasury Thomas Jefferson Coolidge, both of whom participated in at least one of these conferences and both of whom then gave it as their opinion, à la Lew Douglas, that business was on the verge of a revival which would make everything all right soon, if only government did not "interfere." Hardly less staggered was Morgenthau, whose qualms could be overcome only by his worshipful loyalty to Franklin Roosevelt. Ickes and Hopkins, and their respective PWA and FERA staffs, had at once gone to work to develop a highly generalized list of work projects, and Morgenthau had continued to raise what Ickes deemed "stupid, silly" objections which, infuriating to the interior secretary, were for that reason amusing, as well as annoying, to Hopkins.[64]

Then came the elections. In their results Hopkins saw opportunity shining, brilliantly but briefly. Obviously the new Congress would be eager at the outset to ratify and promote a leftward surge by the New Deal—a fact which was, in Hopkins's view, an iron of opportunity glowing white-hot and malleable. But it must be struck at once, this radiant iron, for soon it would either cool under the freezing breath of business reaction or be liquefied in the perfervid breath of a radicalism (revolutionary) born of dashed hopes and physical misery. He brooded over this. And on the Saturday afternoon following election day, while driving with Aubrey Williams and others of his staff to a race track just outside the District,* he suddenly burst out: "Boys—this is our hour! We've got to get everything we want—a works program, social security, wages and hours, everything—now or never. Get your minds at work on developing

---

*Hopkins fancied himself in the role, incongruous for a social worker, of horseplayer and dissipated "hells-bells" hedonist. He was as fond of nightclubs as of the racetrack, though he had little time to devote to such pleasures.

a complete ticket to provide security for all the folks of this country up and down and across the board."[65] There had ensued another burst of intense labor in the Walker-Johnson Building, similar to that which had launched the CWA, and in the St. Regis Hotel in New York City.* From it issued a sweeping, loosely articulated program, including the one Ickes and Hopkins had been working on but including much more beside.

Hopkins carried it in his briefcase when, on the day before Thanksgiving, he left Washington for Warm Springs, having been invited down by the President. It provided the subject matter for informal discussions presided over by Roosevelt in the days after Thanksgiving, at the swimming pool and in the Little White House at Warm Springs, perhaps also on the picnic ground at Dowdell's Knob, and on the special presidential train which left Warm Springs for Washington on December 5—conferences in which Hopkins, Ickes, Tugwell, Morgenthau, and Frank Walker participated. By then the New York *Times,* having somehow got wind of it, had published the gist of the program on its front page. As summarized by reporter Delbert Clark, Hopkins's "EPIA (End Poverty in America) plan" called for: "An expansion of the subsistence homesteads and rural rehabilitation programs to include as many families as need such accommodations or in a position to accept them; a large-scale removal of families from submarginal (unprofitable) land to home sites where they can live on a more civilized scale; federal advances of funds to both categories to equip their homesteads with tools, live stock, etc.; an expansion of the program already in progress on an experimental scale to give factory work to the idle, through what the FERA softly calls "canning centers," "needlecraft centers," or the like; a large-scale, low-cost housing program to shelter those unable for one reason or another to move to subsistence homesteads, since it appears there is no purpose [on Hopkins's part] entirely to depopulate large cities; a social insurance program to give security in the future."[66]

IX

ROOSEVELT was unprepared in mood or mind, as 1934 drew to a close and the new year began, to accept any of these proposals for immediate, vigorous, affirmative action. He confined himself to preparations for the new works relief program and for social insurance legislation, making with regard to the latter, as we shall see, decisions aimed mostly at limiting the scope of the plans being developed.

For he would long continue indecisive regarding overall policy direction, unable to determine the proper angle of departure leftward from what he had formerly deemed the median line. Despite his irritable impatience, and disgust even, with the big business community, he was reluctant to abandon his

---

*Choice of this incongruous locale for social welfare planning was perhaps due to the fact that the St. Regis was in receivership, and Ray Moley was a receiver.

position as President of All the People, his strategy of the "broker state" wherein balance was achieved through a refereed competition of special interests whose representatives were directly actively involved in government. He was even more reluctant to embrace the kind of governmental national planning for which Tugwell continually pressed (he felt it to be a kind of straitjacket planning), as an alternative to broker government, if the latter *must* be abandoned.[67]

And in this state of indecision he gave to those closest to him impressions of basic attitude that differed from one another to the point of contradiction.

Thus Moley, who worked with him on the drafting of the annual message and the budget message to the new Congress, in December 1934, was led to believe that Roosevelt had again (had recovered) a "conciliatory and friendly" attitude toward business. "He had no quarrel with business, as such," remembered Moley. "Certainly he did not regard it as an enemy. He felt that with a suitable educational effort, and with some give-and-take on both sides, a considerably body of business opinion could be brought to accept the New Deal program."[68]

But to others Roosevelt gave the impression that in his conviction, the "give-and-take" favored by Moley could not be even "on both sides," in the circumstances, since business was adamantly insisting upon "take" for itself and "give" for the New Deal.

At a cabinet meeting on Friday, December 14, Secretary of Commerce Roper undertook to assure the President that business was now prepared to "cooperate" with him to achieve economic recovery. "Well, Dan," said Roosevelt with a grim smile, "all I can say is that business will have only until January 3 to make up its mind whether it is going to cooperate or not," January 3 being the date on which his budget message would be delivered and his annual message, to be delivered to Congress next day, would go to the printer. He went on to say he was "tired" of having a few dozen wealthy private individuals determine the "destinies of 120,000,000 people" (he referred to James W. Gerard's 1930 list of sixty-four men who "ran" the United States, only one of whom, Andrew Mellon, held government office); he favored the abolition of their chief means of such control—namely, the holding company.[69]

As regards fundamentals, he was yet in a quandary, sinking ever more deeply in, while he waited, watched and waited, for emergence from the developing "situation" of a clear sign, a definite cue.

II

➜➜✕❮❮

Concerning Social Security:
The First Faltering Steps Toward a Welfare State

I

IN this mood and state of mind, Franklin Roosevelt in the latter half of 1934 and opening months of 1935 dealt with the most important single piece of social legislation in all American history, if importance be measured in terms of historical decisiveness and direct influence upon the lives of individual Americans.

The importance justifies, as our understanding of its nature requires, a swift review of the historical process whereby the social insurance proposal was developed in America and thrust at last, forcibly, into this President's waiting, conservatively shaping hands.

II

WE have already noted that social insurance was far from being a new idea in the world when Governor Roosevelt first publicly espoused it at the Governors' Conference in Salt Lake City on June 30, 1930.* We have remarked how Otto von Bismarck pushed compulsory social insurance laws through the German Reichstag in the 1880s in response to political pressures not unlike, and little, if any, more intense than, those which pushed Roosevelt in the same direction in 1934 and 1935. The German example had been followed by other advanced industrial nations on the Continent and by Great Britain, in the 1890s and early 1900s. In the United States, however, though the western frontier had ceased to exist by 1900, industrialism's vital impact continued to be cushioned by the frontier's lingering economic effects. Frontier attitudes continued to prevail in the popular mind, continued to dominate the business mind. Self-reliance, self-help, and private charity, within limits, were deemed moral goods; conversely, public aid of individual personal welfare was deemed morally reprehensible (it allegedly "sapped" the "initiative" and destroyed the "moral fiber" of the helped individual), and a cult of youth (the frontier placed a premium on youthful hardihood) bred neglect of, if not actual contempt for, the indigent elderly. So it had not been until the second decade of the present century that the United States, this most powerful of industrial nations, even began to consider seriously the need for social insurance which an advanced industrialism necessarily implies.

*See Davis, *FDR: The New York Years,* pp. 164–66.

It did so then, as we have indicated,* largely through the activities of the American Association for Labor Legislation (AALL), established in 1906. AALL's purpose was to shape and lobby for state and federal laws beneficial to American industrial workers. Inspired by the Continental and then-developing British examples of social legislation, it was imbued with Progressivism's belief in the need for social and economic planning in the public interest, with government a participant in the planning process. Most of its charter members were academic economists and political scientists, though there were a few nonacademic economists who were, for the most part, associated with insurance companies. Of the academic founders, two of the most prominent, both from the University of Wisconsin, were political scientist Richard Ely and economist John Commons, the latter of whom secured the appointment of a former Wisconsin student of his, John B. Andrews, as the organization's executive secretary, a post Andrews retained until his death in 1943.

From the outset, therefore, AALL's operations were greatly influenced by what came to be called the Wisconsin Idea of close collaboration between government and university (extensive use of the specialist "expert" was stressed) in the business of the state. It was an idea born of the proximity of capitol and university in Madison and of the fact that Wisconsin politics were then dominated by the elder Bob La Follette, himself a Wisconsin alumnus, at a time when the university had an exceptionally able faculty in the fields of history, sociology, economics, and public administration.† The Idea was essentially pragmatic, empirical in its applications—and most of the founders of AALL were similarly practical-minded men of goodwill, inclined to deal with specific immediate problems in their own specific immediate terms, without great concern for "underlying" purposes or "overall" ideals as unifying, process-determining forces. Commons himself, whose continuing influence upon Andrews was profound, distrusted ideological ("European") approaches to social problems. Though a student and exponent of collective economic action, famous by the 1930s as the father of institutional economics, he was no Socialist. He was emphatically not a Marxist. He was committed to what Holmes called "competition in the marketplace of ideas" as the way toward that efficiency in action which, in the pragmatic view, is the test of the truth of ideas.

But there was also among AALL's charter members a man very different from the Wisconsin contingent in every respect and different, too, from most other association members in his general outlook and mentality.

Isaac M. Rubinow was a Socialist by political conviction and an idealist in both the common and philosophical meanings of the term.[1] Born a Russian

---

*See Davis, *FDR: The New York Years*, p. 165.
†One of La Follette's close friends was Professor Charles R. Van Hise, who in 1912 published a book, *Concentration and Control: A Solution to the Trust Problem of the United States*, which was highly influential on Theodore Roosevelt's New Nationalism. A few years later Van Hise became president of the University of Wisconsin.

Jew, he emigrated to New York in 1893, when he was eighteen, was graduated from Columbia two years later, received an M.D. from New York University's medical school in 1898, and then practiced medicine for several years among the poor of New York. He quickly realized that the horrors he daily encountered, outraging both his practical intelligence and his human sympathies, were in sum not a medical problem but a socioeconomic one, solvable in good part, he was convinced, by socioeconomic means already well developed in Europe. In 1903, having studied political science at Columbia while continuing his medical practice, he abandoned the latter altogether in order to devote himself to the "continuous and obstinate agitation for social insurance" (the words are his) which became his lifework. Within little more than a dozen years, during which he held a number of posts in government and private enterprise (for five years he was chief actuary and statistician for a large insurance firm), he became the author of two classic works in his special field —*Social Insurance* (1913); *Standards of Health Insurance* (1916)—and was everywhere recognized as, in Roy Labove's words, "the outstanding American theoretician of social insurance." Eloquent in argument for social approaches to social problems, Rubinow caustically denied that "voluntarism" or "individualism" had validity as other than subsidiary ways of dealing with the human welfare needs of an advanced industrial society, and he was inclined, always, to see particulars as aspects of the general, was always acutely aware of *connections* between or among things, ideas, acts—which is to say that he viewed every specific problem in his field as an organic element of that field, solvable only (ultimately) in terms of the field as a whole.

It was inevitable that such a mind would often profoundly disagree with the policy line of Commons and Andrews. Rubinow did so with regard to the very first of AALL's major campaigns, that for workmen's compensation, launched in 1911. In the standard compensation law pressed upon the states and in agitation for passage of such laws, the Commons-Andrews leadership placed its major emphasis on the prevention of industrial accident and health hazard rather than on compensation for the individual victim of these. The compensation provisions were designed primarily to induce employers, who bore the costs (passed on to consumers, of course), to reduce their employee accident and sickness rates. This choice of emphasis was the one preferred by industrialists and private insurance companies. They could engage with some enthusiasm in "safety first" and "physical fitness" promotions, for obvious profit reasons, and could accept, if less enthusiastically, laws encouraging such promotions. All the same (or therefore, as he might have said), Rubinow found the relative emphasis mistaken. Prevention and insurance, said he, were "two distinct social efforts," which, tied into the same package, tended to confuse and corrupt each other. Workmen's compensation ought to be conceived primarily, if not exclusively, as an insurance scheme, its concern the protection of the individual's welfare against risks that are "inevitable" in "economic activity." The whole emphasis should be placed on *income maintenance* for

injured workers; the design should be to reduce that financial insecurity of the
wage earner which is inherent in an ill-regulated, profit-oriented, yet technologically advanced industrial society.

Rubinow had the same basic objection to the second of AALL's major
campaigns, that against industrial unemployment, launched in 1914. Here
again the major emphasis was placed by the Commons-Andrews leadership
not on insurance but on prevention, not on income maintenance for the unemployed, but on means of inducing employers to "regularize" their operations
in ways that would increase steady employment and reduce layoffs. AALL's
"Practical Program" (so Commons and Andrews dubbed it) did call for government action to establish labor exchanges or employment offices and to
provide emergency public works to take up the employment slack during hard
times, but the main emphasis was upon unemployment prevention by "scientific management" on the part of "enlightened business leaders." Unemployment insurance was not to be called for until industry had had a "fair chance"
to reduce labor turnover to a minimum on its own initiative. (Ignored, said
Rubinow and others, was the obvious fact that businessmen would long ago
have "rationalized" the labor market and "regularized" their own operations
if [1] their individual enterprise had the power to do so and [2] doing so would
clearly, definitely increase their private profit.)

Only with the third of AALL's major campaigns—that for compulsory
health insurance, launched in 1915—did Rubinow find himself in nearly complete agreement. Here again, AALL's leadership stressed the "prevention of
sickness" as a goal and health insurance as a means of achieving it (such
insurance would "directly stimulate both workman and employer to reduce
the risk of occupational illness," said AALL's official publication). But in the
health field the inadequacy of voluntarism and private initiative was so patent
(horrendous health statistics measured the failure of private medicine to supply
wage earner needs), while binding social action was so clearly the only sensible
solution, that AALL's main emphasis accorded with Rubinow's philosophy.
The standard health insurance law proposed by AALL to the states stressed
the compulsory requirement; by means of it, coverage was rendered universal
instead of partial and the need for expensive reserves was reduced. The model
legislation was also frankly redistributive of income insofar as most of the cost
was to be borne by the employer and the state—an equitable arrangement,
argued AALL, since the state and the employer shared a responsibility for the
general health situation that was far greater than that of the workers.

None of these three campaigns came close to achieving its objectives. Most
states passed workmen's compensation laws, but these had no clearly demonstrable effects upon accident rates, though other factors worked to reduce
accidents, and they inadequately compensated the victims of accident and
occupational illness: The injured worker continued to bear the bulk of the
financial burden imposed by his injury. As for the attack on unemployment,
a mere handful of employers in the whole of the nation ever attempted the
"regularization" schemes proposed by AALL, whereas the need for unemploy-

ment insurance increased, even during the 1920s, when New Era prosperity reigned. Afterward, of course, as unemployment grew catastrophic following the crash of '29, voluntarism and private initiative were utterly discredited as "solutions" to the problem.

But, ironically enough, the greatest failure among the three campaigns was of the one most soundly conceived, in Rubinow's view as in historical perspective—namely, the campaign for compulsory health insurance. It aroused intense national controversy for half a decade. In two states, New York and California, the model legislation seemed at one point close to passage. But in the end the proposal was everywhere decisively defeated and in ways that made its successful revival difficult.

Chief opponent was the organized medical profession itself, whose concern to spread the blessings of medical science to the economically disadvantaged in any efficiently organized way proved to be minimal or, at any rate, to lag far behind the concern for entrepreneurial freedom and private profit. Medical associations—state, local, national—waged ruthless war on the measure, learning and employing as they did so every trick of pressure lobbying and misleading propaganda, including appeals to the mind-befogging patriotic passions aroused by world war. Health insurance was damned as a German conspiracy or (after the autumn of 1917) a Bolshevik one. Consequently, from AALL's point of view, the entire effort seemed ultimately worse than futile. It was counterproductive. The American Medical Association had not theretofore been much involved in politics, but it emerged from this struggle fully and actively conscious of its political potency; it could be counted upon, ever after, to oppose, powerfully, any legislative proposal which might conceivably affect, reduce in the slightest, the private-entrepreneurial nature of American health care delivery.

Small wonder that by the 1920s, as postwar reaction swept America, AALL's leadership was discouraged from further efforts along the same line or, indeed, from any major campaign for the time being. The new decade's principal effort in the field of AALL interest was initiated, not by AALL, though AALL collaborated in it, but by one of America's zoological garden of fraternal associations (Elks, Moose, Lions, et al.)—namely, the Fraternal Order of Eagles (FOE). Local branches of the Eagles were called, with consistency of nomenclature, Aeries, and every state had a goodly number of these, whence came delegates each summer to a national policy-making convention called the Grand Aerie. It was the Grand Aerie of 1921 that at the behest of a "Past Grand Worthy President" named Frank E. Hering committed the Eagles to a campaign for state old-age pensions. The time had come, said Hering, to stop consigning "our unfortunate aged to pauper institutions, humiliated, humbled, and, not infrequently, mistreated."[2]

The subsequent campaign was highly effective in calling popular attention to old-age dependency as a great and growing social problem in America, one that was implicit in "technological progress" and sharply indicated by census statistics. An estimated 2.1 percent of the American population had been sixty-five and older in 1850; by 1900 the percentage had risen to 4.07, and it continued to rise, standing at 4.30 in 1910 and 5.67 in 1920. It was to approach 8 percent by the beginning of the Great Depression. Yet the industrial order had less and less economic use for older people—the average number of years of gainful employment for the individual tended to be reduced—which meant an increase in old-age dependency considerably greater than the increase in the number of elderly in our society. In 1910, 23 percent of the elderly had been dependent upon some form of welfare; 33 percent were so dependent in 1921 (the percentage would climb to 40 by 1929, the peak year of New Era Prosperity), and the public was now reminded by the Eagles that such statistics, as they measured a spreading stain upon our national moral character, stood for myriads upon myriads of preventable human tragedies.[3]

Far less effective were the Eagles in providing solutions to the problem. True, they were largely responsible for the fact that eleven states had old-age pension laws on their books by 1930, whereas no state had had such a law in 1921 (Alaska Territory had one, passed in 1915). Moreover, this was accomplished despite strong opposition from chambers of commerce and manufacturers' associations in a time when businessmen dominated the American scene as never before. But this triumph, alas, was more apparent than real. What opponents could not wholly defeat they might vitiate, and they were aided in doing so by the Eagles' lack of professional expertise and by their willingness to compromise in order to achieve paper victories. Most of the resultant legislation was fatally flawed: It was permissive (county optional), rather than compelling, of local compliance; it required local funding; and it confusedly mingled "moral" concerns with economic need in deciding pension rolls. (Hering's own published belief was that to become a pensioner, one should have a "history of habitual industriousness, habitual loyalty to family obligations and freedom from all crimes involving more than four months imprisonment."[4]) Only six of the state laws were even nominally in effect in 1929, and these produced few actual pensions, none adequate to supply the individual need; of the millions of elderly indigent in America that year, a mere 1,200 or so—and virtually none outside Alaska, Montana, and a few counties in Wisconsin—received pensions totaling $222,000.

Clearly if the old-age problem was to come even close to a solution, a new organized approach to it was needed. And by 1929 such an approach was being made as new, young leaders revived an American social insurance movement that had become virtually moribund when Andrews and Commons lost confidence and interest in it.

Chief among these new leaders was Abraham Epstein, a man whose background was in several ways similar to Rubinow's.[5] Like Rubinow, he was a Russian Jew who had emigrated to New York City when he was eighteen, this in 1910. Like Rubinow, he was intellectually brilliant and avid for education: He took a B.S. and a graduate degree in economics at the University of Pittsburgh. Like Rubinow, he identified with the economically disadvantaged and became passionately committed to social insurance. He differed from

Rubinow in the greater emphasis he placed upon income redistribution as an aim of social insurance, insisting more strenuously and adamantly than Rubinow did that the government as well as the employer and, chiefly for psychological reasons, the employee must contribute to insurance funds. He differed, too, and much more, from Rubinow in temperament, being more impatient, self-centered, abrasive, touchy; his career was marred by bitter quarrels with professional colleagues, including famous ones with Andrews, whose policy line he, of course, like Rubinow, deplored, and with Hering, whose assistant he briefly was when the Eagles' campaign was launched. This undoubtedly made him less practically effective than he, with a different temper, would have been. Nevertheless, more than any other one man, he was responsible for the fact that when the New Era collapsed and the New Deal began, social insurance was again a live idea in America, embodied in a working organization.

The organization was the American Association for Old Age Security (AAOAS), which Epstein launched in 1927, after he had served some nine years as research director of the Pennsylvania Commission for Old Age Pensions, had become disillusioned with the current pension movement, and had tried in vain, through Rubinow, to revive the interest of Andrews and AALL in social insurance. The new organization's first major act was the preparation of a bill introduced into Congress (1927) by New York Representative William I. Sivorich—a bill, of which Epstein was chief draftsman, calling for federal grants-in-aid to states adopting old-age insurance laws. It was never reported out of committee. In the following year Epstein published his highly influential *The Care of the Aged,* which enlarged upon his pioneering *Facing Old Age,* a study of U.S. old-age dependency and old-age pensions which he had published in 1922.

Thus by decade's end the central focus of America's social insurance movement was on old-age security, a problem that had been peripheral to unemployment and health insurance in the movement's earlier years. And old age remained a major concern, increasingly impossible for politicians to ignore, even after the deepening depression had made mass unemployment the nation's most crucial immediate problem.

In 1932, while Herbert Hoover was still in the White House, Senator Clarence C. Dill of Washington and Representative William P. Connery, Jr., of Massachusetts, introduced in Congress a new old-age bill prepared and sponsored by Epstein and AAOAS. It was a revision of the 1927 bill, calling for federal grants-in-aid, totaling one-third of the costs of old-age pensions, to states adopting acceptable old-age laws, to induce passage of such laws. This time the proposal proved politically viable from the outset. The Dill-Connery bill, inherited by the New Deal Congress, was favorably reported out of the Labor Committee of the House and the Pensions Committee of the Senate in early 1934, having gained wide popular support. It would then certainly have passed Congress by a large majority if the President had specifically endorsed it or even indicated that he had no objection to it. He declined to do so, and that was the beginning of the way, the decisive shaping way, in which FDR's mentality, long-term purposes, and political techniques influenced the final development of American social security.

III

ROOSEVELT had himself been influenced in some degree by Rubinow and Epstein, or by their ideas, while yet governor of New York. It was an influence exerted not by his reading of their books (almost certainly he never read them) but through his state industrial commissioner, Frances Perkins, when she persuaded him to come out for mandatory unemployment insurance, in his address to the Conference of Governors at Salt Lake City on June 30, 1930. He also in that address, in language Perkins had originally drafted, called for old-age benefits to be paid out of joint contributions by employers, employees, *and* government. The influence of Epstein and Rubinow is clear. Six months later, at Perkins's urging, Roosevelt assembled a governors' conference of his own, at Albany, to plan concerted interstate action against the rising tide of unemployment, and to prepare for it, it will be recalled,* she summoned Paul H. Douglas to Albany. It was Douglas who briefed Roosevelt in detail on matters the conference would cover. It was Douglas who prepared the annotated agenda which enabled Roosevelt to preside brilliantly over the discussions. And Douglas was a friend and to some degree a disciple of both Rubinow and Epstein.

But this Rubinow-Epstein influence was not the only one brought to bear, largely through Frances Perkins, upon Roosevelt's thinking about social welfare. There was also the influence of the Wisconsin Idea, manifested by the Commons-Andrews leadership of AALL—an influence greatly strengthened in January 1932 when Wisconsin Governor Phil La Follette signed into law an unemployment compensation bill which the state legislature had passed in December.

Drafted by Wisconsin University economics Professors Harold R. Groves, who was a legislator, and Paul A. Raushenbush,† whose wife, Elizabeth, a collaborator in the drafting, was a daughter of Justice Brandeis, the Wisconsin law was a revision of a bill, the Heber Bill, originally drafted by Commons in 1921 and perennially rejected by the legislature throughout the New Era years. It had unemployment prevention as its central theme. It required each firm employing ten or more to establish a reserve fund out of which any of its

---

*See Davis, *FDR: The New York Years,* p. 223. Frances Perkins writes that FDR immensely liked young Douglas, and Douglas was most favorably impressed by Roosevelt's verve and quickness and capaciousness of mind. All the same, Douglas voted for Norman Thomas in 1932.

†Paul Raushenbush was the son of the Reverend Walter Rauschenbusch (the family name had been Americanized by omission of the two c's), a Baptist minister, teacher, and writer whose book *Christianity and the Social Crisis* (1907) had made him the acknowledged leader of the Social Gospel movement in the United States. Son Paul attended Amherst College when Alexander Meiklejohn was its president. Later, at the University of Wisconsin, he took a graduate degree in economics under John R. Commons. He served also on the faculty of Wisconsin's Experimental College during the five years that it operated under the leadership of Meiklejohn.

employees earning less than $1,500 annually would, if thrown out of work, be paid half his weekly wage (up to $10 a week) for ten weeks. Farm workers, loggers, and employees making more than $1,500 were not covered. The rate of required contribution and the size of the individual firm's reserve varied with the firm's employment record: If it had a stable record, its reserve could be relatively small; if its record showed wide fluctuations in the number employed, its reserves must be larger. "Merit rating" this was called. The law was not to go into effect until July 1, 1933, to give employers opportunity to initiate "voluntary plans" along the indicated lines, and it would not go into effect at all if 175,000 Wisconsin employees were covered by acceptable "voluntary plans" before the target date arrived—an unlikely event, which did not, in fact, occur.

This so-called Wisconsin Plan was promptly endorsed by the Governors' Interstate Commission set up the year before at that Albany conference Roosevelt had hosted—an endorsement largely resulting from the fact that Wisconsin's was the only unemployment compensation law then on the nation's statute books. It was greatly and glowingly publicized by its proponents, including AALL's leaders, who laid heavy stress upon its conservative "Americanism," its subordination of income maintenance for the unemployed, as per the much maligned British dole, to employment "stabilization." The measure, said Commons, should appeal to the "individualism of American capitalists who do not want to be burdened with the inefficiencies or misfortunes of other capitalists, and it fits the public welfare policy of a capitalistic nation which uses the profit motive to prevent unemployment."[6]

But the "capitalists" whom Commons was so concerned to propitiate showed no grateful enthusiasm for this effort on their behalf. Quite the contrary. Having strongly opposed the bill's passage, Wisconsin's industrialists resisted the law's application to them for as long as they could, ultimately forcing a year's postponement (until July 1, 1934) of the date it went into effect. Equally negative, for opposite reasons, was the response of intellectual leaders of the social insurance movement. Epstein and Douglas, among others, pointed out that the Wisconsin Plan, with its combine of individual reserves and merit rating, assumed that American "capitalists" operating individually controlled or could control the economic forces which that year produced massive growing unemployment. The assumption was obviously false: The individual business, even when large, now proclaimed itself to be as much a victim of general conditions, and almost as helpless in the face of them, as the individual worker who lost his job.

Nor was the Wisconsin Plan long without a rival in a competition for acceptance as national public policy. It was soon challenged by a clearly defined alternative to it—a so-called Ohio Plan announced in November 1932 as a conclusion, in the form of proposed legislation, by an Ohio Commission on Unemployment Insurance, having Rubinow as its key "idea" member.

Reflecting Rubinow's views, the Ohio Plan differed from the Wisconsin one in that (1) it would establish a single pooled fund under full public control instead of individually segregated funds under employer control; (2) it required contributions to the fund from employee as well as employer, the former contributing 1 percent and the latter 2 percent of the recorded employee wage;* and (3) it would pay the unemployed worker half his weekly wage, but up to $15 instead of Wisconsin's $10, and for sixteen weeks, instead of Wisconsin's ten. The proposal at once gained more adherents among serious students of social welfare than did the Wisconsin Plan; it was soon embodied in more proposed state legislation across the land than was the Wisconsin Plan. In proportion it was more strongly opposed by the business community. The Ohio Chamber of Commerce promptly published, in December 1932, a "critical analysis" in which the proposed legislation was denounced as the "most menacing and revolutionary" in Ohio's history, an "attempt to foist upon the United States foreign ideals and foreign practices" that threatened "complete disruption of our American system of individual responsibility."[7] Other business organizations made similar pronouncements.

There was criticism, too, from an opposite point of view, by leading social welfare economists. Epstein and Douglas, for instance. They immensely preferred the Ohio Plan to the Wisconsin one (indeed, in Epstein's caustic judgment, the latter was worse than useless), but they were sure it did not follow "foreign ideals and foreign practices" closely enough in its funding arrangements—a stricture with which Rubinow privately agreed. The failure to require financial participation by government was, in Epstein's especially strong view, an extremely serious defect, perhaps even a fatal one.

Some of this critical commentary, especially the sharp criticisms of individual plant reserves and merit rating which Epstein made in a personal letter to Raushenbush, had some effect upon this principal author of the Wisconsin Plan and, through him and his wife, upon New Deal planning for social insurance.

Elizabeth Brandeis Raushenbush came to Washington in the week after Christmas 1933 to visit her parents, Supreme Court Justice and Mrs. Louis Brandeis. Hardly had she removed her coat in her parents' apartment when she was told that her father's good friend the wealthy and liberal-minded Boston merchant Lincoln Filene, at her father's behest, had set up a dinner in his daughter's house for January 4, 1934; that the guests at this dinner would include Senator Wagner and Labor Secretary Perkins; and that she, Elizabeth, should be prepared to present the Wisconsin Plan as a model for federal legislation whereby state adoptions of social insurance would be promoted.† Brandeis himself would not be at that dinner. It would be unseemly, if not unethical, for a member of the Supreme Court to involve himself in the making of a law upon whose constitutionality, or lack of it, that court must ultimately

---

*This employer's rate was actually a projected average of rates that varied from 1 to 3½ percent in accordance with a modified merit rating plan which the Ohio commission, in view of the current popularity of the Wisconsin Plan, felt obliged to adopt. Rubinow very reluctantly agreed to it.
†A historical irony attaches to the fact that Filene's daughter was married to Jouett Shouse. Plans which the Liberty League, headed by Shouse, would damn in the months ahead as part of a conspiracy to subvert the Constitution, were laid in Shouse's home on the night of January 4, 1934.

pass. His daughter was his agent; she performed well her assigned task. Also his agent was Lincoln Filene, who, without mentioning Brandeis by name, outlined an ingenious device the Justice had adapted from a law originally drafted in the Treasury Department of Andrew Mellon during the palmiest days of the Coolidge administration. The device was one with which Elizabeth Raushenbush was already familiar. It had been first suggested to her and her husband when they visited in the Brandeis summer home at Chatham on Cape Cod in the summer of 1933 and there complained of the seeming impossibility of inducing other states to follow Wisconsin in the adoption of an unemployment compensation law. The device had later been spelled out in concrete detail to them in a letter from the justice dated September 16, 1933.[8]

Early in the 1920s, Florida, at the urging of its mercantile and real estate interests, amended its constitution to prohibit "forever" the imposition of a state tax on inheritances. The intent was to lure wealthy elderly people into retirement in Florida, there to spend both their "golden years" and a fair amount of actual gold. Naturally this dismayed states that imposed inheritance taxes. The removal from them of their rich elderly citizens would erode their tax bases, would reduce their private business profits, and the extent of possible injury increased as other states having genial climates gave signs of following Florida's lead. Protests and demands for federal corrective action poured into Washington. The upshot was a federal inheritance tax law designed to deprive Florida, and all other states without inheritance taxes, of any profit from their "unfair competition" for the elderly rich. The law provided that 80 percent of the federal inheritance tax collected in a state having an inheritance tax of its own be returned to that state whereas *none* of the federal tax collected in a state without such a tax would be returned. The constitutionality of the act was promptly questioned in the courts, Florida claiming that its sovereign rights, guaranteed by the Constitution, were violated, but the U.S. Supreme Court, with Brandeis on it, ruled unanimously *(Florida* v. *Mellon)* that the law was constitutional. Thereupon Florida repealed its troublesome amendment in order to pass, as it promptly did, its own inheritance tax.[9]

This suggested to Brandeis what Filene explained to an intensely interested Senator Wagner and Frances Perkins on that evening of January 4—a practical means toward two desired ends, one embedded in the other. Brandeis proposed that the federal government levy upon employers a payroll tax equivalent to 5 percent of the total wages paid employees, but with the proviso that in states adopting mandatory unemployment compensation laws meeting certain minimum standards, employers could deduct from the federal tax (that is, would have credited to them as an offset against the 5 percent payroll levy) whatever contributory payments they made under the state acts. Brandeis's tax offset device, it should be pointed out, was not precisely the device ruled constitutional in *Florida* v. *Mellon.* In the federal inheritance tax law the federal government collected the taxes and then returned 80 percent of them as grants to states having acceptable laws of their own. In the Brandeis scheme the "offsetting" was done by the taxpayer himself. This would not only stimulate state adoptions of mandatory unemployment insurance but also protect employers in states having such laws against unfair competition from employers in states *not* having them. For in the former states federal tax moneys which would otherwise go to Washington for unspecified disbursement would be retained locally for local unemployment relief, but in the latter states (those without mandatory insurance laws) the full 5 percent would go into the federal treasury. As for the federally prescribed minimum standards, Brandeis proposed that these be highly flexible, in accordance with his commitment to decentralized government, his hostility to great combinations of power, his view of the states as laboratories for social experiment. Unemployment insurance must be mandatory. Beyond that he would have each state left free to decide for itself between pooled and individually segregated reserves, whether or not the employee as well as employer should contribute, and whether or not the state should also contribute.

The response of Wagner and Secretary Perkins to the Raushenbush-Filene presentation that evening was enthusiastic. They proposed to move at once on the idea. They awaited only a draft bill incorporating it, and before the evening ended, Paul Raushenbush, who remained in Madison, had been recruited by long-distance phone to do the drafting. He came to Washington for the last two weeks of January and worked there with a young Labor Department lawyer named Thomas H. Eliot. In accord with his father-in-law's views and because of Epstein's critical letter, Raushenbush drafted a bill which, in its aim to promote the adoption by the states of mandatory unemployment compensation laws, was considerably less insistent that these laws follow slavishly the Wisconsin model than one might have expected him to be; the states were to have ample leeway for innovation and experiment, after minimum requirements had been met. The bill, several features of which were highly displeasing to Epstein and his organization, was introduced in February 1934 by Wagner in the Senate and Representative David J. Lewis of Maryland in the House.

In the following month Roosevelt endorsed the proposal.

This presidential approval was wholly passive, however—hence without practical effect. The Wagner-Lewis unemployment bill received no more actual White House backing than did the Dill-Connery old-age bill, and like Dill-Connery, it languished in congressional halls, never coming to a floor vote.

IV

WHAT were Roosevelt's motives for thus, in effect, preventing or at least delaying congressional action? The question was earnestly pondered by proponents of the two bills. Some "inside" observers thought he awaited the moment at which, by ostentatiously taking over, he could receive maximum popular credit for social welfare legislation that was in any case inevitable. Others, unpersuaded of this inevitability, worried that Roosevelt was, at heart, opposed to this legislation and so paid it only lip service in the hope that congressional opposition would prevent its ever coming to a vote. Yet others accepted at face value the explanation by White House spokesmen, including Roosevelt himself, that the complex problems required more study before a final decision concerning them was made—this joined to Roosevelt's growing belief that the final decision should be for comprehensive legislation, a single congressional act encompassing all governmental dealings with what was now beginning to be called Social Security. (Use of the term was partly due to Epstein; in 1933 he had broadened the program of his AAOAS to include unemployment insurance, renaming his organization the American Association for Social Security.)

At any rate, the delay continued, and during it, political pressures for far-reaching social welfare legislation grew rapidly toward a point beyond which the White House would be unable to exercise a decisive control over them. There were, outside Congress, as we have seen, Francis Townsend's Old Age Revolving Pension, Huey Long's Share Our Wealth, and Upton Sinclair's EPIC; and within Congress, an increasing Farmer-Laborite, Progressive, and left-wing Democratic pressure toward social welfare legislation more extreme, less rationally conceived, than any proposed by Rubinow or Epstein. It was in, if not also because of, these circumstances that Roosevelt on June 8, 1934, sent to Congress his special message reaffirming the administration's commitment to social insurance. Among New Deal objectives "I place the security of the men, women and children of America first," said he, going on to advocate "some safeguards against misfortunes which cannot be wholly eliminated in this man-made world." He suggested that legislative implementation of the commitment be deferred until early the next year, however, to give time for further study by a special Committee on Economic Security which he would soon appoint and for the preparation by it of definite legislative proposals to be presented to Congress in January 1935.[10]

He established the committee by executive order three weeks later. It was another cabinet committee, consisting of Secretary of the Treasury Morgenthau, Secretary of Agriculture Wallace, Attorney General Cummings, Relief Administrator Hopkins, and Secretary of Labor Perkins, with the last named chairman. The real work would, of course, be done by a full-time professional staff whose appointment, per se revelatory of the administration's intentions, was awaited with mingled eagerness and anxiety by those most knowledgeable of, and dedicated to, social insurance. And at least *some* anxiety was justified by the event. Not one of the major ideological leaders of America's social insurance movement was appointed—not Rubinow, not Epstein, not Douglas.* Instead, economist Edwin E. Witte of the University of Wisconsin, a former student and protégé of John R. Commons, was named executive director; Second Assistant Secretary of Labor A. J. Altmeyer, also from Wisconsin,

---

*Some insight into the process by which Epstein, at least, was excluded is provided in a letter Tom Corcoran wrote Frankfurter on June 18, 1934, ten days after Roosevelt's economic security message was delivered. Corcoran warned Frankfurter, who was preparing to return to America from Oxford, that "the group being formed to work out the social insurance plan" (he assumed that he and Ben Cohen would be members of it) might include "some of the Epstein crowd who will be thoroughly and impracticably wild." He added parenthetically that the Epstein "crowd" had done "their bit toward the shelving of Isaiah's unemployment bill at this session as too tame." "Isaiah" was Corcoran's, and FDR's, code name for Brandeis; the bill was Wagner-Lewis.[11]

was named chairman of the committee's Technical Board on Economic Security; and these two, who had themselves been involved in the Wisconsin Plan, were naturally inclined to choose staff members generally sympathetic to that plan and their views.

The staff finally assembled, however, was large—too large to be of a single mind on any subject. Moreover, it *had* to be chosen to represent a wide range of possible views. It was organized into three major sections, the two largest having to do respectively with unemployment insurance, on which popular attention was focused, and health insurance, on which the baleful eye of the American Medical Association was focused. Much smaller was the section dealing with old-age security in which Witte and the Wisconsin group had relatively little personal interest.

Simultaneously, Witte "proceeded to organize a rather bewildering cluster of advisory committees," as Paul Douglas comments in his *Social Security in the United States,* published in 1936.* There was a general Advisory Council numbering twenty prominent citizens, chaired by the president of the University of North Carolina, Frank P. Graham, its purpose the advising of the top cabinet committee on overall policy. There were also numerous special committees—on child welfare, medicine, public health, dental care, hospitals, and public employment and assistance—plus actuarial and other special consultants in goodly number.

All this would appear on its face to be more conducive to complicated committee politics leading toward compromised conclusions than to swift, clear thinking toward sharply defined, self-consistent goals.

And almost from the moment it began its work in the humid heat of a Washington August, simultaneously with Roosevelt's return to the White House from his *Houston* cruise, the large and cumbrous unemployment insurance section was embroiled in a fundamental controversy, not free of acrimony. It had to do with the administrative setup of the insurance scheme. Should unemployment insurance be administered by the federal government on a national basis? Or should it be administered in separate pieces by the forty-eight states? A national system was known to be favored by Rubinow, Epstein, Douglas, and virtually every other recognized student and theorist of social insurance, none of whom (this was remarked upon at the time) was called in for direct formal consultation on the matter. A national system was also strongly favored by many, if not most, of the professional experts on the committee staff, by several of the best-informed members of the Advisory Council, and by at least one of the top cabinet committee, Henry A. Wallace. Its practical advantages were obvious. Only national administration could insure uniform standards among the states, with fair and equal treatment of workers who moved, as workers now increasingly did, from one state to another. Also, national administration would be more efficient and less costly than state administration.

---

*Douglas dedicated his book "To Robert F. Wagner, Abraham Epstein, I. M. Rubinow, Pioneers in the Movement for Genuine Social Insurance." One senses Douglas's underlining of "Genuine."

But to Witte and the Brandeisians of the Wisconsin group, with their vested intellectual interest in the Wisconsin Plan, the national scheme was anathema. They pressed hard and stood uncompromisingly for a state-federal scheme in which the ingenious "offset" device of Brandeis's invention, incorporated in the 1934 Wagner-Lewis bill, was used to stimulate state adoption of the needed implementing legislation. There was an alternative to the offset device which was greatly preferred by most professional experts on the committee and by nearly all experts having no official connection with the committee—this if they *must* accept state administration. The alternative was direct collection of the payroll tax by the federal government and block allotment of the revenues to states the unemployment insurance of which met federal standards. The block system permitted greater national control and assurance of uniform standards among the states. For this very reason, the Wisconsin group opposed it, and as stubbornly as they did the national scheme itself.

Three immediately practical arguments were employed in support of the state-federal scheme. One was that Congress, because of "state jealousies and aspirations" (Perkins's words), was more likely to adopt legislation for a state-federal system than a purely federal one. Another was the alleged wisdom of giving each state a free choice between the Ohio and Wisconsin approaches; doing so would provide an educative experience for the nation as a whole— a "competition of ideas" in action. The "different states" should be allowed to solve "these different problems . . . according to their own particular genius," said Frances Perkins in a public statement drafted by Witte. The third argument, not publicly made, was the one that darkened and confused every counsel of governmental liberalism and innovation in those years—namely, the need to tailor proposed legislation to the narrow specifications, the narrow minds of the conservatives of the U.S. Supreme Court. A state-federal setup, with state administration, appeared less likely to be declared unconstitutional than a purely national one, and if it were, the state laws would remain on the books, legally protected by constitutionally guaranteed state police powers. A purely national system, on the other hand, would leave nothing behind it if it were struck down. (This constitutional argument was *not* employed by the Wisconsin group in debate upon the subissue of offsets versus block grants; the use of federal grants for a wide variety of purposes had been repeatedly upheld by Supreme Court rulings, whereas the offset device was a legislative novelty as yet untested in the courts.)[12]

The controversy raged unresolved all through the autumn of 1934 and, indeed, until just before the deadline for the presentation to President and Congress of the committee's report and legislative recommendations. "Finally, one day during Christmas week . . . I issued an ultimatum that the Committee would meet at eight o'clock at my house for the evening, and that we would sit all night, if necessary, until we decided the thorny question once and for all," writes Frances Perkins in *The Roosevelt I Knew.* "We sat until two in the morning, and at the end agreed, reluctantly and with mental reservations, that for the present the wisest thing we could do was to recommend a federal-state system."[13]

There remained the issue of individually segregated reserves joined with merit rating, as per the Wisconsin Plan, versus a pooled reserve with no merit rating—an issue which the cabinet committee finally resolved by adopting a compromise proposal by Altmeyer. Notably fair-minded and disinterested, Altmeyer was by this time doubtful of the virtues of the plan to which he had been initially committed (years later he told a congressional committee that merit rating was a bad idea, also that unemployment insurance ought to have been established on a national basis), and his proposal was one that constricted merit rating almost to the point of extinction. The employer, by this proposal, would divide his total contribution between his individual reserve and the pooled reserve, but to the pooled reserve he must contribute a minimum of 1 percent of his payroll—and in no state with an unemployment compensation law had the average overall employer contribution been more than 1.5 percent.

In the end, however, as we may as well anticipate here, this committee-endorsed arrangement foundered on the cautious conservatism of Franklin Roosevelt. At a critical point in the subsequent legislative proceedings, the President backed those congressional conservatives who wished to restore merit rating in full force, and so it was restored, along with segregated reserves, in what would become the final social security bill. The consequences, easily predictable, and predicted, by those best informed on the subject, were in every respect deplorable. "As a result of merit rating," writes Arthur Schlesinger, Jr., "states with low standards and low tax rates tended to enjoy a competitive advantage over states with higher standards. Moreover, merit rating increasingly placed the burden of unemployment compensation on the industries least able to bear it; costs which might better have been socially distributed were instead assessed in a way which further weakened the already weak. And merit rating, by leading to the possibility of tax reductions in times of full employment and tax increases in times of unemployment, could aggravate . . . the swings of the business cycle."[14]

As for the large staff devoted to health insurance, it was beset from beginning to end by a sense of futility in the face of obstacles impossible to overcome. A few staff members professed to believe, with Harry Hopkins, that "with one bold stroke we could carry the people with us . . . for sickness and health insurance" (Hopkins expressed this view in April 1934), yet even these few had to concede at the outset the extreme unlikelihood that any such "stroke" would now be attempted. In the end, relatively innocuous recommendations were made by the committee for federal grants in aid of state public health services. None was made for national health insurance legislation, this being foredoomed by the implacable hostility of the American Medical Association joined with Roosevelt's obvious unwillingness to challenge so formidable a political foe. The President's one public statement on the matter during the period of committee operation was conciliatory to the point of total surrender to private medical interests. He said: "There is *also* the problem of economic loss due to sickness—a very serious matter for many families with and without

incomes, *and therefore an unfair burden upon the medical profession.* *
Whether we come to this form of insurance soon or later on, I am confident
that we can devise a system which will enhance and not hinder the remarkable
progress which has been made and is being made in the practice of the professions of medicine and surgery in the United States."[15]

Far happier in process and outcome were the deliberations of the smallest
of the three staff sections, that dealing with old-age security, and for this the
very smallness of the section was in part responsible. It "proved a great boon,"
writes J. Douglas Brown.[16]

Brown, director of the Industrial Relations Section of Princeton University,
was one of four key members of this section, the other three being Barbara
Armstrong, a law professor from the University of California, who was section
head; Murray W. Latimer, the first chairman of the Railroad Retirement
Board, with whom Brown had worked on a national railroad pension plan; and
Otto C. Richter of the American Telephone and Telegraph Company, who,
according to Brown, "took far broader responsibilities" than those of actuary,
his official assignment. From the first, these four were agreed that any workable old-age insurance plan for the United States must be *compulsory* (experience and logic both argued unanswerably against free choice in this matter);
contributory by both employer and employee, so that benefit payments would
become a legal right of the recipient; and *national* in scope and administration.
They saw no sense whatever in a state scheme for either old-age or unemployment insurance, and they said so to the unemployment section with, one may
be sure, no ingratiating effect upon the Wisconsin group.

They shared with the unemployment section a great worry over the question
of whether the federal government had constitutional authority to do what
clearly should be done, but their response to the question differed from the
Wisconsin group's as idealism differs from pragmatism in the guidance of
action. Said a crucial memorandum, in language excised by cautious editors
from the committee's final printed report: "[T]he [old-age] staff is fully aware
of the limitations imposed upon the Federal Government by our Constitution.
. . . The staff is convinced, however, that it should first seek out the most
constructive proposals for old age security adapted to American conditions
and then, and only then, test as far as possible whether such proposals can be
made effective within our legal system. Since law is a living science, it is
reasonable to assume that if a sound program of old age security can be
projected, our system of constitutional law will evolve in time to support that
program."[17]

Agreed upon fundamentals, members of the old-age section were enabled to
debate in friendly fashion matters of structure and procedure, and as they did
so, they were drawn or pushed together in ever-closing working community
by the feeling that they were faced, if not actually surrounded, by hostile
forces. They were aware when their work began that the executive director had

Emphasis added.

relatively little interest in it, being himself primarily concerned with unemployment insurance. They were soon made aware of his "dismay," as Brown put it, over their "freewheeling tactics."[18] (They exercised a preference for direct approaches over the devious ways of traditional bureaucracy, ways of which Witte as institutional economist was a sympathetic student and experienced practitioner.) Then in mid-November, when their insistence upon a national rather than state scheme of social insurance had been repeatedly stressed, they were brought suddenly, forcibly to realize that the very survival of their project was threatened, not only by the attitudes and priorities of the executive director but also, most fatally, by those of the President of the United States.

This jolting realization came during a National Conference on Economic Security formally summoned by the White House. Attended by some 200 social workers, labor leaders, legislators, federal bureaucrats, and academic economists and sociologists, the Conference was assembled on November 14 in Washington's Mayflower Hotel, under the chairmanship of Frank Graham, for two main purposes. One was to provide public evidence of the administration's concern in an area where Townsend-Long pressures were growing; the other was to provide inspiration for all who labored under the aegis of the cabinet committee. And the latter purpose was well served by Relief Administrator Hopkins in a rousing luncheon address that seemed to commit the administration, once and for all, to a single "bold stroke" (Hopkins repeated the phrase) in which "all phases of social security" would be comprehended. The audience was raised to what newspapers called "a high pitch of enthusiasm." Even the feeble hopes for national health insurance were momentarily revived.

But only momentarily.

For when the President himself addressed the conferees barely three hours later, in the White House, reading a speech of which the initial draft had been prepared by Witte, the sole immediate commitment he made was to unemployment insurance, which, he stressed, must not be allowed to become "a dole" through "a mingling of insurance and relief" but "must be financed by contributions" exclusively. He dismissed health insurance as a present possibility, using words already quoted—a dismissal not totally surprising, if surprisingly ill timed, in the circumstances. His similar dismissal of old-age security, however, astonished and dismayed a substantial portion of his audience. "I do not know if this is the time for any federal legislation on old-age security," said he, going on to deplore "organizations promoting fantastic schemes" whereby hopes impossible of fulfillment were aroused. These had "increased the difficulties of getting sound legislation: but I hope that in time we may be able to provide security for the aged—a sound and uniform system which will provide true security."[19]

Initially stunned ("It's the kiss of death!" cried Barbara Armstrong), members of the old-age section left the White House in flaming anger against what seemed to them a betrayal by Witte. They blamed him bitterly for the speech, knowing he had been asked to prepare the initial draft. But they quickly rallied and fought back with the only weapons they had at hand.

Max Stern, a top editor of the nationally influential Scripps-Howard newspaper chain, was a personal friend of the section leader's, and to him she at once confided her sense of outrage. She and her colleagues did the same with the highly knowledgeable Louis Stark of the New York *Times*. Next day Scripps-Howard papers coast to coast carried an editorial sharply critical of Roosevelt's abandonment of old-age security, and the *Times* carried a lengthy story, played on page one under a three-column headline, telling how great expectations had been aroused by the Hopkins speech only to be dashed when "President Roosevelt chopped the entire social security program down to one subject for early enactment—unemployment insurance."[20] The effects were immediate. Within hours after his breakfast perusal of the *Times,* in bed, Roosevelt let Secretary Perkins know of his unhappiness over the "bad press" the speech was getting. Secretary Perkins promptly informed Witte of the President's displeasure, and Witte, greatly agitated, came to the office shared by Brown and Barbara Armstrong, asking their opinion on why the speech was being reported as it was. (No doubt because the President had said what he said, the two blandly replied; obviously, old-age security had wide popular support.)* In the afternoon of the same day, while key old-age section members were reviewing their tentative insurance plans with Rubinow and Epstein (these two had perforce received invitations to attend the conference; the present meeting was their first and almost only direct involvement in staff planning), Secretary Perkins met with newsmen to express "surprise and annoyance" at the "interpretation" reporters had placed upon the President's remarks. Roosevelt, she said, emphatically, was *not* opposed to old-age legislation in the upcoming session of Congress; old-age insurance was *not* being shelved; a "broad comprehensive program of economic security" remained the administration goal.[21]

V

THE specific subject of the November 15 meeting of Epstein and Rubinow with Barbara Armstrong and her group was a draft "Outline of Old Age Security Program" that had been completed only a few days before (it was dated November 9, 1934). It discussed two ways of establishing benefit payments. One was differential: Benefit payments would bear a percentage relationship to prior individual earnings. The other was integral: Benefit payments would

---

*The "press" of the following days was by no means all "bad." Businessmen were generally relieved, hence pleased, by the speech. They were quoted to this effect. The New York *Times* itself, on November 16, approved editorially the President's "one-step-at-a-time" approach, his evident turning away from "government cure-alls." Goethe's remark that the master worker reveals his mastership by limiting his aims was referred to. (Goethe was an exponent of "pragmatism" a full century before the term was popularized by Peirce and James and Dewey.)

be made on a flat rate, the same for all, regardless of previous earnings. The latter was the simpler of the two. It would be by far the easier to administer. But it would effect some measure of income redistribution, insofar as contributions made by the higher-paid would be shifted to benefit payments to the less well paid, tending to standardize incomes, and for essentially this reason it had been rejected, to Rubinow's and Epstein's regret. It was felt to be un-American. It contradicted what Frances Perkins, writing ten years later, called the "typical American attitude that a man who works hard, becomes highly skilled, and earns high wages, 'deserves' more on retirement than one who has not become a skilled worker." (She added that, in retrospect, "one can see there is much to be said for the flat rate.")[22]

Far harder to decide, and more crucially important, was the matter of longterm financing of the system.

To a degree which to their expert consultants seemed dangerously mistaken, the old-age group's thinking about social security was shaped on private insurance models—this in good part because the President was known to think in this way. ("If I have anything to say about it," Roosevelt was to tell a press conference in 1937, "it [the total financing of social security] will always be contributed, and I prefer it to be contributed . . . on a sound actuarial basis. It means no money out of the Treasury."[23]) Two difficult questions were thus raised. One had to do with the size of the social security reserve fund which a private insurance model implied. The other had to do with the handling of this reserve—that is, with its "investment"—as it accumulated.

The group would have been happy to adopt a pay-as-you-go scheme, wherein current income from contributory payments covered current outgo through benefit payments. But circumstances rendered this impossible. The day on which pension payments began to all in the system who, on that day and after, achieved age sixty-five could not be postponed for more than a half dozen years or so, and the very first pensions must be large enough actually to mean something to their recipients. Political pressures demanded this, as Roosevelt was forced to realize in the aftermath of his economic security conference speech. "We have to have it," said he to Secretary Perkins. "The Congress can't stand the pressure of the Townsend Plan unless we have a real old-age insurance system, nor can I face the country. . . ."[24] And included in the system would be people now in middle age who, with their employers, would make contributory payments for only a few months before retiring— people who, therefore, would have credited to their social security accounts far less than they would extract from the system in benefit payments, even though these last were cut to the smallest practicable amounts.

In other words, the system must assume at the outset a heavy accrued liability, a built-in cumulative deficit. Must this be fully covered by a reserve fund, as in a private insurance enterprise?

It must be if the old-age security system, though using government power to compel individual participation in it, were denied the power to underwrite any part of its operation with the credit of the United States. This reserve must be either built up immediately, through painfully high initial contributory rates, which would probably provoke a contributors' revolt and would certainly further deflate what was at that time an already severely deflated mass market, or built up later through a sudden, equally painful increase of rates. Moreover, the reserve fund must then assume truly awesome, terrifying proportions. Within a few decades it might approximate the size of the total national debt; not enough federal securities would be available to absorb it. How, then, was it to be "invested" without breaking the rules of the "capitalism" which allegedly required it in the first place? These rules presumably prevented any direct purchase of private securities by a government agency, though the Reconstruction Finance Corporation seemed to be doing precisely that; its loans to financial institutions were secured by the preferred stock of those institutions. The rules even more emphatically prohibited a government agency's using its money *as* capital—that is, to fuel a profit-making enterprise —though TVA as maker and distributor of fertilizer and electricity seemed to be doing precisely that.

The "Outline" which Barbara Armstrong's group reviewed with Epstein and Rubinow proposed a compromise solution to the thorny problem, one that fused pay-as-you-go with governmental deficit financing. There would be no immediate draft upon the federal treasury; neither would the initial contribution rates be set shockingly high. Instead, the rates were to begin at half of 1 percent each for employer and employee, gradually increasing to (in 1956) 2½ percent each. At that point the federal government would be called upon to supply whatever additional money was needed to maintain a reserve of $11 billion. This, the "Outline" argued, was the only possible way of paying reasonably high benefits in the early years while avoiding the buildup of impossibly huge reserves. According to Otto Richter's projections, if the proposal were accepted, a federal treasury contribution to the old-age system of approximately $1.4 billion annually might be required by 1980.[25]

Neither Epstein nor Rubinow could approve this compromise on grounds of pure logic or justice, and Epstein even found it impossible to accept, as Rubinow was inclined to do, on grounds of pure expediency (which here meant assumed political necessity). To Epstein, the proposal appeared a "compromise" of contradictions, vitiating logic with absurdity, justice with injustice.

He could concede the practical wisdom of some direct employee contribution to the system, though he was inclined to deplore use of the euphemistic "contributory payment" for what was in brute fact a special payroll tax, and he was convinced that employee payments should be relatively small. The reasons for having them at all were "more psychological than economic." Such contribution was the "best means of taking away whatever stigma is attached to governmental relief," and it made the workers' "claim to participate in the administration of the system more justifiable."[26] But surely fairness, humanity, and sound democratic social policy demanded that the federal government be from the outset a full and at least equal financial partner in this enterprise. Why, under the present proposal, for the next several decades at least, the wealthy, deriving their incomes from investments, would actually have a smaller proportionate obligation for poor relief than they had had under the ancient poor laws of England and the Continent! The burden of such relief would be borne, almost wholly, by the poor themselves. For in the absence of contributions from general revenues derived from the graduated income tax,* social security was to be financed altogether by a highly regressive special tax which the employee, in effect, paid twice, first as employee and second as consumer; the so-called employer contribution would be at once passed on to consumers in higher prices, and the employee, perforce, spent virtually all his income on consumer goods.† Thus the system would perpetuate, or even increase, that gross maldistribution of total national income which was a root cause of the current depression. It would also increase the disadvantage of small business in market competition with big business and hence encourage the growth of a Fascist corporate state; big business could bear the cost of social insurance more easily than small business could.

The argument was powerful, was, indeed, unanswerable in its own terms.

But there were other terms in which Barbara Armstrong and her colleagues felt forced to think.

Even after the administration had been obliged publicly to recommit itself to old-age insurance, the old-age section leaders had as major worry the distinct possibility that their plan for a *national* old-age system would be rejected by the cabinet committee, acting on advice from the executive director. Acute anxieties would attend their recruitment in the weeks ahead of what ultimately proved to be decisive support on this point from big business executives (Walter C. Teagle of Standard Oil, Marion Folsom of Eastman Kodak, Gerard Swope of General Electric, et al.) who were members of the Advisory Council, had had experience with large industrial pension plans, and were convinced by it that only national old-age insurance would work.[27] So on November 15, and after, the section leaders dared not increase their risks by incorporating in their proposal a financing scheme that was bound to provoke strong conservative opposition and that Roosevelt himself was known to oppose. They rejected Epstein's advice. They stuck to their uneasy joining of pay-as-you-go with a partial reserve and a future partial funding annually from general revenues, including this combine in the final report to the executive director, which they made in late December 1934. It then became part of the final full report and legislative recommendation to the cabinet committee—the report and recommendation, covering both unemployment insurance and old-age security, along with a few token gestures in the field of public health,

---

*Actually *some* income tax money had to go into the system in any case, for the government would pay interest on bonds bought by the system. This interest would come from general revenues.
†The employee would pay the tax *three* times if the employer not only raised prices but also reduced wages to cover his contribution to the system. By the 1970s there was considerable agreement among economists that the social security tax did depress wages.

which, after minor changes, was signed by every member of the Committee on Economic Security and submitted to the President on January 15, 1935.

V

IF the President gagged at the compromise old-age funding scheme when it was first presented to him, he was evidently in process of swallowing it anyway, as a political necessity, by mid-January; for it was part of the draft social security bill which he sent to Congress on January 17 with a special message stressing the need for it. At once it was introduced in the Senate by Robert Wagner, in the House jointly by Representatives Lewis and Robert L. Doughton of North Carolina,* then assigned, as a tax measure, to the conservative Finance Committee of the Senate, the conservative Ways and Means Committee of the House. Many proponents of social security thought the bill should have been classed a welfare measure and assigned to the liberal labor and pensions committees of the two houses. Some close political observers were convinced it would have been but for White House fears that its provisions would then be greatly liberalized by the time it was reported out for floor vote. What is certain is that the opposite happened in Ways and Means. Emasculating wounds were there soon inflicted upon it, rendering it as conservative a measure as it could possibly become in that season of multiplying Townsend and Share Our Wealth Clubs. Moreover, these wounds were inflicted for the most part, though it was an administration bill, by the administration itself.

Indeed, Roosevelt personally inflicted them insofar as he, having placed himself, as always, at the balance point between opposing forces in his administration, now tipped the final scale toward mutilation of the measure.

In late January, after hearings on the bill had opened (they began on January 21 in the House, on the following day in the Senate), the secretary of the treasury came to the President to confess a troubled conscience: He, Morgenthau, had signed his name to recommendations of which he now, upon further reflection, profoundly disapproved. And he found in Roosevelt a highly sympathetic listener as he explained his change of heart and mind, then reviewed the revisionary testimony he wished to present when he appeared as a witness before Ways and Means a few days hence. There were two key revisions. One of them repudiated the principle of universal coverage which the Economic Security Committee had adopted after full discussion; Morgenthau now proposed to exclude from old-age benefits precisely those in most dire need of these—namely, farm laborers, transient workers, and domestics—and he pro-

---

*In fact, four social security bills were introduced that day—one by Senator Pat Harrison of Mississippi and one by Doughton, who was chairman of Ways and Means (neither had evinced any prior concern for social security), in addition to those by Lewis and Wagner, whereupon, according to Frances Perkins's *The Roosevelt I Knew* (pp. 296–97), the President decided that for political strategy reasons the measure should be dubbed the Harrison-Doughton bill. It never was, however, nor could it have been in simple justice. It was known at the time and remains in history the Wagner-Lewis bill, with "Doughton" only sometimes added.

posed to exclude from unemployment compensation everyone working for an employer of fewer than ten. In other words, he would exclude from social security coverage those who, of all workers, had the least economic security and were the most ruthlessly exploited. His stated reason was the difficulty of collecting payments from and for people in these categories. (But the "whole administration of the act" was "going to be difficult," Frances Perkins protested, this part no more than other parts.[28]) The other key revision scrapped the compromise funding arrangement which the old-age staff section had so painfully devised and maintained against Epstein's strictures. Morgenthau proposed a reserve fund to built up to a maximum not of $11 billion, as in the original draft bill, but of $50 billion (later reduced to $47 billion) by 1980, with not a dollar of it coming from the federal treasury. This, of course, involved increases in contributory costs. The initial rate would be double that originally proposed, a full 1 percent each for employer and employee instead of the original half of 1 percent, and the rate would rise by half of 1 percent for two successive three-year periods, following which it would jump a full percentage point and remain at 3 percent thereafter. There would also be a reduction in annuities paid during the early years of the system. None whatever were to be paid during the first five years after the law went into effect.

What did the President think of this? Morgenthau wanted to know.

Roosevelt seems to have accepted without much argument Morgenthau's restriction of coverage, though he had himself proposed an extreme universality of coverage in private talk with others on the Economic Security Committee. ("[T]here is no reason why everybody in the United States should not be covered," he reportedly said to several cabinet members. "I see no reason why every child, from the day he is born, shouldn't be a member of the social security system."[29]) He did express some concern over the financing revision; he wondered if so rapid a buildup of so large an old-age reserve might not have deleterious effects on the general economy. He was soothed when Treasury Department economists told him it would not. He found exhilarating some of Morgenthau's suggestions on how the reserve might be used in the business of government. The social security system might become the sole source of federal borrowings, the sole customer for government bonds, forever freeing the government of any dependence whatever on private lending institutions! The reserve might even be used, somehow, to reduce the national debt!

So Roosevelt's hesitation was not prolonged. The original funding proposal was the "same old dole under a new name," said he to the labor secretary, and Frances Perkins understood that the word "dole," or any other word meaning a governmental transfer of money from the affluent who had allegedly "earned" it to the poor who, for whatever reason, didn't have it, was a synonym for "sin" in Franklin Roosevelt's lexicon. "It is almost dishonest to build up an accumulated deficit for the Congress of the United States to meet in 1980," he went on. "We can't sell the United States short in 1980 any more than in 1935."[30] He therefore quickly approved what Morgenthau wished to do.

And Morgenthau's testimony was at once assumed by the public to be administration policy when it was presented on February 5, two days after hearings had begun. It caused a furor. Morgenthau's fellow members of the Economic Security Committee were angered by what they deemed a breach of faith on his part. Others, long and fervently committed to genuine social insurance and doubtful from the first that the administration shared this commitment, had their doubts reinforced—a skepticism that grew toward a sense of betrayal as, for many weeks after the hearings had ended on February 12, the bill languished in Ways and Means with administration forces exerting no evident effort on its behalf. When it was finally reported out favorably, on April 5, it was in a revised form that incorporated the substance of the Morgenthau testimony as regards funding and coverage while also curtailing the authority of the federal government to force the states to adopt "desirable standards with regard to old-age pensions," as the *Nation* editorialized.[31] The original bill had said that minimum old-age pensions must be sufficient to assure "a reasonable subsistence compatable with decency and health." The revised bill said this need be done only so far as practicable under the conditions in each state—a concession to southern congressmen who feared the original phrasing might force payment of higher pensions to aged blacks than local white southerners deemed "desirable."[32]

Public controversy now swirled around the measure. It was attacked from the left for not going anywhere near far enough toward that "security for the men, women, and children of the nation" which the President had announced last June as the primary objective of his administration. It was compared unfavorably, by such leftist publications as the *Nation* and the *New Masses*, with the workers' unemployment and social insurance bill introduced by Representative Ernest Lundeen of Minnesota, on which hearings proceeded in the House Labor Committee simultaneously with those on Wagner-Lewis in Ways and Means. (The Lundeen bill, which may have been drafted by the American Communist party and certainly had Communist support, called for unemployment benefits to be paid over lengthy periods at the full prevailing wage to *every* unemployed worker, the payments to be made out of federal income and corporate tax receipts. The system's administration was to be through commissions of workers elected by labor and farm organizations.[33]) It was also compared unfavorably, by masses of nonideological people, with the proposals of Townsend and Huey Long. At the same time the very idea of social security continued to be attacked from the right (various business leaders testified strongly against it) on the usual grounds that it would discourage thrift, encourage shiftlessness, destroy individual initiative, and in general raise hell with the moral character of the citizenry and the workings of the economy.

But as the weeks passed, right-wing attacks became increasingly perfunctory. Conservatives were forced to realize that on this matter the tide of history flowed overwhelmingly against them. Some form of social welfare legislation seemed bound to be enacted in the present session of Congress. It would either be Wagner-Lewis or something "worse"—and Wagner-Lewis became more palatable to conservatives with every revision that was made of it. In the end, as members of Congress gauged the mood of the electorate in terms of their chances for reelection in 1936, conservative opposition simply collapsed.

On April 19 the House passed the bill, 371 to 33, in substantially the form in which it had been reported by Ways and Means.

In the Senate, however, the bill remained in the Finance Committee as April gave way to May. It was reported out favorably on May 13, but no floor action was taken on it as week after week slipped by and the first session of the Seventy-fourth Congress drew toward an expected adjournment in June.

→≫✕≪←

12

Work Relief and Its Dubiously
Legitimate Offspring

I

INDEED, by mid-May 1935, almost seven months after a popular endorsement of his leadership so emphatic as to give him unprecedented authority over both the legislative and executive branches, or so it seemed at the moment to the general public, Franklin Roosevelt had obtained passage of but a single piece of major legislation through a Congress overwhelmingly dominated by his own party. In the eyes of its most sympathetic observers, the New Deal appeared to have stumbled almost to a halt—and this for lack of executive direction. In the eyes of New Dealers themselves the White House appeared to have become a place where creative proposals and energies were frustrated, dissipated, instead of being stimulated, assimilated, focused programmatically, as they formerly had often been. The President marked time as winter gave way to spring, still seemingly unwilling or unable to make up his mind on fundamentals, while others, outside government, moved swiftly toward ends hostile to his own. The political potency of populist demagogues, especially Huey Long and Father Coughlin, grew at an alarming rate; the attraction which the Communist party had for despairing people, especially young intellectuals, evidently markedly increased (on college campuses there was an expanding enrollment in the John Reed Clubs, the Young Communist Leagues); and the assault by big business upon the constitutionality of every New Deal statute which displeased it began to be devastatingly effective in the courts. In sum, Franklin Roosevelt's personal prestige and leadership were in question and under threat as they had not before been since the inauguration.

The one piece of adopted legislation—the single legislative proposal to which Roosevelt had thus far applied, in that session, the full force of his authority—was of a scope and substantial impact greater than that of all the legislation passed in the entire lifetime of many a Congress. Critical observers recognized the fact. But this had done little or nothing to improve Roosevelt's standing. The event seemed less the result of bold leadership than a forced response to circumstance and, moreover, an inadequate response, in the view of those most committed to stated New Deal aims. The *manner* of the legislation's passage, the injurious amendment of it in the legislative process, and the way in which it was executively implemented when finally passed—these things fed a growing sense of executive weakness, of White House indecisiveness among the public at large and, most definitely, among those best informed.

In his State of the Union message on January 4 the President emphatically told the new Congress that the federal government "must and shall quit this business of relief," that "work must be found for able-bodied but destitute workers," and that this work must be useful—"useful in the sense that it affords permanent improvement in living conditions or that it creates new wealth for the nation." He said: "I am not willing that the vitality of our people be further sapped by the giving of cash, of market baskets, of a few hours of weekly work cutting grass, raking leaves, or picking up papers in public parks. We must preserve not only the bodies of the unemployed from destruction but also their self-respect, their self-reliance and courage and determination."* He spoke vaguely of uniting "all emergency public works . . . in a single new and greatly enlarged plan," superseding FERA "with a coordinated authority . . . charged with the orderly liquidation of our present relief activities and the substitution of a national chart for the giving of work." (This vagueness of speech sent power-hungry Ickes into a tizzy of anxiety; he confided to his diary his fear that power-hungry and administratively incompetent Richberg would be named coordinator of the whole emergency public works program and promised himself that if this happened, he would get out of public works altogether.[2])

Guidelines for the new program were listed. The wage rate for this public employment "should be larger than the amount now received as a relief dole, but . . . not so large" as to encourage the leaving of private for public employment or to discourage the leaving of public for private employment. The projects selected should be highly labor-intensive and "planned so as to compete as little as possible with private enterprise." They should be located in areas having the "greatest unemployment needs as shown by present relief rolls." As for "the work itself," it would "cover a wide field," the description of which in the message seemed to readers of the New York *Times* obviously reflective of the program Harry Hopkins had carried in his briefcase to Warm Springs in late November. Implied was another omnibus bill involving another huge grant of legislative power to the executive. No single item of the project program would be mandated; every item would be, instead, of a "permitted" or "enabled" nature. Which is to say that insofar as the bill contained work program specifics, these would be no more than indications of areas of possible activity, areas of free choice for the executive. Mentioned in the message were slum clearance where private capital could not or would not do the job; rural housing where, again, the necessary private capital was not forthcoming; rural electrification; watershed reforestation to reduce flood-making runoff; soil erosion control; reclamation of "blighted areas"; "extension and enlargement of the successful work of the Civilian Conservation Corps"; and improvement of

*Listening to these words, Ickes deemed them an implied criticism of Hopkins's CWA operation and was greatly pleased by this presumed fact. Actually, unknown to Ickes, Hopkins had helped draft the speech and had contributed some of the specific language which Ickes found so maliciously satisfying.[1]

"existing road systems" along with the construction of new "national high-ways designed to handle modern traffic."[3]

The grand new departure, which would place on the government's payroll some 3.5 million people, or approximately one-third the total number currently unemployed,* bore the price tag of approximately $5 billion with which the public had become familiar during the last two months. Asked for was a new deficit appropriation of $4 billion, to which would be added $880 million already authorized for relief but as yet unspent. This dollar figure provoked immediate critical response. Jouett Shouse, speaking the mind of the Liberty League, thought the figure outrageously high, of course—ruinously high, even, for the national economy—and was sure that the government's massive employment of labor to produce truly valuable goods and services meant the end "of the form of government under which we have lived."[4] Many liberals, on the other hand, thought the figure too low to meet the relief need with any such "useful work" program as the President had outlined, while economists of the Keynesian persuasion were very sure the figure was *far* too low to fuel that burst of mass purchasing which was required if the national economy was to be nudged off dead center into self-renewing, self-expanding activity. Young Bob La Follette spoke the liberal view and pleased the Keynesians when he said that a figure of $9 billion would be more nearly commensurate with the obvious need and stated aim, though some fully converted Keynesians were of the opinion that even the La Follette figure was "dangerously" low, being barely sufficient, if sufficient at all, to assure a real recovery absolutely.

In early January, however, there was little doubt in the public mind that this proposal by an overwhelmingly popular Democratic President, when introduced as a joint resolution, would be swiftly adopted, and substantially as introduced, by an overwhelmingly Democratic Congress. This indeed happened in the House. But in the Senate, with its tradition of unlimited debate, there was a delay of many weeks, during the latter part of which federal relief had to be financed by another transfer to FERA of money originally scheduled for expenditure by PWA. Organized labor protested the proposed wage scale, a so-called security wage averaging $50 a month per worker, claiming it would have a lowering effect upon wages paid by private employers. Liberals protested the proposed scale on humane grounds, claiming that it was inadequate to maintain worker families in decent living conditions. And Nevada's Senator Patrick McCarran, in seeming response to these protests, promptly introduced an amendment substituting the "prevailing wage" for the administration's "security wage." His motive was unclear (certainly McCarran was no liberal), but it probably accorded with that of the conservatives, who, rather surprisingly, joined senatorial liberals in support of the amendment: The conservatives hoped that the amendment's passage through the Senate would encourage

*It was believed or hoped that this would stimulate the private employment of millions more, while business recovery completed itself.

defeat of the whole works relief measure by the House when the Senate version of it went there. And thanks to a remarkably adroit parliamentary maneuver by Huey Long, who was a leader of the fight for it, the McCarran amendment *did* win initial passage by one vote through the Senate despite the strongest possible opposition by administration forces. It was defeated in the end only by a skillful employment of Roosevelt's political power, including the threat of a presidential veto coupled with that of a presidential radio appeal to the people over the heads of Congress. (Long made rueful comment upon Roosevelt's handling of this affair. "Hoover is a hoot owl and Roosevelt is a scrootch owl," said he. "A hoot owl bangs into the nest and knocks the hen clean off and catches her while she's falling. But a scrootch owl slips into the roost and scrootches up to the hen and talks softly to her. And the hen just falls in love with him, and the next thing you know there ain't no hen."[5])

This narrow victory for the President was offset by his forced acceptance of two other amendments which were only somewhat less obnoxious to him, this as the price he had to pay to ensure the relief bill's passage. One of the amendments, sponsored by Idaho's fervently isolationist Senator Borah, said: "No part of the appropriations . . . shall be used for munitions, warships, or military or naval materiel."[6] (Under construction at the time, funded by the assignment of PWA funds made in 1933, were two aircraft carriers, to be named *Enterprise* and *Yorktown,* which were destined in the Battle of Midway to prevent domination of the Pacific by a power hostile to the United States, just seven years hence.) The other amendment was a resentful reaction by congressional Democrats against the administration's handling of patronage, insofar as this had been determined by Roosevelt's "above-the-battle" stance, and especially against Harry Hopkins's refusal of patronage in the appointment of FERA and CWA field administrators. The amendment required that "any Administrator receiving a salary of $5,000 or more per annum in this Program shall be appointed by the President by and with the advice and consent of the Senate." This meant that Hopkins, in his administration of whatever portion of the new program was assigned him, had to clear every major new personnel appointment with Jim Farley and the Democratic National Committee and with the Democratic senator or senators of the state of which the appointee was a citizen. (He came close to resigning his government post over this requirement, was talked out of it by Roosevelt personally, and ultimately decided that being forced to become a political operator against his will, he would become as tough and skillful a one as there was in Washington —this in service of his social welfare ideals and also, for some time ahead, of a burgeoning personal political ambition.[7])

Thus encumbered, after a struggle which had tested and now left in question the President's ability to manage this new Democratic Congress, the joint resolution, known to history as the Emergency Relief Appropriation Act of 1935, went on Friday, April 5, from Congress to White House.

But Roosevelt was not then in the White House to sign the bill at once into law. To the dismay of his wife and others of the innermost circle and at grave risk to his public standing, or so Press Secretary Steve Early believed, he had gone south twelve days before, to Jacksonville, Florida, there to board the *Nourmahal* for another Caribbean cruise with Vincent Astor and the *"Nourmahal* Gang." What made this holiday so questionable, and seemingly indicative of a desperately felt need on Roosevelt's part to get away, to relax away from anxious pressures born of his basic indecision, was the fact that Louis Howe, his closest, dearest friend, lay near death in the White House. Howe's always precarious health had begun to fail alarmingly in early autumn of 1934. He insisted stubbornly upon maintaining his position as secretary to the President, he continued to exert influential power at the topmost level of the administration, but he did so ever more feebly and, more and more, from his bed. His appearances at his office became increasingly infrequent; it became impossible for him, even on his best days, to walk more than a few, slow steps without gasping for breath. And this bad condition became worse still in January 1935; a bad cold developed into pneumonia, making it impossible for him to perform his traditional role as impresario and skit author for the annual Cuff Links Club festivities. These were canceled by the Roosevelts, for the first time in thirteen years. Then, in early March, while still suffering the aftereffects of his pneumonia, Howe collapsed completely. He lay in a coma, under an oxygen tent, for many days, his death expected at any moment. Roosevelt postponed his departure for Florida, originally scheduled for mid-March; Eleanor canceled all plans that would have taken her out of Washington; Howe's wife and children gathered at his bedside. But as he had so often done before, the little man rallied astonishingly, awaking on the morning of March 19 clear-eyed, clear-minded, to address those at his bedside in his normally deep, resonant voice. "Why in hell doesn't somebody give me a cigarette?" he asked. His condition remained serious, it could become critical at any time, but the chances were good that he would survive for several weeks, said the doctors to Roosevelt. Thereupon Roosevelt, on March 25, in pursuance of his postponed vacation plans, boarded his special train and headed south. He was accompanied by Harry Hopkins, (Hopkins was to leave the train at Savannah, Georgia) causing newsmen to speculate in print that the federal relief administrator was slated to head the whole of the new works program. (In Washington empire builder Ickes darkly fumed, malice in his heart, and Early and McIntyre worried about what they would do if Louie died while his great, good friend the President enjoyed himself aboard a multimillionaire's luxury yacht. "I'll just not permit it to be announced!" said Early at one point, in grim half jest.)[8]

So it was to Jacksonville that the adopted congressional resolution traveled by airplane on the morning of Monday, April 8, and it was in Jacksonville, where the *Nourmahal* had just docked, that Roosevelt "affixed his signature" to the document at four o'clock that afternoon. Within an hour thereafter he had signed two allocations from funds made available by the new act, one for $125 million to the federal relief administrator, to keep relief going during the changeover period and one for $30 million for continuation of the "emergency conservation work," meaning the "maintenance of the Civilian Conservation Corps camps."[9]

Returned to Washington, he at once requested and received two specific organization plans for the works relief program, one from Ickes, one from Hopkins. The plans were very different. Hopkins's was a perhaps deliberately elaborate, complicated diffusion of the power he intended, operatively, to take into his own hands and *then* organize coherently in terms of his conception of the job to be done. Ickes's was a streamlined compartmentalization of power, with clear lines of authority between the compartments under a representative board presided over by the President—a plan designed for administrative efficiency but also, more so, to keep Hopkins from becoming, as Ickes put it in his diary, "cock of the walk."[10] Roosevelt chose neither plan. Instead, he wove them together in a pattern so intricate that when he announced it in the last week of April, few people had any notion of how it would work in practice, and many doubted it would work at all. Why this intricacy? some asked. Did the President have a hidden purpose?

Established in the National Emergency Council were three new divisions— a Division of Applications and Information, a Works Allotment Division, and a Works Progress Division—each equal in authority to the others, according to the organization chart. The first-named division, which was to receive and screen "all suggested plans for the useful expenditure of Works Relief funds, no matter what the source of these suggestions may be," would be headed by the affable Frank Walker, whom everybody liked. Walker was evidently chosen for this very reason; his warm, friendly personality might lubricate the working relationships (unlubricated, these were bound to be harshly frictional) between Ickes and Hopkins, each of whom was to head one of the other two divisions and each of whom Roosevelt was anxious to retain in his administration.

Ickes was to preside over Works Allotment. This division would "receive the lists of projects sent to it from the Division of Applications and Information after the various projects have been studied and reported on by the agencies under which they fall"—lists accompanied by information on project costs, locations, percentages of direct labor to be employed, economic justification, and the like. "With all this information in its possession," Works Allotment would "be able to recommend the projects to the President by districts, for his approval," doing so in "round-table conferences" which were to be held "at least once a week for the next few months." A very sizable "round table" would be needed; this division would have as members "a large number of persons"—so great a number, in fact, as virtually to assure its inability to come to any decision on any matter of controversy. The initial appointees, "subject to later additions," numbered no fewer than two dozen individuals, each accustomed to the exercise of power and, most of them, ambitious for more of it. Included were three cabinet secretaries (agriculture and labor as well as interior); the budget director; the executive director of the National Emergency Council; the chiefs of the Forest Service, Soil Erosion (soon to become the Soil Conservation Service), the Bureau of Public Roads; several emergency agency heads; the Business Advisory Council of the Commerce Department; and, outside the federal government altogether, a representative each from organized labor, organized agriculture, the American Bankers Association, and the United States Conference of Mayors.

The third and last of the new divisions to be announced, which Hopkins was to head, was also the least important of the three, as Roosevelt initially described it. The Works Progress Division would be, it appeared, not an operating agency but a record-keeping one. It was to "be in charge of" the figures, the statistical data, needed for allotment decisions; it was to "keep the other divisions informed at all times" on "the actual number of employables whose names are on existing relief rolls." After allotments had been made, Works Progress was "to see that the actual persons . . . employed on the separate projects . . . come from" those named on the relief rolls. "Finally, the Progress Division will be charged with keeping in touch at all times with all projects and reporting on the progress made." The only hint in this first announcement that Works Progress might engage in something more than bookkeeping was the statement that Hopkins "will act as *Administrator*" of it (Ickes was to "act as Chairman" of his division; Walker was to "direct the activities" of his) while continuing as administrator of FERA, "the work of which will, however, diminish in proportion to the number of persons on the relief rolls given employment under the Works Relief program."[11]

It is difficult to believe that Roosevelt did not design this complicated machinery with tongue in cheek and malice aforethought, following as he did so the lead given by Hopkins in *his* organization plan and counting, too, very heavily, upon his own ability, through personal force and charm, to prevent the escalation of an intensely competitive rivalry into totally destructive warfare. At any rate, or in actual fact, the cumbrous complexity was essentially an avoidance of choice, a refusal of decision. It had the effect of substituting for executive direction a trial by combat between Ickes and Hopkins, though a combat in which the odds for victory, from the very first, greatly favored Harry Hopkins.

On May 6 was issued the specific executive order under which Hopkins was to operate and in the preparation of which he had a hand. Between it and the administrative arrangement originally announced were significant differences. What had been the Works Allotment Division was now an Advisory Committee on Allotments, chaired by Ickes. What had been the Works Progress Division was now the Works Progress Administration. (Both changes displeased Ickes mightily. The latter actually infuriated him, for he was convinced that Hopkins made the name change in order to confuse PWA with WPA in the public mind, thereby cloaking Hopkins's reckless, spendthrift ways [so Ickes deemed them] with the reputation for probity, prudence, and sound constructive planning which PWA had earned under Ickes's management.) By then, too, the announced primary role of the agency Hopkins was to head was no longer that of bookkeeper; it was to "be responsible to the President for honest, efficient, speedy, and coordinated execution of the work relief program as a whole . . . in such manner as to move from the relief rolls to work on such projects or in private employment the maximum number of persons in the shortest time possible." One clause of the order required Hopkins to certify the availability of needed and needy skilled and unskilled labor in any area for which a work project was being considered. Another clause authorized him to "recommend and carry on small useful projects designed to assure a maximum of employment in all localities."[12] These were levers of power which Hopkins had only to recognize and grasp to assure his obtaining a lion's share of the available money. He did recognize them, of course, having helped place them there. He did grasp them. In short order, WPA became the largest employer of labor in American history, the means whereby a minimum of decent living and self-respect was maintained for millions of Americans, its ubiquitous enterprise generally financed by money Ickes believed should go to PWA, and even, on occasion, by transfers of funds already budgeted for PWA but as yet unspent.

Thus the bitter quarrel between Ickes and Hopkins, already well under way by the time the work relief bill was introduced in Congress, became now more bitter still, especially for Ickes, who was to lose most of the battles and be brought thereby, again and again, to the verge of resigning his PWA post, if not from government altogether. Hopkins was endlessly in quest of more money for WPA; he proved fertile in schemes for getting it. Sometimes he would deliberately overspend his budget, then go to Treasury for an emergency appropriation from general reserves, demonstrating with facts and figures that his failure to get it would mean great hardship for destitute people across the land. Almost invariably the compassionate Morgenthau would yield to the plea, for all his anxious desire for a balanced budget. This happened so often that an infuriated, anxiety-ridden Ickes became convinced that Morgenthau and Hopkins were joined in deep, dark conspiracy against him. And soon, of course, the quarrel became blatantly public; it repeatedly made the blackest of headlines in the national press as it raged on for more than a year, with intervals of uneasy truce. Perhaps it was stimulative of human energies that would otherwise have lain dormant (we have already noted this claim by some historians), but it was certainly wasteful of these and other energies, being highly absorptive of time and effort that could otherwise have gone into useful work. This would be true for Franklin Roosevelt himself; he would be required to exercise to the full his personal charm, his personal authority, his empathy-nourished ability to manipulate human beings, in time-consuming conferences and written communications—this to prevent the quarrel's getting completely out of hand, with ruinous effect upon the administration. Moreover, the extra strain would tell upon the health of the combatants. It would adversely affect the mental health of Ickes: His natural suspiciousness of other people, joined with his conviction of his own perfect righteousness, became at times, under the quarrel's pressures, almost clinically paranoid. It would take a most heavy toll on the physical health of Hopkins: His gay insouciance of manner and seeming ability to drown his troubles in social pleasures failed adequately to relieve wrenching inner tensions, and in the summer of 1935 he developed a dangerous duodenal ulcer. Never again thereafter would he be a truly well man.

Clearly this monumental feud would have been reduced to modest proportions, it might well have been avoided altogether, if Roosevelt had made at the outset a firm, clear-cut decision and then explained his reasons to Ickes and Hopkins, frankly, before announcing it to the public. And this recognized fact, in early May 1935, encouraged a further waning of confidence at that time, in Roosevelt's capacity to choose, his ability to lead.

II

A similar indecisiveness, productive of turmoil, was at the heart of Roosevelt's implementation of another enabling phase of 1935's Emergency Relief Appropriation Act.

On the face of it, as formal event, this implementation was decisive indeed. It amounted to an assertion, a *creation* by simple assertion, of an executive power very vaguely implied, if implied at all, by the language of the act itself. A paragraph of the act's Section 1 authorized the President to make from the works relief appropriation, on terms to be prescribed by himself, "loans to finance, in whole or in part, the purchase of farm lands and necessary equipment by farmers, farm tenants, croppers, or farm laborers," with the loans to be repaid "in such manner as the President may determine." Nothing was said about how the loans were to be made, or about income status as a determinant of loan eligibility, or about the governmental organization through which the loan program was to be carried out. It therefore required boldness of interpretation, a writing in of words *not* said by Congress, for Roosevelt to find statutory justification in Section 1 for the executive order he issued on May 1, 1935. This order established as "an agency within the Government" a Resettlement Administration. It was to engage in three general types of activity: One, it was to resettle "destitute or low-income families from rural and urban areas" and establish "in such connection . . . communities in rural and urban areas"; two, it was to "initiate and administer" an extensive land use program which, on its face, would duplicate work being done by other federal agencies (the Forest Service, the Bureau of Reclamation, the Soil Conservation Service, et al.), for it had to do with erosion control, flood control, stream pollution control, and "forestation" as well as reforestation; and three, it was to make the loans explicitly authorized by the language of Section 1 quoted above. As administrator of the new agency, the executive order named Rexford G. Tugwell, undersecretary of agriculture.[13]

But the decisiveness and bold assertiveness with which the new agency was launched had to do only with manner of launching. The agency itself represented, on Roosevelt's part, a fairly mindless response to pressures strongly felt but ill defined. It was in substance a hodgepodge, truly astonishing in its variety, of discordant elements, including unsolved problems and failed projects, resulting from a long process of executive vagueness, of executive refusal to make clear-cut choices or firm commitments precisely defined. Tugwell himself described his new responsibilities as "everybody else's headaches."[14]

In this process of Rooseveltian indecision, Tugwell had been very much involved.

When, in early 1933, he definitely knew that he would go to Washington as assistant secretary of agriculture and become administratively responsible for the department's old-line bureaus, Tugwell noted in his diary that one of his first "problems" would be the Food and Drug Administration. ("I'll do what I can for the consumer regardless of politics," he vowed; "I won't compromise on this."[15]) Established in Agriculture by the Food and Drug Act of 1906, itself a response by Theodore Roosevelt's administration to the popular furor occasioned by Upton Sinclair's *The Jungle,* this bureau had been handicapped from the outset by deficiencies in its organic act. The legislation made no provision for the regulation of package fill or standards designation. It contained loopholes and ambiguities whereby lawyers prevented enforcement of rules against fraudulent labeling and against the marketing of fruits and vegetables having upon them, in injurious amounts, the residues of poisonous sprays. Most important, it failed to protect the public against false or misleading advertising in newspapers and magazines and in posters or signs placed in drugstore windows. These deficiencies had become more glaring as cosmetics, a small enterprise in the first decade of the century, grew into big business by the 1920s; as new commercial pesticides and herbicides were developed in growing number; and as the advertising industry grew enormous, while also becoming, in its techniques, more sophisticatedly effective. Meanwhile, the FDA had been neglected, when its operations were not actively hindered, by a succession of business-dominated Republican administrations.

In March 1933, armed with data on the need for it, Tugwell went to the White House to plead for Roosevelt's support of a new, much tougher food and drug law. He appealed, "unscrupulously, I'm afraid," to "Mr. Roosevelt's sense of continuity from T.R.," as he later remembered. He also referred to a book entitled *100,000,000 Guinea Pigs,* by F. J. Schlink and Arthur Kallet, published just two months before and currently near the top of the nonfiction best-seller list, a muckraking book which exposed in ghastly parade, with an abundance of terrifying specifics, the risks to their health, even their lives, which consumers ran by using numerous highly advertised drugs, cosmetics, and processed foods. Tugwell's argument was effective. Roosevelt manifested an eagerness to make on this matter a record comparable to TR's in 1906; he told Tugwell to go ahead.[16] But he seems not to have promised to endorse the bill personally, publicly, much less to place it on the list of must legislation for that special session or for later sessions. At any rate, he did not do these things. There was some delay in the bill's drafting, by two law professors chosen by Tugwell. When the proposal was introduced in the Senate by New York's Royal S. Copeland, himself a doctor of medicine, on June 6, only ten days remained of 1933's Hundred Days, and for *twenty-one months* thereafter the bill was not so much as mentioned in public statement by the President of the United States. A natural conclusion on the public's part was that Roosevelt did not approve what was promptly dubbed by its opponents the Tugwell Bill. (Copeland was known personally to be as conservative politically as the bulk of his medical colleagues.) This encouraged a raining down upon Tugwell's handsome, unprotected head of such clubs of malicious fury, such liquid fires of abuse undiluted by cooling kindness, as few men in national public life have ever had to endure.

For the bill as introduced would indeed have made a difference in the production and marketing of a considerable portion of the total volume of American consumer goods, eliminating from these operations much lucrative chicanery, much profitable lying. It would have required grade labeling and a listing on labels of all active ingredients, with warnings against those which were habit-forming. It would have mandated the secretary of agriculture to establish standards of identity and quality for all products except fresh fruits and vegetables. It would have authorized compulsory inspections, with a federal licensing of factories on the basis of these, if a system of voluntary inspections failed to work, as well as the use of injunctions, under the Federal Trade Commission Act, as an enforcement procedure. Finally, it would have imposed stiff penalties for "false advertising," which was defined in sweeping terms. "An Advertisement . . . shall be deemed false if it is misleading in any particular," said the bill, and any "representation concerning any effect of a drug shall be deemed false . . . if such representation is not sustained by demonstrable scientific facts or substantial and reliable medical opinion." False on the face of it, the bill went on to say, would be any claim for any commercial product that it would cure or have therapeutic effect upon cancer, tuberculosis, syphilis, Bright's disease, or the crippling effects of poliomyelitis.[17]

Clearly this proposed "new charter of honesty and fair dealing in the manufacture and sale of products in everyday use" (Tugwell's words) was an attack, annihilative, if successful, upon the "sacred right of a freeborn American to advertise and sell horse liniment as a remedy for tuberculosis" (George Seldes's words), and as such it utterly horrified drug and cosmetics manufacturers, the owners and employees of advertising agencies, and the proprietors of newspapers and magazines whose profits derived from the sale of advertising space. They promptly formed an exceedingly powerful lobby against the measure, consisting of eight national organizations of drug manufacturers, cosmetics manufacturers, retail druggists, and beauty parlor and barbershop operators, along with three national media organizations—namely, the American Newspaper Publishers Association, the National Editorial Association, and the National Publishers Association. These lobbyists made little effort to debate the bill on its merits. As a matter of fact, they strove to deny to the public any accurate knowledge of it (there was evidently a deliberate suppression by the press of straight news about hearings, resolutions adopted by supportive organizations, Eleanor Roosevelt's endorsement of the measure, etc.). They chose, instead, to identify the bill with Tugwell and then to destroy Tugwell, who, up till then, since his first fame as brain truster, had been given at least as much favorable as unfavorable publicity. He now became, abruptly, in the mass media portrait of him which was blasted day after day into the popular mind, an academic theorist with no common sense, an arrogant intellectual snob, a Red or (less frequently) a Fascist whose purpose was to destroy the "American Way" and establish a totalitarian America.[18]

Against such blinding, deafening onslaught only a determined stand for the bill by Roosevelt could have obtained its passage in anything like its original strength through the congressional session of 1934, though there is little doubt that given such support, in view of the bill's popularity among informed consumers, it *would* have passed. Far from taking such a stand, Roosevelt, while maintaining his public silence about the bill, encouraged a drastic weakening of it by Copeland in early 1934, or so it seemed, at least, to Tugwell, who said in a letter to the President (February 21, 1934) that Copeland apparently believed "he had a mandate from you to kill every provision of the Food and Drug bill which would be of any use."[19] And the weakening of it failed to secure its adoption; it remained in limbo when the regular session ended. It gave every sign of remaining there through the session that opened in January 1935, despite the more leftish cast of the Seventy-fourth Congress over the Seventy-third.

Tugwell stood up manfully under the incessant lambasting. He made no recorded complaint to Roosevelt about the latter's failure to support him on a measure that was, in his view, of some importance to the New Deal's overall success. Yet the lambasting was not without psychological effect. It induced in Tugwell what he himself described as "a certain numbness and cynicism about it all";[20] it weakened a morale which had sunk by the late autumn of 1934 and, in early 1935, was so low that Tugwell went to the White House and there, in face-to-face meeting with the President, sought to resign his Agriculture post.

The immediate incitement of the latter event was another development out of fundamental New Deal indecisiveness—in this case a failure by the executive to make, in 1933, a definite agricultural policy choice between McNary-Haugenism and domestic allotment or, more generally, between a policy clearly aimed at preservation of the family farm (farming as "a way of life") and a policy aimed at or determined by economic (technological) efficiency only.* The family farm policy implied a shaping subordination of technological change, especially the development of farm machinery, to a conscious human purpose: that of maintaining in American life what many, including Roosevelt, regarded as uniquely *rural* virtues, beauties, cultural values. The "efficiency" policy was essentially but a yielding to current social and economic trends basically determined by technological change. (One adversary

*See pp. 69–72, 76.

described it as the policy of "pathetically short-sighted doctrinaires" who "think of the farm as having no value except to turn out low-priced food for the nation just as a steel mill has no function except to turn out low-priced steel. . . ."[21]) Linked with this fundamental indecision between the conception of agriculture as a business and the conception of it as a way of life had been a failure or, perhaps, on the level of Rooseveltian "intuition," a *refusal* to recognize potential sources of political power as distinct from actually existent ones in American agriculture, this as prerequisite to the shaping and guiding of such power through governmental channels toward general welfare ends. The effect of this failure or refusal was to stimulate a further concentration of power in organizations already powerful, which meant a further strengthening of an already strong tendency toward corporate agriculture.

It will be recalled that Tugwell had opposed in the summer of 1933 the use of the Extension Service's county agricultural agents as field staff for AAA because such use would inevitably give to the American Farm Bureau Federation a disproportionate influence over AAA policy making and execution.* It will be recalled, too, that Tugwell had been instrumental in placing Jerome Frank in the office of general counsel of AAA, had protected him against the wrath of George Peek, and, in line with his determination "to do what I can for the consumer regardless of politics," had encouraged the establishment within the general counsel's office of a Consumers' Division headed by Fred Howe. The effect had been a sharp, quarrelsome division between a liberal wing within AAA, headed by Frank, and a conservative wing headed first by Peek and then, after Peek's departure and from a more nearly centrist position, by Chester Davis as AAA administrator. The liberals saw the farm crisis as a historic demand and opportunity for social change in the direction of income equalization and increased economic democracy. The conservatives, as per the definition of conservatism, were primarily concerned to prevent any important structural change—any shift of money and power away from those now in possession of these—within American agriculture.

In 1934 Tugwell was actively sympathetic with the efforts of Frank and the bright young men of Frank's staff to revise drastically the standard AAA cotton production control contract which had been hastily drafted, on the basis of a very limited knowledge of the South's cotton economy, by (chiefly) Alger Hiss in June 1933.[22] It was a rental agreement. The AAA "benefit" or "parity" payment was in the form of rent paid the landowner for acreage taken out of cotton production. But most of the actual cotton production was the work of tenant farmers aided by field hands, some of them cash tenants, some of them sharecroppers. The latter received for their labor half the cash value of the crop produced minus the advances made to them, as also often to cash tenants, for seed, equipment, groceries, and household necessities purchased in some cases from planter-owned stores, the prices of which tended to be inflated. The typical tenant farmer of the South and Southwest was chronically in debt to

*See pp. 271–73.

the landlord and chronically in fear of him. Hence it was easy for the planters, the landowners who were in full firm control of local AAA administration, to circumvent the clauses in the 1933 contract designed to assure tenants a fair share of the AAA checks, clauses requiring the landowner to split the benefit payment fifty-fifty with his sharecroppers and 25 to 75 percent with his cash tenants. In the event, of the myriad millions of dollars paid out by AAA for the great cotton plow-up of that year, no more than 10 to 12 percent was estimated to have found its way into the pockets of tenants. Worse still by far was the fact that the Cotton Acreage Reduction Contract of 1933 gave no protection against the tendency of planters to reduce the number of their tenants in proportion to the reduction in acreage planted.

The human consequence of this last began to be evident even before the last of 1933's cotton crop had been picked; it had become a social calamity of major proportions within a few months thereafter. Thousands of former tenants with their families, abruptly forced off land they had farmed, began to crowd into already jammed city slums. Many more thousands of them took to the road, joining there yet other thousands who had been driven off dust-shrouded plains farms by the combined effects of drouth, tractor,* and AAA. (AAA production control policies also disadvantaged small independent farmers in their competition with big farmers, thereby encouraging the trend toward fewer, larger farms. "The small farmer who has only been growing enough cotton or tobacco to provide decent American standards of living for a family should not be required to reduce production of money crops to the same extent as big commercialized farms," said an article in *Progressive Farmer* magazine in August 1934.[24]) These people headed west, most of them, their few pitiful belongings strapped to the running boards, the tops, the rear trunks of battered jalopies, men, women, and children hoping desperately to find the Golden West of dreams but destined to find, instead, many of them, the "west" of "going west" in frontier parlance. "Steinbeck . . . in *The Grapes of Wrath*," commented Norman Thomas decades later, "never brought out the fact that it wasn't just the tractor turning up the land that drove people out; it was the deliberate displacement of the AAA."[25]

Thomas himself became greatly exercised over the plight of these dispossessed very shortly after the process of dispossession began. He responded to a plea from Harry K. Mitchell (a "white man," as Thomas found it necessary to point out), who in Tyronza, Arkansas, in July 1934 organized a Southern Tenant Farmers' Union, the membership of which was black as well as white and which, in marked contrast with Reno's Farmers' Holiday tactics, employed passive resistance joined with court action against the brutally violent attempts of landowners to crush it. Thomas encouraged Mitchell's organiza-

---

*By 1939 there were 1,626,000 tractors on American farms, nearly twice the number in 1930, and almost "every one of these tractors has pushed a few tenants, sharecroppers, or hired hands out of jobs," a USDA publication, *The Farm Security Administration*, reported in 1941. This report referred to a typical Mississippi delta plantation the owner of which bought twenty-two tractors and promptly turned off his land 130 of the 160 sharecrop families that had formerly farmed it.[23]

tional effort during an investigative and speaking tour he made of Arkansas in early 1934. Returning east, he made horrifying report to Wallace and Tugwell of what he had seen in the bailiwick of Arkansas's Joe Robinson (Huey Long's bête noire), the Senate majority leader. And what Thomas reported was backed up by Dr. W. R. Amberson, a physiologist working at the University of Tennessee Medical School in Memphis.* Amberson, shocked by the number and pitiable condition of the displaced people he saw moving through Memphis day after day, "organized among his students and others a scientific study of what was happening [because of AAA] on some of the big plantations" and made written reports of his findings to the highest officials he could reach in the Department of Agriculture.²⁶ Thus stimulated were two governmental field investigations, one by Wallace's office, one by AAA itself, each of which abundantly confirmed the truth of what Thomas and Amberson said.

By that time Frank and the bright young men of his legal staff had attempted to alleviate the situation by inserting in the Cotton Acreage Reduction Contract of 1934–1935 a clause unequivocally requiring landowners, as a condition of their receipt of benefit payments, to retain on their land the tenants who were there when the contract was signed. This attempt had run head-on into Oscar Johnston, the wealthy Mississippi plantation manager whom Peek had placed in authority over AAA's enforcement and financial procedures, the man from whose shrewd brain, stimulated by Frank's conception of the Federal Surplus Relief Corporation, had sprung the idea for the Commodity Credit Corporation. Johnston, representing the big planters, stubbornly opposed the clause's purpose, which, in his view, was a violation of a "natural right" of property, and when he was through with it, the clause was considerably longer, much more qualified, and far less clear of meaning than it had originally been. The compromise language, which finally became that of Section 7 of the standard contract, was open to a widely various interpretation. It said that the landowner was obligated (legally obligated or morally obligated?) to retain upon his land for the life of the contract the *same number* of tenants, cash or sharecrop, insofar as this was "possible," and to retain the same *individuals,* insofar as was "consistent" with "discipline."† Chester Davis interpreted this to mean that the landowners "cannot move people off the farms as a result of this campaign."²⁷ But since the practical interpretation of the clause, along with its enforcement, continued to be the province of AAA field officials who were dominated by local landowners and local mores, the eviction of tenants and the denial to those who remained of their share of the benefit payments continued at the same rate as before.

By late January 1935 the situation, threatful to every stated social purpose of the New Deal, had become absolutely intolerable to Jerome Frank and his

---

*Amberson did some of the basic research leading to the development and use of blood plasma. He was a member of the Socialist party.

†Implied by "discipline" would seem to be a continued passive submission to the landlord's dictates by tenants, especially "nigger" tenants.

young men. They plotted rebellion. Alger Hiss prepared an interpretation of the crucial contract clause whereby its pristine purity was restored to it: The landlord was explicitly required to retain not only the same *number* of tenants but also the same *individual* tenants, with obvious circumstantial exceptions, as a condition of receiving AAA payments under the contract he had by then, in many cases, already signed. Frank incorporated this interpretation, along with an order for its strict enforcement, in a telegram to be sent as an administrative directive to AAA field offices, then waited for a day when Chester Davis was out of town, on a field trip through the Midwest. On that day the acting administrator was a former Farmer-Laborite congressman from Minnesota named Victor Christgau who, being thoroughly sympathetic with the Frank group, promptly authorized issuance of the directive.

It went out by wire on Friday, February 1.

Alas for the liberals, its effect was the precise opposite of its intention. Frank had badly miscalculated. Having been close to Henry Wallace for nearly two years, having been repeatedly assured by Wallace that the two of them fought side by side for social reform, he had believed that what he now did was what Wallace in his secret heart wanted done. He had counted heavily upon the support he would receive from the secretary and, ultimately, the White House. At the same time he had grossly underestimated the determination, the fighting quality of Chester Davis, and the momentum of those conservative forces which Davis represented and which had been predominantly operative within AAA's administrative structure since its inception. There was an unexpectedly loud explosion of wrath in the South within hours after the telegram had been received. Its noise reached Davis's ears shortly thereafter. He was infuriated by this flouting of his authority, was grimly determined to reassert this authority. He was also intellectually convinced that the new interpretation would have disastrous "revolutionary effects" in the South and, in view of the fact that almost every major committee in House and Senate was chaired by a southerner who represented the planter interest, would force Wallace "out of the cabinet within a month" were it allowed to stand. He rushed back to Washington, arriving there Friday night. Next morning he canceled the directive. He also presented Wallace with an ultimatum: He would resign at once unless Wallace authorized him to fire at once Jerome Frank, Lee Pressman, Gardner Jackson, Fred Howe, Francis Shea (he had helped Hiss draft the Section 7 interpretation), and one or two others.* The choice Wallace then

*But *not* Alger Hiss! Hiss, whom Frank himself regarded as able and charming but rather "gutless," had evidently charmed Davis into a belief that he, handsome young Hiss, was more dupe than full-fledged ally of Lee Pressman, his closest friend and, according to later sworn testimony by Whittaker Chambers, comrade in a secret Communist cell. As a matter of fact, Davis a little later offered Hiss the post Frank had held, and Hiss seems to have considered accepting the offer. He was dissuaded when Frank told him that if he accepted, Frank's dismissal would be interpreted as a consequence not of policy disagreement but of Frank's *personal* obnoxiousness —an interpretation that might increase an already considerable anti-Semitism among the conservatives of the USDA. (See Jerome Frank's interview transcript in Columbia University Oral History Collection.)

made, if excruciatingly painful to him, was also inevitable for one whose idealism had always been heavily discounted by pragmatism, who seemed recently to have begun to nurse secret presidential ambitions, and who was at that moment freed of such immediate influence as Undersecretary of Agriculture Tugwell could exert upon him (Tugwell was in Florida recuperating from a bout with influenza).[28]

Dismissal notices, bluntly phrased, were on the desks of Frank and the others on Monday morning, February 4. Even then Frank continued to believe and told his fellow purgees that Davis took this action solely on his own authority and would be overruled by the secretary, with whom Frank sought an interview. Confidence waned, however, and doubts grew strong, during the hours that passed before Frank, accompanied by Hiss, was at last admitted, in late afternoon, to the secretary's office.

Wallace was obviously suffering. He greeted Frank with outstretched hand, fixing upon him a troubled gaze as he said, in a voice trembling with emotion, how much he admired the valiant fight Frank and the others had made in a righteous cause. But he dropped his gaze and his voice sank low, as if under a burden of shame, as he went on to say that nevertheless, it was necessary for Frank and the others to go. They had incurred the implacable hostility of both processors and farm leaders. They had been grossly insubordinate, as they themselves had to admit. If they were now permitted to remain, the entire agricultural adjustment program would collapse. Feeling helpless, abandoned, Frank made one last plea: that he and his companions in woe be allowed to resign, avoiding the ignominy of a public firing. He asked for three days in which to submit written resignations and have them accepted. This would enable him and his companions to make their case publicly since he and they would, of course, state their reasons for resigning, and in three days' time his group's supporters, though lacking in politically potent organization, just might protest so loudly that the administration could and would reverse itself on this matter. Wallace hesitated, then said the request did not seem to him "unreasonable." He asked Frank to "wait a minute" and left the office. He did not return that day.

Frank later learned that Wallace went to Davis's office, presented to Davis the proposal Frank had made along with his own inclination to accept it, and was met by Davis's flat refusal to rescind the dismissal notices already issued.[29] Perhaps it was too late for this in any case; reporters had got wind of this "purge of the liberals," as they were to call it, and were clamoring for a meeting with Wallace and Davis.

Roosevelt was informed of the dismissals by Wallace next morning, when Wallace was in the White House for a meeting of the National Emergency Council. He made no protest, no comment of any kind. Later, after the public announcement had been made by Wallace and Davis in a press conference that afternoon, he let it be known that he would not "interfere" in an "internal" AAA affair.

Tugwell, in Palm Beach, was informed by long-distance phone of the firings at about the same time as Roosevelt first heard of them. C. B. "Beanie" Baldwin, assistant to the secretary, called from Wallace's outer office in a highly agitated state, giving the news, including the fact that Mordecai Ezekiel and Louis Bean of the USDA's Bureau of Agricultural Economics, two men for whom Tugwell had high regard, were furiously indignant and that he, Baldwin himself, was about to resign in protest. To this last Tugwell expressed opposition; he counseled calmness and patience, saying that "the fight is just beginning, you should save yourself for another day."[30]

Yet Tugwell himself was in no calm, patient mood as he at once cut short his recuperative rest in the sun (he had been in Florida for only three days) and boarded a plane for Washington, hoping to arrive in time to save Frank and the others.

While he flew northward, he brooded.

For some time after AAA's launching, despite his aversion to the agency's organic links with the land-grant colleges, the Extension Service, the Farm Bureau, he had been "taken in" (so he now saw it) by the democratic procedures which M. L. Wilson had devised for the implementation of AAA programs. There were the local AAA committees elected by farmers who had "signed up" as "cooperators"; there were the national referendums in which "cooperators" voted on proposed acreage reductions of major crops. But to what end did this "democracy" work? Did not the procedures actually facilitate, at the same time disguise, the domination of AAA by big farmers and processors? Certainly these groups were the only ones now being truly, profitably served by this agricultural "pillar" of New Deal recovery. Eighty percent of the farmers on the land were being hurt by AAA, in long-term effect—so badly hurt, many of them, that their long continuance upon the land was unlikely. As for Henry Wallace, Tugwell was as disillusioned and disgusted with him as Frank was at that moment. He remained so for a long time. Wallace had a brilliant, if quirky, mind but a sadly flawed character, in Tugwell's view. Within him raged a bloody civil war (mysticism versus logic, religion versus science, personal ambition versus ideal commitment) which rendered him incapable of making up this brilliant mind of his about who he was, or what he meant in the total scheme of things, or where he was heading as government official or private person. It also rendered him fertile in rationalizations whereby any compromise that served ambition was likely to become "obedience to the voice of God," his knowledge of God's will presumably "arrived at through one of those mystical channels he so assiduously cultivates," as Tugwell later remarked to Norman Thomas.[31] As secretary of agriculture, therefore, Wallace had become a pliant tool of the powers that be in American agriculture, had become, in effect, their ally as they assaulted acquisitively the vital interests of the Little Man, the Average Man, the Common Man, the Forgotten Man. Why, then, should Tugwell remain as undersecretary? He saw no good reason why, in that long moment of brooding; he saw several reasons why he should not.

By the time his plane slanted down to a landing in Washington, he had reached a decision. If he were too late or otherwise unable to block this purge from AAA of its liberal component, a purge he saw as part of a studied campaign by conservatives to gain total control of the Department of Agriculture, he would resign from the administration. He would return to his faculty post at Columbia.

He *was* too late to save Frank, of course.

He *did* go to the White House to tell the President of his wish to resign, giving reasons.

And the face-to-face meeting that ensued became a major event in a causal sequence leading not only to the establishment of the Resettlement Administration but also, beyond that, to a resolution of the basic dilemma whose paralyzing effect upon Roosevelt, persisting since the summer of 1934, had by the spring of 1935 brought the New Deal close to death.

Roosevelt expressed personal sympathy with Tugwell's concerns; indeed, he said he shared them. He acted at once upon Tugwell's insistence that Jerome Frank, whose only "crime" was a possibly overzealous pursuit of New Deal goals, must now be protected against personal financial hardship. He phoned Corcoran at RFC. "Tommy," he said, "you've got to find a place right away for Jerry Frank." (The word was passed to Stanley Reed, the RFC general counsel, who promptly offered Frank a job as special counsel on railroad reorganization, this having been Frank's specialty on Wall Street. Having accepted the offer, Frank remained with RFC until late 1935.) Roosevelt made at least passing reference to political realities which the executive must take account of when dealing with farm policy—notably, the fact that Marvin Jones of Texas chaired the House Agriculture Committee, that Cotton Ed Smith of South Carolina chaired the Senate's Agriculture Committee, and that both men, having great power within the legislative process, were adamantly opposed to AAA's engaging in what Chester Davis called the "reform business." Especially were they opposed to any agricultural policy which might result in "uppity niggers" in their region. They would fight to the last ditch for white supremacy, side by side with Joe Robinson of Arkansas, Pat Harrison of Mississippi, and other southern stalwarts without whose support no administration legislation was likely to be passed, in the prevailing circumstances.

But the main thrust of Roosevelt's side of the talk that day was toward a retention of Tugwell in government. When Tugwell weakened to the extent of saying he might be willing to stay if he could get out of Agriculture (away from Wallace) into Interior, there to be an undersecretary or assistant secretary in charge of conservation, as Ickes had suggested, Roosevelt protested even this change. The President would take it as a personal favor, an act of personal friendship, if Tugwell would just sit tight where he was for the time being, talking things over frankly, of course, with "Henry," who, Roosevelt was sure, wanted "Rex" to stay. Tugwell finally agreed to do this.

On this tentative note, having in it a vague promise of some new arrangement suitable to Tugwell in the near future, the interview ended.[32]

Meanwhile, in Arkansas, the Southern Tenant Farmers' Union, its organization efforts aided by "outside agitators" and encouraged by Gardner Jackson of AAA's Consumers' Division, had attracted a surprisingly large and well-disciplined membership. The resort to the Arkansas courts was unrewarding, however. When union leaders sued to force an absentee landlord, a Kansas City lawyer, to take back twenty-seven tenants evicted from his 5,000-acre plantation, their claim being that the eviction violated Section 7 of the contract the landlord had signed, the judge ruled against them. They fared no better when they carried their case to the secretary of agriculture. Wallace, pressed to do so by Paul Appleby, gave Harry Mitchell and a group of Mitchell's friends a half hour of his time, listened unhappily to their recital of grievances, then promised them that the matter would be "looked into" and "action taken" in some unspecified future. Returning, disappointed, to Arkansas, Mitchell and the others promptly called a mass meeting at Marked Tree. A principal speaker there was the Reverend E. B. McKinney who told his listeners that he personally "could lead a mob to lynch every landlord in the county if these people are not fed" but that "we do not wish to resort to violence" and would instead appeal to the courts. McKinney was roughly seized by police as soon as his speech ended and hauled into court on a charge of "anarchy, attempting to overthrow and usurp the Government of Arkansas, and blasphemy." Convicted, he was sentenced to six months in jail.[33]

Thereafter the landlords and their governmental minions, outraged by this "uprising" of "no-account, shiftless people," especially by this organized "mistering" of "niggers," instituted a reign of terror against the union and those it sought to organize. Meetings were routinely broken up; organizers, routinely beaten up. There were flogging, maimings, hundreds of false arrests, and several murders. When fearless Norman Thomas marched into this mortally dangerous scene again, in early March 1935, to speak at a union-sponsored mass meeting in the village of Birdsong, some five miles from Harry Mitchell's hometown of Tyronza, the meeting was broken up by a mob of planters accompanied by sheriff's deputies, who struck Thomas with their fists, knocking him off the speaker's platform, then hustled him across the county line, threatening him with worse violence if he ever dared come back. No "Goddamned Yankee" was going to tell *them* "what to do with our niggers."[34]

Thomas went to Washington. He sought an interview with Wallace, who refused to see him. He talked with Tugwell, and with Aubrey Williams, each of whom had special reasons at that moment to avoid antagonizing hot-tempered Joe Robinson. He asked for audience with the President, was promptly granted it, and went to the White House armed with a copy of the 1934–1935 cotton contract.

He was warmly greeted by the President as "Norman," an old friend, and then, seated before Roosevelt's desk, he found himself overwhelmed by a tide of Rooseveltian volubility—a flood of words into which he could inject no word of his own while minute after minute of his precious allotted time slipped by. ("If you ever had dealings with Mr. Roosevelt," said Thomas to an interviewer many years later, "you know that he really handled interviews in his own way. He tried to keep the conversation in his own hands. He did it rather charmingly. He'd reminisce. He'd tell you stories and you'd sit there and wonder how in the world you were going to get to the point.") Finally Thomas simply bluntly interrupted the President of the United States. He asked what Roosevelt thought of the cotton contract. Was it designed to clarify or to obscure relationships between landlord and tenant?

"I haven't read it," Roosevelt replied.

This astonished Thomas—after all, the contract was "one of the basic documents" of New Deal farm policy—and he at once leaned across the desk to place in Roosevelt's hand his contract copy, calling particular attention to sentences in Section 7 which Thomas had underlined. Roosevelt read these.

"That can mean anything or nothing, can't it, Norman?" he said, with genial smile, and was about to embark on another diversion when Thomas again interrupted.

"Nothing, Mr. President," said Thomas. "In this case, the words mean nothing. The experiences of certain men in the Agriculture Department [thus obliquely did he refer to the firing of Frank and the others] have shown that. . . ."

And he went on to describe forcefully the disastrous effect this calculated meaninglessness was having upon hundreds of thousands of American citizens.

He even made so bold as to suggest an alternative to the present overall New Deal policy line as it affected the South—an alternative truly aimed, as the present policy emphatically was not, toward social justice. This alternative was a carefully designed strategy for actualizing what was now a merely *potential* political power throughout the South. There would be an at least tacit encouragement of such movements as the Southern Tenant Farmers' Union, movements which aimed to replace the prevailing brutal feudal relationships between southern planter and tenant, southern white man and black, with genuine political and economic democracy. There would be, in general, a consistent administration support of efforts to restore to southern blacks the constitutional rights, especially the right to vote, which they had briefly exercised during Reconstruction but had since been denied by terrorist Jim Crow. Certainly there would be full administration support of the antilynching bill which, drafted by lawyers for the National Association for the Advancement of Colored People (NAACP), had been introduced in Congress by Senator Costigan and Senator Wagner in January 1934. By making lynching a federal crime, the bill aimed to deprive white southern terrorists of a principal horrible means of keeping the "nigger" in his "place," and it had been reported out favorably in February 1934 by the Senate Judiciary Committee.* A clear majority of both houses of the Seventy-third Congress had favored the bill; the same was true of the Seventy-fourth Congress. The measure was certain of passage if it came to floor vote. But it was prevented from coming to a vote

---

*Strangely enough, only three of the eighteen members of the powerful Senate Judiciary Committee of the Seventy-third Congress were southerners.

by the threat of prolonged filibuster by southern senators, a minority tactic which could be overcome only by strong presidential pressure for cloture. No such pressure had been exerted.*

Roosevelt "didn't much like this" line of argument, Thomas later recalled. He thought aspersions were being cast upon his political acumen, and he reacted peevishly. "Now, come, Norman," he said, "I'm a damn sight better politician than you are."

Thomas at once drew back, nodding, smiling in the realization that he had pushed a little too hard. "Certainly," he agreed. "You are on that side of the desk, and I on this."

Well, then, Roosevelt went on, Thomas should respect and heed the President's judgment on what was politically possible in the prevailing circumstances and what was needed to change those circumstances. He repeated in essence the argument that Chester Davis made in defense of current AAA policy and that he, Roosevelt, had made last May when, at Eleanor's urging, he had granted a personal interview to Walter White, the NAACP secretary, at Hyde Park. "I did not choose the tools with which I must work," he had said to White. "Had I been permitted to choose them I would have selected quite different ones." As it was, "Southerners, by reason of the seniority rule in Congress, are chairmen or occupy strategic positions on most of the Senate and House committees. If I come out for the anti-lynching bill now, they will block every bill I ask Congress to pass to keep America from collapsing. I just can't take that risk." But White could and should go ahead on his own, Roosevelt had added. "Whatever you can get done is okay with me, but I just can't do it." (After White had left, Eleanor, who was present during this interview, said to her husband, "Well, what about me? Do you mind if I say what I think?" "No, certainly not," he replied. "You can say anything you want. I can always say, 'Well, that's my wife. I can't do anything about her.' ")

Since then there had been several atrocious lynchings, one of them especially so: On an October day in 1934 a black man had been taken from an Alabama jail across the state line to Marianna, Florida, by men whose actions were unprotested by law enforcement officers in either state, and had then been put to death "by unspeakable torture and mutilation" before a crowd of "thousands of men, women and children," the event having been "advertised hours in advance," as a telegram from the Committee on Interracial Cooperation reported to the White House. When, in another case, a fleeing black man was pursued from Mississippi into Tennessee, captured there, and transported back to Mississippi by a lynch mob, which then killed him before another large crowd, Walter White called for invocation of the Lindbergh Law, which made kidnapping with transport across state lines a federal crime, a capital offense. Roosevelt referred the request to Attorney General Cummings, who obliged him by ruling, in an unofficial opinion, that the Lindbergh Law did not apply

---

*Nor would it ever be, during the ten years in office which yet remained to Franklin Roosevelt.

to this case since the kidnapping had not been done for financial gain.) Said Roosevelt now to Norman Thomas: "You can't do better until you get a better lot of Southern leaders." But "I know the South" and the South *was* changing, a new and better leadership *was* coming along, and of the consequent expanded opportunity, whenever it presented itself, Roosevelt intended to take full advantage. . . ."[35]

Yet Roosevelt himself was, at that very moment, in process of change. He shifted ground, and the shift was leftward, a fact for which these reported interviews with Tugwell and Thomas were in some part responsible. These interviews sharpened his awareness that the distress, the desperation of the totally impoverished in rural areas, especially in the South, was, under the spur of New Deal hopes and expectations, generating social energies different in kind and in directional force from the corn belt furies, the dairy state furies, of 1933 and 1934. The corn-hog and dairy farmers had had, generally speaking, no quarrel with the profit system as such. They still felt they had a stake in it. Their quarrel was with what they perceived as distortions of the system's workings, as an unfair advantage taken of it by exploitive "others," with consequent hardship to themselves. But what of these tenant farmers, these migratory laborers, these freshly dispossessed who now thronged the road to elsewhere, or nowhere? What stake did they have in the "system"? It behooved a prudent, intelligently conservative administration to give them one, through prompt federal action, if their anguish was not to become, through political organization, a destructive force directed toward social revolution or toward war and fascism. Right now, as Roosevelt had been informed, several bills were being readied for early introduction in Congress—bills dealing with land tenure, rural rehabilitation, resettlement, production-for-use in agriculture—and some of them were radical indeed.

On March 22 the President broke his long public silence about the food and drug bill. He sent to Congress a special message endorsing the proposal, if in language that indicated a personal aloofness from it, language carefully tailored for appeal to the business mind and notable, in consequence, for non sequitur. He said:

Every enterprise in the United States should be able to adhere to the simple principle of honesty without fear of penalty on that account. . . . The honor of the producers in a country ought to be the invariable ingredient of the products produced in it. . . . In such a situation as has grown up through our rising level of living and our multiplication of goods, consumers are prevented from choosing intelligently and producers are handicapped in any attempt to maintain higher standards. Only the scientific and disinterested activity of Government can protect this honor of our producers and provide the possibility of discriminating choice to our consumers. . . . It is time to make practical improvements [in the law of 1906]. A measure is needed which will extend to advertising also the controls formerly applicable only to labels; which will extend protection to the trade in cosmetics; which will provide for a cooperative method of setting standards and for a system of inspection and enforcement to reassure consumers grown hesitant and doubtful; and which will provide for necessary flexibility in administration as products and conditions change. I understand this subject has been studied and discussed for the last two years and that full information is in the possession of the Congress. . . . It is my hope that such legislation may be enacted at this session of the Congress.

But he still did not place the bill on his list of must legislation, nor would he do so two months hence, when such a list was most emphatically presented. (The congressional session of 1935 adjourned with the bill unenacted.)[36]

Then, on May 1, came Roosevelt's executive order establishing the Resettlement Administration, with Tugwell its administrator.

III

As has been suggested, the new agency was less a rationally coherent response to challenging problems than it was a repository for these problems unsolved, a lumping together of them under a sign of hope that, somehow, solutions to them would be found or, as Roosevelt might have put it to himself, would "work themselves out" of the existing situation through a "logic of events." As such it included several projects and proposals to which Tugwell was ardently committed, but it also included projects to which he was almost as ardently opposed. Among the latter were the projects of the Subsistence Homesteads Division of Interior, including Eleanor's "baby," Arthurdale (Ickes, for all his empire-building proclivities, was glad to be rid of it), which were transferred to Resettlement by executive order on May 15.

The highly complex vision of America that animated Rex Tugwell's national planning doctrine had in it no rosy view of the family farm or of farming as a way of life in the third and fourth decades of this twentieth century. "A farm," he said in a 1930 book, "is an area of vicious, ill-tempered soil with a not very good house, inadequate barns, makeshift machinery, happenstance livestock, tired, overworked men and women . . . a place where ugly, brooding monotony, that haunts by day and night, unseats the mind."[37] It was so because agriculture, an enterprise the function of which in national economic life was the efficient production of food and fiber, persisted in chaotically individualistic ways of production and marketing that were inimical to any rational planning of its activities, any proper use of the methods and tools made available by scientific technological advances in agronomy, animal husbandry, land management, agricultural engineering, etc. What was needed was a reorganization and reform of agriculture along essentially the same lines as had been drawn for industry in Tugwell's *Industrial Discipline.* Yet he was no more an advocate of the kind of corporate farming, the "factories in the field" of California and Florida, toward which prevailing trends pointed through all the major farming areas, than he was of "sentimental" back-to-the-land movements. We have seen his strong opposition to that mindless response to technological imperatives which the organized selfishness of NRA and AAA, each a sad distortion of the kind of planning called for in *The Industrial Discipline,* represented. Personally he yearned toward the rural small-town America, a virtually classless society (no one very rich, no one miserably poor), in which he had grown up. "I'm for decentralization, for simplicity of life, *along with** a recognition of the complexity of industrial and scientific civilization," he said in one of his syndicated columns. Scientific technology should, he thought, "make it possible for all of us to approximate that no-riches, no-poverty kind of life in which I grew up. I'd certainly set the sleighbells ringing in thousands of village streets if I could."[38]

Thus it was in the service of a traditional American dream, it was toward a preservation and restoration in new forms of what would always be for him personally the "real" America of friendly community, of economic equality that national planning for agriculture would be done, if Tugwell had his way. As for the planning itself, it would be no making of rigid patterns to be forcibly imposed on social process. Tugwell's reading of John Dewey's *Reconstruction in Philosophy* had confirmed him in an evidently natural aversion to what Dewey condemned as "radical finalism"—that assumption of final ends inherent in first beginnings which amounts to a denial of real change, or of any possibility of real change, and results in the "closed world" of scholastic philosophy as opposed to the "open world" of modern science. "Planning," in Tugwell's vocabulary, meant the shaping of logical hypotheses to be tested in and by social process. He was, as he often proclaimed, an "experimentalist." His planning would proceed by and through experiment. And it was the opportunity presented by the Resettlement Administration for large-scale and various experiment in scientific land use, in massive retirement from production of marginal and submarginal land, in rural and urban resettlement of people who had been living miserably on such land, in cooperative farming, in the development of "greenbelt" communities wherein town and country living were mingled,† that was happily contemplated by the newly appointed Resettlement administrator.

He regretted the assignment to him of a cluster of responsibilities that had

---

*Emphasis added. Tugwell's social philosophizing never settled upon a solution of the basic problem of the One and the Many. He was never able to decide clearly, in terms of relative emphasis, between the values of freedom and the values of organization (atomism and organism), much less arrive at a balanced synthesis of the two.

†There would be, in the event, three greenbelt towns whose inhabitants were families having incomes of $1,200 to $2,000 per year: Greenbelt, Maryland, adjacent to Washington, D.C.; Greenhills, Ohio, adjacent to Cincinnati; and Greendale, Wisconsin, adjacent to Milwaukee. A fourth such project, Greenbrook, near Bound Brook, New Jersey, was aborted when a group of local citizens, fearing it would attract a "low class of people" and would lower property values, instituted legal proceedings and won a ruling from the Court of Appeals of the District of Columbia that the executive order which established Resettlement had no statutory authorization. Each established town was a true community of from 570 to 885 families, with its own stores, post office, schools, etc., surrounded by a "green belt . . . a girdle of farm and woodland. . . ." The projects anticipated and to some extent established the pattern for the vast suburban developments of later decades, and they, with TVA, were the most interesting to foreign visitors of all concrete New Deal developments.[39]

no logical relationship to his own main concerns. But he was not daunted. He set to work with a will, swiftly assembling a staff notable for intelligence and youthful energy and idealistic commitment (among those he recruited as key subordinates was Beanie Baldwin, who became RA's assistant administrator in charge of program operations), and by the fall of 1935 Tugwell had managed to impose some measure of administrative order upon the maze and chaos of programs with which he perforce began.

He, of course, realized that he ("Rex the Red") carried with him into his new job the press hostility and conservative fury which his sponsorship of the food and drug bill had focused upon him. He realized that this furious hostility would be a major hazard to RA's success. Hence his heavy stress, at the very outset, upon what he called public information and his enemies called propaganda. A key element of his organization was an information division initially headed by John Franklin Carter, the brilliant journalist who commonly used as his signature "Jay Franklin" or "Unofficial Observer."

And this was fortunate for history.

Resettlement's information service, staffed with writers and photographers of extraordinary talent and creative energy, accomplished "a revolutionary innovation in the character of governmental information work," generating "a flood of descriptive materials," as Sidney Baldwin has written. They virtually invented a new kind of literature or art form—the documentary. Especially was this true of the photographic section under Roy E. Stryker, who had been a student of Tugwell's, and later a faculty colleague, at Columbia.[40] It operated on a small budget, it never had more than a half dozen photographers on its staff at any one time, but these included over the years young photographers whose names remain famous in American cultural history, though not always as photographers. Among them were Arthur Rothstein, Walker Evans, Dorothea Lange, Ben Shahn, Gordon Parks, Carl Mydans, Margaret Bourke-White —and much of their greatest work was done on roving field assignment for RA and its successor, the Farm Security Administration. They took more than 272,000 photographs of the people, the villages and towns and cities, the eroding landscape of America in the 1930s, making in sum a national portrait which will forever remain the dominant visual remembrance of our Great Depression. They stimulated the creation of many books wherein their photographs were joined with prose or verse to produce upon the reader a single powerful impression. Several of these achieved over the years the status of minor classics: Dorothea Lange's and Paul S. Taylor's *An American Exodus,* Erskine Caldwell and Margaret Bourke-White's *You Have Seen Their Faces,* Sherwood Anderson's *Home Town,* Archibald MacLeish's *Land of the Free,* Richard Wright and Edwin Roskam's *12 Million Black Voices,* and James Agee and Walker Evans's *Let Us Now Praise Famous Men.* (The last of these came out of an assignment to Agee and Evans from *Fortune* magazine and was shaped by Agee's agitated hands into a kind of "anti-documentary," being composed of a frenetic Faulknerian prose-poetry that was decidedly *not* of a kind the Government Printing Office was ever likely to publish.)[41]

Far less successful than its information division was RA as a whole in its attempt to carry out its multifarious, ill-defined assignment. The fundamental incoherence proved a crumbling hazard to the edifice reared upon it. The agency was compelled toward too many widely differing goals; it was forced to try to do far too much with far too little in the way of financial resource; it was under incessant attack from first to last by the business community, the mass communications media which business controlled, and the Farm Bureau whose dominant members, with the notable exception of Murray Lincoln and his Ohio Farm Bureau, could hardly have cared less what happened to their less fortunate neighbors (especially the tenants, the migrant workers) upon the land; and it was destined to achieve not one-tenth of what Tugwell originally hoped for it.

Indeed, it achieved less than 1 percent of Tugwell's original resettlement goal. He had proposed at the outset, as *immediate* goal, to purchase some 10 million acres of submarginal land and resettle some 20,000 families now living on that land. His ultimate goal had been the resettlement of a half million rural families, or approximately 2 million people—some 8 percent of the entire farm population in 1935. Actually, or in the end, RA resettled fewer than 4,500 families. One reason was that the resettlement idea encountered, in practice, unexpected and powerfully hostile subjective factors. Impoverished rural folk proved to be fearfully reluctant to abandon homes which, however miserable, *were* their homes, in a familiar landscape, with familiar associations, in order to embark upon a journey into the unknown. There was soon forced a shift of emphasis from land reform and resettlement to rural rehabilitation, the latter a program which was inherited from FERA but which in RA aimed not only to provide emergency subsistence to client families in their present locations but also to elevate their material standards of living, enhance the aesthetic and cultural quality of their lives, and increase their long-term economic security. By June 1936 the number of rural rehabilitation client families totaled 536,302, thus equaling the number Tugwell had originally hoped to resettle.[42]

The shift from resettlement to rehabilitation meant increased reliance upon low-interest long-term loans to enable tenants to purchase family farms, an operation Tugwell was inclined to view as an ill-conceived "experiment" since, in his view, the small family farm was inherently incapable of economic competition with farms large enough to employ large and expensive farm machinery. He favored, instead, a major effort: the development of cooperative farms along with new kinds of community, whereby both economic and cultural improvements were facilitated; after all, he pointed out, the farm tenant problem directly involved but 10 percent of the nation's rural poor, and rural poverty as a whole was RA's target. But he was compelled as a practical matter to support legislation which enabled an enlarged tenant loan-purchase program. In any case, as we may as well anticipate here, Tugwell's connection with RA was to be severed in the late autumn of 1936. Shortly before he left, he with others would take Wallace on an educative tour of the rural South, the South of Erskine Caldwell's *Tobacco Road,* a tour from which Wallace would return shaken, horrified by what he had seen,* and determined to accept incorporation of the Resettlement Administration in the Department of Agriculture, a move he had resisted when Tugwell initially proposed it as an agency-protective measure. The transfer was to be made on January 1, 1937. Following enactment in the summer of 1937 of the Bankhead-Jones farm tenant bill, which legitimized RA operations theretofore conducted under an executive order of dubious constitutionality, the agency became the Farm Security Administration. It continued the innovative, idealistic effort RA had begun, but always with grossly inadequate funding, always under attack from the conservative establishment, and never with the kind of all-out risk-taking support from the White House which might have enabled it to develop a constituency (what John Kenneth Galbraith calls countervailing power) of its own. Its only important organized support of the kind effective in congressional halls was to come from the Southern Tenant Farmers' Union, and this was meager compared to the opposition power exerted by the Farm Bureau and the bureau's allies.

By and large, the New Deal's attack on rural poverty must be counted a failure.

IV

THE third new federal agency to be created by Roosevelt's executive order, in implementation of 1935's Emergency Relief Appropriation Act, was the Rural Electrification Administration, established on May 11. Its announced purpose was: "To facilitate, formulate, administer, and supervise a program of approved projects with respect to the generation, transmission, and distribution of electric energy in rural areas."[44] And of all New Deal agencies, none other save the Federal Deposit Insurance Corporation was destined to accomplish so nearly perfectly what it set out to do.

There were two main reasons why this was so.

One was Roosevelt's own considerable and bitter experience of utility corporations, his mental grasp of public utility problems, and his firm belief that the generation of electricity for people *must* take precedence over the generation of profit for business in the overall employment of the electric technology. As governor of New York, in the fall of 1929, he had considered the possibility of establishing a state rural power authority to facilitate a bestowal of the blessings of electricity upon farms now denied these by the workings of the profit system. When he won his legislative battle for the New York Power Authority, in the spring of 1931, he saw to it that rural electrification was one of the goals, a major goal, which the authority kept in view.

---

*"I have never seen among the peasantry of Europe poverty so abject as that which exists in this favorable cotton year in the great cotton states," wrote Wallace in an article published in the *New York Times Magazine* for Sunday, January 3, 1937. "[T]he city people of the United States should be thoroughly ashamed" of the fact that a third of the farmers in the United States lived "under conditions . . . much worse than the peasantry of Europe."[43]

A second reason for REA's success was the man whom Roosevelt appointed its first administrator. This man was sixty-three-year-old Morris L. Cooke, the Philadelphia management engineer, a Taylorite efficiency expert with a social conscience, whom Roosevelt had named a trustee of the New York Power Authority in May 1931.*

Cooke quickly discovered, if he did not know to begin with, that REA could not operate as a relief agency if it were to pursue successfully its main goal of rural electrification. If it expended at the very least 25 percent of its budget on labor, drawing 90 percent of the labor from relief rolls, as the relief agency guidelines required, it could do little to electrify rural America. Cooke therefore proposed that it become primarily a lending agency, using funds supplied by the Reconstruction Finance Corporation to make low-interest loans to facilitate the construction of transmission lines into the electricity-starved countryside, a proposal to which Harry Hopkins agreed and which Roosevelt approved, in August 1935. To whom, then, were these low-interest loans to be made? Their natural recipients would seem to be the operating companies of the utilities corporations. These were in a position to extend rapidly into the country the lines already serving towns and cities, and Cooke tried to persuade utilities executives to accept federal loans for this purpose while lowering rates sufficiently to enable farmers to pay them. His persuasive effort failed. The utilities executives were satisfied with things as they were, though only 10.9 percent of all U.S. farms had electricity at the end of 1934 (less than 1 percent of the farms in states like Mississippi were so served), whereas in Germany and France nearly 90 percent of the rural community was wired, in consequence of systematic government policy. The executives pointed to the undeniable fact that the existent market for rural electricity in America was already abundantly supplied; they refused to believe that they would inevitably create an expanding market simply by extending their lines into new areas at affordable rates, as the westering railroads had done, with government subsidy, in the nineteenth century. So Cooke turned to the model provided by the Alcorn County Electric Power Association which TVA sponsored in Mississippi. He set about stimulating farmers to organize consumer cooperatives, nonprofit rural electric cooperatives, to which the REA low-interest loans (3 percent, with a twenty-year amortization period) could be made—an enterprise which boomed following enactment of the Norris-Rayburn bill in late May 1936. Norris-Rayburn not only gave REA a statutory base of its own, removing it altogether from the relief category, but also required RFC to prefer nonprofit cooperatives over profit-making business enterprises in the allocation of loan money.

The utilities companies did their best, or worst, to prevent this extension of electric energy to human beings in dire need of it. They employed every device and dirty trick they could think of to thwart the formation of rural electric cooperatives and to keep rates high. But they were definitely overmatched and

*See Davis, *FDR: The New York Years,* p. 100.

overwhelmed for almost the first time, so far as truly large-scale effect was concerned, in all their long history of arrogant, exploitive chicanery. Cooke and John M. Carmody, who succeeded Cooke as REA administrator in 1937, were firmly supported by the White House, as was Lilienthal in his TVA power policy, at every crisis point (there were a great many) of their administrative effort, while REA's field operations created for it a growing, politically potent constituency as they brought more and more light into the darkness of country night. Utilities corporations were forced to lower their rates, sometimes by the threat that electric cooperatives would build generating plants of their own, using RFC loans supplied through REA, as the latter announced it was prepared to do, if necessary. In the end, the private utilities themselves greatly profited from this implementation of New Deal policy. . . .

Nearly half the farms in America had been electrified by 1942; nearly all were to be in the following decade. And REA remains in American history as a shining instance of successful application of the cooperative idea to a socioeconomic problem.[45]

13

-→>×<<-

Decision, at Last!

I

IT was on Tuesday night, May 14, 1935, or three days after the executive order establishing REA had been issued, that Franklin Roosevelt at last made up his mind on the direction he would go in his leadership of the New Deal into election year 1936.

This, at least, is a conclusion strongly suggested by the evidence.

Certainly it was on the night of the fourteenth, during a carefully planned and wholly unpublicized meeting in the White House, that Roosevelt for the first time indicated to those around him a mind made up in this regard; certainly there had been, during the preceding two weeks, a convergence of three main lines of force which focused, fused into a single pressure, upon Roosevelt's mind and will. And these two facts, considered in the light of our knowledge of the man, point toward a high probability that the fundamental choice so long postponed was actually made by Roosevelt during the meeting in which it was announced—perhaps in the very process of its announcement.

II

ONE of the three determinative lines of force had been the continuing growth in national influence and political power of Huey Long and Father Coughlin and the increasing use of these against the administration, against Roosevelt personally.

As we know, Long's dangerous effectiveness had been recognized by presidential candidate Roosevelt in the summer of 1932*—and within a few months after his inauguration, when it was clear that Long could never be harnessed into the administration team, Roosevelt the President began to use the coercive powers of his high office, covertly, to reduce Long's power. Federal patronage had been denied the Kingfish, had been used whenever possible to strengthen Long's political enemies in his home state. Ickes had refused to authorize PWA projects in Louisiana on the ground, from which he had soon to retreat, that the state's enabling legislation was defective. One of Henry Morgenthau's first acts as treasury secretary (January 1934) had been to order a full-scale investigation by Internal Revenue agents of Long's federal income tax returns and those of his subordinates in the Louisiana machine. Scores of agents had come swarming into the state, and from their months of labor had come indictments

*See Davis, *FDR: The New York Years*, p. 352.

of four of Long's top lieutenants by the end of 1934. In early February 1935, at a meeting of the National Emergency Council, Roosevelt issued to members of the top echelon of his administration a most emphatic oral order: "Don't put anybody in and don't help anybody that is working for Huey Long or his crowd! That is 100 percent! . . . Everybody and every agency." All to no avail! The pudgy, curly-haired, dimple-chinned, bright-button-eyed "Huey"—with his gaudy shirts, his pongee suits, his sailor straw hats; with his impudence, his buffoonery, his audacity, his penetrating shrewdness, his ruthlessness, his outrageously flaunted contempt for conventions and the conventionally power-ful; with, above all, his flamboyant yet consistent championing of the "lower" against the "upper" orders, especially of the lower middle class—had con-tinued his rise, and at accelerating pace. He had become not only the idol of millions who were convinced he spoke and acted for them against their exploit-ers but also the delight of influential (opinion-making) thousands, including literary intellectuals, who used him often, or their impression of him, to disparage Franklin Roosevelt. (Thus Gertrude Stein, on a lecture tour of America in the spring of 1935, when asked her impression of Long, replied that he had "a sense of human beings, and is not boring the way Harding, President Roosevelt, and Al Smith have been boring." H. G. Wells, visiting the United States in that same season, described him admiringly as "a Winston Churchill who has never been at Harrow" and gave it as his opinion that Roosevelt, of whom he had given a glowing account during the New Deal's first year, was losing his grip, that Long was taking the play away from him.[1]) His national political organization, the Share Our Wealth Society with its hundreds of local units, provided a personal power base that continued to expand, continued to solidify.

It had done so all through 1934, and that accounts for the White House concern when, four days after the first session of the Seventy-fourth Congress had opened, in a Senate chamber jam-packed for the occasion, announced three days in advance, Huey Long declared full-scale war on the administra-tion in an uncharacteristically serious, closely reasoned address. Ingratitude, deceit, betrayal—these characterized Roosevelt's performance in the White House, cried Long. The President owed his election to such progressives as Long proclaimed himself to be, but once in office, far from consulting these progressives or following the policy line they proposed, he had set out to destroy them. A special malice had been reserved for Huey Long, who now reviewed efforts the administration had made and was making to crush him. They were efforts which, in a closing vivid burst of defiance, he vowed to resist and overcome. The speech, from the administration's point of view, was quite alarmingly persuasive of the multitude. "It is more and more evident in Wash-ington that many Democrats feel he [Huey Long] is getting ready to pounce upon their party and absorb all or a large part of it in 1936," commented Arthur Krock in the New York *Times* on January 10, 1935.[2]

A week later, in an attempt to offset in some degree the long series of highly nationalistic acts by his administration in a world the peace of which was increasingly disturbed by aggressive nationalism, Roosevelt proposed a gesture, a largely symbolic gesture, toward internationalism. He sent to Congress on January 16 a special message calling for U.S. entrance into the World Court. He did so with every confidence of success, despite expected furious opposition from Borah, Hiram Johnson, and other western and midwestern isolationists. Of the Senate's ninety-six seats, Democrats occupied five more than the two-thirds needed to ratify treaties, a more than normally careful survey of Senate opinion indicated more than enough Republicans favoring the proposal to cancel out the few Democrats opposed to it, and all signs were that a considerably majority of the American people approved this gesture, if with no great enthusiasm.

But when Borah and Johnson were joined in leadership of the Senate opposition by Huey Long, as they at once were, the balance shifted drastically. Huey's interest in foreign relations was slight, though such opinions as he had in this field were consistently isolationist, but his interest in putting down the President of the United States was enormous, and he now implemented it with speeches and adroit parliamentary maneuvering that helped greatly to prolong a fierce debate through ten long days. During these days the Hearst newspapers did all they could to rouse popular sentiment against this "entangling alliance" and the unpatriotic, if not actually traitorous, Americans who favored it. By the time the debate ended on Friday afternoon, January 25, there was evident an erosion of support for the proposal among the populace and in the Senate, where the number of undecideds increased. Yet Senate Majority Leader Robinson, who operated vigorously on Roosevelt's behalf during this struggle, was convinced he still had in hand enough votes to ratify with several to spare. Probably he did have them, at that time. He would have done well to press for an immediate vote. Instead, he acquiesced in a long weekend recess, postponing the final verdict until Tuesday.

This proved a fatal error.

For on Sunday afternoon Father Coughlin, who had theretofore been relatively quiet in his opposition to ratification, abruptly, emphatically joined with Long against the proposal—indeed, superseded Long as the most influential opposition spokesman. He devoted the whole of his weekly radio network sermon to "The Menace of the World Court." In his rich, deep, melodious, intimately confiding voice—"one of the great speaking voices of the twentieth century . . . a voice made for promises," as Wallace Stegner described it; also a voice perfectly suited to the lush rhetoric it habitually intoned—the Radio Priest warned his vast audience that the Republic was in mortal danger: The Senate was about to sacrifice "our national sovereignty to the World Court" at the behest of an administration "ready to join hands" with those wicked international bankers (he named the Rothschilds, the Morgans, the Warburgs, the Kuhn, Loebs) who had tricked us into bloody European war in 1917 and now conspired to do it again, for their own profit. He proclaimed the duty of all patriotic citizens in this hour of crisis. "Today," he cried, "—tomorrow may be too late—today, whether you can afford it or not, send your senators telegrams telling them to vote 'no' on our entrance into the World Court." And the patriots responded! Somewhere between 40,000 and 50,000 telegrams, each urging a negative vote and often in frenzied tone, flashed into Washington on Sunday afternoon and evening and on Monday. They were delivered to senators by the wheelbarrow load.

And when the vote was taken on Tuesday morning, January 29, far from being ratified with a comfortable margin beyond the required two-thirds, the treaty was rejected by an embarrassingly wide margin of seven votes, the count being 52 for and 36 against, with seven senators absent.

This, in the circumstances, was no mild rebuff. Coming less than three months after a midterm election in which he had been "all but crowned by the people," it was in some respects the most personally humiliating defeat Roosevelt had suffered since entering the White House. ("I regard this as a decisive defeat of the Administration," wrote Ickes in his diary.* "I have been surprised all along that the President should make this such an issue as he has made it.") And Roosevelt reacted to the event with unwonted bitterness. On the morrow of his defeat, which was his fifty-third birthday, he wrote "Dear Joe" Robinson in appreciation of "the splendid fight you have made"; asked the majority leader "to convey my personal gratitude to your fifty-one colleagues . . . who have kept faith with the Republican and Democratic Party platforms"; then added: "As to the thirty-six Senators who placed themselves on record against the principle of the World Court, I am inclined to think that if they ever get to Heaven they will be doing a great deal of apologizing for a very long time —that is if God is against war—and I think He is." A few days later, writing to Elihu Root, who had been TR's secretary of state (succeeding John Hay) and, in 1920, had helped draft the statute establishing the World Court as an adjunct of the League of Nations, Roosevelt spoke contemptuously of the "twelve or fourteen Senators who" during the court debate "would not commit themselves—most of them because they wanted to see which way the cat was going to jump! You know the type from long personal experience."[3]

Long's exultation was in proportion to Roosevelt's discomfiture. He was encouraged toward further aggressive actions against the administration.

On February 11 he rose in the Senate to proclaim his possession of evidence that Postmaster General Farley's management of the Post Office Department was rife with corruption. Farley, he charged, had made free distribution of stamps to favored individuals, had used the powers of his governmental office to obtain political contributions from people of doubtful character (the fact that Farley was both cabinet member and National Democratic Committee chairman laid him open to such accusations), and had a financial interest in construction companies to which contracts to build post offices, using PWA

---

*Ickes, destined to become one of the most effective of all American spokesmen against Hitler and isolationism, was himself an isolationist in 1935. He regarded the court rejection as "a particular victory" for Hiram Johnson. "I called him up by telephone last night [Tuesday night, January 29] to congratulate him and he was as happy as a boy." (See p. 285, Harold Ickes, *Secret Diary of Harold Ickes: The First Thousand Days.*)

money, had been awarded, though these companies were not the low bidders. Two days later he made the last charge specific, claiming that Farley was financially interested in the firm (James Stewart and Company) that had won the contract to construct an annex to the New York City post office. And on the day after that, Long introduced a resolution to require Interior Secretary Ickes to lay before the Senate any or all reports of a secret investigation made by Ickes's assistant, Louis Glavis, into the post office building contracts. All this provoked much sound and fury which, in the end, signified nothing so far as Farley wrongdoing was concerned. Long had no actual evidence to present; his charges eventually were emphatically dismissed as frivolous by a large majority of the Senate. But the administration was forced to defend itself. The defensive posture did nothing to correct the impression of weakened and weakening presidential leadership. Meanwhile, Huey Long prospered, his power growing as it fed upon the efforts of administration supporters to stunt it.[4]

On the second anniversary of Roosevelt's presidential inauguration Hugh Johnson was guest of honor at a banquet given in New York City's Waldorf-Astoria Hotel by *Redbook* magazine, which was about to publish a portion of the general's forthcoming book, *The Blue Eagle from Egg to Earth,* as he finally entitled it. The title of his address, which was nationally broadcast over NBC, was "The Pied Pipers"—its subject, an alleged partnership between Huey Long and Father Coughlin in a campaign for dictatorial power over the United States. "You can laugh at Father Coughlin, you can snort at Huey Long—but this country was never under a greater menace," cried Johnson, who then lambasted the "Louisiana dictator and this political padre" for nearly an hour, exercising to the full his major talent for colorful invective and vituperation. Long, obviously relishing the opportunity to do so, replied in kind on the Senate floor next day. He paid far more attention to Roosevelt than to Johnson, focusing at last on Roosevelt's "henchman" Joe Robinson, who was up for reelection in 1936. "Beware! Beware!" shouted Long, glaring at the majority leader, whose face reddened with fury. "If things go on as they have been going, you will not be here next year." The gibe provoked Robinson into a tirade during which Long's words were described as the "ravings . . . of a madman," whereupon an impudently grinning Huey Long, again gaining the floor, announced his intention to go into Arkansas next year to campaign against that state's senior senator. He would do so for the sake of the Democratic party, he said, for though the Democracy was "now in the ascendancy," it had not got there "on the doctrines of the Senator from Arkansas."[5]

On the following day, renewing his attack upon Farley, Long said in a Senate floor speech that to prove his charge of corruption in the postmaster general's dealings with a New York City building supply firm, "the testimony of [New York City Park] Commissioner Robert Moses, and the data which he has assembled, will be called. . . ." This caused perturbation in the White House. The very name Moses was in that moment an embarrassment and a reproach to the President of the United States, and if Moses became a witness before a Senate committee investigating Long's charges, or before a House one investigating a notorious PWA order issued by Ickes (the latter investigation was being pressed for by Republican Representative Bertrand H. Snell of upstate New York), his testimony with its "data" could be seriously damaging to the administration. . . .[6]

The story of how this came to be has its beginnings in September 1933, when in city primary elections Fiorello La Guardia was chosen as Republican-Fusion candidate, and John P. O'Brien as Democratic candidate, for mayor of New York City. O'Brien at that time held the office. He had won the special election to fill out Jimmy Walker's unexpired term following Walker's forced resignation on September 1, 1932, but he had proved a weak executive, who, in his weakness, operated as a tool of John F. Curry's corrupt Tammany. The O'Brien nomination, therefore, disturbed Roosevelt, who, from the White House, kept a close eye on the politics of his home state. He asked Edward J. Flynn to urge Joseph V. McKee, a shining star of Flynn's Bronx organization, to enter the mayoralty race as an independent. McKee, after some hesitation, during which private polling showed he could win a three-way contest, *did* enter the race. It was understood, for Roosevelt had promised Flynn, that at an opportune moment during the campaign the President would personally endorse candidate McKee. The promise was not kept. "When I thought a suitable time had arrived, I went to Washington and asked Roosevelt to do something to show the people of New York that he was behind McKee," writes Flynn. "I met with evasion." This was largely due to highly persuasive advice coming to the President from Adolf A. Berle, Jr., who was a key idea man in La Guardia's campaign organization, who became personally enthusiastic about the leadership qualities of the "Little Flower," and who told Roosevelt ("Dear Caesar") that La Guardia as mayor would be a far more valuable ally of the New Deal than McKee could be, and was likely to win in any case, presidential endorsement or no. He begged Roosevelt to keep "hands off." Roosevelt did so. La Guardia won.*[7]

The new mayor had not been informed of the long-standing personal enmity between Roosevelt and Robert Moses, though one might believe the latter had a moral obligation to mention the highly relevant fact when, in February 1934, he asked Moses to head the Triborough Bridge Authority, the agency which was to build the huge city bridge or bridge complex as a PWA project, using $50 million of federal funds. Moses, who had made the Triborough a key element in his "unified plan for park and parkway development for the state" more than ten years before, accepted the appointment with alacrity, also with the stipulation that he continue as park commissioner and in other appointive offices he held. Reading of this in New York's papers as he breakfasted in bed one morning, Roosevelt reacted promptly, strongly, negatively, furiously (if coldly so)—a reaction abundantly shared and encouraged by Louis Howe,

---

*Berle was appointed city chamberlain, the city's chief financial officer, in one of the first official acts of Mayor La Guardia.

whose hatred of Moses was, if anything, more virulent than his chief's. Ickes was told that the Moses appointment was personally obnoxious to the President and could not be allowed to stand ("[T]he President has a feeling of dislike for him [Moses] that I haven't seen him express with respect to any other person," noted Ickes, wonderingly, in his diary). Ickes at once conveyed this information to La Guardia, who, expressing undying devotion to the President and bitter regret for a mistake born of ignorance, promised to see to it that Moses resigned at once from the authority, quietly.[8]

But Moses flatly refused to go quietly. If he left under these circumstances, he said, he would also give up all his other posts and issue a full public statement of reasons why, a statement devastating to La Guardia as mayor (he would stand nakedly exposed as a coward, too weak to protect an extremely valuable public servant against a purely personal vindictiveness) and also gravely injurious to Roosevelt as President. From an agitated Berle to Roosevelt went a telegram warning of what impended unless the pressure upon Moses to resign was relaxed. "I think this is one of the things you cannot do," said Berle bluntly, "unless there are reasons other than personal. . . . Remember the execution of the Duc d'Enghien broke Napoleon."* Roosevelt made written reply next day. He denied that "the case of your friend, the duc," was in any "sense a personal one." It was grounded in sound general policy, if a policy not theretofore mentioned in this connection. "There are," explained Roosevelt, ". . . a good many cases in other cities and counties and states where it has been necessary to lay down and follow the definite principle that where an independent Authority is set up to carry through a public work, the members of this Authority must be divorced from any other government agency." But he added, significantly, "I have no objection to your friend, the duc, continuing for a short time as a member of the Bridge Authority. . . ."[9] This "short time" then extended through many weeks adding up to several months, during which Ickes now and then pressed La Guardia for definite action, La Guardia twisted and turned in artful, stubborn procrastination, and Moses continued to dominate the Triborough Bridge Authority.

There was "a truce," as Ickes called it, "in order to avoid a charge that I was playing politics" in the late summer and autumn of 1934.[10] In that season, Moses, who had switched his party registration from Democrat to Republican only the year before, this so that he could actively support La Guardia in the mayoralty race, permitted himself to become Republican nominee for governor of New York, running against incumbent Herbert Lehman. He ran very poorly. Indeed, his was conceivably the least politic political campaign in all American history. During it he managed, with his arrogance, his overbearing egotism, his vicious aggressiveness, to alienate virtually every individual and

---

*The Duc d'Enghien's execution in March 1804 on a charge of conspiracy to assassinate Napoleon was sometimes said to be cold-blooded murder by Napoleon of a hated rival for the bedroom favors of a famous actress. The outrage felt by Europe's aristocracy contributed to formation of the Grand Alliance, which ultimately crushed Napoleon.

group he dealt with, including especially those initially most admiring and supportive of him. He suffered a defeat of truly colossal proportions in what was, admittedly, a disastrous year for Republicans generally: The margin of his defeat was greater by nearly 100,000 votes than the defeat Charles H. Tuttle had suffered at Roosevelt's hands in 1930. Clearly Moses now had none of that popularity among the citizenry, that political potency, he had been presumed to have a few months earlier, and Ickes, prodded by an "implacable" Roosevelt, not only renewed but sharply increased his pressure upon La Guardia for Moses's removal from the Triborough. When the mayor continued to stall, Ickes refused to approve a request for further funding of PWA projects in New York City (these projects could continue full force for some months ahead on funds already allocated) and, a few weeks later, collaborated with Roosevelt in the drafting of a special PWA administrative order, No. 129, which said that no funds would thereafter be "advanced to any authority . . . created for a specific project wholly within the confines of a municipality" *if* any member of the authority's governing body held "any public office under said municipality." The order, as first issued, was secret. Only La Guardia received a copy, in a letter from Ickes. And it applied exclusively to the Moses case—or so Roosevelt and Ickes believed when they drafted it.*

A day or so later a harried, worried La Guardia, at Ickes's suggestion, went down to Washington to discuss the order. He met not only with Ickes but also with the President, who had worked out a typically Rooseveltian stratagem. La Guardia was told that if he would promise *in writing* not to reappoint Moses to the bridge authority when Moses's current term expired on June 30, which was a full year before the Triborough could be completed, he need not force Moses's immediate resignation as a condition for receipt of further PWA funds. The mayor said he would write this promise into a letter as soon as he was back in his office. He did not do so, however—not then or ever. For he had shown Order No. 129 to Moses before he departed for Washington (*why* did he do so? one wonders), and before he arrived back in New York City, Moses had released the order to the press, along with an explanation of its meaning. Its sole purpose was to force him out of office, he said, not because he was incompetent or dishonest but because he "was . . . not sufficiently friendly to the Administration." Ickes had admitted as much to La Guardia. And Moses had told the mayor that though he would "be glad to retire from his [La Guardia's] administration entirely if he wanted me to, . . . I would not take a back door out of the Triborough Authority merely because there was pressure to get me out for personal or political reasons." Moses felt a moral obligation to make this information public since federal "appropriations for public works and work relief are the funds of all the people of the country.

---

*Actually, as phrased, the order applied also to Langdon W. Post who was tenement housing commissioner for the New York City administration and also a member of the Municipal Housing Authority, which received PWA money and operated wholly "within the confines of" the municipality. La Guardia was subsequently assured that the order would not be enforced in Post's case.

. . . If personal or political considerations are to govern the expenditure of public works and relief funds by the Federal Government, this fact should be known to the public."[11]

This made banner-head news in New York City newspapers, and front-page news elsewhere in the nation, on January 4, 1935. It abruptly restored to Moses, as hero and martyr, much of the popularity, the prestige he had lost through his election campaign. It forced "Honest Harold" to tell an outright lie when reporters asked him if the President had ever talked to him about Moses. And the flood of protest and denunciation it released, from progressive reform groups that had been strongly supportive of the New Deal as well as from groups and individuals that were anti-New Deal, did not abate through January and February but, instead, continued to swirl ever higher about an increasingly miserable Ickes. It also carried with it an ever-stronger, more widespread popular suspicion that the real author of Order No. 129 was not Ickes but the President of the United States. On February 27 Al Smith entered the fray, decisively, with a press conference in which he told reporters it was utterly "ridiculous" not to permit Bob Moses to complete the Triborough, a project of Moses's own conception; that the Ickes order was "narrow, political and vindictive"; and that he, Smith, could not believe that the President had anything to do with it. This last remark, heard in the White House, had an ominous tone, indeed; it compelled the "implacable" Roosevelt to agree, at last, with Ickes that this battle could not be won. A retreat was necessary. So on the day after Smith's press statement was published, Roosevelt and Ickes arranged for a public exchange of letters between Ickes and La Guardia, with the letters predated to hide the fact that they were incited by the Smith blast —an exchange in which Ickes "backed down" completely, as the newspapers put it, saying that Order No. 129 would not apply retroactively. Those already appointed to the governing bodies of authorities could remain as members until their respective projects were completed. Moses would continue to be, on the record, the chief builder of the great Triborough complex. . . .[12]

These, then, were the circumstances which added a threatful weight to the words in Huey Long's Senate floor speech of March 6 linking "Moses" with "Farley."

Long had also demanded and obtained from NBC forty-five minutes of prime time in which to reply to Hugh Johnson's attack upon him, and he made his reply on the evening of March 7. Highly effective was his use of his allotted time. Dismissing Johnson's statements in a few restrained, disdainful sentences (it would "serve no purpose to our distressed people for me to call my opponents even more bitter names than they call me"), he then devoted some forty minutes to a statesmanlike discussion of the evils of concentrated wealth and to an exposition of his Share Our Wealth plan. He had, that night, an audience estimated to number 25 million people—the largest by far he had ever had.

The ultimate effect of the Johnson attack, which the astute political journalist Raymond Gram Swing described as "a demonstration of political feeble-mindedness," was a swift and huge increase of Long's national prominence.[13]

Invitations to address large audiences now poured in upon Long. A few days after his NBC broadcast he spoke to a crowd of 15,000 in Philadelphia, in a meeting sponsored by the predominantly Republican Congress Club in that city, and skillfully catered to the prejudices of his immediate audience by subordinating Share Our Wealth to a vehement attack upon the Roosevelt administration. He was a great hit; a former mayor of Philadelphia told reporters, just after the speech, that Long as presidential candidate would receive at least a quarter million votes in the city. In late March Long made a speaking tour of South Carolina, whose Democratic officialdom, warned covertly but definitely by the White House that any favor shown the Kingfish might be penalized by a cutoff of federal allotments to the state, did all it could to ignore his presence. Again he was a hit, attacking Roosevelt as a defender of concentrated wealth, an enemy of Progressivism. More than 60,000 South Carolinians enrolled in Share Our Wealth Clubs during this tour, announced Gerald L. K. Smith; more than 140,000 of those who heard Long, in a state where Roosevelt support was stronger than in any other, checked "I will" on cards passed out to them (with pencils) bearing the printed choice of "I will" or "I will not vote for Huey Long for President."[14]

Nor was the situation improved—indeed, it was worsened—from the White House's point of view, when Ickes in an April press conference told reporters that "the trouble with Senator Long is that he is suffering from halitosis of the intellect." ("That's presuming Emperor Long has an intellect," Ickes added.) The remark was the biggest news to come out of that press conference—it made headlines on every front page—and at a cabinet meeting next day Roosevelt spoke of it admiringly, saying that it was the "best thing that has been said about Huey Long." But Ickes did not have the last word in this affair. Three days later, Long, who had just returned from a flying trip to Louisiana, where he had rammed laws through a special session of the state legislature with his usual ruthless efficiency, rose in the Senate chamber to reply to the Ickes gibe. His speech had the gallery rocking with laughter and amused millions who read quotations from it in the newspapers. He pungently described leading figures of the government in "this third year of our reigning empire of St. Vitus" as the "Nabob of New York" (Farley), the "chinchbug of Chicago" (Ickes), the "honorable lord destroyer" of food (Wallace, also designated "Lord Corn-Wallace, the ignoramus from Iowa"), and, presiding over this crazy crew, "Prince Franklin," otherwise known as Franklin De-Lay-No Roosevelt (Long sang out the middle name), who did his heavy thinking about the problems of America's distressed while cruising on a millionaire's yacht and should therefore be dubbed the "Knight of the Nourmahal."[15]

Five days later (April 27, 1935), Long was in Des Moines, Iowa, as principal speaker of a convention of Milo Reno's Farmers' Holiday Association, which seemed to be reviving after a period of dormancy. It was a meeting at which there was much talk of the possibility, the desirability of forming a third party to contest the 1936 election. Long spoke to a crowd numbering well over 10,000, seated in the grandstand of the Iowa State Fairground, and was sensationally successful with those who heard him.* He contrasted New Deal rhetoric with New Deal performance (the essence of New Deal liberalism was "It's all right to say it, but be damn sure you don't intend to do it"); he described with an abundance of statistics the prevailing and increasing concentration of wealth in the country; he vividly deplored the distressful consequence of such concentration ("The Lord has called America to barbecue, and fifty million people are starving"); he made a persuasive presentation of his Share Our Wealth scheme; and when, at the end, he asked all in his audience who believed in Share Our Wealth to raise their hands, virtually everyone in the grandstand did so. "I could take this state like a whirlwind," boasted a jubilant Long to reporters as he left the speakers' platform.[16]

By that time the normally optimistic Jim Farley was taking the Long threat very seriously indeed as he prepared for the campaign of 1936. He was receiving private reports that if Long ran as a third-party candidate, his campaign would be richly financed by "a number of very wealthy people who hated Roosevelt" and who assumed, as did Farley also, that every vote gained by Long would be a vote lost by the President. The possible number of such votes, as estimated by Farley and by Emil Hurja, pollster for the National Democratic Committee, was alarmingly great, especially in view of what Farley announced to the cabinet on May 10 as a "decided shift" of voter sentiment away from the administration, away from Roosevelt, since last fall. (". . . Farley spoke for the first time about the political situation in the country," wrote Ickes in his diary on the evening of May 10. "He was plainly worried. He said that . . . it behooved everyone to see that only loyal Administration men were in the [administration's] service.") Indications were that Long might win from 4 to 6 million votes in 1936—enough, perhaps, to wipe out what would otherwise be Roosevelt's margin of victory if the present shift in voter sentiment remained unchanged. And there was the distinct possibility, of course, that the shift away from the administration would increase.

To a few of his closest associates Roosevelt began to hint at the immediate need for a bold new move on his part "to steal Long's thunder."[17]

III

A second determinative line of force, fusing with that of Coughlin-Long as pressure upon Roosevelt in early May 1935, was the swiftly rising curve of hostility to the administration by the business community and of actual personal loathing of Roosevelt by the affluent generally, following his midterm election triumph.

He could hardly have been more hated by the "rich and wellborn" in this

---

*Among those impressed by this performance—and against his will, for he distrusted and feared Long as "American fascist"—was Robert Morss Lovett, the distinguished English professor of the University of Chicago. Writing of the meeting in the *New Republic* for May 15, 1935 (pp. 10–12), Lovett described the Kingfish as "an engagingly boyish figure, jovial and impudent, Tom Sawyer in a Toga."

springtime of the New Deal's third year if he had actually personally done something during the preceding two years to effect a genuine "circulation of the elite" or to eliminate economic elites altogether in some kind of cooperative organization of scientific technology. In fact, as our record shows, he had done precisely the opposite of this. In accord with his unexamined basic commitment to Capitalism-as-Democracy, Capitalism-as-Christianity, he had at every crucially decisive point thrown his weight into the balance *against* structural change. At the outset he had favored banking as private enterprise over banking as public service, though nationalization of the credit system would have been readily accepted by the public at that moment and would have rendered impossible the kind of "banker conspiracy" against the administration he thought he perceived as early as the fall of 1933. Since then, while continuing to speak often in public about the average man as victim of economic injustice, he had sided again and again with business profit against consumer need, big farmer against rural poor, management against labor, in specific situations where a major shift in the balance of power might otherwise have occurred. Surely, looking cold-eyed at his overall performance and judging it with that hardheaded realism upon which business leaders prided themselves, one must conclude he had done his personal best to preserve the existing class structure and to protect the prevailing elite against the onslaught of powerful historic forces.

Why, then, the monumental hatred of him by members of this elite?

It is a psychological phenomenon difficult to understand—if also a phenomenon highly fortunate for Roosevelt's ultimate standing in history. Perhaps the businessman's hatred was in part a resentful reaction to an attitude Roosevelt may not even have known he possessed, much less expressed in subtle but consistent ways—namely, the aristocrat's disdain for the bourgeoisie's "money-grubbing," for its "trader mentality" and "trader morality." (During his own active involvement in the business world in the 1920s he had never quite been able to regard what he was doing as a serious pursuit; he had "played business" as a game, and none too skillfully.) As for the hatred of him by his own "upper-upper" class, it was in part, no doubt, as it was often said to be, the hatred of class loyalists for one whom they perceived as "a traitor to his class," one who betrayed them to their enemies through an ostentatiously democratic public manner and a public rhetoric of appalling egalitarianism. Certainly the hatred had in it a sense of him as traitorous, slippery, devious, as false in essence as his smile was false, for this sense of him was the central thrust of their verbal assaults upon him; and certainly that constant broad, confident smile of his was, in the eyes of his haters, a constantly infuriating visual taunt. He *should* have been crushed by their collective frown or at least have flinched away from it with, at best, a sheepish grin. Instead, he was, or seemed to be, amused by it, insofar as he paid it any heed at all. Which is to say that they, who were accustomed to being treated with deference and who treated one another with grave respect, were being looked upon as children whose trivial petulancies were entertaining! Roosevelt dared laugh *at them*!

At any rate, whatever its explanation, the hostility, the personal hatred, was a fact. A formidable fact. It matched in kind and intensity the fury which men of privilege and property focused upon Jefferson and Jackson in the early years of the Republic. And an ugly manifestation that spring was a rash of stories, allegedly "funny," certainly scurrilous, about Roosevelt's mental and physical incapacity, about toothy Eleanor's high-pitched "do-gooding" among "niggers" and unemployed miners and other worthless trash, about the crooked business dealings and sexual promiscuity of the Roosevelt children (it must be admitted that their greatly publicized behavior was often of a kind that invited popular censure), stories that circulated out of country-club locker rooms and railway parlor cars, out of the cocktail lounges of luxury hotels and social gatherings in private homes of the affluent, out of rich men's clubs, to some of which Roosevelt himself belonged or had formerly belonged (the Knickerbocker, for one; the New York Yacht, for another), stories that inevitably found their way into the White House, sometimes verbatim, oftener in blurred, nasty echo, and there provoked Roosevelt's angry resentment of personal insult, his contempt and disgust for those who spread such filth.

And not only were this business hostility and elite hatred a fact. They were also a force, a growing force, impossible to ignore in political calculation, since its motivating emotion was being implemented by a large control over mass communications, by an abundance of money with which to finance political campaigns, and by powerful legislative lobbies.

Thus, as April ended and May began, the impact of this second line of force upon Roosevelt personally was augmented by what amounted to a formal declaration of war upon him by the business community.

On Sunday, April 28, Roosevelt broadcast his first fireside chat of 1935. In it he reviewed the steps being taken under the Works Relief Act, and reviewed also major items of the rest of his legislative program, none of which had as yet been passed. These items included the social security bill, a bill to extend NRA two years beyond its present expiration date of June 16, a banking bill to make "a minimum of wise readjustments" in the Federal Reserve System, "legislation to provide for the elimination of unnecessary holding companies in the public utility field," and, though this went unmentioned in the chat, legislation to amend the Agricultural Adjustment Act. On Monday, April 29, members of the U.S. Chamber of Commerce assembled in Washington for their annual convention. The tone of the meeting was set in its opening session by future chamber President Silas H. Strawn. "Businessmen," said he, "are tired of hearing promises to do constructive things, which turn out to be only attempts to Sovietize America." Harsher attacks still were made upon the President and his policies by following speakers. And in its closing session the convention adopted by huge majorities resolutions opposing, item by item, the whole of the President's proposed legislation, including the two-year extension of NRA. (This last resolution manifested a shift of sentiment in the business community. Polls taken only a few months before had shown chamber members favoring NRA extension by nearly three to one while members of the National Association of Manufacturers opposed extension three to one; now the two leading employer organizations were in agreement.) Resolved against, too, having been denounced with special vehemence, was a pending bill which the President had neither proposed nor endorsed and of which, as a matter of fact, he yet personally disapproved in early May. This was the national labor relations bill, a revision of Wagner's labor disputes bill of 1934,* which the New York senator had introduced in the Seventy-fourth Congress in February. "Of course, the interesting thing to me," said Roosevelt to his press conference on May 3, "is that of all these [convention] speeches made, I don't believe there was a single speech which took the human side, the old-age side, the unemployment side." He also read to reporters a news story clipped from a morning newspaper about the "frosty reception that greeted . . . [an] attempt" by Francis E. Powell, head of the United States Chamber of Commerce in London, "to bring peace between American merchants and the White House. Hundreds of delegates of the . . . convention sat in grim silence as Powell proposed that a group be notified to call on Mr. Roosevelt and pledge cooperation." Powell expressed himself as "astonished" and "amazed at the stubborn fight being made by business here against the New Deal."[18]

IV

THE third determinative line of force that focused upon Roosevelt in early May 1935 was closely linked with the second. It was, in fact, a highly effective implementation of the business hostility and elite hatred just described, being an exercise of what amounted to decisive (yea or nay) control by big business over the application of the nation's laws.

This control came from a joining together of three factors. First was the U.S. Supreme Court's self-assumed right to review legislation and determine whether or not it accorded with, was permitted by, the fundamental law of the land; if it did not, it was null and void. Second was the necessary generality, the avoidance of precise specifications, in much of the language of the Constitution, the articles of which were thereby opened to a various interpretation (since the final ruling interpretation was made by judges, the Constitution became whatever the judges said it was, as Charles Evans Hughes had remarked years ago with a candor he now, as Chief Justice, regretted[19]). Third was a virtual monopolization of judgeships, including those of the Supreme Court, by former corporation lawyers,† a majority of whom were disposed to interpret the Constitution narrowly, in the property interest only; they were

---

*See pp. 323–26.
†Of the nine justices of the Supreme Court, only one, Benjamin Cardozo, had never practiced commercial law.

as one with the Liberty League's lawyers in their inclination to deny constitutionality to any legislation that displeased men of property.

Distressing to the President, if not surprising in the circumstances, was the pattern of judicial decision which began to unfold on January 7, 1935, when the Supreme Court made its first ruling upon congressional legislation enacted since March 4, 1933. In an eight to one decision, with Cardozo the lone dissenter, the Court then declared unconstitutional Section 9(c) of the National Industrial Recovery Act, which section authorized the President to prohibit the transportation across state lines of oil produced in excess of state production quotas (it was called hot oil, because illegal); the authorization, ruled the Court, was an impermissible delegation of legislative power to the executive. This boded ill for other sections of NIRA, indeed, for the act as a whole, in upcoming Court tests—and the warning sounded loud in administration ears in early May, by which time there immediately impended a Supreme Court decision on the legal validity, the enforceability, of NRA codes in general. Under consideration by the justices was a case having to do with flagrant violations of the Live Poultry Code by a firm, the A.L.A. Schechter Poultry Corporation of Long Island, which provided chickens for ritual killing and delivery as kosher chickens, through retail outlets, to the tables of Orthodox Jews in the New York City area. The four Schechter brothers had been convicted in a lower court on charges of making false sale and price reports to their code authority and, more seriously, of selling diseased poultry, unfit for human consumption—an "unfair" competitive practice, surely. Roosevelt awaited with some anxiety the disposal of this "sick chicken" case, as Hugh Johnson dubbed it.

His anxiety was not soothed by consideration of other decisions the Court had by then made on New Deal legislation. A little more than a month after its dealings with hot oil, the Court (February 18) had handed down three five to four decisions on the abrogation of the gold clause (that is, the promise to settle obligations in gold coin) in private and government contracts, as mandated by Congress on June 5, 1933. The majority ruling was that such abrogation was constitutional for private contracts, being for these a valid exercise of congressional control over the currency, but *un*constitutional for government contracts, being a violation of an unequivocal commitment by government to those from which it borrowed. However, the Court went on to say, the plaintiff, who had sued for gold payment of a Liberty bond, had failed to show he would suffer actual damages from his acceptance of legal tender in lieu of gold; therefore, the government was not obliged to fulfill its obligation to him. This mixed, logically incoherent verdict, which greatly disappointed diehard "sound money" advocates, brought some relief to the administration, the whole of whose monetary policy had been at risk. But it was far too narrow a squeak for any comfort; it, too, by its nature, boded ill for the future.

This future was further darkened on May 6 by another five to four Supreme Court decision, this one declaring unconstitutional the Railroad Retirement Act of 1934. The act had provided for a pooled old-age retirement fund to which all interstate railroads, and all employees of such railroads, were required to contribute. This requirement, according to the Court majority, violated the Fifth Amendment by depriving the railroads of property without due process of law. Moreover, ruled the Court, the pool arrangement could not be justified as a legitimate exercise of the government's power to regulate interstate commerce since old-age retirement and pensioning had "no reasonable relation" to the "business" of interstate transportation. Such ruling, devastating in its own right, was fully as ominous as the preceding ones; it clearly implied an ultimate Court rejection of federal social security, if the Senate passed the Wagner-Lewis social security bill (it yet languished in Senate committee in early May), as the House had already done.[20]

V

IT was on the day of the Court's Railroad Retirement ruling, also the day that WPA was established by executive order, that arrangements were completed for that White House night meeting, held eight days later, at which Roosevelt probably made and certainly announced his long-postponed fundamental decision.

The meeting's initial stimulant was a letter addressed to Felix Frankfurter on April 22 by David K. Niles, who had been active in the La Follette presidential campaign of 1924, was currently director of the liberal Ford Hall Forum in Boston, and was also, in Frankfurter's words, "one of the most devoted of . . . [Roosevelt's] followers."* Frankfurter sent the letter on to the White House within an hour or so after he'd received it, for he thoroughly agreed with the advice it contained and knew it to be most happily phrased to obtain Roosevelt's acceptance of that advice. "I am quite disturbed at the way our cock-eyed liberals are permitting themselves to be used in the campaign to discredit the Administration," Niles wrote. "I think it is fair to assume that most of them are misled by their inability to grasp fully what it is the President is up against. . . . After all, trying to satisfy a hundred and twenty-five million people is a somewhat different problem from trying to please the relatively few thousand readers of the *Nation* and *New Republic*. . . ." Niles, looking forward to the election year, was worried about the "different so-called progressive and liberal organizations that are cropping up all over the country" in opposition to a New Deal that seemed to them to be veering more and more to the right. Niles went on:

> It occurs to me that a frank talking-things-over between the President and these liberal and progressive leaders from all over the country should be of real help. It should be a kind of executive session from which all reporters are barred and during which these liberal and progressive leaders could tell the President what it is that disturbs them about his program and have him explain to them why it is so difficult

---

*Niles later became a principal assistant to Harry Hopkins as WPA administrator and, later still, a White House assistant to both Roosevelt and Truman.

to progress as rapidly as he and they would like. . . . I for one believe, of course, that the President has a definite program [most of the "liberal and progressive leaders" were definitely *not* convinced of this, as Niles implied], the carrying out of which depends on proper timing. If these people could be assured, as I think the President can assure them, that it *is* only a question of timing and that he is not going back on them, you will find that they are just as anxious to support him as they were when he first went into office.[21]

A few days later Frankfurter, in the White House, talked over this suggestion with Roosevelt, who told him to go ahead, with Niles, to arrange the meeting. On May 2, shortly after receiving a telegram from the White House definitely scheduling the affair for eight-thirty Tuesday evening, May 14, in the Oval Room, Frankfurter discussed the matter with George Norris, who happened to be in Boston that day. As the professor reported to the President in a letter on the following day, Norris stressed the "importance of a small gathering for an effective interchange," whereupon Niles, drastically scaling down his original idea, "had the happy thought of including only those Senators who were members of the National Progressive League for Franklin D. Roosevelt in 1932. This means, alphabetically, Costigan, Cutting, [Hiram] Johnson, La Follette, Norris, and Wheeler. It draws . . . a relevant line against the inclusion of men like . . . [Gerald] Nye. . . . Two members of your Cabinet, Wallace and Ickes, were also members of the Progressive League. What are your wishes with regard to their inclusion?" If they were included, the conferring group would number eleven, counting Frankfurter, Niles, and Roosevelt himself—just the right number, Frankfurter thought, for the purpose to be served. Roosevelt thought so, too, and said so in a telegram he sent Frankfurter from the Executive Office a few minutes after he had arrived there on Monday morning, May 6. The appropriate White House invitations were then promptly dispatched and as promptly accepted, with eagerness, by their recipients.[22]

Not every one of them, however, was received. Bronson Cutting never saw his.

Early in the morning of that eventful Monday the New Mexico senator was riding an airplane, a TWA DC-2, back to Washington from his home state. He had been forced to go there for affidavits in support of his election of last November—that is, to defend his Senate seat against the challenge being made by Dennis Chavez, the Democratic candidate he had so narrowly defeated, a challenge Roosevelt had initially encouraged. Only a few days before, Cutting had celebrated his forty-seventh birthday. He was a strangely lovable man, for all his darkly brooding taciturnity, with brilliant abilities and an absolute integrity, as everyone recognized. (Though so ill with tuberculosis that he did much of his studying and writing in bed, he at Harvard had won a Phi Beta Kappa key and had been graduated with honors.) His health had been good now for several years, had improved over the last two. He seemed assured of future greatness; many predicted for him a place among the supreme statesmen of American history, provided he surmounted this immediate obstacle which Franklin Roosevelt had put in his way.

But over Kansas, at three o'clock in the morning, his plane flew into thick fog; near Kansas City it crashed. Five persons, among them Bronson Cutting, died in the wreckage.

A few hours later this death was announced in the Senate chamber, where it shocked Norris, La Follette, Borah into tearful breakdown.[23]

At about the same time Steve Early brought the news to the President at his desk in the Executive Office.

And Roosevelt might deem it divinely significant, providential in the sense of its being a frown of disapproval from on high upon his management of this affair, that he was at that moment in conference with Harold Ickes, a friend and great admirer of Cutting's. He must respond to the fatal news in what became at once an *accusing* presence, as he felt. He responded defensively. He greatly regretted this tragic occurrence, he said, for he was "mighty fond of Bronson," whom he had "known since he was a boy." He had not wanted "to do anything to hurt him." He had opposed Cutting's reelection only because "a lot of Bronson's retainers in New Mexico are not considered especially nice citizens." But Ickes, who "felt very keenly" in that moment the loss of this "forceful, independent, and progressive" man, "one of the strong men of the Senate," was in no forgiving mood. "Mr. President," said he, "no one can come out of New Mexico into political life who doesn't have a bad crowd somewhere in his background, and his [Cutting's] crowd was not a bit worse than the Democratic crowd in that state."

On Thursday of the same week Ickes lunched with the President and son James Roosevelt on the open porch just outside the Executive Office. It was a lovely spring day. The White House grounds were a vivid green; the great overarching trees were in full leaf; the air the three men breathed was sweet with the fragrance of freshly blooming flowers. But for the President, evidently, the new eager life he saw and breathed, a yearning, hungering, thirsting life, was a deeply reproachful reminder of untimely death, of cold, indifferent death, for he spoke again, in terms Ickes heard as conscience-stricken, of the demise of Bronson Cutting. He understood, he said, that Senator Norris was "very bitter" about this death and was inclined to blame him, Roosevelt, for it. Ickes's reply was hardly conducive to presidential ease of mind. Such reaction, he indicated, must be expected in the circumstances.

One must assume that it was in an at least somewhat penitential mood that Roosevelt faced Bronson Cutting's personal friends and great admirers— Senators Norris, Borah, Johnson, Costigan, Wheeler, and La Follette, with Harold Ickes—along with Wallace and Frankfurter and Niles, in the Oval Room on the following Tuesday night. Certainly he, in his opening remarks to his guests, virtually invited verbal chastisement, for he stressed that they had been invited here to voice with complete candor their views on the current legislative and political situation, their views on what should be done about it. He said he hoped they would do precisely that. Certainly the talk which followed was frank. It was, at the outset, almost brutally so.

Burt Wheeler and Bob La Follette "did most of the talking," according to Ickes, "but they did a pretty good job of it."[24]

Wheeler, who had introduced the holding company bill in the Senate (Rayburn had introduced it in the House), condemned in the strongest terms the President's repeated compromisings of liberal principles in a vain effort to appease and conciliate the very men, big businessmen, whose insatiable, stupid greed had plunged America into its current troubles. He spoke with a bitterness that matched Huey Long's (Wheeler was almost the only senator who was on personally friendly terms with Huey) of the betrayal of progressives whose leader the President professed himself to be. He deplored the President's failure to exercise any leadership at all, to put it bluntly, in recent months. Roosevelt broke in at one point of this harangue to ask why Wheeler hadn't come to him weeks or months ago to voice these opinions in face-to-face meeting. Because, replied Wheeler with some heat, he had been denied access to the White House. Roosevelt never asked him in, and whenever he sought an appointment, he was told by Marvin McIntyre that the President was "bogged down," his schedule absolutely filled. Roosevelt protested this. "You can get in to see me any time within twenty-four hours," he said. Replied Wheeler, emphatically: "I can't get in at all." Thereupon Roosevelt suggested that Wheeler, in future, seek his appointments through Missy LeHand.[25]

Bob La Follette, if less bitter than Wheeler, was equally condemnatory of the President's recent performance. He described as "fortunate" the attack the United States Chamber of Commerce had just made upon the President, for it demonstrated the futility of efforts to obtain big business cooperation with the administration at the expense of New Deal aims. Never would these businessmen support the President, not even if he abandoned or tailored to their narrow self-interest every administration bill now pending before Congress, and if he attempted such appeasement, he would lose the country to the likes of Long, Coughlin, Townsend. The administration bills added up to "a fine legislative program," in La Follette's estimation; the "best answer" to Huey Long was that program's enactment by Congress in its current session. And this, put in Wheeler, would require vigorous leadership by the President himself. He could not count upon Joe Robinson and Pat Harrison to do the job. Wheeler conceded that the President had "gotten a great deal out of Robinson"—an astonishing amount, in fact—but he, of course, knew that neither Robinson nor Harrison had the slightest sympathy with the New Deal as a liberal, progressive enterprise. La Follette then "reminded the President," significantly, "that Theodore Roosevelt did not hesitate on occasion to take open issue with members of his own party. . . ."[26]

To all this, and more like it, the President listened courteously, sympathetically, deferentially, with a show of gratitude for wholesome candor, yet without surrendering an iota of his control over the situation in that room (from first to last he dominated by force of personality). And to it all he replied at last along the lines Niles had suggested in his April 22 letter. He spoke of the importance of timing, of awaiting patiently the opportune moment, then recognizing it when it came. A wise leader must know when not to lead actively but, instead, to stand aside while things "work themselves out" as far as possible toward a desired end, or far enough to demonstrate absolutely that they are not working in that direction at all. (At the dining table a couple of hours ago, Roosevelt had told Frankfurter with "tender sadness" of his failed hope "that the big leaders of finance and business would learn something"—words which Frankfurter repeated to Brandeis a day or so later. The grand old judge "very gravely shook his head and said, 'I understand truly his feeling. We have all had that hope from time to time, but apparently they just can't.' ") But now, said Roosevelt with dramatic, inspiring effect upon the men before him, "the time has come" to move ahead again, decisively, vigorously, toward New Deal goals. There would be leadership action in the days just ahead, lots of action.[27]

It was an inspired and invigorated group of men, again enthusiastically committed to Franklin Roosevelt, who left the Oval Room shortly before midnight. "There is no doubt about the high success of the Tuesday night session," wrote Frankfurter from Cambridge two days later. "I have heard from all the Senators except Norris and Hiram Johnson, and they all were truly happy. According to Bob La Follette 'it was the best, the frankest, the most encouraging talk we have ever had with the President. I know Burt felt the same way about it for I went home with him. . . . The President was fair, and frank, and I felt greatly encouraged that he is going into the stride of his old aggressive leadership.' "[28]

And so, in effect, the fundamental choice was at long last made.

It was certainly no clear-cut choice between national planning and Brandeisian piecemeal reform, or between government spending as a means of recovery and government economy as a necessity for recovery, or between inflationary and hard-money policies, or between either side of other equally flat and basic alternatives. It meant no drastic, immediately obvious change of direction. As a practical matter it amounted to little more than a shift of emphasis among programs and proposals already in hand, with some shrinkage of the margin of indeterminacy between opposing principles or opposing categories or classes of action. The margin would remain wide enough, would provide plenty of operating room, for Roosevelt's peculiar brand of pragmatism. But the choice *did* mean abandonment of a major portion of the strategy of broker government which Roosevelt had theretofore employed—the portion which had involved him to a politically dangerous extent in practical contradictions of his own New Deal rhetoric, practical compromisings of his own New Deal aims. From now on he would do what the advocates of liberal reform had advised: He would accept business hostility as the price he must pay for doing what was good for the American people as a whole. And out of this acceptance there came to him a sudden expansion of freedom. A release. He was enabled to emerge from the land of quandary with its quagmires of doubt and irresolve, its dark forest of uncertainties, into an open country where maneuver was again possible. Indeed, he now burst out into the open, propelled by an energy that had been dammed up, unspent, for nearly nine months; he emerged into a leadership activity as intense as that of 1933's Hundred Days, and far more consistent in its motives and aims.[29]

VI

ON the night of his meeting with the liberals, during which he convinced them anew of his basic commitment to liberalism, there lay on his desk, awaiting signature or veto, a veterans' bonus bill. This was the bill, with its provision for financing an immediate bonus payment with fiat money, which Texas's Wright Patman had pressed for in every congressional session since 1931.* It had passed the House of the Seventy-fourth Congress with a huge majority and, on April 28, had gone through the Senate by a vote of 55 to 33. Every senator invited into the Oval Room on May 14 had voted for it. Garner, the practical politician, was advising Roosevelt to veto it, then tacitly acquiesce in a congressional override of the veto; the issue would thus be out of the way and forgotten by election year 1936. Morgenthau, the voice of Roosevelt's conservative conscience in this matter, was urging him to veto forcefully and fight forcefully against an override. For days before and after the May 14 meeting Roosevelt wavered between the two options. Under Morgenthau's prodding he prepared a veto message which was, in Morgenthau's estimation, the "most forcible and striking" statement of the President's "since his inauguration." He also encouraged Morgenthau to build what the treasury secretary described as a "bonfire of support for you in your veto message," inside and outside Congress. Yet when Patman with twenty-one of his colleagues called upon him on the morning of May 10 to ask if he had closed his mind absolutely against the bill, he said he had not. There was, he hinted, a possibility of compromise. And he teasingly reported this to Morgenthau when the two men lunched alone together on that same day. Morgenthau was horrified. Should he then go ahead with this "bonfire" he was building? Oh, of course, said Roosevelt, but without mentioning "bonfire" to him again. He promised in return not to mention "compromise" again to Morgenthau. "In other words," he added, with mischievous grin, "never let your left hand know what your right hand is doing." Morgenthau, trying to adapt to the President's mood, then asked which "hand" *he* was. "My right hand," replied Roosevelt promptly. "But I keep my left hand under the table."[30]

In the end, Roosevelt plumped for Morgenthau and conscience. He did so dramatically. In as complete a departure from precedent as had been his flight to Chicago to accept the presidential nomination in person, he went before Congress on May 22 to deliver his veto message in person. He also arranged to have the proceedings broadcast by network radio, the first radio broadcast ever made from the House chamber, where he spoke. The essential argument

*See Davis, *FDR: The New York Years,* pp. 344–45.

made in this speech, which was more closely reasoned than most he gave, was such as Herbert Hoover might have made. It was not at all persuasive of House members; a few hours later they voted 322 to 98 to override the veto. Nor was it overwhelmingly persuasive of the Senate, which next day voted 54 to 40 to override. But the Senate vote fell short of the two-thirds needed, the veto was sustained, and the manner in which Roosevelt had won this narrow victory, the demonstration he had made of courageous commitment to principle, restored to him some of the prestige, the confidence in him as bold, forceful leader, which had been lost over the last half year. *Time* magazine for that week reported an alleged consensus among "newshawks" covering the White House that "Franklin Roosevelt's mood had changed," that the "irritability which had marked his recent actions" had "suddenly . . . dropped from him." His "winter peeve" was over, said *Time,* and he was now once more "the President of two years past, taking the political initiative, breaking precedent with verve and satisfaction."[31]

Then, on May 27, 1935, the Supreme Court handed down its decision on *Schechter* v. *United States.*

The government's side of the case had been argued by Stanley Reed, newly elevated from the post of RFC general counsel to that of solicitor general of the United States, and by Donald Richberg himself, had been argued so much more eloquently and cogently than had the other side* that New Dealers assembling in the courtroom at noon on the fateful Monday had considerable hope mingled with their apprehension.† They were kept in suspense as long as possible, for Chief Justice Charles Evans Hughes had arranged the reading of opinions, with obvious concern for dramatic effect, in an order of ascending importance.

First, those assembled had to listen to an opinion on a relatively minor case involving the New York Life Insurance Company, read by Justice Pierce Butler. Then came an opinion, read for a unanimous Court by Justice George Sutherland, saying that President Roosevelt had been in gross violation of the Constitution when he removed from the Federal Trade Commission, without cause, one William E. Humphrey, a Republican appointee and vehement partisan who had used his FTC position to obstruct administration policies. (The opinion seemed to New Dealers a gratuitous slap in the face for Roosevelt insofar as Sutherland's language made the President's action seem a willful, arrogant, unprecedented abuse of power. Actually a Court majority had ruled in 1926 that the executive had such removal power as Roosevelt in this case exercised.) Third was an opinion on the Frazier-Lemke amendment to the National Bankruptcy Act, designed to provide relief for farm mortgagors in default. This was not, strictly speaking, a New Deal measure; the administra-

---

*The other side was presented by corporation lawyer Frederick H. Wood, whose principal argument (that government regulation of an industry as small as live poultry implied government regulation of all business and, ultimately, all human activity) was not the one on which the Court grounded its decision.
†The courtroom was the Senate chamber of the Republic's early years in the Capitol. The marble palace which was to house the Supreme Court in the near future had not yet been completed.

tion had not introduced it or pressed for its passage, but when it did pass in June 1934, the President had signed it without demur. Now it was ruled unconstitutional, a violation of "due process" as guaranteed by the Fifth Amendment, in an opinion prepared for a unanimous Court by Justice Louis Brandeis. ("If the public interest requires, and permits, the taking of property of individual mortgagees in order to relieve the necessities of individual mortgagors," said Brandeis, "resort must be had to proceedings in the eminent domain; so that, through taxation, the burden of relief afforded . . . may be borne by the public.")[32]

Came then the climactic moment.

The heavily bearded and often beard-stroking Chief Justice of the United States was always Jove-like in appearance and generally aloof of manner, as if above and beyond the interests and passions of ordinary mortals. He seldom evinced much warmth of feeling. But as he read the argumentative opinion he had prepared for a unanimous Court on the *Schechter* case, his voice had throbs of emotion, his manner grew animated, his delivery became almost oratorical. Obviously he savored this moment in history's spotlight; obviously he felt strongly what he was saying.

And what he was saying was, in one major portion, an enlargement of the legal ground upon which he had stood with seven of his brethren in the hot oil case. The Live Poultry Code, he said, was but an instance of an NRA code-making authority that was flagrantly unconstitutional, being a legislative power that Congress had no right to delegate to the executive. (In a concurrence which Justice Stone also signed, Cardozo distinguished the hot oil case, wherein he had been the lone dissenter, from *Schechter,* saying that the legislative power delegated by NIRA's Section 9(c) had been precisely defined, whereas the "delegated power of legislation which has found expression in this [live poultry] code is not canalized within banks that keep it from overflowing. It is unconfined and vagrant." The appalling number of codes, hundreds upon hundreds of them, each to be enforced through the courts, was "delegation running riot.") NIRA was, therefore, in its code-making provisions, null and void.

But this was not all, nor was it from the White House point of view the most devastating part, of what the Chief Justice had to say. He went on to state or unmistakably imply a very broad definition of "local" as an adjective for "industry" and a very narrow definition of "interstate" as an adjective for "commerce," while also making a distinction between "direct" and "indirect" effects upon interstate commerce. He seemed to be saying (he quoted a statement from an earlier Court ruling to the effect) that virtually every economic activity—construction, mining, manufacturing, agriculture—was "local," simply because it happened someplace, and, as such, was not subject to federal legislation under Section 8 of Article I of the Constitution* unless it had a *direct* effect upon interstate commerce. If the effect was indirect, the federal

---

*This section says, in its relevant part, "The Congress shall have Power . . . To regulate Commerce . . . among the several States. . . ."

government could do nothing about it, no matter how great that indirect effect might be. (With this last, if not with Hughes's initial distinction, Cardozo, and Stone, disagreed. "The law," said Cardozo in the otherwise concurring opinion, "is not indifferent to considerations of degree.") Since the Schechter firm was engaged in local industry having no direct effect on interstate commerce,* its violations of the wage and hour provisions of the code were not violations of federal law; NIRA's wage and hour provisions were in general as null and void as its code-making provisions—and so would be, presumably, any other attempt by the federal government to regulate such matters.[33]

The news of this striking down of one of the twin "pillars" of the New Deal's recovery program had shocking impact upon the national consciousness. It produced relief and anxiety, exultancy and despondency, hope and despair, anger and gratification, but in relative proportions, over the nation and the economy as a whole, impossible to assess. The business community might have been expected to react with unalloyed joy to this slapping down of the New Deal, this judicial insurance against further federal encroachments upon the freedom of "free enterprise." Instead, this community's emotional, interested reaction was mixed. New England textile manufacturers, for instance, feared with good reason a renewed competition with cheap-labor southern mills, though they realized that NRA had provided very imperfect defense of them against such competition. Prescient industrialists in other areas of the economy feared with good reason the wave of strikes which, as AFL's William Green predicted, would now flood high against their factories.

And there is reason to believe that Franklin Roosevelt's emotional reaction was equally mixed, that it had in it no small component of relief.

Marion Dickerman was a guest in the White House on that Black Monday of the New Deal. By her own account, she and Eleanor "dreaded going down to dinner that night" and tried to think of things to say that would cheer up the President, for they expected to find him plunged deep into the slough of despond. But he wasn't! Or if he was, he gave not the slightest sign of it. He seemed, if anything, more than normally zestful and buoyant. The Supreme Court was not so much as mentioned at the dinner table! And when Marion went later into his bedroom, as was customary, to bid him good night, he "was sitting up in bed with his old sweater on, working on his stamps," and, to all appearances, was "perfectly happy and at peace with the world." A day or so later, talking with Frances Perkins, he frankly confessed that the "whole thing [NRA]" had become "a mess" of which he was not unhappy to be relieved. He said that "some of the things done in NRA" had been "pretty wrong," that

*Only a year before, ruling on a case of racketeering in New York's live poultry industry, the U.S. Supreme Court had upheld a federal court injunction aimed at the racketeers, rejecting the argument that live poultry was a strictly local industry and hence not subject to federal regulation under the commerce clause. The Court had then said explicitly that the live poultry industry *did* affect interstate commerce, and this statement had been a major factor in the decision by Homer Cummings and Donald Richberg to use *Schechter v. United States* as the NIRA test case before the supreme tribunal.

"perhaps NRA has done all it can do," and that he definitely did not "want to impose a system on this country that will set aside the anti-trust laws on any permanent basis." As long ago as the last of August 1934, having just failed in his effort to prevent the great textile strike, which was essentially a strike against NRA labor policy, he had told Frankfurter that he wished now to retain of NIRA "only (1) minimum wage, (2) maximum hours, (3) collective bargaining and (4) child labor" provisions, as Frankfurter had then reported to Brandeis in a handwritten note.[34]

But he *was* disturbed, and profoundly disturbed, by the Court's ruling with regard to the commerce clause, and it was upon this that he focused in what became one of the most memorable of all his press conferences, on Friday morning, May 31, 1935.[*]

By then he had received through Corcoran an oral communication from Brandeis, "Old Isaiah," as Roosevelt called him, given to Tommy Corcoran and to Ben Cohen in the justices' robing room a few minutes after Black Monday's opinion reading had ended. Highly unusual and of dubious propriety, in view of the constitutional separation of powers, was the giving of direct advice, warning, threatening advice, by a Supreme Court justice to a chief executive regarding the latter's future legislative policy, but this is what Brandeis had emphatically done. The seventy-eight-year-old justice was "visibly excited and deeply agitated" as he "gasped" out that the President "has been living in a fool's paradise," that the three decisions just handed down by a unanimous Court meant that "[e]verything that you [the administration] have been doing must be changed," that an extensive redrafting of existent and pending legislation would be necessary. "This is the end of this business of centralization, and I want you to go back and tell the President that we're not going to let this government centralize everything. It's come to an end." By then, too, Roosevelt's desk had been inundated by letters and telegrams of advice on the situation the Court had created. (". . . I suppose we have had about fifty different suggestions," remarked the President to the first of his press conferences to be held following Black Monday; it was held on Wednesday of that week. "They go all the way from abolishing the Supreme Court to abolishing the Congress, and I think abolishing the President. That is, to make it complete. . . .") Actually the truly thoughtful advice divided fairly evenly between those who favored new legislation, devised by them, which they believed would meet the Court's objections, and those who favored a constitutional amendment rendering the general welfare clause specific, unequivocally giving Congress national economic regulatory power. Moley and Frankfurter both favored an amendment but differed concerning the timing of the proposal. Moley believed it should be pressed for *now*. Frankfurter, in a letter which Roosevelt had talked over personally with its author, for the law

---

[*]In his first presidential press conference (see p. 44). Roosevelt had announced that he would regularly hold a conference on Wednesday morning and Friday afternoon, but this had been changed to Tuesday afternoon and Friday morning.

professor with his wife, Marion, were houseguests at the White House on that press conference Friday, expressed his belief that the "fighting out" of the issue between Court and President might well be postponed until decisions in other cases "accumulate popular grievances against the Court on issues so universally popular that the Borahs, the [Bennett Champ] Clarks, the Nyes, and all the currents of opinion they represent will be with you in addition to the support you have today." Frankfurter himself, it should be pointed out, as a Brandeis disciple, had had no use for NRA. He went on:

> That is why I think it is so fortunate that the Administration has pending before Congress measures like the Social Security bill, the Holding Company bill, the Wagner bill, the Guffey [coal] bill. Go on with these. Put *them* up to the Supreme Court. Let the Court strike down any or all of them next winter or spring, especially a divided Court. *Then* propose a Constitutional amendment giving the national government adequate power to cope with national economic and industrial problems. That will give you an overwhelming issue of a positive character arising at the psychological time for the '36 campaign, instead of mere negative issue of being 'agin' the Court which, rising now, may not be able to sustain its freshness and dramatic appeal until election time.[35]

Frankfurter, not wishing it to appear to the public or to his patron, Brandeis, that he had any responsible connection with what the President had to say, declined Roosevelt's invitation to attend the press conference of May 31, but as the reporters assembled in the Oval Room at ten o'clock, more than 100 of them, filling the room in dense crowd pressed against the President's desk, Marion Frankfurter was there, seated at one side and behind the desk, and Eleanor Roosevelt was there beside her, busily plying her knitting needles upon blue yarn, making a sock. The President himself, almost unprecedently, was late—twenty minutes late—clearly indicating a far greater than normal concern and preparation. Yet the usual broad smile was upon his face when he at last arrived and, as usual, opened the meeting with persiflage.

"What's the news?" he asked.

"That's what we want," one of the reporters replied, going on to ask if he would "care to comment any on NRA."

"Well, Steve, if you insist," said Roosevelt. "That's an awful thing to put up to a fellow at this hour in the morning just out of bed."

And he continued in light humor as he suggested that "we make this background and take some time because it is an awfully big subject to cover, and it is just possible that one or two of you may not have read the whole twenty-eight or twenty-nine pages of the Supreme Court decision."

His smile faded, however, and his manner became grave, as he went on to discuss a decision whose "implications . . . are . . . more important than [those of] any decision probably since the Dred Scott case" since they raised a question of profound historic importance—namely: "Does . . . the United States Government . . . have control over any national economic problem?" Or were governmental economic controls the exclusive province of the forty-eight states, despite the obvious fact that the sovereign power of no single state was able to effect such controls in any of the major areas of national economic life?

First he read in whole or in part fifteen telegrams he had received from businessmen since last Monday (". . . all from businessmen, every one") expressing dismay over the renewed cutthroat competition, "sweatshop competitions," which must follow any obliteration of "fair competition" codes. The telegrams, he said, were representative of a "huge pile" received from anxious small businessmen, each a plea that he "do something" right away.

Then he reviewed that portion of the decision which dealt with improperly delegated powers. The Court had mentioned "in passing that . . . [NIRA] was passed in a great emergency" but had gone on to say that this "did not make any difference." According to Hughes, "Extraordinary conditions do not create or enlarge constitutional power." And surely this statement had "a very interesting implication" when considered in relation to, say, the war emergency legislation of the spring of 1917. "[A] great deal of that [1917] legislation was far more violative of the strict interpretation of the Constitution than any legislation that was passed in 1933." To the extent that it was legislation needed for success in the war effort, one must be grateful for the fact that it was not brought before the Supreme Court while the war emergency was on. If it had been, and the Court of that time had been of the same mind as the Court of today, the process of winning the war would have been declared unconstitutional, hence impossible!

But "in this particular case," Roosevelt went on, the Court's ruling upon the "delegation of legislative power" was "not so very important" because the Court had cited "with approval" such delegation as was made by law to the Federal Trade Commission and had indicated that NIRA's deficiency in this regard could be supplied by some fairly easy changes in the "language of the Act."

Far more important was the portion of the decision "that relates to interstate commerce." Here the Court had seemingly "gone back to the old Knight case of 1885, which in fact limited any application of [the] interstate commerce [clause] to goods in transit—nothing else!" Various Court decisions since 1885 had "enlarged on the definition of interstate commerce" so that it "applied not only to the actual shipment of goods but also to a great many other things that affected interstate commerce. . . . The whole tendency over these years has been to view the interstate commerce clause in the light of present-day civilization. The country was in the horse-and-buggy age when that clause was written. . . . There wasn't much interstate commerce at all [in 1787]—probably 80 or 90 percent of the human beings in the thirteen original states were completely self-supporting within their own communities." How totally different the situation today! "We are interdependent—we are tied together," and so closely that virtually no economic activity of any importance in any locality was without effect upon economic activities in other localities.

He took emphatic exception to the definition of "local" implied by a citation Hughes had made, approvingly, from an earlier Court decision, that of *Indus-*

trial Association v. *United States,* wherein it was said that "building is as essentially local as mining, manufacturing or growing crops" and was, therefore, "outside the reach of the Sherman Act" unless its effect on "interstate trade" could be shown to be definite and direct, not "a fortuitous consequence . . . remote and indirect. . . ." What this implied outraged common sense! Though a completed building was assuredly "a part of the land," its construction was of materials (steel, stone, cement, lumber, etc.) which came to the building site, in large part, through interstate commerce. Most of the raw materials and finished products of manufacturing were articles in interstate commerce. The farm machinery and fertilizers employed, and the crops and dairy products and livestock produced, in agriculture, all were articles in interstate commerce. So were the machinery and products of mining—the coal, oil, iron, copper, etc.* Surely economic facts so perfectly obvious must be taken account of in any sensible, realistic definition of the "interstate commerce clause"; surely Congress in its drafting of legislation should be able to "depend on an interpretation that would include not only those matters of direct interstate commerce, but also those matters which indirectly affect interstate commerce."

But the Supreme Court in this case, setting a precedent for future decisions, said No!

"We have been relegated," said Franklin Roosevelt, "to the horse-and-buggy definition of interstate commerce."

As for what he intended to do about it, he had nothing to say. Suggestions were pouring in, but no final decisions were in process of being made save those having to do with the dissolution of NRA in compliance with the Court's decision. These would be announced within the next few days. (In early June was announced the abolition of seven labor boards created under NRA; three presidential advisory agencies created under NRA, including the Office of Special Adviser to the President on Foreign Trade which George Peek had held and used to the maximum extent possible to frustrate and obstruct Cordell Hull's reciprocal trade program; and all the huge and intricate bureaucratic apparatus of NRA save a "skeleton organization" the primary function of which was the classification and analysis of voluminous records, invaluable to future historians.)[36]

This hour and a half of uninterrupted discourse greatly impressed its immediate audience with Roosevelt's command of factual detail, his grasp of logical implication, his general philosophical mood derived from, sustained by, strong emotions under control. It influenced what newsmen and columnists wrote and so affected the great constitutional debate which now began and continued

---

*With regard to mining, an unsmiling Roosevelt found it "rather interesting" but not at all amusing "that in the past, when mine operators sought injunctions against labor . . . the Supreme Court has tended to approve mining injunctions on the ground that the coal was going into interstate commerce. This case, however, seems to be a direct reversal in saying that where you try to improve the wages and hours of miners, the coal suddenly becomes a purely local intrastate matter and you can't do anything about it. Of course, here the shoe is on the other foot."

with varying intensity for two years. But all of it remained "background," unquotable and unattributable, save for a single phrase. "Can we use the direct quotation on that horse-and-buggy stage?" asked one of the reporters as the conference drew to a close. "I think so," said Roosevelt, turning to Press Secretary Early. "Just the phrase," said Early.[37] And this quoted phrase, stripped of context, gave the general public a false impression of the tone of this press conference and of the President's personal reaction to the judicial setback of the New Deal. He was made to seem rancorous—not only furious with the decision but also with the justices who rendered it. For inevitably, the phrase became detached in the public mind from that interpretation of the commerce clause which Roosevelt had intended it to describe; it became attached instead to the Court itself. Roosevelt was widely believed to have said, in effect, that the nine members of the supreme tribunal were old fogies who were trapped mentally in the horse-and-buggy era in which they had been reared.

The general public reaction to this was by no means wholeheartedly approving. Many who were sympathetic to the New Deal and who deplored the NRA decision were inclined to deplore equally, if not more, Roosevelt's presumed contempt of court. In press and radio commentary were expressed a good deal of cold disapproval and not a little outrage over an ill-tempered attack upon a sacred institution—and these were expressed, too, in those samplings of the presidential mail which were periodically sent up from the White House mailroom for Roosevelt's review. There was enough of this to give Roosevelt pause as he considered the possibility of pressing at once an attack upon the judicial roadblock and the constitutional issue it raised. He presided noncommittally over a series of highly agitated White House conferences; he listened to hours of vehement and conflicting advice as May ended and June began. His conclusion was that the best thing he could do with regard to Constitution and Court was, for the moment, nothing at all.

-»>X«-

Breakthrough:
The First New Deal Gives Way to the Second

I

YET there was nothing passive or yielding in the response he now made to the challenge he faced.

To those who cried out in tones of anguish or jubilation that the New Deal had been shattered beyond repair, that it was dead or dying, his answer was the veritable storm of executive-directed legislative action known to history as the Second Hundred Days, though by actual count the days numbered eighty-five, whereby was launched the Second New Deal.

It began in the first week of June 1935.

Members of Congress were preparing to wind up their work for that session in three or four weeks and then to adjourn, escaping the humid heat which now settled over Washington (though air-cooling devices had just been installed in the Capitol) and leaving much of the administration's legislative program unenacted, when, abruptly, congressional leaders were summoned to the White House and there told by a grimly determined, desk-thumping President that what they contemplated doing was impossible. They must remain in session until they had enacted *every* major administration bill that had been introduced, bills they had been dawdling over for months now, and on his list of absolute must legislation he placed social security, the Wagner labor bill, a banking bill making important changes in Federal Reserve, and the Wheeler-Rayburn utilities holding company bill. A fortnight later, on June 19, he placed a fifth item on the must list. In a special message that caused more consternation among the economic elite than any other he had thus far delivered, he called for major tax reform in a bill (a "soak-the-rich" bill the rich called it) frankly designed to alleviate "social unrest and a deepening sense of unfairness," wherefrom Huey Long prospered, by increasing taxes on high incomes and accumulated wealth.

By that time, using Ben Cohen and Tommy Corcoran as his principal bill draftsmen and Corcoran as his chief operating agent in dealings with Congress, the President was exerting unremitting pressure and employing all his leadership skills and tools—he charmed, he cajoled, he promised, he threatened, he tricked (on occasion), he made ruthless use of such patronage power as remained to him (it was, of course, considerably less in 1935 than it had been in 1933 and 1934)—to get his program through. There was no letup. He labored with a vengeance (literally vindictively, in the belief of some weary congressmen and virtually all the affluent), filling every minute between his breakfast tray and his midnight bed, save for sharply curtailed cocktail and dinner hours, with conferences, phone calls, missive dictation, face-to-face negotiations, planning sessions. A strategy was devised for each bill and pursued tactically with dodges and turns and shifts of pressure that confused and divided opponents. On constant display were his zestfulness, his incredibly good-humored patience, his tenacity, his persistence, his driving forcefulness, and, throughout and overall, a radiant energy, extravagantly spent from some seemingly inexhaustible inner source, whereby everything and everyone around him were galvanized.

When Congress at last adjourned on August 27, ending the longest session (225 days) since 1922, Roosevelt had pushed through, or permitted to be enacted in addition to his must legislation, "the most comprehensive program of reform ever achieved in this country in any administration," as a reluctantly admiring Walter Lippmann wrote in a letter to a friend.[1]

Let us consider, item by item, the legislative history of these measures.

II

THE Wagner-Lewis social security bill was well along toward passage when the Second Hundred Days began. Having gone through the House with a huge majority in April and been reported out of Senate committee for floor debate in mid-May, it required no more than a nudge from the President to make its way to passage through the Senate by a vote of 76 to 6 on June 19. There was attached to it in the Senate, however, a troublesome amendment. Proposed by Bennett Champ Clark, the intermittently conservative Democrat from Missouri, it would exempt from the payment of the social security payroll tax all employers who had their own private pension schemes. Only after weeks of wrangling in joint conference committee, during which the administration employed arguments of principle and logic and (most effectively) constitutionality, did the Senate conferees give in. With the amendment removed, the bill went back to House and Senate for swift final action and was ceremoniously signed into law by the President on August 14.

This Social Security Act of 1935 was, in several respects, "an astonishingly inept and conservative piece of legislation," as William E. Leuchtenburg has said.[2] It excluded from coverage those most direly needful of it. Its initial benefit payments to the aged who were covered were low (they ranged from $10 to $85 a month), even by depression standards. Its hodgepodge of state and federal jurisdictions made it an administrative nightmare, especially with regard to unemployment insurance. It made no provision for health insurance. Its financial "self-sufficiency," insisted upon by Roosevelt, involved complete dependence upon a regressive tax which was to do grave damage to the economy only two years hence. (In June 1937 the coincidence of a drastic slash in government spending and the collection of $2 billion in social security payroll taxes triggered, in August, what became justly known as the Roosevelt Recession; there then were sharp declines in industrial production and security values, equally sharp rises in unemployment.) Indeed, Roosevelt's flat opposition to any general revenue financing of the system would become a root cause of social security's dangerous financial crisis of the 1970s and 1980s.

Nevertheless, the ceremonial signing of the act marked one of the major turning points of American history or, to employ a metaphor more apt, the removal of a major obstacle to that history's "natural" course as it flowed through the twentieth century. This obstacle was the "rugged individualism" which stubbornly insisted (it could never again insist with total effectiveness) that government, though "morally" obliged to provide a "climate" favorable for business profits, had no responsibility whatever for the welfare of mere human beings, common folk of modest abilities and aspirations, who did the work from which profit, as surplus value, was reaped. The flood thus loosed was of irresistible weight and irreversible direction.

Moreover, much that was deplorable in the act was offset by the quality of its initial administration.

John R. Commons used to tell his college students that given a choice between imperfect legislation well administered and perfect legislation poorly administered, they should not hesitate to choose the former, and the operations of Roosevelt's 1935 appointees to the three-member Social Security Board* were as if designed to prove the wisdom of Commons's admonition. For chairman, Roosevelt chose John G. Winant, the Progressive Republican who had sponsored much advanced social legislation while governor of New Hampshire (1925–26, 1931–34) and had done yeoman service as a member of the Advisory Council of the Economic Security Committee, the committee that had drafted social security. Lincolnesque in appearance and temperament, conscientious to a fault, inclined toward melancholia, Winant possessed marked leadership qualities that included an ability to inspire in subordinates and associates a disinterested devotion to the common good. He himself was obviously a good man, selfless, with great sweetness of character. The other two appointees were Vincent Miles, an Arkansas lawyer otherwise unknown to history but an able man, and, most important, Wisconsin's Arthur Altmeyer, who promptly demonstrated a rare genius for organization and administration. It was largely due to Altmeyer that despite the enormous administrative complexities and myriad invitations to disaster presented by the act he had helped shape, sound patterns of procedure were soon established, along with policy precedents that would ever after be followed.

Within two years every one of the forty-eight states passed the necessary implementing legislation. Within two years Social Security became what it would still be a half century later: a governmental agency remarkable for the smooth efficiency with which it performed immensely complicated tasks. No

---

*It was set up as an independent agency, an element of the administrative chaos encouraged by Roosevelt's penchant for blurred delegations of authority and overlapping assignments of responsibility, so that the final decision would be always his. But in this case the independence was fortunate. The original Economic Security Committee proposal was to place the board in the Labor Department, but this ran afoul of conservative hostility to the views and person of Frances Perkins.

private insurance company operated in the late 1930s, or would operate fifty years later, with so small a proportionate overhead cost.

III

WAGNER'S national labor relations bill was also well along toward passage by early June 1935. This redraft by Wagner and Leon Keyserling of the labor disputes bill Roosevelt had sidetracked in June 1934 differed from the earlier bill in several respects. Abandoned was the notion that the three-member labor relations board should consist of a labor representative, an employer representative, a "public" representative. All three members were now to be "public." Abandoned, too, was the notion that the board should have as its major function the mediation or arbitration of labor-management disputes. Its exclusive purposes now were to be a defense of labor against "unfair labor practices," which were given detailed definition, and a practical assurance to labor of its right to organize and bargain collectively, a right spelled out in specific detail. "Thus," as J. Joseph Huthmacher has written, "the new measure made clearer than ever the difference between Wagner's approach to labor relations and the 'get them back to work at any price' approach shared by people like Hugh Johnson and, to some extent, the President himself."[3]

This President, certainly, had done nothing to encourage the redraft, the bill's introduction in the Senate on February 21, or its passage through the Senate thereafter. Neither had Secretary of Labor Perkins, who had not even been consulted during the redrafting process and who told the President, when the bill was about to be introduced, that it was unlikely to be enacted because the AFL would balk at the requirement of proof by a union that it represented a majority of the workers before being accredited by the board as collective bargaining agent. (She quickly learned better: The AFL officialdom was enthusiastically supportive of the Wagner bill.) During the hugely publicized hearings on the proposal, held by the Senate Labor Committee in March and April—hearings in which the assault on it was spearheaded by Henry I. Harriman of the U.S. Chamber of Commerce and James Emery of the National Association of Manufacturers—Roosevelt maintained public silence, refusing even off-the-record commentary when asked about it in his press conferences. Secretary Perkins testified in favor of the bill, but she did so with no enthusiasm; most of what she had to say was an argument in favor of revising the bill so as to place the National Labor Relations Board in the Department of Labor instead of establishing it as an independent agency, a revision Wagner resisted. Yet, at hearings' end, the bill was promptly reported by the Labor Committee for floor action, this on May 2, with only such amendments as its author favored. Indeed, the committee report was actually written by Wagner and Administrative Assistant Keyserling at the behest of committee Chairman David I. Walsh of Massachusetts.

Consternation ensued in the opposition camp. Big business opponents conceded among themselves that if the bill "comes to a vote, it will undoubtedly pass" (the words are those of NAM's Emery) and that only White House intervention could now prevent this dreadful event. They, therefore, worked through Majority Leader Robinson and Finance Committee Chairman Pat Harrison to press Roosevelt to intervene, as he had a year ago when he blocked passage of Wagner's labor disputes bill.

They had reason to hope he would do as they wished. . . .

Last fall one Dean Jennings, top rewrite man on Hearst's San Francisco *Call-Bulletin,* had been summarily fired from his job, obviously solely because of his organizing activity on behalf of the American Newspaper Guild, which columnist Heywood Broun had launched in 1933. Jennings appealed to the San Francisco Regional Labor Board, local unit of the National Labor Relations Board established by Roosevelt, in June 1934. The San Francisco board, in pursuance of Jennings' plea, filed a complaint of antiunion discrimination, as presumably authorized under NIRA's Section 7(a), and asked the newspaper as employer to appear before it. The newspaper refused. The Regional Labor Board had no jurisdiction in this case, the publisher claimed, because a special labor board had been established under the NRA Newspaper Code Authority to deal with such cases. This was standard operational procedure for employers in those industries which had special labor boards set up through their NRA codes or for which other boards of this nature had been established. The newspaper code had been drafted by publishers at a time when the Newspaper Guild was far too weak to be consulted, save out of a sense of fairness which the publishers notably lacked, and its special labor board was therefore stacked in favor of the publishers. Jennings knew his case to be hopeless if dealt with by NRA. So he persisted in his appeal to NLRB, now headed by Francis Biddle of Philadelphia,* who had accepted the appointment when the first chairman, Lloyd Garrison, resigned to return to deanship of the law school at the University of Wisconsin in the fall of 1934. The *Call-Bulletin* also persisted in its contention that NLRB had no jurisdiction. It refused to introduce evidence supportive of its side of the dispute. Thereupon "brash young Biddle," as Broun admiringly called him, ordered the newspaper to reinstate Jennings in ten days' time or be cited for removal of the Blue Eagle, with the order to be sent to the Department of Justice for enforcement in the courts. The virtually unanimous response of the publishers was a loud protest based on alleged violation of the First Amendment (that is, "freedom of the press")—a protest in which even the normally prudent and reasonable New York *Times* emphati-

---

*Also of Groton-Harvard. He was destined for a cabinet post in Roosevelt's administration. Biddle's eldest brother, Moncure, had entered Groton, aged twelve, in the same year as Roosevelt entered at age fourteen and had been described by Roosevelt in a letter to his parents as "quite crazy, fresh and stupid"; his next oldest brother, George, who was among the most famous of American artists by the 1930s, was among those Grotonians who had a decided and permanent aversion to the domineering personality of Headmaster Endicott Peabody; and Francis himself had been a second former when Roosevelt was a sixth former, a fact of which Roosevelt reminded him sometimes when a felt subordination on his part was wished for. (See Davis, *FDR: The Beckoning of Destiny,* pp. 110–111; Francis Biddle, *In Brief Authority,* pp. 4–5.)

cally joined—and the summoning of a convention of all 1,200 publishers who had signed the newspaper code. It was to meet on January 28, 1935, to decide what action to take regarding the "gravest problem with which the press of this country has yet been confronted." The implication was that the publishers would resign from the code in a body.

The publishers were joined in this protest, if on different ground, by slippery, turncoat, excessively ambitious Donald Richberg, who, when NRA was reorganized at the time of Hugh Johnson's departure, had become chairman of the National Industrial Recovery Board and, as such, the effective administrative head of NRA. Richberg in those months was riding high. In the press he was sometimes described as "Assistant President," and certainly he had, that fall and winter, entrée to the White House on a more frequent and seemingly intimate basis than almost any other Washington official. But like Hugh Johnson, if with greater operative efficiency, he seemed to regard his role not as that of government official serving the general public but as top administrator of an agency controlled by, and representing within the executive, the business interest. He continued adamantly to oppose the majority-rule principle in the determination of labor's representation in bargaining negotiations with employers, he continued to favor pluralistic methods which drastically weakened labor's side in such bargaining (this in flat opposition to declared NLRB policy), and he now tried desperately "to get us to drop the [Jennings] case," as Francis Biddle has written. His desperation was "perhaps accounted for by the fact that, with or without the nod of his chief [Roosevelt], he had induced the newspapers to come into the code by assuring them that complaints from the Guild would go to the code [labor] board," Biddle goes on to say. Whatever his motive, Richberg in December 1934 used his entrée to the White House to impress upon Roosevelt his view of Biddle and NLRB as arrogantly self-assertive and traitorously disregardful of Roosevelt's wishes, and his view of Newspaper Guild "representatives" as men "not acting in good faith, but simply trying maliciously to make trouble."

In January 1935 Roosevelt was persuaded to intervene in the Jennings case on Richberg's (the publishers') side of the dispute: He sent the NLRB chairman a letter—"a curious document, half casual, half peremptory"; also "clumsy," lacking in "frankness," and factually inaccurate, according to Biddle—ordering NLRB to stay out of cases where machinery for the "final adjudication" of labor disputes had been established in the industry code. Biddle's two colleagues on the board wanted to resign at once; all of Biddle's persuasive power and all of Roosevelt's charm in a face-to-face meeting with them were required to keep them from doing so. The publishers' convention was then called off, and a disgusted Heywood Broun, confirmed in his opinion that Roosevelt lacked courage and honesty, "told reporters that the newspaper publishers had cracked down on the President of the United States and Franklin D. Roosevelt had cracked up."[4]

Hence the not unreasonable hope with which big businessmen awaited the outcome of efforts by Robinson and Harrison to persuade the President to act against Wagner's bill, at least to the extent of postponing a Senate vote upon it.

But it was now early May, when the several lines of force were converging to focus as a single pressure upon Franklin Roosevelt. Harrison and Robinson were a good deal less persuasive as they argued their case during a tense meeting in the White House than they would have been a few months earlier, especially since Wagner, in the same meeting, argued the opposite case much more powerfully and in urgent pleading tone. At meeting's end Roosevelt continued to refuse to endorse the bill, but he told Robinson, Harrison, and a vastly relieved Wagner that he would do nothing against the bill either. He would let it come to a vote.

A few days later, on May 15, in response to a question from a reporter about his attitude toward the proposal, Roosevelt told his press conference that he had not "given it any thought one way or the other."[5]

On that same day Wagner brought his bill onto the Senate floor with a powerful speech in its behalf, a speech far more persuasive of its disinterested hearers and readers than it was pleasing to the White House, for it was in part and effect a bitter indictment of New Deal labor policy thus far. The failure to sustain Section 7(a) while permitting price-fixing and production quotas by industry had "driven a dagger close to the heart of the recovery program," he declared. Such improvement as there had been in wage and hour conditions for labor, under NRA, were limited to those industries in which labor was sufficiently well organized to force its way into the writing of codes. Otherwise, and in general, "unemployment is as great as it was a year ago. Average weekly hours of work, which stood at 37¼ when the codes were established in the fall of 1933, stand at 37½ today. The real income of the individual worker employed full time is less than in March, 1933. The average worker's income in 1934 was $1,099, or $813 less than the amount required to maintain a family of five in health and decency." Far from correcting the income imbalance between labor and industry, the New Deal through its NRA had greatly increased it, and Wagner, be it remembered, had had his name on the national industrial recovery bill and been its chief Senate sponsor. Ruefulness was therefore implicit in what he went on to say: "In December, 1934, payrolls registered only 60 percent of the 1926 level, while dividend and interest payments were fixed at 150 percent of that level. Total wages have risen only 28 percent in the last two years, while 840 corporations have increased their profits from $471,000,000 in 1933 to $673,000,000 in 1934, a gain of 42 percent. Net profits of 1,435 manufacturing and trading companies increased from $64,000,000 in 1933 to $1,071,000,000 in 1934, or 64 percent, while their annual rate of return rose from 2.7 percent to 4.5 percent." And this manifest "failure to maintain a sane balance between wages and industrial returns" was bound to "be attended by the same fatal consequences as in the past." It was responsible for the aborting of the several "recovery booms" that had seemed to begin in 1933 and 1934; there "had been built up" no mass purchasing power "adequate . . . to sustain" recovery. Hence the dire need for adoption of his national labor relations bill, legislation which would go far toward the restoration of economic balance, legislation which was, in fact, "the only key to the problem of economic stability if we intend to rely upon democratic self-help by industry and labor, instead of courting the pitfalls of an arbitrary or totalitarian state."[6]

Next day, after only desultory debate, every one of the crippling amendments of the bill prepared by NAM was voted down by a huge majority (the major one, introduced by Maryland's Millard Tydings, went down 50 to 21), and the Senate passed the bill 63 to 12.

There was no doubt the House would follow suit, regardless of the White House attitude, when House leaders conferred with Roosevelt on the matter. He interposed no objection to a report of the measure to the House floor for action, and on May 20 the bill was reported. Four days later he announced his support of the "principles" of the bill, and in early June, after the Supreme Court ruling on *Schechter* had destroyed Section 7(a) along with the rest of NIRA, he finally placed the bill on his must list, as has been said. The House passed it without even a roll-call vote in late June, and the President signed it on July 5.

Thus was enacted what many historians came to regard as one of the twin pillars of the Second New Deal, social security being the other, though, alas for any truly sharp distinction between successive historical "periods," both pillars had been substantially constructed long before the First New Deal came to an end and, moreover, would almost certainly have been erected (enacted) even if Roosevelt had failed to make that fundamental choice out of which came the Second Hundred Days. But there can be no question that the Wagner Act rivaled social security in importance; it was one of the very few New Deal measures which actually made a difference in the politicoeconomic power structure of America.

IV

THE public utilities holding company bill, unlike social security or the labor bill, was in serious trouble in early June and required for its passage thereafter all the force of leadership that Roosevelt could and did apply to it.

Introduced by Wheeler and Rayburn on February 6, it had been longer under consideration by the Seventy-fourth Congress than any other administration bill and had encountered far stronger opposition than any other. It also had the longest gestation period, having begun to be conceived at the very height of the New Economic Era. In 1927 there had been loud popular outcry against utilities holding companies, accompanied by demands for increasingly strict regulation of them, following disclosures by a special Senate Committee on Campaign Fund Expenditures of the corruptive use of money by Middle West Utilities, Western United Gas and Electric, and other similar corporations during the 1926 midterm elections. In that same year William Z. Ripley published his highly popular and influential *Main Street and Wall Street*, almost a fourth of which was devoted to the dubious character of much utilities financing and to the social dangers consequent upon the rash of mergers that had occurred in the utilities field since 1925. In the following year, defying "the mightiest lobby ever assembled in Washington" up to that time, the Senate had voted for a full-scale long-term investigation of holding company activities, to be conducted by FTC. Subsequently, the House Commerce Committee had voted an investigation of its own in the same area, through the Federal Power Commission. And Roosevelt referred to both these ongoing investigations in a letter of July 5, 1934, which ordered Ickes to establish within PWA a National Power Policy Committee and asked Ickes to serve as its chairman. The committee, whose eight members included David Lilienthal and Morris L. Cooke, was "to develop a plan . . . whereby . . . electricity may be made more broadly available at cheaper rates to industry, to domestic and, particularly, to agricultural consumers." More specifically, since "legislation on the subject of holding companies and for the regulation of electric current in interstate commerce" would "undoubtedly" be required, the committee "should consider what lines should be followed in shaping this legislation." Such "consideration" and "shaping" became the committee's prime function. Ben Cohen, who was appointed the committee's general counsel, was assigned in late 1934 the task of drafting the needed holding company legislation. He did so, of course, in collaboration with Tommy Corcoran, and the two men had an abundance of factual information, along with a plethora of specific legislative proposals, to draw upon when the FTC and Power Commission investigative reports were completed, and when the ICC and the Treasury Department developed recommendations of their own for reform of the utilities by means of the taxing power.[7]

The final draft bill, which Wheeler and Rayburn introduced, consisted of two titles. Title II empowered the Federal Power Commission to coordinate and integrate operating companies into regional systems that made sense in terms of efficient delivery of light and power, this in place of the systems now prevailing which had been determined in large part by the greed of organizers. But it was upon Title I that controversy focused, for it contained what became at once known as a death sentence or death clause for superfluous holding companies in the utilities field—holding companies established for the sole purpose of "leverage," enabling financiers to control vast utilities "empires" with a minimum of capital investment; holding companies that imposed phony "service" charges upon operating companies, artificially inflating costs for rate-making purposes while, at the same time and in the same way, "milking" the companies that actually made and distributed electricity; holding companies that corrupted the public mind with huge lying propaganda campaigns, campaigns that equated "patriotism" and "Americanism" with acquiescence in the utilities' peculiar brand of "free enterprise" and that went so far as to insert falsehoods into school textbooks and other teaching materials through bribery of authors, publishers, state education officials; holding companies that, in sum, were productive of nothing but profit and corruption through the manifold devices of their organizers for gouging, cheating, deceiving the general public. Title I authorized the Securities and Exchange Commission (SEC) to work with the utilities companies toward a stripping down of their enormously complex organization into administratively efficient simplicity. If the companies cooperated in this beneficent enterprise, well and good. But if they did not, as most assuredly they would not voluntarily, SEC was empowered to compel by January 1, 1940, the dissolution of all holding companies which were unable to prove, on sound economic grounds, their right to exist.

Inclusion of this mandatory "death sentence" had been insisted upon by Roosevelt. Cohen in his first draft of the bill had relied upon strict federal regulation and the taxing of companies in proportion to their holdings of stock in other companies as the means of eventual elimination of superfluous corporations. It was the man who had headed the House Commerce Committee's investigation of the power industry, Walter M. W. Splawn, formerly of the University of Texas, now of ICC, who proposed the outright abolition of holding companies. And at the decisive White House conference on Cohen's initial draft, Roosevelt had plumped for the Splawn approach, which was then written into the final Title I by the Cohen-Corcoran team.[8]

When the bill was introduced, however, it was without the President's specific formal endorsement.

There followed five bitter winter weeks during which the utilities, with Wendell Willkie of Commonwealth and Southern as principal spokesman, raised such hue and cry as had not been raised against a single measure, perhaps, since Stephen Douglas's Kansas-Nebraska bill was before Congress in 1854. The number of utilities lobbyists in the capital soon exceeded by nearly one-fourth the number of senators and representatives assembled in the two legislative chambers. Public speakers, newspaper editorials, columnists, and radio commentators proclaimed the proposed legislation to be the most pernicious, the most threatful to "our system of government" ever to come before Congress. Telegrams and letters descended by the thousand, day after day, upon Senate and House desks, and the humane concern they expressed for widows and orphans whose livelihoods depended upon holding company dividends was of heart-wringing intensity.

Clearly there was need for the most emphatic presidential endorsement of this bill if its passage was to be achieved, and on March 12 Roosevelt provided it in a special message transmitting to Congress the final report of the National Power Policy Committee.

Title I of Wheeler-Rayburn, said the President, "drafted under the direction of Congressional leaders, incorporates many of the recommendations of this [attached] report." He went on:

> I have been watching with great interest the fight being waged against public utility holding-company legislation. I have watched the use of investors' money to make the investor believe that the efforts of Government to protect him are designed to defraud him. I have seen much of the propaganda prepared against such legislation —even down to mimeographed sheets of instructions for propaganda to exploit the most far-fetched and fallacious fears. I have seen enough of it to be as unimpressed by it as I was by the similar effort to stir up the country against the Securities

Exchange bill last spring. . . . We seek to establish the sound principle that the utility holding company so long as it is permitted to continue should not profit from dealings with subsidiaries and affiliates where there is no semblance of actual bargaining to get the best value and the best price. If a management company is equipped to offer a genuinely economic management service to the smaller operating utilities companies, it ought not to own stock in the companies it manages, and its fees ought to be reasonable. . . . But where the utility holding company does not perform a demonstrably useful and necessary function in the operating industry and is used simply as a means of financial control, it is idle to talk of the continuation of holding companies on the assumption that regulation can protect the public against them. Regulation has small chance of ultimate success against the kind of concentrated wealth and economic power which holding companies have shown the ability to acquire in the utility field. . . . Except where it is absolutely necessary for the continued functioning of a geographically integrated operating utility system, the utility holding company with its present powers must go."

He concluded: "I am against private socialism of concentrated private power as thoroughly as I am against governmental socialism. The one is equally as dangerous as the other; and the destruction of private socialism is utterly essential to avoid governmental socialism."[9]

But this emphatic statement did nothing, of course, to diminish the strength of the utilities' attack on the bill. Quite the contrary. Working with the public relations firm which Ivy Lee had founded, the Committee of Public Utilities Executives and the American Federation of Utility Investors organized the expenditure of some millions of dollars in a concerted effort to destroy not only the bill but also its sponsors, especially That Man in the White House, against whom, with or without the blessing of the top organizers, a vicious whispering campaign was launched. (Roosevelt was alleged to have suffered a complete mental breakdown, to have become subject to maniacal fits of laughter, to have collapsed into hysteria when the Supreme Court's NRA decision was handed down.) And the attack, having gathered momentum during the weeks of continued basic indecisiveness and seeming abrogation of leadership on Roosevelt's part, had become by early June dangerously effective.

On the eve of the Senate vote on a crucial amendment to the bill, proposed by Democratic Senator William H. Dieterich of Illinois, who was under tremendous pressure from the utility interests in his state—an amendment which would substitute regulation for the dissolution of holding companies—the rumor spread that Roosevelt himself was succumbing to the attack, that he had agreed to accept Dieterich's proposal. Burt Wheeler found the rumor so plausible that he phoned Missy LeHand to obtain at the earliest possible moment an interview with the President. This earliest moment proved to be during Roosevelt's breakfast hour next morning. The senator was greeted with calm good cheer by a President who yet lay abed, propped against pillows, and who at once "turned on the charm and reassured me that he was standing pat," Wheeler recalled long afterward. "I suggested that he make a public statement to clear the air. He didn't want to do that, but he called for a pencil and paper and scrawled out a short statement. 'You can show this to the boys,' he said, giving the sheet of paper to me. He did not intend for me to make it public

—I suspected he was being very careful in what he was saying to the utility people privately."

But shortly before the amendment vote was taken on June 11, Dieterich rose on the Senate floor to insist that Roosevelt had clearly indicated his willingness to strike the "death sentence" from the bill's Section 11. Wheeler promptly countered by reading aloud Roosevelt's "Dear Burt" note verifying "my talk with you this morning," the note saying: ". . . I am very clear in my own mind that . . . any amendment which goes to the heart of the major objectives of Section 11 would strike at the heart of the bill itself and is wholly contrary to the recommendations of myself." The note's reading obviously decided the vote's outcome. For the administration's victory margin here was as thin as it could possibly be. The amendment was defeated by a single vote, 45 to 44. Eight Progressive Republicans voted against it. Voting for it were twenty-eight Democrats, including twenty who had theretofore been unwavering (if sometimes grumbling) in their support of New Deal legislation. Roosevelt could and did see here the first manifestation of a development he had expected with no little anxiety, and done all he could to prevent—namely, an organized coalition of Republicans and conservative Democrats which could become a frustrating hazard to the New Deal. In the present instance, however, after their narrow amendment defeat, most of the conservative Democrats gave up. When the Senate voted upon the bill as a whole with the "death sentence" in it, the measure went through easily, 56 to 32.[10]

More serious and stubborn, and more ominous in its manifestation of developing conservative coalition, was the utilities-sponsored revolt against administration leadership in the House, which up till then had been almost wholly docile in its submission to White House dictates.

In part, the change was due to the removal of Alabama's William B. Bankhead from the chairmanship of the powerful House Rules Committee, a post he had held in 1933 and 1934. As Rules chairman he had consistently made or approved parliamentary rules favorable to the administration, including the gag rules which greatly aided swift House adoption of every major measure of the First New Deal. But now Bankhead was majority leader of the House; he had been elevated to that post following the death of House Speaker Rainey in late 1934 and the elevation of former Majority Leader Joseph T. Byrns to the speakership. The chairmanship of the Rules Committee had then devolved, through operation of the congressional seniority system, upon abrasive, aggressive, conservative (or reactionary) John J. O'Connor, a Tammany Democrat.* O'Connor had in the past been generally, if unenthusiastically, supportive of the administration. To the "death sentence," however, he was strongly op-

---

*He was a brother of, though differing in personality from, Basil O'Connor, Roosevelt's former law partner and present agent in the management of the Warm Springs Foundation. Basil O'Connor was himself no fervent New Dealer, despite his membership in the original Brain Trust and continuing warm personal friendship with Roosevelt. In November 1934 he had represented in litigation Howard C. Hopson's Associated Gas and Electric Company, a giant holding corporation wherein was concentrated every evil against which Wheeler-Rayburn was aimed.

posed. And in a White House conference on June 13 he urged a compromise on this issue, pointing out that the House Commerce Committee was at that moment deadlocked over an amendment to the bill akin to the one Dieterich had proposed in the Senate, that there was every likelihood the reported bill would include this amendment, and that the present temper of the House favored the adoption of this amendment. House members, after all, were more vulnerable than senators to the kind of pressure the utilities now exerted, facing as they did an election campaign every two years. Hence, if the President continued to stake his prestige without reservation upon the success of his view of this matter, he risked a defeat on the House floor as damaging to his leadership as it would be humiliating to him personally. The argument failed to persuade—was, indeed, almost contemptuously rejected by a President who increasingly disliked O'Connor personally. There was no cause for worry, said Roosevelt, flatly. In a record vote on a measure support for which was a clearly designated requirement of party loyalty on the part of Democrats, any obnoxious amendment was bound to go down to decisive defeat; the bill would then sail through the House in the form the President desired.

But this didn't happen. And one important reason why it didn't was John J. O'Connor in his role as Rules chairman.

The bill which was at last reported out of committee on June 20 had the mandatory "death sentence" removed from its Title I. Substituted was a clause saying that SEC, while possessing the power to dissolve holding companies, could exercise that power in the case of any particular holding company only if it proved dissolution to be clearly in the public interest. On the face of it, the difference between this reported bill in the House and the one the Senate had passed seemed of no truly crucial importance. It amounted simply to a shift of the burden of proof. The Senate version required holding companies to prove their right to exist, the House-committee version required SEC to prove its right to dissolve, and in either case the worst evils of the present setup would, it seemed, be eliminated. This, however, was not the way in which the difference was perceived by either side of what now became a bitter congressional quarrel. Administration supporters at once proposed an amendment restoring the "death sentence"; Roosevelt moved at once to ensure that the vote on this amendment was a roll-call vote, so that loyalty could be recognized, disloyalty punished; and Rayburn, at Roosevelt's urging, went in person before the Rules Committee to plead for the special rule which, under House procedures, a recorded vote on an amendment to a bill would require. Rayburn pleaded in vain. A now thoroughly antagonized O'Connor persuaded his committee colleagues to join with him in denying to the administration the wished-for special dispensation.[11]

So when the vote was taken on the amendment, it was a teller vote, not a roll call. It was taken on July 1, after days of heated debate, during which animosity to the White House was openly displayed for the first time to any significant extent on the House floor by members of the President's own party. Congressman George Huddleston of Alabama, who in committee had led the fight to strike out the "death sentence," was actually cheered by scores of fellow Democrats when proclaiming himself an exponent of the "old-fashioned Southern Democracy of Thomas Jefferson," he excoriated Corcoran and Cohen as "bright young men brought down from New York to teach Congress how to shoot" and damned the bill they had drafted for a complexity beyond the capacity of "a Philadelphia lawyer" to understand and interpret. The vote subsequently taken went overwhelmingly against the administration. Restoration of the "death sentence" was defeated, 224 to 152, the first truly major defeat Roosevelt had ever suffered in the House, and when administration stalwarts then proposed to substitute for the House version of the bill the Senate version in its entirety, they went down to defeat in a recorded vote, 258–147. Next day the committee-reported bill was passed, 323 to 81, an outcome whose announcement was also cheered in the House chamber, long and loudly, according to the New York *Times*.[12]

The battle now shifted to the joint conference committee, where for a long time all attempts to reconcile the chief difference between the House and Senate versions failed. "I will do what I think right and all hell cannot stop me from it," Huddleston had cried, with "hell" clearly identified with White House pressure, and in this rebellious mood the House conferees, of whom Huddleston was one, refused to yield an inch to Senate conferees (they even barred bill author Ben Cohen from conference sessions!) with the result that the wrangling continued from early July well into August.

But meanwhile, sensational public disclosures were being made of the nature of the lobbying campaign the utilities had mounted, disclosures whose impress upon the popular mind had effect upon the ultimate fate of the legislation in question. They were made by a special Senate Lobby Committee, chaired by Hugo Black, which had been appointed after the authenticity of signatures to a number of telegrams received by legislators, urging defeat of the bill, had been tested and found to be nil. There was a lobby investigation by the House, too, but its conduct was assigned, cynically, one suspects, to the Rules Committee, which, under O'Connor's chairmanship, was not disposed to conduct it openly or vigorously. Black *was* so disposed. He would fight fire with fire, as he had done in his airmail investigation, making no pretense of judicial impartiality but proceeding, instead, as a prosecuting attorney or a muckraking journalist bent on exposing and convicting malefactors. The tactics he employed, including extensive use of dragnet subpoenas, whereby all messages between specified individuals within specified time limits were required to be delivered to him, provoked loud protest from defenders of the Bill of Rights, notably the American Civil Liberties Union and, in a much-quoted column, Walter Lippmann, as well as from the utilities and their supporters. None could deny, however, that his tactics served well his immediate purpose; they spread before the public a great deal of relevant information that would otherwise have remained hidden.

Black's agents descended one morning, without warning, upon the chief utilities lobbyist in Washington, Philip Gadsden, chairman of the Committee of Public Utilities Executives, who was then rushed before the committee and forced to answer Black's probing questions without benefit of prepared testimony; the lobbyist admitted the expenditure of more than $300,000 in a few weeks in efforts to influence Congress and told enough of how the money was spent to guide Black's future research. Roused at midnight to receive a subpoena, then brought before the committee a few hours later was an advertising man who admitted under oath, since Black had in hand the evidence, that he was the one who had initiated and helped spread coast to coast the rumor that the President had gone insane. The Western Union manager at Warren, Pennsylvania, was brought before the committee to testify that on orders from his company's headquarters in New York City, he had cooperated with the top local official of Associated Gas and Electric in the preparation and dispatch to the congressman for that district of 1,000 telegrams signed by names selected, in part, from the city directory and that the originals of these messages had then been burned, in violation of FCC and Western Union regulations. The top local utilities official in Warren confirmed this testimony (he was under orders from *his* corporation's headquarters to do as he did). When Howard C. Hopson, chief organizer and head of Associated Gas and Electric, went into hiding for a fortnight to escape service upon him of a Black subpoena, then presented himself before O'Connor's committee, which proposed to hear his testimony in secret, Black made such public issue of the matter that House Rules Committee members overruled their own chairman and turned Hopson over to Black. He, Hopson, was an unusually slimy type even in an area of corporate endeavor that abounded in slimy types (Insull, Doherty, Doheny, Sinclair, et al.)—in 1940 he was to go to jail for defrauding his stockholders—and his self-damaging, utilities-damaging testimony, expertly forced by Black's questioning, capped the climax of Black's exposé. A few days later, in a national network radio broadcast, Black summarized what he had discovered about what he described as a "high-powered, deceptive, telegram-fixing, letter-framing, Washington-visiting, five-million-dollar lobby."[13]

By these disclosures, the persuasiveness of arguments by Senate members of the joint conference committee were greatly strengthened. Still, however, Huddleston as leader of the House conferees remained adamant, though by this time a compromise formula generally acceptable to both sides, if very reluctantly agreed to by a Franklin Roosevelt whose "Dutch was up," had been worked out by Felix Frankfurter and presented on behalf of the Senate conferees by Alben Barkley of Kentucky. It required SEC to abolish by January 1, 1940, utilities systems having more than three layers of holding company and to limit two-tier systems to those that could prove the arrangement to be essential to operating company efficiency. Other regulatory features of the original bill remained intact: Holding companies were required to register with SEC, to make reports to the commission at stated intervals, and to cease issuing or selling securities, or acquiring securities or utilities assets, without SEC permission. At last there prevailed a combination of congressional weariness, a wish to escape the relentless humid heat of a Washington August, and the pressure of a public opinion fed on Black's exposures of lobbying practice. By a vote of 219 to 142, with fifty-nine Democrats (including Huddleston) joining eighty-three Republicans in stubborn last-ditch opposition, the House authorized its conferees to accept the compromise. On August 25 the bill went at last through both houses. On the following day Roosevelt signed it into law.

It was, in sum, a great and astonishing victory for Franklin Roosevelt. Never before had the utilities lobby been met head-on and knocked down in national legislative halls.

V

ROOSEVELT, having permitted the banking bill to be introduced as an administration measure in February, did not then personally endorse it or do anything afterward in active support of it until, in early June, he abruptly made it must legislation for the current session. By then, without having occasioned any such popular controversy as swirled about the holding company bill, it was in equal danger of emasculation or total defeat. Twenty thousand words in length, highly technical in content, it was yet another omnibus bill. Sandwiched between two slices of conservative bread, one of which liberalized requirements for membership in the Federal Deposit Insurance Corporation, the other of which provided for unified bank examinations and extended the term of loans made by banks to their own offices, the meat of the bill was a drastic revision of the Federal Reserve Act of 1913, the first that had ever been attempted.

The bill's principal author and promoter was a highly successful Ogden, Utah, banker and corporation executive, also a devout Mormon, named Marriner S. Eccles. He was a physically small man in his mid-forties, sharp-eyed, sharp-featured, intense, possessed of his full share of that peppery combativeness which small men often develop in compensation for lack of size in a competitive world; but possessed also of a remarkably acute intelligence and sensitive concern for social good. He was destined to become a major influence upon the later development of the Second New Deal. His entrance into government ranks had been initially facilitated by Rex Tugwell. In late February 1933, having just testified brilliantly, as few others did, before the Senate Finance Committee during its lame-duck inquiry into the causes and cure of the Great Depression, Eccles had gone up to New York City from Washington, at the suggestion of Stuart Chase, to meet and talk with Tugwell. In the following October Tugwell had invited him to come to Washington to talk with leading New Dealers, presenting to them his recovery ideas. These last were deficit-financing ideas that accorded well, insofar as they were not identical, with those of John Maynard Keynes, though Eccles had arrived at them through his mind-jolting experiences as big banker during the 1929 crash and following depression, his thought being then guided not by Keynes, whom he had not read, but by "consumption economist" William Trufant Foster, whom he had read closely. Governmental deficits in bad times (to prime the pump of mass purchasing power by means of public works, unemployment relief, slum clearance, farm relief, housing construction, etc.), a rapid retirement of this deficit and an accumulation of surplus in good times (by means of whatever progressive tax increases were necessary)—these were the twin and complementary devices for restoring and maintaining prosperity, in Eccles's view as in Keynes's.*[14]

This was not a view that accorded well with that of budget-balancing, economy-minded Henry Morgenthau. Nevertheless, Morgenthau, recognizing Eccles's obviously great ability and concern for the general welfare, invited him to become assistant to the secretary of the treasury, specializing in housing finance—an invitation which Eccles accepted in early 1934. Five months later, when a vacancy occurred on the Federal Reserve Board, Eccles was proposed by Morgenthau to fill it, a proposal strongly seconded by Tugwell. Roosevelt, in order to determine for himself the nature of Eccles's qualifications, asked the banker what changes should be made in Federal Reserve. Eccles responded with a lengthy, closely argued memorandum, written in collaboration with Treasury economist Lauchlin Currie, who was an avowed Keynesian—a memorandum having as one basic motive and aim, implied rather than explicated in the language employed, the facilitation of government spending through an increased control by government over money supply and credit. Roosevelt was impressed by the argument and attracted by the increase of presidential power it proposed, but he was also concerned about the opposition which any attempt to legislate the memorandum's recommendations was bound to arouse. In November 1934 he sent Eccles's name to the Senate for confirmation as Federal Reserve Board member, with the understanding that his first order of business on the board would be the drafting of a banking reform bill.

Roosevelt did this, strangely enough, without prior consultation with Carter Glass, an omission that could hardly have been an oversight. The crusty, vain, conservative, seventy-seven-year-old Virginia Democrat, whose psyche was torn in that year between his attraction toward Franklin Roosevelt personally and his profound aversion to most of the New Deal, was famous as the Father of the Federal Reserve System.† For two decades he and the system had been so closely identified with each other as to constitute virtually a single force in

---

*The Keynsians would seem in retrospect to have paid insufficient heed to the kind of "human nature" that becomes politically decisive within the profit system they were so concerned to preserve in democratic form against totalitarian threats. It is a "human nature" that generally stubbornly resists the degree of increased taxation, for deficit retirement, which the Keynes-Eccles prescription calls for in good times.

†The title is somewhat dubious, viewed historically. The bill Glass drafted in late 1912, to head off a proposal for centralized banking under private banker control, called simply for a *decentralized* system of reserve banks under private banker control. A highly conservative measure, it was strongly opposed by western and southern Democrats, by Samuel Untermyer of Pujo Committee fame, by Secretary of the Treasury McAdoo, and by progressives generally. These favored a bill drawn up by Oklahoma's Senator Robert L. Owen, providing for full governmental control of banking. The compromise measure, which issued from this clash as the Glass-Owen bill and was signed into law as the Federal Reserve Act of 1913, was very different in important ways from Glass's original conception and desire.

American political life. Why, then, did Roosevelt now bypass him in a way bound to hurt and anger him, being perceived by him and, indeed, by people generally as a deliberate snub? None can say with any certainty. But the unfortunate effect was clear enough. Glass, who would in any case have objected to Eccles's appointment, came out now so strongly against it that Morgenthau had to work hard to get it through the Senate. Nor was this the end of the trouble. Once Eccles had been confirmed, Glass prepared to do battle against whatever the new board member proposed in the way of banking legislation. The bad situation was then worsened, inadvertently, by Eccles himself. In an uncharacteristic attempt at appeasement, he promised Glass that he would show the banking bill to him before it went to Congress; he then failed to do so because of circumstances beyond his control. Glass was furiously convinced of Eccles's bad faith.

As for the bill itself, many saw it as a typically New Dealish half measure. It was wholly unsatisfactory to those who favored nationalization of the banks, as did Father Coughlin most vociferously in that season. It failed to please those who favored central banking on, say, the Canadian model. It enraged those who were accustomed to managing the money market in their own interest and had come to believe they had a God-given or "natural" right to do so. But it was a thorough overhaul of the organic act of 1913, guided by Eccles's published conviction that "laissez faire in banking and the attainment of business stability are incompatible" since variations in the money supply, if they were "to be compensatory and corrective rather than inflammatory and intensifying," must be under "conscious and deliberate control."[15] Eccles proposed neither to do away with banking as private enterprise nor to deprive private bankers of all control over the money supply and consequent interest rates, but he did propose (1) to reconstitute the Federal Reserve Board in ways that made it more representative of the public interest and more responsible to the President, who would have power of removal over the board's chairman and vice-chairman and whose administration would be represented on the board itself by the treasury secretary and the comptroller of the currency, these being *ex officio* board members, as they had been from the first; (2) to give the board power to double by majority vote the size of the reserves against deposits which member banks must maintain as well as more power over member bank changes in rediscount notes; and (3) to assign to the board as a whole, and not to some banker-appointed committee, the "most important single instrument of control over the volume and cost of credit," as Eccles put it—namely, open-market dealings in government bonds, notes, Treasury certificates, and other obligations. For the last dozen years, ever since it became evident that the war-swollen public debt was large enough to make open-market operations in government securities a potent means of control over the money market in general, these operations had been handled by a special committee appointed by the Federal Reserve Banks—a committee, in other words, of bankers representing bankers.

The bill had smooth passage through the House, despite Father Coughlin's rabble-rousing radio assaults upon it. This was due in good part to Eccles himself. His was the first testimony called for by Alabama's Henry B. Steagall, chairman of the House Banking Committee; he was in the witness chair for eleven days; and when he left that chair, at last, every question put to him had been answered with remarkable fullness and persuasiveness. The House testimony that followed was generally supportive of the bill—even that of representatives of the American Banking Association, though these pressed for banker representation in whatever board agency engaged in open-market operations and for limitation of the board's power to increase reserve requirements. California's A. P. Giannini again demonstrated his distrust and dislike of Wall Street, along with his gratitude to the administration for its rescue of his Bank of America in March 1933, by testifying strongly in favor of this administration measure. The bill which Steagall's committee reported in mid-April remained in all essentials the bill Eccles had drafted, and a little more than three weeks later, on May 9, the House passed it, 271 to 110.

But in the Senate, instead of being dealt with by the Banking and Currency Committee under the relatively benign leadership of Duncan Fletcher, the bill was assigned to a subcommittee chaired by an infuriated, Eccles-hating Carter Glass. The Virginian had maneuvered to force this assignment. He then played for time, so that the inevitable opposition of big New York City bankers to a measure designed to reduce their power, an opposition that was initially very weakly and cautiously expressed, could grow strong, well prepared, and bold. Not until mid-April, when House hearings were ending, did Senate hearings begin.

And they then began, not with testimony from the proposal's author and supporter, as was customary and logical, but with testimony from the opposition. This last was typically doomful, characteristically apocalyptic. A committee of distinguished academic economists, several Wall Street bankers, and some former high Treasury officials (Ogden Mills for one, James P. Warburg for another) described the bill as a move to "politicize" Federal Reserve, giving dictatorial authority over money markets into the hands of a power-hungry executive. It was "the most dangerous . . . most unwarranted . . . most insidious" of all New Deal measures. Its passage would create immediate havoc, "invite ultimate disaster," and, according to Mills, "throw us [the United States?] back five hundred years"—that is, to the year 1435.[16] Simultaneously Carter Glass strove to divide the omnibus bill into its three component parts, making each a separate bill. In such case only the conservative bills would pass, he was assured, and he assured others that the deposit insurance and unified bank examination proposals were all the President wanted passed. Roosevelt had told him as much. (Roosevelt was forced to admit, privately, to Morgenthau that he had indeed said this to Glass last January; he had since changed his mind.) The proposed Federal Reserve reform must therefore be regarded as strictly "an Eccles bill," Glass insisted.[17] Nor was what the senator said contradicted in public statement by the President. Roosevelt, as a matter of fact, made no public statement of any kind about bank reform as April gave way to May and May to June.

And so the bill was in serious trouble by the time Roosevelt put it on his must list. It remained in trouble for weeks thereafter. Glass's effort to divide up the measure was frustrated, but he then proceeded to rewrite completely Section II (the reform portion), producing a version which, if by no means as substantially different from Eccles's bill as he evidently believed it to be, did significantly reduce the power the administration could exert over the Federal Reserve System. One section removed the secretary of the treasury and the comptroller of the currency from *ex officio* positions on the board. Another provided for participation by banker representatives in open-market decisions. Struck from the bill was the section empowering the President to remove the board chairman and vice-chairman, and somewhat curtailed was the board's power to alter reserve requirements. In general, however, this Glass version, which the Senate adopted, concentrated in the national board powers formerly diffused among the twelve Federal Reserve Banks, and did so in essentially the way Eccles had originally proposed. Hence the Senate and House versions were not so far apart as to render very difficult their fusion by the joint committee into a single compromise measure. This then went easily through both houses to the President's desk. Roosevelt signed it on August 24, 1935, handing one of the signature pens to Glass, another of them to Eccles.

The final measure was publicly praised by all that had had a hand in its shaping, including the American Banking Association. In the act the Federal Reserve Board, consisting as before of seven members, was officially designated the Board of Governors of the Federal Reserve System, the governors each appointed by the President for a fourteen-year term at a cabinet minister's salary, with the terms so staggered that there would be no more than one regular vacancy every two years. To be established as of March 1, 1936, was a Federal Open Market Committee the membership of which included all seven of the national governors plus five regional representatives of the twelve Federal Reserve Banks. The national board could approve or reject the appointment of any president or vice-president of any Federal Reserve Bank, these being selected for five-year terms by the boards of directors of member banks.[18] In sum, the legislation's overall effect was what Eccles had originally intended. It was now easier than it had been before to launch government spending programs. No longer would the New York Federal Reserve Bank have more power over money and credit than the system's national board. Dominant power over the system, and over monetary matters in general, was shifted from Wall Street to Washington.

This is not to say, however, that the power so shifted was wholly lost to Wall Street's bankers; these remained more than adequately represented in Washington.

VI

THE special tax message which Roosevelt sent to Congress on June 19, calling for a steep federal inheritance tax, a gift tax designed to plug or shrink a large tax loophole much used by the wealthy, a graduated corporate income tax

whereby the existing flat rate of 13.75 percent was replaced by rates ranging
from 10.75 to 16.75 percent, a tax on intercorporate dividends, and an increased
surtax rate on all large personal incomes, appeared to be the sudden fruit of
an abrupt decision on Roosevelt's part. On June 7 he had told his press
conference that he hadn't "thought of taxes, or looked at taxes for a month."[19]
The decision seemed also, to some who were close to him, an impulsive one,
with far less thoughtfulness in it than was required by prudence for so drastic
a change of policy. But actually, on that intuitive level where so much of
Roosevelt's work was done, the decision, though certainly abrupt of implementation, was not sudden at all; it was the outcome of a lengthy grinding process.

As 1935 began, and as we have seen, an undecided Roosevelt was in a
conservative mood. The impulse behind his acceptance of Hopkins's work
relief proposals was wholly conservative. He continued to hope against hope,
and against an increasingly overwhelming weight of evidence to the contrary,
that the business community would soon have a change of heart and mind,
becoming then cooperative with the administration in its recovery efforts. He
wanted at the time no new departures. Thus, as regards taxation, Roosevelt
in his annual budget message (January 3) had recommended the extension
through fiscal 1936, at current rates, of the "miscellaneous internal-revenue
taxes [excise taxes, nuisance taxes] which under existing law" would expire at
midnight on June 30, the end of fiscal 1935, but "I do not consider it advisable
at this time to propose any new or additional taxes for the fiscal year 1936."
He had not changed his mind about this during the immediately following
weeks, despite strong pressures to do so exerted upon him by such Senate
progressives as Norris, La Follette, Cutting, Nye, Borah, and Hiram Johnson.
All these pointed to the rapid growth of Huey Long's Share Our Wealth
movement, and the threat this posed for the New Deal in 1936; they urged
administration espousal of legislation in the current session to increase graduated income taxes sharply and to impose new estate, inheritance, and gift taxes.
Burton Wheeler, who looked upon Long with more affection than alarm, being
himself utterly disillusioned with Rooseveltian "liberalism" as 1935 began,
introduced in the Senate, in February, a Brandeisian "antibigness" bill
whereby the taxing power would be used to discourage corporate growth
beyond "safe" socioeconomic limits. He proposed a graduated tax on corporate incomes, beginning at 2 percent on incomes of $3 million and rising to 25
percent on incomes of $50 million or more; he also proposed, in his bill, an
FTC study of the true relationship of corporate size to economic efficiency,
with recommendations from FTC on the most efficient size within each area
of corporate endeavor.[20]

In that same month of February a Treasury Department tax-study group
appointed by Morgenthau submitted to the President, in the form of a proposed special message to Congress, recommendations that accorded closely
with those of the Senate progressives. Roosevelt "read the message to me one
night in February," writes Moley, "and I . . . urged against it as a whole and
in detail. Particularly I . . . opposed it as an attempt to put over dubious social

reforms in the guise of tax legislation. . . . F.D.R. . . . finally tossed the draft message aside."[21]

And Roosevelt remained publicly of the same mind still on May 22, when he delivered his bonus bill veto message. "In accordance with the mandate of the Congress, our budget has been set," he then said. ". . . That budget asked for appropriations in excess of receipts to the extent of four billions of dollars. The whole of that deficit was to be applied for work relief for the unemployed [in actual executive practice, as we have seen, "work relief" was given a very broad definition]. That was a single-minded, definite purpose."[22] This should mean that the administration's tax program was also finally "set" for the fiscal year ahead, being a part of the budget proposal.

But during the very time he was preparing this veto message he conferred with Hearst newspaper editor in chief E. D. Coblentz, and to him he conveyed a very different message as regards taxation. Coblentz came to the White House in acceptance of a specific Roosevelt invitation. It was an invitation issued in an attempt—the very last attempt, as it turned out—to bridge a widening gap, filled with rancor, which had opened since the first of the year between William Randolph Hearst and the man Hearst had helped put into the White House. The Lord of San Simeon, increasingly uneasy about the direction in which the New Deal was going during the first half of 1934, became definitely critical of the administration during and after the San Francisco general strike, for which he held NIRA's Section 7(a) responsible, and he was, of course, further alienated by the rise of the Newspaper Guild under the aegis of that same 7(a). The last straw for him was the liberal rhetoric which Roosevelt deliberately employed in his 1935 annual message to offset the unrelieved conservatism of his budget message, delivered the day before. Especially was Hearst aggrieved by Roosevelt's statement that "[w]e have . . . a clear mandate from the people, that Americans must forswear that conception of wealth which, through excessive profits, creates undue private power over private affairs and, to our misfortune, over public affairs as well." The great publisher seems to have felt that he personally was being singled out for censure and personally threatened. He immediately ordered his newspapers to open fire upon the New Deal. And it was in the hope of mitigating, if not ending, this fire that Roosevelt arranged the meeting with Coblentz. During it the talk was unwontedly frank on Roosevelt's part—and hardly conciliatory, curiously enough, as if the hope which had inspired the invitation had faded by the time Hearst's emissary came into his presence. "I am fighting Communism, Huey Longism, Coughlinism, Townsendism," he reportedly said, and if he were "to save our system, the capitalistic system," as he wished and strove to do, he must "give some heed" to demands for a more equitable "distribution of wealth." To "combat" successfully such "crackpot ideas" as Long was peddling, "it may be necessary to throw to the wolves the forty-six men who are reported to have incomes in excess of one million dollars a year. This can be accomplished through taxation." He therefore proposed a sharp increase of taxation on large incomes and fortunes, a proposal which struck Coblentz and

Hearst as a yielding to, rather than a struggle against, communism. Coblentz dubbed it "neo-Communism."[23]

There immediately followed for Roosevelt, in early June, the exhilaration of his emphatic assertion of authority over Congress, and it was in this new mood, described by Moley as a "sense of regaining the whip hand," that he accepted wholly the Treasury tax-study group proposal which he had "tossed aside" in February. Moley's descriptive metaphor is, on the evidence, remarkably accurate: A species of flagellating sadism would seem to have been involved in Roosevelt's employment of Moley as one of the three final draftsmen (Frankfurter and Morgenthau were the other two) of a tax message every salient feature of which was, as Roosevelt well knew, abhorrent to him. Surely a more sympathetic speech technician could have been more easily employed! Nor was sadism absent from the way in which the message's delivery was managed. Early in the third week of June, as he worked with his helpers to put the draft message into final shape, Roosevelt savored the effect his words would have upon a Congress that already felt itself grievously overburdened, amid the summer heat, by must legislation. Gleefully he anticipated the shocked reaction of the Senate Finance Committee's chairman. "Pat Harrison is going to be so surprised he'll have kittens on the spot," said he with booming laugh.[24]

As for the message itself, it was replete with phrases which, in the process of "stealing thunder" from Huey Long, were as lashes of lightning across the back of William Randolph Hearst and of every other scion of enormous wealth. Roosevelt said:

> Our revenue laws have done little to prevent an unjust concentration of wealth and economic power. . . . Wealth in the modern world does not come merely from individual effort: it results from a combination of individual effort and the manifold uses to which the community puts that effort. The individual does not create the product of his industry with his own hands; he utilizes the many processes and forces of mass production. . . . The transmission from generation to generation of vast fortunes by will, inheritance, or gift is not consistent with the ideals and sentiments of the American people. . . . Such inherited economic power is as inconsistent with the ideals of this generation as inherited political power was inconsistent with the ideals of the generation which established our Government.

Ickes happened to be in conference with the President when word came that the social security bill had passed the Senate and that the tax message was at that very moment beginning to be read.* Remarking that he thought the message "the best thing I have done as President," Roosevelt proceeded to read much of it aloud to the interior secretary. Upon the portion quoted above, he made comment to Ickes. *"That,"* he said, "is for Hearst."[25]

The effect upon press and public was pretty much what Roosevelt had

---

*Historically suggestive is this simultaneity of event; it reminds of the lost opportunity to effect a genuine redistribution of wealth and income, in equalizing and democratic ways, by means of general revenue financing of social security and the employment of social security reserve funds to finance productive cooperative enterprise.

expected. Moderates deplored the evident motive for this seemingly abrupt new departure—a motive that seemed in equal parts vindictive and political. The proposed taxation seemed likely to increase by only a small fraction the general revenue; it would contribute insignificantly to a balancing of the budget. Obviously its design was to retain for the New Deal, or return to it, voter support otherwise lost to the "crackpot" demagogues while punishing big business for being big and an elite class for being hostile to the administration. Such motive and aim were deemed ignoble.

This was the published view of the highly respected journalist Raymond Clapper, who also condemned the taxation proposal as bad economics. "It looks to some like an effort to drive business back to the horse and buggy stage by penalizing large units . . ." wrote Clapper. William Randolph Hearst, immediately inflamed, was immediately inflammatory. He promptly wired his editors that "President's taxation program is essentially Communism," properly attributable to "a composite personality which might be labelled Stalin Delano Roosevelt." Shortly thereafter the Hearst newspapers were directed by Editor in Chief Coblentz, acting on the publisher's orders, to call the tax proposal a Soak the Successful scheme and, in describing the administration, to substitute "Raw Deal" for "New Deal." (A copy of this directive found its way into Roosevelt's hands, provoking one of his now increasingly frequent private tirades against a mendacious, viciously unfair, special-interest press.) But Felix Frankfurter, who as Brandeisian welcomed this attack upon concentrated private economic power, wrote Roosevelt: "My Boston newspaper friends who keep most track of the press of the country—[Frank] Buxton of the *Herald* and Larry Winship of the *Globe*—tell me that your tax message has had the most favorable response possible from the press throughout the country, as well as among people whose views do not get into the press."[26] And by the time Roosevelt read this he knew from samplings of the letters and wires pouring into the White House mailroom that the message had been most gratefully received and heartily approved by the populace in general.

As for the effect in Congress, it, too, was pretty much what Roosevelt had expected. Huey Long strutted self-importantly about the chamber as the reading proceeded, pointing to himself with impudent grin as the real author of the proposals made. At the reading's close he spoke a loud "Amen!" (Said Will Rogers in his syndicated column next day: "I would sure like to have seen Huey's face when he was woke up in the middle of the night by the President, who said, 'Lay over, Huey, I want to get in bed with you.'"[27]) La Follette, Norris, Borah, and the other senators who had participated in the night meeting in the White House on May 14 enthusiastically welcomed this seeming acceptance of their wealth tax program, this evident confirmation of the commitment to the liberal way which Roosevelt, during that meeting, had made. But upon the conservative congressional leaders who had to push through the implementing legislation—upon Joe Robinson and Pat Harrison in the Senate; upon Ways and Means Chairman Doughton in the House—the message fell not as the ripe welcome fruit of a maturing process in which they had been properly involved but as a bombshell explosively delivered, with no warning, from alien ground. They resented it as personally humiliating. They were constrained by party loyalty, and by the immediately evident popularity of the proposal among the electorate, to "go along," but they did so sullenly, reluctantly, vowing among themselves that this was the last time they'd submit passively to such treatment.

And this feeling, wherein were embedded the seeds of future conservative coalition revolt against the New Deal, was augmented a few days later by what Robinson and Harrison, with their many friends, perceived to be Rooseveltian double-dealing with them, if not an actual double cross.

This last came about because the congressional progressives who initially loudly applauded the tax message had some sobering second thoughts about it on the morrow of its delivery.

The message did not clearly, definitely indicate a presidential desire for the immediate introduction of a wealth tax bill to be enacted in the current session. A rumor spread that Roosevelt, having made his "thunder-stealing" gesture, would be satisfied if only a modest inheritance tax were enacted that summer. Huey Long began voicing a suspicion that the tax message was as phony as the man who had delivered it. (Within two weeks Long was declaring apropos of the wealth tax that Roosevelt was "a liar and a fake."[28]) And it was in part to "test the sincerity" of the President, as Gerald Nye would say, that Wisconsin's La Follette on June 20 announced his intention to attach a rider to the nuisance tax extension bill which was reported out by the Senate Finance Committee that day, a rider incorporating not only the whole of the message's tax program but also his own bill to increase revenue by reducing tax exemptions within the middle-income level.* This would ensure immediate consideration of both tax proposals, the President's and La Follette's own, for the presently mandated excise taxes would end on June 30, and until new excise tax legislation was adopted, the federal revenues would thereafter be reduced daily by some $1.5 million. On the following day La Follette organized a round robin, signed by twenty-two progressive senators of both parties, declaring that Congress should remain in session until the President's tax proposals were enacted.

Whatever Roosevelt's original intentions regarding the implementation of his tax message, his hand was now forced. He summoned congressional leaders to the White House for a strategy conference on June 24. Not only did he then make it clear that he wanted his tax program enacted now, but he also accepted

---

*La Follette was neither a Brandeisian nor a Keynesian. He was animated by no such hostility toward bigness per se as seemed manifested by Roosevelt's words about corporate taxation, and his advocacy of large government spending to stimulate recovery was joined with no willingness to incur equally large deficits. By the end of the summer of 1935 La Follette saw that holding company legislation, social security, Eccles's banking reform, and the wealth tax measure "constituted a whole governmental economic policy" which "was emerging as an alternative to the collectivism in which he believed," as Tugwell writes in his *Democratic Roosevelt* (p. 376). "I recall his talking to me about it in a disappointed way," Tugwell continues. "He thought the new policy hopelessly insufficient."

as his own the tactic La Follette had devised, later approving it as tacit order in a memorandum to Majority Leader Robinson. Reporters pressed around Robinson and Harrison as they left the White House, asking how the new tax bill would be handled, and Robinson told them frankly it would be added to the nuisance tax bill. This June 24 was a Monday, and the current excise tax mandate was to expire on Saturday; this meant the administration proposed to rush through Congress in fewer than six days a complex and highly controversial tax bill, evidently without even holding hearings on it! By the time Pat Harrison made his first move in the Finance Committee to effect the agreed strategy, on Tuesday, the twenty-fifth, a storm of published protest was rising and swirling about the preposterous idea.

And on the day after that, in his press conference, Roosevelt pulled the rug out from under his lieutenants by agreeing with the protesters. The idea *was* preposterous! "What made you think that there was any possibility of passing a completely new tax measure . . . by Saturday?" he chided a questioning reporter. The reporter said he assumed it because Harrison had indicated as much. "Did he say it would be passed on Saturday?" asked Roosevelt, feigning incredulity. Harrison had said he hoped it would be, the reporter replied, and other reporters chimed in that they had heard him say it, too. "I did not know he had said it," said the President, who then hurried on to compound his mendacity. He himself had "never said anything to that effect and you can go back and look at the record." In any case, "I am not Congress. I am just a person down here to make recommendations. I feel I must make this clear in fairness to myself." Such "fairness" to himself was manifestly unfair to Robinson and Harrison, of course, each of whom was made out to be in this matter a liar or a fool, or both, and it required a great deal of immediate effort by White House emissaries to soothe a furious Joe Robinson sufficiently to prevent his publicizing the aforementioned presidential memorandum, which would have proved to the public that Roosevelt was the liar here. By the time reporters reached Robinson for comment, he had his temper under control; he "retreated into an attitude of humor on the whole proceeding," as the New York *Times* put it, "and simply laughed at the suggestion that the course of events was curious." Pat Harrison, a much smoother, more ingratiating operator than Robinson, was able to react "correctly" within a few minutes after he had been surprised by the Roosevelt press statement—and surprised while in the very act of defending the agreed strategy against protesting senators. "Whatever erroneous impression may have gone out to the country," he said to reporters magnanimously, "do not blame the President. I take it upon my shoulders. So let's close this page and not talk any more about it."[29]

In the end it required not five days but nine and a half weeks to get the wealth tax through both houses. The bill which emerged for House floor action from Doughton's Ways and Means Committee on July 30, after six weeks of mostly hostile testimony counteracted by powerful supportive testimony from Robert H. Jackson, Internal Revenue's general counsel, retained little more than the "principle" of the graduated corporate income tax. The intercorporate dividend tax was removed, and an excess profits tax was added, in response to the clamor for increased revenue. It was passed by the House on August 5 by a vote of 282 to 96. In Harrison's Senate Finance Committee, the intercorporate dividend tax was retained, but the proposed inheritance tax was removed; substituted were provisions increasing personal income and estate taxes. On the Senate floor La Follette tried but narrowly failed to obtain an increase of the already much-increased surtax rates. The bill then passed the full Senate, on August 15, by a vote of 57 to 22. In joint conference the Senate version largely prevailed. The intercorporate dividend tax, which the House had cut out, was put back in; efforts to restore the individual inheritance tax failed, but estate taxes were increased; the top surtax rates on individual incomes, rates increased from 59 to 75 percent, the highest in history, were retained. In this form the bill was quickly approved by both houses. The President signed it into law on August 31.

Again Roosevelt had triumphed. But it was a costly triumph insofar as it further encouraged the developing split in the congressional Democracy and the drawing together of right-wing Democrats and Republicans in future conservative opposition to the administration; it was also a decidedly imperfect triumph—it might even be deemed a failure—when measured against the stated ultimate aims of the June 19 special message. The Wealth Tax Act of 1935 did nothing, in the event, to dissolve or prevent dangerous concentrations of private economic power or to change in any important way the pattern of income distribution. The great family fortunes remained at least as great, in comparison with the fortunes of ordinary folk, as they had been before; the upper-income groups continued to obtain for themselves that percentage of the total national income which they had obtained before. Indeed, as William E. Leuchtenburg has pointed out, "the share of the top 1 percent even increased a bit [through the remainder of the 1930s] after the passage of the Wealth Tax Act."[30]

VII

There were two other enactments of this historic first session of the Seventy-fourth Congress which were of major importance.

One of these was of the Guffey-Snyder bituminous coal bill, drafted by John L. Lewis's United Mine Workers and introduced, shortly after the session's opening, by Pennsylvania's Senator Joseph F. Guffey. Thanks in good part to the strength and vitality of Lewis's union, the Bituminous Coal Code of NRA had been so written and administered as to stabilize to a considerable degree an industry that, in the spring of 1933, was being ground down into highly inflammable coal dust by lawless, ruthless competitions within a severely contracted market. The Guffey bill was designed, in effect, to detach this coal code from NIRA, the continuance of which beyond fiscal 1935 was increasingly in doubt, and to establish it as separate and permanent legislation. It called for a national commission for the soft coal industry to administer a code covering wages and hours, trade practices, minimum prices, and collective bargaining; it provided for an excise tax of 15 percent on all coal sold, with a 90 percent rebate of this to those producers who became members of the code. This last was, of course, a powerful inducement to become a code member.

Roosevelt had had nothing to do with the bill's drafting or with its introduction and early legislative history. He had not placed it on his must list in early June. But he effectively did so a few weeks later, when Lewis threatened a paralyzing national coal strike if the bill was not passed and when doubts about the bill's constitutionality threatened to prevent its being reported out by the subcommittee of the House Ways and Means Committee which had it in charge. On July 6 he addressed to the subcommittee's chairman, Representative Samuel B. Hill, a letter which was at once loudly damned by conservatives in Congress, and by the conservative press, as a virtually impeachable offense on the part of the President in that it allegedly deliberately encouraged a flouting of the Constitution, and a contempt of court, by the legislative branch. Wrote Roosevelt:

> Manifestly, no one is in a position to give assurances that the proposed act will withstand constitutional tests, for the simple fact that you can get not ten but a thousand differing legal opinions on the subject. But the situation is so urgent and the benefits of the legislation so evident that all doubts should be resolved in favor of the bill, leaving to the courts, in an orderly fashion, the ultimate question of constitutionality. A decision by the Supreme Court relative to this measure would be helpful as indicating, with increasing clarity, the constitutional limits within which this Government must operate. [Evident here is Roosevelt's disposition to challenge the Supreme Court in the way Felix Frankfurter suggested in his letter of May 29, 1935 to the President.*] . . . I hope your committee will not permit doubts about constitutionality, however reasonable, to block the proposed legislation.[31]

The phrase "however reasonable" in the closing sentence was especially unfortunate. It lent plausibility to the charge that Roosevelt aspired toward dictatorial power. He himself regretted it as soon as he felt the reaction to it. (Three years later, when the 1935 volume of his public papers and addresses was published, he was at pains to defend himself in a way that betrayed an unease of mind. In an explanatory note to his published letter to Hill he cited in justification of his position one of the early decisions of the Supreme Court apropos of its asserted right of judicial review. Justice Bushrod Washington, in his majority opinion in *Ogden* v. *Saunders* (1827), said, and Roosevelt quoted: "It is but a decent respect due to the wisdom, integrity, and the patriotism of the legislative body, by which any law is passed, to presume in favor of its validity, until its violation of the Constitution is proved beyond all reasonable doubt." Roosevelt also complained, in his note, that "certain newspaper publishers and columnists have quoted only the last sentence of the [Hill] letter, taken completely from its text, so as to give a wholly false impression of the letter. This is perhaps typical of methods now prevalent among certain newspaper owners and publishers.")[32]

But there was no doubting the urgency of the "situation" to which Roose-

*See pp. 517–18.

velt, in his letter, referred. By mid-August he had had twice to persuade John Lewis to postpone the effective date of a strike call already issued, doing so with personal assurances that the measure would at least come to a vote during this session; it would not be allowed to remain bottled up in committee.[33]

And on August 20, after a debate which accentuated the split between the conservative and liberal wings of the Democratic party, the bill went through the House by a vote of 194 to 168. On August 23 it went through the Senate on a vote of 45 to 37. Roosevelt promptly signed it into law.

The other major enactment of the session, aside from those proposals placed on the "must" list in June, was of a bill the introduction of which had been urged by Roosevelt himself, evidently on sudden impulse and from devious motive, shortly before his departure for his *Nourmahal* vacation in late March, but concerning which he developed grave doubts during the summer and which he signed at last reluctantly, with published misgivings.

The bill was an outgrowth of a sensationally publicized investigation of the armaments industry authorized by Senate resolution in April 1934 and conducted by a special Munitions Committee under the chairmanship of North Dakota's Gerald P. Nye. This investigation was, in turn, an outgrowth of the tide of pacifistic emotion which swept across America, as it did over Europe, all through the 1920s, in revulsion against the mass slaughters of the Great War and the subsequent betrayals of principle and common sense at Versailles. There was a flood of antiwar novels and "now-it-can-be-told" publications* exposing the ugly realities of the war (the murderous stupidity of generals, the blunderings of politicians, the profiteering of businessmen)—realities that had been hidden behind a wall of censorship while the war was being fought, a wall that was itself plastered over with vividly false propaganda. The tide was at its highest in the early 1930s. Every college campus then had its student pacifist organization, to protest the "militarism" of the Reserve Officers Training Corps (ROTC) and, in land-grant colleges, the two years of military training which all male students were required to take. There abounded national peace organizations—among them the National Council for the Prevention of War, the Methodist Commission on World Peace, World Peaceways, the Fellowship of Reconciliation, the World Alliance for International Friendship Through the Churches, the U.S. section of the Women's International League for Peace and Freedom—which circulated petitions, published leaflets and pamphlets, held public meetings, and actively lobbied Congress regarding legislative proposals relevant to their cause. Increasingly this pacifist agitation focused upon the armaments makers, who, since they obviously made money out of wars and war scares, must be presumed to foment them, a presumption not

---

*Now It Can Be Told, by former British war correspondent Philip Gibbs, was among the most widely read and influential of these publications. The most influential of all, and by far, was the German Erich Maria Remarque's novel *All Quiet on the Western Front*, which, upon its publication in 1929, became one of the great international best-sellers of all time. More than 2 million copies, in some fifteen languages, were sold worldwide in less than two years, and its influence was multiplied by the highly successful motion picture soon made of it.

without substantial merit, as the notorious case of William B. Shearer* clearly showed. Nor was the presumption unshared by public figures who were very far from being pacifist agitators. If efforts toward peace "are not to be frustrated," wrote Secretary of State Henry Stimson to President Hoover in January 1933, "the international traffic in arms must be supervised and controlled by national and international action." And Stimson's immediate predecessor as secretary of state, Frank B. Kellogg, said in a 1934 letter to Nye that "in my opinion, there is no question whatever that the world munition manufacturers are adding their influence and in every way trying to prevent disarmament."[34]

Hence the potency of a resolution adopted by the U.S. section of the Women's International League for Peace and Freedom in annual convention in 1932, and again in 1933, calling for a Senate investigation of the private munitions trade and citing, in support of this call, numerous published reports that the munitions makers and their salesmen did indeed deliberately increase international tensions to the best of their ability, did indeed corrupt public officials, did indeed do everything they could to frustrate disarmament conferences—all this to maintain and expand a profitable market for their lethal products. The Fellowship of Reconciliation, the National Council for the Prevention of War, and World Peaceways also called for governmental investigation and action to control the arms traffic, but it was the Women's International League's resolve which actually triggered the Senate investigation, thanks to the energetic persuasiveness of that organization's executive secretary, Dorothy Detzer. She it was who buttonholed some twenty senators in an effort to find one who would propose the necessary Senate resolution and finally, with the help of George Norris, persuaded Nye to do so.

He, Nye, introduced his resolution in early February 1934. It was referred to the Foreign Relations Committee, whose chairman, Key Pittman, refusing to consider it, managed to get it transferred in early March to the Military Affairs Committee, where it could be expected to die, quietly, under the hostile glare of a promilitary membership. But at that point the astute Dorothy Detzer had a bright idea. She proposed to join the Nye resolution to one Michigan Republican Arthur H. Vandenberg had introduced sometime before, a resolution which had the support of the American Legion.

Since 1920 the Legion had been agitating for legislation to prevent in any future war the excessive business profits which, during the Great War, had substantially reduced industrial efficiency and lowered the morale of combat troops, according to the Veterans' organization. In the early months of the Great Depression various peace organizations, naturally suspicious of any proposal put forward by the superpatriotic, militaristic, generally reactionary Legion, suddenly found merit in this one Legion proposal; they, too, began to agitate for legislation that would "take the profit out of war." In response to this pressure Congress in 1930 established a War Policies Commission to study

*See Davis, *FDR: The New York Years*, p. 141.

the problem of war profits and make recommendations for its legislated solution. This commission consisted of four cabinet members, four senators, four congressmen. It had a decidedly conservative orientation, as any body so constituted might be expected to have during the Hoover administration. And after listening to sixteen days of frequently impassioned and variously informed testimony from proponents and opponents of antiwar profiteering during hearings in the spring of 1931, it acted at last in accordance with the testimony of Bernard Baruch, who professed to find it impossible to believe "that any human being [much less an American big businessman] could be persuaded by the prospect of personal gain, however magnificent, to invoke the horrors of modern war."[35] Moderate, indeed, were the commission's legislative recommendations. They included giving government the authority to fix prices and to impose an excess profits tax in wartime, but they also gave "legitimate profit" a generous definition, one hard to justify in terms of classical economics (the professed economics of conservatives), wherein "profit" is defined as a proper reward for taking risks. Corporations would be permitted to "keep earnings equal to the three-year prewar average plus 5 percent," as John Edward Wiltz has summarized.[36] But big business was inclined to deny to government any profit-restricting power whatever, and the Congress of 1931 and 1932 took no action on the commission's recommendations.

Vandenberg's 1934 resolution was for a congressional review of the findings of the War Policies Commission for the purpose of developing legislation based on these, and both Vandenberg and Nye promptly acceded to Dorothy Detzer's suggestion that their two proposals be joined together in a single Nye-Vandenberg resolution. Roosevelt gave it his endorsement, though only after Secretary of State Hull had expressed himself in favor of it, a massive lobbying campaign had been mounted in its behalf by the national peace movement, and the resolution's premise had been powerfully reinforced by a lengthy, seemingly carefully researched, and certainly highly sensational article entitled "Arms and the Men," published in the March 1934 issue of *Fortune* magazine.

Fortune was, on the face of it, an unlikely publication for any essay against big business practices. A Henry Luce enterprise, financed initially by *Time* magazine profits, it was a large-format, lushly produced periodical which sold for what, in those depression years, was the astronomical price of $1 per copy. Its subscribers were, by and large, businessmen of much higher than average incomes. Yet "Arms and the Men," which was unsigned because it was the composite effort of staff writers (Archibald MacLeish was one of them that year), was the harshest possible indictment of such American big business as E. I. du Pont de Nemours and Company. The munitions manufacturers were true internationalists, the article charged, in that they never permitted national patriotism to inhibit their profit making; they were as willing to sell their weapons to a potential or actual enemy of their country as they were to sell to their own government, and they were joined in an international conspiracy to keep the world in profitable turmoil. "Detail upon detail, incident upon incident, illustrate how well the armament makers apply the two axioms of their business: when there are wars, prolong them; when there is peace, disturb it."[37] Gerald Nye promptly inserted the article in the *Congressional Record.* It was reprinted in abridged form in the May 1934 issue of *Reader's Digest.*

And by that time two books which shared and expanded upon the article's central thesis had been published. One was *Iron, Blood and Profits: An Exposure of the World-Wide Munitions Racket,* by George Seldes. The other was *Merchants of Death: A Study of the International Armament Industry,* by Helmuth C. Engelbrecht and Frank C. Hanighen. The latter was the more influential of the two: It was the April 1934 selection of the Book-of-the-Month Club, it received glowing notices from the most distinguished book reviewers, and it became a major best-seller. Its central charge was specific, sensational, and seemingly supported by an abundance of authoritative evidence (upon close examination, a good deal of this evidence proved to be little more than plausible inference sustained by quoted rumor, gossip, individual assertions)—namely, that six huge munitions manufacturers in six different countries were joined in secret alliance to promote their nefarious businesses at the expense of world peace, the six being Vickers-Armstrong of Great Britain, Schneider-Creusot of France. S. A. Bofors of Sweden, Krupp of Germany, Skoda of Czechoslovakia, and E. I. du Pont de Nemours of the United States.[38]

By that time, too, largely on the impetus given it by "Arms and the Men," the Nye-Vandenberg resolution had been adopted by the Senate, this on April 12, 1934. It authorized the establishment of a seven-member committee "to investigate the activities of individuals, firms, associations and of corporations and all other agencies in the United States engaged in the manufacture, sale, distribution, import or export of arms, munitions or other implements of war; the methods used in promoting or effecting the sale of arms, munitions or other implements of war imported into the United States and the countries of origin thereof, and of the quantities exported from the United States and countries of destination thereof." The committee was also to review the War Policies Commission's findings, as per the Vandenberg portion of the joint resolution, study all existing legislation and treaties having to do with armaments, and come up with legislative recommendations for wartime industrial mobilization, elimination of war profiteering, and, possibly, the nationalization of the armaments industry. Committee membership included, in addition to Vandenberg and Chairman Nye, Missouri's Bennett Champ Clark (he became Nye's second-in-command), Washington's Homer T. Bone, Idaho's James P. Pope, Georgia's Walter F. George, and New Jersey's W. Warren Barbour. Of these, only one, Pope, was definitely an administration man; he alone reflected all of the White House's shifts of attitude and tactic as the investigation proceeded, though he joined the majority of the committee in a final report with which the White House most emphatically disagreed.

Indeed, from the first, this committee's operation was regarded with a suspicious eye, a wary dislike, by Franklin Roosevelt. He privately deplored much of the testimony presented in public hearings after the committee had begun these in late September 1934: testimony that high officials of Latin American governments had accepted bribes from American arms makers (these governments promptly lodged protests with the State Department; Good Neighbor relations seemed threatened); testimony that President Wilson and Secretary of State Robert Lansing had lied to the American people when they claimed they had no knowledge of Allied secret treaties until 1919 (actually this mendacity had been common knowledge among the well-informed for a decade and a half); testimony that the loans American bankers made to Allied governments in 1914 and after had had something to do with America's ultimately becoming actively involved in the Great War; testimony that the armaments industry exerted influence upon the implementation, if not the making, of U.S. foreign policy. But it was the Vandenberg portion of the joint resolution—that part of the committee's assignment having to do with industrial mobilization, war profits limitations, and a possible nationalization of the arms industry—which Roosevelt most regretted and even viewed with alarm as, in December 1934, the committee turned its attention to these matters. Difficult to defend in argument was armaments manufacture as a private enterprise. Even Alexander Hamilton, that great benefactor of big business and hero of big businessmen, had counseled against private speculations in the field of national defense; in his historic *Report on the Subject of Manufactures* (December 5, 1791) he had exempted arms making from his general rule against government manufactures. Equally difficult to counter in argument was the assertion that if young men must be conscripted to risk wounds and death on the battlefield, capital, too, must be conscripted for the duration of the war, and in such way as to render impossible all special private profit. Why must self-sacrificing patriotism be confined to soldiers? Why was it necessary, as certainly it was morally outrageous, to bribe businessmen to do their plain duty to their country in times of desperate national need? The questions struck increasing numbers of people as purely rhetorical in late 1934 and early 1935; there could be no doubting the magnitude of the energies of popular opinion which then flowed, through prepared channel, toward a truly radical change in the way America managed its national defenses and, if war came, mobilized its economic resources to fight it. Certainly there was no doubt of it in the White House, and it behooved a President who opposed such change, yet feared the political consequences of doing so openly, to devise a stratagem for preventing it. Somehow the energies of change had to be diverted from their present concentrating channel and scattered in futility over the political landscape.

So at his press conference on December 12, 1934, Roosevelt announced in his most dramatic fashion that "the time has come to take the profit out of war!" To achieve this purpose, he had, he said, just appointed a committee with which he would be meeting within an hour or so. The committee was to prepare the needed legislation for presentation to the Seventy-fourth Congress when it opened its first session, just two and a half weeks hence. The shortness of time allotted for the performance of a drafting task so difficult and important was astonishing, to say the least. Even more so was the committee's membership when viewed in terms of the committee's announced assignment. On it, and obviously intended to dominate it, were Bernard Baruch and the currently unemployed General Hugh Johnson. Serving with these would be General Douglas MacArthur, Army chief of staff; George Peck, foreign trade adviser; Joseph Eastman, federal coordinator of transportation; Henry Latrobe, assistant secretary of the navy; and the secretaries of state, treasury, war, navy, agriculture, and labor.[39] But not in the least surprising, and not in the least new in idea content, was the recommended legislation which allegedly emerged from the committee's allegedly careful deliberations. It was introduced in the House on the first working day of the Seventy-fourth Congress by South Carolina's John S. McSwain, who had for years been a leading congressional spokesman for the American Legion and had, over these years, repeatedly introduced the antiprofit legislation which the Legion favored, knowing full well it had no chance of passage. The present McSwain bill's provisions were mild indeed, measured against the need which the Nye committee was preparing to define in public hearings within the next few weeks. The bill made no provision for capital conscription, labor conscription, or an excess profits tax. Its only important provision was for mandatory price freezing by the executive upon a declaration of war or of war emergency, the frozen price to be that of the day of the declaration, or of some earlier day, with discretionary power by the President to raise or lower legal prices thereafter.[40]

Announcement of the formation of the Baruch-Johnson Committee, as it was called, provoked expected reactions.

The business community was in general delighted by what it at once interpreted as a presidential undercutting, a shutting off, of the munitions investigation. The maneuver "takes the punch out of the inquisition," reported *Business Week;* it "steals the show, saves the War and Navy departments some embarrassment regarding their relations with munitions makers and forestalls the Senate committee's recommendation for nationalization of the industry."[41] Nye and his committee were in proportion dismayed. The initial funding of the investigation was nearly exhausted, and an appropriation of $50,000 to enable the investigation to continue was being requested. The granting of such appropriation seemed now unlikely; it would be impossible if the White House definitely disapproved it.

But Roosevelt may *not* have expected as great an outpouring of popular support of the munitions investigation, joined with expressed fear and indignation that it was being deliberately cut short by the White House, as at once ensued. Some 150,000 wires and letters urgently requesting a full continuance of the investigation were received by the committee within two weeks after the presidential announcement, Nye reported to the press, and expressions of support poured also into the White House mailroom. To this pressure, Roosevelt made typical response. He held a warm, friendly personal conference with Nye on the day after Christmas 1934. From it Nye emerged, "smiling and happy," to tell reporters that he and his fellow committee members "had misunderstood the purpose of the Baruch-Johnson Committee." Far from wishing to terminate the Senate committee's effort, the President sought to reinforce it. He wanted Congress to give the Munitions Committee the $50,000 asked for, and he wanted Baruch-Johnson to cooperate with Munitions in the shaping of a legislative program "to take the profit out of war."[42]

The committee thereafter forged ahead in ways that did nothing for Roosevelt's own happiness and much for his covert unease. On February 6 Bennett Champ Clark defined the issue between the Nye committee and Baruch-Johnson, with its McSwain bill, by introducing in the Senate no fewer than seven bills which, in sum, would enable the President to socialize the economy to whatever extent he deemed necessary in time of war. They provided the executive with the authority to conscript not only all male citizens of age eighteen or over but also real and personal property and to fix prices and wages. The bills were submitted, Clark admitted, not in any expectation that they would pass but for purposes of discussion. In following days the committee explored in public hearing the war profits of American corporations from 1914 to 1918, discovering no new facts but making popular knowledge of facts theretofore known only to a small minority of the general public, such facts as that, on a total capitalization of $10 million, the Savage Arms Company had made a profit of $6 million in 1917; that Bethlehem Shipbuilding's profits, which averaged $6 million annually from 1910 to 1914, had averaged $49 million from 1914 through 1918; that an even greater increase of profit had come to E. I. du Pont de Nemours; and that top executives of these and other companies had routinely received huge bonuses in addition to their high salaries, often voting them to themselves when they were members of boards. (The bonus payments made to Bethlehem's Eugene Grace received special mention; they totaled $2 million during the war years.)[43]

Simultaneously the Brandeisian economic journalist John T. Flynn, a member of the committee's advisory council,* was working on a war mobilization plan which became the subject of public hearings when the committee resumed these on March 15, 1935. The Flynn plan permitted government price-fixing but placed no reliance on it to prevent war profiteering. A firm's overall profit, Flynn pointed out, is not determined by the profit margin per individual item sold but by this margin multiplied by the total number of items sold, meaning that huge excess profits could be made in an assured war market on a margin considerably smaller than the 5 or 6 percent which the McSwain bill would permit. Control or reduction of war profits could be achieved only by direct attack upon them, Flynn averred, and he proposed to use the taxing power to limit a corporation's annual profit during wartime to 3 percent of its actual

---

*Flynn had been asked to become the Munitions Committee's chief investigator but had refused the post, which went, instead, and fortunately, to the remarkably competent, likable, and fair-minded Stephen Raushenbush, a liberal and a pacifist who had made himself an authority (he had published three books) on the social problems of the coal and public utilities industries. Aged thirty-eight in 1934, he was the brother of Paul Raushenbush (see p. 444).

capital value; to permit no individual income higher than $10,000 annually (on incomes up to $10,000, individuals would pay income taxes at the preceding peacetime rate); and to employ the federal revenues thus obtained to finance the national war effort on an approximately pay-as-you-go basis. Flynn, too, cited the huge salaries, plus bonuses, which corporation executives were paid (paid themselves) out of what was, ultimately, tax money. Representative, said Flynn, was the case of a steel company executive whose pre-1914 salary had been $17,000 but became $61,000 in 1915, an increase of some 360 percent, while the wage paid by that company to its labor increased only 1½ cents an hour, from 18½ to 20 cents, or 8 percent. Two years later, doughboys who were fighting, bleeding, dying on the western front were being paid $1 a day. Flynn's plan, therefore, called for the conscription of business management, the drafting of business executives into government service, for the war's duration. Clearly the sacrifice this plan would impose upon businessmen was not "serious," opined the plan's author in testimony before the committee (at any rate "not as serious as being hit by a high-explosive shell," suggested Senator Clark); it was no greater than all other civilians would be compelled to make, according to Flynn. (This last, in its implications, disturbed officials of the AFL and the railroad brotherhoods; though Flynn did not call for the conscription of labor, the omission was glaring and likely to be supplied in the event of war, if not during the current legislative process. Organized labor therefore supported the mild McSwain bill.)

On March 19, only a few days after Flynn's hearings testimony, the committee members came to the White House for a conference with the President on industrial mobilization plans. Roosevelt expressed general sympathy with the Flynn proposals; he gave committee members the impression that he might actually support some of them effectively.

But he had other things on his mind, as he soon made clear to the conferees.

Dark clouds, thunderous with threats of war, gathered over Europe and Africa. Just three days before, in Berlin, Adolf Hitler had startled the world with his announcement that Germany had developed an air force in defiance of the Versailles Treaty and would no longer be bound by those clauses of that treaty which decreed German disarmament; as Führer and chancellor he proclaimed a new law providing for universal military service and a standing army of over a half million men (twelve corps, thirty-six divisions). Britain and France were protesting strongly. Would they act? Would their action be military? In Rome, Benito Mussolini, following a clash between Italian and Ethiopian troops on the Ethiopian-Somaliland frontier in early December 1934, had reversed his former policy of friendship with Addis Ababa (he had supported Ethiopia's entrance into the League of Nations) and was now concentrating armed forces in Eritrea in obvious preparation for a war of conquest against Ethiopia—this despite large concessions made by France, during conversations conducted by Pierre Laval, to Italy's African claims. What would the League do? Would it impose sanctions that triggered general war? And what could the United States do to prevent the developing world catastrophe?

Roosevelt's immediate reaction to the Hitler announcement had been to outline next day, to Morgenthau and others of his inner circle, a scheme which
struck most who learned of it as unrealistic to the point of absurdity, in view
of the natures of the governments of Britain and France and the current temper
of the American people. According to Morgenthau's diary, Roosevelt proposed

> England, France, Italy, Belgium, Holland, Poland and possibly Russia . . . get
> together and agree on a ten-year disarmament program which would look forward
> to doing away with all methods of warfare other than what a soldier can carry on
> his back or in his hand. His thought was that these countries would sign this pact
> themselves and would then approach Germany and ask her to sign. If she refused,
> these countries would then establish a two-way blockade around Germany, not
> permitting anything at all to enter or leave Germany. . . . We would send an admiral
> abroad who would assist in seeing that our ships did not run through this blockade.

If some such effort were not made, "the chances are we will have a world
war."[44]

Very different from this, and in seemingly flatly contradictory ways, was
Roosevelt's inspiration as he faced the Nye committee members on March 19.
Evidently it was a sudden inspiration. Certainly Nye and the others were
surprised by the President's abrupt suggestion that they turn their attention
to the problem of maintaining U.S. neutrality if war broke out overseas.
Nothing in the Nye-Vandenberg resolution authorized this special committee
to study and report on neutrality, a matter lying well within the domain of the
Senate Foreign Relations Committee. But the committee members, most of
whom were fervent isolationists, accepted the suggestion eagerly and acted
upon it promptly. By March 27, when the State Department tried to persuade
the committee to delay work on neutrality until the President returned to
Washington (he had left for his *Nourmahal* vacation three days before), it was
already too late; the committee was nearing agreement on a neutrality draft
bill. To Foreign Relations Committee Chairman Pittman's loud protests
against this invasion of his committee's legislative territory, Nye, who was not
likely to forget how Pittman had dealt with the original Nye resolution proposal, made bland reply: He sincerely wished he *could* be rid of the neutrality
problem; it was not one the committee had thought of dealing with until "the
President laid it on our doorstep."[45]

By then Roosevelt may well have begun to wish he had not done so. A large
part of his purpose, obviously, had been to divert or distract the Nye committee's attention, and the public's attention, from a line of legislative action
leading toward arms manufacture nationalization and subversion of the profit
system in general. This aim was only partially achieved, at an increasingly
threatened excessive cost in terms of executive control over foreign affairs, as
became clear from events now crowding in upon one another within this field
of legislation.

On April 1, while the House was debating the McSwain bill, Nye's committee issued a report endorsing every major element of the Flynn plan. On April

6, the eighteenth anniversary of America's entrance into the Great War, 50,000 veterans paraded through the streets of the capital in a "march for peace" while pacifist organizations conducted public meetings in which the "tragic error" of 1917 was deplored; commemorative wreaths were laid upon the graves of three members of 1917's Congress who had voted against the declaration of war. And on that day pacifist oratory was loud in the House of Representatives as congressmen, in a veritable frenzy of antiwar sentiment, attached one sweeping amendment after another to the McSwain bill, transforming it into something very like what Flynn proposed. The frenzy quickly subsided. Sobriety returned. On April 9, having made its gesture of deference to organized pacifism, the House, again under the control of administration forces, quietly voted down every radical amendment that had been adopted and then passed the McSwain bill in approximately its original form, 367 to 15.

Three days later a one-hour "strike against war" was staged by some 175,000 college students across America; in public speech and document they demanded the abolition of ROTC, called for "schools, not battleships," and warned, in at least one instance, that the strike was "a dress rehearsal of what students intended to do should war be declared."[46]

On that same April 12, in a statement filed with the Nye committee and released to the press, Baruch directly attacked the Flynn proposals for the first time, and in the strongest terms, damning them as utterly subversive of capitalism. "I am not debating here whether the profit motive is right or wrong," he said. ". . . I *am* saying that the advent of modern war . . . when the fate of the people depends on the efficient operation at high-speed pressure of its industrial system, is *not* the moment . . . to switch from the fundamental base of our economic system to a new and wholly experimental system which was never adopted at any time in the world's history in peace or war without an immediate result of collapse or ruin." To this, and to Baruch's more specific statements to the effect that only the desire for profit could motivate the productive effort needed in wartime, Nye made reply in a national radio broadcast three days later, saying that Baruch, who in his first testimony before the committee had called for a "drastic program" to take the profit out of war, was now "hedging." A sufficiently drastic program having been presented, Baruch opposed it, claiming "that we would be defeated in another war under such legislation because business wouldn't do its share of fighting . . . when profits were so restricted." Cried Nye: "I've expected someone to say that. But, Mr. Baruch, I never expected it from you. So American business won't produce what is needed in war if it can't have its profits! So American business will not go to war on the same basis that the boys go when they are called!" And Vandenberg, in the garbled rhetoric typical of his public speech, expressed the same idea: He was "everlastingly opposed to the collectivist state," but "God help capitalism if it won't defend a common national crisis without its pound of flesh."[47]

And the Nye committee was not so involved with neutrality legislation as to permit the House action on the McSwain bill to go unchallenged. When the

Senate began consideration of the House-passed bill, on May 3, Nye promptly introduced amendments which would transform it into a Flynn type of measure.

It became necessary for the White House to come out definitely in favor of the House version of the McSwain bill, meaning White House opposition to the Flynn plan. Against such opposition that plan had no chance of adoption. By midsummer it was a totally lost cause. So was the proposal to nationalize the arms industry. In its final report, issued the last of June 1935, the special Munitions Committee unanimously recommended adoption of the Flynn proposals but divided four to three with regard to armaments nationalization. The majority (Nye, Clark, Bone, Pope) favored nationalization. Said Nye in public speech: "The will of the munitions industry for profit has so totally blinded it to ordinary decency, and our committee's record reveals so clearly that the industry breeds hate, fear, and suspicion among peoples and nations to the end that there may be more profit for it, that no mere control [regulatory control, such as the administration deemed sufficient] would be sufficient." Cited by the committee were two instances in which government production of ammunition, and government building of warships, could be directly compared as regards cost. In 1928 the government's Frankford Arsenal Plant near Philadelphia was producing cartridges for two-thirds the price per thousand charged the government by private manufacturing firms (Remington Arms, Western Cartridge, Peters, Winchester Repeating Arms)—and this cost data had been obtained by a committee representing the private manufacturers! Government documents showed that two cruisers built in U.S. Navy yards cost $9,331,337 and $9,635,747, whereas four virtually identical cruisers, as regards design, built in private shipyards, cost $11,543,432, $11,689,975, $11,-596,146, and $11,569,831. Nevertheless, three of the committee (Vandenberg, George, Barbour) went along with the administration in its argument that nationalization would reduce the efficiency of arms production.[48] And in Congress, on this matter, the administration prevailed. There was thus lost, as some would say in a later year, an opportunity to gain a measure of sane humane control over what, in the absence of such control, was destined to grow through new world war and its aftermath into a "defense" industry, a so-called military-industrial complex, of awesome size, minimal or nonexistent ethical standards, and terrifying power over the nation's domestic and foreign affairs.

Roosevelt was less successful—indeed, he was hardly successful at all—in his effort to guide and shape the fused pacifist-isolationist energies he had released with his evidently impulsive neutrality legislation proposal. All through that long, hot summer, amid the abundance of his other concerns, he struggled against passage of legislation stemming from three Nye-Clark bills introduced by the two senators on their own responsibility, but obviously with committee support, in April. One of these prohibited loans by American citizens or the government to belligerent governments or to citizens of belligerent nations. Another prohibited the issuance of passports to U.S. citizens for entrance into war zones. The third required the President to embargo all arms shipments to belligerent nations. The effect was a denial to the President of a needed flexibility in the conduct of foreign relations; he would be unable to discriminate in any practical way between an aggressive nation whose victory would be detrimental and possibly fatal to U.S. interests and a victim nation whose survival was of supreme importance to the well-being of the United States. The administration wanted, instead, a measure giving the President a wide range of discretionary power, one that would permit him to take sides between aggressor and victim, joining other nations in collective action against aggressors when doing so would preserve or restore a peace clearly identical with America's good. Perhaps Roosevelt could have prevailed in this had his case been presented to the country in a carefully prepared fireside chat, but the hot summer of 1935 was no time for firesides, and as it happened, he was overwhelmed by organized pacifist and isolationist sentiment, reinforced by events abroad. By August it was clear that Mussolini was determined to annex Ethiopia to a new "Roman Empire" and that the League of Nations could oppose him effectively only at the risk of general war. On August 18 conversations among Britain, France, and Italy, aimed at preventing Italo-Ethiopian war, collapsed. The effect in the United States was to raise to its highest pitch the tide of isolationism, a passionately fearful opposition to any involvement of any kind in a seemingly imminent European conflict. When administration forces then moved to block any neutrality legislation whatever in that session of Congress, they were frustrated by Nye's threat of a filibuster to keep the session going until the neutrality legislation was acted upon.

What emerged from this, on August 24, was Senate passage of a measure, already approved by the House, which mandated the prohibition of the export of arms, though not the prohibition of other war material exports (oil, steel, copper, etc.), by any American to any nation involved in war. It also provided that Americans who traveled to nations at war or into war zones must do so at their own risk; established the National Munitions Control Board to license exporters and importers of munitions (the government could not refuse a license, however, unless the President had embargoed munitions to the country that wished to buy them); and restricted the use of American ports by the submarines of belligerents. The arms embargo was to go into effect automatically upon the President's declaration of the existence of a state of war, and the one concession the White House could wring from isolationism with regard to it was a time limit. The embargo provision was to expire the last of February 1936.

Signing the bill into law on August 31, 1935, Roosevelt declared its "purpose" to be "wholly excellent" but also declared "that no Congress and no Executive can foresee all possible future situations. History is filled with unforeseeable situations that call for some flexibility of action," he went on. "It is conceivable that situations may arise in which the wholly inflexible provisions . . . of this Act might have exactly the opposite effect from that which was intended. In other words, the inflexible provisions might drag us into war instead of keeping us out," for they might prevent effective cooperation by the United States "with other similarly minded Governments to promote peace."[49]

VIII

WHEN this signature statement was issued, the long and almost incredibly productive first session of the Seventy-fourth Congress had at last come to an end. The end had been stormy. A single measure remained to be acted upon, and a joint resolution to adjourn at midnight had already been adopted, upon the President's insistence, when the Senate assembled at six o'clock on that hot, steamy evening of Monday, August 26. This measure was a deficiency appropriations bill which included funds to launch social security. It had already passed the House, but the Senate had added amendments providing for large increases in subsidies, through AAA, to cotton and wheat farmers. Since these amendments could not possibly be sent back to the House for its consideration before midnight, Majority Leader Robinson moved to strike them from the measure. Huey Long objected. Having claimed the floor, he vowed to hold it, filibustering, until the Senate and House leadership agreed to permit the cotton and wheat amendments to be acted upon by the House. This might postpone adjournment for a day or two. So what? Why should the United States Senate roll over and play dead just because the President wanted it to? And Long did hold the floor, against loud cries that he would "deprive crippled children of benefits by defeating this bill," until midnight, when with angry bang of gavel, Vice President Garner declared adjournment.

Actually, as Huey Long told reporters soon thereafter, defeat of this bill did no harm whatever to the launching of the social security program. The Social Security Act, which Long deemed ridiculously inadequate (an "abortion" he called it), was "signed, sealed, and delivered, and that feller's got enough money to polish the North Star if he wants to." As for that "feller" in the White House, he was utterly contemptible, in Long's vividly expressed opinion, and would not be in the White House much longer. "This is his last term."[50]

The "feller" himself waited in growing irritation and exasperation that night for news of the session's end. His patience and good humor, normally immense, were by then as exhausted as his mind, his body. When news of the adjournment came through at last, in the first minutes of Tuesday, August 27, he was "so tired," as he later said to Morgenthau, "that I would have enjoyed seeing you cry, or would have gotten pleasure out of sticking pins into people and hurting them."[51]

Yet even then he could not but have felt, deep down, a glow of personal triumph. Against considerable odds, he had won from a Congress that was at times in open rebellion against his leadership some 80 percent of what he had requested. He who just three short months before had appeared confused, futile, helpless to defend his tottering New Deal against death at the hands of its enemies, must now be perceived to stand upon a very high pinnacle of success, though it remained to be seen whether that success was truly popular. And as he surveyed the political landscape from this lofty perch, he saw the menacing figure of Huey Long as much smaller than it had been last May, when he, Roosevelt, had stood on low ground—though Long was still menacing enough, God knew!

BOOK FOUR

————⟫×⟪————

The Man Becomes
the Issue

15

->>X<<-
Into 1936, Under Gathering Clouds of War

I

IT was a warm, lazy, golden-lighted afternoon at Hyde Park, this Sunday, September 1, 1935. The broad bosom of the Hudson was serenely reflective of an intensely blue, cloudless sky; there was just a hint of tawny autumn color in the green of the long grassy slope leading down to the remnant of pine forest that stretched along the riverbank, beside railroad tracks, on Roosevelt land. And through the open windows of the spacious, comfortably furnished library of the Big House, where Franklin Roosevelt sat, alone for the moment, awaiting a visitor, came on a mild breeze the mingled scents of flowers, fresh-cut grass, and apples rotting on the orchard floor, having fallen green from the boughs. On such a day Roosevelt would have loved to have been out of doors, would have loved to have driven over his estate in his specially built, wholly hand-controlled Ford, pausing here and there to see how trees he had planted were doing, would have loved to have gone over to Val-Kill Cottage and there sunned himself beside the swimming pool in the relaxing company of Missy LeHand, Nancy Cook, Marion Dickerman. Instead, confined to the library, he pondered problems of rough texture and heavy weight which pressed harshly upon his mind, his spirit.

The normally pale brown half-moons below his eyes were now almost black. There was a greater than normal trembling of his hands, especially noticeable when he lit a cigarette. His temper had become again as short, his irritability as great and frequently manifested, as it had been last winter and spring (even so, as others remarked of him, he was more patient and forbearing than many are in their most restful, happy times). To himself and his most intimate associates he admitted that his weariness was bone deep and aching, that he desperately needed the long ocean-cruising holiday he had planned to begin a month from now. If only he could put off until after his vacation his dealings with the problems he faced! But the problems must be dealt with at once; the pressures upon him during the days just ahead would be but little less intense than those of the final weeks of the congressional session. At a time when his reserves of energy were very nearly, if not quite, exhausted there was demanded of him a major expenditure of energy—an effortful exercise of his charm, his persuasiveness, his manipulative ingenuity, and possibly, as last resort, painfully, the coercive punitive powers of his office.

There was, for instance—and a major instance—the quarrel between Hopkins as WPA administrator and Ickes as PWA administrator, the quarrel made inevitable by the blurred and complicated way in which the Emergency Relief

Act of 1935 had been executively implemented. The quarrel had reached crisis stage within the last week.

On Monday afternoon, August 26, the last day of the congressional session, there had come to Ickes's desk a letter from the President that had been designed to lighten the President's administrative load, reducing his direct involvement with this bitter interagency rivalry. The letter said: "[W]ith respect to public works funds available for carrying out the purposes of the National Industrial Recovery Act, as amended [the amendment was a response to the Supreme Court's NRA ruling], I desire that all future applications for allocations and all cancellations, rescissions, and modifications of previous allocations be submitted to the Advisory Committee on Allotments, to be acted upon in the same manner and to the same extent as that committee acts with respect to allocations made under the Emergency Relief Appropriation Act of 1935." It had been Roosevelt's hope that this administrative change would be made palatable to Ickes by the fact that he, Ickes, was chairman of this Advisory Committee on Allotments. But through some mischance or deliberate leak the letter had been published in full in an early-afternoon edition of that Monday's Washington *Star,* as part and basis of a front-page interpretative news story—and this before the letter had been delivered into Ickes's hand. So, at least, Ickes would always claim; a historian must recognize the possibility that the letter was leaked by Ickes himself, for in his endless, relentless struggle for power he often engaged, clumsily, in Machiavellian strategies, and he was on especially friendly terms with a key member of the *Star*'s editorial staff. At any rate, the headline for the *Star*'s story, ICKES IS SHORN OF PWA POWER, was precisely Ickes's immediate interpretation of what the letter meant.

Theretofore, as an agency the statutory base of which was Title II of the Industrial Recovery Act, and insofar as it was funded by appropriations made under that act, PWA had been wholly separate and independent, administratively, of the machinery set up to implement the Emergency Relief Act. Ickes had been accustomed to dealing directly with the White House on all important PWA matters. Now it appeared that his future operation as public works administrator would be subjected to the decisions of an excessively large, cumbersome committee, and the fact that he was its chairman did nothing to ease his pain. The chairmanship, he had found, was a post without power; it condemned him to preside over committee sessions in which virtually everything Hopkins asked for WPA was granted without question whereas PWA proposals were closely scrutinized and often rejected—a galling experience. What this letter meant then, to Ickes's mind, was in practical effect the absorption of Ickes's public works enterprise into Harry Hopkins's expanding empire, and within hours after Ickes had read the letter, he drafted one of his own to the President in which he expressed his sense of outrage and proposed to give up both his PWA administration and his membership on the Allotments Advisory Committee. Let Hopkins run the whole show, nominally as well as actually, if that is what the President wanted! But the letter remained unsent. For having written it, Ickes phoned the White House to obtain an immediate personal interview with the President, though it was then quite late at night, and Roosevelt then "sidetracked me," as Ickes noted, sourly, in his diary. "It is almost impossible to come to grips with him."

What happened was that a weary Roosevelt, insisting upon dealing with this matter over the phone, endured, first, a lengthy tirade, an outpouring of hurt feelings and anger, which Ickes himself described in his diary as a tongue-lashing. Roosevelt had expected some such outburst. In some ways he knew Ickes better than Ickes knew himself, was more accurately aware of Ickes's basic motivations than was Ickes himself, and he had realized from the first that the interior secretary's frequent threats to resign were not to be taken at face value. They were intended to be bargaining counters. They were moves in a power play. They were designed to force showdowns. And as such they were considerably less effective than Ickes thought they were, being heavily discounted by Roosevelt's knowledge of how greatly Ickes loved his position in the administration (it would almost kill him if he actually lost it) and of how emotionally dependent Ickes had become upon Roosevelt personally. A presidential frown could cast him down into deepest depression; a presidential smile could lift him to the heights. He was easy to handle, and normally Roosevelt rather enjoyed doing so. But not now. He was too tired. Wearily he asserted that night that the newspaper report was simply "cockeyed," repeatedly he assured Ickes that no change in his status as public works administrator had been made or was contemplated, and he ended the conversation at last with a promise to issue at once a "clarifying" press statement saying as much. He had then to dictate such a statement, for Steve Early to read back to Ickes and to prepare for release in the morning.[1]

Nothing was settled by this. The problem, for Roosevelt, remained unsolved, with a dangerous blowup in the offing.

But then, only yesterday, there had occurred an event whereby he was helped toward a solution, or at least given some extension of the time in which a solution might be found, insofar as his problem was one of handling Ickes.

Late in the afternoon of Saturday, August 31, 1935, Anna Wilmarth Thompson Ickes, wife since 1911 of Harold Ickes, was killed in an automobile accident on the road from Taos to Santa Fe, New Mexico, where she had been on vacation for several weeks. The event, as Roosevelt may or may not have privately suspected,* was not for Ickes a great personal tragedy. It was more in the nature of a release and relief from emotional bondage and turmoil. The marriage had been from its very beginning bitterly unhappy for psychologically complicated reasons which need not here be explored. It had totally failed as a sexual relationship, else the puritanical Ickes would never have become

---

*That Roosevelt did have such suspicion seems indicated by his immediately subsequent dealings with his interior secretary.

involved in the affair which placed at grave risk his public career during the New Deal's first year.* And Ickes, "Honest Harold," would make no pretense of being emotionally devastated. Roosevelt, however, acted at once upon the assumption that Ickes had suffered grievous personal loss. Tommy Corcoran had dined alone with Ickes that Saturday evening and then gone to the White House while Ickes returned to his office to dictate that day's diary entry; Corcoran was with the President when word of the fatal accident came through. Roosevelt immediately sent him to Ickes's office to give such aid and comfort as he could, Ickes and Corcoran having by this time become close friends. Roosevelt also phoned Ickes to offer condolences and ask what he personally might do to help. He had been about to board for the journey northward to Hyde Park, his special train, aboard which he planned to sleep, but he offered to put this off if he could be of any service at all by remaining in the capital. Ickes was deeply touched. His ill will toward the President was completely overwhelmed for the time being, his blazing anger quenched by this manifestation of personal friendship, personal sympathy. And Roosevelt intended to follow through on this, out of genuine human concern quite as much as from considerations of policy. He wrote Ickes a letter of warm sympathy; he asked Felix Frankfurter to call upon Ickes, while in Washington, as Roosevelt's personal emissary; he asked Eleanor to go to Chicago for Mrs. Ickes's funeral. (Four years later, while discussing the Roosevelt family with Betsy Cushing Roosevelt, whose marriage to the President's son James was then breaking up, Ickes suddenly recognized similarities between his wife and Eleanor, whom he had come to dislike and distrust. Like his wife, Eleanor was impressively effective as public figure but "impossible" in her private life, from Ickes's point of view, being a miserable failure as wife and mother.[2])

From all this came, for Roosevelt, a relief from tensions. But he knew it to be temporary. The Ickes-Hopkins quarrel remained on the verge of explosion.

And that explosion might well occur within the next two weeks, when Roosevelt must preside over a conference of Frank Walker, Ickes, Hopkins, Tugwell, and Acting Budget Director Bell, probably here at Hyde Park, to decide finally the division of the $4 billion emergency relief appropriation among WPA, PWA, and Resettlement. Hopkins was going to get most of it, Ickes but a small fraction of it. This was inevitable in view of the continued high rate of unemployment, the length of the relief rolls, and the fact that Ickes's "sound, worthwhile public works" were far less labor-intensive, far more limited to highly skilled labor than were Hopkins's WPA projects; men must be given work *now*, not in some indefinite future as a problematic "secondary" or "indirect" effect of large federal constructions. Also inevitable, therefore, was a yet more bitter and wrathful Harold Ickes. And this time he must be handled with special care, for this time his threat to resign would have a special weight and leverage. For one thing, as Roosevelt knew and regretted, Ickes was sleeping badly, his nerves were shot; he just might carry out his

*See pp. 203–4.

threat in a spasm of sick despair; and if he did, the administration would suffer a severe blow and Roosevelt, who was fond of the "Old Curmudgeon," as Ickes fondly called himself, would be personally hurt. Not only was Ickes a remarkably able administrator and an incredibly hard, productive worker, who had become in the public eye a vivid personification of absolute honesty and devotion to the public weal, but he was also, as public speaker and writer of articles and books, the most widely persuasive single spokesman for the administration save only Roosevelt himself. He was as much a master of the pungent phrase, the memorable epigram, as Ray Moley; he was a greater master of blisteringly effective invective than Hugh Johnson; he had wit and humor (when he forgot himself). No man could do a more effective hatchet job on political opponents than he. In this capacity he was greatly needed now, and would be increasingly needed as next year's election campaign got under way.

For despite, if not in part because of, the presidential triumphs of the Second Hundred Days, the New Deal remained in trouble politically. The unhappy fact had been impressed upon Roosevelt's consciousnes by his reading in that morning's newspapers of the latest Gallup Poll. The prolonged intense acrimony of the congressional session just ended, the incessant attacks upon Roosevelt personally in the conservative press, portraying him as an aspirant toward dictatorship who was surrounded by a "radical" and "un-American" Brain Trust, had evidently taken a heavy toll of his popularity in the nation as a whole.* Only 50.5 percent of the American people currently approved of him as President, according to Gallup—the lowest rating he had received since entering the White House.[3] The poll added point and force to a letter Roosevelt had received five days ago from hard-driving, power-hungry Roy W. Howard, head of the Scripps-Howard newspaper chain, who had a penchant for manipulative "inside" politicking and, since 1924, had been gradually transforming into typically conservative organs the formerly liberal "people's papers" launched by E. W. Scripps. Howard, however, supported Roosevelt in 1932 (he had backed Newton D. Baker during the struggle for presidential nomination) and had been generally friendly to the administration; he wrote as a personal friend of the President's, his letter dated August 26, the day of congressional adjournment. Said Howard:

> As an independent editor keenly interested in the objectives of the New Deal I have been seeking reasons for the doubts and uncertainties of those businessmen who are

---

*In the judgment of one historian, a major causal factor in this momentary shrinkage of popularity was public reaction to Roosevelt's dealings with the armaments manufacturing, antiwar profits, and neutrality legislative proposals emanating from the Nye committee investigations. The wave of pacifistic isolationism was then at its highest, and those who rode its crest (they numbered in the millions) were encouraged to perceive Roosevelt as militaristic and war-minded—a Big Navy man, an advocate of belligerent "collective action," who was likely to embroil his country in the new world war which seemed to be brewing. This perception heavily discounted the approval Roosevelt gained, through his wealth tax and social insurance proposals, from, roughly, this same group.

skeptics, critics, and outright opponents of your program at a time when there is no commensurate dissatisfaction being evidenced by others of the electorate [the Gallup Poll seemed to indicate, alas, that a "commensurate dissatisfaction" among these "others" was developing]. . . . So long as this hostility emanates from financial racketeers, public exploiters, and sinister forces spawned by special privilege, it was of slight importance. No crook loves a cop. But any experienced reporter will tell you that throughout the country many businessmen who once gave you sincere support are now, not merely hostile, they are frightened. Many of these men . . . have become convinced and sincerely believe:

That you fathered a tax bill that aims at revenge rather than revenue—revenge on business;

That the Administration has side-stepped broadening the tax base to the extent necessary to approximate the needs of the situation;

That there can be no real recovery until the fears of business have been allayed through the granting of a breathing spell to industry, and a recess from further experimentation until the country can recover its losses. . . .

I know you feel as I do [Roosevelt, who often employed this form of words himself, was well aware that such assertion of certainty was a belying of doubt]—that with all its faults, and the abuses it has developed, our system has in the past enabled us to achieve greater mass progress than has been attained by any other system on earth. Smoke out the sinister forces seeking to delude the public into believing that an orderly modernization of a system we want to preserve is revolution in disguise.[4]

How should this letter be answered? Should the letter exchange be published, as Howard in a cover note suggested?

These questions constituted the problem uppermost in Roosevelt's mind, since it must be immediately dealt with, as he sat, momentarily alone, in the library on this late-summer Sunday afternoon. The visitor he awaited was Raymond Moley, who was driving up from New York City. Moley was bringing with him a draft reply to Howard, prepared at Roosevelt's request. And Roosevelt knew what, in general, the reply would say, the conciliatory tone it would have, since Moley had been pressing for months for precisely such administration attitude and policy as Howard called for.

Then Moley entered the room.

He received cordial greeting from a President who seemed to him "more tranquil, generous, indulgent, than he had been for eight months." True, Roosevelt made teasing reference to Moley's "fears over the storm and fury of last summer," and the teasing had a sting in it. He also made acid comment upon the business view of his taxation policy, as described by Howard; he revised and added to what Moley had written in reply to this portion of Howard's epistle.[5] But he was generally approving of what Moley had written, the two quickly put the reply into final shape, and Roosevelt as quickly decided that the exchange should indeed be released to the press in a few days. The reply sent to Howard said:

I appreciate the tone and purpose of your letter, and fairness impels me to note with no little sympathy and understanding the facts which you record. . . . I can well realize . . . that the many legislative details and processes incident to the long and arduous session of the Congress should have had the unavoidable effect of promoting some confusion in many people's minds. . . . The tax program of which you speak is based upon a broad and just social and economic purpose. Such a purpose, it goes without saying, is not to destroy wealth, but to create a broader range of opportunity, to restrain the growth of unwholesome and sterile accumulations and to lay the burdens of Government where they can best be carried. . . . Congress declined to broaden the tax base because it recognized that the tax base had already been broadened to a very considerable extent during the past five years. . . . What is known as consumers' taxes, namely, the invisible taxes paid by people in every walk of life, fall relatively much more heavily upon the poor man than on the rich man. In 1929, consumers' taxes represented only 30 percent of the national revenue. Today they are 60 percent, and even with the passage of the recent tax bill the proportion of these consumers' taxes will drop only 5 percent.

Then came the portion of the letter which would become immediately famous and remain historically memorable, being analogous to the public letter Woodrow Wilson addressed to William Gibbs McAdoo in November 1914 announcing, prematurely, completion of *his* administration's program of reform. Said Roosevelt:

This administration came into power pledged to a very considerable legislative program. It found the condition of the country such as to require drastic and far-reaching action. . . . It seemed to the Congress and to me better to achieve these objectives as expeditiously as possible in order that not only business but the public generally might know those modifications in the conditions and rules of economic enterprise which were involved in our program. This basic program, however, has now achieved substantial completion and the "breathing spell" of which you speak is here—very decidedly so.[6]

He meant that last, with profound sincerity. He personally needed rest even more than the business community said it did.

With the Howard letter disposed of, Roosevelt and Moley chatted about the presidential trip which was scheduled to begin on September 26, a train trip across the continent to San Diego, where Roosevelt would board the USS *Houston* for his cruising and fishing holiday. Roosevelt deemed recreative even the first days of this journey, during which he would deliver three major speeches and some dozen informal talks—he always drew energy, as a recharging electric current, from the audiences he faced and was revivified by them —but he would need Moley's help in the preparation of speech material. Perhaps Moley could return to Hyde Park in a couple of weeks to help plan these speeches?

Moley agreed to do so and took his leave.

II

WHEN Moley came again to Hyde Park, in mid-September, with speech notes and fragments of speech drafts in his briefcase, he found the President in an even more "generous" and "indulgent" mood than he had been on September 1, a finding doubtless influenced by Moley's own relief over the fact that Roosevelt followed, for the moment, a policy line Moley favored.[7] Yet there was objective truth in Moley's observation: Roosevelt was somewhat less weary and tense than he had been a fortnight ago. He had been refreshed, as he always was, by his return to his environmental roots—to the fields, the woods, the river, the house of his growing up. He had found time to drive for happy hours around the estate, renewing acquaintance with great trees he had known since earliest childhood and with the extensive tree plantations he himself had made. He was again with his mother, with whom he had a complex emotional relationship involving spark-engendering clashes of opposing will on many occasions, but a relationship dominated by love and mutual need. He had swum in the Val Kill pool. He had picnicked on the Val Kill picnic ground, beside the big outdoor fireplace designed by Nancy Cook. He had drawn vitality from crowded, fun-filled hours spent with people he had known intimately for a long, long time, people who accepted him unquestioningly as the center of their world, made no demands upon his mind, wanted nothing for themselves save his friendship.

At the same time three developments in public affairs had contributed to an easing of inner tensions.

One had been the reaction to his "breathing spell" announcement.

The letter exchange with Howard was published on Friday morning, September 6. On the New York Stock Exchange, where prices including utilities prices, despite the furor over holding company legislation, had been climbing slowly but steadily on moderate trading volume since March, there was that day a steep rise on a volume of 2,100,000 shares, which was considerably larger than the average daily volume in that year, and the sharp rise continued next day, on the largest Saturday volume (1,289,000 shares) since February 10, 1934. Business analysts universally attributed the bullishness to Roosevelt's pronouncement. On Monday, September 9, the stock price rise continued; on Wednesday, the eleventh, the average price was the highest since September 14, 1931, and trading was the heaviest since July 26, 1934.[8] Gratifying also, more so, was the volume of approving communications which poured into the White House mailroom and into Hyde Park. By the weekend of Moley's return to Hyde Park, thousands of enthusiastic telegrams and letters had been received from all over the country, and the latest Gallup Poll showed that Roosevelt's national popularity had risen precipitously from its lowest point.

By all this, the outlook toward 1936 was greatly brightened.

And it was brightened even more by another development or event, one which Roosevelt had promptly publicly deplored but which enormously simplified his political problems as he headed into an election year.

On Sunday night, September 8, in the marble corridor of the new Louisiana Capitol for whose construction he was responsible, and where the legislature was at that moment in working session, enacting laws he had ordered, Huey Long, the Kingfish, though accompanied as always by a bevy of heavily armed bodyguards, was approached and shot at close range in the abdomen, with a .32 caliber automatic pistol, by a young Baton Rouge medical doctor named Carl Weiss. Weiss paid at once for his deed with his life: He was gunned down by the bodyguards, who then stood over him, emptying their guns into his dead body as he lay facedown in a spreading pool of blood upon the marble floor. He had been an intellectually brilliant, emotionally tense, highly idealistic young man, a son-in-law of a Louisiana district judge who, impregnable in his district (he had been elected and reelected for twenty-eight years), had long been one of the bitterest political enemies of Huey Long and the Long machine. On that very day, Long pushed through his legislature a bill redefining two judicial districts in a way that made this judge's victory in the next election contest virtually impossible.

Rushed to the hospital, Long was operated on in the early-morning hours of Monday, September 9. Immediately upon its completion the operation appeared to have been successful. Long, it seemed, would recover. And Roosevelt at Hyde Park was so informed when, while yet abed that Monday morning, he dictated a press statement saying, "I deeply regret the attempt made upon the life of Senator Long of Louisiana. The spirit of violence is un-American* and has no place in a consideration of public affairs, least of all at a time when calm and dispassionate approach to the problems of the day is so essential." But before this statement was published, the discovery was made by consulted physicians, in the Baton Rouge hospital where the wounded senator lay, that the inexperienced surgeon who had operated upon him had failed to catheterize his patient before beginning the surgical procedure, to determine if the bladder contained blood. If it did, it meant that a kidney had been injured by the bullet and must be tied off. When the catheterization was at last done, hours after the surgery, it revealed much blood in the urine. Long was bleeding to death internally. Nothing could be done about it since he was now far too weak to survive another operation. His death was staved off for a brief time with massive blood transfusions (he had five on September 9), but he grew steadily weaker, was often out of his head, often unconscious, and died a little after four o'clock in the morning of Tuesday, September 10. He was lucid for a few moments before lapsing into his final coma, and those gathered at his bedside heard him plead in a weak voice, as his last words, "God, don't let me die! I have so much to do!" He had celebrated his forty-second birthday a little more than a week before.[9]

At the moment of Long's death Father Coughlin was sleeping on a train running from Detroit to Albany, where, shortly before dawn, he was met at the railway station by his friend and coreligionist Joseph P. Kennedy. Two days before, while dining at his home in Royal Oak, Michigan, a suburb of Detroit, only an hour or two before Long was shot, Coughlin had received a phone call from Kennedy, who was visiting at Hyde Park and who at once put on the line the President of the United States. "Hiya, Padre?" said Roosevelt, who always addressed the priest in this way. "Where have you been all the time? [Coughlin had sent no communication to the White House, nor come there himself, for many months.] I'm lonesome. Come on down and see me."[10]

---

*Actually, Americans are more prone to fatal violence than citizens of any other advanced industrial nation, according to comparative murder statistics.

Roosevelt's dislike and distrust of the Radio Priest had from the first been great. He was privately maliciously amused by Hugh Johnson's attack upon the "political Padre" last March and by Ickes's contemptuous description of Coughlin as a man "whose rich but undisciplined imagination has reduced politics, sociology, and banking to charming poetry which he distills mellifluously into the ether for the enchantment of mankind"—this in a nationally broadcast address by the interior secretary to the annual luncheon of the Associated Press, in New York City, last April 22. Yet he also regretted the Ickes attack; he told Farley it was "unwise." And he sent Michigan Catholic Frank Murphy, ex-mayor of Detroit, as his personal emissary to the priest to "sweeten him up" and try to work out some kind of accommodation with him. For he had been latterly concerned to insure *absolutely* against any effective political alliance between Long and Coughlin. He knew such an alliance to be unlikely. Since the first of the year the approach of the two demagogues to each other had been as the attempted coming together of two subatomic particles bearing the same electrical charge. There had been mutual repulsion. Neither of these two colossal egos was willing to accept the other as equal partner; each insisted upon dominating whatever arrangement they entered into. Nor was there sufficient programmatic agreement to provide a firm basis for practical cooperation between Share Our Wealth and Coughlin's National Union for Social Justice. The priest had let it be known that in his opinion Share Our Wealth was "unspeakable radicalism" (he was quoted as saying so in the Detroit *Free Press* on May 13, 1935), also that he could not trust Long to act upon the principles of social justice which Coughlin had proclaimed. And Long had let it be known that in his opinion Coughlin's prime prescription for depression cure—namely, inflation and monetary reform—was mere nostrum: a real cure required that "we get down to the basic and fundamental" problem, which was the maldistribution of wealth and income. Moreover, and conclusively, Long was put off by the priest's oily manners and lush rhetoric. After one frustrating meeting in Long's Washington apartment, the Kingfish reportedly shouted angrily to his associates that "Coughlin is just a political Kate Smith"* of whom the public was bound soon to tire.[11] Roosevelt had been informed of the gist of all this. He joined this information with an awareness that a very considerable portion of the Catholic Democracy which was the core of Coughlin's constituency was also strongly supportive of himself as President. He had been told that, every time the "Padre" made strong, direct attack on him, a distressing volume of protesting wires and letters poured into the Shrine of the Little Flower, in consequence of which Coughlin's increasing hostility toward him and the New Deal, unlike Long's hard, consistent line, had been wavering and uncertain of expression. No, an effective alliance be-

---

*A woman of such physical weight that some cruelly described her as "fat," Kate Smith possessed a soprano voice of sweetness and great clarity, though lacking depth and resonance, which she used to express a severely limited range of emotion as she sang popular songs. She was one of the most famous radio entertainers of the 1930s.

tween Coughlin and Long was highly unlikely. But the possiblity was one whose realization could be so disastrous that a prudent politician must take precautions.

Hence the phone call to the Little Flower's parsonage in Royal Oak.

Before dawn Coughlin stepped down from his Pullman onto the Albany station platform, where Joe Kennedy awaited him, and as he did so, he glimpsed, at a newsstand across the way, the banner headline of a just-issued newspaper extra. HUEY LONG DEAD, it said. A newspaper reporter came up to him as he bought a copy of the paper. Did Father Coughlin have any comment on the news? "The most regrettable thing in modern history," replied the priest promptly. Then he and Kennedy entered Kennedy's Rolls-Royce for the drive down to Hyde Park.

They arrived at the Roosevelt home before their host had risen from his bed. And it was from Coughlin, or the newspaper Coughlin carried under his arm, that Roosevelt learned of Long's death. It was news which reduced somewhat the urgency with which Roosevelt, in hours of talk with the priest that day, strove to bring him back into the New Deal fold or at the very least to deter him from any third-party attempt in 1936. The talk was inconclusive. "Don't be so innocent as to think that the President of the United States can also be the Congress of the United States," said Roosevelt in reply to Coughlin's plea that he greatly inflate the currency and abolish the Federal Reserve System. "I'm only the President." And when Coughlin and Kennedy departed in late afternoon, having declined an invitation to stay for dinner, the priest had made no commitment whatever. Neither had Roosevelt.[12]

Next day began the third development the issue of which had eased Roosevelt's tensions.

Ickes, summoned from Washington, arrived at Hyde Park late in the afternoon of Wednesday, September 11. He had no chance for personal conference with the President that day; he was instead at once caught up in a celebration of Missy LeHand's birthday,* at Val-Kill Cottage, where he went with Roosevelt, Roosevelt's mother, and the First Lady among others, for "a very pleasant dinner, with movies and some talk afterward." He was very tired: Since his wife's death his insomnia had grown worse, and he shared a bedroom in the Big House that night with Frank Walker whose stentorian snoring would have prevented his getting much sound sleep in any case. He was, therefore, not in good shape nervously, as he had longed to be and as Roosevelt wished him to be, when he conferred with the President in the latter's study at half past ten next morning. Nor were his taut nerves relaxed, or his outlook upon the world brightened, by the substantial conclusions of that conference. He had convinced himself "thoroughly" that Harry Hopkins "is a lawless individual bent on building up a reputation for himself as a great builder, even at the

*Her actual birthday was two days hence; but she would be in Boston then for family celebration of it, and upon that soft, warm September night shone a full moon, the harvest moon of 1935. The party at Val Kill was al fresco.

expense of the President and the country. I think he is the greatest threat today to the President's re-election." He had last weekend written the President a letter in which he "temperately and courteously, but firmly [the descriptive words are his], pointed out the political implications involved in Hopkins's methods." He now repeated this argument, saying that the work relief program "as at present outlined" had him "scared," that he had "no faith" in it, that he "believed it might jeopardize" Roosevelt's reelection. But he made, he realized, no persuasive impact whatever upon a President who, though "in a friendly mood," had his mind already made up on the matter in question, who now consulted Ickes solely for reasons of personal psychology, and whose evident principal purpose for this *tête-à-tête* was to invite Ickes to accompany him on his western trip and on the long sea voyage which would follow. It was an invitation which Ickes knew he was bound to accept, since Harry Hopkins was also being invited, though he told himself he didn't really want to go.

By the time the brief interview ended, Hopkins, Tugwell, and Bell had arrived, accompanied by a member of Ickes's staff and two of Hopkins's, among them Lee Pressman, now WPA's general counsel. There immediately followed, in the library, the decisive conference in regard to allocation of the $4 billion, a conference which turned out to be simply a session in which an imperious Roosevelt announced the decisions he had made on where the money would go; listened, unmoved, to Ickes's anguished protests; and then sternly, pointedly warned those in the room *not* to talk to reporters about these allocations. He indicated his displeasure over the huge publicity being given the feud between Ickes and Hopkins, also over the flood of telegrams and letters the White House had been receiving in protest against the alleged "scuttling" of PWA. He knew very well that such publicity and such floods were orchestrated by deliberate leaks to the press and to interested parties by members of Hopkins's and Ickes's staffs; he wanted the process halted. When the meeting ended, Hopkins had been assigned billions of dollars, Ickes less than $500 million (Tugwell received some $150 million), and it was a miserably unhappy public works administrator who left Hyde Park by train that night, having sourly refused the President's invitation to stay over until next morning.[13]

But the difficult task was done, a crisis in Roosevelt's relations with Ickes had been reached and passed, with no damage done the administration, and this was a great relief to the President who again conferred with Ray Moley, in mid-September. He told Moley of his plan to take both Hopkins and Ickes with him on his ocean voyage. There would be, he predicted, a death and burial at sea of the quarrel between the two, for he had immense confidence in the healing, soothing power of salt air and ocean spray, of seascapes and deep-sea fishing, and of the camaraderie of a ship's company, especially a ship over which he himself presided. Certainly his own peace of mind would be served by having both men constantly in his sight as he vacationed: he would not have to worry about what they were doing to each other, and to the administration, back in Washington.

It was peace he now longed for. He told Moley that in the speeches he was to make on his way to the Pacific he wanted again "to strike the note of peace and unity and harmony." And he seemed to Moley to be again his old buoyant self, "with his old winsome enthusiasm."[14]

A very different impression of him was made upon Walter Lippmann fewer than twenty-four hours later, when Lippmann came to Hyde Park to lunch with the President.

For many weeks Lippmann had been "deeply troubled about Roosevelt personally," as he had put it in a letter to his friend Edward Sheldon just the last week. In his syndicated column he had wondered if the President was prepared to return to the people "the extraordinary powers they granted him in a moment of grave danger for the single purpose of recovery" or if, instead, he was intent upon using these powers to substitute "some kind of planned collectivism" for the "free economy" to which Lippmann himself was committed. "He has a good heart, though not a great one," Lippmann went on to say in his letter to Sheldon. "And he certainly hasn't a great mind. And his best virtues—which are sensitiveness and zeal and courage—are not qualities with which to withstand the corroding effects of authority. . . . I am afraid that he is not thoroughly matured and that he is more suited to a crisis than to longer efforts." Lippmann fully shared with Moley and other conservatives the conviction "that the particular crisis that made him [Roosevelt] great is no longer with us" and that the "test" of Roosevelt between now and the convening of Congress next January "will be whether he recognizes" this alleged fact. The journalist was somewhat reassured by his hours of private talk with the President on this Monday, September 16; when he left Hyde Park, in the late afternoon, it was with the belief that he and the President were truly agreed upon the need for a "breathing spell," that Roosevelt was himself convinced "that he has gone as far as he should go with reforms that require important mental adjustments by the people." But Lippmann had definitely *not* found the President to be his usual buoyant, zestful self; instead, he seemed "edgy," restlessly ill at ease, notably lacking his usual self-assurance. When Eleanor Roosevelt entered the study where the two men discussed tax reform and interjected comments of her own on this matter (they were silly comments, in Lippmann's view), Roosevelt actually lost his temper.

"Oh, Eleanor, shut up!" he barked. "You never understand these things anyway."

Three days later, in another letter to Sheldon, Lippmann described Roosevelt as "dangerously tired," so tired "that if he were confronted with difficult decisions at this moment [Lippmann was greatly concerned over the imminent invasion of Ethiopia by Fascist Italy and the threat of general European war which it posed] his judgment couldn't be depended upon"; there was even the possibility that a serious challenge now "might lead to a nervous breakdown." "He will be put to a very severe test in the next few months because the attack upon him will be relentless," concluded Lippmann, worriedly, "and I don't know whether his inner reserves are sufficient to meet it."[15]

III

THE presidential special, carrying the President and First Lady, Hopkins and Ickes, and some seventy-five other people, pulled out of Washington's Union Station shortly before midnight of Thursday, September 26, 1935. Aboard were Marvin McIntyre and Steve Early, Missy LeHand and Grace Tully, military aide Colonel Edwin M. "Pa" Watson, and naval aide Captain Wilson Brown, personal physician Dr. Ross T. McIntire, and bodyguard Gus Gennerich—the whole of the President's personal staff save Louis Howe, who, by mid-August, had become again so ill that he could not be properly cared for in the White House and had been moved to an air-conditioned room in the Naval Hospital.

Two days later, in Fremont, Nebraska, the President delivered the first of three major addresses, its subject the New Deal's farm program. "The burden of agricultural debt . . . has been decisively and definitely lessened," he said. Loans totaling more than $1.8 billion had been made through the Farm Credit Administration to nearly half a million farmers since May 1933, most of them "used to refinance existing farm indebtedness" at the "lowest rate" of interest "in the whole history of our country." The disparity between farm and industrial prices—the "gap that was the measure of the farmer's despair and distress"—had been "in large part closed." The drouth was partially responsible for the rise in farm prices, of course, but so were the administration's monetary policy, the increased demand for farm products resulting from the "economic revival," and the "operations of the Agricultural Adjustment Administration." Farmers need not be told how AAA had worked:

> They know from the contents of their own pocketbooks that their income has been increased. The record is there to prove the case—an increase of $1 billion in farm cash income in 1933 over the year 1932; an increase of $1.9 billion in 1934 over 1932 and an estimated increase of $2.4 billion in this year of 1935 over 1932. Yes, that makes a total increase of $5.3 billion over what the farmer's income would have been if the 1932 level had been continued. Is it surprising, in the light of this improved income, that the farm implement factories in Illinois and New York, the automobile factories of Michigan, the steel mills of Pennsylvania, are springing into renewed life and activity?[16]

On September 30 he spoke at the dedication of Boulder Dam on the Colorado River, ceremonies presided over by Ickes, in whose department was the Bureau of Reclamation, which had built the dam. "We are here to celebrate the completion of the greatest dam in the world, rising 726 feet above the bed-rock of the river and altering the geography of a whole region; we are here to see the creation of the largest artificial lake in the world*—115 miles long, holding enough water . . . to cover the State of Connecticut to a depth of ten feet; and we are here to see nearing completion a power house which will

---

*The lake would be named Lake Mead, after Elwood Mead, the commissioner of reclamation who had administered this great construction and who died in office four months after its dedication, in January 1936.

contain the largest generators and turbines yet installed in this country, machinery that can continuously supply nearly two million horsepower of electric energy." Thus spoke the President, with genuine enthusiasm. He went on to say:

> We know that, as an unregulated river, the Colorado added little of value to the region this dam serves. When in flood the river was a threatening torrent. In the dry months of the year it shrank to a trickling stream. For a generation the people of the Imperial Valley had lived in the shadow of disaster from the river which provided their livelihood, and which is the foundation of their hopes for themselves and their children. Every spring they awaited with dread the coming of a flood, and at the end of nearly every summer they feared a shortage of water would destroy their crops. The gates of these great diversion tunnels were closed here at Boulder Dam last February. In June a great flood came down the river. It came roaring down the canyons of the Colorado, through Grand Canyon, Iceberg and Boulder Canyons, but it was caught and safely held behind Boulder Dam.

Had the dam been completed a year earlier, the $10 million crop loss in Imperial Valley last year, caused by drouth, would have been prevented. Moreover, the taming of the river had made feasible the construction of a $220 million aqueduct across the San Jacinto Mountains by the cities of Southern California "for the purpose of carrying [the Colorado's] regulated waters . . . to the Pacific Coast 259 miles away."[17]

The presidential special pulled into Los Angeles at eight o'clock in the morning of Tuesday, October 1. An estimated 1 million people saw Roosevelt as he made a fifty-mile automobile tour of the city; some 75,000 packed the Coliseum to hear him speak briefly and informally. He said that President Wilson had told him years ago:

> [T]he greatest problem that the head of a progressive democracy had to face was not the criticism of reactionaries or the attacks of those who would set up some other form of government, but rather to reconcile and unite progressive liberals themselves. The overwhelming majority of liberals all seek the same end, the same ultimate objectives. But because most liberals are able to see beyond the end of their own noses, they are apt to want to reach their goal by different roads. People who do not want to move forward in the improvement of civilization are perfectly content to stand in one spot, and those people find it easy to remain united in demanding inaction. Liberals, therefore, in order to make their efforts successful, must find common ground and a common road, each making some concession as to form and method in order that all may obtain the substance of what all desire. . . . Democracy is not a static thing. It is an everlasting march.[18]

The most important of his addresses on this western trip was delivered next day at the San Diego Exposition. He began by recalling that "twenty long years" ago he had "stood here in company with Vice-President Thomas Marshall when the first exposition was held here in San Diego. At that time the flames of a world war were spreading and two years later we ourselves were to take part in that great catastrophe to mankind." He spoke then most soberly of "fierce foreign war" which, with "malice domestic" (the phrases were from Shakespeare), constituted "the two most menacing clouds that hang over human government and human society. . . ." Of "malice domestic" he had little fear, but "fierce foreign war" appeared at that moment to be a very real immediate threat, and confronting that threat, he sought to soothe the popular fears it bred, using language that nationalistic, isolationist Raymond Moley had given him. "In the face of this apprehension [of general European war sparked by Mussolini's aggression against Ethiopia] the American people can have but one concern—the American people can speak but one sentiment: despite what happens in continents overseas, the United States of America shall and must remain, as long ago the Father of our Country prayed that it might remain—unentangled and free. . . . We not only earnestly desire peace, but we are moved by a stern determination to avoid those perils which will endanger our peace with the world." There followed qualifying words, perhaps inserted by the flexible Roosevelt into Moley's rigidly isolationist script. "Our national determination to keep free of foreign wars and foreign entanglements cannot prevent us from feeling deep concern when ideals and principles that we have cherished are challenged," he said. ". . . Our flag for a century and a half has been the symbol of the principle of liberty of conscience, of religious freedom and of equality before the law; and these concepts are deeply ingrained in our national character." Hence Americans could not but deplore and con- demn violations by governments abroad of these "ideals" and "principles" and "concepts." These violations, however, "are beyond our jurisdiction." All that we could do with regard to them was "assert for ourselves complete freedom to embrace, to profess and to observe the principles for which our flag has been so long the lofty symbol" and hope that other peoples would choose to follow our example. He returned then, through words evidently his own, to the Moley line:

> As President of the United States I say to you most earnestly once more that the people of America and the government of those people intend and expect to remain at peace with all the world. In the two and a half years of my presidency, this government has remained constant in following this policy of our choice. At home we have preached, and will continue to preach, the gospel of the good neighbor. I hope from the bottom of my heart that as the years go on, in every continent and in every clime nation will follow nation in proving by deed as by word their adher- ence to the ideal of the Americas—I am a good neighbor.[19]

Then began Roosevelt's real vacation, the long-awaited ocean cruise.

He and the men who were to accompany him boarded the heavy cruiser *Houston* shortly before three o'clock in the afternoon of Wednesday, October 2, at San Diego's Municipal Pier, while Eleanor Roosevelt, Missy LeHand, Grace Tully, and the others who had been on the train but were not sailing looked on, waving their farewells. There was, of course, another huge and often cheering crowd at hand.

Again, as in the summer of 1934, the President occupied the admiral's quarters, consisting of two large well-lighted rooms, with private bath. One room contained his bed. The other, with bookcases, easy chair, and writing desk, was where Roosevelt and his immediate party (Hopkins, Ickes, Ross

McIntire, Pa Watson, Wilson Brown) dined each evening, and lunched, too, each day, save those days on which the President was out in his fishing launch. Again, special ramps had been installed for the presidential wheelchair. He had to be wheeled up and down these, had, when he went fishing, to be carried sideways down a lowered companionway by two brawny men to the platform at its foot and there handed over, as if he were a monstrous infant, to two other brawny men standing on the launch deck (Captain Brown was one of them; the other, a sailor detailed to the *Houston* because of his expert knowledge of deep-sea fishing), and these in their turn effortfully lifted and deposited him, a heavy weight, in one of the two swiveled armchairs at the launch's stern, where he sat side by side with whomever he had chosen as his companion for the day, manipulating his rod and reel. This last he did skillfully, also with unusual strength and endurance, making joyous use of his superbly muscled arms, shoulders, torso, whenever big fighting fish were on his line. The moment of transfer from platform to launch was always a moment of risk. The risk increased when seas grew choppy. A sudden lurch might then tumble him down in a heavy fall, severely injuring him. But he manifested not the slightest concern over this—never flinched or gave any other sign of fear or even of awareness that danger existed. He commonly talked a steady stream while being carried; he laughed, he joked with those who carried him. All in all, through a marvelous alchemy of character and personality, which included his constant patient good cheer, his joyous openness to experience (to *all* experience), his seeming total lack of self-consciousness or sense of embarrassment, he managed to transform personal helplessness into personal power, passive submission into effortless domination, over those who physically handled him and those who watched him being so handled. What could have been pity tinged with contempt became an admiration wholly respectful; what would have been for another a series of humiliations became for him a series of triumphs.

On the first day out of San Diego, after coasting barren, mountainous Lower California for hours, so near the shore that the very few and poor and far-spaced dwellings upon it could be clearly seen from her deck, the *Houston* dropped anchor off barren, mountainous Cerros Island, where Ickes, at Roosevelt's invitation, boarded the presidential launch with his host and fished with him through the early afternoon. Ickes caught the largest fish of that day, a twelve-pound yellowtail, which, baked in the *Houston*'s galley, became the main dish at the President's table when they dined that evening.

And on the same day, halfway around the world, in a climate and landscape not greatly dissimilar to that viewed from and environing the *Houston,* Italian troops massed on Eritrea's border began, at Mussolini's order, their long-awaited invasion of Ethiopia, driving southward and westward against impotent resistance by primitively armed Ethiopians (the bulk of them had only spears with which to fight) toward Aduwa, where in 1896 an Italian army had been virtually annihilated by grandfathers of these same Ethiopians. Alarm bells rang in every major capital of the world. Coded radio messages were flashed from Washington to the *Houston* and, decoded, were delivered to Roosevelt upon his return from his fishing. In Geneva the Council of the League of Nations prepared to meet for special action. Clearly the League now faced a final test: If it proved as helpless in its dealings with the present crisis as it had been in its handling of crisis in the Far East, it was doomed.

Next day, in Magdalena Bay of Baja California and in choppy seas, the *Houston*'s presidential party fished for and caught yellowtail and mackerel and tuna. Soft-spoken, humorous, courteous Pa Watson, a southern gentleman as beloved by all who knew him as westerner Frank Walker was, if for different reasons and in a different way, landed a sixty-five-pound tuna that day; he impressed all who heard him with the persuasive eloquence, the linguistic ingenuity, with which he talked the hooked fish, in prolonged, uninterrupted monologue, into his landing net. And on that day, half a world away, Italian forces pushed on south and west through increasingly mountainous country, pushed also north and west from Italian Somaliland across the eastern Ethiopian plain, slaughtering human beings as they went. Warplanes roared overhead. In one of these rode or would soon ride Vittorio Mussolini, son of the Duce, who would subsequently edify the world with his description of dive-bombing as a "magnificent sport." According to aesthetic sportsman Vittorio, the bombs bloomed as sudden red roses, abrupt and beautiful, when they fell among swarming, dusky, lance-carrying horsemen "and blew them up."

At the President's dining table on the evening of Saturday, October 5, when the *Houston* sailed past Cape San Lucas, the southern tip of Baja California, and so beyond the sight of land, all the talk, being dominated by the President, was about the Italian-Ethiopian conflict. There had been no formal declaration of war, either in Rome or in Addis Ababa. But clearly what was happening was "war" within the meaning of the Neutrality Act which Roosevelt had signed on August 31. And Roosevelt now insisted upon immediate issuance of the proclamation, implementing this act, which, in anticipation of the event, had been prepared before he left Washington on this trip. It was at that very moment being published to the world. It declared "that a state of war unhappily exists between Ethiopia and the Kingdom of Italy" and, as mandated by Congress, prohibited the American export of arms, ammunition, and implements of war to the belligerents. It also specifically defined the prohibited matériel in six different categories, listing as implements of war aircraft, submarines, and surface war vessels of all kinds.

But could not and should not there be a considerably broader definition of "implements of war" than the present proclamation made? The question was raised during the talk at the President's dining table, that Saturday evening, and Ickes was reminded that there had been a lengthy discussion of it by Secretary of State Hull at the last cabinet meeting, on Tuesday afternoon, September 24. The arms embargo would operate exclusively against Italy, of course, since Ethiopia had no means of buying or transporting arms or any capacity to use them effectively were they placed in its hands. But by the same token the embargo had no force whatever as a deterrent to continued Italian aggression since Italy already had in hand a dozen times the amount of modern weaponry needed to crush a spear-wielding Ethiopian army. What *would* be effective was an interpretative extension of the Neutrality Act—an extension which seemed no greater, on the face of it, than had been made with regard to many other pieces of legislation since March 1933—whereby vital raw materials were defined as implements of war and so placed on the embargo list. This would deny Italy the American oil, copper, steel, scrap iron, cotton, etc., which it had to have in steady or increasing supply to sustain its military effort. It would render effective, as they could not otherwise be, the economic sanctions which the League must be expected to attempt to impose upon Italy as the aggressor in this conflict. Hull had indicated an inclination to do this, during his talk at the cabinet meeting, but Roosevelt had demurred. The President had doubted, and he continued now at the *Houston* dining table to doubt, that either the "letter" or the "spirit" of the Neutrality Act would permit him "to stretch it that far."

Indeed, he had good reason so to doubt. The sponsors and supporters of the act clearly meant by "neutral" what dictionaries said the word meant—to wit: "Not inclining toward or actively taking either side in a matter under dispute." Effective implementation of League sanctions against Italy would be a definite taking of side against Italy. Moreover, during Senate debate on the neutrality bill on August 21, Key Pittman of the Committee on Foreign Relations had undertaken specifically to define "implements of war" within the meaning of the bill and, in his definition, had made no mention of oil or steel or any raw material. Finally, certainly, pacifism and nationalistic isolationism, joined together, constituted a much more potent political force in American life at that time than pacifism linked to internationalism, with its proposals for collective action. Very active educative leadership by the President, a risk-taking leadership, would be required to transform the prevailing blind fear of war involvement, on the part of Americans, into clear-eyed, rational judgments on the best way, the most probably successful way to prevent a general war in which America must almost certainly become eventually involved. And in his present "breathing spell" mood, during which his dominant vital need was for rest and relaxation, Roosevelt was not disposed to provide such leadership; he would not have been even if he had been clear in his own mind as to what U.S. foreign policy at this juncture ought to be. Instead, to his dinner companions this Saturday evening he spoke of applying a "moral embargo" whereby the government would appeal to the conscience and patriotism of American businessmen to prevent their profitable export to Mussolini's Italy of the stuff of war.

There was also talk at table, and afterward, among Wilson Brown and Ickes and Hopkins, about the advisability of the President's cutting short his holiday and returning at once to Washington. Brown and Ickes were agreed he should do so, and Hopkins seemed to be, if only for the effect on public opinion; but the President dismissed the proposal out of hand when it was broached to him next day, Sunday, October 6, a day on which the *Houston* pitched and rolled on a heavy ground swell from morning to night. Episcopal church services were held for the President and his party on the cruiser's well deck that morning. News was received through ship's radio that Italian troops had taken Aduwa and were driving on toward the fortress of Makale. And Roosevelt approved for immediate publication a statement prepared by Hopkins saying he remained in constant touch with Washington by radio, regarding the war crisis. Ickes wanted him to add that he was prepared to return to Washington at any time, but this he refused to do.[20]

And so the holiday continued.

There was no fishing on October 7 and 8 as the *Houston* sailed southward at a leisurely pace through a continuing heavy ground swell and news flashed in from Geneva that the League Council had formally declared Italy the aggressor in the Ethiopian conflict and was preparing to impose sanctions upon it. On the morning of the ninth the *Houston* anchored off Cocos Island, the jungle island where the original of Robinson Crusoe had suffered shipwreck. Ickes was that day the fishing companion of the President, who, with a light rod and no shoulder straps, managed to land the largest fish yet caught by the party—a 109-pound sailfish. Two days later, with Hopkins his fishing companion, Roosevelt caught a 134-pound sailfish, landing it after two hours and twenty minutes of skillful, strenuous play, though by that time of that same day Gus Gennerich had landed a 148-pound sailfish, the largest fish caught during the whole cruise. News from Geneva was that the League might invite non-League members to join in the upcoming discussion of sanctions by the League Assembly, news to which the President, again aboard the *Houston*, responded promptly by approving a private message from Hull to League officials begging them *not* to invite the United States. If they did, the administration would be compelled by public opinion to refuse the invitation; there would be embarrassment all around.

Thereafter, for two full weeks, during which the representatives of fifty-one nations in the League Assembly voted for the imposition of economic sanctions on Italy and preparations were made to effect this, Roosevelt dismissed public affairs almost completely from his mind.

The black circles faded from beneath his eyes, his skin acquired a healthy glow of suntan, the bone-deep tiredness was drained out of him through fun and relaxation, as the *Houston* loafed along the coast of Central America for several days, anchoring frequently for fishing. This last, however, became increasingly unsatisfactory the farther south they sailed. It was so poor in the Gulf of Panama that the President decided to transit the Panama Canal on Wednesday, October 16, instead of on the seventeenth, as originally scheduled. And in the evening of that Wednesday, when the *Houston* was anchored behind the breakwater off Cristóbal at the Caribbean end of the canal, the President was presented with clear evidence of the success of his stratagem in inviting Hopkins and Ickes to join him in this holiday.

A special edition of the *Blue Bonnet,* the cruiser's weekly newspaper, was distributed to those at the presidential dinner table. It featured two "news" articles. Neither was signed, but all at the table knew that Hopkins must have written both of them. His denial that he had done so was not convincing. One article told of Hopkins's seasickness while Roosevelt was struggling to reel in his 134-pound sailfish, an episode which had made Hopkins the butt of much good-natured kidding. "Hopkins . . . stripped for action, moved from one side of the boat to the other, then like a cat moved back again—he looked sternly fore and aft and finally saw a school of sharks about to attack the sailfish. He leaned over the boat—looked intently into the blue sea," and then with "his fine features sharply drawn . . . went manfully about his" task of drawing the sharks away from Roosevelt's catch by providing them with other food. The other article reported:

> [The] feud between Hopkins and Ickes was given a decent burial today. With flags at half mast . . . the President officiated at the solemn ceremony which we trust will take these two babies off the front page for all time. Hopkins, as usual, was dressed in his immaculate blues, browns and whites, his fine figure making a pretty sight with the moonriffed sea in the foreground. Ickes wore his faded grays, Mona Lisa smile, and carried his stamp collection. . . . Hopkins expressed regret at the unkind things Ickes had said about him and Ickes on his part promised to make it stronger . . . as soon as he could get a stenographer to take it hot. . . . It was soon over. The President gave both of them a hearty slap on the back—pushing them both into the sea. 'Full Steam Ahead," ordered the President.

Three days later, when the *Houston* was anchored among coral islands in San Blass Bay, off the northern coast of Panama, Hopkins, Ickes, and Pa Watson, just the three of them, went out in a whaleboat on a warm, muggy, showery morning. They fished in desultory fashion for a few hours, during which they were soaked to the skin by intermittent showers, then went ashore on an uninhabited island to eat their picnic lunch under coconut palms. There they were caught in a torrential downpour which, since it gave no sign of letting up, drove them at last, in midafternoon, back to the cruiser. They arrived happy and sopping wet, also soaked through with camaraderie, each having thoroughly enjoyed himself and his companions during their shared adventure. Thereafter, in his diary, Ickes spoke of Pa Watson as "one of the best fellows I have ever known," a man who "simply bubbles with good humor and one cannot be grouchy or dispirited when he is around," and of Hopkins with a warmth which, if considerably less than Watson aroused (Hopkins "fitted in well with his easy manners and keen wit"), was more remarkable, in view of Ickes's earlier attitudes. Thus was developed between the PWA and WPA administrators a personal friendship which would not prevent but would reduce the acrimony of future public feuding between them as rival government officials.

In late afternoon of that Saturday, October 19, the *Houston* weighed anchor and headed north across the Caribbean toward Charleston, South Carolina, and the holiday's end. The travel schedule included a day's pause for fishing off Crooked Island in the Bahamas, but as they entered the Windward Passage off Haiti, a radiogram from Washington warned them of a hurricane developing behind them and moving northward. The Crooked Island stop was canceled, the sailing speed markedly increased, as the skies darkened and the seas grew rough. For a couple of days the ship "kept bowling along," as landlubber Ickes recorded, "at about twenty-one knots an hour [*sic*]." It reached Charleston Harbor and dropped anchor there, near Fort Sumter, at ten o'clock on the night of Tuesday, October 22.

Next day, before boarding his train for Washington, Roosevelt spoke extemporaneously to a large crowd at Charleston's famed military school, The Citadel, saying that "on landing" he had been "told the same story about South Carolina" as had been told him about the other states he had passed through during "my trip across the continent"—a story of economic recovery the truth of which was evident to his own eyes and ears. "Yes, we are on our way back," he said, in words that came back to haunt him two years later "—not by mere chance. We are coming back more soundly than ever before because we planned it that way, and don't let anybody tell you differently." He also reiterated the promise he had made in his San Diego address. "I shall make it my great and earnest effort to keep this country free and unentangled from any great war that may occur in the countries across the seas." His "very happy three weeks" aboard the *Houston* had revived him, renewed his energy. "I have come back very sunburned, full of health and ready to tackle a great ɪ.   hings."[21]

IV

A chief one of the "things" he had to "tackle," as he returned to the White House for a week, then went up to Hyde Park for a few days, then went down from Washington to Warm Springs for a two-week stay beginning on November 21, was the continuing problem of American policy with regard to Italian aggression against Ethiopia.

On October 30 he issued a statement warning American citizens that the Neutrality Act was in effect and that American citizens who engaged in "transactions of any character with either of the belligerent nations" did so "at their own risk." He went on to propose his "moral embargo," though without using that phrase. "[I]n the course of the war, tempting trade opportunities may be offered our people to supply material which would prolong the war," he said. "I do not believe that the American people will wish for abnormally increased profits that temporarily might be secured by greatly extending our trade in such materials; nor would they wish the struggles on the battlefield to be prolonged because of profits accruing to a comparatively small number of American citizens. Accordingly," he concluded on a note of vague threat, "the American Government is keeping informed as to all shipments consigned for export to both belligerents."[22]

This had the usual effect of appeals to conscience, which is to say it had none at all, upon those businessmen who profited from the commercial transactions which were deplored. During October the American shipments to Italy of oil, refined copper, and iron and steel scrap more than doubled the amount shipped in October 1934; the volume of such sales continued steadily and greatly to increase during the days following the President's statement, and so, in proportion, did the seriousness and difficulty of Roosevelt's foreign policy problem.

On the day after the presidential statement went out, the League definitely committed itself to the sanctions which the Assembly had recommended on October 11. There were four of these, scheduled to go into effect on November 18: an arms embargo, an embargo on credits, a boycott of Italian imports, and an embargo on certain raw materials. Oil was not included. But on November 6 the League Coordination Committee voted to extend sanctions to oil and some other previously unlisted materials, provided that simple guarantees of cooperation in this action were obtained from nonmember states. As regards oil, American cooperation was obviously absolutely essential. The United States in that year produced well over half of all the world's oil, the American oil industry thought itself plagued by market surpluses, and one could be sure that American oil companies, unless restrained by governmental action, would eagerly supply whatever Italian needs might result from a cutoff of the oil produced by League nations.

Thus a painfully sharp-horned dilemma was thrust upon Roosevelt. He was now convinced that a swift and effective imposition of economic sanctions would force Mussolini to abort his Ethiopian adventure if this were not very soon concluded, in view of Italy's lack of natural resources and of stockpiles of strategic materials sufficiently large to sustain even a relatively modest war effort for more than a few weeks. He was fully aware of the need for American cooperation with the League's "sanction movement," as he called it, if this was to succeed. He knew, too, that failure of this "movement," which meant triumph for fascism, was bound to encourage further aggression in contemptuous defiance of a moribund League, leading almost inevitably to a new world war. But he also knew—he was being continuously warned by politicians supportive of the administration—that his political opponents were "hoping and praying" that he would do something "in the present world crisis . . . which may be distorted into an endeavor on the part of our country to be a part of the League of Nations or of England's policy," as Senator Hiram Johnson was soon to say in a letter to him.[23] Even the appearance of permitting his foreign policy to be in any degree determined in Geneva would be construed by isolationists, who made up a large majority of the electorate and probably an even larger majority of his own supporters, as a "foreign entanglement" violative of George Washington's dictum and of the congressional will expressed in neutrality law. If he were not very careful, he would hand his political opposition an issue on which it might defeat him in 1936.

Nor were the horns of his dilemma at all blunted—they were, on the contrary, further sharpened—by the military situation in Ethiopia following the fall of Aduwa. The advance toward Fortress Makale was unexpectedly slow as Italian forces proved to be poorly organized and led and to have little stomach for fighting, while the Ethiopians, avoiding direct confrontations,

resorted to ambushes and hit-and-run attacks in which their primitive armament was often surprisingly effective. And at Makale, which was at last taken
on November 8, the Italians were stalled while changes were made in their top
command and they were completely reorganized. They must now drive due
south toward Addis Ababa through wild, mountainous country far better
suited to guerrilla warfare than to the swift movement and effective maneuver
of a large modern army. The preparations for this advance would evidently
take weeks. Obviously Mussolini could not quickly present his Ethiopian
conquest to the world as a *fait accompli,* and this meant that the Italian
economy became daily more vulnerable to sanctions.

"I know I'm walking a tight rope and I'm thoroughly aware of the gravity
of the situation," said Roosevelt to a worried Jim Farley on November 14. "I
realize the seriousness of this from an international as well as a domestic point
of view."[24]

It was with the feeling that he was going as far as he could go that he, next
day, approved the immediate issuance of a bluntly worded, implicitly threatful
recognition by Cordell Hull that the "moral embargo" was not working. More
and more of such essential war matériel "as oil, copper, trucks, tractors, scrap
iron, and scrap steel" were "being exported" by Americans to Italy "for war
purposes," though such trade "is directly contrary to the policy of this government . . . as it is also contrary to the general spirit of the recent neutrality act,"
said the secretary of state.[25] His words did nothing, as it turned out, to increase
compliance with the declared governmental policy. The volume of basic raw
material exports to Italy continued to swell. For the last quarter of 1935 the
amount of American oil shipped to Italian ports totaled thrice the amount
shipped during the last quarter of 1934.

What the Hull statement did do was increase the anxieties, politically hazardous to the administration, of those whose interpretation of the neutrality
law's "general spirit" was diametrically opposed to Roosevelt's and Hull's.
The public's reaction was by no means wholly unfavorable. Of some 3,000
letters received by the State Department from citizens strongly supporting
neutrality, during this period, a "significant minority" praised the administration's "tacit cooperation with the League," and a *Fortune* poll published in
December showed 47.9 percent of the citizenry in favor of economic cooperation with other nations to preserve peace.[25] But on the specific issue of cooperation with the League in economic sanctions against Italy, a large majority of
the American people were clearly opposed to doing so. They saw such cooperation as a war-risking taking of sides against Italy. Of course, American failure
so to cooperate, and especially the great increase in U.S. oil exports to Italy,
were an active and decisive taking of sides against Ethiopia, with whose cause
Americans in general were deeply sympathetic, as Roosevelt might have
pointed out in risky educative public speech, but Ethiopia, however hurt and
angered it might be by American actions, could not retaliate effectively,
whereas Italy, it was believed, could. And would. This belief might be false,
as Britain's Winston Churchill was sure it was. "Mussolini would never have

dared to come to grips with a resolute British Government" even in response to a naval blockade, Churchill later said, adding, "If ever there was an opportunity to strike a decisive blow in a generous cause with a minimum of risk, it was here and now."[26] But true or false, the popular perception of Mussolini's determination and Italy's potency was a powerfully operating political energy in the America of late 1935, and Roosevelt, heading into an election year, dared not defy or attempt to change it.

Warning letters now poured in upon him from his supporters. They continued to do so as November gave way to December. Representative was one from the publisher of the New York *Post* who wrote: "I believe that an overwhelming majority of Americans care more about keeping out of war than about any other one thing. If the average citizen suspects . . . that your administration is backing up the League or Great Britain, it would cause a most unfortunate reaction."[27] In Warm Springs on December 2 Roosevelt read a lengthy, argumentative letter from a highly agitated Moley, written on Thanksgiving Day and mailed two days later. Moley was very sure that the administration's recent foreign policy was a disastrous departure from the line taken by the President in the San Diego speech:

> [I]t requires little demonstration to show that the instruments you are using—that is, the men in whom the delicate job of preserving neutrality is vested—are, almost without exception, of that school of thought that believes that participation in international coercive movements can save us from war. They are of that mistaken group that guided Wilson along the road, first to war and, beyond that, to bitter disillusion. . . . Apparently they are still firmly in the saddle, some of them in person, some of them through protégés (i.e., as Bingham or House), others, career men trained under the old dispensation—all of them the intellectual brethren of the naïve Lansing with one foot at Broad and Wall and the other at Geneva.

Moley quoted at length from an editorial he had composed for publication in the upcoming (December 7, 1935) issue of *Today:*

> In Europe the opinion apparently prevails that economic sanctions on the part of the League to coerce Italy will be ineffective unless the United States "cooperates." . . . [And] with the growing disposition on the part of our government to restrict the export of . . . articles not included in the statutory embargo . . . the tension in Europe has become acute. It has become apparent that the coercing nations of Europe will move against Italy with respect to such items as these only if the United States takes the lead. . . . This has definitely made us a determinant factor in the general effort to coerce Italy. . . . I cannot say with too much seriousness that taking sides in this fashion will almost automatically make us a party to the wider war that might easily develop out of the present small war.[28]

But even as Roosevelt read these words, there was taking place in Paris and London an event which, if tragic in its world consequences, provided some relief for him from his immediate dangerous political embarrassment.

The League Coordination Committee had been scheduled to meet on November 29 and was expected then to declare an oil embargo, despite the lack of a prior guarantee of U.S. cooperation. Such was the mood in Geneva at that time. This League action would have forced the Roosevelt administration to take a definite, unequivocal stand regarding U.S. oil exports. The meeting, however, was postponed at the request of Pierre Laval, French premier and foreign minister, who then met with Sir Samuel Hoare, the British foreign secretary, to shape a proposal for ending the Italo-Ethiopian conflict. The agreement reached during this meeting, when revealed through the French press on December 7, outraged public opinion on both sides of the Atlantic. For what Hoare-Laval proposed to do, in total betrayal of the League of Nations, was reward Mussolini for his naked aggression by giving him, either outright or as a "zone of economic expansion and development," all of Ethiopia's territory that had any economic value. Hoare was said to believe that this would prevent Mussolini from forming an alliance with Hitler and induce him instead to ally himself with Britain and France, but there began now to develop a widespread suspicion that Hoare and Laval and the right-wing forces they represented were themselves Fascists at heart, and probably pro-Nazi also, and were committed to a deliberate policy of building up Mussolini and Hitler for a drive to the east against Soviet Russia. The popular revulsion in Britain was so great that Hoare was forced to resign his office, to be replaced by strongly anti-Fascist Anthony Eden, with a resultant serious worsening of relations between London and Rome, while in France the Laval ministry was so undermined that it collapsed in late January 1936, opening the way to the radical redirection of French politics that occurred in the spring of that year.

In America the effect was a wave of angry disgust with the British and French governments, a virtually total destruction of whatever faith had remained in the League's capacity to deal with major crises, and a renewed, emotionally charged determination to remain wholly aloof from all "foreign quarrels." Roosevelt himself now feared that a new world war might break out within a few months. He said so on the day (December 10) of his return to Washington from Warm Springs, while lunching with Ickes. At his cabinet meeting two days after Christmas, held in the Oval Room because he had a heavy cold, he spoke gloomily of a letter he'd just received from his ambassador to Germany, William E. Dodd, saying it was "the most pessimistic letter he had ever read." Dodd believed European civilization to be tottering "on the brink of the precipice," not solely or even chiefly because of Mussolini's aggressiveness but because "nothing can restrain Hitler."[29] Yet Roosevelt knew that Hoare-Laval had so strengthened isolationist sentiment in the United States that he no longer had any practical choice between a broad or narrow interpretation of "implements of war" as he executed the Neutrality Act, and there was no further public talk, by White House or State Department, of embargoing under that act oil shipments or shipments of other strategic materials to Italian ports.*

---

*Standard Oil executive James A. Moffett, by then resigned from his post as federal housing administrator (see pp. 431–32), informed the State Department at this time that Japan, no longer a member of the League and therefore not bound by League actions, "will deliver oil to Italy in any volume needed by Italy." This oil would be American-produced, shipped to Japan under contracts with U.S. oil companies. According to Moffett, such contracts "legally have to be filled

Greatly lessened, too, was the possibility of obtaining from Congress a larger grant of discretionary presidential power with regard to trade with belligerents when the embargo provisions of the Neutrality Act of 1935, due to expire on February 29, 1936, were reinstated in the new neutrality bill the swift enactment of which was a foregone conclusion. The political danger of an attempt by Roosevelt to obtain such power became extreme, and he made the attempt, feeling bound to do so, with extreme caution. This was manifest in the wording of that portion of his 1936 annual message, delivered on January 3, having to do with international affairs. He told Congress that "the people of the Americas must take cognizance of growing ill-will, of marked trends toward aggression, of increasing armaments, of shortening tempers—a situation which has in it many of the elements that lead to the tragedy of general war." He insisted that the "policy of the United States" in this sadly worsening situation "has been clear and consistent," a key element of it being "a two-fold neutrality toward any and all nations that engage in wars that are not of immediate concern to the Americas. First," he went on, "we decline to encourage the prosecution of war by permitting belligerents to obtain arms, ammunition, or implements of war from the United States. Second, we seek to discourage the use by belligerent nations of any and all American products calculated to facilitate the prosecution of war in quantities over and above our normal exports of these in time of peace. I trust that these objectives thus clearly and unequivocally stated will be carried forward by cooperation between the Congress and the President."[31]

On the same day a neutrality bill drafted in the State Department with White House cooperation was introduced by Samuel D. McReynolds in the House and by Pittman in the Senate. It continued the mandatory provisions of the 1935 act as regards armaments, ammunition, loans to belligerents, and items obviously exclusively intended for war use; but it also gave the President power to prohibit exports of such strategic raw materials as oil and cotton to any belligerent in excess of the amount "normally" exported to that nation in time of peace, and it left the President free to determine for himself what the "normal" rate of export was.

The negative reaction to this proposal by isolationists in Congress and throughout the country was immediate and strong, the objection being to the discretionary power which the bill would grant the executive. At Nye's and Clark's request, counterlegislation had been prepared by Stephen Raushenbush, the able secretary and chief investigator of the Munitions Committee, and on January 6 this legislation was introduced by Nye and Clark in the upper chamber and by Maury Maverick of Texas in the House. It would meet the obviously true charge that American oil and other materials were fueling

---

regardless of the ultimate disposition of the oil by Japan." But Moffett's special business interest may have inclined him to exaggerate the difficulty of cooperating in a League oil sanction should the League ever declare one. Certainly his stated view raises a pertinent question. Presumably Japan, an industrial nation heavily dependent on oil, had contracted for American oil it itself needed. How, or from what source, could it satisfy this need if it sold its American oil to Italy?[30]

Mussolini's war machine by adding to the mandatory arms embargo a mandatory embargo of virtually all other goods (oil, cotton, iron, steel, copper), including food, clothing, and medical supplies. The President would have, in these concerns, no discretionary power whatever, once he had recognized formally the existence of a state of war.

The quarrel between supporters of Pittman-McReynolds and supporters of Nye-Clark-Maverick sounded loudly in congressional halls through January and early February, with White House forces fighting as strongly as they dared for Pittman-McReynolds. But as it turned out, the truly decisive quarrel was not between the rival bills but between those who supported one or the other of them and those who opposed both—commercial exporting interests that protested bitterly the imposition of nonmunitions embargoes of any kind, whether mandatory or discretionary on the part of the executive. Hiram Johnson, whose California constituency included major oil and cotton producers, spoke at vehement length, in the Senate Foreign Relations Committee and upon the Senate floor, against this threatened sacrifice of traditional neutral rights, "freedom of the seas." He was powerfully aided by the Lion of Idaho, William Borah, whose isolationism had a religious fervor but included no disposition to "give up the sea to the exclusive use of belligerents." Neutrality did not mean that "a neutral has . . . [no] right to trade and to use the sea for trade in non-contraband goods," he thundered. "Neutrality is not synonymous with cowardice."[32]

Pittman, whose initial enthusiasm for the administration bill he had introduced was minimal, indicated to the White House in the first week of February a readiness to give up the fight for it. He said in a letter to Moley on February 5 that "the necessity for foreign commerce is so great and political pressure at this particular time is so strong that possibly it is advisable to avoid weeks of acrimonious debate with probably no accomplishment, and simply extend the existing law for one year."[33] And this is substantially what happened, Roosevelt feeling forced to abstain from active personal battle for his proposal. Neither Pittman-McReynolds nor Nye-Clark-Maverick was reported out of Pittman's Foreign Relations Committee. Instead, on February 12 the Senate committee voted unanimously to extend the 1935 act's principal provisions, with a few unimportant changes, until May 1, 1937. Two days later the House Foreign Affairs Committee, which had reported Pittman-McReynolds on January 28, rescinded this action and voted unanimously for a measure virtually identical with the Senate committee's. And three days after that, on February 12, the full House adopted the committee-recommended proposal by a vote of 353 to 27, the familiar gag rule having been imposed to prevent amendments and severely limit debate. The Senate then passed the bill on voice vote, after only four hours of debate, and sent it to the President, who signed it into law as the Neutrality Act of 1936 on February 29.

In his signature statement Roosevelt tacitly regretted, by simply mentioning the fact, that "the high moral duty I have urged on our people of restricting their exports of essential war materials to either belligerent to approximately the normal peace-time basis has not been the subject of legislation. Nevertheless," he continued, ". . . greatly to exceed that basis, with the result of earning profits not possible during peace, and especially with the result of giving actual assistance to the carrying on of war, would serve to magnify the very evil of war which we seek to prevent."[34]

And war-profiteering exports to Italy continued unabated.

V

EVENTS in Europe now swiftly followed a downward path to the edge of the abyss.

At almost the very moment of Roosevelt's signing of 1936's Neutrality Act, Adolf Hitler in Berlin was reaching a final decision upon the greatest gamble of his career thus far, one whose loss would mean the end of his regime and, probably, his life.

Two days earlier the French Chamber of Deputies, reflecting the leftward swing of French political sentiment after the collapse of the Laval ministry, had approved a Franco-Soviet mutual defense pact, which had been negotiated in the spring of 1935 and promptly ratified in Moscow but had since languished in the climate of anti-Soviet opinion that dominated France's ruling circles. The probability was now high that the treaty would be finally ratified by the French Senate in a few weeks. Hitler seized upon this as a pretext, while also taking advantage of the confusion and League disarray consequent upon the Italo-Ethiopian conflict, to order German troops into the Rhineland. The move was made at dawn on March 7, with three battalions of the Reichswehr* then marching southwestward across the Rhine bridges in violation not only of the Versailles Treaty, which Hitler had already renounced, but also of the Locarno Pact of 1925, whereby Germany had joined with France and Belgium, with Britain and Italy as guarantors, in agreement that the Rhineland would remain a demilitarized zone after the French forces which had occupied it since the close of the Great War were withdrawn. A few hours later, in a lengthy, impassioned address to a delirious Reichstag, the Führer declared that the Locarno Pact had been invalidated by the Franco-Soviet Pact and that his military occupation of the Rhineland was now absolutely essential to the defense of the Fatherland. He also pledged "that now, more than ever, we shall strive for an understanding among the European peoples, especially for one with our Western neighbor nations. . . . We have no territorial demands to make in Europe! . . . Germany will never break the peace!"[35]

Said Hitler in private conversation some years later: "The forty-eight hours after the march into the Rhineland were the most nerve-racking in my life. If the French had then marched into the Rhineland, we would have had to withdraw with our tails between our legs, for the military resources at our

---

*Jittery Allied intelligence officers promptly overestimated this token force vastly, claiming it consisted of three divisions.

disposal would have been wholly inadequate for even a moderate resistance."[36]

Indeed, the troops that had crossed the Rhine were under definite secret orders to retreat at once if they encountered French opposition. But France did not march. It sought desperately for assurances of support from London should it do so. None was forthcoming. The British Foreign Office, which, under Eden, might have been expected to act in this situation as the plain wording of the Locarno Pact required Britain to do, denied instead that any "flagrant aggression" or "unprovoked act of aggression" had been committed by Germany. David Lloyd George, Britain's wartime prime minister, went so far as to say that "there was provocation" on the Allies' part for Hitler's "breach of a treaty." He did not say what the provocation was. And after all, as was pointed out by many popular spokesmen in Britain and by most of the British press, the Rhineland *was* a part of Germany; its occupation by the Reichswehr was no invasion of foreign soil and was accompanied by Hitlerian avowals of a love of peace.

Less than two months later, on May 2, Italian troops at last occupied Addis Ababa, having made extensive use of poison gas during the last stages of their southward drive. By May 5 all Ethiopian resistance had collapsed, and the Ethiopian emperor Haile Selassie had fled his capital to "avoid the extermination of the Ethiopian people," as he said in a wire from Jerusalem to the secretary-general of the League of Nations a few days later. When the League's Assembly met for five days in Geneva, beginning on June 30, 1936, the exiled emperor appeared in person before it. "I decided to come myself to testify against the crime perpetrated against my people," he said, "and to give Europe warning of the doom that awaits it if it bows down before the *fait accompli.*
. . . If a strong government finds that it can with impunity destroy a weak people, then the hour has struck for that weak people to appeal to the League of Nations to give its judgment in all freedom. God and history will remember your decision. . . . What answer am I to take back to my people?"[37]

The League's answer was felt to be utterly disgraceful by most of those who shaped it. On July 4 the Assembly rescinded the sanctions it had voted last October to impose on Italy. The Ethiopian conquest was simply accepted as a *fait accompli* about which nothing could, or would, be done; the most ancient of all Christian nations became a part of Mussolini's new Roman Empire.

Two weeks later bloody civil war began in Spain—a conflict which had from its outset grave international implications.

In February 1936, after years of increasing and often violent political unrest throughout Spain, especially in industrialized Catalonia, Spanish voters in free national elections were presented with a choice between a government of the right, made up of conservative republicans, clericals, monarchists, and a government of the left, a Popular Front coalition of liberal republicans, Socialists, syndicalists, Communists. They chose the Popular Front government by a large majority. The new government at once took steps toward land reform, the secularization of education, and the curbing of the power over national affairs of army and church. Simultaneously, ranking officers of the army, with the support, if not the active cooperation, of the Spanish hierachy of the Catholic Church, began to plot the overthrow of the elected government by armed force and its replacement by an avowedly Catholic Fascist dictatorship. The army revolt was launched in Spanish Morocco on July 17, 1936. It quickly succeeded there. It was far less successful in Spain itself, to which it spread on July 18. The rebels seized Cádiz, Seville, and other garrison towns but were defeated in Madrid and Barcelona by government forces—the Republican or Loyalist forces, as they were called—despite the latter's deficiency in arms and military training.

Spain was thus doomed to a prolonged and savage internal struggle in which the legitimate government, though continuing to be favored by a substantial majority of all Spaniards, was gravely disadvantaged. For not only did the Fascist rebels, led by General Francisco Franco, have in their hands at the outset the bulk of Spain's armament and munitions, but they were also assured of abundant supply by Nazi Germany and Fascist Italy, and they constituted, of course, the bulk of the nation's trained fighting men. Five days after the army revolt had begun, Count Galeazzo Ciano, the Italian foreign minister, pledged his country's aid to it; Italian bombers took off for Morocco. Three days later Hitler, meeting at midnight with a Spanish rebel emissary personally pledged Nazi aid to Franco; soon thereafter German transport planes were flying troops from Morocco to Spain, the first such mass airlift in history, and Hermann Göring began to use Spain as testing and training ground for the German air force. This international Fascist support of Spanish totalitarianism was not matched by international democratic support of Spanish democracy. Britain, whose immediately announced dominant concern was to prevent the Spanish conflict from expanding into general European war, proposed a policy of total nonintervention, with an embargo on shipments to either side of the civil war, and pressured France, which by then had its own Popular Front government, into acceptance of this policy. Hitler and Mussolini also formally committed their countries to this policy while, with their usual respect for their pledged word, continuing and increasing their active support of Franco. Loyalist Spain was thus, in actual practice, discriminated against by the democracies; it was denied desperately needed war supplies.

And so it was that Franklin Roosevelt was presented in August 1936 with another grave problem of foreign relations. It was greatly complicated for him by three salient facts: First, the Spanish conflict was a *civil* war during which the United States continued to maintain diplomatic relations, through Ambassador Claude G. Bowers, with the duly elected Spanish government in Madrid; secondly, the Neutrality Act of 1936 said nothing whatever about "internal conflicts" and so did not automatically apply, if it applied at all, to the Spanish situation; and thirdly, and the overriding consideration for Roosevelt at that moment, the election campaign of 1936 was then about to shift into its highest gear. It cannot be said that the gravity of the problem was matched by the seriousness with which it was studied or the care with which the responses to it were considered. Roosevelt's "solution" was simply to go along with the

British policy of complete nonintervention, including the embargo—a policy which amounted to a throwing of Spanish democracy into the claws and jaws of the Fascist wolves. Within a few hours after the civil strife began, Ambassador Bowers and his staff in Madrid had been informed by Secretary Hull that "in conformity with its well-established policy of non-interference with internal affairs in other countries, either in time or peace or in the event of civil strife, this Government will, of course, scrupulously refrain from any interference whatever in the unfortunate Spanish situation." And when the Spanish government sought to buy eight warplanes from the Glenn L. Martin Company, and that company asked for guidance on the matter from the State Department, Roosevelt, in sharp departure from conventional international practice, instructed State "to intimate that any such sale would not be in line with the policy of the government."[38]

16

A Rendezvous with Destiny

I

THE campaign of 1936 was the first of Roosevelt's election campaigns since 1910 in which Louis McHenry Howe played no effective part, though he certainly tried to do so, despite his fatal disabilities.

He was not again able to descend to his White House office after his miraculous return from the brink of death in the spring of 1935. Bedridden in his room upstairs, a room Abraham Lincoln had used as sitting room, he was able to work only in fits and starts, haphazardly, often complicating with ineffectual interferences work which would otherwise have been simply, easily done by others. But these others were generally under strict orders from the President to deal always with Howe respectfully, patiently, kindly, and they did so. If he was now only nominally the secretary to the President, he remained the President's oldest, closest friend and confidant; the busiest of cabinet secretaries came to him when he summoned them and listened deferentially to what he had to say. His physical weakness remained extreme, so extreme that even reading a book, holding it in his hands, was too much for him over any extended period. When his wife, Grace, moved into the White House to help care for him in the summer of 1935, coming down then from the Howe home in Fall River, Massachusetts, her major chore was to read aloud to him. For hour after hour she read, until she herself was dead tired. Sometimes he demanded more of this than she found it possible to give, and he grew churlish with her when she, pleading fatigue, laid down the book in hand. For he was no easy patient; he had been furiously rebellious against the death that was close to him through nearly all his life, he refused to give in to pain, and this rebellion continued, with consequent irritability and irascibility. After his removal in late August from White House to Naval Hospital, the task of reading aloud to him devolved upon young Navy medical corpsmen, each of whom became immensely fond of him, greatly admiring the robust, if acid, humor with which he defied the frailties of his body. They, too, read to him for hours on end—from P. G. Wodehouse, whose brilliant wordplay over light subjects especially delighted him; from Agatha Christie and other mystery writers; from such romantic favorites of his youth as Anthony Hope's *Prisoner of Zenda* and *Rupert of Hentzau.* Indeed, most of this reading was a rereading, a recapturing of his mental past, from Dickens, Kipling, Stevenson, and, most exhaustingly to the readers aloud, from the endlessly assertive and exclamatory Thomas Carlyle, whose *On Heroes, and Hero-Worship, and the Heroic in History* had had a shaping influence upon his vital attitudes when he was a young man-about-town in Saratoga Springs. Almost constantly now he wheezed and gasped for breath. Often he was racked by paroxysms of coughing that dangerously strained his weak heart. Yet he continued to smoke incessantly, scattering cigarette ashes over the bedclothes.[1]

He had accepted his removal to the hospital with unexpected calm, to the great relief of Eleanor Roosevelt, who had been his chief nurse in the White House and who accompanied him on this unhappy journey, but when he discovered that there was no telephone in his hospital room, nor any intention to install one, his hurt anger was boundless. He exploded. He absolutely would not accept this shunting aside. He remained convinced of the importance of his advice to his beloved Franklin as preparations were made for the upcoming campaign, advice less on issues (he had substantially yielded this point, in forced self-immolation, during the campaign of 1932) than on campaign organization and tactics. He was especially concerned about Roosevelt's psychological response, his emotional reaction, to the challenge he faced. Roosevelt might yield too much to his enemies, or as was equally likely, he might overreact to them and "go off on a tangent" or "fly off the handle." As Howe had once said with regard to his relationship with Roosevelt, "My job is to supply the toe-holds." And it may well have been Roosevelt's sharing of this conviction of Howe's at least as much as his compassionate concern for the feelings of a devoted friend, which caused him to order a phone installed in Howe's hospital room, though with the stipulation that Howe use it only between the hours of 10:00 A.M. and 4:30 P.M. It was a stipulation not rigidly adhered to by the sick man. Roosevelt was also a frequent visitor in Howe's hospital room, where the talk between the two was in its tone much as it had always been—a bantering frankness involving an interchange of genuine personal feeling, an intimate knowledge of each other, not possible between Howe and anybody else or between Roosevelt and anybody else.[2]

All through the fall of 1935 Howe paid close attention to foreign affairs, warning Roosevelt again and again that Mussolini's imperialistic ambitions would cause a new world war. He followed closely the arms embargo controversy of those months; he gave copious advice on how best to deal with it, the precise nature of which is unknown but which almost certainly accorded more closely with Moley's rigid isolationism than with the views of the European desk of the State Department. By this time Hugh Johnson had traveled to the border of the country of the Liberty League, if he had not actually crossed that border, and when he published in an October 1935 issue of the *Saturday Evening Post* an article* providing an abundance of ammunition for anti-New Dealers to use against the administration, Howe peremptorily demanded of the general an "explanation." He received it, which is a measure of Howe's continued perceived potency in that late season. "Bernard Baruch phoned," said a memorandum from Margaret "Rabbit" Durand to her hospitalized boss in mid-December. ". . . The General 'phoned him and told him of your conversa-

---

*In this article Johnson asserted that Felix Frankfurter was the "most influential single individual in the United States," having artfully "insinuated" his "boys," whom Johnson dubbed "happy hot dogs," into "obscure but key positions in every vital department" of the Roosevelt administration.

tion. He told Mr. Baruch that he had explained several things to 'your' satisfaction. Incidentally, Mr. Baruch suggested that no one answer the articles Johnson is writing. . . . He wants very much to talk to you and I have told him that you would 'phone him about 4:00 today."[3] At the same time Howe, in a lengthy letter to Roosevelt, gave advice on the tone, the line to be taken in the President's state of the Union message to Congress. He urged a strong line. "You have a lot to brag about, nothing to apologize for," he wrote. "Let 'em have it. They'll lap it up."[4] When Eleanor Roosevelt visited Howe in the hospital a day or so after the message had been delivered, he seemed "like himself" of old, as she wrote to Lorena Hickok, adding: "I only hope F. [Roosevelt] goes over tomorrow. L.H. feeling better is because he feels F. followed his advice in his speech."[5]

In the following weeks Howe made elaborate plans for the coming campaign. He prepared organization charts, gathered campaign materials, ordered the updating of devices used four years before, talked of going to New York City to direct the campaign from his bed in a hotel room, as he had directed much of the battle for nomination in Chicago in 1932. But when an aide, one day, pretended to accept such talk at face value and spoke of Howe's soon moving northward, Howe's mood changed abruptly.

"No, I will not be there," he said sadly, and then, in a flare of wistful pride, a boastful pride in what he had done, a loving pride in the man in whom he had invested the whole of his life, he added, "Franklin is on his own now."[6]

This was a momentary lapse, however; in general, he maintained unflawed the pretense that he not only would "be there" but also functioned in the meantime effectively as campaign organizer—a pretense actively kept up by the President and Eleanor and all who operated under the President's direct orders with regard to the upcoming election. On a Wednesday afternoon in early April, when Howe phoned the secretary of the interior requesting an interview, Ickes went at once to the sick man's hospital room. Three days later Ickes wrote in his diary:

> He presented a strange figure. The President said on one occasion recently that Louis looked like a goat and this was an accurate description. He has let his hair and beard grow and his beard has never been trimmed. It is as ragged and unkempt as that of a goat, only more luxurious. . . . The condition of his heart makes it more comfortable for him to spend his time on his elbows and knees atop his bed and this was the posture he maintained throughout my call. . . . He wanted to discuss certain campaign plans. Mrs. Howe was with him and, shortly after I arrived, Henry Wallace came in. It seemed to me that Louis' plans were not very practical in most instances. . . . He presented me with a long list of questions and asked me for my answers to such as came under my purview. I don't know what he expects to do after he gets these answers. He also wanted me to send him pictures of the principal PWA projects in Michigan, and this I promised to do.[7]

Ten days later, on the afternoon of Saturday, April 18, 1936, Roosevelt came for the last time to Howe's room, where he found his old friend no better but seemingly no worse in health than he had been for a long time. On the same day Eleanor Roosevelt wrote Jim Farley, saying, "The President tells me that everything is to clear through both you and Louis and anything you are not entirely sure about is to come to him."[8]

Nothing thereafter "cleared" through this sick room into campaign action, however, for shortly after eleven o'clock on that Saturday night, Louis McHenry Howe, aged sixty-four, died in his sleep while his beloved Franklin, a mile or so away, was addressing to the assembled newsmen at that year's Gridiron Club dinner an off-the-record speech replete with sarcastic commentary upon the self-asserted omniscience of political columnists. Eleanor wrote Hick next day: "They [in the hospital room] just noticed that his [Louis's] breathing was changing, called the doctor who did what he could but he never responded & was never conscious."

This death had, of course, been long expected. Yet somehow, when it came, it was a shocking surprise to both Roosevelts. "I think I felt Louis would always be an invalid but still always there . . ." wrote Eleanor, wonderingly, to Hick, who had her own reasons for loving, as she did, this gnomelike, bittersweet little man. And the President, writing two weeks later to his ambassador to the Court of St. James's, was to say of Louis's death that "the end was very unexpected and sudden."[9]

There was a state funeral in the East Room of the White House on Tuesday, April 21; flags on all government buildings flew at half-mast. A special funeral train, with the President and First Lady aboard, then carried the body overnight to Fall River. There, next morning, the weather, in sharp contrast with the capital's, was cloudy and cold. Patches of snow yet lay beside the flower-strewn open grave in Oak Cemetery, and a raw breeze brushed Roosevelt's bowed head, as he stood in motionless silence for a long moment after the coffin had been lowered. He "appeared oblivious to everything around him, both during the [graveside] service and when he returned to his car for the ride back to the station," reported the New York *Times* on the following morning.

A subtle but profound and permanent change in the Roosevelts' lives ensued, a difference that had been developing in proportion to Howe's long, slow fading away and was now completed. For Howe had been at the very heart of these lives. In every major crisis during the last twenty-three years (Roosevelt's typhoid in 1912, which would probably have nipped in the bud his political career had not Howe come to his rescue; the passionate affair with Lucy Mercer, the denouncement of which would almost certainly have been different, and fatal to Roosevelt's career, had the weight of Howe's influence not gone into the narrow balance; the dangerous estrangement of Roosevelt from Josephus Daniels and Woodrow Wilson during a dark time of troubles in late 1919 and early 1920; the ghastly polio crisis of 1921 and the repeated crises requiring vital decisions during that illness's long and agonizing aftermath; the battle back into national political life for Roosevelt in 1924; the repeated crises of the last years of struggle toward the White House) Louis Howe had been centrally, actively *there,* his thought and feeling and effort so closely intertwined with those of Franklin Roosevelt that it would be hard for future historians to determine precisely where one man left off and the other began. Howe's devotion and the loving trust invested in him had been the vital glue holding the innermost Roosevelt circle in such community as, without him, could not have become nor long continued. Now he was gone, and there would be, inevitably, a falling apart. Soon would come a disintegration of that friendship of Eleanor Roosevelt and Nancy Cook and Marion Dickerman out of which had come Val-Kill Cottage, Val-Kill Industries, Todhunter School, and, with Howe's active assistance, the *Women's Democratic News.* There would be a widening of psychic distance between Eleanor and her husband; for Louis Howe, their dearest, closest mutual friend, had long been a main bridge of trust and emotional understanding between these two.

As for Roosevelt himself, his wife wrote thirteen years later:

> Louis Howe's death left a great gap in my husband's life. I have always felt that if Louis had lived the number of people drawn closely but briefly into the working and social orbits of Franklin's life would have been fewer. For one reason and another, no one quite filled the void which unconsciously he was seeking to fill, and each one in turn disappeared from the scene, occasionally with a bitterness which I understood but always regretted. There are not many men in this world whose personal ambition it is to accomplish things for someone else, and it was some time before a friendship with Harry Hopkins, somewhat different but similar in certain ways, again brought Franklin some of the satisfaction he had known with Louis Howe.[10]

One can only speculate upon the influence Howe would have had upon Roosevelt's personal conduct of the election campaign of 1936 had Howe been then restored to such vigor as he had had in the 1920s. One can be sure that Roosevelt's conduct would then have been significantly different from what it actually was, and different in ways that would have lessened the probability of the disastrous errors of judgment, psychologically motivated, which in the event followed hard upon the election's outcome. Never had Roosevelt more needed at his side than during the last half of 1936 a Louis Howe capable of saying No! to him, emphatically, and of persisting in such naysaying until it stuck—something which Howe had often done in the past and which no one else would ever be able to do with equal effectiveness.

II

FOR Roosevelt personally, the campaign began very early; it began with his delivery of the presidential annual message to Congress on January 3, 1936.

He insisted upon delivering it to a night session, so that its national radio broadcast would reach tens of millions of voters, an insistence that was loudly but futilely protested by congressional conservatives.

Two weeks before, he had told Moley, who as "speech technician" crafted this address while wholly disagreeing with its tone and strategic implications, that he wanted a "fighting speech." He thus followed Howe's advice. He also shared Ickes's expressed belief that "the general sentiment of the country . . . is much more radical than that of the Administration," as Ickes had said

to him during an Oval Room lunch on December 10, and he proposed to appeal
to this sentiment in ways that would inspire and rally his left-wing support.
But he had also indicated to Moley a disposition to confine his "fighting"
pretty much to the formal, the rhetorical. He had no sweeping new legislation
to propose; there would be, as regards substance, a continuation of the "breathing spell." And in view of this, Moley had protested the approach. What good
would it achieve? To the extent that the rhetoric inspired the left it would anger
the right, and while the left was bound to support his reelection in any case,
or at least not oppose it, since it had no valid alternative to him, the right's
opposition was dangerous, yet might be reduced by a reaffirmation of the
attitude expressed in his recent letter to Roy Howard. What Roosevelt proposed to do would pose "a threat of . . . further undefined changes" to the lately
soothed businessmen, thereby reducing their willingness "to take risks" that
were necessary for "production and reemployment."

It seemed to Moley that a "fighting speech" was now justified only if it
specifically aimed to achieve some "great objective."[11]

It might be justified, for instance, if it aimed toward a constitutional amendment that explicitly endowed Congress with power to legislate national social
and economic concerns, a power now only implied by the Constitution's
"general welfare" language and so vaguely that a conservative Supreme Court
could plausibly deny its existence. The possibility was one which Roosevelt
had had before him, as we know, ever since the NIRA invalidation. Since his
return from his *Houston* cruise he had talked with various people about an
amendment which would give the attorney general the right to demand directly from the Supreme Court a ruling on the constitutionality of any legislative enactment that seemed to him questionable in this regard. But if the Court
ruled the act unconstitutional, said the amendment, and the next succeeding
Congress, with the Court's decision before it, reenacted the legislation, this
would purge the act of its unconstitutionality. The reenactment would stand
as the law of the land. Other possible amendments that dealt more directly
with the problem of increasing federal powers without destroying the state
system had also been discussed.

Roosevelt, however, more than doubted that this constitutional question
was one he should accept as a central issue in the upcoming campaign. His
political intuition told him, and a good deal of objective evidence supported
his conclusion, that this matter, like the issue of the executive budget which
he had faced as New York governor, was too technical and complicated to be
readily understood by the general electorate. People in general had little wish
to understand those subtleties of constitutional law which the lawyers of the
Liberty League, whose large incomes derived from the manufacture and manipulation of such subtleties, found so fascinating. And Roosevelt *knew* that
common folk could not be "led and instructed" into a blind "worship" of the
Constitution as sacred document in any way that would cause them to prefer
constitutionality to practical efficacy in governmental programs that greatly

benefited them. The basic premise of the Liberty League's current anti-New Deal propaganda campaign was wholly false.

Late last summer Roosevelt had engaged in some trial ballooning of his own on this subject. While in the very midst of the launching of the Second New Deal, so called, he had found time to collaborate with George Creel in the preparation of a *Collier's* magazine article entitled "Looking Ahead with Roosevelt." He had then dictated a couple of paragraphs about the Court problem which, according to Creel's later testimony, appeared verbatim in the published piece. One of the two was the opening paragraph. "It is the deep conviction of Franklin D. Roosevelt that the Constitution of the United States was never meant to be a 'dead hand,'" this paragraph began, "but that the founding fathers conceived it as a living force for the expression of the national will with respect to national needs." The other paragraph closed the article with the assertion that if the Supreme Court continued to interpret the Constitution in ways rendering "the present generation . . . powerless to meet social and economic problems" of today, "then the President will have no other alternative than to go before the country with a constitutional amendment that will lift the Dead Hand. . . ." Both Roosevelt and Creel had expected these portions of the article to provoke widespread public comment. They provoked none at all. "[N]othing was more plain," said Creel later, "than the lack of public interest." This popular uninterest or indifference continued, and Roosevelt was content that it should until the Court issue had been further developed by pending decisions on New Deal measures and he himself had definitely decided how to proceed in this matter.[12]

Hence his total lack of receptivity to Moley's hint that if a "fighting" stance was to be taken with regard to the current state of the Union, it might well be taken on the need to curb the judiciary's present power to frustrate democratic government. He dismissed, too, Moley's argument that moderate supporters of the New Deal would be alienated by the line and tone he proposed to take in his address. He confidently assured Moley that the moderates would understand and approve his essential strategy. They could not but be aware of the leftward surge of national public sentiment and of the urgent need for a presidential response to it if the administration were to remain in office. They must surely recognize and be grateful for the fact that the response now made was bold and sweeping only in its rhetoric, being unaccompanied by concrete leftish proposals or, indeed, specific proposals of any kind.

The address as delivered, having opened with a review of the darkening world situation, followed by a reiteration of the national will to remain neutral and uninvolved in any war overseas, then made a neat thematic transition to domestic affairs. The President said:

> Peace is threatened by those who seek selfish power. The evidence before us clearly proves that autocracy in world affairs endangers peace and that such threats do not arise from those nations devoted to the democratic ideal. If this be true in world affairs, it should have the greatest weight in the determination of domestic policies.

Within democratic nations the chief concern of the people is to prevent the continuance or the rise of autocratic institutions that beget slavery at home and aggression
abroad. Within our borders, as in the world at large, popular opinion is at war with
a power-seeking minority.

He then directly named the enemy, the target of this "fighting" speech:

In these latter years we have witnessed the domination of government by financial
and industrial groups, numerically small but politically dominant in the twelve years
that succeeded the World War. . . . In March, 1933, I appealed to the Congress of
the United States and to the people of the United States in a new effort to restore
power to those to whom it rightfully belonged. . . . Now, after thirty-four months
of work . . . we have returned the federal government to the City of Washington.
To be sure, in doing so, we have invited battle. We have earned the hatred of
entrenched greed.

And the bulk of the remainder of the speech was a rhetorical lambasting of
the denizens of the land of greed:

They seek the restoration of their selfish power. . . . They steal the livery of great
national constitutional ideals to serve discredited special interests. As guardians and
trustees for great groups of individual stockholders they wrongfully seek to carry the
property and the interests intrusted to them into the arena of partisan politics. They
seek—this minority in business and industry—to control and often do control and
use for their own purposes legitimate and highly honored business associations; they
engage in vast propaganda to spread fear and discord among the people—they would
"gang up" against the people's liberties. The principle that they would instill into
government if they succeed in seizing power is well shown by the principles which
many of them have instilled into their own affairs: autocracy toward labor, toward
stockholders, toward consumers, toward public sentiment. Autocrats in smaller
things, they seek autocracy in bigger things. . . . Give them their way and they will
take the course of every autocracy of the past—power for themselves, enslavement
for the public. Their weapon is the weapon of fear. I have said, "The only thing we
have to fear is fear itself." That is as true today as it was in 1933. But such fear as
they instill today is not a natural fear, a normal fear; it is a synthetic, manufactured,
poisonous fear that is being spread subtly, expensively and cleverly by the same
people who cried in those other days, "Save us, save us, lest we perish."[13]

Long before Roosevelt reached his peroration it was abundantly clear to his
congressional listeners that this alleged message on the state of the Union was
in actual fact a campaign speech, the opening gun of the election battle of 1936.
As such it distressed thoughtful molders of left-wing opinion almost as greatly
as it infuriated big businessmen. The *Nation* and *New Republic* both condemned it editorially in their issues of January 15, 1936. Roosevelt, said the
New Republic, "cannot hope to hold the masses . . . by expressions of sympathy
which . . . give hardly an inkling of what, after nearly three years of office, he
proposes to do for them." The *Nation* condemned him for speaking not as "a
statesman" but as "pure politico," converting "what was supposed to be a
thoughtful discussion of the nation's ills into a political diatribe."[14] But the
"diatribe" was immediately immensely effective with a majority of the Americans who heard it on the radio or later read it. Appreciative letters and
telegrams poured into the White House "from all over the country," as Roose-

velt said in a Jackson Day Dinner broadcast five days later. ". . . I think it will interest you to know that within a few hours I received more of these than at any time since the critical days in the spring of 1933."[15]

And the message's effectiveness with the majority was increased by the public response big business made to it three weeks later.

Roosevelt in his message had warned against the danger that the "new instruments of public power" which the New Deal had created and which were "wholesome and proper" when in the hands of "a people's government" might fall into the hands of "our resplendent autocracy," which would use them to "provide shackles for the liberties of the people." On the night of January 25, 1936, as if they were so many puppets on Roosevelt's strings, Liberty League members and fellow travelers, resplendent in formal evening dress, gathered 2,000 strong in the luxurious banquet room of Washington's Mayflower Hotel to eat an expensive meal and hear Alfred E. Smith (to call him Al seemed now incongruous; he wore white tie and tails) speak such words as Roosevelt might have given him to say at such a time and place. To the delight of his audience of multimillionaires, including a considerable portion of the Du Pont family as well as such former administration figures as Warburg, Acheson, and Douglas, Smith inveighed against the New Deal's violations of states' rights, its spending of tax money "the way they throw sawdust on a barroom floor," its continuous subversion of the Constitution in the service of radical un-Americanism. "The young Brain Trusters caught the Socialists in swimming and they ran away with their clothes . . ." said Smith, and while it was "all right" with him "if they want to disguise themselves as Norman Thomas, or Karl Marx, or Lenin, or any of the rest of that bunch," he absolutely would "not stand for . . . allowing them to march under the banner of Jefferson, Jackson, or Cleveland." In his impassioned peroration he employed that very "weapon of fear" which Roosevelt had described in his message as the one the big business interest continuously used in public appeals. Smith cried out that the country faced a desperate choice between "Washington and Moscow," the "pure air of America or the foul breath of communistic Russia," the "stars and stripes or the red flag of the godless . . . Soviets."[16]

III

ON Monday, January 6, just three days after the congressional session opened, the U.S. Supreme Court made another devastating assault upon the New Deal. Having last May struck down in its NRA ruling what Roosevelt had deemed the industrial pillar of his administration's recovery program, the Court now struck down the agricultural pillar by declaring Agricultural Adjustment Act unconstitutional. The ruination of the basic structure of the New Deal seemed complete.

The vote of the justices this time was not unanimous, as it had been on the NIRA, or five to four, as it had been in a lengthening series of cases involving liberal-conservative disagreement. It was, instead, six to three. Chief Justice

Hughes went over to the conservative majority's side, while Stone, Cardozo, and Brandeis dissented. Hughes, however, made this move less out of personal conviction, it would seem, than for political reasons: He feared the adverse popular reaction to his Court, the popular demand for a limitation of the judicial power, which might result from a five to four ruling on so important a matter. Certainly his lack of enthusiasm for the verdict seemed indicated by the fact that he himself did not write the majority opinion, as a Chief Justice usually did when voting with the majority in a major case. Instead, he assigned this historic task to Justice Roberts.

And Roberts accepted the assignment, despite the highly dubious propriety of his doing so in the circumstances.

The circumstances were these:

The suit against AAA had been brought by William M. Butler, who had been a lavish contributor to Calvin Coolidge's election campaigns, the manager of Coolidge's presidential election campaign, and subsequently the chairman of the Republican National Committee. He brought the suit on behalf of the Hoosac Mills, a Massachusetts cotton textile manufacturing firm which had made him wealthy but had now fallen on hard ground as a result of southern competition. Recently Butler, through a clever and (for him) fortune-saving maneuver, had managed to throw his company into bankruptcy and obtain court appointment as its coreceiver, the other receiver being a senior executive of the great meat-packing firm of Armour and Company. Armour was a large purchaser from Hoosac of stockings for sausage and hams, and the biggest stockholder of Armour, who also owned much stock in Armour's principal rival, Swift and Company, was the Boston financier Frederick H. Prince, whom we last encountered during the Hundred Days when he, president of a couple of railroads, proposed the consolidation of all the nation's rail lines into seven or eight regional systems.* Prince's base of operations was the First National Bank of Boston, of which he was reported to be the largest stockholder, and from First National Butler had borrowed $1 million to tide over the Hoosac Mills Corporation. The inevitable conclusion of knowledgeable observers, therefore, was that Butler, when he went to court to prevent the government's collection of the $20,000-a-month AAA processing tax levied on Hoosac Mills, was acting as front man for Prince, who wanted to outlaw this tax, on behalf of his meat-packing interests, without appearing publicly to be involved in the process.

Hired to argue Butler's case before the Supreme Court was George Wharton Pepper, a former U.S. senator. And surely not irrelevant to the selection of Pepper for this job, or to the size of the fee he commanded for the performance of it (it reportedly totaled $1 million), was the fact that he was an intimate personal friend of Justice Owen J. Roberts, who had already become known as the chief swing man on the Court in that he had sometimes voted with the liberal justices, if more often with the conservatives. Roberts and Pepper had

*See p. 113.

been close ever since the two were undergraduates together at the University of Pennsylvania. Pepper, indeed, was in large measure responsible for Roberts's rise from affluent obscurity as a Philadelphia corporation lawyer into national prominence, for it was Pepper who had persuaded Coolidge to appoint Roberts to the post of government prosecutor in the Teapot Dome oil cases, and it was Pepper who most forcefully had urged Hoover to name Roberts a Supreme Court justice.[17]

Hence the considerable cynicism with which the knowledgeable noted the closeness of Roberts's line of argument, in his majority opinion, to that taken by Pepper before the Court.

Pepper contended first:

> that the processing exaction is not in its nature the exercise of the taxing power of the United States, but is wholly regulatory in character, and is part of a nation-wide scheme for the federal regulation of local agricultural production; and second, that if that scheme as a whole is unconstitutional as an invasion of the reserved powers of the states, then the whole scheme falls with it. . . . Congress has said in so many words, "We exact from the processor a sum equal to our estimate of what the farmer should be receiving in addition to his present income [the addition being a benefit payment to the farmer for nonproduction]." . . . If it is going to be possible for the federal government to offer pecuniary reward to the farmer under conditions such that he cannot very well afford to decline, you get a situation where he sells his freedom for a mess of pottage and disavows his allegiance to that state which, under the Tenth Amendment,* is entitled to control his production.

The government, speaking through Solicitor General Stanley Reed, contended that Section 8 of Article I of the Constitution (it says Congress "shall have Power to lay and collect Taxes, Duties, Imposts and Excises, to . . . provide for the . . . general Welfare of the United States") should be construed broadly to include whatever was conducive to the national welfare, which is to say that it should not be limited to the specific powers enumerated in Section 8 immediately following the general welfare clause. Congress, argued Reed, may therefore not only raise taxes but also appropriate the proceeds to promote the general welfare, including among the objects of its spending those which lie outside the national regulatory power or which, to put it another way, lie within the regulatory powers of the states. The federal government's taxing and spending power, in other words, exceeds its regulatory power. Implicit in this was the right of the federal government to impose contractual obligations upon those who accepted federal money for specified purposes. The purposes of the Agricultural Adjustment Act were, in fact, national welfare purposes, the agricultural problem being a national problem. In any case, it was the prerogative of Congress to determine what was the general welfare and what were the national purposes; it was *not* the prerogative of the courts to do so.

Roberts's lengthy majority opinion (it ran to something more than 7,000

---

*The Tenth Amendment says, "The powers not delegated to the United States by the Constitution, nor prohibited by it to the States, are reserved to the States respectively, or to the people."

words) agreed with this to the extent of saying that Congress did indeed have broad taxation powers, was not limited in this regard to the specifications listed under Section 8, Article I. But he asserted that federal power over the spending of federal tax money was as severely limited by the Tenth Amendment as was the federal power to regulate commerce. Agriculture, he insisted, was *not* a national problem; agricultural production was "a purely local activity" lying wholly within the regulatory power of the states. The processing tax, he insisted, was *not* a revenue-raising device; it was a mere incident of a scheme for the regulation of agriculture, something the federal government had no constitutional right to do. It was also unconstitutional in that it taxed one segment of the economy for the benefit of another segment. And Roberts went on to delineate the horrific consequences of this kind of unconstitutional legislation. "It would be possible to exact money from one branch of an industry and pay it to another in every field of activity which lies within the provinee of the states." It would make of the welfare clause an "instrument for total subversion of the governmental powers reserved to the individual states." In the end, "the independence of the individual states [would be] obliterated, and the United States converted into a central government exercising controlled police power in every state of the Union."

On behalf of the Court minority, Justice Harlan Fiske Stone presented a powerful, scathing dissent. Neither he nor Brandeis approved of AAA. Had they been members of Congress they would almost certainly have voted against the bill creating it (Cardozo would probably have voted for it). But Stone was very sure that on principle, "courts are concerned only with the power to enact statutes, not with their wisdom. . . . For the removal of unwise laws from the statute books, appeal lies not to the courts but to the ballot and to the processes of democratic government." It was not "the business of courts to sit in judgment on the wisdom of legislative action." Nor was a "tortured construction of the Constitution" justified by such "recourse to extreme examples" as Roberts had indulged in the majority opinion. Stone stressed in contemptuous language the absurdities implied by Roberts's expansive definition of the federal taxing power when conjoined with his constrictive definition of the federal spending power. "The government may give seeds to farmers, but may not condition the gift upon their being planted where they are most needed or even planted at all. The government may give money to the unemployed, but may not ask that those who get it shall give labor in return, or even use it to support their families. . . . It may aid state-reforestation and forest-fire-prevention agencies, but may not be permitted to supervise their conduct. It may support rural schools, but may not condition its grant by the requirement that certain standards be maintained."

His most crushing indictment of Roberts's reasoning, however, had to do with what was clearly, in Stone's view, a disastrous usurpation by the judicial branch of powers constitutionally assigned to the legislative and executive branches. He said:

Courts are not the only agency of government that must be assumed to have the capacity to govern. Congress and courts may both unhappily falter or be mistaken in the performance of their constitutional duty. But interpretation of our great charter of government which proceeds on any assumption that the preservation of our institutions is the exclusive concern of any one of the three branches of government, or that it alone can save them from destruction, is far more likely "to obliterate the constituent members" [he quoted Roberts] . . . than the frank recognition that language, even in a constitution, may mean what it says: that the power to tax and spend includes the power to relieve a nation-wide economic maladjustment by conditional gifts of money.[18]

Stone's powerful dissent was without immediate practical effect, of course. The majority opinion stood; the Agricultural Adjustment Act of 1933 was null and void.

But the dissent seemed to some outside observers to have effect upon the Court's next major ruling.

This came on February 17, 1936, in *Ashwander* v. *Tennessee Valley Authority*. The case had been initiated by a small minority of the preferred stockholders of the Alabama Power Company who sought an injunction to prevent that corporation from effecting its side of a contract it had signed with TVA, a contract the terms of which were admittedly highly favorable to the company. Involved was the sale *to* TVA by the company of transmission lines leading from the authority's Wilson Dam and the purchase *from* TVA by the company of electric power transmitted through those lines. The handful of preferred stockholders charged that entrance into such a contract was beyond the company's legal authority because TVA as government agency had no constitutional right to sell electricity. The first question before the Court had been whether or not to hear the case, and on this the decision had been five to four in favor of doing so, with Roberts joining with Stone, Cardozo, and Brandeis to deny that the preferred stockholders were entitled to raise the constitutional issue in a suit against a company of which they themselves were part owners. Chief Justice Hughes, on this initial issue, again switched to the conservative side. His doing so, and then very narrowly defining the issue here involved, no doubt had something to do with the fact that three of the conservative justices, all save Justice McReynolds, joined with him and the liberals in an eight to one decision upholding TVA's constitutional right to enter into this agreement. The decision was at once and everywhere hailed as a victory for the administration.

It was, however, a dubious victory, if one at all, in that Chief Justice Hughes, in his majority decision, very carefully avoided the broad constitutional question which the stockholders had raised. He confined himself to the sale of electricity to this particular company from this particular dam, saying:

[T]hese transmission lines lead directly from the dam, which has been lawfully constructed, and the question of the constitutional right of the Government to acquire or operate local or urban distribution systems is not involved. We express no opinion as to the validity of such an effort, as to the status of any other dam or

power development in the Tennessee Valley, whether connected with or apart from
the Wilson Dam, or as to the validity of the Tennessee Valley Authority Act or of
the claims made in the pronouncements and program of the Authority apart from
the questions we have discussed in relation to the particular provisions of the
contract of January 4, 1934, affecting the Alabama Power Company.[19]

Thus floodgates were opened to a torrent of anti-TVA litigation, crucial elements of which would inevitably come before a Supreme Court that, as presently constituted, was more likely ultimately to deny than to affirm TVA's
right to exist.

And if, after observers had read this majority opinion, there remained any
real hope on their part that the Court's conservative majority was undergoing
a change of heart or mind, the hope was snuffed out on May 18, 1936, when,
in a decision more complicated than usual, the Court struck down the Bituminous Coal Conservation Act (the Guffey Act). This law, it will be recalled, had
been adopted barely nine months before as a "little NIRA" for a coal industry
which, with the outlawing of NRA's Bituminous Coal Code, was threatened
with a renewal of what Justice Cardozo characterized as "anarchic riot." It
will be further recalled that Roosevelt, in a letter urging passage of the Guffey
bill, had frankly admitted to "doubts about constitutionality" while insisting
that a Court decision on the matter "would be helpful as indicating . . . the
constitutional limitations within which this Government must operate." As in
the TVA case, the case against Guffey originated in a stockholder suit. This
time, however, the stockholder was a single person: James W. Carter sought
to enjoin his own Carter Coal Company of West Virginia from acceptance of
the conditions imposed by the Coal Commission which the act had established.
Carter charged that such compliance was illegal because the act creating the
commission was unconstitutional.

Three facts complicated the Supreme Court's dealings with this case: first,
the Guffey Act divided into two main parts, one dealing with price stabilization
and fair trade practices, the other with wages and hours and collective bargaining, the latter being the portion to which Carter and employers in general were
strongly opposed; secondly, Congress had stipulated in the act, as was customary, that the invalidation of any one portion should not per se invalidate other
portions; and thirdly, only the first part of the act had actually gone into effect
when the case came before the Court—the labor portion's execution was yet
in preparation.

Hence the Court had to decide whether or not the price and fair competition
section of the law was separable from the labor section. And on this issue the
vote was five to four. Roberts agreed with the diehard conservatives (Sutherland, McReynolds, Butler, Van Devanter) that the two parts of the act were
inseparable and that its labor provisions were unconstitutional, meaning that
the act as a whole was null and void, including the pricing and fair practice
portion, upon which the majority passed no judgment. Chief Justice Hughes
agreed with the majority that the labor provisions were indeed unconstitutional, but he held that this portion of the legislation was separable from the

other portion and that the latter, the pricing and fair competition portion, *was* constitutional. He agreed on this last with Brandeis, Stone, and Cardozo but seems not to have agreed with their contention that the labor portion of the act could not properly be considered at all by the Court at this time since it was not in effect when the challenging suit was filed.

Justice George Sutherland spoke for the majority. He accepted as true the the contention of a Carter lawyer, in agreement with the decision in *Industrial Association* v. *United States,* which Hughes had approvingly cited in his NRA majority opinion, that coal mining "is just as much a local activity as is farming or manufacture." It was therefore not subject to federal regulation under the commerce clause, this despite the undisputed fact that 97 percent of the coal Carter mined went into interstate commerce. It followed, according to Sutherland, that the "evils which come from the struggle between employers and employees" over wages, working conditions, collective bargaining were "all local evils over which the federal government has no legislative control," no matter how great the national effects of these evils might be. "The relation between employer and employee is a local relation. At common law, it is one of the domestic relations. Wages are paid for doing local work. Working conditions are obviously local conditions. . . . And the controversies and evils, which it is the object of this Act to regulate and minimize, are local controversies and evils affecting local work. . . . Such effect as they may have upon [interstate] commerce, however extensive, is secondary and indirect. An increase in the greatness of the effect adds to its importance. It does not alter its character." Congress, therefore, could do nothing about the problem.[20]

Fervently did Justice Benjamin Cardozo argue, on behalf of the dissenters, that Congress "was not condemned" by the Constitution "to inaction in the face of price and wage wars," the effects of which upon interstate commerce and upon the relationships between government and people were "pregnant with disaster" for the nation as a whole. The legislation in question had been undertaken, said Cardozo, because commerce in coal "had been choked and burdened; its normal flow had been diverted from one state to another; there had been bankruptcy and waste and ruin alike for capital and for labor. The Fifth Amendment* does not include the right to persist in this anarchic riot. . . . An evil existing, and also the power to correct it, the lawmakers were at liberty to use their own discretion in the selection of the means."[21]

But it was Sutherland's opinion that prevailed.

Be it noted that in all these major negative judgments upon the New Deal, rendered by the Court in its 1936 term, a majority of the justices had explicitly or implicitly reserved to the states exclusively the power to deal in legislative regulatory ways with economic enterprise. Agriculture, construction, mining, manufacturing, and, indeed, as it seemed, any economic activity whatever, save only the physical transportation of people and goods across state lines,

*This is the amendment, cited by Sutherland, which says: "No person shall be . . . deprived of life, liberty, or property, without due process of law. . . ."

was a *local* activity the effect of which upon interstate commerce was wholly "secondary" and "indirect." As such it was subject only to state control; it was beyond the jurisdiction of the federal government. So, too, were the labor relations incident to such activity, including such matters as the wages and work hours of employees. And surely this emphatic assertion of the inability of the federal government to legislate economic concerns carried with it an equally emphatic assertion that state government *did* have the ability to do so. So it seemed, at least, to simple, direct minds who were convinced that economic concerns must be legislated.

But in this, as in so much else, simple and direct minds were mistaken, according to the Court majority. For on June 1, 1936, in another five to four decision, the Supreme Court declared unconstitutional that New York State minimum wage law for women which had gone through the legislature shortly after Governor Roosevelt's second term had expired and which President Roosevelt, shortly after entering the White House, had recommended to all states as model legislation. State government, it now appeared, was as hamstrung by the Constitution as federal government was in the face of the evils of economic exploitation and of growing problems in labor-management relations.

The decision was made in the case of *Morehead* v. *Tipaldo,* a case that came to the Supreme Court on appeal from a four to three decision by the New York Court of Appeals (March 1935). The court of appeals had said that the minimum wage law was unconstitutional because it was indistinguishable from a District of Columbia statute struck down by the Supreme Court, as a violation of due process,* in *Adkins* v. *Children's Hospital,* back in 1923. The court of appeals decided, in other words, that *Tipaldo* was ruled by *Adkins;* it rejected the contention of New York's solicitor general and of the lawyer (Dean Acheson) who represented the Consumers' League "that further data and experience and additional facts," as Justice Roberts would later put it, rendered *Tipaldo* a case substantially different from *Adkins.* Hughes was the only member of the Supreme Court who, in March 1936, accepted this argument of distinction and proposed to grant certiorari (i.e., to hear the case) on the basis of it. Brandeis, Stone, and Cardozo rejected the distinction. They voted with Hughes to grant the writ but they did so precisely *because* they believed

---

*The due process clause here invoked is the one in Section 1 of the Fourteenth Amendment, as interpreted by a highly property-minded Supreme Court in the late nineteenth century. Congress's clear intent in proposing this amendment immediately following the Civil War was to protect newly enfranchised blacks against attempts by southern whites to prevent their exercise of the rights of citizenship. It was not until 1882 that Roscoe Conkling discovered, in a theretofore unknown journal of the proceedings of the committee which had drafted the amendment (Conkling had been a member of it), that he and his fellow draftsmen had intended the word "person" to apply to corporations as well as people when they wrote: ". . . nor shall any State deprive any person of life, liberty, or property, without due process of law; nor deny to any person within its jurisdiction the equal protection of the laws." This somewhat incredible interpretation was unanimously affirmed by the Supreme Court in 1886, and ever since the Fourteenth Amendment had been the most sacred portion of the sacred Constitution, in the view of big businessmen.

Tipaldo to be ruled by *Adkins* and viewed *Tipaldo* as a long-awaited opportunity to overrule *Adkins*. The four conservative stalwarts, on the other hand, voted against the grant because they rejected the argument for distinction and, of course, fervently wished to perpetuate *Adkins* as fundamental law. "When my turn came to speak," Roberts later explained, "I said I saw no reason to grant the writ unless the Court were prepared to re-examine and overrule the Adkins case. To this remark there was no response around the table [one suspects that the point had already been made by the liberal justices] and the case was marked granted."[22] This means, surely, that Roberts then voted to grant the writ, though in his later written remembrance he seems to be at some pains to blur perception of this fact. And one can understand why! For Roberts, after evidently voting with Hughes and the liberals in a five to four decision to grant the writ—and voting in this way *because,* as he indicates, he wanted to overrule *Adkins*—then proceeded to vote with the four conservatives to invalidate the New York law. The resultant decision, if not originally technically grounded on *Adkins,* since the petitioner distinguished the New York law from the District of Columbia one, became in the hands of Justice Pierce Butler, who wrote the majority opinion, a sweeping reaffirmation of the principle enunciated by the Court in *Adkins* and a seeming denial to the states of any power to legislate a minimum wage of any kind, ever.

The "dominant issue in the *Adkins* case was whether Congress [which legislates for the District of Columbia] had power to establish minimum wages for adult women in the District . . ." said Butler. "The opinion directly answers in the negative. . . . [I]t was held that Congress was without power to deal with the subject at all." And so, by the same token, were state legislatures, for these dealt with state matters as Congress did with District matters. Butler had much to say about "liberty of contract" as a fundamental freedom "protected by the due process clause." He said, "In making contracts of employment, generally speaking, the parties have equal rights to obtain the best terms they can by private bargaining." He also condemned the act for the effects it would have in the marketplace, giving no credence whatever to the "factual background" which had been recited in the opening section of the New York law. He asserted:

> While men are left free to fix their wages by agreement with employers, it would be fanciful to suppose that the regulation of women's wages would be useful to prevent or lessen the evils listed in the first section of the Act. Men in need of work are as likely as women to accept the low wages offered by unscrupulous employers. . . . It is plain that, under such circumstances as those portrayed in the "Factual background," prescribing of minimum wages for women alone would unreasonably restrain them in competition with men and tend arbitrarily to deprive them of employment and a fair chance to find work.[23]

In his dissenting opinion Chief Justice Hughes contended that in view of the differences between the New York statute and the District of Columbia one, *Tipaldo* was *not* ruled by *Adkins,* but he made no extended argument supporting this contention. He pointed to the fact that the Court had validated legislation regulating work hours for women and argued: "If liberty of contract were viewed from the standpoint of absolute right, there would be as much to be said against a regulation of the hours of labor of women as against the fixing of a minimum wage. Restriction upon hours is a restriction upon the making of contracts and upon earning power. But the right being a qualified one, we must apply in each case the test of reasonableness in the circumstances disclosed. . . . In the statute before us, no unreasonableness appears. The end is legitimate and the means appropriate. I think that the Act should be upheld."[24]

Stone on behalf of himself, Cardozo, and Brandeis presented a separate dissent—a much stronger and more widely quoted dissent:

> While I agree with all the Chief Justice has said, I would not make the differences between the present statute and that involved in the Adkins case the sole basis of decision. . . . The vague and general pronouncement of the Fourteenth Amendment against deprivation of liberty without due process of law is a limitation of legislative power, not a formula for its exercise. It does not purport to say in what particular manner that power shall be exerted. It makes no fine-spun distinctions between methods which the legislature may and which it may not choose to solve a pressing problem of government. It is plain too, that . . . the liberty which the amendment protects is not freedom from restraint of all law or of any law which reasonable men may think . . . appropriate means for dealing with any of those matters . . . with which it is the business of government to deal. There is grim irony in speaking of the freedom of contract of those who, because of their economic necessities, give their services for less than is needful to keep body and soul together. But if this is freedom of contract no one has ever denied that it is a freedom which may be restrained, notwithstanding the Fourteenth Amendment, by a statute passed in the public interest.

And Stone again inveighed, in language as scathing as that he had employed in his AAA dissent, against the usurpation of legislative power by the judiciary. "It is not for the courts to resolve doubts whether the remedy of wage regulation is as efficacious as many believe, or is better than some other, or is better even than the blind operation of uncontrolled economic forces," said he. "The legislature must be free to choose unless government is to be rendered impotent. The Fourteenth Amendment has no more embedded in the Constitution our [he meant the justices'] preference for some particular set of economic beliefs than it has adopted, in the name of liberty, the system of theology which we may happen to approve."[25]

Next day, at his press conference, Roosevelt was asked if in view of the "Supreme Court's series of opinions about New Deal objectives," he saw "any way in which those objectives can be reached within the present framework of the Constitution." He refused to answer the question, making comment, instead, upon *Morehead* v. *Tipaldo* only. The American people "should read all three opinions," he said, "the opinion of Justice Butler, the opinion of the Chief Justice, and the opinion of Justice Stone, because it is the combination of the three that [has] . . . made one fact fairly clear." That fact was the existence of a "no-man's-land," defined by the "present majority of the Court," where no government could function, whether state or federal. "How can you meet that situation?" persisted the reporter. Roosevelt again sidestepped the question, this time with an expressiveness that provoked laughter. "I think that is about all there is to say about it," said he.[26]

Among the public at large there was much comment on this decision, virtually all of it highly disapproving. Even staunch conservatives expressed alarm. They saw as possibly portentous of grave social unrest such property worship at the expense of humane feeling by the nation's highest tribunal while millions, including the women "wage slaves" now specifically ruled against, yet wallowed in the miseries of depression. The decision "plays into the hands of radical change," said the conservative Catholic magazine *America*. It "has had big effect in causing criticism of the Court in quarters formerly defensive of it," reported *Kiplinger's Letter*. It was "a shocking blow to enlightened conservatism," editorialized the Boston *Herald*. It was a "new Dred Scott decision," declared Republican Representative Hamilton Fish of New York, who was "frankly shocked" by it.[27]

IV

By that time nearing its end was the second session of the Seventy-fourth Congress, a session which, meeting in the shadow of the impending election campaign, was almost as remarkable for unproductiveness as the first session had been for production. Nothing specific had been asked of it by the President in his message, almost nothing was asked of it by him later, and when it adjourned on June 21, it had enacted, in addition to the Neutrality Act of 1935, a mere five pieces of legislation which might be termed major, only one of them as historically important as the least of the major enactments of the preceding session.

First came the passage through both houses by voice vote, with little debate, of a bill for payment in 1936 of the veterans' bonus originally scheduled for payment in 1945. It went to the White House on January 20. It differed from the Patman bill of the preceding year in that the bonus would be paid not in fiat money but in interest-bearing bonds, which, however, could be cashed in at any time. The difference was trifling. Roosevelt promptly vetoed the bill. But it is a measure of his change of attitude that he did so in perfunctory fashion. Instead of presenting the veto message in person, dramatically, as he had unprecedentedly done last year, he sent to the House on January 24 a brief handwritten note in which he "respectfully" referred "the members of the Senate and the House . . . to every word" of what he had said on the earlier occasion. "My convictions are as compelling today as they were then," he said. "I therefore cannot change them."[28] Thus did he tacitly concede the congressional override of his veto which at once occurred, by a vote of 325 to 61 in the House and of 76 to 19 in the Senate.

The second of the five enactments was wholly a response and the third was in important part a response to the Supreme Court's new assaults upon the New Deal.

On February 27 both houses passed, and two days later the President signed, a Soil Conservation and Domestic Allotment Act designed to fill the gap left in the administration's recovery program by the striking down of the Agricultural Adjustment Act. The substitute measure had been in preparation by Department of Agriculture officials in consultation with farm organizations, chiefly the Farm Bureau, almost from the moment the original AAA began its operations, for from the first, Henry Wallace, Tugwell, Jerome Frank, and others had been unhappy about the sloppy draftsmanship of the originating bill and also doubtful of the wisdom as well as the constitutionality of the processing tax. The new enactment continued essential features of the original domestic allotment plan but stated new purposes for it while redesigning the machinery through which the purposes were to be achieved. The purposes were now declared to be:

> (1) preservation and improvement of soil fertility; (2) promotion of the economic use and conservation of the land; (3) diminution of exploitation and of wasteful and unscientific use of national soil resources; (4) protection of rivers and harbors against the results of soil erosion in aid of maintaining the navigability of waters and water courses and in aid of flood control; and (5) reestablishment . . . of the ratio between the purchasing power of the net income per person on farms and that of the income per person not on farms that prevailed during the five-year period August 1909–July 1914, inclusive, and the maintenance of this ratio.[29]

States were required to submit to the federal government by January 1, 1938, plans acceptable to the secretary of agriculture for use of federal grants-in-aid of a diversion of land from "soil-depleting surplus cash crops" to soil-conserving crops, this as a condition for receiving such grants. Until January 1, 1938, the federal government would make direct grants to individual farmers for this purpose.

The act must not be used to restrict agricultural production below the amount needed for normal domestic use, this being the gist of an amendment consumer-minded Bob Wagner had introduced in the Senate. The House adopted it after the Senate had rejected it, and it was retained, thanks largely to Wagner, by the conference committee. The House also adopted an amendment designed to ensure that tenants, sharecroppers, and small farmers received their fair share of the federal subsidies, but the conference committee revised this into a form sufficiently meaningless to be acceptable by southern planters, landlords generally, and farmers of large acreages generally. The final enactment said merely that the secretary of agriculture should protect "so far as possible" the interests of tenants, sharecroppers, and small producers.[30]

In practice, Agricultural Adjustment would continue uninterruptedly its encouragement of the process whereby the small family farm was eliminated, replaced by ever-larger and -fewer farmers operating ever-larger, more expensive farm machinery.

On the day he signed this new farm bill, Roosevelt had in preparation a supplemental budget message to Congress which he sent up the Hill three days later (March 3, 1936). In it he pointed out that the outlawing of the processing tax by the Supreme Court, the expenditures to be made under the Soil Conservation and Domestic Allotment Act, and the immediate payment of a veterans' bonus formerly due in 1945 threw badly out of balance a budget that had been balanced, save for the "item of relief" (a huge item, certainly), when he delivered his annual budget message last January. "We are called upon, therefore, to raise by some form of permanent taxation an annual amount of $629,000,000," he said. Of this, $500 million "represents substitute taxes in place of the old processing taxes." Only $120 million "represents new taxes not hitherto levied." He suggested that the needed revenue come from a tax on the undistributed profits of corporations. The proposal was one Marriner Eccles had been pressing for since 1932 as a means of restoring effective purchasing power. A powerful case for it was made in Keynes's *General Theory of Employment, Interest, and Money* (1936); Keynes saw it as one of the devices for saving and stabilizing capitalism without sacrificing democracy. But Roosevelt now considered and probably understood it only as a revenue-raising scheme which would "remove . . . inequalities in our tax system, and stop 'leaks' in present surtaxes."

Said the President:

The accumulation of surplus in corporations controlled by taxpayers of large incomes is encouraged by the present freedom of undistributed corporate income from surtaxes. Since stockholders are the beneficial owners of both distributed and undistributed corporate income, the aim, as a matter of fundamental equity, should be to seek equality of tax burden on all corporate income whether distributed or withheld from the beneficial owners. As the law now stands our corporate taxes dip too deeply into the shares of corporate earnings going to stockholders who need the disbursement of dividends; while the share of stockholders who can afford to leave earnings undistributed escape current surtaxes altogether. . . . The evil has been a growing one. It has now reached disturbing proportions from the standpoint of the inequality it represents and of its serious effect on the Federal revenue. Thus the Treasury estimates that, during the calendar year 1936, over four and one-half billion dollars of corporate income will be withheld from stockholders. If this undistributed income were distributed, it would be added to the income of stockholders and there taxed as is other personal income. But, as matters now stand, it will be withheld from stockholders by those in control of these corporations. In one year alone, the Government will be deprived of revenues amounting to over one billion three hundred million dollars.[31]

In addition to this permanent tax, the President suggested a couple of temporary taxes: First, a tax on the "windfall" received by "certain" processors "who shifted to others the burden of processing taxes which were impounded and returned to them or which otherwise have remained unpaid"; secondly, an "excise on the processing of certain agricultural products," a processing tax which, since it was wholly designed to obtain general revenue and not to benefit any one segment of the economy, had to be deemed constitutional even by the conservative majority of the present Supreme Court. It was, in effect, a consumers' tax and, as such, vulnerable to charges of inequity, but Roosevelt defended it on grounds of expediency, saying, "By increasing the number of commodities so taxed, by greatly lowering the rates of the old processing tax, and by spreading the tax over two or three years, only a relatively light burden would be imposed on producers, consumers or processors."[32]

There ensued, in Congress and in the corporate world, much sound and fury signifying, in the end, little more than the establishment in law of the principle of taxing corporate surpluses.* The House Ways and Means Committee quickly rejected the proposed new processing taxes but otherwise reported out a complicated measure closely similar to the bill that had been drafted in the Treasury Department. It would impose a graduated tax of up to 42½ percent on corporation net income and an "unjust enrichment tax" of 80 percent on the windfalls to processors which Roosevelt had mentioned. The reported bill then sailed through the House, after only desultory debate, on April 20, the vote being 267 to 93. But in the Senate Finance Committee, a more conservative body than its House counterpart, the bill encountered strong opposition; it was, indeed, completely rewritten, a process during which the tax on undistributed profits was lowered to only a nominal amount. The reported bill then went through the Senate, 38 to 24, after considerable heated debate on June 5. In the joint conference committee much that the Senate had struck out of the House-passed bill was restored to it, though application of the undistributed profits tax was so modified that it effected relatively little of what Eccles had hoped for it. The final measure, passed by the House on June 19, 223 to 99, and by the Senate next day, 42 to 29, *did* raise additional revenue, an estimated $785 million during its first year of operation. It could be, and was, deemed a victory for the President, who signed it into law on June 22.

The fourth of the major bills to be enacted in that session was the Robinson-Patman price discrimination bill, which went through the Senate on April 30, through the House on May 28, and was signed into law on June 30—a delayed signing (more than three weeks intervened between the bill's arrival on Roosevelt's desk and his formal approval of it) indicative of a lack of enthusiastic support for this measure by the administration. Indeed, neither the Tugwell national planning wing of the administration, which had largely influenced the First New Deal, nor the Brandeisian-Frankfurter small-unit free-competition wing, which was largely influential in the Second New Deal, took much interest in this proposal in that spring of 1936, though the Brandeisians were mildly in favor of it. Drafted by counsel for a national wholesale grocer organization in the immediate aftermath of the Supreme Court's NRA decision and vociferously promoted by independent merchants, the measure was designed to protect the independents against that unfair competition from chain stores which NRA mercantile codes had been supposed to prevent. As

---

*Actually the principle had been partially established in law as long ago as the Civil War, when a personal income tax was applied not only to people but also to corporations—a tax on their total earnings, whether distributed to stockholders or not. This was a kind of anticipation of the 1880's definition of corporations as legal persons, though not a kind likely to be cited as precedent by the corporation lawyers of the 1930s.

enacted, having been considerably revised under heavy pressure from chain-store lobbyists during the legislative process, this measure prohibited price discrimination, "by any person engaged in interstate commerce," between large-bulk and small-bulk producers, "where either or any of the purchases are involved in commerce and where the effect of such discrimination may be to lessen competition or create a monopoly in any line of commerce." The act was to be administered by the Federal Trade Commission.[33]

The fifth major enactment of the session was of a deficiency appropriation bill to fund work relief. As originally drafted and introduced under White House auspices, the bill assigned $1.5 billion, virtually without strings, to WPA Administrator Harry Hopkins. No provision was made for funding PWA, the continuance of which as an independent agency was thus placed in doubt; it appeared that all public works, large as well as small, were soon to come under Hopkins's jurisdiction. Inevitably this revived that quarrel between Hopkins and Ickes which Roosevelt had hoped to drown in tropical seas during last October's ocean cruise. It was somewhat less acrimonious than it would have been if the cruise had not occurred, but the acrimony remained great enough, and the threat it posed politically for the administration in an election year was sufficiently strong, to require of Roosevelt a considerable effortful attention. He had at last to exercise fully his human management skills, mingling coercive power judiciously and intuitively with personal charm.

Ickes, having persuaded himself that WPA under spendthrift Hopkins's recklessly wasteful direction had become the major hazard to Roosevelt's reelection, now found it easy to agree with Farley and Garner and other administration conservatives that Hopkins himself had become, among the general electorate, the most unpopular man in Washington. PWA, on the other hand, along with CCC, was now the most popular of New Deal agencies among this general electorate, in Ickes's view, because of the prudent, efficient way in which it was run, meaning that Ickes himself was one of the most popular men in Washington. Operating on this assumption, known by Roosevelt to be false, Ickes encouraged, if he did not help instigate, the introduction of an amendment to the deficiency bill earmarking for PWA $700 million, or nearly half the total deficiency appropriation, an amount soon scaled down to between $300 million and $400 million. Furthermore, he encouraged friendly senators to invite his appearance before a subcommittee of the Senate Appropriations Committee, to present a review of PWA's accomplishments and work in progress. He then prepared testimony which tacitly supported the proposed amendment by stressing the favorable cost-benefit ratio of PWA's projects compared, by implication, with WPA's. A major benefit, statistically described in the prepared testimony, was the alleged large "indirect employment" resulting from large-scale public works.

Roosevelt, who saw the proposed amendment as a fatal threat to the whole of his relief program, was warned of Ickes's impending testimony (perhaps by Hopkins) only a day or so before it was scheduled to be presented. He moved at once, forcefully, to prevent what amounted from his point of view to an act of sabotage. At a cabinet meeting on May 14, he sternly ordered Ickes to present to the subcommittee no statistics that had not been cleared with him in advance (he added that the figures Ickes had shown him a few days before were "all wrong") and no statistics whatever regarding indirect employment. Ickes, hurt and angered by what he described in his diary as a "spanking" administered before his cabinet colleagues, retorted with some heat that there was no point in his testifying at all if he could give no figures on indirect employment; the stimulation of such employment was a major stated purpose of PWA's organic legislation. Roosevelt remained adamant. He made perfectly clear to all in the room his awareness that Ickes's prepared report on PWA was in intention and effect an attack on WPA, made perfectly clear also his own intention to prevent any such attack. He said flatly, coldly that if the deficiency bill were amended to earmark for PWA any of the money originally assigned to WPA, he would veto it.

Having returned to his office after the cabinet meeting, Ickes spent the rest of that day, until midnight, writing and rewriting, with his closest advisers, a letter of resignation so unequivocal and bitter in tone that Roosevelt could hardly do other than accept it. But early next morning, after some hours of sleepless tossing and turning upon his bed, he decided that "it would be a mistake to send that particular letter" precisely because it was "simply a knockout and left him [the President] no recourse." So he rewrote. The letter actually delivered at the White House by special messenger an hour or so later was far more succinct and less bitter than the earlier draft. It said that passage of the pending deficiency bill "as written will destroy the Public Works Administration," that Roosevelt in "recent press conferences" had "in effect . . . repudiated PWA and indicated a lack of confidence in me as Administrator," that Roosevelt's statement at "the cabinet meeting today [the letter was dated May 14] . . . made it impossible for me" to testify before the committee, and that he, Ickes, had therefore "no option except to tender my resignation both as Secretary of the Interior and as Administrator of Public Works."

But Roosevelt, having now put the interior secretary in his proper place, proposed to keep him there. He had no wish to part with Ickes the man or with Ickes as remarkably effective government official and political campaigner. And so, clearly anticipating some such missive as Missy LeHand placed upon his desk shortly before eleven o'clock on that morning of May 15, he issued to Ickes through Marvin McIntyre an invitation to lunch with him at one o'clock. Ickes, not wanting McIntyre to know what was afoot, accepted, then phoned LeHand, after he knew his letter had been delivered, to find out if the President still wanted him to come. The President did. He greeted Ickes "with an expression of mock reproach and then, without saying a word . . . handed me a memorandum in his handwriting," as Ickes recorded in his diary. The memorandum said: "Dear Harold—1. PWA is not 'repudiated.' 2. PWA is not 'ended.' 3. I did not 'make it impossible for you to go before the committee.' 4. I have not indicated lack of confidence. 5. I have *full* confidence in you. 6. You and I have the same big objectives. 7. You are needed, to carry on a big common task. 8. Resignation *not* accepted! [signed] Your affectionate friend, Franklin D. Roosevelt."

During the luncheon talk that followed, Roosevelt was at pains to seem regretful if not apologetic, for his harshness of the day before. He encouraged a full venting by Ickes of grievances, the causes of which he seemed anxious to remove. He spoke with evident, tentative approval of an arrangement that had already been suggested to Ickes by Tommy Corcoran whereby RFC loans, augmented by specific grants from the $1.5 billion WPA fund, would finance a considerable continuing PWA program. He also listened sympathetically to Ickes's protest against the immense grant of power to Hopkins personally which the deficiency bill as presently worded would provide.

Ickes, his anger overcome, his hurt feeling assuaged, stayed on.

And the deficiency appropriation bill finally signed into law on June 19 assigned full power over the appropriated $1.5 billion not to the WPA administrator but to the President of the United States. It also, despite Roosevelt's initial opposition to any such amendment, assigned $300 million to PWA, a sum which, with the addition of RFC loans, specific WPA grants, and money already in hand, would enable it "to put through a program of about $600 million, which isn't so bad," as Ickes told his diary. "The important thing is that PWA is recognized as a going concern."[34]

On June 21, 1936, the Seventy-fourth Congress adjourned.

V

THE congressional session had absorbed far less of the nation's political attention than had any other since Roosevelt entered the White House, and now the whole of this attention shifted to the preparations for, the beginnings of that year's great drama of presidential election, with its accompanying congressional and state elections. By June's end the drama's central themes had been established, its cast of main characters selected.

In 1932 Alf* M. Landon of Independence, Kansas, who had made a modest fortune as an independent oil producer before actively entering Republican state politics, was elected governor of his state, narrowly defeating his Democratic opponent, the incumbent Governor Harry Woodring. The vote was 278,581 to 272,944. His victory was due to the running for governor as an independent in that year of a quack medical doctor and radio personality named John R. Brinkley, notorious for his "goat gland" operations to restore virility to impotent males; of Brinkley's 244,607 votes, far more came from normally Democratic than from normally Republican ranks in that (historically) monolithically Republican state. All the same, the event made Landon the only Republican to be elected governor of a state west of the Mississippi in 1932, and two years later he became the only Republican governor in all the land to win reelection. Inevitably he became a focus of such hopes of recaptur-

---

*His full name was Alfred, of course, but he himself seldom used it.

ing the White House in 1936 as could remain in Republican breasts after the huge Democratic triumph of the midterm elections. His candidacy began to be quietly but very actively promoted in early 1935 by Roy Roberts and Lacy Haynes of the Kansas City *Star,* a paper long accustomed to power over Kansas Republican politics. These two were joined some months later in this enterprise by the Republican national committeeman for Kansas, John D. M. Hamilton, an adroit politician of extreme conservative views who took over the practical management of the campaign. They were also joined by Emporia's William Allen White, whose national fame was greater than any other Kansan's and who was notoriously in the party's liberal wing. Then, in the fall of 1935, the newspapers and magazines of the Hearst publishing empire began to publicize Landon as a plain man of the people who was also a heroic defender of sound conservative policies, a budget-balancing "Kansas Coolidge" who had also the qualities of Abraham Lincoln. In the last month of the year William Randolph Hearst grandly descended in person upon Topeka, with an entourage that included Arthur Brisbane, Cissy Patterson, and former screen star (also longtime Hearst mistress) Marion Davies to call upon Landon in the executive mansion and size him up face-to-face. Hearst approved what he saw and heard. So did his companions. They all loudly proclaimed their approval in the public prints. And if Hearst's blessing upon Landon was far from being a true blessing, politically, in the long run, Hearst having made himself one of the most hated men in America, it did have the immediate effect of a huge and favorable national publicity which, in early 1936, made Landon the man most widely and frequently talked of as potential Republican president. He thereafter won the open support of one after another of the most respectable molders of Republican opinion, the most effective leaders of that party's politics. By the time the Republican National Convention opened in Cleveland on June 10, Landon was clearly the front-runner for the nomination, with only Frank Knox, publisher of the Chicago *Daily News,* as a rival possessed of even a slight chance of snatching the prize away, and Knox was known to be willing to run for the vice presidency on a Landon ticket.

Landon was fairly young for a presidential aspirant. He was forty-eight years old. He was certainly no commanding presence. A man of middle height, he was bland of countenance, neither handsome nor homely, with little sparkle to his personality and no manifest brilliance of intellect. He appeared to be what in fact he was: a decent man, a shrewd, kindly, prosperous, mild-mannered small-town Middle American businessman of moderate passions and generally conventional opinions, who instinctively shied away from extremes and sought, instead, in almost all concerns, a middle ground as flat, as featureless, as arid as the Kansas plain. He spoke in a flat, rather twangy tone of voice, with a midwestern accent. He looked out upon the world through rimless spectacles with a flat, mild gray-eyed gaze. His imagination neither soared into the heavens nor plunged into the abysmal depths; when it took flight, it rose to a moderate height above the hard flat country of common sense and there maintained itself in level flight until it descended to that same hard ground.

He was not without wit, but his humor was in a low key, dry and understated. In temperament, background, personality, vital attitude he was a sharp contrast with Franklin Roosevelt—a fact that refreshed and enhanced his appeal to Roosevelt haters. They hoped it would recommend the prairie statesman to millions who had voted for Roosevelt in 1932 but were now weary of Rooseveltian histrionics, worried about the direction the New Deal was taking, and nostalgic for the tranquillity of the White House in the golden years of Calvin Coolidge.

In his political and economic views Landon was considerably less conservative than the majority of his own party and far less so than the Liberty League, the aggressive propaganda of which he deplored as a hazard to Republican victory in November. Like Frank Knox and William Allen White (also Harold Ickes) he had bolted the Republican party to follow TR into the Bull Moose campaign. He had bolted the Kansas Republican party in 1924 to join White in successful protest against Ku Klux Klan influence over party affairs. He was more deeply and consistently committed to First Amendment freedoms than Roosevelt personally was. He demonstrated his commitment when Norman Thomas spoke in Topeka in the spring of 1934, introducing the Socialist to a large audience with a graceful personal tribute and a ringing endorsement of the principle of free speech.[35] He was no such bitter enemy of the New Deal, root and branch, as Herbert Hoover was and as most of his influential supporters wished him to be. As governor he had indeed displayed extreme fiscal conservatism. He had made drastic cutbacks in essential state services (some college faculty salaries had been cut back one-fourth; other state salaries were cut almost as much) at a time of dire popular need and so had maintained a balanced state budget. But he was virtually compelled to do this by Kansas law, and he personally recognized that he could do it without provoking dangerous social unrest only because of the $100 million or so of federal money poured annually into his state through New Deal relief and other programs. He had publicly recognized in 1933 and 1934 the need for broad executive powers in Washington to deal with the national emergency, and he had since endorsed in general terms the stated general purposes of the New Deal, confining his criticisms to detail and method—to the *way* in which the purposes were being pursued. If he became President, the "breathing spell" would continue through four years so far as the initiation of great new programs was concerned, but those four years would be devoted, if he had his way, not to tearing down what the New Deal had built but to a consolidation of the gains it had made and to the repair or replacement of faulty governmental machinery.

He exerted upon the drafting of the party platform, to the limit of his ability to exert, a moderating influence. And as adopted by the convention in Cleveland on June 11, that platform was far more extreme in its general rhetorical attacks upon the administration than it was in its specific substantive proposals for dismantling and providing alternatives to the New Deal.

The platform preamble damned the Roosevelt administration in fervent language written by, and designed to please, haters of Roosevelt and all his works. The most sacred "American traditions" had been "dishonored," and so had been the government's "most sacred obligations." The dignity, the integrity, the authority of the Supreme Court had been "flouted." The state system was in process of destruction as dictatorial powers were concentrated in Washington. Personal liberties had been "violated"; private citizens had been "harassed" and "intimidated by investigative proceedings. Instead of confidence, the administration had "bred fear and hesitation in commerce and industry"; instead of appealing to "reason and tolerance," the New Deal appealed to "passion and class prejudice." But in its specific program planks, the platform subscribed to most of the central programs of the New Deal while insisting that these could be better carried out by state and local governments with the "encouragement" of the federal government in the form of grants-in-aid and in other ways.

For instance, society had an obligation "to promote the security of the people by affording some measure of protection against involuntary unemployment and dependency in old age," but social security as established by the act excluded too many needy people from its benefits, decreed an administrative machinery that was "unworkable," and should be replaced by a more effective system under state control. Similarly, the "necessities of life must be provided for the needy," but relief should be administered through nonpolitical local bodies, and federal public works must be totally divorced from relief activities. For agriculture, the Republicans outlined a program of submarginal land retirement, benefit payments to farmers for soil conservation, and so on that was not substantially different from the current farm program. (There was sharp difference from the administration, however, over farm surplus disposal abroad. The Republicans embraced the George Peek proposals which the New Deal had rejected along with their author, Peek having resigned his government posts in a huff in late November 1935.) Labor's right "to organize and bargain collectively through representatives of its own choosing without interference from any source" must be protected. (The statement was deemed deliberately ambiguous by labor leaders, who pointed out that its practical meaning depended upon the definitions given "interference" and "any source." The latter might be construed to mean the newly formed Committee for Industrial Organization, the AFL, or even the National Labor Relations Board. If so, the chief, if not sole "right" to be "protected" was that of forming company unions.) As for labor exploitation, there must be state legislation and interstate compacts to abolish child labor and sweatshops and to protect women and children against starvation wages and intolerable working conditions. "We believe this can be done within the Constitution as it now stands," asserted the Republicans, unconvincingly, since the Supreme Court had said just eleven days ago, in *Morehead* v. *Tipaldo,* that the thing could *not* be done.

This last greatly disturbed Alf Landon himself, so much so that he felt compelled, "as a matter of private honor and public good faith," to state his own position with regard to it. He sent a telegram to Cleveland, to be read to the assembled delegates before his name was placed in nomination. In it he sincerely "hoped" that within the Constitution "as it now stands," the promise to protect women and children against exploitive employers could be kept, but, he went on to say, if it could not, he favored adoption of a constitutional amendment specifically authorizing this kind of legislation.[36]

The telegram did nothing to diminish the expressed delegate enthusiasm for him. Within a few hours after it was read, he was nominated by acclamation, all others having withdrawn from the race. Frank Knox was chosen as his running mate.

VI

THE Democratic National Convention met in Philadelphia for five days beginning on June 23.

Why it remained in session so long when it had so little real business to transact (its assigned labors could easily have been concluded in a single day; its exuberant enthusiasm for Roosevelt and the Democratic cause could have been sufficiently demonstrated to the nation in a couple of days) was a question cynically but accurately answered by those who knew how hugely Philadelphia's merchants had contributed to the Democratic campaign treasury in return for the choice of their city as convention site. Jim Farley, who was to take leave of absence from his cabinet post in order to manage the campaign, deemed it "good politics" to assure the merchants of a profit on their investment. He may even have promised them and the merchants of other cities a profitable prolongation of the proceedings when he was accepting competitive bids for the convention.

For this was how Farley understood and practiced politics, as a competitive game of bargains, deals with those who could deliver something wanted, brokerage operations aimed directly at winning votes. He remained very much an organization man. He continued to place heavy emphasis upon big-city Democratic machines, upon Curley of Boston, Hague of Jersey City, Pendergast of Kansas City, Kelly-Nash of Chicago—a heavier emphasis than did Ed Flynn, whose Bronx machine was among the most efficient. He failed to realize, as Flynn did, that the machine's importance in the nation as a whole, and even in the big cities, steadily declined. If Farley was now somewhat more interested in issues, governmental program ideas, and underlying historical trends than he had been in 1932, the increase of interest was very slight and wholly due to the fact that he, like Wallace, Hopkins, Ickes, had secret presidential ambitions growing in him. His understanding of basic issues was no greater than before, was, indeed, less than before insofar as the New Deal, as governmental response to the socioeconomic challenges of an advancing scientific technology, developed beyond his ken. The combine of secret ambition with lack of understanding of the political world in which he operated made Farley a less reliable instrument of Roosevelt's purposes than he had been when he first entered the Roosevelt camp. He remained extremely valuable, but he needed more guidance, required more restraints than before.

Thus in the spring of 1936 he did considerably more public speaking than Roosevelt thought desirable; he was far less well equipped for the role of leading spokesman for the New Deal in an election year than was Ickes, in the President's opinion. Parochial in his attitudes, Farley made mistakes—a bad one on May 20, when, speaking in Michigan, he predicted that Landon would become the Republican presidential nominee and described him denigratively as "governor of a typical prairie state." At once greatly publicized, the remark insulted mid-America and angered Franklin Roosevelt, who promptly sent Farley a blunt memorandum: "I thought we had agreed that any reference to Landon or any other Republican candidate was inadvisable. . . . [A] good rule which should be passed down the line to all who are concerned with speech material is that no section of the country should be spoken of as 'typical' but only with some laudatory adjective. If the sentence had read 'One of those splendid prairie states,' no one would have picked us up on it. . . ."[37]

Some three months later Roosevelt again issued what amounted to a rebuke of Farley when the latter attempted to muzzle Harry Hopkins for the duration of the campaign. Hopkins during a western trip made several speeches extolling WPA and the President. When he returned to Washington, Farley phoned him to say bluntly that "about 75 percent of the complaints we [at national campaign headquarters] were receiving were about WPA," that Hopkins himself was about the most unpopular man in the administration (he had said this often enough to Ickes, in agreement with Ickes's assessment), and that he wanted Hopkins to stop making speeches or holding press conferences until after election day. Hopkins responded to this angrily, defiantly. He promptly told Roosevelt about it. And Roosevelt's response was to take Hopkins with him on a tour of the drouth areas of the Midwest during which Hopkins made a number of speeches along the same line he had earlier followed.[38]

For it was Roosevelt who actually ran the campaign in its every major phase and form. To some of his worried associates in late July and early August it would seem that he, deprived of the naysaying Howe's views and counsels, became as overoptimistic and -confident as Farley often was, hence disinclined to exert the strenuous effort required to assure election triumph. Even Eleanor Roosevelt, whose letters to Lorena Hickok during the summer expressed her emotional aloofness from her husband, her personal indifference to the election's outcome, provoking from Hick angry and anguished responses, felt obliged to chide her husband on occasion for a carelessness of communication which resulted sometimes in no communication between himself and top officials of his campaign. "I hear from outside sources that the Landon headquarters are set up and ready to work full time," she reported in a memo to her husband and others in mid-July, when Democratic headquarters seemed in sad disarray. "They have continuity people writing for the radio, they have employed advertising people to do their copy, and the whole spirit is the spirit of a crusade. My feeling is that we have to get going and going quickly. . . ."[39] But in actual fact, Roosevelt, who felt acutely the need which Howe's death left unsupplied, paid a closer attention to the details of the campaign and dominated its whole to a greater degree than he had done during the campaign of 1932.

Clear to his perception, and determinative of his overall strategy, was the emergence in this election year of a coalition of economic class interests and regional loyalties, of agrarian West and Midwest and Solid South with key portions of the industrial urban North, of farmers, industrial workers, service employees, and professional people, all joined by a common denominator of progressivism. It was an emergent reality somewhat different from that grand coalescence into a Roosevelt Democracy which he had intuitively envisaged and begun definitely to plan and work toward in 1925,* for there were two major elements of it which he had *not* foreseen—not, at any rate, in the form and force of their actual development—and done little or nothing personally, directly, to bring about. Indeed, he had often acted in ways that discouraged their development.

One of the two was the black American as voting bloc.

In his identification of himself with Georgia through his Warm Springs connection, Roosevelt had emphatically not embraced the racial bigotry, the viciously paranoid fear of "nigger" equality which characterized the poor white farmers of Meriwether County and elevated Herman Talmadge to Georgia's governorship. But neither had he embraced the cause of those white progressives of Georgia, centered in Atlanta, who were concerned to assure the black man of his constitutional rights as U.S. citizen. He developed and maintained unflawed his warmly friendly relations with his Warm Springs neighbors in part by remaining discreetly silent about the "race question." He had maintained the same silence in the White House; references to black Americans and the injustice they continually suffered were notably absent from his presidential utterances. He had also maintained an aloofness that amounted to a siding with southern planters against black tenants and share-croppers during the great crisis over AAA policy in early 1935, as we have seen.

Eleanor Roosevelt, on the other hand, having no liking for Warm Springs and a distinct aversion to the typical southern white's racial attitudes, had done what she could, privately, to aid the efforts of the Southern Tenant Farmers' Union to unite blacks and whites in common cause, breaking down racial barriers. She had been outspoken in support of the NAACP and of federal antilynching legislation; she had got her husband's permission to be so, though he cautiously retained the option of dissociating himself from her stands whenever negative reactions to them grew strong, as we have also seen. In social situations, as in her public speech and published writings, she had consistently demonstrated her abhorrence of race prejudice, her conviction that all men, black and white, are "created equal" in the sense in which the Declaration of Independence uses these words. And it was with her support, which included influential appeals to her husband's conscience (or to his calculating sense of the practical potency of her kind of moral feeling in New

*See Davis, *FDR: The Beckoning of Destiny,* pp. 779–85.

Deal politics), that both Harry Hopkins and Harold Ickes had insisted from the first upon an antiracial discrimination policy in their administration of federal relief and public works, thereby assuring southern blacks of a higher percentage of available welfare funds and public works jobs than they had ever received before.

Louis Howe, too, in his operations as Roosevelt's right hand in setting up the Civilian Conservation Corps and establishing CCC policy, had stressed equal access and treatment for blacks. True, prevailing prejudice in North as well as South dictated the assignment to segregated camps of the great bulk of the 200,000 blacks enrolled in CCC from first to last. Only 30,000 of them entered integrated camps, mostly in the West and New England. But young blacks who were enabled to escape from dire misery into a healthy, secure, well-fed outdoor life, doing useful work in forest and field for pay as high as white boys received, were not disposed to be critical of CCC. They were immensely grateful for it. Admittedly, other New Deal agencies adopted discriminatory policies that were harshly unfair in traditional ways. Black leaders protested them bitterly. TVA, operating in a region where race prejudice was as high as personal incomes were low, accepted the white South's mores when dealing with black people. Even Eleanor's "baby," Arthurdale, in West Virginia, felt compelled to restrict admission to "white native stock," refusing the applications of more than 200 blacks, according to Arthur Schlesinger, Jr.[40] Yet the feeling among blacks, justified by evidence, was that the New Deal did care more about them than any earlier administration had done, and was far more actively concerned for their welfare.

The result of all this, politically, had been a massive shift of party allegiance by voting black Americans. Insofar as they had voted at all in the past, they had voted Republican since Republicans were allegedly the party of the Great Emancipator,* while Democrats were, certainly in the Solid South, the party of Jim Crow. A great majority of the black ballots cast in the presidential election of 1932 had been cast for Herbert Hoover. But now, when and where blacks were permitted to register for the primaries (they were not permitted to do so in the South, of course), they were registering in overwhelming majority as Democrats. They were Roosevelt Democrats. And this was no mean accession of Democratic strength at the polls in those big northern cities into which some 2 million blacks had moved from the South since the beginning of the Great War.

The other element of the grand coalition which Roosevelt had not foreseen in its present dimensions and nature was organized labor.

Under the aegis of Section 7(a) and with no help from Roosevelt personally —quite the contrary at crucial moments—there had been a tremendous growth of labor union membership since 1933, a growth that continued apace after NRA had been struck down by the Supreme Court. By the summer of

---

*Actually the Republican party as history knows it was born five years after Abraham Lincoln's death. It had its beginnings in the Grant administration.

1936 total union membership approached 5 million. All unions had grown, but the growth had been most spectacular in the industrial unions, of which there were four within the AFL, a fact that rendered increasingly unrepresentative of total membership the federation's prevailing conservative craft union leadership. There was a natural anxiety on the part of this old-line skilled-craft leadership to retain unimpaired its jurisdictional power, and this anxiety was increased by the aggressive determination of John L. Lewis of the United Mine Workers (UMW), David Dubinsky of the International Ladies' Garment Workers' Union (ILGWU), Sidney Hillman of the Amalgamated Clothing Workers (ACW), and others to organize, on an industry basis, not a craft basis, the workers in such mass-production industries as automobiles, steel, aluminum. A pious wish to unionize this unorganized labor force had been expressed from time to time by AFL President William Green. But nothing effective had been done in that direction, or could be done under the present dispensation.

Proposal of a policy of industrial unionism had been made in the form of a resolution during the annual convention of the AFL at Atlantic City in October 1935. The debate was prolonged and stormy, with Lewis the leading spokesman for it. He was at his oratorical best, at once thunderous and lyrical, declamatory and logical, metaphorical and literal, in his grandest Shakespearian manner. Nevertheless, the resolution was voted down, and by a huge majority. Within weeks thereafter, in defiance of the AFL executive council, Lewis and other industrial unionists had formed a Committee for Industrial Organization (CIO); with Lewis its chairman, and both he and Dubinsky resigned their posts as AFL vice-presidents. Within months, in the spring of 1936, an intensive drive to organize the steel industry was under way, launched by CIO. By mid-June this drive was under the direction of the remarkably able Philip Murray, long one of the most effective of UMW organizers, who now headed a newly formed and aggressive Steel Workers Organizing Committee. And by August the AFL executive council had formally expelled the ten of its unions which were affiliated with CIO, among them the UMW, the United Textile Workers, the United Rubber Workers, the ILGWU. The labor movement was split in two. John L. Lewis emerged as the most powerful labor leader in American history. And the CIO grew into one of the truly important historical forces in American life in that it would make actual changes in the basic power structure of the nation.

It was a force that worked strongly for Roosevelt's reelection that year. Most of the membership of AFL craft unions voted for him; on May 5 William Green came out personally for him and urged other union members to do the same. But the support from CIO unions was stronger, more substantial. The 200,000-member ILGWU declared for Roosevelt on June 14 and made a considerable contribution to the Roosevelt campaign chest. So did Sidney Hillman's ACW. Lewis declared for Roosevelt on July 9, and his UMW contributed a whopping $469,870 to the Roosevelt campaign. By October unions having an estimated membership of 3 million had come out for Roosevelt, and many of them made campaign contributions.[41]

To hold his grand coalition together, or as a major component of the common denominator among its disparate elements, Roosevelt had already plumped heavily for the feeling provoked, the opinion aroused, by the common enemy he had defined last January in his annual message—namely, that "minority of business and industry" that strove from their positions of "entrenched greed" for a "restoration of their selfish power," a power they would use to establish an "autocracy." Implied by this strategic common enemy, who was repulsive, hateful, fear-inspiring in cohesive mass effect, was a common hero who was attractive, lovable, hope-inspiring in cohesive mass effect—a Champion of the People or Knight in Shining Armor, who marched forth bravely, victoriously against the evil foe. And for this role of hero, he felt himself to be cast by God and history. He, Franklin Delano Roosevelt, personified the New Deal. He was the living embodiment of all the historic forces that had transformed government, in its relations with individual Americans, since March 1933, which is to say, as he did say to Moley in the Oval Room on an evening in late May 1936, that he personally was the "one issue in this campaign" and that "people [including Ray Moley] must be either for me or against me." He meant, of course, that he himself was the single overriding or summary issue, for in that same conversation he talked of "specific" issues (the administration's current tax program, for instance, salient features of which outraged Moley) as "details" in which he was "not interested" at that moment.[42]

Yet even as he said this, he knew he would have to make campaign policy decisions about these "details." He must choose to emphasize or ignore any one of them as he waged his heroic battle. And now, in June, it was imperative that he decide once and for all whether to make a "specific" campaign issue of the common enemy's most potent weapon, which was the Constitution as interpreted by the present Supreme Court majority.

Jim Farley was very sure he should not do so. "Mr. President," he said, in Frances Perkins's hearing, ". . . the people of the United States don't understand it [i.e., the problem of Court and Constitution]. You could not possibly get a sufficient excitement among the people about it."[43] Roosevelt had of course, been led toward the same assessment by his own trial ballooning on this subject last summer. But since then there had been the AAA decision, the Guffey coal decision, the *Tipaldo* decision, each provoking published anger against the judges, each spreading more widely a popular belief that the Court was not truly judicial but simply, primarily, a tool of big business. "It is a tragic and ominous commentary on our form of government when every decision of the Supreme Court seems designed to fatten capital and starve and destroy labor," John L. Lewis had commented ominously when the *Guffey* decision was handed down.[44] Hence the question: Was the public's indifference or unconcern about the Court, its lack of understanding of the constitutional issue still as great as Farley believed it to be? If so, would this state of affairs continue after Roosevelt had accepted the Liberty League's challenge? If he had been convinced that it would, he might for that very reason have decided to make a critical reference to the Court issue in his nomination acceptance speech and to devote at least one major campaign address to possible ways of overcoming Court obstructionism. Doing so would enable him to claim that his election victory, which he regarded as inevitable, provided he made no bad mistakes, included a mandate to move directly against Court intransigence. Or if he had been convinced that the populace would rally behind him in solid majority as he attacked the Court as a tool of property, and proposed judicial reforms that would restore power to the people's elected representatives, he might, he certainly would have done so. The mandate would then have been absolute, unquestionable. He was *not* so convinced, however. The negative popular reaction to his "horse-and-buggy" remark in May 1933, as reported in the press, still rankled, and gave him pause. The air above the league's chosen battleground just might be as charged with inchoate yet powerful emotions, the ground itself just might be as suited to defensive warfare, full of quicksands and pitfalls, as the league's perpetrators believed it to be. If so, the direct assault invited by the league could become for Roosevelt the bad mistake that offset disastrously all he had now going for him, triumphantly, toward November.

In the end he decided to make no mention of Court or Constitution in his acceptance speech. He would devote no campaign speech to the subject, though this meant a passing up of opportunity to educate the public on a momentous issue of government. He also rejected the urgings of several advisers that he incorporate in the party platform, which was essentially dictated by the White House, a plank forthrightly proposing a constitutional amendment, one that spelled out the meaning of "general welfare" in ways that definitely, unequivocally permitted the federal legislation of national economic concerns. He would go no farther on this matter than Landon had said he would go, in the telegram sent to the Republicans in Cleveland. "We know that drouth, dust storms, floods, minimum wages, maximum hours, child labor and working conditions in industry, monopolistic and unfair business practices cannot be adequately handled exclusively by forty-eight separate state legislatures, forty-eight separate state administrations, forty-eight separate state courts," said the Democratic platform in direct answer to the Republican platform's proposal to solve pressing national problems only through state action. "Transactions which inevitably overflow state boundaries call for both state and federal treatment. We have sought and will continue to seek to meet these problems through legislation within the Constitution." But if they could not "be effectively solved within the Constitution, we shall seek such clarifying amendment"* as would permit state and federal legislation "adequately to

---

*The word "clarifying," inserted by Don Richberg, was intended to imply that the Constitution in its present form gave Congress the needed power but that judges were too obtuse or perverse to read it accurately.

regulate commerce, protect public health and safety, and safeguard economic security. Thus we propose to maintain the letter and the spirit of the Constitution."[45]

Only in the keynote address to the convention, delivered by Kentucky's mighty orator, Senator Alben Barkley, was the issue between Court and people boldly faced and clearly stated. Barkley's flaming words, heartily approved in advance by the President, roused the delegates in Philadelphia to a frenzy. The senator began with an impressive summary of the administration's achievements. Then, he said: "But we are told by the smug and cynical apostles of the status quo that the Supreme Court has nullified some of the acts of this administration. And while anxious farmers ponder their fate, and laboring men scan the heavens for a rainbow of hope, and women and children look in vain for preservation of their lives and health, a voice from the grave at Palo Alto [i.e., Herbert Hoover's voice] shouts: 'Thank God for the Supreme Court.' I make no attack on the Supreme Court. As an institution I respect it. . . ." But when the nine justices of the Court could not agree among themselves on what the Constitution meant, when five said it meant one thing and four who were "equally eminent, learned, and sincere" said it meant the opposite, surely "we are at least relieved of the obligation to underwrite the infallibility of the five whose views prevail." He posed questions, dramatically: "Is the Court beyond criticism? May it be regarded as too sacred to be disagreed with?" And to each of these the great crowd replied in a roar of negatives.[46]

Roosevelt's nomination acceptance speech caused him more trouble during its preparation than Rooseveltian speech drafting usually did.

By late spring it had become as clear to Roosevelt as Moley claims it was to him that these two, Roosevelt and Moley, could no longer work together. Their attitudes, their opinions diverged too widely, Moley's to the right, Roosevelt's to the left, and Moley was no docile, submissive personality who could, even by design, subordinate himself wholly to another's will. Roosevelt, therefore, on the last of May, called for help from Sam Rosenman, who had served him so well as speech draftsman and information file during the gubernatorial campaigns of 1928 and 1930. To be Rosenman's aide in this drafting enterprise, Roosevelt called in a well-known Protestant churchman named Stanley High, a divinity school graduate and former *Christian Herald* editor who had written for the Republicans in 1932 and would do so again in future election campaigns. He had a facile pen, flexible convictions, and an affable personality; Rosenman liked him personally, and they worked well together. But at the same time, without informing Rosenman and High of the fact, Roosevelt asked Tommy Corcoran to prepare a draft. This was Corcoran's first speech-writing assignment, and, according to Moley, he was so jittery about what he produced (it was 12,000 words long! says Moley) that he begged a reluctant Moley, as personal friend, to help him cut and revise it. Moley did so, meeting with Corcoran in a Philadelphia hotel on Monday, June 22, the day before the Democratic National Convention opened. From Philadelphia

Moley went down to Washington next day in response to a phone call Roosevelt had made to him some days before, a call which may have been made, as Rosenman believed, mostly to ease the hurt Moley must have felt at being now shunted aside, but which Moley preferred to believe was made out of a genuine, if not actually desperate, need for help.

The event would seem to indicate that Rosenman's belief was true, Moley's false.

On the morning of Wednesday, June 24, Moley and Corcoran met in the Oval Room with Roosevelt, who told them he wanted a speech "only fifteen minutes long," which rose "to a serious note." When Moley predictably suggested that the "note" be a conciliatory one, conciliatory toward business, and that it be sounded upon a theme of "Serenity and Service" which Baruch had proposed, Roosevelt accepted the suggestion with a show of enthusiasm. "Splendid!" he said, adding that he'd like also to "bring in reference to Hope, Faith, and Charity—with Charity being interpreted as Love."[47] Thereupon Moley and Corcoran retired to the Mayflower Hotel where, by evening, they had carved and revised out of the original Corcoran manuscript several pages of soothing sweetness and light. The two then went back to the White House as the President's dinner guests, the other guests being Rosenman and High, with Missy LeHand presiding (she almost always did, in the First Lady's absence) as hostess.

That dinner, served in the small family dining room, was effectively the end of the relationship between Roosevelt and Moley, though the two had three or four meetings and a phone conversation or two during the immediately following weeks. "[F]or the first and only time in my life, I saw the President forget himself as a gentleman," Rosenman remembered sixteen years later. Stanley High, sensing an opportunity to curry favor with the President, who had given him and Rosenman speech-drafting guidelines far different from those given Moley, made a teasing remark about Moley's associating these days exclusively with the wealthy, a remark that provoked laughter around the table and visibly annoyed Moley. Roosevelt then took up the theme and pursued it with a vengeance. According to Rosenman:

> He [Roosevelt] began twitting Moley about his new conservatism and about the influence of his "new, rich friends" upon his recent writings, which had been very critical of the Administration. Moley responded with what I thought was justifiable heat. The President grew angry, and the exchanges between them became very bitter. We all felt embarrassed; Missy did her best to change the subject but failed. The words became acrimonious. . . . While I knew how deeply Roosevelt had been stung by the unfriendly attacks on his policies by Johnson and Moley, I thought that his temper and language were particularly unjustified, not only because there were other people present, but because they were all his invited guests. It was an ordeal for all of us. . . .[48]

Next day the Moley-Corcoran draft—"a very moderate, conciliatory speech," as Rosenman described it—was completed and delivered to Roosevelt, who made joking reference, in his exchanges with Moley, to the rough talk of the night before. The draft was accepted as the speech to be given three days hence, or so Moley then believed, Roosevelt having indicated as much. But by then—indeed, several days before—Roosevelt had accepted with genuine enthusiasm the speech which Rosenman and High had written, a draft having "very little in it that was conciliatory," being, instead, "a militant, bare-fisted statement . . . intended to give battle to the reactionaries in both parties who were out in full force to stop the New Deal." And it was to Rosenman and High that the President now turned for preparation of the truly final draft. Into their hands he confided the Moley-Corcoran manuscript with the request that they "work it into" the draft they had prepared, a weaving together of discordant strands that failed, in their hands, for all their trying, to produce a smooth and single fabric.

Roosevelt himself managed to do some smoothing out through redictation on Friday, June 26. (In the convention hall in Philadelphia that day, Roosevelt's name having been placed in nomination in an uninspired speech by John E. Mack of Poughkeepsie, who had done the same thing in Chicago four years before, the seconding speeches and the noisy, inane demonstrations went on and on and on.) But the truly effective smoothing out was done some thirty hours later by Roosevelt in the very process of delivering the speech, was done through his varying of the tones of his wonderfully vibrant voice, through his distribution of emphases, through his speeding up and slowing down in ways that slurred over the rough spots. Ickes, personally witnessing the performance from the speakers' platform in Philadelphia, thought it "the greatest political speech I ever heard . . . a strong and moving statement of the fundamental principles underlying our politics today. . . ."[49]

The nomination acceptance ceremony was held not in the convention hall but outdoors in Franklin Field, a sports stadium with a seating capacity of 100,000. All that Saturday afternoon rain had fallen in intermittent showers from lowering skies, and showers continued into the evening. Yet by eight o'clock, two hours before the President was scheduled to speak, the stadium was filled to overflowing—by a vast throng whose mood during the waiting time was exalted by the lyrical romanticism of Tchaikowsky, rendered by the Philadelphia Symphony under Leopold Stokowski, and by the glorious singing of the lovely, petite operatic coloratura Lily Pons. Sometime after nine o'clock the rain ceased, the skies began to clear. A half-moon shone down through veils of mist as Roosevelt appeared on the speakers' platform to receive a thunderous ovation.

Thereafter, through a long quarter hour, he was, measured by the standards properly applicable to such an occasion, nothing less than magnificent.

"Here, and in every community throughout the land, we are met at a time of great moment to the future of the nation," he said to the myriads in sight of him, the millions within range of his radio voice. "It is an occasion to be dedicated to the simple and sincere expression of an attitude toward problems, the determination of which will profoundly affect America. . . . Philadelphia is a good city in which to write American history. . . . Political tyranny was wiped out in Philadelphia on July 4, 1776." But since that day "man's inventive genius" had "released new forces in our land." There had come the "age of machinery, of railroads; of steam and electricity; the telegraph and the radio; mass production, mass distribution. . . ." And these things

> combined to bring forward a new civilization and with it a new problem for those who sought to remain free. For out of this modern civilization economic royalists [the phrase was Stanley High's] carved new dynasties. New kingdoms were built upon concentration of control over material things. Through new uses of corporations, banks and securities, new machinery of industry and agriculture, of labor and capital—all undreamed of by the fathers—the whole structure of modern life was impressed into this royal service. . . . It was natural and perhaps human that the privileged princes of these new economic dynasties, thirsting for power, reached out for control over Government itself. They created a new despotism and wrapped it in the robes of legal sanction. . . . Against economic tyranny such as this, the American citizen could appeal only to the organized power of Government. The collapse of 1929 showed up the despotism for what it was. The election of 1932 was the people's mandate to end it. Under that mandate it is being ended.

He had to drag in by main force, and with the aid of no lubricating oil of transition, his reference to "faith, hope and charity." He simply abruptly asserted that these were not unattainable ideals.

> Faith—in the soundness of democracy in the midst of dictatorships. Hope—renewed because we know so well the progress we have made. Charity—in the true meaning of that grand old word. . . . In the place of the palace of privilege we seek to build a temple out of faith and hope and charity. . . . Governments can err, Presidents do make mistakes [Moley's words], but the immortal Dante tells us that divine justice weighs the sins of the cold-blooded and the sins of the warm-hearted on different scales. Better the occasional faults of a Government that lives in a spirit of charity than the consistent omissions of a Government frozen in the ice of its own indifference.

Came then the words for which this speech would be most remembered: "There is a mysterious cycle in human events. To some generations much is given. Of other generations much is expected. This generation of Americans has a rendezvous with destiny."*[50]

VII

HERBERT Lehman, to the dismay of the national Democracy, since it might mean the loss of New York in the national referendum, had announced that for personal reasons, he would not run for reelection as governor of his state. Roosevelt, in a public appeal, a private letter, and a three-hour talk with Lehman at Hyde Park on June 29, managed to change the governor's mind. A day or so later Roosevelt told Ickes, in response to the latter's question, that he wanted him to make "attack" speeches in the campaign. Apart from these two things, he did at that time almost nothing political. Until Landon had

---

*Tommy Corcoran contributed the phrase "rendezvous with destiny."

made his formal acceptance speech in Topeka on July 23, and for some time after, he seemed to dismiss the campaign wholly from his mind.

He was vigorously presidential for a couple of weeks, his primary presidential concern being the great drouth which had become a catastrophe for the Midwest and much of the Southwest by July of that year. Its human miseries were increased by the fact that the farm belt had by no means completely recovered from the drouth of two years before. A six-member Great Plains Drouth Area Committee was appointed—Morris Cooke was chairman; Rex Tugwell and Harry Hopkins were members—to survey the situation and designate specific drouth emergency areas. Hustled into being with an efficiency that recommended the administration highly to normally Republican farmers was an emergency drouth area program which provided federal relief to destitute families, feed for starving livestock, and financing for farm operations in the late summer and fall, which is sowing time for winter wheat.

On July 11 Roosevelt was principal speaker at the dedication of the great Triborough Bridge in New York City, a ceremony that must have been something of an ordeal for him in that it was a ceremony of triumph for Robert Moses, who presided over the proceedings. Moses did not introduce Roosevelt to the huge audience, however, for the President refused to permit it; Mayor La Guardia intoned the traditional words "Ladies and gentlemen, the President of the United States."

A few days later Roosevelt departed for a sailing vacation with his sons on a chartered schooner yacht, the *Sewanee,* embarking at Rockland, Maine, and sailing at leisurely pace to Shelbourne, Nova Scotia, and thence to Campobello, where he arrived on June 27.

His seeming total unconcern with the election, his seeming lack of personal attention to campaign detail all through July, provoked acute anxieties in Jim Farley, Stanley High, Ickes, and others of his associates, who saw Landon gaining strength day by day. The press, predominantly Republican, was clearly inclined to play the news in ways favorable to Landon, while, of course, promoting the Landon candidacy in editorials and feature articles. The bias was outrageous in such papers as the Hearst chain, the Kansas City *Star,* and (worst of all) Colonel Bertie McCormick's Chicago *Tribune.* And the impression of growing Landon strength conveyed by the press was given objective support by a poll scientifically conducted by the Washington *Post* and reported in that paper's "America Speaks" column on Sunday, July 12. It showed a sharp decline in Roosevelt support: He still received slightly more than 50 percent of the vote, but his support was so distributed that Landon led in electoral votes. A poll conducted for the Democrats by Emil Hurja just before the "America Speaks" results were published accorded precisely with these results. Hurja himself expressed grave concern. Wrote an indignant Ickes in his diary on July 18: "[T]he President smiles and sails and fishes and the rest of us worry and fume. . . . [T]he whole situation is incomprehensible to me. It was loudly proclaimed that Louie Howe had supplied most of the political strategy that resulted in the nomination and election of President Roosevelt and I am beginning to believe that this must have been true."[51]

There was thunder on the right and thunder on the left as radical populism continued its erratic movements under demagogic leadership. Gerald L. K. Smith, deeming himself successor of Huey Long, announced on June 17 the formation of a Union party, the presidential candidate of which was North Dakota's Congressman William Lemke. The party was an amalgam of Lemke's Nonpartisan League support, Share Our Wealth, Coughlin's followers, and, said Smith, the Townsend movement. Two days later in a nationwide CBS broadcast, Father Coughlin came out for Lemke, saying that the Union party "has raised a banner of liberty" for all to follow who would drive the "money changers' servants" from White House and Congress and "eradicate the cancerous growths from decadent capitalism" while also avoiding the "pitfalls of red communism." Dr. Townsend, however, did not endorse the Lemke candidacy until mid-July in Cleveland, where a monster national convention of his followers was held. Both Smith and Coughlin addressed rabble-rousing speeches to this immense gathering of the elderly, and both were carried away on the tides of their own rhetoric. Coughlin was carried the farthest. The reverend father, voice screaming, perspiration streaming, tore off his priestly coat and clerical collar before proclaiming to the thousands in the hall, the millions before their radio sets that "Franklin Double-crossing Roosevelt" was the "great betrayer and liar" of the United States.[52]

And, as Ickes recorded in his diary forty-eight hours later, there was not a word of reply from any administration figure! "The President is having too much fun sailing and fishing to resent a gross insult or to designate somebody else to resent it," commented Ickes disgustedly, adding that everybody was worried about the way things were going except the President, who "seems to be up in the clouds with his mind fixed on more spiritual things than his own election."[53]

Yet Roosevelt continued unperturbed, imperturbable.

And on the day after Roosevelt's disembarkation from the *Sewanee,* Father Coughlin, under Vatican pressure exerted through his own Bishop Michael J. Gallagher, publicly apologized to the President for having called him a liar. He had been overwhelmed by the passions of the moment when he made these "intemperate" statements, explained Father Coughlin. Roosevelt did not deign to notice either the insult or the apology.

He continued to be energetically presidential.

While drouth plagued the plains, floods plagued New England. On his way back to Washington from Campobello, he made news by touring briefly the flood-damaged areas in Vermont, New Hampshire, Massachusetts; he held conferences with the highest officials of the governments of those states.

He responded promptly, effectively to the new wave of war fear that swept the country as civil war began in Spain, a fear that this conflict would spark a general conflagration into which the United States would be drawn. On August 14, at Chautauqua, New York, where a discussion of the "subject of peace" was "eminently appropriate," he delivered a carefully crafted address designed to qualify an appeal to pacifist sentiment with hints of the hard realities of foreign affairs. Having reviewed his Good Neighbor policy toward the "American republics south of us," he stressed that though "we shun political commitments which might entangle us in foreign wars . . . we have cooperated wholeheartedly in the social and humanitarian work [of the League of Nations] at Geneva." This indicated that "we are not isolationist except insofar as we seek to isolate ourselves completely from war. Yet we must remember that so long as war exists on earth there will be some danger that even the nation which most ardently desires peace may be drawn into war." The country could rest assured that he personally would do all that was humanly possible to prevent such calamity. He employed language that identified him with the passionate revulsion toward the Great War's slaughters that were manifest in the novels *All Quiet on the Western Front* and *A Farewell to Arms,* in the plays *Journey's End* and *What Price Glory?* saying, "I have seen war. I have seen war on land and sea. I have seen blood running from the wounded. I have seen men coughing out their gassed lungs. I have seen the dead in the mud. I have seen cities destroyed. I have seen two hundred limping exhausted men come out of line—the survivors of a regiment of one thousand that went forward forty-eight hours before. . . . I hate war!" He was absolutely determined to maintain American neutrality "in case of war." This must mean, however, the denial of war profiteering on the part of Americans, and such denial would require strong leadership from an administration truly, profoundly committed to peace, an administration ready and able to prevent the kind of war profit that leads to war involvement.[54] Would a business-dominated Republican administration be so committed? was the question implicitly raised in the public mind.

In late August he toured the drouth-stricken states of Indiana, Illinois, Iowa, of North and South Dakota, Nebraska, Missouri. He held five major conferences and several smaller ones with governors and other state officials, the most important of these in Des Moines on September 1. Invitations to meet with him in Des Moines went to the governors of Iowa, Nebraska, Kansas, Oklahoma, Missouri on August 21 and were released to the press. Each governor, including Landon, felt obliged to accept. And so the two contenders for the presidency were in greatly publicized conference together on a blazing hot Tuesday morning, a friendly conference during which Landon impressed everyone with his poised self-possession, his courtesy, his concern for drouth victims, yet a conference at which the President was the dominant figure, to whom Landon perforce deferred. Roosevelt returned to the White House on September 5. Next day, a Sunday, in the evening, he presented the first fireside chat he had made since the spring of 1935: a report of what he had seen and learned during his drouth area tour. "We are going to conserve soil, conserve water and conserve life," he said. "We are going to have long-time defenses against both low prices and drouth." He also reminded his millions of radio listeners that "tomorrow is Labor Day," a national holiday, not a class holiday. "Anyone who calls it a class holiday challenges the whole concept of American democracy. The Fourth of July commemorates our political freedom—a freedom which without economic freedom is meaningless indeed.

Labor Day symbolizes our determination to achieve an economic freedom for the average man which will give his political freedom a reality."⁵⁵ He gave "nonpolitical" speeches in North Carolina on September 10 and at the Harvard University Tercentenary Celebration on September 18.

Then, finally, on September 29, he formally opened his presidential campaign with an address before the New York State Democratic Convention in Syracuse. He reminded his listeners of the state of the nation when he assumed office in March 1933—not, he added, that most people needed reminding. Most people vividly remembered that "starvation was averted, that homes and farms were saved, that banks were reopened, that industry revived, and that the dangerous forces subversive of our form of government were turned aside." There were a few people, however, who were "unwilling to remember." And he went on to tell about "a nice old gentleman wearing a silk hat" who in the summer of 1933 "fell off the end of a pier. He was unable to swim. A friend ran down the pier, dived overboard and pulled him out; but the silk hat floated off with the tide. After the old gentleman had been revived, he was effusive with his thanks. He praised his friend for saving his life. Today, three years later, the old gentleman is berating his friend because the silk hat was lost." By that time the Republican press and Republican speakers, including Al Smith, had injected "communism" into the campaign as major issue. Roosevelt and the New Deal, they charged, were leading the way to a Soviet America. Replied Roosevelt at Syracuse: "Conditions congenial to Communism were being bred and fostered throughout this nation up to the very day of March 4, 1933. Hunger was breeding it, loss of homes and farms was breeding it, closing banks were breeding it, a ruinous price level was breeding it. Discontent and fear were spreading throughout the land. The previous national Administration, bewildered, did nothing. . . . Lacking courage, they evaded. Being selfish, they neglected. Being short-sighted, they ignored. When the crisis came—as these wrongs made it sure to come—America was unprepared."⁵⁶ The New Deal had saved America from revolution.

On October 1 he made a half dozen campaign speeches in West Virginia and Pennsylvania, the major one an address in Pittsburgh, where, four years before, he had made vehement attack upon Herbert Hoover as a spendthrift and pledged himself to a balanced budget. "To balance the budget in 1933 or 1934 or 1935 would have been a crime against the American people," he now said. "To do so we should either have had to make a capital levy that would have been confiscatory, or we should have had to set our face against human suffering with callous indifference. When Americans suffered, we refused to pass by on the other side. Humanity came first." Indeed, New Deal spending had not really been spending in the sense of a diminishment of substance.

President Hoover's Administration increased the national debt in the net amount of $3 billion in three depression years; and there was little to show for it. My Administration has increased the national debt to the net amount of about $8 billion, and there is much to show for it. . . . Over a billion and a half went for payment of the World War Veterans' Bonus this year instead of in 1945. That payment is now out of the way, and is no longer a future obligation. . . . As for the other six and a half billions of the deficit, we did not just spend money; we spent it for something. Americans got something for what we spent—conservation of human resources through CCC camps and through work relief; conservation of natural resources of water, soil and forest; billions for security and a better life. While many who criticize today were selling America short, we were investing in the future of America.[57]

A week later he began a speaking tour that took him through Iowa, Minnesota, Nebraska, Wyoming, Colorado, Kansas, Missouri. Most remembered by history of all this talking were a few remarks made extemporaneously from the rear platform of his special train in Emporia, Kansas, on October 13. Emporia was the home of William Allen White, who had been the most prominent of Landon's few liberal-minded supporters. White had published several magazine pieces and Emporia *Gazette* editorials portraying the Kansas governor in the most favorable light that White, having grave doubts about Landon's ability, found it possible to play upon him; some of these writings had been gathered together in a book recently issued, entitled *What It's All About: Being a Reporter's Story of the Early Campaign of 1936*. And Roosevelt's first remark was that he was "very glad to be in Emporia. But I do not see Bill White." White, he explained was "a very old friend of mine" and "a very good friend of mine for three and a half years out of every four." Actually White *was* present, lurking in the far fringes of the crowd; he was pointed out to the President, who beckoned him forward, calling out, "Come on up, I want to see you a minute," and White was pushed forward, to stand within a few feet of Roosevelt during the latter's innocuous little talk. Landon's campaign managers were furious with White for being in the crowd at all.[58]

But by that time White, along with every other prominent member of the Republican party's slender liberal wing, had either removed himself or been shoved aside from the controlling center of the Landon campaign. The nominally Republican George Norris of Nebraska, now running by petition as an independent, had come out for Roosevelt, and White was supporting Norris for reelection that year. Gifford Pinchot's personal antipathy to Roosevelt had driven him into the Landon camp, but he, as campaign warrior, languished there, unemployed. Borah, antagonized by Landon's espousal of a return to the gold standard, did not come out for Roosevelt but refused to endorse Landon. Raymond Gram Swing, who had early lent his considerable journalistic talents to Landon's cause, became totally disaffected when Landon badly misused some information about the operations of social security which Swing had supplied him—this in a speech in Milwaukee on September 26. Week by week, under the leadership of the reactionary John Hamilton, Landon's tactics and speeches had themselves become more stridently reactionary. (As early as July White had complained to a Topeka newspaper publishing friend that Hamilton "has a seven-devil lust to live and shine under the blessing of the rich and he has turned over what ought to have been a good middle-of-the-road campaign to the hard-boiled political reactionaries . . . and their financial supporters."[59])

Landon's attack on social security was his greatest single error, as he himself readily admitted in retrospect. The information Swing had given him was from a preliminary report, hence unpublished, which Swing had helped prepare for the Twentieth Century Fund. It was a report, generally favorable, upon social security as a whole but critical of the reserve fund—of the size to which it would grow and of its probable handling. Upon this weak foundation Landon, whose flat-voiced speeches and campaign style were falling flat upon his audiences and who was desperately in search of an electrifying issue, based a direct attack upon social security as "unjust, unworkable, stupidly drafted and wastefully financed," its contributory features "a cruel hoax." Three days later John Winant resigned his post as Social Security Board member and chairman in order to mount a public defense of the Social Security Act against Landon's gross misrepresentations.

Yet the attack did have upon Landon's right-wing support something of the electrifying effect he desperately longed for, joined as it was with an increasingly broad and gaudy smear of Roosevelt and the New Deal as communistic. And as October wore on, with Roosevelt now steadily gaining ground in every poll scientifically conducted (the absurdly flawed *Literary Digest* poll predicted every week a landslide Landon victory), Republican campaign strategists, with Landon's full cooperation, moved to capitalize upon the uncertainties which Landon's Milwaukee speech had bred in the popular mind regarding social security—and to capitalize in ways ruthlessly disregardful of truth and decency. The most serious weakness of the Social Security Act was indeed its financing arrangements, as we have seen, thanks to Roosevelt's adamant refusal to permit any part of the scheme to be financed out of general revenues. The alternative to this, which Congress perforce accepted, was total financing out of contributory taxes upon employer and employee. These contributory taxes became now the target of Republican fire. In their weekly pay envelopes employees of many an industrial plant found enclosed a warning that beginning on January 1, 1937, the employer would be "compelled by a Roosevelt 'New Deal' law" to deduct 1 percent from each employee's paycheck, that this deduction might in years ahead go as high as 4 percent, and that the money so deducted might or might not be eventually returned to the worker. "Decide before November 3—election day—whether or not you wish to take" the chance of making this contribution and receiving no return for it. On the weekend before election day Landon, in a major speech in St. Louis, spoke of social security as an invitation to federal tyranny, destructive of individual liberty. For how was the federal government to maintain records of the millions of people enrolled in the program? Were they to be fingerprinted and have "mug shots" taken of them for file in Washington? "Or are they going to have identification tags put around their necks?" John Hamilton promptly asserted that this was precisely what they would "have" to do and that the tags would be of metal, the kind of tags placed on the collars of dogs. The Hearst press, on the day before the election, printed pictures of this alleged "dog tag" on its front pages.[60]

The assault, the cynically timed climax of which came so near the campaign's end that effective answer to it was difficult, aroused anxious fears in Democratic campaign headquarters.

It infuriated Franklin Roosevelt.

And on Saturday night, October 31, in New York City's Madison Square Garden, he struck back in one of the great political speeches in American history.

So eager was he to begin that he became almost angry with the huge crowd before him as it prolonged for a quarter hour the ovation that had greeted his appearance at the lectern. But once he was permitted to begin, he delivered his speech superbly, in wonderfully various, vibrant tones, and with rhythms perfectly suited to the achievement of maximum dramatic effect. He opened with the assertion that the issue of 1936 was the "preservation" of the people's victory that had been won in 1932. The "hopes" of the people in 1932 have "become our record" in 1936, he said. He went on:

> For twelve years this nation was afflicted with hear-nothing, see-nothing, do-nothing government. The nation looked to government but government looked away. Nine mocking years with the golden calf and three long years of the scourge! Nine crazy years at the ticker and three long years in the breadlines! Nine mad years of mirage and three long years of despair! Powerful influences strive today to restore that kind of government with its doctrine that the government is best which is most indifferent.
> . . . Never before in all our history have these forces been so united against one candidate as they stand today. They are unanimous in their hatred of me—and I welcome their hatred. I should like to have it said of my first administration that in it these forces of selfishness and lust for power met their match. I should like to have it said of my second administration that in it these forces met their master.

Again he had to wait for a frenzied crowd response to die down.
Then:

> Only desperate men with their backs to the wall would descend so far below the level of decent citizenship as to foster the current pay-envelope campaign against America's working people. Only reckless men, heedless of consequences, would risk the disruption of the hope for a new peace between worker and employer by returning to the tactics of the labor spy. . . . Every message in a pay envelope, even if it is the truth, is a command to vote according to the will of the employer. But this propaganda is worse—it is deceit.
> They tell the worker his wage will be reduced by a contribution to some vague form of old-age insurance. They carefully conceal from him the fact that for every dollar of premium he pays for that insurance, the employer pays another dollar. That omission is deceit.
> They carefully conceal from him the fact that under the federal law, he receives another insurance policy to help him if he loses his job, and that the premium of that policy is paid 100 percent by the employer and not one cent by the worker. They do not tell him that the insurance policy that is bought for him is far more favorable to him than any policy that any private insurance company could afford to issue. That omission is deceit.
> They imply to him that he pays all the cost of both forms of insurance. They carefully conceal from him the fact that for every dollar put up by him his employer puts up three dollars—three for one.

But they are guilty of more than deceit. When they imply that the reserves thus created against both these policies will be stolen by some future Congress, diverted to some wholly foreign purpose, they attack the integrity and honor of the American Government itself. Those who suggest that are already aliens to the spirit of American democracy. Let them emigrate and try their lot under some foreign flag in which they have more confidence.

And what of the New Deal's plans for the future?

Of course, the administration would continue to battle for better working conditions for labor, the abolition of sweatshops and child labor, collective bargaining, the elimination of unfair competition, cheaper electricity for homes and farms, low interest rates, better banking, regulation of securities issues, slum clearance, higher incomes for farmers, reduction of agricultural surpluses, soil and water conservation, flood control, reforestation, useful work for the unemployed.

"For all these we have only just begun to fight."[61]

VIII

THE great river of his life, the mighty Hudson, rising and falling with the tides of the sea and of history, flowed slowly but powerfully south toward triumph that weekend as he went northward along its eastern shore to Hyde Park. There, in the house of his birth, he read and heard news of the latest public opinion polls while consulting his own secret signs and portents. The sun shone. Every prospect was fair.

All the polls predicted his reelection by a large majority of the popular vote and an even larger one in the electoral college—all of them, that is, save the direct-mail poll of the *Literary Digest* (it continued to predict a landslide victory for the Republicans), in the accuracy of which virtually no one now believed. Certainly Alf Landon did not. Gallup and Roper listed only three states—Maine, Vermont, and New Hampshire—as "sure" for Landon but listed several other states as "possible" for him. Jim Farley, on the basis of Hurja's polling and his own information sources, was convinced, and told Roosevelt on November 2, that the President would carry every state in the Union, save Maine and Vermont. Roosevelt didn't believe it. He did now estimate a wider margin of victory for himself than he had done last January 10, when he had deemed probable an electoral college outcome of 325 for himself, 206 for his opponent; he now gave himself 360 electoral votes, compared to 171 for Landon. But there remained imponderables. No one could be sure what effect had been produced upon the electorate by the greatly amplified Republican lies about social security, especially by the huge surge of blatant lying during the last forty-eight hours. Nor could anyone be sure of the effect of Roosevelt's threat of "mastering" the "forces" opposed to him, language that had an ominous sound even in the ears of some of Roosevelt's friends. Certainly the Republicans, these last two days before the election, made the most of such fears of dictatorship as these words might arouse. Some Democrats had begged Roosevelt to make, on Monday, a "clarifying" statement. He refused to do anything of the sort, either in his formal talk to a friendly crowd in Poughkeepsie that day ("I was thinking this afternoon about the first political speech I made, in this city, way back in 1910 . . . a terrible speech") or in his final campaign radio speech an hour or so later at his home in Hyde Park.

Instead, in his Hyde Park talk he laid heavy stress upon his democratic faith and made oblique reference to the Republican pay envelope campaign and other Republican efforts to intimidate voters. He hoped that every one of the 55 million Americans eligible to vote would vote:

> I like to think of these millions as individual citizens from Maine to the southern tip of California, from Key West to Puget Sound—farmers who stop their fall plowing long enough to drive into town with their wives—wage earners stopping on the way to work or the way home—business and professional men and women— town and city housewives—and that great company of youth for whom this year's vote will be a great adventure. . . . And when you go to the ballot box tomorrow, do not be afraid to vote as you think best for the kind of world that you want to have. . . . No one will know how you vote. And do not let anyone intimidate you or coerce you by telling you otherwise. In the ballot booth we are all equals.[62]

Next morning, Tuesday, November 3, 1936—a bright, almost summerlike day along the Hudson River—the Roosevelt family—Franklin, his mother, and Eleanor—drove up from the Big House to Hyde Park's town hall to cast their ballots. They spent the rest of the day in relative peace and quiet.

Night fell.

The first radio returns came chattering in over teletypes set up in the library of the Big House at Hyde Park and over radio sets, of which there was at least one in every room.

Roosevelt wheeled himself into the small room he used as study and closed the door, there to chart in solitude with pencil on pad of paper, and with frequent reference to a voting chart, the path of his victory or defeat.

There was little real suspense, and that little did not last long: From the first the returns ran strongly in Roosevelt's favor.

Soon he flung wide open the study door and joined his family and closest associates to read and hear the development of the greatest presidential triumph in all history up till then—a triumphant parade of growing numbers that marched to the music of Tommy Corcoran's accordion and warm tenor voice singing and playing, again and again, "Happy Days Are Here Again." By nine o'clock only the dimensions of this victory remained as yet unknown, and as night wore on and the margin widened, these dimensions became stupendous. Not until two o'clock on Wednesday morning, November 4, however, did Roosevelt receive Landon's concession telegram. "The nation has spoken," it said. "Every American will accept the verdict and will work for the common cause of the good of the country." To it a gloriously happy Roosevelt made prompt reply: "I am grateful to you for your generous telegram and I am confident that all of us Americans will now pull together for the common good."[63]

Farley's election eve prediction, seemingly so extravagantly optimistic, proved to be precisely accurate.

Nearly 46,000,000 Americans, some 83 percent of all who were eligible to vote, had voted. Of these, 44,156,256 had voted for one or the other of the two major party candidates. Roosevelt had received 27,476,673 votes, and Landon 16,679,583. Roosevelt's plurality of 10,797,090 was the largest in presidential history, and his electoral college victory of 523 to 8 was proportionately the largest since James Monroe's Era of Good Feeling triumph of 1820. He had indeed carried every state save Maine and Vermont! He had carried into office with him larger House and Senate majorities than had been achieved two years before: More than 75 percent of the membership in each House would be Democratic when the Seventy-fifth Congress assembled in January 1937. And there could be no doubt that he was largely responsible for the reelection to the Senate of George Norris of Nebraska—a victory second only to the President's own as a source of Rooseveltian pleasure—for Norris's reelection had been very much in doubt when his independent candidacy was emphatically endorsed by Roosevelt, and the Norris victory was a narrow one.* Of the thirty-three races for state governorships that year, the Democrats had won twenty-six, and of two others, the victors (Farmer-Laborite Elmer Benson in Minnesota, Progressive Philip La Follette in Wisconsin) could be deemed New Deal allies.

As for the third-party threat, which had loomed so ominously in the fall of 1935, it had ceased to exist by October 1936. In mid-August Father Coughlin had dramatically announced that he would never broadcast again "if I don't deliver 9,000,000 votes to Lemke," but by then his rhetorical excesses, especially his branding of Roosevelt as "liar" and "betrayer" and "Communist," had already drained away much of the potency of that radical populism which the new Union party was supposed to organize. In late September the Catholic archbishop of Cincinnati and in early October, Monsignor John A. Ryan of Catholic University publicly rebuked the radio priest for repeatedly insulting the President of the United States. Coughlin was forced into evasive, ambiguous apology. On election day the vote for Lemke was less than one-tenth that which Coughlin had said he personally would deliver to him. It totalled 892,763. Equally catastrophic was the defeat inflicted upon socialism as a political force in American life. The election statistics showed all but a fraction of the once-growing strength of the Socialist party to be absorbed now into the Roosevelt coalition. Norman Thomas had won approximately 900,000 votes in 1932, nearly four times the number he had won in 1928. In 1936 he won a mere 187,342. The Socialist program was indeed being "carried out" by the New Deal, but "on a stretcher," as Norman Thomas himself would say rue-

---

*The Norris vote was 258,700, compared with 223,276 for the Republican candidate and 108,901 for the Democratic.

fully. The Communist party, on the other hand, had evidently gained a little in popularity, if far too little to worry those committed to democracy. Earl Browder, the Communist presidential candidate, had won something over 80,000 votes, compared with the 70,000 the Communist presidential candidate had won in 1932. He might have won considerably more from the unemployed and dispossessed had he campaigned directly, exclusively for American communism, attacking the New Deal as an economically destructive operation which had accomplished nothing (so party propagandists had claimed in 1933) that a huge earthquake would not have done better. Instead, following the new line adopted by Moscow in the face of the growing Nazi threat, he had waged a popular front campaign the slogan of which was "Communism is Twentieth Century Americanism" and the strategic aim of which was not to win votes for himself but to build a centrist bulwark against right-wing reaction. Browder and the Communists had, in deliberate effect, worked for the reelection of Roosevelt.

And Franklin Roosevelt himself stood now at the highest pinnacle of political power ever occupied by an American in time of peace.

He dominated the national consciousness, every phase of it, as no man had ever done before.

All things, it seemed, were possible for him.

17

‑>>X<<‑

Concerns and Anticipations:
November, December 1936

I

FROM this heightened pinnacle of power, he could not but take a more distant view in space and time and derive from what he saw a sense of enlarged, more important historic role. For the election's enhancement of his influence, his potential for leadership was evidently not confined to the domestic scene.

ROOSEVELT TOWERS IN THE IMAGINATION OF EUROPE, said a headline in the New York *Times* over a story filed by a correspondent in England on the day after the election. "Each country in its exaggerated nationalism pictured the triumphant President as one of its own heroes . . ." wrote this correspondent. The dictatorships saw him as a "voluntarily chosen dictator over 125,000,000 people," his administration a demonstration of the validity of authoritarian principles; the democracies saw him as a warrior for freedom whose reelection effected "a renewal of faith in popular government" in a time of doubt, confusion, and despair. The dictatorships applauded what they saw as his policy of strict neutrality with regard to European controversies; the democracies deplored this isolationism but saw it as a policy initially forced upon him which he would now, with his vastly augmented power, soon change. "Somehow the President's personality has crossed the ocean, leaped all Europe's barriers of language and tradition and made the common man here believe in him," the *Times* correspondent said. "If the election has given him vast responsibilities and colossal power for good or evil in the United States, it has also given him prestige in Europe such as no President has enjoyed since Woodrow Wilson landed on his peace mission seventeen years ago." The *Neue Zürcher Zeitung* of Zurich, the *Völkischer Beobachter* of Munich, the *Zeitschrift für Politik* of Berlin, the *Corriere della Sera* of Milan, and the *Giornale d'Italia* of Rome—all these, on the morrow of the election, printed glowing descriptions of Roosevelt the man and lengthy assessment of his importance in history.[1]

Some of the European interpretations of the election's significance appeared strange in the eyes of knowledgeable Americans. Thus a writer in the December issue of the *Revue de Paris* found "[o]ne of the most interesting aspects of the November 3 election" to be "that Roosevelt was reelected by no particular class but by all classes. Any of the groups could have passed entirely into the camp of his opponent without changing in any way the final result." This was true because the electorate had voted not for the man Roosevelt but for a set of principles, a philosophy of government. "In 1932," said this writer, "the Americans elected a Savior, a bit blindly. This year they affirmed a sum of principles that were upheld by the man and his philosophy but surpassed them by far. After four years of trial and experience the Americans simply recognized that Roosevelt represented better than anyone else . . . the great currents of their national destiny."[2]

More in tune with well-informed American opinion was a writer in the *Observer* of London who, in that periodical's November 8 issue, though sure that the American electorate had indeed voted for the New Deal, was equally sure it had done so because the New Deal was personified by "Roosevelt the man" with his "courage, his infectious gaiety, his capacity for intimate personal contacts, his consummate political strategy, his dynamic leadership, the unquestionable sincerity of his belief in social reform and that it is the duty of the state to help the victims of depression. . . ." And still more in tune with well-informed American opinion was the *Economist* of London in a report in its issue of November 21 headed "A Class Election," a report wholly contrary to the *Revue de Paris* interpretation. The *Economist* reported the mood in the Iridium Room of the fashionable St. Regis Hotel in New York City on the night of election day:

[O]nly dance music relieved the gloom as results flashed in on an improvised screen. The elegantly dressed clientele grew more and more morose. . . . At one table sat a party of New Dealers [they included Harry Hopkins, WPA executive Lawrence Westbrook, and newspaper columnist Dorothy Thompson, wife of Sinclair Lewis, whose commitment to Roosevelt and the New Deal soon proved fragile]. . . . After the election had been conceded the woman [Dorothy Thompson] arose, lifted her glass and proposed a toast to the President of the United States. The companions at her table promptly stood and lifted their glasses. But though a painful silence fell over the assemblage not a person stirred, not another glass was lifted. . . . The scene depicts to what extent the election was fought, and certainly felt, along class lines. A scattered handful of men above a given income level voted for Roosevelt, and a similar scattered handful below that level were for Landon. But on the whole, the poor won the election from the well-to-do.[3]

And the *Economist* went on to refute, through analysis, the notion that the reelected President now had power unlimited or even that his capacity to work his will in national government was at all commensurate with the magnitude of his election triumph:

Not since the Civil War have the Republicans fallen to such low representation [in Congress], and only once, just after the war, were the Democrats reduced to so pitiful a handful. The danger of this result is obvious. The majority is too large for efficient service. It is bound to deteriorate into factionalism. And as the Solid South sent 101 representatives into the lower house, most of whom cannot by wild exaggeration be described as New Dealers, they will constitute an immediate conservative influence. . . . The public so far has not paid much of a price for the new doctrine of unionization [under the Wagner Labor Relations Act]. If strikes and riots, and, later on, gross inconvenience to the public become the order of the day, Mr. Roosevelt may topple from his place as labour's Messiah. He may have to treat labour more "objectively" than he did on occasion during the last four years. And once he has chilled the enthusiasm of his labour following, his second honeymoon will have ended. President Roosevelt is more enviable today than he is likely to be a year hence.[4]

From William C. Bullitt also, in two long "personal and confidential" communications to the President, came glowing reports of the European reaction to Roosevelt's reelection. They were accompanied by a warning against any mistaking of this surge of European popularity for a practically efficacious "moral authority" over European affairs, the mistake Woodrow Wilson made in 1918 and 1919, Bullitt alleged, with world-catastrophic results.

To review in some detail the contents of these Bullitt epistles is to review one of the two concerns uppermost in Roosevelt's mind in the immediate aftermath of his election triumph—namely, the swiftly developing threat of new world war.

II

BULLITT'S tenure as the first U.S. ambassador to the USSR, which had opened in December 1933 with a warm sympathy on his part for the Soviet "experiment" and the men who directed it, had ended in bitter disillusionment with Stalin and Stalin's Russia in the summer of 1936, when Bullitt relinquished his Moscow post. Indeed, his disillusionment had by that time hardened into a hostility toward the Soviet regime which rendered his reports and policy recommendations from Moscow flatly contradictory of Roosevelt's view of Soviet-American relations or of what they could and should be. His successor in Moscow was to be the multimillionaire Wisconsin Democrat Joseph E. Davies, who knew nothing of Russia but did know what Roosevelt wished to hear and would begin to say it at once; he continued to do so, with great emphasis, in utter disregard of the advice of his own embassy staff (it included the brilliant and scholarly George Kennan) and of many signs that his reported "facts" and conclusions were probably untrue.[5] Meanwhile, Bullitt had been appointed U.S. ambassador to France, succeeding Jesse I. Straus. He had taken up these new duties in early October. It was from Paris, therefore, that Bullitt wrote the President to say:

> [T]he wave of enthusiasm in France which greeted your election was really phenomenal. No American President ever received such a tornado of praise. . . . Blum [Léon Blum, French premier, whose Popular Front ministry, a coalition of Radical Socialists and Socialists supported by Communists, had taken office in early June] came [to the American Embassy] personally to express his congratulations. This is unheard of. . . . You have, of course, received . . . the resolution adopted by the Chamber of Deputies and the resolution of the town of Lannoy which claims to the honor of your ancestors.* . . . The cause of this outburst is that the French regard you as a

---

*When what is now French Flanders was part of the Roman Empire, members of an already ancient Roman patrician family called the Actii established themselves near what is now Lille in a place called Alnetum, according to Roosevelt genealogists. Through the centuries this place-name became L'Aulney, then L'Annee, then Lanney, and finally Lannoy. Near the end of the eleventh century one of the family claiming descent from the town's original Actii settlers sufficiently distinguished himself to be granted a title of appellation. He became Hugues de Lanney. The title descended through male heirs until, in 1300, there was none. Only a female, Demoiselle de Lanney, remained in the ancestral manor. In 1310 she married one Jean de Franchiment, who

national leader who has succeeded in giving the lower classes a greater proportion of the national income without disturbing any of the ancient liberties. The French are all praying for such a man. Blum, himself, said to me he felt his position had been greatly strengthened because he is attempting in his way to do what you have done in America. In addition, the French all feel . . . that you will somehow manage to keep Europe from plunging again into war. [For] there is a universal belief that Europe is drifting toward war, and that no man on the continent has imagination enough to devise any method of reconciliation. Every minister of a small European state who has yet called on me has expressed the hope that you might intervene, saying that if you did not, his country would certainly be destroyed by the inevitable conflict. I have asked how you could intervene, what you could do to prevent war, how you could be certain that anything you did would not produce a fiasco similar to the London Economic Conference. The reply invariably has been that no one in Europe can think of any way in which you can intervene effectively—but you might be able to think of some way yourself. You are, in other words, beginning to occupy the miracle man position. And I am strongly reminded of the sort of hope that for a time was reposed in Woodrow Wilson.

Bullitt himself believed, in a wishful blinking of evidence daily generated in Hitler's Berlin and Blum's Paris, that "reconciliation between France and Germany," a reconciliation which remained (despite the "explosions of Mussolini") the "nub of the problem of European peace," was "still" possible. He refused to take note of the price which, in view of Hitler's personality and power, would have to be paid by France for such "reconciliation." France would have to become itself essentially Fascist, an authoritarian state ruled by men willing and even eager to subordinate themselves to Hitler's will. Bullitt wrote:

> The essential thing the Germans must have is the development of their economic relations with central Europe and the Balkans. . . . Indeed, it is perfectly obvious that whether the French want it or not, it will come to pass. It is in the logic of economic facts, for example, that Rumania should exchange her wheat and oil for German machines and construction material. Similarly, the Germans need the products of Yugoslavia, Hungary, Bulgaria, and Turkey, and these countries need German products. No one can invent any legitimate reason for trying to prevent this German economic development. The reason why so many people are afraid of it is because [sic] they fear that economic domination will lead to political domination and the realization of the old Berlin-to-Bagdad bloc.

But Bullitt refused to believe that political domination must inevitably follow economic domination. He chose to believe instead:

> It may be possible to get together the French and Germans on the basis of an economic agreement which would give the Germans a chance to develop Central Europe and the Balkans economically: provided such an agreement should be accompanied by an agreement with regard to limitation of armaments and a general revival of a feeling of European unity. That sounds like a large order. It is a large order; but the events in Spain have made most people in most European countries

---

assumed her name along with her estate. Their children were De Lanneys, who, as the generations passed, became De la Noyes. One of them, Philippe de la Noye, a Huguenot fleeing religious persecution, emigrated to Leyden, Holland, and from there with a party of Puritans to Plymouth, Massachusetts, in 1621. The name was Americanized as Delano.[6]

realize that there is such a thing as European civilization which reposes on certain very old civilized principles that may be destroyed by war or Bolshevism. I do not mean that people are anxious to start a crusade against Bolshevism or that anyone (even Germany) intends to invade the Soviet Union, but I do mean that there is beginning to be a feeling that if the nations of Western Europe do not hang together, they will hang separately.

Bullitt's conclusion: "If we can assist diplomatically in laying the basis for reconciliation between France and Germany, I think we should help. If we get anywhere diplomatically and see a fair chance of success, you could then come forward with some stupendous public announcement. But I feel emphatically that you should not let yourself be persuaded to make some great gesture until you have prepared the ground with great care."[7]

On November 24 Bullitt wrote again to the President from Paris, emphasizing once more the passionate desire of Europeans for Roosevelt's intervention in European affairs to prevent the great war, totally destructive of European civilization, which was deemed otherwise inevitable. But what could Roosevelt do? How could he intervene effectively? To these questions, Bullitt reiterated, the Europeans themselves had no answer; they simply insisted that "the President must have some idea." And to this Bullitt by his own account "invariably" replied that Roosevelt was not God, had "no authority to bend the rulers of Europe to his will," and was certainly "not going to send the American Navy and American soldiers to Europe," though it became more and more clear "that our money, ships and men are the things that are wanted." The situation was bound to grow worse. As it did so, "you will hear more and more flattery about your moral prestige and your duty to civilization. The pressure of one sort or another will not be easy to handle."[8]

He turned his attention to the civil war in Spain, where the U.S. ambassador was Claude Bowers, a man widely different from Bullitt in almost all respects but addicted, like Bullitt, to the writing of long, long personal letters to the President he represented. Bowers's sympathies lay wholly with the duly elected government of Spain to which he was accredited, though he was also committed, or easily accommodated himself to Roosevelt's prompt commitment, to a "complete neutrality in regard to Spain's internal affairs," as the President himself put it in a letter to Bowers on September 16. "The rebels," the latter had said to Roosevelt soon after the civil war began, "are the same element as that opposing your administration"—were, in other words, of the type of the American big businessman who was the bulwark of the American Republican party—and like the Republicans of the United States, they were bound by history to fail. "I really think the thing will be over soon," Bowers predicted in a letter of August 26 to Roosevelt.[9] Bullitt saw things differently. The Spanish conflict had "become an incognito war between the Soviet Union and Italy," he wrote on November 24, though he also took note of the fact that German aviation was a major portion of Franco's air force. At that moment Franco's Fascist rebels were locked in a stalemated battle with Loyalist troops before Madrid. They had been for weeks, and they would be for bloody months and years ahead. But implicit in Bullitt's letter was his conviction that the Madrid government was doomed. "My . . . impression is that Mussolini has decided to put Franco through whatever the cost may be. I think the cost will be very high. . . . I believe that before the Spanish Civil War is over it may bring Europe to the very edge of war." He did not believe this general war would "spring directly out" of Spain, however. Instead, because of the Spanish turmoil, a "situation may arise . . . which will give Hitler a chance to make some move against Czechoslovakia. Czechoslovakia, clearly, is the next item on Hitler's menu."[10]

And what would France do, if Hitler sent troops into Czechoslovakia? It was sworn by solemn treaty to come at once to Czechoslovakia's aid. But would it? "The Belgian ambassador here [in Paris] is an able man of long experience. . . . He predicted that France would ask Belgium and England what they would do. He said that he was certain that both his country and England would refuse to do anything; that the French would then be faced with the problem of attacking Germany alone, unsupported, or allowing Czechoslovakia to be swallowed and denying their pledged word. He added that the French, under the circumstances, would not march." Bullitt made no mention of the treaty of alliance between France and Russia signed in the spring of 1935 or of the treaty between Czechoslovakia and Russia signed in that same spring. The latter's effectiveness was contingent upon that of the treaty between France and Czechoslovakia: Russia was obligated to come to Czechoslovakia's aid in the event of an attack *only* if France did so. Clearly Bullitt did not believe that the Russian treaties would influence France to honor its pledged word in the crisis which Hitler's aggressive ambition seemed certain to create. But he did give some credence to the opinion of "a number of Frenchmen" with whom he had talked about the dire "eventuality" and who had told him that France *would* march, "knowing perfectly well that, when France began to be beaten by Germany, England would have to come in on the side of France." Bullitt's "own guess is that there will be a hair's breadth decision, and that no one can predict with certainty" what France would do.

Of "all this intellectual chaos and impending doom, the underlying truth is that the development of the airplane has made Europe an absurdity," Bullitt concluded, on a note indicating that he deemed bolshevism, not nazi-fascism, the greatest ultimate danger to European civilization. "Last year, flying from Munich to Venice, I crossed Austria in fifteen minutes. When you and I were children, it took that long to drive from the Place de la Concorde to the Bois de Boulogne. These dinky little European states cannot live in an airplane civilization. Today they have the alternative of submerging their national hatreds and national prides sufficiently to unify the continent or of destroying themselves completely and handing Europe over to the Bolsheviks. There is as yet no sign that there may be an outbreak of common sense."

Bullitt's closing words were: "I hope you are having a grand trip to South America."[11]

III

FOR this letter of Bullitt's, having arrived in Washington, was to be carried by mail plane from Washington to Roosevelt aboard the USS *Indianapolis* and be read by the President as he sailed northward along the coast of South America, returning from a voyage to Buenos Aires.

Nearly a year before, on January 30, 1936, in pursuance of plans initiated by Secretary of State Cordell Hull seven months earlier, Roosevelt had formally proposed to the twenty-one Latin American states that they send representatives to "an extraordinary inter-American conference . . . to assemble at any early date, at Buenos Aires . . . to determine how the maintenance of peace among the American Republics may be best safeguarded. . . ." In August 1936, after an agenda had been agreed upon, Argentina formally invited the other Latin American states to meet in Buenos Aires for a conference beginning on December 1, 1936. On November 4, the day after the election, Roosevelt in Hyde Park let it be known that he had decided some weeks before to attend in person the opening session of this conference. Doing so would focus world attention upon a demonstration of cooperation among democratic states to achieve disarmament and mutual understanding and upon Roosevelt personally as agent and symbol of a strong vital democracy, a powerful force for peace, who was available for international leadership if circumstances made his effectiveness likely in that role. It would also provide Roosevelt with the kind of vacation he most enjoyed, a relaxing and recreative 12,000-mile ocean voyage with occasional stops for deep-sea fishing and abundant opportunities for careless fun.[12]

He embarked on the USS *Indianapolis* at Charleston, South Carolina, on the morning of November 18, 1936. With him were his son James ("Jimmy will be a great comfort on the trip and it will do him good," wrote Roosevelt to his mother on November 17); his physician, Ross McIntire; his naval aide, Captain Paul Bastedo; his military aide, Pa Watson; and, of course, the indispensable Gus Gennerich. With him, also, as part of his luggage, was tangible evidence of the second of his two predominant postelection concerns, his concern over the U.S. Supreme Court as presently constituted.

For he viewed the Court majority's class-biased interpretation of the nation's fundamental law as the chief hazard—indeed, almost the only serious hazard, in view of the size and character of his election triumph—to the success of a bold and sweeping attack on poverty in America which he intended to be the central theme of his second term, though his program plans for dealing with poverty were as yet very vaguely defined. Two massive bound volumes had been prepared for him, at Homer Cummings's instigation, in the Department of Justice. One contained all the constitutional amendments that had been proposed to overcome judicial obstructionism, along with "expert" commentary upon each of them. The other, and much the larger, contained all the bills that had been proposed in Congress to that same end, also with commentary. But it cannot be said that he devoted any large percentage of his time during this long voyage to a perusal and pondering of these volumes or to the perusal of other "expert" documents from Cummings that awaited him, as prearranged, at every port of call. A glance through these materials sufficed to confirm certain tentative conclusions he had arrived at during the two weeks of almost daily tête-à-têtes with Cummings that had preceded his sailing, tête-à-têtes kept secret even from those whom, one would have thought, Roosevelt would have wished to involve deeply in this matter. He now, there-fore, put the Court problem aside as one already largely solved in essence; he devoted himself almost wholly for days at a time to the recreative activities, interspersed with long periods of no activity at all, which he so desperately needed—the sunbathing, the trolling, the relaxing pleasures of what he de-scribed in a letter to his wife ("Dearest Babs") as an unusually "happy ship."

He was at Trinidad, "anchored alongside a tanker three miles from shore," on the morning of November 21, remaining there until two o'clock that after-noon, having had four "restful days" during which "sleep and sunlight" had "done all of us good," as he said in a letter to his mother in Hyde Park. (He was reminded "of one day [in Trinidad] . . . 32 years ago!" he said to his mother, referring to some unspecified event that had occurred during the Caribbean cruise on which he was taken by his mother in 1904, a cruise arranged by the iron-willed and possessive Sara Delano Roosevelt as part of her strategy for delaying, if not preventing, her son's marriage to Eleanor.) By then he had been "warned" by "King Neptune" that he approached the equator, had received a "subpoena" for appearance before "King Neptune's Court" when the *Indianapolis* crossed the line, as had 200 others aboard ship who had never before entered the Southern Hemisphere. The line crossing occurred on November 24 and was, wrote Roosevelt to Eleanor in the White House two days later (Thanksgiving Day), "Great fun . . . —Marvelous costumes in which King Neptune and Queen Aphrodite and their court ap-peared. The Pollywogs were given an intensive initiation lasting two days, but we have all survived and are now full-fledged Shellbacks."[13]

The first of his scheduled "goodwill" appearances was in Rio de Janeiro, whose harbor ("The harbor—the harbor, the colors and the *orchids*—common as sweet peas!" he wrote to "Dearest Babs") was entered at seven-thirty in the morning of November 27. The U.S. ambassador to Brazil, career diplomat Hugh Gibson,* came aboard at the harbor entrance. The ship docked at nine, with Roosevelt going ashore then to be formally greeted by Brazil's notoriously dictatorial President Getúlio Vargas at the quay. A madly cheering crowd was gathered there. He had an early lunch at "a country place" with Vargas, going from there to the Brazilian Capitol, where he addressed to Brazil's Congress

---

*Hugh Gibson, who had been ambassador to Belgium during the Hoover administration and had long been, as he would remain, one of Hoover's closest personal friends, was by that token no favorite of Roosevelt's. He eventually was forced out of the Foreign Service by Cordell Hull, at Roosevelt's behest.

words of slight distinction but immense goodwill and optimism, saying that the "fine record of our relations [those of Brazil and the United States] is the best answer to those pessimists who scoff at the idea of true friendship between Nations. Let us present a record which our Hemisphere may give the world as convincing proof that peace lies always at hand when Nations, serene in their sovereign security, meet their current problems with understanding and good will."[14] He received from Brazil's congressmen, much of whose legislative power had been taken over by the Brazilian executive, a stupendous ovation.* He then again rode through Rio's streets in an open car, side by side with Vargas, to the U.S. Embassy, where there was a reception in his honor, rode then to a banquet elsewhere. It was well after dark when he returned to the *Indianapolis,* which sailed at ten for Buenos Aires.

Every street through which he rode that day was jammed with people who hailed him in frenzied fashion with shouts of *"Viva la democracia! Viva Roosevelt!",* and Vargas, who could not but interpret this ecstatic popular approval of Roosevelt and what Roosevelt stood for as an equally emphatic disapproval of himself and what *he* stood for, grew uneasy, embarrassed. At one point along the madly cheering streets he turned to Roosevelt to whisper a comment that was also a question. "Perhaps you've heard," he said, "that I am a dictator?" To which Roosevelt, while acknowledging the plaudits of the multitude with broad smile and lifted hand, made soothing reply: "Perhaps you've heard that I am one, too."

No less fervently enthusiastic than his reception in Rio was his reception in Buenos Aires when he landed there at 1:00 P.M. on November 30.

Some 2 million Argentines, "packed in every conceivable point of vantage, greeted . . . [him] with wild acclaim and showered him with flowers as he passed," said one eyewitness report of the events of that bright spring day. The reception "by the citizens of Buenos Aires exceeded in warmth and spontaneity anything that has ever occurred in Argentina," the same eyewitness said. Roosevelt himself, in a letter to his wife, described that Monday as "a jumpy sort of day—a vast surging throng all the way, 4 miles from the ship to the Embassy—then another equally long trip to the Presidential Palace and back again—crowds, tossed flowers, cheers, people running out, balconies filled." It was past midnight when, after a formal Delegation Dinner which, in accordance with Argentine (Spanish) custom, did not begin till 9:00 P.M., he went at last to bed in the embassy. He was very tired. He was also very happy. For by the events of the day he was further confirmed in his belief, expressed in his letter to Eleanor following the Rio visit, that "the moral effect of the Good Neighbor policy is making itself definitely felt," that this policy had made a "complete change" in a Latin American public opinion which "three years ago . . . was almost violently against us" (so he was soon to say in a letter to James

*The welcoming spokesman for the Brazilian Congress spoke of Roosevelt as "the *Man*—the fearless and generous man who is accomplishing and living the most thrilling political experience of modern times."[15]

M. Cox), and that the change was likely to become "a permanent fact." He slept soundly until eight o'clock next morning.[16]

And on this next morning, that of Tuesday, December 1, came the climax, the accomplishment of the major stated purpose, of his South American trip. He formally opened the Inter-American Conference for the Maintenance of Peace with an address calling upon the delegates to develop through their deliberations "mechanisms of peace" that would make "war in our midst impossible" and enable the nations of the New World to unite to help the Old World "avert its impending catastrophe of war." The union of American states which, he hoped, would emerge from this conference should and would, he said, "stand firm" against any aggression by the Old World against any part of the New.

He thus indicated the nature of the resolutions which Hull, as head of the United States delegation, would present to the conference. They would require the American republics to consult with one another whenever war was threatened in any of the Americas, would establish a permanent inter-American consultative committee for this purpose, and would commit the republics to a policy of strict neutrality toward international conflicts elsewhere on the globe, thus bringing Latin America into accord with the U.S. Neutrality Act. In the event, these resolutions failed of adoption. They were stubbornly, angrily opposed by the head of the Argentine delegation, Foreign Minister Carlos Saavedra Lamas, who was persuasive of a considerable group of delegates from Central America. If not personally sympathetic with the Loyalists in Spain and concerned lest they be deprived of offsets to the aid being given Franco by Mussolini and Hitler, Saavedra was profoundly committed, personally as well as officially, to Argentine supremacy in Latin American affairs. He bitterly resented the bland assumption of such supremacy by the Colossus of the North, was sure the Hull resolutions were "nothing more nor less than a means by which the United States hoped to extend its power and influence over the smaller nations of the hemisphere." He was also profoundly committed to the League of Nations as arbiter of international quarrels and guarantor of world peace (he had just returned from Geneva, where he had presided over the League Assembly) and saw the Hull resolutions as limitations upon the League's power to impose sanctions upon aggressor nations or to aid the victims of aggression with arms shipments. The policy disagreement soon degenerated into a bitter personal quarrel between Saavedra and Hull, with the conference finally adopting a "compromise" of the Saavedra and Hull positions that was in effect a repudiation of the latter. The permanent consultative committee idea was dropped, the republics merely promising to consult with one another whenever the peace of the hemisphere was threatened from within or without (the promise was nonbinding; each nation was left free to consult or not in any situation that might arise). The idea of a common neutrality policy was likewise dropped, the conference merely saying that neutrality was a general objective but that each nation was free to act as its prior treaty obligations and domestic legislation indicated.[17]

Thus the conference as a whole proved a failure from Hull's point of view,* a flat contrast in this respect with the shining public relations triumph scored by Roosevelt personally in Rio de Janeiro, Buenos Aires, and, finally, Montevideo, Uruguay, where he paused for seven crowded hours on December 3 in the last of his ceremonial appearances in South America. (". . . then a long rest—8 days before we get to Trinidad," he wrote "Dearest Mama" aboard the *Indianapolis* as it made the crossing of La Plata, from Buenos Aires to Montevideo. "We need it!")[18]

But to return to the events of December 1 . . .

The weather in the streets to which Roosevelt descended, a final ovation by the delegates ringing in his ears, from the building in which the conference assembled, was dismal. Dark skies lowered. From them fell heavy rain. This seemed not to dampen the enthusiasm of sidewalk multitudes—great throngs of people who "braved the weather to show President Roosevelt this last evidence of their unbelievably deep admiration for him," as an eyewitness reported[19]—but it accorded perfectly, this weeping of gloomy skies, with the pall that hung over everything that happened that day for Roosevelt and his immediate entourage; it harmonized perfectly with the mood that underlay every surface excitement, exhilaration, stimulated in Roosevelt himself by the popular responses to his public appearances. This basic mood was one of grief, of sadness. He spoke of it in the first sentence of the letter he addressed to his wife within an hour after his boarding of the *Indianapolis* that afternoon for his brief voyage to Uruguay.

"The tragedy of poor Gus," he wrote, "hangs over us all."[20]

James Roosevelt and Ross McIntire had broken the news to him while he yet lay abed on that morning of December 1, each of them having had a virtually sleepless night. Gus Gennerich, they told him, was dead! The news was as great a shock to him as the event had been to those who witnessed it.

There had been no warning.

Indeed, Gennerich had seemed rather more than normally "happy and well" to Roosevelt through all the day before (November 30) as he helped the President in and out of automobiles, into and out of buildings, with his usual swift, unobtrusive efficiency. A physically tough, husky man, he was only fifty years old. A bachelor, he had, since coming to Washington, "lived quietly in the Mayflower Hotel, devoting practically his entire time to accompanying the President when he left the White House or sitting quietly in the Executive Office," as the New York *Times* later said, adding that he "apparently had no other interest in life than service to" Roosevelt. But he *did* have another interest in these closing months of 1936. He was buying a farm to which he expected to retire when the Roosevelt presidency ended, and he "was really

---

*Sumner Welles saw things differently; he was always to maintain that the conference was a great success in that it laid foundations for future inter-American meetings from which important substantive action emerged.

living for that farm," as Roosevelt said to Eleanor "—he thought about it day and night and was buying things for it in Rio and B.A." After Roosevelt had gone to bed following the Delegation Dinner last night, Gennerich, who had eaten nothing during the evening, had gone with two shipboard friends to a café where he dined and danced. He had just returned to his table after a dance and made a joking comment to one of his table companions when he suddenly pitched forward, unconscious. "They did everything to revive him," Roosevelt told his wife, "but he died without knowing he was ill. There was of course no question that it was a straight heart attack."* His body had been taken to a funeral parlor upon the orders of James Roosevelt and of Ross McIntire after they, routed out of bed at 2:15 A.M., had notified authorities and dealt with the necessary formalities.

On the morning of December 2, in the large reception room of the embassy, there was a simple funeral service conducted by Chaplain C. V. Ellis of the *Indianapolis.* It was described to his wife by Roosevelt in broken words, as if with sobs: "There was a detail of marines and all the secret service men acted as pallbearers and were very much affected—the Embassy staff—and mine— lovely flowers on and beside the flag covered coffin—also flowers and a special representative from [Argentine] President [Agustín] Justo. The coffin was taken on board ship."[22] He cabled orders to Washington for another service to be held in the White House when the coffin arrived there.

He was far more deeply affected by this death, emotionally, than an outsider would have deemed likely. Almost from the first day of Gennerich's service to him, in Albany, he had regarded him not as servant or subordinate but as close personal friend, "the kind of a loyal friend who simply cannot be re- placed," as he said to his wife. He had spoken of Gennerich to others as his "ambassador to the man in the street" and "my humanizer"; he had often tried out speech language and ideas on him, to get the reaction of the "common man." Herbert Lehman, aware of this relationship, and himself very fond of Gennerich, sent condolences from Albany as soon as he heard of the death. "It was good of you to cable me," Roosevelt replied, "and I felt sure that you also would be distressed. . . . He was a true and loyal friend and I shall miss him greatly."[23]

The return voyage was uneventful and restful. The President relaxed in a continuing satisfaction with his personal reception in South America and a continuing optimism about Latin American affairs, despite gloomy reports that came to him from Hull in Buenos Aires. He was, however, "still most pessimistic about events in Europe," as he said in his letter to Cox on Decem-

---

*But it was *not* a heart attack, according to James Roosevelt. It was a cerebral hemorrhage. During the "hijinks" of the protacted "pollywog" initiation incident upon the *Indianapolis*'s crossing of the equator, the "roughhousing got a little out of hand and Gus hit his head rather hard," James said in print forty years later. "He complained of headaches from then on."[21]

ber 9, "and there seems to be no step we can take to improve the situation. Therefore until there is something I can hang my hat on, I must keep away from anything that might result in a rebuff of an offer to help."[24]

As the *Indianapolis* approached Trinidad, a British colony, on December 10, word came to him via ship's radio that King Edward VIII of Great Britain had abdicated his throne, to be succeeded by his brother George, after Parliament had refused to accept as his queen the American divorcée Wallis Warfield Simpson. "Awful dilemma," wrote Roosevelt sarcastically to his wife, referring to the fact that tomorrow he would go ashore at Trinidad for a formal luncheon with the island's governor and must then deal with the question "Do I or do I not propose 'the health of the King'?" He was mildly amused by the agitation this aroused among the formalists of diplomacy. It was a question to be answered, he said, "by good manners and not by State Dept. protocol."[25]

Of greater immediate interest to him was another news item that came in over ship's radio that day. The National Association of Manufacturers had held its annual dinner last night in the Grand Ballroom of the Waldorf-Astoria in New York City. It was "the largest ever." Some 1,800 people had attended. And from it came the startling announcement that the NAM had decided to "drop its fight on the administration and agreed to cooperate to end unemployment throughout the nation." E. T. Weir, chairman of the National Steel Corporation, told those assembled that industry "should undertake the solution of human problems arising out of the depression because it was best equipped to do so." Lewis Brown, president of the Johns-Manville Corporation, advocated in his address "a wider appreciation and understanding of the social responsibilities of business" on the part of businessmen.[26]

Big business, obviously, had read the election returns.

Roosevelt smiled, broadly.

As symbolism the news might be deemed of a piece with a recent social note involving Roosevelt's own family, a social note that had astonished and delighted scores of millions of people, including the President himself, while simultaneously annoying and even dismaying scores of thousands, all across America. This note was the announcement in Wilmington, Delaware, by Mr. and Mrs. Pierre S. du Pont, that their daughter Ethel (she was a beautiful girl, a leading debutante of her year) was engaged to marry Franklin D. Roosevelt, Jr., the wedding to take place after young Roosevelt's graduation from Harvard, in June 1937. Such joining together in familial relationship of the chief financial angel of the Liberty League (under duress by circumstance, surely!) with That Man in the White House, of whom people like the Du Ponts could now hardly speak without sputtering, struck most other people as delicious humor. It was as if Venus and Clio conspired to play an outrageous joke upon the whole class of affluent reactionaries.

And Roosevelt laughed aloud.

Some thirty-five miles north of Trinidad, on Saturday, December 10, he went fishing in the Caribbean, off tiny Bird Island, in shallow waters so clear that schools of fish could be seen on the ocean floor, twenty-five feet down. He caught thirty-four of these fish (pompano, barracuda, other varieties) in three hours that day and deepened his suntan.

The *Indianapolis* then headed at twenty-five knots for Charleston, where Missy LeHand and Grace Tully and Marvin McIntyre came aboard as soon as the ship dropped anchor on Tuesday, December 15. The weather was vile in Charleston. The air was chilly; a cold rain was falling. And there was no public ceremonial greeting of him, by his own strict order (he had also canceled a planned stopover at Warm Springs on his way home) in deference to the memory of his late great friend August Adolf Gennerich.

It was not until he was again in the White House that he was told of a family crisis that had occurred during his absence.

His newly engaged namesake son had been gravely ill, so ill that for a time his life had been despaired of. Eleanor Roosevelt had radioed her husband on Thanksgiving Day that she "was going to Cambridge to see F., Jr., on account of his sinus," as Roosevelt had written on that same day to "Dearest Mama," adding, "I hope it is not a bad attack." But she had not informed him that the attack was indeed bad, very bad, spreading to young Franklin's throat as a streptococcus infection which caused his temperature to soar dangerously high and would have killed him, doctors told reporters on December 16, but for a new sulfa drug, prontosil, which had been given him despite the fact that its therapeutic value was still being tested and it had not yet been approved for general use. He was now on the mend, but still very weak, in the Massachusetts General Hospital in Boston, where he had been since the day before Thanksgiving. Ethel du Pont had come to Boston to be with her fiancé and had stayed there nearly three weeks following his admission into the hospital, had shared anxious bedside vigils with his mother, had only just returned to her home in Wilmington. Doctors were quoted as saying that the patient was "expected to be sufficiently recovered to celebrate Christmas at the White House."[27]

IV

It was well that Roosevelt had been spared this anxiety over his son, well that he was enabled to return to his office tanned, refreshed, and zestful; he had a great deal of hard work to do and very little time in which to do it. Thanks to the final ratification of the Twentieth Amendment in February 1933, the presidential inauguration would be on January 20 instead of March 4, for the first time in history. (The ceremonies would be "simple," at the President's request, "because of the cold season," announced Rear Admiral Cary T. Grayson after conferring with the President on December 16; Grayson was in charge of inaugural arrangements, as he had been in 1933.[28]) This meant that Roosevelt, within just two January weeks, must deliver three major addresses: his state of the Union message to Congress; his budget message; then his inaugural. Each must be a policy statement having close internal relations with the other two, and the three together must not only point the way but also chart the course, generally, for his second term. The process of preparing these speeches was, therefore, a process of fundamental decision making with regard to domestic and foreign affairs.

He had already decided not to deal with the problem of the Supreme Court in any specific way, either in his annual message or in his inaugural. He would deal with it later, specifically, in a special message. He had also decided upon a slowdown of government spending. He proposed a moderate reduction in the spending authorized under the budget for 1937, though the fiscal year would not end till July 1, a full half year ahead. He would follow this with a sharp reduction in spending, to bring the budget into balance, in fiscal 1938. It appeared to him, and his view seemed sustained by statistical data, that recovery was now so well under way that it could continue under its own momentum. Industrial production had climbed almost to the 1929 level. Agricultural prices were sharply higher than they had been, having been boosted in some degree by AAA production controls and more by the great drouth and the fact that people in general had more money to spend for food and clothing. Increased corporate and personal incomes meant increased federal tax revenues, and these had rapidly increased during the last year; they seemed bound to do so at the same or more rapid rate as recovery continued. The only dark spot in the otherwise bright picture was unemployment. It persisted stubbornly at between 15 and 20 percent of the work force. But this percentage could be reduced, taking up the slack between production figures and employment figures, by reducing the size of the labor force, and Roosevelt had a ready ear for those who proposed to do this by more retirement of workers at age sixty-five (social security encouraged this), by prolonging the average time spent by young people in school (more young people should be encouraged to complete high school, to go on to college), and by reducing the hourly workweek.

Secretary of the Treasury Morgenthau heartily approved this tendency of the President's mind when Roosevelt revealed it at a White House conference with him and with Marriner Eccles, chairman of the Federal Reserve Board, on December 17. But Eccles most emphatically disapproved. To reduce government expenditures before full employment had been reached would be to abort recovery once again, said he. The recovery now under way was directly and almost solely due to government spending, he went on to say—due, that is, to the $14 billion or so of overall federal expenditures that had had impact upon the consumer market (expenditures for relief primarily, but also for public works) and to the $1.7 billion that had been paid out as a lump sum to veterans in implementation of the veterans' bonus bill that had been passed over Roosevelt's veto. To cut off this stimulus to the economy now would be to send the economy again downward into depression. Eccles also doubted the validity of the projections of economic growth and consequent tax revenue increase upon which Roosevelt proposed to base federal economic policy. Evidently left out of account, in these projections, was the rash of strikes that had already begun to occur and would certainly spread as the new industrial unions, under the aegis of the Wagner Act, proceeded with their announced intention to organize the workers of the automobile, steel, and other mass production industries. These efforts ran hard against the employers' determination to prevent any such organization and to crush the new unions, a determination they were prepared to implement with brute force. Strikebreakers were already being recruited, stockpiles of weapons and ammunition were already being accumulated, in unprecedented magnitude by the big industrialists; they worried not at all about their patent violations of the Wagner Act, being convinced the Supreme Court would soon declare this act unconstitutional. There thus impended a full-scale, bloody war between the industrial unions and the management of the industries they proposed to organize, and this would certainly prevent any such climb in overall production figures as Roosevelt was counting on.[29]

This strong oral objection to what Roosevelt planned to do, jarring to him, was followed by an Eccles memorandum spelling out the objection in close argumentative detail. The argument, if independently conceived by Eccles, was essentially the same as that of Keynes's just-published *General Theory of Employment, Interest, and Money.* Any serious attempt to achieve a balanced budget in 1938 would not merely fail, but "put the country into an economic tailspin," Eccles asserted, according to a summary of the memorandum in Morgenthau's diary. "The popular analogy between the debt of an individual and the debt of a nation [an analogy Roosevelt had repeatedly used in public speech] was false. The crucial consideration was not the size of the deficit but the level of national income. It would be unsafe to slash federal expenditures until the expansion of private enterprise took up the whole slack of employment. Meanwhile, deficit expenditures were a necessary compensatory form of investment which gave life to an economy operating below capacity." If the administration ignored this fact and attempted a balanced budget next year, there would certainly be "a new wave of deflation," a reversal of "the processes of recovery thus far set in motion," and this "would spell the doom of the Democratic party, perhaps even pave the way for totalitarianism."[30]

Roosevelt may or may not have been impressed by this argument per se (probably he was not; he remained convinced of the iniquity of deficit financing, the moral rectitude of balanced budgets), but he was certainly impressed, and strongly, by the force, the vehemence, with which Eccles made it. He sought to reassure himself by sending the memorandum to Morgenthau, asking for Morgenthau's advice. He knew his treasury secretary would advise him to reject the Eccles argument, root and branch, as Morgenthau promptly did. Simultaneously Budget Director Daniel Bell presented to the White House revised budget estimates indicating that the budget for fiscal 1938 could be brought into balance with a cut of only 3 percent in total federal expenditures! Bell's arithmetic was glowingly optimistic. Recovery, as it continued, would increase by $1.4 billion the treasury revenues derived from income taxes (corporate as well as individual) and from excise taxes during the next fiscal year; an additional $450 million would be collected in social security taxes; and this would reduce from $2.2 billion to $800 million the deficit that would be incurred if spending for fiscal 1938 were the same as that for fiscal 1937. But of this deficit of $800 million, $564 million had resulted from payment in 1937 of the remainder of the soldiers' bonus, an expenditure that would not be repeated. Ergo 1938's budget could be brought into perfect balance through a reduction of only $250 million in federal expenditures! Such reduction, if not a considerably larger one, could be achieved by the cut in relief which would result, in any case, from increased employment, for though employment presently lagged far behind other recovery factors, it was bound to catch up with them during the months ahead. Eccles was convinced that this cheerful arithmetic was as inaccurate as it was optimistic—it derived from assumptions that were at best highly dubious (Eccles saw them as patently false)—but Roosevelt promptly, happily accepted what Bell told him as a solid ground for fiscal policy, the policy he would announce in his budget message.[31] Government spending would be reduced significantly during the months ahead.

In the area of foreign affairs the major immediate decision the President had to make was whether or not to continue the policy with regard to the Spanish Civil War which he had adopted last summer, amid the pressures and excitements of his reelection campaign. At that time he had accepted as America's own the policy of nonintervention in Spain's "internal conflict" which Britain and France promoted, and to which Germany and Italy formally agreed, though they were already committed to aiding Franco's Fascist rebels. The administration, in other words, went along as far as it could (it was limited in the action it could legally take by the fact that the Neutrality Act contained no provision for civil wars) with the embargo on arms shipments to Spain which Britain and France sought to impose by international agreement and to which these two governments, with a few minor exceptions by Blum's France, rigidly officially adhered. Nevertheless, in late August 1936, the State Department had informed the legitimate democratically elected Spanish government that the United States "would insist on the right of American ships and American exporters to land supplies of all sorts in Spanish ports held by rebels unless the Madrid Government should be able to establish a complete blockade." This had promptly elicited a protesting letter to Roosevelt from Norman Thomas. He wrote:

> There may be a basis for this in international law, but in fact it makes Americans potential allies in the Fascist triumph which threatens the peace of the whole world. . . . The Spanish war is not a war between nations with both of which America is on terms of peace. It is not an uprising of the exploited masses against autocracy. It is a singularly cruel and dangerous military revolt engineered by the economic royalists of Spain. What its success will mean to any genuine democracy in Western Europe I need not tell you, neither need I urge upon your consideration the difficulty which every American government will find in keeping clear of new World War. Hence I urge you to reverse the ruling of the Department of State so as to discourage rather than encourage exports of supplies useful in war to ports held by Spanish rebels.[32]

To this, Roosevelt made no known reply. He ordered no published reversal of the State Department ruling. But he did do all he could to discourage arms and war matériel shipments by American businessmen to Spain, as we have seen in the case of Glenn Martin.*

He had persisted in this policy long after it was made abundantly clear to him by press dispatches and diplomatic reports from abroad, notably those of Claude Bowers, that Fascist Italy and Nazi Germany actively and massively intervened in Spain on Franco's side; that without their aid Franco would by now have been defeated, since he had little popular support in Spain; and that nonintervention by the democracies therefore worked wholly against the Loyalists and for the Fascist Rebels. He stubbornly persisted in the belief that his nonintervention policy contributed to a confinement of the Spanish conflict within Spain's boundaries, preventing its spread into general war. Such prevention was his primary concern. To it he sacrificed, fairly painlessly, it would seem, the personal sympathy for the Loyalist cause which he privately avowed.

Should he continue to do so?

There is no evidence that the doubt which this question expresses even arose in him during these last two weeks of 1936. But if it did, he crushed it, answering the posed question, in action, with a resounding "No!"

On the day before Christmas one Robert Cuse, president of the Vimalert Company, a New Jersey firm dealing in used aircraft, applied to the State Department for licenses to export nearly $3 million worth of planes and parts to the Spanish (Loyalist) government. Under existing law the licenses had to be granted, and they were, but R. Walton Moore, acting secretary of state in the absence of Hull, at once denounced Cuse in a public statement for violating the "moral embargo" which Cuse knew to be government policy and which other businessmen, almost without exception, had respected. As for Roosevelt, he moved at once toward a revision of the Neutrality Act which would extend its application to civil wars, and in his December 29 press conference he, too, denounced Cuse, without specifically naming him, as "one man" who "does what amounts to a perfectly legal but thoroughly unpatriotic act."[33]

This provoked another protesting letter to Roosevelt from Norman Thomas:

It is true that necessarily the sale of implements of war to the Spanish Government at this juncture means that some Americans are making a profit out of another nation's civil war, but nevertheless in vital respects the situation that now confronts the United States is very different from that created by a war between nations. The Spanish Government is a duly constituted, democratically elected government, recognized by the United States. It is fighting against a military, fascist revolt. The effective rebel soldiers are mercenaries and foreigners, and they are well equipped with the most modern weapons of war by their friends among the European Powers. It is the legitimate democratic government which, despite the gallantry of the Spanish workers and other Loyalists, has been almost strangled by "non-intervention" agreements in Europe which have worked mostly to the advantage of the rebels. The Powers which now request American cooperation in non-intervention have not, so

*See p. 598.

far as the public knows, consulted the United States upon the terms of their agreement or the way in which it is to be enforced. Apparently they offer no assurances whatsoever that they will stop the continuing stream of supplies to the rebels whose victory would menace the peace of the world by the encouragement it would give to fascist aggression. The victory of the Spanish Loyalists will have no such ill effects. That victory would have been won long ere this except for foreign aid—and this includes, according to report, the aid of British capitalist interests in Spain—to the rebels. . . . We* plead for recognition of the possibly disastrous effect of your action in disarming the Spanish Government in the face of well armed and ruthless rebel armies.[34]

Roosevelt was unmoved.

V

COMING event cast no dark shadow upon holiday festivities in the White House during the last week of 1936. It was in a radiance of past event and present glory that Franklin Roosevelt basked as—serenely confident, secure, and wholly outward-looking—he celebrated what the press described as an "old-fashioned" family Christmas and New Year's.

The weather since mid-December in Washington, and along the whole of the middle Atlantic seaboard, had been unseasonably warm, with temperatures often hovering near sixty degrees at midday, even in New York City. And the weather continued so. The dusk of Christmas Eve was actually balmy as Roosevelt with most of his family crossed the street at five o'clock to attend the lighting of the national Christmas tree, a tall, perfectly formed fir that had been erected in Lafayette Park in accordance with tradition. More than 3,000 people were assembled in the park, and Roosevelt spoke briefly to them, and to the nation over a national radio hookup, quoting the Christmas pledge made by Scrooge near the conclusion of Dickens's *Christmas Carol* and referring to the Buenos Aires conference as a manifestation of the Christmas spirit. After dinner that night he and his family gathered in the East Hall on the second floor of the White House, where the traditionally decorated family tree had been placed. (There was a much larger tree downstairs in the East Room which the public could view daily during the holiday season between the hours of 10:00 A.M. and 2:00 P.M. It was trimmed with snow-white streamers and white lights but with no other ornament.) Seated before the tree, Roosevelt as paterfamilias read aloud to those assembled virtually the whole of *A Christmas Carol,* acting out each character in it with great histrionic skill and enormous gusto, as he did every year.[35]

The next day, Christmas Day, remained bright and springlike. Roosevelt spent it "in the bosom of his family," as newspapers reported. Some members of the family were not there. Eleanor Roosevelt was not, nor Franklin, Jr. The latter yet remained in the Boston hospital, where his reported recovery obviously proceeded more slowly than doctors had predicted and where he was

*Thomas wrote as spokesman for the Socialist party's Public Affairs Committee, which he chaired.

attended by his mother, who would also be with him on New Year's, remaining in Boston through the whole of the holiday week. Daughter Anna was not in the White House, either, that Christmas: she and her husband, John Boettiger, remained in Seattle, where Boettiger had just taken over as publisher of the *Post-Intelligencer.* [36] But Anna's children by her first husband, Curtis Dall, were there—Eleanor and Curtis, Jr., who had become known to all the nation, during the time they had lived with their divorced mother in the White House, as Sisty and Buzzy. John Roosevelt, down from Harvard, was there, and Elliott, with his second wife and their two children, Elliott, Jr., and Ruth Chandler (she was generally called by her middle name, Chandler). James and his wife, Betsey, with their two daughters, Sara Delano and Kate, were there. And of course, the President's mother, Sara Delano (Mrs. James) Roosevelt, was there, was, in fact, the presiding presence among the women, as she always was, in the White House as in the Big House at Hyde Park, whether or not Eleanor Roosevelt was there. Accompanied by many of his family houseguests, the President attended church services on Christmas morning, an interdenominational service at the Church of the Covenant. Also on Christmas morning were the distribution and opening of the children's presents, with Roosevelt handing out the gifts and making of each bestowal an event delightful and memorable for each child. The adults exchanged their gifts, in joyous, noisy fashion, that afternoon.

What the President and his houseguests ate during their Christmas dinner was known to the world, the menu having been published in the newspapers days before:

> Blue points and saltines, with calf's head soup
> Turkey with chestnut dressing and giblet gravy, sausages, cranberry jelly
> Cauliflower, beans, candied sweet potatoes
> Fresh pineapple salad
> Plum pudding with hard sauce
> Eggnog ice cream, with coffee

A wholly traditional Christmas dinner it was, traditionally prepared and served under Mrs. Nesbitt's direction to a President who would doubtless have preferred a more imaginative feast in which he at least sampled some of the gifts of food that had been sent to him. They had been pouring into the White House mailroom for days from admirers all over the land—venison, pheasant, grouse, duck, geese, great juicy hams, puddings, cakes, and breads of all kinds —only to be intercepted there by the Secret Service and sent to laboratories for testing against poison, ground glass, and other life-threatening substances. None of this food, alas, would ever reach the President's table. [37]

A week later Roosevelt in the White House greeted the New Year "quietly," according to the newspapers, though it was certainly a noisy quiet, being full of shouts and laughter and romping of children and of the incessant, mutually interruptive talk, always animated and often loud, which constituted conversation in the Roosevelt household. The President remained surrounded by his children and grandchildren, though still without his wife and Franklin, Jr. He entered the new year in excellent health, reported Navy Captain Ross McIntire, the White House physician. He had lost some weight, as he needed to do, during his South American trip; he was now a trim and fit 180 pounds, and his suntan had not yet faded.[38]

By then it had been announced that son James was to become part of the official White House family, assuming many of the functions, though not as yet the title, of a White House secretary. James and Betsey Roosevelt would not live in the White House; they had rented a house in Georgetown, a few blocks away. But Betsey Roosevelt would be in the White House most of every day while her husband labored in what had formerly been Steve Early's office in the Executive Office wing, Early having moved into Louis Howe's old office. The arrangement was made against the strong protest of the First Lady, one so strong, in fact, that it became a quarrel and may have been as much a reason for her spending Christmas week in Boston as was young Franklin's hospitalization. She was sure this arrangement would lead to charges of nepotism and would focus upon James a savagely hostile attention which could be gravely injurious to his career and mental health. The President had brushed the objection aside irritably. "Why should I be deprived of my eldest son's help and the pleasure of having him with me just because I am the President?" he asked, paying no heed to the cogent reply which she promptly, forcefully made.[39]

It may be said here that her dire predictions would be abundantly fulfilled in the months and years just ahead. Upon James would be concentrated the venomous wrath and hatred aroused by Roosevelt and the New Deal in conservatives who had ownership control over the bulk of the nation's mass communications facilities. He would be viciously attacked for business dealings in which he allegedly capitalized hugely and dishonestly upon his father's position. And the incessant drumfire of highly personal criticism would prove, in the end, more than he could bear. The stomach ulcers from which he had suffered off and on since his youth would flare up dangerously, forcing him into major surgery at the Mayo Clinic. His marriage, too, would be shattered by the stresses and strains of life too close to immense radiant power—or so James himself would indicate. Many years later he would say of his by then long-divorced first wife: "She [Betsey] moved into the White House and practically took over, assuming many of the functions that normally would have been mother's. Mother disapproved, though she seldom was there to fulfill these functions. Father approved because Betsey delighted him. She was pretty, playful, a teaser. She flattered him, and he adored her." James began to side with his mother on this matter, becoming jealous of the attentions his wife paid to his father and resentful of them. "I wanted her to do for me, not for father. We began to move in different circles and make different friends. We didn't like each other's friends, and we began to bicker."[40]

But no more than other coming events did this one cast shadows on Roosevelt's mood on this New Year's Day 1937. What he anticipated from the arrangement with James was an assuagement of an ache of personal loneliness he had felt increasingly in recent months, despite and amid the crowded activity that filled his days. The nearness to him of James and Betsey would supply some of the need for human warmth and relaxed easy companionship of which he had been deprived by the deaths of Louis Howe and Gus Gennerich.

This happy anticipation added to the zest, the eagerness with which he faced the future.

EPILOGUE

❧ ⫸✕⫷ ❧

A Summing-up,
January 1, 1937

A CENTRAL thesis of this work is the obvious truth that the basic causal force operating in Western history since the early seventeenth century has been the accelerating advance of science and technology, with its increasingly strong impact upon social, cultural, economic, and political institutions and upon the lives of individual men and women. Virtually every major decisive event in political history over the last two centuries, including the major wars between nations and the Civil War in America, has had at its heart the dynamic relationship, that of challenge and response, between man's personal and institutional life, on the one hand, and the growing power of his technology, on the other. But since the latter has been increasingly the prime mover of the whole process, there arises the question of whether man's technology, involving as it does vast environmental forces, is truly his in the sense of ownership and control.

Does he possess this technology and control it—or does it possess and control him?

The question was by no means wholly fanciful when Mary Shelley published her *Frankenstein*. It had become wholly realistic by the time Henry Adams published his *Education*. We have referred in an earlier volume of this history* to Adams's account of how he had sailed up New York Harbor at the end of an Atlantic crossing from Cherbourg, in November 1904, and had seen the "outline of the city" as "frantic." Vast new forces were on the loose. And when Adams had debarked and was again upon the streets of New York, the city seemed to him to have the "air and movement of hysteria," with its citizens "crying, with every accent of anger and alarm, that the new forces must at any cost be brought under control."[1]

But they were not brought under control. Instead, they continued to grow out of control, distorted by the political and economic arrangements of a preindustrial age. They imposed intolerable strains upon social walls and overflowed economic channels that had never been designed to contain them. They created global interdependencies that were increasingly frustrated by the prevailing system, or anarchy, of national sovereignties. Blind responses to them increasingly submerged individual lives and personalities and liberties in vast collectives, essentially mindless in their direction, giant organizations of which the nominal administrator was more puppet than master, organizations determined almost solely by the machine's laws of operation. The gap which has generally existed throughout history between power and intelligence was

*See *FDR: The Beckoning of Destiny, 1882–1928,* p. 550.

now greatly widened. Out of this gap came the Great War of 1914–1918, the Russian Revolution and the rise of totalitarian communism, the Fascist reaction in Italy and the Nazi reaction in Germany, the mad speculative fevers of the 1920s in the United States, the stock market crash of 1929, the Great Depression, and the doom of every effort to mitigate national sovereignty, through collective, cooperative international action, to the extent needed for a making and keeping of world peace.

By the time of Franklin Roosevelt's first inaugural in March 1933, Western civilization, as the Prologue to this book describes, was in a parlous state indeed.

Three of the five great powers of Europe, and most of the smaller ones, were dictatorships. In Italy and Germany, especially in Germany, where Hitler won dictatorial powers in a Reichstag election on the morrow of Roosevelt's inauguration, a barbarism armed as no earlier barbarism had been by industry and science was well on the way to crushing human freedom and even the possibility of it in the area of its rule while initiating a ruthless, relentless march toward new world war. In Soviet Russia, Stalin, using the Nazi threat as excuse, soon was to consolidate his absolute personal power by imposing upon his own people, more heavily than had ever been done before, an all-pervasive murderous terror. Democracy still survived in England and France, but its government was in the hands of men of special privilege who were too timid, too selfish, and too confused to launch effective attacks upon growing domestic economic problems or to stand firm against the rising barbarism abroad, men who were prepared, many of them, to acquiesce in fascism for their own countries rather than to permit radical change in the prevailing national power structure, change that would reduce their own privileges. Organizations dedicated to the overthrow of democratic government and the replacement of it by Fascist or Communist dictatorship were marching, and would march in growing strength, the Fascist forces especially, through the streets of Britain, the streets of France.

As for America, during the three years preceding Roosevelt's inauguration it had ceased to be, either in its own eyes or in those of the world, that exemplary land of freedom and promise and hope which it had been throughout its history. Among leading opinion makers, as among millions of the dispossessed, there was a growing despair of democracy, a growing demand for a suspension of constitutional limits upon the executive, enabling the new President to rule by decree. In the last days of the interregnum every channel of effective action and socially unifying communication seemed hopelessly clogged. Fear and despair dominated the national mood.

All this was changed for Americans with incredible swiftness in ways inspiriting to devotees of democracy abroad, by the new President through exercise of a marvelously acute sensitivity to the mood of the people and through an almost miraculous exercise of temperament and projection of personality. Within three days after the inauguration the national mood had become a reflection and extension of Roosevelt's own confidence, his own buoyant optimism. Channels became unclogged. Wheels began to turn. Government began to govern. And it governed in blithe disregard of the Hoover-conservative view that it could not and must not attempt to assume responsibility for the economic welfare of ordinary human beings. Awesome thereafter was Roosevelt's manifest genius—a unique blend of intuition, calculation, confidence, charm, personal force—for locating, seizing, then actively holding the focal points of countervailing political power, a genius whereby he had achieved and maintained through nearly four crisis years a decisive centrality in the historical process of America and now aspired to achieve it in the historical process of the world. He was central to everything. Wherever he happened to be seemed the capital of the universe simply because he was there.

Clearly he had kept the worst from happening, if the "worst" be defined as a totalitarian American state operating in a world of totalitarianism the only possible issue of which was a global war which civilization could not survive. He had kept open options that had been on the verge of being closed forever. He could rightly proclaim himself the savior of the "system of private profit and free enterprise," as he had said in a mid-October campaign speech.[2] He had dissipated or turned into hopeful creative channels historic forces that had been driving swiftly and hard toward social revolution and dictatorship, had proved in action that democracy could "work" in a crisis, had become what John Maynard Keynes described him as being in his public letter of New Year's Eve 1933, "the Trustee for those in every country who seek to mend the evils of our condition within the framework of the existing social system" without resort to "intolerance, tyranny or destruction."[3]

But he had also greatly helped at decisive moments to keep the best from happening, if that "best" be defined as a peaceful world order in which America played its part as a truly participatory democracy, a truly cooperative commonwealth, the technology of which was wholly subject to the general mind and will of the citizenry and used to enlarge human freedom and enhance the quality of individual lives. The "best," thus defined, could have happened only through basic, power-shifting changes in the structure of American society which, though they were called for by a sizable portion of the American intellectual community and were acceptable and even expected by great masses of ordinary citizens, were opposed by Franklin Roosevelt. It would have required Roosevelt to enter upon his presidency with those attitudes toward finance-capital and big business which his first inaugural address had at least implicitly expressed but which he personally did not actually hold until 1935. It would have required a broad, consistent legislative program, carefully designed beforehand to achieve definite goals, thus avoiding that hodgepodge of frequently contradictory legislative proposals, improvised in response to specific challenges according to instincts basically conservative, which became the substance of the First New Deal. It would have required a shaping of this program in terms of a clear understanding of the forces that worked inexorably toward new world war and a foreign policy also shaped in terms of this understanding and, therefore, perfectly consistent with the domestic policy.

Opportunities were open, possibilities were present in the spring of 1933 that would not come again within the lifetime of anyone then alive.

In late February 1939, a little more than two years hence, came a night when Adolf Berle presided over an American Youth Congress meeting honoring Eleanor Roosevelt. She was that night in a somber mood as she chatted with Berle for a few minutes before she rose to give her prepared address. She wondered aloud if instead of this speech, "she should tell the truth," as Berle wrote in his journal, "the truth being that we had still to solve the fundamental problem" which was "economic and not political." The New Deal "had bought time to think," she said, "but the thinking had not been done." Berle commented: "I was really excited about this because I have been thinking so myself from the very beginning."[4]

But we need not here further anticipate.

Suffice it now to say that Franklin Delano Roosevelt, on this first day of 1937, came near the end of the years when profound world-changing opportunities were not merely open to him but actually thrust upon him by history. He was about to enter a time of diminishing opportunity, of shrinking freedom of choice, of increasing necessity. All the same, great opportunities would yet shine through the stormy dark into eyes prepared to see them.

How would he respond?

What would be, for him, the final reckoning of destiny?

Notes

Prologue: The State of The World, March 2, 1933

1. José Ortega y Gasset, *The Revolt of the Masses* (New York, 1932; paperback edition, 1950), pp. 7, 10, and 102 of paperback edition.

2. *Ibid.*, p. 137.

3. According to Robert Conquest, *The Great Terror* (New York, 1968), p. 23, "[o]nly one famine listed in the ENCYCLOPAEDIA BRITANNICA (that of China in 1877–1878) is cited as more destructive" than the Russian famine of 1932–1933.

4. Ivan Stadnyuk, *People are Not Angels,* serialized in the Soviet periodical *Neva* and quoted by Conquest, *op. cit.,* p. 23.

5. Stalin confided the 10 million figure to Winston Churchill during World War II. See Churchill, *The Hinge of Fate* (Boston, 1950), p. 498. Others have put the figure at considerably more than this, according to Stephen E. Cohen, *Bukharin and the Bolshevik Revolution* (New York, 1973), p. 463.

6. It was Franklin Roosevelt who pasted the "big smile" on the face of presidential politics, where it has remained every since. Never before had a presidential candidate smiled as constantly, broadly, showing his teeth—not even Theodore Roosevelt in 1904 and 1912—as did FDR in 1932. In fact, an unsmiling, if not actually stern, countenance seems to have been almost obligatory for successful aspirants to the nation's highest office until the first Roosevelt came along and then to have become so again until the second Roosevelt came along. Rarely is a broad smile upon the photographed faces of Cleveland, McKinley, Taft, Wilson, Harding, Coolidge—and rarer still is a photograph of FDR *not* smiling.

7. Actually Lincoln used the word "Confederacy" rather than "Union" in the quoted sentence because, one more than suspects, the seven southern states which had declared their secession from the United States called the government they had formed the Confederacy, short for Confederate States of America, and Lincoln was determined to do all in his power to persuade them they could *not* secede —it was physically as well as constitutionally impossible for them to part—from the great Confederacy (Union) to which they already belonged.

Book One: **The New Deal Begins**

One. Inauguration Amid Crisis

1. Walter S. Myers and Walter H. Newton, *The Hoover Administration,* p. 356, quoting the letter that confirmed the telephone conversation between Rand and Theodore G. Joslin, written by Hoover to Rand, February 28, 1933.

2. James A. Farley, *Behind the Ballots* (New York, 1938), pp. 207–8.

3. New York *Times,* March 4, 1933.

4. Grace Tully, *F.D.R., My Boss* (New York, 1949), p. 64. James Roosevelt and Sidney Shalett, *Affectionately, F.D.R.* (New York, 1959), p. 252.

5. Raymond Moley, *After Seven Years* (New York, 1939), p. 147. Moley, *First New Deal* (New York, 1966), p. 151

6. Moley, *Seven Years,* p. 155.

7. *Time,* (March 13, 1933), p. 11. Frank Freidel, *Franklin D. Roosevelt: Launching the New Deal* (Boston, 1973), p. 198. New York *Times,* March 5, 1933.

8. Moley, *First New Deal,* p. 160.

9. Tully, *op. cit.,* pp. 67–68.

10. Samuel Rosenman, *Working with Roosevelt,* pp. 90–91. Beatrice Bishop Berle and Travis Beal Jacobs, eds., *Navigating the Rapids, 1918–1971, from the Papers of Adolf A. Berle,* pp. 83–84, quoting BBB diary, March 5, 1933. New York *Times,* March 5, 1933.

11. Rosenman, *op. cit.,* p. 91. Moley, *First New Deal,* p. 119.

12. *The Public Papers and Addresses of Franklin D. Roosevelt, 1933* (hereafter *PPA, 1933*), pp. 11–16. Moley, *First New Deal,* reproduction of FDR-copied draft of inaugural address, inserted between pp. 120–21.

13. New York *Times,* March 5, 1933. Freidel, *op. cit.,* pp. 208–12.

14. New York *Times,* March 6, 1933. Freidel, *op. cit.,* p. 214, 217. *PPA, 1933,* pp. 17–18.

15. Ronald Steel, *Walter Lippmann and the American Century,* p. 300. Lippmann's "Today and Tomorrow" columns for January 17, February 14, 1933. New York *Times,* February 8, 1933. Arthur M. Schlesinger, Jr., *The Coming of the New Deal* (Boston, 1958), p. 3.

16. *PPA, 1933,* pp. 22–23.

17. Quoted by Freidel, *op. cit.,* pp. 207–8.

18. Lorena Hickok, RELUCTANT FIRST LADY, p. 103. New York *Times,* March 5, 1933.

19. Leo Tolstoy, *War and Peace* (New York, 1942), p. 831.

20. Rexford G. Tugwell, *The Democratic Roosevelt,* pp. 270–71. Freidel, *op. cit.,* pp. 213–14, quoting and commenting on Tugwell's account.

Two. A Week of Fateful Decision

1. Edward Robb Ellis, *A Nation in Torment,* p. 276, quoting Thurman W. Arnold, *The Folklore of Capitalism.*

2. *Ibid.,* p. 276, quoting Will Rogers column.

3. *PPA, 1933,* pp. 30–40. Transcript of this in Franklin D. Roosevelt Library for remark about "these two boys."

4. Graham J. White, *FDR and the Press,* p. 7, quoting Walter Davenport, "The President and the Press," *Collier's,* vol. 115 (1945), p. 12.

5. *Ibid.*

6. Ira Smith, *Dear Mr. President,* (New York, 1949), p. 214. Leila A. Sussman, *Dear FDR,* (Trenton, N.J., 1963), p. 60.

7. Ernest K. Lindley, *The Roosevelt Revolution,* p. 85. Freidel, *op. cit.,* pp. 225–26.

8. *PPA, 1933,* pp. 37–38.

9. Susan Estabrook Kennedy, *The Banking Crisis of 1933,* (Lexington, Ky., 1973), p. 164.

10. Moley, *Seven Years,* p. 148.

11. *Ibid.,* p. 149. Berle says, in his diary entry for July 27, 1939, commenting on the Moley memoirs, then running in the *Saturday Evening Post,* that his "Colonel House" remark "related to my insistence that the Brain Trust was at an end; and that the only way any of us could properly function, if at all (which was doubtful), was through the Cabinet officers to which we were assigned." But this meant, of course, that Berle's remark was a direct criticism of Moley, who could not possibly have functioned as he did at this time, and as FDR wanted him to do, "through" Cordell Hull. (See Berle and Jacobs, *op. cit.,* p. 232.)

12. *Ibid.,* p. 150. Moley, *First New Deal,* p. 169. Kennedy, *op. cit.,* p. 167. Kenneth Burke, *A Grammar of Motives,* p. 394.

13. Kennedy, *op. cit.,* p. 167. Henry J. Rosner, "Nationalize the Banks," *World Tomorrow,* (March 22, 1933), pp. 279–81. Bronson Cutting, "Is Private Banking Doomed?" *Liberty* (March 31, 1934). Rexford G. Tugwell, "Bankers' Banks," *New Republic* (December 12, 1928). Norman Thomas and fellow Socialist Morris Hillquit had a conference with Roosevelt in the White House on March 14, 1933, being greeted by the President "with a geniality not ordinarily accorded Socialists," according to W. A. Swanberg, *Norman Thomas, the Last Idealist* (New York, 1975), p. 140. The two visitors urged upon Roosevelt a $12 billion bond issue to finance relief and public works and, as follow-up of the Emergency Banking Act, the nationalization of the banks.

14. Moley, *Seven Years,* p. 151. Moley, *First New Deal,* p. 171.

15. Marquis W. Childs, *I Write from Washington* (New York, 1942), p. 21. Freidel, *op. cit.,* p. 227. A. Schlesinger, *op. cit.,* p. 5.

16. Kennedy, *op. cit.,* p. 173. Jackson Reynolds, Columbia University Oral History Collection (hereafter COHC). Moley, *Seven Years,* p. 152; Moley repeats the story, correcting portions of his earlier account, in *First New Deal,* p. 172.

17. Jesse H. Jones and Edward Angly, *Fifty Billion Dollars,* (New York, 1951), p. 27. Freidel, *op. cit.,* p. 235.

18. Max Freedman, *Roosevelt and Frankfurter: Their Correspondence, 1928–1945* (Boston, 1967), pp. 111–114, from memorandum dictated by Frankfurter on March 15, 1933. "It [the memo] is, I believe, a very accurate account of what transpired between the President and me, for the interview lay, of course, very vividly in my mind, and I repeated it promptly to Brandeis and to Marion [Mrs. Frankfurter] on my return."

19. Tully, *op. cit.,* p. 65. Catherine Drinker Bowen, *Yankee from Olympus* (Boston, 1946), p. 414. Of the "form your battalions and fight" quotation Mrs. Bowen writes in her notes (p. 429): "I include it [the story] because it is a recognized part of Holmes's history. But I don't like it. It is out of character. It smacks of the grandiose, and I suspect the witnesses of blowing it up because they loved the Justice." The present author finds the quote perfectly consistent in tone with at least one famous speech Holmes gave about his war experience.

20. James MacGregor Burns, *Roosevelt: The Lion and the Fox* (New York, 1956), pp. 156–57. Burns cites a "confidential source" for the Holmes quotation. Schlesinger, using the same quote, *op. cit.,* p. 14, cites as source his interview with Thomas G. Corcoran, October 21, 1957.

21. *PPA, 1933,* pp. 45–46.

22. Kenneth S. Davis, *Invincible Summer: An Intimate Portrait of the Roosevelts* (New York, 1974), based on recollections of Marion Dickerman, p. 114.

23. *PPA, 1933,* pp. 45–46.

24. Lindley, *op. cit.,* pp. 90–91. New York *Times,* March 13, 1933. Freidel, *op. cit.,* p. 245. Earle Looker, *The American Way* (New York, 1933), p. 67.

25. Moley, *First New Deal,* pp. 194–95. This account differs somewhat from the one in his *Seven Years,* wherein he says (footnote, p. 155) that Roosevelt merely "edited" the Ballantine draft "before delivery." In his diary entry for September 19, 1939 (Berle and Jacobs, *op. cit.,* p. 257), Berle says FDR "was thoroughly angry" that day about Moley's memoirs *(After Seven Years)* then being serialized in the *Saturday Evening Post,* asserting that he himself wrote the first fireside chat. "He [FDR] said he told Grace Tully to sit behind him; he sat and looked at the wall, trying to imagine a painter on a scaffold at work on the ceiling, a fellow repairing an automobile on the other side of the room, and a clerk working a cash register, or some similar person, in the other corner of the room, all of them saying: 'All our money is in the Poughkeepsie bank, and what is this all about?' He then dictated just as it came to him. . . ."

26. On January 25, 1982, Robert Trout, involved in the preparation and presentation of a three-hour TV "retrospective" on FDR to be broadcast by ABC, gave reporters the story of how FDR's first fireside chat was introduced by him. In the late 1920s Harry Butcher went to Washington as editor of the *National Fertilizer Review* and there became a close friend of Milton Eisenhower, then director of information for the U.S. Department of Agriculture. Through Milton he became a close friend of Dwight D. Eisenhower, and when the United States entered World War II, he, then a vice-president of CBS, having enlisted in the Naval Reserve before Pearl Harbor, became Lieutenant Commander Butcher of the Navy. Unprecedentedly for a naval officer, he became principal aide to a general not long thereafter; he went in this capacity to Europe with General Eisenhower when Eisenhower took command of the European Theater of Operations in late June 1942. See Kenneth S. Davis, *Soldier of Democracy* (New York, 1945), pp. 224, 301–4.

27. *PPA, 1933,* pp. 63–65.

28. *Ibid.,* p. 60.

29. Moley, *Seven Years,* p. 155. Having remarked that "when the Roosevelt administration began, the country was quite prepared for socialization of the banking structure," Kenneth Burke, *op. cit.,* p. 394, goes on to say: "Yet it was precisely here that Roosevelt's 'collectivism' [he being then regarded widely as a collectivist] made its most important contribution to individualism, in that he drew upon the government credit, not to introduce a new collectivist step . . . but to underwrite the traditional modes of private investment insofar as the changes in the situation itself permitted. And since banking is the very essence of a monetary economy, the whole logic of his administration followed from this act. . . . For in a capitalist economy, a decision about banking is a decision about the very core of motivation, and in its substantiality it is the ancester of a whole family of policies."

30. Quoted by Freidel, *op. cit.,* p. 236.

31. Moley, *Seven Years*, p. 154. Moley, *First New Deal*, pp. 191–93.

32. Jones and Angly, *op. cit.*, pp. 19–20. Freidel, *op. cit.*, pp. 233–34.

33. Lindley, *op. cit.* p. 91. *PPA, 1933*, pp. 66–67.

34. Lindley, *op. cit.*, p. 94.

35. Freidel, *op. cit.*, p. 247, quoting Arthur Krock in New York *Times.*

36. Freedman, *op. cit.*, pp. 114–20. Steel, *op. cit.*, pp. 301–2.

Three. Improvisations upon Discordant Themes: The Opening Rush of the Hundred Days

1. *PPA, 1933*, pp. 67–68, 71.

2. *Ibid.*, p. 74.

3. Russell Lord, *The Wallaces of Iowa* (Boston, 1947), p. 330. Freidel, *op. cit.*, p. 308, quoting Moley diary entry for March 21, 1933.

4. Freidel, *op. cit.*, p. 91.

5. *Ibid.*, p. 95, quoting Tugwell diary.

6. Rexford G. Tugwell, *The Brains Trust* (New York, 1968), pp. 80, 190–91. Moley, *First New Deal*, pp. 252–53. Freidel, *op. cit.*, pp. 94–95, quoting Tugwell diary entries for January 12, 13. Schlesinger, *op. cit.*, p. 42, quoting Milo Reno, "What the Farmer Wants," *Common Sense* (February 1934). John Morton Blum, *From the Diaries of Henry Morgenthau, Jr, Years of Crisis, 1928–1938* (Boston, 1959), pp. 38–42.

7. Freidel, *op. cit.*, p. 85, quoting John A. Simpson letter to FDR, January 11, 1933.

8. Van L. Perkins, *Crisis in Agriculture: The Agricultural Adjustment Administration and the New Deal*, p. 38.

9. *PPA, 1933*, p. 74. Perkins, *op. cit.*, pp. 66–67. Freidel, *op. cit.*, p. 312.

10. Perkins, *op. cit.*, p. 62. Freidel, *op. cit.*, p. 315.

11. *PPA, 1933*, p. 111.

12. Freidel, *op. cit.*, p. 317, citing Hugh Johnson letter to FDR, March 30, 1933.

13. Dedication of Ernest K. Lindley, *The Roosevelt Revolution.* In his Preface to this work, Lindley writes: "The primary purpose of this book is to bring order out of confusion—insofar as there has been order instead of confusion." That there

was a great deal of the latter he abundantly demonstrates in a work of immense permanent value to historians.

14. *PPA, 1933*, pp. 80–81. One of those appearing before the Senate Labor Committee in opposition to the bill was a spokesman for John Dewey's Joint Committee on Unemployment who found in the bill's language evidence that the CCC was intended to become an integral part of the Army. "Wagner helped devise changes that eliminated some of the . . . objectionable wording," says J. Joseph Huthmacher, *Senator Robert E. Wagner and the Rise of Urban Liberalism* (New York, 1968), p. 140.

15. John A. Salmond, *The Civilian Conservation Corps, 1933–1942* (New York, 1967), pp. 40–45. Freidel, *op. cit.,* p. 264.

16. Joseph P. Lash, *Eleanor and Franklin* (New York, 1971), p. 367. Ellis, *op. cit.,* pp. 303–4.

17. Frances Perkins, *The Roosevelt I Knew* (New York, 1946) pp. 183–84.

18. Schlesinger, *op. cit.,* pp. 264–65.

19. Unofficial Observer (Jay Franklin), *The New Dealers* (New York, 1934), pp. 179–84. Childs, *op. cit.,* pp. 22–23. Henry H. Adams, *Harry Hopkins* (New York, 1977), p. 51–54. Robert E. Sherwood, *Roosevelt and Hopkins,* p. 51. The direct quote of Hopkins is from Sherwood, who reports the remark as made to "someone" who came to Hopkins when the latter was CWA administrator with a project idea that would work out well "in the long run."

20. *PPA, 1933*, p. 80.

21. Lindley, *op. cit.,* p. 105.

22. Michael E. Parrish, *Securities Regulation and the New Deal* (New Haven, 1970), pp. 44–46.

23. Lindley, *op. cit.,* p. 106. Moley, *Seven Years,* pp. 176–78. Moley, *First New Deal,* pp. 310–11.

24. Moley, *First New Deal,* p. 311. *PPA, 1933,* p. 93.

25. Moley, *Seven Years,* p. 180. Moley, *First New Deal,* p. 312.

26. Franklin, *op. cit.,* pp. 155–56, 321. Moley, *First New Deal,* p. 313. Parrish, *op. cit.,* p. 64.

27. Parrish, *op. cit.,* p. 69. Freidel, *op. cit.,* p. 147, says that when "on May 5, Thompson learned the full truth" regarding the Frankfurter involvement (". . . that from the time Frankfurter appeared I was apparently superseded," quoting Thompson's diary, May 5, 1933), "he took it philosophically." But

Parrish derives a very different impression from the same Thompson diary entry, from which I quote, and so do I.

28. Parrish, *op. cit.*, pp. 74–75.

29. *Ibid.*, p. 89, quoting Herbert Feis memo to Louis Howe, May 10, 1933, and FDR letter to Duncan Fletcher, May 20, 1933; p. 90, quoting Hiram Johnson letter to Hiram Johnson, Jr., May 14, 1933. For full story of "The Strange Death of Title II" see Parrish, Chapter IV, *op. cit.*, pp. 73–107.

30. *PPA, 1933,* p. 122.

31. Lindley, *op. cit.*, p. 112.

32. Schlesinger, *op. cit.*, p. 323. Arthur E. Morgan, "Bench-Marks in the Tennessee Valley," *Survey Graphic* (January 1934).

33. Edgar B. Nixon, *Franklin D. Roosevelt and Conservation, 1911–1945,* (Hyde Park, 1957), vol. I (1911–1937), p. 152.

34. Freidel, *op. cit.*, p. 351. Harold Ickes, *The Secret Diary of . . .: The First Thousand Days, 1933–1936* (New York, 1953), p. 15. Schlesinger, *op. cit.*, p. 325–26.

35. *PPA, 1933,* p. 123. Schlesinger, *op. cit.*, p. 329.

36. Lindley, *op. cit.*, p. 113.

37. Moley, *Seven Years,* p. 185.

38. *Ibid.*, pp. 185–86. Freidel, *op. cit.*, pp. 151–52.

39. Schlesinger, *op. cit.*, pp. 91–92. Bernard Bellush, *The Failure of the NRA* (New York, 1975), pp. 6–7. Gerald T. Dunne, *Hugo Black and the Judicial Revolution,* (New York, 1977), p. 145.

40. Frances Perkins, *op. cit.*, p. 194. Moley, *First New Deal,* p. 287.

41. Quoted by Freidel, *op. cit.*, pp. 409–10.

42. Frances Perkins, *op. cit.*, pp. 230–31.

43. Freidel, *op. cit.*, quoting Earl Latham, *The Politics of Railroad Coordination, 1933–1936,* p. 23, which in turn quotes Eastman letter to FDR in January, 1933.

44. Moley, *Seven Years,* p. 187. *PPA, 1933,* pp. 133, 135. Freidel, *op. cit.*, p. 418. New York *Times,* April 14, 1933.

45. Huthmacher, *op. cit.*, p. 144.

46. Moley, *Seven Years*, p. 188.

47. Moley, *First New Deal*, p. 288.

Four. Improvisations Continue as Pressures Increase: To the End of the Hundred Days

1. Lindley, *op. cit.*, p. 119. Moley, *Seven Years*, pp. 158–59. Moley, *First New Deal*, pp. 300–01. James F. Byrnes, All in One Lifetime, (New York, 1958), p. 77. Freidel, *op. cit.*, pp. 332–33.

2. Orville H. Bullitt, ed., *For the President, Personal and Secret: Correspondence Between Franklin D. Roosevelt and William C. Bullitt*, (Boston, 1972), pp. 18–33.

3. Lindley, *op. cit.*, p. 120. Moley, *Seven Years*, pp. 159–60. Moley, *First New Deal*, p. 302.

4. *PPA, 1933*, p. 119.

5. Steel, *op. cit.*, pp. 302–3.

6. Lippmann column, "Today and Tomorrow," New York *Herald Tribune*, April 18, 1933. Lindley, *op. cit.*, pp. 120–21.

7. *PPA, 1933*, pp. 137–40.

8. *Ibid.*, p. 166.

9. *Ibid.*, p. 176.

10. Lindley, *op. cit.*, p. 131.

11. Claude M. Fuess, *Joseph B. Eastman, Servant of the People*, (New York, 1952), p. 203.

12. *PPA, 1933*, p. 153.

13. Huthmacher, *op. cit.*, p. 146. Frances Perkins, *op. cit.*, pp. 198–99.

14. Lindley, *op. cit.*, p. 158.

15. Ickes, *op. cit.*, p. 32.

16. *PPA, 1933*, p. 164.

17. Ernest K. Lindley-by-lined story of industrial recovery bill preparation, New York *Herald Tribune*, May 8, 1933.

18. *PPA, 1933*, pp. 156–57.

19. *Ibid.*, pp. 202–3.

20. New York *Times*, May 15, 16, 1933. Freidel, *op. cit.*, p. 433.

21. *PPA, 1933*, pp. 185–86. Robert Dallek, *Franklin D. Roosevelt and American Foreign Policy, 1932–1945*, (New York, 1979), p. 42. John D. Hicks, *A Short History of American Democracy*, (Boston, 1943), p. 790.

22. William L. Shirer, *The Rise and Fall of the Third Reich*, (New York, 1960), p. 200.

23. *Ibid.*, p. 202.

24. *Ibid.*, p. 241. New York *Times*, May 11, 1933.

25. New York *Times*, May 15, 1933. Freidel, *op. cit.*, p. 401.

26. Freidel, *op. cit.*, p. 377, quoting Paul Claudel's direct quotation of FDR in Claudel's final dispatch as French ambassador to the United States to Paris.

27. Moffat diary, May 15, 1933, quoted by Freidel, *op. cit.*, p. 401.

28. Moffat diary, May 16, 1933, Freidel, *op. cit.*, p. 372. A year before, May 1932, Winston Churchill in the House of Commons poured scorn and ridicule upon the notion, advanced by the foreign secretary in the MacDonald government, that weapons could be classified in exclusive categories of "offensive" and "defensive," a notion put forward as a basis for what the foreign secretary called "qualitative disarmament." The foreign secretary had admitted that such classification was difficult. "It certainly is," said Churchill, "because almost every conceivable weapon may be used for defense or offense. . . . To make it more difficult for the invader, heavy guns, tanks, and poison gas are to be relegated to the evil category of offensive weapons. The invasion of France by Germany in 1914 reached its climax without the employment of any of these weapons. The heavy gun is to be described as an 'offensive weapon.' It is all right in a fortress; there it is virtuous and pacific in its character; but bring it out into the field— and of course, if it were needed, it would be brought out into the field—and it immediately becomes naughty. . . ." See Winston S. Churchill, *The Gathering Storm*, (Boston, 1948), pp. 71–72.

29. The whole of the appeal is in *PPA, 1933*, pp. 185–88.

30. *PPA, 1933*, pp. 195, 197.

31. New York *Times*, May 18, 1933. Shirer, *op. cit.*, pp. 209–10.

32. Morgenthau diary ("Farm Credit Administration Diary"), May 22, 1933, quoted by Freidel, *op. cit.*, p. 404.

33. Freidel, *op. cit.,* pp. 404–5, quoting San Francisco *Chronicle* and *Christian Science Monitor.*

34. New York *Times,* May 18, 1933.

35. Moley, *Seven Years,* pp. 208, 406.

36. *Ibid.,* p. 210.

37. Ickes, *op. cit.,* pp. 44–45.

38. Moley, *Seven Years,* p. 216.

39. *Foreign Relations of the United States,* (Washington, D.C., 1950) vol. I, pp. 607–11. Dallek, *op. cit.,* p. 46.

40. Cordell Hull, *Memoirs,* vol. I, pp. 250–51.

41. The quoted Republican congressman was James Beck of Pennsylvania who, in a 1932 book, *Our Wonderland of Bureaucracy,* condemned Hoover as a "big government" man. During the brief House debate on the farm relief bill Beck had dismissed the "emergency" justification for that bill as the "same excuse" with which "in Germany . . . they are voting power today to Hitler." His reference was to the fact that on the day he spoke, the Reichstag was in process of passing the Enabling Act whereby Hitler was granted dictatorial powers until April 1, 1937. For the Chamber of Commerce and other quotes, Ellis W. Hawley, *The New Deal and the Problem of Monopoly*, (Princeton, N.J., 1966), p. 26; *Business Week* (May 24, 1933), p. 3; and New York *Times,* May 18, 1933.

42. Freidel, *op. cit.,* p. 446.

43. Frances Perkins, *op. cit.,* pp. 200–201.

44. Ickes, *op. cit.,* p. 48.

45. Freidel, *op. cit.,* p. 445, quoting Henry Morgenthau, Jr., Farm Security Administration diary entries for May 22, 29, 1933.

46. *Ibid.,* again quoting Morgenthau diary (entry for April 28, 1933), p. 445.

47. New York *Times,* May 25, 26, June 1, 1933. Lindley, *op. cit.,* (New York, 1939) pp. 139–41. Charles A. Beard and Mary R. Beard, *America in Midpassage,* pp. 185–87. Schlesinger, *op. cit.,* (New York, 1939), pp. 435–36. Broadus Mitchell, *Depression Decade,* (New York, 1947), pp. 155–56.

48. Quoted by Schlesinger, *op. cit.,* p. 436.

49. Quoted by Beard, *op. cit.,* p. 169.

50. Quoted by Schlesinger, from Kansas City *Times, op. cit.,* p. 437.

51. T. Harry Williams, *Huey Long,* p. 633.

52. Ickes, *op. cit.,* p. 46. Somewhat less inclined than FDR to forgive and forget this exercise of special privilege, on the assumption that businessmen's "ethics" had undergone a "radical change" since 1929, were members of the U.S. Senate Committee on Banking and Currency. Said the hearings report, *Stock Exchange Practices,* pp. 101, 107: "The 'preferred lists' strikingly illustrate the methods employed by bankers to extend their influence and control over individuals in high places. . . . The granting of these preferential participations on the one hand and their acceptance on the other created a community of interest and similarity of viewpoint between donor and donee which augured well for the mutual welfare and ill for that of the public. . . . Implicit in the bestowal of favors of this magnitude is a pervasive assumption of power and privilege. Implicit in the acceptance of such favors is a recognition of that power and privilege. The 'preferred lists,' with all their grave implications, cast a shadow over the entire financial scene."

52. Ickes, *op. cit.,* p. 46.

53. Lindley. *op. cit.,* p. 162.

54. Quoted by Bellush, *op. cit.,* p. 19.

55. *Ibid.,* p. 20–21. Williams, *op. cit.,* p. 635. Hawley, *op. cit.,* p. 30. Early in the special session Long had introduced three bills implementive of his program for the "redistribution of wealth." One, which would have imposed a capital levy on all fortunes of more than $1 million (it was to be a graduated levy—1 percent of a fortune of more than $1 million, 2 percent of one of more than $2 million, and so on, making it impossible for anyone to have more than $100 million), was subsequently withdrawn by him. The other two—a proposal to raise the graduated income tax to make it impossible for anyone to have an income of more than $1 million a year; a proposal to increase the inheritance tax to the effect that no individual could inherit more than $5 million—went down to resounding defeat (50 to 14 or, since there were four paired votes, 54 to 18) in mid-April. See Williams, *op. cit.,* pp. 632–33.

56. Hawley, *op. cit.,* p. 30, for quotes of big business protest to the White House.

57. Bellush, *op. cit.,* pp. 23–25.

58. Schlesinger, *op. cit.,* p. 10. Moley, *First New Deal,* p. 352.

59. Freidel, *op. cit.,* pp. 452–53, for Johnson judgment of Douglas, *PPA, 1933,* p. 99.

60. *PPA, 1933,* p. 168.

61. Moley, *Seven Years,* p. 191.

62. Bascom N. Timmons, *Jesse H. Jones,* p. 182, quoted by Moley, *First New Deal,* p. 319.

63. *PPA, 1933,* pp. 246, 252–53.

64. Frances Perkins, *op. cit.,* pp. 201–2.

65. *Ibid.,* pp. 202–3.

66. Morgenthau ("Farm Security Administration") diary, June 12, 1933.

67. National Industrial Conference Board, "The Gold Standard: Recent Developments and Present Status," a mimeographed memorandum dated May 5, 1933. Franklin D. Roosevelt Library.

68. *Ibid.*

69. *PPA, 1933,* p. 245.

70. Moley, *Seven Years,* pp. 228–29.

71. FDR to Colonel Edward M. House, May 15, 1933. Franklin D. Roosevelt Library.

72. Freidel, *op. cit.,* p. 464, quoting Warburg diary, May 29, 1933.

73. Moley, *Seven Years,* pp. 229–30.

74. *Ibid.,* p. 231.

Five. The Wrecking of the London Conference

1. Eleanor Roosevelt, *This I Remember,* (New York, 1949), p. 25.

2. Charles Hurd, *When the New Deal Was Young and Gay,* (New York, 1965), p. 155.

3. *Foreign Relations of the United States, 1933,* vol. I, p. 649, quoted in full by Moley, *First New Deal,* p. 479.

4. Byrnes, *op. cit.,* p. 81, quoted by Moley, *First New Deal,* p. 437.

5. Moley, *Seven Years,* pp. 235–37. FDR to William Phillips, June 19, 1933, in *Foreign Relations,* vol. I., p. 650. The memorandum by Herbert Bayard Swope, June 20, 1933, is in Edgar B. Nixon, ed., *Franklin D. Roosevelt and Foreign Affairs,* (Cambridge, Mass., 1969), vol. I, pp. 248–50. Roosevelt used some phrases and all the essential argument of this memo in his later message rejecting the joint declaration cabled to him from London by Moley on June 30, 1933, adding a certain bitter irony to the discomfiture Moley then suffered.

6. Moley, *First New Deal*, p. 442. That the stated "conscious act of will" was required is my own interpretation, but it is strongly suggested by Moley's overly emphatic way of denying that he was "disturbed" by Kennedy's "admonition." He protests too much. "I had never believed nor could believe that Roosevelt regarded me as anything but a faithful packhorse in his great affairs [a chapter of *After Seven Years* is entitled, "A Packhorse in His Great Affairs"]," he writes. "For eighteen months he had intrusted me with confidences and had imposed upon me very serious reponsibilities, and I felt that in the present instance I was acting with full assurance of successfully carrying out his wishes. I also made mental note of the fact that at that time Kennedy grievously resented the fact that Roosevelt had not yet recognized his support and financial outlay in the 1932 campaign . . . in the form of an appointment in the new Administration. I was also quite well acquainted with the in-fighting in politics, which so often characterizes itself in driving discordant wedges between allied individuals. My sleep that night and later was not disturbed by that warning, and I cannot accept it today as valid."

7. The Warren convert was B. H. Inness Brown, whose letter to House, dated June 19, 1933, is in Nixon, *Foreign Affairs*, pp. 244–47. Schlesinger, *op. cit.*, p. 219. Dallek, *op. cit.*, pp. 51–52.

8. Dallek, *op. cit.*, p. 52.

9. FDR to Phillips, June 26, 1933, in *Foreign Relations, 1933*, vol. I, p, 657, quoted by Freidel, *op. cit.*, p. 474.

10. Author interviews with Marion Dickerman, 1973–1974, Davis, *Invincible Summer*, pp. 115–16.

11. Washington, D.C., *Herald*, April 5, 1933. Quoted by Lash, *op. cit.*, p. 378.

12. *Ibid.*, p. 354

13. Author interview with Anna Roosevelt Halsted, 1974.

14. Lash, *op. cit.*, p. 355. Roosevelt had reason to feel kindly toward Bernarr Macfadden, who, upon acquiring the weekly *Liberty* magazine (it was already a going concern) in 1931, promptly made it the leading mass-magazine promoter of Roosevelt's presidential candidacy. "There Will Be No Dole!," the first of nineteen articles signed by FDR (ghosted by Earle Looker) which would appear in *Liberty* by the late spring of 1932, was published in the issue of December 12, 1931, only a few months after the magazine had become Macfadden property. One motive for Macfadden's hiring of Eleanor Roosevelt as editor of *Babies—Just Babies* is said to have been his hope that she would influence her husband to establish a Department of Health, with Macfadden as the first secretary of health. See Theodore Peterson, *Magazines in the Twentieth Century* (Urbana, Ill., 1957), pp. 243–44.

15. Lash, *op. cit.*, pp. 355–56.

16. Frances Perkins, *op. cit.,* p. 69.

17. Hickok, *op. cit.,* pp. 71–75. Doris Faber, *The Life of Lorena Hickok,* (New York, 1980), p. 139. Doris Faber was the first researcher to examine the Lorena Hickok papers, deposited by Hickok herself, in the Franklin D. Roosevelt Library. There are ten boxes of Hickok-ER correspondence in the library, containing more than 2,000 letters from ER to her friend.

18. New York *Times,* June 7, 1933 (letter by Will Rogers), quoted by Lash, *op. cit.* p. 368.

19. Hickok, *op. cit.,* p. 62.

20. *Ibid.,* p. 86.

21. Lash, *op. cit.,* p. 376.

22. James Roosevelt (with Bill Libby), *My Parents, a Differing View* (Chicago, 1976), pp. 213–14. James Roosevelt and Shalett, *op. cit.,* p. 237. Sherwood, *op. cit.,* p. 214. Lash, *op. cit.,* p. 501.

23. Frances Theodora Parsons, *Perchance Some Day* (Privately Printed, New York, 1921) p. 340, quoted by Lash, *op. cit.,* p. 369.

24. Hickok, *op. cit.,* pp. 82–83. New York *Times,* March 16, 1933. Lash, *op. cit.,* p. 368.

25. New York *Herald Tribune,* March 20, 1933. Lash, *op. cit.,* p. 366.

26. New York *Herald Tribune,* April 25, 1933. Lash, *op. cit.,* p. 363.

27. Hickok, *op. cit.,* pp. 44, 46–49.

28. Faber, *op. cit.,* pp. 61–63, 69, 71–72, 79.

29. Hickok, *op. cit.,* pp. 64–65.

30. Faber, *op. cit.,* pp. 53–54, 110.

31. *Ibid.,* p. 113.

32. *Ibid.,* pp. 114–15. Hickok, *op. cit.,* pp. 89–92.

33. Faber, *op. cit.,* pp. 110, 119–20, 121

34. Hickok, *op. cit.,* p. 96.

35. *Ibid.,* p. 134.

36. Nixon, *Foreign Affairs*, pp. 253–54.

37. Moley, *Seven Years*, p. 244, quoting New York *Times* and United Press dispatches.

38. *Foreign Relations, 1933*, Vol. I, pp. 660–61. Freidel, *op. cit.*, pp. 476–77.

39. Hurd, *op. cit.*, pp. 165–71. New York *Times*, July 1, 1933.

40. Morgenthau diary, June 30, 1933. Freidel, *op. cit.*, p. 480

41. *Ibid.*, Nixon, *Foreign Affairs*, p. 264.

42. Moley, *Seven Years*, pp. 245–46.

43. *Ibid.*, pp. 246–47. Nixon, *Foreign Affairs*, pp. 266–67.

44. Moley, *First New Deal*, p. 456. Moley, *Seven Years*, p. 255.

45. Nixon, *op. cit.*, pp. 264–66.

46. Moley, *Seven Years*, pp. 256–58.

47. Nixon, *Foreign Affairs*, pp. 268–69. *PPA, 1933*, pp. 264–66. In his explanatory note, in the latter volume, Roosevelt claims that the "gold bloc nations" had "in effect" issued an "ultimatum: that if the United States did not enter the proposed narrow agreement" regarding stabilization, they, the gold bloc nations, "would not discuss the other matters on the agenda." He describes his message as "realistic at a time when the gold bloc nations were . . . unwilling to go to the root of national and international problems." What the "root" was he does not say.

48. Schlesinger, *op. cit.*, p. 224, quoting Snowden article entitled "Roosevelt the Laughing Stock."

49. Moley, *Seven Years*, p. 263.

50. *Ibid.*, pp. 270–71. Lindley, *op. cit.*, pp. 217–18.

51. Ickes, *op. cit.*, p. 59.

52. Moley, *First New Deal*, p. 469.

53. *Foreign Relations, 1933*, vol. I, p. 688. Freidel, *op. cit.*, p. 490. Moley, *First New Deal*, p. 559, which is opening page of a complete transcript of the telephone conversation between Roosevelt, Moley, and Hull, July 5, 1933, printed as Appendix C of Moley's volume.

54. Moley, *First New Deal,* pp. 495–96. Schlesinger, *op. cit.,* pp. 230–31, citing James P. Warburg, "Reminiscences," COHC, p. 1060.

55. Nixon, *op. cit.,* pp. 298–300, gives complete text of Hull's message.

56. Moley, *Seven Years,* pp. 274–76, 423.

57. Mitchell, *op. cit.,* p. 140.

Book Two: A Pattern Emerges From the New Deal's Initial Surge

Six. The Personality and Mind of the New Deal

1. Mitchell, *op. cit.,* p. 125.

2. David E. Lilienthal, *The Journals of . . . , the T.V.A. Years, 1939–1945* (New York, 1964), vol. 1. p. 66. Dean Acheson writes of FDR on p. 165 of his *Morning and Noon:* "[H]e could charm an individual or a nation. But he condescended. Many reveled in apparent admission to an inner circle. I did not. . . . To me it was patronizing and humiliating. . . . It is not gratifying to receive the easy greeting which milord might give a promising stable boy and pull one's forelock in return." It might be added that Acheson's own ego was large, his arrogance notorious, and that one senses an element of condescension, and a patronizing tone, in the "affection and devotion" he expresses toward Truman in his memoirs. Acheson goes on to say that the "essence" of Roosevelt "the man and the impression he made" was "force. He exuded a relish of power and command."

3. A full account of the affair was written by Ickes himself in a lengthy memoir of his private life included among the Ickes papers in the Library of Congress. He refers to the woman only as "X" though other documents identify her by name. See Graham White and John Maze, *Harold Ickes of the New Deal* (Cambridge, Mass., 1985), pp. 121–28.

4. Paul Appleby transcript, COHC.

5. Lilienthal, *op. cit.,* pp. 44–45. Ickes, *op. cit.,* pp. 421–22. Ernest Hemingway, a dinner guest at the White House in 1937, "later reported without sympathy on the amount of careful maneuvering that was required to get the paralyzed President from room to room or even into a chair," writes Carlos Baker, *Ernest Hemingway,* (New York, 1969), pp. 315–16. Professional "he-man" Hemingway found Eleanor Roosevelt "thoroughly charming" but disliked FDR, whom he thought " 'sexless' and even somewhat womanly in appearance, like a great woman Secretary of Labor."

6. Moley, *Seven Years.* p. 192.

7. Rosenman, *op. cit.,* p. 151.

8. Schlesinger, *op. cit.*, p. 579, quoting a Garner interview in *U.S. News & World Report* (March 8, 1957).

9. Lilienthal, *op. cit.*, pp. 48–49. On December 13, 1933, as recorded on p. 40, *op. cit.*, Lilienthal came to the Oval Room for an appointed conference with the President and "got something of a shock" to find Jo Davidson mounted on "a crude wooden platform in the middle of the oval room" modeling the President's head in "a large lump of dark clay. . . . While Davidson, with his whiskers bristling, kept punching away at the clay, we [FDR and Lilienthal] got to talking about the plan I had worked out with [Wendell] Willkie just that morning. . . ."

10. Eleanor Roosevelt, *op. cit.*, p. 117.

11. Schlesinger, *op. cit.*, p. 525, quoting Mary W. Dewson papers.

12. Ickes, *op. cit.*, p. 132. Lilienthal, *op. cit.*, p. 95.

13. Ickes, *op. cit.*, p. 195.

14. Joseph P. Lash, *Love, Eleanor*, p. 230.

15. Rosenman, *op. cit.*, pp. 150–51.

16. Schlesinger, *op. cit.*, p. 585. "I remember saying to Mrs. Roosevelt, 'You know Franklin is really a very simple Christian.' " writes Frances Perkins. "She thought for a moment and, with a quizzical lift of her eyebrows, said, 'Yes, a *very simple* Christian.' " Roosevelt himself once said to Perkins: "I can do almost anything in the 'Goldfish Bowl' of the President's life, but I'll be hanged if I can say my prayers in it." See Frances Perkins, *op. cit.*, pp. 141, 144.

17. Actually, as Donald J. Hughes points out in his *The Neutron Story* (New York, 1959), pp. 37–38, the name "neutron" was "not new; scientists had been speculating for years about the possibility of an uncharged particle with a mass about that of the proton. The most tempting possibility for the origin of such an entity had been that an electron might combine with a proton in a stable configuration—something like a compressed hydrogen atom. This purely imaginary structure had been referred to as the 'neutron' some dozen years before Chadwick's discovery. We know, however, that the neutron is definitely *not* a combination of a proton and an electron. . . . [but] is actually a fundamental particle, existing in its own right, and constituting a basic component of matter."

18. Leon Cammen, associate editor of *Mechanical Engineering* magazine, in his contribution to the *American Year Book* for 1934, writes: "No discussion of power generation today would be complete without some reference to the possibility of obtaining new sources of power either from sunlight or from so-called atomic forces. . . . In both directions only laboratory work is available but the recent advances in the knowledge of the structure of the atomic nucleus bear promise of advancement in this art" (p. 670 of *1934 Year Book*).

19. Einstein quoted by Clayton Fritchey of *Newsday* in column published in Worcester (Massachusetts) *Telegram*, Sunday, November 28, 1982. In 1938, when asked by William L. Laurence of the New York *Times* whether men would *ever* be able to harness the power of the atom, Einstein replied: "No. We are poor marksmen, shooting at birds in the dark in a country where there are very few birds."

20. Ben J. Wattenberg, compiler, *The Statistical History of the United States* (U.S. Bureau of the Census reports), (New York, 1976), pp. 809–10. Morris L. Ernst, *The First Freedom*, (New York, 1946), p. 62. Oswald Garrison Villard, *The Disappearing Daily* (New York, 1944), p. 3.

21. Kenneth Burke, *Permanence and Change*, p. 213. Alexander Meiklejohn, *What Does America Mean?* (New York, 1935), pp. 239–40. Meiklejohn goes on to say (pp. 240–41): "I know that this suggestion will be bitterly resented. I shall be accused of trying to take away freedom from the press. And to this I must answer very bluntly that those who say this do not seem to me to know what freedom means in our American scheme of life. We demand that our news be free from any external domination. And on this ground it is essential that the commercial connections of the press be broken. Selling has no right to freedom. Men who sell news are merchants and must be treated as such. Their activities, being external, are open to regulation, to control, to prohibition, in whatever forms the public interest may require. As seekers for economic gain, they are concerned, not with inner values, but with outer arrangements. And the spirit of our institutions forbids that they be free and unhindered in the use of our common intellectual heritage for their own private, selfish advantage."

22. *Statistical Abstract of the United States, 1931*, Lewis Corey (Louis Fraina), *The Decline of American Capitalism* (New York, 1934), p. 471.

23. Beard and Beard, *op. cit.*, p. 824. New York *Times*, June 28, 1933; December 16, 1933.

24. *Recent Social Trends in the United States* (Washington, D.C., 1933), vol. 1, p. 133.

25. J. G. Brainerd, "Electrical Engineering," *American Year Book*, 1933, *Brainerd*, p. 697.

26. New York *Times*, February 24, 1934

27. If, as seems to me to be true, the substance or meaning of an idea is always something felt, not something logically thought, and if one function of logic is to freeze fluid intuitive feeling into discrete static shapes that can be used as the building blocks of larger concepts, then a more precise statement here would be "who insisted upon applying logic to their emotional reactions, thereby transforming these into distinct ideas." Suggested is an equation of thought and feeling, of idea and emotion, somewhat akin to Einstein's mass-energy equation, ideas being concentrated, solidified emotion in somewhat the same way as matter is concentrated, solidified energy.

28. Reinhold Niebuhr, "After Capitalism—What?," *World Tomorrow*, vol. XVI (March 1, 1933) pp. 203–5.

29. Ernest Gruening, "Capitalist Confiscation," *Nation*, vol. CXXXVI (February 1, 1933), pp. 116–17, reprinted in Howard Zinn, ed., *New Deal Thought* (Indianapolis, 1966), pp. 110–16.

30. Friedrich Engels, *Anti-Duhring*, the most comprehensive philosophical statement of the Marxist position, cites with approval Hegel's definition of freedom as the appreciation of necessity. "Freedom . . . consists in control over ourselves and over external nature which is founded on knowledge of natural necessity; it is therefore necessarily a product of historical development," writes Engels. Lenin in his *State and Revolution* repeats Marx's assertion that the advent of communism will mean the "inevitable withering away of the State" and claims that until this happens, freedom is impossible. ("While the State exists there is no freedom. When there is freedom there will be no state.") Elsewhere Lenin describes freedom in exclusively negative terms, chiefly as the absence of "bourgeois" ownership and control of the press and of capital goods. See pp. 225, 752, 829 of *A Handbook of Marxism*, an official anthology of basic Marxist literature, issued by International Publishers in 1935.

31. Lawrence Dennis, *Is Capitalism Doomed?* (New York, 1932), pp. 91–93, 316. Ronald Radosh, *Prophets on the Right*, (New York, 1975), p. 277. From Dennis's *Coming American Fascism*, (New York, 1936) and later *Dynamics of War and Revolution*, (n.p., 1940), Charles A. Lindbergh would derive some of the language and much of the basic argument of his America First speeches and articles in the early 1940s. Pound arrived at his hatred of Jews and love of Mussolini (or believed that he did) by way of monetary theory. Usury was the root of all evil and the Jews were identified with usury. See Earle Davis, *Fugitive Vision: Ezra Pound and Economics* (Lawrence, Kansas, 1968), pp. 172–78.

32. John Chamberlain, *Farewell to Reform* (New York, 1932), p. 323. Schlesinger, *op. cit.*, p. 210.

33. Chamberlain, *op. cit.*, p. 310.

34. Niebuhr, *op. cit.*

35. Stuart Chase, "The Age of Distribution," *Nation*, vol. CXXXIX (July 24, 1934), pp. 93–94, reprinted in part in Zinn, *op. cit.*, pp. 22–27.

36. Stuart Chase, *The Economy of Abundance* (New York, 1934), p. 315.

37. John Dewey, "The Future of Liberalism," *Journal of Philosophy*, vol. XXII, no. 9 (1935), pp. 225–230.

38. Bruce Allen Murphy, *The Brandeis-Frankfurter Connection* (New York, 1983), p. 42.

39. The "original suggestion that there were *two* New Deals," a suggestion followed by most historians of the period, was made in "an article by a journalist in about 1937, which defies efforts to locate it," writes Basil Rauh in the Preface to his pioneering *The History of the New Deal*. (New York, 1944), Rauh describes the First New Deal as ending in 1934, with the Second launched by the President's annual message to Congress on January 4, 1935.

40. Henry A. Wallace, *America Must Choose*, (New York, 1934), pp. 11, 26, 27.

41. Paul H. Douglas, "Rooseveltian Liberalism," a review of Rexford G. Tugwell's, *Industrial Discipline*, *Nation* (June 21, 1933), pp. 702–3.

42. Rexford G. Tugwell, *The Industrial Discipline* (New York, 1933), p. 215.

43. Douglas, *op. cit.,* p. 703.

Seven. Recovery Through Planned Scarcity: NRA and AAA

1. Schlesinger, *op. cit.,* pp. 284–85, quoting transcript of the meeting of the Special Board of Public Works, July 1, 1933. Frances Perkins, *op. cit.,* pp. 270–71, summarizes Douglas's arguments against public works and says: "There is no doubt in my mind that Roosevelt did give him [Douglas] grounds to believe that he wanted a balanced budget and that he was at least doubtful of the wisdom of a public works program if it could not be achieved without throwing the budget out of balance. This was one of the conflicts in Roosevelt's nature and in his thinking. He wanted a balanced budget, but he also wanted to do the right thing by his unemployed fellow citizen." He also wanted to win elections.

2. *Statistical Abstract of the United States, 1934,* p. 730. *American Year Book, 1933,* p. 360.

3. *Statistical Abstract, 1936,* p. 298.

4. Michael R. Beschloss, Kennedy and Roosevelt (New York, 1980), p. 82.

5. Special Industrial Recovery Board, *Proceedings,* July 18, 1933, quoted by Schlesinger, *op. cit.,* p. 113.

6. *Ibid.,* p. 285

7. In hearings before the Senate Committee on Finance on the national industrial recovery bill, Senator Wagner said: "[T]he expenditure of large amounts of public moneys upon public works will inevitably induce the investment of substantial amounts of private funds. The construction of a waterworks may make a whole area suitable for residential development. The improvement of a traffic facility may invite the reaction of a business enterprise. The fundamental fact to remember is that the distribution of purchasing power and the resumption of investment which this bill involves will have a stimulating effect and help revive all forms of business activity." Quoted by Mitchell, *op. cit.,* p. 236.

8. Ickes, *op. cit.,* p. 54.

9. Harold L. Ickes, "My Twelve Years with F.D.R.," *Saturday Evening Post* (June 12, 1948). Schlesinger, *op. cit.,* p. 287.

10. Tugwell, *Democratic Roosevelt,* p. 320.

11. Huthmacher, *op. cit.,* p. 155.

12. Frances Perkins, *op. cit.,* p. 206.

13. *Ibid.,* p. 206.

14. Schlesinger, *op. cit.,* p. 93, quoting Donald Richberg, *Tents of the Mighty* (New York, 1930). Jerome Frank's view of Richberg and Richberg's performance differs from mine, derived from such published reactions as Clarence Darrow's and Ickes's, among many others. Frank believes that Richberg was simply a weak character, essentially, who was "overawed" by Johnson's "brilliant superficiality" and *seeming* force of character. He expresses this opinion in COHC.

15. *PPA, 1933,* p. 202.

16. Bellush, *op. cit.,* p. 45.

17. *PPA, 1933,* p. 275.

18. New York *Times,* June 24, 1933. Schlesinger, *op. cit.,* p. 123.

19. Bellush, *op. cit.,* p. 44.

20. *Ibid.,* p. 43.

21. Special Industrial Recovery Board, Proceedings, July 18, 19, 1933, quoted by Schlesinger, *op. cit.,* p. 113.

22. *Ibid.,* p. 113.

23. *PPA, 1933,* pp. 300, 301.

24. New York *Times,* September 14, 1933.

25. *PPA, 1933,* p. 316.

26. Lindley, *op. cit.,* p. 239. Actually Eugene Grace received as much as $1,623,753 in bonuses in a single year. A handful of Bethlehem Steel directors and executives were granted $6,800,524 in bonuses in the three years of 1925–1928, though Bethlehem's common stock paid no dividends during those years. Schwab and his fellow directors did not bother to inform stockholders of these bonus payments. All in all, between 1917 and 1930, Bethlehem's board voted to corporation

officials, several of whom were themselves board members, bonuses totaling 80 percent of the amount of money distributed to all of Bethlehem's stockholders in dividends. Such revelations might encourage simpleminded folk to conclude that if there was any moral difference between a Bethlehem board member executive and a common thief, that difference favored the latter. A common thief at least ran some personal risk as he did his stealing, and his thefts were infinitesimal compared to those of the executives. See chapter 8 of John T. Flynn, *Graft in Business* (New York, 1931).

27. Frances Perkins, *op. cit.,* p. 232.

28. *PPA, 1933,* p. 318.

29. Sidney Fine, *The Automobile Under the Blue Eagle* (Ann Arbor, Mich., 1963), pp. 55, 60. Bellush, *op. cit.,* pp. 94–97.

30. Irving Bernstein, *Turbulent Years: A History of the American Worker, 1933–1941,* (Boston, 1970), quoted by Bellush, *op. cit.,* p. 92.

31. The company-house company-store requirement had long been a particularly vicious exploitive device. Norman Thomas reports on a visit he made in the fall of 1932 to a representative company house in a West Virginia coal town—an unplastered rotten-floored three-room shack with a rickety front porch. "The householder showed me slips to prove that he had been making from $16 to $21 a month. From this the company had held out, that month, $12.80 to pay rent and various fixed charges for accidents and hospital services. . . . He was actually in debt to the company for advances made to him in the form of scrip, good only at the company store. At these company stores we found that prices averaged at least 25 percent above prices in the so-called free stores where, however, miners dependent upon advances could not pay in cash, and where miners in fear of their jobs did not always dare to trade. At the time of our visit a particular sack of a particular brand of flour, which the relief committee had been able to buy in some quantity for 49 cents a bag, was selling at the company store for $1.10." Norman Thomas, *Human Exploitation* (New York, 1934), pp. 100–101.

32. *PPA, 1933,* p. 255.

33. *Ibid.,* p. 302. General Johnson made the same point more strongly when he addressed the American Federation of Labor convention on October 10, saying, "Labor does not need to strike under the Roosevelt plan. . . . The plain stark truth is that you cannot tolerate the strike. . . . In the codes you are given complete and highly effective protection of your rights." New York *Times,* October 11, 1933. The general was considerably less persuasive of labor than the President was.

34. *American Year Book, 1933,* p. 359.

35. Schlesinger, *op. cit.,* pp. 148–49.

36. Richard Lowitt and Maurine Beasley, eds., *One Third of a Nation: Lorena Hickok Reports on the Great Depression* (Urbana, Ill., 1981), p. 117.

37. *PPA, 1933,* p. 524.

38. *Ibid.,* pp. 166, 167.

39. Hawley, *op. cit.,* pp. 57–58. George Terborgh, *Price Control Devices in NRA Codes.* Mitchell, *op. cit.,* pp. 247–48.

40. *American Year Book, 1933,* p. 490.

41. *Statistical Abstract,* 1934, pp. 730, 304.

42. Sumner H. Slichter, "Employment Condition," *American Year Book,* 1933, p. 621.

43. *Ibid.,* p. 730.

44. Data on prices presented to NRA price hearings by E. J. Condon for Mail Order Association of America, January, 1933. Bellush, *op. cit.,* pp. 72–73.

45. Tugwell, *Democratic Roosevelt,* p. 311.

46. Special Industrial Recovery Board, *Proceedings,* November 13, 27, and Dec. 12, 1933, cited by Schlesinger, *op. cit.,* p. 127.

47. Johnson speech to National Retail Dry Goods Association January 18, 1934, quoted by Schlesinger, *op. cit.,* p. 131; and by Hawley, *op. cit.,* p. 81.

48. Hawley, *op. cit.,* p. 77. Bellush, *op. cit.,* p. 66. Schlesinger, *op. cit.,* pp. 130–31.

49. *PPA, 1933,* pp. 514–15.

50. Quoted from Wallace speech by Schlesinger, *op. cit.,* p. 61. Wallace's troubled conscience and attempt to ease it by disclaiming personal responsibility for what he "had" to do was abundantly manifest on pp. 174–75 and 200 of his *New Frontiers.* (New York, 1934) "[T]o have to destroy a growing crop is a shocking commentary on our civilization," he writes, adding that he himself could "tolerate it only as a cleaning up of the wreckage from the old days of unbalanced production. . . . The plowing under of 10 million acres of growing cotton in August 1933, and the slaughter of 6 million little pigs in September . . . were not acts of idealism in any sane society. They were emergency acts made necessary by the almost insane lack of world statesmanship during the period from 1920 to 1932."

51. Gladys L. Baker, *The County Agent,* (Chicago, 1939), pp. 15–16.

52. M. L. Wilson made the quoted statement to Christianna McFadyen Campbell in August 1959 as she interviewed him while gathering material for her *The Farm Bureau and the New Deal,* (Urbana, Ill., 1962) the first chapter of which deals with the "Origins and Functions" of the Farm Bureau.

53. *PPA, 1933,* pp. 259, 260. Photograph is one of group between pp. 84 and 85 of Wayne D. Rasmussen and Gladys L. Baker, *The Department of Agriculture* (New York, 1972). Mitchell, *op. cit.,* p. 179, remarks that "the farmer who symbolized the campaign to destroy growing cotton" may have "had to borrow the money to buy a decent shirt in which to appear for his award." Certainly clothing, mattresses, bed sheets, and other cotton goods were in horrifyingly short supply when winter swept into the northern Great Plains that year, as Lorena Hickok recorded in her reports to Harry Hopkins and her letters to Eleanor Roosevelt. See Lowitt and Beasley, *op. cit.*

54. Quoted from Wallace speech by Schlesinger, *op. cit.,* p. 63.

55. U.S. Department of Agriculture, *Agricultural Adjustment, 1933–1934,* (Washington, D.C., 1935), p. 22 ff., 74, 97 ff., gives official version of the production-destruction program.

56. Frank transcript, COHC.

57. Appleby transcript, COHC.

58. Henry Wallace to FDR, May 15, 1933, cited by Schlesinger, *op. cit.,* p. 48.

59. *PPA, 1933,* p. 260.

60. Cited by Schlesinger, *op. cit.,* p. 50.

61. Kenneth S. Davis, *The Politics of Honor. A Biography of Adlai E. Stevenson,* (New York, 1967), p. 117.

62. Frank transcript, COHC.

63. J. Franklin, *op. cit.,* p. 36.

64. *PPA, 1933,* p. 370.

65. *Ibid.,* p. 372.

66. Frank transcript, COHC.

67. *PPA, 1933,* p. 407.

68. John L. Shover, *Cornbelt Rebellion: The Farmer's Holiday Association* (Urbana, Ill. 1965), p. 160, citing stories in Sioux City (Iowa) *Journal,* November 25, 26, 1933.

Eight. A Hazardous Passage Across Winter into Spring and Summer 1934

1. Lowitt and Beasley, *op. cit.,* pp. 55–57.

2. *Ibid.,* pp. 59–61.

3. *Ibid.,* p. 79. According to Whittaker Chambers's testimony during the Alger Hiss libel and perjury trials, also Chambers's *Witness* (New York, 1952), pp. 275–443, Harold "Hal" Ware, son of Ella Reeve Bloor, "Mother" Bloor to the whole American Communist Party, organized a highly secret Communist party cell in the U.S. Department of Agriculture in 1933. In the 1920s Ware had managed state farms in the Soviet Union, introducing dry-farming techniques (ironically enough, these had been introduced to the American Great Plains by Mennonite emigrants from Russia in the late 1890s) and demonstrating new American agricultural machinery. Members of the Ware cell in Washington were several of the bright young men (Lee Pressman, John Abt, Nathan Witt, allegedly Hiss) whom Jerome Frank recruited for the AAA's Legal Division. (Frank was most emphatically *not* a Communist himself; he was profoundly ideologically opposed to Marxism.) Since none of these secret Communists exerted any influence on policy that was not a matter of record at the time, nor were they in any position to convey to the Soviet Union secret information detrimental to U.S. national security, I pay no attention to their cell activities in the main body of my text. But it should be noted here that Ware, masterminding Communist agrarian agitation, *did* have some influence upon the Farmers' Holiday movement, chiefly through front man and field agent Lem Harris. Mother Bloor presided over, and Ware attended, a meeting of some fifty farmers during a mass Farmers' Holiday demonstration in Sioux City on September 9, 1932, and one may be sure that midwestern Communists thereafter did what they could to incite violent protest on the part of the farmers. See Shover, *op. cit.,* pp. 65–85.

4. Lowitt and Beasley, *op. cit.,* pp. 51–52.

5. *Ibid.,* p. 54.

6. *Ibid.,* p. 69.

7. Rexford G. Tugwell, syndicated newspaper column, October 22, 1933. Bernard Sternsher, *Rexford Tugwell and the New Deal,* (New Brunswick, N.J., 1964) p. 195.

8. Quoted by Edwin G. Nourse, *Marketing Agreements Under the AAA* (Washington, D.C. 1935), p. 38, cited by Sternsher, *op. cit.,* p. 196. Peek made the statement on May 15, 1933.

9. Nourse, *op. cit.,* Chapter 2. Schlesinger, *op. cit.,* pp. 56–57.

10. Henry Wallace to FDR, September 11, 1933, Official Files, Agriculture, Franklin D. Roosevelt Library. On September 7, Wallace had written FDR: "Undoubtedly the agricultural situation is becoming more tense day by day."

11. Reno to FDR, September 26, 1933, quoted by Shover, *op. cit.,* p. 151.

12. Shover, *op. cit.,* pp. 151–52.

13. New York *Times,* October 22, 1933. Shover, *op. cit.,* pp. 154–55.

14. Shover, *op. cit.,* p. 157, quoting news story in Des Moines (Iowa) *Register,* October 31, 1933.

15. Warburg to FDR, September 20, 1933; Warren to FDR, September 20, 1933. Cited by Schlesinger, *op. cit.,* pp. 237, 238.

16. Ickes, *Secret Diary,* pp. 108–9.

17. FDR to Woodin, September 30, 1933, cited by Schlesinger, *op. cit.,* p. 238.

18. Warburg transcript, COHC. cited by Schlesinger, *op. cit.,* p. 239.

19. Moley, *Seven Years,* pp. 281–83. Moley, according to his own testimony, gave Roosevelt the description of the gold purchase program as "a policy and not an expedient." When Moley made the suggestion "quietly," he says, "the old ease came into our collaboration . . . as if, after months, some mental log jam had broken."

20. *PPA, 1933,* pp. 420–27.

21. Blum, *op. cit.,* p. 46. Daily gold prices are from *American Year Book, 1933,* pp. 438–42.

22. *PPA, 1933,* pp. 490–491.

23. New York *Times,* November 22, 23, 1933. James P. Warburg, *The Money Muddle,* p. 121. O. M. W. Sprague, *Recovery and Common Sense,* pp. 70–71. Schlesinger, *op. cit.,* pp. 245–46.

24. Blum, *op. cit.,* p. 49. Tully, op. cit., p. 178, says it was Morgenthau who "decided," that Acheson "was responsible for the leak." She adds: "It was learned subsequently that the break in secrecy had come through Lewis Douglas."

25. Blum, *op. cit.,* pp. 50–51.

26. John M. Blum, *From the Morgenthau Diaries: Years of Crisis, 1928–1938,* p. 72.

27. Shover, *op. cit.,* Sioux City, Iowa, *Journal,* November 3, 1933. George H. Mayer, *The Political Career of Floyd B. Olson,* pp. 153–54.

28. Shover, *op. cit.,* p. 159, footnote 29, citing Sioux City (Iowa) *Journal,* October 23, 1933.

29. Ickes, *Secret Diary*, p. 108. Blum, *Morgenthau and Roosevelt*, p. 36.

30. Sherwood, *op. cit.*, p. 51. Adams, *op. cit.*, p. 57.

31. Wallace, *America Must Choose*, p. 9.

32. Roosevelt reiterated this "conviction" in a letter to Olson, April 16, 1934, cited by Schlesinger, *op. cit.*, pp. 66–67.

33. Lowitt and Beasley, *op. cit.*, p. 88.

34. Mayer, *op. cit.*, p. 154. Shover, *op. cit.*, p. 162.

35. Lowitt and Beasley, *op. cit.*, p. 87.

36. Shover, *op. cit.*, p. 163. New York *Times*, November 7, 1933.

37. Shover, *op. cit.*, pp. 165–66. In footnote 40 on latter page, Shover cites interview with Donald R. Murphy as source for statement that front rows in auditorium were reserved for Farm Bureau members.

38. Schlesinger, *op. cit.*, 58,

39. Appleby transcript, COHC.

40. Rexford G. Tugwell, "A New Deal Memoir: Early Days, 1932–1933" Tugwell Papers, Franklin D. Roosevelt Library Chapter 4, cited by Schlesinger, *op. cit.*, p. 38. Writes Tugwell in his *Democratic Roosevelt*, p. 313: ". . . Franklin, still exhibiting political caution and with a wary eye on Baruch, sought to ease Peek's departure by giving him a post in the Department of State. . . . But since his scheme of selling more products abroad was totally antithetical to Hull's determined sponsorship of most-favored-nation treaties, it could be seen that presently more trouble would erupt."

41. Wayne S. Cole, *Roosevelt and the Isolationists* (Lincoln, Neb., 1983) pp. 100–101, citing William Phillips diary, which is in Houghton Library, Harvard University.

42. Franklin, *op. cit.*, pp. 83–84.

43. *PPA, 1933*, p. 516.

44. Hull, *Memoirs, op. cit.*, vol. 1, p. 370.

45. Freedman, *op. cit.*, gives full text of the Oxford economists' letter, pp. 168–73.

46. *Ibid.*, pp. 177–83, gives full text of Keynes letter. Also New York *Times* for Sunday, December 31, 1933. *The Public Papers and Addresses of Franklin D. Roosevelt, 1934.* (hereafter *PPA, 1934*), pp. 40–45.

47. Freedman, *op. cit.,* pp. 170, 180.

48. *Ibid.,* pp. 183–84.

49. *PPA, 1933,* p. 457.

50. Sherwood, *op. cit.,* p. 51–52. *PPA, 1933,* p. 457.

51. Ickes, *Secret Diary,* p. 116.

52. *PPA, 1933,* pp. 457–58.

53. Sherwood, *op. cit.,* p. 55.

54. Lowitt and Beasley, *op. cit.,* pp. 92, 106, 112.

55. Sherwood, *op. cit.,* pp. 54–55. Schlesinger, *op. cit.,* p. 271, citing Lt. Col. J. C. H. Lee, "The Federal Civil Works Administration: A Study Covering Its Organization in November 1933 and Its Operations Until 31 March, 1934."

56. Ickes, *Secret Diary,* pp. 119–120.

57. Sherwood, *op. cit.,* p. 57. Jerre Mangione, *The Dream and the Deal: The Federal Writers' Project, 1935–1945,* (Boston, 1972), p. 33.

58. Alfred E. Smith, "Civil Works," *New Outlook* (December 1933), Emily Warner Smith, with Hawthorne Daniel, *The Happy Warrior,* (New York, 1956), p. 269.

59. Thomas, *op. cit.,* p. 275.

60. *Fortune* magazine (October 1933), cited by Sherwood, *op. cit.,* p. 57, and Adams, *op. cit.,* p. 61.

61. Robert E. Wood to Henry A. Wallace, June 29, 1934, cited by Schlesinger, *op. cit.,* p. 274.

62. Lowitt and Beasley, *op. cit.,* pp. 187–88.

63. *Ibid.,* p. 188.

64. *PPA, 1933,* p. 458.

65. John Edward Wiltz, *In Search of Peace: The Senate Munitions Inquiry, 1934–36,* (Louisiana State Press, 1963), p. 30. Bellush, *op. cit.,* pp. 66–67.

66. *PPA, 1934,* p. 65.

67. Bellush, *op. cit.,* p. 70, citing Consumers' Advisory Board Report, *Suggestions for Code Revision.*

68. *PPA, 1934*, pp. 126–29.

69. Bellush, op. cit., pp. 145–46. Hawley, *op. cit.,* p. 96. Schlesinger, *op. cit.,* p. 133.

70. *PPA, 1934*, p. 137.

71. Hugh Johnson to FDR, May 15, 1934, cited by Schlesinger, *op. cit.,* p. 134. Paul Y. Anderson, "The Darrow Report," *Nation,* May 30, 1934.

72. Freedman, *op. cit.,* pp. 213–215. That Frankfurter's mention of Keynes's wife had some persuasive impact upon Roosevelt seems indicated by a chit attached to the note for Missy LeHand from Frankfurter, dated May 7, 1934, which Keynes forwarded along with his Washington visit schedule and which is now in the Franklin D. Roosevelt Library. Said this chit: "Missy: I want to see him and get him in some time at tea alone. When you get ahold of Keynes, ask him to bring his wife."

73. Freedman, *op. cit.,* pp. 216–17, 222. Frances Perkins, *op. cit.,* pp. 225–26.

74. R. F. Harrod, *Life of John Maynard Keynes* (London, 1951), p. 20. Robert Lekachman, *The Age of Keynes* (New York, 1966), p. 30.

75. *PPA, 1934*, pp. 274–75.

76. Ickes, *Secret Diary,* pp. 197–98.

77. Franklin, *op. cit.,* p. 36.

78. Hugh S. Johnson, "The Future of NRA," *Saturday Evening Post* (July 21, 1934).

79. Huthmacher, *op. cit.,* p. 165.

80. "It does appear that during the automobile strike [*sic*] Roosevelt and Johnson used Wagner's bill as a club in persuading the auto makers to accept the General's [it was equally Roosevelt's] settlement of March 25 . . ." writes Huthmacher on p. 166, *op. cit.*

81. *Ibid.,* p. 169.

82. *Ibid.,* pp. 170–71. *Congressional Record,* Seventy-third Congress, 2nd session, p. 12016 ff. Bellush, *op. cit.,* pp. 110–14.

83. Herbert Solow, "War in Minneapolis," *Nation* (August 8, 1934). Schlesinger, *op. cit.,* pp. 385–88. Eric Sevareid, *Not So Wild a Dream,* (New York, 1946), p. 58.

84. Frances Perkins, *op. cit.,* p. 316.

85. Bellush, *op. cit.,* pp. 119–20. New York *Times,* July 6, 1934.

86. Hiram Johnson to Harold Ickes, July 16, 1934. Julius Meier to FDR, July 16, 1934, quoted by Schlesinger, *op. cit.*, pp. 391–92. Bellush, *op. cit.*, p. 121.

87. *PPA, 1934*, pp. 333–34.

88. Bellush, *op. cit.*, pp. 122–25. New York *Times*, July 16, 18.

89. PPA, 1934, pp. 398–399 (excerpt of transcript of 141st press conference, September 5, 1934). Frances Perkins to FDR, July 15, 1934. Louis Howe to FDR, July 15, 1934. Schlesinger, *op. cit.*, p. 392.

Nine. The View from Russian Hill: An Interlude and Retrospect

1. Hickok, *op. cit.*, p. 172.

2. Lorena Hickok to Eleanor Roosevelt, July 3, 1933. Reprinted in part in Lowitt and Beasley, *op. cit.*, pp. 304–305.

3. Lash, *Love, Eleanor*, p. 192.

4. Dallek, *op. cit.*, pp. 78–81. Bullitt, *op. cit.*, p. 49–50. Ickes, *Secret Diary*, pp. 123–24.

5. Quoted in Lash, *Love, Eleanor*, p. 272.

6. Faber, *op. cit.*, p. 152.

7. *PPA, 1933*, pp. 519–20. Lash, *Love, Eleanor*, pp. 174–75.

8. Lash, *Love, Eleanor*, p. 175.

9. *Ibid.* p. 174.

10. *Ibid.*, pp. 175–76. Faber, *op. cit.*, pp. 155–56. Faber, having told of the close friendship which developed between Anna and Hick during this time of trouble for Anna, opines that it would have been unlikely for Anna to "have approved of a relationship between her mother and Hick such as their private letters may seem to imply. Indeed, to the staff at the F.D.R. Library, screening the Papers of Lorena Hickok before opening the collection, the closeness between Anna and her mother at this period provided persuasive evidence that the relationship between E.R. and Hick must have been more naive [*sic*] than their correspondence suggests." See p. 155 of Faber. I myself think it distinctly possible that Anna suspected a lesbian relationship between her mother and Hick, knowing as she did how many of her mother's closest friends had such relationships, and was not shocked or dismayed by it at all, was only concerned about the risk of scandal which was being run. I think so because of a lengthy interview I had with Anna in 1973 during which she talked with remarkable frankness, and sympathetic understanding, about her mother's attitudes toward sex as these were expressed to her during her late adolescence and after. She struck me as a woman possessed of a rare depth of understanding of human beings and their relation-

ships, and of wholly "liberated" attitudes toward sex, did Anna Roosevelt (Dall, Boettiger) Halsted, and she seems to have been so when young.

11. Lash, *Love, Eleanor,* pp. 176–77.

12. Lowitt and Beasley, *op. cit.* pp. 164–65. Lash, *Love, Eleanor,* p. 181.

13. Lash, *ibid.,* p. 182.

14. Ickes, *Secret Diary,* p. 31.

15. Theo Lippmann, Jr., The Squire of Warm Springs (Chicago, 1977), pp. 203–4. Turnley Walker's *Roosevelt and the Warm Springs Story* (New York, 1953), gives a very full account of the history of the birthday balls.

16. *PPA, 1934,* p. 63.

17. Davis, *Invincible Summer.* Thanks to Mrs. Mary Belle Starr, who with some difficulty persuaded Miss Dickerman that the statute of limitations had run out on Steve Early's order of 1934, there was published in *Invincible Summer,* as the lead photograph of a portfolio selected from the still and motion pictures taken by Nancy Cook, the now rather famous photo of Roosevelt as "Caesar" surrounded by his "court," at the 1934 Cuff Links party. Wrote Early to fellow members of the Cuff Links Club, in February 1934: "The photographs made at the birthday dinner this year are given to each member of the gang with the understanding that each of the pictures shall be safeguarded against duplication. . . . It is respectfully requested that none of these photographs be exhibited or that their existence be discovered by any outsider. These photographs belong to the gang and to the gang alone. Should they escape from your care and keeping, dire punishment will be imposed. Be warned, be careful, or be banished to the regions where the faithless, false, fraudulent, deceitful, unscrupulous, and perfidious felons abide." Quoted in *Invincible Summer,* p. 112. Lash, *Love, Eleanor,* p. 182 (for quote from Eleanor's letter.)

18. Faber, *op. cit.,* p. 167. Lash, *Love, Eleanor,* p. 188. Both quoting letter from Eleanor Roosevelt to Lorena Hickok, April 18, 1934.

19. Lash, *ibid.,* p. 196.

20. Lowitt and Beasley, *op. cit.,* p. 200.

21. Ickes, *Secret Diary,* p. 505.

22. Anne O'Hare McCormick, "Roosevelt Surveys His Course," New York *Times Magazine,* July 8, 1934.

23. *PPA, 1934,* p. 349.

24. Hickok, *op. cit.,* p. 136

25. *Ibid.*, p. 138.

26. Alfred B. Rollins, Jr. *Roosevelt and Howe,* (New York, 1962), p. 407. According to Rollins, the script is dated August 20, 1933 (it is in Group XXXVI in the FDR Library), but the delivery must have been on Sunday, August 22, 1933, Sunday being the weekly broadcast time.

27. New York *Times,* October 14, 1933. Lash, *Eleanor and Franklin,* p. 398.

28. Alan Brinkley, *Voices of Protest: Huey Long, Father Coughlin and the Great Depression,* (New York, 1983), p. 145. Brinkley provides an excellent account of "The Dissident Ideology," which Long and Coughlin articulated, on pp. 143–68 of his book, his point being that "the Long and Coughlin ideologies" were not mere demagogic artifacts but "rested on some of the oldest and deepest impulses of American life."

29. Davis, *Invincible Summer,* pp. 122–23.

30. Lash, *Eleanor and Franklin,* p. 399.

31. *Ibid.,* p. 399.

32. New York *Times,* February 21, 1934.

33. Kenneth S. Davis, *The Hero: Charles A. Lindbergh and the American Dream,* p. 294. Henry Ladd Smith, *Airways, the History of Commercial Aviation in the United States* (New York, 1942), covers in detail the story of Brown's airmail operations on pp. 156–248.

34. Schlesinger, *op. cit.,* pp. 450–51.

35. Davis, *The Hero,* pp. 332, 338.

36. Schlesinger, *op. cit.,* p. 455. Emile Gauvreau and Lester Cohen, *Billy Mitchell,* (New York, 1942), p. 211. New York *Times,* March 12, 1934.

37. New York *Times,* January 11, 12, 13; February 12, 1934. Davis, *The Hero,* pp. 333–34.

38. *PPA, 1934,* p. 141.

39. Davis, *The Hero,* p. 336. New York *Times,* February 14, March 15, 16, 1934.

40. Schlesinger, *op. cit.,* p. 454.

41. *PPA, 1934,* p. 139.

42. Parrish, *op. cit.,* p. 110.

43. Moley, *Seven Years,* p. 285.

44. *PPA, 1934,* p. 91.

45. Parrish, *op. cit.,* pp. 113–15.

46. Felix Frankfurter to FDR, Feb. 22, 1934, quoted by Parrish, *op. cit.,* p. 121.

47. *Ibid.,* p. 122.

48. *Ibid.,* p. 124.

49. Fred I. Kent to FDR, March 23, 1934, quoted by Parrish, *op. cit.,* p. 129.

50. *PPA, 1934,* pp. 169–70.

51. Tugwell, *Democratic Roosevelt,* pp. 322–323. Schlesinger, *op. cit.,* pp. 457–59. Lash, *op. cit.,* p. 400.

52. Tully, *op. cit.,* p. 22.

53. Freedman, *op. cit.,* pp. 220–21.

54. Ickes, *Secret Diary,* p. 173. Beschloss, *op. cit.,* says on p. 85 that Louis Howe strongly opposed the Kennedy appointment when rumor that it might be made got about, saying "that assigning Kennedy to police Wall Street is like setting a cat to guard pigeons," and that Roosevelt subsequently asked Frank Walker "to talk Kennedy out of the chairmanship," Walker being a fellow Roman Catholic. Writes Beschloss: "Night after night, during walks through the deserted streets of the capital, the president's man [Walker] reasoned with Kennedy, but to no avail. 'You go back and tell him I don't want to be a member of the commission,' Kennedy ordered, 'I'm going to be chairman—or else.' "

55. Davis, *Invincible Summer,* pp. 128–29.

56. Parrish, *op. cit.,* p. 179. Beschloss, *op. cit.,* p. 92. New York *Times,* July 26, 1934.

57. Schlesinger, *op. cit.,* pp. 469–70. Beschloss, *op. cit.,* p. 94.

58. Parrish, *op. cit.,* pp. 179–80.

59. Freedman, *op. cit.,* p. 382.

60. *PPA, 1934,* pp. 317–18. Actually the "blending" of the new structure "with the essential lines of the old" White House was largely the doing of architect Eric Gugler. Roosevelt initially approved plans for the Executive Office wing enlargement which, Gugler protested, on behalf of the Fine Arts Commission, "were an outrage against both history and architecture, being "a complete departure from Jefferson's careful, tasteful designs for possible future additions to the

White House, and they would produce a monstrosity totally destructive of the building's symmetry, flatly contradictory of its basic original design." An annoyed Roosevelt had grumbled that people like Gugler cared "more for appearances than you do about your country's government." Roosevelt had, in fact, been sufficiently annoyed to make reference (something he practically never did) to his physical handicap whose difficulties for him were increased by the lack of adequate office space for assistants adjacent to his living quarters. Gugler did not back down. Instead, he made a bold suggestion: "If you need, as you say, three times the office in addition to the major rooms, and I can show you that this space can be provided without increasing the apparent size of the building —no change to the eye, as to size—will you consider my plan?" Roosevelt promised somewhat grumpily to do so, provided Gugler had the design plans ready within five days. Gugler met the challenge, and it was his design which was used for the renovation. See Davis, *Invincible Summer,* pp. 132–34.

61. Berle and Jacobs, *op. cit.,* pp. 103–4.

62. Ickes, *Secret Diary,* p. 152.

63. Wesley W. Stout, "The New Homesteaders," *Saturday Evening Post* (August 4, 1934). The story of Lorimer's declaration of war upon the New Deal is told by John Tebbel, *George Horace Lorimer and the Saturday Evening Post,* (New York, 1948), pp. 198–99.

64. Hickok, *op. cit.,* pp. 172–76.

Book Three: The New Deal Ebbs, Then Flows to Its Highest Tide

Ten. Into a Land of Quandary: The Elections of 1939, and After

1. *PPA, 1934,* p. 353.

2. Ickes, *Secret Diary,* p. 182.

3. *Ibid.,* p. 184. Lash, *Love, Eleanor,* p. 198; quoting letter to Lorena Hickok, October 5, 1934.

4. *PPA, 1934,* pp. 360, 361, 363, 365.

5. Wellington Brink, *Big Hugh, the Father of Conservation* (New York, 1951), p. 5., quoting testimony by H. H. Bennett before U.S. Senate Committee on Public Lands and Surveys, April 1935. Paul Bonnifield, in his *The Dust Bowl,* (Albuquerque, N.M., 1979) p. 43, says Bennett was woefully laggard in his recognition of wind erosion as a serious soil conservation problem. In an article entitled "Land Impoverishment by Soil Erosion," which Bennett contributed to the 1931 Biennial Report of the Kansas State Board of Agriculture, writes Bonnifield, "the nation's foremost exponent on preventing erosion did not mention the dangers of wind to soil." Bonnifield seems to deny that the plowing up of the rangeland and planting of it to wheat was an important cause of the 1930's dust storms, citing dust storms

that occurred during drought years when the buffalo grass carpet was yet intact. But Bonnifield shows a strong bias against the federal government in all its shapes and forms, as these affected the high plains; is obviously a very rugged individualist, in the old-fashioned sense (he is an executive in a Colorado coal company); and does not, in my judgment, prove his case.

6. Nixon, *Conservation,* vol. 1, pp. 201–2.

7. *PPA, 1934.* pp. 366–67.

8. The fourteen-page speech draft, of which three pages are in Roosevelt's hand and the rest typewritten, is in the Franklin D. Roosevelt Library at Hyde Park. An extended excerpt from it is in Nixon, *Conservation,* pp. 17–19.

9. Brink, *op. cit.,* pp. 82–83. The direct quotes from Bennett are here, though Brink, whose book is neither indexed nor footnoted, doesn't say where he got them. His book was read by Bennett in manuscript.

10. *Ibid.,* p. 89.

11. Nixon, *Conservation,* pp. 363, 364.

12. Ickes, *Secret Diary,* pp. 326, 339.

13. *Ibid.,* pp. 343–44.

14. Brink, *op. cit.,* pp. 6–7.

15. *Ibid.,* pp. 95–97. With the Coon Valley project during these years I was personally intimately acquainted, being information officer, in 1936 and 1937 for the U.S. Soil Conservation Service regional office for Wisconsin-Minnesota, in La Crosse, Wisconsin.

16. Quoted by Kenneth S. Davis, *River on the Rampage,* (New York, 1953), footnote, p. 163. The Dern letter is excerpted at length in Arthur Maass, *Muddy Waters, the Army Engineers and the Nation's Rivers.* (Cambridge, 1951).

17. *PPA, 1934,* p. 371.

18. Elliott Roosevelt, ed., *F.D.R., His Personal Letters, 1928–1945,* (hereafter *PL, 1928–1945),* p. 394.

19. *PPA, 1934,* pp. 371–74.

20. Lash, *Love, Eleanor,* p. 199, quoting Eleanor Roosevelt letter to Lorena Hickok, written from Chicago.

21. Moley, *Seven Years,* quotes (p. 292) with approval these words he'd written, to bolster his argument (against contrary evidence) that FDR yet remained in a mood to conciliate the business community in August 1934.

22. Schlesinger, *op. cit.,* p. 486.

23. Alpheus T. Mason, *Harlan Fiske Stone: Pillar of the Law,* (New York, 1956), p. 433, quotes this memorandum, of which he must have obtained a copy, for he cites no source. Captain W. H. Stayton of the Baltimore Steamship Company had been, with John J. Raskob, Pierre S. du Pont, Jouett Shouse, and other big businessmen, a founder in the 1920s of the American Association Against the Prohibition Amendment, which had a double motive or purpose: (1) to reduce corporate and income taxes by substituting for them taxes on legalized alcoholic beverages; (2) to keep focused upon the "safe" Prohibition issue popular attention that might otherwise be focused on social and economic matters.

24. White editorial in Emporia (Kansas) *Gazette,* August 15, 1934, quoted by Walter Johnson, *William Allen White's America,* (New York, 1947), p. 444.

25. Herbert Hoover, *Memoirs: The Great Depression, 1929–1941,* (New York, 1952), pp. 454–55.

26. Williams, *op. cit.,* p. 692, says the Share Our Wealth program "was completely" Long's "own creation, the idea coming to him, according to one account, at three o'clock one morning in his rooms at the Mayflower Hotel." Long's plan was not "Socialistic" in his own conception or in fact. He did not advocate government ownership of wealth, "which was equivalent to destruction of wealth," and he would retain the profit motive. His sole aim was to obtain an equitable distribution of wealth, preventing its piling up in dangerous concentrations.

27. Leon Harris, *Upton Sinclair, American Rebel* (New York, 1965), pp. 297–98.

28. *Ibid.,* pp. 299–300. Upton Sinclair, *I, Governor of California and How I Ended Poverty* (Los Angeles, 1933).

29. Harris, *op. cit.,* p. 303.

30. Blum, *Roosevelt and Morgenthau,* p. 110. Ickes, *Secret Diary,* p. 174.

31. Blum, *Roosevelt and Morgenthau,* p. 111.

32. Davis, *Invincible Summer,* pp. 130–31.

33. Harris, *op. cit.,* p. 303. New York *Times,* September 5, 1934. Upton Sinclair, *I, Candidate for Governor—and How I Got Licked.* (Pasadena, 1935). Sinclair said in his New York *Times* quotes, and in his book, that FDR had told him that his (Roosevelt's) mother had "read *The Jungle* aloud to him at the breakfast table" when he "was young." In 1906, when *The Jungle* was published, Roosevelt was twenty-four years old, married, the father of a child, and enrolled as a law

student at Columbia. Harris, *op. cit.*, pp. 303–4, wonders if Sara Roosevelt might not have read Rudyard Kipling's *Jungle Books* to Franklin as a child, a memory of which led him to confuse Kipling's Mowgli stories with the very different *Jungle* of Sinclair. Schlesinger, *op. cit.*, p. 116.

34. Josephus Daniels to FDR, September 17, 1934, quoted in Schlesinger, *op. cit.*, p. 394.

35. New York *Times,* September 16, 1934.

36. New York *Times,* September 15, 1934. Bellush, *op. cit.*, pp. 132–33.

37. Freedman, *op. cit.*, pp. 236–37.

38. *Ibid.*, p. 237.

39. Ickes, *Secret Diary,* pp. 198–99.

40. The letter from FDR to Hugh Johnson, August 20, 1934, is printed in *PL, 1928–1945,* p. 412.

41. Berle and Jacobs, *op. cit.*, pp. 102–3.

42. The Hutchins story is most fully told in Ickes, *Secret Diary,* pp. 198, 200–201, 208–11, 219–20, 236. *PPA, 1934,* pp. 405–7.

43. *PPA, 1934,* pp. 417–19.

44. Schlesinger, *op. cit.*, pp. 505–6, quoting, *Proceedings,* National Emergency Council, August 21, 1934.

45. *Ibid.*, pp. 501–2. Moley, *Seven Years,* pp. 293–95.

46. Ickes, *Secret Diary,* pp. 195–96.

47. Moley, *Seven Years,* pp. 295–98.

48. *PPA, 1934,* pp. 436–37.

49. Moley, *Seven Years,* p. 298.

50. Ickes, *Secret Diary,* p. 217.

51. *Ibid.*, p. 217.

52. Schlesinger, *op. cit.*, p. 507, citing quotes in New York *Times,* November 7, 11, 1934, and *Time* magazine (November 19, 1934).

53. Garner to FDR, November 8, 1934. On November 13, 1934, FDR wrote Garner: "I am very anxious to talk with you about our plans—not only the general line of policy, but also the handling of the general situation in the House and Senate." *PL, 1928–1945*, p. 430.

54. Frances Perkins, *op. cit.*, p. 124. Arthur Schlesinger, Jr., *The Politics of Upheaval*, (Boston, 1960), p. 117. Moley, *Seven Years*, p. 299.

55. Moley, *Seven Years*, p. 299. Schlesinger, *Upheaval*, p. 120. *PL, 1928–1945*, p. 426.

56. Schlesinger, *Upheaval*, p. 120.

57. *Ibid.* Ickes, *Secret Diary*, p. 217.

58. Harris, *op. cit.*, p. 314.

59. Wattenberg, op. cit., pp. 135, 224. Frederick Lewis Allen, *Since Yesterday, 1929–1939* (New York, 1940), p. 149, *PPA, 1934*, p. 491.

60. Lilienthal, *Journals*, p. 43. *PPA, 1934*, pp. 459–60. *PL, 1928–1945*, p. 433.

61. *PPA, 1934*, pp. 485, 486, 488, 489.

62. Ickes, *Secret Diary*, pp. 230–34, 236. *PPA, 1934*, pp. 479–84. William E. Leuchtenburg, *Franklin D. Roosevelt and the New Deal*, p. 135.

63. *PPA, 1934*, pp. 466–71, 473–75.

64. Ickes, *Secret Diary*, pp. 203, 239, 240.

65. Sherwood, *op. cit.*, p. 65.

66. *Ibid.*

67. Readers of Burns, *op. cit.*, will recognize my debt to his description of "broker government" in Chapter 10 of his fine book. Burns, in turn, acknowledges his debt to Max Lerner's "The Broker State," one of the essays in Lerner's *Ideas for the Ice Age*, and to Pendleton Hering, *The Politics of Democracy* (New York, 1940) in which, as Burns writes, Hering "favors the ambiguous, non-doctrinaire quality of American politics." The latter value judgment is also made by, among others, Daniel J. Boorstin in his three-volume *The Americans*. (New York, 1958, 1965, 1973). I myself am unable to share the enthusiasm these writers seem to have for muddle headedness as the stuff and guarantee of individual freedom— for "ideas" that are little more than physical reactions to physical stimuli. Surely one can deplore and reject tendencies toward straitjacketing ideology without making a virtue of the incapacity or unwillingness to think clearly. Ideology and ambiguity are alike failures of mind, and out of both comes a loss of freedom, in my opinion.

68. Moley, *Seven Years,* p. 300.

69. Ickes, *Secret Diary,* pp. 244–45.

Eleven. Concerning Social Security: The First Faltering Steps Toward a Welfare State

NOTE: Though not cited for specific items, Edwin E. Witte, *The Development of the Social Security Act* (Madison, Wis., 1962) was much used as a reference work for this chapter. I am also indebted to Wilbur J. Cohen, secretary of Health, Education and Welfare during the Johnson administration, currently professor of Public Affairs at the LBJ School of Public Affairs, University of Texas, for interviews and correspondence which did much to educate me in the history of social security and, indeed, of the New Deal. He, as a young man just graduated from the University of Wisconsin (he was one of Alexander Meiklejohn's students in the university's short-lived but highly influential Experimental College), played a very active role in the launching of social security and, in his conversation and writings, conveys the *feel,* the excitement, of those years in Washington.

1. Biographical data on Rubinow is from Roy Lubove, *The Struggle for Social Security, 1900–1935,* (Cambridge, Mass., 1968) pp. 34–44. Also in David Hackett Fischer, *Growing Old in America,* (New York, 1930), p. 172.

2. Frank E. Hering, "Awakening Interest in Old Age Protection," *American Labor Legislation Review,* vol. 13 (June 1923), p. 143.

3. Lubove, *op. cit.,* p. 114. Wattenberg, *op. cit.*

4. Frank E. Hering, "We Are on the Firing Line," *Eagle Magazine,* March, 1923, pp. 26–27, quoted by Lubove, *op. cit.,* p. 141.

5. Lubove, *op. cit.,* p. 130 ff., gives biography of Epstein. Also Fischer, *op. cit.,* p. 173.

6. John R. Commons, "The Groves Unemployment Reserves Law," *American Labor Legislation Review,* 20 (December 1930), pp. 21–23, quoted by Lubove, *op. cit.,* p. 170.

7. Ohio Chamber of Commerce, *Critical Analysis of the Report of the Ohio Commission on Unemployment Insurance* (Columbus, 1932), pp. 5, 6, 24.

8. Paul A. Raushenbush and Elizabeth Raushenbush, *Our "U.C." Story,* pp. 176–78. Privately published by its authors in Madison, Wisconsin, this work consists for the most part of transcriptions of interviews the authors conducted for COHC. Murphy, *op. cit.,* pp. 166–67.

9. Paul H. Douglas, *Social Security in the United States,* (New York; Da Capo Press [reprint], 1971) pp. 21–23, gives story of *Florida* v. *Mellon* as basis for Brandeis proposal.

10. *PPA, 1934,* pp. 288, 292, 321–22.

11. Freedman, *op. cit.,* pp. 224, 225–26. The letter is signed "Tom, Ben," but Corcoran is obviously its author.

12. Douglas, *op. cit.,* pp. 48–49.

13. Frances Perkins, *op. cit.,* p. 292.

14. Schlesinger, *Coming of the New Deal,* p. 314. In a letter to me dated July 12, 1979, Paul A. Raushenbush and Elizabeth B. Raushenbush brand this interpretation as "nonsense" but don't say how or why it is. I am very grateful for their helpful critical review of this chapter in manuscript.

15. *PPA, 1934,* p. 454.

16. J. Douglas Brown, *An American Philosophy of Social Security* (Princeton, 1972), p. 8.

17. *Ibid.,* p. 13.

18. *Ibid.,* p. 17.

19. *PPA, 1934,* p. 454.

20. Brown, *op. cit.,* pp. 16–17. New York *Times* (Louis Stark by-line), November 15, 1934.

21. New York *Times* (Louis Stark by-line), November 16, 1934.

22. Frances Perkins, *op. cit.,* p. 292.

23. FDR press conference, April 17, 1937.

24. Frances Perkins, *op. cit.,* p. 294.

25. Brown, *op. cit.,* pp. 18–19. Schlesinger, *Coming of the New Deal,* pp. 309–10.

26. Abraham Epstein, "Financing Social Security," *Annals of the American Academy of Political and Social Science,* 183 (January 1936), pp. 212–16.

27. Brown, *op. cit.,* p. 21.

28. Frances Perkins, *op. cit.,* pp. 297–98.

29. *Ibid.,* p. 282.

30. *Ibid.,* p. 294.

31. "Defeat the Wagner-Lewis Bill," editorial, *Nation,* 140 (April 17, 1935), p. 433.

32. Douglas, *op. cit.,* pp. 100–101, 110–11.

33. Maxwell S. Stewart, "Congress Discovers the Class Struggle," *Nation,* 140 (February 27, 1935), pp. 247–49. Schlesinger, *Coming of the New Deal,* pp. 295–96.

Twelve. Work Relief and Its Dubiously Legitimate Offspring

1. "I thot [*sic*] it was a good speech and particularly because I had worked on it with him . . ." noted Harry Hopkins in his very intermittently kept diary, on January 4, 1935. Hopkins Papers, Box 6, Franklin D. Roosevelt Library. Adams, *op. cit.,* pp. 72, 73. Ickes, *Secret Diary,* p. 293.

2. *Public Papers and Addresses of Franklin D. Roosevelt, 1935* (hereafter *PPA, 1935*), pp. 20, 21. Ickes, *Secret Diary,* pp. 264–65.

3. *PPA, 1935,* pp. 21–23. On May 18, 1936, ruling on a suit brought against Rex Tugwell as resettlement administrator, the Court of Appeals for the District of Columbia decided that the whole of the Emergency Relief Act of 1935 was unconstitutional because of its failure to specify the programs to be funded by moneys appropriated under the act. It was, said the court, "delegation running riot"—this in reference to the huge grant of legislative authority which the act gave to the President. Attorney General Cummings ruled that the decision applied only to the specific case in which it was made and so avoided a Supreme Court test of this act.

4. New York *Times,* February 5, 1935.

5. Williams, *op. cit.,* p. 812.

6. Sherwood, *op. cit.,* p. 67.

7. *Ibid.,* p. 68.

8. Rollins, *op. cit.,* p. 442–43. Lela Stiles, *The Man Behind Roosevelt: The Story of Louis McHenry Howe,* p. 279. Ickes, *Secret Diary,* pp. 329–30.

9. *PPA, 1935,* p. 118.

10. Ickes, *Secret Diary,* pp. 337, 340–41.

11. *PPA, 1935,* pp. 126–29.

12. Sherwood, *op. cit.,* p. 69.

13. *PPA, 1935,* p. 143.

14. Sidney Baldwin, *Poverty and Politics* (Chapel Hill, N.C., 1968), p. 93, quoting letter from Tugwell to Lewis C. Gray, Nov. 14, 1935.

15. Tugwell, "Notes from a New Deal Diary," Sternsher, *op. cit.,* p. 225.

16. Sternsher, *op. cit.,* p. 225.

17. *Ibid.,* p. 226, quoting S.1944, introduced June 6, 1933.

18. *Ibid.,* pp. 231–32. Schlesinger, *Coming of the New Deal*, pp. 357–58.

19. Tugwell to FDR, February 21, 1934. Quoted by Schlesinger, *Coming of the New Deal,* p. 358.

20. Sternsher, *op. cit.,* p. 243, quoting Tugwell, "The Preparation of a President," *Western Political Quarterly* (June 1948), p. 152.

21. Clarence Poe, editorial in *Progressive Farmer,* (August, 1934), p. 26.

22. Kate Louchheim, ed., *The Making of the New Deal,* (Cambridge, 1983), p. 237, which begins Alger Hiss's contribution to the anthology, discussing his experience of the AAA.

23. U.S. Department of Agriculture, *Technology on the Farm; Report of Interbureau Committee, 1940,* pp. 9–11. U.S. Department of Agriculture, *The Farm Security Administration,* 1940, pp. 5–6. Mitchell, *op. cit.,* pp. 220–21.

24. Poe, *op. cit.,* p. 26.

25. Norman Thomas interview transcript, COHC.

26. *Ibid.*

27. Schlesinger, *Coming of the New Deal,* p. 78.

28. Lord, *The Wallaces of Iowa,* (Boston 1947) pp. 303–09. Baldwin, *op. cit.,* pp. 81–2. Sternsher, *op. cit.,* p. 204.

29. Frank transcript, COHC. Writes Alger Hiss in Louchheim, *op. cit.,* p. 239: "Those of us in charge of cotton contracts felt we were representing Secretary Wallace's view" when they made their Section 7 interpretation order. He adds: "We felt that Wallace had backed down on his own principles. It was a terrible shock to Jerome, who was very close to Wallace."

30. *Time* magazine, (February 18, 1935). Sternsher, *op. cit.,* p. 204. Baldwin, *op. cit.,* p. 82.

31. Thomas transcript, COHC.

32. Frank transcript, COHC. Schlesinger, *Coming of the New Deal,* p. 80. Baldwin, p. 83. Ickes, *Secret Diary,* pp. 302–3.

33. Baldwin, *op. cit.,* p. 80. Thomas transcript, COHC. Harry L. Mitchell transcript, COHC. Schlesinger, *Coming of the New Deal,* p. 377.

34. Thomas transcript, COHC. Schlesinger, *Coming of the New Deal,* pp. 377–78.

35. Thomas transcript, COHC. Lash, *Eleanor and Franklin,* pp. 515–16. Walter White, *A Man Called White,* (New York, 1948), pp. 179–80. Frank Freidel, *F.D.R. and the South,* pp. 82–86.

36. *PPA, 1935,* pp. 110–11.

37. Rexford G. Tugwell, Thomas Munro, and Roy E. Stryker, *American Economic Life and the Means of its Improvement* (New York, 1930), pp. 85–90, quoted by Baldwin, *op. cit.,* p. 88.

38. Sternsher, *op. cit.,* p. 242, quoting syndicated Tugwell columns.

39. *PPA, 1935,* p. 154. Baldwin, *op. cit.,* p. 112.

40. Baldwin, *op. cit.,* pp. 117–18. Stryker, head of Resettlement Administration photography, had collaborated with Tugwell in the authorship of the 1930 book cited in note 37, above.

41. Baldwin, *op. cit.,* p. 118. Alfred Kazin, *On Native Grounds* (New York, 1942), pp. 493–95. MacLeish said of his *Land of the Free* (Boston, 1938), that it was "the opposite of a book of poems illustrated by photographs. It is a book of photographs illustrated by a poem. . . . The original purpose had been to write some sort of text to which these photographs might serve as commentary. But so great was the power and the stubborn living inwardness of these vivid American documents that the result was the reversal of the plan." Wrote Agee in *Let Us Now Praise Famous Men:* "[E]verything is to be discerned [by the camera], for him who can discern it, and centrally and simply, without either dissection into science, or disgression into art . . . all of consciousness is shifted from the imagined, the revisive, to the effort to perceive simply the cruel radiance of what is." I have no clear notion what this means (it's the kind of boozy rhetoric which Faulkner indulges in, say, *Absalom, Absalom!* and, as such, has been much praised in Agee by numerous academic critics); I suppose it means what Margaret Bourke-White said when she spoke of the perfect simplicity and direct objectivity of the camera's vision. "Whatever facts a person writes have to be colored by his prejudice and bias," she once wrote. "With a camera the shutter opens and closes and the only rays that come in to be registered come directly from the object in front of you."

42. Baldwin, *op. cit.,* p. 108.

43. *Ibid.,* p. 122.

44. *PPA, 1935,* p. 172.

45. Schlesinger, *Coming of the New Deal,* pp. 383–84.

Thirteen. Decision, at Last!

1. Forrest Davis, *Huey Long,* (New York, 1935), p. 125. Schlesinger, *Upheaval,* p. 66. Williams, *op. cit.,* p. 759.

2. Williams, *op. cit.,* p. 794. New York *Times,* January 10, 1935.

3. Brinkley, *op. cit.,* pp. 135–37. *PL, 1928–1935,* pp. 449–50, 451. Williams, *op. cit.,* p. 800.

4. Williams, *op. cit.,* pp. 803–7. Ickes, *Secret Diary* pp. 294–98. Farley, *op. cit.,* pp. 244–48.

5. Hugh S. Johnson, "The Pied Pipers," *Vital Speeches,* March 11, 1935. New York *Times,* March 5, 6, 1935. Schlesinger, *Upheaval,* pp. 244–46. Williams, *op. cit.,* pp. 808–9, 813.

6. New York *Times,* March 7, 1935. Robert A. Caro, *The Power Broker: Robert Moses and the Fall of New York* (New York, 1974), p. 437.

7. Edward J. Flynn, *You're the Boss,* p. 136. Berle and Jacobs, *op. cit.,* pp. 88–89.

8. Ickes, *Secret Diary,* pp. 148–49, 229.

9. Berle and Jacobs, *op. cit.,* pp. 92–93.

10. Ickes, *Secret Diary,* p. 229.

11. Caro, *op. cit.,* pp. 430–31. Ickes, *Secret Diary,* pp. 307–8.

12. Caro, pp. 439–40. Ickes, pp. 267–69, 317.

13. Williams, *op. cit.,* pp. 810–11. Schlesinger, *Upheaval,* pp. 247–48.

14. Williams, *op. cit.,* pp. 815–16.

15. Ickes, *Secret Diary,* p. 346. Williams, *op. cit.,* p. 813.

16. Williams, *op. cit.,* p. 817. New York *Herald Tribune,* April 28, 1935.

17. Ickes, *Secret Diary,* p. 360.

18. *PPA, 1935,* pp. 162–63.

19. What Hughes actually said, in an extemporaneous speech on May 7, 1907, when he was governor of New York, was that "we are under a Constitution, but the Constitution is what the judges say it is, and the judiciary is the safeguard of our liberty and our property." He essentially repeated this idea in a formal address, September 5, 1908, saying: "The Constitution, with its guarantees of liberty and grants of Federal power, is finally what the Supreme Court determines it to mean." According to Samuel Hendel, *Charles Evans Hughes and the Supreme Court*, (New York, 1951), p. 12, Hughes was not disparaging or deploring the power of judicial review but simply being "realistic" about it, the plain fact being "that constitutional interpretation depended, in the final analysis, not upon some inexorable mandate of the Constitution as law, but upon the qualities of judges as men." In a campaign speech on behalf of presidential candidate William Howard Taft in 1912, Hughes's appeal for votes was grounded on the probability, as he put it, "that the next President will appoint at least four judges of the Supreme Court," adding: "Upon the learning, wisdom, and character of the judges rests . . . to a very large degree the course of our political history and the development and security of our institutions."

20. Chief Justice Hughes dissented from the majority ruling in the Railroad Retirement Act case, saying: "The gravest aspect of the decision is that it does not rest simply upon a condemnation of particular features of the . . . Act, but denies to Congress the power to pass any compulsory pension act for railroad employees." See Percival E. Jackson, *Dissent in the Supreme Court*, (Norman, Oklahoma, 1969), p. 182. See also *PPA, 1935*, pp. 7–9.

21. Freedman, *op. cit.*, pp. 260–62. According to Murphy, *op. cit.*, pp. 153–54, "the message in this letter and its careful timing had hardly been chance occurrences. Niles was an old Frankfurter ally who was accustomed to doing favors for the professor. . . . Niles occasionally acted as a spokesman for Frankfurter's (and hence Brandeis's) political views. Niles would send his political commentary to Frankfurter, and when the professor was impressed with the latter's message, but not completely satisfied with its style, he would attach his own comments and return it to Niles for redrafting. Once completed, Niles would send the rewritten letter back to the professor, who would then forward it to Roosevelt."

22. Freedman, *op. cit.*, pp. 269–70.

23. New York *Times*, May 7, 1935; Schlesinger, *Upheaval*, p. 141.

24. Ickes, *Secret Diary*, pp. 358–59.

25. *Ibid.*, p. 364.

26. *Ibid.*, p. 363.

27. Freedman, *op. cit.*, p. 271.

28. *Ibid.*

29. William James in his *Principles of Psychology* (pp. 531–33 of v. II of the original edition, issued by Henry Holt and Company in 1890) describes "Five Types of Decision." Of these, a compound of the second and third types seems descriptive of the kind of decision making in which Franklin Roosevelt here engaged. Writes James: "In the *second type* of case our feeling is to a certain extent that of letting ourselves drift with a certain indifferent acquiescence in a direction accidentally determined *from without*, with the conviction that, after all, we might as well stand by this course as by the other, and that things are in any event sure to turn out sufficiently right. *In the third type* the determination seems equally accidental, but it comes from within, and not from without. It often happens, when the absence of imperative principle is perplexing and suspense distracting, that we find ourselves acting, as it were, automatically, and as if by spontaneous discharge of our nerves, in the direction of one of the horns of the dilemma. But so exciting is this sense of motion after our intolerable pent-up state, that we eagerly throw ourselves into it. 'Forward now!' we inwardly cry, 'though the heavens fall.' This reckless and exultant espousal of an energy so little premeditated by us that we feel rather like passive spectators cheering on the display of some extraneous force than like voluntary agents, is a type of decision too abrupt and tumultuous to occur often in humdrum and cold-blooded natures. But it is probably frequent in persons of strong emotional endowment and unstable or vacillating character. And in men of the world-shaking type, the Napoleons, Luthers, etc., in whom tenacious passion combines with ebullient activity, when by any chance the passion's outlet has been damned by scruples or apprehensions, the resolution is probably often of this catastrophic kind. The flood breaks quite unexpectedly through the dam. That it should so often do so is quite sufficient for the tendency of these characters to a fatalistic mood of mind. And the fatalistic mood itself is sure to reinforce the strength of the energy just started on its exciting path of discharge."

30. Morgenthau diary entry for May 20, 1935. Commented Morgenthau: "This is the most frank expression of the real F.D.R. that I ever listened to and that is the real way he works—but thank God I understand him." Quoted by Blum, *Roosevelt and Morgenthau,* p. 127.

31. *Time,* May 27, 1935. Schlesinger, *Upheaval,* p. 290. James T. Patterson, *Congressional Conservatism and the New Deal* (Lexington, Ky., 1967), p. 36, quotes a letter from Senator Charles L. McNary to John H. McNary, February 26, 1935, saying, "The President has lost considerable of his influence with his party and has developed a rather childish peevishness which should not be a part of the big fellow. . . ."

32. Jackson, *op. cit.,* p. 183. Drew Pearson and Robert S. Allen, *The Nine Old Men* (New York, 1937), pp. 270–71.

33. Mason, *op. cit.,* p. 397. Schlesinger, *Upheaval,* p. 282.

34. Murphy, *op. cit.,* p. 144. In his note for the quotation I use, Murphy says it is from a letter by Brandeis to Frankfurter, August 31, 1934, but this is plainly an error. It was, as his text says, Frankfurter to Brandeis.

35. *PPA, 1935*, p. 200. Moley, *Seven Years*, p. 306. Moley writes: "I, over the telephone, took the position that I didn't see how an effective measure to achieve the permanent objectives of the N.I.R.A. could be constructed in the light of the Court's obiter dicta on the interstate-commerce clause. I argued for a constitutional amendment, enlarging Congress' powers to regulate industry. Frankfurter strongly opposed my idea of a constitutional amendment." But the letter I quote, from Freedman, *op. cit.*, p. 272, clearly indicates that what Frankfurter opposed was not the idea of a constitutional amendment but Moley's proposal to press for such an amendment *now*.

36. *PPA, 1935*, pp. 200–22

37. *Ibid.*, p. 221.

Fourteen. Breakthrough: The First New Deal Gives Way to the Second

1. Walter Lippman to Hamilton Fish Armstrong, June 25, 1935, quoted by Steel, *op. cit.*, p. 312.

2. Leuchtenburg, *op. cit.*, p. 132.

3. Huthmacher, *op. cit.*, p. 191.

4. Francis Biddle, In Brief Authority (New York, 1962), quotes Heywood Broun, p. 38. His comments on Roosevelt's letter to him are on p. 36. He gives a brief history of the Jennings case, pp. 31–38. Writes Biddle of Donald Richberg: "I doubt whether Donald Richberg had any [convictions]. Like a number of Americans who seem at a certain age to lose the direction of their lives and make a complete circle from left to right, he changed, when ambition touched him, from a supporter of liberal labor policies to an instrument to prevent their success. I could not trust him, and I do not think his influence upon the President was Healthy. But it was brief." Arthur Schlesinger, Jr., deals with the Jennings case on pp. 399–400 of his *Coming of the New Deal.*

5. FDR press conference transcript, May 15, 1935. Huthmacher, *op. cit.*, p. 197.

6. Huthmacher, *op. cit.*, pp. 194–95.

7. *PPA, 1934*, pp. 339–40. In his note to this item Roosevelt says the letter "was prepared before my departure on my trip to the outlying parts of the United States [his *Houston* cruise]; but was not signed until July 9, 1934." Hawley, *op. cit.*, pp. 330–32.

8. Hawley, *op. cit.*, p. 331.

9. *PPA, 1935*, pp. 98–101.

10. Burton K. Wheeler, "My Years with Roosevelt," ed. Rita James Simon, *As We Saw the Thirties* (Urbana Ill., 1969). p. 197. Patterson, *op. cit.*, pp. 39–40.

11. Patterson, *op. cit.*, p. 52–53.

12. New York *Times*, July 3, 1935.

13. Dunne, *op. cit.*, p. 157.

14. Marriner Eccles, *Beckoning Frontiers* (New York, 1951), pp. 114–15. Sternsher *op. cit.*, p. 75. Schlesinger, *Upheaval*, pp. 237–40. Tugwell, *Democratic Roosevelt*, pp. 374–75.

15. New York *Times*, Feb. 9, 1935. Mitchell, *op. cit.*, p. 168.

16. Schlesinger, *Politics of Upheaval*, p. 297.

17. *Ibid.*, p. 299 and quotes Morgenthau diary.

18. Milton Friedman and Anna Jacobson Schwarz, *A Monetary History of the United States, 1857–1961,* (Princeton, 1963), pp. 447–49. Hawley, *op. cit.*, pp. 346–47.

19. FDR press conference transcript, June 7, 1935.

20. *PPA, 1935,* p. 36. Hawley, *op. cit.*, pp. 344–45.

21. Moley, *Seven Years,* p. 308.

22. *PPA, 1935,* p. 191.

23. E. D. Coblentz, *William Randolph Hearst* (New York, 1952), p. 178. According to Schlesinger, *Upheaval,* p. 333, Roosevelt in a press conference gave the figure 58 as the number of persons in the United States with annual incomes in excess of $1 million.

24. Moley, *Seven Years,* pp. 312, 310. "Do let Pat Harrison have his kittens," wired Frankfurter from Cambridge to the White House, June 10, 1935. "He will find them as did Baron Munschausen [*sic*] the lions in his path stuffed and harmless while our people will find through you new hope for the traditional Democratic promise of American life by curbing excessive concentration of plutocratic power." See p. 276, Freedman, *op. cit.*

25. *PPA, 1935,* pp. 271–72, Ickes, *Secret Diary,* pp. 383–84.

26. Freedman, *op. cit.*, p. 280.

27. Williams, *op. cit.*, p. 836. Long quoted the Will Rogers column in his Senate speech of June 22, 1935.

28. Schlesinger, *Upheaval,* p. 329.

29. Patterson, *op. cit.*, pp. 66–67, citing Washington *Post,* June 28, 1935.

30. Leuchtenburg, *op. cit.*, p. 154.

31. *PPA, 1935*, pp. 297–98.

32. *Ibid.*, p. 298.

33. Schlesinger, *Upheaval*, p. 336.

34. Wiltz, *op. cit.*, p. 17. I have leaned very heavily upon Wiltz's book in my account of the Nye committee investigation and the legislation stemming from it; the book was exhaustively researched and is written with admirable clarity and precision. I disagree, however, with certain of the author's judgments on what should have been done and what was politically possible at that time—a disagreement rooted in my personal experience of the "peace movement" in the 1930s. As a Kansas State undergraduate I organized an anti-ROTC, anti-compulsory-military-training campaign on that campus and was, of course, deeply immersed in the pacifist mood and literature of the period.

35. Quoted by Wiltz, *op. cit.*, p. 15.

36. *Ibid.*, p. 15.

37. "Arms and the Men," *Fortune* (March 1934).

38. Helmuth C. Engelbrecht and Frank C. Hanighen, *Merchants of Death* (New York, 1934), p. 9.

39. Wiltz, *op. cit.*, pp. 119–20. New York *Times*, December 13, 1934.

40. Wiltz, *op. cit.*, p. 131.

41. *Ibid.*, p. 120, quoting "War Profits," *Business Week* (December 22, 1934), p. 22.

42. Wiltz, *op. cit.*, p. 121. New York *Times*, December 27, 1934.

43. Wiltz, *op. cit.*, pp. 122–23.

44. Dallek, *op. cit.*, pp. 102–3. Morgenthau diary entry for March 16, 1935.

45. Wiltz, *op. cit.*, p. 175.

46. Dallek, *op. cit.*, p. 101.

47. Wiltz, *op. cit.*, pp. 139–40.

48. *Ibid.*, pp. 95–96, 97.

49. *PPA, 1935*, pp. 345–46.

50. Williams, *op. cit.*, p. 843.

51. Blum, *From the Morgenthau Diaries*, p. 257.

Book Four: The Man Becomes the Issue

Fifteen. Into 1936, Under Gathering Clouds of War

1. Ickes, *Secret Diary* pp. 424–25. I deem it unlikely that Ickes failed to learn of the news story until late afternoon, and quite likely that he himself leaked the letter through his good friend James W. Fawcett, the Washington *Star*'s chief editorial writer.

2. *Ibid.*, pp. 429–31. White and Maze, *op. cit.*, pp. 134, 141, 142. The daughter of a wealthy Chicago family, Anna Wilmarth, born in 1897, married James Westfall Thompson, a distinguished historian, in 1897 and was divorced from him in 1909, two years before her marriage to Ickes. Her three terms in the Illinois state legislature were from 1928 to 1934. In 1933, her book *Mesa Land*, dealing with the life and problems of the Pueblo Indians of New Mexico, was published.

3. Moley, *Seven Years*, p. 318.

4. *PPA, 1935*, pp. 352–53.

5. Moley, *Seven Years*, p. 318.

6. *PPA, 1935*, pp. 354–57.

7. Moley, *Seven Years*, p. 318.

8. *American Year Book, 1935*, pp. 354–55.

9. *PPA, 1935*, p. 358. Williams, *op. cit.*, pp. 873–76. A. J. Liebling, *The Earl of Louisiana*, p. 14.

10. Sheldon Marcus, *Father Coughlin*, (Boston, 1973), pp. 98–99, based on Marcus's interview of Coughlin, April 11, 1970. Beschloss, *op. cit.*, p. 118.

11. Marcus, *op. cit.*, p. 85. Benjamin Stolberg, "Dr. Huey and Mr. Long," *Nation* (September 25, 1935).

12. Marcus, *op. cit.*, pp. 99–100. Beschloss, *op. cit.*, p. 119.

13. Ickes, *Secret Diary*, pp. 435–38. Sherwood, *op. cit.*, pp. 78–79.

14. Moley, *Seven Years*, p. 318.

15. Steel, *op. cit.*, pp. 316–17.

16. *PPA, 1935,* pp. 381–83.

17. *Ibid.,* pp. 397–99.

18. *Ibid.,* p. 404.

19. *Ibid.,* pp. 405, 410–12.

20. Ickes, *Secret Diary,* pp. 446–51. *PPA, 1935,* pp. 412–18. In a letter to W. Russell Bowie, October 30, 1935, Roosevelt spoke of the "difficulty . . . that under ordinary and normal circumstances wheat, cotton and copper ingots are not implements of war. The letter of the law does not say so and the trouble is that the spirit of the law, as shown by the debates during its passage, does not allow me to stretch it that far out—no matter how worthy the cause." See p. 514, *PL, 1928–1945.*

21. Ickes, *Secret Diary,* pp. 451–60, 589–94. Nixon, *Foreign Policy,* Vol. III., pp. 14–15. Dallek, *op. cit.,* p. 113. *PL, 1928–1945,* pp. 512–13. *PPA, 1935,* pp. 424–25.

22. *PPA, 1935,* p. 440.

23. Dallek, *op. cit.,* p. 115.

24. James Farley, *Jim Farley's Story,* pp. 55–56.

25. Dallek, *op. cit.,* p. 115.

26. Churchill, *op. cit.,* p. 177.

27. Dallek, *op. cit.,* p. 115.

28. Moley, *Seven Years,* pp. 326–29.

29. Ickes, *Secret Diary,* pp. 479, 494.

30. *PL, 1928–1945,* p. 536.

31. *Public Papers and Addresses of Franklin D. Roosevelt, 1936* (hereafter *PPA, 1936*), pp. 9, 11–12.

32. Cole, *op. cit.,* pp. 184–85.

33. *Ibid.,* p. 185, quoting Pittman letter.

34. *PPA, 1936,* p. 90.

35. William L. Shirer, *Berlin Diary,* pp. 53–54.

36. Paul Schmidt, *Hitler's Interpreter*, (New York, 1951), p. 211, cited by Shirer, *The Rise and Fall of the Third Reich*, p. 293.

37. Churchill, *op. cit.*, p. 194. Frederick L. Schuman, *International Politics* (New York, 1937), p. 680.

38. Dallek, *op. cit.*, p. 127.

Sixteen. A Rendezvous with Destiny

1. Rollins, *op. cit.*, pp. 444–45. Lash, *Love, Eleanor*, p. 227.

2. Rollins, *op. cit.*, p. 445

3. *PL, 1928–1945*, p. 534.

4. Stiles, *op. cit.*, p. 293, quoting Howe letter to Roosevelt.

5. Lash, *Love, Eleanor*, p. 236.

6. John Keller and Joseph Boldt: "Franklin's on His Own Now—The Last Days of Louis McHenry Howe," *Saturday Evening Post* (October 12, 1940), p. 47.

7. Ickes, *Secret Diary*, pp. 551–52.

8. Lash, *Love, Eleanor*, p. 236.

9. *Ibid. PL, 1928–1945*, p. 587.

10. Eleanor Roosevelt, *This I Remember*, p. 145.

11. Moley, *Seven Years*, pp. 330–31.

12. George Creel, *Rebel in Politics*, p. 291.

13. *PPA, 1936*, pp. 12–17.

14. Quoted by Moley, *Seven Years*, in footnote, p. 331.

15. *PPA, 1936*, p. 42.

16. New York *Times*, January 26, 1936. Matthew and Hannah Josephson, *Al Smith: Hero of the Cities* (pp. 457–59.) Schlesinger, *Politics of Upheaval*, p. 519.

17. Pearson and Allen, *op. cit.*, pp. 139–40, 277–78. Beard and Beard, *op. cit.*, pp. 270–71.

18. Thomas Reed Powell, "The Supreme Court and Constitutional Law," *American Year Book, 1936,* pp. 38–43. Louis H. Pollak, ed., *The Constitution and the Supreme Court,* pp. 334–35. Schlesinger, *Upheaval,* pp. 471–74.

19. Powell, *op. cit.,* pp. 47–51.

20. *Ibid.,* pp. 44–46. Schlesinger, *Upheaval,* pp. 476–77.

21. Powell, *op. cit.,* p. 47–48. Jackson, *op. cit.,* p. 186. Beard and Beard, *op. cit.,* p. 279. Schlesinger, *Upheaval,* p. 477.

22. Freedman, *op. cit.,* p. 393. The quote is from a memorandum given Felix Frankfurter by Owen Roberts, November 9, 1945.

23. Powell, *op. cit.,* p. 53.

24. *Ibid.,* p. 53.

25. *Ibid.,* pp. 53–55.

26. *PPA, 1936,* pp. 191–92.

27. Quoted from *America* (June 13, 1936), p. 217; Boston *Herald;* and *Congressional Record,* June 5, 1936, p. 9040, by Mason, *op. cit.,* pp. 424–25.

28. *PPA, 1936,* p. 67.

29. *PPA, 1936,* p. 97 footnote.

30. George C. S. Benson, "The Year in Congress," *American Year Book,* 1936, p. 20.

31. *PPA, 1936,* pp. 103–6.

32. *Ibid.,* pp. 106–7. Benson, *op. cit.,* pp. 31–32.

33. Benson, *op. cit.,* p. 32. Schlesinger, *op. cit.,* p. 510.

34. Ickes, *op. cit.,* pp. 588–97, 620. Graham White and John Maze, *Harold Ickes of The New Deal* (Cambridge, 1985), pp. 173–75.

35. I vividly remember this occasion, having driven over to Topeka from Manhattan, Kansas, home of (as it was then named) Kansas State College of Agriculture and Applied Science, to obtain from Norman Thomas a statement of support for the anticompulsory-military-training campaign we were conducting at Kansas State. Landon, though he would not, of course, publicly endorse our campaign effort, *seemed* sympathetic to it.

36. New York *Times*, June 12, 13, 1936. Beard and Beard, *op. cit.*, pp. 305–10. Schlesinger, *op. cit.*, pp. 542–43.

37. Elliott Roosevelt, ed., *op. cit.*, pp. 591–92.

38. James A. Farley, *Jim Farley's Story*, (New York, 1948), pp. 63–64. Henry H. Adams, *Harry Hopkins* (New York, 1977), pp. 105–6.

39. Elliott Roosevelt, ed., *op. cit.*, p. 598.

40. Schlesinger, *op. cit.*, p. 432.

41. New York *Times*, May 6, June 15, July 10, 1936. *American Year Book*, 1936, p. 75.

42. Moley, *op. cit.*, p. 342.

43. Frances Perkins, "Reminiscences," Oral History Research Office, Columbia University, p. 3390. Quoted by Schlesinger, *op. cit.*, p. 582.

44. Beard and Beard, *op. cit.*, p. 280.

45. *Ibid.*, pp. 316–17.

46. New York *Times*, June 25, 26, 1936. Beard and Beard, *op. cit.*, pp. 318–20.

47. Moley, *Seven Years*, pp. 344–45. It should be noted that Moley's account of these events is designed to make him appear always master of the situation, and of himself; and that other accounts, notably Rosenman's, portray Roosevelt as being here chiefly concerned to "let Moley down easy." Surely Roosevelt's naïveté was considerably less than Moley would have his reader believe.

48. Rosenman, *op. cit.*, p. 105. Moley, *Seven Years*, pp. 345–46 covers the same episode, doing so by quoting Joseph Alsop and Robert Kintner, *Men Around the President*, p. 104. The Alsop-Kintner account is substantially the same as Rosenman's, and Moley says, "It is misleading chiefly insofar as it suggests that the episode was the occasion of a final 'break' between us"—suggesting that *otherwise* the account is accurate. And the fact remains that Moley's relationship with the President did at this point end, Moley's later invitations to Hyde Park being obviously and clearly, in retrospect, an attempt by Roosevelt to ease Moley's hurt at being shunted aside.

49. Ickes, *Secret Diary*, p. 626.

50. *PPA, 1936.* pp. 230–35.

51. Ickes, *Secret Diary*, pp. 636, 640.

52. New York *Times*, June 18. Marcus, *op. cit.*, pp. 118–19.

53. Ickes, *Secret Diary,* p. 645.

54. *PPA, 1936,* pp. 285, 288–89, 291.

55. *Ibid.,* pp. 336, 339.

56. *Ibid.,* pp. 385–86.

57. *Ibid.,* pp. 404–5.

58. *Ibid.,* pp. 465–66. Johnson, *op. cit.,* pp. 460–61.

59. Johnson, *op. cit.,* p. 460, quoting White letter to Oscar Stauffer, July 29, 1936.

60. Schlesinger, *Upheaval,* pp. 636–37. New York *Times,* Nov. 3, 4, 1936.

61. New York *Times,* November 1, 1936. *PPA, 1936,* pp. 568–71.

62. *PPA, 1936,* pp. 578, 580–81.

63. *Ibid.,* p. 582.

Seventeen. Concerns and Anticipations: November, December 1936

1. Nicholas Halasz, *Roosevelt Through Foreign Eyes* (New York, 1961), pp. 74–76, 326.

2. *Ibid.,* p. 77, quoting *Revue de Paris* (December 1936).

3. *Economist* (November 21, 1936); Marion K. Sanders, *Dorothy Thompson: A Legend in Her Time* (Boston, 1973), p. 221.

4. *Economist* (November 21, 1936).

5. George F. Kennan, *Memoirs, 1925–1950* (New York, 1967), pp. 82–83. Charles E. Bohlen, *Witness to History,* pp. 44–45.

6. Daniel W. Delano, Jr., *Franklin Roosevelt and the Delano Influence* (Pittsburgh, 1946), whose genealogical researches supplied facts recounted on pp. 36–37 of Davis, *FDR: The Beckoning of Destiny.*

7. Bullitt, *op. cit.,* pp. 178–81. Nixon, *Foreign Affairs,* vol. III, pp. 471–76.

8. Bullitt, *op. cit.,* pp. 184–88. Nixon, *Foreign Affairs,* pp. 499–502.

9. Nixon, *Foreign Affairs,* p. 400.

10. Bullitt, *op. cit.,* p. 186. Nixon, *Foreign Affairs,* pp. 500–501.

11. Bullitt, *op. cit.*, p. 188. Nixon, *op. cit.*, p. 502.

12. New York *Times*, November 5, 1936. Dallek, *op. cit.*, p. 132.

13. *PL, 1928–1945*, pp. 631, 632.

14. Ibid., pp. 634–35, Dallek, *op. cit.*, p. 133.

15. Dallek, *op. cit.*, p. 558.

16. *Ibid.*, pp. 132–33. *PL, 1928–1945*, p. 635.

17. Nixon, *Foreign Affairs*, has full speech, pp. 516–21. Dallek, *op. cit.*, pp. 133–34. *PL, 1928–1945*, p. 639.

18. *PL, 1928–1945*, p. 637.

19. Dallek, *op. cit.*, p. 133.

20. *PL, 1928–1945*, p. 635.

21. James Roosevelt (with Libby), *op. cit.*, p. 215.

22. *Ibid.*, p. 636. New York *Times*, December 2, 1936.

23. *PL, 1928–1945*, p. 639.

24. *Ibid.*, p. 638.

25. *Ibid.*, p. 641.

26. New York *Times*, December 10, 1936. The headline said: INDUSTRY GIVES UP FIGHT ON NEW DEAL; TO AID UNEMPLOYED.

27. *PL, 1928–1945*, p. 633. New York *Times*, December 17, 1936.

28. New York *Times*, December 17, 1936.

29. Sidney Hyman, *Marriner S. Eccles* (Stanford, Calif., 1976), pp. 222–23, 226. This is a remarkably fine book, accurately researched and well written, with a keen sense of historical values, sound psychological insights, and a firm grasp of economic issues and theory.

30. Blum, *From the Morgenthau Diaries*, p. 280. Hyman, *op. cit.*, p. 226.

31. Hyman, *op. cit.*, pp. 226–27.

32. Nixon, *Foreign Affairs*, p. 409.

33. *Ibid.*, p. 563. New York *Times*, December 30, 1936. Roosevelt spoke the quoted words in his December 29, 1936, press conference, held in the afternoon in the Executive Office.

34. Nixon, *Foreign Affairs*, pp. 565–66. See also pp. 592–93 of *op. cit.*, printing Roosevelt's reply to Norman Thomas, dated January 25, 1937. The reply, drafted by R. Walton Moore in the State Department, denied that U.S. policy with regard to Spain was in any way tied to British and French policy but had been independently determined as a result of "our policy of non-intervention and from the spirit of the recent neutrality laws." The reply went on to say, "Furthermore, the very circumstances which you set forth so fully in your letter must make it clear that the civil conflict in Spain involves so many non-Spanish elements and has such wide international implications that a policy of attempting to discriminate between the parties would be dangerous in the extreme. Not only would we, by permitting unchecked the flow of arms to one party in the conflict, be involving ourselves in that European strife from which our people desire so deeply to be aloof, but we would be deliberately encouraging those nations which would be glad of this pretext to continue their assistance to one side or the other in Spain and aggravating those disagreements among the European nations which are a constant menace to the peace of the world." Thomas could not but have deemed this argument sophistical in the actually existing circumstances.

35. New York *Times*, December 25, 26, 1936.

36. The *Post-Intelligencer* was a Hearst paper, and Hearst with his newspaper chain had viciously attacked the President and New Deal all through the 1936 election campaign. But the election returns had chastened the publisher, had also suggested to him a possibility of not only building a bridge to the evidently virtually omnipotent White House but also restoring to profitability a paper that had been crippled by a strike by the Newspaper Guild. He quickly acceded to most of the demands of the guild, settling the strike, and then offered Boettiger the job of publisher of the paper—a three-year contract stipulating that Boettiger would have full authority to direct the "editorial and business policies of the paper." Boettiger's pay, handsome indeed for that year, was $30,000 per annum. In that same contract, Anna was given the job for the same three-year period of "contributor to women's pages . . . and in connection with all matters of interest to women." Her salary was $10,000 per annum. See John R. Boettiger, *A Love in Shadow*, (New York, 1978), p. 204. This book, by the son of Anna, is a very good one, with remarkable psychological insights into the tragic effects an attraction into the circle of power radiating from such as FDR can have upon highly intelligent and sensitive human beings. John and Anna were eventually divorced, at his instigation, after misfortunes in journalism convinced him he was a failure and cast him into deep depression. He committed suicide in 1950.

37. New York *Times*, December 24, 1936.

38. New York *Times*, January 1, 1937.

39. James Roosevelt (with Libby), *op. cit.,* p. 238. Eleanor Roosevelt, *This I Remember,* p. 165.

40. James Roosevelt (with Libby), *op. cit.,* pp. 223–24, 317–18.

Epilogue: A Summing-up, January 1, 1936.

1. Henry Adams, *The Education of Henry Adams,* (Modern Library edition), p. 499.

2. *PPA, 1936,* p. 480.

3. New York *Times,* December 31, 1933.

4. Berle and Jacobs, *op. cit.,* pp. 197–98.

Index

Acheson, Dean, 139, 153, 163, 183, 210, 291, 292, 295–96, 497, 607, 614. *See also* London Conference

Adams, Charles Francis, 140*n*

Adams, Henry, 180, 673

Agee, James, 488

Agricultural Adjustment Act, 70, 71, 72–76, 110, 118, 132; declared unconstitutional by Supreme Court, 607–11

Agricultural Adjustment Administration (AAA), 75–76, 269–83, 580; and destruction of food and fiber, 269–75; dispute over cotton production control in, 475–81; impact of policies, 284–86; linkage with Extension Service, 272–74; organization of, 275–81; and Peek-Wallace conflict, 299–302; and price controversy, 287–88; and Surplus Relief Corporation, 281

Agricultural policies: and drought, 384–86; in 1937, 663; Roosevelt's indecision on, 474–85; Wallace's proposals for, 235–36. *See also* Farm legislation

Airmail, investigation of government contracts for, 355–62

Alcorn County Electric Power Association, 430, 432–33

Altmeyer, Arthur J., 449–50, 452, 524

Amalgamated Clothing Workers (ACW), 98, 243, 631

Amberson, Dr. W.R., 477

American Association for Labor Legislation (AALL), 438–41, 444, 445

American Association for Old Age Security (AAOAS), 443

American Association for Social Security, 449

American Banking Association, 149, 419–20, 540, 541

American Civil Liberties Union (ACLU), 535

American Farm Bureau Federation, 70, 93, 272, 273, 475

American Federation of Labor (AFL), 36, 77, 78, 98, 306, 525, 631

American Federation of Utility Investors, 532

American Friends Service Committee, 350, 353

American Legion, 58, 64, 147, 551–52

American Liberty League. *See* Liberty League

American Medical Association (AMA), 441, 450

American Newspaper Guild, 526–28

American Tobacco Company, 221

American Youth Congress, 676

Anderson, Carl D., 215, 217

Anderson, Sherwood, 226, 275, 488

Andrews, John B., 438, 439, 440, 442, 444

Antilynching legislation, 483–85, 629

Antitrust laws, Industrial Recovery Act and, 87, 116, 118, 120, 142–43, 151, 244–45

Antiwar organizations. *See* specific peace organizations

Appleby, Paul, 204, 276–77, 278, 300, 482

Argentina, Roosevelt's visit to, 656–57

Armaments industry, investigation of, 550–60

Armaments legislation, 550–62; Flynn plan, 556–59; McSwain bill, 559–62; Nye-Vandenberg resolution, 551–54; and peace organizations, 558–59, 561; and Roosevelt, 553–55; and threat of World War II, 557–58; and War Policies Commission, 551

Armour and Company, 608

Armstrong, Barbara, 453, 454–55, 457, 458

Arnold, Thurman W., 42, 279

Arthurdale project, 352–54, 361, 362, 368, 373–75, 488, 629–30

Associated Press (AP), 179, 180

Astor, Vincent, 196, 209, 243*n*, 367, 467

Atomic research, during New Deal, 214–19

Automation, 224–27

Automobile industry: and NRA codes, 257–58; strike of 1933, 263–64

Avery, Sewell L., 400

Awalt, F.G., 49

Baird, J.L., 219

Baker, Gladys, 272

Baker, Newton D., 36, 92*n*, 140*n*, 571

Balanced budget. *See* Federal deficit

Baldwin, C.B. "Beanie," 480, 488

Baldwin, Sidney, 488

Ballantine, Arthur, 26, 49, 59

Bankers, Banks: and Eccles's banking bill, 537–41; farmers' movement and, 291; and Roosevelt's monetary policies, 108–109. *See also* Banking crisis of 1933

Bankhead, John H., 91

Bankhead, William B., 533

Banking crisis of 1933, 21–22, 35, 49–53; bank closures, 13, 26–28; Roosevelt-Hoover meeting and, 24–26; farm crisis and, 72; and Glass-Steagall bill, 150; passage of emergency banking bill, 55–56; proposals for nationalization of banks, 50; and Roosevelt's first fireside chat, 60–61. *See also* National bank moratorium

Barbour, W. Warren, 553, 560

Barkley, Alben, 536, 634

Baruch, Bernard, 69, 76, 100, 112, 132, 133, 140*n*, 163, 183, 188, 196, 555, 600–601;

About the Author

A biographer of Eisenhower, Lindbergh, and Adlai Stevenson as well as a novelist, KENNETH S. DAVIS was awarded the prestigious Francis Parkman Prize for *FDR: The Beckoning of Destiny,* which was also a nominee for the National Book Award. He has received a Guggenheim Fellowship among other awards and fellowships.

A graduate of Kansas State University, with a master of science degree from the University of Wisconsin and an honorary doctor of letters degree from Assumption College, Mr. Davis has been a journalism instructor at New York University, a war correspondent attached to General Eisenhower's personal headquarters, special assistant to the president of Kansas State University, a member of the State Department's UNESCO Relations Staff, editor of the *Newberry Library Bulletin* in Chicago, an adjunct professor of English at Clark University, and a visiting professor of history at Kansas State University.

He and his wife now live in Princeton, Massachusetts.

OSWEGO CITY LIBRARY